Licensed Premises: Law, Practice and Policy

Second edition

D1610307

Licensed Premises: Law, Practice and Policy

Second edition

Philip Kolvin QC, MA (Oxon), FRSA
Barrister, Cornerstone Barristers
Patron, Institute of Licensing
Chairman, Best Bar None
Chairman, Purple Flag

Bloomsbury Professional

Bloomsbury Professional Ltd, Maxwelton House, 41–43 Boltro Road, Haywards Heath, West Sussex, RH16 1BJ

A CIP Catalogue record for this book is available from the British Library.

ISBN: 978 1 84592 288 7

Typeset by Columns Design XML Ltd, Reading, Berkshire
Printed and bound in Great Britain by CPI Group (UK) Ltd, Croydon, CR0 4YY

Dedication

Dedicated to the memory of
Prof. Israel Kolvin
(1929–2002)
my father,
who taught me partnership.

Preface to the Second Edition

Judging when to bring out the second edition of this book has been like working out when to jump onto a moving train. The first edition was printed just as the Licensing Act came into force and the absence of most of the operative regulations, case law or day to day licensing experience presented the most delightful of vistas for the legal commentator: a stationary, blank canvas upon which to imprint one's views.

Now, the exercise is altogether more difficult. There has been a plethora of legislation impacting on licensing regulation – the Violent Crime Reduction Act, the Police Reform and Social Responsibility Act, the Equality Act and the Provision of Services Regulations, to name but some. Cumulative impact policies have moved from being rare, exotic, rather metropolitan creatures to populous beasts bestriding all manner of towns and cities. New species have been created: early morning restriction orders, summary reviews, late night levies, persistent sale closure notices all spring to mind and one – the unloved, ill-fated Alcohol Disorder Zone – has already joined the dodo. New life forms have sprung up as counterpoints in the regulatory jungle – Purple Flag, Best Bar None, Community Alcohol Partnerships and Business Improvement Districts. And, of course, there is far greater experience of living in this brave new world: policies to dissect, sub-committees to negotiate and a wholly new breed to reckon with – the expert licensing officer. Nor have we time to catch breath. Even as I write on this, the first day of summer 2013, the Licensing Act 2003 (Descriptions of Entertainment) (Amendment) Order 2013 awaits the Parliamentary gift of life. Meanwhile the Government continues to haver over new alcohol health measures such as minimum pricing and the introduction of health as a material factor in the decision to designate cumulative impact policies.

What there has not been amidst all this frenetic activity is a pause for contemplation. It is as though, somewhere in government, there is a voice which says 'we must be seen to **do** things about alcohol.' Most practitioners feel that there are more powers than you can shake a stick at. What we need now is mature analysis of what works, resources to make it work, and better training of the main protagonists in the system – licensing officers, committee members and magistrates – so that this most crucial aspect of our national life and economy is regulated by those with appropriate levels of skill and knowledge.

This book does not purport to have all the answers. But it does set out to encourage those with their hands on the levers of power to ask the right questions. It does try to ensure that the answer to each licensing problem is not just a binary yes or no, but is informed by a full understanding of the myriad possibilities which lie between these polarised extremes. It does try to broaden the horizon of those involved in the system by setting out systematically the full range of regulatory and non-regulatory means by which the chosen goals may be attained, so that resources may be prioritised in the pursuit of initiatives which are most likely to achieve something worthwhile. It does try to respond to the experience of the system in operation by setting out standards for regulators and answering some of the commonly arising questions and issues. For me, success would be that readers feel engaged in a debate, agree or fiercely disagree with the views expressed, but leave the book energised with ideas of their own, and the motivation to implement them. If we are to build a new leisure economy, fit to leave to our children, driven by more than alcohol and directed at more than a single age group and demographic, we need actors, agitators, thinkers, makers and doers across the land, utilising all the regulatory and non-regulatory tools at their disposal. It cannot be done from Whitehall. It is a task performed bar by bar, street by street, neighbourhood by neighbourhood. It is my fervent hope that this book may, for some, be a *vade mecum* along the way.

The book bears some limited resemblance to the first edition, although there is a new word – policy – in the title reflecting that this is a practical policy volume, not a law book. The policy chapters have been brought to the fore, and whole parts of the book – in particular part B4 and most of parts C, D and E are new. It has never been my intention to treat the book as sacred text, encrusting the hallowed words with new footnotes and nuances of interpretation in subsequent editions – in fact I cannot bear the thought. When it comes to write a third edition, it might be necessary to throw it all out and start again: come to think of it that would be the best time – and reason – to do so.

Now, thanks. Some people have had a huge influence on this book, maybe without even knowing it. Others, too numerous to mention, have helped me with snippets of text, advice or kindness – they know who they are. Let me confine myself to this. My huge appreciation goes to the many contributors to this book, who have brought diversity, expertise and vivacity to the text. This is my first collaboration with Bloomsbury Professional who, if there were BAFTAs for legal publishing, would get one. Thanks to my methodical, unflappable, hawk-eyed editor Tom Prince, and to Martin Casimir, Leanne Barrett, Jenny Burdett and Victoria Daniels. Tender thanks to Jessie and Eilah – who manage to be a delight in spite of – or is that because of? – paternal absence. And, as always, thanks to Laurie for her insightful commentaries on my drafts, for coaxing me up the mountain and, well, everything.

The law is stated at 1st January 2013 but I have tried to incorporate changes since. For the errors, I accept ministerial responsibility.

Philip Kolvin
Grays Inn
June 2013

Foreword to the First Edition

From the end of 2005 our existing archaic licensing legislation will be swept aside and replaced. The fixed 11pm call of 'time at the bar' will become a thing of the past and people will have more choice about how they spend their leisure time.

This represents the most radical shake up of our licensing laws in 40 years.

Underpinning the new system are four crucial objectives: the prevention of crime and disorder, public safety, the prevention of public nuisance and the protection of children from harm.

Six regimes will be turned into one, which will be the responsibility of one local, accountable authority – a licensing authority. They will licence the sale of alcohol, the supply of alcohol by clubs, the provision of regulated entertainment and the provision of late night refreshment. This will cut out significant amounts of red tape at a stroke.

The new system will give authorities a range of powers to tackle venues where the law is flouted, where problems are occurring or if the local community is being disrupted. The current system provides only two options – either do nothing or revoke the licence.

Local businesses and residents will be among those who will be able to ask for a review of a licence, which could result in its suspension or revocation. In addition, local businesses and local residents can have their say on many applications, giving the local community more opportunity than ever before to have their say in the licensing decisions that affect them.

Each licensing authority has drawn up their own policy which will complement the local authority's wider strategy to prevent crime and disorder, as well as looking at the impact on transport, regeneration and tourism.

As we approach full implementation of the Act it remains important that all parties concerned with its practice and its administration – industry, licensing authorities, the police and other responsible authorities – continue to work closely together. The adoption of consistent professional standards is vital to the success of the new system.

Publications, such as this one, make an important contribution to the development of good practice and partnership working under the new regime.

Tessa Jowell
Secretary of State for Culture, Media and Sport

Preface to the First Edition

A tavern chair is the throne of human felicity.

Samuel Johnson

The Licensing Act 2003 is one of the largest revamps in our licensing laws for half a millennium, but the arguments surrounding it are no different to those which have been debated in Parliament and pubs, with varying degrees of eloquence, for centuries. Individual Liberty v Collective Restraint; Personal Responsibility v State Control; Pleasure for the Masses v the Demon Drink; Free Trade v Temperance; National Rules v Local Democracy; Licensing as Regulator of the Public or Merely the Private Realm? The outcome of such debates is neither certain, universal nor permanent, for which reason the pendulum has frequently swung towards greater or lesser regulation. On 7th February 2005, the pendulum will swing once again.

This book proceeds from the notion that those who learn nothing from history are destined to repeat it. Its main thesis is that licensing is a matter for local control depending on what is necessary in an individual case to promote the licensing objectives. That aim is easier to state than to attain. It is essential to build evidential data-bases, locally and nationally, to identify the problems and test the solutions, as a foundation for the formulation of policy and individual decision-making. It is time to articulate clear standards and to revise them in the light of experience. It is time to cease licensing control based on political proclivity, whim, well-meaning guesswork or amorphous concepts such as 'saturation' and 'binge drinking'.

The book calls for a new approach on the part of statutory and non-statutory stakeholders. Licensing is not a free-standing discipline, but part of a complex web of regulation of (principally) the night time economy. Licensing authorities should not stop at regulation, but must play their part in recognising their potential as agents of positive change – harnessing industry innovations and investment to the wider social agenda of the community in terms of regeneration, tourism, transportation and employment. So they must look beyond their departmental walls and work in tandem with other agencies in the town hall. More than that, they must promote partnership across civil society, involving other statutory agencies, and the business and residential community in working to create a thriving, yet peaceful night time economy.

In this book, of course we describe the new law. We also set out some lessons from history, other regimes and international experience generally. We describe the professional disciplines which bear on the management of the night time economy, outline the partnerships necessary to make it work, and articulate the standards to which both industry and the statutory agencies should aspire.

We hope that the book is read by all those whose job brings them into contact with the new regime. Operators need a clear understanding of modern standards so as to reflect them in their operating schedules. Police and other regulatory authorities need such understanding so as to decide whether to make representations. Councillors and magistrates require the same understanding so as to decide whether particular conditions are necessary to promote the licensing objectives. But more than ever, the industry, working hand in hand with other stakeholders, needs to forge common approaches based on accepted standards beyond the coercive reach of licensing control. We hope that this book will assist in developing a language for communication.

In that the book is opinionated, we expect it to be criticised. If it provokes no debate, it will have failed. Any standards it articulates are suggested without the experience of the new regime actually in operation. We therefore consider this to be work in progress. Successive editions will benefit from our growing understanding, remembering the old cowboy adage that good judgment comes from experience, and experience comes from bad judgment.

We have aimed to have this book on the shelves in time for the First Appointed Day, 7th February 2005. We have therefore had to go to print before the procedural and fees regulations are finalised. The law is stated as at 31st August 2004, but subsequent material has been incorporated wherever possible.

Philip Kolvin
Grays Inn
November 2004

List of contributors

Editor
Philip Kolvin QC, MA (Oxon), FRSA
Barrister, Cornerstone Barristers

Contributors
Lewis Aldous BA (Hons)
Licensing Officer, London Borough of Hammersmith and Fulham

Nick Arron LLB (Hons)
Solicitor, Poppleston Allen

Stephen Baker, PGCert & PGDip Community Safety & Crime Prevention (UWE)
Chair, National Pubwatch

Josef Cannon LLB (Hons) (London)
Barrister, Cornerstone Barristers

Rory Clarke MA (Cantab)
Barrister, Cornerstone Barristers

Dale Collins MA
Solicitor-Advocate (Criminal Proceedings), Senior Associate, Bond Dickinson

Paul Davies BArch DipArch DipTP RTPI
Consultant, Association of Town Centre Management

Dr Martin Elvins PhD
Lecturer in Politics and International Relations, University of Dundee

James Findlay QC, MA (Cantab)
Barrister, Cornerstone Barristers

Gerard Forlin QC, LLB (Hons) LLM (LSE) MPhil (Cantab), PGDASL (London)
Barrister, Cornerstone Barristers

Carlo Gibbs
Policy and Public Affairs Manager, Wine and Spirit Trade Association

Robin Green LLB (London)
Barrister, Cornerstone Barristers

Andy Grimsey LLB (Hons)
Solicitor, Poppleston Allen

Ryan S Kohli MA (Oxon)
Barrister, Cornerstone Barristers

Sanju Manji (DTS, MTSI)
Trading Standards and Licensing Manager, London Borough of Hammersmith and Fulham

Martin O'Brien (DTS)
Trading Standards Officer, London Borough of Hammersmith and Fulham

Adrian Overton
Licensing Officer, London Borough of Hammersmith and Fulham

Clare Parry BA (Oxon)
Barrister, Cornerstone Barristers

Asitha Ranatunga MA (Cantab) MPhil (Cantab)
Barrister, Cornerstone Barristers

Jacquie Reilly
Former Director, UK BIDs

Robin Room PhD
Director, AER Centre for Alcohol Policy Research, Turning Point Alcohol & Drug Centre, and Professor, School of Population and Global Health, University of Melbourne

Valerie Simpson (DTS, MTSI)
Bi-borough Head of Environmental Health (Licensing and Trading Standards), London Borough of Hammersmith and Fulham

Louise Smail BSc (Hons) PhD, CMIOSH, MBCS, CITP
Health and safety law specialist, Ortalan Ltd

Jonathan Smith LLB (Hons)
Solicitor, Poppleston Allen

Alistair Turnham BA (Hons), MSc
Principal, MAKE Associates

Cathy Thornton
Deputy Team Leader (Planning), London Borough of Hammersmith and Fulham

Nick Walton LLB (Hons)
Solicitor, Poppleston Allen

Lisa White
Licensing Officer, London Borough of Hammersmith and Fulham

Somayya Yaqub (MCIEH)
Environmental Protection Manager, London Borough of Hammersmith and Fulham

Contents

Page

Table of Statutes

Table of Statutory Instruments

Table of Cases

Introduction

Before the Roman came to Rye or out to Severn strode,
The rolling English drunkard made the rolling English road.
A reeling road, a rolling road that rambles round the shire,
And after him the parson ran, the sexton and the squire.

GK Chesterton, *The Rolling English Road*

1

Challenges

This pudding has no theme.

Winston Churchill

A THE BIBULOUS GENE

1.01 English literature begins in a pub[1], the Tabard Inn in Southwark, whose merry host, Harry Bailly, moots a prize of a free feast for the pilgrim who tells the best tale on the pilgrimage and thus inspires the Canterbury Tales. Throughout literature, the pub, inn, tavern, alehouse and gin palace are placed at the heart of our social culture: a canvas against which the drama of our daily lives is played out. Relationships are made and broken, sorrows bemoaned and drowned, successes toasted. The literary references in the chapter headings of this book underline this point.

The corollary is that we are a nation which likes to drink. At the time of the Norman conquest, William of Malmesbury wrote of us: 'Drinking in particular was a universal practice, in which occupation they passed entire nights as well as days ... They were accustomed to eat till they became surfeited, and drink till they were sick.'[2] The English defeat at the hands of the Norman invader was put down to drink, the natives fighting 'more with rashness and precipitate fury than with military skill'. This bibulous gene has driven our linguistic evolution: we now have over 800 words and phrases for 'drunk'.[3] As the modern beer expert Pete Brown notes, 'Drunkenness is such

---

[1]   Steven Earnshaw, *The Pub in Literature* (Manchester University Press, 2000).
[2]   Andrew Barr, *Drink: An Informal Social History* (Bantam Press, 1995).
[3]   Jonathan Green, *The Cassell Dictionary of Slang* (Cassell, 2000).

an important part of our culture that it compels us to push our facility with language to new limits.'[4] This proclivity is not without consequences. The writer and presenter Jeremy Paxman mourns that the English: 'far from being ashamed of their behaviour ... see fighting and drunkenness as part of their birthright. It is the way they proclaim their identity.'[5] While it would be remiss to fail to acknowledge the historic role of the English drinking establishment as a place of entertainment, accommodation and the transaction of commerce,[6] it is the service of alcohol, and its results, which has principally occasioned regulatory intervention.

1.02   Over the last half millennium, the political response to our national trait has been ever-changing and contradictory. There are many reasons for this. On a simple level there has been a basic lack of knowledge and evidence as to how best to confront it. Despite a far greater understanding of the pharmacological properties of alcohol and the social mechanisms through which it is mediated,[7] that gap remains. More than that, however, alcohol has been a political football which all kinds of bodies have wanted to kick about for their own diverse reasons: the clergy, the justices, the exchequer, the puritans, the temperance movement, the big brewers, the small brewers, the gin-makers, the wine makers, the agriculturalists and the monarchy to name but a few. Thus, the treatment of alcohol has often turned on which of these interests holds centre stage for the time being. This in turn has led to a complicated mesh of competing considerations – moral, religious, social, economic – all vying for primacy in the political discourse.

1.03   Into this maelstrom, one which has been known to bring down governments, the Labour Government of 1997–2010 chose to boldly go, promulgating the most radical change in our licensing laws for 400 years. The main structural plank of the changes was to streamline liquor, entertainment, night café, theatre and cinema licensing into a single system, and to pass it to local authorities for administration, stripping from local justices the main role in licensing which they had held since Edward VI bestowed it upon them in 1552.[8] National guidance emanated from government for the first time, with local authorities required to promulgate their own local policy having regard to national policy, bringing the process of licensing into line with town and country planning.

---

4   Pete Brown, *Man Walks into a Pub: A Sociable History of Beer* (Macmillan, 2003).
5   Jeremy Paxman, *The English: A Portrait of a People* (Penguin, 1999).
6   See Kumin and Thusty (eds), *The World of the Tavern: Public Houses in Modern Europe* (Ashgate, 2002).
7   For the importance of socially-inculcated patterns of behaviour amongst intoxicated persons, see MacAndrew and Edgerton, *Drunken Comportment: A Social Explanation* (Aldine, 1969). See also Chapter 23 (The Operation of Licensed Premises), paras 23.3 and 23.4.
8   The Act of 1552, 5 and 6 Edw VI, c 25, introduced the three distinct forms of control which are the basis of modern licensing: the power of selection, withdrawal and the imposition of conditions. See Wilson, *Alcohol and the Nation* (Nicholson and Watson, 1940).

1.04 One of the greatest benefits of the new legislation was that it compelled scrutiny of the reason for having a licensing system at all. The Licensing Act 2003 asked and answered the question by setting out, again for the first time, clear licensing objectives. These are the prevention of crime and disorder and public nuisance, public safety and the protection of children. While all of these considerations have been part of the armoury of licensing justices for centuries, the licensing objectives perform the valuable function of reminding both decision-makers and parties to focus on the policy end in view. More importantly, the objectives state by implication what licensing is not about. Those practitioners who, representing burger chains wanting an extra 30 minutes on their night café licence, were subjected to hours of emotive but extraneous evidence from politically motivated objectors regarding the sacking of the rainforests, breathed a sigh of relief.

1.05 But the most fundamental alteration in the law was the removal of the universal terminal hour for sale of liquor. Once the licensing objectives are understood, there is no intuitive or logical reason why there should be uniformity of licensing hours within a single place, let alone across the country. Yet the system laboured under such uniformity, partly because the idea of closing hours was ingrained in our national consciousness and embedded in our culture, and partly because licensing has long been hedged about with notions of morality and temperance. Once such notions are supplanted by the libertarian model of free choice subject to not harming other interests (as embodied by the licensing objectives), the need for uniformity falls away. To understand the importance and possible implications, of this deregulatory measure, it is instructive to consider its ancestry.

B A HISTORY OF TIME

1.06 As the 16th century drew to a close, behaviour in alehouses moved the Puritan Philip Stubbes to rail: 'How they stutter and stagger and reel to and fro, like madmen, some vomiting, spewing and disgorging their filthy stomachs, othersome pissing under the board as they sit ... ' [9] The tension between the Puritan and the carouser is reflected in Malvolio's admonishment of his masters and betters, Belch and Aguecheek, in Shakespeare's *Twelfth Night*: 'Do ye make an ale-house of my lady's house, that ye squeak out your coziers' catches without any mitigation or remorse of voice,' provoking Belch's riposte: 'Dost thou think, because thou art virtuous, there shall be no more cakes and ale?' [10]

1.07 The dichotomy between an England at drink and at prayer reached the ears of James I, who set out to cure the problem. In 1606 alone he passed two pieces of legislation, for the licensing of alehouses and the suppression of

[9]   Andrew Barr, *Drink: An Informal Social History* (Bantam Press 1995).
[10]   Shakespeare, *Twelfth Night*, 1600.

drunkenness.[11] The title of the latter proclaimed its noble purpose: 'Act for Repressing the Odious and Loathsome Sin of Drunkenness'. Its preamble set out the scale of the endeavour: 'Whereas the loathsome and odious sin of drunkenness is of late grown into common use in this realm, being the root and foundation of many other enormous sins, as bloodshed, stabbing, murder, swearing, fornication, adultery, and such like, to the great dishonour of God, and of our nation, the overthrow of many good arts and manual trades, the disabling of divers workmen, and the general impoverishing of many good subjects, abusively wasting the good creatures of God ... ' The legislation conspicuously failed, because further legislation in 1609, An Act for the Reformation of Alehouse Keepers, commenced: 'Whereas notwithstanding all former laws and provisions already made, the inordinate and extreme vice of excessive drinking and drunkenness doth more and more abound ... '

1.08   Undeterred, the monarch continued his programme of reform, which lead to the first recorded example of licensing hours: the Newmarket Proclamation of James I in 1618. This required all inns and alehouses to close at 9 pm and also during Divine Service on Sundays.[12] There is no evidence that this suppressed the nation's enthusiasm for alcohol: whereas in 1577 the number of alehouses per capita was 1:120, by 1636 it had risen to 1:95.[13] The failure of the legislation may have reflected trickle down from an overflowing aristocratic goblet. When King Christian of Denmark visited the court of James I in 1606, he recorded: 'Those whom I never could get to taste good liquor now follow the fashion and wallow in beastly delights. The ladies abandon sobriety, and are seen to roll around in intoxication.'[14] During his Protectorate (1653–1658), Oliver Cromwell imposed closure throughout Sundays,[15] but the restrictions seem to have lapsed thereafter.[16] While justices took it upon themselves to impose closing times, no national hours or days of trade were set again until 1839.[17]

---

[11]   This was not the first attempt to control the sale of liquor. By Acts of 1495 (11 Henry VII c 2) and 1504 (19 Henry VII c 12) any two justices were authorised summarily to repress useless ale-houses in their neighbourhood, with the first legislation to create a licensing system coming in 1552 (5 and 6 Edward VI c 25). For an early history see Sidney and Beatrice Webb's treatise 'The History of Liquor Licensing in England', English Local Government (1903).

[12]   See *Paterson's Licensing Acts 2003* (Butterworths, 111th ed), Part 2, for an illuminating history of licensing hours.

[13]   Brown.

[14]   Peter Haydon, *Beer and Britannia: An Inebriated History of Britain* (Sutton Publishing, 2003).

[15]   Andrew Barr, *Drink: An Informal Social History* (Bantam Press, 1995).

[16]   The licensing system was formalised by an Act of 1729 (2 George II c 28) when the Brewster sessions was instituted, whereby all licences had to be granted at an annual general session of the justices rather than, as formerly, by any two justices at any time. The justices were local so that they might inform themselves of the 'occasion or want' of licensed premises, thus implying a test of need.

[17]   Although the Beer Act of 1830 did in fact impose opening restrictions on the new unregulated beer shops.

1.09 However, an interesting interlude appeared in Dorchester during Cromwell's era, when a Puritan group came to dominate the town corporation – taking a multi-faceted approach to dissolution and licentiousness, with moral police pillorying the rapist, stopping up the mouths of the profane, closing the riotous taverns or evicting their keepers, cancelling the festivals and press-ganging the populace into church attendance. It is recorded that the beneficial social changes in terms of crime, health, education and sexual morality were dramatic.[18] This experience highlights that licensing restraint by itself is an uncertain instrument for social control – rather a number of instruments of social control need to work in harmony.

1.10 By the end of the seventeenth century in particular, there was very little control of the supply of liquor, with licences freely granted by the justices and rarely withdrawn,[19] causing the number of licensed premises to burgeon and consumption of beer to increase by 1722 to 36 gallons a year for every man, woman and child, a figure never exceeded before or since.[20] Not that beer was the only issue. Following his accession to the throne William of Orange pursued commercial warfare upon the French, placing heavy tariffs on the importation of brandy, and in 1690 passing an Act granting a general permission to distil and retail spirits grown from patriotic English corn.[21] By the early eighteenth century, there was no licensing restraint on 'punch houses' and 'dram shops' selling this commodity, which was in any case subject to very low rates of duty. In case one could not obtain an adequate supply in the six or seven thousand dram shops in London, one might obtain gin in lieu of wages at work, from barrow boys and market girls, pedlars, watermen and chandlers until 'one half of the town seems set to furnish poison to the other half.'[22] In one shop, the trader provided a back room 'where, as his wretched guests get intoxicated, they are laid together in heaps, promiscuously, men, women and children, till they recover their senses, when they proceed to drink on ...'[23] Parliament stood by, confining itself to formalising the process of licensing by an Act of 1728[24] and sought belatedly to control the growth in the spirit trade through heavy taxation, which was met with, at best, total disregard and, at worst, riots. Manufacture of spirits

---

[18] Simon Schama, *A History of Britain, The British Wars 1603 – 1776* (BBC, 2001).

[19] Webb and Webb recount that the supervision by the Privy Council of the justices was broken by the outbreak of the Civil War, and that no serious attempt was made either during the Protectorate or after the Restoration to reconstruct the centrally supervised administrative system aimed at by James I. By the end of the 17th century, local Justices of the Peace were abandoned to their own devices.

[20] Webb and Webb.

[21] Webb and Webb.

[22] Theophilus, cited in Webb and Webb.

[23] *Distilled Liquors: the Bane of the Nation* (1736), cited in Webb and Webb.

[24] 2 George II c 28, instituting the Brewster sessions, whereby all licences had to be granted at an annual general session of the justices rather than, as formerly, by any two justices at any time. The justices were local so that they might inform themselves of the 'occasion or want' of licensed premises, thus implying a test of need.

in 1742 ran to 7,160,000 gallons,[25] largely unchecked by a further Act of 1736 which required gin traders to purchase a licence for an exorbitant fee of £50 and imposed still more swingeing taxes.[26] The Act was evaded by a series of measures, including the sale of spirits under the guise of medicine.[27] Parliament thus reversed the policy in a further Act of 1743, drafted by a Kentish distiller, lowering both the licence fee and tax on spirits. This experience again underscores that single measures (whether regulatory or deregulatory) are but pebbles strewn in the river – most unlikely to alter its course or flow.

1.11 A more imaginative measure, the Gin Act of 1751, prevented distillers selling to unlicensed retailers, and made drinking debts irrecoverable at law, thus removing the credit upon which much of the trade depended.[28] As the London Evening Post of March 1751 put it: 'This wicked gin, of all Defence bereft/ And guilty found of Whoredom, Murder, Theft/ Of rank Sedition, Treason, Blasphemy/ Should suffer Death, the Judges all agree'. There is some evidence of a fall in gin consumption thereafter, but also of a rise in demand for licences, which were freely dispensed by the justices. The net effect was that by 1752 the London suburbs 'abounded with an incredible number of public-houses, which continually resounded with the noise of riot and intemperance ... the haunts of idleness, frau, and rapine, and the seminaries of drunkenness, debauchery, extravagance, and every vice incident to human nature.'[29] Clearly justices, entrusted with the control of licensing, were not doing so, and tales abounded of justices and their clerks profiteering from the grant of licences, or well-meaning magistrates granting licences merely in order to keep the licensee off the poor rate, and without regard for the needs of the neighbourhood.

1.12 At the end of the eighteenth century, licensing curtailments were re-imposed by Pitt's Government at the instance of Wilberforce[30] in the Royal Proclamation Against Vice of 1787, passed against growing concern that licensed premises were becoming dens of iniquity, as well as places for the unemployed to plan their crimes.[31] The Proclamation was sent by the Home Secretary to all lord lieutenants to ask the justices to flex their muscles. It declared the royal intention to punish 'all manner of vice, profaneness and immorality'. It forbade gambling on Sundays. It urged strict

---

25   Webb and Webb.
26   The pre-amble to the Act warned grimly that the 'ill consequences of such liquors are not confined to the present generation but extend to future years and tend to the destruction of the United Kingdom.' The sentiment was real but the prophecy not.
27   Griffith Edwards, *Alcohol: the Ambiguous Molecule* (Penguin 2000).
28   Haydon.
29   Smollett, cited in Webb and Webb.
30   Who recorded in his diary that 'God has set before me as my object the reformation of manners' (Webb and Webb).
31   Barr. See also Webb and Webb, describing a village near Leeds in 1786, containing 30–40 alehouses, 'the rendezvous of ... nocturnal villains, where they plan their depredations ... divide their spoil.'

enforcement of laws against 'excessive drinking, blasphemy, profane swearing or cursing, lewdness, profanation of the Lord's day, or other dissolute, immoral, or disorderly practices ... public gaming houses ... unlicensed public shows, interludes, and places of entertainments, loose and licentious prints, books and publications' and supplying refreshments during divine service. The Home Secretary sent a covering letter referring to 'the depredations which have been committed in every part of the kingdom, and which have of late been carried to such an extent as to be even a disgrace to a civilised nation.' He urged justices to act 'for the preservation of the lives and properties of His Majesty's subjects.' This was a national alcohol strategy and national guidance rolled into one.

1.13 The justices began to exercise their powers zealously, with licences revoked for, amongst other things, suffering tippling on Sundays or during divine service, or keeping late or irregular hours, and conditions routinely imposed to similar effect. Justices were also wont to suppress licences on the simple ground that they were superfluous, thus stimulating the consumption of alcohol. On one day in 1787, local justices shut every dram shop in Sheffield.[32] In the following three years 3,825 spirits licences disappeared nationally and the Excise was complaining of its losses.[33] The Fabian writers Sidney and Beatrice Webb[34] argue that crime and disorder fell in the quarter century following the Royal Proclamation, and that the limitation of the opportunities for drinking was an important contributory cause, more important in their estimation than the absorption of disorderly characters by the armed forces and factories.

1.14 The balance of evidence is that the high degree of regulation introduced through Pitt's initiative became attenuated over time, for no apparent reason other than that the justices lost the will to go on, their ardour increasingly dampened by the free trade movement, which had it that unrestricted competition would drive up the quality of the product and standards of competition and drive down price. A House of Commons Committee of 1816–1817 reflected the philosophy of the age by recommending that the function of the justices ought to be confined largely to a ministerial exercise of statutory provisions, celebrating 'the long-undisputed and exercised right enjoyed by the victuallers to conduct their houses, and to sell ale, beer, wine and spirits, in the manner and after the mode as suited best to the character of their respective customers.'[35] The effect of its report was to inculcate in justices a sense of duty to grant unconditionally.

1.15 Consequently, the early part of the 19th century saw a vast increase in alcohol consumption, particularly gin, inimical to the need for a sober workforce to power the industrial revolution. The number of spirit licences

[32] Webb and Webb.
[33] Haydon.
[34] Webb and Webb.
[35] Webb and Webb.

increased in the first quarter of the century by 8,500, exacerbated still further by a large reduction in the cost of a spirit licence in 1825.[36] One commentator in 1824 depicted an England sodden in spirits: 'In every broad thoroughfare, and in every close alley, there was drunkenness abroad: not shamefaced drunkenness creeping in maudlin helplessness to its home by the side of the scolding wife, but rampant, insolvent, outrageous drunkenness.'[37]

1.16 This vista lead to the passage of the Duke of Wellington's Beer Act 1830 which abolished duty on beer and provided mandatory grants of licences for beer shops, in the hope of weaning the working classes off the demon spirits[38]. This optimistic instrument of social engineering had predictable and immediate results. On day one, hordes of 'Tom and Jerry shops' or 'tiddlywinks' opened their doors. Within a fortnight, the essayist Sydney Smith complained: 'Everybody is drunk. Those who are not singing are sprawling. The sovereign people are in a beastly state.'[39] To take one example, in Leeds, convictions for drunkenness more than trebled in the first 31 months of the legislation.[40] An amazing 24,000 new beer shop licences were granted in the first year of the Act,[41] rising to 46,000 by 1836, one for every 32 people in the country![42] Given that justices had no control over this proliferation, they started granting full licences to beer shops, to enable them to bring some control to bear. So the number of public houses increased 15% within the decade after the 1830 legislation. This had the effect, contrary to the purpose of the 1830 legislation,[43] of driving up consumption of gin to levels hitherto unattained.

It is worth pausing to reflect on the Webbs' salutary critique of this deregulatory measure:

> 'No attempt was made to inquire what would be the effect of the measure on drunkenness and disorder. No one recalled the experience of Free Trade in liquor between 1689 and 1729; or that of the indiscriminate granting of licences and neglect of regulation between 1753 and 1787. ... The decision to allow Free Trade in beer, momentous ... in its consequences, may indeed be cited as the leading case of legislation based on abstract theory – on axioms deduced from first

---

[36]   Webb and Webb.
[37]   Haydon.
[38]   Although the measure also sat well with agricultural interests in the Tory party, and with the Radicals' desire for universal freedom.
[39]   Webb and Webb. While the Rev. Smith's reaction is oft-cited, it contained an irony, in that when writing for the Edinburgh Review four years earlier he had glorified beer drinking for labourers, denounced the justices for attempting to regulate the number or conduct of pubs and demanded absolute freedom of competition in liquor traffic (Wilson).
[40]   Wilson.
[41]   According to the Bishop of Bath, 'every third or fourth house in some of the country towns had become a beer shop' (Webb and Webb).
[42]   Haydon.
[43]   The number of fully-licensed houses in fact increased by 40% between 1830 and 1872 (Wilson).

principles – without investigation of previous experiments, without inquiry into the existing facts, and even without any clear conception of the state of society which it was desired to bring about.'

The picture, therefore, in the first half of the 19th century is of a country struggling to bring consumption under some kind of control. By 1853, Lord Palmerston was driven to the melancholy observation that 'The words "licensed to be drunk on the premises" are by the people interpreted as applicable to the customers as well as the liquor.' The failure of the 1830 legislation provides apt warning that deregulatory measures can sometimes have the opposite effects to those intended.

1.17 The first substantial legislative reaction to these developments was the Metropolitan Police Act 1839 which stipulated midnight closing in London on Saturdays, and re-opening only at 1 pm on Sundays. The measures seeped northwards to Liverpool, Manchester, Newcastle upon Tyne and Sheffield, finally being extended to the whole of England and Wales by legislation in 1848, whose preamble proclaimed that the 1839 legislation had 'been found to be attended with great benefits.' This was not unjustified, for it had had the effect of immediately reducing public drunkenness and a 35%-plus reduction in arrests for drunk and disorderly conduct.[44] In the meantime, Sunday closing was extended by the Sale of Liquors on Sunday Act 1854 to between 2.30 pm and 6 pm and then relaxed in the following year to 3–5 pm and a terminal hour of 11 pm.

1.18 The extended Sunday closures were politically justified by a war effort – that troops fighting in Crimea were fighting drunk heightened the movement at home to curb excessive drinking. It is said that the closures produced a reduction in gin consumption of an astonishing four million gallons per annum.[45] But, with the war over, there is no evidence that the measures continued to be effective. Well-intentioned legislation in 1860, the Refreshment Houses and Wine Licences Act,[46] extended the opportunities for consumption through the establishment of a wine licence and an off-licence for wine to grocers' and other shops. Gladstone explained that this would promote the consumption of weaker beverages and encourage the taking of wine with meals: 'I recommend the present bill as one which will have a decided tendency to the promotion of habits of sobriety among the people by offering the means of reasonable access to the refreshing influence of liquor in conjunction with their meals.'[47] Gladstone was not the last to express this hope, but it was in vain. Fyodor Dostoevsky, visiting London in 1862,

---

44 According to Wilson, the number of arrests for drunk and disorderly behaviour in London from midnight on Saturday to midnight on Sunday fell from 12,357 per 10,000 population in 1838, to 12,178 in 1839, to 7,919 in 1840, and then remained at or below this level (1841: 7,088, 1842: 5,708, 1843: 4,936).

45 Haydon.

46 23 and 24 Vict c 27.

47 Lord Askwith, *British Taverns: their history and laws* (Routledge, 1928).

admittedly to garner evidence for his theory that Western ideas were corrupting Russia, recorded his impressions of a London pub: 'Everyone is drunk, but drunk joylessly, gloomily and heavily, and everyone is strangely silent. Only curses and bloody brawls occasionally break that suspicious and oppressively sad silence ... Everyone is in a hurry to drink himself into insensibility ... wives in no way lag behind their husbands and all get drunk together, while children crawl and run among them.'[48]

1.19   A further attempt in 1863 to prevent Sunday drinking altogether was unsuccessful, Parliament provoked by the growing temperance movement but no longer girded by Crimea. Still more controversial was the Licensing Bill 1871, which proposed a raft of regulatory measures including yet further restrictions on closing hours and Sunday trade. This Bill was withdrawn amidst public opposition, and a tamer version was published the following year. In London, terminal hours were midnight, save on Sundays and holidays when opening hours were restricted to 1–3 pm and 6–11 pm. Outside London, the hours were dependent on the discretion of the justices, but closure was between 10 pm and midnight on weekdays; on Sundays one could drink from 12.30 pm (or 1 pm if the justices so ordered) to 2.30 pm and between 6 pm to 9–11 pm at the justices' discretion. Even this measure was deeply unpopular, and Gladstone lost the 1874 election, in his words 'borne down in a torrent of gin and beer.' Disraeli understood the politics, and soon delivered an extra half an hour of trade to a grateful nation.

1.20   An attempt to resuscitate national Sunday closure, last imposed by Cromwell, came in a Bill in 1889, and evaporated after a withering leader in The Times which richly exposed the importance of using measures other than just licensing control to enforce proper conduct, and questioned whether it is the role of licensing to enforce a moral code. To the editor, the Bill was:

'... an invertebrate measure, supported by flabby arguments, based upon a narrow, vulgar and retrograde theory of ethics, and condemned by our experience of analogous enactments ... To hedge people round with petty restrictions instead of teaching them nobility of conduct and a worthy use of liberty is the perennial resource of shallow and incompetent reformers. A small minority occasionally injured themselves with bad liquor on Sunday, and these reformers can think of nothing better to do than to forbid the entire community to drink on Sunday at all. To punish the swindlers who supply poisonous liquor, to provide alternative resorts to the public house, and to give men better employments and amusements for their leisure than idle talk in front of a bar, would be worthy objects for a paternal government. But these

---

[48]   Fyodor Dostoevsky, *Winter Notes on Summer Impressions* (1862, translated in Northwestern University Press, 1997), cited in Paxman.

things are too hard and not sufficiently sensational for the mechanical moralists who provide the grandmotherly legislation of the present day.'[49]

Nobody attempted further restrictions on licensing hours for a further 25 years. It is right to interpolate that the Times' appeal for regulation based on individual responsibility rather than national restriction neatly foreshadows modern debates.

1.21 While there had been many attempts at terminal hours throughout the preceding three centuries, the modern system of terminal hours really took root with World War I. In a series of ratcheting measures, terminal hours were pegged back, first in harbours, then in certain districts and then countrywide, to 10 pm. Just as the behaviour of the British soldier in the Crimea had resulted in truncated hours, now the behaviour of the munitions workers did the same thing. Lloyd-George announced: 'Drink is doing more damage in the war than all the German submarines put together', followed shortly after by: 'We are fighting Germany, Austria and Drink, and the greatest of these deadly foes is drink.'[50] The imposition of terminal hours was part of a raft of measures, including the establishment of a central Liquor Control Board, with wide powers to regulate supply of liquor. In certain areas, including in particular Carlisle (which contained a large munitions factory), the Board took over the licensed premises and breweries themselves.

1.22 The effect of these measures was radical – convictions for drunkenness nationally fell 84% between 1914 and 1918, while deaths from cirrhosis and alcoholism fell 58% and 84% respectively.[51] As if to presage the child protection objective, suffocation of infants fell 55%. Meanwhile, consumption of beer dropped 63%.[52] In an interesting counterpoint to the legislation of 2003, the general perception was that earlier closing hours produced less not more disorder. The Brewers Gazette wrote:

'A transformation of the night scenes of London has followed from the closing of the public houses at 11.[53] Great traffic centres, like the Elephant and Castle, at which immense crowds usually lounge about until 1 a.m., have suddenly become peaceful and respectable. The police, instead of having to "move on" numbers of people who have been dislodged from bars at 12.30 at night, found very little intoxication to deal with, the last hour and a half [to 12.30 a.m.] being responsible for much of the excess of which complaint is made. Many of the houses were half-empty some time before closing time. Journalists, who are necessarily out late, have quickly noted the effects of the

[49]   Barr.
[50]   Barr.
[51]   Shadwell, Barr.
[52]   Wilson.
[53]   Instead of 12.30 am. It was later reduced even further, to 9.00 or 9.30 pm.

change upon public conduct, and have been spared the sounds of ribald songs, dancing and quarrelling which have hitherto marked "closing time" since war began.'[54]

But the evidence suggests that the curtailment of licensing hours was not, indeed could not have been, solely responsible for the social transformation at home. Instead, the centralisation of the production, distribution and sale of alcohol enabled the sale of lighter beers, while increased price, dilution of alcohol, non-alcoholic drinks and the encouragement of women as a moderating influence in bars in the areas of the munitions plants were significantly contributory factors. Even then, of course, these beneficial changes occurred while the nation was at war, and its youth defending the realm in Flanders. Such conditions never will, or ought to, be repeated. It is poignant, however, to note that the licensing hours which became as natural to the English as nine to five originated with the national emergencies of Crimea and World War I.

1.23   The Licensing Act 1921 introduced the concept of 'permitted hours', setting out a complicated series of provisions governing the times of the day within which permitted hours might be set by the licensing justices. In the metropolis, the maximum weekday hours were nine hours between 11 am and 11 pm with at least a two hour break after noon, and on Sundays and holidays there were to be no more than five hours in two tranches ending at 10 pm. Outside the metropolis, an hour less was permitted on weekdays and last closure was 10 pm. Within these hours, the precise times were to be set by the justices. Special arrangements were allowed for an extra 'supper hour' on weekdays, where a table meal was supplied to the customer and the alcohol was ancillary to the meal. Finally, the justices were entitled to extend the permitted hours outside the metropolis by 30 minutes and to 10.30 pm on weekdays, and to permit opening as early as 9 am, where there were 'special requirements.' In Greater London,[55] the extension of hours had a dramatic effect: convictions for drunkenness rose 39% in the first four months after implementation of the new legislation, as compared to the last four under the previous regime.[56]

1.24   By now, generations of English people had grown up with terminal hours as an intrinsic part of their way of life. So, when the Royal Commission sat in 1929–30, it is no surprise that it refrained from tampering. It was told by one witness:

'The present opening hours have met with extraordinary acceptance by the British public ... The earlier closing hour has been a reform of the first magnitude for the whole country. The last hour in the evening is

---

[54]   Arthur Shadwell, *Drink in 1914 – 1922: A Lesson in Control* (Longmans, 1923).

[55]   The Licensing (Permitted Hours) Act 1934 permitted such special requirements to apply for part only of the year.

[56]   Shadwell.

always the worst, whatever the period of opening is, and to get the streets cleared at least an hour earlier than used to be the case has been an enormous benefit. The health of the working classes must also have benefited through getting more sleep.'[57]

But, in a resounding parallel to the debates which accompanied the 2003 Act, the Commission was told by another witness that just before closing time:

'... customers may be seen clamouring at the bar to gulp down two or three drinks where, in a free country across the channel, they would have been perfectly content to sit at their leisure over one.'[58]

1.25 Following the second World War, a substantial liberalising measure occurred in the Licensing Act 1949 in relation to certain parts of the metropolis. The Act provided for the grant by the justices of a special hours certificate to hotels and restaurants with a music and dancing licence, and to registered clubs with a music dancing certificate. The special hours certificate extended the permitted hours from 12.30 pm to 2 am on weekdays with a break from 3 pm to 6.30 pm. The Act also amended the 1921 Act by preventing the justices fixing the terminal hour before 10.30 pm on weekdays. This, then, was the forerunner of the modern night time economy which has culminated in the current legislation. In particular, the linking of later hours to music and dancing was predominantly responsible for shaping the demographic and style of the night time licensing landscape.

1.26 The Licensing Act 1961 was a major general revision of licensing laws. Permitted hours on weekdays were set at 11 am to 10.30 pm with a break from 3 pm to 5.30 pm, and on Sundays noon to 10.30 pm with a longer break of 2 pm to 7 pm. The special position of London was recognised with an extra half an hour in the evening, and individual licensing districts elsewhere were empowered to adopt the concession. All districts were also entitled to modify the licensing hours locally, within certain parameters. The drinking up period was introduced, although it was only ten minutes long. The machinery of special hours certificates for premises providing music and dancing was extended to the nation as a whole. These changes were carried through to the Licensing Act 1964.

1.27 The Erroll Committee, which reported in 1972, recommended abolition of the afternoon break and extension of the licensing hours, but its proposals were shelved, in the teeth of opposition, principally from the medical profession, but also, strangely, from the trade, which was concerned about longer working hours. The trade also opposed a liberalising measure in a bill introduced in 1976 by the then opposition Tory MP Kenneth Clarke, who stated 'I take the view that our licensing laws are among the most

---

[57]   Barr.
[58]   Barr.

complicated, archaic, uncivilised and restricted parts of our legal system.'[59] Be that as it may, his Bill failed. But 12 years later, the Licensing Act 1988 allowed premises to open throughout the day, and even extended Sunday opening from 2 to 3 pm, following a manifesto pledge by the Tories, whose Home Secretary, Douglas Hurd, described the measure as 'a common-sense Bill designed to remove an absurdity that has come into our law as a result of history rather than logic.'

1.28 It was another Tory, and proponent of warm beer, John Major, who was responsible for finally consigning Sunday day-time restrictions to history by the Licensing (Sunday Hours) Act 1995, condemning them as 'old-fashioned, out of date, patronising, Government-knows-best regulations'[60] which returned the position to that obtaining before 1854. This brave measure unleashed no grave social consequences. As one commentator puts it: 'Sunday afternoon is not the same as Friday night drinking. Most people don't drink simply to get drunk, and even if they do, there are different paths, different arcs of drunkenness, and the Sunday afternoon one is about steady, sitting down, having-a-laugh and wasting-the-day blatheration, rather than adrenaline-fuelled, hedonistic, "It's the weekend!" twattedness.'[61] No-one who purports to write or enforce social policy should be ignorant of these nuances.

C LESSONS FROM HISTORY

1.29 This walk through the history of licensing curtailment demonstrates that the imposition of a terminal licensing hour is no panacea to social ills. Equally, the removal of a terminal hour by itself is most unlikely to produce significant social benefits, and there is no historical evidence at all that deregulation is an effective method of social control. History has demonstrated that we are a nation that sees drunkenness as a consummation devoutly to be wished. Fiddling with the hours at which alcohol can be publicly purchased is a very blunt instrument indeed for reversing the diktats of our ancestry.

The only periods in which one can discern a significant social improvement as a concomitant of licensing curtailment is when it has been accompanied by other measures. Dorchester of 1620 is probably about as far-removed from Carlisle of 1914 as it is possible to be in one country, but what they had in common was a multi-lateral approach which brought together every instrument of social control at their disposal. They were also fortunate to carry out their social engineering against a disciplinary backcloth: the strictures of the Puritan movement and a world war respectively, and enforcement measures far greater than would ever be tolerated today. Similar

[59] Barr.
[60] Barr.
[61] Brown.

effects appear to have been achieved through the draconian clamp-down following the Royal Proclamation of 1787.

1.30 The Parliament of 2003 was perfectly sensible to the reality of what might be achieved legislatively: no less a figure than the Parliamentary Under-Secretary of State in the Department for Culture, Media and Sport acknowledged: 'This is not a Bill to reduce crime. This is not a Bill to convert the morals of the English and Welsh people. That cannot be done ... '[62]

However, the Labour Government believed that the terminal hour caused binge drinking and a mass exodus into our sleeping streets with which the public infrastructure could not cope. It hoped that removal of the terminal hour would help to cure those evils, by promoting a more organic drift away from licensed premises. It is fair to say that the research evidence for the proposition was somewhat wanting, and there was an inevitable element of experiment in the legislation.

Furthermore, since the legislation came at a time when planning policy was to bring more residents back into town centres in order to promote a mixed economy, enhance sustainability, reduce dependence on the motor car and protect the rural areas, the opportunities for conflict between drinker and sleeper were obvious. On the other hand, the pub trade was able to argue persuasively that the ability to operate late at night was confined to the nightclubs, which alone were placed to obtain special hours certificates, and whose demographic promoted a narrow, youth-driven, alcohol-led monoculture. Only the deregulation of the late night market could achieve a greater cultural diversity and age range into our licensing landscape, so producing a moderating influence on its effects.

It cannot pass without mention that, as is so often the case in licensing, there was a double measure of political expediency involved in the deregulation of licensing hours, evidenced by the Labour Party's text message to students before the 2001 general election: 'Cdnt give a XXXX 4 lst ordrs? Then vote Labour for extra time.'

D THE LICENSING ACT 2003: SUCCESS OR FAILURE?

1.31 As one would expect, analysis of the outcomes of the 2003 legislation has assumed a political dimension. In 2010, the Coalition Government delivered this indictment of the Licensing Act 2003:

> 'The "café culture" that the Licensing Act 2003 was expected to deliver has failed to materialise and instead our town centres have become blighted by crime and disorder driven by irresponsible drinking. We are committed to overhauling licensing in England and Wales so that

---

[62] Lord McIntosh, HL Deb 26 November 2012, Col 733.

alcohol is no longer the driver of violent crime and anti-social behaviour that it is today.'[63]

There is in fact no evidence that the irresponsible drinking has increased since the Licensing Act 2003 was implemented in November 2005, or that the level of drink-related crime and disorder has generally risen since that date. However, that statement – more credo than evidence-based analysis – underpins the re-regulation of licensing inherent in the Police Reform and Social Responsibility Act 2011.

1.32   The statement contrasts markedly with the Department for Culture, Media and Sport's analysis published under the Labour Government in 2008.[64] There, a 'mixed picture' was suggested: the Licensing Act 2003 had not led to widespread problems, with serious violent crime and alcohol consumption down, and some improvement in dispersal from licensed premises in some areas, but with evidence of some displacement of crime later into the night.

The Health Select Committee, on the other hand, was rather more scathing of the achievements of the Act:

'Alcohol-related crime and anti-social behaviour have increased over the last 20 years, partly as a result of the development of the night time economy with large concentrations of vertical drinking pubs in town centres. The DCMS has shown extraordinary naivety in believing the Licensing Act 2003 would bring about "civilised cafe culture". In addition, the Act has failed to enable the local population to exercise adequate control of a licensing and enforcement regime which has been too feeble to deal with the problems it has faced.'[65]

1.33   Perhaps closest to the mark was a report for the Alcohol Education and Research Council[66] which stated:

'Assessing the impact of the Licensing Act 2003 will require time. Furthermore, in the light of other interventions – such as the development of local alcohol policies and strategies and encouragement to mount partnership, multi-agency responses to prevention and harm reduction – it is unlikely that change can be attributed to any one kind of intervention.'

This last statement merits elaboration, since it rises above the somewhat crude tub-thumping which often accompanies debate concerning the alcohol economy, and recognises the nuances of the arguments regarding cause and effect. The truth was that the Licensing Act 2003 was not an exercise in

---

[63]   'Responses to Consultation: Rebalancing the Licensing Act' (Home Office, 2010).
[64]   'Evaluation of the Impact of the Licensing Act 2003' (DCMS, March 2008).
[65]   'Health Select Committee report on Alcohol', HC 151-I (2010).
[66]   'Implementation of the Licensing Act 2003: A national survey' (AERC, January 2008).

unexpurgated deregulation at all, but was intrinsically balanced by a series of preventive and control measures to maintain control over the licensed sector. Moreover, both before and after the Act was implemented, the government moved to dilute the deregulatory effects and increase control over licensees.

1.34 First, the Act introduced the requirement for both personal licensees and designated premises supervisors on alcohol-licensed premises, a salutary measure intended to place responsibility for licensing compliance on those with licences, careers and reputations to lose.

1.35 Second, it created review powers, whereby a range of statutory bodies ('responsible authorities') and local residents and businesses ('interested parties') could bring licences in for review at any time, whether on grounds of non-compliance with licensing conditions or any other threat to the licensing objectives, with sanctions ranging from adjustment of hours or other conditions to suspension and revocation. This had the dual effect of curtailing miscreants and promoting compliance.

1.36 Third, the Secretary of State's original Guidance in 2005 pursuant to section 182 of the Act clearly advocated longer licensing hours as a means of reducing late night alcohol-related crime and disorder. Paragraph 3.29 stated: 'The Government strongly recommends that statements of policy should recognise that longer licensing hours with regard to the sale of alcohol are important to ensure that the concentrations of customers leaving premises simultaneously are avoided', while paragraph 6.6 stated: 'The aim through the promotion of the licensing objectives should be to reduce the potential for concentration and achieve a slower dispersal of people from licensed premises through longer opening times.'

1.37 However, the Secretary of State Tessa Jowell was forced into a retreat from this position by a loose alliance of bodies including ACPO, the British Medical Association and the Council of Circuit Judges, who expressed acute misgivings about the policy. Those views were fortified at governmental level by the Home Affairs Select Committee which, in its March 2005 report on anti-social behaviour,[67] stated:

> 'We conclude that there is no clear-cut evidence as to whether more flexible licensing hours will make current problems worse or will improve the situation. We accept that there is unlikely to be wholesale moves towards 24 hour opening as such, but it is to be expected that many licensed premises will after a time apply to stay open longer, and in some cases much longer than currently. Moreover, once one place does extend its opening hours then others in the area are likely to follow suit because of competition. Staggered drinking hours may reduce some flashpoints, but the changes may make it more difficult for the police in an operational sense to predict where and when officers need

---

[67] 'Fifth Report of Session 2004–2005', HC 80-I, para 330.

to be deployed. We recommend that local licensing authorities work closely with police to ensure that this is addressed. In the meantime, we urge the Government to monitor the situation on the ground extremely closely and to seek to change the law if necessary.'

This political pressure, together with a concerted press campaign, saw the Secretary of State resile from the position adumbrated in national Guidance even before the Act was implemented. In a letter to local authorities on 23 September 2005, she wrote:

'The Licensing Act gives power to local communities to decide on closing times, and to co-ordinate licensing with other policies like fighting crime and disorder. It replaces a national closing time, handed down by Whitehall, with local decisions about flexible closing times ... I want to be absolutely clear; where an application for longer hours would undermine those objectives, the public interest should win hands down.'

1.38 This statement, which purported to be no more than clarificatory, was in fact a *volte face*, reducing the status of longer hours from a credo to a statement of good practice to be taken into consideration when appropriate. As early as April 2006, the High Court was able to state that the Act 'neither promotes nor prohibits' longer hours.[68] Over a series of reincarnations, national Guidance watered down its original exhortation to longer hours. The 2010 version[69] appealed not to longer but to 'flexible' licensing hours,[70] while reminding decision-makers that the licensing objectives remain paramount considerations at all times.[71]

1.39 Fourth, as early as 21 January 2005, DCMS, ODPM and the Home Office jointly published 'Drinking Responsibly, the Government's Proposals' announcing a series of new measures for tackling alcohol-related disorder. These included the alcohol disorder zone, closures for persistent sale to underage drinkers, fixed penalty notices to cover young people attempting to buy alcohol under age and staff in licensed premises who serve people who are drunk; a review of penalties for alcohol-related offending; and a voluntary code of practice dealing with irresponsible drinks promotions.

These proposals crystallised into the Violent Crime Reduction Bill in 2005, which passed muster in Parliament in 2006. The alcohol disorder zone theoretically enabled authorities to levy a charge on licensees to pay for initiatives designed to combat alcohol-related crime and disorder provided that the authority in question could tolerate the political stigma of the

---

[68]   *R (JD Wetherspoon plc) v Guildford Borough Council* [2006] EWHC 815 (Admin) at [56].
[69]   October 2010.
[70]   Paras 1.18, 10.19.
[71]   Para 10.20. The April 2012 version finally abandoned even a vestige of approbation of longer hours. The approach is now one strictly based on the merits – see eg para 10.20.

nomenclature. The power was vigorously contested as, variously, unworkable, unjust, discriminatory and counter-productive, including by some police officers, and was never in fact utilised before being euthanased by the Coalition in the Police Reform and Social Responsibility Act 2011. However, the Bill also contained other proposals, including drink banning orders, summary reviews and closure for persistent sale to minors which remain on the statute book.

1.40 Fifth, the Criminal Justice and Police Act 2001 (Amendment) Order 2005 added two more offences to the fixed penalty notice scheme, these being selling alcohol to a drunken person and buying or attempting to buy alcohol by a person under 18.[72]

1.41 Sixth, in July and August 2004, the Police Standards Unit of the Home Office together with ACPO launched the first of its alcohol misuse enforcement campaigns involving multi-agency inspections of licensed premises, together with test purchase operations and confiscations of alcohol from children. The purpose of the campaigns has ostensibly been to improve enforcement practice at local level, with the side benefits of keeping licensees on their toes while publicising the role of the enforcement authorities.

1.42 It is important to stress that all of these initiatives originated even before the Licensing Act 2003 came into effect on 24 November 2005. They reflected an acknowledgment by government that simple deregulation of hours was no silver bullet, and that any deregulation would need to be balanced by far-reaching enforcement measures. This is no doubt sensible but produces an occluded picture which is resistant to such simplistic statements as 'longer hours do/don't work.'

1.43 Legislative rebalancing continued with the introduction by the Policing and Crime Act 2009 of a mandatory code, in fact a set of mandatory conditions on licences,[73] including a condition preventing irresponsible promotions.

1.44 Further still, recent years have seen the inception or spread of a number of worthy national measures which have been designed to ameliorate the detrimental effects of the alcohol economy in various ways. Some, such as the Best Bar None and Purple Flag scheme, set standards for local areas, the former in terms of bar safety and the latter in terms of the quality of the night time realm. Some represent joint working by pubs and bars, for example Pub Watch and nite net radio, which permit the sharing of information between operators for their mutual benefit. One, the Street Pastor scheme, is a voluntary initiative whereby local individuals work

---

[72]   SI 2005/1090.
[73]   The Licensing Act 2003 (Mandatory Licensing Conditions) Order 2010 (SI 2010/860).

together to help people on the streets at night whose drinking or participation has made them vulnerable.

1.45   Finally, in recent years patterns of drinking have changed quite radically. The volume of alcohol purchased for consumption outside the home decreased by 39% from 733 millilitres of alcohol per person per week in 2001/02 to 446 ml per person per week in 2009. This reduction was mainly due to a 45% decrease in the volume of beer purchased from 623 ml to 342 ml per person per week over the same period.[74] Furthermore, as a proportion of total expenditure on alcohol, purchases from pubs fell 12% between 1998 and 2007, while supermarket purchases rose 18%,[75] due at least in part to the ability of the latter to engage in deep price discounting, which is reported to have resulted in the dual phenomena of public drinking by teenagers and pre-loading, whereby individuals do some or most of their drinking at home before they even get to the pub or club, thus throwing the problems of drunkenness onto premises which were not responsible for the state of those seeking admission. Overall, the total consumption of alcohol per person per week fell from 1379 ml per person per week in the last year before the implementation of the Licensing Act 2003, namely 2004/5, to 1190 ml in 2009.[76] It is likely that the drop has been a combination of the recession and changing attitudes, the latter including, among certain elements of the population, the pursuit of healthier lifestyles and a preference for fewer nights out and the consumption of lower volumes of premium products in preference to higher volumes of standard products.

1.46   Social science is by its nature imprecise, but when applied to human behaviour nationally, with no control group and a mass of variable factors, almost any and no conclusion can be justified. To the question 'do longer licensing hours work?', the sensible response is 'from what base level, to what level and under what social, economic and regulatory conditions?' Logically and intuitively, it may be stated with confidence that the Licensing Act 2003 may have had some limited effect in reducing peaks of disorder at closing time, but logic and intuition are not scientific tools of measurement. Approaching the matter more rigorously, it must be concluded that there is simply no conclusive evidence that longer hours do work. The sheer quantum of variable factors, including the regulatory measures passed by the government, the concerted enforcement activity since implementation and the range of voluntary measures designed to alleviate the worst potential consequences of longer hours, mean that the effect of longer hours *per se* cannot be analysed in any scientific way.

---

[74]   'Statistics on Alcohol: England, 2011' (NHS, Health and Social Care Information Centre), paragraph 2.3.

[75]   'Health Select Committee report on Alcohol', HC 151-I (2010).

[76]   'Statistics on Alcohol: England, 2011' (NHS, Health and Social Care Information Centre), Table 2.7.

1.47 What is more, any proper analysis would need some thorough evidence as to how much longer licensed premises are in fact opening. The British Beer and Pub Association reports that the average pub opens only 27 minutes longer than previously.[77] While that average may conceal a tendency for urban pubs to open later than their rural counterparts, that statistic alone recasts the debate as one concerning whether licensing flexibility, rather than longer hours, is an effective tool for reducing the fallout from the alcohol economy. After half a millennium of experience, the best answer that may be given is: it depends.

E POST GRANT ENGINEERING

1.48 The Coalition Government did not come into power anxious to conduct thorough-going assessment of the evidence-base as to the costs and benefits of differing forms of regulation. Both parties in the coalition had promised further regulatory measures. The Coalition was ready to publish its consultation 'Rebalancing the Licensing Act – a consultation on empowering individuals, families and local communities to shape and determine local licensing'[78] in July 2010, within three months of coming to power. Despite claiming to follow the principles of the Government's own 'Code of Practice on Consultation',[79] the consultation allowed only six weeks for reply, half of that recommended by the Code, and even then during the summer holidays, to the concerted outrage of the industry. Remarkably, the Government was then able to consider 1,089 formal responses and 2,938 campaign responses to the consultation and present the Police Reform and Social Responsibility Bill to Parliament on 30 November 2010, less than three months after the consultation closed. During the ensuing Parliamentary debates, there was precious little discussion, let alone controversy, regarding the proposals themselves, the coalition as determined to hit the ground running as the Labour opposition was neutralised by the view of its leader Ed Miliband that the Labour Government had failed to give local people adequate protection against the onward march of commercialisation, including in relation to the alcohol economy.[80] The brake on the Bill's chronology had nothing to do with alcohol and much to do with its far-reaching reforms in relation to the police, with the Bill finally receiving Royal Assent on 15 September 2011. Nevertheless this was a remarkable achievement on a matter of such far-reaching importance – from first consultation to the statute book in just 14 months.

1.49 As it transpired the measures in the Bill had little to do with individual responsibility or the role of the off-trade whose influence over the inebriated behaviour of many coming into town centres at night is now no longer

[77] Licensing Act 5th anniversary – pub trade association comments (24 November 2010).
[78] ISBN: 978-1-84987-245-4.
[79] July 2008.
[80] Telegraph, 11 March 2011.

doubted. The measures, rather, were squarely directed at the on-trade. One block of provisions was designed to rebalance licensing powers both on application and review, away from the industry and towards authorities. So, in both applications and reviews, there was to be removal of the geographical restrictions on individual participants in licensing issues, and an ability for the licensing authority to become involved as a 'responsible authority'. Moreover, the threshold for regulatory intervention was to be significantly lowered, from 'necessary' to 'appropriate'. These are largely matters of process, albeit their impact should not be underestimated.

1.50 However, the revolutionary aspects of the new legislation are concerned with what in this book is loosely described as 'post grant engineering'. Hitherto, the ability of licensing authorities to control the activities of licensed premises once the licence has been granted has been strictly limited. Before a review may be brought, for example, the premises must in practice have been breaching its licence conditions or in some other way harming the licensing objectives. This resulted in the system operating as a one way valve, able to expand at will but only able to contract on a case by case basis.

1.51 Now, licensing authorities may impose early morning restriction orders in relation to all or part of their areas, on all or any days of the week, forcing premises to stop serving alcohol at any time between midnight and 6 am. The Labour Government had placed a prototype on the statute book through the Crime and Security Act 2010, but these could only operate from 3 am and in any case were never supported by the requisite secondary legislation. The ability for the authority to impose a curfew on all premises without actually interfering with their licences is unprecedented in licensing terms. Furthermore, the threshold for such imposition is set deliberately low – it needs merely to be appropriate for the promotion of the licensing objectives. It might be noted, with the enjoyment of the historian in political contradictions, that we have now come full circle in under a decade: the Licensing Act 2003 promoting a move away from fixed licensing hours and the Police Reform and Social Responsibility Act 2011 encouraging a move towards them, in neither case with any serious underpinning evidence or justification.

1.52 Licensing authorities may now also impose a late night levy on all alcohol providers who supply after midnight, to be shared between the police and the local authority to pay for measures to reduce or prevent late-night alcohol-related crime and disorder. The levy will be payable whether or not the premises involved causes any crime and disorder and whether or not any resources are targeted on the area in which the premises operates. This has been a matter of acute concern to those representing rural pubs, which will inevitably be made to pay through the levy for police operations targeted upon town centres.

1.53 Local authorities will also have the ability to recover all their costs of the licensing system, including enforcement and their own responsible authorities' costs, subject to a national cap. This has the effect of enabling a higher level of enforcement work, as well as passing the cost of the entire licensing exercise from local people to alcohol providers, on the 'polluter pays' principle.

1.54 The *cri de coeur* of the industry has traditionally been that as payers of business rates, excise duty and corporation and income tax they cannot be expected to be responsible, morally or economically, for the policing of the public realm. However, the industry has comprehensively lost that debate and, ironically, has lost it to a Government which is bred in the bone to deregulate. Novel powers have been targeted at the on-trade which deliberately go much further than any similar power in history. Just as the first edition of this book asked whether the deregulatory bent of the Licensing Act 2003 would achieve worthwhile public benefits, so this edition comes to be published against the question of whether these measures are useful additions to the armoury and whether, in the hands of the unwise, they will achieve their regulatory purpose without excessive collateral damage to the diversity and vitality of our town centres.

1.55 The Government's thirst for alcohol measures has by no means been assuaged by the fountain of palliatives contained in the Police Reform and Social Responsibility Act 2011. Rather, it elected to ape the illogicality of its Labour forebears by passing primary legislation first and its Alcohol Strategy[81] afterwards. The Strategy promised a series of yet further measures, including minimum unit pricing, sobriety schemes to be enforced through conditional cautions, and promoting the alcohol treatment requirement imposed by courts as part of a community sentence. No matter that the strategy is based upon a somewhat tendentious view of the evidence base. For example, it records the British Crime Survey as reporting that there were almost one million alcohol-related violent crimes in 2010/11 alone (the true figure is 928,000), without noting that this is a dramatic decrease from 1,656,000 in 1995 and 1,105,000 the year prior to the implementation of the Licensing Act 2003 in 2005. True to tradition, the national response to alcohol and its consequences is politically rather than forensically motivated. What is clear is that the present Government's will to assail alcohol harms is greater than that of any administration since the First World War.

1.56 The Strategy sits alongside the Responsibility Deal,[82] which pledges a series of voluntary measures by industry including improved labelling, improved communication of health harms from drinking, more rigorous age controls and stronger industry support for voluntary schemes such as Best

---

[81] 'The Government's Alcohol Strategy', Cm 8336 (April 2012).
[82] 'The Public Health Responsibility Deal' (Department of Health, March 2011).

Bar None, Purple Flag, Community Alcohol Partnerships and Business Improvement Districts.

Furthermore, in its amended national Guidance, published in April 2012, the Government abandoned any lingering exhortation to longer licensing hours, thus removing the last of the philosophy underpinning the Licensing Act in the first place. Now, the question of hours is, as a matter of government policy, governed by the individual merits of the case.[83]

F THE UNIFYING PHILOSOPHY

1.57 It is against this historical background that the second edition of this book comes to be written. The modest part of its aim is to state the law briefly but accurately and comprehensibly. The more ambitious part of its aim is to capture and define in one place best practice in management, policy and enforcement relating to the night time economy.

The fundamental thesis of this book is that licensing in general, and restrictive licensing in particular, can be no more than a single limb in the body politic. A society which wishes to promote mixed use economies must employ every social tool at its disposal to enable night-time businesses to flourish while protecting other stakeholders from harm. In the first edition, it was predicted that subsequent editions would contain many revisions, as the new regime allows empirical experience to replace theory. This has proved to be the case.

1.58 The plethora of new law and best practice over the last decade runs the risk of weaving a stimulating patchwork quilt of measures lacking an underlying theme. The following is humbly suggested as a single 'unifying philosophy' to provide a reference point from which local regulatory work might flow. It is also the philosophy of this book. The philosophy is as follows:

> The Licensing Act 2003 places licensing in the hands of local authorities, which already exercise functions in terms of community strategies, planning strategies and crime reduction strategies, giving them the opportunity to take a joined up approach to the night time economy.

> The Act requires the publication of licensing policy, which involves extensive consultation with the police, other statutory agencies, business and residents, and which ought positively to guide licensing proposals to the right places, and set out the standards which will minimise the risk to the environment of licensing proposals.

> The Act also involves the industry putting forward operating plans, which should reflect best practice in operation and management of premises.

---

[83] Para 10.20.

The unifying philosophy requires that local authorities, working in partnership with the industry, statutory agencies and local businesses and residents, employing all regulatory and non-regulatory measures at their disposal, should foster a climate in which our city centres become safe and attractive places in which to live, work and play. The business of licensing should be much more than saying no to licensing proposals, but should facilitate a regime in which the industry knows what is needed, in terms of location and other operating conditions, to obtain the licence it needs with which to trade, and other stakeholders are clear as to what is likely to be tolerated, where and under what terms.

Licensing, shorn of moral connotations and issues of demand, and directed towards clear licensing objectives, is hence brought into the modern era.

The philosophy is deliberately exhortative, if not aspirational. Its principal aim is that there should be a paradigm shift from the formerly adversarial, court-based system based on 'development control' to a more co-operative system based on 'forward planning'. The new system does not guarantee that this will occur, but provides real opportunities to enable it to do so.

The paradigm shift

1.59 Prior to the Licensing Act 2003, licensing was an adversarial exercise taking place in a setting of conflict dominated by lawyers. Decisions were taken on a case by case basis without regard to any overall framework or aspiration for the town centre involved. Other policies which spoke to an application, such as planning policy, crime and disorder reduction strategies, economic policies for the locality etc were rarely before the licensing justices. The justices could not or did not attach conditions to mitigate any adverse impacts of the proposal, and were left blissfully unaware of modern thinking eg regarding designing out crime. The practice before local authority licensing committees formerly charged with the duty of deciding public entertainment licence applications actually suffered from many of the same defects, and the bifurcation of the system between justices and local authority was a recipe for a fragmented hotchpotch of decisions.

The Licensing Act 2003 provided the opportunity to all players to produce a far better system for the benefit of business, the customer, the residents and the environment. However, for the new system genuinely to work, there needs to be a paradigm shift, characterised by policy-based decision making and a partnership between all stakeholders for the promotion of the licensing objectives. This is well understood by the most competent and enlightened local authorities.

The benefits of the transfer to local authorities

1.60 The shift of licensing decision-making from the criminal courts to the local authority has presented a key opportunity to change the approach to licensing decision-making from the black and white 'yes or no' response to a more sensitive and proactive approach. For example, planning committees are well-used to considering whether the application of conditions might render acceptable an otherwise unacceptable proposal; indeed such consideration is part of their development control function. Furthermore, the development of licensing policy finds its analogy in the forward planning function of planning authorities, whereby the positive aspirations of an area are set out in development plan policy, so that development control decisions are taken against that broad aspirational framework. The best licensing authorities have adopted that approach and made it their own.

1.61   Much of the debate in recent years has proceeded on the assumption that the role of policy is to refuse that which would otherwise have been permitted. This is because the case law has largely concerned negative rather than positive policies.[84] However, there is considerable scope for policy to play a positive role in the location, disposition and management of premises. Nothing requires licensing policy to act only as the executioner of worthwhile proposals, or prevents it from straying into the realms of exhortation. There is no reason why licensing policy may not direct applicants to sites which tend to promote the statutorily defined licensing objectives, or to manage their premises with that end in mind. Well-formulated licensing policy ought also to inform applicants of the considerations or criteria applied by the licensing authority when determining licensing applications, so aiding certainty and moulding a licensing regime comprehensible to all those who work within it or are affected by it. In that way, licensing policies may continue to play a positive role in the development of attractive, peaceful and safe environments for business, residential and leisure uses.

Partnership

1.62   The word 'partnership' has come to be a leitmotif of government policy. The challenge is to translate the aspiration into practice. Often it is understood as entailing little more than membership of the Pubwatch scheme. However, partnership can and should arise in many new and different ways for the benefit of all stakeholders.

The shift in licensing from the justices to the local authorities produced, for the first time, the possibility for partnership between both relevant stakeholders and the regulatory body itself. Previously, involvement by justices was confined to an annual yes or no to an application. The involvement of local authorities permits the setting of policies which, if well-drafted, can promote a positive pattern of licensing, setting out the goals to be attained by the system, and the means by which they are to be attained. It ought to encourage liaison between local authorities and other statutory agencies responsible for the licensing system, including the police and fire authorities.

---

[84]   See eg *R (Westminster City Council) v Middlesex Crown Court and Chorion plc* [2002] LLR 538.

Furthermore, the new enforcement provisions in the Licensing Act 2003, including the wide discretion afforded upon review, permitted a graded response to licensing breaches, to enable a more sensitive approach to be utilised than was ever possible when the only remedy was revocation. The abolition of annual licensing, and therefore annual licensing inspections, enable greater targeting by enforcement authorities of miscreant operators, and a greater risk assessment-based approach by both authorities and operators.

But what opportunities for partnership does the new regime present?

Partnerships within local authorities

1.63 The licensing objectives (crime and disorder, nuisance, public safety and children) mirror existing local authority functions in the fields of crime and disorder reduction, health and safety, environmental protection and education. They also go hand in hand with other local authority strategies, e g the crime and disorder reduction strategy, community strategies under the Local Government Act 2000, community safety partnerships and planning policies, which in turn look to national guidance, e g the Home Office guidance on safer clubbing and the National Alcohol Strategy. There is an opportunity for licensing to pull together the strategic thrust of these disparate functions so as to become the nerve centre of the night time economy.

Licensing officers ought to be the experts within the local authority as to the opportunities afforded by the night time economy and as to best practice regarding proportionate enforcement. That in turn involves acquisition of expertise. In that regard, the development of bodies such as the Institute of Licensing, which sets out to provide an educational and professional net-work, perform a key role in the development of expertise within the system. On the other hand, the inability, until recently, for licensing officers to make representations on licence application or to bring reviews, and the self-denying ordnance of licensing officers in making recommendations on licence applications, has significantly retarded their development as a profes-sion. Their new role as responsible authorities ought to produce a catalytic effect on their expertise and professionalism, for the good of local com-munities. The best officers will seize these opportunities so as to play a leading role in the development of safe, diverse night time economies, just as their counterparts in planning have done for the retail economy.

On a practical level, local authorities which understand that licensing is only one element of control of the night time economy will reap dividends. An imaginative menu of control should be devised incorporating, for example, alcohol by-laws, alcohol referral schemes, safe havens, use of mobile urinals, social marketing, safer glass campaigns, promotion of standards of design and management, town centre design, CCTV etc. All of these activities may have at least as great an effect on levels of night time crime and disorder as a licensing refusal.

Partnerships between statutory agencies

1.64 In the real world of scarce resources, it is important that statutory agencies create partnerships so as not to duplicate each other's efforts or, worse, to permit effective regulation to fall between (bar) stools. Thus, for example, clear enforcement protocols between police and local authorities will be of great importance.

Partnerships between residents and industry

1.65 Under the current regime, residents have a potential for disruptive power, not just at the application stage, where there is a right to object and appeal, but because of their power to initiate reviews which may ultimately lead to revocation of the licence. It will be increasingly important to establish systematic interface with those who have the potential to threaten one's livelihood, eg through local licensing forums. This is more of an issue with larger operators, since it is the all too frequent complaint of residents that they have no idea who the manager is and s/he seems to change every couple of months. An audit trail of contact is needed, both to show the licensing committee and to enable incoming managers to assimilate the drift of the dialogue. The operators who develop diplomacy as a core skill will continue to reap dividends in the form of fewer reviews, better reputations and happier relationships with neighbours.

Partnerships between local authorities and industry

1.66 Many industry figures, having wanted longer hours, went on to resist the Licensing Act 2003 on the grounds that handing licensing to local authorities will produce increased regulation, bureaucracy and political decision-making. Whether or not this is so, it is true that local authorities may be unaware of what the market really wants, so there is a disjuncture between their thinking and the thinking of applicants. Councillors need knowledge of the beneficial effects of good design and management of premises on the licensing objectives, principles of good town centre design and policing as tools for the reduction of crime and disorder, and protective conditions which might be applied as an alternative to licence refusals. Without knowledge of all of these things, councillors risk approaching their decision-making in the mind-set that this is a 'yes' or 'no' debate. They may approach the job of formulating policy in the same unreconstructed way. It has been an article of faith for many in local authorities that licensing officers should not make recommendations to committees. The sooner that ends, the better. Licensing officers should of course accumulate expertise and impart it whenever they can: that is their job. Their new status as responsible authorities will accelerate that process.

1.67 In time, local authorities will undoubtedly ensure that their licensing officers have all acquired all the skills necessary to plug learning and skills gaps, as planning officers have in the half century since the town and country planning legislation of 1948. But for the time being the industry can do a great deal to set the agenda for local authorities. It is suggested that the industry take a pro-active role in the formulation of policies, and a lead in ensuring that policies reflect best practice as they understand it. If an operator is convinced that his high quality management practices are such as to create no impact on the locality, he would presumably wish to ensure that his competitors have to incur the expenditure to reflect the same practices so as to gain entry to, or stay in, the market. He would also wish to avoid being tarred with the same brush as his neglectful neighbour. The best way for operators to ensure that their own high standards are matched by their competitors so as to provide a better trading environment for all is by driving licensing policy, and ensuring that it reflects their own aspirations. In short, the industry should work towards being seen not as part of the problem but as part of the solution. Their motivation to do so is now increased by the fact that the poor practices of their competitors may result in the use by local authorities of the draconian post grant engineering tools, so that they may genuinely be answerable for the sins of their brothers. Compliance by all has therefore become the concern of all.

Partnerships with other operators

1.68 Operators already co-operate on a number of levels – pub and club watch schemes and nite net radio being good examples. Stripping away the arguments, the key question for operators is whether and to what extent they wish to take responsibility for the public realm. Almost all debates in licensing committee and courts come back to that fundamental question.

1.69 As stated above, it is a long-cherished notion in many trade quarters that they have no responsibility for the public realm, that their liability ceases on the forecourt, and that they pay enough through rates, taxes and excise duty to expect public authorities to meet the responsibility for what happens thereafter. The argument has some logic. However, the contrary case may equally appertain: if the very nature of the business concerned has the consequence of disgorging noisy people into the environment, the operator's responsibility is no different from that of the factory disgorging smoke.

1.70 In fact, the operator should no more run the street than the licensing officer the pub. But the symbiosis needs to be recognised. There is a commonality of objective: to produce a safe environment which provides leisure in safety for the user, and maximises the business and employment opportunities of the operator, while minimising the fall-out for the local residents. It is imperative that the tools for attaining these objectives come to be understood on all sides, refined over time, and utilised judiciously.

1.71 However, leaving aside questions of social responsibility (the polluter pays issue), there needs to be a better informed debate as to whether there are commercial reasons for operators to exercise a wider role, in collaboration with neighbours. There are small examples around the country of this happening. A group of operators pays for a community warden in their street. A burger chain sponsors some dustbins. Two operators lend a member of their door supervision team to keep order at a cab rank. Operators subscribe to a minimum pricing scheme in return for generally longer hours.

It is submitted that there should be no *a priori* positions in this debate. Local authorities are not entitled to look to trade as a first resort. But nor should trade expect that local authorities have the resources or ability to produce the perfect operating environment. The notion of contributing economically to the public realm in order to procure a consent is not new. Contributions, for example to transport provision, are regularly made in planning cases, pursuant to section 106 of the Town and Country Planning Act 1990 in order to procure a planning consent. Business have worked together to create Business Improvement Districts, resulting in the levying of an extra business rate to fund public realm improvements, including in the night time economy. If there is economic benefit for operators in pooling resources to produce an urban backcloth which opens new markets, procures longer hours and fends off objections/reviews before they arise, then they should not rule out the proposition on philosophical grounds.

It is appreciated that in a competitive economic environment, the idea of positive collaboration with competitors, let alone contribution to lessening the public impact of one's activities, may be anathema. But the truth is that the best judges of what the market requires, and how best to tap it, are the operators themselves. They are also the drivers of that market. If they can work together to create the conditions in which to develop those markets free from restraint or interference, there is a strong pragmatic argument for them to do so.

The motivation for operators to work with authorities to create a safer public realm has again been considerably strengthened by the introduction of the new post grant engineering powers. Operators who are deaf and blind to alcohol-related disorder on our streets are liable to find themselves clipped and mulcted by early morning restriction orders, late night levies and higher fees. Those who exercise active citizenship in relation to the public realm ought to find themselves rewarded by a more permissive and less costly operating environment, together with better business returns. Therefore, whether used or not, the mere presence of post grant engineering powers may come to have a salutary effect.

Voluntary schemes

1.72 Reference has been made above to voluntary schemes such as Best Bar None, Business Improvement Districts, Pub Watch and Purple Flag. Others such as Community Alcohol Partnerships, which target the causes of youth drinking, have come into being to good effect. The benefit of these schemes is that they involve the pooling of local expertise and the bringing of concerted will to finding solutions to problems in the alcohol economy. Where they work, they reduce the need for policing and general enforcement activity, to the benefit of the whole community, and at negligible cost to public authorities. It is suggested that authorities who, through political expedience or lack of knowledge, reach for the blunt instrument of enforcement rather than the more lucid tools of voluntary engagement will deprive themselves of opportunities to construct better and more diverse economies, and so serve their communities less well than they might. Post grant engineering measures such as the early morning restriction order and the late night levy, may be relevant in some cases, but the best authorities will treat them as measures of last resort.

G CONCLUSION

1.73 History has demonstrated that a coercive, restrictive licensing regime is not sufficient by itself to yield sustainable social benefits. The aim has long been clear. A century ago the then Prime Minister Lord Balfour said:

> 'What then should you aim at? Surely at this ideal, that the public house should be kept respectably, should be kept by respectable persons and should be kept in such a manner as will make those who frequent it obey the law and conform to the dictates of morality.'[85]

The problem has never been the objectives, but the means to attain them and the evidence to justify the means. Just as the Webbs criticised the lack of a proper evidence base informing the legislature in 1830, so Lord Askwith bemoaned uninformed legislative intervention in the two centuries before then, stretching back to James I[86]:

> '... As the bad results of excessive drinking from time to time became apparent or recrudesced ... legislation was attempted, inconsistent, on no fixed or understood principles.'

1.74 The Licensing Act 2003 has transferred responsibility for the night time economy to locally accountable bodies who already exercise powers in allied fields of planning and environmental protection, and are used to exercising their powers against the strategic backdrop of policy. They have

---

[85] Askwith, see fn 47 above.
[86] Askwith. See fn 47 above.

also been armed to the teeth with coercive powers granted by the Act and its legislative successors. The new regime brings opportunities for a more professional, policy-led system of licensing. There is the prospect that licensing could harness a range of thinking across the local authority realm, from the fields of crime and disorder reduction, community strategies and town and country planning, providing a focus for the development of the night time economy. This will require enhancement of expertise within dedicated licensing departments, which in turn raises questions of resources. Local policy should promote a positive pattern of licensing, setting out the authority's aspirations, stimulating cultural diversity, and establishing broad standards of design and management in furtherance of the licensing object-ives. Operators should ensure they are not part of the problem but part of the solution, working in partnership with local authorities over policy and implementation, so as to secure the operating backcloth they require. They should also work on the basis that effective partnership with residents is not only politically expedient, but economically wise. A key issue will be the extent to which operators are prepared to work with each other so as to take responsibility for the public realm, or whether they will maintain that it is nothing to do with them. In the latter case, they may increasingly find that their foothold on the ledge of later licensing hours becomes precarious, rendering them vulnerable to exercises in post grant engineering.

1.75 While none of the recent legislative measures can credibly be said to have been in response to strong evidence bases, in a recessionary economy it will be necessary for licensing authorities, whether in formulating policy or in making individual licensing decisions, to 'regulate smart' by deciding how to target their limited resources so as to achieve the regulatory end in view and so as not to damage local businesses business more than necessary. In many cases, this will involve using collective voluntary measures rather than post grant engineering tools.

Licensing authorities need to maintain an evidence base which they can share with their partners, so that problems can be analysed and rational responses formulated and justified. Otherwise, how could an authority decide whether its cumulative impact policy, Purple Flag scheme or early morning restriction order had succeeded or failed, or should be retained or discontinued? While at a national level there has been a strong political component to licensing legislation, at local level policy and control should be driven by facts and inference from facts, rather than belief and prejudice.

England and Wales have been fortunate to acquire both national licensing Guidance and a national alcohol strategy. There is now an urgent need for new learning as to how these two seminal instruments may complement each other, and how local licensing policy may be formulated so as to play its proper role in advancing the national alcohol agenda.

1.76 Standing back, the Licensing Act 2003 was the greatest social experi-ment in licensing for half a millennium. The permissive element of the regime still remains, but it has been balanced by an unprecedentedly strong cadre of powers to bring the night time economy under control. To make the entire machinery work, there needs to be a paradigm shift in the thinking of all stakeholders, leading to a collaborative, more systematic and evidence-based – and less adversarial – approach, with legal intervention only when, and to the extent, necessary. Where that happens, there is the prospect that the regime will pay dividends, in the form of a more vibrant, profitable, culturally diverse yet peaceful night time economy. The practical mechanisms through which that may occur constitute the theme of this book.

2

Unifying philosophy

We got to the pub and stared through the windows.
The bar seemed on fire with its many lamps.
Rose-coloured men, through the rain-wet windows
seemed to bulge and break into flame.
They breathed out smoke, drank fire from golden jars,
and I heard their great din with awe.

Armistice Day in *Cider with Rosie*
Laurie Lee

A JOHN AND JANE'S BIG NIGHT OUT

2.01 John and Jane go for a night on the town to celebrate Jane's 30th birthday. They've not been there for ages, what with all the newspaper reports of trouble, and they don't have much idea of where to go. Most of the venues look the same anyway, with few people their age milling around. But they see a big queue outside a club, so plump for that. The punters are making quite a din, which the door staff are ignoring. When they reach the front they are not searched and inside the standard tipple is shots, mostly served to groups by the dozen. The noise is deafening and the crush worrying. There's nowhere to sit and staff aren't collecting glasses and bottles – they're too busy doling them out, even to the near-legless, and the atmosphere is hot, loud and not a little intimidating. The odd row goes un-noticed by the door staff but puts John and Jane on edge. Suddenly the music stops, the lights go on and they are out on the street, surrounded by youngsters, some carrying bottles. There are few police, and some people are urinating in dim alleys. Passing by the disorderly melee for the kebab shop they wait in vain at the single taxi rank, pushed past by angry young men, give up eventually on the night bus and walk home. For John's birthday they stick to a DVD and a pizza.

2.02 The picture is deliberately exaggerated, but the message clear. The job of giving John and Jane a good, safe night out, and ensuring they actually want to return, is one which involves proper planning by all of the relevant agencies, working hand in hand with management. That makes not only good regulatory sense, but good economic sense for the town and good business sense for its operators. But what are the main principles?

Unifying philosophy

2.03 The first edition of this book was underpinned by a 'unifying philosophy' developed to inform the writing process. The philosophy, drafted in mid-2002, remains true today and is retained in this edition with only slight amendments as a reminder of the purpose of the system. It is to be found in Chapter 1 Section F.

2.04 The philosophy is perhaps something about which we can all agree. The issue is how to advance it in the complex arena of the night time economy, with its myriad players, interests and priorities. That is the theme of this book.

2.05 Nobody would think of staging a rock festival without concerted planning, and bringing together the expertise and resources of the relevant statutory and non-statutory organisations to ensure the event passes off safely and without undue disturbance. But every Friday and Saturday night similar numbers of people converge on our larger towns and cities; the same web of organisation must be in place. The principles equally apply to smaller towns, where often residents live in closer juxtaposition to the night time economy and there is less infrastructure in place to handle its impacts. The job is not to ask the negative question: 'how shall we control the night time economy?', but the positive question: 'how shall we provide for an entertaining, safe night out for all demographics, whatever their preferences, without harming others?'

2.06 The dedicated reader will note that throughout the chapters, whether they are dealing with crime, noise, health and safety or policing, the same themes re-emerge time and again. In this chapter, we term those themes the 'six-pack'. The themes are noted but not explored in any depth – for that the reader must visit the relevant chapters themselves.

B   THE SIX-PACK

2.07   The six-pack is as follows:

(1)   Local challenges, local strategies
(2)   Partnership
(3)   Evidential data-base
(4)   Risk assessment and prevention

(5)   Targeted enforcement
(6)   Development of good practice

It would be wrong to pretend that these are the only themes, but they are recurrent ones, and serve as an educational tool and model for future debate. What follows is a brief exposition of each of the themes.

(1) Local challenges, local strategies

2.08   The Licensing Act 2003 confers jurisdiction on local authorities, which are best-placed to understand local concerns, and to produce a concerted response by marrying their varying functions in an environment of democratic accountability.

The menu

2.09   Both authorities and operators will wish to have regard to:

Best practice sources

- National guidance.
- Standards and practices set out in local licensing policy.
- Industry codes of good practice, such as those in the appendices to this book.
- Established technical standards.
- Model national conditions.
- Examples of good practice from elsewhere, see eg Appendix 2 to this volume.

2.10   Hopefully, this book will help to indicate the main tenets of current good practice. But it should be taken as given that there is no blueprint for solving licensing issues. They must be solved having regard to the problems, aspirations and priorities of the communities where they arise, and also the nature, precise location, style and clientele of the individual operation. An *a priori* approach is the wrong approach. While the menu of controls and practices is seemingly infinite, it is for those whose actions determine the outcome – the operators and authorities – to select judiciously from it. The question is not 'what works?', but 'from what I have learned, what will work here?' The controls necessary in a suburban wine bar are different from those of a city centre super-pub; hence standard conditions are anathema in a modern licensing regime.

2.11   While this book contains critique of government policy, the text is not anti-government or party political: it is an analysis of the legal and policy basis for current national guidance, and an argument for local discretion, based on good practice, evidence and risk prevention.

Strategies

2.12   It is of cardinal importance that communities take a strategic approach to issues concerning the night time economy, so that decisions are not made *ad hoc*, but are made against a framework of objectives and priorities that are clearly articulated and understood. These strategies include:

Strategies

- Licensing policy
- Planning policy
- Community strategy
- Local transport plan
- Crime and disorder reduction strategy

2.13   The role of licensing policy merits brief elaboration here. Licensing policy is not merely a filter to weed out unworthy proposals. It should set standards, lay out criteria, orchestrate the pattern and disposition of the leisure economy, and promote diversity (in cultural provision, typology and target age) to serve the needs of all sectors of the community.

Measures

2.14   Guided by the strategies, drawing from the menu, and taking a risk assessment/prevention approach, the stakeholders may put in place the measures required to achieve the licensing objectives, and indeed the wider cultural and economic objectives of the area. The measures are described throughout this book. But it is important to note that they go far beyond the mere imposition of entry criteria through licensing and planning conditions and building control. Many of these measures are simply incidents of good management of the public and private realm by authorities and operators respectively.

They include the following:

Public realm

- Guardianship
- High visibility policing
- Door-staff outside premises
- Street pastors

- Community wardens
- 'Capable guardians', e g local residents
- Taxi marshalls

Infrastructure

- CCTV
- Transportation improvement
- Safe transport corridors
- Save havens
- Dispersal/design/supervision of taxi-ranks
- Pedestrianisation
- Lighting
- Bottle bins
- Urinals

Powers

- Fixed penalty notices for low level disorder
- Alcohol free zones
- Confiscation of alcohol from young drinkers
- Magistrates area closure orders
- Local authority closure orders (ASBO Act 2003, s 40)
- Licensing and planning conditions to control public realm impacts
- Targeting illegal taxis
- Dispersal areas (ASBO Act 2003, s 30)
- ASBOs
- Litter control areas
- Street litter control notices
- Directions to leave
- Table and chairs licensing

Private realm

- Planning and licensing conditions
- Police closure of individual premises (Licensing Act 2003)
- Police closure notices (Criminal Justice and Police Act 2001)
- Responsible management
- Health and safety
- Noise controls/limitation
- Design, layout and lighting of premises
- Chill-out rooms
- Responsible server training
- Door supervision
- CCTV
- Admissions policy
- Search policy

- Drug policy
- Pricing policy/promotions
- Plastic bottles/glasses or toughened glass
- Anti-spiking measures
- Anti-theft measures
- Trading hours
- Winding down periods
- Late food service
- Dispersal policy
- Dedicated taxis

Partnership measures

- Purple Flag
- Best Bar None
- Pub Watch
- Community Alcohol Partnerships
- Business Improvement Districts

There is a wide variety of means of funding such strategies:

- Licence fees
- Section 106 agreements
- Late night levy
- Community Infrastructure Levy

2.15   The lists above are clearly not exhaustive. But they help to underline the sheer breadth of measures at the fingertips of stakeholders, whose responsibility it is to implement those which are necessary for the protection of the public and the promotion of their business. It goes without saying that no single measure will do, and that the measures may cut across different objectives, so that for example an efficient drugs policy can help to serve all four licensing objectives.

2.16   But it is also important that these potential measures are understood by licensing authorities themselves, both officers and members. At the policy stage it will their responsibility to decide whether the area's objectives are best served by growth, diversification or managed decline, whether the best route is a partnership measure such as a Purple Flag or a coercive measure such as a late night levy, whether the course chosen may result in negative unintended consequences and whether the risk is justified by the reward. In contested cases it will their responsibility to consider whether such measures may be imposed as licensing conditions in preference to licensing curtailment such as refusal or the imposition of terminal hours. All of this implies a proper training programme for committee members, a continued dissemination of best practice within authorities, and continuing professional development for licensing officers, whose job it is to give professional advice to members as necessary.

(2) *Partnership*

2.17 The list of stakeholders in the night time economy is a long one.

Stakeholders in the night time economy:

Statutory

Licensing authority
Police
Fire and rescue authority
Health authority
Health and safety authority
Planning authority
Environmental health authority
Child protection authority
Neighbouring licensing authority
Weights and measures authority

Other public functions

Town centre managers
Tourism authorities
Transport providers and authorities
Councillors and MPs

Industry

Operators
Chamber of commerce

Trade associations

Pub Watch
Door supervisors
Business improvement district members
Performers

Community

Local residents
Civic and amenity societies
Tenants and residents associations

Partnerships

Crime and Disorder Reduction Partnerships
Community Alcohol Partnerships
Local licensing forums
Business crime reduction partnerships

2.18   Just as important are the **kind** of partnerships these stakeholders can form. Consider the following:

- Consultation on licensing/planning policy involving dialogue within a democratic legal framework.
- Pub and club watch schemes.
- Business Improvement Districts.
- Local licensing forums.
- Joint working arrangements and protocols between local authorities and police and/or other authorities.
- Protocols between police and door supervisors.
- Crime and Disorder Reduction Partnerships.
- Local strategic partnerships.
- Community safety partnerships.
- Informal advice networks between operators and police/local authorities.
- Partnerships between management and staff, eg through supervision by DPS, involvement in health and safety procedures, server and door-supervisor training and the promotion of a licensing-compliant culture.
- Co-option of customers to the safety/environmental agenda, eg through posters/announcements/marketing/education dealing with coping strategies/responsible drinking/anti-spiking/anti-noise.
- Trade organisations, eg BEDA, BII, BBPA, for dissemination of good practice and strategic dialogue with authorities.

2.19   It need hardly be said that if an authority set out to cultivate all of the above partnerships, the outcome would not be strategic but flaccid and would soon lead to overload, initiative fatigue and disintegration. The authority should rather lead a debate as to what partnerships are needed to achieve the strategic objectives for the area and to ensure, through leadership, exhortation and, if possible, funding, that they arise and prosper.

(3) Evidential data-base

2.20   The UK was once a world leader in evidence-based alcohol policy development, but has in more recent times tended to proceed by intuition. It is a recurrent theme of this book that licensing needs to be evidence-driven. To take any other approach is to waste resources, frustrate the social objectives and impose unnecessary or irrelevant controls on the commercial freedom of operators.

Evidential sources

- At local level, the accumulation of evidence, concerning for example crime, noise, injuries, visitation (and times thereof), will help to:
  - inform local policy, eg regarding cumulative impact/terminal hours, to support either tightening or relaxation;
  - judge its success;
  - inform local decision-making;
  - develop best practice;
  - drive future strategy.
- At national level it is for government departments and researching bodies to disseminate best practice based on evidence. There is a welter of DCMS and Home Office literature directed at this.[1]
- England is not an island. But awareness, let alone influence, of international evidence-based research and experience is almost wholly lacking in some quarters.

2.21 In order for a proper evidential data-base to emerge, a common language is crucial.[2] If a police force records a crime at a bus stop outside a night club as 'Crime at Licensed Premises' it will skew research about good practice at the premises themselves. If A & E and police have different definitions of 'alcohol-related', the resultant data will be misleading. A common language needs to be built not just locally but nationally, so that ideas and best practice may cross-fertilise.

(4) Risk assessment and prevention

2.22 Risk assessment is a structured method for analysing risk and the causes underlying it, and devising commensurate responses. As is recognised by modern regulatory practice, systematic risk assessment and prevention is a

---

[1]   See eg 'Good Practice in Managing the Evening and Late Night Economy: A Literature Review from an Environmental Perspective' (ODPM, 2004, http://www.communities. gov.uk/documents/communities/pdf/131197.pdf). See also 'The Practical Guide for Preventing and Dealing with Alcohol Related Problems: what you need to know' (Home Office, 3rd ed, November 2010). NB this guide was withdrawn by the Home Office because of legal errors in the text relating to closure notices; in other respects it is a helpful guide. See also Appendix 11: Bibliography.

[2]   See Chapter 1 of the first edition for a discussion of the various definitions of 'binge drinking'.

far more competent mechanism for handling risk than merely invoking penal sanctions when harm occurs. The principle of risk assessment is a seam running through the management of the night time economy, for example:

- Pre-application licensing risk assessments focusing on harms to the licensing objectives, to inform the contents of the operating schedule and thereafter the licence conditions.
- Statutory health and safety risk assessment.
- Statutory noise assessment.
- Environmental noise assessment.
- Risk assessments by police, to inform an intelligence-led policing approach.
- Risk assessment by local authorities and fire authorities to prioritise the allocation of resources for inspection/enforcement.

(5) Targeted enforcement

2.23 The main purpose of enforcement is not (or is rarely) to punish the miscreant: its main purpose is to secure compliance for the protection of the public. It is for authorities to consider the following menu and consider what action, if any, is necessary and the most effective and economical to achieve protection.

Enforcement

Premises

- Inspections and structured visits: targeting high risk premises
- 'Top ten' enforcement schemes
- Test purchasing
- Licence review
- Summary review
- Early morning restriction orders
- Closure orders (Licensing Act 2003)
- Closure for persistent sale to minors
- Area closure orders
- Closure notices (Criminal Justice and Police Act 2001)
- ASBO Act drugs closure
- ASBO Act noisy premises closure
- Planning enforcement notice
- Planning stop notice
- Statutory nuisance abatement notices
- Health and safety improvement and prohibition notices
- Injunctions

- Street litter control notices
- Prosecution of management/directors etc for:
  - Licensing offences, including breach of condition
  - Health and safety/fire safety offences
  - Breach of enforcement notice
  - Breach of abatement notice
  - Prosecution for offence under Noise Act 1996
- Prosecution of staff for:
  - Licensing offences, eg serving drunks or children
  - Breach of licence conditions

Individuals

- Directions to leave
- Confiscation of alcohol
- Prosecution for
  - drunken/disorderly behaviour
  - buying alcohol for children
  - Persistent possession of alcohol
- ASBOs
- Drink banning order
- Drug/alcohol referral schemes
- Prosecution of illegal taxis

2.24 Consideration of the above list re-emphasises the importance of a partnership approach between the various agencies involved. It also serves to emphasise, as the licensed industry has been at pains to point out for decades, that they must not be made the scapegoats for the depredations of others. They may provide the premises for alcohol to be purveyed, but they did not bring up the young people who visit them, or design the townscape into which their customers are disgorged at closing time. To target only operators may be a less than surgical response to the real difficulties.

Above all, enforcement needs to be applied with a degree of sensitivity, in order to maintain the partnership which it is rightly a cornerstone of government policy to foster.

(6) Development of good practice

2.25 The natural end of a risk assessment approach on the part of the operator and an evidence-based policy approach on the part of the authorities is to build and refine a bank of good practice. It is for national, local and enforcement authorities, institutions such as the Institute of Licensing, trade organisations, professionals and academics to propagate good practice. The message is through national guidance, local policy, codes of good practice, industry codes, regulations, model national conditions, technical standards and so on. The medium is books, the licensing press, the world wide web, published research and seminars.

For anybody involved in the night time economy, be they operator or regulator, it is essential that they have ready access to helpful material, written in a way which will be of actual assistance to them.

So, as good practice informs local initiatives, so the experience of such initiative moulds good practice, creating a virtuous circle. See Figure 1.

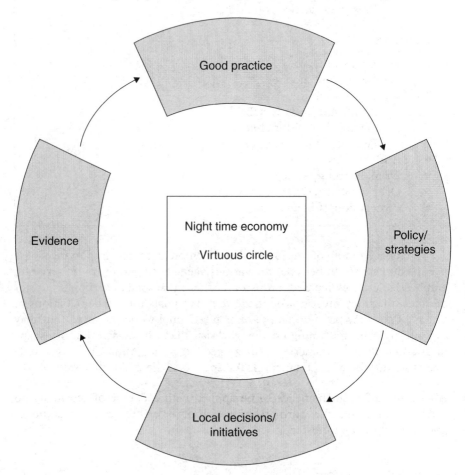

Figure 1

C COMING HOME

2.26 At root this book is about the promotion of sustainable leisure economies. That is a partnership endeavour with cross-cutting themes of planning, environmental, health and safety control, and the development and implementation of various economic, cultural and tourism strategies.

Crucially, in this picture, the licensing authority is far more than a referee of contested applications, once conflict has arisen. It writes the agenda through its policy which promotes its vision and standards. It co-opts the players to its agenda. It prepares the field, in everything from lighting its streets to providing public sanitary facilities. It uses non-statutory carrots such as Purple Flag to sticks such as multi-agency licensing visits. It can raise funds through a multitude of means. In short, it pulls every policy lever at its disposal in the realisation of its vision.

The system simply cannot work unless there is a place where all of the ideas come together, which acts as a hub of the policy wheel. The thesis of the book is that licensing, and more particularly the licensing policy for the area, should occupy that place.

2.27 That is not to say that licensing should dominate any other regime, far from it. But the range of issues raised by the licensing objectives gives licensing a vantage point from which to survey the night time economy, and to bring together the various local authority and other disciplines to respond to its challenges. The conferment of licensing upon local authorities, which already exercise control across the field of community development and protection, facilitates that role. Licensing, in short, has come home.

3

A strategic approach to the night time economy

Behold the rain which descends from heaven upon our vineyards;
there it enters the roots of the vines, to be changed into wine;
a constant proof that God loves us, and loves to see us happy.

Benjamin Franklin

A INTRODUCTION

3.01 It is unthinkable that a local authority would leave to chance the development of the day time retail economy, or its provision of housing, education or open space. But when it comes to the night time economy, the principal determinants of the type, density and location of licensed premises have tended to be the market and *ad hoc* decision making. This chapter advocates a strategic approach and describes how this may be achieved.

3.02   If one is to take such an approach, it is as well to have in mind certain key factors which will affect the leisure economy in the coming decades.[1]

3.03   First, the population of England and Wales will grow. Current estimates are that it will increase from 55 to 65 million between 2010 and 2036.[2] This indicates a need to plan for further leisure provision.

3.04   Second, the population as a whole will continue to age. The only age groups which will grow as a proportion of the population overall are the 60–74 year olds (14.7% in 2010 to 16% in 2036) and 75 and overs (7.9% to 12.4%). Even now, 15–29 year olds make up only 20% of the population and this is set to fall to 18.6%. Current employment data and economic indications are that this age group is likely to be poorer than its forebears. Targeting a town centre night time economy exclusively or even substantially at young people therefore appears to be bad economics, bad town planning and bad crime and disorder reduction strategy.

3.05   Third, global warming has the potential to carry catastrophic consequences. However, over the next 30 years it is likely to render the UK climate more hospitable[3] and the Mediterranean climates significantly less so, making the UK a more attractive destination for domestic and international tourism. Fourth, the emergent middle class in the Asian nations provide rich tourism potential for UK towns and cities. Chinese visitors to the UK increased by 50% between 2009 and 2011, and the trend continues to rise.[4] Fifth, and conversely, the increasing price and scarcity of fossil fuels may dampen the demand for foreign travel, rendering the UK a still more important destination for domestic travellers and those from Western Europe.

3.06   The most successful towns and cities will be those which plan for these new circumstances. They will create and improve leisure destinations which work for all sectors of the community and all age groups, including visitors, workers and residents, and are capable of attracting a tourist market, whether from home or abroad. They will compete effectively with other towns and cities in the region and promote the attraction of their areas as places to live, work and invest.

3.07   The Licensing Act 2003 has been augmented by the Violent Crime Reduction Act 2006, the Policing and Crime Act 2009 and now the Police Reform and Social Responsibility Act 2011. These, together with other powers described below, give authorities greater powers than ever before to

---

[1]   For an excellent, though now aged, analysis of these and other factors see 'Planning for Leisure and Tourism' (ODPM, 2001): http://www.communities.gov.uk/documents/planningandbuilding/pdf/158391.pdf.

[2]   2010-based 'National Population Projections' (Office for National Statistics, 2011).

[3]   See DEFRA's climate change projections: http://ukclimateprojections.defra.gov.uk.

[4]   'Visit Britain' press release, 21 November 2011.

shape and direct the night time economy, control the activities of operators and recover the costs of doing so from operators and their customers. The key for authorities is to use the powers judiciously and creatively to promote a sustainable economy, to reward diversity and responsibility, and to control the errant, rather than to stifle the economy.

3.08 There is no doubt at all that in the name of regulation, authorities now have the scope to depress their night time economies, in some cases severely. That makes it the more important to reiterate that the true nature of the exercise is not simply to regulate the night time economy but to promote a sustainable economy. That certainly involves targeting enforcement on operators who are not compliant or who are otherwise harming the licensing objectives. However, regulation is not an end in itself, but a means of attaining the end, which is a leisure economy which works both for its visitors and also for the statutory agencies and residents who are the receptors of its negative consequences.

B STARTING OUT: THE EVIDENTIAL DATABASE

3.09 In planning the night time economy, inspired leadership is a beneficial asset, but without an evidence-base leadership could direct a town centre a long way in the wrong direction. The maintenance of an evidential basis performs a number of crucial functions.

Table 1: The Value of Evidence

- Evidence defines the baseline.
- Evidence informs the choice of strategic objectives.
- Evidence explains how to achieve such objectives.
- Evidence informs whether the strategy is working and the objectives are being achieved.
- Evidence drives licensing policy, eg a cumulative impact policy.
- Evidence informs whether the policy is working.
- Evidence informs whether the policy is still required or should be changed.
- Evidence justifies departures from national guidance.
- Evidence drives local initiatives, eg youth drinking, polycarbonates.
- Evidence informs whether the initiatives are working, or whether resources should be directed in a different way or to different areas.
- Evidence drives decisions in individual cases. Applicants, responsible authorities and the public should have access to a pool of shared data.
- Evidence drives consultation options, which drive policy, and so on.

What kind of evidence may be valuable? The following table provides an indication of types and sources of evidence.[5]

Type of data	Content/value	Source
Licences: number, type, terminal hours, capacity, clustering/ density, diversity	1. Identifies gaps in provision, overall or for particular sectors 2. Identifies balance between alcohol-led and other premises 3. Identifies over-concentration or supply 4. Identifies pattern of closing times and therefore propensity to cause nuisance or peaks of disorder 5. Helps to identify potential for cumulative impact 6. Identifies where there may be capacity to grow 7. Identifies changes in the above over time, to help explain trends and any need for future restraint.	Licensing register maintained by licensing authority
Planning data	1. Location of A3, A4, A5 and D2 use class premises 2. Indication of locations, trends, likely future growth and capacity	Planning department.
Residential population: type, density, dispersal, location.	1. Growth of population or particular sectors may indicate gap in provision 2. Identifies liability to be affected by proximity to leisure economy	Planning authority

---

[5] For useful data sets, see also M Elvins and P Hadfield, 'West End "Stress Area", Night Time Economy Profiling: A Demonstration Project' (2003); and Dr Phil Hadfield and Dr Andrew Newton, 'Alcohol Crime and Disorder in the Night Time Economy' (Alcohol Concern, September 2010).

Type of data	Content/value	Source
	3. Type of housing (eg public or private sector) may indicate whether juxtaposition is elective 4. Population projections may indicate need for growth	
Crime: amount, type, hours, location, inside or outside premises, alcohol-related, by/on customers	1. Relationship of crime and night time economy 2. Types of crime, eg glassing, causing particular concern 3. Identification of hot spots 4. Indications of cumulative impact 5. Identification of troublesome premises or types of premises 6. Implications for police resources 7. Trends may relate to development of night time economy 8. Data may highlight causes of crime, eg bad management (customers drunk), narrow demographic of visitors (victims, perpetrators and witnesses consistently from narrow age band), inadequate policing or enforcement (eg youth drinking), poor town centre design (eg overcrowded taxi ranks, bad lighting)	Police recorded crime data Police incident data British Transport Police Town centre CCTV incident logs Transport providers Local licensing forums Pub Watch Accident and emergency data Ambulance data[6]

---

6   For a more complete list of sources of criminal data, see 'Home Office Guidance for Local Partnerships on Alcohol-related Crime and Disorder Data', Home Office Development and Practice Report No 6 (2003), and Tierney and Hobbs, 'Alcohol-related Crime and Disorder Data: Guidance for Local Partnerships' (Home Office, 2003).

Type of data	Content/value	Source
Hospital admissions	1. Amount of alcohol-related injury 2. Percentage of all admissions overall and at night which are alcohol-related 3. Type of injury, eg glassing, or type of victim, eg women or minors, may indicate need for targeting 4. Times/days of admission indicates particular problems 5. Location of incident may indicate cumulative impact, hot spot or troublesome premises 6. Trends in data may relate to development of night time economy	Accident and emergency data Ambulance data
Noise	1. Number of complaints 2. Location of complaints 3. Time/day of complaints 4. Type of complaints, eg noise breakout, noise from departing customers 5. Trends in complaints may relate to development of night time economy 6. Normal noise assessments may show breach of levels in World Health Organisation Guidelines on Community Noise[7] and the Night Noise Guidelines for Europe[8]	Environmental health department: Noise complaints Noise mapping Any other noise studies

[7]   Berglund et al (World Health Organisation, 1999).
[8]   World Health Organisation, 2009.

Type of data	*Content/value*	*Source*
Transport provision	1. Number of hackney carriages operating at night.	Licensing department
	2. Number of private hire vehicles operating at night	Transport providers
	3. Number/capacity of night buses operating at night	Highway department
	4. Number of car parking spaces	
	5. Data may be matched to capacity/usage of town centre to assess adequacy of provision and ability to disperse customers efficiently now and if there is growth in premises or custom in the future	
	6. Is there illegal provision? Why? Undercapacity? Underenforcement?	
Pedestrian count	1. Use of town centre at different times of day and night	Formal pedestrian surveys
	2. Indication of cumulative impact	
	3. Capacity of transport infrastructure	
	4. Capacity of street cleansing to function	
	5. Trends indicate success of, or pressure on, night time economy and public infrastructure	
Policing resources	1. Number of officers on different days/times	Police
	2. Ability to cope with existing/anticipated levels of usage/crime	

Type of data	Content/value	Source
Street cleaning	1. Times/days of operation 2. Ability to cope with existing/anticipated levels of usage.	Street cleaning department

In addition to the compilation of the above data sets and their maintenance over time to show trends, there is great value in survey work. At least three different types of survey might be conducted.

Street survey

3.10 A survey of this nature involves researchers standing on the street at night and recording what they see, according to pre-set instructions. Eg they may record incidents of music noise, incidents of drug dealing, fighting, shouting, vomiting, other crime and disorder, taxi touting, littering and fouling, rubbish, illegal parking, queues, numbers of police officers and response by the emergency services. Such survey work is apt to provide evidence of hot spots, flash points and indications of cumulative impact.

Resident survey

3.11 A survey of local residents would be designed to uncover the environmental effects of the night time economy, be it noise breakout, noise from departing customers, general street noise including sirens and car horns, and fear of (and actual) crime and disorder. Undertaken periodically it provides good data on the success or otherwise of mixed use economies, and provides impetus for policy and enforcement responses.

User/non-user survey

3.12 This type of survey is effectively market research to uncover attitudes to the night time economy. Questions would uncover:

- Who is using the town centre at night by reference to days, hours, frequency, income group, age, gender, ethnicity, sexuality, disability, distance from town centre, spending power.
- What attracts them specifically to the town centre? What deters them? What would make them visit/spend more often? What could be improved?
- Who is not using the town centre at night?

● Why not? Market offer? Transport? Other users? Fear of crime? Better alternatives in catchment?

3.13 Matching survey results to the evidential data will help build a picture of what is and is not working in the town centre, and what has to change to enable the town centre to provide and compete adequately. It may show results that indicate a need for substantial infrastructure planning, eg that the range of leisure facilities in a neighbouring town has sucked trade out of the town centre. Equally, it may demonstrate deficiencies which could relatively easily be remedied. Perhaps older people do not come in because it is impossible to get cabs home, which may be remediable by encouraging venues to work with dedicated cab firms. Perhaps under 18 year olds do not come in because they perceive there is nothing to do or because drinking in public spaces is more fun. This may indicate a need to encourage premises to lay on alcohol-free music and dancing earlier in the evening. Female groups may avoid the town centre because of fear of harassment in public areas, which may be remediable through provision of community wardens or better lighting. Or customers may fear violence in clubs, the solution to which may be a policy regarding use of scanning facilities and CCTV. Users and non-users may fear street crime. If their perceptions of crime are exaggerated, the solution may simply be to market the town centre better. The possibilities, of course, are infinite, but the message is the same: solutions are a waste of time and money unless they are directed at known problems and aspirations.

C INTEGRATING STRATEGIES

3.14 Authorities should take care not to reinvent the wheel when developing their strategies for the night time economy. In many cases they may take inspiration from other corporate strategies, namely:

● Tourism.
● Culture.
● Regeneration.
● Crime and disorder reduction.
● Transport.
● Community.
● Equality and diversity.

3.15 Together these strategies set out the vision for communities, by defining what kind of society we wish to live in locally. It is certainly important that a strategy for the night time economy is informed by, and coheres with, allied strategies of the promoting authority.

D   BUILDING THE VISION

3.16   It is suggested that, armed with the above information, the Council is in a position to consult stakeholders as to a 10 or 25 year vision for leisure in town centres. This may be done by a general consultation exercise or by assembling key individuals from each strategic field, eg planning, regeneration, town centre management, residents, business etc. The objective is to ask and answer the questions:

- What sort of town centre do we want in 10 or 25 years?
- How can we set about achieving that?
- What steps can we take now?
- What steps can we inspire in others?
- How are we going to fund it?

The vision may be zonal or infrastructural, so as to:

- Promote a cultural quarter.
- Promote a food-led zone.
- Develop a Gay Village.
- Develop a family leisure area.
- Protect living conditions in residential or mixed use areas.
- Build a late night leisure economy in a zone next to the bus station.
- Develop conferencing facilities with leisure opportunities attached.
- Develop safe parking facilities.
- Pedestrianise the town centre.

The vision may also be concerned with promoting uses, so as to:

- Use the town square for live entertainment.
- Promote theatre, cinema or arts-led entertainment.
- Promote a better age or ethnicity mix.
- Promote live entertainment above pubs.
- Promote outdoor eating areas (eg area with no stand-up drinking outside).
- Promote facilities for local bands.
- Promote dance facilities for 15–17 year olds.

E   FROM VISION TO POLICY

3.17   The vision may then be articulated and promoted through the Council's Development Planning Documents and its Licensing Policy, both of which are subject to public consultation. The objective should be for planning and licensing policy to work hand in glove.

Licensing policy helps to integrate strategies by:

- Setting out the vision. Ie it describes the night time economy to which the authority aspires, both in the public and private realm.

- Encouraging operators to make applications which will further the vision, in terms of the 'what, when, where and how' of licensing, and discouraging them from making applications which will not do so.
- Doing all it can to secure the achievement of the vision through licensing decisions, eg by setting out the standards of management and control which are desired.

3.18 In this way, policy acts not just as an instrument of regulation but as a positive hub for the ambitions of the town to be recorded so as to influence future applications and decision-making.

F SHAPING THE INFRASTRUCTURE

3.19 The licensing authority has little power to shape the infrastructure of the town centre. But planning authorities have powers to do so through planning policy, the use of compulsory purchase powers and regeneration initiatives. The introduction of Community Infrastructure Levy[9] also gives authorities powers to pass the costs of their infrastructure needs onto developers.

G VOLUNTARY INITIATIVES

3.20 The last decade has seen the development of far-sighted voluntary initiatives for excellence in the leisure economy.

3.21 Purple Flag, run by the Association of Town Centre Management, is a means of accrediting the quality of the leisure economy as a whole, in terms of its qualities as safe, welcoming, diverse and accessible. The process of obtaining the Purple Flag requires partnership working and proper reflection on the role and function of the town centre.[10]

3.22 Best Bar None, run by the British Institute of Innkeeping, is a programme for accreditation of safe bars, and has produced startling results in terms of reduction of alcohol-related crime and disorder.[11]

3.23 Community Alcohol Partnerships (CAPs) are partnerships of retailers, trading standards officers, police, health and education professionals and other local stakeholders to tackle the problem of underage drinking and associated anti-social behaviour. The partners share information and training to encourage risk-based enforcement and resolution of problems.[12]

3.24 Street Pastors is a scheme inspired and run by the church to engage with users and others in the night time economy who need assistance.

---

[9]   See Chapter 63.
[10] See Chapter 53.
[11] See Chapter 55.
[12] See Chapter 56.

Although street pastors are voluntary and have no statutory powers, their presence has been praised by policy makers and enforcers as of assistance in reducing crime and fear of crime, and in providing assistance to vulnerable people.

3.25   Local authorities may seek to run individual events or promote initiatives by others to raise the profile of the night time economy and attract new users. The concept of the *notte bianca* has been used to good effect in certain areas, as have 'Purple Flag Weeks' in which a series of linked events occur to celebrate the award. But just as important are attempts to promote late nights at libraries, galleries and other services, so as tempt into the urban realm at night those who may once have come or have never come, so as to dispel any negative myths surrounding town centres at night.

3.26   For local authorities, voluntary initiatives tend to be relatively cheap, but equally they can be time-consuming to administer. The wrong initiative can crowd out more apt programmes, frustrate participants and deter future involvement. The right initiative, however, is likely to strengthen communities and forestall the need for far more expensive and onerous enforcement activity later.

3.27   The role of voluntary measures in the policy mix is consistent with the Coalition's approach to regulation, described in its guidance document 'Reducing Regulation Made Simple'.[13] This states:

> 'At the core of the new framework is a focus on helping policy-makers to identify the most effective approach to achieving a desired policy outcome by ensuring alternative approaches to regulation are thoroughly explored, and that traditional "command and control" regulation is seen as the last, not first, resort.'

H   STAFFING UP THE PUBLIC REALM

3.28   Any casual observer of town centres will see that the heterogeneous mix of users during the day is replaced at night by a much narrower demographic band, often characterised by being young and alcohol-driven. The effects of that are obvious in terms of crime and disorder. More subtly, however, the social norms which are observed during the day tend to be diluted or absent at night. The reasons for that are concerned with alcohol. However, they are also concerned with the reduction in natural guardianship which the day-time economy affords.

One challenge for authorities, therefore, is restoring natural guardianship to the night time economy. The means of achieving that are as follows.

---

[13]   Better Regulation Executive, 2010.

3.29 First, and most obviously, guardianship is provided by police officers. The major constraint, equally obviously, is funding. The availability of the late night levy may provide some redress in that regard, although both the fairness and the benefits of the levy are open to question.[14]

3.30 Second, community support officers provide high visibility patrol with the purpose of reassuring the public, increasing orderliness in public places and being accessible to partner agencies at local level.[15] They are police appointments, and therefore could be funded through the late night levy.

3.31 Third, community wardens are generally local authority employees who provide a uniformed presence, act as the eyes and ears of the public and liaise with police officers when required to do so. As local authority appointees, they could be funded through the late night levy or even through BIDs.

3.32 Fourth, local authority enforcement officers, while unlikely to be as numerous as police officers, provide a presence in the night time economy, principally concerned with late night inspections of premises. Their role ought to be funded or subsidised by licence fees.

3.33 Fifth, street pastors are the example par excellence of guardianship of the public realm, without power but trusted by the public and the police act and therefore carrying natural authority, usually linked by radio with each other and patrolling police officers.

3.34 Sixth, door supervisors are increasingly used to patrol in front of premises, rather than merely in the reception area. They provide a visible presence, are badged, uniformed and often linked with each other through common employers or nite net radio. In certain areas, door supervisors are deployed to act as taxi marshalls. Funded by operators, they act as indispensable partners to police in town centre night time economies.

3.35 Seventh, the successful town centres will manage to attract back a wider demographic mix of citizens into the night time economy, thus reintroducing the diversity and social expectations prevalent during the day. While this cannot genuinely be characterised as 'staffing up', its effects may transpire to be as if not more effective.

3.36 The aim of making the streets at night not only safer but also feeling safer is a central challenge for public authorities, crucial not only for the reduction of crime and disorder but also business growth and development and market diversification. A key element of that is to reintroduce a sense of guardianship of the streets, through all the levers available.

[14] See Chapter 62.
[15] For further reading on role and effectiveness, see 'A National Evaluation of Community Support Officers' (Home Office, 2006).

I FUND RAISING POWERS

3.37 There are more ways of raising funds to develop and control the night time economy than there have ever been before.

3.38 The Police Reform and Social Responsibility Act 2011 enables authorities to set out to recover all their costs of administering the system, including enforcement, through the licence fee. This ought to enable authorities to provide stronger enforcement teams to promote compliance and reduce drunkenness and disorder.[16]

3.39 Authorities may raise money for infrastructure improvements through the Community Infrastructure Levy.[17]

3.40 Authorities may also raise money from late night alcohol providers by way of a late night levy, to spend on schemes which reduce crime and disorder in the night time economy.[18]

3.41 Authorities may also enter into section 106 agreements with developers for the provision of funds for expenditure rendered necessary by the development of schemes which have been granted planning permission. This might, for example, include something as minor as a new taxi rank opposite a new nightclub, or as major as a highway link or new bus service serving a new late night entertainment complex.[19]

3.42 Finally, operators may themselves work together to create a Business Improvement District, whereby businesses within the District pay a supplemental rate to fund a programme, which might be for physical provision such as CCTV or for a service such as community wardens.[20]

3.43 These disparate sources of funding add up to a significant opportunity for entrepreneurial town centre managers, councils and operators to create safer and more attractive town centres. It is fundamental that there are individuals who understand and can advise on pursuit of the most apposite funding streams for the programmes desired.

J CONTROLS AT POINTS OF ENTRY

3.44 Both planning and licensing policy should ensure that desirable developments are directed to the right place and that undesirable development is deterred. In this, they should work symbiotically.

---

[16] At the time of writing, the requisite secondary legislation has not been published.
[17] See Chapter 63.
[18] See Chapter 62.
[19] See Chapter 64.
[20] See Chapter 57.

3.45 Allied regimes deal with sex establishments[21] and gambling premises,[22] both of which afford grounds for refusal on grounds of location, and which should be governed by policies which explain the authority's desired locations (if any) for such activities.

K PLANNING THE STREET

3.46 Although it is obviously more difficult to control behaviour in the street than in a licensed premises, there are various means of doing so.

3.47 Designated public places orders control street drinking, whether by those who would be known as street drinkers or by revellers seeking to pre-load. Properly enforced, they have an important effect in reducing exterior drinking.[23]

3.48 The Highways Act 1980 provides for 'table and chairs licences' which are also an important means of controlling outside drinking.[24] Policies in this regard are sometimes included as appendices to the statutory statement of licensing policy under the Licensing Act 2003.

3.49 Premises licence conditions often contain conditions regarding exterior drinking and also dispersal, which assist in protecting the immediate environment of such premises.

3.50 Traffic orders and pedestrianisation schemes can be used to calm the environment and provide the correct balance between the needs of vehicular uses and those on foot.

3.51 CCTV provision, depending on its quality, can be an important source of evidence in the night time economy, and may also act as a deterrent. Licence conditions requiring premises to install exterior cameras can play a key role in detecting crime and identifying offenders who would otherwise go unapprehended.

3.52 Schemes such as safe transport corridors and safe havens can provide important protection for those who are vulnerable as they leave licensed premises and make their way home.

L PROMOTION OF STANDARDS

3.53 Policy plays a key role in promoting standards in the night time economy, and dealing with problems which have been identified and evidenced. Such standards may be set out in terms of handling of those arriving

---

[21] See Chapter 33.
[22] See Chapter 32.
[23] See Chapter 37.
[24] See Chapter 34.

at licensed premises, the operation of the interior of premises, management of the exterior of the premises (eg smoking terraces and beer gardens) and handling of dispersal. Particular issues, eg use of knives or drugs, may be met by special control policies.[25]

M ENFORCEMENT STRATEGIES

3.54 Local authorities and police have an overwhelming armoury of enforcement powers which are briefly summarised in Chapter 1 and which are dealt with at greater length in later chapters of this book. Clearly, a strategic approach needs to be taken in relation to questions of enforcement so as to achieve the maximum effect for the minimum expenditure of resources, and so as to ensure that enforcement is proportionate and transparent. Authorities' enforcement policies ought to be published, and again the natural repository for such policies in relation to the night time economy is in licensing policy.

N POST GRANT ENGINEERING

3.55 The Police Reform and Social Responsibility Act 2001 gave licensing authorities three key new powers.

3.56 First, authorities now have the power to recover the full cost of their licensing functions through the licence fee, subject to the national cap.[26]

3.57 Second, they have the power to raise a levy from those supplying alcohol after midnight to fund police and authority work to combat crime and disorder.[27]

3.58 Third, they have been given the power to impose an early morning restriction order, or curfew, on alcohol providers, or at least on their ability to serve alcohol, after midnight.[28]

3.59 Well-used, such powers may well bring useful controls to bear on the night time economy otherwise unavailable to licensing authorities. Poorly used, they may stultify the night time economy or worse, and perpetuate existing problems without targeting and rooting out the poor operators. They are important new tools, but before authorities use them, they ought to consider not only their necessity in licensing terms, but also their likely socio-economic consequences, and their propensity to further or foil the authority's ambitions for their town centres.

---

[25] See Chapter 45.
[26] See Chapter 61.
[27] See Chapter 62.
[28] See Chapter 40.

O POLICY AS THE HUB

3.60 The sheer array of powers and functions briefly canvassed in this chapter makes it clear that successful towns and cities must bring together their thinking about their development into one place. Logically, that place is the licensing policy of the authority, where all may look to understand the ambitions for the night time economy and the strategic means of achieving them.

P A NIGHT TIME ECONOMY CHAMPION

3.61 Successful towns and cities depend on good policy and good partnerships, of course. But if licensing policy is to be the hub, this needs to be mirrored at political level. For the system to work effectively, there needs to be high-level political support, both to bring forth adequate funding and to drive the agenda. Most of all, the system requires leadership.

3.62 Within the night time economy, good leaders perform two functions. First, they need the power and charisma to bring statutory and non-statutory stakeholders together and get them working to a common agenda. Second, they need the ability to see the entire regulatory and voluntary landscape and the intellect to drive discussion and consensus on the appropriate levers to meet the aspirations of the area. This might be a job for a town centre manager, but in general a councillor is likely to enjoy better political connections and greater influence. This could be seen as an incident of a Cabinet post. But there is a strong argument for creating a bespoke role for a councillor of 'night time economy champion'.

3.63 The need for individuals with a more complete understanding of the policy options was well-expressed in 'Reducing Regulation Made Simple'.[29]

'It is critical that policy-makers develop the skills and knowledge to creatively consider and implement non-regulatory solutions to policy issues. Equally, it is important that Whitehall provides the incentives to encourage policy-makers to do so. An additional challenge for policy-makers in exploring alternative approaches will be to create the necessary 'breathing space' in which stakeholders can be effectively engaged, evidence properly reviewed and alternatives thoroughly assessed before a commitment to a specific course of action is made.'

Q CONCLUSION

3.64 The agenda set out in this chapter is a challenging one. However, it is a necessary one if authorities wish to evolve from relatively passive recipients

---

[29] Better Regulation Executive, 2010.

of licence applications to dynamic, entrepreneurial creators of safe, welcoming, diverse, accessible leisure economies.

4

Policy as the hub

Up the street, in the Sailors Arms, Sinbad Sailors, grandson of Mary Ann Sailors, draws a pint in the sunlit bar. The ship's clock in the bar says half past eleven. Half past eleven is opening time. The hands of the clock have stayed still at half past eleven for fifty years. It is always opening time in the Sailors Arms.

Under Milk Wood
Dylan Thomas

A INTRODUCTION

4.01 The theme of this book is that licensing can play an important role, not only in the narrow promotion of the licensing objectives, but in the advancement of a wider community, cultural and economic agenda. In this chapter, I consider the crucial role of policy in that agenda. Legal issues concerning policy are touched on but lightly, because they are dealt with in Chapter 10.

4.02 The development of licensing policy finds its analogy in the forward planning function of planning authorities, whereby the positive aspirations of an area are set out in development plan policy, so that development control decisions are taken against that broad aspirational framework. There is no reason why the same approach should not be adopted to licensing functions.

4.03 The shift of licensing decision-making from the criminal courts to the local authority presented a key opportunity to change the approach from a black or white yes or no to a more sensitive, graded and pro-active response. For example, planning committees are well-used to considering whether the application of conditions might render acceptable an otherwise unacceptable proposal: indeed such consideration is an integral part of their development control function.

4.04 As was pointed out in Chapter 1 (Challenges), much of the industry's suspicion of licensing policy derives from the fact that it is rarely a document which promotes a scheme: its usual role has been negative. But under the new regime, there is no reason why policy should not stake out a role as an advocate or, better still, instrument of positive change. Licensing policy can and should usher applicants towards sites or areas where their proposals will be consistent with the promotion of the licensing objectives, encourage operation at times acceptable in the given area, and set out standards of management and other matters of concern to licensing authorities which applicants may then address in their proposals. Licensing policies should thus become the progenitor of a well-ordered, peaceful, safe and thriving night time economy.

B POLICY AS THE HUB

4.05 Effective management and development of the night time economy requires a partnership approach. The list of potential partners is long. It includes licensing and responsible authorities, the licensed trade, local people and businesses, town centre managers, Crime and Disorder Reduction Partnerships, performers and local transport authorities and operators. Many of those bodies will have policies of their own, which may themselves pull in different directions. It is a Herculean task to expect such partnerships simply to arise.

4.06 It is suggested that there needs to be a place in which the expertise, experience and agendas of these disparate groupings can come together to be rationalised into a driving philosophy for the local night time economy. The most logical repository for such pooled thinking is licensing policy. Individual agencies exercise control only over certain elements of the night time economy. The police control crime, the environmental health department nuisance, the health and safety authorities public safety and so on. Licensing policy can speak to all of the objectives of the community, in so far as they are affected by the operation of the night time economy. In short, licensing policy should operate as the hub of the public policy wheel.

If this approach is adopted, it means that anybody who wishes to discover the agenda for the night time economy, be they investor, resident, operator, politician, court or statutory agency, has a single place of reference, the licensing policy. There is no reason why in a matter as economically, socially and culturally important as leisure, which engages the attention of so much public interest, discourse and concern, any person should have to embark on a paper chase through myriad strategy and policy documents to find out what their authority thinks and hopes to achieve. It ought to be discoverable instantly, in a way which informs, reassures, motivates and inspires.

4.07 It is suggested that licensing policy should perform at least four key functions.

THE CORNER STONE OF LICENSING POLICY

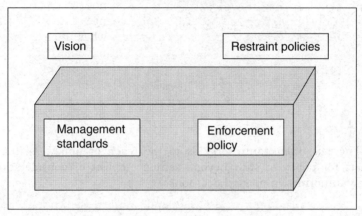

Figure 1

4.08 The first function is to set out the vision for the night time economy. What is it that the authority is trying to achieve over a period of 10 or 25 years so as to make their town and city centres places of delight where people of all ages and types want to visit, interact, play, live, work and invest?

4.09 The second function is to promote standards, which it does by setting out its expectations and seeking to translate those into business practices through licence conditions.

4.10 The third is, where necessary, to set out restraints, which may be locational, in the form of cumulative impact policies, or temporal, in the form of expected terminal hours. Where this is done, it needs to be balanced by zonal policies so that the policy sets out affirmatively where particular forms of investment or hours of operation are actually encouraged or at least not opposed, so as to nudge the area over time towards a consistent, coherent pattern of operation.

4.11 The fourth is to make clear what the authority's enforcement policy is, setting out a transparent position to which it and any appellate court may pay heed, to deter transgression and to give confidence to non-transgressors that their compliance will be reinforced by condign action against those who flout the rules.

THE REACH OF POLICY

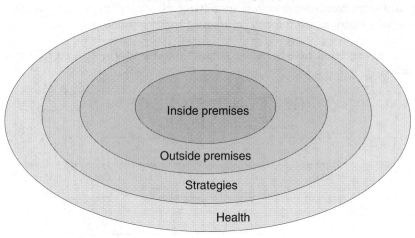

Figure 2

4.12   There is often controversy as to the reach of policy. Is it actually legitimate for policy to stray beyond setting out lists of considerations for licensing authorities in making decisions?

The reach of policy	
Inside	Policy reaches, subject to licensing objectives
Outside	Policy reaches, subject to: – licensing objectives – direct impact or cumulative impact
Town centre strate-gies	– Policy may **implement** strategies relevant to licensing objectives, eg crime and disorder reduction strategy – Policy must **integrate** with other strategies – Policy sets out the vision for the town centre as a point of reference
Health	Health stands outside the purview of the regime The sum total of other policies may impact to some degree

Figure 3

4.13   Policy is, of course, fully able to deal with the way the premises themselves are operated so as to comply with the licensing objectives.

4.14   So far as the exterior of premises are concerned, this has been subject to a nagging debate due to indications in national Guidance that licence conditions cannot seek to manage the behaviour of customers once they are beyond the direct management of the licence holder and their staff or agents.[1] This is obviously true. In the same way, a factory owner cannot fly into the sky to gather up smoke emitted from its chimneys. But, perfectly obviously, conditions may be placed on the factory's planning permission to stop it belching out smoke, and planning permission may be refused altogether if the factory seeks to site itself in an environmentally sensitive location.

4.15 A licensing policy can set out a presumption of refusal of a licence where it is sought in an environmentally sensitive area and is liable to breach the licensing objectives, an example being a nightclub in the heart of a residential area. The basis of the policy, and of a subsequent refusal, would be that the nightclub would cause harm to the licensing objectives, not by virtue of noise breakout, or even mismanagement, but because the mere fact of its hours of operation is likely to cause its departing customers to wake up sleeping residents.

4.16 Similarly, a licensing policy can reflect an identified concern that the concentration of licensed premises is causing 'cumulative impact', whereby nuisance and disorder on the street is not the fault of any individual premises, but is the function of the sheer weight of people on the street at particular times of the night, and the inability of the public infrastructure to cope with and disperse them.

4.17 As regards town centre strategies, one will not find in the Licensing Act 2003 an exhortation to set out such strategies in the town centre. However, this is not to say that, at the very least, they should not be recorded there as a point of reference.

4.18 In some respects it is obvious that the policy may deal with strategies. The policy may actually help to implement a strategy which is relevant to the promotion of the licensing objectives. For example the crime and disorder reduction strategy may focus on drug supply and use. The licensing policy may help to further the strategy by expecting drug searching on entry, regular inspection of WCs, drug swabs of surfaces and the maintenance of drug safes for confiscated substances.

4.19 In other respects, the policy may integrate with other strategies. If the cultural strategy for the town is to focus on the area's reputation for producing live bands, the policy-makers ought to ensure that adequate provision is made for live bands in the policy, by creating a favourable policy environment for such activities, or by nominating zones or areas in which favourable consideration is likely to be given. Or, a transport provider may have decided to lay on a night bus to take customers back to outlying estates. This may gel with a police desire to disperse individuals quickly from the town centre so as to reduce nuisance and flashpoints. The policy may then

---

[1]   Para 1.16.

encourage operators to inform their customers about how to get home, including by using the night bus.

4.20   In all of these ways, and many others, the policy is not merely an instrument which sets out ways for venues to prevent crime and disorder, nuisance, accidents and harm to children. It is an instrument which co-opts the licensed industry to the job of furthering the macro-objectives of the community. These themes will now be explored a little further.

C   LEVERING IN THE WIDER AGENDA

4.21   It is not immediately obvious from a reading of the 2003 Act why an authority should take into account any considerations going beyond the four licensing objectives when formulating its policy, far less when making licensing decisions. For instance, given the phraseology of sections 4(1) and 18(3)(b) of the Act, it is at least arguable that to bring in considerations other than the licensing objectives themselves would be ultra vires as taking account of a matter which is legally irrelevant under the Act. Fortunately, it is not necessary to give the Act such a narrow reading.

4.22   To take a practical example, the Guidance[2] suggests that statements of licensing policy should provide clear indications of how the licensing authority will secure the proper integration of its licensing policy with tourism strategies. Assume that when reviewing its licensing policy, the authority receives a report that indicates a pressing need for late night facilities to serve a burgeoning late night tourist economy, which would otherwise drain away to a neighbouring district. How should this be reflected in licensing policy?

If licensing policy is simply a document which sets out the circumstances in which applications will be refused, and describes the kind of conditions which are likely to be imposed, the answer is that the needs of the tourist economy cannot be reflected in licensing policy. This would mean that the exhortation in the Guidance would be so much seed cast on stony ground.

4.23   The example given serves to make an important point. Licensing policy is not just a document which says no. It should make a positive contribution by stating not just what will or will not be tolerated, but what the authority positively wishes to foster, and where. In doing so, the authority is not guided solely by an arid application of the licensing objectives. The policy might positively state that it wishes to promote the tourist economy, or a particular type of tourist economy, subject to the safeguards of the licensing objectives.

4.24   It is the common experience of licensing authorities that not all licensable activities produce the same level of risk to the licensing objectives.

---

[2]   Para 13.54.

Pubs, clubs, restaurants, wine bars, concert halls, night cafes, theatres and cinemas act on the public realm in different ways. Even to categorise licensed venues in that way is potentially invidious, since premises within the same category are infinitely various in terms of size, character, target clientele, operating style and so on. Nor do premises any longer fall into neat categories. A chameleon venue can consistently serve coffee and croissants in the morning, and cater for an office lunch time crowd, the early evening drinker, the smart diner and the night time reveller. It is up to licensing authorities to keep pace with these commercial developments and reflect them in their licensing policy and decisions.

4.25 The variety of types of venue gives the authority a much greater possibility of producing a positive licensing policy, focussed on how it wishes to strike a balance between promotion of the night time economy in general (or the tourist economy in particular) and environmental considerations. For example, the authority may have received representations pointing out the high residential density in the area, or the juxtaposition of sensitive residential uses with a rapidly growing night time economy. The retrogressive authority will publish a policy designed to halt the progress of the economy in its tracks. The progressive authority will publish a policy positively promoting the kind of premises which it believes will develop the economy with less risk to the environmental expectations of the community.

4.26 The heterogeneity of licensed premises is hardly a new concept. As long ago as 1946, W Bently Capper was writing that the café system 'entirely justifies the Continental policy of perfect freedom in respect of the sale of liquor' which furnished 'a model for us in our development of the ideal of the public house', married to the 'traditional idea of hospitality which was the boast of the old time inn.'[3] For him, the owner should strive for not just a 'drinking saloon', but an 'eating house, a place of comfort and a recreative centre with a healthy atmosphere which no man – or woman – need be ashamed to visit.' And so, more than half a century ago, came the call to arms for diversity in provision, curing a drinking monoculture not through choking it off but by developing it.

4.27 Not only may the policy state what it supports, but it may also state where it supports it. An incoming investor will be particularly interested to know what sort of proposal is likely to receive the least friction, or even be positively supported by the licensing authority. But he will be even more assisted to know where his investment should be directed. That place may be defined either by a map or by locational criteria or considerations set out in the policy, eg that the proposal should be well-situated for late night transport. The notion of showing policy preferences on a map may be redolent of zoning, considered by some to be anathema in licensing terms. But the Guidance does not, indeed never has, set its face against expressing

[3]   *Licensed Houses and Their Management* (Caxton, 4th ed, 1946).

policy preferences in locational terms. It is not only permissible, but arguably highly beneficial, for a policy to state with clarity that particular proposals in particular areas will be welcomed.

4.28 Taking a positive approach may also help to mediate out harms that are identified as already occurring within particular town centres. The current licensing regime has tended to fossilise the disposition and hours of licensing. Thus, a typical town centre will tend to consist of pubs shutting the bars between 11 pm and midnight, restaurants trading until midnight and clubs trading until 2 am, 3 am or 4 am. This pattern has caused enforcement agencies to identify a youth drinking monoculture in the early hours of the morning. Further, once the pub has closed, the only real opportunity to continue the night's entertainment is to pay to go into a club, which may induce the customer to drink up until closing time so as to get value for the admission fee. Thus, peaks of disturbance may arise at midnight and then later on closure of the clubs, with the streets dominated by young people who have been drinking.

4.29 Confronted with this situation, the licensing authority may be tempted to choke off further growth. This might be the right policy response, but it might also be a counter-productive one. The enlightened authority may ask itself whether a pro-active licensing response might be a better one. For example, if pubs, which charge no entrance fee, were permitted to extend their hours, the clientele may be more inclined to stay for a last drink before drifting away from the town centre rather than going on to pay an admission fee at the club. If the authority positively promotes other forms of late night entertainment which are not drink led, such as comedy and performance venues, late night cafes in galleries and libraries, and cinemas, it may find that drink-fuelled problems dry up or at least diminish. If it does this, it may also begin to tempt more older people back into the town centre at night, so that the emergent phenomenon (or perception) that town centre streets have become the night time domain of the young drinker is reversed, with a better age-mix acting as a deterrent to low level disorder.

4.30 While the above thoughts are no blueprint, and the examples are given merely to illustrate the point, the point itself is of cardinal importance: the licensing policy should be a tool with which the pattern and disposition of licensing which the licensing authority considers apt is positively promoted. Furthermore, a negative approach to licensing is not only likely to engender conflict rather than partnership, it may also in licensing terms be positively harmful to the wider agenda. It may, in short, fossilise the existing problems rather than growing out of them in diverse and creative ways. In order for a licensing authority to say no to particular proposals in particular places, it should be positively encouraging that or other proposals in that or other places.

D LEVELS OF CONTROL

4.31   The question is how to translate the above considerations into the wording of the policy. There will be some proposals which clearly fall in line with the authority's policy aspirations, which should be encouraged, just as there will be some which clearly conflict with the licensing objectives as expressed through local policy, which should be firmly discouraged. But between these polar opposites, there is a wide spectrum of possibilities. There may be proposals, for example, which would normally be welcome, unless outweighed by other factors, which may or may not be specified. A sensitive policy, concerned to set out a graded approach, will reflect such nuances in its wording.

4.32   Quite clearly, a policy cannot cater specifically for every proposal which may come forward in the future. But what it can do is to set out the criteria which it will apply in consideration of the proposal. A criterion is a consideration non-satisfaction of which would normally result in refusal of the application. Setting out clear criteria will give certainty, most of all to the operator, as to the pre-requisites which must be satisfied to obtain a grant. Such criteria might relate, for example, to the location, content, style or clientele of the operation, or the protective measures to be put in place.

4.33   It is sometimes argued that a well-defined criteria-based policy is all that is required, because a proposal which satisfies all of the criteria must by definition be one which operates without the negative consequences which the Act seeks to avoid. The clear problem with such an approach is that it results in a piece-meal development of the night time economy, which is as unlikely to accord with any wider vision as it is likely to result in a disorderly development of the night-time landscape to the disadvantage of the community and the enforcement agencies. Criteria policies have a major role to play in licensing control, but they are a single player in what should be a more concerted approach.

4.34   However, to include every single material consideration in policy as a criterion is likely to result in an inflexible, draconian document. There will be some factors which may be taken into account by the licensing authority but will not necessarily cause the application to fail if not satisfied. To include those factors in the policy as considerations will assist the operator to direct his proposal towards their satisfaction, and will help over time to nudge the late night landscape into one which fulfils the authority's expectations. A simple example would be to include as a material consideration 'the measures proposed by the applicant to control queues'. If, on the other hand, long queues were a notorious cause of disturbance, the consideration could be elevated to a criterion: '... provided that adequate measures are proposed to avoid disturbance caused by queues.'

4.35   With the above in mind, it is suggested that there are at least six levels of control, in descending order of regulation. These can be expressed in licensing policy as follows:

Levels of control

- The authority will actively encourage [x form of activity in y sort of location].
- There will be a presumption in favour of [x form or activity in y sort of location] unless outweighed by other [specified or unspecified] factors.
- The authority will grant a licence for [x form or activity in y sort of location] subject to satisfaction of [specified] criteria.
- The authority will take into account the following [specified] matters when considering [all or some activities in all or some locations]. (Note, those matters can conveniently be grouped according to the licensing objectives.)
- There will be a presumption against [x form or activity in y sort of location] unless exceptional circumstances are shown. (Note, exceptional circumstances can be defined or undefined.) The policy may also indicate that certain exceptional circumstances, eg the good character of the applicant, will not ordinarily be treated as an exceptional circumstance.
- The authority's policy is to refuse [x form or activity in y sort of location] except in [defined or undefined] exceptional circumstances.

Figure 4

4.36   A similar, hierarchical, approach may be taken to licence conditions. The possibilities include:

- The policy is to impose condition X.
- There will be a [strong] presumption in favour of condition X.
- Condition X will normally be imposed unless the applicant demonstrates exceptional circumstances.
- Condition X will be considered.

As will be explained later, the authority only has discretion where there has been a relevant representation, which the policy needs to make clear. However, having done that, it may then proceed to create a hierarchy of control in the manner stated above.

E   THE GOLDEN THREAD OF LICENSING POLICY

4.37   The importance of promoting high standards of operation in the night time economy cannot be overstated. Whether one is dealing with the

prevention of drunkenness, the detection of drugs, the protection of customers from violence, the safety of clientele, the prevention of nuisance from
external smoking areas or the safe and quiet dispersal of crowds, good
practice is key to the advancement of the public interest protected by the
Licensing Act 2003.

4.38 It is of course necessary to remember that conditions impose burdens
and restraints on operators. In some cases, a carelessly applied condition can
make a venue inoperable or uneconomic. Furthermore, not all venues are the
same: a knife arch may be necessary at some nightclubs but not usually at the
opera. Clearly, licensing authorities should not apply standard conditions
without regard to the merits of the individual case. Nor should they attach
conditions which simply replicate the effect of other regimes. Not only does
the Guidance make it clear that such duplication should be avoided[4], but a
condition could hardly be justified under section 18(3)(b) of the Act as
appropriate for the promotion of the licensing objectives when it simply
duplicates a legal requirement under a different regime. Books of standard
conditions applied without individual consideration are not only likely to
result in a weight of unnecessary and possibly irrelevant regulation around
the operator's neck, but are most unlikely to be read or understood by the
staff responsible for actually implementing them.

4.39 With that caveat in mind, the importance of having appropriate
standards attached to the licence by way of condition, and then properly
enforced, is fundamental to the operation of the system. The licence acts as a
kind of contract between the operator and the licensing authority, which in
turn is there to protect the interests of the wider community, including those
using the premises themselves. Like all contracts, it should clearly spell out
its requirements so that all is understood and nothing is left to chance. It is a
fact of life that personal licence holders and designated premises supervisors
come and go, and that larger companies will contain levels of management
who do not come into regular contact with the enforcement agencies. It is
essential that all those who work in, manage or supervise the management of
premises can readily see in one document what standards are considered
necessary for the protection of the public, be they visitors, residents or
adjoining businesses.

4.40 The key question is how to ensure that the necessary standards do
come to be incorporated into the licence.

Here, a crucial distinction may be discerned between planning and licensing
procedures. In deciding individual planning applications, planning authorities may attach such conditions as they think fit.[5] The value of this is that
while a planning application may look innocuous to the unversed, the

---

4   Para 13.55.
5   Town and Country Planning Act 1990, s 72(1).

planning authority may realise that it will only be innocuous if some limitation or requirement is bonded on to the planning permission by way of condition.

4.41   The power of licensing authorities is far more constrained. Where a duly made application is not subject to any relevant representations, the licensing authority is bound to grant the application, subject only to such conditions as are consistent with the operating schedule and mandatory conditions under sections 19, 20 and 21.[6] The lack of discretion afforded to licensing authorities absent relevant representations has the potential to cause an unregulated night time economy which undermines rather than promotes the licensing objectives. While such difficulties may of course be cured on review, the objective of the licensing regime should, it is submitted, be to close the stable door before the horse has bolted. For example, one should not need to wait for a bad accident to occur before imposing a condition to aid public safety.

4.42   In this connection, it is key to the operation of the entire regime that the policy sets out the standards which are to be expected, and the kind of operation (whether in terms of type of venue, location or hours) from which they are expected. This then operates at each stage of the system so as to bring about the desired outcome, namely that the standards are incorporated into the licence by way of condition.

It is for the policy to set out with absolute clarity the management standards which may or will be required so as to promote the licensing objectives.

4.43   While the policy is intended to assist the licensing committee in deciding whether those standards are met by the proposal, the policy has a prior, and equally important, effect.

4.44   An applicant for a licence is required to submit an operating schedule which must set out the steps which it is proposed to take to promote the licensing objectives. If the licensing authority clearly sets out in its policy the steps which it considers relevant, it enhances the prospects that those steps will come to be incorporated in the operating schedule. Such incorporation will guarantee that those steps will crystallise as licence conditions, since in the absence of objections the authority is bound to grant the application as submitted, subject to the mandatory conditions.[7]

4.45   The policy is not entitled to <u>require</u> the applicant to incorporate particular conditions. However, it can use persuasive language short of requirement, such as 'expect', 'strongly expect', 'encourage' and 'exhort'. It may not tell the applicant that if a particular standard is not included then

---

[6]   Licensing Act 2003, s 18(2).
[7]   Licensing Act 2003, s 18(2).

THE GOLDEN THREAD

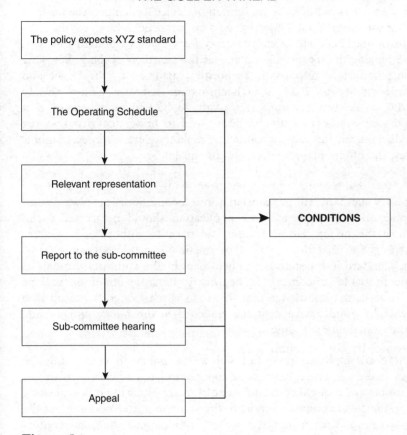

Figure 5

the licence will be refused, because that is not legally true.[8] If nobody objects, then the licence must be granted as applied for, subject to the mandatory conditions. But the policy may explain to the applicant that if the condition is not proposed, then a relevant representation is likely to be made, which will result in a hearing, adding cost and delay to the process, at the end of which the standard is likely to be imposed, subject to the merits of the individual case.

4.46 Of course, it is still open to an applicant to take their chances and decide not to incorporate such steps in the operating schedule. That takes the thread to the next stage. The Act permits a wide range of people to make representations, including statutory agencies, known as responsible authorities, and residents and businesses. Here, the policy ought to provide a benchmark for the content of representations. A representation that a local resident is concerned at noise breakout will of course carry such intrinsic

---

8   As explained in *R (BBPA) v Canterbury City Council* [2005] EWHC 1318 (Admin). See further Chapter 10.

weight as it deserves. But a representation that states that, contrary to the policy, the venue has neither a noise limitation device to dampen the noise of amplified music, nor double-glazing nor an acoustic lobby, so that the resident fears nuisance, will obviously carry far greater weight. In this way, the person making the representation acts as the guardian of the policy. One of the most important responsible authorities, made so by the Police and Social Responsibility Act 2011, is the licensing authority itself. The licensing officer, who speaks for that authority, ought to be vigilant to ensure that applications are consistent with the policy and to bring departures to the attention of the licensing sub-committee by making relevant representations. In this way, the officer plays a crucial sentinel role.

4.47   The fact that a representation has been made by no means guarantees that the policy standard will be translated into a condition. It is always open to the applicant to explain why the application should be treated as an exception to the policy. However, the law permits authorities to phrase policies strongly so that the ambit of permissible exceptions is restricted.[9] Where the standard in question is one held dear by the authority through its policy, the probable outcome of a hearing is that the condition will be imposed. Indeed, the knowledge that this is so is what ought to result in a culture whereby applicants accept the standard in the policy and include them in their operating schedule.

4.48   Where an applicant does not follow the policy in composing the operating schedule and a representation has been made, a hearing ensues. A licensing officer (who ought to be different from any licensing officer making a representation) will compile a report to the sub-committee pointing out the content of the application and the representations and the legal context within which the application falls to be judged. Crucially, however, it is up to the officer to set out with clarity the contents of the policy and the respects in which the application falls short.

4.49   Following the golden thread through, the licensing sub-committee which hears the contested application ought to do so with the licensing policy at their elbow, so that the question of whether the policy ought to be followed or departed from becomes the subject matter of the discussion. Where they impose the standard, they should explain why it was that they have not departed from the policy. If they do decide to depart from the policy, they should explain why they have done so in the individual circumstances of the case: usually this will involve an explanation of how the objectives of the policy are nevertheless served by the application. There will be exceptional cases, but in the case of the central tenets of the policy one would expect the relevant standard to be imposed more often than not: otherwise one should be questioning the rationale for the policy. It is to be reiterated that it is up to

[9]   *R (Westminster City Council)* v *Middlesex Crown Court* [2001] LLR 621. See further Chapter 10.

the sub-committee to place the policy centre-stage in the hearing. A policy which languishes in filing cabinets is not performing its role in guiding and directing the night time economy.

4.50 If an applicant decides to contest the imposition of the condition, then an appeal may be made to the magistrates' court. The magistrates' court must stand in the shoes of the licensing authority in applying the policy[10] and the question for the court is whether the decision of the authority is 'wrong'.[11] Where an authority has imposed a condition as a result of the application of its own policy, this ought rarely to be so. Therefore, it is crucial, once more, that the policy context of the application is correctly presented to the justices, so that they can see, from the policy itself, the representations, the report to the sub-committee, the minutes of the sub-committee, the written reasons for decision and the witness statements and live evidence on appeal that the policy lies at the heart of the case. All of this makes it more likely that justices will wish to endorse the underlying strategy of the authority by helping it to promote better standards of licensed operation for the area.

4.51 The golden thread of licensing therefore works to ensure that the promotion of standards does not occur on an *ad hoc* basis according to the whim of the operator, but that at every stage of the process the system provides and argues for the incorporation of such standards as legally enforceable conditions.

4.52 Once the crucial pathway from policy to licence condition is appreciated, it will be obvious that the requisite step needs to be defined in specific rather than vague or aspirational terms. One licensing objective is the prevention of public nuisance. The policy needs to do much more than say that the premises should be managed to avoid public nuisance. That is likely to lead to measures suggested in the operating schedule in equally vague terms which, if incorporated as conditions, would be void for uncertainty.[12] The policy should suggest particular means of achieving the objective in question. For example, the policy might say: 'Signs should be posted on all exit doors asking customers to depart quietly.' If that wording is used, it is likely to travel into a licensing condition via the operating schedule. Following this reasoning, the suggested form of wording is obviously better than 'There should be notices in the premises asking customers to leave quietly', since this gives no clarity at all as to where or how many notices are required. While such specificity may be thought over-burdensome, it is of course always open to the operator to suggest alternative means of achieving the same ends which, if as efficacious, are likely to be accepted.[13]

---

[10]   *R (Westminster City Council) v Middlesex Crown Court.* See further Chapter 20.
[11]   *R (Hope and Glory Public House Limited) v City of Westminster Magistrates' Court* [2011] EWCA Civ 31.
[12]   See Chapter 17.
[13]   A copy of the model pools is at Appendix 3 in this book.

F THE STANDARDS

4.53 So far, the discussion has been about the promotion of standards without descending into any detail as to what kinds of standards are being referred to.

4.54 Model pools of conditions were formerly found in in Annex D of national Guidance but are now published as good practice guidance on the Home Office web-site, and good practice points will be found throughout this book. The following represents a brief resume of the kind of standards which might be promoted in the policy, arranged as standards on arrival, the exterior, the operation of premises and dispersal.

Arrival

- Queue management, barriers
- Numbers or ratios of door supervisors to customers
- Door supervision companies to be members of Security Industry Authority's Approved Contractor Scheme
- Door supervisors to wear high visibility jackets
- Door supervisors to use nite net radio/bodycams
- Challenge 25/PASS card
- Random search policies
- Club scan/knife arch/search wands
- Drug detection/confiscation
- Last entry times (how to handle returning smokers?)

Figure 6

At the premises

- Designing out crime[14]
- Presence of DPS/personal licensees
- Records of door staff on duty
- Incident records
- Bar refusals logs
- Risk assessment
- CCTV: all cameras set to record, duration of retention, production of images to authorities
- Notifying police of promoted events
- Notifying police of criminal incidents
- Staff training/records
- Polycarbonates
- Internal patrols

---

[14] See Appendix 7 for BBPA guide to Security in Design.

- Inspection of WCs
- Safe capacities/counting customers
- Noise leakage – acoustic lobbies, double glazing, noise limitation devices[15]
- Anti-spiking measures
- Glass collections
- Designated driver schemes
- Off-sales – till prompts/refusal logs/inspection
- Server training
- Polycarbonates/no glass outside premises
- Drug controls: staff training, monitoring, swabbing, inspection of WCs, confiscation, drug safes.[16]
- Emergency contact numbers for management

Figure 7

Exterior areas (beer gardens, forecourts, smoking areas)

- Delineation of area. Rope barriers?
- Supervision
- No drinks to be taken outside at all/from x o'clock
- Curfew
- How many customers allowed out simultaneously?
- CCTV
- Cleaning
- Times of deliveries and refuse collection
- Dropping glass in outside bins

Figure 8

Leaving

- Neighbour courtesy notices
- Get home safely posters
- Dispersal policies[17]
- Winding down period
- Dedicated taxi service
- Instruction of taxi companies on hooting, queuing, idling
- Door supervisors
- Exterior clean-up

Figure 9

[15]   See Appendix 5 for BBPA guide to Noise Control
[16]   See Appendix 4 for BBPA guide to Drugs and Pubs.
[17]   See Appendix 3 for NOCTIS guide to Dispersal Policies

G RESTRAINT POLICIES

4.55 The term 'restraint policies' is not found in the Act or the Guidance. It is a catch-all phrase here used for:

- Cumulative stress policies, which presume against applications to a greater or lesser degree because of cumulative impact, whereby a concentration of premises is collectively causing intractable harm to the licensing objectives.
- Zonal policies, which presume against particular types of premises, or particular hours, in particular zones, eg residential or family leisure areas.
- Terminal hours policies, which set presumptions or guidelines as to terminal hours.

4.56 National Guidance initially set out to limit the reach of such policies, largely as a concomitant of the Labour Government's core licensing philosophy: longer hours good, fixed hours bad. It said that fixed terminal hours policy would cut across the exhortation to longer hours. Zonal policies would create peaks of disturbance at closing time and impose fixed terminal hours by the back door. Cumulative impact policies should not be used to fix terminal hours, restrain off-licences or influence the result of reviews. The formulation of the first national Guidance was also influenced by the view, later discarded, that licensing did not speak to activities of customers once they had left the licensed premises.

4.57 These arguments and policy positions were all canvassed, dissected and contested at length in the first edition of this book, to which the reader is respectfully referred.[18] It was argued that national Guidance was largely misguided, that such policies may indeed be apposite, and could be imposed, if need be as departures from Guidance, where this was necessary to promote the licensing objectives. It was suggested that authorities ought to take the steps which were appropriate to promote the licensing objectives locally, to create certainty and confidence among residents and businesses, and to promote positive patterns of licensing across our administrative areas. Certain authorities did expressly depart from national Guidance, and no such policies were challenged, let alone successfully.

4.58 As time passed, the Guidance was diluted in several respects, and ultimately the Coalition indicated that authorities should be free to create such policies as they see fit. The net effect is that, where appropriate, such policies may be imposed with the blessing of the Guidance rather than in defiance of it. As to that, some pertinent observations may be made.

4.59 First, it is absolutely right that an authority which has a mind to promoting the leisure economy while protecting local residents should be

---

[18] See the first edition of this book, Chapter 22.

able to create locational and hours policies to set out its likely attitude to applications. This helps operators to decide where to place their investments, and gives residents the confidence to move into particular locations in the safe knowledge of what is, and is not, likely to be tolerated.

4.60 Second, however, every restraint policy potentially deters investment, frustrates legitimate business aspirations and reduces the economic potential of the area.

4.61 Third, therefore, restraint policies should go no further than is genuinely appropriate for the promotion of the licensing objectives. In some cases, they will not be needed at all. The concern to achieve a particular objective may be satisfactorily achieved through a criteria-based policy.

4.62 Fourth, authorities which are minded to impose restraint policies should balance the negative aspects of policy with positive enthusiasm for that which they wish to see developed. So it would be a major disappointment to lose the investment, jobs and leisure and tourism potential associated with a major entertainment complex because of a zonal policy which set its face against such developments in one part of the town, unless in another part of the town the policy welcomes that form of development.

4.63 Similarly, in a cumulative impact area, the problem may have been identified of a surfeit of alcohol-led premises. So be it. But that is not a reason for the policy to operate in a blanket manner so as to set its face against performance venues. Or the stress in a cumulative impact area may have been identified to arise after public transport ceases at midnight. Therefore, the logical policy response is to permit applications with closing hour up to midnight.

4.64 These considerations lead to the proposal of a matrix approach, where the following questions are asked:

- What type/category of activity is proposed? Is it one that policy encourages?
- Where is it proposed? Is it in area that policy encourages?
- At what times is it proposed? Is it at a time that policy encourages?

The type of activity, location and hours would then be dealt with in a policy which uses the hierarchy of control discussed earlier from encouragement to discouragement.

An example of how the policy matrix might work is as follows:

Matrix example			
Activity/Time	**Stress area**	**Leisure area**	**Other**
Pubs up to midnight	Must demonstrate will not add to cumulative impact	Will be granted provided they do not harm licensing objectives	Will be judged according to the following criteria ...
Pubs beyond midnight	Will be refused except in exceptional circumstances	Will normally be granted provided they do not harm the licensing objectives	Will be refused unless they satisfy the following criteria
Restaurants	Will generally be granted, subject to the relevant criteria	Will be granted unless it is proved that they will harm the licensing objectives	Will normally be granted, subject to satisfaction of the relevant criteria

Figure 10

4.65 Of course, it is not suggested that an actual matrix must be set out in the policy, although it could be used to summarise the policy framework. The purpose of the matrix is to avoid a blanket approach, but to ensure that the policy asks the fundamental questions of licensing – what? where? when? and how? – and then allocates the application spatially and temporally according to the answer. In this way, the vision for the area is pursued while unacceptable harm is avoided.

Cumulative stress policies

4.66 The steps towards adoption of a cumulative impact policy are described in national Guidance.[19] The potential sources of material justifying the policy are set out, many of which, such as crime and disorder data and environmental health complaints, will be readily accessible to the licensing authority. Authorities should take care to ensure that policies are properly directed and do no more than is necessary to address the problem identified. So, if issue of stress arise after midnight, there is no policy justification for restraining trade before midnight. If the issues are caused by customers of nightclubs, there is no justification for restraining the proliferation of performance venues. If the issues occur in one area of the town centre, that

[19] Para 13.23 et seq.

does not in and of itself justify the spread of the policy to the entire centre, and so forth. Furthermore, restraint policies should be balanced by positive policies which state where particular types of venue and hours of operation are likely to be welcomed, so as to promote investment, create diversity and produce an entertaining, attractive leisure-mix.

4.67 The 2012 Guidance does not exhibit the vices of its forebears by preventing terminal hours policies as a response to cumulative impact. That was always likely to have the opposite effect to that intended, by restraining investment in harmless premises which wished to trade to an earlier hour, which hoped to provide alternatives to those venues which were the cause of concern, and which aspired to attract back to the town centre those put off by the existing offer.

4.68 The 2012 Guidance also moves away from the stance that a concentration of off-licences may not justify a cumulative impact policy. Dependent upon the local circumstances, they may well do so. Some off-licences may be responsible for pre-loading, street drinking, youth drinking and even parallel loading (drinking alternately pub-bought and shop-bought alcohol). Further, a concentration of off-licences may result in price competition which acts as a magnet to drinkers. Where there is cumulative impact caused by off-licences, there is no reason why there should not be a policy response, provided that the reason for the policy is clearly articulated.

4.69 The Guidance, however, still exhibits a confusion which equally beleaguered its ancestors. It correctly states that the effect of a cumulative impact policy is to create a rebuttable presumption that applications contrary to the policy will be refused if relevant representations are made. However, it then states:

> 'If the licensing authority decides that an application should be refused, it will still need to show that the grant of the application would undermine the promotion of one of the licensing objectives and that appropriate conditions would be ineffective in preventing the problems involved.'[20]

4.70 This approach spins the evidentiary burden onto the licensing authority to show that there would be harm to one of the licensing objectives. This is inimical to the concept of presumptive policies, which presuppose that it is for the party seeking a departure from the policy to show why the proposal would not harm the objectives of the policy. If a refusal to grant an application which breaches the policy is appealed, the question of the burden assumes real importance. If the authority is obliged to present all the data and thinking which underlay the adoption of the policy in the first place, this is liable to lead to an undue proliferation of evidence and argument before the magistrates' court, leading to repeated scrutiny of the merits of having

---

[20] Para 13.35.

the policy. This in turn will place a strain both on the resources of the licensing authority and the court.

Furthermore, the court, unlike the licensing authority, is neither elected nor appointed under the legislation to weigh the considerations which mould and inform a statutory licensing policy. The authority should rather be able to adduce its policy in answer to the proposal, leaving it to the applicant to show how the proposal will not harm the objectives of the policy, and therefore will not harm the statutory licensing objectives. This is consistent with the role of negative policies in licensing and administrative law generally, whereby it is open to an authority to create a rebuttable presumption in its policy, which casts the onus onto the applicant to demonstrate reasons why there ought to be a departure. It is also consistent with the nature of the rebuttable presumption described in the Guidance itself. It is therefore suggested that in this respect the Guidance does not correctly state the law.

Zonal policies

4.71   The 2012 Guidance has completely abandoned the previous discouragement of zonal policies. It is suggested that zonal policies may play an important role in creating a sustainable pattern of licensing in modern, mixed-use urban environments. Indeed, as society moves towards a 24 hour economy they may become the most important element of licensing policy. Many people may choose to move into a residential area simply because it is quite at night, and wish to have confidence in doing so that the licensing authority will set its face against late operating premises there. Others may choose to live in the town centre so as to be able to access a vibrant night time economy. Even those people, however, may blanch at the thought of round-the-clock revels. So there may be room for a leisure zone where, due to the absence of residential occupiers, nuisance is simply not a problem. A competent licensing authority may be moved, following consultation, to promulgate a licensing policy which respects these distinctions through differential terminal hours, protecting the residential areas, allowing for a balanced approach in town centres and exercising much greater freedom in leisure zones. Investors may well be grateful for the certainty which such an approach brings, so that they may target their proposals in the right area, and so as to attract assent and not opposition. In this way, authorities will play a key role in promoting a diverse, well-ordered night time economy. Leaving the matter to an *ad hoc,* case by case approach is, arguably, a dereliction of responsibility which will leave the authorities and the community to see licensed premises as a threat, and to spend their time fighting against the tide rather than channeling commercial demand for later hours to the right locations.

Terminal hours

4.72 Once the mantra of longer licensing hours which underpinned so much of the discourse during the passage of the Licensing Bill is abandoned, it becomes clear that authorities can take an approach as to hours which is most suited to their area. This may result in a case by case approach, with principles or criteria by which to judge the application if objection is made. It may state that applications up to a particular hour will normally be granted while applications beyond that hour would need to carry a higher level of justification and/or positively demonstrate that they will not offend the licensing objectives and/or satisfy policy criteria. It may set different thresholds for different activities, e g food-led, performance-led or drink-led premises. It may result in the setting of zones over part or all of the administrative area. It may similarly result in cumulative impact policies. Or it may result in a mixture of the three. These are all pre-eminently a matter for the licensing authority, which has been entrusted by Parliament to make these kind of balanced judgments, informed by local experience, evidence and consultation.

4.73 At its most basic level, the mantra of longer hours was misguided. It was nourished by the thought that giving people longer hours in which to drink may result in a more organic departure from premises and a reduction of conflict accompanying mass departure. Those ills no doubt occurred, or still occur, in many premises. But they are not universal. Where there is no mass departure, there is no policy imperative to longer hours. So far as nuisance is concerned, residents may be disturbed by noise upon departure, but prefer that it is all contained within a fixed period rather than being dispersed throughout the night. Responsible authorities may indeed have no trouble coping with the impact of departure at a fixed hour, while being unable to muster sufficient resources to police the town throughout the night. They may therefore regard an earlier terminal hour as preferable. There is no universal answer to these issues: all will turn on the individual circumstances of individual locations.

4.74 Therefore, while the licensing authority is not obliged to set a terminal hour, it may do so for all or particular types or locations of premises where it considers this appropriate to promote the licensing objectives. The freedom of authorities to do that which is expedient for their own local areas is embodied in the Guidance:

> '10.11 The Government acknowledges that different licensing strategies may be appropriate for the promotion of the licensing objectives in different areas. The 2003 Act gives the licensing authority power to make decisions regarding licensed opening hours as part of the implementation of its licensing policy statement and licensing authorities are best placed to make decisions about appropriate opening hours in their areas based

on their local knowledge and in consultation with responsible authorities. However, licensing authorities must always consider each application and must not impose predetermined licensed opening hours, without giving individual consideration to the merits of each application.'

H JUSTIFYING THE POLICY

4.75   A licensing policy is, at very least, a starting point for the consideration of a licensing application, whether by the authority itself or by the magistrates court on appeal. This carries various benefits, such as a consistent approach to decision-making, clarity and transparency. It also means that the licensing authority is not required to unfurl the evidential base which was the original justification for the policy on each occasion when an application is contested.

4.76   For example, police evidence that there is a serious problem of crime and disorder in the town centre may have been the product of research from many different sources. It would place an intolerable burden on police to have to bring forth all of the underlying research every time a licensing decision falls to be made. Nor should residents' groups, who have compiled the evidence of nuisance which led to a terminal hours policy, have to reheat their evidence for every application. Instead, the policy can and should set out the underlying concern, so that it can be readily understood by applicant, objector or decision-maker alike. In most cases, this will lead to speedier and more efficient decision-making, avoiding the need to rake over evidence which informed the evolution of the policy.

4.77   The corollary of this is that a policy which fails to set out the underlying rationale, particularly where the policy is restrictive, is liable to receive less weight by the decision-maker. If the decision-maker cannot understand the reason for having the policy, he is unlikely to allow it to lead him by the nose: the policy is the servant and not the master of good decision-making.

4.78   More than this, the policy is not an end in itself, but a means of attaining a set of objectives. When confronted with a proposal which amounts to a departure from policy, a key consideration for the decision-maker is whether the objectives of the policy would be met by the proposal.[21] Of course, in order for applicants to be able to direct their proposals at alleviation of a particular concern, they need to know clearly what the concern was which justified the inclusion of the policy in the first place. Thus, it is good sense for the policy, and a restrictive policy in particular, to spell out the underlying concern and to summarise the evidence underpinning it. If it does that, it is more likely to achieve 'buy-in' to the policy

---

[21]   See further Chapter 15.

objectives by relevant stakeholders and decision-makers, and to ensure that even departures from policy are rational and responsive to the policy objectives.

I THE EVIDENTIAL BASE

4.79 Clearly, the exercise of licensing powers, both in the formulation of licensing policy and the making of licensing decisions, involves some ordering of political priorities. The desire for a good night's sleep and the desire for a good night out cannot be nicely weighed and balanced in grams. But this is no excuse for acting on political whim.

4.80 To the extent that licensing powers are exercised so as to restrict the commercial freedom of operators, they need to be objectively justified so far as possible. So far as some incursion is to be made on the peace of adjoining occupiers, such incursion should be objectively measurable, to the extent achievable.

4.81 But prior even to the formulation or review of licensing policy, there should be an evidential base. The purpose of such a base is, initially, to inform licensing policy. Following promulgation of the initial policy, ongoing development of the base enables the licensing authority to monitor the success of the policy. If the policy has been adopted, for example, because of a concern regarding crime, the authority should be able at any time to say whether the crime figures which led to adoption of the policy in the first place are improving or worsening.

4.82 Further, departures from national Guidance are permissible, provided of course that there is reasoned justification for the departure, as the Guidance itself recognises.[22] Where the justification for the departure can be proved by evidence, that evidence should be summarised in the policy itself as part of the justification.

4.83 This is very far from saying that each tenet of policy needs to be underpinned by evidence which would satisfy a judge or jury that the policy was needed. The entity which must make judgments of that sort is not the court, which is not a public authority, but the licensing authority itself which is steeped in the business of making policy decisions, and of balancing out the various considerations which prompt such decisions. There is no legal requirement that policy has to backed by a particular quantum of evidential material. It is no part of the court's function to judge the merits of the policy. Indeed, the magistrates have no power to quash the policy at all. The only body which may do that is the High Court, and then only if the policy is unlawful or irrational. That imposes a very high burden on the party challenging the policy, which goes far beyond demonstrating that on balance

---

[22] See Guidance para 1.9.

the policy is not justified by the evidence. It would require a party to demonstrate that the policy was actually contrary to the law or that no reasonable licensing authority could have adopted the policy on the basis of the material before it. That has not happened since the inception of the Licensing Act 2003.

4.84 The point made here is different. Where there is an evidential underpinning for policy, this should be clearly stated. Where it is, it establishes a baseline for a policy, justifies its rationale, builds its credibility, achieves buy-in, and helps decision-makers to understand the circumstances in which a departure might be permitted. An authority which can provide no proper rationale for its policy is more likely to find that mere lip service is paid by all those who have to use it.

J ENFORCEMENT

4.85 The Licensing Act 2003 does not require the authority's enforcement policy to be set out in its licensing policy. However, once again, on the basis that the licensing policy is the hub of thinking about the night time economy, it makes good sense for the enforcement policy to be included as an appendix. Enforcement policies are dealt with further in Part E of this book.

K CONCLUSION

4.86 In this chapter, I have stressed the importance of a pro-active licensing policy, acting as the hub of thinking about and control of the night time economy, setting appropriate standards and acting as much as a motivator of the right proposal in the right place as the filter through which inappropriate proposals are weeded out, so as to foster and promote the night time economy best suited to the needs and priorities of the area. I have also reiterated the need for the establishment of a far-reaching evidential database to inform formulation and review of policy, so that policy is a living document which is rooted in the actual circumstances of the locality and responds to those circumstances with resolution and vision.

5

Evidence and inference in licensing[1]

I like to have a martini,
Two at the very most.
After three I'm under the table,
after four I'm under my host.

Dorothy Parker, *The Collected Dorothy Parker*

A INTRODUCTION

5.01 In Chapter 4 we saw that evidence of the kind which would pass muster in a court is not necessary in order to underpin a licensing policy, provided that the policy is based on considerations which are rational. This chapter concerns the kind of material which would justify regulatory intervention, for example the refusal or revocation of a licence or the imposition of conditions on an application or a review. Does such material need to be 'evidential', in the sense that this is understood in courts of law? Obviously, the matter is of seminal importance for licensing authorities.

5.02 Since the decision of the High Court in *Daniel Thwaites plc v Wirral Borough Magistrates' Court*[2] it has become fashionable to seek to dissuade licensing sub-committees from imposing restraints on licence applicants under the 2003 Act on the grounds that there is no 'evidence' that a particular harm will occur. In this chapter, it will be demonstrated that *Thwaites* created no rule of law that evidence of prospective harm of the type which would be admissible in a court of law is necessary before conditions or other curtailments are imposed. Further, if *Thwaites* had purported to invent such a rule of law, it would have been contrary to binding Court of Appeal authority.

---

[1]   This chapter first appeared as an article in the Licensing Review.
[2]   [2008] EWHC 838 (Admin).

5.03   The chapter will start by describing the general rule in licensing. Then it will consider the position under the Licensing Act 2003 and demonstrate its consistency with the general rule. It will then show that *Thwaites* leaves the general rule neither shaken nor stirred.

B   THE GENERAL RULE

5.04   Licensing is a species of administrative decision-making. While that statement may appear uncontentious, part of the reason for the debate as to what constitutes 'evidence' in licensing hearings is a repeated refrain that licensing committees are 'quasi-judicial bodies' and therefore have to pretend that they are judges. They are not. In *R (Hope and Glory Public House Limited) v City of Westminster Magistrates' Court*[3] Toulson LJ stated:

> 'As Mr Matthias rightly submitted, the licensing function of a licensing authority is an administrative function. By contrast, the function of the district judge is a judicial function. The licensing authority has a duty, in accordance with the rule of law, to behave fairly in the decision-making procedure, but the decision itself is not a judicial or quasi-judicial act. It is the exercise of a power delegated by the people as a whole to decide what the public interest requires.'[4]

5.05   So, the licensing decision is one taken by an administrative body. Such bodies have no inherent jurisdiction – their powers are derived wholly from statute. They are charged with furthering the objectives of the legislation in the decisions that they make. They are able to formulate policies to guide them in their decision-making. They are not bound by the Civil or Criminal Procedure Rules. They work by considering the material which has been placed before them and making a decision which appears to them to be sensible and apt to advance the policy of the legislation in their local area. Their decision may involve some fact finding (Did the cabbie swear at the customer? Was the CCTV working?) but usually the outcome of the case turns on a value judgment. Parliament has not appointed professional judges to make such judgments, but has been content to leave them to experienced local individuals representative of their community.

5.06   Put that way, it would be illogical to suggest that only particular sorts of material – which in a different forum entirely would satisfy rules of evidence – can be taken into account by the decision-maker. And indeed, when one looks at the judgments of the higher courts on the issue, one finds no such rule. In fact, one finds the opposite approach entirely.

5.07   We start – for reasons which will shortly become obvious – with the dictum of Diplock LJ in an old case concerning adjudication on a claim for

---

[3]   [2011] EWCA Civ 31.
[4]   Para [41].

industrial injuries benefit: *R v Deputy Industrial Injuries Commissioner, ex p Moore.*[5] Dealing with hearsay evidence, His Lordship stated:

> 'These technical rules of evidence, however, form no part of the rules of natural justice. The requirement that a person exercising quasi-judicial functions must base his decision on evidence means no more than it must be based on material which tends logically to show the existence or non-existence of facts relevant to the issue to be determined, or to show the likelihood or unlikelihood of the occurrence of some future event, the occurrence of which would be relevant. It means that he must not spin a coin or consult an astrologer, but he may take into account any material which, as a matter of reason, has some probative value in the sense mentioned above. If it is capable of having any probative value, the weight to be attached to it is a matter for the person to whom Parliament has entrusted the responsibility of deciding the issue.'

5.08 That decision, now nearly half a century old, has repeatedly informed decisions of the higher courts in the field of licensing.

5.09 In *Kavanagh v Chief Constable of Devon and Cornwall*[6] the Court of Appeal was dealing with a submission that on an appeal from a refusal of a shotgun licence, Quarter Sessions (the then equivalent of the Crown Court) should not receive hearsay evidence. Their Lordships dismissed with a judicial exocet the appellant's observations that there was no authority on evidential requirements under firearms legislation by observing that no-one had been brave enough previously to advance the submissions being made before them! The Court upheld the judgment of the Divisional Court which, in applying the dictum of Diplock LJ cited above, held that hearsay evidence was indeed admissible. Lord Denning made it clear that neither the decision-maker nor the magistrates or Crown Court on appeal are bound by the strict rules of evidence. They were all entitled to act, he said, on any material that appears to be useful in coming to a decision, including their own knowledge. They may receive any material which is logically probative even though it is not evidence in a court of law. Agreeing with him, Lord Roskill added that the decision-maker 'is entitled and indeed obliged to take into account all relevant matters, whether or not any reports and information given to him would be strictly admissible in a court of law.'

5.10 Perhaps the only surprising matter is the frequency with which that clear statement of the law has had to be reiterated over the succeeding decades.

5   [1965] 1 QB 456, 488.
6   [1974] QB 624.

5.11 The statement was revisited in the 1980's, when Pill J delivered judgment in *Westminster City Council v Zestfair*[7] which concerned night cafes, holding hearsay evidence to be admissible. It enjoyed a reprise in the 1990s in the Court of Appeal in the taxi licensing case of *McCool v Rushcliffe*[8] in which Lord Chief Justice Bingham said:

> 'I conclude that, in reaching their respective decisions, the Borough Council and the justices were entitled to rely on any evidential material which might reasonably and properly influence the making of a responsible judgment in good faith on the question in issue. Some evidence such as gossip, speculation and unsubstantiated innuendo would be rightly disregarded. Other evidence, even if hearsay, might by its source, nature and inherent probability carry a greater degree of credibility. All would depend on the particular facts and circumstances.'

5.12 There was a repeat performance at the turn of the millennium in *R v Licensing Justices for East Gwent ex parte Chief Constable of East Gwent*[9] in which the Justices had refused to admit evidence from local residents of rowdy behaviour in a neighbouring public house and were held to have been wrong to do so. Shortly thereafter, the rule was adduced by Davis J in *R (Brogan) v Metropolitan Police*[10], which concerned evidence given on applications for special orders of exemption under the Licensing Act 1964.

5.13 This amounts to a simply overwhelming cadre of authority that a licensing decision-maker is entitled to act on any material which appears to him to be logically probative, including his own local knowledge. The only boundaries are rationality – a decision to admit evidence must not be perverse – and fairness, in the sense that a party must have the opportunity to comment on that which is being relied upon by others. It is no exaggeration to say that the opposite case – that only evidence admissible in a court is admissible before a licensing authority – is unarguable.

5.14 Not only is the position plain, but there is a good reason for it. Whether the decision-maker is making a judgment on whether a person should be allowed to wield a shotgun, drive a member of the public in his car, run a late night burger stall or operate a nightclub, the judgment fundamentally involves an evaluation of risk. If there is no risk, there is no need for interference. If there is a significant risk – whether of physical harm or nuisance to the neighbours – then some form of interference, be it by the imposition of conditions or outright refusal, may be merited. The evaluation of risk can never be weighed as a matter of fact, as though one is weighing sugar for a recipe. It is a value judgment. Furthermore, it is a value judgment

---

[7]   (1989) 88 LGR 288.
[8]   [1998] 3 All ER 889.
[9]   2001 LLR 693.
[10] [2002] EWHC 2127 (Admin).

about what <u>might</u> happen in the future, with or without the regulatory control under consideration.

5.15 Every human activity involves risk, whether it is crossing the road or changing a light bulb. Some risks we are not prepared to take. Others we take only with precautions. Others we deem acceptable even without precautions. Licensing is the process of making such judgments in the public interest, for the protection of others. There is rarely a right answer. It is an exercise of local discretion, applying common sense and judgment to the material as it has been presented. To dismiss material from consideration because it would not pass muster in a court of law is to abandon common sense, wisdom and judgment, and to place the public at risk by ignoring material which may well be probative.

5.16 In many instances, there will be very little primary material – the case will turn almost entirely on a value judgment. Imagine a large capacity nightclub wants to open until 3 am in a quiet residential street. What evidence would an experienced local councillor need before reaching a judgment that those departing the club in the middle of the night would be liable to awaken the neighbours? The answer may well be none, other than the primary facts just described. Certainly, it would not be necessary to await the opening of the club in order to test the proposition empirically, any more than a person carrying out a fire risk assessment needs to await an inferno before advising on the installation of sprinklers.

5.17 Therefore, once it is understood that the job of licensing is not to respond to harm once it has occurred, but to make rational judgments to avert risk, it becomes still clearer that to require evidence, in the sense understood by courts, is to encrust the system with rules which are liable to expose the public to unnecessary risk and work contrary to the pursuit of the objectives of the legislation conferring the discretion.

5.18 So far, we have reached a very clear position based on a consistent line of authority over the last half century. Has anything in the Licensing Act 2003 altered that?

C THE LICENSING ACT 2003

5.19 Decisions under the Licensing Act are driven by a common engine – that no action is warranted unless it is appropriate for the promotion of the licensing objectives. So, when making applications for new licences or club premises certificates where representations have been received, sub-committees may only act – whether to impose conditions or refuse outright – where such action is considered appropriate to promote those objectives.[11]

---

[11]   Licensing Act 2003, ss 18, 72.

Again, when considering an application for review of licences and certificates, the authority is obliged to take such action, whether altering conditions, curtailing the permitted activities, suspending or revoking, as it considers appropriate for the promotion of those objectives.[12] In none of these cases is the authority punishing for past behaviour. It is not a retrospective sentencing exercise, but a prospective exercise as to what the promotion of the licensing objectives requires. Furthermore, no facts adverse to the licensee or prospective licensee need necessarily be established. It is simply a question for the authority to ask itself whether, on the basis of what is placed before it, some interference is warranted in order to promote the licensing objectives in the future.

5.20   In this regard, the language of the legislation is particularly instructive. The job of the decision-maker is to promote the objective – be it crime or nuisance prevention, or the protection of children or the pursuit of public safety. It is not to act only when harm has occurred to one of those objectives – in the case of a new application that could not be done. It is not even to act only when harm will demonstrably occur, even on balance of probabilities. Imagine objection were to be taken to a large temporary structure at a concert. It could not seriously be suggested that the authority could only impose a condition requiring the safety of the structure to be certified when satisfied on the balance of probabilities that it will collapse. No, the ability to take preventive measures arises when the authority is satisfied that this is appropriate in the interests of public safety.

5.21   On what material may an authority make a judgment that there is a risk which requires to be averted? Why, on any material which appears to it to be rational. Nothing in the Act, or indeed the Regulations made under the Act, alters the position which has been applied by administrative bodies since time immemorial.

5.22   The position may be tested thus. Authorities are charged with the duty of publishing licensing policies.[13] It is well-established in law[14] that such policies may contain presumptions against grant in particular circumstances. The effect of a presumption is that where the statutory discretion arises then, absent evidence justifying a departure from the policy, an application made contrary to the policy is to be refused. But on what basis is it justifiable to refuse a licence based on policy, without actual evidence that the grant of the licence will cause harm? The answer must be that the policy itself leads to the inference of harm, unless such an inference can be rebutted in an individual case. Put slightly differently, the policy is the means by which the authority promotes the licensing objectives as required by the Act.[15] If that analysis is

---

[12]   Licensing Act 2003, ss 52, 88.
[13]   Licensing Act 2003, s 5.
[14]   *R (Westminster City Council) v Middlesex Crown Court* [2002] LLR 538.
[15]   See *R (A3D2 Limited t/a Novus Leisure) v Westminster Magistrates' Court* [2011] EWHC 1045 (Admin) at paras [56]–[57].

correct, it means that the statutory test is satisfied, and an inference that harm to the licensing objectives will result is justified, not by evidence, and certainly not by live evidence, particular to the individual case, but by a piece of paper drawn up months or perhaps even years before the application is made. This serves to emphasise that the inference of prospective harm can come from any source and can be adduced in any way. It does not draw sustenance only from evidence sufficient to satisfy a court. It can even arise as a result of the general policy of the administrative body charged with making such judgments.

5.23 It may also be pointed out that this view of the effect of the Act accords with that of the Government at the time. In 'The Evening Economy and the Urban Renaissance'[16] the ODPM Committee suggested that residents may find difficulty proving cumulative stress. In response, the Government stated[17]:

> 'The Licensing Act makes no reference to "evidence". This recommendation appears to misunderstand the role that will be played by the licensing authorities when their regulatory decision-making function is engaged by the receipt of representations under the Licensing Act 2003 and the nature of the hearings that will occur in these circumstances. Under the 2003 Act, where relevant representations are received by the licensing authority, the authority is bound to hold a hearing to consider them. However, in holding such a hearing, the licensing authority will not be performing a judicial or even quasi-judicial role, but instead will be engaged in a balancing exercise in the public interest on the basis of what is necessary for the licensing objectives.'

5.24 In short, therefore, the requirement that the licensing authority act so as to do what is appropriate for the promotion of the licensing objectives does not lead to a departure from the general rule. It is wholly consonant with the rule. The authority should act on any material which it considers plausible and apt to influence its judgment.

The remaining question is whether anything in *Thwaites* disturbs that general rule.

D DANIEL THWAITES V WIRRAL BOROUGH MAGISTRATES' COURT

5.25 In this case, the claimant had sought to vary a premises licence to obtain longer hours. A police objection was resolved through negotiation, so

---

[16] 'Twelfth Report of Session 2002–03', HC 396-I (Office of the Deputy Prime Minister: Housing, Planning, Local Government and the Regions Committee) http://www. publications.parliament.uk/pa/cm200203/cmselect/cmodpm/396/396.pdf.

[17] 'The Government Response to Office of the Deputy Prime Minister Housing, Planning, Local Government and the Regions Committee's Report on the Evening Economy and the Urban Renaissance', Cm 5971 (2003).

that the police were able to withdraw their objection. No representations had been made by the environmental health authority, leaving only local residents as objectors. The licensing sub-committee granted the licence as asked and the residents appealed. However, by the time the appeal came to be heard, the premises had been operating to the hours sought, with no evidence that harm to the licensing objectives had arisen, but the appellants spoke of their fears of future harm. Nevertheless, the Justices allowed the appeal and removed the extended hours granted to the premises by the authority.

5.26 The licensee successfully judicially reviewed that decision. Mrs Justice Black criticised the Justices for disregarding what had happened in the past as an aid to predicting what would happen in the future. She was also critical of the way the Justices used their local knowledge, saying 'There can be little doubt that local magistrates are also entitled to take into account their own knowledge, but ... they must measure their own views against the evidence presented to them.' She particularly made that point because the evidence was that the responsible authorities were untroubled and that the history of the premises when operating to the longer hours did not substantiate the Justices' fears.

5.27 In her conclusions, Black J stated that the Justices should have looked for 'real evidence' that greater regulation was required in the circumstances of the case. Their conclusion that it was required was, in her judgment, not a conclusion to which a properly directed bench could have come. Here, it was said, they proceeded without proper evidence, gave their own views excessive weight and the police views none at all.

5.28 These dicta are the high water mark of arguments regularly addressed to licensing sub-committees that they cannot act to impose restraint. But the arguments are quite wrong.

5.29 It is plain from Black J's judgment that she was saying that the conclusions of the Justices were irrational. In other words it was not rational of the Justices to say there would be future harm when (a) there had not been any harm in the past and (b) the responsible authorities were not suggesting that there would be such harm. This was plainly a decision on the facts. She was not saying that restraint may never be imposed at the instance of local residents, or that authorities might never act on their own knowledge, or that hearsay evidence was inadmissible, or that only evidence admissible in a court is admissible before the authority. She was just saying that, on the facts, it was a stretch too far for the Justices to find harm when there was empirical evidence – over a period of months – showing that there had been none. The licensee might have considered itself fortunate to find a judge prepared to delve so far into the facts on a judicial review. Be that as it may, the case did not concern what amounts to evidence, but what findings were open to the Justices in the individual case.

5.30 Still more resonant is that Black J was not referred, and did not refer, to any of the Court of Appeal cases set out above, dealing with what kind of evidence may be admitted before administrative bodies. In truth, there was no need for such reference, for nobody was contending that there are particular types of evidence which are and are not probative. The case did not concern that matter at all, but whether the finding made was justifiable on the evidence given. Black J would, no doubt, have been gravely concerned by any suggestion that her judgment amounted to a tacit departure from the consistent utterances of the Court of Appeal over a period of decades. But the fact is that nothing in the judgment amounts to a departure, and if it did it would have been without reference to such authorities and therefore *per incuriam* and of no binding effect.

E CONCLUSION

5.31 In this chapter, I have tried to debunk the shibboleth that licensing authorities are 'quasi-judicial' and are thereby constricted as to what may guide them in their decision-making. The general position in licensing is that authorities may act on any material appearing to them to be relevant, whether or not the material would be admitted evidentially in a court. Nothing in the Licensing Act 2003 alters that position. The judgment of Black J in *Thwaites* is often submitted to create an evidential threshold for regulatory intervention, but in fact it was no more than a decision on the individual facts. The learned Judge certainly did not intend to depart from several decades of binding Court of Appeal authority, and of course could not have done so.

5.32 While the result in *Thwaites* was arguably correct on the facts, if it has had the effect of weakening the resolve of licensing decision-makers to act with common sense on the material placed before them, that would be most unfortunate. For the system to function as intended, it is imperative that licensing decision-makers grasp that they are not judges but democratically elected individuals charged with making sensible decisions in the public interest. Technical rules of evidence simply stand in the way of that process.

5.33 Put shortly, Parliament has given the job of deciding licensing applications to lay councillors, who can act on anything upon which they think it sensible to act. They should not leave their common sense at the door when deciding licence applications, but must use their wisdom gained through the years to take the steps which they consider right, having regard to what they have seen and heard at the meeting in question.

The Licensing Act 2003

Fifteen men on the dead man's chest-
Yo-ho-ho, and a bottle of rum!
Drink and the devil had done for the rest-
Yo-ho-ho, and a bottle of rum!

Treasure Island
Robert Louis Stevenson

The Licensing Act 2003: Concepts

Drink today, and drown all sorrow;
You shall perhaps not do it tomorrow;
Best, while you have it, use your breath;
There is no drinking after death

Ben Johnson

The Licensing Act 2003 framework

Come my good friends, you are welcome to me, and I am glad that I have a house to entertain you in; and while supper is making ready, if you please, let us entertain one another with some good discourse.

Gaius the innkeeper
Pilgrim's Progress
John Bunyan

A INTRODUCTION

6.01 The purpose of this chapter is to provide a broad overview of the regime in the Licensing Act 2003, to assist navigation through this part of the book. It is not a full statement of the law and should not be treated as such. It is an aerial photograph to the more detailed land surveys which follow.

It should also not be confused for a complete statement of the law relating to the licensing of licensed premises. These include the following:

(1)   Statutes which bear on decision-making under the Licensing Act 2003, such as the Crime and Disorder Act 1998, the Human Rights Act 1998, the Equality Act 2010 and the Provision of Services Regulations 2009.

(2)   Statutes which provide enforcement mechanisms against licensed premises such as closure notices under the Criminal Justice and Police Act 2001, prohibition and improvement notices under the Health and Safety at Work Act 1974, abatement notices under the Environmental Protection Act 1990 and closure orders under the Anti-Social Behaviour Act 2003.

(3)   Statutes which provide parallel consent regimes, eg the Gambling Act 2005 which provides for premises licences for casinos and betting offices and the Local Government (Miscellaneous Provisions) Act 1982 which creates the need for licences for sexual entertainment venues. In general, these kinds of premises will have licences under the Licensing Act 2003 for their bars and under the other legislation for their main activity.

(4)   Planning legislation, which creates the need for planning consent for all forms of licensable activity.

B THE FRAMEWORK

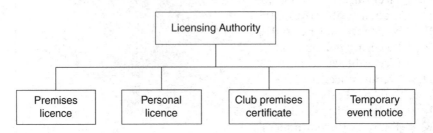

Figure 1: Framework

6.02   The framework of the new regime is:

- A single licensing authority.
- Acting with a view to promoting the licensing objectives
- Guided by national Guidance and its own licensing policy.
- A single licensing regime for all licensable activities
- A single premises licence to cover one or more licensable activities.
- A system of portable personal licences for the sale of alcohol in premises with premises licences.
- Club premises certificates for qualifying members' clubs, subject to a lighter regulatory regime.
- A simple procedure of temporary event notices to authorise occasional events.
- A wide range of sanctions, including review, closure and criminal offences.
- A single tier of appeal, available to all.

Now for a closer look at the terrain.

C LICENSING AUTHORITIES

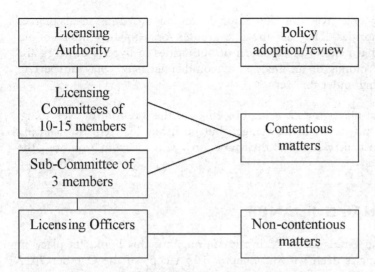

Figure 2: The licensing authority

6.03 Licensing authorities are dealt with in Chapter 7.

In general, licensing authorities are district or borough councils.

The job of adopting a local licensing policy is exercised by the authority itself. Otherwise, nearly all functions are delegated to a licensing committee of ten to fifteen members, who may in turn delegate to sub-committees usually, but not necessarily, of three. Further delegations may be made to officers, of non-contentious matters.

6.04 Licensing authorities exercise functions previously exercised in piecemeal manner by local authorities and licensing justices. The harmonisation promotes an integrated approach to the night time economy hand in hand with other local authority functions.

D LICENSING OBJECTIVES

- The prevention of crime and disorder
- Public safety
- The prevention of public nuisance
- The protection of children from harm

Figure 3: The licensing objectives

6.05   The licensing objectives are covered in detail in Chapter 10.

The licensing objectives are the rationale for all the decision-making of licensing authorities. They are the sole ground for regulatory intervention. This means that matters the concern of authorities in bygone days, eg the promotion of morals or an analysis of commercial need, play no part in decision-making under the Act.

6.06   The Act places the licensing objectives at the forefront of everything. They are not just to be acknowledged but positively fostered. So licensing authorities must carry out all of their functions 'with a view to promoting the licensing objectives.'

E NATIONAL GUIDANCE

6.07   National Guidance is dealt with throughout this book. Its place in decision-making is dealt with in Chapter 10. A copy of the October 2012 iteration of the Guidance is set out at Appendix 9 of this volume.

This is the first time that licensing guidance has been issued under statute. In this book, we call it Guidance or national Guidance for short. Licensing authorities are to have regard to Guidance both when adopting their policy and when making individual decisions.

The Guidance performs four main functions:

(1)   It offers guidance to licensing authorities in exercising their functions. Authorities are not bound to follow the Guidance but departures should be for good reason, otherwise legal challenge is risked.
(2)   It sets out good practice for all statutory and non-statutory stakeholders in the night time economy, in particular promoting partnership approaches.
(3)   It offers menus of model licensing conditions from which selection might be made where necessary to promote the licensing objectives in individual cases.
(4)   It acts as a guide to the Licensing Act 2003 itself. But it does not change the law and is at most one interpretative tool.

F LICENSING POLICY

6.08   Prior to the Licensing Act 2003, some local authorities and magistrates had adopted licensing policies as to the exercise of their functions, but their status and weight was sometimes contentious. The Act placed local licensing on a statutory footing for the first time.

6.09 The Act does not define what should go into policies. But policies should broadly relate to the exercise of licensing functions, and how the licensing objectives are to be promoted. Policies need not follow national Guidance provided that good reason is given for departure.

Policies under the Act have covered a wide spectrum from:

• a faithful rendition of national Guidance, without much reference to the local area, to
• statements of the specific standards to be expected of operators, to
• the articulation of a clear vision for the night time economy, covering the type, mix, pattern, location, hours and target clientele of licensed premises so as to promote both the licensing objectives themselves and the wider cultural and economic strategies of the town.

6.10 Licensing authorities must consult widely before adopting their policy. The policy has a shelf-life of five years, but within that period is to be monitored and revised as appropriate. If it is reviewed within that period, its shelf life is unaffected. If it is replaced within that period its shelf life starts afresh.

Licensing authorities must have regard to their policy when making licensing decisions.

6.11 The Act sets out no order of precedence between national Guidance and local policy. But where a licensing authority has expressly departed from national Guidance in its policy, then on that matter the policy would hold sway.

6.12 The policy does not relieve the licensing authority of the duty to consider the individual merits of an application. But the policy may create a presumption one way or the other, capable of being displaced in the individual circumstances.

G LICENSABLE ACTIVITIES

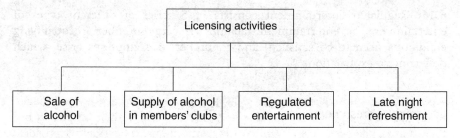

Figure 4: Licensable activities

6.13   Licensable activities are explained in Chapter 8.

The activities are culled from the former liquor, entertainment and late night refreshment house/night cafe regimes.

Alcohol

6.14   The Act regulates the sale of alcohol, not its consumption. So for example a terminal hour on a licence will not control later consumption without a specific condition to that effect.

Supply of alcohol in clubs

6.15   Club members already own the contents of the bar between them so when they are served with alcohol they are not actually buying it. Hence such supply is made a separate licensable activity.

Regulated entertainment

Entertainment	
A	Performance of a play
B	Exhibition of a film
C	Indoor sporting event
D	Boxing or wrestling entertainment (indoor and outdoor)
E	Performance of live music
F	Playing of recorded music
G	Performance of dance
H	Entertainment similar to E–G

Figure 5: Regulated entertainment

6.16   Regulated entertainment consists of a series of different types of entertainment or entertainment facilities. A large number of qualifying conditions need to be satisfied, and a number of exemptions arise, which defy concise explanation.

Late night refreshment

6.17   Late night refreshment mostly consists of supplying hot food or drink to members of the public between 11 pm and 5 am, whether eat in or take away. It also involves supplying to others where members of the public are admitted. So a private works canteen is not caught, but would be if the public were admitted. Various exemptions are provided for.

H PREMISES LICENCES

Premises licence:

- Authorises licensable activities
- Indefinite, subject to review
- Sources of conditions:
  - Mandatory statutory conditions
  - Conditions proposed in operating schedule
  - Conditions imposed by licensing authority where relevant representations made

Figure 6: Premises licences

6.18 Premises licences are covered in Chapter 15.

Premises licences authorise one or more licensable activities.

To obtain a premises licence, an applicant must submit an application with an operating schedule which must include a description of the proposed licensable activities and the times of operation of each, together with the steps proposed to promote the licensing objectives.

6.19 Relevant representations, which must be about the effect of the grant of the licence on the licensing objectives, may be made by responsible authorities (statutory agencies named in the Act and regulations) or any other person or body, whether local or not. Representations from any other person or body may be disregarded if they are frivolous or vexatious.

6.20 Where there are no representations (or all representations have been withdrawn) the licensing authority has no discretion. It must grant the licence subject only to:

- conditions consistent with the operating schedule.
- mandatory conditions (see Figure 7).

Mandatory conditions:

- No supply of alcohol under premises licences where there is no designated premises supervisor
- Supply of alcohol under premises licence to be made/authorised by personal licensee

- Door supervisors under premises licence to be Security Industry Authority-registered
- Observance of age classification in films
- Observance of mandatory code

Figure 7: Mandatory conditions

6.21 The mandatory conditions set out above create base minimum requirements for premises licences where these provide for the service of alcohol, the use of door supervisors or for the exhibition of films, as the case may be. The following is added to the above brief description.

Designated premises supervisor

6.22 The designated premises supervisor is a person in managerial control of the premises. He does not need to be on the premises at all times. However, his absence may render him unsuitable to be the designated premises supervisor in which case the police may object to his appointment or apply to have him removed on a review of the licence. There is no reason in law why the premises licensee, the personal licensee and the designated premises supervisor should not all be the same person.

Personal licensee

6.23 There is no limit to the number of personal licensees who may be on the premises. While sales need to be made or authorised by the personal licensee, authority does not necessarily equate to presence. For example, a personal licensee on their lunch hour may still authorise sales in their absence. At the other extreme, sales made while the personal licensee was on sabbatical would contravene the condition. It is good practice for personal licensees to authorise individuals to make sales in writing, so as to avoid doubt.

Community premises

6.24 The Act gives the licensing authority power to dispense with the mandatory conditions in relation to the designated premises supervisor and personal licensee for community premises such as church, village or community halls, and substitute a condition that every sale of alcohol must be made or authorised by the management committee.

Door supervision

6.25 The Private Security Industry Act 2001 regulates the door supervision industry through the Security Industry Authority. This is dealt with in Chapter 35.

Age classification

6.26 Age classification of films is carried out by the British Board of Film Classification. Although a licensing authority could in theory depart from the BBFC for licensing purposes, few if any will do so.

Powers where relevant representations made

6.27 Where relevant representations are made, there will normally be a hearing as a result of which the licensing authority may take such of the following steps as it considers necessary for the promotion of the licensing objectives:

- Grant licence as asked, subject to conditions in operating schedule and mandatory conditions.
- Augment, change or delete conditions in operating schedule.
- Reject a proposed licensable activity.
- Refuse to accept the proposed designated premises supervisor.
- Refuse to grant the licence.

Figure 8: Powers where relevant representations made

Provisional statement

6.28 Where premises are not yet built, the applicant may apply for a provisional statement to enable him to proceed with greater confidence. If the provisional statement is granted, the scope for subsequent objections to the premises licence is limited. If his plans are sufficiently detailed, he may apply for a full premises licence without needing to apply for a provisional statement.

Duration

6.29 A premises licence, unless granted for a limited period, is indefinite, subject to provisions for review or if the licence lapses eg through death or liquidation.

Review

6.30 A key safeguard of the Act is the ability of a responsible authority or other person to apply for a review of the premises licence at any time. An application by the latter may be summarily rejected if frivolous, vexatious or repetitious.

The licensing authority has wide powers upon review to reflect the concerns expressed. It may take such of the following steps as necessary for the promotion of the licensing objectives:

Review powers:

- Augment, amend or delete conditions
- Exclude a licensable activity
- remove the designated premises supervisor
- Suspend the licence for up to three months
- Revoke the licence

Figure 9: Review powers

6.31   There are also procedures for:

- Summary review of the licence in urgent cases concerning serious crime and disorder, which are quicker than ordinary reviews, and where the authority is given power to impose interim steps pending final determination of the review. This is dealt with in Chapter 42 Section C.
- Reviews following a closure order on premises made by the police. This is covered in Chapter 43.

I PERSONAL LICENCES

Personal licences:

- For sale of alcohol under premise licences
- Fully portable
- Duration ten years unless forfeited

Figure 10: Personal licences

6.32   Personal licences are dealt with in Chapter 18.

All supplies of alcohol under premises licence must be made or authorised by a personal licensee, except where the alternative licence condition has been applied to community premises (see above). A personal licence is not needed for supplies under the auspices of a club premises certificate or a temporary event notice.

6.33   The personal licence is fully portable, allowing the holder to ply his trade anywhere. Only a personal licensee may be a designated premises supervisor. An applicant who meets the statutory criteria is entitled to a grant.

Personal licence criteria:

A   Aged 18 or over
B   Recognised licensing qualification
C   Has not forfeited a personal licence in the last five years
D   Has not been convicted of relevant or foreign offence

Figure 11: Personal licence criteria

6.34 If the applicant does not meet criteria A, B or C, refusal is mandatory. If he fails on criterion D, the police may object on crime prevention grounds, with a power of refusal by the licensee if appropriate to promote the crime prevention objective.

The licence lasts for ten years unless forfeited by a court on conviction for a relevant offence listed in Schedule 4 of the Act.

J   CLUB PREMISES CERTIFICATES

- Members' clubs
- Subject to qualifying conditions
- Lighter regulation

Figure 12: Club Premises Certificates

6.35 Club premises certificates are dealt with in Chapter 16. The premises covered are the members' clubs previously licensed under Part II of the Licensing Act 1964. Under the 2003 Act, classification as club premises involves satisfaction of a series of qualifying conditions. They are subject to considerably lighter regulation than that applying to premises licences in that they need neither a designated premises supervisor nor a personal licensee for the supply of alcohol. In other respects, the provisions for application and grant are analogous to those governing premises licences.

K   TEMPORARY EVENT NOTICES

6.36 Temporary event notices ('TENs') are dealt with in Chapter 19.

TENs allow licensable activities to take place on a temporary basis, which could otherwise only be carried on under premises licences or club premises certificates. They might be used to augment a current licence for a brief period, eg two hours extra for a pub to host a party, or to allow an event, eg a travelling circus, to take place on an unlicensed site.

There are two sorts of TENs, standard TENs and late TENs, which are taken in turn.

Limits	Control Mechanism
168 hours	Not a temporary event under the Act
499 people	Not a temporary event under the Act
21 days per annum per premises	Counter-notice
24 hours between events	TEN is void
12 events per annum per premises	Counter-notice
50 standard/10 late TENs per annum for personal licensees	Counter-notice
5 standard/2 late TENs per annum for others	Counter-notice

Figure 13: Temporary Event Notice limits

Temporary event notice limits

6.37   The standard TEN procedure may be used for temporary events satisfying the above criteria.

6.38   The TEN contains details, dates and times of the licensable activities and the maximum numbers attending at one time. It is served on the licensing authority at least ten days before the event. The police and environmental authority are served by the licensing authority (if it has been served electronically) or by the applicant (if not). The police and environmental health authority then have three working days to object to the notice on the grounds of any of the licensing objectives. If they do, this leads to a hearing at which the authority may either effectively permit the event to proceed, permit the event to proceed but subject to conditions where there are already conditions on the licence, or refuse consent for the event by serving a counter-notice. In each case, its discretion is governed by what it considers to be appropriate for the promotion of the licensing objectives. Both applicants and the objecting authorities have rights of appeal to the magistrates' court.

6.39   A late TEN may be served between five and nine working days before the event. In this case, however, the police and environmental health authority have an absolute veto over the event, no conditions may be added and there is no right of appeal. There are also much lower limits on the number of late TENs that can be served, and if the lower limit is reached then no more TENs of any sort, whether late or standard, can be served in the same calendar year (and vice versa).They are, therefore, an exceptional course to take where for whatever reason there is insufficient time to serve a standard TEN prior to the desired event.

L CLOSURE

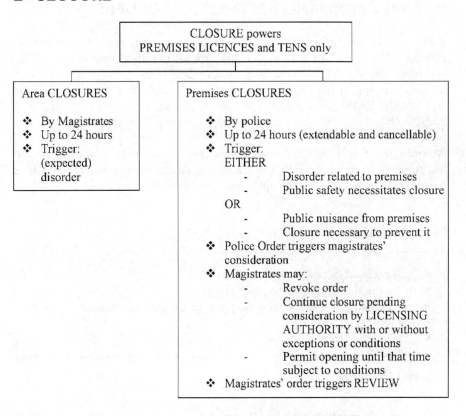

Figure 14: Closure

6.40   Closure is dealt with in Chapters 41 and 43.

The powers fall into two parts.

6.41   Magistrates may on application by the police close all the licensed premises in an area in which disorder is occurring or expected for up to 24 hours, where they are satisfied that closure is necessary to prevent disorder. The power might be exercised where the police fear violence associated with a particular event such as a demonstration or sporting event.

6.42   The police may unilaterally close individual premises on grounds relating to disorder or nuisance. Police action, which is necessarily a last resort measure, triggers consideration by magistrates and thence review by the licensing authority, which may result in loss of the licence. It is therefore both a protective and a deterrent measure, amounting to a key safeguard under the Act.

There are other closure powers under other legislation which are dealt with in Chapters 44 to 46.

M   EARLY MORNING RESTRICTION ORDERS

6.43   A licensing authority may make an early morning restriction order, or EMRO, in any or all of its area for any time of the night between midnight and 6 am, any day of the week, and for any time of the year, provided that it considers it appropriate for the promotion of the licensing objectives. The effect of the EMRO is to outlaw the sale of alcohol during those hours. The EMRO therefore trumps whatever may be stated to the contrary on a premises licence, club premises certificate or temporary event notice. Accordingly, it is a powerful tool which, though not only a weapon of last resort, is only to be brandished when the circumstances warrant it. It is considered further in Chapter 40 (Early Morning Restriction Orders).

N   APPEALS

- Nearly all decisions appealable.
- Single tier of appeal to magistrates.
- Magistrates' orders following police closure appealed to Crown Court.
- Universal right of appeal.

Figure 15: Appeals

6.44   Appeals are dealt with in Chapter 20.

The Act introduced the right of appeal for those who made relevant representations, ie even a grant of a licence may be appealed.

6.45   Practically all appeals go to the magistrates' court. An obvious exception is where the magistrates have themselves made an order following police closure of individual premises, where the appeal is to the Crown Court. Unusually, area closures by magistrates are not appealable.

O   BALANCED PACKAGE OF SAFEGUARDS

6.46   Much of the public debate regarding the Act concerned later terminal hours. In fact, the Act itself is silent on the question. The matter has only ever arisen in the Guidance. Even then, concerns that the Guidance, trammelled by political neo-liberalism, promoted trading hours which frustrated proportionate environmental control were always wide of the mark.

There could be no genuine concern about allowing local authorities to make judgments about closing hours having regard to the licensing objectives. Indeed, it is conceivable that in an individual case the licensing authority could set a terminal hour earlier than the formerly permitted hours. The gravamen of the concern was that, in its earliest editions, the Guidance encouraged not just flexible hours, but also later hours. By degrees, the Guidance has slid back from that extreme view. However, the correct terminal hour was always and remains pre-eminently a matter for licensing authorities according to the individual merits of the case.

6.47 The narrow focus of much of the debate around licensing hours did serve to obscure the wider picture. It would be wrong to depict the new legislation as anything other than a balanced package of freedoms and safeguards. There are numerous features of the Licensing Act 2003 regime which testify to that.

The deregulatory measures include:

- Removal of statutorily fixed terminal hours.
- Removal of the licensing authority's discretion where there has been no objection to the grant.
- Premises licences of unlimited duration.
- Discouragement of burdensome standard conditions rather than conditions tailored specifically to promote the licensing objectives.
- Light touch regulation for temporary events.

The counter-point to these features now includes:

- Placing of control in the hands of local authorities, enabling a more pro-active administrative involvement harnessed to wider local government strategies, in contrast to the tri-annual, formal, judicial involvement of the licensing Justices.
- The need for an operating schedule to outline proposed activities with some specificity.
- The requirement for operating schedules to set out the steps proposed to promote the licensing objectives, which then translate into licence conditions.
- For premises licences, the requirement for qualified personal licensees and designated premises supervisors where alcohol is served.
- The right for local people and statutory agencies to appeal grants of premises licences and club premises certificates.
- The power of review, whose existence alone exerts a disciplinary effect, and whose exercise is wont to carry severe consequences for businesses.
- The closure powers of police and magistrates.
- Increased penalties for a number of offences concerned with licensed premises.
- New offences, particularly concerning children, for example requiring under-16s to be accompanied by adults in alcohol-led premises. (Formerly over-14s could go in alone.) Children may no longer be supplied

alcohol in qualifying clubs, and the myriad exceptions to the prohibition on the sale of alcohol to under-18s outside licensed premises (eg on river and 'booze cruises') disappeared.

- The ability for authorities to impose late night levies on operators serving alcohol after midnight.
- The ability for authorities to impose curfews on alcohol providers after midnight through the medium of the early morning restriction order.

6.48   However, the thesis of this book is that merely having in place statutory mechanisms for the control of the night-time economy does not guarantee beneficial results. For example, the offence of sale of liquor to a drunken person[1] practically fell into desuetude in the years preceding the new Act, principally because of lack of police resources, and has been severely underused since. It is fair to say that rigorous enforcement of this provision alone may have served to combat at least some of the town disorder which perennially exercises national and local government and police.[2] However, it is use of the new statutory mechanisms alongside other statutory and voluntary measures which are most likely to yield peaceable town centres while allowing night time economies to thrive in the hands of responsible operators.

P   INTERPRETATION OF THE LEGISLATION

6.49   The Act has given rise to a number of issues of interpretation, which tend to be aired in front of licensing sub-committees and justices. For lawyers, it is tempting to rely on a series of interpretative 'aids', including ancient cases under previous licensing regimes, the contents of the Explanatory Notes published with the Act, and the contents of Guidance.

While a complete explanation of the law of statutory interpretation is beyond the compass of this book,[3] it is suggested that the following approach should be taken to interpretation of the Act.

(1)   There is a presumption that the meaning of the Act is to be ascertained by reference to the natural or ordinary meaning of the words concerned.[4]

(2)   The presumption may be displaced where necessary, for example where:

---

[1]   Licensing Act 1964, s 172.
[2]   Since the Act came into force, penalty notices for this offence still total only about 70 per year (Office for National Statistics: Number of Penalty Notices for Disorder issued to offenders aged 16 and over by offence, 12 months ending June 2005 to 12 months ending June 2011) and prosecutions about 2 per year (Hansard HL WA 61010 Col WA8).
[3]   See Bennion, *Statutory Interpretation* (Lexis Nexis, 5th ed, 2007) for a comprehensive approach to the subject, from which the following principles are culled.
[4]   *Pinner v Everett* [1969] 1 WLR 1266, 1273.

(a) Displacement is necessary to remedy the 'mischief' towards which the Act is aimed. For example, Parliament has clearly discerned a 'mischief' that it is not always possible to identify who is supposed to be in charge of premises and that that person may not be genuinely supervisory. Therefore, the expression 'designated premises supervisor' would be construed in a manner which ensured that such individual is an actual supervisor rather than a remote figurehead.

(b) The legislative purpose would otherwise be undermined. For example, since one of the licensing objectives is to protect children from harm, if a part of the Act is susceptible to two constructions, the literal one of which harmed children but another of which protected them, the latter would prevail.

(c) A literal construction would yield a result which is absurd, eg because it is unworkable or impracticable. Even then, Parliament may in fact have intended that result, and care is necessary to avoid a departure from the plain and obvious meaning of the words just because they are inconvenient.

(3) Where the Act retains and reproduces sections from the previous legislation, case law as to the meaning of such sections may be cited and is binding according to the usual rules of precedence. Where the language or context differs, case law is of limited, if any, assistance.

(4) Since 1999, government departments have published Explanatory Notes to most Public Acts. The Licensing Act 2003 is no exception.[5] The Notes are admissible aids to construction, in so far as they 'cast light on the objective setting or contextual scene of a statute, and the mischief at which it is aimed.'[6] However, they do not replace the statutory words:

> 'What is impermissible is to treat the wishes and desires of the Government about the scope of the statutory language as reflecting the will of Parliament. The aims of the Government in respect of the meaning of clauses as revealed in Explanatory Notes cannot be attributed to Parliament. The object is to see what is the intention expressed by the words enacted.'[7]

In short, while the Notes may be used in order to invoke the 'mischief' or 'purpose' aids to construction set out in paragraphs 2(a) or (b) above, they do not supplant the actual statutory words or the intention which those reveal.

The matter was put still more pointedly by Lord Rodger:

> 'In interpreting [the statutory provisions] ... I pay no attention whatever to the explanatory notes as an indication of their

---

5   http://www.legislation.hmso.gov.uk/acts/en2003/2003en17.htm.

6   *Westminster City Council v National Asylum Support Service* [2002] 1 WLR 2956, per Lord Steyn, para 5.

7   *Westminster City Council v National Asylum Support Service*, para 6.

meaning. In this case the notes do not identify the mischief behind the enactments. Nobody outside government knows who drafted them, or revised them or on what basis. They cannot be regarded as any kind of authoritative guide to the meaning of the provisions. The focus must be on the words of the provisions themselves.'[8]

(5)   A similar question is raised by the use of side-notes which, since 2001, due to a change in practice brought about by the Parliamentary Counsel Office, were moved so that they now appear in bold type as headings to each section in the version of the statute which is published by The Stationery Office. In *R v Montila*[9] the House of Lords dealt with the status of side-notes and their role in interpreting the legislative text. Their Lordships held:

'Account must, of course, be taken of the fact that these components were included in the Bill not for debate but for ease of reference. This indicates that less weight can be attached to them than to the parts of the Act that are open for consideration and debate in Parliament. But it is another matter to be required by a rule of law to disregard them altogether. One cannot ignore the fact that the headings and side notes are included on the face of the Bill throughout its passage through the Legislature. They are there for guidance. They provide the context for an examination of those parts of the Bill that are open for debate. Subject, of course, to the fact that they are unamendable, they ought to be open to consideration as part of the enactment when it reaches the statute book.'[10]

(6)   The Guidance is often cited before sub-committees as to the legal meaning of the provisions of the Act. However, the Guidance itself is only intended to guide as to the discharge of functions under the Act, and not as to the meaning of the Act itself.[11]

Further, Guidance may simply be wrong as to the meaning of legislation, and it has been said that 'there are great dangers in treating government pronouncements, however helpful, as an aid to statutory construction'.[12]

There are many reported instances in which the higher courts in licensing cases have either refused to be guided by statutory or non-statutory guidance, or have simply found guidance to be an inaccurate statement of the law. Most pertinently, in *R (4 Wins Leisure*

8   *Mucelli v Government of Albania* [2009] UKHL 2.
9   [2004] 1 WLR 3141.
10   *R v Montila*, para 34.
11   Licensing Act 2003, s 182.
12   *R v DPP ex parte Duckenfield* [1999] 2 All ER 873, 895.

Limited) v the Licensing Committee of Blackpool Council[13] Sullivan J held that the statutory guidance under section 182 was wrong as to the interpretation of a later-repealed provision and stated: 'It is important to remember that, whilst regard must be had to the guidance, it should not be allowed to usurp the clear language of the legislation.'[14]

Finally, the Guidance itself issues its own health warning:[15]

> 'The Guidance does not in any way replace the statutory provisions of the 2003 Act or add to its scope and licensing authorities should note that interpretation of the 2003 Act is a matter for the courts. Licensing authorities and others using the Guidance must take their own professional and legal advice about its implementation.'

(7) If the meaning of the Act is ambiguous or obscure, or where its literal meaning leads to an absurdity, reference may be made to Hansard reports of Parliamentary debates on the Bill if, but only if, the following applies:

    (a) The report must be of a statement made by the Minister promoting the Bill.

    (b) The statement must disclose the mischief aimed at by the Act, or the legislative intention underlying the words.

    (c) The statement must be clear.[16]

6.50 In summary, while reference may in certain circumstances be made to subsidiary documentation in order to construe the primary legislation, the primary task is to ascertain the plain and ordinary meaning of the legislative language, aided where necessary by principles of construction, including those relating to the mischief aimed at by the legislation, the purpose of the legislation and the avoidance of absurdity.

Q CONCLUSION

6.51 The Licensing Act 2003 provides a balanced package of freedoms and safeguards which amount to important but not sufficient conditions for the night time economy to thrive in a manner conducive to the promotion of the licensing objectives. The attainment of that end is also dependent on the co-ordinated use of other regulatory regimes, together with proactive measures on the part of the key stakeholders.

---

[13] [2007] EWHC 2213 (Admin), at para [15].

[14] See also *R (Betting Shop Services) v Southend-on-Sea Borough Council* [2008] EWHC 105 (Admin) at para [26] (Gambling Act 2005); R (TC Projects) *Limited v Newcastle Licensing Justices* [2008] EWCA Civ 428 at para [51].

[15] Para 1.10.

[16] *Pepper v Hart* [1993] AC 593.

7

The licensing authority

You hope, because you're old and obese,
To find in the furry civic robe ease?
Rouse up, sirs! Give your brains a racking
To find the remedy we're lacking,
Or, sure as fate, we'll send you packing!

Robert Browning, Pied Piper of Hamelin

A INTRODUCTION

7.01 Most licensing authorities are local authorities and one of the more contentious changes wrought by the Act was the transfer of liquor licensing decision making from magistrates to local councillors. Since then the leisure sector and others, who had been less than complimentary about the abilities of local authority officers and councillors and the supposed advantages of democratic accountability, have had to get used to working with them and within the local government framework. Indeed, in order to operate under the Act effectively and successfully it is necessary to understand how the licensing scheme fits into the more general local government framework within which those very officers and councillors are used to working.

7.02 The judgments in the well known *Hope and Glory* case[1] – of which more in Chapter 20 on appeals – confirm the importance of this change. The Court of Appeal confirmed that the licensing function of a licensing authority is an administrative function (like most other local authority

---

[1]   [2011] EWCA Civ 31.

functions) and stressed that it is to local authorities that the power is delegated to decide what the public interest requires in any particular case requiring determination under the Act. It is for that reason that even on appeal a magistrates' court should pay careful attention to the reasons given by the licensing authority for any decision, which itself should only be reversed if the court is satisfied the licensing authority is wrong.[2] This emphasis on local determination would seem to accord with the current Coalition Government's approach to decision making in other spheres, eg planning, and is consistent with the identification (since 25 April 2012) of the licensing authority as a responsible authority.

7.03   This chapter therefore seeks to provide an overview of the licensing authority as it sits within that framework and to draw attention to those matters to which anyone seeking to navigate within the licensing system should have regard.

7.04   The most important new matter to note (at least as far as licensing in England is concerned) is Part 1 of the Localism Act 2011, which received Royal Assent on 15 November 2011. The Coalition Government has made substantial changes to the local government framework and has sought to provide new freedoms and flexibility for local government which include providing local authorities with a general power of competence, abolishing the Standards Board, making statutory intervention into the law of predetermination and further shaking up the governance of such authorities, with committee systems coming back into favour. These matters are considered in greater detail below. The position in Wales remains largely unchanged by that Act.

7.05   It is too early to predict what impact these changes will have and it is not the purpose of this chapter to deal in any particular detail with the changes or, indeed, to provide a general discourse on local government law. For a fuller exposition on the law relating to such bodies reference should be made to the relevant textbooks.[3] Further, the more specific procedural provisions relating to each type of application are dealt with in the relevant chapters

B   THE LICENSING AUTHORITY

7.06   Licensing authorities are clearly identified by section 3 of the Act. In England they primarily comprise (a) district councils, (b) county councils in which there are no district councils, (c) the councils of London Boroughs and (d) the Council of the Isles of Scilly. In Wales they comprise the council of a county or county borough.

---

[2]   *Hope and Glory,* paras 44–6.
[3]   Eg *Butterworths Local Government Law; Cross on Local Government Law.*

7.07 In addition, the following bodies are also licensing authorities: the Common Council of the City of London, the Sub-Treasurer of the Inner Temple and the Under-Treasurer of the Middle Temple.

7.08 In each case, the licensing authority's area of jurisdiction is the same as the area for which each relevant council acts,[4] i e it will be coincident with that council's normal boundaries, which should be well known or easily ascertainable, being defined by legislation. They are identified in a number of documents, e g OS maps usually show local government boundaries, and, if there is any doubt, reference can be made to the council to ascertain whether the land concerned is within or without its area.[5]

7.09 The licensing authority's jurisdiction within its own area is almost unlimited. It covers all Crown Land, land vested in but not occupied by Her Majesty in the right of the Duchy of Lancaster and land which is vested in but not occupied by the possessor for the time being of the Duchy of Cornwall. It also applies to all persons in the public service of the Crown. However, there can be no criminal liability of the Crown and nothing in the Licensing Act 2003 affects the Queen in her private capacity.[6]

7.10 Moreover, there are no general privileges or exemptions accorded to any bodies as there were under the Licensing Act 1964,[7] albeit that there are a number of specific exemptions to licensable activities set out in Part 2 of Schedule 1 and paragraphs 3–5 of Schedule 2 to the Act. (These are dealt with later in Chapter 8 on Licensable Activities.)

The remainder of this chapter will concentrate upon those bodies referred to in paragraph 7.06.

C LICENSING AUTHORITY AS LOCAL AUTHORITY

7.11 As noted above, in order to understand how licensing authorities themselves function it is necessary to consider the legal framework within which local authorities operate, as all the main licensing authorities are local authorities. That framework is primarily provided by the Local Government Act 1972 (as amended). There is, however, a considerable amount of other material legislation, both primary and subordinate, including, in particular, the Local Government Act 2000 (as amended) and the Localism Act 2011.

---

[4]   Licensing Act 2003, s 3(2).
[5]   Licensing Act 2003, s 12 provides that the relevant licensing authority in relation to an application for a premises license is the authority in whose area the premises are situated. If premises straddle the border, then, for the purposes of the premises licence, s 12(3)–(4) identifies the relevant licensing authority in respect of the application for a premises licence (s 68 makes similar provision for clubs.) For temporary events, the approach is similar but in case of overlap both authorities are relevant authorities: s 99.
[6]   For the provisions as to Crown Land, see s 195, and as to the exceptions sub-ss (3) and (5).
[7]   Section 196.

Corporate status, power and the Localism Act 2011

7.12 One feature common to all local authorities is their corporate status. However section 1 of the Localism Act, in force from 18 February 2012, has provided all local authorities in England with a general power of competence, which itself has replaced the general power of well-being previously provided for by section 2 of the Local Government Act 2000. The 2000 Act continues to govern the position in Wales.

7.13 The Localism Act gives local authorities the same power to act that an individual generally has and provides that the power may be used in innovative ways, that is, in doing things that are unlike anything that a local authority – or any other public body – has done before, or might previously have done, ie to go where no local authority has gone before, although probably not to infinity and beyond. It defines the meaning of an 'individual' so as to avoid referring to the reduced powers exercised by for example a child. Section 1(4)–(6) further defines the extent of the power. Where the authority can do something under the power, the starting point is that there are to be no limits as to how the power can be exercised. For example, the power does not need to be exercised for the benefit of any particular place or group, and can be exercised anywhere in the UK or elsewhere and in any way, including for a commercial purpose with or without charge.

7.14 This does not mean, however, that all existing controls are swept away. Section 2 requires local authorities to act in accordance with statutory limitations or restrictions. Limitations that apply to existing powers that are overlapped by the general power are applied to the general power. So, for instance, if an existing power requires a particular procedure to be followed before it can be exercised, the same procedure will apply to the use of the general power to do the same thing. Likewise, if a power can only be exercised having regard to, say, the four licensing objectives, that will remain the case even if reliance is placed on the general power to undertake the same act. It also applies any express prohibitions, restrictions and limitations within primary or secondary legislation, to the use of the general power. A distinction is drawn between restrictions in pre-commencement legislation and those in post-commencement legislation. Restrictions in post-commencement legislation will only apply to the general power where they are expressed to do so. The general power does not apply to governance functions.[8]

7.15 It has to be borne in mind that local authorities are given greater powers than individuals, eg to administer a licensing system. The Localism Act does not innovate on the extent of the power to undertake such a role, but what it does is affect the manner in which – and the freedom with which – such a role is undertaken.

---

[8]   Localism Act 2011, s 3.

Charging powers

7.16 As to local authority powers to charge for providing services, there is further control. Section 3 restricts the ability of a local authority to charge for providing a service to a person using the general power, or where they are using an overlapped power. Local authorities can charge up to full cost recovery for discretionary services – that is those services that they are not required by legislation to provide – unless specific charging powers exist which provide for a different approach. Likewise section 4 restricts the ability of a local authority to do things for a commercial purpose using the general power. The power does not authorise authorities to trade in a service with a person to whom they are already statutorily obliged to provide it. Also, they must only trade commercially through a company. Further, the provision of the service must be cost-neutral when assessed annually. These provisions reflect broadly – with some changes – the previous trading provisions in sections 93 and 95 of the Local Government Act 2003 (which are themselves amended by the Localism Act) and could become relevant if, as some planning authorities do, any licensing authorities sought to charge for pre-application advice etc. A recent example is Westminster City Council, which has started to charge for pre-application licensing advice.

7.17 The Minister (Mr Eric Pickles) summarised these changes during the Second Reading of the Localism Bill as follows: 'All those fun-loving guys who are involved in offering legal advice to local authorities, who are basically conservative, will now have to err on the side of permissiveness.' Not the permissive society (given certain restrictive changes to the Licensing Act discussed elsewhere), but certainly permissive local government! Put more formally, whereas in the past local authorities could only do things that were permitted to them by legislation, that approach has been 'inverted', and they can do anything that isn't forbidden by legislation.

7.18 There has been little time for case law to develop on the impact of the general power of competence. The first case was *Manydown Co Ltd v Basingstoke and Deane BC* [2012] EWHC 977 Admin, but its impact was limited as the judge determined that section 1 was not available to rescue an authority from the consequences of unlawful actions taken before it came into effect. He did not have to consider the boundaries and limits on the general power. However, it is likely that the courts will pay considerable regard to the desire to free local authorities from unnecessary control. The onus now will be on a challenger to demonstrate there is no power or only a restricted power to do something rather than on the local authority having to point to a power to authorise whatever step/decision is in dispute.

7.19 What does this mean for local authorities as licensing authorities? In carrying out any licensing function, it is suggested that they are still primarily limited to doing that which the framework provided for by the Licensing Act 2003 (and attendant subordinate legislation) permits them to do (and in the manner in which they are permitted to do it).[9] Given that the Licensing Act 2003 provides (or intends to provide) for a self-contained and, arguably, highly prescriptive code it is unlikely that licensing committees, in their exercise of their licensing functions under the Act, will be found to have any (or any need for) substantive, as opposed to procedural, powers beyond those set out in Licensing Act. However, in so far as the Licensing Act framework does not provide for any particular matter they have a free hand provided what they do is not inconsistent with the Licensing Act framework or other provisions which govern local authority conduct.

7.20 For a practical licensing example of the need to rely upon a more general power outside a specific statutory framework, consider the case of registration schemes for nightclub bouncers in the context of public enter-tainment licences and the Local Government (Miscellaneous Provisions) Act 1982 – which made no express provision for them. The Court of Appeal held it was lawful to impose such a system of registration without express powers to that effect but unlawful to charge separately for registration.[10]

7.21 On the other side of the coin is the case of *R* (*on the application of Harpers Leisure International Ltd*) *v Chief Constable of Surrey*[11] where the court declined to imply a power in the licensing authority to refuse to consider an application for a review on the basis that it constituted an alleged abuse of process. Whether or not such a power existed was a matter of statutory construction and, having regard to the underlying purpose and nature of the scheme, the court held that no such implied power existed. There is no reason to consider that the Localism Act would lead to a different conclu-sion.

7.22 Further, case law, such as *Westminster City Council v The Albert Court Residents' Association* [2011] EWCA Civ 430, will no doubt continue to illustrate the point that a local authority has to act in accordance with the express terms of any relevant statutory provision – in that case to grant a licence if no relevant representations were received. They are still good law and consistent with the provisions of sections 1 and 2 of the Localism Act 2011.

Requirement to act within the scope of authority

7.23 In general terms, however, it is still the case that if a licensing authority were to act outside the scope of its authority, its actions would be *ultra vires* and unlawful and capable of being struck down by the High Court

---

9   See the approach of the court in *R* (*BBPA*) *v Canterbury CC* [2005] EWHC 1318 (Admin).
10   *R v Liverpool City Council, ex parte Barry* [2001] LGR 361, [2001] LLR 310, CA.
11   [2009] EWHC 2160 (Admin).

exercising its supervisory function in judicial review proceedings.[12] Furthermore, the presence of such an unlawful act may well be capable of being used as a defence to any action, eg a prosecution, by the authority.[13] The status of an unlawful act or decision which has not yet been struck down is however not entirely clear.[14]

7.24 Moreover and more particularly, the Localism Act does not displace the more general principles which will apply to local authority actions although it may affect some of them. For example:

(a) An authority may still not exclude or limit the future exercise by it of its powers.[15]

(b) If an authority asks itself the wrong question or misinterprets its powers or makes a mistake of fact, it may unlawfully fetter its discretion.[16]

(c) An authority generally has a duty to consider whether it should exercise its powers.[17]

(d) An authority may not enter into any contract, or take any action, incompatible with the due exercise of its statutory powers or the discharge of its functions.[18]

(e) In applying relevant policy, the decision-maker must understand the policy correctly. If he departs from policy he must acknowledge that fact, and set out cogent reasons for doing so.[19]

(f) Importantly, the Supreme Court has clarified that policy statements are to be interpreted objectively in accordance with the language used, read in its proper context.[20] The decision maker will err if a false interpretation is applied even to a policy created and adopted by that very decision maker, such as a licensing policy, even if it was one that appeared to the court to be reasonable even if mistaken.

7.25 However, some pre-existing general principles will require to be reconsidered in the light of the 'inverted' approach to local authority powers referred to above.

---

[12] As to Administrative Law generally, see Wade and Forsyth, *Administrative Law* (OUP, 2009); De Smith, Woolf and Jowell, *Judicial Review of Administrative Action* (Sweet & Maxwell, 2006).

[13] See eg *Boddington v British Transport Police* [1999] 2 AC 143.

[14] See *Boddington*, pp 164, 165, 172, 175; and *Clockfair Limited v Sandwell MBC* [2012] EWHC 1857 (Admin).

[15] See *R v Secretary of State for the Home Department, ex parte Venables* [1998] AC 407, in particular the speech of Lord Browne-Wilkinson at p 496G to p 497B.

[16] See *R v Secretary of State for the Home Department, ex parte Fire Brigades Union* [1995] 2 AC 513, in particular the speech of Lord Browne-Wilkinson at p 551D–E.

[17] See *Stovin v Wise* [1996] AC 923, in particular the speech of Lord Hoffmann at p 950B.

[18] See *Birkdale District Electric Supply Co v Southport Corporation* [1926] AC 355, in particular the speech of the Earl of Birkenhead at p 364.

[19] See, for example, the judgment of Purchas LJ in *Carpets of Worth Ltd v Wyre Forest District Council* (1991) 62 P&CR 334, at p 342.

[20] See the judgment of Lord Reed in *Tesco Stores Ltd v Dundee City Council* [2012] UKSC 13, at paras 17 to 21.

(a) When a public body is entrusted with an apparently unfettered discretion, it must exercise its power reasonably and in accordance with the relevant statutory purpose.[21] As to the second limb of that requirement, consideration would have to be given in any case to the impact of section 1 of the Localism Act and the extent to which 'statutory purpose' is given expression to by way of a limitation or restriction.

(b) Powers conferred on a local authority by statute can, again subject to the Localism Act, validly be used only in the way that Parliament, when conferring the power, is presumed to have intended.[22] Parliament has clearly intended section 1 to provide a broad power but when a limitation or restriction exists this principle will remain relevant.

(c) An authority must discharge its functions so as to promote – and not so as to thwart or act contrary to – the policy and objects of the legislation conferring the power under which the land was acquired and is held.[23] The same comment can be made as per (b) above.

Procedural failure

7.26 Further, as noted above, the exercise of some powers can often be contingent upon fulfilment of various procedural requirements. Failure to comply with such requirements will not, though, necessarily result in any action being rendered ultra vires. Consideration will be given as to whether or not there has been substantial compliance, whether or not any non-compliance should be waived and as to the consequences of non-compliance.[24]

D EXERCISE OF FUNCTIONS GENERALLY

7.27 Once the particular composition of a local authority is established by election, it is for that local authority to determine how it will then exercise its functions. In the absence of specific statutory provision to the contrary, the power lies with the authority itself, exercise being at meetings of full council. (Consequently, the first step a 'new' council takes is, or should be, to elect a chairman and vice-chairman.)

---

[21] See *Smith v East Elloe RDC* [1956] AC 736, in particular the speech of Lord Radcliffe at p 767.

[22] See *Porter v Magill* [2002] 2 AC 357, in particular the speech of Lord Bingham of Cornhill at p 463D–H.

[23] See *Padfield v Minister of Agriculture Fisheries and Food* [1968] AC 997, in particular the speech of Lord Reid at p 1030B–D, p 1033A, and p 1045G.

[24] See *London & Clydeside Estates Ltd v. Aberdeen District Council* [1980] 1 WLR 182 (HL) and *Regina v. Secretary of State for the Home Department, ex parte Jeyeanthan* [2000] 1 WLR 354 (CA) as applied most recently in *Rochdale BC v Dixon* [2011] EWCA Civ 1173, paras 55–6 and, in a licensing context, *R (TC Projects Ltd) v Newcastle upon Tyne Justices* [2006] EWHC 1018 (Admin).

7.28 Section 7 of the Licensing Act 2003 requires that each licensing authority must establish a licensing committee which must consist of between 10 and 15 members of the authority.[25] It is that committee which will take the vast majority of decisions under the Act.

7.29 Local authorities have historically been run by committees or sub-committees on a day to day basis. These committees are in turn serviced by the officers, who provide the material upon which they make their decisions, most commonly in the form of reports to the committee. Matters of lesser importance (or great urgency) are commonly delegated to officers, some-times with a proviso that decision should be taken after consulting the Chair of any relevant committee or sub-committee. Matters of greater importance, such as general policy, are commonly reserved for determination by full council.

7.30 At meetings of full council each member has a vote and will exercise their vote and contribute to the debate as they see fit. In committees, membership is restricted to particular nominated councillors (non-councillors can be co-opted but they cannot vote), but most councils permit non-committee members to address/attend the committee if they wish to do so. Thus the views of any local member in whose ward premises under consideration may lie will be made known and may well carry considerable weight. This can work both in favour of and against any particular proposal.

Political balance

7.31 The Local Government and Housing Act 1989 has introduced a requirement that appointments by 'relevant authorities' (and committees of relevant authorities) to committees, sub-committees and other bodies achieve a political balance.[26] In broad terms, the political make-up of committees must reflect that of the full council. However, it would appear to be the aim of the Licensing Act 2003 to avoid such controls.

7.32 The provisions of the 1989 Act apply[27] to 'ordinary' committees of an authority.[28] 'Ordinary' committees are later defined to include a council's social services committee and all others appointed under section 102(1)(a) of the Local Government Act 1972, which section provides for appointments pursuant to arrangements under section 101 of the same Act.[29] It would appear clear that the licensing committees are appointed under the Licensing Act 2003 (see further below), and not under the general powers of the Local

---

[25] Save for the Sub-Treasurer of the Inner Temple and the Under Treasurer of the Middle Temple, see s 6(2) of the Licensing Act 2003.
[26] Local Government (Committees and Political Groups) Regulations 1990 (SI 1990/1553), as amended, regs 15–17 and Sch 1.
[27] Sections 15(1) and (7).
[28] Local Government and Housing Act 1989, Sch 1, para 1.
[29] Local Government and Housing Act 1989, Sch 1, para 4.

Government Act 1972, and so are more in the nature of social services committees, which are appointed pursuant to a separate enactment. However, unlike social services committees, they have not been included in the definition of ordinary committee. This interpretation is reinforced by the consequential amendments enacted as part of the Licensing Act 2003, which add a new subsection to section 101 of the Local Government Act 1972 to the effect that the section does not apply to any function under the 2003 Act of a licensing authority.[30] There are no consequential amendments to Schedule 1 of the Local Government and Housing Act 1989. For these reasons, there is no requirement of political balance on licensing committees, but licensing authorities would be well-advised to reflect the political make-up of the local authority on their licensing committees if possible, as a matter of good governance.

Executive arrangements

7.33 When Part II of the Local Government Act 2000 came into force all local authorities were, with limited exception, obliged to adopt 'executive' arrangements. These arrangements were meant to provide for more efficient and effective government – a reaction against the somewhat cumbersome committee system described above. However, the Localism Act has in Part 1, Chapter 5 made wholesale changes to that structure and, perhaps not before time, committees are now back in favour.[31] A local authority must now operate either executive arrangements[32] – which broadly comprise either an elected mayor or leader plus two or more councillors – or a committee system,[33] or prescribed arrangements under any regulations which may in due course be made. These new arrangements will gradually come into play.

7.34 Executive action remains overseen by Overview and Scrutiny committees made up of ordinary members. Whilst the executive is likely to be of one political leaning the Overview and Scrutiny committees must be politically balanced so as to reflect the balance of full council.

E EXERCISE AND DELEGATION OF FUNCTIONS UNDER THE LICENSING ACT 2003

7.35 As stated above, section 7 of the Licensing Act provides that all licensing functions are to be discharged by the licensing committee, with only four exceptions:

---

[30] Schedule 6, para 58.

[31] See the Localism Act 2011, s 21 and Sch 2, which provides for a new Part 1A to the Local Government Act 2000.

[32] As provided for in Chapter 2 of the new Part 1A of the Local Government Act 2000.

[33] See Chapter 3 of the new Part 1A of the Local Government Act 2000.

First exception – adoption of licensing policy

7.36 First, functions concerning the statement of licensing policy under section 5 of the Act have to be carried out by the licensing authority itself. Even if an authority has executive arrangements, it is full council which should exercise functions relating to policy.[34]

Second exception – overlapping functions

7.37 Secondly, if a licensing function overlaps with another function of the licensing authority under the remit of another committee, the particular matter may be referred from the licensing committee to that other committee. (Alternatively, the licensing committee may discharge both functions. In either case, unless the matter is urgent, the committee that is going to take the decision must receive a report from the other relevant committee.[35])

Third exception – impossibility

7.38 Thirdly, if it is impossible for the licensing committee to discharge a function because of the number of its members who cannot take part in its deliberations, ie because of conflict of interest, the particular matter concerned has to be referred back to the licensing authority and the authority may discharge that function.[36]

The licensing committee may also discharge other functions which relate to but are not themselves licensing functions if appropriate arrangements have been made by the licensing authority. If such arrangements are not made, before determining any matter that is related to a licensing function the licensing authority must, unless the matter is urgent, have before it a report of the licensing committee with respect to the relevant matter.[37]

It is not clear whether this would permit licensing committees to perform other licensing duties – eg hackney carriage licensing. The intention would appear to be to create a stand-alone separate committee. However, in practice, the problem could be solved by the same body of members reconstituting itself as an ordinary committee before determining other types of application.

Fourth exception – early morning alcohol restriction orders

7.39 The Police Reform and Social Responsibility Act 2011 made provision for such orders, effectively curfews on alcohol providers, which are dealt with

---

[34] See the Local Authorities (Functions and Responsibilities) (Amendment No 3) Regulations 2004 (SI 2004/2748).
[35] Licensing Act 2003, s 7(2), (5)–(8).
[36] Licensing Act 2003, s 7(9).
[37] Licensing Act 2003, s 7(3)–(4).

in Chapter 40 of this book. Given the importance of such orders, the intention is that they should be made only by the full council.

Powers of delegation

7.40 As to the licensing committee and how it conducts its business, express provision is made for the establishment of one or more sub-committees consisting of three members of the licensing committee[38] and the normal powers of delegation provided for by section 101 of the Local Government Act 1972 do not apply.[39]

7.41 The recent case of *The Queen (Raphael) v Highbury Corner Magistrates Court & London Borough of Islington*[40] demonstrates the importance of ensuring that powers are properly delegated. Whilst the challenge in that case failed on its particular facts and the court indicated that, even if there had been some technical flaw, it would not have granted any relief, it should not be assumed that such a benevolent approach will be taken in all cases, particularly if other errors of law are involved.

7.42 While section 9(1) of the 2003 Act states that sub-committees are to consist of three members of the committee, it does not make requirements as to the quorum. Section 9(2) allows there to be regulations as to the proceedings of sub-committees, but section 9(3) states that subject to such regulations the licensing committee may regulate its own procedure and that of its sub-committees. The upshot is that, in the absence of regulations, a licensing committee may provide for a quorum of fewer than three members of its sub-committees.

7.43 So far as committees are concerned, there is no limit on the number of members who may sit simultaneously. It is the practice of certain committees to sit en masse for contentious matters, eg reviews, and while this may be somewhat intimidating for the attending parties it is perfectly lawful.

7.44 Express provision is also made for sub-delegation either to sub-committees or, subject to certain exceptions, to officers.[41] The exceptions are listed in section 10(4) but, in essence, officers cannot take decisions in respect of matters which are controversial, eg where representations or police objections have been made, nor in respect of revocation under section 124(4).

7.45 Sub-committees can themselves, subject to the same exceptions and any direction given by the licensing committee, delegate further to officers.

---

[38] Licensing Act 2003, s 9(1).
[39] See Local Government Act 1972, s 101(15).
[40] [2011] EWCA Civ 462.
[41] Licensing Act 2003, s 10(1).

Moreover, authorities are permitted to have arrangements which provide for delegating the same matters to both a sub-committee and any officer concurrently. In such circumstances there will no doubt be some scheme of delegation distinguishing which business should be directed where.

7.46 Indeed, the current version of the Guidance[42] states that statements of licensing policy should indicate how, in terms of allocation of decision making duties, any particular licensing authority intends to approach its functions. A recommended scheme of delegation is provided at paragraph 3.63 of Guidance. A three tiered approach is suggested. Officers should deal with non-contentious and enforcement matters. Sub-committees should deal with most contentious matters, whilst the full committee should deal with reviews of premises licences and specific cases where there are police representations. The Guidance notwithstanding, under section 7 it is for the licensing committee itself to delegate functions, and therefore anything stated by the full council in the licensing policy can be no more than a general indication or, more usually, a reflection of that which the committee has determined.

7.47 It is also common within local government for certain powers to be delegated to officers acting in consultation with a specified member, eg in cases of emergency. Such arrangements are lawful provided the officer does not act under the dictation of the member. However, a decision made without that consultation would probably be held unlawful.

F THE CONDUCT OF BUSINESS

7.48 Rules as to the conduct of licensing committees is provided for by the Licensing Act 2003 (Hearings) Regulations 2005[43] and are dealt with in the chapter on hearings, see Chapter 21.

7.49 However, notwithstanding the specific rules, such hearings will also continue to be governed by the normal rules governing administrative hearings, provided that they are not inconsistent with express provisions. Eg an applicant must be told what is said against him. In basic terms he must usually be given a copy of any officer's report which is before the decision making body and notice of any other representations against his case. Moreover, it will be important that the licensing authority clearly distinguishes between its functions, particularly now that it is a responsible authority as well. Therefore, steps should be taken to ensure that its decision making is not infected by its other roles. So, for example, the officers who sit with the committee to administer the licensing function should be different from officers participating in the hearing eg by seeking or supporting a

---

[42] October 2012, paras 13.59–13.61.
[43] SI 2005/44.

review of a licence. The need for separation of responsibilities is noted at paragraphs 9.17–19 and 9.31–2 of the Guidance.

7.50   Two further issues require more detailed discussion – the general rules as to conduct of members and, secondly, the burgeoning case law on bias and predetermination.

Councillor conduct

7.51   A further major change wrought by the Localism Act 2011 is the repeal of Part III of the Local Government Act 2000 and the abolition of the Standards Board for England. In its stead there is now Chapter 7 of the Localism Act.

7.52   Under the new provisions all relevant local authorities '*must promote and maintain high standards of conduct by members and co-opted members of the authority*',[44] and in order to discharge this duty it is a mandatory requirement that the authorities adopt a code dealing with the conduct of members expected of them when acting as members.[45] The underlying ethos behind the changes is that councils, who are democratically accountable to their own electorates, should be free to decide how they promote and maintain high standards of conduct among all their members.

7.53   Relevant authorities however are not given an entirely free hand as to the content of their codes. They are obliged[46] to secure that their code, when viewed as a whole, is consistent with the principles of: (a) selflessness (b) integrity (c) objectivity (d) accountability (e) openness (f) honesty and (g) leadership. (Absent from this list are duties to respect others and uphold the law which were previously present in a broadly equivalent list of principles.) The code must provide for registration and disclosure of pecuniary and non-pecuniary interests.[47] If an allegation of a breach of a code is made in writing, the authority must, having involved an independently appointed person, take a decision on whether or not to investigate the allegation and, if it is considered that an investigation is warranted, investigate in any way the authority sees fit. Enforcement of the code, apart from certain limited but specific criminal offences,[48] is in effect left to the local authority but it cannot exclude members from meetings or suspend them. Perhaps most importantly, for these purposes, it is expressly stated that a decision is not invalidated by a failure to comply with the code.[49]

---

[44]   Localism Act 2011, s 27(1).
[45]   Localism Act 2011, s 27(2).
[46]   Localism Act 2011, s 28(1).
[47]   Localism Act 2011, s 28(2).
[48]   Localism Act 2011, s 34.
[49]   Localism Act 2011, s 28(4).

7.54 Whether this more relaxed control of councillors will produce better decision making whilst adequately controlling poor behaviour is arguable, but time will tell.

Predetermination

7.55 In parallel with the abolition of the Standards Board, Parliament has used the Localism Act to attempt to clarify the rules on 'predetermination'. In basic terms, predetermination occurs where someone has a closed mind, with the effect that they are unable to apply their judgment fully and properly to an issue requiring a decision. There is a clear and crucial distinction between predisposition and predetermination. The former is acceptable, the latter is not. A finding of predetermination or apparent predetermination would normally lead to a decision being quashed. The concept was developed out of the rules relating to bias (ie no decision maker should be biased or appear to be biased towards a particular outcome) to ensure that councillors came to council discussions – on, for example, planning or licensing applications – with an open mind.

7.56 However, the government considered that these rules had been interpreted in such a way as to reduce the quality of local debate and stifle valid discussion. In some cases councillors were warned off doing such things as campaigning, talking with constituents, or publicly expressing views on local issues, for fear of being accused of bias or facing legal challenge. The new provision[50] therefore provides that a decision-maker is not to be taken to have had, or to have appeared to have had, a closed mind when making the decision *just because* (a) the decision-maker had previously done anything that directly or indirectly indicated what view the decision-maker took, or would or might take, in relation to a matter, and (b) the matter was relevant to the decision.

7.57 Yet it has been observed, with some justification, that this section creates at least as much uncertainty as it resolves, and will probably make no difference at all to the previous situation. In particular, the words 'just because' are a pressure point: it is inconceivable that previous expressions of very strong opinion would not be relevant and admissible in showing that someone had a closed mind, just as it always was inconceivable that a mere previous expression of a provisional opinion would have been seen as conclusive evidence of a closed mind. So whether or not a decision-maker has an open mind will be required to be judged in the light of all the circumstances and available evidence, including previous opinions, in exactly the same way as it would have been before the enactment of this section.

7.58 Perhaps more importantly, the courts have taken an increasingly restrictive view as to the issue of predetermination – see in particular the

---

[50]   Localism Act 2011, s 25(2).

Court of Appeal's decision in *R (Lewis) v Redcar and Cleveland BC*.[51] First, the court endorsed the view that the approach to predetermination in administrative context is quite different from that in judicial or quasi-judicial contexts, albeit that the underlying test is the same. In particular, it endorsed the view that the importance of appearance of predetermination is generally more limited in administrative contexts. There is express recognition that democratically accountable decision makers are not expected to be as independent or impartial as if they were judges or quasi-judges, and that they should be trusted to abide by the rules and to take decisions with open minds. Indeed, recently the Court of Appeal has emphatically endorsed its approach in *Lewis* and taken it further – disapproving an earlier expressed view that the apparent predetermination of one councillor would taint the remainder of the committee.[52] The point appears to have been obiter in that case and there is no real guidance how to approach the impact of apparent predetermination of one councillor when assessed against the views of others. If it transpires that it is necessary to show that the votes of those 'guilty' of predetermination were essential to the decision under challenge being taken it will be very much more difficult to challenge a decision in the future. In the light of these two cases, earlier decisions, particularly on apparent predetermination, will need to be reconsidered.

7.59 That said, in general terms, councillors should not approach matters with closed minds and the following principles still hold good. Councillors should be careful to ensure that they approach the matter with open mind and not to give the impression they have made their minds up before the decision is taken.

(a) As to voting and party loyalty, an individual councillor may be influenced, but his discretion should not be fettered, by party loyalty and party policy. It is the responsibility of the councillor alone to decide what view to take on any question which he has been called upon to decide.

(b) In terms of party political policy generally, public powers given to a local authority, such as powers under the Licensing Act 2003, should only be exercised for the public purpose for which they have been conferred. Those who exercise powers for some other purpose behave improperly. Councillors do not act improperly or unlawfully if, exercising a power on behalf of a council for its proper purpose, they hope to obtain the electorate's support and strengthen their electoral position. Also they may lawfully support party policy so long as they do not abdicate responsibility to exercise personal judgment. However, powers conferred on a local authority may not lawfully be exercised to promote the electoral advantage of a political party.[53] Thus a party in power

---

[51]   [2009] 1 WLR 83.
[52]   *R (Berky) v Newport City Council* [2012] EWCA Civ 378 in particular per Sir Richard Buxton at paras 58–59 and Pill LJ at para 30.
[53]   See *Porter v Magill* [2002] 2 AC 357.

must exercise its functions properly and not resist any and every application in order to further its political purpose.

7.60 Officers who are involved in any investigations etc which result, for example, in action against the licensee obviously should not take part in the deliberations of the committee,[54] although of course they may give evidence before the committee.

7.61 If these rules are breached then, provided the decision is appealable to the magistrates' court, that avenue rather than judicial review is likely to be the preferable approach. Judicial review is a remedy of last resort, and permission to proceed by judicial review is refused where there is an effective alternative remedy. The impact of any breach is likely only to be relevant to the weight the court may attach to the decision. However, where such an appeal is not available the above concepts will assume greater importance.

G LIABILITY IN TORT ETC

7.62 The issue of liability in tort (eg negligence) for actions of local authorities when administering schemes, such as under the Licensing Act 2003, is beyond the scope of this book. However, the following general points should provide a useful starting point for any consideration of the matter.

- There is no general right of damages for maladministration[55] although the tort of misfeasance in public office provides redress where there is targeted malice or an officer knowingly acts without power in the knowledge that such act is likely to injure another party. Therefore, mere delay in dealing with an application leading to late opening of a business could not found a claim for damages under normal common law principles.[56]
- The Local Government Ombudsman has no power to order, as opposed to recommend, compensation consequent upon a finding of maladministration, although payment of some compensation is a common outcome.
- It used to be thought either that no liability could arise for the actions of officers and/or authorities in carrying out functions in processing licence applications or, if it did, it would be limited to the most extreme circumstances. (Eg an officer of a licensing authority may negligently give misleading advice about the ambit, say, of a condition attached to a licence.) Such a general proposition can no longer be advanced with

---

[54] See *R v Barnsley MBC ex parte Hook* [1976] 1 WLR 1052 CA at 1057F–G, where the court held that a market manager who terminated a licence should not have taken part in a subsequent internal appeal decision.

[55] *R v Knowsley MBC, ex p Maguire* (1992) 90 LGR 653.

[56] E.g. *Haddow v SOSE* [2000] Env LR 212.

confidence and consideration would have to be given to the particular circumstances of any case.

Whilst a number of planning cases suggest that informal responses by planning officers will not give rise to liability there are increasing exceptions to that rule. A senior building control officer has been held liable for telling a claimant that he could go ahead with building works notwithstanding that the question of whether a planning permission required to be amended remained unresolved.[57]

Furthermore, in *Kane v New Forest District Council*[58] a local planning authority failed in its application to strike out a claim founded upon a condition requiring a footpath to be constructed in a location which was dangerous given lack of adequate sightlines. It was subsequently found liable in damages for an accident that occurred. An analogous situation might arise in a licensing situation if particular building requirements are imposed on a licence which give rise to danger rather than minimise it.

[57] *Lambert v West Devon BC* (1997) 96 LGR 45.
[58] [2001] 3 All ER 914 CA.

8

Licensable activities

No sweeter inn could be found in all Nottinghamshire than that of the Blue Boar. None had such lovely trees standing around, or was so covered with trailing clematis and sweet woodbine; none had such good beer and such humming ale; nor, in wintertime, when the north wind howled and snow drifted around the hedges, was there to be found, elsewhere, such a roaring fire as blazed upon the hearth of the Blue Boar. At such times might be found a goodly company of yeomen or country folk seated around the blazing hearth, bandying merry jests, while roasted crabs bobbed in bowls of ale upon the hearthstone.

The Merry Adventures of Robin Hood
Howard Pyle

A INTRODUCTION: THE FRAMEWORK

8.01 Part 1 of the Licensing Act 2003 consists of two commendably short sections which provide the cornerstones upon which the entire edifice of the Act rests. While section 1 defines licensable and qualifying club activities, section 2 sets out the need for authorisations for such activities, whether a premises licence, a temporary event notice or a club premises certificate. But the brevity of section 1 is deceptive, for it ushers in Schedules 1 and 2, which elaborate on the primary definitions.

8.02 Section 1 of the Act sets out definitions of licensable activities and qualifying club activities. The latter is a sub-set of the former, so that all

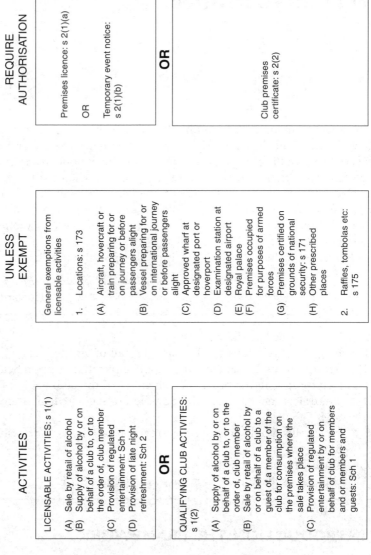

Figure 1: Licensable activities framework

qualifying club activities are also licensable activities. The purpose of the distinction is that different forms of authorisation apply to each.

8.03   Licensable activities are defined as follows:[1]

(a)   the sale by retail of alcohol;[2]

---

[1]   Licensing Act 2003, s 1(1).
[2]   See Section B below.

(b)   the supply of alcohol by or on behalf of a club to, or to the order of, a member of the club;[3]
(c)   the provision of regulated entertainment;[4]
(d)   the provision of late night refreshment.[5]

8.04 Meanwhile, qualifying club activities, which are all also licensable activities, are defined as:

(a)   the supply of alcohol by or on behalf of a club to, or to the order of, a member of the club;
(b)   the sale by retail of alcohol by or on behalf of a club to a guest of a member of the club for consumption on the premises where the sale takes place;
(c)   the provision of regulated entertainment where that provision is by or on behalf of a club to a guest of a member of the club for consumption on the premises where the sale takes place.[6]

8.05 It is not possible to argue under the Act that premises upon which a licensable activity is being carried out are not being 'used' for that activity, thus avoiding the need for an authorisation, for example on the grounds that the activity is a merely ancillary part of another use. It is expressly provided that premises are 'used' for a licensable activity if that activity is carried on or from the premises.[7]

8.06 Section 2 sets out the need for authorisations for licensable and qualifying club activities. There are three types of authorisation available under the Act: premises licence, club premises certificate and temporary event notice.[8] A licensable activity may be carried on under and in accordance with a premises licence pursuant to Part 3 of the Act[9] or, in circumstances where the activity is a permitted temporary activity,[10] by virtue of Part 5.[11] A qualifying club activity may be carried on under and in accordance with a club premises certificate.[12]

8.07 The Act specifically provides that two or more authorisations may be held in respect of the whole or part of the same premises or in respect of the same person.[13] So, for example, if a club which trades under a club premises

---

[3]   See Section C below.
[4]   See Section D below.
[5]   See Section E below.
[6]   Section 1(2). See further below.
[7]   Section 1(6). But note Schedule 1 para 7 which excludes incidental musical entertainment from the definition of regulated entertainment.
[8]   Section 2(4).
[9]   See Chapter 15 (Premises Licences).
[10]   As to which see s 98.
[11]   See Chapter 19 (Temporary Events).
[12]   See Chapter 16 (Clubs).
[13]   Section 2(3).

certificate is holding a temporary event which falls outside the definition of a qualifying club activity, it could do so under the terms of a temporary event notice or a premises licence. Or a pub which wishes to trade beyond the hours permitted by the licence may do so under the terms of a temporary event notice.

8.08   Certain activities are expressly excluded from the definition of licensable activities, even if they fall within the above definitions.[14] These general exclusions from licensable activities are considered below.[15]

8.09   The Live Music Act 2012 created important changes to the regulation of entertainment. In short, it entirely removed the provision of entertainment facilities from the definition of regulated entertainment. Further, it relaxed the licensing requirement for unamplified live music, and also for amplified music taking place on alcohol-licensed premises. These changes, which were designed to support the creative industries, are considered further below.

8.10   It is now necessary to consider the definitions of licensable activities and qualifying club activities in greater detail. As indicated above, there are four separate categories of licensable activities and three categories of qualifying club activities. Naturally, a single premises may be used for any one or more of the categories, whether at the same or at a different time. However, use for any one of the categories at any time will give rise to the need for the relevant authorisation.

B   FIRST LICENSABLE ACTIVITY: THE SALE BY RETAIL OF ALCOHOL

8.11   The first licensable activity is the sale by retail of alcohol.[16]

8.12   The Act is intended to encompass all forms of retail sales of alcohol in its purview. Exceptions are provided only for off-sales from business premises to a trader for the purposes of his trade or to the holders of authorisations under the Act for the purposes of making sales permitted by their authorisations.[17] However, a sale otherwise made to a member of the public in wholesale quantities is for the first time a licensable activity.[18]

8.13   Where the contract for sale is made elsewhere than where the alcohol is 'appropriated to the contract', the Act treats the latter venue as the place where the alcohol is sold.[19] Thus, for example, if a trader executes contracts for sale of wine in his office, which is then selected and despatched from his

---

14   Section 1(7).
15   Section G below.
16   Section 1(1)(a).
17   Section 192
18   See Guidance, para 3.3.
19   Section 190.

shop, then no licensable activity would occur in his office, and so no premises licence would be required for that place. This is further explained in the Guidance:[20] where payment is made on the internet or direct to a call centre handling sales, the sale is treated as being made at the premises from which the alcohol is assigned to the purchaser. Therefore, the call centre would not require a licence, but the warehouse from which the despatch is made would do so.

8.14 It is to be noted that the mere supply of alcohol without sale is not a licensable activity, unless it falls within s 1(1)(b), which governs the supply of alcohol in a club setting.[21] This, however, is not carte blanche for retailers to attempt to avoid the need for a licence by supplying alcohol free with the purchase of some other product or service. The courts have been astute to hold that such 'wheezes' amount to the sale of alcohol.[22] The reason for making a supply of alcohol in the club setting a licensable activity is that it has been generally held that in a true club the member already partly owns the alcohol, so that when he appropriates it on payment of a sum he does not so much buy it as balance his equity in the club's assets.[23]

Alcohol

8.15 The term 'alcohol' embraces spirits, wine,[24] beer,[25] cider[26] or any other fermented, distilled or spirituous liquor.[27] There are certain minor exclusions,[28] namely: alcohol below 0.5%, perfume, certain flavouring essences,[29] Angostura bitters, alcohol comprising or included in a medicinal product, denatured alcohol,[30] methyl alcohol, naphtha and alcohol contained in liqueur confectionery.[31]

---

[20]   Para 3.8.
[21]   See Section C below
[22]   See e g *Horgan v Driscoll* (1908) 42 ILT 238 – daily bottle of porter included in charge for board and lodging.
[23]   See *Graff v Evans* (1882) 8 QBD 373, 378.
[24]   The term 'wine' includes both wine and made-wine within the definition of the Alcoholic Liquor Duties Act 1979: Licensing Act 2003, s 193. For definitions of wine and made-wine see sections 1(4) and (5) respectively of the 1979 Act.
[25]   'Beer' has the same meaning as in the Alcoholic Liquor Duties Act 1979: Licensing Act 2003, s 193. See 1979 Act s 1(3).
[26]   'Cider' has the same meaning as in the Alcoholic Liquor Duties Act 1979: Licensing Act 2003, s 193. See 1979 Act s 1(6).
[27]   Section 191.
[28]   See s 191(1)(a)–(i).
[29]   Namely, those recognised by the Commissioners of Customs and Excise as not being intended for consumption as or with dutiable alcoholic liquor, as defined by the Alcoholic Liquor Duties Act 1979. 'Dutiable alcoholic liquor' means spirits, beer, wine, made-wine and cider: 1979 Act s 1(1).
[30]   'Denatured alcohol' has the same meaning as in s 5 of the Finance Act 1995: Licensing Act 2003, s 191(2).
[31]   'Liqueur confectionery' means confectionery containing alcohol in a proportion not greater

C SECOND LICENSABLE ACTIVITY: THE SUPPLY OF ALCOHOL BY OR ON BEHALF OF A CLUB TO, OR TO THE ORDER OF, A MEMBER OF THE CLUB

8.16   The second licensable activity is the supply of alcohol[32] by or on behalf of a club to, or to the order of, a member of the club.[33] This licensable activity puts in a further appearance in the guise of a qualifying club activity in section 1(2)(a).

8.17   The term 'club' is not defined in section 1, or indeed anywhere else in the Act. This is because the types of club which can avail themselves of the lighter touch regulation applied to clubs are limited to those which are 'qualifying clubs' within the meaning of section 61.[34] Thus, the type of club does not affect whether the activity in question is a licensable activity, but does affect whether the operator can apply for a club premises certificate rather than a premises licence.[35]

D THIRD LICENSABLE ACTIVITY: THE PROVISION OF REGULATED ENTERTAINMENT

8.18   The third licensable activity is the provision of regulated entertainment.[36] The definition of 'regulated entertainment' is revealed in somewhat complex fashion in Schedule 1 to the Act. For an activity to amount to 'regulated entertainment' it must satisfy three fundamental tests:

---

than 0.2 litres of alcohol (of a strength not exceeding 57%) per kilogram of the confectionery and either consists of separate pieces not weighing more than 42g, or is designed to be broken into such pieces for the purposes of consumption: Licensing Act 2003 s 191(2). 'Strength', for these purposes, is to be construed in accordance with s 2 of the Alcoholic Liquor Duties Act 1979: Licensing Act 2003, s 191(2).

[32]   For meaning of 'alcohol' see para 8.15 above.

[33]   Section 1(1)(b).

[34]   See Chapter 16 (Clubs).

[35]   Paragraph 28 of the Explanatory Notes to the Act which accompanied the Bill stated that supplies of alcohol by clubs which are not within the ownership or control of members are sales within s 1(1)(a), and that s 1(3) ensured that references to the supply of alcohol by clubs to members do not include supplies by such clubs. If this was the draftsman's intention, it has not been carried through properly. Section 1(1)(b) does not distinguish membership clubs and proprietor's clubs, and s 1(3) states simply that references to supplies to or to the order of club members do not include references to sales. Further, contrary to the Notes, not all supplies by proprietor's clubs to members are sales – they may be supplies made without consideration. In practice, this drafting deficiency may not matter, because of the need for a club to be a qualifying club within s 60 in order to obtain a club premises certificate in relation to the supply of alcohol.

[36]   Section 1(1)(c).

(1)   It must fall within one of the descriptions of 'entertainment'.[37]
(2)   The general conditions set out in Schedule 1 Part 1 must be satisfied.
(3)   The activity in question must not be exempted by Schedule 1 Part 2.

These three tests shall now be examined.

Descriptions of 'entertainment'

8.19   A total of eight types of entertainment are set out in the Act.[38] They have in common the need for an audience,[39] which includes spectators.[40] Furthermore, Parliament deemed it necessary to provide that the entertainment had to be provided inter alia for the purpose of entertaining the audience.[41] 'Entertaining' is not defined by the Act, but its Oxford English Dictionary definition of engaging the attention agreeably or amusing is likely to be accepted. Conceivably, this may mean that if the purpose of the 'entertainment' is only to instruct or proselytise the audience rather than divert it, then the activity would not be categorised as regulated entertainment. There may be refined questions as to whose 'purpose' is relevant. If a performance of Richard III is in fact entertaining, but is mounted by a political radical expressly for the purpose of provoking hostility against the system of monarchy, would this be considered entertainment? What if the director's purpose is political but the producer's is entertainment? Whose purpose prevails? What of the performance for schoolchildren who are there only to revise for their GCSEs and who cannot conceive of being moved or amused by the drama? It is thought that the word 'purpose' must be objectively considered – the need for a licence cannot turn on the psychological make-up and motivation of the production team or the audience.[42]

8.20   We must now consider the eight types of 'entertainment' defined in the Act.

(a)   'A performance of a play'[43]

8.21   This is defined as a performance of any dramatic piece, whether involving improvisation or not, which is given by one or more persons actually present and performing and in which the whole or a major

---

[37]   Schedule 1, paras 1(1)(a) and 2.
[38]   Schedule 1, para 2(1)(a)–(h).
[39]   Schedule 1, para 2(1).
[40]   Schedule 1, para 2(2).
[41]   Schedule 1, para 2(2).
[42]   This turns on an interpretation of the term 'purpose' in this particular context. In other contexts, purpose has been given both an objective and subjective meaning. See *IRC v Mills* [1975] AC 38 (objective) and *Department of Transport v Gallacher* [1994] ICR 967, 975 (subjective).
[43]   Schedule 1, para 2(1)(a).

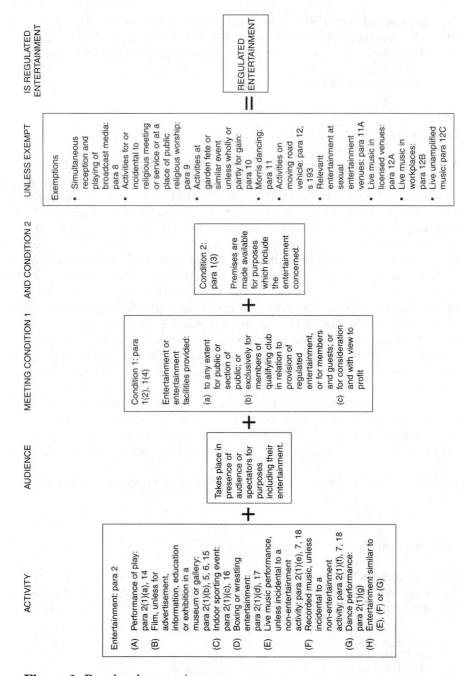

Figure 2: Regulated entertainment

proportion of what is done by the performer(s), whether by way of speech, singing or action, involves the playing of a role.[44] This definition is clearly sufficiently wide to comprehend scripted or improvised drama, opera or mime. Rehearsals are expressly included within the definition.[45]

(b) 'An exhibition of a film'[46]

8.22 An 'exhibition of a film' means any exhibition of moving pictures,[47] but it excludes exhibits put on show for any purposes of a museum or art gallery.[48] This exemption would not avail a museum which wished to use its facilities to show commercial films. The exemption is rather directed at the museum or gallery which shows moving pictures as part of a particular exhibit on display. Also excluded are films whose sole or main purposes are to demonstrate products, advertise goods or services or provide information, education or instruction.[49] Thus a primarily educational film which sets out to ensure that the attention of its audience is held through, for example, amusing commentary or lively music would remain exempt. There will clearly be questions of degree as to when an educational film becomes an entertaining one, which would need to be judged on a case by case basis.

(c) 'An indoor sporting event'[50]

8.23 An indoor sporting event is defined as a sporting event which takes place wholly inside a building and at which the spectators present at the event are accommodated wholly inside the building.[51] The term 'sport' is widely defined to include any game in which physical skill is the predominant factor and also any form of physical recreation which is also engaged in for purposes of competition or display.[52] Thus, it seems that activities such as darts, shove halfpenny, snooker, pool and ten-pin bowling could all come within the meaning of 'sport', provided of course that the activity was being watched by an audience and was being provided for purposes which included their entertainment.[53] Furthermore, activities which do not consist of games at all, but nonetheless consist of physical recreation engaged in competitively or for display are embraced in the definition. This might include gymnastics or indoor athletics events. It is not necessary for there to be winners and losers for an event to qualify as an indoor sporting event, because a 'sporting

---

44   Schedule 1, para 14(1).
45   Schedule 1, para 14(2).
46   Schedule 1, para 2(1)(b).
47   Schedule 1, para 15.
48   Schedule 1, para 6.
49   Schedule 1, para 5.
50   Schedule 1, para 2(1)(c).
51   Schedule 1, para 16(1).
52   Schedule 1, para 16(2)(a).
53   See para 8.19 above.

event' is defined as 'any contest, exhibition or display or any sport'.[54] The term 'building' is given an extended definition, being 'any roofed structure (other than a structure with a roof which may be open or closed) and includes a vehicle,[55] vessel[56] or moveable structure.'[57] It is unclear why the draftsman has chosen to exclude buildings with retractable roofs, unless this is intended to exclude sports stadia with retractable roofs, which may be subject to regulation under the Safety of Sports Grounds Act 1975, and would in any event require a premises licence if any other form of licensable activity was taking place there. It is thought that the inclusion of moveable structures is not confined to structures which are moved in their constructed state, but is apt to include structures which can be dismantled and carted away, such as marquees: at least there would be no sensible reason to exclude such structures from control.

(d)   'Boxing or wrestling entertainment'[58]

8.24   It may be wondered why boxing and wrestling entertainments are given a category of their own, rather than falling within the previous category of indoor sporting events. It is thought unlikely that the draftsman was trying to state that these activities do not constitute sport, as that term is defined. Indeed, the definition accorded to the term – 'any contest, exhibition or display of boxing or wrestling'[59] – serves to underline their sports-like nature. Rather, the position appears to be that, of all sports, outdoor boxing and wrestling require to be licensed under the Act. Why these particular sports have been selected for special treatment is not entirely clear, but is probably concerned with the pugilistic nature of the event and the febrile atmosphere which this may generate.

(e)   'Performance of live music'[60]

8.25   Music is defined to include 'vocal or instrumental music or any combination of the two'.[61] The definition is obviously not exhaustive, and it is perhaps surprising that it should be focused on the mode of production of the music rather than its constituent elements, eg sound, pitch, rhythm or beat, or how this is heard. Modern music can be generated in a great variety of ways, eg electronically or by computer. More outlandishly, the 19th century performer, Joseph Pujol, 'Le Petomane', created musical notes by

---

54   Schedule 1, para 16(2).
55   This means a vehicle intended or adapted for use on roads: s 193.
56   This includes a ship, boat, raft or other apparatus constructed or adapted for floating on water: s 193.
57   Schedule 1, para 16(2).
58   Schedule 1, para 2(1)(d).
59   Schedule 1, para 17.
60   Schedule 1, para 2(1)(e).
61   Schedule 1, para 18.

passing wind, far out-earning Sarah Bernhardt at the Moulin Rouge. While this would not qualify as instrumental music, it was incontestably 'music' within the Act's definition.

INCIDENTAL MUSIC

8.26 As a concession to the Musicians Union, which was concerned at the loss of the 'two in a bar' exception to the requirement for a public entertainment licence in section 182 of the Licensing Act 1964, the 2003 Act expressly excludes live musical performances or the playing of recorded music which are incidental to a non-entertainment activity.[62] The Bill was originally drafted to exclude only incidental recorded music, but was amended so as to broaden the exemption. The effect is that the restaurant can hire a pianist or the pub a fiddler without requiring the provision of regulated entertainment to be reflected on its licence.

The issue of what amounts to 'incidental' music is liable to give rise to interesting questions in practice. It is suggested that the following matters may be relevant:

(1) The volume of the music, both absolutely and in relation to the ambient noise.

(2) Whether those present are permitted to talk during the performance, or whether the expectation (by management and others present) is that they will listen during the performance.

(3) Whether a charge has been made for the performance.[63]

(4) The extent of advertising of the event. For example a note on an exterior board may be viewed differently from fly-posting, or even newspaper advertisements.

(5) Are those present arranged as an audience or as, for example, diners?

(6) Viewed in the round, are the public there in order to watch the performance or is the performer there to entertain the public while they are engaged in another activity?

(f) 'Any playing of recorded music'[64]

8.27 The playing of recorded music[65] is licensable under the Act. However, the 'incidental music' exemption[66] applies equally here. A pub juke box, for

---

[62] Schedule 1, para 7.

[63] The Guidance (para 15.32) says that it is not normally relevant to inquire whether the performance is pre-arranged and whether a charge is made. However, it is respectfully submitted that this is wrong. It is most unlikely that the music will be incidental where an audience has paid to listen to a particular performer.

[64] Schedule 1, para 2(1)(f).

[65] For definition of 'music' see para 8.25 above.

[66] See para 8.26 above.

example, will almost always be incidental music.[67] Further, it is rare for recorded music to be played before a live audience. The main setting in which recorded music will actually be licensable, therefore, is a nightclub, where the music is very much the point of the exercise and may in fact be played by a DJ who has attained celebrity status for his ability to entertain the audience in question.

(g) 'Performance of dance'[68]

8.28 This definition speaks for itself.

(h) 'Entertainment of a similar description to that falling within paragraph (e), (f) or (g)'[69]

8.29 This is obviously intended to be a catch-all provision, to ensure that more esoteric performances which are on the margin of music or dance will be captured by the Act. However, the Act has not swept up a number of performances which might be thought logically to require a licence. These are stand-up comedy and magic performances. Most comedy clubs are unlikely to escape the need for a licence because of the service and consumption of alcohol within the auditorium. But the omission of magic performances from the licensing requirement is somewhat surprising.

HYPNOTISM

8.30 The Act does not regulate hypnotism, but this continues to be governed by the Hypnotism Act 1952.[70] Section 2 of that Act prevents hypnotism for the purposes of public entertainment without an authorisation from the controlling authority, which is the same as the licensing authority under the 2003 Act.

Modification of definitions by Secretary of State

8.31 The definition of entertainment may be enlarged, varied or removed by the order of the Secretary of State, who is given express power to amend the Schedule itself.[71] This power may come to be exercised as the market

---

[67] See further para 8.26 above. The Guidance suggests that if played at high volume it would not qualify for exemption (para 15.31). However, the volume of the music can only be one part of the test, and it is hard to contemplate any case in which the juke box would be the point of the evening, rather than being incidental to some other activity.
[68] Schedule 1, para 2(1)(g).
[69] Schedule 1, para 2(1)(h).
[70] By virtue of amendments to the 1952 Act contained in Sch 6, paras 25–27.
[71] Schedule 1, para 4.

throws up new forms of entertainment, or it comes to be appreciated that certain forms of entertainment have been omitted from the scrutiny of the Act, or no longer require regulation. A draft deregulation order was before Parliament at the time of publication of this volume.[72]

The general conditions for regulated entertainment

8.32 In order for entertainment to amount to regulated entertainment, it is not sufficient that it complies with the definitions of those terms. They must also satisfy two general conditions.[73]

First general condition

8.33 This condition may be met in three alternative ways, as shown in Figure 2. The condition is designed to ensure that only entertainment which is provided for the public, or club members or for profit can become regulated entertainment. It is apparently designed to exclude the purely private event. It does not exclude the charitable event, unless that event is private. It works by stating what is included within the condition, rather than by excluding that which is not intended to be covered.

PUBLIC NATURE

8.34 The first part of the first general condition relates to provision of the activity 'to any extent for members of the public or a section of the public.'[74]

8.35 Much of the pre-existing case law concerned operators who wished to avoid the need for a licence by establishing a nominal club so as to argue that customers were club members and had thus ceased to be members of the public. The argument has turned upon whether there is a sufficient degree of segregation to convert the member of the public into a genuine club member. Procurement of a form of membership does not guarantee success. For example, in *Lunn v Colston-Hayter*[75] membership was obtained by completion of an application form countersigned by an existing member, but there was no rule book, constitution or limitation on numbers. Application had to be made 24 hours before the offending event, and no tickets were on sale on the night. Simon Brown LJ held:[76]

'... nothing about gaining membership of these clubs involved a sufficient degree of segregation or selection ... to translate the innumerable successful applicants from being members of the public to being

---

[72] The Licensing Act 2003 (Descriptions of Entertainment) (Amendment) Order 2013.
[73] Schedule 1, para 1(1).
[74] Schedule 1, para 1(2)(a).
[75] (1991) 155 JP 384.
[76] *Lunn v Colston-Hayter*, p 388.

instead, rather than in addition, club members. It is not necessary to go so far as to characterise these clubs as a sham. It is sufficient to see them for what they are: transparent devices designed to achieve the effect of circumventing the licensing requirements for this sort of entertainment.'

The court was, respectfully, quite right to look beyond the formal nature of the structure to see whether it satisfied the trappings of the club, by asking itself whether in fact the purpose of the venture was to run a membership club or merely to circumvent licensing requirements. One important element in that consideration will plainly be whether there is a genuine selection procedure, or rather whether the club is in fact open to all-comers.

8.36   There is a respectable line of 19th century authority that there does not need to be a charge for admission to be made in order for the event to be 'public'.[77] However, the fact that admission is charged does not necessarily make the event public. In a case in which a single person had procured entry on payment of the admission fee, it was held that:

> '... the test ... is not whether one, two or three or any particular number of members of the public were present, but whether, on the evidence, the proper inference is that the entertainment was open to the public in the sense that any reputable member of the public on paying the necessary admission fee could come into and take part in the entertainment.'[78]

In that case, it was held that while it might be open to draw the inference from a single admission of a member of the public that public entertainment was being provided, that was not the only possible inference. The inference may well be easier to draw under the 2003 Act, because it is only necessary to show that the entertainment or facilities are provided 'to any extent' either for members of the public or a section of the public.[79] Where a group of friends club together to hire a hall, inviting only their own friends, each contributing to the expenses through purchasing tickets, this is not to be considered as entertainment of members of the public or a section of the public. If, however, they admit members of the public beyond their circle, whether free or for a charge, then the event satisfies the first condition.[80]

'SECTION OF THE PUBLIC'

8.37   The addition of the term 'or a section of the public' requires some examination.

---

[77]   See eg *Archer v Willingrice* (1802) 4 Esp 186; *Gregory v Tuffs* (1833) 6 C & P 271.
[78]   *Gardner v Morris* (1961) 59 LGR 187, 189 per Lord Parker of Waddington CJ.
[79]   Schedule 1, para 1(2)(a), see paras 8.38–40 below.
[80]   The issue of the 'subscription ball' was discussed in *Maloney v Lingard* (1898) 42 SJ 193, although the decision itself was on the facts.

8.38 Use of an expression of this nature, rather than merely 'members of the public' was roundly criticised by Viscount Dilhorne in *Race Relations Board v Dockers Club*[81] as being conducive to litigation. It apparent purpose was explained by Lord Diplock[82] as being designed to exclude the situation in which the relationship between the provider and the seeker of the relevant services is of a private or personal character.

8.39 In *Dingle v Turner*[83] the House of Lords had to consider whether a trust fund for employees and ex-employees of a large company was for a section of the public, and therefore charitable. While the decision turned on somewhat arcane principles appertaining to charity law, the speech of Lord Cross of Chelsea was more generally illuminating. In particular, Lord Cross rejected the notion that the public/private fault-line is along the question of whether the individuals in question were bound by common ties to a particular person or body. Rather, it was necessary to stand back and ask whether they were a section of the public. He said:[84]

> 'For my part I would prefer to approach the problem on far broader lines. The phrase a "section of the public" is in truth a vague phrase which may mean different things to different people. In the law of charity judges have sought to elucidate its meaning by contrasting it with another phrase: "a fluctuating body of private individuals." But I get little help from the supposed contrast for as I see it one and the same aggregate of persons may well be describable both as a section of the public and as a fluctuating body of private individuals. The ratepayers of the Royal Borough of Kensington and Chelsea, for example, certainly constitute a section of the public; but would it be a misuse of language to describe them as a "fluctuating body of private individuals"? After all, every part of the public is composed of individuals and being susceptible of increase or decrease is fluctuating. So at the end of the day one is left where one started with the bare contrast between "public" and "private." No doubt some classes are more naturally describable as sections of the public than as private classes while other classes are more naturally describable as private classes than as sections of the public. The blind, for example, can naturally be described as a section of the public; but what they have in common – their blindness – does not join them together in such a way that they could be called a private class. On the other hand, the descendants of Mr. Gladstone might more reasonably be described as a "private class" than as a section of the public, and in the field of common employment the same might well be said of the employees in some fairly small firm. But if one turns to large companies employing many thousands of men and women most of whom are quite unknown to one another and to

81 [1976] AC 285, 295E.
82 *Race Relations Board v Dockers Club*, p 297E.
83 [1972] AC 601.
84 *Dingle v Turner*, pp 616–617.

the directors the answer is by no means so clear. One might say that in such a case the distinction between a section of the public and a private class is not applicable at all or even that the employees in such concerns as I.C.I. or G.E.C. are just as much "sections of the public" as the residents in some geographical area. In truth the question whether or not the potential beneficiaries of a trust can fairly be said to constitute a section of the public is a question of degree ... '

8.40 So, provision of entertainment facilities only to pensioners, or supporters of a particular football club, would amount to provision to a section of the public. But provision by a parent teachers association to parents at a particular school would most probably not come within the condition, since such parents could not be considered to be a section of the public. Nor would staff at a small office party. However, were the Civil Service to hold an annual ball, to which all its workers and their spouses were invited, it would be very hard to argue that the guest list did not amount to a section of the public.

QUALIFYING CLUB

8.41 The second part of the first general condition deals with provision 'exclusively for members of a club which is a qualifying club in relation to the provision of regulated entertainment, or for members of such a club and their guests'.[85] The question of whether a club is a qualifying club according to that definition is dealt with in sections 62–64, and involves satisfaction of a series of tests in relation to the bona fides and membership of the club.[86]

8.42 The Act produces the curious situation that if entertainment is provided to persons who are genuinely club members, and therefore not members of the public, but the club is not a qualifying club, then the entertainment is not regulated at all. This appears to be a lacuna in the legislation. The gap is partly filled by the third part of the first general condition, which sweeps up profit-making enterprises. But it seems to be the case that, at least in relation to entertainment, some non-profit making clubs can side-step regulation altogether. This is in contrast to the provisions concerning non-recognised clubs in the context of late night refreshment.[87]

CONSIDERATION AND VIEW TO PROFIT

8.43 The third part of the first general condition is one in which neither the first nor the second part applies and the activity is provided 'for consideration and with a view to profit'.[88]

---

[85]   Schedule 1, para 1(2)(b).
[86]   See further Chapter 16 (Clubs).
[87]   See Sch 2, para 6.
[88]   Schedule 1, para 2(c).

8.44 It seems tolerably clear that the consideration may be provided in cash or kind. However, the consideration must be by way of a charge paid by or on behalf of those enjoying the entertainment.[89] Further, the charge must be made by or on behalf of certain persons. These are a person concerned in the organisation or management of the entertainment.[90] This is not satisfied where the charge is made by a person who simply manages the venue but without managerial control over the actual entertainment.[91] The logic of that is not easy to discern. However, in most cases, the situation will be catered for by one of the first two parts of the first general condition.

8.45 A further qualification is that where the entertainment consists of performing live or recorded music, the performer or player is not concerned in the organisation or management of the entertainment by reason only that he chooses the music or decides how to play it.[92] This has the effect of excluding the disc jockey or musician who is not himself responsible for the organisation or management of the performance. Clearly, if a musician charges the host of a private event for his services, where the host is not charging his guests with a view to profit, the event is unlicensable.[93]

8.46 The requirement that there be a view to profit should be taken to refer to the objective of the enterprise. For example, a classic members' club, in which the members themselves are the owners and run the club through trustees or a committee and hold any trading surplus for the benefit of the club, is not conducted with a view to profit.[94] This may be contrasted with a proprietor's club where the proprietor owns the premises and its stock in trade, and conducts the enterprise with a view to profit, albeit entrusting much of the organising and decision-making to a committee of members.[95] The expression 'view to profit' does seem to focus on the subjective intention of the operator. However, while a not for profit constitution, or avowedly non-commercial intentions, of the operator may carry considerable weight, the fact that the operation does continually turn in profits may well drive one to the view that the operation is being carried out with that end in view.

8.47 During the Parliamentary debates, the House of Lords originally inserted, and then deleted, a provision that entertainment provided with a view to raising money for a charity was provided with a view to profit. The purpose of the removal of the provision was to accord with the Government's view that a private event held by a charity which was intended to cover its costs without making a profit was not within the purview of Schedule 1

---

[89]   Schedule 1, para 1(4).
[90]   Schedule 1, para 1(4)(a).
[91]   *R (Aksu and Yazgan) v London Borough of Enfield* [2013] EWHC 29.
[92]   Schedule 1, para 1(6)
[93]   See Guidance, para 15.6.
[94]   See *Tehrani v Rostron* [1971] 3 All ER 790, 793.
[95]   *Tehrani v Rostron*, p 794.

paragraph 1(2)(c).[96] The effect, however, seems to be that private charitable events which are designed to make a profit do fulfil the third part of the first general condition.

Second general condition

8.48   The second general condition focuses on the premises themselves. It requires that the premises on which the entertainment is provided should be made available for the purposes which include the purpose of enabling the activity to take place.[97] It should be respectfully observed that this provision is a nearly perfect tautology. If the operator of the premises did not make them available for entertainment, it is hard to see how or why they would ever come to be licensed for entertainment.

The general exemptions from regulated entertainment

8.49   Twelve exemptions from regulated entertainment are specified in the Licensing Act 2003.[98] The first three exemptions are in fact qualifications upon the relevant categories of entertainment, and are so shown in Figure 2.

First general exemption: films for advertising, informing or educating[99]

8.50   Films whose sole or main purpose is to demonstrate a product, advertise goods or services or provide information, education or instruction, even if they simultaneously entertain.

Second general exemption: film exhibitions in museums and art galleries[100]

8.51   Films in museums and galleries are exempt when part of an exhibition, again even if they amount to the provision of entertainment.

Third general exemption: incidental music[101]

8.52   The incidental music exemption takes out of licensing control all music to the extent that it is incidental to some other activity which is neither

---

[96]   HL Debs 11 March 2003, Cols 1275–1276
[97]   Schedule 1, para 1(3).
[98]   Schedule 1, paras 5–12.
[99]   Schedule 1, para 5.
[100]   Schedule 1, para 6
[101]   Schedule 1, para 7.

entertainment nor the provision of entertainment facilities, even if such music is provided for the purposes of entertainment.

Fourth general exemption: use of television or radio receivers[102]

8.53 The simultaneous reception and playing of a programme included in a programme service[103] within the meaning of the Broadcasting Act 1990 is deemed not to be regulated entertainment. Despite oft-expressed concern that wide-screen television broadcasting of major sporting events in pubs is far more likely to cause trouble (inside the pub or later) than a flute duet, the position remains that the former does not require a licence.

Fifth general exemption: religious services[104]

8.54 The Act excludes activities for the purposes of, or for purposes incidental to, a religious meeting or service, or at a place of public religious worship. The first part of the exemption is easy to understand. Choral or organ performances, gospel singing and the like which take place during, before or after a religious meeting or service do not require to be licensed, wherever the service occurs. The second part provides a wide exemption from licensing. Effectively, it means that a church which decides to host weekly discos or concerts to pay for the new roof would not need to apply for a licence. It may well be that the legislators considered that the priesthood ought to answer to a higher authority than the licensing authority, and that the commandment to love thy neighbour entirely supplants the licensing objective to prevent public nuisance. Be that as it may, it is perhaps perplexing why entertainment in churches is excluded, while entertainment in other public buildings such as schools does not receive exemption.

Sixth general exemption: garden fetes etc[105]

8.55 This exemption applies not only to garden fetes, but also to functions of a similar event or character.[106] The term 'garden fete' is not defined in the Act, and the extension of the exemption to events of a similar character compounds the amorphous nature of this exemption. The fact that judgments will need to be made in advance of the event, both by the operator and the licensing authority, may heighten the potential for disagreement. The

---

[102] Schedule 1, para 8.
[103] This includes a television broadcasting service or other television programme service; a sound broadcasting service or licensable sound programme service; a digital sound programme service; and certain services conveyed by telecommunication: Broadcasting Act 1990, s 201.
[104] Schedule 1, para 9.
[105] Schedule 1, para 10.
[106] Schedule 1, para 10(1).

word 'fete' connotes an outdoor function at which goods are sold and amusements are provided. The word 'garden' appears to have been added to distinguish the event from, say, a boot fair or amusement fair. However, that might have the effect of excluding from the exemption the fund-raising fair which is held on the hard play area of an inner city school. It is hoped that the licensing authority would exercise latitude and treat that as a function of a similar character. The protection from commercial exploitation of the exemption is that the event must not be promoted with a view to applying the whole or part of the proceeds for the purposes of private gain,[107] the meaning of 'private gain' being construed in accordance with section 19(3) of the Gambling Act 2005.

During the Parliamentary debates, it was suggested that there was no real difference between a garden fete making a profit and a village hall or community centre making a profit, but the Government helpfully explained that whereas events at the former might get out of hand, the latter 'is a rather different matter'.[108] Social anthropologists and lawyers will no doubt speculate why, and how.

Seventh general exemption: morris dancing[109]

8.56 At the eleventh hour, morris dancers and their music were taken out of the description of regulated entertainment.[110] Parliament has therefore arguably decreed that morris dancers are not entertaining, as a matter of law.

Eighth general exemption: vehicles in motion[111]

8.57 This exemption applies to activities on premises consisting of or forming part of a vehicle when the vehicle is not permanently or temporarily parked. The expression 'vehicle' means a road vehicle,[112] so this exemption is principally directed to entertainment for coach parties.

Ninth general exemption: relevant entertainment at sexual entertainment venues[113]

8.58 The purpose of this exemption is to provide a proper demarcation between the regime for the control of regulated entertainment under the Licensing Act 2003 and the regime for the control of sexual entertainment

---

[107] Schedule 1, para 10(2).
[108] HL Debs 11 March 2003, Cols 1277–1278.
[109] Schedule 1, para 11.
[110] The exemption was widened slightly by the Live Music Act 2012, s 2.
[111] Schedule 1, para 12.
[112] Section 193.
[113] Schedule 1, para 11A.

under Schedule 3 of the Local Government (Miscellaneous Provisions) Act 1982. The mechanism is that any entertainment qualifying as sexual entertainment under the 1982 Act[114] is exempt under the 2003 Act, whether the entertainment falls to be licensed under that Act, or whether it would be licensed but for the fact that it happens sufficiently rarely to fall within the frequency exemption under that Act.[115] To the extent that sexual entertainment is exempt under the 2003 Act, so is music which is integral to that entertainment.[116]

Tenth general exemption: live music in licensed venues[117]

8.59   This exemption applies to live music played in venues which benefit from a premises licence or club premises certificate authorising the supply of alcohol for consumption on the premises, where the music is played between 8 am and 11 pm or during the hours permitted by a licensing hours order under section 172 of the Act, and the premises are open for the purpose of being used for the supply of alcohol for consumption on the premises. In addition, the music must either be unamplified or be performed to an audience not exceeding 200 persons. This exemption, which was introduced by the Live Music Act 2012, is intended to promote musical performance in licensed venues. However, if the exemption proves unsuccessful in that in an individual case the licensing objectives are harmed, there is provision for the exemption to be removed upon review.[118] Where this happens, the exemption no longer applies[119] and the musical performance falls to be licensed in the same way as any other licensable activity.

Eleventh general exemption: live music in workplaces[120]

8.60   This exemption, also introduced by the Live Music Act 2012, deregulates live music in workplaces. To be exempt, the premises must be a workplace within the meaning of the Workplace (Health, Safety and Welfare) Regulations 1992,[121] the performance must be to no more than 200 persons and must take place between 8 am and 11 pm on the same day. It does not appear to matter for the purpose of this exemption whether the performance is actually to the workers at the workplace. This would seem to permit any employer to promote a concert for profit without any regulation under the Act.

---

[114]   Schedule 3, para 2A(2).
[115]   Schedule 3, para 2A(3).
[116]   Schedule 1, para 11A(3).
[117]   Schedule 1, para 12A.
[118]   Section 177A(3)–(4).
[119]   Schedule 1, para 12A(b).
[120]   Schedule 1, para 12B.
[121]   Regulation 2(1).

Twelfth general exemption: live unamplified music[122]

8.61   This exemption was also introduced by the Live Music Act 2012. It exempts live unamplified music between 8 am and 11 pm, subject again to the ability of the licensing authority on review to remove the exemption in the case of premises benefiting from a premises licence or club premises certificate.[123]

E   FOURTH LICENSABLE ACTIVITY: THE PROVISION OF LATE NIGHT REFRESHMENT

8.62   Late night refreshment receives a relatively brief definition, and is then made subject to a series of exemptions, which need to be considered in turn.

Late night refreshment: background

8.63   The Act performs the valuable task of harmonising control of late night refreshment premises as between London and the provinces. Previously, control in London was through the London Local Authorities Act 1990,[124] and applied to restaurants operating after 11 pm and takeaways operating after midnight. Control outside London was under the Late Night Refreshment Houses Act 1969 which applied to restaurants operating after 10 pm, but was silent on the question of takeaways, which could only be controlled through closing orders imposed under the Local Government (Miscellaneous Provisions) Act 1982.

Definition of late night refreshment

8.64   The definition falls into two parts.

8.65   The first part stipulates that a person provides late night refreshment if at any time between 11 pm and 5 am he supplies hot food or drink to members of the public, or a section of the public, on or from any premises, whether for consumption on or off the premises.[125] The meaning of the public and section of the public has been considered above, and is intended to exclude supply on a private basis. It is specifically provided that supplies to a member or guest of a member of a club which is not a recognised club[126] is

---

[122]   Schedule 1, para 12C.
[123]   Section 177A(3),(4).
[124]   Which was adopted by all but two boroughs.
[125]   Schedule 2, para 1(1)(a).
[126]   Ie a club which satisfies conditions 1 to 3 of the general conditions in s 62: Licensing Act 2003, s 193. For discussion of these conditions see Chapter 16.

ACTIVITY

- Supply of hot food or drink
- Between 11 p.m. and 5 a.m.
- To public or a section of public
- On or from premises
- For consumption on or off the premises

Para 1(1)(a)

OR

- Supplies or holds himself out as willing to supply hot food or drink
- Between 11 p.m. and 5 a.m.
- To any persons, or persons of a particular description
- On or from premises
- For consumption on or off the premises
- At a time when members of the public or a section of the public are admitted

Para 1(1)(b)

IS PROVISION OF LATE NIGHT REFRESHMENT

PROVISION

OF

LATE

NIGHT

REFRESHMENT

UNLESS EXEMPT

Clubs, hotels and employees

Entrance to premises and consumption is restricted to:
- (A) Members of recognised club
- (B) Residents of hotel, guest house, lodging house, hostel, caravan or camp site or similar for night in question
- (C) Employees
- (D) Engagement in particular trade, profession or vocation
- (E) Guest of person within (A)–(D)

Para 3

OR

Supply is on premises licensed under:
- (A) Greater London Council (General Powers) Act 1966 s 21 (public exhibitions)
- (B) London Local Authorities Act 1995 s 16 (near beer premises)

Para 4

OR

Miscellaneous supplies:
- (A) Hot drink containing/consisting of alcohol
- (B) Hot drink from vending machine
- (C) Hot food or drink free of charge
- (D) Hot food or drink by, or authorised by, registered charity
- (E) Hot food or drink from road vehicle in motion

Para 5

Figure 3: Late night refreshment

to be taken as a supply to a member of the public.[127] In the same vein, the admission of any person as being such a member or guest is to be taken to be the admission of a member of the public.[128]

The expression 'on or from any premises' brings into play the serving hatch or even the kebab van, given that 'premises' is defined to include any place and includes a 'vehicle, vessel or moveable structure'.[129]

Shoddy service is not rewarded under the Act, in that lukewarm food or drink qualifies as hot: the term being defined as 'above ambient temperature.' The food or drink may be supplied already hot or the intention may be to heat it on the premises, but the purpose of the exercise must be to enable it to be consumed hot, whether on or off the premises.[130] So, for example, the supply of a loaf of hot baked bread from an all night bakery would probably not qualify as late night refreshment, whereas the supply of a hot filled roll probably would. It should be noted that the limitation of regulation to the supply of hot food or drink amounts to a substantial deregulatory measure. It means that the supply of cold food or drink is taken out of licensing altogether.

8.66   The second part of the definition widens the reach of the Act when public access to premises is concerned. It arises where at any time between 11 pm and 5 am when members of the public or a section of the public[131] are admitted to any premises, the provider supplies, or holds himself out as willing to supply, hot food or drink to any person, or to persons of a particular description, on or from the premises, whether for consumption on or off the premises. The point of the provision is two-fold. It allows the licensing authority to find that late night refreshment is being provided even where there is merely a holding out by the operator. Second, it extends the ambit of the Act to cases where only private individuals are actually being served with refreshment, provided that members or a section of the public are admitted. So, for example, while a works canteen would normally be excluded from licensing, if the canteen started to admit members of the public too, it would be covered, whether or not it served them.[132]

General exemptions from late night refreshment

8.67   The Act provides for three sets of exemptions from late night refreshment,[133] which are taken in turn.

---

[127]   Schedule 2, para 6(a).
[128]   Schedule 2, para 6(b).
[129]   Section 193.
[130]   Schedule 2, para 2.
[131]   For meaning, see paras 8.38–40 above.
[132]   Unless they are a guest of the employee: see Sch 2, para 3(2)(e).
[133]   Schedule 2, paras 3–5.

First general exemption: clubs, hotels, staff and traders.

8.68   The supply of hot food and drink is not licensable when all those admitted to or served on or from the premises fall within certain categories.[134] Those categories are:

(a)   members of a recognised club;[135]

(b)   residents of hotels, guest houses, lodging houses, hostels, caravan sites, camping sites or similar overnight residential establishments;[136]

(c)   employees of a particular employer;

(d)   those engaged in a particular trade or following a particular location, or members of a particular profession;[137]

(e)   guests of persons within (a) to (d).

In most cases, service and admission confined to those categories will in any event prevent the activity falling within the primary definition of late night refreshment, because the customers will not be members of the public. However, this exemption makes the matter clear.

Second general exemption: premises licensed under certain other Acts

8.69   This exemption concerns London premises already licensed for public exhibition under section 21(1) of the Greater London Council (General Powers) Act 1966 or as near beer premises under section 14 of the London Local Authorities Act 1995. The supply of hot food and drink is immune from licensing under the 2003 Act if it takes place during the licensing hours under one of those licences.[138]

Third general exemption: miscellaneous

8.70   There are five miscellaneous exemptions. These are:

(a)   The supply of hot drink which consists of or contains alcohol.[139] This is because it is caught by the provisions relating to the sale or supply of alcohol.[140]

(b)   The supply of hot drink by means of a vending machine.[141] This exemption only applies to fully automatic machines, where the machine

---

[134]   Schedule 2, para 3(2).

[135]   Ie a club which satisfies conditions 1 to 3 of the general conditions in s 62: Licensing Act 2003, s 193. See further Chapter 16.

[136]   Schedule 2, paras 3(2)(b) and 3(3).

[137]   Schedule 2, para 3(2)(c).

[138]   Schedule 2, para 4.

[139]   Schedule 2, para 5(1)(a). For meaning of 'alcohol' see para 8.15 above.

[140]   See Guidance, para 3.16.

[141]   Schedule 2, para 5(1)(b).

dispenses the drink after payment is inserted.[142] Note that the exemption does not apply to hot food dispensed by machine.[143]

(c) The supply of hot food or drink free of charge.[144] The supply must be genuinely free, in that if, to procure the refreshment, it is necessary to pay for admission to the premises or for some other item, the exemption does not apply.[145]

(d) The supply of hot food or drink by a registered charity or a person authorised by a registered charity.[146]

(e) The supply of hot food or drink on a moving road vehicle.[147] This effectively exempts non-alcoholic refreshment on coaches, since of course the supply of cold food and drink is not licensable in any event.

F QUALIFYING CLUB ACTIVITIES

8.71 Section 1(2) of the Act sets out three qualifying club activities. It is important to note that all qualifying club activities are also licensable activities, although of course the reverse is not also the case. The section stresses the point by stating that for the purposes of the Act the 'following licensable activities are also qualifying club activities.' Therefore, qualifying club activities may be regarded as a subset of licensable activities.

8.72 The purpose of specifying qualifying club activities is that such activities may potentially entitle the operator to apply for a club premises certificate rather than a premises licence. The entitlement is only potential, because in order for the entitlement to arise the club must satisfy a series of further conditions which test whether the club is a 'qualifying club' in relation to the qualifying club activities.[148]

8.73 The advantage of being able to apply for a club premises certificate rather than a premises licence is that clubs receive lighter regulation. Most importantly, there is no need for a personal licence or a designated premises supervisor as there is in the case of a premises licence.[149]

8.74 There are three qualifying club activities. These are:

(a) The supply of alcohol by or on behalf of a club to, or to the order of, a member of the club. This replicates the wording of the licensable activity in section 1(1)(b).[150]

---

[142] Schedule 2, para 5(2).
[143] See Guidance, para 3.14.
[144] Schedule 2, para 5(1)(c).
[145] Schedule 2, para 5(3).
[146] Schedule 2, para 5(1)(d).
[147] Schedule 2, para 5(1)(e). For definition of road vehicle, see s 193.
[148] Sections 61–64. See Chapter 16.
[149] Section 19.
[150] See Section C above.

(b)   The sale by retail of alcohol by or on behalf of a club to a guest of a member of the club for consumption on the premises where the sale takes place.[151] This effectively preserves the dispensation for clubs when sales takes place to guests of members, though it will be noted that off-sales are excluded from the dispensation. Any off-sale to a guest is a licensable activity as a sale by retail of alcohol.[152]

(c)   The provision of regulated entertainment[153] where that provision is by or on behalf of a club for members of the club or members of the club and their guests.

G   GENERAL EXCLUSIONS FROM LICENSABLE ACTIVITIES

8.75   The Act provides two blocks of exclusions from licensable activities, taking the activities in question out of the licensing regime. These are activities taking place in certain locations,[154] and incidental non-commercial lotteries.[155] These are considered in turn.

First general exclusion: excluded locations

8.76   Section 173 of the Act specifies eight locations where activities will not be considered licensable.

(a)   'Aboard an aircraft, hovercraft or railway vehicle engaged on a journey.'[156] This includes the period preparatory to departure and the period after arrival and before the occupants alight.[157]

(b)   'Aboard a vessel engaged on an international journey',[158] where vessel includes a ship, boat, raft or other apparatus constructed or adapted for floating on water.[159]

(c)   'At an approved wharf[160] at a designated[161] port or hoverport.'[162]

---

[151]   Section 1(2)(b).
[152]   Section 1(1)(a).
[153]   For meaning of 'regulated entertainment' see s 1(4), Sch 1 and Section D above.
[154]   Section 173.
[155]   Section 175.
[156]   Section 173(1)(a).
[157]   Section 173(2).
[158]   Section 173(1)(b).
[159]   Section 193.
[160]   'Approved wharf' has the meaning given by s 20A of the Customs and Excise Management Act 1979: Licensing Act 2003, s 173(6).
[161]   The Secretary of State may designate a port, hoverport or airport for these purposes if it appears to him to be one at which there is a substantial amount of international passenger traffic: s 173(3). Any port, airport or hoverport already designated under s 86A or 87 of the Licensing Act 1964 is to be treated as designated under this section: s 173(4).
[162]   Section 173(1)(c).

(d) 'At an examination station[163] at a designated[164] airport.'[165]

(e) 'At a royal palace'.[166]

(f) At premises permanently or temporarily occupied for the purposes of the armed forces.[167]

(g) 'At premises in respect of which a certificate issued under s 174 (exemption on grounds of national security) has effect.'[168] Section 174 enables a Minister of the Crown[169] who is a member of the Cabinet or the Attorney General[170] to issue such a certificate if he considers it appropriate to do so for the purposes of national security.[171] The certificate may later be cancelled by that Minister or any other who fulfils the above criteria.[172]

(h) 'At such other place as may be prescribed.'[173] While the list of exemptions may not be narrowed without primary amending legislation, it seems that it may be widened by secondary legislation.[174]

Second general exclusion: raffles and tombolas

8.77 The purpose of this exemption is to permit sealed containers of alcohol to be given away as prizes in raffles and tombolas at non-commercial, usually charitable, events which are not organised for the purposes of private gain. The raffles and tombolas are categorises as incidental non-commercial lotteries and are exempt from regulation under the Gambling Act 2005, and if one of the prizes is, say, a bottle of wine the supply of alcohol is exempt from regulation under the Licensing Act 2003 too.

---

163 'Examination station' has the meaning given by s 22A of the Customs and Excise Management Act 1979: Licensing Act 2003, s 173(6).
164 See note 159 above.
165 Section 173(1)(d).
166 Section 173(1)(e).
167 Section 173(1)(f).
168 Section 173(1)(g).
169 As defined by the Ministers of the Crown Act 1975: Licensing Act 2003, s 174(7).
170 Section 174(6).
171 Section 174(1).
172 Section 174(5)–(6).
173 Section 173(1)(h).
174 See ss 193 and 197.

9

The general duties of
licensing authorities

It is not about domestic violence, unprotected sex, smoking, sex discrimination, gambling, sexual attraction in birds, or the taxation of alcohol and cigarettes.

Lord McIntosh of Haringey, House of Lords, 26 November 2002

A INTRODUCTION: DESTINATIONS AND SIGNPOSTS

9.01 Section 4 of the Licensing Act 2003 is the nerve centre for the exercise of all licensing functions. It delimits and defines the very reason for existence of licensing authorities. It lays down the objectives to be attained, and maps out the recommended routes to attain them. Section 4 provides:

'4 General duties of licensing authorities

(1) A licensing authority must carry out its functions under this Act ("licensing functions") with a view to promoting the licensing objectives.
(2) The licensing objectives are –
    (a) the prevention of crime and disorder;
    (b) public safety;
    (c) the prevention of public nuisance; and
    (d) the protection of children from harm.
(3) In carrying out its licensing functions, a licensing authority must also have regard to –
    (a) its licensing statement published under section 5, and
    (b) any guidance issued by the Secretary of State under section 182.'

9.02   At face value, the section appears to set out an order of priorities. Chief in the hierarchy are the licensing objectives themselves. It is mandatory for licensing authorities to carry out licensing functions with a view to promoting such objectives. The objectives may thus be termed destinations. Subordinate to these are the licensing statement and Secretary of State's Guidance, which are matters to which a licensing authority must also have regard. These may therefore be termed signposts.

National Guidance → Local Policy → Licensing objectives

Figure 1: Relationship of objectives, Guidance and policy

9.03   This short section apparently sets out to defuse any argument as to what licensing is actually for. To take one example, the section would appear to preclude any contention that licensing any longer performs a moral function, rather than the pragmatic function of assisting in the attainment of the prescribed objectives, which are the designated destinations. Similarly, its effect would appear to be to excise from the argument any considerations of need or demand, which have exercised licensing justices and committees in the past. By ranking both licensing statements and national Guidance as matters merely to which regard must be had, that is to say signposts rather than destinations, the section appears to make such documents the servants rather than the masters of decision-making.

9.04   But in codifying not only what licensing authorities do but also how they are supposed to do it, the section creates a tension between, on the one hand, the conferment of discretion and, on the other, the trammelling of its exercise. This tension frequently simmers below the surface of licensing debates. A licensee might argue on a review that the premises licence should not be revoked because 50 jobs are at stake. Or the event should be allowed to proceed in Hyde Park, notwithstanding the likely nuisance, because it is part of the Olympic celebrations. The unasked, certainly unanswered, question is whether the code set by the licensing objectives is exclusive or whether it is open to licensing authorities simultaneously to promote other objectives through the exercise of their licensing functions. In other words, are the discretionary powers conferred on licensing authorities under the Act open or closed? What is more, despite the best efforts of the parliamentary draftsman, there remain for future debate many issues relating to the status and role of, and interplay between, the licensing objectives, licensing statements and national Guidance.

B   THE LICENSING OBJECTIVES

9.05   The Act sets out four licensing objectives, being the prevention of crime and disorder, public safety, the prevention of public nuisance and the protection of children from harm.[1] None of these expressions receives further definition in the Act. However, the expressions are tolerably clear. They are neither technical terms nor terms of art, and there is no reason to displace the legislative presumption that the expressions should be given their literal meaning.[2] However, the extent to which the objectives are directed at certain activities, for example indecent activities within premises and noisy activities outside, remains somewhat controversial. These objectives are considered in turn.

The prevention of crime and disorder

9.06   This objective is termed the 'crime prevention objective'.[3]

On its face, the objective is to prevent both crime and disorder, ie the expressions 'crime' and 'disorder' are disjunctive. So, the crime prevention objective extends to the prevention of acts which are criminal, even if they do not involve disorder. *In R (Blackpool Council) v Howitt* [2008] EWHC 3300 (Admin), a District Judge had allowed the licensee's appeal against revocation of the licence where the licensee had criminally flouted the smoking ban, holding that 'crime and disorder' was essentially directed at 'drunken, yobbish, alcohol-related behaviour … ' and not at crimes which involved no disorder at all. The expression 'crime and disorder' was to be read conjunctively, and unlawful smoking was therefore not relevant to the crime prevention objective because it did not involve disorder. The Administrative Court disagreed. The expression 'crime and disorder' is to be read disjunctively. His Honour Judge Denyer stated:

> '18. … one goes back to the wording of section 4. It is true, and indeed is the case, that it is hard to think of any disorderly behaviour which would not in fact be criminal. Equally though, as the Secretary of State's guidelines show, there may be many examples of serious criminal behaviour, serious crimes, which do not involve disorder. To give the section the meaning for which the respondent contends and the Deputy District Judge gave it might effectively lead to an authority having to ignore that guidance from the Secretary of State, which by definition the licensing authority and indeed the court has to have regard to by virtue of section 4. Like the respondent I agree that to regard smoking in a public place such as his pub as a serious crime on a par with dealing in heroin, gun running or even flogging counterfeit videos is an absurdity. Nevertheless, it is a crime.
>
> 19. Given the respondent's convictions and his stated intention to carry on the permitting of smoking, the licensing authority were entitled to

---

[1]   Section 4(2).
[2]   See Chapter 6: The Licensing Act 2003 Framework, Section P (Interpreting the legislation).
[3]   Section 193.

say that the revocation of his licence did promote the licensing objective of preventing crime.'

9.07   Conversely, the objective plainly goes further than the mere prevention of crime, whether inside or outside the premises. It extends to the prevention of disorder. Prior to the decision in *Howitt* one might perhaps have argued theoretically that the legislature intended to add nothing to the word 'crime' when using the word 'disorder'. But even then one should not ascribe to the Parliament the sin of using two synonymous words when one would do. This is particularly so when the expression is found in the title of an Act of Parliament: the Crime and Disorder Act 1988. That Act directs certain public authorities, which clearly includes licensing authorities, to formulate and implement strategies for the reduction of crime and disorder[4] and to exercise their functions with that end in view.[5] Consequently it would be unrealistic to suggest that the word 'disorder' is no more than surplusage. It must, therefore, be accorded some meaning and effect of its own.

9.08   The difficulty with the expression is that it is easier to decide retrospectively whether particular conduct is to be classified as disorderly than it is to define the term in advance. In *Chambers and another v Director of Public Prosecutions*[6] the Divisional Court held that whether behaviour is properly to be characterised as disorderly for the purposes of section 5 of the Public Order Act 1986 is a question of fact for the trial court to determine, and that there need not be any element of violence, present or threatened, for there to be disorderly behaviour. The difficulty for licensing authorities is that they must go further than the criminal courts which have to decide whether behaviour was disorderly, and consider prospectively what is encompassed by the term 'disorder', because their interpretation will be the foundation for the exercise of their licensing functions, for example in granting or refusing, or attaching conditions to, a premises licence. It is, therefore, important to develop some broad idea of what is meant by disorder. The following guiding principles are suggested.

(1)   The disorder which the section is designed to prevent need not be criminal in nature, for the reasons given above.
(2)   Nor does it have to be actually or prospectively violent.
(3)   The disorder may be individual or collective. Nothing in section 5 indicates that it is only the conduct of a crowd which is under consideration.
(4)   The disorder may be inside or outside the premises. The section draws no distinction. Furthermore, much conduct outside the premises is already catered for by the remaining objectives, and to construe the provision as confined to disorder in the streets is unnecessarily restrictive.

---

4   Crime and Disorder Act 1988, s 6.
5   Crime and Disorder Act 1988, s 17.
6   [1995] COD 321.

(5)   Disorder is not the same as nuisance. If it were, then it would simply replicate the third licensing objective. Therefore, it is possible for disorder to occur without the need for a member of the public to be disturbed by it.[7]

(6)   Whether conduct is disorderly must be judged in the context of its time and location. Crowd behaviour which is perfectly acceptable on, say, the football terraces may be completely unacceptable in a shopping street. Standards of dress normal in a lap-dancing venue may be apt to shock in a tea-room.

(7)   Nevertheless, in a society which is increasingly heterogeneous, great care needs to be taken by decision-makers not to characterise as disorderly conduct which is simply different from theirs.

Is disorder a moral issue?

9.09   The sixth principle above will be seen to take the Act close to the formulation of moral judgments. This is a practically inevitable consequence of the use of the word disorder, and not only because of the necessity of finding a meaning for it separate from the meaning of the remaining objectives. The word 'disorder' has itself acquired a connotation in English law as contrary to public morality or decency. For example, in *Moores v DPP*,[8] the Divisional Court was considering the common law offence of keeping a disorderly house, where a licensee was promoting a male exotic dancer in a public house. Bingham LJ said:

> 'Moreover, it appears to me that the mischief at which the common law offence is aimed is the mischief of keeping a house to which members of the public resort for purposes of the disorderly recreation – if one can so describe it – which is available there, whether it takes the form of indecency or illicit pugilism or cock fighting or whatever.'[9]

9.10   Nonetheless, the common law conception of a disorderly house is confined, for the most part, to conduct at the extreme end of the spectrum. In *R v Tam*[10] the Court of Appeal eschewed an exhaustive definition of 'disorderly house' while holding that a house is disorderly where the services provided amount to an outrage of public decency or are otherwise calculated to injure the public interest to such an extent as to call for condemnation and

---

[7]   In the context of the Gambling Act 2005, which includes the prevention of crime and disorder amongst the licensing objectives, the Gambling Commission's Guidance to Local Authorities (4th ed, 2012) states at para 5.16 that: 'disorder is intended to mean activity that is more serious and disruptive than mere nuisance. Factors to consider in determining whether a disturbance was serious enough to constitute disorder would include whether police assistance was required and how threatening the behaviour was to those who could see or hear it. There is not a clear line between nuisance and disorder ...'.

[8]   [1992] QB 125.

[9]   Page 132.

[10]   [1983] 1 QB 1053.

punishment.[11] While the term 'disorder' is clearly sufficiently wide to extend beyond behaviour amounting to a crime or a nuisance, it is submitted that its use in this statute is not intended to refer to conduct about whose morality reasonable people might differ. While conditions may be added concerning film exhibitions and children are to be protected from harm, the content of regulated entertainment is a matter which is addressed by existing laws governing indecency and obscenity.[12] If conduct is not criminally indecent and does not amount to crime, an actual or perceived threat, harassment, a nuisance, or a risk to children or public safety, it is very hard to see how it could be condemned under modern licensing legislation as disorderly. In this context, the sixth principle above merits close consideration.

Public safety

9.11   This objective relates to the safety of members of the public both inside and outside the premises, in so far as that may be affected by the operation of the premises under the licence. Public safety is involved where the physical integrity of members of the public is at stake. Public safety extends beyond protection against physical trauma. It would seem that the detrimental consequences of, say, loud noise and stroboscopic lighting effects, are encompassed in the objective. On the other hand, the term 'safety' is to be distinguished from the term 'health'. Thus, for example, the Guidance makes it clear that conditions are not to be imposed on licences which relate to cleanliness or hygiene.[13] Similarly, the safety which is dealt with in this objective is of the public variety. The objective is not designed to protect the safety of the licensee himself or his employees. However, conditions which protect members of the public are likely also to protect staff members,[14] and staff are also entitled to protection under the crime prevention objective. Thus the concentration on the safety of the public is not likely to produce any practical disadvantage for employees.

The prevention of public nuisance

9.12   This expression, comprising five short words, has probably occasioned more debate than any other in the Act, principally due to Parliament's misconception as to the meaning of the term 'public nuisance' in the common law. Those disinterested in the highways and byways of the debate may look no further than the definition of nuisance in the Guidance, the better part of which has received judicial approval. This states:

[11]   Page 1062, per Parker J.
[12]   Guidance para 10.15.
[13]   Para 2.8.
[14]   Employees are of course protected in any event by the duties imposed upon employers by the Health and Safety at Work Act 1974 and associated legislation, see further Chapter 47 Section D.

'2.18 The 2003 Act enables licensing authorities and responsible authorities, through representations, to consider what constitutes public nuisance and what is appropriate to prevent it in terms of conditions attached to specific premises licences and club premises certificates. It is therefore important that in considering the promotion of this licensing objective, licensing authorities and responsible authorities focus on the effect of the licensable activities at the specific premises on persons living and working (including those carrying on business) in the area around the premises which may be disproportionate and unreasonable. The issues will mainly concern noise nuisance, light pollution, noxious smells and litter.

2.19 Public nuisance is given a statutory meaning in many pieces of legislation. It is however not narrowly defined in the 2003 Act and retains its broad common law meaning. It is important to remember that the prevention of public nuisance could therefore include low-level nuisance, perhaps affecting a few people living locally, as well as major disturbance affecting the whole community. It may also include in appropriate circumstances the reduction of the living and working amenity and environment of other persons living and working in the area of the licensed premises. Public nuisance may also arise as a result of the adverse effects of artificial light, dust, odour and insects or where its effect is prejudicial to health.[15]

Those with a deeper interest in the topic may read on.

9.13 The starting point for the consideration of this objective is that where the word 'nuisance' appears in a statute it is normally given its common law meaning.[16] It is noteworthy that the objective apparently relates to public rather than private nuisance. In *Attorney General v PYA Quarries Ltd*,[17] Romer LJ held:

' … any nuisance is "public" which materially affects the reasonable comfort and convenience of life of a class of Her Majesty's subjects. The sphere of the nuisance may be described generally as "the neighbourhood"; but the question whether the local community within that sphere comprises a sufficient number of persons to constitute a class of the public is a question of fact in every case. It is not necessary, in my judgment, to prove that every member of the class has been injuriously affected; it is sufficient to show that a representative cross-section of the class has been so affected … '[18]

---

[15]   The final sentence was added by the October 2012 edition of the Guidance.
[16]   *National Coal Board v Thorne* [1976] WLR 543
[17]   [1957] 2 QB 169.
[18]   Page 184.

9.14   It is right to say that the categories of public nuisance at common law are not closed, and a wide variety of incidents have been held to amount to public nuisance. For example, in the *PYA Quarries* case itself, they related to dust, vibration and flying debris from a quarry. In *Wandsworth London Borough Council v Railtrack plc*,[19] pigeon droppings falling from a railway bridge to the pavement below so as to affect the passage of pedestrians were held to be a public nuisance. In *R v Clark No. 2*[20] an obstructive assembly on the highway was held to qualify. However, of more importance than what public nuisance may potentially cover is the question of what it does not cover. The answer is that at common law public nuisance is conceptually distinct from private nuisance.

9.15   In the *PYA Quarries* case itself, Denning LJ would not prescribe a certain dividing line between private and public nuisances, beyond holding the latter to be 'so widespread in its range or so indiscriminate in its effect that it would not be reasonable to expect one person to take proceedings on his own responsibility to put a stop to it, but that it should be taken on the responsibility of the community at large.'[21] But the distinction is nevertheless a real one, being encapsulated by Watkins J in *National Coal Board v Thorne*:

'A public nuisance at common law has been expressed to be an act or omission which materially affects the material comfort and quality of life of a class of Her Majesty's subjects. A private nuisance has often been defined in this way: private nuisances, at least in the vast majority of cases, are interferences for a substantial length of time by owners or occupiers of property with the use or enjoyment of neighbouring property.'[22]

9.16   Wherever the dividing line may be, what may unequivocally be said is that the adjective 'public' must be taken to add something to the noun 'nuisance' when used in section 4(1)(c). Taking the common law approach arguably denudes neighbours from protection by acts amounting to a mere private nuisance. If that were right, the absence of protection in the Act for neighbouring occupiers against direct environmental impact, unless they can be held to be part of a class of Her Majesty's subjects, would be an extremely surprising one. Of course, such occupiers may retain rights to sue for private nuisance, or rely on statutory remedies under Part III of the Environmental Protection Act 1990, which would not be precluded merely by the grant of a licence for the offending activity.[23] The question, however, remains: is the intention of the legislature, as expressed through the term 'public nuisance', to remove or retain protection for neighbouring occupiers afforded by the licensing system? In other words, does the common law presumption that

---

[19]   [2002] 2 QB 756.
[20]   [1964] 2 QB 315.
[21]   Page 191.
[22]   Pages 546–7.
[23]   *Blackburn v ARC Ltd* 1998 Env LR 469.

public nuisance is to be given its common law meaning prevail, or may a wider approach be taken? The answer to the question turns both on a brief consideration of the remainder of the Act, human rights, the legislative history and the Guidance.

The Act

9.17 The Act contemplates that interested parties, namely, those living or involved in businesses in the vicinity of the relevant premises, or bodies representing such individuals,[24] should have a say in the granting of licences. By terming environmental protection departments 'authorised persons'[25] it also contemplates that those departments have relevant material to contribute to the decision-making process. Given the rarity of the occurrence of events which disturb entire neighbourhoods of people and the commonplace circumstance that more limited number of people are disturbed by nuisance, it seems most unlikely that the Act is genuinely intended to guillotine the voice of neighbours unless they constitute a tribe. Not only would that lack common sense, but it would also fail to accord with the obviously protective purpose of the legislation.

Legislative history

9.18 Initially, the use of the word 'public nuisance' was chosen by the Government in order to limit the circumstances in which behaviour by customers after they had left the premises could be taken into account. But as the debate progressed the Government came to accept that it was unrealistic for licensing law to blind itself to such conduct either when occurring in the vicinity of the premises or by an agglomeration of licensed premises. Given the evolutionary nature of the Government's approach, it is both difficult and unproductive to find a ministerial statement which would survive the *Pepper v Hart*[26] requirement of clarity.[27] In the early debates, the Government's attention was directed to *PYA Quarries*. Speaking for the Government, Baroness Blackstone stated that the Government did expect case law developed to date to be applied, but simultaneously stated that the word 'nuisance' in the Bill referred to noise and other nuisance caused directly from the premises concerned, which is more likely to give rise to private nuisance. The Government appeared more concerned with the origin rather than the effect of the nuisance, maintaining that the licensee was not

---

[24] Section 13(3).
[25] Section 13(4).
[26] 1993 AC 593.
[27] See Chapter 6 (The Licensing Act 2003), Section P (Interpretation of the legislation).

to be held responsible for any disturbance caused by customers outside the premises, since such behaviour was a matter of personal responsibility.[28]

9.19   That, however, could not stand with the crime prevention objective, let alone the objective in question: if the result of opening licensed premises is crime and disorder or public nuisance on the streets, the licensing authority could not ignore that in the exercise of its functions.

9.20   At the report stage in the House of Lords, Baroness Buscombe moved an amendment to the objective in the following terms: 'The prevention of unreasonable diminution of the living and working amenity and environment of interested parties in the vicinity of the premises balancing those matters against the benefits to be derived from the leisure amenity of such premises.'[29] The amendment was agreed to. In the debate preceding the amendment, Baroness Blackstone referred to the common law definition of nuisance and stated: 'I understand that the expression "public nuisance" has been chosen in the Bill as it is well known, flexible and capable of application in a huge range of circumstances.'[30] She went on to say:

> 'It would not be desirable to set in stone in the Bill what will constitute a public nuisance, partly because it is not possible to cover every eventuality, and partly because what constitutes a public nuisance will vary from place to place and neighbourhood to neighbourhood. The licensing authority, informed by the experts, needs to be in a position to determine what constitutes public nuisance in each individual case. In certain circumstances it may well be that some lower-level nuisance – such as the slamming of car doors by patrons leaving the premises late at night – has to be taken into account. I say to the noble Lord, Lord Phillips of Sudbury, that public nuisance is not just about acid-house parties or raves, as was argued in Committee and as he repeated tonight, although it might include those types of nuisance. However, it includes many others as well.

> The Bill allows for that necessary flexible approach. As was stated in the guidance[31] that we have made available to the House,

>> "the 2003 Act requires licensing authorities and responsible authorities to make objective judgements about what constitutes nuisance and what is needed, in terms of conditions attached to premises licences and club premises certificates to prevent it. These will not be easy judgements"—

> my noble friend Lord McIntosh made this point earlier—

---

[28]   See 642 HL Official Report (5th series) Cols 545–561, 17 December 2002, particularly Cols 560–561.

[29]   HL Debs, 24 February 2003, Col 79.

[30]   HL Debs, 24 February 2003, Col 76.

[31]   Ie the draft Guidance.

"as one man's enjoyable music is another man's irritating noise. It is therefore important that in applying the relevant objective tests, licensing authorities and responsible authorities focus on impacts of the licensable activities at the relevant premises on people living, working and sleeping in the vicinity that are unreasonable" '. [32]

9.21 While Baroness Blackstone's speech probably attributed a wider meaning to 'public nuisance' than had hitherto been accepted by the judiciary, what is noteworthy is the absence of any avowed intention to excise from the purview of this legislation acts amounting to a private nuisance. The distinction does not appear at all. Rather, the intention seems to have been to use the term 'public nuisance' flexibly, so as to allow appropriate balances to be drawn on a case by case basis.

9.22 Further support is given for a flexible interpretation of 'public nuisance' by the subsequent debates in the House of Commons, in which the Government successfully overcame Baroness Buscombe's amendment and restored the original formulation of the public nuisance licensing objective. Speaking for the Government, Dr Kim Howells stated:

'We believe that replacing the idea of public nuisance with the idea of amenity significantly weakened the Bill, particularly in terms of the protection that it offers local residents in relation to the carrying on of licensable activities. That was not the intention of the amendment in another place, but it was its effect.

In the debate in another place, an impression was given by some contributors that "public nuisance" was a narrow concept that would not cover some of the problems that might be caused to residents living near licensed premises. That was because those contributors had regard to the narrow definition of "nuisance" in the Environmental Protection Act 1990. That definition is misleading in the context of the Licensing Bill. The Bill does not define "public nuisance" and it therefore retains the wide meaning it has under common law, rather than that in the 1990 Act or any other statutory definition. The term "public nuisance" therefore retains the breadth and flexibility to take in all the concerns likely to arise from the operation of any premises conducting licensable activities, in terms of the impact of nuisance on people living or doing business nearby.' [33]

9.23 Again, with respect, the Minister appeared to misunderstand the difficulty. It is not that the meaning of public nuisance at common law is wide and under the 1990 Act narrow, but precisely the reverse. Be that as it may, the statement acknowledges that the use of the term 'public nuisance' is intended to have a wide definition.

---

[32] HL Debs, 24 February 2003, Col 76.
[33] HC Debs, 8 April 2003, Cols 155–156.

9.24 This was echoed when the Bill returned to the House of Lords. Lord McIntosh of Haringey stated:

> 'The Bill does not define "public nuisance". It retains the wider meaning that it has under common law; not that in the 1990 Act or in any other statutory definition. "Public nuisance" therefore retains the breadth and flexibility to take in all the concerns likely to arise from the operation of any premises conducting licensable activities in terms of the impact of nuisance on people living or doing business nearby.'[34]

9.25 Later in the same debate he illustrated his point by stating that loud music in the early hours of the morning, car doors slamming and people coming and going all amount to a public nuisance.[35] Therefore, while the concept of public nuisance clearly evolved during its sojourn in Parliament, by the end of the Parliamentary debates it was abundantly clear that the Government conception of the term was sufficiently wide to embrace disturbances to the public operating at a low level perhaps to a few individuals only.

Guidance

9.26 While only very limited weight can normally be given to the Guidance as a direct interpretative tool, particularly since it emerged in final form nearly a year after the Licensing Act 2003 was passed,[36] the Guidance has the particular imprimatur in this instance of judicial endorsement in *R (Hope and Glory) Public House Limited v City of Westminster Magistrates' Court*.[37] Nothing in the Guidance suggests, or indeed has ever suggested, that nuisance caused directly and solely to sleeping neighbours is beyond the reach of the Act. From its inception, Guidance has treated the scope of public nuisance in the way set out at the beginning of this discussion – the language has not changed at all.[38]

9.27 The nature of the evolution in the Government's thinking on the subject is exemplified by its approach to litter. In the early House of Lords debates, Lord Davies stated on behalf of the Government that fast food outlets should not be responsible for litter dropped in the street by departing customers.[39] However, national Guidance acknowledges, and always did, that in relation to the public nuisance prevention objective: 'The issues will mainly concern noise nuisance, light pollution, noxious smells and litter.'[40]

---

[34]   HL Debs, 19 June 2003, Col 913.
[35]   HL Debs, 19 June 2003, Col 917.
[36]   See Chapter 6: The Licensing Act 2003 Framework, Section P (Interpreting the legislation).
[37]   [2009] EWHC 1996 (Admin).
[38]   See para 7.40 of Guidance issued July 2004.
[39]   HL Debs, 17 December 2002, Cols 617–618.
[40]   Para 2.33.

Hope and Glory

9.28 The scope of public nuisance was a regular source of debate in licensing cases, until it was largely laid to rest in *Hope and Glory*.

9.29 There, a Soho public house allowed outside drinking which disturbed the neighbours and on a review application the licensing authority forbade the activity after 6 pm, a decision upheld by District Judge Snow. The High Court refused permission to challenge the District Judge's approach to public nuisance, and the Court of Appeal refused permission to challenge that decision. On what was it based?

The Learned District Judge had found the following facts:

'I have already found that noise nuisance was caused, by the patrons of The Endurance gathered in Kemps Court to Miss Schmidt, at 17b Berwick Street, and to Miss Rhys-Jenkins Bailey and her students at Westminster College on Hopkins Street. In addition, I note that although they have not given evidence before me, complaints were made about noise caused by the customers of Kemps Court by Tamara Berton of 17 Berwick Street, Mr Estranero of Ingestre Court and at least one other person who has not been identified had made complaint. In addition Walter Rigby had made a complaint ... I find, on the balance of probabilities, that given the number of residents, students and teachers affected and given the geographical spread, the nuisance clearly is a public nuisance.'

9.30 In so finding, the District Judge had applied the Guidance now contained in paragraph 2.19, as cited above. This was now challenged as legally incorrect, on the grounds that a low level nuisance affecting a few people living locally did not amount to a public nuisance within its common law meaning.

Burton J took as his lodestar the dictum of Romer LJ in *Attorney General v PYA Quarries Ltd*:[41]

'I do not propose to attempt a more precise definition of public nuisance than those which emerge from the textbooks and authorities to which I have referred. It is, however, clear, in my opinion, that any nuisance is "public" which materially affects the reasonable comfort and convenience of life of a class of Her Majesty's subjects. The sphere of the nuisance may be described generally as "the neighbourhood"; but the question whether the local community within that sphere comprises a sufficient number of persons to constitute a class of the public is a question of fact in every case. It is not necessary, in my judgment, to prove that every member of the class has been injuriously affected; it is

---

[41]   [1957] 2 QB 169, 184.

sufficient to show the representative cross-section of the class has been so affected for an injunction to be issued.'

9.31   Burton J went on to analyse the treatment of Romer LJ's judgment in the House of Lords case of *R v Rimmington, R v Goldstein*[42] and also the treatment of Denning LJ's judgment in *PYA* which had not received universal approbation by the House of Lords. This led him to conclude:[43]

'... what is a public nuisance is a question of fact, namely and in particular whether, by reference to Romer LJ, there is effect on a sufficiently large number of members of the public by reference to one act or a series of acts, or, by reference to Denning LJ, such effect was sufficiently widespread or indiscriminate ... I do not read Denning LJ's words as meaning that the effect of the public nuisance must be very indiscriminate or very widespread. It simply needs to be sufficiently widespread and sufficiently indiscriminate to amount to something more than private nuisance.'

9.32   Applying that to the facts, Burton J was not prepared to hold that the District Judge's approach was wrong, even though the majority of the complaints came from a single set of premises.

9.33   From this, it is clearly the law that unreasonable disturbance to a few people, even earlier in the evening, and even if living in a single building, amounts to a public nuisance.

9.34   If there is room for further argument, it is whether the very same degree of disturbance, but occurring to a single person who is sufficiently unfortunate (in legal if not social) terms to live alone, can complain of public nuisance. That is not decided by *Hope and Glory*. However, it is striking that the case largely centred on the pre-penultimate sentence in what is now paragraph 2.19 of Guidance. It did not deal with the penultimate sentence: 'It may also include in appropriate circumstances the reduction of the living and working amenity and environment of other persons living and working in the area of the licensed premises.' The word 'also' obviously implies a different factual scenario from the pre-penultimate sentence. It is submitted that in the great majority of cases, if only a single person is disturbed by noise, it is unlikely to be a nuisance, whether public or private. But it does not follow as a matter of law that the mere fact that only one person is disturbed prevents the nuisance from amounting to a public nuisance. Take the *Hope and Glory* case. Imagine that Miss Schmidt's tenants could not stand it any more and had moved out, leaving Miss Schmidt locked in to the nuisance by dint of her property ownership. Could it seriously be said that the very same noise ceased to be a nuisance because it had driven her

---

[42]   [2005] UKHL 63.
[43]   Para [59].

tenants, her income and her livelihood away, so that she was entitled to no protection from the Act?

9.35 The answer resides in a consideration of the degree of disturbance constituting a nuisance. This involves analysis not just of the level but also the character of the noise (eg impulsive, grating, shrill, sporadic, repeated), the hour, the duration and the frequency. Where, taking account of these factors, one can credibly say that the nuisance is of a sufficient level to amount to an unreasonable disturbance to neighbouring occupiers then as a matter of fact it is sufficient to amount to a public nuisance. It is not necessary for the licensing sub-committee to hear from all (or indeed any) of the local residents in order to make that judgment, provided that it can draw an inference on the facts which it has heard, which may include the opinion of an experienced noise or licensing officer.

Conclusion on public nuisance

9.36 In *Hope and Glory*, the court arrived, through learned judicial reasoning, at a common sense approach to the statute as explained in the Guidance, which supports the interpretation based on the legislative history and purpose of the statute. The Act was not intended to prevent a person complaining at the volume of the pub juke box next door, the litter strewn outside a take away restaurant, of loud voices heard through an open window of commercial premises late at night or of car doors slamming and radios playing as customers drive away. Rather, all matters resulting from the operation of licensed premises which impinge unreasonably on the living and working conditions of those in the vicinity of the premises are to be considered by the licensing authority when raised before them.

The protection of children from harm

9.37 This objective is drafted in recognition of the special vulnerability of children in licensed premises. It does not imply that adults are less deserving of protection from harm, or that licensing authorities should not concern themselves with the well-being of adults. The harm to which the objective is directed clearly extends beyond physical hazards, for that is protected by the first and second objectives. The Guidance suggests, correctly, that it extends to moral, psychological and physical harm.[44] Therefore, for example, it covers protection from:

- emotional harm caused by witnessing activities or performances to which they ought not to be exposed;
- predatory conduct on the part of adults or even other children;
- harm caused to themselves through illegal or excessive consumption of alcohol or drugs;

[44]   Para 2.25.

- harm from smoke;
- exposure to strong language and sexual expletives.[45]

9.38   The term 'children' is not susceptible of precise definition[46] and receives no general definition in the Act. However, section 146 of the Act, whose sidenote is 'Sale of Alcohol to Children', prohibits the sale of alcohol to those under 18. From this, it is probable that the reference to children in the licensing objective refers to those under 18. Of course, the protective requirements for 17 year olds are likely to differ from those for 7 year olds, which will be reflected in differential conditions attached by licensing authorities.

C THE PROMOTION OF LICENSING OBJECTIVES

9.39   Section 4(1) of the Act is a mandatory provision governing the exercise of all licensing functions. It provides that licensing authorities must carry out their functions under the Act 'with a view to promoting the licensing objectives'. Quite clearly, the obligation upon licensing authorities goes beyond merely having regard to those objectives. As stated previously, the licensing objectives are destinations in their own right, not merely signposts to the attainment of some other objective. However, there is an issue as to the necessity or otherwise of attaining the objectives in any particular case.

9.40   The issue can be illustrated thus. Suppose there is a quiet residential area with no licensed premises and which is largely asleep by 11 pm. An application is made for a new premises licence for a public house. It is frankly acknowledged that the influx of people to the public house will produce some increase in crime and disorder, because currently there is none. Ought the licence to be refused on the grounds that it will not actually prevent crime and disorder? Reduced to a single question, ought the licensing application to be granted (a) only if it positively assists in the prevention of crime and disorder, or (b) only if it does not add to crime and disorder, or (c) only if it does not add unreasonably to crime and disorder?

9.41   Those who argue in favour of (c) might point out that the purpose of the Act is not to attain the licensing objectives; its purpose is shown by the long title: 'to make provision about the regulation of the sale and supply of alcohol, the provision of entertainment and the provision of late night refreshment, about offences relating to alcohol and for connected purposes'. In achieving that purpose, the licensing authority is to promote the licensing

---

[45]   See Guidance, para 2.25. Although Guidance refers to such language in the context of film exhibitions and adult entertainment, the protection must logically extend to hearing such language used by customers themselves.

[46]   In *R v Cockerton* 1901 1 KB 340, it was suggested that for practical purposes a 16–17 year old person is beyond childhood.

objectives. But, as Lord McIntosh of Haringey put it during the passage of the Bill: 'Licensing authorities will, or will not, be able to promote those objectives to the best of their ability. But this is not a Bill to reduce crime.'[47] On the other hand, while the purpose of the Act might not be to prevent crime, it is arguable that the purpose of the regulation of licensable activities is to prevent crime. To argue otherwise is to relegate the licensing objectives from destinations to signposts, from matters to be promoted to matters to which regard must be had, but which can be ignored in appropriate circumstances. Proponents of that view would argue in favour of (a) or (b).

9.42 The solution to this seemingly intractable problem is found in the expression 'with a view'. The courts have tended to use this expression synonymously with 'purpose' or 'intention'.[48] In other words, licensing authorities, when carrying out their licensing functions, must do so with the purpose of attaining the licensing objectives. But while it is mandatory to have that purpose, it is not mandatory to attain the objective. It must be recognised that any large gathering of people, particularly if alcohol is involved, will have some implications for, say, crime and disorder. It is highly unlikely that granting a licence will actually prevent crime and disorder. But in determining the application, it would be wrong to refuse the licence just because a grant would not actually guarantee the absence of crime, let alone the prevention of crime which is already occurring. Rather, the licensing authority should exercise its powers with those ends in view. This implies that the answer to the example given above is (c).

9.43 Why, then, did the legislature draw section 4(1) in mandatory terms, rather than making the licensing objectives merely material considerations? It seems that the legislative stance has two central purposes. The first is to underline the importance of the licensing objectives themselves. They are not merely factors to be taken into account in the overall balance. They are to be the focus for the exercise of every licensing application. Second, by listing them as mandatory considerations, they clearly take precedence over any other consideration.

9.44 Similar conclusions have been reached in the world of waste management licensing. In *R v Leicester County Council ex parte Blackfordby & Boothorpe Action Group Limited*[49] Stephen Richards J was dealing with the Waste Management Licensing Regulations 1994,[50] regulation 2 of which obliged the competent authorities to 'discharge their specified functions, insofar as they relate to the recovery or disposal of waste, with the relevant objectives.' This may be considered slightly less directive than the Licensing Act's command to carry out functions with a view to 'promoting' the

---

[47] HL Debs, 26 November 2002, Col 733.
[48] See eg *The Trustee of the Property of New Prance and Garrard v Hunting & Others* [1897] 2 QB 19, 27, per Lord Esher MR.
[49] Unreported, 15 March 2000.
[50] SI 1994/1056.

licensing objectives, but nevertheless the language is sufficiently similar to command attention. In that case, the claimant's counsel accepted, as the Judge put it, that:

> ' ... the objectives are not absolute requirements in the sense of requiring a local planning authority in each case to <u>achieve</u> the result pursued by the objective. That would amount to a requirement to refuse planning permission if there were <u>any</u> risk to human health or the environment, which would in turn lead to refusal of planning permission for any or almost any landfill site ... '[51]

The Judge held:

> 'What matters is that the objectives should be taken into consideration (or had regard to) <u>as objectives,</u> as ends at which to aim. If a local authority understands their status as objectives and takes them into account as such when reaching its decision, then it seems to me that the authority can properly be said to have reached the decision 'with' those objectives. The decision does not cease to have been reached with those objectives merely because a large number of other considerations have also been taken into account in reaching the decision and some of those considerations militate against the achievement of the objectives.'[52]

9.45   Richards J's approach was followed by Maurice Kay J in *R v Derbyshire County Council ex parte David Murray*[53]. There, the council had acted on advice that 'the Article expresses a series of objectives to be achieved, which the Authority should follow, but does not create an absolute duty of that kind. If such a strict interpretation were to be followed then as a matter of logic it is difficult to see how permission could be granted for any means of disposing of waste; none can be shown to be entirely risk free.' The Learned Judge held that to be an entirely correct approach.

9.46   In a yet further waste management case, *R (Thornby Farms Limited) v Daventry DC*,[54] Pill LJ ruled more generally on the meaning of the word 'objective':

> 'An objective in my judgment is something different from a material consideration. I agree with Richards J that it is an end at which to aim, a goal. The general use of the word appears to be a modern one. In the 1950 edition of the Concise Oxford Dictionary the meaning now adopted is given only a military use: "towards which the advance of troops is directed". A material consideration is a factor to be taken into account when making a decision, and the objective to be attained will be such a consideration, but it is more than that. An objective which is

---

[51]   Para [42].
[52]   Para [49].
[53]   2001 Env LR 494.
[54]   [2003] QB 503, at para [53].

obligatory must always be kept in mind when making a decision even while the decision-maker has regard to other material considerations. Some decisions involve more progress towards achieving the objective than others. On occasions, the giving of weight to other considerations will mean that little or no progress is made. I accept that there could be decisions affecting waste disposal in which the weight given to other considerations may produce a result which involves so plain and flagrant a disregard for the objective that there is a breach of obligation. However, provided the objective is kept in mind, decisions in which the decisive consideration has not been the contribution they make to the achievement of the objective may still be lawful. I do not in any event favour an attempt to create a hierarchy of material considerations whereby the law would require decision-makers to give different weight to different considerations.'

9.47 To Pill LJ, therefore, in the context of waste management, an objective is more than a material consideration. It is the end in view, to which the decision-maker should endeavour to direct his decision. At very least, he should not set out to make decisions which point away from the objective, albeit that the contribution in individual cases may be limited or neutral.

9.48 While the statutory language is not identical to that under the 1994 Regulation, and the Licensing Act imposes a stronger duty of acting with a view to promotion of the objectives, the linguistic thrust, and the analysis, are the same. It is not necessary to refuse a licence merely because the licensing objectives may not actually be furthered by a grant. The end result of the system, however, should be to promote the licensing objectives. How that is achieved is in part a function of the totality of individual decisions of licensing authorities.

9.49 Lest this be thought to be too dilute an approach to the licensing objectives, it requires a modicum of qualification. Take a case in which it is established that private nuisance is actually occurring, and the matter comes to a review. Section 52 (3) of the Act requires the authority to take the steps as are considered appropriate for the promotion of the licensing objectives. In such a case, it appears clear that the combined effect of the duties in sections 4 and 52 is to require the authority to take steps, if appropriate, to abate the nuisance. It cannot simply stand by and allow the nuisance to continue. Reasoning from that basis, if the authority is satisfied on balance at the application stage that the result of the application will actually be that public nuisance will occur, its duty is no different – it should act to prevent it, it cannot just stand by.

9.50 The reconciliation of these difficulties is that licensing is a species of risk aversion whereby the authority must act to promote the objectives specified. It is preventive rather than reactive legislation. This does not mean that it has to avert all risk: there will always be some risk, and the authority should do what is reasonable, proportionate and practical to avert it. If it had to act to ensure that risk never materialised, it would never grant a licence. On the other hand, if it can see that the risk actually will materialise or worse, if it has materialised, then it should act to prevent its occurrence or recurrence.

Exclusivity of objectives

9.51   This discussion gives rise to a further important question. In carrying out its functions, may a licensing authority have in view any objectives other than the licensing objectives? Section 4(1) states that the authority must carry out its functions with a view to promoting the licensing objectives. It does not state that the authority may not promote other objectives simultaneously. It would be anathema for the authority to set out to promote objectives which actually conflicted with the licensing objectives. But what if the authority bore in mind objectives which supplemented the licensing objectives without actually derogating from them? The Government clearly intended that the licensing objectives should be exclusive rather than part of a menu, as the quotation at the head of this chapter graphically demonstrates. But nothing in the section would appear expressly to exclude other considerations. However, in *R v Secretary of State for the Environment ex parte Lancashire County Council*,[55] Jowitt J held that where a statute required the Local Government Commission to recommend boundary changes having regard to certain considerations, those considerations were exclusive.[56] Further, when the Act is read as a whole, it is plain that the licensing objectives are intended to be amount to exclusive destinations. See, for example, section 18(4)(a) (attachment of conditions to premises licences), and section 51(7) (representations on review to be relevant to licensing objectives).

9.52   From this, it is concluded that the licensing objectives may not be supplemented by other objectives of licensing authorities' own devising. To take one example, imagine that a building had an established planning use as a pub so that it did not need planning permission for that purpose, but the current development would have resulted in a refusal had planning permission been needed, because the area is being promoted for other uses. The owner applies for a licence, and there are no grounds based on the licensing objectives to refuse the licence. It would clearly be unlawful for the licensing authority to refuse the licence application in order to promote the planning objectives of the area. In summary, the authority may not impose constraint upon a licensee, be it by adding a condition to a licence or refusing or revoking it, in order to promote objectives other than the licensing objectives.

---

[55]   [1994] 4 All ER 165.
[56]   Page 172. The distinction of this case in *R (Hestview Limited) v Snaresbrook Crown Court* 2001 LLR 214 at [64], in the context of betting legislation, is unconvincing.

9.53   But may an authority ameliorate its stance, by imposing less draconian regulation, in order to promote an objective other than the licensing objectives? For example, may it refrain from requiring double-glazing in a listed building on grounds of expense to the licensee? May it take account of the benefits of a community pub in deciding to grant it a licence? It is submitted that, in drawing an overall balance, a licensing authority may have regard to the <u>benefits</u> of a proposal, and the fact that, or extent to which, it meets a wider strategic objective of the town, for example under its cultural, tourism or economic strategy. It is also submitted that it may take account of the costs of regulation to the licensee. Conversely, if a proposal is not consonant with the wider aspirations of the community, it is possible that a correspondingly larger weight will be attributed to discerned harms to the licensing objectives. These are somewhat controversial propositions and require justification.

9.54   Licensing is not an end in its own right, but a tool to achieve a social agenda. Nor does it operate in a vacuum, but exists alongside other policies designed to achieve the same agenda. For example, licensing operates in a field already occupied by health and safety, planning and environmental legislation. The Guidance sets out ways in which these regimes may complement each other without duplication or treading on each other's toes. That is a function of proper management and application of the licensing regime. What is more contentious is when licensing strays into territory which it is not its statutory objective to control.

9.55   As stated above, the powers of the licensing authority are firmly circumscribed by the licensing objectives set out in the Act. It must act with a view to promoting those objectives in all that they do.[57] It may only refuse a licence application if it considers it appropriate to do so for the promotion of the licensing objectives, and may only attach such conditions as are appropriate for the promotion of those objectives.[58] What an authority clearly may not do is to refuse a licence or attach conditions on grounds which have nothing to do with the licensing objectives. But what of factors which weigh in favour of a more lenient approach?

9.56   Take a village without a pub or even a convenience store. It is moribund during the day and dead at night. A licensing application is made for a pub which will bring some life to the village at night, provide investment and a little local employment, and give an opportunity for some local musicians to enhance the cultural life of the area. It is unquestionable that there will be a greater potential for nuisance once the pub opens its doors since the only noise currently experienced at night is the odd dog bark. Since the village suffers no crime at present, the pub is liable to bring some potential for crime and disorder, but not much.

[57]   Section 4(1).
[58]   Section 4(4).

9.57   A licensing authority which takes a strict approach to the application of the licensing objectives may approach the matter in this way. If the licence is refused, there will be no harm to the licensing objectives, for the village will continue to be dead at night. If the licence is granted, there will be some threat to the licensing objectives, for drinking and music will come to a village where none existed before. Therefore, the course most conducive to the promotion of the licensing objectives is to refuse the licence. On the facts given, that would be the wrong approach.

9.58   The proper approach would be for the licensing authority to recognise that there may indeed be some limited harm to the licensing objectives, but this does not require the licensing authority to exercise its discretion against the proposal. The authority is still entitled to consider the benefits to the community which the pub would bring, and reflect that consideration in the weight which is attached to the harm to the licensing objectives. In similar vein, the authority may have a policy that there should be door supervision at pubs. The applicant may, however, plead that the cost of door supervision would kill his fledgling business and prevent his obtaining finance for the project at all. The licensing authority may, it is submitted, weigh this in the balance when deciding whether it is appropriate to impose the requirement. In this way, positive strategies can influence the result of a licensing application even though not expressed to be material in the Act itself.

9.59   Undoubtedly, this argument is strengthened by the transformation of the threshold test in the Act from 'necessary' to 'appropriate'. Where a particular form of regulation is necessary, it is more challenging to argue that it should not be imposed. Where, however, the test is appropriate, this admits more scope for importing considerations militating in favour of a more permissive approach. The Guidance appears to support this approach, by admitting the relevance of the burden of the condition on the licensee and the benefit of the activity to the community, although is arguably internally contradictory on the issue.[59]

9.60   Therefore, while a licensing authority may only refuse a licence or impose conditions for reasons going to the promotion of the licensing objectives, the question of whether the activity is or is not consistent with the wider public agenda may be reflected in the weight which is given to the actual or anticipated harm to the licensing objectives in the individual case and the regulatory response to such harm.

The order of priority of objectives

9.61   The Guidance indicates that each objective has equal importance.[60] However, given that section 4(1) makes it clear that all of the objectives are

---

[59]   See paras 2.20, 9.40 and 10.10.
[60]   Para 1.4.

to be kept in view, there would appear to be no need to rank them in order of importance in any event. Certain activities may cause greater or less concern in terms of individual objectives, but this is not to say that any individual objective is subordinate to any other. For example, if an application fails because the licence is liable to cause children harm, it would be no riposte that it did not after all cause a public nuisance. Thus, it is better to say that all of the objectives are at the heart of this legislation, but that not all will necessarily be in play in every licensing application. In other words, while the objectives are of equal importance, they will not necessarily be of equal weight when judged against individual licensing applications.

D THE ROLE OF LOCAL AND NATIONAL POLICY

9.62 Section 4(3) of the Act provides that in carrying out its licensing functions, a licensing authority must also have regard to its licensing statement published under section 5 and Secretary of State's Guidance issued under section 182. Detailed consideration is given to local policy in Chapters 4 and 10. The Guidance impinges on all aspects of licensing authority and police powers and is therefore dealt with as relevant topics arise.

The policy hierarchy

9.63 In the Parliamentary debates on the Licensing Bill, Lord McIntosh set out the Government's intentions as follows:

> 'It is a hierarchy of obligations. The licensing objectives ... are common for all local authorities and are obligatory on all local authorities. The statement of licensing policy ... is designed to take account of local circumstances and is produced by licensing authorities themselves. The guidance ... is designed to provide help for local authorities in producing consistency between licensing authorities and to give guidance on what should be in licensing policies.'[61]

Having regard to licensing statements

9.64 It is clear from the context of section 4(3) that the licensing authority's regard to its licensing statement is not to be exclusive. This is not only because it must also have regard to national Guidance, but also because the entire exercise of licensing functions is to be carried out with a view to promoting the licensing objectives. In fact, the production of the statement of licensing policy is itself a licensing function, and therefore to be carried out with a view to promoting the licensing objectives. Naturally, the policy is

[61] HL Debs, 17 December 2002, Col 631.

likely to contain procedural sections and exhortations to licensees to behave in a particular way, but this does not affect the central proposition as to the purpose of the document. Since the licensing statement is produced expressly to play its part in an interlocking policy mechanism, it is clear that the statement itself is intended to carry very considerable weight in the determination of applications. That weight may be increased by strong wording within the statement itself.[62]

However, where it is shown that there is a different, better way of meeting the objectives than is set out in the licensing statement, a licensing authority could not shut its eyes to such considerations. Further, a licensing statement may become outdated, or in conflict with subsequent national Guidance, so that to follow it would be no longer to promote the licensing objectives. Again, it could not be contended that regard might not be had to such circumstances. Therefore, while a licensing authority must always have regard to its own licensing statement, such regard cannot be exclusive, far less conclusive of the outcome of a particular case.[63] On the other hand, where a licensing authority departs from its own policy in an individual case, then unless it gives reasons for so acting, it risks its decision being quashed for failure to have regard to a relevant factor, namely, its own policy.[64] It is arguable that this is so even where the policy is unlawful, since if it is not challenged within the period allowed for judicial review[65] it remains a material consideration in the exercise of licensing functions.[66] This issue is explored further in Chapter 20 (Challenging Licensing Decisions).

Having regard to Guidance

9.65   Section 182 of the Act provides that the Secretary of State may issue, and from time to time revise, Guidance to licensing authorities on the discharge of their functions under the Act. The same considerations apply to the duty to have regard to Guidance as have just been discussed in relation to local policy. The distinction is that while the contents of local policy are constrained both by the licensing objectives and Guidance, the formulation of Guidance is constrained only by the terms of section 182. However, since the Guidance must be directed towards the discharge of licensing functions, and licensing functions are by section 4(1) to be exercised with a view to the promotion of the licensing objectives, in practice it follows that national

---

[62]   See *R (Westminster City Council v Middlesex Crown Court and Chorion plc* [2002] LLR 538 at [34].

[63]   See further Chapter 10 (Licensing Policy).

[64]   See *R v London Borough of Croydon ex parte Jarvis* (1994) 26 HLR 195, 209–210; *Gransden & Co Ltd v Secretary of State for the Environment* (1987) 54 P & CR 86, 94.

[65]   The requirement is to apply promptly and in any event not later than three months after the grounds to make the claim first arose: CPR Rule 54.6, and see *R v Hammersmith & Fulham LBC ex parte Burkett* [2002] 1 WLR 1593.

[66]   *R (Westminster City Council) v Middlesex Crown Court and Chorion plc* [2002] LLR 538 at [21].

Guidance is most unlikely to direct itself at anything other than the attainment of the licensing objectives. If, on analysis, it is clear that the Guidance represents a departure from the licensing objectives, then of course the licensing authority would be free to depart from it in the exercise of its licensing functions, although it should explicitly state both that it is doing so and why. The Guidance itself states for the avoidance of doubt that nothing in it is intended to override any requirement of licensing law in general or the Act in particular.[67]

Order of priorities between local policy and Guidance

9.66 Since the production of the licensing statement is itself a licensing function, the licensing authority must have regard to national Guidance when carrying out that task.[68] In a number of areas, national Guidance sets out matters for inclusions in local policy. To that extent, local policy is subordinate to national Guidance. However, a licensing authority is free to depart from national Guidance for good reason.[69] As a matter of good law and practice, where it does so, it should say explicitly in the statement that it has done so and explain why. When this occurs, it cannot then be said that the local policy has subordinate status: rather the reverse is true. Conversely, if after the licensing statement has been published, national Guidance is altered so that the two documents are in plain conflict, it is submitted that the latter should normally have primacy, unless the licensing authority determines otherwise for good reason. Confronted with this situation, the licensing authority ought to review its policy to decide whether it wishes to bring it into conformity with national Guidance, or whether there are good reasons to depart from it.

Licensing policy: requirements set out in national guidance

9.67

Guidance paragraph	Requirement
8.7	Identification of body competent to advise on child protection objective, with contact details.
13.9	State licensing objectives.
13.12	State that licensing is about regulating licensable activities, and conditions will be focussed on matters which are within the control of those with authorisations, ie the premises and its vicinity.

---

[67] Para 1.10.
[68] See Guidance para 1.12.
[69] This matter of common sense is acknowledged in Guidance para 1.7.

13.13	State that licensing is not the primary mechanism for controlling anti-social behaviour away from premises and beyond direct control of operators. However, it is a key aspect of such control and licensing law is part of the holistic approach to the management of the evening and night time economy in town and city centres.
13.39	Indicate the mechanisms that are available for addressing cumulative effect: planning, partnership working to create safe and clean town centre, CCTV, alcohol-free zone designation and enforcement, police of enforcement of criminal law, including fixed penalty notices, prosecution for serving drunks, exercise of closure powers under Part 8 of Act, review of licence/certificate, early morning alcohol restriction orders.
13.15	Include a firm commitment to avoid attaching conditions that duplicate other regulatory regimes as far as possible.
13.16	Describe joint enforcement protocols with police and other enforcement agencies.
13.43	Set out the licensing authority's approach regarding licensed opening hours and the strategy it considers appropriate for the promotion of the licensing objectives in its area. The statement of licensing policy should emphasise the consideration which will be given to the individual merits of an application.
13.49	Make clear the range of alternatives which may be considered for limiting the access of children where that is appropriate for the prevention of harm to children.
13.50	Make clear that conditions requiring the admission of children to any premises cannot be attached to licences or certificates.
13.52	Indicate which body the licensing authority judges to be competent to act as the responsible authority in relation to the protection of children from harm.
13.53	Make clear that in the case of premises giving film exhibitions, the licensing authority will expect licence holders or clubs to include in their operating schedules arrangements for restricting children from viewing age-restricted films classified according to the recommendations of the British Board of Film Classification or the licensing authority itself.

13.54	Provide clear indications of how the licensing authority will secure the proper integration of its licensing policy with local crime prevention, planning, transport, tourism, equality schemes, cultural strategies and any other plans introduced for the management of town centres and the night-time economy.
13.55	Indicate that planning permission, building control approval and licensing regimes will be properly separated to avoid duplication and inefficiency.
13.57	Recognise that the Equality Act 2010 places a legal obligation on public authorities to have due regard to the need to eliminate unlawful discrimination, harassment and victimisation; to advance equality of opportunity; and to foster good relations between persons with different protected characteristics.
13.58	Refer to the duty to publish information at least annually to demonstrate compliance with the Equality Duty, and explain how the Equality Duty has been complied with.
13.59	Explain the authority's scheme of delegation of its licensing functions.

Understanding policy and guidance

9.68 It is well-established that where a public body applies a relevant policy document, it must understand the policy. If it does not, then its decision will be treated as defective, in the same way as if no regard had been paid to the policy.[70] Policy documents, however, are not statutes, and are often capable of more than one meaning. The question therefore becomes who is to be the arbiter of the correct meaning.

Until recently, the position in the analogous field of planning law was as follows:

(1) It is for the court to determine as a matter of law what the words in a policy are capable of meaning.[71]

(2) Where the words are capable of more than one meaning, the correct meaning in the particular context will be a matter for the licensing authority, and not susceptible to legal challenge.

(3) Where the licensing authority adopts a meaning for the words which they could not possibly have, they will err in law.[72]

---

[70] *Gransden & Co Ltd v Secretary of State for the Environment* (1987) 54 P & CR 86, 94.

[71] *R v Derbyshire County Council ex parte Woods* [1997] JPL 958, 967. See also illuminating article by James Maurici: 'The Meaning of Policy: A Question for the Court', 1998 JR 85.

[72] *Northavon District Council v Secretary of State for the Environment* [1993] JPL 761.

9.69 As to licensing, these themes came to be discussed in *R (JD Wetherspoon plc) v Guildford Borough Council*,[73] which concerned the interplay between a local licensing policy and national Guidance on the question of whether a cumulative impact policy applied as a matter of interpretation to a variation in terminal hours. Wetherspoons said it could not because national policy was to favour longer hours, and the council's interpretation would have cut against the grain of that presumption. Beatson J, in an important judgment as to the meaning of policy documents, the justiciability of interpretations of such documents by decision makers and the interplay of guidance and policy, rejected the argument.

9.70 As to the interpretation of Guidance, Beatson favoured an approach which eschewed a strict reading as though the document is a statute in favour of a reading which had regard to the purpose of the document. He said:

' ... guidance such as this is not drafted in the tight way in which a statute is drafted. It has similarities to the planning policies and development plans considered by Davis J in *Cranage Parish Council v First Secretary of State* [2004] EWHC 2949 (Admin). At paragraph 49 of the judgment his Lordship stated:-

"For one thing, in the planning field of policies and development plans of this kind are commonly drafted by planners for planners and often are very loosely drafted. They are not, putting it broadly, intended to be legally binding documents in the strict sense. For another, the relevant phrases used will often be hardly sensible bearing a strict hard edged interpretive approach and resort will be needed to elements of value judgment ... "

... Similarly, in *R v Rochdale Metropolitan Borough Council, ex p Milne* [2001] Env. LR 406 at paragraph 51 Sullivan J stated that "a legalistic approach to the interpretation of development plan policies is to be avoided" '.

9.71 Beatson J then went on to note that when reading policy documents, it would be unusual to find all policies pulling in the same direction, so that the question 'is the proposal in accordance with the policy' may not admit of a single, simple answer. He approved a further dictum of Sullivan J in *R v Rochdale Metropolitan Borough Council, ex p Milne*[74] in which Sullivan J had stated:

'It is not at all unusual for development plan policies to pull in different directions. A proposed development may be in accord with development plan policies which, for example, encourage development for employment purposes, and yet be contrary to policies which seek to protect open countryside. In such cases there may be no clear cut answer to the question: "is this proposal in accordance with the plan?"

---

[73] [2006] EWHC 815 (Admin).
[74] [2001] Env. LR 406, at para [48].

The local planning authority has to make a judgment bearing in mind such factors as the importance of the policies which are complied with or infringed, and the extent of compliance or breach.'

9.72   In the context of this case, Beatson J pointed out that policies favouring longer hours may jar with policies seeking to prevent an augmentation of cumulative stress. How these were to be reconciled in an individual case was a matter for the decision-maker. Furthermore, he held that on matters of interpretation of policy, the court would not hold an interpretation unlawful unless the interpretation applied is one which is unreasonable. Where the document is capable of more than one meaning, then provided the authority adopts a meaning which the document is capable of bearing, its decision will not be struck down as unlawful.

9.73   The effect of the *Wetherspoon* case was to elide the approach to policy in planning and licensing law which, since both are species of administrative law is right and to be expected. In particular, the courts do not encourage a highly legalistic approach to policy and Guidance. These documents are drafted by non-lawyers for non-lawyers, and are to be applied and interpreted by local decision-makers having regard to their purpose. The lawyers' instinct for setting out to ascertain a single meaning for an instrument is an improper approach. Rather, provided that the decision-maker applies and interprets it in a rational manner, the approach is not justiciable, that is to say it will not be overturned as unlawful by the court.

9.74   That apparently settled position, however, was apparently shaken by the Supreme Court in a Scottish appeal named *Tesco Stores Limited v Dundee City Council*.[75] There, it was held that the meaning of a policy is a matter of law, and therefore susceptible of a single meaning which may be reviewed by the court, while its application may produce a number of possible results, as to which a margin of discretion is accorded to the planning authority.

As to the meaning of the policy, Lord Reed held:

'The development plan is a carefully drafted and considered statement of policy, published in order to inform the public of the approach which will be followed by planning authorities in decision-making unless there is good reason to depart from it. It is intended to guide the behaviour of developers and planning authorities. As in other areas of administrative law, the policies which it sets out are designed to secure consistency and direction in the exercise of discretionary powers, while allowing a measure of flexibility to be retained. Those considerations point away from the view that the meaning of the plan is in principle a matter which each planning authority is entitled to determine from time to time as it pleases, within the limits of rationality. On the contrary, these

[75]   [2012] UKSC 13.

considerations suggest that in principle, in this area of public administration as in others (as discussed, for example, in *R (Raissi) v Secretary of State for the Home Department* [2008] QB 836), policy statements should be interpreted objectively in accordance with the language used, read as always in its proper context.'[76]

However, when it comes to the application of the policy, the authority's approach is not justiciable unless perverse. Lord Reid stated:

> 'That is not to say that such statements should be construed as if they were statutory or contractual provisions. Although a development plan has a legal status and legal effects, it is not analogous in its nature or purpose to a statute or a contract. As has often been observed, development plans are full of broad statements of policy, many of which may be mutually irreconcilable, so that in a particular case one must give way to another. In addition, many of the provisions of development plans are framed in language whose application to a given set of facts requires the exercise of judgment. Such matters fall within the jurisdiction of planning authorities, and their exercise of their judgment can only be challenged on the ground that it is irrational or perverse (*Tesco Stores Ltd v Secretary of State for the Environment* [1995] 1 WLR 759, 780 per Lord Hoffmann). Nevertheless, planning authorities do not live in the world of Humpty Dumpty: they cannot make the development plan mean whatever they would like it to mean.'[77]

9.75   The *Tesco* case clearly represents a recovery by the courts of jurisdiction over the interpretation of licensing policy, so that challenges may in theory be brought on the grounds that an authority misinterpreted its own policy, even if its interpretation was rational. However, on the question of the application of the policy, authorities are given a margin of discretion with judicial interference occurring only where the authority exceeds the bounds of rationality.

Changes in policy and guidance

9.76   It frequently happens that, after an application is made but before it is determined, the policy relevant to the decision changes. Should the old or the new policy be applied? The starting point is that the new policy should be applied. In *London Borough of Newham v Secretary of State for the Environment & Another*[78] it was held that circular advice which comes into existence after a planning inquiry has been held but before a decision has been delivered is a

---

[76]   *Tesco Stores Ltd v Dundee County Council*, para [18].
[77]   *Tesco Stores Ltd v Dundee County Council*, para [19].
[78]   (1987) 54 P & CR 98.

material consideration. It follows that the licensing authority is to have regard to any policy or guidance which comes into force before a decision has been made.[79]

9.77   Nevertheless, it may sometimes be argued that the previous policy or guidance should be applied as an exception to the general rule, although the mere lapse of time between application and decision could not, it is submitted, amount to an exceptional circumstance. Published Guidance may, of course, state that it is not to have retrospective effect, and indeed that is the case with the October 2012 edition of the Guidance.[80] In the absence of such a statement, the duty is to have regard to the versions of policy and guidance which are current at the time of the decision.[81]

E CONCLUSION

9.78   This chapter has considered the meaning of the licensing objectives, together with the interrelationship between the objectives and national and local policy. While much of the debate rehearsed in this chapter will not arise in the great majority of straightforward licensing applications, it has arisen and will continue to arise in litigation of the harder cases. As a result it is expected that a still clearer understanding will emerge of the general duties of licensing authorities.

---

[79]   See also *Jefferson v National Assembly for Wales* [2008] 1 WLR 2193.

[80]   Para 1.6.

[81]   In one case, a District Judge upheld this approach after hearing full argument on the matter: *Gurgur v London Borough of Enfield* (Haringey Magistrates Court, 23 Nov 2012. See Local Government Lawyer, 27 November 2012). At the time of publication, the decision is subject to a case stated appeal to the High Court.

10

Licensing policy

At noon I went to the Sun tavern; on Fish Street hill … where we had a very fine dinner, good musique, and a great deal of wine. We staid here very late, at last Sir W. Pen and I home together, he so overcome with wine that he could hardly go; I was forced to lead him through the streets and he was in a very merry and kind mood. I home … my head troubled with wine, and I very merry went to bed, my head akeing all night.

Diary of Samuel Pepys, 22 December 1660

A INTRODUCTION

10.01 Section 5 of the Act placed licensing policy on a statutory footing for the first time. In order to understand the effect licensing policy has under the Act, it is necessary to trace the common law relating to licensing policy. Decision making by licensing authorities is no more than a species of administrative decision-making. However, the law relating to licensing policy has developed separately from the law relating to administrative policy generally, with the courts taking a less interventionist approach in the latter case. In recent years, the administrative and licensing 'orthodoxies' have been fused into a hybrid 'new orthodoxy' which is likely to govern licensing policy into the future (see Figure 1).

10.02 For obvious reasons, nearly all the case law regarding licensing policy concerns negative policies, which create presumptions against particular types of activity. Nothing in the Act or the early case law under it prevents

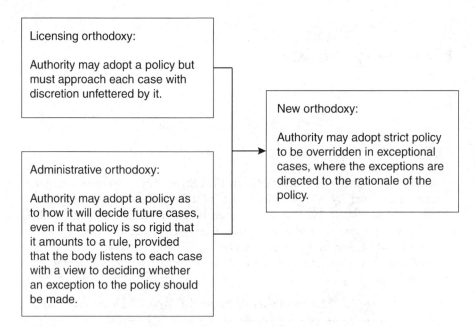

Figure 1: The new orthodoxy

policies creating such negative presumptions. The only theoretical constraint is that policies may not purport to prohibit certain activities, because of course if there has been no objection to an application it must be granted, whatever the policy may say on the matter. In the climate introduced by the Police Reform and Social Responsibility Act 2011, in which licensing officers can object to applications and are likely to do so where the application rubs up against the policy, that is no real constraint at all.

10.03 However, the driving theme of this book is that just because it is legally possible to write policies with strong negative presumptions does not obligate an authority to do so. Negative presumptions deter investment, diversity, choice and growth, and should only be used where there is a good regulatory purpose. This should always be balanced by the use of licensing policy as a pro-active instrument of positive change in the licensing environment, guiding applicants to the most suitable locations and setting consistent standards of management and operation for the benefit of licensees, users and local occupiers alike. These themes are explored in greater depth in Chapters 3 and 4. In this chapter, we concentrate on the law of licensing policy.

B THE ADMINISTRATIVE ORTHODOXY

10.04 In administrative law, the legal position is relatively settled and well-defined. It is perfectly in order for an administrative body to adopt a policy as to how it will decide future cases, even if that policy is so rigid that it amounts to a rule, provided that the body listens to each case with a view to deciding whether an exception to the policy should be made. In *R v Port of London Authority, ex parte Kynoch Limited*[1] Bankes LJ said:

> 'There are on the one hand cases where a tribunal in the honest exercise of its discretion has adopted a policy, and, without refusing to hear an applicant, intimates to him what its policy is, and that after hearing him it will in accordance with its policy decide against him, unless there is something exceptional in his case. I think counsel for the applicants would admit that, if the policy has been adopted for reasons which the tribunal may legitimately entertain, no objection could be taken to such a course. On the other hand there are cases where the tribunal has passed a rule, or come to a determination, not to hear any application of a particular character by whomsoever made. There is a wide distinction to be drawn between these two classes.'[2]

10.05 In *British Oxygen Co Ltd v Minister of Technology*[3] the House of Lords took the position still further. In that case, the Board of Trade refused grants under a statutory scheme partly because the cylinders in respect of which application was made cost under £25, and it was therefore contrary to government policy as to the minimum threshold cost for the award of grants. The House of Lords adjudged that approach to be lawful. The appellants relied on the judgment of Bankes LJ to support the proposition that an authority which makes a fixed rule is not exercising a discretion, and that it is not open to an authority to build into a statutory scheme an exclusion which is not contained in the statute. This argument was rejected. Lord Reid referred to the dictum of Bankes LJ and stated:

> 'I see nothing wrong with that. But the circumstances in which discretions are exercised vary enormously and that passage cannot be applied literally in every case. The general rule is that anyone who has to exercise a statutory discretion must not "shut his ears to an application" (to adapt from Bankes L.J. ...). I do not think there is any great difference between a policy and a rule. There may be cases where an officer or authority ought to listen to a substantial argument reasonably presented urging a change of policy. What the authority must not do is to refuse to listen at all. But a Ministry or large authority may have had to deal already with a multitude of similar applications and then they will almost certainly have evolved a policy so precise that it could well be called a rule. There can be no objection to that, provided the authority is always willing to listen to anyone with something new to say – of course I do not mean to say that there need be an oral hearing ... '[4]

1   [1919] 1 KB 176.
2   Page 184.
3   [1971] AC 610.
4   Page 625.

10.06   Viscount Dilhorne went still further, and wondered whether the dictum of Bankes LJ was really applicable to a case of this kind. He said:

> 'It seems somewhat pointless and a waste of time that the Board should have to consider applications which are bound as a result of its policy decision to fail. Representations could of course be made that the policy should be changed.'[5]

10.07   This pragmatic yet bold approach did not commend itself to the remainder of their Lordships, who contented themselves with agreeing with Lord Reid: it cannot therefore be considered part of the *ratio decidendi* of the case.

10.08   The upshot is that the House of Lords comfortably contemplated a framework in which a rigid policy is adopted, with the authority doing no more than listening to the application and considering whether anything is raised which could amount to an exception to the policy.[6]

C   THE LICENSING ORTHODOXY

10.09   While the exercise of a licensing jurisdiction is no more than a species of administrative decision making, the leading authorities cited above, with their endorsement of highly directive policies, were not historically cited in licensing cases. The effect was that a series of old licensing cases came to be understood as authority for the proposition that licensing authorities may not adopt strong licensing policies. In fact, the old cases tended to be authority for nothing more than that licensing authorities must afford applicants the courtesy of a hearing in which all material matters are taken into account.

10.10   In *R v The Licensing Justices of Walsall*[7] the justices had come to a general resolution not to hear any application for a new licence, so that when the applicant came armed with his attorney to the annual licensing meeting he was turned away with his application for a new licence unheard. The High Court granted an order of mandamus requiring the justices to determine the application. Lord Campbell, CJ held that if an applicant 'wishes to be heard he is entitled to be heard' and that justices must hear before they determine. This case is not authority against the adoption of a rigid licensing policy, but

---

[5]   Page 631.
[6]   See also *Cummings v Birkenhead Corporation* [1971] 2 WLR 1458. The Privy Council has been prepared to go further. In *Ng Enterprises Limited v The Urban Council (Hong Kong)* [1996] 3 WLR 751, it held that where a Council had the power to issue licences to two categories of hawkers – those operating from fixed sites and itinerant hawkers – it was entitled to prohibit one category, itinerant hawkers, absolutely. However, the case is better viewed as one concerning the power to regulate, rather than licence, activities.
[7]   1854 24 LTOS 111.

turns on the duty of a judicial body to hear both sides of the argument.[8]
Similarly in *R v London County Council ex parte Corrie*[9] the Council resolved
that no new permits should be granted for the sale of literature in parks, and
so refused to hear an application for a permit. The Divisional Court granted
mandamus, ordering the Council to hear the application, Sankey J holding
that 'The right to be heard is one of those public safeguards which we should
always struggle to preserve'[10], while Avory J concurred with reluctance,
doubting whether their decision would be of any value since 'when the
application for permission is considered, the Council will probably refuse to
give it'.[11] In *R v Port of London Authority, ex parte Kynoch Limited*, Bankes LJ
characterised this case as one which turned not on the adoption of a policy in
exercise of a discretion but as a refusal to exercise any discretion.[12] These
cases, therefore, have nothing to say on the adoption of licensing policies, but
turned on the outright refusal on the part of the licensing authority to hear
the application at all.

10.11 Subsequent cases also failed to resolve the position as to the
lawfulness of rigid licensing policies. In *Sharp v Hughes*[13] a public house lost
its licence on police evidence that the premises were the habitual resort of
prostitutes. Williams J expressed a misgiving that the justices may simply
have applied a ban where prostitutes had been served, holding that 'To lay
down any such hard and fast line would be inconsistent with anything like a
judicial decision'. However, the case is equally explicable as one in which the
basis of the justices' finding was unclear. *R v Flintshire County Council
Licensing (Stage Plays) Committee ex parte Barrett*[14] is a further example of
justices taking a hard line. The Queen's Theatre, Rhyl had enjoyed the ability
to sell tobacco and alcohol for over half a century and had done so without
incident. But in 1956, the local authority committee prohibited such sales, in
accordance with long-standing rules which had been waived in favour of the
theatre since its inception. The Court of Appeal struck down the decision,
Jenkins LJ holding that the committee had wrongly pursued consistency at
the expense of individual cases.[15] However, again it would be wrong to view
this case as authority for the proposition that a committee may not adopt a
rigid policy, for the rules in question were made under section 9 of the
Theatres Act 1843, which confined the purpose of the rules to ensuring
order and decency. The Court held that the application of the rule to the
instant case could not have had such a purpose, in the light of the blameless

---

8   This was recognised by the Divisional Court in *R v Torquay Licensing Justices ex parte
     Brockman* [1951] 2 KB 784, 789, per Lord Goddard CJ.
9   [1918] 1 KB 68.
10   Page 75.
11   Page 74.
12   [1919] 1 KB 176, p 185 (and see para 10.04 above).
13   1893 57 JP 104.
14   [1957] 1 QB 350.
15   Page 368.

record of the theatre.[16] In fact, in *R v Birmingham City Council, ex parte Sheptonhurst Ltd*[17] O'Connor LJ explained the decision as being no more than an application of the principle that all material matters must be taken into consideration.

10.12 In *R v Rotherham Licensing JJ, ex parte Chapman*[18] the issue of whether it was lawful to adopt a strict policy was specifically considered. The licensing justices had adopted what was variously termed a rule or principle that the number of occasional licences granted to the same promoters in a single year should not exceed two, in consequence of which an application was refused. The chairman's affidavit that the justices had not agreed to exclude the consideration of exceptional circumstances did not save the decision from being quashed by the Divisional Court. Lord Hewart LCJ stated:

> 'It may well be that justices of discretion and experience might prescribe for themselves a general rule of that nature as a counsel of perfection, intending, and being able, to apply an unfettered discretion to the consideration of the merits of each particular case. The rule itself, however, or the principle, if that word be preferred, seems plainly designed to prevent the application of an unfettered judgment to the individual case, and to prescribe in advance a hard-and-fast rule, save in exceptional circumstances – a phrase to which the Licensing Act itself in this connection is a stranger – and so exclude any more than two applications ... in the course of 12 months. That seems to me to be an abdication of the duty of the duty of the justices impartially to consider upon the facts the merits of each individual application.'[19]

10.13 The refusal by the court to countenance the adoption of a rule or policy, to be applied save in exceptional cases, was a departure from the principles set out in *R v Port of London Authority, ex parte Kynoch Limited*.[20] That case, being a decision of the Court of Appeal, bound the Divisional Court. Unfortunately, however, *Kynoch* was not cited. This resulted in a much stricter position being adopted towards the formulation and implementation of policies than was the case for other branches of administrative decision-making. This stricter approach, here termed the licensing orthodoxy, continued throughout the second half of the twentieth century.

10.14 In *R v Torquay Licensing Justices ex parte Brockman*[21] the Divisional Court had to consider the justices' policy that 'in the future, circumstances would have to be very exceptional before they would grant full in place of

16   See also, on similar facts, *R v Cardiff Corporation ex parte Westlan Productions Ltd, New Theatre (Cardiff) Ltd and Moss Empires Ltd* (1929) 73 SJ 766.
17   [1990] 1 All ER 1025, 1035.
18   [1939] 2 All ER 710.
19   Page 712.
20   [1919] 1 KB 176 (and see para 10.04 above).
21   1951 2 KB 784.

restricted licences.' The applicant fell foul of the policy, but failed to persuade the court to overturn the decision, because the evidence showed that the justices had considered whether they were prepared to apply an exception in this case. Lord Goddard CJ stated:

> ' ... no fault can be found with the justices' determining that, as a general rule, they would look with disfavour on persons who had come before them and obtained a restricted licence and who subsequently applied for a full licence, and would consider that in such a case there was a very considerable onus thrown upon the applicant. We think that that is well within their powers; but, when an application is made ... the justices are bound to hear it and consider whether, on the facts of the particular case, there is enough to take it out of the general rule which they have laid down. That is what we think that the justices have done in the present case.'[22]

10.15   While no cases from the administrative field were cited to, or by, the court, the decision smacks of an application of a classic administrative orthodoxy.[23] However, in its subsequent application, the case has sometimes been used to justify overturning decisions where the appeal court has been unable to envisage circumstances in which an exception could arise, so that the policy is indistinguishable from a rule.

10.16   The dichotomy between the administrative and licensing orthodoxies was confronted head-on by the Court of Appeal in *Sagnata Investments Ltd v Norwich Corporation*.[24] There, the local authority adopted a general policy not to permit amusement arcades. Sagnata's application for a licence was refused, after a full hearing, on the grounds of undesirable effects on young people and the sufficiency of amusement with prize machines in Norwich. The decision was reversed on appeal to Quarter Sessions, the recorder stating:

> 'I am forced to the conclusion that in this case, where the application met with all the ordinary requirements as to suitability of site, premises and management, the general policy must have been applied. In other words, no application to the local authority, however suitable, would succeed.'[25]

10.17   The matter eventually came before the Court of Appeal. Phillimore LJ pointed out that no evidence had been called to support the assertion that amusement arcades harmed young people, and the chairman of the committee had told Quarter Sessions that the decision had been

---

[22]   Page 791.
[23]   A similar approach was taken by Wien J in *R v Torbay Licensing Justices ex parte White* [1980] 2 All ER 25.
[24]   [1971] 2 QB 614.
[25]   Page 639.

reached solely on the basis of the policy. Having quoted from the Recorder's decision, he said:

> 'In other words the council had not exercised any form of discretion. They had simply dismissed this application after going through the necessary motions without regard to its individual merits or demerits. I take this to be a finding of fact with which this court is in no position to interfere.'[26]

10.18 So Phillimore J's judgment turned on the factual conclusion that the council had not paid attention to the merits of the individual case. Similarly, Edmund Davies LJ accepted that it was open to the council to adopt a general policy of refusing applications provided that it was prepared to depart from the policy where the justice of the individual case required.[27] But he was equally swayed by the finding of the Recorder that no application, however suitable, would succeed. Under the administrative orthodoxy, of course, that is not problematic, but under the developing licensing orthodoxy, a policy which was hard to rebut was impeachable on appeal. In a powerful dissenting judgment, Lord Denning MR attempted to unite the administrative and licensing orthodoxies. He stated that both *R v Port of London Authority, ex parte Kynoch Limited*[28] and *R v Torquay Justices ex parte Brockman*[29] needed to be read in the light of modern cases including *British Oxygen Co Ltd v Board of Trade*[30] He continued:

> 'I take it to be perfectly clear now that an administrative body, including a licensing body, which may have to consider numerous applications of a similar kind, is entitled to lay down a general policy which it proposes to follow in coming to its individual decisions, provided always that it is a reasonable policy which it is fair and just to apply. Once laid down, the administrative body is entitled to apply the policy in the individual cases which come before it. The only qualification is that the administrative body must not apply the policy so rigidly as to reject an applicant without hearing what he has to say. It must not "shut its ears to an application"; see 1971 AC 610, 625, per Lord Reid. The applicant is entitled to put forward reasons urging that the policy should be changed, or saying that in any case it should not be applied to him. But, so long as the administrative body is ready to hear him and consider what he has to say, it is entitled to apply its general policy to him as to others.'[31]

10.19 Applying the administrative orthodoxy, Lord Denning MR considered that it was perfectly in order for the council to apply its policy, provided

26   Page 639.
27   Page 632.
28   [1919] 1 KB 176 (and see para 10.04 above).
29   1951 2 KB 784 (and see para 10.14 above).
30   1971 AC 610 (and see para 10.05 above).
31   Page 626.

that it listened conscientiously to what the applicant had to say. However, the majority applied the developing licensing orthodoxy, and held it unlawful for the council to adopt a rigid policy. To some extent, the decision may be seen as turning on its facts, in view of the explicit factual findings that the policy would have been applied whatever the merits of the individual case. But it clearly represented a trend of aversion by the courts to decisions taken by licensing authorities in accordance with policy and without other supporting evidence justifying refusal.

D THE NEW ORTHODOXY

10.20 In a series of modern decisions, the courts developed a new jurisprudence on the circumstances in which policy should be disapplied, so concentrating less on the formal flexibility or rigidity of the policy. This is the new orthodoxy.

10.21 In *R v Chester Crown Court, ex parte Pascoe and Jones*,[32] the Chester justices had adopted a policy that liquor should be only be supplied from a 'shop within a shop' and not by self-service. The policy contained the following proviso, of the sort frequently found in licensing policies to avoid accusation that they operate as a rule:

'The justices emphasize that the policy is general but not invariable. Each application which they receive will be considered on its own merits, and if they are satisfied that circumstances warrant a deviation from their general policy, then they will make the appropriate deviation.'

10.22 The justices refused an application for an off-licence for a Tesco's supermarket whose self-service liquor section would have violated the policy, and the Crown Court upheld the refusal, holding that nothing it had heard justified a departure from the policy. The Divisional Court overturned that decision. In doing so, it reiterated the law as laid down inter alia in *Brockman*,[33] that while an authority may lay down a policy, it must always consider whether the policy is applicable, or should be applied, to the facts of the instant case.[34] Indeed, this was no more than the justices' policy itself stated. But the court went further in stating, for the first time, which matters were relevant to whether an exception to the policy applied. Glidewell LJ stated:

' ... where there is a general policy and an applicant is seeking to persuade a court ... to make a proper departure from that general

---

[32] (1987) 151 JP 752, followed in the similar case of *R v Licensing Justices at North Tyneside, ex parte Todd and Lewis* (1988) 153 JP 100. See also *R v Windsor Licensing Justices ex parte Hodes* [1983] where the vice was that the justices had failed to give individual consideration to the merits of the application – see p 695.

[33] 1951 2 KB 784 (and see para 10.14 above).

[34] Page 755, per Glidewell LJ.

policy, then amongst the most important of the matters which the court or the justices must consider is the reasons for the policy and whether, if they were to grant what is sought by way of exception, those reasons would still be met.'[35]

10.23 Here, where the reasons for the policy were to deter crime and under-age purchase, it was found that the Crown Court had not sufficiently addressed its mind to whether those concerns were adequately met by the Tesco proposal.

10.24 The decision represents a subtle hybrid of the administrative and licensing orthodoxies. In that it accepts that the licensing authority may apply the policy unless an exception is shown, it follows the administrative orthodoxy. In stating that, absent direct evidence of harm the policy cannot hold sway, it follows the licensing orthodoxy. The subtlety is the introduction of a principle that the licensing authority, when considering whether the policy should prevail, must ask itself whether a departure would harm the rationale of the policy.[36] This may be termed the 'new orthodoxy'.

10.25 The new orthodoxy has been developed in succeeding cases. In *R v Sheffield Crown Court ex parte Consterdine*[37] the justices' policy was normally to refuse new applications for justices' licences in the absence of proven need or demand that was not met by existing premises. A disappointed applicant appealed to the High Court and submitted that it was necessary for the licensing authority to justify its decision to apply the policy.[38] Turner J disagreed. While an authority should always consider whether the facts merit a departure from the policy, it is not necessary for it to revisit on each occasion the reason why it adopted the policy. He said:

'Given that it is, in general, reasonable for there to be a policy, and that there is no challenge to it, the question then arises whether it is incumbent on the committee (or the crown court, as the case may be) to have to justify its decision to apply the policy, or is it for the applicant to demonstrate, if it can, that in the circumstances appertaining to its application, the policy should not apply for reasons which it has advanced and made good? ... [I]f the proposition that it is for the committee to prove that the policy or the reasons which underpin it will be jeopardised unless the application is refused, this appears to stand

---

[35] Page 757.
[36] For other cases turning on failure to give adequate consideration to whether an exception to policy should be applied, see *R v Chester Justices ex parte Cecchini* (1997) 29 Licensing Review 19; *R (Thompsett) v Croydon Crown Court* [2001] LLR 714; *R (Chorion plc) v Crown Court at Middlesex Guildhall* [2001] LLR 621], although here Turner J mistook the reasons for the policy, as being related to management of the premises and nuisance in the immediate area, whereas the policy was directed at cumulative stress over a wider area.
[37] 1992 Licensing Review 19.
[38] Following the decision of Hutchison J in *R v Sheffield Crown Court ex parte Mead* [1992] 8 LR 19.

the rationale of having a policy on its head. ... [I]t is for the party seeking to persuade the committee to depart from its policy to show that it can be done without imperilling it or the reasons which underlie it.'[39]

10.26 Under the new orthodoxy, then, the courts are less concerned with the strictness of the policy than the question of the rationale for the policy, emphasising that consideration is always needed as to whether an exception has been shown to the policy which is directed towards that rationale, the onus of demonstrating the exception lying on the applicant.[40]

The Westminster litigation

10.27 The adoption of restrictive licensing policies by Westminster City council generated widespread dissent within the licensing trade, and copious litigation, one by-product of which has been to clarify and crystallise modern principles regarding licensing policy. The background was the proliferation of public entertainment venues and night cafés in the West End of London which, according to the council, had generated problems of cumulative stress. These included criminal offences on, and by, visitors, nuisance to residents by noise, litter and fouling, attraction of unlicensed minicabs and traffic noise and congestion. The council claimed that these problems could not be attributed to individual premises, and certainly not to mismanagement by individual licensees, and so collective restraint was called for. The council's solution was to adopt a policy which contained a presumption against the grant or extension of licences in what it termed the 'stress areas'. While the adoption of the policy was not challenged by judicial review[41], on appeal against licensing decisions made in accordance with the policy, courts were routinely invited to disregard/disapply the policy on the basis that the premises were well managed and the applicant was fit and proper. These decisions gave rise to important questions as to what, if any, force a policy

[39] Page 23. The notion that it is not for a committee to produce probative evidence to justify a policy is consistent with the decision of the Court of Appeal in *R v Torbay Borough Council ex parte Cleasby* (unreported, 31 July 1990), although if a committee fails to do so it is more likely that a court on appeal will hold that such reasons as underlie the policy have been met in the instant case, thus justifying an exception.

[40] The new orthodoxy has also been followed in Scotland: see *Calderwood v Renfrewshire Council* 2004 LLR 171. See further *R v City & County of Swansea, ex parte Jones* (unreported 28 November 1996) which held that an inflexibly worded policy might be cured by evidence that it could be flexibly applied. Such an approach, however, may fall foul of the principle that a policy which means something other than what is intended is unlawful: see *R (Chorion plc) v Westminster City Council* [2002] LLR 27 at para 25. It is submitted that the better view is that a policy should always allow for at least the possibility of exceptions: *Attorney General ex rel Tilley v London Borough of Wandsworth* [1981] 1 WLR 854.

[41] Save for a judicial review complaining that the policy appeared to apply to variations which did not amount to extensions, which resulted in a voluntary clarification of the policy: see *R (Chorion plc) v Westminster City Council* [2002] LLR 27.

enjoyed both at first instance and on appeal. The matter came to a head in *R* (*Westminster City Council*) *v Middlesex Crown Court and Chorion plc*[42] In that case, the applicant, who traded as 'Delicious' in the West End of London, applied to the council for a public entertainment licence with a terminal hour of 3 am but was granted a licence only until 1 am. The stipendiary magistrate allowed the applicant's appeal on the grounds that the applicant was fit and proper and that the premises would be well managed. The council appealed to the Crown Court, contending that its policy should prevail over the individual circumstances. The Crown Court dismissed the appeal, because it found 'no evidence specific to these premises or this [licensee] that permits us to support the otherwise entirely laudable attitude of the local authority.' The council might have responded that had the applicant been a rogue who could not control his visitors, and whose premises leaked noise and odours, it would not have needed a policy in order to deny the terminal hour sought. It applied to judicially review the decision.

10.28   The Judge, Scott Baker J, adopted the new orthodoxy, by following *British Oxygen Co Ltd v Minister of Technology*.[43] He held that the council could adopt a policy provided that it considered in each case whether an exception was justified, and absent exceptional circumstances was entitled to rely on the policy.[44] As had Turner J in *R v Sheffield Crown Court ex parte Consterdine*,[45] he held that in considering whether to disapply a policy, the decision-maker should ask itself whether the object of the policy would be damaged.[46] Furthermore, he held that a court hearing an appeal should apply the policy as it would be applied by the council. He said:

> 'How should a Crown Court (or a magistrates' court) approach an appeal where the council has a policy? In my judgment it must accept the policy and apply it as if it was standing in the shoes of the council considering the application. Neither the magistrates court nor the Crown Court is the right place to challenge the policy. The remedy, if it is alleged that a policy has been unlawfully established, is an application to the Administrative Court for judicial review.'[47]

10.29   To that extent, therefore, Scott Baker J merely brought together the developing principles concerning the role of policy in licensing decision-making. On the facts, he held that Westminster's then policy suffered from the vice of being sufficiently flexible to permit a departure even where the reasons for the departure did not go to the reasons for the policy, namely cumulative stress. In particular, one paragraph of the policy specifically stated that it was unlikely that applications would be refused on policy

---

[42]   2002 LLR 538.
[43]   1971 AC 610 (and see para 10.05 above).
[44]   Page 543.
[45]   1992 Licensing Review 19 (and see 10.25 above).
[46]   Page 544.
[47]   Page 543. In this, Scott Baker J followed Glidewell LJ in *R v Chester Crown Court ex parte Pascoe and Jones* (1987) 151 JP 752, p 756 (see para 10.21 above).

grounds alone – this reduced the policy to a mere factor in the equation and so justified the Crown Court as treating it accordingly.

10.30   Scott Baker, however, went on to prescribe how the policy might in future be drawn so as to achieve greater presumptive effect:

'It is both understandable and appropriate for the claimant to have a policy in the light of the problems it has identified in the West End. The policy needs to make it clear that it is not directed at the quality of the operation or the fitness of the licensee but on the global effects of these licences on the area as a whole. If the policy is not to be consistently overridden in individual cases it must be made clear within it that it will only be overridden in exceptional circumstances and that the impecca-ble credentials of the applicant will not ordinarily be regarded as exceptional circumstances. It should be highlighted that the kind of circumstances that might be regarded as exceptional would be where the underlying policy of restricting any further growth would not be impaired. An example might be where premises in one place would replace those in another. The guidance document needs to be redrawn so as to eliminate inconsistencies and ambiguities.'[48]

10.31   In this passage, Scott Baker J outlined a licensing policy regime which would enable licensing policy to enjoy the same force as policies in other areas of administrative law. To achieve that position, however, it is necessary for the policy to be robustly phrased, and expressly narrow the circumstances potentially considered exceptional. The instant policy failed to achieve that, so though phrased as a presumption it was in law no more than a pebble in the scales. Thus, while the Crown Court was bound to take the policy into account, its duty extended no further than that. But Scott Baker J clearly contemplated a world in which policy could be sculpted to enjoy a far more powerful profile on the licensing landscape.[49]

---

[48]   Page 546.
[49]   To complete the picture, following Scott Baker J's judgment, Westminster City Council did revise its policy so as to achieve the robustness referred to in the judgment. In brief, the policy was:

'The City Council's policy is to refuse applications ... within the West End Stress Area ...'

'The City Council will not ordinarily treat the following considerationsas justifiable exceptions to [the above]:

(1)   That the premises will be well managed.
(2)   That the applicant is of good character.
(3)   That the premises, or the capacity, or the size of the increase applied for, is small.'

'Where applications are granted ... as an exception to City Council policy, the Council will set a terminal hour for licensed premises having regard to the impact of the premises on the area, both individually and cumulatively with other premises.'

'The City Council's guideline terminal hours for new applications and applications to increase the terminal hour are (West End Stress Area): 1 a.m.'

10.32   The effect of Scott Baker J's decision on the law of licensing policy prior to the promulgation of the Licensing Act 2003 is of obvious importance. It may be summarised thus:

- Policy may state that it is to be overridden only in exceptional circumstances.
- The rationale for the policy may be stated in the policy – where it is, exceptions must be directed to the rationale.
- Policy may exclude particular exceptional circumstances.
- Appeal courts to apply policy as if they are licensing authority
- Policy may not be challenged in appeal court

The question now is: what role does policy play in the new licensing regime?

E   POLICY UNDER THE LICENSING ACT 2003

10.33   While previously, licensing policy was a document produced by licensing authorities to guide and inform their decisions pursuant to statute, under the Licensing Act, the policy itself is an emanation of the statute. This alone confers a new status on licensing policy, perhaps in recognition of the fact of the increasingly prominent role that policy has come to play in licensing decision-making. Section 5 provides:

'(1)   Each licensing authority must in respect of each five[50] year period –
  (a)   determine its policy with respect to the exercise of its licensing functions; and
  (b)   publish a statement of that policy ("a licensing statement") before the beginning of the period.'

10.34   Before determining its policy for a five year period, the licensing authority is obliged to consult a comprehensive list of consultees.[51]

10.35   During the five year period the licensing authority is under a positive obligation to keep its policy under review and make such revisions to it as it considers appropriate[52]. Doing so does not alter the shelf life of the policy.

While the policy was challenged by judicial review, the claim was withdrawn before it reached a hearing. Subsequent incarnations of thepolicy have similarly escaped challenge.

[50]   The period specified in the Licensing Act 2003 was three years, which was extended by the Police Reform and Social Responsibility Act 2011. The five year period commences on 7 January 2011: Police Reform and Social Responsibility Act 2011, s 122(8).

[51]   Licensing Act 2003, s 5(3). These are the chief officer of police, the fire and rescue authority, the health authority and such persons as the authority considers to be representative of existing holders of premises licences, club premises certificates, personal licences, and of businesses and residents.

[52]   Licensing Act 2003, s 5(4).

The authority may also elect to replace its policy during the five year period, in which case the period begins to run afresh from the date specified in the policy.[53] There is no statutorily defined difference between a revision and a replacement: an authority may term a minor change a replacement and so re-set the shelf life of the policy. Whether the change is a revision or a replacement, the authority is obliged to consult the statutory list of consult-ees.[54]

The role of policy

10.36   The role of the statement of licensing policy is relatively undefined by the Act, but its place in the hierarchy of licensing considerations may provide some clue as to what Parliament intended. For clarity, it is necessary to set out section 4 of the Act in full:

'4 General duties of licensing authorities

(1)   A licensing authority must carry out its functions under this Act ("licensing functions") with a view to promoting the licensing objectives.

(2)   The licensing objectives are –
(a) the prevention of crime and disorder;
(b) public safety;
(c) the prevention of public nuisance;
(d) the protection of children from harm.

(3)   In carrying out its licensing functions, a licensing authority must also have regard to –
(a) its licensing statement published under section 5, and
(b) any guidance issued by the Secretary of State under section 182.'

10.37   It will be seen that the licensing authority is under a mandatory duty to carry out its licensing functions with a view to promoting the licensing objectives. That is the legislative end in view which must govern everything the licensing authority does. If it acts with promotion of some other end in view, it is acting ultra vires. In contrast, there is no compulsion on the licensing authority to follow its licensing statement: the obligation is merely to have regard to that document. If, in an individual case, the licensing statement and promotion of the licensing objectives pull in the same direction and would lead to the same result, then the licensing statement serves merely to reinforce a decision already dictated by the licensing objectives. In cases in which adherence to the licensing statement would yield a different result from that indicated by the licensing objectives, the intention of the legislature would clearly seem to be that the licensing objectives must hold sway and there should be a departure from the policy.

---

[53]   Licensing Act 2003, s 5(6A)–(6C).
[54]   Licensing Act 2003, s 5(5)–(6B).

10.38 However, if that is the whole story, then the licensing policy would exert no influence over the result of the application. It would simply act as a weathervane of licensing decisions, informing the observer whether the decision was or was not in accordance with the policy.

10.39 The true position, however, is qualitatively different. First of all, a presumption in a licensing policy reverses the evidential burden, so that it falls to an applicant to demonstrate why an exception should be made to the policy in an individual case, rather than to the objector to the application (be they local resident or responsible authority) to explain why the application should be refused.

10.40 Second, policies are treated by the court as the means by which the licensing objectives are promoted, not only case by case but in terms of the overall strategy for the area. For example in *R (A3D2 Limited t/a Novus Leisure) v Westminster Magistrates' Court*,[55] the appellant suggested to the Administrative Court that by asking itself only whether an exception to the policy had been established, the magistrates' court had lost sight of the true question, which was whether the licensing objectives would be promoted. This was rejected by Cranston J, who stated:

> 'In my judgment, there is no reviewable flaw in the judge's analysis of the issues presented to her in question 3. Under sections 18(3) and (4) of the Licensing Act 2003, the test in considering whether to grant or refuse an application for a premises licence is whether it is necessary in order to promote the licensing objectives. Westminster's licensing policy is the background under section 4(3) against which individual licensing decisions should be made, applying that statutory test. Westminster has adopted a policy of refusing applications for new public houses and bars in the so-called Stress Areas – where it is considered there is already a saturation of such establishments, the cumulative impact of which has led to problems of crime, disorder and public nuisance – other than for a variation of hours within the prescribed core hours. The policy recognises exceptional cases, although it makes clear that a case is most unlikely to be considered exceptional unless it is directed at the underlying reasons for having the policy.'

10.41 In other words, by answering the question whether the policy applies and whether exceptional circumstances have been demonstrated, so the question posed in section 18(3) of the Act is answered. Were there to be any different approach, the policy would be demoted to nothing more than a pebble in the scales, contrary to the new orthodoxy described above.

10.42 Third, this analysis is consistent with the wider role of the policy in setting the framework for future licensing decisions. The licensing objectives themselves are broadly cast, presumably so as to broaden the discretion of

---

[55]   [2011] EWHC 1045 (Admin).

licensing authorities when applying them. Furthermore, the Act does not state that there needs to be a demonstrable breach of the licensing objectives before refusing or attaching conditions to a licence. Rather, the Act recognises the necessity of a broader based policy approach. Section 4(1) enjoins authorities to carry out their functions 'with a view to promoting' the licensing objectives. Section 18(3)(b) requires them, when relevant representations have been made, to take the steps mentioned in section 18(4), including the attachment of conditions or outright refusal, 'as it considers appropriate for the promotion of the licensing objectives.' It is clear that the pre-condition for a refusal is not that a grant would actually breach the licensing objectives, but that a refusal is considered appropriate to promote the objectives. In cases such as these, the policy has very considerable influence in determining the outcome of the case.

10.43 This may be demonstrated. If a council identifies a family residential area and wishes to ensure that it does not become a late night destination, it may say so in its licensing policy. For the sake of argument, the policy may indicate that the council wishes to guard against late night alcohol-led licensing in a particular residential area, and that a much stricter approach will be taken to the prevention of nuisance objective in that area. By those means, the policy would operate to create a much lower threshold of evidence of risk of nuisance necessary to found a refusal. If an application for a late night destination venue comes before the licensing authority, it is not apparently necessary for the licensing authority to be satisfied on balance of probabilities that a public nuisance will be caused before refusing the licence. It is only necessary for it to consider refusal to be a necessary step to promote the objective of preventing public nuisance. Thus, the decision can be justified on the basis that the authority is preventing the risk of nuisance, rather than needing to be justified on the basis that a grant would cause a nuisance. In that way, the policy, by taking a strict approach, exerts clear influence on the outcome of the case.

10.44 The matter cuts both ways. The authority may consider that late night licensing should be positively promoted in its cultural quarter or in its town centre generally. In those locations there may still be a risk of nuisance occasioned by late night licensing, but if the policy has acknowledged that risk but encourages such outlets there in any event, it would take a much higher threshold of evidence of risk of nuisance before a refusal could be considered appropriate. Thus, in its approach to the licensing objectives, policy can play a key role in the character, disposition and hours of operation of licensed premises across the authority's domain.

10.45 This can be demonstrated by a still simpler example, also given elsewhere in this book.[56] Take a small village with one pub and no crime, disorder or nuisance after 11.30 pm. The pub operator applies to extend

---

[56]   Chapter 9.

trading hours to 1 am. It would be impossible to conclude that this gives rise to no risk of crime, disorder or public nuisance. Clearly, where late night drinking activity is introduced to an area where there has previously been done, there is almost bound to be some crime committed during the course of the year, by or on customers, and some disturbance to neighbours. The statutory formulation of the licensing objectives and the tests for their exercise in sections 4(1) and 18(3) do not state how much crime or nuisance is too much. That is a matter for local control having regard to the needs and priorities of the particular area. It is for the licensing authority to spell out those needs and priorities through its licensing policy and to reflect these through its licensing decisions. Thus, the fate of the pub's application may largely be determined, one way or the other, by the wording of the policy.

10.46   In general, therefore, a well-framed policy may often bring to bear practically conclusive influence when weighed against other material considerations. In this regard, the advice given by Scott Baker J as to the formulation of policies[57] remains good law.[58]

10.47   Furthermore, the licensing objectives themselves describe the ends but not the means. No doubt they may be attained in a number of different ways. For example, it is sometimes argued that crime and disorder would be diminished if premises closed earlier (so as to get people out of the town centre) or later (so as to aid gradual dispersal). Which might be the more effective approach is a matter which the local authority may consider jointly with other agencies and stakeholders. The result of such consideration may feed into the council's licensing policy. In that way, the policy will inform consideration in individual cases of what the licensing objectives require, and where that is uncertain the policy may be expected to be determinative. Therefore, while under the Licensing Act licensing policy is theoretically subordinate in each case to the attainment of the licensing objectives, the policy itself, particularly if underpinned by thorough-going research and consultation, may come to define what is required by those objectives. In short, while the licensing objectives are the destination, the local licensing policy is the signpost by which the destination is reached.

Canterbury: the frontiers of policy

Context

10.48   As the first paragraph of Chapter 1 relates, English literature starts in a pub on a pilgrimage to Canterbury. So, the fact that the first important case under the Licensing Act 2003 concerned Canterbury creates some pleasing symmetry. In *R (British Beer and Pub Association et al) v Canterbury City*

---

[57]   See para 10.30 above.
[58]   See also *British Oxygen Co Ltd v Minister of Technology* (para 10.05 above).

Council,[59] the BBPA together with other trade associations representing the great majority of the licensed retail sector brought their collective might to bear on the licensing policy of one council, Doncaster and Gloucester having decided to amend their policies in the teeth of the BBPA's parallel claims against them. Canterbury was the tail wagging a large dog, as the High Court was told that at least 30 other authorities had received letters from the BBPA complaining about their policies, which made this a test case.

10.49 The case was of importance in that it clarified the extent to which a policy may direct applicants as to the contents of their operating schedules, and the extent to which it may contain expressions of presumption for or against a particular approach to decision-making.

10.50 To summarise the procedural position, the scheme of the Licensing Act is relatively straightforward. An applicant for a new or varied premises licence or club premises certificate puts in an operating schedule which must include any steps which the applicant proposes in order to promote the licensing objectives of the prevention of crime and disorder, the protection of children from harm, public safety and the prevention of public nuisance. If no responsible authority (ie statutory agency) or other person makes a relevant representation (ie objection) then the council must grant the application on the terms of the operating schedule proposed by the applicant. If there is a relevant representation, the authority must hold a hearing, at the end of which it is obliged, having regard to the representation, to take such steps as it considers necessary to promote the licensing objectives. This may include adding to or modifying the proposed conditions or rejecting some or all of the application.

10.51 Under the previous regime, many councils had adopted non-statutory licensing policies as to their approach to decision-making. As explained above, it had been held in *R (Westminster City Council) v Middlesex Crown Court and Chorion plc*[60] that such policies could set out strong presumptions against particular forms of licensed activity or trading hours, by geographical sector or otherwise. The Licensing Act 2003 placed such policies on a statutory footing for the first time. The question was how prescriptive the new policies were entitled to be.

The three stages

10.52 There are three stages in the licensing process. The first is when the applicant completes the operating schedule. The second is when council officers process the application. The third is when the licensing sub-committee makes a decision on an application following receipt of relevant

---

[59]   [2005] EWHC 1318 (Admin).
[60]   2002 LLR 538.

representations. It is helpful to analyse what *Canterbury* has to say about each stage in that process.

Stage one: the operating schedule

10.53 At stage one, the applicant has to complete the operating schedule. The applicant has carte blanche to decide what, if any, steps he proposes in order to promote the licensing objectives. If there are no objections to what he proposes, the steps will become licence conditions. But may the policy set out what steps the council would <u>like</u> him to propose? The answer is provided by the Secretary of State's Guidance:

> '8.34 In completing an operating schedule, applicants are expected to have regard to the statement of licensing policy for their area. They must also be aware of the expectations of the licensing authority and the responsible authorities as to the steps that are appropriate for the promotion of the licensing objectives, and to demonstrate knowledge of their local area when describing the steps they propose to take to promote the licensing objectives.'

10.54 As may be seen, therefore, the Secretary of State contemplates that policies will set out the expectations of the licensing authority and responsible authorities as to best practice. Given that the policy is by definition the product of a consultative effort involving a range of stakeholders, it ought to reflect a collaborative view of the best means of promoting the licensing objectives. To the extent to which an applicant incorporates that collective view in his operating schedule, he is less likely to encounter objection to that which he proposes.

10.55 So if, for example, the licensing authority has a strong view about particular standards of safety, or noise insulation, or anything else, it may state that it expects proposed conditions on the matter to be set out in the operating schedule.

10.56 In the *Canterbury* case, the BBPA accepted that the policy could 'advise' or 'strongly recommend' the steps to be proposed. The Judge, Richards J, held that policies may go further than advice and set out expectations: indeed they would be better and clearer for doing so. He stated: 'For a policy to indicate a decision-maker's general expectations is acceptable in principle and, in this particular context, is also in accordance with the Guidance.'[61] He dealt with the benefit of a policy which sets out expectations as follows:

> '82. A policy relating to the decision-making stage under section 18(3) not only guides the decision-maker but also serves to inform an applicant about what he should consider in preparing his application.

---

61   Para 80.

Far from being objectionable, that is one of the purposes of having such a policy. As the Secretary of State recommends at paragraph 5.47 of the Guidance,[62] in preparing an operating schedule "applicants should be aware of the expectations of the licensing authority ... about the steps that are necessary for the promotion of the licensing objectives". An application that takes account of the matters set out in the policy, for example by including what is referred to in the policy or by giving a reasoned justification for not doing so, is less likely to give rise to relevant representations and more likely to be granted without additional conditions, whether under the administrative procedure in the absence of relevant representations or on a decision by the council under section 18(3) in the event of relevant representations.'

10.57 However, and this was really the crux of the *Canterbury* decision, the language of expectation is the limit of the power of councils to specify the steps to be included in an operating schedule. If a council goes further and positively misleads applicants into thinking that a particular step is mandatory or, worse, that the application would automatically be rejected if the step is not included, the council goes too far. As the Judge said:

'If a policy creates a different impression, and in particular if it misleads an applicant into believing that he must meet certain requirements in relation to his application and that he lacks the freedom accorded to him by the Act and Regulations, the policy is contrary to the legislative scheme and is unlawful on *Padfield* grounds (*Padfield* v. *Minister of Agriculture, Fisheries and Food* [1968] AC 997).'[63]

10.58 On this matter, therefore, there was little difference between the cases of the respective parties. The only real question was whether the *Canterbury* policy crossed the forbidden line.

10.59 The matters criticised by the claimants were not adjudicated upon individually by the Judge. Some of those contained no more than the language of expectation. However, a formulation in mandatory language which plainly had the potential to fall foul of the Judge's analysis of the law was:

'When addressing the issue of crime and disorder, the applicant must demonstrate that those factors that impact on crime and disorder have been considered.'

10.60 In a number of places, the policy set out a list of control measures and stated that these were 'considered by the council to be among the most essential that applicants should take account of in their Operating Schedules ... ' By itself, this may not have been objectionable, but coupled with the

---

[62] The then Guidance was to the same effect as the current edition.
[63] Para 85.

criticisms of how the policy dealt with stage two of the process it was held to create a potentially misleading impression.

10.61   A related issue in the case was the extent to which the council is entitled to demand information from the applicant in the operating schedule. One of the claimants' criticisms concerned a requirement that 'In respect of each of the four licensing objectives applicants will need to provide evidence to the council that suitable and sufficient measures, as detailed in their operating schedule, will be implemented and maintained, relevant to the individual style and characteristics of their premises and events ... ' In similar vein was a criticism of references to the requirement to conduct risk assessments, such as: 'The council will expect the selection of control measures to be based upon a risk assessment of the premises.'

Now, national Guidance encourages the applicant to risk assess their operation and use the results to inform the content of his operating schedule. It states:

> '10.4 The conditions that are appropriate for the promotion of the licensing objectives should emerge initially from the risk assessment carried out by a prospective licence or certificate holder, which they should carry out before making their application for a premises licence or club premises certificate. This would be translated into the steps recorded in the operating schedule or club operating schedule, which must also set out the proposed hours during which licensable activities will be conducted and any other hours during which the premises will be open to the public.'

10.62   The Judge did not adjudicate specifically on the point, because he took the view that the policy overall was overly prescriptive as a matter of 'overall impression'. However, consonant with the tenor of national Guidance and the remainder of the judgment, it is submitted that it is in order for a policy to 'expect' that risk assessments will be carried out and that information regarding the outcome would be included in the operating schedule. It is regrettable that the prescribed form for operating schedules does not lend itself to the provision of information rather than the tendering of conditions. However, many operators, in order to avert relevant representations, append or refer to their risk assessments or other information, such as the presence of conditions on a fire safety certificate. This is a helpful attitude and there is no reason why a policy may not encourage it.

10.63   National Guidance has evolved to emphasise that in completing an operating schedule an applicant should take a risk assessment approach, with the primary material for the assessment being contained in the policy, supplemented by his own research and collaboration with statutory agencies all feeding through into the proposals and information contained in or submitted with the operating schedule. National Guidance now provides:

'8.34 In completing an operating schedule, applicants are expected to have regard to the statement of licensing policy for their area. They must also be aware of the expectations of the licensing authority and the responsible authorities as to the steps that are appropriate for the promotion of the licensing objectives, and to demonstrate knowledge of their local area when describing the steps they propose to take to promote the licensing objectives. Licensing authorities and responsible authorities are expected to publish information about what is meant by the promotion of the licensing objectives and to ensure that applicants can readily access advice about these matters. However, applicants are also expected to undertake their own enquiries about the area in which the premises are situated to inform the content of the application.

8.35 Applicants are, in particular, expected to obtain sufficient information to enable them to demonstrate, when setting out the steps they propose to take to promote the licensing objectives, that they understand:
- the layout of the local area and physical environment including crime and disorder hotspots, proximity to residential premises and proximity to areas where children may congregate,
- any risk posed to the local area by the applicants' proposed licensable activities; and
- any local initiatives (for example, local crime reduction initiatives or voluntary schemes including local taxi-marshalling schemes, street pastors and other schemes) which may help to mitigate potential risks.

8.36 Applicants are expected to include positive proposals in their application on how they will manage any potential risks. Where specific policies apply in the area (for example, a cumulative impact policy), applicants are also expected to demonstrate an understanding of how the policy impacts on their application; any measures they will take to mitigate the impact; and why they consider the application should be an exception to the policy.

8.37 It is expected that enquiries about the locality will assist applicants when determining the steps that are appropriate for the promotion of the licensing objectives. For example, premises with close proximity to residential premises should consider how this impact upon their smoking, noise management and dispersal policies to ensure the promotion of the public nuisance objective. Applicants must consider all factors which may be relevant to the promotion of the licensing objectives, and where there are no known concerns, acknowledge this in their application.

8.38 The majority of information which applicants will require should be available in the licensing policy statement in the area. Other publicly available sources which may be of use to applicants include:
- the Crime Mapping website;
- Neighbourhood Statistics websites;
- websites or publications by local responsible authorities;
- websites or publications by local voluntary schemes and initiatives; and
- on-line mapping tools.

8.39 Whilst applicants are not required to seek the views of responsible authorities before formally submitting their application, they may find them to be a useful source of expert advice on local issues that should be taken into consideration when making an application. Licensing authorities may wish to encourage co-operation between applicants, responsible authorities and, where relevant, local residents and businesses before applications are submitted in order to minimise the scope for disputes to arise.

8.40 Applicants are expected to provide licensing authorities with sufficient information in this section to determine the extent to which their proposed steps are appropriate to promote the licensing objectives in the local area. Applications must not be based on providing a set of standard conditions to promote the licensing objectives and applicants are expected to make it clear why the steps they are proposing are appropriate for the premises.

8.41 All parties are expected to work together in partnership to ensure that the licensing objectives are promoted collectively. Where there are no disputes, the steps that applicants propose to take to promote the licensing objectives, as set out in the operating schedule, will very often translate directly into conditions that will be attached to premises licences with the minimum of fuss.'

10.64 This formulation of best practice in the preparation of a licence application represents a significant advance on the earlier incarnations of the Guidance. Just as it ill behoves a licensing authority to reach for the formulaic response of standard licence conditions when confronted with a licensing issue, so applicants should ensure that their application responds to the particular impacts attendant upon their proposal. It is here that the licensing policy plays a crucial role, not just in setting out the operating standards expected, but also in giving factual information about the general location and issues arising there, so that applicants are guided in the formulation of their proposals. Where the system works as intended, there ought to be far less scope for objection, costly hearings and lengthy appeals. The role of licensing policy in driving and informing the preparation of licence applications is an important aspect of the golden thread of licensing described in Chapter 4 of this book.

Stage two: processing the application

10.65 At stage two, the council must process the application. If there are no objections, the council must grant it. If there are representations it must refer the case for a hearing by the licensing sub-committee. *Canterbury* does not change the law regarding stage two. No-one suggested that the council might actually refuse an application or attach further conditions even where there had been no objections. Of course, the policy must not say that the council would interfere with an operating schedule in the absence of objections. That, again, was common ground.

10.66 References in the Canterbury policy which were criticised by the claimant on this account included:

'The incorporation of measures for ensuring the safe and swift dispersal of patrons away from premises and events without causing nuisance or public safety concerns to local residents is vital in seeking approval for an Operating Schedule by the council.'

10.67 Specifically, the concern expressed was that this implied that the council might exercise some independent judgment on the operating schedule, and reject it or attach further conditions even in the absence of relevant representations.

10.68 At a more extreme level, the claimants criticised the first sentence in the policy as exhibiting this flaw: 'All applications will be considered on their merits as well as against the relevant policy and statutory framework.' In the past, statements such as these were routinely included in most licensing policies in England and Wales. Yet it does not strictly represent the law, because those applications which are not met by relevant representations will not be considered on their merits at all.

10.69 It is here that the interrelationship between stages one and two in the policy becomes centrally important. There is no difficulty with a policy setting out strong expectations, recommendations and advice at stage one, provided that the policy makes clear that at stage two the council will have no discretion absent relevant representations. But if the policy, when read fairly and as a whole, leaves the reader with the impression that the council can or will interfere unilaterally at stage two, then even the language of expectation at stage one may tip the policy into a document that prescribes rather than advises. This is because an applicant, fearing unilateral interference, may be misled into including material, and therefore potentially onerous conditions, in his operating schedule which he would not otherwise have wished to include.

10.70 On that question, Richards J held that the claimants' case was 'substantially overstated'. He said that, after adoption of a 'health warning' at the start of the policy setting out the law (see below), the policy was 'unlikely seriously to mislead applicants' and there was no evidence that any applicants had actually been misled. However, he did find the policy to be over-prescriptive in parts.

10.71   The Judge made the important point that a policy which is unlawfully over-prescriptive and one which is lawfully exhortative is likely to have the same effect. This is because in either event an applicant whose operating schedule departs from the policy is likely to be met with relevant representations and to face an uphill struggle. He is therefore likely to want to comply with the substance of the policy.[64]

Stage 3: Powers at the hearing

10.72   Stage three is where there have been relevant representations so that an application is referred for a hearing. At the hearing, the licensing sub-committee is obliged to have regard to its policy. The previous law, arising from the case of *R (Westminster City Council) v Middlesex Crown Court and Chorion plc*[65] is that authorities are entitled to adopt policies with strong presumptions, provided that they give consideration to the merits of the individual case. In Westminster, that has involved a strict approach to new or later operations in the West End of London. But it is not confined to stress areas: there could be strict policies on drug or noise control or prevention of crime and disorder. The law is unchanged by *Canterbury*: it is still open to a council to adopt a strong policy where it considers it necessary to promote the licensing objectives. So, when it comes to the exercise of discretion by the council in its decision-making capacity, *Canterbury* changes nothing. The Judge held:

> 'In so far as the council's policy applies to the decision-making stage under section 18(3), there is little to object to in it. All the matters dealt with are relevant and legitimate considerations, as is supported by the passages in the Guidance to which Mr Lowe took me. The council's decision-making can properly be guided by the policy, provided that there is a willingness to consider individual applications on their merits, which the policy emphasises will be done ... '[66]

The health warning

10.73   *Canterbury* proposed to adopt a 'health warning' at the start of is policy so as to clarify its meaning and intent. A modified version of the health warning is set out below. The purpose is to make the distinction between stages one, two and three clear, namely that:

---

[64]   Para 86.
[65]   2002 LLR 538 (and see para 10.27 above).
[66]   Para 81.

- At stage one, an applicant is free to compile the operating schedule as he wishes, albeit that expectations are set out in the policy.
- At stage two, the council is bound to grant absent relevant representations.
- At stage three, the council will have regard to the policy, including any presumptions set out in it.

The Judge held:

'89. The proposed addendum, on the other hand, represents a substantial improvement in the policy. It sets out clearly the different stages in the procedure and explains at what point the matters covered in the policy can bite on applications. If the rest of the document is read in the light of the addendum, a careful reader may understand that the prescriptive language of, or impression conveyed by, later passages is not to be taken at face value. But even with the addendum the policy is far from ideal. The objectionable passages remain in place, and there is at the very least a marked tension between them and the addendum. There is a risk that applicants will focus on particular parts of the policy without taking the time to read the document as a whole and without understanding how the objectionable passages are to be read subject to the addendum ...

91. ... It would obviously be better if the rest of the policy were recast so as to reflect the correct approach set out in the addendum.'

Canterbury: *the result*

10.74 The Judge held that there was a sufficiently strong assurance that the health warning would be adopted as to make it unnecessary and inappropriate to grant any relief in respect of the policy in its then form. Given the delay in bringing the proceedings and the chaos that would be caused by quashing the policy at such a delicate stage in the transitional period, with the vast majority of conversion and variation applications still to be submitted but with only six weeks remaining for submission, he refused to quash the policy or give any form of relief to the Claimants. Instead, he expected Canterbury to review its policy to carry the sentiments in the health warning through to the rest of the text.

Lessons from *Canterbury*

10.75 A key aspect of the Secretary of State's Guidance is its exhortation to partnership. The benefit of policies is that they represent a partnership view, after consultation with the industry, the public and the regulatory authorities, as to how best the licensing objectives may be promoted locally. Clearly, it is an advantage to operators to know that if their operating schedule does not conform to the policy, there are likely to be objections. While the BBPA complained that the mere existence of the policy might cause objections to come forward, the judge saw nothing wrong with that. The purpose of the policy is to bring certainty and clarity, so that if an operator wants to avoid objections the policy gives him a clear guide as to how to go about it. *Canterbury* therefore reaffirms that a clear policy is not an undesirable deterrent to investment, but a promoter of proper standards, a guide for the operator and a touchstone by which applications may be judged.

10.76   On analysis, the *Canterbury* decision changes little, and the Claimants' counsel was probably right to say that the case concerned the form and not the substance of policies. For example, there was argument as to whether the policy might refer to a level of training of personal licence holders. Arguments which have arisen elsewhere include whether a policy might specify that in nightclubs there must always be a personal licence holder on the premises, even though the Act does not formally require this. The situation remains that a policy may express a view on any matter whose purpose is to further the licensing objectives. The Act provides a slender but robust legal framework upon which policy considerations and best practice provide the cladding. The fact that the Act does not require a step to be taken does not prevent the authority from declaring as a matter of policy that it expects the step to be proposed in operating schedules or is likely to require the step to be taken when its discretion is engaged. On these matters, the outcome of *Canterbury* is clear.

10.77   In the event, there was little dispute on the law. Indeed, it was common ground that licensing policy is now to be tested by reference to well-established principles of public law. The case mostly concerned the application of the law to the facts of the instant policy. Nevertheless, it is important that councils get these things right, and if the decision causes council policies to reflect more exactly the councils' powers at stages one, two and three of the process, it is very welcome.

10.78   Finally, lurking in the shadows of the case was a far more pressing issue. May a council refuse an application or attach conditions for reasons which go beyond the representations which have been made? This is canvassed further in Chapter 17.

Drafting policies in a post-Canterbury world

10.79   It is fair to say that most policies do not create a clear demarcation between stages one, two and three of the licensing process. This is at least in part because national Guidance itself frequently fails to make that distinction. For example, paragraph 13.10 of the Guidance states:

'While statements of policy may set out a general approach to making licensing decisions, they must not ignore or be inconsistent with provisions in the 2003 Act. For example, a statement of policy must not undermine the right of any person to apply under the terms of the 2003 Act for a variety of permissions and to have any such application considered on its individual merits'.

10.80 Many policies have expressly included a statement along these lines, but such a statement may give the misleading impression that each application will be considered on its merits, when of course this will not be true unless there are relevant representations.

10.81 While there are innumerable ways of drafting policies so as to comply with *Canterbury*, the following represents some possible approaches.

A health warning

10.82 It is recommended that policies should include a health warning at the beginning so that the regulatory context of the policy is clear. A suggested form is as follows:

'How this policy applies

All applications for new premises licences or variations need to be supported by an operating schedule. The schedule must specify (among other things) the steps which the applicant proposes to promote each of the licensing objectives.

If no responsible authority or other person lodges an objection (known as a "relevant representation") to the application, the licensing authority must grant the application as set out in the operating schedule, subject only to mandatory conditions under the Licensing Act 2003. The steps proposed by the applicant will become licence conditions. The licensing authority will have no discretion to refuse the application or to alter or add to the conditions arising from the operating schedule.

Where, however, there are relevant representations, then a hearing of the opposed application before a licensing sub-committee will normally follow. After the hearing, the sub-committee must, having regard to the representations, take such steps as it considers appropriate to promote the licensing objectives.[67] These may include refusing the application, or adding to or modifying the conditions proposed in the operating schedule.

In exercising its discretion, the licensing sub-committee will have regard (amongst other things) to this licensing policy. Therefore, in drawing up their operating schedule, applicants would be well advised to read

---

[67] This represents a change from the *Canterbury* health warning which referred to a council having 'full discretion', which gave rise to a debate as to the extent of the discretion, related in Chapter 15.

this policy carefully. Where an operating schedule complies with this policy, it is generally less likely that responsible authority or other person will object to it, or that any objection will succeed. Therefore, compliance with this policy is likely to assist the applicant to avoid the delay and expense of a contested licensing hearing, and the risk of a refusal or the addition of unwanted licence conditions.

This is not to say that an opposed application which complies with the policy will necessarily be granted or that an opposed application which does not comply with it will necessarily be refused. Where there have been relevant representations, the licensing authority will always consider the merits of the case, and interfere with the operating schedule only when, and to the extent, appropriate to promote the licensing objectives. Nor will blanket or standard conditions be applied without regard to the merits of the individual case. So, for example, the licensing authority will not interfere with an operating schedule which does not comply with this policy where the steps proposed are sufficient to meet the licensing objectives in the individual circumstances of the case.

However, the policy represents the licensing authority's view of the best means of securing the licensing objectives in most normal cases. It has been drawn up in consultation with other expert bodies and responsible authorities, together with community stakeholders. While the contents of the operating schedule are a matter for the applicant, where there is objection to a schedule which departs from the policy, the licensing sub-committee hearing an opposed application will normally expect to be given a good reason for the departure if it is to be asked to make an exception to the policy.

In this policy, there are a number of references to the licensing authority's expectations of applicants. As explained above, the policy is only engaged where the licensing authority has a discretion following the receipt of objections. In such cases, the licensing authority will not apply the policy rigidly, but will always have regard to the merits of the case with a view to promoting the licensing objectives.

Further, the licensing authority may use this policy when exercising other licensing functions. For example, when considering an application for review of a licence, the licensing authority is likely to view with concern premises which are being operated in clear breach of the terms of this policy.

The contents of this section apply both to premises licences and club premises certificates.'

10.83   The adoption of such a health warning makes it much less likely that a challenge to a policy could be successfully mounted. Nonetheless, the health warning will not cure unlawful expressions in the remainder of the policy, so much as provide a proper context when other parts are susceptible to more than one meaning. While the Judge in *Canterbury* accepted the submission that policies need to be read as a whole,[68] he saw the risk that a policy may mislead by containing starkly different approaches in different parts. It is, therefore, advisable to reflect stages one, two and three more clearly in the body of the policy.

Possible formulations

10.84   Take a statement of policy which, on the *Canterbury* judgment, might be considered unlawful: 'The licensing authority's policy is to attach a condition to the licence requiring toughened glass save in exceptional circumstances.' That gives the impression that the authority may unilaterally interfere with an operating schedule in all cases.

One way of overcoming that problem would be to qualify the sentence as follows:

> 'When the licensing authority's discretion is engaged following the receipt of relevant representations, its policy is to attach a condition to the licence requiring toughened glass save in exceptional circumstances.'

10.85   That cures the unlawfulness in the policy, but it results in an unwieldy sentence. Furthermore, the qualification would have to be repeated in respect of every single statement of policy in the document.

10.86   To some extent, this may be overcome by reference back to the health warning, for example by including a text box or similar at the head of every chapter: 'For how this policy is intended to apply, see [health warning].'

10.87   While that would plainly help, it may still be exposed to the criticism that it presupposes a level of sophistication in the reader that not all may possess.

A further possibility would be to include, in addition to the health warning, some introductory text in each chapter, such as:

> 'Where there are no relevant representations, the licensing authority will grant the licence or club premises certificate on the terms of the operating schedule, together with any mandatory conditions. Where, however, there are relevant representations, the Council's discretion will be engaged and it will have regard to this policy when making its decision.'

While that is preferable to no text at all, it does not adequately distinguish between stages one, two and three.

---

[68]   Para 87, following *R v Rochdale Borough Council ex parte Milne* [2001] Env LR 22, paras 50–51.

A suggested approach

10.88 With the above in mind, the following suggestion is made as to how *Canterbury* may be carried forward into a licensing policy. The example given is, of course, no more than a bare bones outline.

THE CRIME PREVENTION OBJECTIVE

Best practice in crime prevention

The licensing authority strongly encourages the implementation of best practice in licensed premises in its area in order to promote the crime prevention objective.

Examples of best practice include:

- Use of toughened glass in pubs and nightclubs to prevent use of glasses as weapons and danger from broken glass on dance floors etc.

Operating schedules

Before preparing their operating schedules applicants are encouraged to carry out a risk assessment of their premises by reference to the above items of best practice.

Applicants are expected to include the above items of best practice in their operating schedule. Where they elect not to do so, they are strongly advised to include information explaining the omission. This might be because a risk assessment has shown the step to be unnecessary or because the item is already the subject of another consent, eg a planning permission or a statutory obligation. If such information is not included, it is more likely that a relevant representation will be made, leading to the cost and delay of a hearing before the licensing authority.

Opposed applications

If a relevant representation is made, the licensing authority will have discretion to take such steps as are appropriate to promote the licensing objectives. In exercising its discretion, its policy is to attach [or, there will be a strong presumption in favour of attaching] [or, it will normally attach] conditions requiring toughened glass in pubs and nightclubs, save where the applicant can demonstrate exceptional circumstances why such a condition should not be applied.

10.89 The benefit of the above formulation is not only that it properly separates out stages 1, 2 and 3, but also that it enables the licensing authority to attach such weight to the policy considerations as it considers apt, without altering the format. So, an authority which attached less importance to toughened glass could state simply:

> 'In exercising its discretion, it may where relevant take into account whether the applicant proposes to follow the best practice set out above.'

Conclusion on Canterbury

10.90 The main outcome of *Canterbury* is that licensing authorities will need to take care to ensure that their policies do not give a misleading impression (a) that applicants are obliged, rather than merely expected, to include particular material in their operating schedules, or (b) that licensing authorities may interfere with operating schedules absent relevant representations.

10.91 Provided that policies observe that base minimum requirement, there is no reason why they cannot expect or strongly encourage particular conditions to be proposed in operating schedules. Nor is their ability to include strong presumptions in their policies affected by the *Canterbury* judgment, provided that it is clear to the reader both that the presumptions may only be applied where the authority's discretion has been engaged by the receipt of relevant representations and that the individual merits of the case will always be considered.

F JUDICIAL REVIEW OF POLICY

10.92 It has been held that the court will not entertain judicial review of a policy *in vacuo*, and that an applicant should wait instead to exercise his right of appeal if dissatisfied with the decision made in accordance with the policy.[69] However, in *R (Westminster City Council) v Middlesex Crown Court and Chorion plc*, Scott Baker J specifically indicated that the proper forum for a challenge to the policy was the Administrative Court.[70] Given the potential importance of policy to licensing decisions, it would seem a considerable injustice to applicants and others affected that they should be shut out from calling attention to unlawfulness in the policy itself or its manner of adoption. It also appears to promote uncertainty if the status of policy should remain unchallenged until considered, perhaps years later, by the local

---

[69] *R v Halton Borough Council, ex parte Poynton* (1989) 1 Admin LR 83. A similar decision was made in the Scottish case *of Inverness Taxi Owners & Drivers Association v Highland Council* TLR 5/5/99.

[70] See para 10.28 above.

bench. Now that the adoption of a licensing policy is a public function carried out under primary legislation following a statutory procedure, it is submitted that it is clearly permissible for any statutory consultee to challenge the adoption or review of a licensing statement on conventional judicial review grounds.[71]

10.93   The question of whether the policy may be challenged is of particular importance to policies appearing to advocate derogations from existing licences. It is well-established that a licensing authority has an unfettered discretion on renewal of licences, albeit that it must take into account the fact that the applicant has previously traded without incident, and may have expended money in reliance on the previous grant.[72]. But there is a dearth of authority as to the effect that the adoption or revision of licensing policy may have on already trading licences. In *Laker Airways Limited v Department of Trade*[73] Mr Laker's airline had expended considerable sums establishing Skytrain to operate between London and New York, in reliance on positive guidance and the issue of a licence under the relevant legislation. But in 1975 a new Government reversed the guidance and promulgated policy advocating removal of competition with the state-owned airline, which resulted in revocation of the licence. The airline sought to judicially review the new policy. It succeeded on a number of grounds, but unsuccessfully argued that it had a legitimate expectation that the policy would remain unchanged. Lawton LJ held that the airline 'had been the victims of a change of government policy. This often happens. Estoppel cannot be allowed to hinder the formation of government policy.'[74]

10.94   Therefore it is most unlikely that the fact of an existing licence could afford grounds for a challenge to a policy which threatens the continued existence of the licence. Nor has it previously been a requirement that full reasons be shown for a change in licensing policy. In *R v Torbay Borough Council, ex parte Cleasby*[75] the Court of Appeal held that a change of policy in relation to the award of licences to operate pleasure boats, in contrast to a decision of fact, was not required to be based on probative evidence. These cases may impinge less on operators now that premises licences will mostly be granted in perpetuity. But upon review, the licensing authority is still bound to have regard to its licensing policy, so that even existing operators will have reason to be concerned as to the content of policy as it evolves over time.

---

[71]   For which see Chapter 42.
[72]   *Sharpe v Wakefield* [1891] AC 173.
[73]   [1977] QB 643.
[74]   Page 728. The position is still clearer, in the light of the decision of the Court of Appeal in *South Bucks District Council v Flanagan* [2002] 1 WLR 2601, that there is no longer a place for the private law doctrine of estoppel in public law or for the attendant problems which it brings with it (per Keene LJ at para 16).
[75]   Unreported 31 July 1990.

10.95 However, the statutory requirement for widespread consultation under the Act introduces rigour into the adoption and periodic formulation of policy. See Chapter 11 for the content of the duty to consult under the Act. The likely consequences of any consultation are that the interests of existing licence holders will at least be a material consideration before the licensing authority which, if not taken into account, will found an application for judicial review. Indeed, the right to bring a judicial review challenge is not confined to those who responded to the consultation exercise. In *R (on the application of David Edwards) v The Environment Agency and the First Secretary of State*,[76] Keith J rejected the argument that the failure on the part of a local resident to reply to a consultation exercise deprived him of standing to judicially review a permit granted to a cement company. He held:

> 'You do not have to be active in a campaign yourself to have an interest in its outcome. If the consultation exercise ends with a decision which affects your interests, you are no less affected by that decision simply because you took no part in the exercise but left it to others to do so. You should not be debarred from subsequently challenging the decision on the ground of inadequate consultation simply because you chose not to participate in the consultation exercise, provided that you are affected by its outcome.'[77]

10.96 Furthermore, since the formulation of licensing policy is one of the functions of a licensing authority, the authority must do so with a view to promoting the licensing objectives.[78] Thus, the policy will potentially be reviewable on the grounds that part or all of the policy would counter the promotion of those objectives. In these ways, at least potentially, the courts have control over the procedures for adoption of policy, together with the content of policy itself.

G THE MEANING OF THE POLICY

10.97 There is sometimes disagreement as to the true meaning of a policy, for example whether, properly read, a cumulative impact policy is intended to apply to off-licences. In such cases, the question may arise whether the meaning of a policy is a 'hard-edged' question to be decided as a matter of law by the courts, or whether it is a 'soft' question to be determined by the decision-maker, subject only to limited judicial intervention if the meaning attached to the policy is perverse. This is not least because policies are not framed as precisely as statutes, and may contain shades of meaning upon which reasonable persons may differ. Recent authority *Tesco Stores Limited v Dundee City Council*[79] establishes that the meaning of a statutory policy is a

---

[76]   [2004] 3 All ER 21.
[77]   Judgment para 16.
[78]   Licensing Act 2003, s 4(1).
[79]   [2012] UKSC 13.

hard-edged question to be determined by the court as a matter of law, while the application of the policy to the facts is a matter for the decision-maker, with judicial interference only if the approach is irrational. This is considered at greater length in Chapter 9.

H STATUS OF POLICY IN APPEALS CASES

10.98 The Act is silent as to the status of policy in appeal cases. However, it is submitted that the approach of the court in *R (Westminster City Council) v Middlesex Crown Court and Chorion plc*[80] continues to bind appellate courts. That is to say, it is not open to an appellate court to refuse to have regard to a policy on the grounds of its alleged unlawfulness, when that policy has not been challenged in the proper manner by judicial review. Instead, the appellate court must have regard to the policy in the same manner as if the court itself were the licensing authority.

10.99 An interesting example of this arose in *R (Portsmouth Borough Council) v 3D Entertainment Group (CRC) Limited*[81] in which Supperstone J held the magistrates to have committed an error of law by requiring the police and the council to adduce evidence that there would be a negative cumulative impact, when a cumulative impact policy created a presumption against grant. In other words, the approach to a cumulative impact policy by the magistrates must be as rigorous as that which one would expect of the licensing authority itself.

These matters are explored further in Chapter 20 (Challenging Licensing Decisions).

I CONCLUSION: THE FUTURE OF POLICY

10.100 This chapter has concerned the law of licensing policy. It has shown how under the 2003 Act, it is possible for licensing authorities to adopt robust policies, provided that they articulate the rationale for the policy and remain prepared to consider whether a departure from the policy would damage that rationale.

10.101 Most appeal cases result from licence refusals or the contested addition of conditions and, where policy is relevant at all, the negative component of such policies. For this reason, reported cases tend to give a distorted view of the positive role which licensing policy can and should play in achieving a pattern of licensing growth which is beneficial to the individual licensee, the economy of the town and the leisure interests of inhabitants,

---

[80] 2002 LLR 538 (and see para 10.27 above).
[81] [2011] EWHC 507 (Admin).

without damaging the living and working conditions of neighbours. It is worth reiterating that licensing policy not only can but should do far more than operate as a filter through which non-conforming proposals are rejected, but should itself stimulate the right type of investment in the right place, promoting high standards of management to ensure a diminished environmental footprint. This theme is explored in depth in earlier chapters of this book.

Licensing policy consultation

I know a house of antique ease
Within the smoky city's pale,
A spot wherein the spirit sees
Old London through a thinner veil.
The modern world so stiff and stale,
You leave behind you when you please,
For long clay pipes and great old ale
And beefsteaks in the Cheshire Cheese.

John Davidson

A INTRODUCTION

11.01 In 'Modern Local Government: In Touch with the People'[1] the government emphasized its wish to improve local accountability, one way of achieving which was to increase the obligations on local government to consult with its electors. Consistently with that, and also with the aim of the Licensing Act 2003 to enhance accountability within the licensing process, the Act imposes a consultation requirement on licensing authorities prior to the publication of their initial and each succeeding licensing policy. However, the Act does not specify how such consultation is to be carried out. This chapter concerns itself with the minimum legal requirements of consultation on public authorities, describes best practice from related fields, and makes some suggestions for best practice in licensing.

B THE ACT

11.02 Section 5 of the Act requires an authority in respect of each five year period to determine its policy with respect to the exercise of its licensing

---

[1]   Cm 4014: 1998.

functions and publish a statement of its policy (a licensing statement) before the beginning of that period. It may revise or replace its policy during that period, the latter action causing the period of five years to start afresh. Before doing any of these things it has to consult with responsible authorities, and those it considers to be representative of licence and certificate holders, businesses and residents. Obviously, other bodies may also be consulted, as Guidance acknowledges,[2] and bodies which the authority may voluntarily elect to consult include health authorities, crime and disorder reduction partnerships, tourism authorities and the British Transport Police.

Beyond stating that the authority must consult, and stating whom it must consult, the Act makes no requirements as to the consultation process.

C THE FOUR MAIN PRINCIPLES OF CONSULTATION

11.03 It is generally recognised that fair consultation involves four main principles. In *R v Gwent County Council ex parte Bryant*,[3] Hodgson J described them as follows:

Fair consultation means:

(a) consultation when the proposals are still at a formative stage;
(b) adequate information on which to respond;
(c) adequate time in which to respond;
(d) conscientious consideration by an authority of the response to consult-
     ation.

11.04 In *R v British Coal Corporation and Secretary of State for Trade and Industry ex parte Price*,[4] Glidewell J followed Bryant and summarised the position as follows:

'Another way of putting the point more shortly is that fair consultation involves giving the body consulted a fair and proper opportunity to understand fully the matters about which it is being consulted, and to express its views on those subjects, with the consultor thereafter considering those views properly and genuinely'.

11.05 In *R v North and East Devon Health Authority ex parte Coughlan*[5] the Court of Appeal reiterated the modern principles of consultation:

'To be proper, consultation must be undertaken at a time when proposals are still at a formative stage; it must include sufficient reasons

---

2   Para 13.5.
3   [1988] COD 19. The formula has been extensively applied in the employment context, see
     Rowell v Hubbard [1995] IRLR 195, *Mugford v Midland Bank plc* [1997] ICR 399 and, in
     Scotland, *King v Eaton Ltd* [1996] IRLR 199.
4   [1994] IRLR 72.
5   [2000] 2 WLR 622.

for particular proposals to allow those consulted to give intelligent consideration and an intelligent response; adequate time must be given for this purpose; and the product of consultation must be conscientiously taken into account when the ultimate decision is taken: *Reg. v. Brent London Borough Council, Ex parte Gunning* (1985) 84 L.G.R. 168.[6]'

These principles each merit some further analysis.

The first principle: proposals at formative stage

11.06 The first principle involves the proposition that at the time when the proposals go out to consultation, the outcome must not be a foregone conclusion. They must be capable of change, and the consulting body must be ready, willing and able to have its mind changed by the consultation responses. That does not mean that the proposals cannot go out in an advanced stage of preparation. Indeed, it is possible, though perhaps unlikely, that the ultimate document will prove to be unchanged from the consultative draft. An obvious parallel is town and country planning, where local planning authorities consult on a fully-formulated version of their proposed development plan. Indeed, if the proposal is evanescent, it may itself be criticised as lacking substance: in *Gunning*[7] Hodgson J said that the proposals should be 'of some specificity into which those consulted can get their teeth, whether the proposals be framed in general policy terms or in terms of specific options'.

11.07 The position was summarised in *Rollo v Minister of Town and Country Planning*[8], in which Bucknill LJ approved of the words of the Judge at first instance, dealing with consultation of local authorities by a Minister, but directly analogous to consultation of local people by a licensing authority:

'The holding of such consultation with local authorities as appear to the Minister to be concerned is, in my judgment, an important statutory obligation. The Minister, with a receptive mind, must by such consultation, seek and welcome the aid of advice which those with local knowledge may be in a position to proffer in regard to a plan which the Minister has tentatively evolved.'[9]

The requirement that the consultation occur when the proposal is at a formative stage was underscored in *R (Montpeliers & Trevors Association) v*

---

6   Page 661.
7   (1985) 84 LGR 168, p 189.
8   [1947] 2 All ER 488.
9   *Rollo v Minister of Town and Country Planning*, p 17. The dictum was applied to a local authority consulting local residents on a Controlled Parking Zone in *Cran v Camden London Borough Council* [1995] RTR 346, 374.

City of Westminster.[10] There, a consultation exercise on a traffic order was quashed where the council did not consult upon one important option, having already discounted it. The case is of importance because it demonstrates that omission of a single option may be sufficient to vitiate a consultation exercise, even where consultation proceeds on various other options.

The second principle: adequate information

11.08 It will be noted that the Court of Appeal's judgment in *Coughlan* slightly re-casts the second principle set out above, in that it seems to require not only adequate information about the matters the subject of consultation, but reasons for the particular proposal. It appears to be saying that a consultation proposal must state not only what a council is proposing to do but why it is proposing to do it. The distinction did not actually arise for consideration in *Coughlan* and was not therefore argued.

11.09 In *Middlesborough Borough Council v TGWU*[11] the Employment Appeal Tribunal held that there was no duty to give reasons for proposed redundancies, in reliance on *ex parte Price*.[12] However, these decisions should be understood in their context – the judgment being that the financial reasons for redundancies need not be given for large scale redundancy consultations pursuant to section 188 of the Trade Union and Labour Relations (Consolidation) Act 1992. Section 188(2) stated the matters which did need to be included in the consultation: these did not include reasons. The cases cannot be taken as authority for the proposition that reasons need never be given.

11.10 Clearly, not every line of text of a consultation draft licensing policy need be supported by reasons, particularly where the policy is merely reiterating matters of good practice set out in national Guidance. However, it is thought that the main strands of policy should be supported by reasons, and particularly where the policy, if applied, would amount to an obvious restraint on trade or incursion on the comfort or living conditions of residents, or where the policy amounts to a departure from Guidance.

The following statement of the position in *Coughlan* expresses the true position cogently:

'Its obligation is to let those who have a potential interest in the subject matter know in clear terms what the proposal is and exactly why it is under positive consideration, telling them enough (which may be a

10 [2005] EWHC 16 (Admin)
11 [2002] IRLR 332.
12 [1994] IRLR 72, and see para 11.03. The decision was followed in *Securicor Omega Express Limited v GMB* [2004] IRLR 9.

good deal) to enable them to make an intelligent response. The obligation, although it may be quite onerous, goes no further than this.'[13]

11.11 Where an authority gives reasons for proposing to take a particular course, is it obliged to set out the other side of the argument? In *R (Beale) v London Borough of Camden*, Munby J stated:

'... there is nothing [in *Coughlan*] to suggest that consultation involves as a legal requirement an articulation of both sides of the argument. Proper consultation requires sufficient reasons to be given for the particular proposals to enable those consulted to give intelligent consideration and an intelligent response to the proposals. But it is not said that consultation requires sufficient information to be given about any objections to the proposals to enable those consulted to give intelligent consideration and an intelligent response to the objections.'[14]

From this it is clear that an authority is not bound to argue the other side of the case. As was said in *Coughlan*[15]: '... consultation is not litigation: the consulting authority is not required to publicise every submission it receives.'

The third principle: adequate time to respond

11.12 What is an adequate time in which to respond must depend on the circumstances. However, HM Government's Code of Practice on Consultation 2008 suggested a twelve week period.[16] While it is clearly not unlawful to afford less time than that, the period in question must be sufficient to enable the consultee to formulate proper responses. Many consultees will be representative bodies or groups, who will wish to consult their own members through meetings or newsletters. The fact that they have their own cycles for contact with their members would need to be respected. The licensing authority will need to bear that in mind. It would, it is submitted, be a rare case in which less than, say, eight weeks is afforded for consultations on licensing policy.

The fourth principle: conscientious consideration of response

11.13 If an authority has clear views about how it wants its licensing policy to go and sets them out in its consultation draft policy, can it claim to be giving 'conscientious consideration' to the responses? In *Cran v Camden London Borough Council*, McCullough J stated:

---

13 Page 662.
14 [2004] BLGR 291, para 19.
15 Para 112.
16 Criterion 2, and see further below.

'... the consulting party must consider responses with a receptive mind and a conscientious manner when reaching its decision.'[17]

11.14   This was explored in *Coughlan* itself, in which it was alleged that a letter of consultation revealed a pre-judgment as to the outcome. Rejecting the argument, Lord Woolf MR stated:[18]

'We accept, too, Mr. Goudie's submission that the letter went from an officer of the authority and not from any of its decision-makers. It did undoubtedly reveal an anticipated outcome, but the mind was not that of a decision-maker. It may well be, as Mr. Gordon suggests, that Dr. Clark would have had little difficulty in deducing which way Mrs. Jefferies, who wrote the letter to him, would prefer his advice to go; but this is a long way from a case of prejudgment in either the authority or the adviser.'

11.15   Similarly in *R (Dudley) v East Sussex County Council*[19] it was held that a predisposition to a particular result does not equate to pre-judgment. Even when an unequivocal recommendation is put before members by officers, this does not affect the fairness of the consultation.

11.16   From these cases can be deduced the proposition that it is not improper for a consultation draft policy to go out with a clear predisposition to a particular result. The fourth principle in fact flows from the first – when the policy goes out to consultation it must still be 'formative' in the sense that it is genuinely capable of being changed. Then, after analysis of the consultation response there is nothing wrong with officers advising the licensing authority of their preferred outcome and making a clear recommendation, provided of course that the authority is clear as to the nature and content of the consultation response and the arguments on both sides. What the 'conscientious consideration' requirement involves is an open mind, not a blank one.

11.17   The most efficient way of demonstrating that consultation responses have been conscientiously considered is for each response to be summarised in a table, with the officer's views and recommendations placed alongside it. The table should then be appended to the post-consultation report placed before the licensing authority. As was observed by McCullough J in *Cran*: 'Even submissions which are believed to be unsound are entitled to receptive consideration and objective reporting.'[20]

[17]   [1995] RTR 346, 374. See also *Rollo v Minister of Town and Country Planning* [1947] 2 All ER 488, 496.
[18]   Page 662.
[19]   2003 ACD 353.
[20]   [1995] RTR 346, 374, p 402.

Extent of consultation

11.18 As to the extent of the consultation, this is pre-eminently a matter for the consulting body, and the supervisory courts offer a very wide margin of discretion. As was stated in *Cran*[21]: 'The process of consultation must be effective; looked at as a whole it must be fair.' Beyond that, the courts are not wont to interfere. In *R (Wainwright) v Richmond upon Thames LBC*,[22] Clarke LJ, having set out the four principles, stated:

> 'Provided that the notification and consultation satisfy the principles set out above, it appears to me that councils must have a comparatively wide discretion as to how the process is carried out. The council cannot be in breach of duty unless the extent of the consultation process was such as to be outside the ordinary ambit of its discretion. In short, in order to be unlawful the nature and extent of the process must be so narrow that no reasonable council, complying with the principles set out above, would have adopted it.'

11.19 Hence, while clearly the duty to consult extends to those mentioned in the Licensing Act 2003, in practice it is only where the licensing authority has effectively failed to consult them at all or its consultation was so narrow that no reasonable council could have adopted the process that a challenge could legitimately be upheld.

11.20 In conclusion, the following principles may be stated in relation to consultation upon licensing policy.

Fair consultation means:

(a) Consultation when the proposals are still at a formative stage. This means ensuring that the consultation draft policy is capable of being changed once consultation responses have been considered. The policy may be put out for consultation with the preliminary views of the licensing authority clearly expressed.

(b) Adequate information on which to respond. This involves setting out the reasons for the main strands of policy, particularly those liable to act as a restraint on the trade of the operator or interfere with the living conditions of residents, or those which depart from national Guidance.

(c) Adequate time in which to respond, bearing in mind the exigencies under which business and voluntary organisations and community groups and bodies work.

(d) Conscientious consideration by an authority of the response to consultation. Each consultation response should be summarised for the benefit

[21] [1995] RTR 346, 374, p 374.
[22] *Times*, 16 January 2002.

of the licensing authority. It is acceptable for the post-consultation draft policy to go to the licensing authority with a clear officer's recommendation.[23]

D CONSEQUENCES OF FAILURE TO CONSULT PROPERLY

11.21   The courts have tended to take a relatively strict view of a failure to consult properly, tending to quash the resultant instrument, on the grounds that the court cannot second-guess what course the decision maker would have taken had there been proper consultation. Therefore, a failure to consult properly over licensing policy is liable to lead to the policy being quashed.

11.22   In *R v Chief Constable of Thames Valley Police ex p Cotton*[24] Bingham LJ adumbrated the principles:

'While cases may no doubt arise in which it can properly be held that denying the subject of a decision an adequate opportunity to put his case is not in all the circumstances unfair, I would expect these cases to be of great rarity. There are a number of reasons for this:

1.   Unless the subject of the decision has had the opportunity to put his case it may not be easy to know what case he could or would have put if he had the chance.
2.   As memorably pointed out by Megarry J in *John v Rees* [1970] Ch 345 at page 402, experience shows that what is confidently expected is by no means always that which happens.
3.   It is generally desirable that decision-makers should be reasonably receptive to argument, and it would therefore be unfortunate if a complainant's position became weaker as the decision-maker's mind became more closed.
4.   In considering whether the complainant's representations would have made any difference to the outcome the court may unconsciously stray from its proper province of reviewing the propriety of the decision-making process into the forbidden territory of evaluating the substantial merits of a decision.
5.   This is a field in which appearances are generally thought to matter.
6.   Where the decision-maker is under a duty to act fairly the subject of the decision may properly be said to have a right to be heard, and rights are not to be lightly denied.'

11.23   From this it may be seen that a person seeking to quash an instrument on grounds of a failure of consultation need show only a very low

---

[23]   See further Olley, 'The Principles of Proper Consultation' 2001 JR 99.
[24]   [1990] IRLR 344, 352, subsequently approved by the Court of Appeal in *R v Broxtowe Borough Council ex p Bradford* [2000] IRLR 329.

probability that proper consultation would have made a difference. This was accepted in *R (Wainwright) v Richmond upon Thames London Borough Council*,[25] in which Clarke LJ referred approvingly to a test at first instance in *Cotton* of whether there was a 'real, as opposed to a purely minimal, possibility that the outcome would have been different'. This was further underscored in *R v Secretary of State for the Environment ex p Brent London Borough Council*,[26] in which Ackner LJ stated:[27]

> '... it would of course have been unrealistic not to accept that it is certainly probable that, if the representations had been listened to by the Secretary of State, he would have nevertheless have adhered to his policy. However, we are not satisfied that such a result must inevitably have followed ... It would in our view be wrong for this court to speculate as to how the Secretary of State would have exercised his discretion if he had heard the representations ... we are not prepared to hold that it would have been a useless formality for the Secretary of State to have listened to the representations ... '

11.24 In *Wainwright*, Clarke LJ implied that the court may take a more benign approach when the failure was in consulting the general public properly as opposed to when the failure was at individual level where individual rights were at stake.[28] However, it is difficult to know where to draw the line. In licensing policy consultations, individual licensees may be potentially gravely affected by a policy phrased in one way rather than another. The mere reference to the possibility of a restriction may have an effect on the value of their business, as it may, at least potentially, affect the value of a home nearby or the quality of life of occupants.[29] Therefore, while the fact that individual rights are not at stake may be relevant, it is unlikely to be determinative in most cases. If, however, the view which the consultee would have expressed is similar or identical to others which were given little weight or dismissed, the court may safely conclude that the single consultation response would have made no difference.

11.25 To summarise, while the licensing authority is given a wide margin of discretion as to how it consults, if it falls short of the minimum standards the Administrative Court is unlikely to exercise its discretion to uphold the policy unless it is clear that the prospects of a different result ensuing would have been purely minimal.

---

[25] *Times*, 16 January 2002, and see para 11.14.
[26] [1982] QB 593.
[27] Page 647.
[28] Para 52. There, the decision was to approve a toucan crossing and associated works outside the claimant's home.
[29] This is not to say that human rights are engaged by the promulgation of a licensing policy (see Chapter 27), simply that the Court is unlikely to be heavily swayed in the exercise of its discretion to quash a licensing policy by a plea from a defaulting licensing authority that the claimant is merely one local trader or resident out of many.

E GOOD PRACTICE IN CONSULTATION

11.26 In 2008, the government published an updated Code of Practice on Consultation ('the Code') The Code did not have the force of law, and does not expressly apply to local authorities, although it indicated that public sector organisations in general were free to make use of the Code for their consultation purposes. Experience suggests that the Code is heavily relied upon at local level.

11.27 In 2012, the Government replaced the Code with a brief document named 'Consultation Principles' ('the Principles'). Its rationale was that the Principles were more proportionate and targeted, so that the type and scale of engagement would be proportional to the potential impacts of the proposal. The emphasis was said to be on understanding the effects of a proposal and focussing on real engagement with key groups rather than following a set process.

Because the Code is so ingrained in local government thinking, and so many of its tenets are reflections of common law principles, in this section we shall continue to set out the criteria in the Code, while also stating the contents of the Principles by way of comparison. In considering either document, however, it should be recognised that neither has the force of law.

11.28 The Code sets out seven consultation criteria. In this Section, each of the criteria is recited, followed by suggestions as to how the criteria may translate into a licensing context.

Criterion 1: When to consult

Formal consultation should take place at a state when there is scope to influence the policy outcome.

11.29 Licensing policies tend to be published in their intended final form. This is not unlawful, but it does limit the scope for effective participation. The earlier the consultation occurs, the more chance that alternative solutions will emerge which may suggest a better set of objectives for the policy or a more creative means of achieving them. Given that the leisure economy is a complex mosaic of human behaviour, temporal and spatial factors, and business and regulatory practice, with regulation by a large number of public authorities, it is obvious that there cannot ever be a single possible policy approach. Given this, the earlier the consultation process begins, the more chance that the licensing authority can begin the process of refining and moulding options to meet the exigencies of the particular locality.

11.30 Nor should it be thought that consultation needs to be a one-off exercise. It can be an iterative process whereby strategies for the night time economy are developed through consultative dialogue before a draft policy is formulated for consultative purposes. Early consultation might, for example, take the form of a survey, whereby priorities for the town centres at night are identified or deterrents to use discovered. This might then lead to a second round survey which seeks to ascertain how the priorities should be secured. For example, should late night congregation in town centres be cured by lengthening licensing hours and so helping people to drift away, or shortening them so that the town centre is clear at an earlier hour? This might then lead to a draft policy upon which further consultation may occur.

11.31 The Principles build on this approach, by encouraging consultation early in policy development, and advising that it may be appropriate to engage in different ways at different stages.

Criterion 2: Duration of consultation exercises

Consultations should normally last for at least 12 weeks with consideration given to longer timescales where feasible and sensible.

11.32 There is an understandable tendency to plan consultation exercises around the meeting cycles for local authorities. They should be planned sufficiently early so that pressures on communities are properly taken into account. Many of the most thoughtful responses to consultation come from residents', civic and amenity groups. They may only meet every three months and may have to canvass their own members before discussing the policy at a meeting (public or otherwise) and formulating a response. They may have to do this simultaneously over matters of local planning policy and local planning applications. A consultation of 12 weeks is an appropriate period. There ought to be justification for a shorter period, and the justification ought not to be that insufficient forward planning occurred. If the period of 12 weeks includes a summer holiday, in many cases that will affect the quality of the response.

11.33 As much as the period for consultation, it is important for authorities to raise awareness that a consultation exercise is pending, through the local media, its own web-site, its e-mail database and through councillors. This will enable local people to take advantage of the entire consultation period when it starts, without being caught by surprise.

11.34 The Principles state that timeframes should be proportionate and realistic to allow stakeholders time to provide a considered response, with the amount of time dependent on the nature and impact of the proposals. They advise that this may typically vary between two and twelve weeks. It is submitted to be very unlikely that a two week consultation on licensing policy would ever be justifiable, particularly given that many of those who will wish to respond will not be seasoned professionals, but local residents with limited time available to read through lengthy consultation documents.

Criterion 3: Clarity of scope and impact

Consultation documents should be clear about the consultation process, what is being proposed, the scope to influence and the expected costs and benefits of the proposals.

11.35   The consultation should make it clear what stage has been reached, what has already been decided and what, therefore may still be influenced. It should also state how the consultation exercise will be run and how responses to the consultation will be evaluated.

The consulting body should also be transparent about what facts it has taken into account and what assumptions it has made. The consultation questions should be given prominence so that the consultee can readily see where their views are, and are not, sought.

The consultation questions should themselves be clearly stated. In some instances it may be good practice to put open and closed questions.

For example, consultation on a licensing policy could do all or any of the following.

(1)   Simply put out the policy for consultation and seek views upon it.
(2)   Include closed questions, such as: 'Baines Town Centre is proposed for designation as a cumulative impact zone. Do you agree or disagree with the proposal?'
(3)   Include open questions such as: 'What are the most important measures for reducing nuisance late at night?'

However the consultation is framed, there should always be the opportunity to express views on issues not specifically addressed in the consultation questions.

11.36   The Principles concur that the objectives of the consultation process should be clear, and that any aspects of the proposal that have already been finalised and will not be subject to change should be clearly stated. It also states that every effort should be made to make available the evidence base at an early stage to enable contestability and challenge.

Criterion 4: Accessibility of consultation exercises

Consultation exercises should be designed to be accessible to, and clearly targeted at, those people the exercise is intended to reach.

11.37   The purpose of consultation is to reach all those who may wish to contribute to the debate. These will almost certainly go beyond statutory consultees. It is particularly important actively to engage other departments within the same authority and the members themselves whose role should go beyond receiving the outcomes from the process.

11.38   Some members of the public will present their views whether asked or not. Others may be harder to reach, and may be diffident when reached. Amongst the hard to reach groups in some areas may be children, consumer groups, disabled people, black, minority and ethnic groups, faith/belief groups, lesbian, gay, bisexual and transgender groups, older people, those on low incomes, small businesses and third sector organisations. In some cases, it will be appropriate for the authority to seek advice from local representative bodies as to how to reach particular groups. Certain groups may not speak English as a first language. In some cases, written consultation may be supplemented by discussion groups or public meetings.

11.39   More generally, in conducting dialogue with a community, written consultation may not be the only or the most effective means of consultation. Other forms of consultation may be as if not more helpful, including:

- stakeholder meetings;
- public meetings;
- web forums;
- public surveys;
- focus groups;
- targeted leaflet campaigns.

It is essential to identify a baseline constituency for focused consultation work, so as ensure that all sections of the community, including under-represented groups, are reached. Once identified, the challenge then become to reach them in a constructive way. For example, this might be through existing groups or structures or by building capacity to ensure the involvement of under-represented groups.

11.40   The Principles share the concern that the consultation should be formulated to ensure that the full range of affected stakeholders is captured, and that the format of the consultation is accessible and useful to them. It also encourages the informal methods of consultation, rather than defaulting to written consultations.

Local licensing forum

11.41   In Scotland, where local authorities have been responsible for licensing since 1976, most of the major towns and cities have a local licensing forum. These tend to meet up to six times a year, with membership comprising licensees, police, the licensing standards officer, health, education or social work professionals and local residents including young people. While individual consultations can obtain no more than a snapshot view of the community, a forum can help shape policy over the longer term through a building of expertise and a sharing of views, enabling more focused and detailed work to be achieved.

Children

11.42   Children are frequently ignored in consultation exercises, but there is no reason why this should be so, either morally or legally. Article 3 of the United Nations Convention on the Rights of the Child[30] provides that in all actions concerning children undertaken by (inter alia) administrative authorities, the best interests of the child shall be a primary consideration. In turn, Article 12 provides:

> 'State Parties shall assure to the child who is capable of forming his or her own views the right to express those views freely in all matters affecting the child, the views of the child being given due weight in accordance with the age and maturity of the child.'

Children's needs for leisure opportunities are no less than adults', and they may be as if not more affected by some of the fall-out from the leisure economy in terms of crime, disorder and nuisance.

11.43   The right of children to be consulted is now routinely recognised at governmental level. For example, in 2001, the government established the Children and Young People's Unit[31] to influence policy in all government departments in the interests of children. In 2001, the Unit published 'Learning to Listen, Core Principles for the Involvement of Children and Young People.'[32] The Core Principles were:

- A visible commitment is made to involving children and young people, underpinned by appropriate resources to build a capacity to implement policies of participation.
- Children and young people's involvement is valued.
- Children and young people have equal opportunity to get involved.
- Policies and standards for the participation of children and young people are provided, evaluated and continuously improved.[33]

11.44   The main messages of relevance emerging from recent work is that there is no set way in which to consult children effectively, and that different forms and methods of dialogue need to be explored with children themselves. For example, an authority may consult through formal and informal settings, actively listening to children speaking to each other, or through informal or

---

[30]   1990. http://childrensrightsportal.org/convention/text/.
[31]   Later part of the Department for Education and Skills.
[32]   DfES, 2001.
[33]   See also 'Building a Culture of Participation, involving children and young people in policy, service planning, delivery and evaluation' (DfES Publications, 2003). https://www.education.gov.uk/publications/eOrderingDownload/DfES-0827–2003.pdf.pdf.

more focused dialogue. Visual presentations are likely to assist, and feedback may occur through suggestion boxes rather than more formal face to face settings. Consultation may occur through youth forums, school councils, group meetings, circle time within class, creative youth groups or youth researchers, and so on.[34]

11.45 As an example of good practice, in one study, 'Citizenship: young people's perspectives'[35], researchers managed to consult focus groups comprising children aged between 5 and 15, who described how lack of attractive and safe leisure facilities was an inducement to anti-social behaviour, articulated their fear of crime by others, and expressed a loathing of litter and other detritus on the streets. The report concluded that consultation with the community should include consultation with children of different ages, who often have a different perspective about the problems of an area and how to address them.

Criterion 5: The burden of consultation

Keeping the burden of consultation to a minimum is essential if consultations are to be effective and if consultees' buy-in to the process is to be obtained.

11.46 Plainly, any consultation exercise involves some trespass into the time of local citizens. Hence, consultation papers should be no longer than necessary, consultation should not occur more often than is necessary, and the burden of replying to the consultation should be minimised.

11.47 Because of the large quantity of material contained in national Guidance which needs to be covered in licensing policies, policies tend to be bulky documents. Necessarily, much of it is uncontentious, explanatory material. The crux points likely to give rise to controversy are likely to be few and far between, eg terminal hours, stress areas or treatment of proposals in residential areas. For this reason, it would be good practice for the authority to summarise its key policy proposals, either in an executive summary at the start of the document, or separately.

11.48 The accessibility of a policy would certainly be enhanced by publishing its key tenets in a short leaflet form. While it is not practicable to deliver the whole policy to every household in a local authority area, it may conceivably be practicable to disseminate a leaflet in this way. If not, the main points may be summarised in local press advertisements.[36]

---

[34] See also Fajerman et al, 'Children are Service Users Too' (Save the Children, 2004).
[35] Home Office Development and Practice Report 10, 2004. http://www.homeoffice.gov.uk/rds/pdfs04/dpr10.pdf.
[36] The authority will need to bear in mind the 'Code of Recommended Practice on Local

11.49 The proposed policy should be posted on the authority's web-site from day one, and consultees should be allowed to answer by e-mail.

Where written responses are requested, the following pro forma may be considered:[37]

Please use this form to set out your objection to, or representation in support of the XYZ Council proposed licensing policy. Please **use a separate form for each policy or paragraph you wish to object to.** You may photocopy this form or obtain further copies free of charge from the Planning Authority.
Please complete all sections in block capitals, using black ink.

1 Name and Address	Agents's Name and Address (if applicable)
Organisation (if applicable) **Telephone**	
2 Which policy/paragraph are you commenting on? Policy Number: Paragraph: Subject:	Are You: (please tick as appropriate) Objecting: Supporting:
3 Please state fully and clearly the reasons you are objecting or supporting this part of the plan, using a continuation sheet if necessary.	
Signature	Date

Please return all completed forms to: **[insert appropriate address]**, no later than **[insert date]**. The result of this consultation will be posted on the Council's web-site www.xyz.gov.uk/licensingpolicy after xyz 2005.

Figure 1: Model form for objecting to, or supporting, a local licensing policy

11.50 An alternative or supplementary approach would be to describe each policy and then ask questions to elicit the degree of support or opposition to

Authority Publicity' (DCLG, 2011). http://www.communities.gov.uk/documents/local government/pdf/1878324.pdf.

[37] Adapted from 'Local Plans and Unitary Development Plans, Guide to Procedures', Department of Environment, Transport and the Regions. http://www.odpm.gov.uk/stellent/ groups/odpm_planning/documents/source/odpm_plan_source_606149.doc.

the policy. The question may be as simple as whether the respondent agrees/disagrees with the policy. Or it may ask for the extent of disagreement by asking whether the respondent strongly agrees, agrees, neither agrees nor disagrees, disagrees or strongly disagrees. Such closed questions may be particularly effective when the key policies are few in number, but are interspersed in a much larger document.

Criterion 6: Responsiveness of consultation exercises

Consultation responses should be analysed carefully and clear feedback should be provided to participants following the consultation

11.51 The authority should publish a document or documents which summarises the consultation responses, explains the authority's view of the response and states what action the authority is taking in consequence. Under the Licensing Act 2003, it is of course the full council which decides the contents of the licensing policy. The council is advised by officers in a written report. It is recommended that the consultation responses be analysed in a grid, such as the following:

Represent-ation Number	Name of respond-ent	Policy Num-ber	Represent-ation	Officers' response	Recommend-ation
1	Dixie Dean	MD8	All pubs should have sound limitation devices on their sound systems	The policy advises that where there have been relevant representations, the authority will consider whether a sound limitation device is necessary. Each such case should be considered on its merits to avoid unnecessary regulation	No change

11.52 The covering report may then provide a general summary of the consultation responses and recommendation, but the use of a grid ensures that each responses has received individual consideration, which is important from the point of view of democracy, encouragement of a sense of public ownership of the policy, effective policy-making and avoidance of legal challenge.

Criterion 7: Capacity to consult

Officials running consultation exercises should seek guidance in how to run an effective consultation exercise and share what they have learned from the experience.

11.53 The Code recommends the appointment of a consultation co-ordinator, who should be the policy lead and the point of contact for enquiries. Those creating the policy should look to the co-ordinator for advice. The co-ordinator should ensure that best practice is being followed, and the co-ordinator should share lessons learned across the authority, so as to build the authority's capacity and expertise over time.

11.54 In particular, the effectiveness of the consultation should be evaluated. Which methods worked, and which didn't? How did responses clarify the policy options and affect the final decision? Were consultees satisfied with the process?

Examples of good practice

11.55 No two cases are alike, and it would be invidious to attempt to design a licensing policy consultation exercise without reference to individual facts. The Directgov web-site carries many examples of current UK consultations carried out in accordance with the Code of Practice.[38] The Annex to this chapter contains four examples of recent consultation exercises carried out in order to elicit general opinions about a particular subject matter, the results of which could then be used to inform the process of policy development. The range and type of questions provides a useful model for policy-makers here, particularly when policies are being reviewed and replaced.

F   CONCLUSION

11.56 In this chapter, consideration has been given both to law and good practice in relation to consultation on licensing policy. While the law is tolerably clear, best practice as to consultation techniques is developing apace.

Even if some of the wider strategic thinking advocated in this book is not undertaken, consultation during the life as a policy might include as a minimum:

- Establishment baseline data, eg regarding criminality and noise.
- Continual up-dating of data to appraise the success of the policy.

[38]   http://www.direct.gov.uk/en/Governmentcitizensandrights/UKgovernment/PublicConsultations/DG_170463.

- Through local licensing forum, discuss trends and priorities.
- Conduct public opinion survey work within the community:
  - What are the strengths of the night time economy?
  - How can these be improved?
  - What are the problems?
  - How can these be solved?
  - Has the authority got the policy balance right on particular issues?
  - What changes would they like to see?
- Through local licensing forum, discuss public views and consequent policy options and formulate draft policies.
- Consult on draft policies.

11.57 The suggested process involves ascertaining the views of the trade and statutory agencies through the local licensing forum, which presupposes that the forum is genuinely representative of all shades of opinion. If it is, then the authority is likely to get a higher degree of buy-in, as a result of developing policies by consensus rather than diktat. At all costs, authorities should avoid the waste and frustration associated with a 'Decide-Announce-Defend' approach to policy making. As it has been aptly put: 'This is clearly an area where best practice must be disseminated and any success in getting the public, especially the previously unheard voices, to participate in local democracy should be heralded.'[39]

ANNEX EXAMPLES OF GOOD PRACTICE

Example 1: Scottish licensing

11.58 As part of its review of Scottish licensing law, the Nicholson Committee commissioned research to test public opinion on alcohol-related issues.[40] The survey was of 1,003 people across various regions, age-groups and social classifications.

Q1 Thinking about the number of bars, restaurants, clubs and other licensed premises in which you can buy alcohol to consume on the premises, do you think there are too many, too few, or about the right amount of licensed premises?

A   Too many/too few/about right/unsure

Q2 In Scotland, most licensed premises are open between the standard permitted hours of 11:00 am to 11:00 pm Mondays to Saturdays, and between 12:30 pm and 2:30 pm, and 6:30 pm and 11:00 pm on Sundays. Do you think that these opening hours should be further restricted, extended, or are they about right?

---

[39]   Thompson, 'General duties to consult the public: how do you get the public to participate?', Nottingham Law Journal 33 (2002).

[40]   Scottish Executive Social Research 2003. http://www.scotland.gov.uk/library5/justice/ostp.pdf. Crown Copyright acknowledged.

A   Further restricted/extended/about right/unsure

Q2a   Why do you say that opening hours should be restricted?

A   Alcohol too readily available/need tighter controls on consumption/to reduce public drunkenness/to enhance public safety/to reduce health issues/other/unsure.

Q2b   Why do you say that opening hours should be extended?

A   Should be able to purchase at any time/discourages binge drinking/less people coming out of pubs/clubs at same time/other/unsure

Q3   Thinking about the number of off-licenses, shops, supermarkets and other outlets from which you can purchase alcohol to take away, do you think there are too many, too few, or about the right number?

A   Too many/too few/about right/unsure

Q4   In Scotland, it is possible to purchase alcohol from off-licenses, shops, supermarkets and other outlets between the hours of 8:00 am to 10:00 pm Mondays to Saturdays, and between 12:30 pm and 11:00 pm on Sundays. Do you think that these licensing hours should be further restricted, extended, or are they about right?

A   Further restricted/extended/about right/unsure

Q4a   Why do you say that licensing hours should be restricted?

A.   Alcohol too readily available/need tighter controls on consumption/ availability increases consumption in home/availability increases crime/ disorder in home/to reduce health risks associated with drinking/other/ unsure

Q4b   Why do you say that licensing hours should be extended?

A   Should be able to purchase at any time/would reduce numbers going to pubs/other/unsure

Q5   In your opinion, how much disturbance, or problems of crime and disorder occur in Scotland's cities, towns and villages at night?

A   A lot/a little/none/unsure.

Q6   And how much of the disturbance and crime and disorder problems occurring at night in Scotland's cities, towns and villages do you think is linked to alcohol consumption?

A   A lot/a little/none/unsure

Q7   Would you say that the levels of drunkenness and drunken behaviour in Scotland have increased, decreased or remained the same in the last 5 years?

A   Increased/decreased/stayed the same/unsure

Q8   What is the ONE thing that concerns you most about public drunkenness and drunken behaviour?

A   Violence/disorderly behaviour (eg urinating in the street)/vandalism/ being a victim/other/have no concerns/unsure.

Q9   How do you think public drunkenness could be controlled?

A   Reduce licensing hours/extend licensing hours/fewer licensed premises/ ban happy hours and drinks promotions/more police officers on street at night/make alcohol more expensive/reduce size of measures/stricter policies/laws on serving those intoxicated/other (specify)/unsure

Q10 Many pubs, clubs and licensed premises now run 'Happy Hours' or special drinks promotions, such as '2 for 1'. How strongly do you agree or disagree with the idea of running 'Happy Hours' and drinks promotions in pubs and clubs?

A   Agree strongly/agree slightly/neither agree nor disagree/disagree slightly/disagree strongly

Q11 What do you think are the problems associated with licensed premises using 'Happy Hours' or special drinks promotions?

A   Increased levels of drunkenness/drunken behaviour/encourages a culture of binge drinking/increases alcohol-related crime and disorder/ increases alcohol-related health problems/domestic violence/no problems/unsure/other (specify)

Q12 Do you think there is a problem with underage drinking in Scotland?

A   Yes/no/unsure

Q13 Where do underage drinkers in Scotland obtain their alcohol?

A   Buy it themselves at off-licences/buy it themselves at supermarkets/buy themselves in licensed premises (eg pubs and clubs)/friends/parents/ older siblings/strangers/take it from home/other (specify)/don't think they do/unsure

Example 2: Twickenham

11.59 In 2000 Richmond LBC consulted the public as to its attitudes to Twickenham Rugby Stadium. The exercise again demonstrates that a broad range of opinion may be elicited from a few well-chosen questions.

Q1   Thinking about the stadium generally, to what extent are you favourable to it?

A   Very favourable/fairly favourable/neither favourable nor unfavourable/ fairly unfavourable/very unfavourable/no opinion

Q2   Why do you say you are favourable to Twickenham Rugby Stadium?

A   (Answers included) boost local economy; historical/landmark/famous; rugby/sports fan; causes no problems; convenient for sports; local jobs; attracts visitors; convenient for other events; like look of stadium; other.

Q3   Why do you say you are unfavourable to Twickenham Rugby Stadium?

A   (Answers included) traffic congestion/road closures; general inconvenience to public/residents; noise on match days; large crowds on match days; litter; parking problems; unreliable/inadequate public transport; behaviour of fans; traffic noise; poor access for private transport; increased demand on local facilities; poor access from central London; traffic pollution; poor access for public transport/pedestrians; not enough policing; too much policing; stadium puts house price up; opposed to stadium generally; dislike stadium/pre-match entertainment.

Q4   On balance how would you rate the impact of Twickenham Stadium on your local area?

A   Very positive/fairly positive/neither positive nor negative/fairly negative/ very negative/no opinion

Q5   To what extent do you feel each of the following issues are a problem for you personally? (Traffic congestion on event days; on-street parking on event days; behaviour of visitors to the stadium; noise on event days)

A   Not a problem/minor problem/major problem

Q6   At recent matches a licence has not been granted to public bars at the Stadium to open after the game. To what extent do you think it would be better or worse for local residents if these bars were open after the game?

A   Much better/a little better/makes no difference/a little worse/much worse/no opinion

Q7   The local police have opposed the granting of a post match licence to the bars on grounds of public safety, disruption and noise to the local area and extended traffic congestion. The Council has supported the police in their opposition. To what extent do you support or oppose the position taken by the police and the Council?

A   Strongly support/support to some extent/neither support nor oppose/ oppose to some extent/strongly oppose/no opinion

Q8   Which, if any, of the problems listed below have you experienced by supporters after events at the Stadium?

A   Supporters trespassing on your property; damage to your home/garden; damage to other property eg car; anti-social behaviour from supporters eg verbal abuse/urinating in public; littering; graffiti; difficulties in gaining easy access to and from your property; other; none.

Example 3: householder survey

11.60   The following sample questionnaire is an adaptation of questions asked of householders in surveys in Swansea and the West End of London regarding their attitudes to potential sources of environmental stress related to the night time economy.

	Agree Strongly	Agree	Disagree	Disagree Strongly
There is heavy traffic in the area I live between the hours of 10pm and 4am				

I experience a considerable amount of noise from traffic in my own home between the hours of 10pm and 4am			
Many people who visit the area I live between the hours of 10pm and 4am			
Park their vehicles near to my home			
I am uneasy about the safety of my car when it is parked near to my home between the hours of 10pm and 4am			
There are problems of noise coming directly from restaurants/bars/pubs/clubs in the area I live between the hours of 10pm and 4am			
There are problems of littering and street fouling in the area I live between the hours of 10pm and 4am			
There are problems of vandalism and anti-social behaviour in the area I live between the hours of 10pm and 4am			
There are problems of street crime, such as robbery, in the area I live between the hours of 10pm and 4am			
I would never go out alone in the area I live between the hours of 10pm and 4am			
I don't think the area I live is particularly dangerous between the hours of 10pm and 4am			

A more obvious police presence in the area I live between the hours of 10pm and 4am would increase my feelings of safety				
I feel safe to go out in the area I live between the hours of 10pm and 4am if I am in the company of others				
I am deterred from using buses in the area I live between the hours of 10pm and 4am by fears for my personal safety				
There are problems relating to the presence of homeless people in the area I live between the hours of 10pm and 4am				
There are problems relating to the presence of drug dealers in the area I live between the hours of 10pm and 4am				
There are problems relating to the presence of street vendors in the area I live between the hours of 10pm and 4am				
There are problems relating to the presence of prostitutes and sex establishments in the area I live between the hours of 10pm and 4am				

Methodological note:
To obtain more precise results, questions might be broken down into smaller portions of time, for example 10pm–Midnight; Midnight–2am; 2am–4am; etc. Further questions might ask respondents to nominate days of the week upon which such problems are experienced.

Example 4: City of London survey regarding sexual entertainment venue licensing policy

11.61 In 2010 the City of London conducted an extensive survey of City residents and workers as to its proposed sexual entertainment venue licensing policy. The questionnaire is replicated below.

CITY
OF
LONDON

Questionnaire - Licensing Sexual Entertainment Venues in the City of London

The City of London Corporation now has the power to regulate sexual entertainment venues (SEVs) in the City. Sexual Entertainment Venues are defined as commercial venues offering live performance or stripping, pole dancing, peep shows, live sex shows, lap- and/or table-dancing which are designed for the purpose of sexually stimulating the audience.

The City of London Corporation is considering adopting a SEV policy. If it does, all applications will be judged on their merits in accordance with the policy. If it does not, applications will be judged on a case by case basis.

Please tick the answers that reflect your views. Thank you.

1.   **Do you think that the City of London Corporation should**

☐ *Adopt a Sexual Entertainment Venue (SEV) policy?*

☐ *Have no Sexual Entertainment Venue (SEV) policy?*

2.   **If the City adopts an SEV policy, please indicate below which issues the policy should address:**

	Yes	No	Don't Know
The suitability of the applicant and those connected to them to own and manage a SEV	☐	☐	☐
Detailed operating rules for the management of a SEV if a licence is granted	☐	☐	☐
The interior layout of the premises and the facilities available	☐	☐	☐
The character of the localities and their compatibility with SEV	☐	☐	☐
Compatibility of SEVs with particular neighbourhood uses	☐	☐	☐

3. In general, are there any localities within the City of London boundaries that you consider to be appropriate for Sexual Entertainment venues?
(Another word for "localities" is "neighbourhoods", which you might think of as areas such as Smithfield, Barbican, Bow Lane or Crosswall)

☐ Yes *(go to Q4)*   ☐ No *(go to Q7)*   ☐ Don't know *(go to Q7)*

4. Which localities within the City of London boundaries do you consider appropriate for Sexual Entertainment Venues? Please be as specific as possible.

5. The City of London Corporation can use the policy to set maximum numbers of Sexual Entertainment Venues for individual localities within the City's boundaries. This number could be zero.
Do you think that the City should set a figure for the maximum number of SEVs within any particular locality?

☐ Yes   ☐ No, there should be no limits set

If yes, state which locality or localities, and how many. Please be as specific as possible.

6. Are there any localities within the City of London boundaries that you consider to be inappropriate for Sexual Entertainment Venues?

☐ Yes   ☐ No

If yes, please state which locality or localities. Please be as specific as possible.

7. **We would like your views on whether SEVs should be allowed to open near particular areas and types of building, for example, residential areas or banks. Please state how compatible an SEV would be near to the following types of area or building.**

	Highly compatible	Quite compatible	Neither	Quite incompatible	Highly incompatible
Mainly residential	☐	☐	☐	☐	☐
Historic buildings	☐	☐	☐	☐	☐
Schools	☐	☐	☐	☐	☐
Financial institutions such as banks	☐	☐	☐	☐	☐
Family leisure facilities e.g. Barbican, Golden Lane Leisure Centre, children's play areas	☐	☐	☐	☐	☐
Mainly retail	☐	☐	☐	☐	☐
Areas with lots of night-time entertainment or late-night shopping	☐	☐	☐	☐	☐
Cultural facilities such as galleries and museums	☐	☐	☐	☐	☐
Youth facilities e.g. youth hostels	☐	☐	☐	☐	☐
Places of worship	☐	☐	☐	☐	☐

8. **How important are each of the following features in deciding whether or not to grant a licence for a Sexual Entertainment Venue?**

	Very important	Fairly important	Neither	Fairly unimportant	Very unimportant
The quality of the venue	☐	☐	☐	☐	☐
The ability to supervise activities in the premises	☐	☐	☐	☐	☐
Safety and treatment of the men and women working in SEVs	☐	☐	☐	☐	☐
Community safety issues	☐	☐	☐	☐	☐
Disabled access	☐	☐	☐	☐	☐
Safety and treatment of customers	☐	☐	☐	☐	☐

PERSONAL INFORMATION
The City of London Corporation is keen to ensure that all sections of the working and residential populations of the City are well represented in this survey. It will help us to do this if you provide the following information. This information will be treated in the strictest confidence, will only be processed on an anonymous basis and will never be passed onto third parties. Sharing your personal information is optional but we would strongly encourage you to do so, as this will help us to make sure everyone's voice is heard.

Which of the following applies to you?

☐ *Work in the City of London*   ☐ *Live in the City of London*   ☐ *Both*

Other (e.g. visitor), please state:

☐

Please provide the first half of your postcode (e.g. EC4):-

☐

What was your age last birthday?

☐ *16-24*   ☐ *35-44*   ☐ *55-64*
☐ *25-34*   ☐ *45-54*   ☐ *65+*

Are you male or female?

☐ *Male*
☐ *Female*

Do you consider yourself to be disabled?

☐ *Yes*
☐ *No*

Ethnicity: To which of these groups do you consider you belong?

Asian or Asian British

☐ *Indian*
☐ *Pakistani*
☐ *Bangladeshi*

Any other Asian background (please specify)

☐_____

Black or Black British

☐ *Caribbean*
☐ *African*

Any other Black background (please specify)

☐_____

Chinese

☐ *Chinese*

Irish

☐ *Irish*

Mixed heritage

☐ *Asian & White*
☐ *Black & White*

Any other mixed heritage (please specify)

☐_____

White

☐ *White British*
☐ *White European*

Any other White background (please specify)

☐_____

Other Ethnic Group *(please specify)*

☐_____

Sexual orientation: Which of the following best describes your sexual orientation?

☐ *Bisexual*   ☐ *Gay woman/lesbian*   ☐ *Prefer not to say*
☐ *Gay man*   ☐ *Straight/heterosexual*

Other (please specify)

☐_____

Faith: What is your religion, faith or belief even if you are not currently practising?

☐ *No religion*   ☐ *Hindu*   ☐ *Sikh*
☐ *Buddhist*   ☐ *Jewish*   ☐ *Prefer not to say*
☐ *Christian*   ☐ *Muslim*

Any other religion (please specify)

☐_____

Thank you for your time!

12

The appropriateness test

What must become of the infant who is conceived in gin?

Henry Fielding (1751)

I never drink anything stronger than gin before breakfast.

W.C. Fields

A INTRODUCTION

12.01 In this chapter, we consider a major change to the test for licensing intervention introduced by the Police Reform and Social Responsibility Act 2011. Whereas the Licensing Act 2003 permitted regulatory interventions only where necessary, the new legislation lowered the legislative threshold to 'appropriate'. Here, we shall consider the legal and philosophical basis of the necessity test, and the implications and lawfulness of the new lower threshold.

B THE NECESSITY TEST

12.02 The necessity test underpinned all of the regulatory powers under the Licensing Act 2003. The word 'necessary' appeared in the Act on more than forty occasions. The political philosophy which underpinned the test might be characterised as neo-liberal in origin, that is to say that business should be allowed complete freedom to operate and develop except to the extent that regulation is required in order to protect some defined elements of the public interest. The test was also consistent with concepts of necessity and proportionality emanating from the European Convention on Human Rights, which was incorporated into our law by the Human Rights Act in 1998. For example, Article 1 of the First Protocol of the Convention stressed the right of the State to enforce such laws as it deems necessary to control the use of property in accordance with the general interest. The same approach was taken in ensuing regulatory legislation. Section 21 of the Legislative and Regulatory Reform Act provided that any persons exercising a function to which that section applied should have regard to the principle that regulatory activities should be targeted only at cases in which action is needed. Similar sentiments were expressed in section 5 of the Regulatory Enforcement and Sanctions Act 2008, which obliged the Local Better Regulation Office,[1] in exercising its functions, to secure that local authorities exercised their relevant functions so that regulatory activities should be targeted at cases in which action is both proportionate and needed. This, then, is what came to be known as 'light touch' regulation.

12.03   As expressed in Guidance, in many licensing policies and by practitioners in their day to day work, this meant that before imposing any form of regulatory intervention, be it a condition on a new licence or revocation of an existing licence, the authority should ask itself whether the intervention was both necessary and proportionate, in the sense that no lesser step would suffice in order to promote the licensing objectives. This is not, it will be noted, some kind of constraint upon what kind of evidence may be admitted by the licensing authority, or a measuring device of the quantum of evidence which is necessary before intervention is justified. Properly understood, it is a test which sets the threshold for regulatory intervention itself. Put in another way, it controls the exercise of the discretion, and forces the licensing authority before imposing the sanction to ask itself: is this really necessary? Would a lesser step suffice?

C TRANSMOGRIFICATION

12.04   The consultation exercise preceding the Police Reform and Social Responsibility Bill[2] posited, without analysis or rigorous evidence, that the presumption in favour of grant under Licensing Act 2003 made it difficult for local authorities to turn down applications. It stated that the necessity test placed a 'significant evidential burden' on licensing authorities, and that the Government was considering amending the Act 'to reduce the burden on licensing authorities from the requirement to prove that their actions are "necessary" to empowering them to consider more widely what actions are most appropriate to promote the licensing objectives in their area.'

---

[1]   Although that body was dissolved by the Local Better Regulation Office (Dissolution and Transfer of Functions, Etc) Order 2012, Sch 1 para 3, the obligation, which now falls on the Secretary of State and the Welsh Ministers, remains.

[2]   'Rebalancing the Licensing Act: a consultation on empowering individuals, families and local communities to shape and determine local licensing' (Home Office, 2010).

12.05 The amending provisions in the Police Reform and Social Responsibility Bill were entitled 'Reducing the evidential burden on licensing authorities'. This is of course a misnomer: the Act does not place an evidential burden on authorities; rather it sets a test for the exercise of their discretion.

12.06 At the Committee stage in the House of Commons, the Home Office Minister James Brokenshire was challenged to justify the loosening of the test and the commensurate broadening of powers of licensing authorities to impose regulatory burdens even where these were not necessary. He stated that the Government's 'sense' was that local authorities had been defensive about imposing regulatory requirements for fear that upon appeal their actions would not be regarded as necessary.[3] He considered that a wider discretion was necessary in order to 'enable communities to assert themselves properly', stating:

> 'A decision that is "appropriate" for the promotion of the licensing objectives provides some flexibility to consider the effects of the decision on the promotion of the objectives. It may therefore be decided to take steps that are suitable for, rather than necessary to, the promotion of the objectives. It provides an element to deal with that reluctance or resistance, to enable local communities to assert themselves properly in relation to this particular approach.'

12.07 The Minister was therefore comfortable about regulation being imposed even when it is not necessary. Indeed, that was the very inspiration for the change.

12.08 The Minister was also challenged on whether imposing regulation on an existing business in the absence of any necessity for such intervention was compliant with the European Convention on Human Rights. He stated that the Government's legal advice was that the measure was compliant because of legal rights of appeal.[4] With respect, it is difficult to understand that position, because rights of appeal might resolve procedural issues such as bias, but they cannot resolve any substantive non-compliance of a legal test with fundamental human rights. If a test which permits an authority to impose regulation in the absence of necessity breaches the European Convention, that cannot be cured by permitting an appeal to a court which is governed by the same test.

12.09 Be that as it may, the appropriateness test has replaced the necessity test throughout the Licensing Act 2003, including for the grant and review of premises licences and club premises certificates, for personal licences and for temporary event notices.[5]

---

[3] HC Deb, 10 February 2011, Col 549.
[4] HC Deb, 10 February 2011, Col 552.
[5] Police Reform and Social Responsibility Act 2011, ss 109–111.

D NATIONAL GUIDANCE

12.10 As presaged in the Parliamentary debates, the Government has sought to elucidate the appropriateness test through national Guidance. This states:

> '9.38 Licensing authorities are best placed to determine what actions are appropriate for the promotion of the licensing objectives in their areas. All licensing determinations should be considered on a case by case basis. They should take into account any representations or objections that have been received from responsible authorities or other persons, and representations made by the applicant or premises user as the case may be.

> 9.39 The authority's determination should be evidence-based, justified as being appropriate for the promotion of the licensing objectives and proportionate to what it is intended to achieve.

> 9.40 Determination of whether an action or step is appropriate for the promotion of the licensing objectives requires an assessment of what action or step would be suitable to achieve that end. Whilst this does not therefore require a licensing authority to decide that no lesser step will achieve the aim, the authority should aim to consider the potential burden that the condition would impose on the premises licence holder (such as the financial burden due to restrictions on licensable activities) as well as the potential benefit in terms of the promotion of the licensing objectives. However, it is imperative that the authority ensures that the factors which form the basis of its determination are limited to consideration of the promotion of the objectives and nothing outside those parameters. As with the consideration of licence variations, the licensing authority should consider wider issues such as other conditions already in place to mitigate potential negative impact on the promotion of the licensing objectives and the track record of the business. Further advice on determining what is appropriate when imposing conditions on a licence or certificate is provided in Chapter 10. The licensing authority is expected to come to its determination based on an assessment of the evidence on both the risks and benefits either for or against making the determination.'

12.11 It will immediately be seen that the Guidance equates appropriateness and suitability, while expressly discarding the test that 'no lesser step will suffice.' This latter test is, however, one way of expressing the principle of proportionality which is avowedly retained. What, then, does proportionality bring to the party? Further guidance is given on the issue of proportionality in Chapter 10 of the Guidance:

> **'Proportionality**

> 10.10 The 2003 Act requires that licensing conditions should be tailored

to the size, type, location and characteristics and activities taking place at the premises concerned. Conditions should be determined on a case by case basis and standardised conditions which ignore these individual aspects should be avoided. Licensing authorities and other responsible authorities should be alive to the indirect costs that can arise because of conditions. These could be a deterrent to holding events that are valuable to the community or for the funding of good and important causes. Licensing authorities should therefore ensure that any conditions they impose are only those which are appropriate for the promotion of the licensing objectives. Consideration should also be given to wider issues such as conditions already in place that address the potential negative impact on the promotion of the licensing objectives and the track record of the business.'

12.12 The role of proportionality here seems to involve a consideration of the costs of imposing the proposed step, which may be the direct costs upon the licensee of compliance, eg of employing extra door staff, and the indirect costs upon the community, eg of being unable to attend an event for which there is demand. This appears to widen the scope of the inquiry in a way which cut across the grain of what the Government apparently intends by the legislative change. Rather than asking simply whether a step is necessary to promote the licensing objectives, the authority would now need to carry out a cost benefit exercise in which the costs of the measure – which may be economic or qualitative – are weighed against the benefits of the measure, which are almost certain to be subjective. If this is the true nature of the exercise, the Guidance is self-contradictory because in the same breath it advises: 'However, it is imperative that the authority ensures that the factors which form the basis of its determination are limited to consideration of the promotion of the objectives and nothing outside those parameters.' If that is right, then questions of the cost of the measure and the benefit to the community may not be taken into account.

E CRITIQUE

12.13 From the foregoing discussion, it will be seen that far from making the test simpler and broadening the ability of authorities to intervene, the change has made the test confusing and legally suspect. There are five areas which merit comment.

12.14 The first is the supposition that the necessity test imposed a constraint on authorities which caused them to fight shy of imposing effective regulation. There is no evidence for this. The root of the supposition is that the necessity test imposed a threshold which was too high in the ordinary run of cases. Not so. The necessity test was not predicated on proof that if the step was not imposed the feared consequence would certainly or even be likely to happen. It was simply predicated on evidence that the required step was necessary to promote the licensing objectives. In the same way that a smoke detector may be thought necessary in a home without needing to prove that in its absence the house will burn to the ground, so a search arch might be considered necessary in a nightclub without proof that without it someone will be stabbed. It is simply a necessary precaution. And, if it is necessary, it should be imposed. Therefore, the threshold was not so high that it required to be lowered at all.

12.15   Support in the case law for an interpretation of the necessity test as requiring something short of indispensability may be found in *R (Clays Lane Housing Co-operative Limited) v The Housing Corporation*[6], in which the Court of Appeal held that, depending on the context, necessary may be interpreted as meaning merely 'reasonably necessary'.[7]

12.16   Second, assuming that the threshold did need to be lowered, 'appropriate' is not a valuable test. Indeed, it is not a test at all, let alone an objective one. In the context of licensing, it is vacuous. It means no more than that the licensing authority should do what it thinks right. It is most unlikely that any authority would do otherwise. It provides no ascertainable measure against which the justifiability of the regulatory intervention may be gauged.

12.17   Third, if it results in regulation being imposed on licensees which is unnecessary, it has the potential to do great damage. If, for example, a door supervision requirement is imposed with which the publican does not have the economic means to comply, s/he may well be moved to ask whether the authority thinks it necessary to impose it. If the answer is no, the publican may well ask why then it was imposed, and rue the day that a discretion was conferred to impose unnecessary measures.

12.18   Fourth, the legal basis of the dilution is at best unclear and at worst unfounded. Treating a licence as a property right,[8] Article 1 Protocol 1 of the European Convention on Human Rights clearly operates to permit control of the use of property where this is necessary. In this case, control has been sanctioned even where it is unnecessary. If the only way to comply with the Convention is to interpret 'appropriate' as 'necessary' then the shift has achieved nothing other than to raise expectation (of communities) and alarm (of licensees) in equal measure. If, however, regulatory intervention is imposed merely where it is considered appropriate, without its being necessary, then there is a real argument that the intervention is non-compliant with the human rights obligations of the State.

6   [2005] 1 WLR 2229.
7   *R v The Housing Corporation* at paras [21]–[23]. See also *Pascoe v First Secretary of State* [2007] 1 WLR 885 at para [70] and *Handyside v United Kingdom* (1976) 1 EHHR 737 at para 48.
8   *Tre Traktorer v Sweden* (1989) 13 EHRR 309; *Catscratch Limited v City of Glasgow Licensing Board* [2001] LLR 610.

12.19 A little elaboration is necessary so that the argument does not repose at the level of generalisations. In *Samaroo v Secretary of State for the Home Department*[9] Dyson LJ stated that in considering proportionality, there are usually two distinct stages: (i) can the objective be achieved by a less intrusive measure; and (ii) if not, does the measure proposed have an excessive or disproportionate effect on the interests of affected persons.[10] The first of these stages is expressly disavowed in the Guidance.

12.20 However, the *Samaroo* approach is not universal. In planning cases, where a balance is to be struck between the rights of landowners to use their land as they wish and the rights of others affected by their use of the land and of the community in general. In such cases, the Court of Appeal in *Lough v First Secretary of State*[11] held that the requirement of proportionality is met by the decision-maker setting out to strike a fair balance. In *McCarthy v First Secretary of State*[12] the Court of Appeal held that the approach in *Lough* may be applicable more widely in the planning context and not merely when the essential dispute is between two or more sets of private interests, although it is fair to point out that in that case the decision which was upheld was that it was necessary to refuse planning permission.

12.21 The approach in *Lough* was applied by the Court of Appeal in *R (Clays Lane Housing) v Housing Corporation*[13]which held that in the context of deprivation of property, which domestically is governed by a test of 'compelling case in the public interest', the test is met in terms of proportionality by asking not whether deprivation is the least intrusive measure but whether it is reasonably necessary.[14] In both cases, the Court of Appeal held that the 'least intrusive measure' test is effectively restricted to cases where there is a direct interference with rights rather than where there is a conflict between more than one private interest.[15]

12.22 In licensing, decisions of an authority may have an expropriatory effect, particularly when licences are being reviewed. Clearly, any decision on review may involve balancing interests. Those interests may not all be private interests. They might involve balancing the rights of the licensee to trade on the one hand and the community interest in the prevention of crime and disorder on the other, but this remains a balance. However, if there is to be a reduction in, or qualification or removal of, the right to trade, then the case nears the situation canvassed in *Samaroo* of a direct interference with rights.

9   [2001] EWCA Civ 1139.
10   *Samaroo* at para [19]. See also *R (Daly) v Secretary of State for the Home Department* [2001] 2 AC 532 at para [27].
11   [2004] 1 WLR 2557 at paras [49] and [55].
12   [2007] EWCA Civ 510.
13   [2005] 1 WLR 2229.
14   See para [26]. Followed in *Pascoe v First Secretary of State* [2007] 1 WLR 885 and *Smith v Secretary of State for Trade and Industry* [2008] 1 WLR 394.
15   See *Lough* at para [55] and *Clays Lane* at para [21].

If that is right, then a test which does not even ask whether the measure proposed is reasonably necessary, let alone whether it is the least intrusive available measure, seems to fall well short of the standard required by proportionality. While it is acknowledged that even in the case of compulsory purchase the latter test is not applied, there remains in that case a test of 'compelling interest' translated in rights terms into 'reasonable necessity'. It is hard to see why expropriation of land requires that standard, while expropriation of a business does not. Accordingly, it is submitted that, as a minimum, in the case of review applications, proportionality involves at least a test of reasonable necessity, a test which is not contained in the Guidance at all.

12.23 Fifth, similarly, the Provision of Services Regulations 2009, which implement the Services Directive,[16] require that authorisation schemes for the provision of services must be based on criteria which preclude the competent authority from exercising its power of assessment in an arbitrary manner. Further, the criteria must be (a) non-discriminatory, (b) justified by an overriding reason relating to the public interest, (c) proportionate to that public interest objective, (d) clear and unambiguous, (e) objective, (f) made public in advance, and (g) transparent and accessible. While one might say that the licensing objectives meet the test of being non-discriminatory, justified, clear, objective and transparent, the ability to use them to prevent activities taking place or to impose constraints even where this is not necessary would appear to encourage behaviour which is arbitrary, disproportionate and unjustified by an overriding reason relating to the public interest. Therefore, there is an argument that the test, or conceivably its application in individual cases, may breach domestic and European law.

12.24 Sixth, section 21 of the Legislative and Regulatory Reform Act imposes an obligation on licensing authorities to have regard to two principles, the first of which requires regulatory activities to be carried out in a way which is proportionate. For all practical purposes, this makes proportionality in regulation a legislative requirement.[17]

12.25 Seventh, if the solution to these difficulties is to broaden the picture as is seemingly suggested by the Guidance, so as to encompass the cost of the measures and the benefit of the proposal, the effect is arguably to convert the licensing authority from a regulator with a defined, narrow but important role to that of an economic and cultural arbiter, a role which it is likely to be ill-equipped or at least untrained to perform.

---

[16] Directive 2006/123/EC on services in the internal market.
[17] This is canvassed further in Chapter 29 (The Legislative and Regulatory Reform Act 2006).

F RESOLUTION

12.26 Some trenchant criticisms of the test governing licensing disputes have been set out in the previous section. The criticism is in essence that in an attempt to broaden the discretion of licensing authorities, Parliament has succeeded in giving a discretion to impose unnecessary regulation in a manner which will create uncertainty and a possible breach of domestic, European and human rights law. While it seems pretty clear that the gap between appropriateness and necessity is narrowed by the superimposition of the requirement of proportionality, it is not fully closed.

12.27 It is suggested that there may be a route out of the imbroglio for licensing authorities, without needing to await adjudication on the new provisions in the High Court. While the range of possible responses under the necessity test was relatively narrow, the range of potential responses under the appropriateness test is relatively large. There may not be many steps which are really necessary, but there are many more arguably appropriate means of promoting the licensing objectives. These may range from steps which are merely good practice to steps which are genuinely necessary in the circumstances of the case. However, acting sensibly, a licensing authority may consider it inappropriate to impose draconian regulation on an operator unless it is genuinely necessary to do so. In this way, while the legal test remains 'appropriate', the discretion will not be exercised to impose burdensome regulation unless there is a demonstrable necessity. The term necessity may not imply that the measure is indispensable, merely that it is 'reasonably necessary'. But for an authority to impose a burden on a business if it is not even reasonably necessary to do so invites criticism that this is a paradigm of disproportion.

12.28 This may be demonstrated by a simple example. Imagine a case in which a review is brought because customers of a nightclub have been disturbing local residents on their departure. By the time the case gets to a hearing of the licensing sub-committee, the problem has been cured through the adoption of a competent, well-thought through dispersal policy. The licensee says that a curtailment of hours is no longer necessary because the problem has been solved. The applicants for the review, however, continue to press for an earlier terminal hour, arguing that they do not need to show that the step is necessary. It is submitted that the licensing authority would be quite at liberty to find that a condition of a dispersal policy is appropriate, but that an earlier terminal hour is not appropriate <u>because it is not reasonably necessary.</u>

12.29 It is accepted that the resolution of the problem has a tendency to conflate the appropriateness test and necessity test, when the Government clearly wanted to impose a diluted test. There is much truth in that. However, the reason for this is that, in holding the balance between local communities and local businesses, it is unlikely to be considered appropriate to regulate more than is reasonably necessary to meet the objectives of the regulation. While adoption of this solution may well reduce the gap between appropriate and necessary to a semantic one, it will have the virtue of legality, fairness, justice and common sense.

Licensing and proximity

Then this mead-hall was in the morning
this noble hall stained with gore when the day lightened,
all of the benches smeared with blood
the hall battle-gory. I had friends the fewer,
cherished old battle-retinue, for these Death took them away.

Beowulf

A INTRODUCTION

13.01 The purpose of this chapter is to slay a shibboleth, that licensing may not be used as a tool to cure nuisance and disorder away from licensed premises. The fallacy of the proposition will be demonstrated through a basic analysis of the Act itself, case law and Guidance.

13.02 In essence, the fallacy has arisen because two concepts have been conjoined so as to produce an illogical conclusion. The first is that licensees cannot control the behaviour of their guests once they have left the premises. The second is that there are other measures which may be effective to control behaviour in the public realm. The undoubted truth of these two concepts does not entail, however, that constraints may not be placed upon the licence where this is appropriate to promote the relevant licensing objectives. To the contrary, where appropriate and proportionate measures can be imposed to promote the licensing objectives, it does not matter whether the potential harm to those objectives arises on or off the premises, provided that they are causally linked to the licensable activities.

B THE ACT

13.03 The Act is designed to protect against harm to the licensing object-ives caused by licensable activities. It is disinterested in the medium by which such harm arises, whether on or off the premises. Section 18(3) of the Act, for example, requires the licensing sub-committee at a hearing of an application to have regard to the application and any relevant representations, and to take such of the steps mentioned in subsection (4) (if any) as it considers appropriate for the promotion of the licensing objectives.

13.04 Imagine that the case concerns a proposed nightclub at which the main direction of travel for departing customers will be along a residential street. The residents have no evidence that customers will be guilty of crime and disorder but fear, and the sub-committee accepts, that a large number of customers walking down a residential street in the middle of the night are liable to wake up the residents, which they consider will amount to a nuisance. There are apparently no other powers to prevent the anticipated nuisance. The sub-committee therefore determines that some curtailment of hours is appropriate for the promotion of the licensing objectives. It is difficult to see how, given the terms of the section, this is an unlawful application of the section 18(3) test. There is nothing in the wording of the test which entitles the sub-committee to take into account noise emanating from the premises but not noise emanating from customers who have emanated from the premises. Any suggestion of such a restriction would amount to an unjustified gloss on the statutory language.

C THE CASE LAW

13.05 In *Sharp v Wakefield*[1] the Kendal licensing justices refused to renew a liquor licence for the Low Bridge Inn in Westmorland, which refusal was upheld by the Court of Quarter Sessions, not on the grounds of the unfitness of the licensee or disorder within the premises, but on the grounds of remoteness from police supervision and the character and necessities of the neighbourhood. The refusal was appealed all the way to the House of Lords, which unhesitatingly held that it was open to the court to refuse on such grounds. The Lord Chancellor, Lord Halsbury, held that while on renewal the inquiry would be likely to be limited to the conduct and condition of the premises and the character of the licensee, that does not preclude a wider inquiry as to the wants and needs of the neighbourhood.[2] This clearly established that, notwithstanding the good character of the licensee and the exemplary conduct of the premises, not only a new licence but also a renewal may be refused on the grounds of the impact of the licence on the public realm.

13.06 The issue recrudesced in *Lidster v Owen*[3], in which Lidster was the licensee of the Stateside Centre in Bournemouth, one of three discotheques with a joint capacity of over 3,000 with music and dancing licences until

---

[1] [1891] AC 173.
[2] *Sharp v Wakefield*, p 181.
[3] [1983] 1 WLR 516.

1 am. The police objected to renewal on the grounds of crime and disorder, bringing forth clear evidence of vandalism, violence, excessive noise, disorder and indecent behaviour. However, there were no incidents of disorderly behaviour inside the Stateside Centre, very little direct evidence that any disorder had been caused by Stateside customers, and clear evidence of good management practice in excluding undesirables. The justices pegged back the licences for all three to midnight and Lidster appealed to the Divisional Court and then to the Court of Appeal. The Court of Appeal unanimously held that the justices had been entitled to take into account considerations of public order, even though the premises themselves were well-conducted. Slade LJ considered the Stateside operators rather unlucky, bearing in mind that theirs was the first of the three discotheques on the scene, and their running of the premises was beyond reproach:

> 'Nevertheless, the evidence ... showed that ... a quite unacceptable degree of public disorder existed ... and the principal factor creating this disorder was the number of persons leaving the applicants' prem-ises and the other discotheque premises ... at one o'clock in the morning. I have no doubt that the justices were entitled to take these factors into account when considering whether or not to renew the applicants' licence.'[4]

13.07 The issue arose in the context of the Late Night Refreshment Houses Act 1969, in *Surrey Heath Borough Council v McDonalds Restaurants Limited,*[5] in which justices had allowed McDonalds' appeal against the imposition of an 11 pm closure on the renewal of its licence. The evidence showed that the management of its premises was good with few incidents within, but the justices had acceded to a submission that it was beyond their purview to consider incidents in the public realm, holding that to penalise the restaurant for its success in the absence of fault would be wrong, especially as there was adequate legislation to deal with public disorder outside. Nolan LJ held:

> 'The danger of unreasonable disturbance to residents may arise even in the case of a thoroughly well-run restaurant. It may be that such a restaurant, through no fault of its proprietors, has become a focus for unruly behaviour ... [T]here may be such a situation ... in which the proprietors of the restaurant would be bound to accept a restriction upon their ability to conduct their business in the interest of the community as a whole and to accept that there were times when the restaurant would have to remain closed. That could not properly be described as penalising the restaurant for its success.
>
> The existence of legislation dealing with public disorder outside again, it seems to me, is not really crucial to the sole question before the justices (which is that stated in s. 7 of the Act), that is, the desirability of avoiding unreasonable disturbance to residents. This could occur no

---

4 *Lidster v Owen*, p 524.
5 (1991) 155 Loc Gov Rev 232; (1991) 3 Admin LR 313.

matter how stringent the legislation dealing with public disorder outside and no matter how assiduous the police are in seeking to enforce that legislation.'[6]

13.08   So far as the High Court was concerned, the dividing line was whether the events relied upon related to an unreasonable disturbance to residents properly attributable to the restaurant being kept open after 11 pm.

13.09   What of the situation where it could not be proved that the customers were themselves causing crime and disorder, but when aggregated with those coming from other premises caused a nuisance or other issues in the neighbourhood? A partial answer was given by *Lidster*: the licensing authority is plainly entitled to consider the aggregate effect when considering individual licensing applications. The reason is obvious from both *Sharp* and *Surrey Heath*: the purpose of licensing is not to reward the licensee for good behaviour, but to regulate premises in the interests of the wider community. Therefore, where there is evidence that customers from premises are contributing to a global difficulty, that is relevant material for the licensing authority.

13.10   Support for that suggestion arose in *R (Westminster Council) v Middlesex Crown Court and Chorion plc*[7] which concerned the declaration by the Council of a 'stress area' in Soho and Covent Garden and the promulgation of a policy leaning against further late night licensing there, on the grounds that it was 'saturated'. In the instant case, the Crown Court had decided to grant a licence contrary to the policy, with whose purposes it declared sympathy, on the grounds that there was no evidence specific to the premises or its management militating against the grant. However, invited by counsel, it stated that notwithstanding that the applicant was a fit and proper person and the premises would be well-managed, a public entertainment licence could be refused on the sole ground that the area was already saturated with licensed premises and that the cumulative effect of the existing premises was impacting adversely on the area to an unacceptable degree. However, on the facts it appears to have found that the grant of a licence was not going to exacerbate the situation.

13.11   The council appealed to the High Court. Scott Baker J held that there was ambiguity in the policy, and that therefore the Crown Court could not be criticised for regarding the particular applicant's credentials and the fact that the grant would not significantly add to the problem as overriding the policy presumption.

However, the learned judge added:

'34. It is both understandable and appropriate for the Claimant to have a policy in the light of the problems it has identified in the West End.

[6]   *Surrey Heath*, p 234.
[7]   [2002] LLR 538.

The policy needs to make it clear that it is not directed at the quality of the operation or the fitness of the licensee but on the global effect of these licences on the area as a whole. If the policy is not to be consistently overridden in individual cases it must be made clear within it that it will only be overridden in exceptional circumstances and that the impeccable credentials of the applicant will not ordinarily be regarded as exceptional circumstances. It should be highlighted that the kind of circumstances that might be regarded as exceptional would be where the underlying policy of restricting any further growth would not be impaired. An example might be where premises in one place would replace those in another. The guidance document needs to be redrawn so as to eliminate ambiguities and inconsistencies.'

13.12 To complete the history, Westminster City Council took up the judge's invitation, amending its policy so as to declare plainly that its policy in the stress area was to refuse further entertainment or night café licences (or increases in terminal hours or capacities or material variations), that the good character or conduct of the licensee or the minor nature of the grant or variation application would not ordinarily be treated as exceptions, and that if the application was granted as an exception to policy, guideline terminal hours would normally be followed.[8]

13.13 The policy stated that a series of difficulties had arisen from a concentration of licensed premises, the 'cumulative effect' of which was that large numbers of people were in the streets at night causing a number of problems, including large gatherings of people, crimes both on and by visitors, noise nuisance caused by people and vehicles, attraction of unlicensed minicabs, traffic congestion, parking difficulties, littering and fouling. The policy stressed that most of the disturbance was not illegal. Further, it was not only cumulative but largely non-attributable to customers of particular premises. For example, a loud noise may be transient, part of a larger noise and some way from premises, and would almost certainly not be due to an identifiable lapse on the part of an individual operator. The council pointed out that it had put in place a raft of measures to deal with the deteriorating public realm, but that these had not succeeded in eradicating the 'stresses' which had occurred to amenity in the West End. The policy had therefore been put in place to prevent further additions to the 'cumulative stress' caused by existing licensed operations.

13.14 While that policy was itself judicially reviewed, the proceedings were withdrawn before they reached a hearing.

Hence, into the lingua franca of licensing law were introduced the expressions 'cumulative effect', 'stress' and 'saturated'. Naturally, none of these terms was rigorously defined, because they were merely convenient labels to describe the concentration of licensed premises in Westminster in general

---

[8] Full details of the policy are noted in Chapter 10 Section D.

and the West End in particular, which was unique in the UK and possibly the world. By using those terms, Westminster was not attempting to circumscribe the circumstances in which licensing authorities were entitled to take account of the effect of licensed premises on the public realm. Far less was it attempting to limit such circumstances according to whether the effect was direct or indirect, or attributable or unattributable to particular premises, or according to whether licensees were behaving exemplarily or poorly, or whether customers were behaving reasonably or unreasonably once beyond the confines of the premises. However, implicit in the notion of a stress policy is the assumption that authorities may use licensing to attenuate the environmental impact of licensed premises.

13.15   Standing back, the following propositions may be derived from the pre-Act case law:

The pre-Act position

(1)   The licensing authority is entitled to take into account impacts on the neighbourhood by customers emerging from particular premises.

(2)   This may lead to a refusal of a licence or the attachment of conditions even if the premises themselves have been or will be run impeccably.

(3)   The relevant impacts may be taken into account even though individual customers are behaving reasonably, if the cumulative impact of all the customers is such as to cause harm in licensing terms.

(4)   The impact caused by customers from a particular premises may also be aggregated with impacts caused by customers of other premises, provided that it is reasonable to infer that the customers from the particular premises contribute to the overall impact.

(5)   The overall impact may be considered even if individual incidents are unattributable to particular premises.

(6)   The licensing authority may formulate a policy containing a strong presumption against expansion, and expressly limiting the circumstances which may be characterised as exceptional.

13.16   It is important to note that prior to the *Chorion* case, there was over a century of authority for the proposition that licensing authorities might take into account the effect of a licence on the public realm, and no-one seriously doubted that to be the case. Viewed with an historical eye, *Chorion* did no more than legitimise the notion that cumulative impact could be considered in licensing, and that licensing authorities could put in place presumptive policies to deal with it. It certainly did not originate the notion that licensees might have to accept restrictions on their commercial activities in the community interest: that had been decided by the House of Lords over a century before. Nor did either *Westminster* or *Chorion*, by the adoption of 'cumulative stress' terminology, seek to limit the circumstances in which an impact on the community of licensed premises might be taken into account.

13.17 The issue has been revisited since the implementation of the Licensing Act 2003 in *Luminar Leisure Limited v Wakefield Magistrates' Court* [2008] EWHC 1002 (Admin), in which the first question stated by the magistrates' court for the opinion of the High Court was 'Was it open to the court to take into account issues relating to crime and disorder away from the proposed premises and beyond the direct control of the licensee?' However, when the case was ultimately argued in the High Court, counsel for the appellant did not argue that it was not open to the magistrates' court to do so, but merely argued that the latter had attached too much weight to events away from the premises, a proposition which was held not to amount to a point of law at all. It is submitted that counsel was right not to trouble the High Court with the point – there would have been no warrant for the proposition either in the Licensing Act 2003 or in the case law.

13.18 Conversely, there is no authority which states that the exterior activity of departing customers may not be taken into account by the licensing authority in deciding whether any and if so what steps are necessary to promote the licensing objectives. The question, in effect, is how it ever came to be thought that the Licensing Act 2003 was intended to reverse a century of thinking regarding the role of licensing legislation. The answer resides in the evolution of national Guidance.

D THE GUIDANCE

13.19 The above set of authorities, decided in the context of what are now the main licensable activities under the Licensing Act 2003 (liquor, entertainment and late night refreshment), demonstrated clearly that licensing authorities were entitled to refuse or attach conditions to licences on the grounds of the effect of the existence of premises on the public realm, even if there is no issue as to the character of the licensee or the management of the premises.

13.20 Much debate, however, stemmed from the Government's original insistence that licensing should not concern itself with the public realm at all, undoing over a century of thinking on the matter. Its eventual *volte face* on that position caused it to borrow terms such as cumulative stress from the experience of a single local authority, when such terms in any event describe only one of the issues arising in the public realm.

13.21 In early Parliamentary debates, the Government was asked to explain why it had chosen the term 'public nuisance' in the third licensing objective, given the restrictive definition of that term at common law.[9] Baroness Blackstone explained that the word nuisance in the Bill:

> '... refers to noise and other nuisance caused directly from the licensed premises concerned.'[10]

13.22   Baroness Blackstone went on to explain that the Government's intention was that bad behaviour outside the premises fell under the control of other regimes and that it would be wrong to require licensees to deal with such behaviour which was beyond their control.[11] She explained that the Government was keen to avoid undermining key policy objectives such as increased diversity of late-night provision and a reduction of disorder associated with artificial fixed closing times.[12]

13.23   Thus, arguably, the fact that the Government had selected a single policy tool for dealing with nuisance and disorder – lengthening terminal hours – was skewing the development of coherent policies in relation to the control of nuisance. In similar vein, Lord Davies explained that litter was not to be a licensing issue, since the licensee had no control over where the customer deposited it. He stated that:

> '... protection of the environment is an important issue. But it does not come within the scope of this Bill.'[13]

13.24   The philosophy, therefore, was to confine the scrutiny of licensing to the interior of the premises. Relaxation of terminal hours was seen as a panacea for most ills, with the remainder to be dealt with under other legislation. While that explained the selection of the term 'public nuisance' over nuisance, it was hard to see how even that could ever have deprived licensing authorities of the right, let alone the duty, of considering the impact of licensed premises on the public realm.

13.25   One pauses to observe that had the Government's intention carried through, it would have reversed what is demonstrated above to have been a consistent line of authority since the 19th century that disturbance in the public realm is a licensing matter. Further, the approach confuses the issue of whether a licence might be refused or conditions imposed to mitigate the harm from those departing premises (which may be appropriate) and whether a licensee can be required to intervene in the street to prevent the behaviour (which is inappropriate).

13.26   During the Committee stages of the Bill, the *Westminster* example arose recurrently, with peers expressing concern that under the new regime

---

9   See Chapter 9 (The General Duties of Licensing Authorities), Section B (The Licensing Objectives).

10   HL Debs, 17 December 2002, Col 559.

11   Col 560.

12   Col 562.

13   Col 618.

cumulative effect would be disregarded.[14] The Association of Chief Police Officers made a telling and influential submission:

> 'There comes a time when saturation point is reached and the addition of any further licensed premises has the potential to considerably exacerbate existing problems of crime and disorder. We feel that both the police and the local authority, bearing in mind its responsibilities under the Crime and Disorder Act, should be able to raise objections based specifically on the additional and cumulative impact of a new premises on the crime and disorder problems in the area'.[15]

13.27 The Government's response was initially that such matters were properly the province of other regimes, particularly planning. However, the Government ultimately conceded the point when the first draft Guidance was published in January 2003. Baroness Blackstone stated:

> 'In effect, we have made it clear in the guidance that licensing authorities will be able to take into account saturation or cumulative effect where it exists. They will be able, for example, to make clear in their statements of licensing policy, which will be subject to consultation, that an area could cope with no more premises of a particular type and that there would be a general presumption against granting any more licences for premises of that type.'[16]

13.28 While that was a victory of sorts for those who had been concerned at the emasculation of licensing, it further skewed the political discourse. For while cumulative effect describes one way in which licensing can affect the public realm, it is not concerned with the more common or garden case of single premises causing a direct impact on a locality, despite the best endeavours of its management. As to that, Baroness Blackstone informed the House:[17]

> 'What the Bill is not designed to address, however, is the behaviour of patrons after they have left the vicinity of the premises. I repeat what I said in Committee: it would be neither practical nor reasonable to expect the Bill to do so. It is pretty easy to see how a licensee might encourage sensible, decent and respectful behaviour as individuals are leaving his or her premises, even when they are getting into their cars and driving away. However, that influence becomes quickly attenuated. It is at that point that the onus for good conduct should fall squarely on the individual, and it is on the individual that enforcement efforts should be focused.
>
> The licensee can and should demand good behaviour from customers while they are on or in the vicinity of the premises. He or she can

---

[14]   See in particular HL Debs, 12, 17 and 19 December 2002.
[15]   HL Debs, 19 December 2002, Col 810.
[16]   HL Debs, 24 February 2003, Col 104.
[17]   HL Debs, 24 February 2003, Col 78.

encourage and request his or her customers to behave when they are beyond the scope of such demands—when they are on the way home or going to another venue. However, he or she cannot exert absolute control over individuals when they have left the vicinity of the premises and are, for example, several hundred yards away. That is why the Government are equipping the police with additional tools to control anti-social behaviour.'

13.29   Reflecting the dividing line in Government thinking between cumulative and non-cumulative effects, the draft Guidance published by the Government in January 2003 did indeed make provision for the consideration of cumulative impact. But it stated that it arose 'in a small number of city centres, where the number, type and density of premises selling alcohol are unusual, [and where] serious problems of nuisance and disorder have sometimes arisen or begun to arise outside or some distance from licensed premises.'

13.30   As to the more usual problem of impact from customers leaving individual licensed premises, the draft Guidance indicated that local policy statements should make clear that licensing law 'is not a mechanism for the general control of anti-social behaviour by individuals once they are beyond the direct control' of the management.

13.31   The effect, therefore, was that the only circumstance in which licensing could exercise influence over the public realm was where impacts from premises were cumulative with impacts from other premises. Given that the purpose of the exercise is to protect the public from harm, the logic behind such a stricture is unclear, but explicable only by reference to the genesis of the draft Guidance.

13.32   Even Baroness Blackstone's concession apparently went unrecognised by the Minister for Tourism, Film and Broadcasting, Dr Kim Howells, who spoke for the Government in the first debate in the House of Commons, stating that:

> 'Providing powers to refuse new licences on the grounds of saturation would provide an undesirable skew in favour of older, established premises, some of which might themselves be the focus of disorder.'[18]

13.33   Notwithstanding that, the limited concession as to cumulative impact remained in all subsequent editions of the draft Guidance, including the final version approved by Parliament in the summer of 2004.[19]

13.34   After further debate, the Government accepted that licensing might have a part to play in the public realm in circumstances falling short of

[18]   HC Debs, 24 March 2003, Col 121.
[19]   HL Debs, 8 June 2004, Col 246.

cumulative stress. On 19 June 2003 Lord McIntosh stated that public nuisance was to have a wide common law definition.[20] This acceptance that the term is to be construed widely was the Government's final concession: that licensing might, after all, concern itself with the public realm. The acceptance that impact in the public realm is a licensing matter was then reflected in the final draft of the Guidance, whose main tenets were as follows:

1. Licensing is about the regulation of licensable activities.
2. Conditions should focus on matters in the control of licensees.
3. Licensing authorities should primarily focus on direct impacts in the area concerned.
4. Licensing is not the primary mechanism for control of behaviour by individuals once beyond the licensee's direct control. But it is a key aspect of such control and licensing will always be part of a holistic approach to management of the night time economy.

These sentiments have remained part of the DNA of Guidance, and can still be found in Guidance today.[21]

13.35 At this stage, it is important to refer to two qualifications. First, the further the distance between the premises and the conduct complained of, the more difficult it is to show that the nuisance has anything to do with the premises, and so the harder it would be to justify any regulatory limitation on the premises' activities. Second, conduct far from the premises is controllable in other ways, for example by police intervention or by better town centre management of dispersal. Therefore it may simply be disproportionate to limit the activities of the premises on the basis of such conduct. However, this goes to the correct balance to be struck in the individual case. It does not go to whether it is appropriate to take such conduct into account at all. Where the premises' activities are the cause or anticipated cause of public nuisance or any other harm to the licensing objectives, then the Act permits authorities to intervene to take the steps appropriate to avert the harm. Nothing in Guidance prevents that conclusion.

13.36 The Guidance has always made it clear that conditions should be focused on measures within the direct control of the licensee. The current Guidance states:

'Conditions attached to various authorisations will be focused on matters which are within the control of individual licence holders and others with relevant authorisations, i.e. the premises and its vicinity.'[22]

13.37 That does not, however, mean that an authority may not require premises to close at an earlier hour or take other measures within the control

---

20 HC Debs, 19 June 2003, Col 913.
21 See Guidance (October 2012), paras 2.24, 13.13.
22 Para 13.12.

of the licensee to prevent nuisance. It means that conditions cannot require the licensee to exercise dominion over the wider public realm. An analogy may be given of a factory emitting smoke. A planning condition could not require the landowner to try to collect up the smoke once it has been emitted. But it could require the landowner not to emit the smoke in the first place. In the case of licensing, Guidance gives an example of placing 'respect the neighbours' notices near the exit, even though the conduct of customers beyond the immediate area surrounding the premises is a matter of individual responsibility.[23]

E CONCLUSION

13.38   An analysis of the Act, the case law and the Guidance demonstrates the fallacy of the proposition that licensing is not concerned with nuisance or other harms to the licensing objectives in the public realm which are caused by the operation of the premises. While there may be other measures available to deal with such harms, the existence of which falls to be taken into account, and while the causal link may be harder to show where the harm does not arise upon the licensed premises, there is no principle of law that requires such harm (or anticipated harm) to be ignored.

13.39   Were it otherwise, much of the effect of the Licensing Act 2003 would be emasculated. Some of the main issues in our towns and cities arise not within the controlled environments of licensed premises but in the relatively uncontrolled environment outside, particularly in mixed use or residential areas where people are trying to sleep during the dispersal period. The Licensing Act 2003 is able to deal with the cause of such problems. Other measures, such as policing and town centre dispersal policies, can only try to mitigate their effect, which is often an uphill task. The conclusion, therefore, that licensing does concern itself with the impact of activities on the local environment whatever the causal link is not only legally correct but carries the imprimatur of common sense.

[23]   See para 2.24.

14

Opening hours under the Licensing Act 2003[1]

HURRY UP PLEASE ITS TIME
Goodnight Bill. Goodnight Lou. Goodnight May. Goodnight.
Ta ta. Goodnight. Goodnight.
Good night, ladies, good night, sweet ladies, good night, good night

The Waste Land
TS Eliot

A INTRODUCTION

14.01 The fact that the status of opening hours under the Licensing Act 2003 could form a credible topic in a licensing textbook is an indictment of the legislative provisions themselves. The lack of clarity in the Licensing Act 2003 is exemplified by section 172, which permits the Secretary of State to extend 'opening hours' for special occasions, one such being the recent royal wedding. However, 'opening hours' is defined in section 172(5) as meaning the times during which the premises may be used for licensable activities. This is to conflate licensing hours and opening hours, when in fact these are different concepts altogether.

14.02 The history of closing times may be briefly stated. Under the Licensing Act 1964, the hours of supply of alcohol were statutory, with a prescribed drinking-up time. During transition to the Licensing Act 2003, in some cases drinking-up times were grandfathered onto premises licences, and in some cases they were not. Under the Licensing Act 2003, there are prescribed forms for new licences, provisional statements and variations, whose Box O asks the applicant what hours the premises are to be open to

---

[1]   This Chapter originally appeared as an article in the Journal of Licensing (Institute of Licensing, 2011).

the public. Applicants will sometimes indicate on the form that they intend to remain open to the public for a short period, perhaps 30 or 60 minutes, following the terminal hours for sale of alcohol. In some cases, this is translated by the licensing authority into a condition regarding opening and closing times. In others it is not. Is it open to an authority to do so?

14.03   The first, and probably last, word on this topic must be the judgment of Black J in *R (Daniel Thwaites plc) v Wirral Borough Magistrates' Court*[2] who made it quite clear that it is open to the licensing authority to regulate hours of opening. She said:

'67. I have considered quite separately the argument as to whether the hours of opening can be regulated as part of the licensing of premises as opposed to the hours during which licensable activities take place. It was suggested during argument that there was no power to regulate the time by which people must leave the premises. I cannot agree with this. Clearly keeping premises open (as opposed to providing entertainment or supplying alcohol there) is not a licensable activity as such. However, the operating schedule which must be supplied with an application for a premises licence must include a statement of the matters set out in section 17(4) and these include not only the times when it is proposed that the licensable activities are to take place but also "any other times during which it is proposed that the premises are to be open to the public". On a new grant of a premises licence, where there are no representations the licensing authority has to grant the application subject only to such conditions as are consistent with the operating schedule. I see no reason why, if it is necessary to promote the licensing objectives, these conditions should not include a provision requiring the premises to be shut by the time that is specified in the operating schedule. If representations are made and the licensing authority ultimately grants the application, it can depart from the terms set out in the operating schedule when imposing conditions in so far as this is necessary for the promotion of the licensing objectives. It must follow that it can impose an earlier time for the premises to be locked up than the applicant wished and specified in its operating schedule. It is important to keep in mind in this regard that the role of the licensing authority and, if there is an appeal, the court, has two dimensions: the fundamental task is to license activities which require a licence and the associated task is to consider what, if any, conditions are imposed on the applicant to ensure the promotion of the licensing objectives. A requirement that the premises close at a particular time seems to me to be a condition just like any other, such as keeping doors and windows closed to prevent noise. I see no reason why a condition of closing up the premises at a particular time should not therefore be imposed where controlling the hours of the licensable activities on the premises (and such other conditions as may be imposed) is not sufficient to promote the licensing objectives.'

14.04 The real issue is not whether it is open to an authority to specify the opening and closing times on the licence, but the legal consequences of having done so.

14.05 Where there is no opening or closing time placed on the licence, then plainly the premises can remain open for whatever hours the licensee wishes. The issue comes where the licensing authority does place opening and closing times on the licence. Particular instances include the following:

(a) The licence has an opening time of 10 am. The licensee wishes to open to serve breakfast, but not to conduct any other licensable activity, at 7 am. Would s/he be committing a criminal offence?

(b) Late night refreshment premises have a licence which permits the provision of late night refreshment from 11 pm to 3 am, and then requires the premises to close at 3.30 am. Would the licensee be committing a criminal offence by remaining open, though not for the provision of late night refreshment, thereafter?

(c) Premises have a premises licence which authorises, say, the sale of alcohol. On some days the licensee does not sell alcohol, eg because s/he rents out a room on a dry hire basis. Is the licensee bound by licence conditions, including closing hours?

14.06 The reason why these situations do not admit of an easy answer is because it is not an offence under the Act to breach a licence condition, much less to open the premises to the public outwith the hours specified on the licence. Instead, section 136 of the Act provides that it is an offence if a person:

'(a) ... carries on or attempts to carry on a licensable activity on or from any premises other than under and in accordance with an authorisation, or

(b) he knowingly allows a licensable activity to be so carried on.'

14.07 Plainly, the *actus reus* under (a) is carrying on or attempting to carry on the licensable activity. Under (b) it is knowingly allowing the activity to be carried on. In other words, it is not *per se* an offence to do something prohibited by a condition. It is an offence to carry on the licensable activity, or knowingly allow the activity to be carried on, in breach of the condition.

14.08 In considering the legal status of opening and closing hours, it is important to state that they could only have legal force as conditions on the licence. A licence confers the right to do something which would otherwise be unlawful, eg selling alcohol. If one does that beyond the hours permitted by the licence, then that is a breach of section 136 because one would be doing so otherwise than <u>under</u> the authorisation. A licence may also impose conditions on the authorisation, eg by preventing the playing of amplified music other than through a noise limitation device. To play amplified music without using such a device would be to do so otherwise than <u>in accordance with</u> the authorisation.

14.09   These seemingly banal points are made to underscore the fact that there is no other way of committing an offence under section 136. Thus, a closing hour need not coincide with the terminal licensing hour. Even where it does coincide it is always specified separately from the terminal licensing hour. Thus closure is a separate concept from the terminal hour for licensing. Therefore, if it has any force, it can only conceivably have force as a condition on the licence.

B   THE LEGAL ENFORCEABILITY OF OPENING HOURS

14.10   With those essentially preliminary comments in mind, we can now approach the question of the legal enforceability of opening hours. The argument proceeds in stages.

14.11   First of all, when there is a condition which specifically limits the licensable activity, then it is plain that this is caught by section 136. For example, a pub has a condition that alcohol must be sold in polycarbonates. An outdoor festival has a licence which prevents music being played above a certain decibel level. In these cases, there is no doubt whatsoever but that the licence is governed by the condition and breach of the condition is an offence under section 136.

14.12   The second proposition is that the condition does not have to circumscribe the licensable activity itself in order for a breach to engage section 136. For example, there is a condition requiring a pub to use door staff to control who comes in. That is not a limitation on the sale of alcohol. It is a control of the circumstances in which alcohol is sold. If alcohol is sold when no door staff are on, that amounts to carrying on the licensable activity otherwise than in accordance with the authorisation.

14.13   The third area for scrutiny concerns conditions which go further in that they do not circumscribe the licensable activity <u>and</u> are not contemporaneous with such activity. For example, there might be a condition preventing emptying of bottles outside at night, or preventing deliveries before a particular time in the morning, or requiring a take away restaurant to sweep up outside after the premises close.

14.14   In all these cases, it is doubtful that anyone would suggest that the conditions are not enforceable. Indeed, were they not to be enforceable, a great many conditions imposed under the Licensing Act 2003 would be ineffective except in terms of their persuasive force and as a basis for the bringing of a review when they are breached. However, that there is a collective consensus that a category of conditions is enforceable and is regularly imposed is not a sufficient basis to say that section 136 is engaged. Those involved with licensing may simply be acting on custom and practice, without specifically turning their mind to the enforceability of the conditions. The question is why such conditions are enforceable. For example if a delivery were to be made at 5 am, 5 hours after the premises closed and 5 hours before it re-opens, could it be said that there are licensable activities being carried on otherwise than under and in accordance with the licence?

14.15 In truth, the enforceability of such conditions under section 136 is somewhat problematic. The argument could be made that section 136 does not require precise contemporaneity between the licensable activity and the condition. So if, for example, premises close at midnight and open the following morning at 10 am but breach their conditions by taking a noisy delivery at 5 am then their offence is carrying out the licensable activities throughout the whole period (ie the day before and the day after). In other words they are selling alcohol while accepting delivery of the alcohol at forbidden times.

14.16 However, that argument might be thought to stretch language quite close to breaking point in significant regards. Imagine that in the situation just described the premises do not in fact open the following day. How could it be said that the premises had traded on the previous day otherwise than in accordance with the licence when at the time they were trading they were not in breach of the licence, the breach of the licence only coming five hours later?

14.17 These arguments are finely balanced. However, it is submitted that a court would come down in favour of enforcement of the condition under section 136. The rationale would be that the premises are in general carrying on licensable activities while not adhering to the conditions subject to which those licensable activities were permitted. Having regard to the mischief at which section 136 is aimed, the construction of the section is sufficiently wide that contemporaneity is not required.

14.18 With those propositions in mind, one may turn to consider one kind of condition – a condition which requires the premises to close at some point following the termination of licensable activities and/or which specifies an opening hour at some point prior to the provision of licensable activities.

14.19 For the reasons just given, it is submitted that on narrow balance a condition of that nature would be enforceable under section 136. To take but one example, what if a licence to sell alcohol is conferred, but subject to the stricture that the customers to whom the product is sold must be off the premises with the doors closed within 30 minutes of the terminal hour? It is submitted that such a condition could be enforced by prosecution.

14.20   However, not all situations are so simple. What of the pub which dutifully closes 30 minutes after selling the last pint, but then wishes to open again to sell coffee and croissants at 8 am the following morning, in other words for an activity which is nothing to do with licensable activities? Probably, this is where the relevant line is to be drawn. Where a condition requires premises to close at the end of trading hours, that is a way of limiting the impact of the licensable activities themselves. Beyond that what the proprietor chooses to do with the premises is not a matter for licensing.

14.21   In reality, it would be rarely if ever that a licensing authority could attach a condition which expressly purported to control the use of premises in general outside the licensing hours in relation to activities which are not licensable activities. Therefore, the question really boils down to whether upon construction a licence which imposes a closing hour imposes require-ments or prohibitions upon a licensee in relation to commercial activities which are not licensable activities at all. It is submitted that it does not. Or, rather, in the absence of some very express language, it does not. The purpose of a licence condition is to provide the requirements and prohib-itions subject to which a party is permitted to provide licensable activities. Without very specific language, it is hard to contemplate that a condition could be construed so as to limit the ability of operators to conduct activities on premises which have nothing to do with licensable activities.

14.22   Coming back to one of the examples above, what of the pub which supplies coffee and croissants in the morning? It does not need anybody's permission to do that. It is hard to see that it could somehow lose permission by virtue of asking for a licence to sell beer in the evening. There may well be some grey shading. What of the pub, for example, which closed but then re-opened five minutes later to serve the coffee and croissants? As it happens, that is arguably an effective breach of the closure condition because the condition is designed to dissipate the clientele who have been purchasing alcohol, and a brief, technical closure does not satisfy the condition. However, the fact that one can think of examples which challenge the application of the rule does not mean that there is no rule. While an attempt to circumvent a condition, e g by closing and then immediately re-opening, may well be considered to be a breach, that does not mean that conducting activity which has nothing whatsoever to do with the licensable activity and at a different hour from the licensable activities would be held to breach a condition which is intended to govern the impact from licensable activities.

C CONCLUSION

14.23   In conclusion, a condition which is designed to control the impact of the licensable activities is enforceable under section 136, even though the condition requires or prohibits action outside the licensing hours. There is a counter-argument that one cannot be charged with 'carrying on licensable activities' at a time when one is not actually carrying on licensable activities;

and that if that conclusion is inconvenient then the remedy lies with Parliament by way of legislative amendment rather than with the courts by way of linguistic distortion. However, for the reasons set out above, the argument that a closing time imposed on a licence is enforceable under section 136 is to be preferred.

14.24 Nevertheless, when directed at activities which are not only outside the licensing hours but which have nothing to do with the licensable activities, a much clearer answer appertains. In that situation, a general closing or opening hour on the licence is designed to control the licensable activities and their impact and it is not appropriate to construe it so as to restrict other activities altogether.

14.25 Therefore, the pub may serve its coffee in the morning without offending the conditions on the licence. The function room can have its dry hire, and if the room is not used pursuant to the licence, the licence conditions do not apply. The late night refreshment premises can operate out of hours. However, it should avoid action which amounts to a thinly veiled attempt to find a loophole to the condition. For example, if the condition is to close at 3 am, the premises should not re-open with the same customers at 3.05 am. However, the operator would have a good argument that nothing prevents it from opening for cold drinks and sandwiches at 4 am, an hour after the customers served hot food have disappeared – ie there is no reason or logic why a licence condition should be construed to place the business at a disadvantage to another premises selling cold food all through the night.

14.26 The Act could have been framed much more simply, permitting authorities to stipulate opening and closing times for licensed premises and making it an offence to open beyond such hours. In the absence of such legislative clarity, it is inevitable that legal argument ensues. However, a conclusion that opening and closing times can never be enforced is not only legally untenable but would drive a coach and horses through the community protection role of the Act, and so would not be contemplated by the appellate courts.

Licensing Act 2003: Regime

'Come Darcy, I must have you dance. I hate to see you standing about by yourself in this stupid manner. You had much better dance.'

'I certainly shall not. You know how I detest it, unless I am particularly acquainted with my partner. At such an assembly as this, it would be insupportable. Your sisters are engaged, and there is not another woman in this room, whom it would not be a punishment to me to stand up with.'

Assembly room in *Pride and Prejudice* (Jane Austen, 1813)

'You dancing?'
'You asking?'
'I'm asking'
'I'm dancing'

Nightclub in Liverpool, *Liver Birds* (BBC, 1969)

The premises licence

'D'you call, Sir?'
'Call Sir? What a plague – Egad 'tis a pretty Girl – Heark you Child, do
you serve Travellers upon the Road here?'
'Yes sir.'
'Kiss me then.'
'That's the Chambermaid's business.'

The Stage Coach, George Farquhar

A INTRODUCTION

15.01 Premises licences account for over 90% of permanent authorisations
for licensable activities in England and Wales. As at 31 March 2012 there
were approximately 202,000 premises licences compared with approximately
15,900 club premises certificates.[1] These proportions have not changed
substantially since 2008 when comparable records began.[2] The nature,
extent and location of premises licences are limited only by the imagination
and finances of their holders and the extent of local opposition by residents
or responsible authorities to the activities proposed. Pubs, nightclubs and
restaurants account for a large proportion, but the list is almost endless.
There are castles, zoos, canal boats, burger vans and corner shops all of

---

[1]   Home Office, 'Alcohol and Late Night Refreshment Licensing England and Wales
       2011/12'.
[2]   Although the number of club premises certificate has decreased by 6% since 2010.

whose activities are authorised by a premises licence. There are holiday parks whose various pubs, nightclubs, shops and other entertainment come under the umbrella of a single premises licence and there are other holiday parks which may possess a licence for each individual location within the park. Some large scale music festivals apply for a completely new premises licence every year; others have a 'rolling' licence where the consultation and preparation process for each annual festival is codified in the conditions of the licence itself. There are premises licences with no conditions whatsoever save for the mandatory conditions, and there are licences with over a hundred conditions which no-one in their right mind could either remember or comply with. Many of these are standard public entertainment licence conditions carried over from the former regime; others are the now confusing 'embedded restrictions' carried over from the old justices' licences and governing such diverse and antiquated concepts as under 14's in a bar and the restricted hours for opening on Christmas day.[3] There are even premises licences whose standard public entertainment licence conditions are not attached by the licensing authority to the licence at all; and areas identified on plans 'edged green' originally referred to on a justices' licence, without a copy being attached to the premises licence!

15.02   There are almost certainly premises licences under which the holder is presently trading that are completely void due to the previous lapsing of the licence during the insolvency of a former premises licence holder. In many of these cases neither the present holder nor the authorities will have the slightest clue that the premises is trading unlawfully – but that does not mean that the premises licence is not void.

15.03   There are premises licences that are considered of little or no intrinsic value *per se* and others that have been sold in their own right (ie disregarding the value of the business) at tens of thousands of pounds. This trend is likely to continue, particularly in areas in which cumulative impact policies are rigidly enforced and extended and where the prospect of obtaining a new licence outside of core hours or activities is virtually nil.[4]

15.04   Despite their limitations, premises licences are generally flexible, essential to those in the commercial licensed trade, and sometimes of a great intrinsic value. The rapid development of case law, legislation and practice reflects this.

B   PLAYERS

15.05   The licensing system exists so as to ensure that licensed premises promote the licensing objectives. The public and private interests involved

---

3   See the first edition of this book, Appendix 9.
4   For an example, see *R (on the Application of A3D2 Ltd (T/A Novus Leisure)) v Westminster Magistrates' Court* [2011] EWHC 1045(Admin).

are represented by the players who are given a stake by the Licensing Act in the promotion of those objectives.

The relevant licensing authority

15.06 The 'relevant authority' is the licensing authority in whose area the premises in question are situated.[5] Where premises straddle two or more licensing authority boundaries, section 12 of the Act makes provision for determining which area the premises are situated in. Where a greater part of the premises is situated in one licensing authority area then this authority is the relevant licensing authority for the premises. In areas where the premises are located equally in two or more areas, the applicant may choose the authority. This is clearly a rarity, but given the ability for licensing authorities to set their own fee levels[6] and the different policies which may apply in adjoining areas, this particular provision may on occasion be scrutinised by operators. The licensing authority plays the central role in the regime, publishing its licensing policy, setting its fee levels, delegating decision-making to the appropriate level, processing applications, making decisions, enforcing the regime and imposing late night levies and early morning restriction orders.

Authorised persons

15.07 'Authorised persons' are bodies empowered by the Act to carry out inspection and enforcement roles and include those persons set out at section 13(2)(a)–(f) of the Act. This includes the police, officers of the licensing authority, Fire Authority inspectors, inspectors responsible for the enforcement of the Health & Safety at Work etc Act 1974 and environmental health officers. In relation to a vessel, an authorised person is an inspector or surveyor of ships appointed under section 256 of the Merchant Shipping Act 1995.

Responsible authorities

15.08 The number of authorities classed as 'responsible authorities' has increased as a consequence of sections 104 and 105 of the Police Reform & Social Responsibility Act 2011. All responsible authorities are public bodies that must be notified of and are entitled to make representations to a licensing authority in relation to applications for a grant, variation or review of a premises licence. They are as follows:

(1)   The chief officer of police.

---

[5]   Licensing Act 2003, s 12.
[6]   Licensing Act 2003, s 197A.

(2) The local Fire Authority.
(3) The local Enforcement Agency for the Health & Safety at Work etc Act 1974.
(4) The local Planning Authority.
(5) The local body recognised by the licensing authority responsible for, or interested in, matters relating to the protection of children from harm.
(6) The local authority responsible for environmental health.
(7) The relevant licensing authority and any other licensing authority in whose area part of the premises is situated.[7]
(8) In relation to a vessel the relevant Navigation Authority, Environment Agency, British Waterways Board, Secretary of State or other person prescribed for the purpose of the Act.
(9) The Primary Care Trust or Local Health Board for any area in which the premises are situated.[8]
(10) The Local Weights & Measures Authority (Trading Standards) for any area in which the premises is situated.[9]

15.09 The new power for the relevant licensing authority to object to applications, and indeed call for reviews, in respect of which it would also sit as the determining authority is seen as another turn of the screw by many operators. However, the position is not a novel one. It has already been trialled under the Gambling Act 2005[10] without apparently adverse consequences. While it is anticipated that the majority of representations will still emanate from other responsible authorities with defined roles such as health and safety and environmental health, this is not to say that the licensing authority itself will not have a positive role to play.

15.10 In particular, first of all, it may act as a guardian of its own licensing policy, drawing the attention of the licensing sub-committee to any proposed departure. This is very much in keeping with the golden thread described in Chapter 4. It may of course be that another stakeholder makes a similar point, but compliance with the policy should not turn on the happenstance of such objection. It is the job of the licensing authority to ensure that its own policy is followed, and if it is not then the licensing sub-committee should be given the opportunity to consider whether there should be a departure or not.

15.11 Second, the licensing authority has a statutory role to play in prosecution for breaches of the licence. It is right that it should also have a role in enforcing licence conditions through licence reviews, and in bringing

---

[7] Licensing Act 2003, s 13(4) as amended by the Police Reform & Social Responsible Act, s 104(1)(2).
[8] Licensing Act 2003, s 13(4) as amended by the Police Reform & Social Responsible Act 2011, s 105(1)(3).
[9] Inserted by the Licensing Act 2003 (Premises licences and club premises certificates) Regulations 2005 reg 7 under the enabling provisions of Licensing Act 2003, s 13(4)(i).
[10] Gambling Act 2005, s 157.

past breaches of licence conditions to the attention of the licensing sub-committee when this is relevant to a decision which it is called upon to make. It may do so through the medium of its new status as a responsible authority.

15.12 Third, it frequently happens that licensing sub-committees lack thorough advice as to possibilities for resolution of licensing conflicts. A licence applicant may not wish to proffer conditions because of the administrative and economic burden such conditions cause. A residential objector may not wish to suggest conditions because they believe it will weaken their case that the licence should be refused. This may mean that the authority refuses a licence which, with proper advice, it may have granted with conditions, leaving the matter to be sorted out at great expense on appeal. The licensing authority, participating in the hearing as a responsible authority, may play a salutary role of advising the sub-committee as to the means by which a perceived harm to the licensing objectives can be avoided.

15.13 The mere fact that the licensing authority is entitled to make representations does not mean that it should in all cases. However, there will be cases where the authority can play a positive, constructive role and it is to be hoped that licensing officers will take up the challenge of bringing their knowledge and experience to bear upon the licensing process, just as their planning colleagues have done in planning applications for many decades. There is a fear amongst industry operators that where the licensing authority chooses to participate in front of sub-committees of councillors who may have appointed the officer in the first place, then the only option for the premises licence holder will be to lie prostrate at the throne of the licensing authority and sue for mercy. However, a better view is that the licensing sub-committee will weigh up the representations of all parties, whatever their status, and reach the conclusion which is most appropriate for the promotion of the licensing objectives.

15.14 One particular consequence of making the licensing authority a responsible authority is that there will need to be a separation of functions between the licensing officer who makes a representation on an application and the officer responsible for processing the application and advising the sub-committee. The officer participating as a responsible authority needs to be kept at arm's length in the same way as any other participant in the licensing process. It is for the licensing authority to establish processes and procedures to make sure this happens and, just as importantly, demonstrate that it happens.[11]

15.15 The prospect of Primary Care Trusts and Local Health Boards being responsible authorities is likely to be a different matter. Such bodies are unlikely to have strong views about particular premises, and are unlikely to possess the sort of records (apart from perhaps ambulance call out notes)

---

[11]   See further Guidance paras 9.17–9.18.

that can usefully be distilled into direct evidence against the premises licence holder without extensive analysis which, due to resourcing limitations, many are unwilling to carry out. This is not to say that health authorities could never play a role in licensing. Accident and emergency departments pick up significantly more incidents of alcohol-related crime and disorder than the police. Were such departments to question patients as to the location of the incident they may well be able to assemble good information as to alcohol-related violence hotspots which could be fed into the licensing process, whether at the policy formulation stage or in response to applications for licences in stress areas. The new national Alcohol Strategy[12] contemplates that a hospital which is regularly dealing with patients at A&E as a result of alcohol-related violence at a particular pub will now be able to instigate a review of the licence at those premises.[13] While the theory holds sound, the accumulation of data at this level of specificity would require a change of practice and a devotion of resources within most health authorities. This is, however, precisely what is contemplated by national Guidance.[14]

15.16   In relation to vessels, a 'responsible authority' means: a Navigation Authority having functions where the vessel is usually moored, or any waters where it is navigated when used for a licensable activity; the Environment Agency; the British Waterways Board or the Secretary of State.

15.17   The police's role as a responsible authority is an important one, because they have a far greater knowledge of what actually happens on the street and in licensed premises at night than any other authority. Accordingly their views, when properly formulated and evidence-based, are entitled to, and for the most part receive, great respect. They are the only authority entitled to object to designated premises supervisors and personal licence applications, and one of only two allowed to object to temporary event notices. This reflects the crucial role they play in the prevention of crime and disorder in and around licensed premises.

15.18   There was a proposal, however, to upgrade their status to that of a 'super authority'; albeit not through statute, but by national Guidance. The original suggestion, contained in the consultation document preceding the Police Reform and Social Responsibility Bill[15] was to amend the legislation to require licensing authorities to accept all representations and notices and to adopt all recommendations from the police, unless there is clear evidence that these are not relevant. By the time of the Government's response to the consultation, the proposal was that the Guidance should be amended to make it clear to licensing authorities that there should be a presumption that

12   Cm 8336.
13   Cm 8336, para 3.17.
14   Paras 9.20–9.21.
15   'Rebalancing the Licensing Act, A consultation on empowering individuals, families and local communities to shape and determine local licensing' (Home Office, 2010), para 5.05.

all reasonable recommendations from the police should be accepted unless there is clear evidence to the contrary.[16] Against continuing disquiet from many quarters, including the police themselves, many of whom do not wish to be given special status, the eventual Guidance was diluted still further, so that it now reads:

> 'The licensing authority should accept all reasonable and proportionate representations made by the police unless the authority has evidence that to do so would not be appropriate for the promotion of the licensing objectives. However, it remains incumbent on the police to ensure that their representations can withstand the scrutiny to which they would be subject at a hearing.'[17]

15.19 The Guidance is now so dilute as to be practically devoid of effect. If any responsible authority made reasonable and proportionate representations, one would expect them to be accepted unless there is evidence suggesting that to do so would not be appropriate for promotion of the licensing objectives. It adds little to the sensible advice contained in the first part of the paragraph, which builds on Guidance which has stood for many years:

> 'In their role as a responsible authority, the police are an essential source of advice and information on the impact and potential impact of licensable activities, particularly on the crime and disorder objective. The police have a key role in managing the night-time economy and should have good working relationships with those operating in their local area. The police should be the licensing authority's main source of advice on matters relating to the promotion of the crime and disorder licensing objective, but may also be able to make relevant representations with regards to the other licensing objectives if they have evidence to support such representations.'

15.20 A system which depends upon the participation and partnership of a large range of stakeholders loses credibility if, other than legislatively, it purports to accord preferential status to any single player. Had the original proposal been carried through, it would not only have skewed the licensing process but gone some way to achieving a delegation of responsibility from the licensing authority to the police. Thankfully, the Guidance as drafted has softened the original proposal to the extent that it cannot be said to have that, or indeed any significant, effect.

Other persons

15.21 The 'Interested Party' is dead, long live the 'Other Person'. The concept of 'vicinity' is buried alongside. The other person is a body or

---

[16] 'Responses to Consultation: Rebalancing The Licensing Act', para 13.
[17] Para 9.12.

individual who is entitled to make representations to licensing authorities on applications for the grant, variation or review of a premises licence. The removal of the requirement to show vicinity means that any person, body or business, whether or not they live in the vicinity or even the local authority area, will be able to make a representation or bring an application for review. The benefit of this is that it will enable the democratic participation in the licensing process of those who use town centres without living or working there, together with others who have a vested interest in their control and development such as civic and amenity groups, prospective investors, tourism authorities, the British Transport Police and so forth. The fear amongst operators is that it will also allow campaigners, including temperance campaigners, to interfere in the process at an industrial scale, according power without responsibility, adding to the length, cost and complexity of hearings and deterring investment. The tool for handling unwanted interference is quite a blunt one, in the form of the ability of the licensing authority to ignore representations which are either frivolous or vexatious.[18] The first of these really only relates to representations which are wholly lacking in seriousness or substance. The second only arises where the purpose of the representation is to inconvenience or annoy rather than to pursue the promotion of the licensing objectives. It is only in an extreme case that either of these criticisms will obtain. Provided that the representation genuinely concerned the promotion of the licensing objectives it would be difficult to rule it out on these grounds. However, in fairness, participation is the price of democracy, and the fear that the system cannot cope remains to be tested. It has not proved to be the case under the planning system, where there is no geographical limit on potential participants.

15.22   In consequence of the ability for any human being to make representations, the specific right for members of the relevant licensing authority to make representations has been abolished.[19] Councillors, for these purposes, now count as other persons.

Designated premises supervisor

15.23   The position of designated premises supervisor ('DPS') was invented by the Licensing Act 2003. The role is not defined by statute, other than the tautologous explanation that s/he is the individual for the time being specified in a premises licence (authorising the sale or supply of alcohol) as the premises supervisor.[20]

---

[18]   See e g Licensing Act 2003, s 18(7)(a), and also Guidance paras 9.5 and 9.6.
[19]   Licensing Act 2003, s 13(3)(e) inserted by the Policing & Crime Act 2009, s 33(1), removed by Police Reform & Social Responsibility Bill, s 105(2)(c).
[20]   Licensing Act 2003, s 15(1).

The following points are worthy of comment:

(1) A designated premises supervisor is required solely in relation to premises where the licensable activities include the supply of alcohol, although community premises may apply for the 'alternative licence condition' to allow the function to be performed by a management committee (see below).

(2) Nothing prevents the premises licence holder also acting as the designated premises supervisor.[21] In small businesses, this is the norm.

3) When there is no designated premises supervisor in respect of a premises licence, no supply of alcohol may be made under that licence.[22]

(4) Where the individual specified as the designated premises supervisor either does not hold a personal licence or his personal licence is suspended, no supply of alcohol may be made under that premises licence.[23]

(5) The designated premises supervisor does not have to be present at the licensed premises at all times.[24]

(6) At any one time, no more than one person may be specified as the designated premises supervisor of particular premises.

(7) A person can be the designated premises supervisor of more than one premises at a time so long as he or she can in practice manage the responsibility for running more than one premises.[25] As the responsible authorities have a legitimate expectation to be able to readily identify – and contact – a named individual in the event of problems, an expectation reinforced by Guidance,[26] the practice of area managers being named a DPS on many licences is not as prevalent as it once was.

(8) Any personal licence holder may authorise the supply of alcohol under the premises licence, not just the DPS; such authorisation to be given in line with the advice set out in the Guidance.[27]

As the Guidance states:

'10.26 The main purpose of the 'designated premises supervisor' as defined in the 2003 Act is to ensure that there is always one specified individual among these personal licence holders who can be readily identified for the premises where a premises licence is in force. That person will normally have been given day to day responsibility for running the premises by the premises licence holder.'

---

[21] Licensing Act 2003, s 15(2).
[22] Licensing Act 2003 ss 19(1), (2)(a).
[23] Licensing Act 2003 ss 19(1), (2)(b).
[24] Guidance para 10.27.
[25] Guidance para 4.24.
[26] Para 4.19.
[27] Paras 10.28–10.34.

15.24   The designated premises supervisor is the premises licence holder's eyes and ears on the premises, the single point of management focus, and the key liaison for the responsible authorities. It is essential that the appointee has effective management control of the premises and is capable of working in a relationship of partnership with statutory agencies so as to ensure the promotion of the licensing objectives.

C APPLYING FOR A PREMISES LICENCE

Who can apply?

15.25   The usual applicant for a licence will be a person who carries on, or proposes to carry on, a business which involves the use of the premises for the licensable activities to which the application relates,[28] but other applicants are listed, including recognised clubs, charities, proprietors of educational institutions, health service bodies and the police. So far as commercial operators are concerned, a 'person' can include both an individual and a company, whether corporate or unincorporated.

15.26   A person 'proposing' to carry on a business involving licensable activities need not establish an actual legal interest in the premises, so long as there is a genuine intention to carry on that business if the application is granted. This is a wide ranging definition. The freehold owner of a corner shop who proposes to run an off-licence will have no problem satisfying this test, nor will the leaseholder of a night club premises who is applying for a new licence as a result of a major refurbishment. Equally, however, freehold owners who have no intention whatsoever of running a business involving licensable activities themselves may still apply for a premises licence if their intention is to lease that premises out to a person who does indeed intend to do so. This position was confirmed by the Administrative Court in *Hall and Woodhouse v The Borough and County of the Town of Poole*.[29] This situation often arises with property owning companies who know nothing about the licensed trade, but wish to market a premises which has the necessary licensing (and no doubt planning) authorisation in order to maximise the interest from potential lessees.

FAQ

Q   Can someone apply for a premises licence even though they can prove no existing or future proprietary interest in the premises in question?

---

[28]   Licensing Act 2003, s 16(1)(a).
[29]   [2009] EWHC 1587 (Admin) at para [24].

A   There is no requirement to establish an actual legal interest in the premises. So long as the individual can satisfy the licensing authority that he proposes to carry on a business which involves the use of the premises for licensable activities to which it relates, s/he should be allowed to make the application.[30] The circumstances of such an application should be looked at broadly by the licensing authority but the decisive factor as to the validity of the application is not any legal interest in the premises, but the intention to use those premises for licensable activities. In the event of a 'hostile' application (perhaps from a former manager or ex-business partner) the lack of ability of that applicant to show (as the case may be) that he has a proprietary interest in the premises and therefore an ability to control what occurs 'on the ground' is likely to result in representations from responsible authorities in any event. Such cases ought to be distinguished from those of contested transfers of premises licences, where the licensing authority may be required to undertake an extensive analysis of the competing interests of the existing premises licence holder and the (hostile) proposed transferee (see below).

Applying for a premises licence

15.27 Applications for a premises licence range from those where full prior, albeit non-statutory, consultation has taken place with responsible authorities and local residents, to urgent applications for existing premises where a previous licence has lapsed and has not been reinstated in time. Despite some operators' hopes to 'stick the application in and hope for the best' the application most likely to result in a premises licence matching the applicants' requirements is one where full pre-consultation has taken place – even with residents. This is certainly envisaged in national Guidance,[31] although a lack of pre-consultation would not invalidate an application.

15.28 In Chapter 4, it was explained that the golden thread of licensing involves the applicant reading the licensing authority's policy when completing the operating schedule, those making relevant representations pointing out any departure from the policy and those judging contested applications using the policy as a benchmark. The 2012 edition of the Guidance takes the matter still further, and positively exhorts the applicant to take a risk assessment approach, to research the local area, analyse how the proposal may impact upon it, and explain to the licensing authority how such impacts are to be ameliorated. It also expects the applicant to explain in the operating schedule how particular provisions in the licensing policy impact on their application; any measures they will take to mitigate the impact; and why they

---

[30]   See also *R v Dudley Crown Court, ex p Roger Pask* (1983) 147 JP 417.
[31]   Paras 8.34–8.42 and 10.4.

consider the application should be an exception to the policy. Those familiar with the preparation of planning statements in the analogous field of town and country planning will not be fazed by this Guidance. It does, admittedly, go far beyond the statutory requirement which is that the operating schedule should merely set out the steps which it is proposed to take to promote the licensing objectives.[32] But in that it involves a far closer initial engagement by the applicant with the policy priorities of the licensing authority and the needs and concerns of the community, it promotes a more competent, sensitive and responsive licensing process, for which it merits commendation. Such engagement ought to lead the applicant to submit operating schedules which identify the risks to the licensing objectives, set out the steps proposed to deal with those risks and explain how local licensing policy impacts upon the proposal. It is not inevitable that the steps will be proffered as licence conditions. An applicant may argue that it can be trusted to take such steps based on its track record without being subject to conditions, or that the steps are already a legal requirement under other legislation. The identification of the requisite measure and the explanation of how it is to be attained is, however, far less likely to attract representations than failure to refer to the measure at all.

15.29   Therefore, in all but the least contentious applications (and perhaps even in those) the applicant would be wise to contact the licensing authority, environmental health officer and the police to explain the nature of the new business and, if necessary, agree conditions to be set out in the operating schedule. Nobody likes a nasty surprise, and for the authorities to receive an application for a 3 am finish nightclub without prior warning is likely to harden their attitude and make compromise less likely. Applicants can often fail to remember that the granting of a premises licence is only the beginning of a long term relationship with the authorities. Equally, the proposal of new conditions during the process to meet the concerns expressed in relevant representations can itself sometimes cause delay for applicants which might easily have been avoided prior to the application going in and diminishes the trust of the licensing authority in the competence of the applicant. Residents often fail to understand the requirements to advertise the full extent of the potential hours of operation (even if these are never intended to be operated), and lack of pre-consultation with neighbours can result in a large number of written representations, many of which are not withdrawn even if post-issue meetings satisfy the residents' concerns. The licensing authority, police and environmental health officer often know the likely main objectors and can assist in such negotiations. No one wants an unnecessary dispute, and co-operation and dialogue are usually the best means of averting one.

---

[32]   Licensing Act 2003, s 17(4).

The application process

15.30 An application for a premises licence must be made in the prescribed form and sent to the relevant licensing authority and be copied to each of the appropriate responsible authorities. The application must be accompanied by:

- the required fee;
- an operating schedule;
- a plan of the premises in a prescribed form; and
- if the application involves the supply of alcohol, the consent of the individual who is to be specified as the designated premises supervisor.[33]

15.31 A notice on pale blue paper must be displayed at or near the premises for a consecutive period of 28 days, and a similar advertisement must be placed in a local newspaper within ten working days commencing on the day after the day that the application is given to the licensing authority.[34]

The operating schedule

15.32 An application for a premises licence is made under section 17 and must be set out in the prescribed form. Where there are no representations, the authority must grant the licence in accordance with the application subject only to such conditions as are consistent with the operating schedule accompanying the application[35] and any mandatory conditions. It is a common misconception by applicants that the operating schedule only commences at Box M where steps are set out to promote the full licensing objectives, and are placed as conditions on the licence. However, the operating schedule actually starts at Part 3 and therefore includes the box requiring a general description of the premises as well as Box K which requires any adult entertainment or services which may give rise to concern in respect of children to be identified. These boxes, together with the boxes in which the individual licensable activities and their hours are set out, form part of the operating schedule and under section 18(2)(a) can legitimately be made conditions so long as they are consistent with that operating schedule. Thus if in Box K an applicant puts 'no' to any adult entertainment or services, this can legitimately be placed as a condition on the licence. Equally, if the box requiring a general description of the premises states that the beer garden will not be used after 2300 hours (even if this is not repeated in the public nuisance box in Box M) then the applicant may find, even in an uncontested application, such a restriction placed as a condition on the licence.

---

[33]   Licensing Act 2003, s 17(3).
[34]   Licensing Act 2003 (Premises Licences And Club Premises Certificates) Regulations 2005, reg 25.
[35]   Licensing Act 2003, s 18(2)(a).

15.33   Common mistakes can include a failure to describe the area where the consumption of off-supplies takes place in the general description, as required in the guidance notes attached to the form. The definition of 'indoors' can include a tent or marquee, a fact which is sometimes overlooked by environmental health officers. The start and finish times should be clearly set out, and if necessary the distinction made between 0000 (the very start of the 24 hour day) and 2400 (exactly the same time, but signifying the end of the 24 hour day) in line with global practice.

15.34   Some applicants for late night licences forget to request the additional hour required when the clocks go forward to protect their existing trading hours. Applicants for hotel licences who may have been out of the trade for some years may be surprised to know that there is no automatic 24 hour drinking for their residents, and this must be specifically applied for.

Live music

15.35   The Live Music Act, which came into force on 1 October 2012, has fundamentally altered the requirements to licence live music in many circumstances.[36] So far as amplified live music is concerned, where a premises licence or club premises certificate permits 'on-sales', is open for the sale or supply of alcohol for consumption on the premises, and live music is taking place between 8 am and 11 pm before an audience of no more than 200 people, then that live music is not a licensable activity and therefore does not require authorisation. Additionally, and subject to the same criteria, any 'live music – related' condition on the licence or certificate does not apply.

15.36   The main beneficiaries of these provisions (which are now set out in a new section 177A and Schedule 1, paragraph 12A of the Licensing Act 2003) are pubs, clubs, night clubs and restaurants. 'Live music' includes any vocal and instrumental music. Any recorded music accompanying this live music (for example backing tracks or sample music in the case of live bands, or music from a karaoke machine) is, in most cases, likely to be considered part of the live music and not therefore requiring separate authorisation as recorded music.[37] An audience will not include performers, technical or security staff, or bar staff.

15.37   The phrase 'live music – related condition' is likely to be interpreted widely given the deregulatory emphasis of the Live Music Act. Conditions which explicitly refer to live music will clearly be suspended, but also conditions which indirectly refer to live music (for example 'all doors and windows to be closed during regulated entertainment') will likewise be suspended if the only form of regulated entertainment taking place is live music. It is important to remember that the provisions of section 177A only

---

[36]   See further on this topic Chapter 8 (Licensable Activities) and Chapter 17 (Conditions).
[37]   Guidance para 15.12.

suspend conditions, so that if any of the relevant criteria are exceeded or breached – if the bar is shut, for example, for a short period, or if the audience in a particular room exceeds 200 – then any live music related conditions will bite.

15.38 A similar exemption exists for workplaces[38] that do not have a premises licence or club premises certificate (unless it is only to authorise late night refreshment).[39] These provisions are intended to allow a similar exemption for schools, factories and hospitals, together with cafés and restaurants that do not sell alcohol but may have a premises licence solely in order to be able to sell hot food after 11 pm. 'Workplace' is a very wide term and includes outdoor spaces.

15.39 The Live Music Act also creates a general exemption that live unamplified music provided anywhere shall not be regarded as the provision of regulated entertainment if it takes place between 8 am and 11 pm, regardless of the number of people in the audience.[40]

15.40 As mentioned above, it is clear from the government's Guidance that karaoke will usually be considered live music for the purposes of section 177A and Schedule 1 paragraphs 12A to 12C.[41] This includes not only the live singing but also the recorded music played by the karaoke machine. The reasoning is somewhat stretched, but it may be useful to consider the justification for karaoke (including the recorded music) as a form of live music. Historically, it has always been accepted that there will often be an element of recorded music in a typical performance by a live band, for example recorded backing tracks or sampled music between sets. Such recorded music of itself has rarely if ever required a separate authorisation as recorded music. Likewise (the reasoning goes) and setting aside issues of the quality of the singing, the recorded music accompanying live singing during karaoke is just as integral a part of that live performance as the sampled music or backing tracks for a live band. In either case there is a requirement that this type of recorded music must be accompanied by an additional (substantial and continual) creative contribution by the live singers or performers.[42] For the implications of this line of argument on DJs and discos, please see the recorded music section below.

---

[38] Defined under section 2(1) of the Workplace (Health, Safety and Welfare) Regulations 1992 as anywhere that is made available to any persons as a place of work.
[39] Schedule 1, para 12B.
[40] Schedule 1, para 12C.
[41] Guidance para 15.24.
[42] Guidance para 15.12.

LIVE MUSIC AND BEER GARDENS

15.41   The exempting provisions of section 177A and Schedule 12A are predicated upon the area authorised to sell alcohol for consumption on the premises, not the 'premises' in general, or indeed the exact location where live music takes place. This has implications for licensed premises and where they can have live music. Many licensed plans have a so called 'red line' delineating the exact area where alcohol can be sold for consumption on the premises. If this red line extends into a beer garden or other outside area, then the outside area can benefit from the exempting provisions. Equally, many licensed plans show the entirety of a building (kitchens, toilets, garden and all) and in effect the whole premises is licensed for the sale of alcohol. In both these cases live music could take place outside. However, in cases where the beer garden or other outside area is shown on the plans but is not authorised to sell alcohol the exempting provisions do not apply. The final scenario involves licensed premises with beer gardens which are not shown at all on the licensed plans. Clearly, such 'premises' cannot benefit from section 177A (they are not authorised to sell alcohol) but they are entitled to benefit from the similar provisions of Schedule 1, paragraph 12B which applies to work places.[43]

15.42   There are a number of mechanisms for the protection of local residents. Upon a review of the premises licence the licensing authority can determine that conditions on the premises licence relating to live music will no longer be suspended between 8 am and 11 pm. If the licence or certificate doesn't presently authorise live music the licensing authority can add conditions to that licence or certificate as though the live music were regulated entertainment, to apply again between 8 am and 11 pm; and it can determine that live music at the premises is a licensable activity that can no longer be provided without explicit authorisation on the licence, certificate or temporary event notice.

Recorded music

15.43   This box has traditionally been completed where there are proposals for a DJ or disco. However, a DJ performing a set consisting largely of mixing recorded music to create new sounds might constitute live music and not require authorisation in certain circumstances.[44] The music played by a karaoke machine is subject to the criteria set out in section 177A and is likely to be considered live music.[45] A juke box is often considered incidental[46] but where it is not, perhaps due to its volume and the fact that customers are dancing, then this should be authorised.

---

[43]   Guidance para 15.26.
[44]   Guidance para 15.12.
[45]   Guidance para 15.24. Also see paras 15.36–15.41 above.
[46]   Where the playing of that recorded music is incidental to some other activity which is not itself regulated entertainment, see Licensing Act 2003, Sch 1, para 7.

Provision of facilities for making music, for dancing and for anything similar (previously Boxes I, J and K)

15.44 The Live Music Act removed the above formerly licensable activities entirely from the licensing regime. Authorisation for facilities for making music was usually required for pub pianos made available for customers to use, microphone stands, and even the element of karaoke machines which enable customers to take part in entertaining themselves. Facilities for dancing most often meant the provision of a permanent or temporary dance floor. Authorisation under the Licensing Act for such diverse activities is now no longer required, although it will be some years no doubt before the last vestiges of these confusing categories have been removed from all licences and certificates. It is to be hoped that licensing officers will excise these otiose authorisations at the first opportunity, perhaps when a licence is transferred, the DPS is varied or a minor variation is processed.

Late night refreshment

15.45 Applications should not be returned simply because the applicant has mistakenly entered the start time for late night refreshment as commencing prior to 11 pm. A substitute page is probably not even necessary. Late night refreshment, unlike other licensable activities, is partly defined by its hours and therefore can only commence at 11 pm whatever is stated in the application.

15.46 Another mistake commonly made is for the applicant to equate the 'indoors' and 'outdoors' boxes for the provision of late night refreshment with the 'on' and 'off' boxes for the supply for alcohol. These descriptions are not the same. Late night refreshment takes place, and therefore needs to be authorised at the place, where it is provided.[47] The supply takes place when the hot food or hot drink is given to the customer, for example handed over a counter at a take away food outlet or served in a restaurant to a customer at a table; not when it is paid for.[48] A pub with an outside terrace that serves hot food after 2300 will need to have that terrace licensed for late night refreshment if the customers are served at a table. Conversely, if customers collect their food from the counter in response to some form of voucher or wooden spoon service inside the premises, then 'indoors only' alone would need to be ticked. Returning to the case of the outdoor terrace with service at a table, this terrace would need to be part of the premises and shown on the licensed plan. If, however, customers collected their food orders from a counter inside the pub and took them outside on the terrace to eat after 11 pm then as the supply had taken place indoors (and assuming the indoors was authorised) the terrace would not need to be shown on the licensed plan by virtue of the late night refreshment provisions alone

---

[47] Licensing Act 2003, Sch 2(1)(1).
[48] Guidance para 3.12.

(although under the regulations it may well have to be shown for some other reason[49]). Take-aways do not have to show where their customers eat, if they don't serve to tables. 'On' and 'off' the premises are irrelevant for the purposes of late night refreshment.

15.47 The position of late night food operators who undertake deliveries after 11 pm is interesting to note. No doubt all of these operations have their premises licensed for late night refreshment where necessary. However, if the supply of the pizza or curry takes place on the doorstep of the customer, and at the time the food is supplied it is above ambient air temperature (one lives in hope), then surely it is the customer's door step that needs to be licensed for late night refreshment? Domestic premises do not appear to fall within any of the exemptions for late night refreshment under Schedule 2 of the Act. The Guidance, whilst adverting to late night take-aways and other food outlets, is silent as to late night deliveries.

Supply of alcohol

15.48 The Act provides that where the place where a contract for the sale of alcohol is made is different from the place where it is appropriated to the contract, the sale of alcohol is to be treated as taking place where the alcohol is appropriated to the contract.[50] The Act assumes a concluded contract for the retail sale of that alcohol in order for this provision to bite. In other words, one would normally expect the order to be placed by the customer and the total price ascertained whether or not it is paid for immediately in order for such a contract to have legal effect.

15.49 In a typical pub or night club the alcohol will be appropriated to that contract by the bar tender pulling a pint or opening the bottle. The area behind the bar therefore needs to be authorised for the sale of alcohol as this is the point at which the alcohol is appropriated to the contract. In cases where alcohol is delivered to table, so long as this is pursuant to a concluded order, then the location of the sale is still treated to be at the point where the alcohol is specifically and physically selected for the particular purchase[51] ie the bar not the table. If the delivery point, as opposed to the selection point, needed to be within the proverbial red line then internet and mail order sellers would all go out of business.[52] The tables where customers are served their drinks may or may not be shown on the plans attached to the

---

[49]   Licensing Act 2003 (Premises Licences and Club Premises Certificates) Regulations 2005, reg 23.

[50]   Licensing Act 2003, s 190. It must follow that where the places are the same then the sale is made from that place.

[51]   Guidance, para 3.8.

[52]   There is, in fact, a plausible argument that, in consequence of section 18 of the Sale of Goods Act 1979 alcohol is only appropriated to the contract at the point of delivery, for that is when the customer intends to assume ownership of the specific goods. However, it has generally been assumed that section 190 operates to make the point of despatch

premises licence (it is generally best if they are not when they do not affect fire routes etc), or indeed within the red line, but the sale (ie the specific selection of the alcohol) must always take place within the red line or on the licensed premises if there is no such line. If customers are served at tables which lie outside the area of the deposited plans, then off-sales will need to be authorised. The distinction between the selection and delivery points similarly makes it academic whether the waiter/waitress has a hand-held ordering terminal. For a discussion of what is on and what is off the premises, the reader is referred to para 15.56 below.

Hours open to the public

15.50 There has been much debate about whether the times set out in this box form conditions on the licence, the non-compliance with which can lead to prosecution under section 136 of the Licensing Act 2003 for carrying out licensable activities otherwise than in accordance with an authorisation. An argument can be raised that where the opening hours are directly related to the provision of licensable activities, for example closing time shortly after the last sale of alcohol, then clearly such closing times are conditions on the licence. In other words, if the last customer is not off the premises by that closing time, there is a breach of condition. There are many conditions on licences, for example relating to the provision of door staff or the mainten-ance of CCTV, which themselves are not directly related to the provision of licensable activities, but are directed at regulating and controlling the way in which those activities are provided, pursuant to the licensing objectives and the licensing authority's duty to carry out all its statutory functions with those objectives in mind.[53] By parity of reasoning, it may safely be said that when proposed closing hours are intended to disgorge customers at the end of the night who have been partaking in the licensed activities, then the closing hours may be enforced by licence condition. These matters are canvassed further in Chapter 14: Opening Hours.

FAQ

Q   If a pub is authorised to open and sell alcohol from 12 midday can it open its doors at 7 am in the morning to provide breakfast and coffee?

A   Yes, it quite clearly can open at 7 am. The question is really whether the premises licence holder or designated premises super-visor will be successfully prosecuted and convicted for an offence under section 136, or that some other enforcement activity will take place for an alleged breach of condition. The issue is not so

---

licensable rather than the point of delivery, and the convenience of that conclusion has protected the assumption from challenge.

[53]   Licensing Act 2003, s 4.

much whether the premises is open to the public during hours which contravene those set out in the premises licence, but whether licensable activities are being conducted other than under the authority of the licence. In this example, there are no licensable activities taking place at that time and nor do the activities on the premises in any way relate to the licensable activities authorised. Further, any enforcement action would have to be proportionate, and it would seem disproportionate to prosecute a licensee for activities which can just as easily be conducted without a licence on the premises at all. However, any risk or confusion can and, it is submitted, should be averted by an application for a minor variation to bring forward the opening hours to 7 am.

Box M – steps intended to promote the four licensing objectives

15.51   As shown above, Guidance is now suggesting that the operating schedule should do more than merely articulate the steps proposed to promote the licensing objectives. It is therefore important that in completing Box M, or in compiling any document referred to in Box M, the applicant distinguishes those steps it is expecting to have incorporated as conditions and other material, such as descriptive or contextual material.

15.52   However, in so far as the applicant is proffering steps as conditions of the licence, the applicant ought to use language which will translate into enforceable conditions. In *Crawley Borough Council v Attenborough*[54] Scott Baker J said:

> 'The terms of a licence and its conditions may of course be the subject of enforcement. Breach carries criminal sanctions. Everyone must know where they stand from the terms of the document. It must be apparent from reading the document what the licence and its conditions mean.'

15.53   If the language, when transposed, would not result in an enforceable condition, then the job of the licensing authority will be to re-write the proposal so as to achieve certainty.[55] A well-advised applicant will not place himself at the mercy of the licensing authority's draftsman in this manner, but will set out his proposals so that they can be cut and pasted into the

---

[54]   [2006] EWHC 1278 (Admin), followed in *R (on the Application of Westminster Council) v Metropolitan Stipendiary Magistrate and Merran* [2008] EWHC 1202 (Admin) and *R (on the Application of Developing Retail Ltd) v East Hampshire Magistrates' Court* [2011] EWHC 618 (Admin).

[55]   See Guidance paragraph 10.5 and 10.7, *R (on the Application of Bristol City Council) v Bristol Magistrates' Court* [2009] EWHC 625 (Admin); *R (on the Application of Westminster Council) v Metropolitan Stipendiary Magistrate and Merran* [2008] EWHC 1202 (Admin). See further Chapter 17 (Conditions).

licence by the authority. This is particularly important when it is considered that conditions are often drafted on the hoof at the end of a late evening licensing hearing: it is far preferable that they be drafted by experienced practitioners from electronic precedent banks.

The plan

15.54 After the application form/operating schedule, the second most important document is the plan of the premises. As the word 'premises' under the Act can mean any place,[56] 'licensed premises' means premises in respect of which a premises licence has effect.[57] The plan is critical to delineating the physical extent of the premises in question.

The plan must show[58]:

(a)   the extent of the boundary of the building, if relevant, and any external and internal walls of the building and, if different, the perimeter of the premises.

The use of the word 'relevant' here must be, it is submitted, seen in the context of the licensing objectives. It may therefore be necessary to show the boundary of the whole building in which the licensed premises is situate if, for example, fire exit routes are intended to take patrons off the licensed premises and out to safety through those other parts of the (unlicensed) building. In practice, licensed premises that form small parts of large unlicensed buildings rarely include plans of those buildings so long as the fire exit routes from the licensed premises themselves are clearly marked on the plan. A fire risk assessment is required under the Regulatory Reform (Fire Safety Order) 2005 and an application may receive a representation from the fire authority if that risk assessment is proved to be inadequate either on site inspection or through lack of detail in the plans accompanying the application.

In a typical case of a stand alone pub, the boundary of the building together with its internal and external walls will have to be shown. Where the perimeter of the premises is different to the boundary of the building then this must be shown. This would seem to suggest that where a pub has, for example, a walled beer garden to the rear, then the beer garden perimeter must be included in the plan of the premises. However, such a view confuses the flexible definition of the word 'premises'. If the beer garden is not shown on the plan, it cannot form part of the premises, and therefore the perimeter wall need not be shown. In other words, the perimeter of the King's Arms from a customer's perspective may include the pub building and the beer garden at the back. However, if only the pub building is shown on the

---

[56]   Licensing Act 2003, s 193.
[57]   Licensing Act 2003, s 193.
[58]   Licensing Act 2003 (Premises Licences and Club Premises Certificates) Regulations 2005, reg 23.

licensed plans, then from a licensing perspective this is the premises. As long as the pub is entitled to off sales and has complied with the other requirements under the plans regulations then there is no requirement to show the beer garden or car park etc (although it should be described in the relevant application).

Conversely, if for some reason the walled beer garden has been shown on granted licence plans, then clearly this is part of the perimeter of the premises. If subsequent changes are made to that perimeter (for example by knocking down the back wall to extend the garden a little into parking spaces owned by the licence holder) then a variation application would be required to show the amended plans. Such an application would not be required had the garden and its perimeter not been shown on the plans in the first place.

(b)   The location of points of access to and egress from the premises and, if different, the location of escape routes from the premises.

(c)   In a case where the premises are to be used for more than one licensable activity the area within the premises used for each activity.

Practice varies around the country and with different operators. Some large pub companies submit plans of premises without any red line denoting where licensable activities take place, in effect licensing the whole premises, kitchens, toilets and all. The best method, it is submitted, is for a red line to be placed around those public areas (to include behind the bar) where licensable activities take place. This red line would normally include all the licensable activities, as much for convenience as for anything else so that recorded music covers exactly the same area as where the sale of alcohol is authorised. In some circumstances, however, this may not be appropriate, for example, where part of the licensed premises lies outside and the playing of recorded music in this area would cause disturbance to local residents. A yellow line could be used to delineate those areas permitted for recorded music, restricting it to the interior of the building, with the red line for the sale of alcohol and late night refreshment covering both inside and outside the premises.

Any area shown on the plan is by definition part of the licensed premises and therefore 'on' the premises unless explicitly excluded. Consumption of alcohol can therefore take place in any of those areas regardless of whether off sales are permitted. As stated earlier, in the case of late night refreshment, every area where hot food or hot drink is supplied must be shown on the premises as there is no such thing as off sales so far as hot food goes. In the case of our fictitious King's Arms, the licence holder may prefer not to show the beer garden and to rely on off sales of alcohol to avoid expensive minor variations every time he moves the tables (if they affect fire escape routes); but if he wishes to provide hot food after 11 pm to a terrace in that beer garden, it would have to be shown on the plan if served to table. If a premises has a mobile bar (which does not affect escape routes) which is not shown on the deposited plans then this bar can be moved around within the 'red line' without the need for a variation.

(d)   Fixed structures (including furniture) or similar objects temporarily in a fixed location (but not furniture) which may impact on the ability of individuals on the premises to use exits or escape routes without impediment.

This horrendous wording has caused no end of practical problems, but can be deciphered if seen through the lens of the licensing objective of public safety. The purpose of this provision is to make sure that those large structures on the premises (be it inside the building or outside, if the outside is licensed) which may hinder customers from escaping in the event of a fire or other public safety emergency are shown. No item, whether fixed or not, or whether furniture or not, need be shown if it will not hinder egress from the premises. A large pool table in the middle of a big room far away from the exits will not need to be shown. Fixed seating which customers could vacate easily in the event of a fire equally does not need to be shown. A gaming machine placed in front of a fire exit would most definitely need to be shown (and no doubt would attract a representation!)

(e)   In a case where the premises includes a stage or raised area, the location and height of each stage or area relative to the floor.

(f)   In a case where the premises includes any steps, stairs, elevators or lifts, the location of the steps, stairs, elevators or lifts.

(g)   Any public conveniences (but the cubicles, urinals or basins do not have to be shown).

(h)   The location and type of any fire safety and any other safety equipment including, if applicable, marine safety equipment (in new developments or provisional applications, the final positioning of such equipment can be agreed with the Fire Authority. The requirement so far as the Plans Regulations go is that if there is any fire safety equipment then it must be shown).

(i)   The location of a kitchen, if any, on the premises.

15.55   The plan may include a legend through which the matters mentioned above are sufficiently illustrated by the use of symbols. There is no requirement that the plan be professionally drawn up, but its contents must be clear and legible in all material respects.

FAQ

Q   What about a large music festival where the final locations and timings of bands and other licensable activities are not known until it is too late to amend the plans by way of minor variation?

A   The Licensing Act 2003 and accompanying regulations are not ideal for large scale outdoor events. However, the regulations are sufficiently flexible to allow for various plans of the licensed site to be attached to the licence to accommodate last minute changes in stages, open-sided lorries and such like. There is no reason why certain areas of a large scale site plan cannot be hatched out to show the general position of the proposed entertainment accompanied by suitably worded conditions on the licence to allow for final sign off by the relevant authority (where necessary) in the days immediately before the event. Indeed, it is perfectly permissible to put the times of certain activities on such plans if this assists all parties in understanding what is going on where. The list of requirements set out in the regulations is not exhaustive and only sets out what is required to be shown. It should never be necessary to rely upon the goodwill of the licensing authority to substitute one plan for another in the week before the event. If the licensing officer is away sick or on holiday, great difficulties may ensue.

Q   I am planning some major refurbishment works at my premises which will require a variation application and that the premises close for some weeks. I don't exactly know when I will be able to re-open. How can I word my application so that I can know it is granted, but I am neither trading under incorrect plans if the work is completed early, nor having to make another variation application if I decide not to go ahead with the refurbishment at all?

A   Many practitioners, in the box where it asks when the application is to take effect (in both the major (section 34) variation and minor variation application forms) use the words 'to take effect upon completion of the works as notified by the applicant to the licensing authority in writing'. This may for some time require the licensing authority to hold two sets of plans on their file, but it seems to be the best way for applicants to deal with the combined vagaries of the Licensing Act and the building trade at once. Another way is simply to apply for a second licence, allowing the applicant complete flexibility.

Service of the application

15.56 It goes without saying that applications must be in writing.[59] The regulations do permit the application to be given electronically. However, where the application has to be accompanied by a fee the application is not

---

[59] Licensing Act 2003 (Premises Licences and Club Premises Certificates) Regulations 2005, reg 21.

treated as given until the fee has been received.[60] Where the application is served electronically, it is the licensing authority's job to forward it to the responsible authorities no later than one working day after it received the application.[61] In other cases, that duty falls upon the applicant who must give the application documents to the authorities on the same day as he gives them to the licensing authority.[62]

Advertisement of the application

15.57 The requirement for advertising the premises licence application is one of those areas where common sense faces squarely up to the black letter of the law. The requirements themselves are simply:

- The application must be advertised for no less than 28 consecutive days starting on the day after the day on which the application was given to the relevant licensing authority;
- By displaying a notice which is:
  - Of a size equal to or larger than A4;
  - Of a pale blue colour;
  - Printed legibly in black ink or typed in black in a font or a size equal to or larger than 16;
  - Prominently at or on the premises to which the application relates where it can be conveniently read from the exterior of the premises and in the case of premises covering an area more than 50 metres square, a further notice in the same form and subject to the same requirements every 50 metres along the external perimeter of the premises abutting any highway; and
- By publishing a notice:
  - In a local newspaper or, if there is none, in a local newsletter or a similar document circulating in the vicinity of the premises;
  - On at least one occasion during the period of ten working days starting on the day after the day on which the application was given to the relevant licensing authority.[63]

Procedural laxity

15.58 All of the above can have their own potential pitfalls. Before turning to the detail, it needs to be pointed out that it is regrettable that the Act

---

[60] Licensing Act 2003 (Premises Licences and Club Premises Certificates) Regulations 2005, reg 21A.
[61] Licensing Act 2003 (Premises Licences and Club Premises Certificates) Regulations 2005, reg 27.
[62] Licensing Act 2003 (Premises Licences and Club Premises Certificates) Regulations 2005, reg 27A.
[63] Licensing Act 2003 (Premises Licences and Club Premises Certificates) Regulations 2005, reg 25.

provides no slip rule in the case of breach of these procedural requirements. To the contrary, section 17(5) of the Act requires the Secretary of State to make regulations requiring the applicant to advertise the application in the proper form and manner, while section 18, which deals with determination, only applies where there has been compliance with section 17(5).[64] The modern approach to procedural non-compliance is to ask, upon construction of the legislation in question, what the legislature intended should be the procedural consequence of non-compliance, rather than asking whether the legislative provision is mandatory or directory, as was the former approach.[65] Here, unfortunately, because of the legislative drafting, the position is clear. If there is compliance, the authority may proceed to determine the application. If there is not, it may not. The rigour of these provisions was demonstrated in *R (Albert Court Residents Association) v Westminster City Council*[66] in which the notion of a discretion to step outside the procedures mandated by the Act (in that case the acceptance of late representations) was firmly scotched. Therefore, one is thrown back onto the long-standing principle that, even where the provisions do not contemplate non-compliance, an exception may be made where there has been substantial performance and where the defect consisted of a slight error or mischance, as expressed in the judgment of Lord Denning in *R v Newcastle-upon-Tyne Gaming and Licensing Committee ex parte White Hart Enterprises Limited*.[67] In the light of this brief procedural canter, we can now return to the practical ramifications of the regulations.

The notice

15.59 As stated above, the notice must be displayed for a period of no less than 28 consecutive days. The notice must be displayed for this whole period.

FAQ

Q   What happens if the notice is ripped down during the 28 days?

A   This depends upon whether you support or oppose the application. If no-one notices, then no-one will raise the point. Equally, if the most prominent and practicable place that an applicant can place their notice is on, for example, a telegraph pole outside the premises then it is quite possible that such a notice will be ripped down during that 28 day consecutive day period. The onus is clearly on the applicant to ensure that a replacement notice is put up as soon as possible. If the applicant

---

64   Licensing Act 2003, s 18(1).
65   *R (TC Projects) v Newcastle Justices* [2006] EWHC 1018 (Admin).
66   [2010] EWHC 393 (Admin); [2011] EWCA (Civ) 430.
67   [1977] 3 All ER 961).

does so quickly, then he will be able to argue that any breach of the regulations is trivial, amounting to nothing more than a slight error or mischance. Indeed, if there are objectors there to argue about the matter, that will rather make the applicant's point for him! No councillor will want the application to fail simply due to the antics of local youths or conceivably even the actions of aggrieved local residents, and if ripping down a notice is sufficient to ensure that an application can never be heard, the purpose of the Act will be stymied. Provided, therefore, that the applicant can show that he has regularly checked the notice and replaced it immediately when it has been removed, then the application should be allowed to proceed. In contentious cases, applicants will be well advised to take regular photographs of their notices so as to prove their position beyond doubt.

Q   What if, due to postal issues, the applicant's notice specifies a 28 day period which is different to that calculated by the licensing authority?

A   The 28 day period commences when the application is 'given' to the licensing authority. As it is ultimately up to the licensing authority to decide whether the regulations have been complied with,[68] if the application sits in the post room for a couple of days then the licensing authority's calculations of when the 28 day period starts (and thus ends) can be different to those of the applicants' (whatever the provisions of section 184 say about 'Giving of Notices etc'). In non-urgent cases (for example where the applicant is not planning a big opening event on a specific day) it may not cause problems, but if the applicant can prove, perhaps by way of special delivery, that the application was given to the authority and signed for at either the principal office of the authority, or any other office of the authority specified by it as one which will accept such documents, then this should be sufficient to persuade the authority that the applicants' start date for the 28 days is correct.[69] Many applicants, in their covering letter to the licensing authority and responsible authorities, indicate that the application will be treated as delivered in accordance with the Magistrates' Courts Rules, ie as having been received the second working day after the application was posted, if sent first class. The 28 day period on the notice is specified accordingly.

As an added precaution, the A4 notice sent to the premises for display can be displayed immediately upon receipt by the premises (perhaps literally the next day) meaning that the pale blue notice is displayed at the premises for a total period of 30 days or so. In the event that the licensing authority treats the application as

---

[68]   Licensing Act 2003, s 18(1)(b).
[69]   Licensing Act 2003, s 184(2)(a)–(b).

having been received the day after it was sent (and thus earlier than the deemed receipt under the Magistrates' Courts Rules) the only possible problem is with a resident who relied upon the final day as stated in the notice as opposed to the licensing authority's own calculation. In practice this tends to cause few problems, although the way the Regulations are drafted makes it difficult for an applicant to be certain that his calculation is the same as the licensing authority's unless he personally delivers the application, agrees the 28 day period and hurries back to prepare his notice accordingly.

Q   My licensing authority requires me to hold back from putting up the notice until my application is received and processed by them. Sometimes this can take quite a few days. Is this right?

A   Not if the application has been submitted in the correct format with the proper accompanying documents. As long as you can prove that the application has been given to the licensing and other authorities in accordance with the Act and regulations, you may display your notice indicating the 28 day period starting with the day after the day that your application was so given.

Pale blue colour

15.60 What starts out as pale blue paper on day one can (even in our changeable climes) have faded in the sunlight to something closer to white by the end of the 28 days. In particularly contentious applications this can pose a difficulty and attention should always be kept on the notice.

Font size

15.61 A typical notice on A4 paper is unlikely to accommodate a font size greater than size 16.

FAQ

Q   What do I put on my notice?

A   The regulations[70] state that for an application for a new premises licence the notice shall contain:-

(1) A statement of the relevant licensable activities which it is proposed will be carried on or from the premises;

(2) The name of the applicant;

---

[70]   Licensing Act 2003 (Premises Licences and Club Premises Certificate) Regulations 2005, reg 26.

(3) The postal address of the premises, if any, or if there is no postal address for the premises a description of those premises sufficient to enable the location and the extent of the premises to be identified;

(4) The postal address and, where applicable, the world wide web address where the register of the relevant licensing authority is kept and where and when the record of the application may be inspected;

(5) The date by which an interested party or responsible authority may make representations to the relevant licensing authority;

(6) That representations may be made in writing;

(7) That it is an offence knowingly or recklessly to make a false statement in connection with an application and the maximum fine for which a person is liable on summary conviction for the offence.

In respect of variation applications, the notice should include all of the above save for item 1, which should be substituted with a brief description of the proposed variation.

Q   Is it sufficient to simply describe 'regulated entertainment' on the notice, or do I have to identify each individual activity, eg live music, boxing and wrestling?

A   It is at least arguable that the licensable activity required to be stated on the notice is regulated entertainment, not its constituent parts[71] but an applicant in any but the least controversial applications would be advised to itemise each of the individual activities listed under the umbrella of regulated entertainment to avoid allegations of bad faith at best and non-compliance at worst.

Q   Should I refer to the opening hours on the notice?

A   Practice varies, and it is not required for a new application. Conversely the regulations do not explicitly state that the hours for the relevant licensable activities should be stated either, although it would be unwise not to put these into an application for fear of non-compliance, so the best advice would be to include the opening hours if space permits. In the case of a variation where the opening hours are being varied this should be stated on the notice (as the requirement here is that the variation shall be 'briefly described').

Prominently at or on the premises.

15.62 The notice should ideally be fixed behind glass to avoid it being removed, and members of the public should not have to cross private land in

---

[71] Licensing Act 2003, s 1(1)(c).

order to read its contents. In the 'building site' scenario, a convenient place is sometimes difficult to find. Common practice has involved fixing the notice where other such notices are already displayed, for example planning notices or on nearby telegraph poles. In cases where there is any doubt a conversation with the licensing authority is essential.

FAQ

Q   I have a pub which is set a long way back from the road with a large car park at the front. Can I display the notice in my pub window?

A   Strictly speaking if the car park did not form part of the premises (ie was not on the licensed plan) then this would comply as the notice could 'be conveniently read from the exterior of the premises'. The requirement that the notice abuts any highway only applies to premises whose area is more than 50 metres square. However, this action is likely to attract more problems than fewer and it would be more advisable to fix a further notice to the bottom of the pub sign at the entrance to the car park or similar location. The licensing authority's discretion under section 18 as to whether the regulations have been complied with must always be borne in mind, as must the potential for a suggestion, however unfounded, that the applicant is trying to pull the wool over the eyes of the public.

The '50 metres square' requirement

15.63 Whilst in the early days this ambiguous wording caused some confusion, it is accepted that this phrase means that the applicant has some additional requirements if its total area (again measured by reference to the plan) is 2500 square metres or more. Some licensing authorities take a far stricter view than others on this point, requiring the siting of notices along footpaths and down the sides of walls that are hardly, if ever, used. A conversation with the licensing authority prior to issue is therefore essential to ensure compliance.

Local advertisement

15.64 Any applicant who does not have access to an approved list of local newspapers should clarify this with the licensing authority prior to issue. A national newspaper, whether the Times or the Racing Post, will not do.[72] The requirement to publish the advertisement during the period of ten working days starting on the day after the day on which the application was given to the licensing authority suffers from the same risks as the 28 day period mentioned above. However, as the advert can appear at any point during those ten working days the applicant is afforded rather more flexibility.

Consent of the designated premises supervisor

15.65 A signed original consent of the designated premises supervisor ('DPS') should be included with the application sent to the licensing authority. An application that includes a request to sell alcohol but does not include details of the DPS or the consent should not be rejected. The soon-to-be-holder of the licence will nevertheless have to make an urgent DPS variation application under section 37 if he wishes to sell alcohol on the day of the grant of the premises licence, however, as there is no provision to name a DPS once the application has been submitted (although an understanding licensing authority may accept substitution of that page of the application).

New premises licences – supply of alcohol from community premises

15.66 The management committee of community premises can, when making an application for a new premises licence, include an application for the 'alternative licence condition', namely that every supply of alcohol under the premises licence must be made or authorised by the management committee. If granted, this has the effect of removing the requirements in section 19(2)–(3) that there be a designated premises supervisor and that every sale of alcohol is authorised by a personal licence holder.[73]

D POST-APPLICATION PROCEDURE

15.67 If an application for a premises licence is validly made and there are no representations, then it must be granted by the licensing authority. If relevant representations are received during the 28 day consultation period and not withdrawn, then the application should go to a hearing in 20 working days starting with the day after the end of the consultation period. If only life was that simple!

Uncontested applications

15.68 Many applications are validly submitted and receive no relevant representations at all. The duty of the licensing authority is then to grant the

---

[72] *R v Westminster Betting Licensing Committee, ex p Peabody Donation Fund* [1963] 2 QB 750.
[73] See Section J below, and also Chapter 17 (Conditions).

licence in accordance with the application subject only to such conditions as are consistent with the operating schedule accompanying the application, and mandatory conditions which must under section 19, 20 or 21 be included in the licence.[74] The transposition exercise is not purely mechanical. The High Court has held that the licensing authority is not obliged to include all of the contents of the operating schedule in the licence. Rather, section 18(2) of the Act gives a power to impose conditions consistent with the operating schedule where this is appropriate to promote the licensing objectives. It does not impose a duty to impose conditions that replicate the effect of the operating schedule. Not only, therefore, may the licensing authority pass over proposals which do not in its view promote the licensing objectives or which are sufficiently covered by other legislation, but it may (and should) rework language which is vague or opaque, so as to produce a set of workable, enforceable and clear conditions.[75] While there is good sense in this judgment, it may work to disadvantage authorities or local residents who decided not to object solely because of the proposals made by the applicant, which proposals may even have been agreed by them prior to preparation of the operating schedule, only to find that such proposals are not carried through into the licence. The message for potential objectors is that they should object and then compromise the case with an agreement that the conditions be included.

15.69 In practice, the applicant's task is to wait patiently for the expiry of the consultation period and, once it is apparent that there have been no representations, to contact the licensing authority at that time. Many applicants make the mistake of thinking that since the 28 day period has expired without representations having been made, then the licence is automatically granted. This is not necessarily the case. The licensing authority must indeed grant the licence, but there is no time limit stated in the Act within which a grant must take place.[76]

15.70 Following the expiry of the 28 day period the licensing authority must physically prepare the licence and add the relevant mandatory conditions together with such conditions as are consistent with the operating schedule accompanying the application. The re-wording of the steps set out in Boxes M (a) to (e), if done well, can sometimes take time. The applicant who had planned his grand opening on the 29th day may therefore come unstuck if the licensing authority is not prepared to state over the phone 'yes, it's granted, the licence will be out soon'. On the rare occasions where licensing authorities take an inordinate amount of time to grant an uncontested application, it seems that the only remedy for the applicant is the threat of judicial review. The instances of licensing authorities adding their own 'standard' conditions which are not themselves consistent with the

[74] Licensing Act 2003, s 18(2).
[75] *R (Bristol City Council) v Bristol Magistrates Court* [2009] EWHC 625 (Admin).
[76] Licensing Act 2003, s 18(2).

operating schedule are thankfully rare, but do sometimes occur. This is clearly outside the authority's discretion and would be considered *ultra vires*.

15.71 Another issue that can cause applicants problems is that of the withdrawal of a relevant representation following an agreement to additional conditions (perhaps with the police or environmental health officer) after issue of the application. Such circumstances frequently arise, where an authority is unhappy with the specific wording on the application and wants it tightened up, or requires additional conditions before they will withdraw their objection. Once all representations have been withdrawn, they are no longer relevant representations[77] so that their withdrawal should result in a mandatory grant. The problem here is that neither the Act nor the Regulations allow for an application to be amended once it has been issued. If licensing authorities stuck rigidly to this principle, the licensing system would collapse. Authorities therefore tend to take a gratifyingly pragmatic stance[78]. Some solutions include the requirement for the submission during the application period of an amended operating schedule either as a full application form or just the page containing Box M. Other licensing authorities have so called 'agreement hearings' where the licensing sub-committee effectively rubber stamps the amended application. Clearly, this latter proposal can cause substantial delays. Moreover, an issue may arise if the if the sub-committee do not like what has been agreed, given that once all representations have been withdrawn there is no power for the authority to add its own conditions.

15.72 These controversial situations are avoided if, rather than withdrawing representations once there has been an agreement, the applicant and objector agree a set of conditions in order to resolve the objection. Provided that the authority and all parties agree that a hearing of the representations is unnecessary then the matter need not go to a full hearing.[79] Instead, the agreement may be placed before a meeting of the licensing sub-committee for the agreement to be endorsed and the licence granted on those terms. While the applicant risks the problem that the sub-committee may not want to endorse the settlement, in practice this is rarely the case, because a knowledgeable sub-committee will be aware that it could not defend its position on appeal unsupported by any of the parties to the application.

Contested applications

15.73 Contested applications are triggered by relevant representations. These are representations which are made by responsible authorities or other persons, which are about the likely effect of the grant of the premises licence

---

[77]   Licensing Act 2003, s 18(7).
[78]   An approach endorsed by the High Court in *Matthew Taylor v 1) Manchester City Council and 2) TCG Bars Limited* [2012] EWHC 3467 (Admin).
[79]   Licensing Act 2003 (Hearings) Regulations 2005, reg 9.

on the promotion of the licensing objectives and which are made on time, that is to say during a period of 28 consecutive days starting on the day after the day on which the application to which it relates was given to the authority by the applicant.[80] Late representations cannot be accepted.[81] Frivolous and vexatious representations made by parties other than responsible authorities are not relevant representations.[82] Furthermore, if the representation concerns the identity of the designated premises supervisor, it may only be made by the police and relate to the crime prevention objective.[83] A representation which is withdrawn ceases to be a relevant representation.[84]

15.74 Subject to the requirement that it relate to the licensing objectives and that it should not be frivolous or vexatious, which is very rare, there is no rule as to the content or detail of a relevant representation. This may disadvantage the applicant in that, without knowledge of the true nature of the objection, it is difficult to prepare any rebuttal. It may also disadvantage the objector, in that if the objection is not elucidated prior to the hearing, they may find themselves precluded from fleshing it out in their evidence. The solution to this is the provision in the regulations for the notice of hearing.

15.75 Where agreement cannot be reached between the parties the application for the new premises licence must go to a hearing unless the authority, the applicant and each person who has made representations agree that a hearing is unnecessary.[85] The hearing must take place within 20 working days beginning with the day after the end of the 28 period for making representations,[86] although there is a power of adjournment, eg due to holidays or illness,[87] or for further information to be provided by the applicant.[88]

Notice of hearing

15.76 At least ten working days before the hearing, the authority is to give the parties a notice of the hearing.[89] The notice must be accompanied by some crucial information:

---

[80] Licensing Act 2003, s 18(6)–(7), Licensing Act 2003 (Premises Licences and Club Premises Certificate) Regulations 2005, reg 22(1)(b).
[81] *R (Albert Court Residents Association) v Westminster City Council* [2010] EWHC 393 (Admin); [2011] EWCA (Civ) 430.
[82] For a discussion as to the meaning of 'frivolous or vexatious' see para 15.21 above, and Guidance paras 9.5–9.9.
[83] Licensing Act 2003, s 18(6)(c).
[84] Licensing Act 2003, s 18(7)(b).
[85] Licensing Act 2003, s 18(3)(a).
[86] Licensing Act 2003 (Hearings) Regulations 2005, Sch 1.
[87] Licensing Act 2003 (Hearings) Regulations 2005, reg 12.
[88] See *R (Murco Petroleum Ltd) v Bristol City Council* [2010] EWHC 1992 (Admin).
[89] Licensing Act 2003 (Hearings) Regulations 2005, reg 6(4).

(a)   the rights of a party provided for in regulations 15 (to attend and be assisted or represented) and 16 (to give clarification where this has been sought in the notice of hearing, to give further information in support of their application, representations or notice; if given permission by the authority, to question any other party; and to address the authority).
(b)   the consequences if a party does not attend or is not represented at the hearing;
(c)   the procedure to be followed at the hearing;
(d)   any particular points on which the authority considers that it will want clarification at the hearing from a party.

15.77 Crucially, at the hearing, the authority may take into account documentary or other information produced by a party in support of their application, representations or notice either before the hearing or, with the consent of all the other parties, at the hearing.[90] The upshot is that documentary or other information given for the first time at the hearing may be admitted only if all other parties consent, and there is no guarantee that they will. If the gloves come off at a hearing, then there is a strong possibility that they won't, and a local objector will be prevented from enlarging on all their all too brief relevant representation.

15.78 The solution to this lies in the notice of hearing. All too often, this is a *pro forma* notice sent out administratively. It ought to be much more. A professional licensing officer ought to read the application, the relevant representations and the council's licensing policy and consider what further information is likely to be needed in order to enable the licensing sub-committee to come to a sensible, well-informed decision. This information should be sought in the notice of hearing. The notice should also warn the parties about the strictures of regulation 18 and invite them to prepare material to be pre-read by the licensing sub-committee. The notice should set a timetable for the service of such material, and should give directions as to the number of copies to be lodged. In this way, the parties will be able to prepare such documents, be they statements, petitions, plans, photographs, correspondence and/or proposed conditions, as will assist them in presenting their case to the sub-committee, and the hearing will proceed more expeditiously, in a more focussed manner, and will yield a more considered result. While, particularly from the point of view of objectors, it results in extra work prior to the hearing, it gives objectors a better chance to put their case and overcome any disparities in advocacy power between the parties. It also enables the sub-committee and advisers to prepare properly for the hearing itself.

15.79 Following receipt of the notice of hearing, and at least five working days before the hearing,[91] each of the parties must give the authority a notice

---

[90]   Licensing Act 2003 (Hearings) Regulations 2005, reg 18.
[91]   Licensing Act 2003 (Hearings) Regulations 2005, reg 8(5).

stating whether he intend to attend or be represented at the hearing, whether he considers a hearing to be unnecessary, and requesting permission to call a witness at the hearing, together with a brief description of the points upon which the witness will speak.[92] Such notice does not have to name any representative of the party.

The licensing sub-committee

15.80   The hearing will generally be delegated to a licensing sub-committee. A common misconception is that the sub-committee must consist of three members actually sitting. In fact, while sub-committees must under section 9(1) of the Act consist of three members, the failure of Regulations to specify a quorum under section 9(2)(a) of the Act leaves the matter of quorum to the discretion of the licensing committee under section 9(3). The committee may in particular wish to specify fewer than three for minor or urgent cases, where parties have reached agreement or to cater for unforeseen circumstances such as illness.

Procedure at the hearing is governed by the Licensing Act 2003 (Hearings) Regulations 2005.

Adjournment, extension, non-appearance

15.81   An authority can extend time for any step to be taken if it is in the public interest and, if it does so, must give notice to the parties of any extension and reasons for it.[93] It can also adjourn hearings to specified dates or arrange additional dates if necessary for the consideration of the representations, giving requisite notice thereof as appropriate.[94]

15.82   There would appear to be a potential conflict between the power to adjourn hearings under regulation 12 to any specified date and the requirement under regulation 5 that if a hearing is to take more than one day it must be arranged to take place on consecutive working days. Two comments can be made. First, the requirement to arrange hearings on consecutive working days is apt to cause considerable administrative upheaval within licensing authorities. Secondly, the provisions probably can be reconciled in this way: if a hearing is known to be likely to last for more than one day before it begins then regulation 5 would apply. If, however, it becomes apparent after notice of the hearing has been given or there is some other change of circumstance (eg the case expands in complexity or a requisite person cannot attend) then regulation 12 applies.

15.83   Provision is also made for what should happen if a party fails to appear. The procedure depends on whether the non-attendance is with or

---

[92]   Licensing Act 2003 (Hearings) Regulations 2005, reg 8(1)–(2).
[93]   Licensing Act 2003 (Hearings) Regulations 2005, reg 11.
[94]   Licensing Act 2003 (Hearings) Regulations 2005, reg 12.

without warning. First, if a party has informed the authority that he does not intend to attend or be represented at a hearing, the hearing may proceed in his absence.[95] This gives an open discretion. The authority would be likely to proceed if the party was simply electing not to attend. If, however, the party had a good excuse for not attending, such as illness or accident, the authority may well exercise its discretion under regulation 12 to adjourn the hearing to a new date. If a party simply does not turn up at the hearing, without having indicated his non-attendance in advance, the authority is only to adjourn where this is considered to be necessary in the public interest.[96] In practice, sub-committees should first adjourn briefly to ascertain any reason for the non-appearance and then decide whether adjournment is necessary in the public interest. Even if the party has a good excuse for not attending, the sub-committee may still decide to proceed, eg because the case is urgent, or because the party's evidence is unlikely to be important, being one objector among many.

The nature of the hearing

15.84 The hearing is to be held in public, save where the authority takes the view that the public interest in excluding the public from all or part of the hearing outweighs the public interest in the hearing, or that part of the hearing, taking place in public.[97] This might happen, for example, if the police are bringing forward matters that are part of an ongoing criminal investigation which would be prejudiced by public discussion of the facts. There is also power to require persons to leave who are disruptive, provided that an opportunity is given to them to make written submissions.[98]

15.85 Parliament was anxious that the licensing sub-committee hearing should not resemble a contested criminal trial. It therefore provided that a hearing shall take the form of a discussion led by the authority and cross-examination shall not be permitted unless the authority considers that cross-examination is required for it to consider the representations, application or notice as the case may require.[99] While this gives advocates less opportunity to sharpen their teeth than some might like, it is consonant with the notion of licensing as a non-adversarial forum intended to arrive at a sensible judgment as to the balance between competing interests rather than a forensic search for the truth. This was expressed succinctly by Toulson LJ in *R (Hope and Glory Public House Limited) v City of Westminster Magistrates Court*:

'Licensing decisions often involve weighing a variety of competing considerations: the demand for licensed establishments, the economic

---

[95] Licensing Act 2003 (Hearings) Regulations 2005, reg 20.
[96] Licensing Act 2003 (Hearings) Regulations 2005, reg 20.
[97] Licensing Act 2003 (Hearings) Regulations 2005, reg 14.
[98] Licensing Act 2003 (Hearings) Regulations 2005, reg 25.
[99] Licensing Act 2003 (Hearings) Regulations 2005, reg 23.

benefit to the proprietor and to the locality by drawing in visitors and stimulating the demand, the effect on law and order, the impact on the lives of those who live and work in the vicinity, and so on. Sometimes a licensing decision may involve narrower questions, such as whether noise, noxious smells or litter coming from premises amount to a public nuisance. Although such questions are in a sense questions of fact, they are not questions of the "heads or tails" variety. They involve an evaluation of what is to be regarded as reasonably acceptable in the particular location. In any case, deciding what (if any) conditions should be attached to a licence as necessary and proportionate to the promotion of the statutory licensing objectives is essentially a matter of judgment rather than a matter of pure fact.'[100]

15.86   Furthermore, Parliament provided that a party may be represented or assisted by another person whether or not that person is legally quali-fied.[101] It is a common occurrence that local councillors, who know their way around the system, come to hearings to assist their constituents, which is a valuable service. In many cases, parties simply appoint spokespersons, which helps to save time and focus the debate. The important point is that parties are heard, without technical points being taken as to the qualifications of the person representing them.

Procedure at the hearing[102]

15.87   While the regulations stipulate certain matters which have to be done, they are not exhaustive, and the licensing authority is given a certain latitude to develop its own domestic arrangements.[103] Usually, the procedure to be adopted by the sub-committee is committed to a *pro forma* document published in advance and sent out with the agenda for the meeting. The agenda typically includes a report pack, containing the officer's report, the application, the representations and any evidence filed by the parties. By the time the parties assemble, all concerned should have pre-read the docu-ments, so that it is not necessary for any party to engage in lengthy recitation of the facts.

15.88   At the outset of the hearing, the authority, usually through the chair, explains to the parties the procedure which it proposes to follow at the hearing and also considers any request made by a party for permission for another person to appear at the hearing.[104] It is difficult to envisage upon what grounds relevant evidence could be excluded. Indeed, it is also provided that such permission shall not be unreasonably withheld (such a provision might be said to be stating the obvious since authorities would be acting

---

[100]   [2011] EWCA Civ 31.
[101]   Licensing Act 2003 (Hearings) Regulations 2005, reg 15.
[102]   See further Chapter 21 (Best Practice in Licensing Hearings).
[103]   Licensing Act 2003 (Hearings) Regulations 2005, reg 21.
[104]   Licensing Act 2003 (Hearings) Regulations 2005, reg 22.

unlawfully if they acted unreasonably.) Conceivably, an authority might refuse permission to call evidence if (a) it merely duplicates evidence to be given by that or another party, or (b) the evidence is agreed, or (c) its prejudicial effect outweighs its probative value. However, given that the licensing authority is entitled to cap the length of time afforded to each party for presentation of their case, the power to exclude relevant evidence which a party wishes to call is infrequently, if ever, exercised.

15.89 Typically, following these opening formalities, a licensing officer makes a brief presentation of their report. Almost always, this summarises the application, informs the sub-committee of the spectrum of possible outcomes allowed by the statute and draws their attention to relevant guidance and policy.

FAQ

Q   Is the presenting officer entitled to make recommendations?[105]

A   The views on this topic are polarised. On the one hand, it is pointed out that local government is founded on the principle of professional and experienced officers giving advice to lay council-lors. On the other hand is the view that the hearing is a quasi-judicial hearing and for an officer to proffer a view would be likely to bias, or at least skew, the sub-committee in one direction or the other. The former view is much to be preferred. As to the latter view, it is wrong to say that the hearing is quasi-judicial in nature. As Toulson LJ stated in *R (Hope and Glory Public House Limited) v City of Westminster Magistrates Court*:[106]

'... the licensing function of a licensing authority is an administrative function. By contrast, the function of the district judge is a judicial function. The licensing authority has a duty, in accordance with the rule of law, to behave fairly in the decision-making procedure, but the decision itself is not a judicial or quasi-judicial act. It is the exercise of a power delegated by the people as a whole to decide what the public interest requires.'[107]

Furthermore, there is no rational basis for stating that an officer's view is liable to create prejudice in the hearing. In the analogous field of planning, it is routine for officers to give their views, and provided that they do so openly, transparently and dispassionately, and provided that the parties have the opportunity to comment on the recommendation, no prejudice results. Far from being preju-dicial, the expression of view is liable to be very helpful. It

---

[105] See further, Chapter 23 (Licensing Officers).
[106] [2011] EWCA Civ 31.
[107] Para 41.

frequently happens that officers, because of their experience in the field, are able to make recommendations as to how particular impediments may be overcome, a perspective which councillors may lack, resulting in a licence refusal rather than a grant on terms. Similarly, applicants may have a tendency to avoid discussion of conditions so as to avoid the burden of such conditions, while objectors may avoid discussion of conditions because they are intent on procuring a refusal and do not wish to discuss compromise. The benefit of an officer's recommendations is that it produces a neutral view, and may result in a compromise which would otherwise only be achieved at great expense at the end of a magistrates' court appeal.

Where there are issues of fact – such as whether a nuisance is likely – the officer may refrain from expressing a view as to the finding of fact. But this does not mean to say that the officer cannot make a recommendation when the primary issue is factual. The officer may advise that if it is determined that a nuisance is likely then the sub-committee might consider solutions A, B and/or C, but if not then such solutions may not be considered proportionate.

Now that the licensing authority is entitled to participate as a responsible authority the debate as to whether an officer may make a recommendation loses some of its urgency. But it does help to remind one that licensing officers, who are experts in their field, can play a useful role at sub-committee hearings and their absence as a protagonist in the guise of a responsible authority does not prevent their attendance in the guise of a neutral adviser to the sub-committee. The distinction is that in the latter guise they ought not to be making representations or bringing matters of fact to the sub-committee's attention, for this is the role of the parties to the application and not the adviser to the sub-committee. In any event, it is strongly recommended that the officer advising the sub-committee does not retire with the sub-committee, so as to prevent any suspicion of preferential access or influence.

The parties' cases

15.90 Following presentation of the report by the officer and any questions arising from the report, the parties are given an opportunity to present their cases in turn.

Each party is given certain limited rights at a hearing: to respond to any notice under regulation 7(1)(d) (ie points set out in the notice of hearing as to which the authority will require clarification), to question other parties and to address the authority.[108] Simple as this may seem, a number of issues arise. This is because Parliament attempted through the regulations to keep the hearings within strict bounds, not trusting, so it would seem, the normal, established rules of fairness that are applied to local authority hearings, in respect of many other local authority functions. It is convenient to approach the matter in stages.

(1)   The authority must allow the parties an equal maximum period of time in which to exercise their rights provided for in regulation 16. This is intended to achieve fairness between the parties, but is very difficult to interpret. If there are 20 objectors, do they each get the same maximum time? In that case, it may be completely unfair to the applicant to be given ten minutes to present the case while his 20 opponents get ten minutes each. The Chair may try to mitigate this by asking the 20 objectors to appoint a spokesperson, but they may not wish to do so, and even if they do they are still each entitled to the same maximum time. A further question is whether the time is calculated in respect of the entirety of the party's presentation. If it is, then is time spent questioning the other party to be deducted from the questioner's or the other party's time? What if the other party is recalcitrant or long-winded in replying to questions? If a party takes a technical point, eg regarding the admissibility of the other's evidence, whose time are they on? Similarly, if the sub-committee asks questions, is this deducted from a party's time? Or are three maximum times allotted per party – for clarification, questions and address each of which must be equal to the maximum time accorded to the other parties?

There is no simple answer to any of the above questions. In reality, the rule is observed in a loose fashion by the Chair keeping an eye on the clock and reminding an over-running party that it may be time to wind up their address. Where this can go wrong is when a party is given an unacceptably short time – five or ten minutes – to present their case. This can leave parties with a genuine sense of grievance when they are applying for a licence for a business which may have cost them a seven figure sum, only to find that they have a few minutes to cover all of the issues raised. Often, this can leave sub-committees bereft of the information that they may need to make a proper decision, and impels the parties to appeal and make costs applications because they were not given an adequate opportunity at first instance. It is recommended that, rather than arbitrarily imposing a time limit on proceedings, sub-committees should first canvass the views of the parties as to how long they need before making a balanced decision as to how the time of the sub-committee is to be allocated.

(2)   Each party is entitled to present their case within the maximum time allotted.

---

[108]   Licensing Act 2003 (Hearings) Regulations 2005, reg 16.

(3)   They may also call a witness to give evidence, provided that they have been given permission to do so.

(4)   In presenting their case, they may refer to the basic content of their application.

(5)   They may also give information in reply to a request for clarification in the notice of hearing.

(6)   They may also refer to documentary or other information which they have submitted before the hearing.[109] The regulation specifies no particular time before the hearing so in theory it could be given immediately before. In such a case, the sub-committee may deal with any prejudice arising to other parties by giving them time to consider the material or even adjourning the hearing. Hopefully, a sufficiently explicit direction in the notice of hearing will discourage parties from late submission of material.

(7)   They may not present documentary or other information produced for the first time at the hearing except with the consent of all other parties at the hearing.[110] This enables a party effectively to stymie the presentation of the other party's case. No reason need be given for an objection and nor does the objection have to be reasonable. It is not clear what purpose is served by the strictness of the rule. While of course late information can cause considerable difficulties, it would have led to a fairer system had the authority simply been given discretion to deal with any application to introduce late evidence on a case by case basis.

It is uncertain whether the problem of new evidence can be overcome by the authority exercising its right to ask questions of the party on the subject, and then admitting the answers into evidence. This is at least an arguable interpretation of the regulations, since it effectively leaves the authority with a discretion as to whether the material should be admitted into evidence through answers to their own questions, thus permitting them a tight rein on proceedings. Regulation 18, it would be said, applies to documents and information produced by a party in support of their case rather than material produced in response to questions from the authority. In similar vein, the regulations expressly permit a party to give further information where this has been sought in the notice of hearing.[111] Regulation 16(a) does not say that answers to the request for clarification have to be given in advance of the hearing. Therefore, the argument would go that regulation 18 has to be read subject to regulation 16(a).

---

[109]   Licensing Act 2003 (Hearings) Regulations 2005, reg 18.
[110]   Licensing Act 2003 (Hearings) Regulations 2005, reg 18.
[111]   Licensing Act 2003 (Hearings) Regulations 2005, reg 16(a).

These solutions serve to highlight inherent tensions in the regulations, and the underlying injustice that a party is prevented from presenting fresh evidence, however innocuous, if his opponent objects, however unreasonably. The final word on the topic is to reiterate that prevention is better than cure, in the form of the notice of hearing warning parties of the rule against the provision of new information at the hearing and making directions for the service of evidence before the hearing so as to avoid its strictures.

(8) The members of the authority are entitled to question any party or any other person such as a witness appearing at the hearing.[112] Not only can they ask questions, but they are entitled to demand answers. If the answers are not forthcoming, the sub-committee can adjourn the hearing to a specified date for answers to be provided. In *R (Murco Petroleum Limited) v Bristol City Council* [2010] EWHC 1992 (Admin) Cranston J rejected a submission to the contrary in trenchant terms:

> '34. Any other construction of the powers of a licensing authority would turn it into a cipher. It would be forced to make a decision on less information than necessary to promote the licensing objectives. A licensing authority must be able to pursue issues of public safety, the protection of children from harm and other objectives of the 2003 Act. The example proffered by Mr Kolvin QC, for the Council, is apposite:
>
> > "Imagine a rock festival. A temporary spectator stand is proposed. A question is raised whether it will be safe or a death trap. On the claimant's showing, the applicant can simply refuse to tell the authority anything about the means of construction, the expertise of the designer or the safety certification process, defying the authority to refuse the application and risk having to respond to an appeal, with all the unnecessary cost and time that that would entail".
>
> The claimant's interpretation of the provisions of the 2003 Act and attendant regulations would make a mockery of the standing of the Council as the licensing authority and its function as the primary decision-maker. It would also be inimical to the aim of the legislation to promote the licensing objectives. Perhaps as important it would frustrate the role which local residents have in making representations under the 2003 Act and would downgrade the role of democratically elected decision-makers.'

(9) A party may question another party with permission.[113] There is an open discretion to give permission. The Act does not provide for any presumption either way. This is to be contrasted with cross-examination, which is not to be permitted unless the authority considers that cross-examination

---

[112] Licensing Act 2003 (Hearings) Regulations 2005, reg 17.
[113] Licensing Act 2003 (Hearings) Regulations 2005, reg 16.

is required for it to consider the representations, application or notice as the case may require.[114] Here, the presumption is very much against, with permission for cross-examination to be given only in defined circumstances. This may include where there is a genuine question of fact the answer of which can only be elicited by those means. What is the difference between questions and cross-examination? This is not stated. However, the intention is presumably to distinguish between open questions where the questioner is trying to elicit an answer and cross-examination where closed questions are asked in order to wrest admissions or to prove a point. A further difference is that cross-examination may well involve pursuit of the person being questioned, whereas questions usually involve a single exchange on the topic at hand. The former is rarely helpful, and can in fact be seriously counter-productive, in licensing hearings. At all costs the Chair must ensure that no person attending the hearing is placed at a psychological disadvantage by the legal armoury available to the other side.

(10) The authority is obliged to disregard any information given by or on behalf of a party which is not relevant to the party's application, representation or notice and the promotion of the licensing objectives.[115] If material is not relevant, it should, of course, be disregarded. However, what of the case of an objection based on prospective nuisance which raises one type of noise nuisance, eg noise escape from a nightclub, but omits to refer to noise by persons after they have left the premises? Is evidence as to the latter relevant to the representation or not? On a literal approach, it is not. However, if the provision is to be read literally it becomes nonsensical. For example, if a party is not entitled to give evidence which is not relevant to their own application, they would be unable to rebut the content of the other party's representations. Further, if a party is not entitled to give evidence which is not relevant to the licensing objectives, an applicant would be unable to give evidence that their operation would create 100 jobs, make a contribution to the transport system in the town and cohere with the authority's transport, tourism, cultural and employment strategy, all of which might be relevant to the proportionality of imposing licensing restraints upon the operation. The purpose of the provision is to narrow the focus of the hearing and to prevent irrelevant evidence being given. The regulations might profitably have left it to the good sense of the committee to reach that conclusion by themselves. To avoid absurdity, it seems correct that the regulation should be given a purposive construction, so that only material wholly unrelated to the application or representation is excluded.

---

[114]   Licensing Act 2003 (Hearings) Regulations 2005, reg 23.
[115]   Licensing Act 2003 (Hearings) Regulations 2005, reg 19.

FAQ

Q   Is hearsay evidence admissible at the hearing?

A   Yes. The sub-committee is not a court of law and may take into account any information which it considers helpful, whether or not the evidence would be admissible in a court of law. This includes hearsay evidence. The topic is dealt with extensively in Chapter 5 (Evidence and Inference in Licensing).

Q   May the sub-committee take into account matters which are not the subject of relevant representations themselves should such material unexpectedly emerge at the hearing?

A   This important point still awaits resolution in the higher courts. Proponents of the view that the sub-committee may roam no further than the relevant representations make several points. First, section 18(3) of the Act states that where representations are made, the authority must 'hold a hearing to consider them' – ie the purpose of the hearing is to consider the representations, no more no less. Second, at the end of the hearing section 18(3) states that the authority must, having regard to the representations, take such of the steps mentioned in subsection (4) (if any) as it considers appropriate for the promotion of the licensing objectives. In other words, the material upon which the authority must act comprises the representations, not considerations going beyond those representations. Third, if there are no representations then there is no hearing; the authority cannot decide to take into account representations of its own devising. The logic is that if there is a hearing, it should only canvass the representations that have been made in due time by the proper parties in the proper manner. Fourth, the rules are designed to provide certainty as to the matters which are to be canvassed and the timing of their introduction. To permit other matters to be canvassed is sure to leave one or another party at a disadvantage. These are all powerful considerations.

On the other side of the argument is a purposive approach to the legislation. The legislation is there to protect the public interest as expressed through the licensing objectives. If a threat to the objectives emerges during the hearing, it would seem damaging to the public interest if the sub-committee were compelled to ignore it. While section 18(3)(b) of the Act refers to the duty to have regard to the representations, there is no reason why this has to be construed as having regard only to the representations. Had Parliament intended such a restrictive approach, it would have said so. It does not follow from the fact that a grant is compelled when there are no representations that when there are representations the authority has no wider remit than to consider them as though they are pleadings in civil litigation. The automatic grant provisions are designed to enable applications to which there is no objection to be granted without further ado. They do not constrain the discretion of the authority when a discretion has been conferred by the making of relevant representations. Furthermore, if the discretion is constrained, how does the constraint work? If there is an objection on grounds of public nuisance, does it mean that the authority cannot consider a type of public nuisance other than that specifically relied upon? Or does it just mean that it cannot consider a different licensing objective from that relied upon? But what if the different objective arises out of the same facts as the objective relied upon? What if questions which the sub-committee ask pursuant to their entitlement to do so reveal a threat to the licensing objectives? Must the sub-committee ignore this, and if so does this not render nugatory the right to ask questions? Are they entitled to take account of any obvious non-compliance with their own licensing policy, or can they only do so if representations have been made on the subject? In the latter case, how does this square with their duty to have regard to their own policy?[116] It will be seen that as soon as one seeks to erect barriers around the discretion of the authority, difficulties ensue.

The issue was in fact argued in *R (British Beer and Pub Association) v Canterbury City Council.*[117] However, in that case Richards J elected to leave the question open to be fought another day, and so the question has been left unanswered for many years since the Act was implemented. In conclusion, it is worth pointing out that national Guidance stops short of saying that the authority is debarred from looking beyond the content of the representations, stating:

> 'As a matter of practice, licensing authorities should seek to focus the hearing on the steps considered appropriate to promote the particular licensing objective or objectives that have given rise to the specific representation and avoid straying into undisputed areas.'[118]

It is considered on balance that that represents a correct statement of the law. While in most cases the hearing will solely concern the relevant representations, and the licensing sub-committee will not seek to conduct a hunt for further issues, nevertheless where a matter of concern arises, the authority, in pursuance of its statutory duty to promote the licensing objectives, is bound to consider it.

---

[116]   Licensing Act 2003, s 4(3)(a).
[117]   [2005] EWHC 1318 (Admin).
[118]   Para 9.33.

The decision

15.91   In the case of licence applications, the authority is given five working days from the last day of the hearing to make its decision.[119] It is often wise for the sub-committee to take this time so as to come to a fully considered view. Authorities are obliged to deliver reasons for their decision.[120] The quality of the written decision is an important factor in the determination of any appeal. In *R (Hope and Glory Public House Limited) v City of Westminster Magistrates Court*,[121] it was stated:

> '43. The statutory duty of the licensing authority to give reasons for its decision serves a number of purposes. It informs the public, who can make their views known to their elected representatives if they do not like the licensing sub-committee's approach. It enables a party aggrieved by the decision to know why it has lost and to consider the prospects of a successful appeal. If an appeal is brought, it enables the magistrates' court to know the reasons which led to the decision. The fuller and clearer the reasons, the more force they are likely to carry.'[122]

Therefore, clearly, the authority should not rush its decision. Some authorities prefer not to keep the parties in suspense and so announce their decision after a brief retirement and state that reasons will follow in due course. While this has its advantages, it can leave the suspicion that the authority has not necessarily thought matters through particularly thoroughly, and will simply have the legal adviser draw up reasons for its conclusions retrospectively. It is considered preferable for the authority to announce its decision only once it has drawn up proper reasons.

15.92   While the sub-committee is deliberating, it may be minded to impose conditions which have not been discussed by the parties. It is good practice for the authority to canvass the conditions with the parties to hear any submissions upon them and to arrive at an agreed form of wording if the conditions are to be imposed. This reduces the prospect of an appeal to the magistrates' court on the basis that conditions were imposed without submissions or that the wording adopted is uncertain or unduly onerous. Such a procedure has been held apposite for the justices,[123] and there is no reason why a different procedure should appertain before the licensing sub-committee.

---

[119]   Licensing Act 2003 (Hearings) Regulations 2005, reg 26(2).
[120]   Licensing Act 2003, s 23(2).
[121]   [2011] EWCA Civ 31.
[122]   Per Toulson LJ.
[123]   *R (Merran) v Metropolitan Stipendiary Magistrate* [2008] EWHC 1202 (Admin) at para [9].

Grant or rejection

15.93 When an application is granted under section 18, the licensing authority must forthwith give a notice to that effect to the applicant, any person who made relevant representations and the chief officer of police.[124] The authority must also forthwith issue the applicant with the licence and a summary of it[125] although note the requirement to do this 'forthwith' relates to the period between grant and the physical issue of the licence, and not the decision to grant in the first place. Forthwith in this context must surely mean not 'immediately, at once' but as soon as is 'reasonably practicable' in line with common sense.

15.94 Where an application has been rejected the authority must forthwith give a similar notice to the same persons mentioned above.

Form of licence and summary

15.95 The premises licence and summary must be in a prescribed form.[126]

E MAINTENANCE OF LICENCE, RIGHTS OF ENTRY, REGISTRATION

Production

15.96 The licensing authority is under an obligation to keep premises licence documents updated and, if necessary, to issue a new summary of a licence. For the purpose of discharging its obligations in this respect, it may require the holder of the premises licence to produce it (or the appropriate part) to the authority within 14 days. An offence is committed if the holder fails, without reasonable excuse, to comply with such a requirement.[127]

Custody and display

15.97 Whenever premises with a premises licence are being used for one or more licensable activity authorised by the licence, the holder of the licence must ensure that a licence or a certified copy of it is kept at the premises in the custody or control of the holder of the licence, or such other person who works at the premises and whom the holder of the licence has nominated in

---

[124]   Licensing Act 2003, s 23(1)(a).
[125]   Licensing Act 2003, s 23(1)(b).
[126]   Licensing Act 2003, s 24.
[127]   Licensing Act 2003, s 56.

writing for this purpose.[128] 2011 saw, under Home Office guidance, multi-agency enforcement visits to so called 'problem premises' in their area. Such visits entailed an on the spot analysis of each and every condition on the licence, and whether those conditions were being complied with. There are, no doubt, operators of licensed premises who do not hold, or do not know where they hold, their premises licence. Operators of licensed premises should ensure that all key personnel are aware of the whereabouts of the licence/certified copy to avoid such enforcement visits getting off to a bad start.

15.98 The holder of the premises licence must ensure that the summary of licence (or a certified copy) and a notice specifying the position held at the premises by the person responsible for the custody of the licence is prominently displayed at the premises.[129] The holder of the licence commits an offence if he fails without reasonable excuse to comply with these requirements. A constable or authorised person[130] may require the person so nominated to produce the licence, or a certified copy of it, for examination. The holder of the licence must additionally retain a list of any relevant mandatory conditions, and must also produce these upon request by a constable or authorised person. Where licensing authorities have not re-issued licences containing all the relevant mandatory conditions and a request is made to see these, the operator would either have to argue reasonable excuse (on the basis that the licensing authority had not issued the licence containing them), or provide his or her own list.

Powers of entry

15.99 A constable or authorised person[131] may, at any reasonable time before the determination of an application for a grant of a licence, provisional statement, variation or review of a licence, enter the premises concerned to assess the likely (or in the case of a review, the actual) effect on the promotion of the licensing objectives. An authorised person in such circumstances must, if so requested, produce evidence of his authority. Reasonable force may be used by a constable or authorised person in the exercise of these powers and intentional obstruction of such a person constitutes an offence.[132]

15.100 Similar powers of entry exist under section 179 even where no application in respect of the premises concerned is pending. In these circumstances, the grounds for entry are that the constable or authorised person has reason to believe that any premises are being, or are about to be,

---

[128] Licensing Act 2003, s 57.
[129] Licensing Act 2003, s 57.
[130] Licensing Act 2003, s 13.
[131] For the definition of 'authorised person' see para 15.07 above.
[132] Licensing Act 2003, s 59.

used for a licensable activity. If so, he may enter the premises with a view to seeing whether the activity is being, or is to be, carried on under and in accordance with an authorisation.

15.101   Further powers exist under section 108 for a constable to enter and search any premises where he has reason to believe that an offence under the Licensing Act has been, is being or is about to be committed. A constable exercising a power under this section may, if necessary, use reasonable force.

15.102   None of the rights of entry conferred above affect a constable's rights of entry under other legislation or common law.

Theft, loss etc of licence or summary

15.103   If the licence is lost or stolen, the holder of a premises licence may apply to the relevant licensing authority for a copy of the licence or summary. A crime reference number will be required in order to re-issue the licence if it has been lost or stolen in line with the requirement under section 25(3)(b).

Registration of interest

15.104   Many pub companies, multiple operators and freehold landlords have no interest in the day to day running of licensed premises, and are content to allow their tenant to be the premises licence holder. The right of the freeholders to do so is now established at law.[133] Nevertheless, as premises licences often have an intrinsic value, any change to that licence (particularly if it is after a review or a variation application) may carry serious economic consequences. A partial solution is provided by section 178 of the Act, which enables a person with a property interest, upon payment of a fee, to be notified forthwith of any changes to the licensing register. Such changes include any applications for variation or review of the licence.[134] While in theory this provides comfort, in practice this may not prove to be the case. While the licensing authority has to notify the freeholder forthwith of any changes to the licensing register, there is no commensurate requirement to update the licensing register forthwith.[135] Therefore, a licensing authority could take some time to amend its register to show that a licence is being reviewed under section 51. Unless the register is updated at the same time as the initial application is processed, the time window for the person who has registered the interest to take action may shrink dramatically, or indeed disappear.

---

[133]   See *Hall & Woodhouse v The Borough and County of the Town of Poole* [2009] EWHC 1587 (Admin) at [24].
[134]   See Licensing Act 2003, s 8, Sch 3.
[135]   See Licensing Act 2003, s 8.

15.105 The matters that must be entered into the register are listed variously both under Schedule 3 to the Act and subordinate legislation.[136]

15.106 A person who is entitled to register an interest in licensed premises includes the freeholder or leaseholder of those premises; a legal mortgagee; someone who is in occupation of the premises or has a prescribed interest in the premises.[137]

F DURATION

15.107 A premises licence has effect until:

(1) It is revoked under section 52;[138]
(2) It is specified to have effect for a limited period and that period expires;[139]
(3) The licensee dies or becomes a person who lacks capacity within the meaning of the Mental Capacity Act 2005 to hold the licence;
(4) The licensee becomes insolvent;
(5) The licensee is dissolved[140];
(6) If it is a club, the holder ceases to be a 'recognised club';[141]
(7) The licence is surrendered.[142]

An interesting discussion of these provisions arose in *Beauchamp Pizza Ltd v Coventry City Council*[143] where the licensee was struck off the register and dissolved by the Registrar of Companies for failing to file documents at Companies House in accordance with its company law obligations. The dissolution caused its premises licence to lapse under section 27(1)(c) of the Licensing Act 2003. The company was later granted administrative restoration to the register under section 1024 of the Companies Act 2006, the effect of which was that pursuant to section 1028 it was deemed to have continued in existence without having been struck off or dissolved. The company successfully argued that that meant that its licence was deemed to have continued in existence notwithstanding section 27(1)(c).

---

[136] Licensing Act 2003, Sch 3, and Licensing Act 2003 (Licensing authority's register) (other information) Regulations 2005.
[137] Licensing Act 2003, s 178(4)(a)–(d).
[138] Interestingly, the provisions of section 26 which set out the period of validity of a premises licence mention revocation under section 52, but not revocations under section 167(6)(e) (Revocation following Closure Order) nor section 53C(3)(e) (Revocation following Expedited Review).
[139] Licensing Act 2003, s 26(1)(a)(b).
[140] Licensing Act 2003, s 27(1)(a)(d).
[141] Ie a club which satisfies conditions 1 to 3 of the general conditions in section 62: see section 193.
[142] Licensing Act 2003, s 28.
[143] [2010] EWHC 926 (Ch).

Surrender of premises licence

15.108   The holder of a licence may at any time surrender the licence by giving the licensing authority a notice to that effect accompanied by the premises licence or if that is not practicable, by a statement of the reasons for the failure to provide the licence.[144]

The surrendered licence can be reinstated upon transfer (see below).

FAQ

Q   Can I surrender a licence immediately before a review where I expect the licence to be revoked, in order to apply to reinstate the licence once the review hearing has been cancelled by transferring it to another person?

A   While it has not been unknown for authorities to proceed to review the licence even after surrender, the better view is that it cannot do so because at the moment of the review hearing the licence is dead. An authority which is concerned that a subsequent application will be made to reinstate the licence would be well-advised simply to adjourn the review until following the last date for reinstatement, so that any reinstatement will be subject to the pending review of the licence.

G   PROVISIONAL STATEMENTS AND 'PROVISIONAL PREMISES LICENCES'

15.109   Provisional statements and the associated procedures set out in sections 29 to 32 of the Act are akin to outline planning consents. They enable applicants to establish the principle of the authorisation before having to work up the detail of their scheme. However, the crucial difference is that a provisional statement limits but does not exclude the possibility of later objection to the principle of the authorisation and so does not afford the certainty that the Government hoped and expected it to afford, for which reason the procedure is unpopular with applicants.

15.110   Rather, despite having to go through an almost identical process as a full premises licence application, including an application form, a schedule of works, advertisement and fending off relevant representations, the provisional statement does not give assurance of a premises licence. In this way, it stands in contrast to the former system, whereby provisional justices' site licences could be obtained and then made final at a later date without the

---

[144]   Licensing Act 2003, s 28.

possibility of further objections. Under the current regime, even if the provisional statement is granted and the substantial funds required are invested in development, a new premises licence must be applied for. When that happens, while certain relevant representations are automatically excluded, others are not.

15.111 The Act provides for the limitation of representations to the full premises licence as follows. Where an application is made for a full premises licence in the same form as the licence described in the application for the provisional statement <u>and</u> the work described in the schedule of works accompanying the application for the provisional statement has been satisfactorily completed, then certain representations to the full premises licence application are excluded.[145] From this it follows that where there is any difference between the provisional statement application and the premises licence application, there is no limit on the scope of relevant representations.

15.112 Where there is no difference then representations are excluded if the person making representations could have made them but failed to do so without reasonable excuse and there has been no material change in circumstances relating to the premises or the vicinity since the provisional statement was made.[146] Both limbs have to be satisfied before representations are treated as excluded. It will immediately be seen that the scope for repeat representations is large. The person making the representations would have a valid excuse if they did not live in the area formerly, or if they were away (eg working abroad, on holiday or in hospital) when the provisional statement application was made. Even if they were, they may still argue that matters have changed in relation to the premises or the vicinity in the intervening period. In the case of a new development, there may be more bars than were originally envisaged or, as often happens in the case of large developments, the built fabric may vary from the original designs. Equally, it may be said that the general vicinity has deteriorated, so increasing the importance of licensing restraint or the authority may have introduced a cumulative impact policy so altering the policy approach to the proposal. Indeed, the myriad possibilities of fresh objections being raised are such that no well-advised developer would be prepared to place substantial reliance on a piece of paper marked 'provisional statement'. It is too provisional a document upon which to rest one's business plans.

15.113 These concerns were in fact raised as the Bill passed through Parliament and Guidance was written to cater for the concerns, which remains to this day:

'Any person falling within section 16 of the 2003 Act can apply for a premises licence before new premises are constructed, extended or changed. This would be possible where clear plans of the proposed

---

[145] Licensing Act 2003, s 32(2).
[146] Licensing Act 2003, s 32(3).

structure exist and the applicant is in a position to complete an operating schedule including details of:

- the activities to take place there;
- the time at which such activities will take place;
- the proposed hours of opening;
- where the applicant wishes the licence to have effect for a limited period, that period;
- the steps to be taken to promote the licensing objectives; and
- where the sale of alcohol is involved, whether supplies are proposed to be for consumption on or off the premises (or both) and the name of the designated premises supervisor the applicant wishes to specify.'[147]

15.114 Acting on that advice, many developers therefore apply for what is sometimes referred to as a 'provisional premises licence'. This raises some practical problems where the premises have not yet been built, but with the co-operation of the licensing authority and other responsible authorities, such hurdles can be overcome. For example, the plan may simply show the shell of a building, without giving the sort of detail one might expect of operational premises. Matters not shown might include the location of the bar, fire safety equipment, fixed seating, pool tables or gaming machines or the heights of any steps or raised platforms, all of which may be required to be shown under the regulations if they impact on individuals' ability to use the exits. However, if none of these items exists, then clearly they need not be shown on the plan. Such details can be dealt with by way of a section 34 or minor variation at a later date. 'Sign off' conditions can be offered in the operating schedule allowing the Fire Authority, the police or environmental health the final say before licensable activities can commence. Additionally, conditions can be offered up thus: 'no licensable activities shall be permitted until this premises licence has been transferred to an operator tenant' and/or 'the Premises shall not trade until a full variation application under section 34 has been submitted which includes full details of the layout of the proposed premises'.

15.115 Such Provisional premises licences tend to be sufficient to persuade interested operators to commit to signing the agreement for lease. So long as a wide interpretation is taken of the requirement under section 16 that the developer or other applicant is someone who is a person who 'carries on or proposes to carry on a business which involves the use of the premises for the licensable activities to which the application relates', then it seems that the trend for provisional premises licences in preference to provisional statements will continue.

---

[147] Para 8.85.

Provisional statements – procedure

15.116 Any person who is interested in the premises[148] and is over the age of 18 and is an individual, may apply for a provisional statement. The requirement of an interest in the premises is far more relaxed than that under section 16(1) for premises licences ('carries on, or proposes to carry on, a business which involves the use of the premises for the licensable activities to which the application relates') and should be construed broadly by the licensing authority. A legal or equitable interest in the premises is not required. The premises must either be, or be about to be, constructed for the purpose of being used for one or more licensable activities, or be or be about to be extended or otherwise altered for that purpose (whether or not they are already being used for that purpose).[149] A provisional statement does not require a plan, just a schedule of works. The application must be advertised in the usual way both at or on the premises and in a local newspaper. The wording of the notice must additionally state that representations are restricted after the issue of a provisional statement and, where it is known, may state the relevant licensable activity which it is proposed will be carried on, on or from the premises. Whilst plans are not required under the Regulations to accompany the application, the application form under Schedule 3 of the Licensing Act (Premises Licences and Club Premises Certificates) Regulations 2005 states 'please give details of the work and please attach plans of the work being done or about to be done at the premises'.

H TRANSFER OF PREMISES LICENCE

15.117 The simplest and most common form of transfer of premises licence is in a consensual commercial transaction where the date of the transfer may be important (for signing of the lease or for the new tenant to start trading), but the application itself is not urgent. Problems for operators, and indeed licensing authorities, occur however when time or consent, or both, are in short supply.

15.118 A basic transfer of a premises licence takes place under section 42. Any person who complies with the criteria under section 16(1) (who can apply for a premises licence) may apply to the licensing authority for the transfer of the licence to him. The applicant must be 18 or over if an individual and the relevant form must be completed. A crucial requirement is that the written consent of the existing premises licence holder is given and included in the application. Such an application can include a request for the

---

[148] Licensing Act 2003, s 29(2)(a); as with applications for premises licences, licensing authorities should look broadly at the circumstances of the individual application, and it is not necessary to import automatically any requirement of an interest in the property, either legal or equitable.

[149] Licensing Act 2003, s 29(1).

transfer to have immediate effect.[150] Where the consent is included, this can result in an almost immediate transfer of the premises licence from one operator to another, so long as the police have been given a copy of the application. The police must be given the application on the same day on which the application is given to the licensing authority.[151] The police have 14 days to object from the date they are notified of the application, and therefore prospective tenants who commit unconditionally to a lease upon the immediate transfer of the premises licence are technically at risk should the police object within those 14 days and subsequently persuade the licensing authority at a hearing to reject the transfer application (although the transfer has effect pending that hearing).

15.119 Where a transfer application has been made which includes a request that the transfer have immediate effect and the requirements of section 43 are met, then the premises licence has effect during the application period as if the applicant were the holder of the licence. The application period itself begins with the date when the application is received by the licensing authority (and also the police) and ends either when the licence is transferred following the grant of the application or, if the application is rejected, when the applicant is notified of the rejection, or when the application is withdrawn. In cases where the application is rejected or withdrawn, the licence will revert to the original premises licence holder. If during this application period the original premises licence holder has become insolvent, then the licence will immediately lapse. An interim authority or an application to reinstate the premises licence would therefore be required within 28 days (see below).

15.120 The police may only object if they are satisfied that the exceptional circumstances of the case are such that granting the application would undermine the crime prevention objective.[152]

15.121 An applicant can appeal against a rejection[153] and the police may appeal against a grant.[154] Unlike decisions by a licensing authority on a review under sections 52 or 53C, the decision of the licensing authority is not 'suspended' during any appeal. Thus upon notification of any rejection of the transfer the premises licence reverts to its original holder. This applies equally whether the application included a request for the transfer to have an immediate effect or not.

---

[150] Licensing Act 2003, s 43(1).
[151] Licensing Act 2003 (Premises Licence and Club Premises Certificate) Regulations 2005, reg 28(2)(c).
[152] Licensing Act 2003, s 42(6).
[153] Licensing Act 2003, s 181, Sch 5, Part 1 para 1(d).
[154] Licensing Act 2003, s 181, Sch 5, Part 6.

FAQ

Q   What happens if a tenant takes over a pub and submits a transfer to have immediate effect only to have it rejected following a hearing?

A   The licence will revert to the original premises licence holder which clearly may cause contractual issues. The original premises licence holder may (due to the new tenant) now have no interest in the running of the premises but would nevertheless have legal responsibilities under the Licensing Act as holder of the licence. If an appeal is lodged, both the tenant and the (unwilling) licence holder may have a tricky period pending any successful outcome. The alternative is to continue to submit 'immediate effect' transfers, thus re-invoking the provisions of section 43(1) until the original appeal is successful. However, if the circumstances of the premises in question are such that the police are resolutely opposed to the transfer, no doubt they would consider issuing a review or even summary review application for revocation of the premises licence which is likely to be heard prior to any appeal.

Transfers, reviews and appeals

15.122   Difficulties are frequently encountered where a transfer is made before or during the review process, or pending an appeal against a review decision. The transfer does not defeat the review, as a review is a review of the premises licence, and not the premises licence holder.[155] A premises licence holder whose licence is being reviewed may, perhaps in desperation, transfer it to another operator the day before the hearing. This may have some effect on the hearing (notification of parties etc) but it will not avoid the review going ahead at some point. Following a review, and within the 21 days permitted to appeal the decision, the premises licence can be transferred in the normal way – in which case the new holder of the premises licence would need to appeal (if so advised).[156] It sometimes occurs that transfers take place after an appeal is lodged. May the transferee stand in the shoes of the original licensee for the purposes of prosecution of the appeal? This eventuality is not contemplated either in the Act or in the Magistrates' Courts Act 1980. Further, the Magistrates' Court Rules deal with appellants and respondents, not with premises licence holders, so that arguably the fact that the latter has changed does not give the incoming licensee the status of respondent. There has certainly been one case in which a District Judge has

---

[155]   See for example Licensing Act 2003, s 51(1) 'May apply to the relevant licensing authority for a review of the licence'.
[156]   See for example Licensing Act 2003, Sch 5 para 8(2)(b) (Review under Section 52) and para 8A(2)(b) (Summary Review) both of which state 'The holder of the premises licence' may appeal against the decision.

refused to permit the new licensee to take over the appeal.[157] Nevertheless, it is generally accepted that the transferee may be substituted as the appellant, provided that this can be done without injustice and subject of course to the assumption of any risk as to costs.

15.123 In certain circumstances the new holder may need the assistance and evidence of the former holder at the hearing of the appeal. However, where the review is based on the mismanagement of the former licensee and the transferee pitches itself as the new broom, it may not want the former licensee involved at all.

Non-consensual transfers

15.124 The circumstances in which an existing premises licence holder might refuse or ignore any requests to sign the consent form are diverse, but most arise from contractual disputes or the fact that the existing licence holder has simply vanished from the face of the earth. In such circumstances both a standard transfer and an 'immediate effect transfer' can be made if the licensing authority has exempted the applicant from the requirement to obtain the holder's consent.[158] In both cases, the applicant must show to the licensing authority's satisfaction that he has taken all reasonable steps to obtain that consent and that he would be in a position to use the premises for the licensable activities or activities authorised by the premises licence. In the case of the absentee licence holder, proof of telephone calls made and more specifically a stamped addressed envelope sent to the holder's usual business address should suffice. Sworn affidavits showing that 'reasonable steps' have been taken have been used on some occasions. It is submitted that some form of proactive action must be shown to have been taken as a decision by the licensing authority to grant the transfer without consent is an important one.

15.125 More frequent perhaps are those situations where there is a contractual dispute and the existing premises licence holder has explicitly refused to sign the consent, perhaps even writing (through lawyers or not) to the licensing authority to that effect. Such refusals can also be accompanied by threats of civil action against the licensing authority if it grants the transfer in light of such a refusal. One interpretation of the requirement to take all reasonable steps to obtain consent is that the express refusal of consent self evidently proves that this requirement has not been met. This interpretation is usually based on two limbs, namely (i) that the provisions were drafted to cover those cases where the applicant to the transfer, despite his best efforts, is unable to obtain a decision on the issue of consent (for example, because the present holder is uncontactable) and (ii) that for a licensing authority to

---

[157] See for example, *Kuldip Singh Bhandal v Walsall MBC and Baljit Singh (Intervener)* (unreported) before DJ Morris, Walsall Magistrates' Court 23 July 2008.
[158] Licensing Act 2003, ss 44(6) and 43(5) respectively.

transfer the licence against the express wishes of the existing licence holder might violate the holder's Convention rights under the Human Rights Act 1998, namely his rights to protection of his property under Article 1, Protocol 1 of the European Convention on Human Rights. Whilst the point has not yet been decided, it would appear that this interpretation takes too restrictive a view of the 'reasonable steps' requirement, and places too much weight on the requirement to obtain consent in preference to the second and conjunctive requirement, namely that the applicant would be in a position to use the premises for the licensable activities authorised by the premises licence. If the licensee is no longer in any position to use the premises but the putative transferee is, then the preferable view is that proof that the latter had sought the consent of the former is all that should be required.

15.126 The licensing authority may choose to sit on the fence, frozen into indecision by the lack of clarity in the Act. The Act, however, *requires* the licensing authority to exempt the applicant from the requirement to obtain the holder's consent if the aforementioned criteria are complied with to the licensing authority's satisfaction. Thus the licensing authority may feel compelled, regardless of any outstanding contractual dispute, to grant the transfer. However, this in itself may cause problems and result in a game of ping pong transfer if, in the light of this grant, the original licence holder himself submits a transfer application. However, the licensing authority is statutorily mandated to scrutinise the relative claims and make a decision. In doing so, it will bear in mind that simply being the premises licence holder (whether on an interim basis or not) does not in and of itself imply a legitimate proprietary interest in the premises. It is submitted that the minimum requirement is that any prospective transferee can prove an extant and valid interest in the premises in order to prove that he will be in a position to use those premises for the licensable activity or activities authorised. It does not matter whether the interest arises through a lease, a tenancy at will or a licence granted by the landlord. However, the tenant who has been kicked out or has handed the keys back should not be able to stop a transfer back to the landlord.

Notification of determination of transfer

15.127 Where a transfer is either granted or rejected under section 42 the licensing authority must give a notice to that effect both to the applicant and to the police.[159] Where the police have objected and the matter goes to a hearing, the licensing authority's notice must state the authority's reason for granting or rejecting the application.[160]

---

[159] Licensing Act 2003, s 41(1)(a)–(b).
[160] Licensing Act 2003, s 45(2).

FAQ

Q   Can I make an application to transfer a premises licence but allow it to take effect at a later date, for example when the completion of a sale takes place?

A   Both the application form and the Act [161] accommodate transfer applications where the grant of the application may differ from the date when the transfer takes effect. It is therefore possible to allow a measure of certainty in sale and purchase agreements of the premises in which the 14 day police objection period has expired, the transfer has been granted, but the transfer does not take effect until perhaps several days later. In such circumstances purchasers of ongoing businesses can sign the completion documents knowing that the transfer is already granted and that the premises licence will pass into their name on the date agreed. This raises interesting questions as to whether, if the sale negotiation collapses, and the original premises licence holder wishes to withdraw, the transfer would still go through. There seems to be no reason why it should not. Such contingencies ought therefore to be addressed in the sale and purchase agreements.

What happens if the date of the transfer of the premises is unknown? Might a licensing authority accept an application to transfer which states 'to take effect upon notification to the licensing authority in writing', in the same way as many plans variations are made? This is questionable at best. The Act requires the authority to specify 'the time when the transfer takes effect.' [162] There has to be a degree of closure from the licensing authority's perspective.

Duty to notify designated premises supervisor of transfer

15.128   The applicant must notify any designated premises supervisor of the transfer application forthwith if the transfer includes a request to have immediate effect [163] in cases where the applicant and the designated premises supervisor are not the same person. Additionally, whether the transfer is immediate or not, upon grant the applicant must forthwith notify the designated premises supervisor of that transfer. [164] These are important

---

[161]   Licensing Act 2003, s 45(3).
[162]   Licensing Act 2003, s 45(3).
[163]   Licensing Act 2003, s 46(2).
[164]   Licensing Act 2003, s 46(3).

provisions for any applicant to bear in mind as an offence is committed if the applicant fails without reasonable excuse to comply with these require-ments.[165]

15.129 It is often the case that the designated premises supervisor stays with the premises on either an immediate or standard transfer application in which case service of either notice can be effected by delivering it to or sending it by post to his proper address (often the premises in question). Where the designated premises supervisor has, however, left the premises then service upon his last known address or his relevant registered address as stated in the licensing authority's register are equally valid.[166]

15.130 As stated above, the transfer itself is not invalid if subsequent inquiries show that proper service upon the designated premises supervisor was not effected, but an offence may have been committed.

Preserving the licence on death, mental incapacity or insolvency

15.131 A licence is a valuable commodity. There is a logic to the provisions causing the licence to lapse on the death, insolvency or mental capacity of the licensee. Otherwise, who is to be charged with the responsibility of upholding its terms? But Parliament wished to enable administrators or successor in title to preserve the licence while arrangements were made for succession. This resulted in two provisions: interim authority notices and reinstatement on transfer governed by sections 47 and 50 respectively. It is necessary first to set out the effect of the provisions briefly before considering their practical effect.

Interim authority notice

15.132 Within 28 days of the lapse of the licence for death, incapacity or insolvency, a person who is connected to the former licensee or a person with a prescribed interest may apply for an interim authority notice.[167] Connected persons are the deceased's personal representative, a person with power of attorney for an incapacitated person or, most usually, an insolvent person's insolvency practitioner. A prescribed interest is defined as a legal interest in the premises as freeholder or leaseholder.[168]

---

[165] Licensing Act 2003, s 46(5).
[166] Licensing Act 2003, s 184(3), (5)–(7).
[167] Licensing Act 2003, s 47(1), (2). Section 47(2) was amended by the Legislative Reform (Licensing)(Interim Authority Notices etc) Order 2010 which extended the 'initial period' from 7 to 28 days.
[168] Licensing Act 2003 (Premises Licence and Club Premises Certificates) Regulations 2005, reg 8.

15.133   If such application is made, the interim authority notice takes effect immediately, so reviving the licence temporarily in the name of the applicant.[169] The applicant must then notify the police by the end of the 28th day, failing which the notice lapses.[170] The police then have two working days to decide whether the exceptional circumstances of the case are such that a failure to cancel the notice would undermine the crime prevention objective, and so give a notice to the licensing authority to that effect. If they do, a hearing ensues[171] at which the authority must cancel the notice if it considers it appropriate for the promotion of the crime prevention objective to do so.[172] The licence will lapse once again in such circumstances.

15.134   If no application to cancel is made, or if such application fails, the interim authority notice remains good for three months from the date it was given or earlier if terminated by the person giving notice.[173] At the end of that period or upon earlier termination, the premises licence lapses again. In essence, therefore, the interim authority gives breathing space of up to three months for the holders to work out to whom they wish to transfer the licence in the meantime. If, within the period of three months a 'relevant transfer application' is made which is given interim effect by section 43 of the Act, then the licence is preserved by virtue of that section.

15.135   If a police objection to the notice is upheld, the person who gave the notice may appeal to the magistrates court, but the interim authority notice will not be reinstated unless and until the court decides to do so.[174] The court has jurisdiction to order the reinstatement of the notice pending the disposal of the appeal or the interim authority period, whichever occurs first.[175] An urgent application ought therefore to be made to the court for reinstatement at the time of the appeal. The court is of course under no requirement to reinstate the interim authority notice but may generally be expected to do so unless there would be immediate harm to the licensing objectives. The police may also appeal against a decision not to cancel the notice, but there are no similar provisions allowing the court to cancel the notice pending the disposal of the appeal or the expiry of the interim authority period.[176]

---

[169]   Licensing Act 2003, s 47(6).
[170]   Licensing Act 2003, s 47(7). Where the interim authority notice is given electronically, it is the licensing authority which has to notify the police: s 47(7A).
[171]   Unless the authority, the relevant person and the police all consider a hearing unnecessary: s 48(3).
[172]   Licensing Act 2003, s 48(3).
[173]   Licensing Act 2003, s 47(7), (10).
[174]   Licensing Act 2003, Sch 5 para 7(1).
[175]   Licensing Act 2003, Sch 5 para 7(4).
[176]   Licensing Act 2003, Sch 5, para 7.

Reinstatement on transfer

15.136 An alternative route to preservation is provided by section 50. Within 28 days of the licence lapsing a person who is within section 16(1) and so would be entitled to apply for a licence may apply for a transfer of the licence and for the transfer to have immediate effect. If he does, then the licence is reinstated from the moment of receipt of the application. The licence lapses if the application is rejected or if the application is withdrawn.

Discussion

15.137 In recent years, trade associations have reported that between 20 and 50 pubs are closing in England and Wales each week. It is therefore unsurprising that interim authority notices have come to be widely used. The usual scenario is that a company which holds many premises licences becomes insolvent and an insolvency practitioner ('IP') is appointed to manage the company's affairs, frequently appointing a management company on an interim basis to run the estate. The primary responsibility of such IPs will be to protect the assets of the company on behalf of its creditors. In many cases, therefore, the IP will want the business(es) involved to continue trading pending negotiations with interested purchasers. Such situations can be urgent in the extreme and often the protection of the premises licence is forgotten when matters such as employees' remuneration and repossession of the premises are being dealt with. Others may be so called 'pre-pack' insolvencies where matters are a little more planned. The other scenarios at which these provisions are directed, namely the death or mental incapacity of the licence holder, are less common. However, in all cases, if the licence is to be preserved an application must be made either for a transfer of the licence or an interim authority within 28 days of the insolvency, death or incapacity.[177]

15.138 It is useful to compare the two sets of provisions. One practical point that is sometimes lost, certainly by operators, is that if a premises licence lapses then there is no licence and the premises cannot trade until that licence is either the subject of an interim authority notice or a reinstatement on transfer. Often, the licensing authority itself may not discover that the licence has lapsed until it has obtained information from Companies House or the IP. The fact that the premises have been trading for days or weeks beforehand, albeit unlawfully, is of course, is no reason to permit that unlawful situation to continue pending remedial action.

---

[177] Licensing Act 2003, s 47(2) as amended by the Legislative Reform (Licensing) (Interim Authority Notices etc) Order 2010 which extended the 'initial period' from seven to 28 days.

15.139   An interim authority notice cannot be made where an application for transfer of the licence has been made under section 50.[178] In similar vein an application for reinstatement of the licence under section 50 can only be made where no interim authority notice has effect.[179] So, to that extent, the provisions are intended to be mutually exclusive. Furthermore, neither interim authority notices nor section 50 applications to reinstate require the consent of the former holder. There are clearly practical reasons for this – directors disappear; dead people can't write.

15.140   What is the practical difference therefore between the two sections? IPs often use interim authority notices as it is difficult for them to meet the requirements under section 16(1) which must be satisfied in order to permit an application for reinstatement on transfer. They will then hold the premises licence under the interim authority notice, pending a subsequent transfer within three months to a trade operator. This may be to an interim pub management company or on a more permanent basis. If the IP wishes to maximise the time to find that trade operator it can submit the interim authority notice towards the end of the 28 day period, in effect giving it nearly a full month to do so. However, as mentioned above, the premises will of course not trade at all (as the licence has lapsed) between the triggering event (in this case insolvency) and the interim authority notice.

15.141   A reinstatement on transfer is more likely to be made either by an interim pub management company with the consent of the IP, or perhaps by the freeholder pending the identification of another tenant. Some large pub companies which hold freeholds and normally lease out some of their estate to tenants may choose to take the licence back under their managed arm (with a temporary manager) whilst a new tenant is found into whose name the licence can subsequently be transferred. Only one application for transfer of the premises licence by way of reinstatement can be made[180] within 28 days of lapse.[181]

FAQ

Q   I am a director of a pub company. One of my tenants is in dispute with us about his lease agreement. I believe he is also about to be made insolvent. The pub isn't trading, but he refuses to sign a consent – I want the licence back. What do I do?

A   Clearly, you can apply to transfer the licence under section 43 without consent and ask the licensing authority to exempt you, having shown that you have taken all reasonable steps to obtain

---

[178]   Licensing Act 2003, s 47(1)(b).
[179]   Licensing Act 2003, s 50(1)(b).
[180]   Licensing Act 2003, s 50(7).
[181]   Licensing Act 2003, s 47(10) of the Act as amended by reg 2(1)(b)(ii) of the Legislative Reform (Licensing) (Interim Authority Notices etc) Order 2010.

that consent. However, if it looks likely that the licensing authority will reject such an application in the light of a commercial dispute then the position is more complicated. You can register an interest to be notified of changes to the licensing register under section 178 of the Act. You can also keep an eye on any insolvency proceedings. If and when the tenant is made insolvent then you can apply, without his consent, to reinstate the licence as you satisfy the requirements of section 50. Alternatively, you could apply to the county court to remove the tenant under the terms of the lease and re-apply under section 42. Neither a possession order in the county court nor any subsequent transfer application would however be guaranteed to succeed. Lastly, there is nothing to stop you making an application for a new premises licence which could clearly be withdrawn if consent is obtained during the application period, or indeed if the tenant becomes insolvent and reinstatement is preferred.

I INSOLVENCY AND DISSOLUTION

15.142 There are almost certainly premises being used for licensable activities by operators even though the licence has lapsed and is void. In many cases, this will be because the licence was transferred after the initial period for applying for an interim authority notice or reinstatement on transfer has expired.[182]

15.143 Neither licensing authorities nor necessarily even licensing lawyers are generally experts in insolvency law, and in addition to this, and sometimes because of this, are not aware of the current state of relevant insolvency proceedings. However, a working knowledge of insolvency law is an essential tool. Definitions of insolvency are set out in section 27 of the Act.

15.144 In brief, an individual becomes insolvent on:

(a)   The approval of a voluntary arrangement proposed by him;
(b)   Being adjudged bankrupt or having his estate sequestrated or;
(c)   Entering into a deed of arrangement made for the benefit of his creditors or a trust deed for his creditors.

A company becomes insolvent on:

(a)   The approval of a voluntary arrangement proposed by its directors;
(b)   The appointment of and administrator in respect of the company;
(c)   The appointment of an administrative receiver in respect of the company; or
(d)   Going into liquidation.

---

[182]   7 days before the Legislative Reform Order of 1 October 2010 and 28 days since.

All of those expressions are given the same meaning as they have in the Insolvency Act 1986.

15.145 A premises licence lapses immediately upon the insolvency of the holder. No notice to the licensing authority or any other individual is required. Every one of the routes to insolvency described above involves different procedures, be they orders from the court or the signed minutes of an Emergency General Meeting, the date of the appointment of an administrator or the coming into existence of a company or individual voluntary arrangement. However, it is not always immediately clear whether there is an insolvency situation, which poses problems for those interested in maintaining the validity of the premises licence following its lapse. Many licensing authorities rely upon entries on the Companies House website, but that website is not updated instantaneously and neither does the basic information it provides necessarily give the exact time and date of the relevant insolvency. Often the only definitive statement of the position can be obtained from the IP itself. Needless to say, any prospective purchaser considering acquiring a premises licence from a holder with a turbulent financial history would be well advised to check in great detail that that premises licence has not lapsed by virtue of section 27 – regardless of what the licensing authority may say.

15.146 With regard to dissolution, as described above, the restoration to the register under section 1028 of the Companies Act 2006, following an administrative striking off, retrospectively undoes the automatic lapsing provisions of section 27(4)(d) of the 2003 Act (license lapses on company going insolvent).[183] This raises issues for both operators and enforcing authorities. Operators, during the period between any administrative striking off and subsequent restoration, will have to make the decision whether they can lawfully trade. The license has lapsed, but it may retrospectively be deemed to have continued during the period since the company was struck off, by virtue of the deeming provisions of section 1028 of the Companies Act 2006. It would, however, be a brave operator who chose to trade during a period when the licence was dead, but if it did, enforcing authorities may be reluctant to institute prosecutions for unlicensed trading if there is a chance that the company will be restored to the Register.

J VARIATIONS TO THE PREMISES LICENCE

Introduction

15.147 Prior to the introduction of the minor variation procedure the only way a premises licence holder could vary the licence was by way of a major

[183] *Beauchamp Pizza Ltd v Coventry City Council* [2010] EWHC 926 (Ch). See para 15.107 above.

variation under section 34 (hereafter called 'a major variation') or a so called informal variation, a variation to the DPS or a change of name or address.

15.148 In the case of an informal variation many licensing authorities forewent the right to an application fee in order to allow the premises licence holder to change certain aspects of the licence or the accompanying plan in uncontroversial cases. Local practices developed where the licence holder may have been requested to obtain the police or the environmental health officer's prior consent or indeed the licensing authority itself may have sought relevant authorities' views upon receipt of the request. This practice, inspired by a mixture of common sense and the seeming inflexibility of the Act and Regulations, has all but died out. Despite initial concerns, the minor variation procedure seems to strike about the right balance between allowing licensing authorities to charge a fee for processing insignificant changes to the relevant licence, and not imposing punitive fees or administrative burdens on licence holders who seek to ensure that their licences are truly reflective of the layout of their premises, and the licensable activities which they undertake. This is quite a success given that the licensing authority's decision is final, and there is no appeal!

15.149 Before looking at the various procedures individually, it is important to clarify when any form of variation application needs to be made. When it comes to the question of licensable activities and the hours during which those activities take place, the position is quite clear – either the licence covers the hours and activities in question or it doesn't. In the latter case, urgent action is required to rectify matters.

15.150 The dilemma for even the innocently mistaken operator in these circumstances is that by varying the licence he or she may be drawing the authorities' attention to a breach (to which they may have been hitherto blissfully unaware). In the case of the operator who has been deliberately flouting the law, proportionate enforcement consequences will follow. For the operator who has made a genuine mistake about the law, perhaps not realising that a particular function room is not licensed for music entertainment even though the rest of the premises is, then clearly the unlicensed activities must cease immediately, but any remedial action to rectify the position could also be dealt with proportionately, and with a degree of common sense. Clearly, the operator who makes a variation application in such circumstances and can say in all honesty to the licensing sub-committee that it was a mistake (together with an explanation why) may well be able to use the periods of unlicensed trading to prove the variation in fact would not undermine the licensing objectives as no noise complaints or incidents of disorder arose during that unlicensed period.

15.151 However, when it comes to the plan attached to the licence, the position is less obvious. There are many plans attached to licences across the country which show a level of detail that is not remotely required by the

Regulations. These include pot plants, computerised images of happy customers sitting at tables, microwave ovens and toilet seats. The author has even seen one plan attached to an application where the applicant, having taken the sensible advice of the licensing authority that the plan did not have to be 'professionally drawn' at face value, submitted a pencil sketch of himself behind his counter proudly displaying his range of cheap beverages.

15.152 Some commentators have indicated that as things such as pot plants (provided they do not impact on individuals' ability to use fire escape routes etc) do not need to be shown on plans, then if such items are removed from the premises, then nothing needs to be done to the plan itself. In other words, since the Regulations do not require these things to be shown then altering them or removing them does not require any form of variation of the licence. This view, it is submitted, confuses the applicants' right to choose any additional items that he wishes to be shown on the plan (for example to assist with the Fire Authority's consideration of the application) with his duties to carry out licensable activities in accordance with an authorisation, failing which he could be liable to prosecution under section 136. Neither section 34 nor section 41A (minor variation) are compulsory – they do not say 'shall apply' but 'may apply'. An operator whose premises (and therefore layout) has undergone a major refurbishment and complete change of style, for example from a restaurant to a nightclub, may choose to take these words at face value. However it will not be long before the police or licensing authority are knocking on the door with a section 19 closure notice[184] or an invitation for an interview under caution. There is no offence of not making a variation – but there is an offence of carrying out licensable activities otherwise than in accordance with an authorisation.

15.153 If, therefore, during the transitional period the licence holder included a very detailed plan with the sort of specific (but not required) details as listed above, what does he do if the pot plant dies, or his customers are no longer interested in microwaved hotdogs, and he removes the offending oven? In strict terms he is carrying out licensable activities otherwise than in accordance with an authorisation, as the plan is part of the licence and the licence is the authorisation. None but the most draconian licensing authorities would commence enforcement proceedings for omitting a pot plant or computer-drawn customer. But what if instead the items were pool tables? So long as pool tables do not impact on fire escape routes, then they are not required by the Regulations to be shown, but many operators would wish to show them. For example, a typical snooker hall may often remove or move such items. Many snooker halls have recorded music and facilities for dancing to cover the odd private event.[185] Showing snooker tables gives responsible authorities assurance that they are not being asked to

---

[184]   Criminal Justice and Police Act 2001.
[185]   Facilities for dancing are now no longer licensable activities by virtue of the Live Music Act 2012.

deal with a nightclub posing as a snooker hall. But if the snooker hall owner is not required to submit any form of variation application with respect to his plans when moving those tables, he could easily turn himself into a nightclub without any of the authorities needing to be notified.

15.154 Whilst the above scenario may sound unlikely, many operators are constantly seeking new income streams in these straitened times. They would also rather not pay a fee if possible.

15.155 The minor variations procedure solves many of these problems. It allows operators whose plans may be too detailed to clear them up with a single 'less is more' plan that shows no more than the Regulations require. Additionally, more detailed plans for information purposes can be provided to the authorities if desired. A snooker hall cum nightclub owner would be well advised to submit a similar minor variation removing any items (including pool tables) which are not required to be shown in the plans regulations. If the licensing authority has any questions when deliberating on such an application, they will no doubt ask.

15.156 Some operators are perfectly happy to continually submit minor variation applications as and when certain aspects of the plans change or are due to change (whether required by the Regulations or not). This is perfectly good practice, since it prevents any suggestion of discrepancy between the plans and the actual layout. However, for those with shallower pockets a more considered approach to the Regulations may be appropriate.

(i) Major variations under section 34

15.157 The timescales and procedures for an application under section 34 are identical to those for a new premises licence application, and will not be repeated here. The application form is similar and self-explanatory, although some problems have been encountered when either applicants or licensing authorities have failed to make clear the distinction between what is staying on the licence and what is changing. The application form states 'please complete those parts of the Operating Schedule below which would be subject to change if this application to vary is successful'. Some confusion has arisen when applicants wishing to add certain licensable activities have deleted other boxes which their licence already authorises them to undertake, but they do not wish to change. On some occasions this has been treated as a request to remove those licensable activities in their entirety. Equally, the question arises as to what to put in the 'times stated' boxes when an applicant is applying to extend existing times. If an applicant can already sell alcohol until 2300, and wishes to extend to 2400 does he state the start time in the variation application as '2300' and the finish time as '2400' or does he complete the boxes on the basis of total hours that alcohol could be sold where the variation application to be granted? The note on the form as stated above is clear, and requests *completions* of those parts of the operation below which would be *subject to change* if successful. Both common sense, and the note itself, therefore indicate that where licensable activities (or indeed opening hours) are to be extended in any way, the entirety of the granted hours should be stated. Where days or indeed whole licensable activities are to remain unchanged, leaving blank should suffice, but for the avoidance of doubt the insertion of the words 'no change' may be preferable.

15.158 It should be noted that section 35, which deals with the grant (or rejection) of a major variation application does not contain the same requirement of its equivalent for a new licence application under section 18, namely to grant the variation subject to such conditions as are consistent with the operating schedule accompanying the application.[186] Section 35(2) simply states as long as there have not been relevant representations and the application is not to extend the period for which the licence has effect, nor to vary substantially the premises to which it relates, it must simply grant the application. This raises the question as to the statutory basis for any 'conversion' by the licensing authority of the measures set out in boxes M (a) – (e) of the operating schedule into conditions. Nonetheless the licensing regime would break down if applicants were not able to add conditions by way of a major variation application, and common practice sees measures set out in those boxes accompanying variation applications converted into conditions in the same way as they are with new premises licence applications.

15.159 As stated above, a licence may not be varied under section 35 to extend the lifetime of the licence nor to substantially vary the premises.[187] The concept of 'substantial variation of the premises' is not defined in the Act, and the Guidance is silent on the point. It is thought, however, that major structural alterations would be classified as substantial and therefore not capable of being authorised through the variation procedures. Where there is doubt as to the correct application, prior consultation with the licensing authority is advisable to avoid unnecessary rejection, not least because the only redress for the failed applicant would be an expensive judicial review.

15.160 Just as for premises licence applications, if there are no relevant representations, the application must be granted. If there are representations, then there needs to be a hearing unless the authority and all parties agree that the hearing is unnecessary.[188] The authority has to have regard to such representations before taking such steps (if any) as it considers necessary for the promotion of the licensing objectives. These are to modify the conditions of the licence or to reject the whole or part of the application.[189] There is sometimes a temptation for licensing authorities to take steps which are not

---

[186]   Licensing Act 2003, s 18(2)(a).
[187]   Licensing Act 2003, s 35(6).
[188]   Licensing Act 2003, s 35(3).
[189]   Licensing Act 2003, s 35(4).

related to the variation sought but which nevertheless appear appropriate. For example, an operator might apply to extend their hours from midnight until 1 am but find themselves with a new door supervision requirement operational from 8 pm. Nothing in the Act specifically prevents that. However, it is submitted to be outwith the purpose of the procedure to impose conditions on a licence which are unrelated to the variation sought. The proper means of imposing such conditions is following a review application.

15.161 Nevertheless, the concern on the part of operators that a variation application may lead to the imposition of burdensome conditions leads some to eschew the variation procedures altogether. Instead, they work on the basis that 'what I have, I hold', and if they want more they simply apply for a new licence altogether. Then at least if the new licence is granted subject to unwanted conditions, they can continue to trade on their old licence while they bring an appeal. If the new licence is granted as asked, then they can simply surrender their old licence. As the costs and procedures for both new and variation applications are similar, it seems some operators will continue to choose this option.

(ii) Minor variations

15.162 The Guidance conveniently points out that minor variations generally fall into four categories: minor changes to the structure or layout of the premises; small adjustments to licensing hours; the removal of out of date, irrelevant or unenforceable conditions or the addition of volunteered conditions; and the addition of certain licensable activities.[190]

15.163 The minor variations process under sections 41A to 41C of the Act, which commenced on 29th July 2009, is designed to provide a straightforward route for formalising uncontentious changes to the licence which could not impact adversely on the licensing objectives. The applicant is not required to advertise the application in the newspaper nor to copy it to responsible authorities. The consultation process is shorter and an application can, in principle, be granted within ten working days commencing with the day after the application was received by the licensing authority. The fee is less than that applicable to major variations. The downsides from the operator's point of view are that the licensing authority has the final say – there is no appeal – and if for some reason the application is not considered within 15 working days, the application will be treated as refused, although the fee should be returned (unless a new application date is agreed between the licensing authority and the applicant).

15.164 The minor variations procedure has generally been a success, but it is not a panacea for all woes. If, for example, a licensing authority takes the

---

[190] Guidance para 8.54.

full 15 working days to grant an application, then, taking into account weekends, the full application period can often be only a few days less than a grant at the expiry of the 28 day consultation period of an uncontested major variation. Moreover, in cases where a re-opening is planned but the minor variation is refused on the 15th day by a licensing officer who on second thoughts feels that all the authorities should be consulted, the applicant's only recourse is to submit a full variation application and start again. This can turn what may have been a ten working day grant period into one of possibly three months, if the major variation goes to a hearing. It seems that pre-issue consultation is necessary therefore in all but the most simple applications, or those where time is not of the essence. Many licensing authorities will engage in such discussions, although some are unwilling until the full minor variation has been received.

15.165   The minor variations process cannot be used to vary a premises licence to:[191]

(a)   Extend the period to which it has effect;
(b)   Vary substantially the premises to which it relates;[192]
(c)   Specify an individual as the designated premises supervisor (covered by section 37)
(d)   Add the supply of alcohol as an activity authorised by the licence;
(e)   Authorise:
    (i) The supply of alcohol at any time between 11 pm and 7 am or;
    (ii) An increase on the amount of time on any day during which alcohol may be sold by retail or supplied; or
(f)   Include the alternative licence condition referred to in section 41D(3) (supply of alcohol from community premises).

The restriction at (d) above prevents any applicant who does not already have alcohol authorised on its licence from using the minor variations procedure to do so. The inference here of course is that the introduction of the sale by retail of alcohol to any existing premises licence could adversely affect the licensing objectives and the licensing authority's discretion should not be engaged. Paragraph (e) renders late night/early morning sales of alcohol off limits even for those with alcohol already authorised on their licence, and additionally restricts a net increase in the overall hours that alcohol can be sold at any time of the day. For example, an operator who wishes to serve champagne breakfasts may therefore have to sacrifice his lunchtime trade if he is to use the minor variations procedure.

Advertisement of minor variation applications

15.166

---

[191]   Licensing Act 2003, s 41A(3)(a)–(f).
[192]   See para 15.159 above.

- The applicant must display a notice which is:
  - White;
  - Of a size equal to or larger than A4;
  - Printed legibly in black ink or typed in black.
- The notice must include:
  - At or near the top of the notice the heading 'Licensing Act 2003; Minor Variation of premises licence';
  - A brief description of the proposed variation or variations (for example 'to amend the layout of the premises in accordance with the plans submitted with this application', or 'to add recorded music Monday to Sunday between the hours of 1900 to 2200');
  - The name of the applicant;
  - The postal address of the premises, if any, or if there is no postal address for the premises a description of those premises sufficient to enable the location and the extent of the premises to be identified;
  - The postal address and, where applicable, the web address where the register of the relevant licensing authority is kept and where and when the record of the application may be inspected.
  - The date by which an interested party may make representations to the relevant licensing authority;
  - That it is an offence knowingly or recklessly to make a false statement in connection with an application and the maximum fine for which a person is liable on summary conviction for the offence.
- The information referred to in sub-paragraph (B)(i) or (ii) above is printed or typed in a font of a size equal to or larger than 32;
- The remainder of the notice is printed in a font of a size equal to or larger than 16.[193]

Display of the notice

15.167   The applicant shall display a notice which complies with the requirements above prominently at or on the premises to which the application relates so that it can be conveniently read from the exterior of the premises. If any part of the external perimeter of the premises is 100 metres or more in length and abuts a public highway or other place accessible to the public, the notice must be displayed at least every 50 metres along that part

---

[193]   Licensing Act 2003 (Premises Licences and Club Premises Certificates) Regulations 2005, reg 26A as amended by the Licensing Act 2003 (Premises Licences and Club Premises Certificates) (Amendment) (Electronic Applications etc) Regulations 2009, regs 2 and 7(a)–(b).

of the perimeter.[194] It is interesting to note the different wording here compared with the applications for new licences or major variations.[195]

15.168   The notice(s) must be displayed for the continuous period beginning on the first working day after the application was given to the licensing authority and ending at the expiry of the ninth consecutive working day after that day.[196] This interesting definition of ten working days does compute so long as the first working day after the licensing authority receives the application is added to the 'nine consecutive days'.

Determination of the application

15.169   The licensing authority may of course take a view on the application well before the expiry of the ten working days during which responsible authorities or any other persons can make their relevant representations. However, because the authority must take into account any such representations in determining the application it must not make such a determination until that full ten day period has expired.[197] Further, the licensing authority has an additional requirement to consult those responsible authorities as it considers appropriate which would normally mean an email to the environmental health officer or the police or a perhaps a request that the applicant sends a copy of the application to such authorities (although of course the applicant would not be required so to do). Having consulted the authorities it considers appropriate, and taking account of any relevant representation, the authority must grant the application if:

(a)   The variation proposed in the application could not have an adverse effect on the promotion of any of the licensing objectives; or

(b)   If more than one variation is proposed, none of them whether considered separately or together could have such an effect.

15.170   The expression 'could not' is important. It is not the same as 'will not'. The latter expression involves a judgment as to what will happen on the balance of probabilities. The former expression asks whether something might happen. If it might, then it is not possible to say that the promotion of the licensing objectives will be unaffected. Furthermore, it is not sufficient that there could not be an adverse effect on the licensing objectives, which entails asking whether the application could actually cause harm. It is necessary that there could not be an adverse effect on the promotion of the licensing objectives, which seems to entail that an application which reduces

---

[194]   Licensing Act 2003 (Premises Licences and Club Premises Certificates) Regulations 2005, reg 26A(1)(b).

[195]   Licensing Act 2003 (Premises Licences and Club Premises Certificates) Regulations 2005, reg 25(a)(ii).

[196]   Licensing Act 2003 (Premises Licences and Club Premises Certificates) Regulations 2005, reg 26A(3).

[197]   Licensing Act 2003, s 41B(2)(a)–(b).

the ability to promote the public interest embodied in the objectives, even if it does not cause actual harm, would have to be rejected. It is, therefore, a high test.[198]

15.171 Further, if but one aspect of the application could adversely impact on the promotion of the licensing objectives then the application in its totality must be rejected. Applicants with uncontroversial changes to the layout of their premises who are also considering adding or extending more controversial licensable activities at the same time may consider that two separate applications are the wiser strategy.

15.172 In any other case the licensing authority must reject the application. There is no right to a hearing. The determination must be made within the period of 15 working days beginning on the initial day[199] and if the licensing authority fails to respond to the applicant within those 15 working days the application will be treated as refused and the fee must be returned to the applicant forthwith.[200] However, the licensing authority and the applicant are permitted to agree instead that the undetermined application be treated as a new application and that the fee originally submitted be treated as the fee for that new application.[201] Section 41B(8) additionally states that the new application 'is to be treated as having been made on the date of the agreement referred to in [subsection 7(a)], or on such other date as is specified in the agreement'. Clearly, this allows an apologetic licensing officer who has just come back from holiday to permit the applicant to start again on the '16th day' without having to send a new fee or resubmit the application.

15.173 However, do the words 'or on such other date as is specified in the agreement' include treating the new application as having been made the day after it was originally submitted, thereby allowing the 15 working day period to be put back a further day during which the licensing officer can grant or refuse the application? Any local residents who had made representation would not be prejudiced, as the licensing authority would have to take into account their representations so long as they were made within the initial ten working days. It seems that neither the Act, the Regulations, nor the Guidance had such a scenario in mind, but in principle this may be a convenient get out for both the over-worked or absent licensing officer and an applicant whose application has failed through no fault of his own.

15.174 Where an application is granted the licensing authority must forthwith give a notice to that effect to the applicant, specifying the variation of the premises licence which is to have effect and the time at which that variation takes effect.[202] That time will be the date stated in the application

---

[198] For specific examples see Guidance paras 8.54 et seq.
[199] Licensing Act 2003, s 41B(5).
[200] Licensing Act 2003, s 41B(6).
[201] Licensing Act 2003, s 41B(7).
[202] Licensing Act 2003, s 41C(2).

where this date is after the notice. Otherwise, the authority must specify a later date.[203] Therefore, if the application relates, say, to a layout change to take effect on 1 May, but the notice is given on 3 May and the date it takes effect is 5 May, the change is not actually authorised until 5 May. In practice, it is unlikely that much attention is given to this provision except in sensitive cases

15.175   Where an application is rejected the licensing authority must forthwith give a notice to that effect to the applicant including a statement by the authority of the reasons for its decision.[204]

15.176   Although the threshold for a grant of a minor variation is a high one, it should not be thought that the procedure is reserved for extreme cases. The procedure is useful for making minor layout changes, removing redundant conditions from licences, and tidying up the wording of unenforceable conditions. The procedure may also be used to add conditions which have been agreed between the applicant and responsible authorities in lieu of a review of the licence. Further, an applicant may, having discussed the matter through with responsible authorities in advance, apply for a minor variation which proposes new activities and conditions to prevent their having any impact. In such a case, if there is no other representation, the authority is on fairly safe ground reaching the conclusion that, in the light of the conditions, the proposed variation could not have an adverse effect on the promotion of the licensing objectives, because there will be no party to challenge it.

(iii) Variation of premises licence: supply of alcohol from community premises

15.177   The provisions of section 41D of the Act[205] are intended to relieve small community premises which are licensed to sell alcohol from the burden and cost of having a designated premises supervisor and personal licence holders. Instead, through the medium of a variation, they may seek an 'alternative licence condition' instead of the usual mandatory conditions set out in sections 19(2) and 19(3) of the Act.[206] The alternative licence condition is that every supply of alcohol under the premises licence must be made or authorised by the management committee, in effect replacing the requirements to have a designated premises supervisor and to have all sales of alcohol made or authorised by a personal licence holder.

---

[203]   Licensing Act 2003, s 41C(3).
[204]   Licensing Act 2003, s 41C(4)–(5).
[205]   As inserted by the Legislative Reform (Supervision of Alcohol Sales in Church and Village Halls etc) Order 2009.
[206]   See further Chapter 15 (Conditions). Similar provisions apply to new applications for premises licences: s 25A.

15.178 This relaxation is applicable to community premises, which are defined as premises that are or form part of (a) a church hall, chapel hall or other similar building, or (b) a village hall, parish hall, community hall or other similar building.[207] While in most cases, it will be obvious whether premises fall within this definition, the meaning of 'community hall' requires some further discussion. For example, what of a school hall which is hired out for private parties from time to time? On this topic, the Guidance suggests that to qualify the premises' predominant use should be considered. If they are genuinely made available for community benefit most of the time, and accessible by a broad range of persons and sectors of the local community for purposes which include purposes beneficial to the community as a whole, the premises will be likely to meet the definition.[208]

15.179 Conversely, school and private halls which are available for private hire by the general public would not qualify.[209] Otherwise, every commercial function room would be a community premises. Furthermore, the Guidance indicates that if the general use of the premises is contingent upon membership of a particular organisation or organisations, this would strongly suggest that the premises in question are not a 'community premises' within the definition – ie it is not the intention that qualifying clubs, which are able to apply for a club premises certificate, should instead seek a premises licence with the alternative licensing condition.[210] In reality, those community premises which qualify are usually multi-purpose including a variety of activities such as playschools, senior citizens' clubs, indoor sports, youth clubs and public meetings.

15.180 For the alternative licence condition to apply, the licensee must be the 'management committee', which is defined as meaning a committee or board of individuals with responsibility for the management of the premises.[211] The Guidance indicates that the intention is that the term is intended to cover any formally constituted, transparent and accountable management committee or structure.[212] It states that such a committee should have the capacity to provide sufficient oversight of the premises to minimise any risk to the licensing objectives that could arise from allowing the responsibility for supervising the sale of alcohol to be transferred from a DPS and personal licence holder or holders. This could include management committees, executive committees and boards of trustees.

15.181 It is clearly insufficient simply to have a committee to hold the licence, but which exercises no genuine oversight of licensable activities. This risk is guarded against by the application form, which requires applicants to

---

207 Licensing Act 2003, s 193.
208 Para 4.39.
209 Para 4.40.
210 Para 4.41.
211 Licensing Act 2003, s 193.
212 Para 4.43.

set out how the premises is managed, its committee structure, how the supervision of alcohol sales is to be ensured in different situations (eg when the hall is hired to private parties), and how responsibility for this is to be determined in individual cases and discussed within the committee procedure in the event of any issues arising. Applicants are required to submit copies of any constitution or other management documents with their applications.

15.182   The alternative licence condition is no soft option. The management committee is the premises licence holder. The Guidance contains a stern reminder that the committee is collectively be responsible for ensuring compliance with licence conditions and may be liable to prosecution if licensable activities are conducted outwith the terms of the licence.[213] The Guidance indicates that that position may be mitigated where the hirers of community premises are provided with a written summary of their responsibilities under the 2003 Act in relation to the sale of alcohol. In such cases, the Guidance states that the management committee is likely to be treated as having taken adequate steps to avoid liability to prosecution if a licensing offence is committed.[214] It is respectfully submitted that this overstates the matter. The committee does not absolve itself of liability by a set of terms and conditions. For example, if it has knowledge of licensing breaches, it may find itself liable for the 'knowingly allowing' offence in section 136(1)(b). Wise advice to a committee would be that it is not sufficient to accept the hirer's signature and then walk away – there ought to be somewhat more scrutiny of the event.

15.183   Only the police may object to the alternative licence condition,[215] and then only on the ground that due to the exceptional circumstances of the case the crime prevention objective would be undermined. Where this happens, it is up to the licensing authority to hold a hearing to determine whether the arrangements for the management of the premises by the applicant are sufficient to ensure adequate supervision of the supply of alcohol on the premises.[216]

(iv) Varying the DPS

15.184   An application to vary a premises licence so as to appoint a new DPS is dealt with on a different basis from major or minor variations (and indeed is prohibited under those relevant provisions). The holder of a premises licence may apply to vary a premises licence under section 37 of the Act only where:

(1)   The licence authorises the supply of alcohol; or

[213]   Para 4.45.
[214]   Para 4.45.
[215]   Licensing Act 2003, s 41D(6)(b).
[216]   Licensing Act 2003, s 41D(5).

(2)   The licence is varied under section 34 so as to authorise the supply of alcohol.

15.185   Though the practice continues in some areas, there is no statutory basis to add a DPS through the medium of a section 34 variation application. The section 34 and 37 applications are discrete.

15.186   An application to vary a premises licence to appoint a new DPS must be made on the approved form and accompanied by payment of the specified fee. An application must also include:

(1)   A form of consent given by the proposed individual in a prescribed form.
(2)   The premises licence (or the appropriate part of it) or a statement of the reasons for failing to provide the licence.

Notice of the application must be served on the police and the existing DPS (if there is one). The notice must state whether the application is to have interim effect.

Interim effect

15.187   Where the holder wishes to vary a premises licence so as to appoint a new DPS, the application can be made to have immediate effect.[217] Where this occurs, then from receipt of the application by the licensing authority the premises licence has effect as if it were varied in the manner set out in the application. (Clearly, however, in cases where a concurrent application under section 34 to add the sale of alcohol as a licensable activity is ongoing, no sale of alcohol can take place until that application is granted.) The existing DPS is therefore temporarily replaced by the new individual, pending the grant of the variation. This interim effect operates until:

(a)   The full application for variation is granted;
(b)   Notification is given to the applicant, where the application is rejected; or
(c)   Withdrawal of the application if it is withdrawn before being determined.

15.188   On those rare occasions where a DPS has deserted the premises just before the start of a busy weekend, before the days of electronic applications the only option was an urgent application to vary the DPS being faxed/emailed to the police and the licensing authority with the fee to follow thereafter, often outside normal working hours. It is questionable whether this practice could ever have effected good service. However, authorities took a pragmatic view, and premises were not closed down over the weekend, if they had otherwise done their best to comply.

---

[217]   Licensing Act 2003 s 38.

15.189 The advent of the ability to submit electronic applications has not significantly changed this position. Firstly, electronic applications are neither the success story they were planned to be, nor are they used widely by either applicants or licensing authorities due to widespread technical problems. Secondly, any application sent to a licensing authority is only deemed to have been given to that authority at the time that all the required documents become accessible to it, and it is questionable whether an application is accessible to a licensing authority over the weekend.[218] Thirdly, the fee must have been received by the licensing authority or again the application is not taken to have been given.[219] Again, however, authorities take a pragmatic view, and do not complain where the new application is sitting on their server and a cheque is in the post.

15.190 Where there is no notice given by the police by way of objection to the application to vary the DPS the licensing authority must grant the application.

15.191 Where the police are satisfied that the exceptional circumstances of the application would mean the grant of the variation would undermine the crime prevention objective, they must within 14 days of being notified of the application give the licensing authority notice setting out their reasons. Such objections by the police should arise only in genuinely exceptional circumstances, and should not be used as a routine mechanism for hindering the portability of a personal licence.[220] Of course, if concerns arise in relation to the individual's management of the premises once he has been installed as a DPS, the police have the power to seek a review of the premises licence on any grounds relating to the licensing objectives. The only example given in the Guidance of such exceptional circumstances is of an individual convicted of selling alcohol to underage persons (but having been allowed by the court to retain his personal licence) who is then proposed as the DPS for premises with a history of underage drinking.[221]

FAQ

Q   Is there anything to prevent a premises licence holder from issuing repeated interim effect DPS variations naming an individual whom the police continue to oppose, in order to permit that proposed individual to remain as DPS ad infinitum?

A   Under the provisions of section 37 and section 38, no. Each application is treated as a supervening event and, if the licence

---

[218] Licensing Act 2003 (Premises Licences and Club Premises Certificates) Regulations 2005, reg 21A(3).
[219] Licensing Act 2003 (Premises Licences and Club Premises Certificates) Regulations 2005, reg 21A(4).
[220] See Guidance para 4.28.
[221] Guidance para 4.26.

holder was prepared to keep paying the application fee (and continued to serve each new application on the same person named in the application) then this unhappy status quo could remain in perpetuity. If the situation was not so bad at the premises that the police were unable to take more immediate enforcement action (under section 161, or section 53A perhaps) then their only option would be to apply to review the licence to remove the DPS (and it is submitted, request a condition that that person should not be permitted on the premises when licensable activities take place).

On objection by the police to the application, the licensing authority must hold a hearing to consider the objection, unless the authority, the applicant and the police agree a hearing is not necessary. The licensing authority considering the objection must confine their consideration to the issue of crime and disorder and must give reasons for their decision.[222] Where the application is granted, the notice must state the time when the variation takes effect. That time will be the time specified in the application or, if that time is before the Applicant is given the notice of grant, such later time as the licensing authority specifies in the notice.[223] Such provisions for the date and time of the grant should not be confused with the interim provisions under section 38, which have effect when the application is received by the licensing authority. Following determination, it falls to the holder of the premises licence to tell the incoming DPS of his appointment or, if the application is refused, the existing DPS of the refusal. Failure to do so constitutes an offence.[224]

---

[222] Licensing Act 2003, s 39(5).
[223] Licensing Act 2003 s 39(6).
[224] Licensing Act 2003 s 40.

16

Clubs

I rose politely in the club
And said 'I feel a little bored;
Will someone take me to a pub?'

Gilbert Keith Chesterton, Ballade of an Anti-Puritan.

A	Introduction 16.01
B	The language of club licensing 16.15
C	Application for club premises certificate 16.29
D	Grant or rejection of application 16.57
E	Duration of certificate 16.80
F	Duty to notify certain changes 16.82
G	Variation of certificate 16.91
H	Review of certificate 16.101
I	Withdrawal of certificate 16.103
J	Production of certificate, rights of entry, etc 16.106
K	Sales to non-members 16.113

A INTRODUCTION

16.01 The history of the private members' club mirrors the industrial and class history of the nation. Established to support particular communities and community groups, such as working men in general or miners in particular, clubs were places where the combined purchasing powers of members enabled them to procure alcohol or entertainment more cheaply, to offer mutual support and to socialise with each other and their families. So powerful did they grow that there were working men's clubs and institutes in the North East which owned and operated their own breweries for the benefit of their members. Clubs were also established to enable other birds of a feather to flock together, be they political (Conservative and Labour clubs), military (Royal British Legion), sporting (golf) or the upper echelons of the establishment communing in the enclave of their St James' clubs. All of these private establishments have historically been treated to a more emollient regime than that extending, say, to the public house. In the main, this has been justified on the grounds that they impose a lower burden on statutory agencies.

16.02   The Licensing Act 1964 made specific provision for the registration of 'members clubs', being a 'society of persons associated together for the promotion of some common object or objects, such as social intercourse, art, science, literature, politics or sport'.

16.03   The 1964 Act divided clubs into 'proprietary clubs' (where the club house, furniture, stores and drink belonged to a proprietor to whom a subscription was paid) and 'members' clubs' (where all of the property of the club vested in the members jointly, with subscriptions being paid to a common fund and managed by an elected committee).

16.04   In a 'proprietary club', stocks of liquor would belong to the proprietor and any supply of liquor, therefore, would be a sale to a member, which would require a Justices' on licence under the 1964 Act.

16.05   In a 'members' club', stocks of liquor are owned jointly by the members and, therefore, the supply of liquor to a member is not regarded as a sale, but rather a release to a member of the ownership rights of his co-owners. Such a supply was governed not by the Justices' on licence provisions of the 1964 Act, but rather by the issue of a certificate of registration for the premises by the magistrates' court.[1]

16.06   The provisions of the Licensing Act 2003 relating to clubs are found in Part 4 of the Act (sections 60–97). Certain of the principles involved in relation to the grant of a club premises certificate are similar, if not identical, to principles involved in relation to the grant of a premises licence. Accordingly, the reader should refer back to discussion of the relevant concepts in Chapter 15, and specific reference will be made at appropriate points within this chapter. However, club premises certificates confer clear advantages on their holders, as set out below.

16.07   Introducing the Licensing Bill during the second reading debate in the House of Lords on 26 November 2002, Baroness Blackstone, the Minister of State, Department for Culture, Media and Sport, set out the Government's intentions in relation to clubs. She said:

> 'We recognise the value to the community of registered members clubs such as working men's or political clubs. We recognise that such clubs are private premises to which access is restricted and where alcohol is not supplied for profit. We intend to protect the special position of such clubs. Although they will have to promote the licensing objectives in the same way as other licensed premises, they will not require the full premises licence. The Bill will, however, bring clubs into line with other premises in relation to sales to and consumption by children.'[2]

[1]   See Licensing Act 1964, s 40 and Sch 5 generally.
[2]   Hansard, HL Debate, vol 641, col 645.

16.08 The Licensing Act 2003 preserves the special treatment of 'registered members clubs' and requires a club to 'qualify' to be outside normal premises licensing arrangements. The new instrument for the supply of alcohol and provision of other licensable activities on qualifying club premises is a club premises certificate. The certificate is issued by the licensing authority and certifies that the club may be used for the licensable activities set out in the certificate and that the club is a 'qualifying club'.

16.09 The grant of a club premises certificate by a licensing authority entitles a qualifying club to a substantial number of benefits, compared with the premises licence regime. These include:

(1) the authority to supply to members and sell it to guests on the premises to which the certificate relates without the need for any member or employee to hold a personal licence;

(2) the absence of a requirement to specify a designated premises supervisor;

(3) more limited rights of entry for the police and authorised persons;

(4) the club premises not being subject to police powers of instant closure on grounds of disorder and noise nuisance (except when being used under the authority of a premises licence or temporary event notice); and

(5) not being subject to potential orders of the magistrates' court for the closure of all licensed premises in the area when disorder is happening or expected.

16.10 Under the 1964 Act, registered members clubs enjoyed the freedom to sell alcohol to minors and allow them to consume it on the club premises. The 2003 Act has removed this privilege and the sale or supply of alcohol to children in such clubs is now unlawful.

16.11 The White Paper published in advance of the Licensing Bill had identified 'unregulated access by children, where children as young as 5 years old can lawfully drink alcohol' as one of three issues upon which the Government was particularly focusing in relation to registered members clubs. The other two were:

(a) the potential for disorder and disturbance in the vicinity of the club premises resulting from excessive drinking, rather than on the premises themselves; and

(b) police rights of entry.[3]

16.12 Whilst explaining the desire 'to preserve the unique and special status of clubs', the White Paper outlined the Government's intentions in relation to these other two issues:

---

[3]   White Paper: Time for Reform – Proposals for the Modernisation of our Licensing Laws (April 2000), para 103.

'Clubs are regarded by many people as extensions of their home, even though they have to be given permission to supply and consume alcohol there. It is not our intention to give the police unauthorised access to such clubs except in exceptional circumstances. These would be essentially where there is an emergency situation requiring immediate attention. For example, this might occur where serious disorder was taking place or where the police could show that they had reasonable suspicion based on information received that a particular club was being used for the supply of alcohol to minors or [*for*] drugs.'[4]

16.13   In fact, the Act, whilst giving the police a right of entry which did not previously exist, does not go quite as far as the White Paper proposed.[5]

16.14   Proprietary clubs which are run commercially by individuals, partnerships or businesses for the purposes of profit are not entitled to register as a qualifying club and require a premises licence under the Act. Even genuine members' clubs would require a premises licence if they decided to hire out their premises to members of the public for parties, receptions and the like other than under the auspices of a temporary event notice.

B THE LANGUAGE OF CLUB LICENSING

16.15   'Club premises certificate' means a certificate granted under Part 4 of the Act by the 'relevant licensing authority' in respect of premises occupied by, and habitually used for, the purposes of a club, and which certifies that the premises may be used by the club for one or more 'qualifying club activities' and that the club is a 'qualifying club' in relation to each of those activities.[6]

16.16   The 'relevant licensing authority' in relation to club premises is the authority in whose area the premises is situated. Where the premises is situated in two or more licensing authority areas, the relevant licensing authority is the authority in whose area the greater part of the premises is situated. In the unlikely event that the boundary line between the two authorities lies directly in the middle of the club premises, the club can nominate one of the licensing authorities as the relevant licensing authority.[7]

16.17   'Qualifying club activities' are:

(a)   the supply of alcohol by or on behalf of a club to, or to the order of, a member of the club (on and off sales);

(b)   the sale by retail of alcohol by or on behalf of a club to a guest of a

---

4   White Paper, para 105.
5   Licensing Act 2003, ss 96–97. See paras 16.121–16.122 below.
6   Licensing Act 2003, s 60.
7   Licensing Act 2003, s 68.

member of the club for consumption on the premises where the sale takes place (on sales only); and

(c)   the provision of regulated entertainment where that provision is by or on behalf of a club for members of the club or members of the club and their guests.[8]

16.18 A club is a 'qualifying club' in relation to the provision of regulated entertainment if it satisfies the 'general conditions'. A club is a qualifying club in relation to the supply of alcohol to members or guests if it satisfies both the general conditions and the 'additional conditions'.[9]

16.19 The general conditions a club must satisfy if it is to be a qualifying club in relation to a qualifying club activity are that:[10]

(1)   under the rules of the club, persons may not be admitted to member- ship, or be admitted as candidates for membership, to any of the privileges of membership, without an interval of at least two days between their nomination for membership and their admission;

(2)   under the rules of the club, persons becoming members without prior nomination or application may not be admitted to the privileges of membership without an interval of at least two days between their becoming members and their admission;

(3)   the club must be established in good faith as a club;[11]

(4)   the club must have at least 25 members; and

(5)   alcohol is not supplied, or intended to be supplied, to members on the premises otherwise than by or on behalf of the club.[12]

16.20 The additional conditions that a club must satisfy if it is to be a qualifying club in relation to the supply of alcohol to members or guests[13] are that:[14]

(1)   the purchase of alcohol for the club and supply of alcohol by the club (so far as they are not managed by the club in general meeting or body of members) are managed by a committee whose members are mem- bers of the club, are 18 years old or over and are elected by members of the club;

---

[8]   Licensing Act 2003, s 1(2). In relation to 'guests' see s 67(1) and paras 16.64–16.72 below.

[9]   Licensing Act 2003, s 61, ie the general conditions in s 62 and the additional conditions in s 64.

[10]   The general conditions are modified for industrial, provident, friendly societies and miners' welfare institutes. See Licensing Act 2003, ss 55–56 in relation to these organisations.

[11]   See definition at paras 16.21–16.25.

[12]   Licensing Act 2003, s 62.

[13]   In relation to 'guests' see Licensing Act 2003, s 67(1) and paras 16.64–16.72 below.

[14]   The additional conditions are modified for industrial, provident, friendly societies and miners' welfare institutes. See Licensing Act 2003, ss 55–56 in relation to these organ- isations.

(2)   no arrangements are, or are intended to be, made for any person to receive at the expense of the club any commission, percentage or payment on, or related to, purchases of alcohol by the club; and

(3)   no arrangements are, or are intended to be, made for any person directly or indirectly to derive any pecuniary benefit from the supply of alcohol by the club to members or guests, apart from any benefit accruing to the club as a whole or any indirect benefit.[15]

16.21 It is interesting that the term 'good faith' has survived the transition from the old legislation to the new, particularly since the White Paper specifically criticised use of the term, stating:

'The law relating to registered clubs once again exhibits unnecessary complexity, using many terms that are imprecise. For example, "good faith" is an unclear way of setting standards of behaviour and propriety that should be required of clubs and their members.'[16]

16.22 This said, the Licensing Act 2003 provides some assistance in relation to interpretation of the term. For the purposes of general condition (3) above, the matters to be taken into account in determining whether a club is established and conducted in 'good faith' are:

(a)   any arrangements restricting the club's freedom of purchase of alcohol;

(b)   any provision in the rules or arrangements under which money or property of the club or any gain arising from the carrying on of the club, may be applied otherwise than for the benefit of the club as a whole or for charitable, benevolent or political purposes;

(c)   the arrangements for giving members information about the finances of the club;

(d)   the account books and other records kept to ensure the accuracy of the premises occupied by the club; and

(e)   the nature of the premises occupied by the club.[17]

If a licensing authority decides for any purpose of the Act that a club is not 'established and conducted in good faith as a club', the licensing authority must give the club notice of the decision and the reasons for it.[18]

16.23 In *City of London Police Commissioner v Little Ship Club Ltd* (1964) the police alleged that the club was not conducted in good faith because it permitted sales to non-members at functions unconnected with the club for the purpose of raising money. It was held that a club could enact a rule permitting sales to non-members without offending the principle of 'good faith', subject to the courts' right to veto in any case not covered by

---

[15]   Licensing Act 2003, s 64.

[16]   White Paper: Time for Reform – Proposals for Modernisation of our Licensing Laws (April 2000), para 101.

[17]   Licensing Act 2003, s 63(1)–(2).

[18]   Licensing Act 2003, s 63(3).

section 49(4) of the Licensing Act 1964. Parker CJ found that whether or not a club is conducted in good faith is a question of fact and degree.[19]

16.24 A major sensitivity in relation to good faith arises around the service of non-members. As to this, the Guidance states:

> '6.8 There is no mandatory requirement under the 2003 Act for guests to be signed in by a member of the club. However, a point may be reached where a club is providing commercial services to the general public in a way that is contrary to its qualifying club status. It is at this point that the club would no longer be conducted in "good faith" and would no longer meet "general condition 3" for qualifying clubs in section 62 of the 2003 Act.'

16.25 The arrangements for giving members of the club information about the finances of the club are also important. If the membership at large (who effectively own the club) have difficulty in obtaining or are refused the opportunity to review details concerning the finances of the club, this too may indicate that the club is not being conducted in good faith.

16.26 An 'authorised person' is a body empowered by the Act to carry out inspection and enforcement roles. The phrase includes officers of the licensing authority, fire and rescue authority, health and safety authority, environmental health authority and officers of the navigational authorities.[20]

16.27 A 'responsible authority' in relation to a club premises certificate application means those public bodies that must be notified of, and are entitled to make representations to a licensing authority in relation to, applications for grant, variation or review of club premises certificates. These include the licensing authority itself and any other authority in whose area the part of the premises is situated, the chief officer of police, the local fire and rescue authority, the health and safety authority, the environmental health authority, the local planning authority, the child protection authority and navigational authorities.[21]

16.28 'Relevant representations'[22] are representations made in relation to an application for a club premises certificate which:

(a) are about the likely effect of the grant of the certificate on the promotion of the licensing objectives;

---

[19] Brewing Tr Rev 702. The *Little Ship* decision was of significant benefit to clubs which were finding it hard to maintain healthy memberships and were increasingly competing with other licensed premises for bookings such as weddings, christenings and birthday parties. However, under the Licensing Act 2003 it is not open to clubs to throw open their doors to the public for licensable activities unless under the aegis of a concurrent premises licence or a temporary event notice.

[20] Licensing Act 2003, s 69(2).

[21] See Licensing Act 2003, s 69(4).

[22] Defined at Licensing Act 2003, s 72(7)–(8).

(b)   were made by a responsible authority or other person within a period of 28 days starting the day after the application was given to the authority;[23]

(c)   have not been withdrawn; and

(d)   in the case of representations made by other than by a responsible authority, are not frivolous or vexatious in the opinion of the licensing authority.

C APPLICATION FOR CLUB PREMISES CERTIFICATE

16.29   A club may apply for a club premises certificate in respect of any premises which are occupied by, and habitually used for the purposes of, the club[24].

16.30   The application is made to the relevant licensing authority[25].

16.31   The application must include:

(1)   an operating schedule;

(2)   a plan, in the prescribed form;[26]

(3)   a copy of the club rules;

(4)   a plan of the premises;

(5)   a prescribed fee;[27] and

(6)   such other matters as may be prescribed by the Regulations[28].

16.32   The applicant is required to advertise the application for at least 28 days, starting the day after the day on which the application was given to the relevant licensing authority, both by displaying a site notice, and also by publishing a notice in a local newspaper at least once during the period of ten working days starting on the day after the day on which the application was given to the relevant licensing authority.[29] The application also needs to be served upon each responsible authority on the same day as it is given to the licensing authority.[30]

---

[23]   The Licensing Act 2003 (Premises Licences and Club Premises Certificates) Regulations 2005, reg 22.

[24]   Licensing Act 2003, s 71(1).

[25]   Licensing Act 2003, s 71(2).

[26]   The requirements for the plan are prescribed by the Licensing Act 2003 (Premises Licences and Club Premises Certificates) Regulations 2005, reg 23.

[27]   The fee is prescribed by the Licensing Act 2003 (Fees) Regulations 2005, reg 6 and Sch 2.

[28]   Licensing Act 2003, s 71(3)–(4). The form of the application and the information it must contain are prescribed by the Licensing Act 2003 (Premises Licences and Club Premises Certificates) Regulations 2005, reg 18 and Sch 9 Part B.

[29]   Licensing Act 2003 (Premises Licences and Club Premises Certificates) Regulations 2005, reg 25. The contents of the notices are governed by reg 26.

[30]   Licensing Act 2003 (Premises Licences and Club Premises Certificates) Regulations 2005, reg 27A. Where the application is given electronically, the licensing authority must serve the responsible authorities no later than the first working day after receipt: reg 27.

16.33 Representations, whether made by responsible authorities or other persons, must be made within 28 days of the day after the day on which the application was given to the licensing authority.[31]

Club operating schedule

16.34 A club operating schedule must be in the prescribed form[32] and must include a statement of the following matters:

(a) the qualifying club activities to which the application relates;

(b) the times during which it is proposed that the relevant qualifying club activities are to take place;

(c) any other times during which it is proposed that the premises are to be open to members and their guests;

(d) where the relevant qualifying club activities include the supply of alcohol, whether the supplies are proposed to be for consumption on the premises or both on and off the premises;

(e) the steps which it is proposed to take to promote the licensing objectives; and

(f) such other matters as may be prescribed[33] by Regulations. The Regulations prescribe a form of declaration to enable the authority to ascertain that it is dealing with a genuine members' club.[34]

16.35 The club operating schedule should include any information which is necessary to allow any responsible authority or interested party to assess whether the steps to be taken to promote the licensing objectives are satisfactory.

16.36 The steps the club intends to take to promote the licensing objectives will be translated into conditions included in the certificate, unless the conditions have been modified by the licensing authority following consideration of relevant representations by responsible authorities or other persons.

Best practice in club registration applications

16.37 The preparation of applications for club premises certificates presents certain challenges, with traps for the unwary, as we shall now proceed to describe.

---

[31] Licensing Act 2003 (Premises Licences and Club Premises Certificates) Regulations 2005, reg 22.

[32] Licensing Act 2003, s 71(5). For the form of the club operating schedule see Regulations, reg 18 and Sch 9.

[33] Licensing Act 2003, s 71(5).

[34] The Licensing Act 2003 (Premises Licences and Club Premises Certificates) Regulations 2005, reg 17 and Sch 9 Part A.

The plan

16.38 Detailed requirements in respect of plans are set out in regulation 23(3) of the Regulations.[35] As might be expected, plans must include the perimeter of the premises. The advent of the no smoking legislation[36] brought with it significant issues for committees of club premises who have to provide external smoking areas for their members. If the external area is not identified as part of the premises on the plan, then the mandatory conditions[37] prevent members taking their drinks with them when they go outside for a smoke. Any clubs in this position ought to redraw their plans at the outset or, after grant, by minor variation, to include the exterior in the premises.

16.39 The Regulations also require the plan to show, in a case where the premises is to be used for more than one licensable activity, the area within the premises used for each activity. For example, the plan might show a red line around the perimeter of both the building and the external areas for the supply and consumption of alcohol, with a key indicating that this is the case. A brown line might then show where regulated entertainment is to occur, which will often be indoors only so as to ward off adverse representations from the environmental health authority.

16.40 The plan also needs to show the location and type of any fire safety and any other safety equipment. It is worth paying considerable attention to these details, which may include fire extinguishers, fire blankets and the position and type of alarm systems, so as to avoid adverse representations from the fire and rescue authority. However, it is advisable to include a note that their position may be altered on consultation with the authority, so as to avoid the need for variation applications every time a small alteration occurs.

16.41 The Regulations are also concerned with fire hazards caused by obstacles to egress. They require the plan to show fixed structures (including furniture) or similar objects temporarily in a fixed location (but not furniture) which may impact on the ability of individuals on the premises to use exits or escape routes without impediment. So fixed booths or high tables will need to be shown on a plan if they may (not will) affect the ability to evacuate the premises. If they are on exit routes or near to exit doors then they must be shown.

The partnership approach

16.42 Responsible authorities are an important resource, whose expertise may be drawn upon in preparation of the operating schedule. For example,

---

[35]   The Licensing Act 2003 (Premises Licences and Club Premises Certificates) Regulations 2005.
[36]   Health Act 2006.
[37]   See paras 16.59–16.62.

an environmental health officer may be able to assist in the wording of conditions on the operating schedule which obviate the need for a representation relating to noise leakage or noise nuisance and a consequent costly hearing before the licensing sub-committee.

16.43 While it may be attractive to avoid representations to offer a condition that under 18s will be excluded, this may significantly reduce the ability of the club to accommodate members' requests for birthdays and weddings. Furthermore, in the case of sports clubs it may be desirable to encourage access by children. The applicant ought to discuss through with the police what controls may be appropriate to protect children and safeguard against nuisance and crime and disorder. This may simply be a Challenge 21 policy or a condition restricting children from entering the bar area unaccompanied by an adult. However, local experience might have shown that it is better to have conditions which prevent the admission of children onto the premises after a certain hour except as part of a pre-booked event. There is no set condition: rather each case rests on its merits. However, an experienced local police officer will be able to assist in formulating the control to meet the requirements of the case.

16.44 Adequate consideration of these matters in partnership with the police and environmental health is particularly important, since any resultant conditions will not just apply to the club premises certificate itself. They may also apply to any temporary event notices subsequently issued for hours extending beyond those on the certificate.[38] Correctly thought out and appropriately identified conditions are therefore extremely important in order to avoid the certificate being a document which removes the opportunity for flexibility rather than enabling a flexible approach to the operation of the premises.

The club rules

16.45 A club premises certificate application must be accompanied by the rules of the club. The club rules typically define the categories of membership, the process for obtaining membership, disciplinary proceedings, rules for governance of the club such as election to and proceedings of committees, financial rules and the conduct of the committee involved in the purchase of alcohol.

16.46 Membership may for example, consist of ordinary members, associate members, temporary members, life members, honorary members and junior members. However, in establishing membership categories and processes, it is important to bear in mind the minimum requirements set out for

---

[38] See Chapter 19 (Temporary Events).

membership in the general conditions.[39] Otherwise, the premises may not qualify for a club premises certificate.

16.47   There are specific requirements in relation to the purchase and supply of alcohol.[40] All of those requirements must be carefully considered when formulating the rules of the club. Section 75(1) of the Act prevents any restriction on the sale of alcohol to an associate member or guest where the rules of the club provide for such sale. Therefore, it is prudent to include such provision in the rules of the club.[41] In doing so, it is important that there is some restraint on admission of members, otherwise there is a danger that the club will be treated as not having been established in good faith.[42]

16.48   There are further requirements in relation to the conduct of the club in terms of handling money, dealing with profits, sharing information regarding finance and keeping proper books.[43] All of these matters must be dealt with in the rules, to ensure that the licensing authority accepts that the club is established and operated in good faith. The rules may for example limit the number of guests who may be introduced on a particular day, require guests to be signed in, prevent expelled members being admitted as guests and require guests to be accompanied during their visit.

16.49   The application process involves the filing of a declaration which requires the specific rule to be identified in relation to a number of these matters.[44] Thus, in formulating the rules, applicants will be well-advised to read sections 60 to 76 of the Act and the declaration, and ensure that the rules are tailored to meet their requirements.

Determination of application for certificate

16.50   The procedure varies according to whether or not there have been relevant representations.

Where there are no relevant representations

16.51   The term 'representations' is used in the Act instead of 'objections'. This is merely a matter of vocabulary. Where no relevant representations are made, the licensing authority must grant the certificate if the application has

---

[39]   Para 16.19 above.

[40]   Para 16.20 above.

[41]   Similar advice applies in relation to regulated entertainment: s 75(2).

[42]   See Guidance para 6.8 (quote at para 16.24 above).

[43]   See para 16.22 above.

[44]   The Licensing Act 2003 (Premises Licences and Club Premises Certificates) Regulations 2005, Schedule 9.

been made in accordance with section 71 of the Act and Regulations have been complied with.[45]

16.52 The licensing authority must grant the application subject only to the imposition of such conditions as are consistent with the club operating schedule accompanying the application and any of the mandatory conditions applicable, as set out in sections 73(2) to (5) and 74 of the Act.[46]

16.53 Where there are no relevant representations, the issue of a club premises certificate should be dealt with as a simple administrative process by licensing authority officials.[47]

Where there are relevant representations

16.54 Where relevant representations are made then the licensing authority must hold a hearing to consider them unless the authority, the applicant and each person who has made representations agree that a hearing is unnecessary.[48]

HEARINGS

16.55 At a hearing, the licensing authority should seek to focus on the steps needed to promote the licensing objectives which has given rise to the specific representation. However, it is not considered that the licensing authority is entirely trammelled by the representations. If it appears to the authority that other relevant matters arise, it may consider them. This is considered further in Chapter 21.

16.56 In determining the application, the licensing authority must give the appropriate weight to:

(1) the representations (including supporting information) presented by all the parties;
(2) the Guidance;
(3) the licensing authority's own statement of policy; and
(4) the steps that are appropriate to promote the licensing objectives.

D GRANT OR REJECTION OF APPLICATION

16.57 Following a hearing, the steps the licensing authority can take are:

---

[45] Licensing Act 2003, s 72(2).
[46] Licensing Act 2003, s 72(2)(a)–(b).
[47] In such circumstances the licensing authority has no discretion. It is obliged to grant.
[48] Licensing Act 2003, s 72(3)(a).

(1) to grant the certificate, subject to the conditions consistent with the club operating schedule and any mandatory conditions that must be included in the certificate by virtue of sections 73(2) to (5), 73A or 74 of the Act;

(2) to grant the certificate subject to modification of the conditions proposed in the club operating schedule as the licensing authority considers appropriate for the promotion of the licensing objectives and any mandatory conditions;

(3) to exclude from the scope of the certificate any qualifying club activities to which the application relates; or

(4) to reject the application.[49]

Conditions

16.58 Conditions can only be imposed on the certificate if they are appropriate for the promotion of the licensing objectives. The licensing authority may grant a club premises certificate subject to different conditions in respect of different parts of the premises or different licensable activities.[50]

Mandatory conditions

16.59 Mandatory conditions arise in relation to supplies of alcohol for consumption off the premises and also the exhibition of films.[51] Further, certain of the 'mandatory code' provisions apply to club premises certificates.[52]

CONSUMPTION OFF THE PREMISES

16.60 Where a club premises certificate authorises supplies of alcohol to a member for consumption on the premises, it may also authorise supplies of alcohol for consumption off the premises. However, a certificate may not authorise supplies of alcohol for consumption off the premises only. A certificate which allows off sales must be subject to three conditions:

(1) that the supply must be made at a time when the premises are open for the purpose of supplying alcohol to members of the club for consumption on the premises;

(2) that any alcohol supplied for consumption off the premises must be in a sealed container; and

---

[49] Licensing Act 2003, s 72(4). Throughout the Act, the word 'reject' is used instead of, for example, 'refuses'.

[50] Licensing Act 2003, s 72(10). Note that under the Licensing Act 1964 magistrates were not empowered to impose any conditions on the registration certificate.

[51] See Chapter 17 (Conditions).

[52] Licensing Act 2003, s 73A. See further Chapter 17 (Conditions).

Grant or rejection of application 403

(3)   that any supply of alcohol for consumption off the premises must be made to a member of the club in person.[53]

EXHIBITION OF FILMS

16.61   Where a club premises certificate authorises the exhibition of films, the certificate must include a condition restricting the admission of persons under 18 in accordance with a recommendation of the film classification body or, where there is no recommendation, the recommendation of the licensing authority.[54]

MANDATORY CODE

16.62   The mandatory code contained in the Licensing Act 2003 (Mandatory Licensing Conditions) Order 2010[55] contains conditions applicable to all club premises certificates. These include conditions relating to irresponsible promotions and service of alcohol, free tap water, age verification and service in smaller measures. These provisions are dealt with further in Chapter 17.

Prohibited conditions

16.63   Two types of condition are to be avoided, the first relating to associate members and their guest and the second relating to plays.

ASSOCIATE MEMBERS AND THEIR GUESTS

16.64   First, where the rules of a club permit sales by retail of alcohol or the provision of regulated entertainment to an associate member of the club or a guest of such member, no condition may be attached to a club premises certificate so as to prevent such sale or provision.[56]

16.65   The provisions within the Act relating to associate members and their guests have caused considerable controversy and confusion. The White Paper published in advance of the Licensing Bill criticised the then existing law[57] in relation to registered clubs as exhibiting 'unnecessary complexity, using many terms that are imprecise.' One of the examples then given was 'that

---

53   Licensing Act 2003, s 73.
54   Licensing Act 2003, s 74.
55   SI 2010/860.
56   Licensing Act 2003, s 75.
57   Ie Licensing Act 1964, Part II (Sale and supply of intoxicating liquor in club premises).

members' guests may be supplied with alcohol on the premises in a variety of circumstances, but there is no clear statutory definition of the term "guest" '.[58]

16.66 The Licensing Act 2003 contains a guide to interpretation of the term 'guest', in that section 67(1) provides that any reference in the Act (other than section 67) to a guest of a member of a club includes reference to:

(a)   an associate member of the club, and

(b)   a guest of an associate member of the club.

16.67 The Act goes on (at section 67(2)) to define 'associate member'. A person is an 'associate member' of a club if:

(a)   in accordance with the rules of the club he is admitted to its premises as being a member of another club, and

(b)   that other club is a recognised club.

16.68 'Recognised club' is defined in section 193 as meaning 'a club which satisfies conditions 1 to 3 of the general conditions in section 62.'[59] Such conditions effectively prohibit instant club membership.

16.69 The provisions clearly create a number of procedural hoops through which a visitor must climb before being able to buy a drink at the bar or enjoy regulated entertainment. By way of contrast, section 49(1) of the Licensing Act 1964 (relating to the sale of intoxicating liquor) by registered clubs clearly authorised such sale to, inter alia, 'persons other than members and their guests', without the requirement for a justices' licence authorising that sale.[60] Pursuant to such authorisation, it was common practice, for example, for visitors to a golf club, who are permitted to use the club's golf course upon payment of a green fee, to additionally use the club's other facilities, including its bar.

16.70 It would appear that such visitors are now permitted to use a club's bar for the purposes of purchasing alcohol only if they can be clearly identified as being a member of another 'recognised club', and the rules of the club that they are visiting provide for admission of such persons.[61] This raises obvious practical questions relating to verification, namely whether:

---

[58]   White Paper: Time for Reform – Proposals for the Modernisation of our Licensing Laws (April 2000), para 101.

[59]   See para 16.19.

[60]   See *Little Ship* case at para 16.23 above.

[61]   Club rules should accordingly be scrutinised to establish whether they need to be altered as regards (a) visitors, (b) associate members as defined in s 67(2), and (c) guests of the club (in relation to which see para 16.71). It may also be that a club which intends to operate solely or principally under the aegis of a premises licence may nevertheless still wish to hold a club premises certificate in order to allow its members the ability to enjoy the facilities of

(a)   a person is in fact a current member of another club; and

(b)   that other club is in fact a 'recognised club'.

16.71   It may be that 'guest of a member of a club' should fall to be interpreted as including reference to 'guest of a club'. Such an interpretation would be more akin to the apparent view of the Government, as stated by the then Minister for Sport and Tourism, Mr Richard Caborn,[62] and use of the word 'includes' in section 67(1) indicates that it is anticipated that others than solely 'an associate member of the club' and 'a guest of an associate member of the club' will fall within the category of 'guest of a member of a club'.

16.72   While it is unsatisfactory that there should be doubt as to the correct interpretation of a key section of the Act, the matter does not appear to have caused much difficulty in practice, not least because members' clubs cause such little regulatory concern in any event.

PLAYS

16.73   Second, where a club premises certificate authorises the performance of plays, no condition may be attached to the certificate which would restrict the nature of plays performed at the premises or the manner of performing such plays. However, this would not prevent a licensing authority imposing conditions that it thought necessary on the grounds of public safety.[63]

Notification of decision

16.74   Where an application for a club premises certificate is granted, the licensing authority must forthwith:

(a)   give notice to that effect to:
   (i) the applicant,
   (ii) any person who made relevant representations in respect of the application, and
   (iii) the chief officer of police for the area in which the premises are situated; and

(b)   issue the club with the club premises certificate and a summary of it.[64]

---

other clubs elsewhere in the country. See Licensing Act 2003, s 2(3)–(4) in relation to two or more authorisations having effect concurrently.

[62]   Hansard, House of Commons 28 June 2004, Col 3.

[63]   Licensing Act 2003, s 76.

[64]   Licensing Act 2003, s 77(1).

The certificate and the summary must be in the form prescribed by the Regulations.[65]

16.75   In accordance with the Regulations,[66] the certificate must:

(a)   specify the name of the club and its registered address;
(b)   specify the address of the premises to which the certificate relates;
(c)   include a plan of the premises;
(d)   specify the qualifying club activities for which the premises may be used;
(e)   specify the conditions subject to which the certificate has effect.[67]

16.76   Where an application for a club premises certificate is rejected, the licensing authority must forthwith give notice to that effect, and state its reasons for that decision to:

(a)   the applicant;
(b)   any person who made relevant representations in respect of the application; and
(c)   the chief officer of police for the police area in which the premises are situated.[68]

16.77   Where relevant representations were made in relation to the application, the notification of the decision must specify the authority's reasons for its decision and, where applicable, reasons for modifying conditions, excluding activities from the scope of the licence or rejecting the application.[69] This would apply whether or not the determination of the application was made after a hearing, or by agreement between the club, the authority and any interested parties that a hearing is unnecessary.

16.78   The flowchart at Figure 1 illustrates the process involved in relation to an application for the grant of a club premises certificate.

Theft or loss of club premises certificate or summary

16.79   Where a club premises certificate is lost, stolen, damaged or destroyed, the club may obtain a certified copy of the licence or summary, on payment of a specified fee to the licensing authority. In order to issue a copy of the certificate, the licensing authority must be satisfied that the certificate has been lost, stolen, damaged or destroyed, and that where it has been lost

---

65   Licensing Act 2003, s 77(1). The form is prescribed by the Licensing Act 2003 (Premises Licences and Club Premises Certificates) Regulations, regs 35, 36 and Sch 13.
66   Licensing Act 2003, s 77(1).
67   Licensing Act 2003, s 78.
68   Licensing Act 2003, s 77(3).
69   Licensing Act 2003, s 77(2). The licensing authority does not have to address each submission made to it but relevant and potentially decisive submissions must be specifically addressed. See *R (Ron Bushell) v Newcastle Licensing Justices* [2004] QBD 26 March 2004.

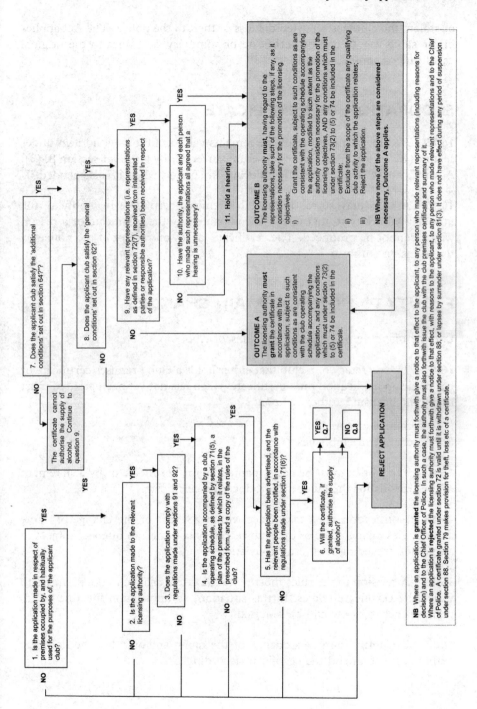

Figure 1: Application for grant of a club premise certificate

or stolen, the club has reported the loss or theft to the police. The Act applies in the same way to a copy certificate or summary as it does to the original certificate or summary.[70]

E DURATION OF CERTIFICATE

16.80 A club premises certificate remains valid until it is withdrawn under sections 88 or 90 of the Act or lapses on surrender by virtue of section 81(3). A certificate does not have effect during any period when it is suspended.[71]

16.81 A club may surrender a club premises certificate by notifying the licensing authority to that effect, accompanied by the certificate or a reason why it cannot be produced. The certificate lapses on receipt of the notice by the licensing authority.[72]

F DUTY TO NOTIFY CERTAIN CHANGES

Change of name or alteration of rules of club[73]

16.82 The secretary of a club that either holds a club premises certificate or has made an application for a certificate which has not yet been granted must notify the licensing authority upon:

(1)   a change of name; or
(2)   a change of club rules.

16.83 The notice must be accompanied by the certificate or by a statement of the reasons for the failure to produce the certificate.

16.84 Notification must take place within 28 days of the change of name and/or rules taking place or the club secretary commits an offence, subject to a fine not exceeding level 2 on conviction.

16.85 A revision to the rules must not authorise a change in the premises to which the certificate relates. In this situation, an application for a new club premises certificate would be required.

16.86 On notification of a change of the name and/or rules, the licensing authority must amend the certificate accordingly.

---

[70]   Licensing Act 2003, s 79.
[71]   Licensing Act 2003, s 80.
[72]   Licensing Act 2003, s 81.
[73]   Licensing Act 2003, s 82.

Change of relevant registered address[74]

16.87 A club may give notice of a change to its relevant registered address so that the licensing authority may alter this information in the licensing register.

16.88 Where a club ceases to have authority to use its current registered address as its address, it must as soon as reasonably practicable notify the licensing authority of the new address.

16.89 The notice must be accompanied by the certificate, or by a statement of the reasons for failure to produce it.

16.90 Failure to comply with this requirement is an offence committed by the secretary and is subject to a maximum level 2 fine on conviction.

G VARIATION OF CERTIFICATE

16.91 It is possible for a club to apply for a variation of the club premises certificate at any time. For example, a club may wish to extend the hours during which its certificate permits the supply of alcohol.

16.92 The application must be accompanied by the club premises certificate, or statement why that cannot be produced.[75]

Where there are no relevant representations

16.93 Where no relevant representations are made, the licensing authority must grant the variation if the application has been made in accordance with section 84 of the Act and Regulations have been complied with.[76]

16.94 Where the licensing authority determines that any representations are frivolous or vexatious, it must explain to the person who made them why it made that decision.[77]

Where there are relevant representations

16.95 Where relevant representations are made then the licensing authority must:

[74] Licensing Act 2003, s 83.
[75] Licensing Act 2003, s 84(3).
[76] Licensing Act 2003, s 85(1)–(2).
[77] Licensing Act 2003, s 86(5).

(a)   hold a hearing to consider the application, unless the authority, the applicant and each person who made representations agree that a hearing is unnecessary;[78] and
(b)   as it considers appropriate for the promotion of the licensing objectives:
    (1) modify the conditions of the certificate,
    (2) reject the whole or part of the application.[79]

Notification[80]

16.96   Following the hearing of an application for variation of the certificate, whether the application is granted or rejected in whole or in part, the licensing authority must forthwith notify:

(a)   the applicant;
(b)   any person who made relevant representations; and
(c)   the chief officer of police.

16.97   The notice must specify the licensing authority's reasons for its decision. Where the application is granted, the notice must state when the variation will take effect.

Vary substantially

16.98   It is not possible to use the variation procedure to vary substantially the premises. The Act does not contain a definition of 'substantially'.[81] However, structural alterations and enlargements of the licensed area are likely to be viewed as substantial and will need to be pursued by making an application for a new certificate.[82]

16.99   The flowchart at Figure 2 illustrates the process involved in relation to an application for variation of a club premises certificate.

Minor variations

16.100   The 2003 Act as originally drafted imposed a heavy bureaucratic burden on those who wished only to make minor variations to their club premises certificates. Therefore, the Legislative Reform (Minor Variations to

---

[78]   Licensing Act 2003, s 85(3)(a)–(b).
[79]   Licensing Act 2003, s 85(4)(a)–(b).
[80]   Licensing Act 2003, s 86.
[81]   It will be a matter for the licensing authority to determine on the particular facts of each relevant application whether an applicant's proposal would represent a substantial variation of the premises for which the certificate has effect.
[82]   See further Chapter 15 (Premises Licences), paras 15.172–15.176.

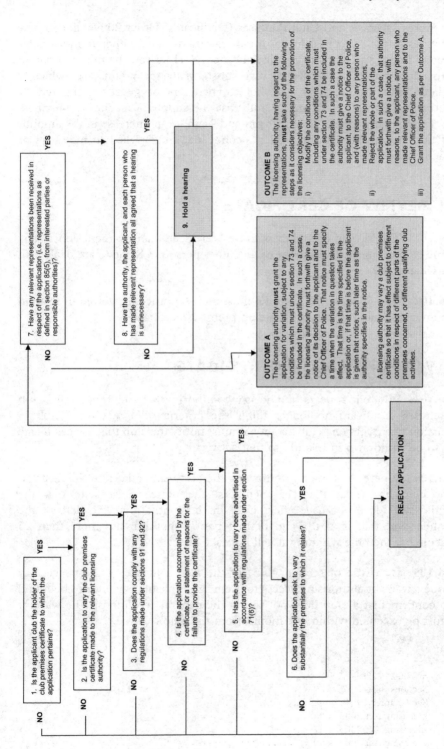

Figure 2: Application for variation of a club premises certificate

Premises Licences and Club Premises Certificates) Order 2009[83] added new sections to the Act[84] to cater for minor variations. These operate in a similar way to minor variations to premises licences.[85] However, the minor variation procedure may not be used to vary substantially the premises to which it relates, add the supply of alcohol to members or guests as an activity authorised by the certificate, or authorise the supply of alcohol to members or guests at any time between 11 pm and 7 am, or an increase in the amount of time on any day during which alcohol may be supplied to members or guests.[86]

H REVIEW OF CERTIFICATE

16.101   The review of a club premises certificate can be requested at any time by a responsible authority or any other person.[87] Reviews are dealt with in Chapter 42.

16.102   The flowchart at Figure 3 illustrates the process involved in relation to an application for review of a club premises certificate.

I WITHDRAWAL OF CERTIFICATE

16.103   Where it appears to a licensing authority that a club holding a club premises certificate no longer fulfils the criteria of a qualifying club in relation to a qualifying club activity, it must notify the club that the certificate is to be withdrawn in relation to that activity.[88]

16.104   Where the notice withdrawing the certificate relates to the fact that the club has fewer than 25 members, the notice must state that the withdrawal does not have effect until three months after the date of the notice, and that if at the end of that period the club has more than 25 members, then the withdrawal will not take effect.[89]

16.105   By virtue of section 90(5) of the Act, a justice of the peace may issue a warrant authorising access to premises to enable evidence to be found to confirm that a club does not satisfy the general conditions. The warrant must be executed within one month from the date of issue.[90]

---

[83]   SI 2009/1772.
[84]   Sections 86A–C.
[85]   See Chapter 15 (Premises Licences).
[86]   Licensing Act 2003, s 86A(3).
[87]   Licensing Act 2003, s 87(1).
[88]   Licensing Act 2003, s 90(1).
[89]   Licensing Act 2003, s 90(2).
[90]   Licensing Act 2003, s 90(5).

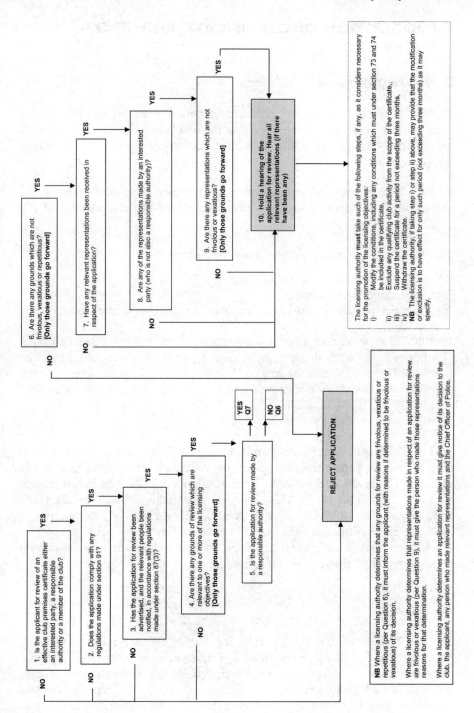

Figure 3: Application for review of a club premises certificate

J PRODUCTION OF CERTIFICATE, RIGHTS OF ENTRY ETC

Duty to keep and produce certificate[91]

16.106 If the club premises certificate authorises a qualifying club activity then the club secretary must ensure that the certificate, or a certified copy, is kept at the premises to which it relates and that a nominated person is responsible for it.

16.107 The nominated person must be nominated by the secretary in writing and the licensing authority must be notified of the identity of the nominated person.

16.108 The 'nominated person' must be either:

(a)   the secretary of the club;
(b)   any member of the club;
(c)   any person who works at the premises for the purposes of the club.

16.109 The nominated person must ensure that both a summary of the certificate, or a certified copy, and a notice specifying the position that the nominated person holds at the club are prominently displayed at the premises. A constable or an authorised person may require the nominated person to produce the club premises certificate, or a certified copy, for examination.

16.110 The club secretary commits an offence if he fails, without reasonable excuse, to ensure that the certificate, or a certified copy, is held at the premises under the control of a nominated person. The nominated person commits an offence if he fails, without reasonable excuse, to display a summary of the certificate, or a certified copy, or a notice. The nominated person also commits an offence if he fails, without reasonable excuse, to produce the certificate, or certified copy, on demand. These offences carry a maximum level 2 fine on summary conviction.

Inspection[92]

16.111 Where an application is made for a club premises certificate, variation of a certificate or review of a certificate, an authorised person or a constable may enter and inspect the premises. Any inspection must take place within 14 days from the date of the application. The inspection period can be extended by up to seven days if the licensing authority believes that reasonable steps have been taken to arrange the viewing but that it has not

91   Licensing Act 2003, s 94.
92   Licensing Act 2003, s 96.

been possible for the inspection to take place within the 14 days allowed. Before an authorised person or constable inspects the premises, at least 48 hours' notice must be given to the club. Any person obstructing an authorised person attempting to inspect the premises is guilty of an offence, liable on summary conviction to a fine not exceeding level 2.

Other powers of entry and search[93]

16.112 Where a club has a club premises certificate, the police may enter and search the premises if a constable has reasonable cause to believe that any offence related to the supply of drugs has been or is likely to be committed, or that there is likely to be a breach of the peace. In these circumstances, reasonable force may be used to gain entry.[94]

K SALES TO NON-MEMBERS

16.113 Under the pre-existing law,[95] it was clear that club rules may provide for a club to admit persons other than members and their guests and to enable the sale to them of intoxicating liquor for consumption on the club premises. Nevertheless were the club rules too widely drawn, the magistrates (who had jurisdiction for registered clubs) were entitled to determine that the premises in question were not established and conducted in good faith as a club. In practice, many club rules have provided that, for example, visiting sports teams, their officials and other clubs or categories of club can be made temporary members provided that their attendance does not lead to existing club members being excluded from the facilities of their club.[96]

16.114 The Licensing Act 2003 permits the sale by retail of alcohol to a guest of a member of a club[97] and also to 'associate members' of the club and their guests.[98] However, it appears to prohibit such sale to other persons

---

93   Licensing Act 2003, s 97.

94   This provides the police with a power of entry which did not previously exist.

95   Licensing Act 1964, s 49, and *Little Ship* case. See para 16.23.

96   In *Coventry Football Club v. Coventry JJ* (1973) 117 Sol Jo 855, DC it was held that a rule that 'visiting teams, officials, sporting, social and invited clubs can be temporary members provided their names be placed on the board at least two days before the date of attendance' will not be interpreted so as to apply the status of membership to members of a visiting club at a function attended by such members to the exclusion of members of the club at which the function takes place (*Paterson's Licensing Acts 2003* (111th ed, Butterworths), see commentary para 2.497). The Good Practice Guide commented that the arrangement adopted by some clubs whereby persons attending the club premises are made 'temporary members' is questionable, and that it would be better for clubs to enact a rule whereby visitors to the club premises may be supplied with intoxicating liquor in certain circumstances. (Justices' Clerks' Society Good Practice Guide, para 7.25).

97   Licensing Act 2003, s 1(2)(b).

98   Licensing Act 2003, s 67. See paras 16.64–16.72.

with the consequence that sales would be unlawful unless a premises licence or temporary event notice has been granted in relation to the premises in question.[99]

16.115 If a club decides to widen its activities (for example, by allowing the general public to hire the club hall for wedding receptions) a premises licence will be needed and a designated premises supervisor would have to be specified. Furthermore, an individual on behalf of a club may give temporary event notices in respect of the premises. On such occasions the club may sell alcohol to the public or hire out their premises for use by the public.[100]

---

[99] For a discussion on this point see paras 16.64–16.72.
[100] See Licensing Act 2003, Part 5 (Permitted temporary activities) and Chapter 19 (Temporary Events).

17

Conditions

Souls of Poets dead and gone,
What Elysium have ye known,
Happy field or mossy cavern,
Choicer than the Mermaid Tavern?
Have ye tippled drink more fine
Than mine host's Canary wine?
Or are fruits of Paradise
Sweeter than those dainty pies
Of venison?

John Keats

A INTRODUCTION

17.01 Under the Licensing Act 2003, conditions arise in three ways:

- Proffered
- Imposed
- Mandatory

17.02 Under the previous regime, local authorities granting public entertainment licences tended to attach lists of standard conditions, together with such special conditions as they thought necessary in the individual circumstances of the case. Therefore late night venues, which needed public entertainment licences in order to procure special hours certificates under section 77 of the Licensing Act 1964, were well-used to operating under standard conditions. By way of contrast, while licensing justices enjoyed the power to impose such conditions as they thought proper in the interests of the public under section 4 of the Licensing Act 1964,[1] the power was not extensively used. Understandably, therefore, pub operators were nervous about the new regime in that it was to be administered by local authorities who have made liberal use of their condition-making powers.

17.03 However, conditions should be seen not only as mechanisms for cutting down the grant of a licence, but as enabling devices to permit a grant where none would otherwise have issued. The existence of the power obliges the licensing authority, before refusing a licence, to consider whether its objections to grant might be overcome by the imposition of conditions. The limitation in the Act, that only appropriate conditions should be imposed, together with exhortations in the Guidance to avoid the routine imposition of standard conditions,[2] should result in a more surgical application of conditions and save the licence from being emasculated by inapposite and burdensome reams of requirements.

17.04 The system requires the operator himself, when making application, to set out the measures which he proposes to promote the licensing objectives. These measures will subsequently become incorporated as conditions of the licence. For the system to work, it requires other relevant experts, both within and without the authority, to ensure that the licensing sub-committee is made aware of the kind of measures which may be taken to avoid harm to the licensing objectives. In this way, the black or white grant/refuse exercise is intended to be a more sensitive process of considering what imaginative measures may be used to overcome any legitimate objections.

17.05 Certain conditions are also added to licences automatically. This is either because they are mandatory conditions expressly specified in the Act, or because they are part of the 'mandatory code'.

B THE STATUTORY SCHEME

17.06 An almost identical mechanism is contained in the Act for both the imposition of conditions on a premises licence and on a club premises certificate (see sections 18 and 72 respectively). The mechanism for imposing conditions envisages two different scenarios.

---

[1]   In *R v Sussex Confirming Authority, ex parte Tamplin & Sons Brewery (Brighton) Limited* [1937] 4 All ER 106 and *R (Sitki) v Inner London Crown Court* (1993) 157 JP 523, the width of the discretion was confirmed.

[2]   Para 1.16.

The first scenario: no relevant representations

17.07 Taking a premises licence by way of example[3], the first scenario is where an application is received (in accordance with s 17) and the relevant licensing authority is satisfied that the applicant has complied with any requirement imposed by way of regulation (section 17(5)). In such circumstances the authority is obliged to grant the licence in accordance with the application subject only to such conditions as are consistent with the operating schedule (section 18(2)(a)) and any mandatory or mandatory code conditions as imposed by sections 19–21.

Conditions which are consistent with the operating schedule

17.08 The Act has been drafted to afford no discretion to authorities in the field of conditions in the first scenario where they have received no 'relevant representations' from a responsible authority or other person.[4]

17.09 The importance therefore, of the content of the operating schedule is self-evident.[5] Sections 17(4) (premises licence) and 71(5) (club premises certificate) stipulate what should be contained in an operating schedule. The list includes (inter alia) the steps which the applicant proposes to take to promote the licensing objectives (which are the prevention of crime and disorder, public safety, the prevention of public nuisance, and the protection of children from harm).

17.10 The Guidance has evolved so as to make it clear that in formulating their proposed measures, they ought to consider the terms of the licensing policy, appraise the needs of the area and consult with responsible authorities. If this is done, then not only are relevant representations less likely to be made and hearings therefore avoided, but if representations are made, the applicant ought to be in a stronger position to overcome them.

17.11 The Guidance on the matter merits reproduction, since it exemplifies the policy-driven, partnership approach which it is the intention of this book to exhort:

'8.34 In completing an operating schedule, applicants are expected to have regard to the statement of licensing policy for their area. They must also be aware of the expectations of the licensing authority and the responsible authorities as to the steps that are appropriate for the promotion of the licensing objectives, and to demonstrate knowledge of their local area when describing the

---

3 See Licensing Act 2003, ss 69–76 for the operation of the regime in relation to club premises certificates.
4 Licensing Act 2003, s 18(7)(a).
5 See Chapter 15 (The Premises Licence), for a detailed discussion of the 'operating schedule'.

steps they propose to take to promote the licensing objectives. Licensing authorities and responsible authorities are expected to publish information about what is meant by the promotion of the licensing objectives and to ensure that applicants can readily access advice about these matters. However, applicants are also expected to undertake their own enquiries about the area in which the premises are situated to inform the content of the application.

8.35 Applicants are, in particular, expected to obtain sufficient information to enable them to demonstrate, when setting out the steps they propose to take to promote the licensing objectives, that they understand:

- the layout of the local area and physical environment including crime and disorder hotspots, proximity to residential premises and proximity to areas where children may congregate;
- any risk posed to the local area by the applicants' proposed licensable activities; and
- any local initiatives (for example, local crime reduction initiatives or voluntary schemes including local taxi-marshalling schemes, street pastors and other schemes) which may help to mitigate potential risks.

8.36 Applicants are expected to include positive proposals in their application on how they will manage any potential risks. Where specific policies apply in the area (for example, a cumulative impact policy), applicants are also expected to demonstrate an understanding of how the policy impacts on their application; any measures they will take to mitigate the impact; and why they consider the application should be an exception to the policy.

8.37 It is expected that enquiries about the locality will assist applicants when determining the steps that are appropriate for the promotion of the licensing objectives. For example, premises with close proximity to residential premises should consider how this impact upon their smoking, noise management and dispersal policies to ensure the promotion of the public nuisance objective. Applicants must consider all factors which may be relevant to the promotion of the licensing objectives, and where there are no known concerns, acknowledge this in their application.

8.38 The majority of information which applicants will require should be available in the licensing policy statement in the area. Other publicly available sources which may be of use to applicants include:

- the Crime Mapping website;
- Neighbourhood Statistics websites;
- websites or publications by local responsible authorities;
- websites or publications by local voluntary schemes and initiatives; and
- on-line mapping tools.

8.39 Whilst applicants are not required to seek the views of responsible authorities before formally submitting their application, they may find them to be a useful source of expert advice on local issues that should be taken into consideration when making an application. Licensing authorities may wish to encourage co-operation between applicants, responsible authorities and, where relevant, local residents and businesses before applications are submitted in order to minimise the scope for disputes to arise.

8.40 Applicants are expected to provide licensing authorities with sufficient information in this section to determine the extent to which their proposed steps are appropriate to promote the licensing objectives in the local area. Applications must not be based on providing a set of standard conditions to promote the licensing objectives and applicants are expected to make it clear why the steps they are proposing are appropriate for the premises.

8.41 All parties are expected to work together in partnership to ensure that the licensing objectives are promoted collectively. Where there are no disputes, the steps that applicants propose to take to promote the licensing objectives, as set out in the operating schedule, will very often translate directly into conditions that will be attached to premises licences with the minimum of fuss.

8.42 For some premises, it is possible that no measures will be appropriate to promote one or more of the licensing objectives, for example, because they are adequately covered by other existing legislation. It is however important that all operating schedules should be precise and clear about the measures that are proposed to promote each of the licensing objectives.'

17.12 As stated above, where there are no relevant representations the duty is to grant the licence subject only to such conditions as are 'consistent' with the operating schedule. But what does this mean? What if the proposed condition is meaningless, unenforceable, illegal, ineffective or inconsistent with another condition?

17.13 The Guidance on this matter states:

'10.7 Consistency means that the effect of the condition should be substantially the same as that intended by the terms of the operating schedule. If conditions are broken, this may lead to a criminal prosecution or an application for a review and it is extremely important therefore that they should be expressed on the licence or certificate in unequivocal and unambiguous terms. The duty imposed by conditions on the licence holder or club must be clear to the licence holder, club, enforcement officers and the courts.'

17.14 However, the Guidance is far from complete, since it deals only with a situation in which the proposed condition is unclear. There are many other reasons, as just stated, why it may be undesirable or improper to carry forward the condition in its proposed form or indeed at all.

17.15 This was considered in *R (Bristol City Council) v Bristol Magistrates*[6] where it was stated:

> '21. Plainly it is desirable that an operating schedule should describe any steps proposed as clearly as possible, so that those considering the application are clear as to what it may involve and whether any other steps are required to promote the licensing objectives. But, if the steps are proposed in language which is general or opaque, the licensing authority may impose a condition describing more specifically and concretely what is proposed if that is necessary to promote the licensing objectives. Such a condition would be consistent with the operating schedule, it would just be more specific.'

17.16 The Learned Deputy Judge went further, however, and held that not only is for the licensing authority to translate the operating schedule into enforceable conditions but that the authority may simply omit to translate particular proposals into licensing conditions. He said:

> '33. The licensing authority have power to impose conditions under those provisions, a power which they must exercise, in accordance with the general duty imposed by section 4 subsection (1), with a view to promoting the licensing objectives. In my judgment there is no legal obligation to impose a condition, in order to promote the licensing objectives, to give effect to anything contained in the operating schedule if, for example, the authority considers that compliance with other legislation is sufficient for that purpose ...
>
> 35. In my judgment, even under section 18(2), there is no obligation to impose a condition to give effect to the operating schedule if that condition is not necessary to promote the licensing objectives. Indeed, if the operating schedule contained matters which would in fact harm the achievement of the licensing objectives, it is hard to conceive that Parliament would have required a licensing authority to impose such a condition.'

17.17 The notion that conditions which are actively harmful or illegal should not be transposed is understandable. However, it is considered that a licensing authority ought to think long and hard about omitting a condition merely because it did not think it was needed. A potential objector may have refrained from making a representation precisely because such a condition was proposed. Therefore, there is a danger that an administrative decision to omit a condition will cause injustice to a party who would otherwise have wished to exercise their democratic right to participate in the licensing process.

---

[6]   [2009] EWHC 625 (Admin).

The second scenario: relevant representations

17.18 The second scenario is where there have been 'relevant representations' made by a responsible authority or other person. In those circumstances the authority's discretion will be engaged following a hearing whereby if it is satisfied that the premises licence ought to be granted, it will have to attach such conditions as are consistent with the operating schedule and modified to such extent as the authority considers appropriate for the promotion of the licensing objectives (see section 18(4)(a)(i) of the 2003 Act).

17.19 'Relevant representations' are defined in section 18(6) as being representations which:

- are about the likely effect of the grant of the Premises Licence on the promotion of the licensing objectives;
- meet the requirements of section 18(7);
- if they relate to the identity of the person named in the application as the proposed premises supervisor, meet the requirements of section 18(9); and
- are not excluded by virtue of section 32 (restriction on making a statement following issue of provisional statement).

17.20 The requirements of section 18(7) (as referred to above) are that the representations are made by a responsible authority or other person within the period prescribed under section 17(5)(c), have not been withdrawn and (in the case of representations made by someone other than a responsible authority) are not in the opinion of the relevant licensing authority 'frivolous or vexatious'. Where the authority determines that such representations are frivolous or vexatious, it must notify the person of the reasons for its determination.

Frivolous or vexatious

17.21 The exercise of the power to dismiss a representation as frivolous or vexatious without a hearing is highly significant both for the maker of the representation and for the applicant. For the maker of the representation, he loses the chance to contribute further to the decision-making process. Where he is the only objector, the licence will then be granted administratively, without further consideration of the merits. Where there are other objectors, he is unlikely to be heard at the hearing of the application. In either case, he will be unable to appeal against a grant, since this right is confined to those making relevant representations.[7] His remedy, therefore, will be confined to judicial review. Given the width of the discretion afforded to the licensing authority to rule out objections as frivolous and vexatious, the judicial review route is fraught with difficulties.

---

[7] Licensing Act 2003, Sch 5 para 2(3).

17.22 Conversely, for the applicant, the exercise of the power by the licensing authority may yield significant commercial benefits. At very least, it saves the applicant the time and expense of having to prepare to meet that objection, and possibly of having to prepare for a hearing at all. It removes the uncertainty which litigating the issue may cause, and also the risk of appeal by the objector. Often, contractual arrangements between the applicant and the landowner involve options requiring the grant of a licence by a certain date, so that removal of an objector from the fray and a speedier grant could actually save the applicant from losing the property altogether.

17.23 There are therefore powerful countervailing interests at play riding on the authority's decision. The decision is likely to be taken by a licensing officer, and there will be no hearing before the decision is made. It is easy to imagine that officers may be put under intense pressure from one or both sides before they make their decision. What are the guiding principles?

17.24 The Guidance, which of course authorities are bound to take into account, offers some general perspectives on the meaning of the term 'frivolous or vexatious'. It states:

> '9.5 ... A representation may be considered to be vexatious if it appears to be intended to cause aggravation or annoyance, whether to a competitor or other person, without reasonable cause or justification. Vexatious circumstances may arise because of disputes between rival businesses and local knowledge will therefore be invaluable in considering such matters. Licensing authorities can consider the main effect of the representation, and whether any inconvenience or expense caused by it could reasonably be considered to be proportionate.
>
> 9.6 Frivolous representations would be essentially categorised by a lack of seriousness. Frivolous representations would concern issues which, at most, are minor and in relation to which no remedial steps would be warranted or proportionate.'

17.25 Some assistance may also be gleaned from case law. In *Ashmore v British Coal Corporation*, Stuart-Smith LJ held that:

> 'A litigant has a right to have his claim litigated, provided it is not frivolous, vexatious or an abuse of the process. What may constitute such conduct must depend on all the circumstances of the case; the categories are not closed and considerations of public policy and the interests of justice may be very material.'[8]

While the context was different, the principle holds. It is not possible to determine in advance what amounts to frivolous or vexatious conduct – but it is a matter which may be readily recognisable on the facts of individual cases.

---

8   [1990] 2 QB 338, 348.

17.26 In its original form, the 2003 Act limited the ability for local people to make representations to those who lived or worked in the vicinity of the premises.[9] However, this limitation was abolished by the Police Reform and Social Responsibility Act 2011, in the interests of local empowerment, so that now anybody may object to a licence application wherever they live and whatever their interest. This inevitably throws a greater importance on the frivolous and vexatious test to act as a filter to weed out meritless objections. Nevertheless, early experience is that there has not been an onrush of objections from distant busybodies, and the pessimism that there would be a flood of politically motivated representations has proved unfounded.

Particularly given that a finding that a representation is frivolous and vexatious disables the maker from participating further in the process, it is considered that the exercise of the jurisdiction should be handled with some caution.

17.27 The licensing authority would no doubt also wish to bear in mind two other circumstances. First, the representation will often not be made by a person who finds it easy to express themselves fully or articulately on paper. Second, representations which look hopeless on paper may turn out to have substance when investigated properly at a hearing.

17.28 For these reasons, while the authority should not shy away from dismissing representations which do meet the test, and should not allow administration of the process to be unnecessarily delayed or frustrated, they should exercise considerable caution before ruling out representations on these grounds. It is suggested that it is only in cases in which the authority can see that the objection is hopeless or obviously without substance that the discretion ought to be exercised. This means not only that a grant is bound to be issued, but that the representations made could not even give rise to sensible consideration of the need for conditions on the licence to supplement those suggested in the operating schedule.

17.29 For the above reasons, it is considered that the Guidance offers sound counsel:

> '9.9 It is recommended that, in borderline cases, the benefit of the doubt about any aspect of a representation should be given to the person making that representation. The subsequent hearing would then provide an opportunity for the person or body making the representation to amplify and clarify it.'

17.30 If representations are in fact ruled out, the Act requires that reasons be given for the determination (section 18(8)). Given that this is an area where the authority will be vulnerable to challenges by way of application for

---

[9]   Section 13(3)(a).

judicial review, it is obvious that any summary rejection of the representation should be accompanied by full reasons which will survive high judicial scrutiny.

17.31 Upon relevant representations being made the authority must hold a hearing to consider them (unless the applicant and those making representations agree that a hearing is unnecessary) and take such steps as set out in section 18(4) as it considers appropriate for the promotion of the licensing objectives.

17.32 The steps as stipulated in section 18(4) are:

- to grant the licence, subject to:
  - conditions which are consistent with the operating schedule accompanying the application, modified to such extent as the authority considers necessary for the promotion of the licensing objectives, and
  - any conditions which must under sections 19–21 be included in the licence;
- to exclude from the scope of the licence any of the licensable activities to which the application relates;
- to refuse to specify a person in the licence as the premises supervisor; or
- to reject the application.

17.33 In adding conditions (whether the grant was mandatory or discretionary), the authority may impose different conditions in respect of different parts of the premises and different licensable activities (section 18(10)).

Conditions: law and practice

17.34 While the Act appears to give a wide discretion to attach such conditions as the authority considers appropriate, in reality the discretion is tempered by a series of considerations, which are neatly summarised in the Guidance:[10]

'Conditions on a premises licence or club premises certificate are important in setting the parameters within which premises can lawfully operate. The use of wording such as "must", "shall" and "will", is encouraged. Licence conditions:

- must be appropriate for the promotion of the licensing objectives;
- must be precise and enforceable;
- must be unambiguous and clear in what they intend to achieve;
- should not duplicate other statutory requirements or other duties or responsibilities placed on the employer by other legislation;
- must be tailored to the individual type, location and characteristics of the premises and events concerned;

---

[10]   Para 1.16.

- should not be standardised and may be unlawful when it cannot be demonstrated that they are appropriate for the promotion of the licensing objectives in an individual case;
- should not replicate offences set out in the 2003 Act or other legislation;
- should be proportionate, justifiable and be capable of being met, (for example, whilst beer glasses may be available in toughened glass, wine glasses may not);
- cannot seek to manage the behaviour of customers once they are beyond the direct management of the licence holder and their staff, but may impact on the behaviour of customers in the immediate vicinity of the premises or as they enter or leave; and
- should be written in a prescriptive format.'

Certain of these principles require a little further commentary.

The requirement of proportionality

17.35 Conditions play an important role in defining the standards expected of the operator so as to promote the licensing objectives in a manner consistent with the licensing authority's policy. Furthermore, businesses change hands, and while a particularly light touch may be appropriate with a known operator, an incoming operator may be unaware of the standards operated by his predecessor. The conditions of the licence therefore speak directly to each new operator to inform them of their obligations. Nevertheless, it is important to recognise that conditions may impose high economic burdens on operators, even to the extent that they make the difference between a viable and a non-viable business. They may even affect the value of the business itself. Therefore, it is insufficient to say that they should be imposed whenever they are considered appropriate. There is an additional requirement, that imposed conditions be proportionate.

17.36 This important concept is recognised in national Guidance, which states:

'1.17 Each application must be considered on its own merits and in accordance with the licensing authority's statement of licensing policy; for example, if the application falls within the scope of a cumulative impact policy. Conditions attached to licences and certificates must be tailored to the individual type, location and characteristics of the premises and events concerned. This is essential to avoid the imposition of disproportionate and overly burdensome conditions on premises where there is no need for such conditions. Standardised conditions should be avoided and indeed may be unlawful where they cannot be shown to be appropriate for the promotion of the licensing objectives in an individual case.'

This theme is developed further in the Guidance, thus:

'10.10 The 2003 Act requires that licensing conditions should be tailored to the size, type, location and characteristics and activities taking place at the premises concerned. Conditions should be determined on a case by case basis and standardised conditions which ignore these individual aspects should be avoided. Licensing authorities and other responsible authorities should be alive to the indirect costs that can arise because of conditions. These could be a deterrent to holding events that are valuable to the community or for the funding of good and important causes. Licensing authorities should therefore ensure that any conditions they impose are only those which are appropriate for the promotion of the licensing objectives.'[11]

17.37   The concept of 'appropriateness' is arguably empty of meaning. It is most unlikely that an authority would ever attach a condition which it considered to be inappropriate. The test therefore provides no benchmark, no objective yardstick by which the value or need of the condition can be measured. This is supplied by the concept of proportionality, which asks whether the regulatory intervention goes further than is really needed for the promotion of the licensing objectives, and whether the intervention is unnecessarily burdensome in the light of all the circumstances.[12] So, to take one example, in acting proportionately, an authority's attention might be focused first on whether management conditions would suffice, before asking itself whether the business itself ought to be curtailed by imposing earlier terminal hours or excluding a licensable activity. If a management condition, such as a requirement for a noise limitation device, could resolve an issue of nuisance, then curtailing terminal hours would be disproportionate.

17.38   To this should be added the important point that the requirement of proportionality is not merely the creation of Guidance. It has deep roots in human rights law, and also in the Legislative and Regulatory Reform Act 2006, which are canvassed elsewhere in this book.[13]

Duplication

17.39   The question of whether conditions may be added which duplicate other statutory requirements has occupied a large amount of committee and court time since the inception of the 2003 Act. The answer may be simply given. If the condition precisely duplicates an enforceable obligation arising elsewhere, it is most unlikely to be appropriate to load the licence with it. For

---

[11]   See also Guidance para 9.40.
[12]   See also *R v Secretary of State for Health ex parte Eastcheap Cheese Company* [1999] 3 CMLR 123, at para [41].
[13]   See Chapter 12 (The Appropriateness Test), Chapter 27 (Human Rights), and Chapter 29 (The Legislative and Regulatory Reform Act 2006).

example, a condition requiring the pub to carry out a health and safety risk assessment, or not to serve alcohol to drunk people, is a waste of time and paper. On the other hand, the fact that there exists another regime capable of controlling the activity ought not necessarily to prevent a condition being applied. For example, the Environmental Protection Act 1990 is an Act to control nuisance, eg through the use of noise abatement notices. The Health and Safety at Work Act imposes criminal liabilities on employers and others to protect the health and safety of those working at and visiting premises. Plainly, the existence of these regimes is not in and of itself a bar to the attachment of conditions concerning nuisance and health and safety. However, the fact that they exist may be taken into account by the licensing sub-committee.

Where, however, precise measures have been identified as appropriate by the sub-committee, it is most unlikely that the sub-committee will consider itself precluded from imposing them as conditions just because parallel protection systems exist. Indeed, if the mere existence of parallel systems barred the use of the Licensing Act 2003, the Act itself would be nugatory.[14] On the other hand, if more general concerns are raised which do not seem particularly pressing in the individual circumstances of the case, the licensing authority may well decide that if such concerns do actually materialise they may be met by enforcement under the parallel regime, or even through licence reviews, and that it would be disproportionate to meet them now through the imposition of licence conditions. The situation is not therefore black and white: the existence of the parallel regime is always likely to be relevant, but in some cases it will obviate the need for conditions and in other cases it won't. An experienced sub-committee, assisted by professional advisers, ought to become adept at recognising which side of the line the instant case falls.

The question of duplication is considered in greater detail in Section F below.

Certainty

17.40 Operating schedules are often not drafted by lawyers. It is a vital function of the licensing authority to translate proposals, which may be phrased quite loosely, into enforceable conditions. As was pointed out by *Scott Baker LJ in Crawley Borough Council v Attenborough*,[15] those operating the licence, those benefiting from its conditions (such as neighbours) and those enforcing it must have a clear understanding of what it means. Most importantly, breach carries serious criminal sanctions, and so it is crucial that everyone knows where they stand from the terms of the document.

---

[14] See further on this topic *Di Ciacca v Scottish Ministers* [2003] LLR 526; *R (Blackwood) v Birmingham Magistrates* [2006] LLR 802.

[15] [2006] LLR 403.

Management of customers off-site

17.41 While conditions cannot require a licensee to go out into the town and ask his customers to behave themselves at the bus station, they can recognise the potential for nuisance or crime and disorder from departing customers. This may result in conditions regarding a dispersal plan, responsible alcohol service, alcohol awareness training, last entry or terminal hours. The licence cannot seek to control the behaviour of customers once they are away from the premises, but it can seek to control the behaviour of the licensee so that customers do not leave at a time, in such numbers or in such a manner as to harm the licensing objectives. This basic principle has often been misunderstood and misapplied by representatives and decision-makers, but it is fundamental to the effective operation of the system.[16]

Good practice

17.42 Debates before the licensing sub-committee can be polarised. On the one hand, there is an applicant who wishes to emerge with as few conditions as possible, and so has an interest in not proposing any. On the other, there may be residents who do not want there to be a licence, and so have no interest in proposing a compromise, and may lack relevant expertise anyway. This may result in an outright grant or refusal which is then subject to a costly appeal, when the application of sensitive conditions may well have been an answer to the case. Often, the outcome of the appeal, whether by consent or otherwise, is the imposition of conditions which ought to have been proposed and imposed in the first place.

17.43 The answer to this lies in gearing the system to the identification and imposition of appropriate conditions. The first source is the licensing policy itself, which ought to set out clearly the kind of conditions which might be considered in individual cases. This gives all parties a set of solutions to which they may refer not only when compiling their operating schedules or relevant representations, but also when in the crucible of debate before the sub-committee.

17.44 The second source is the licensing officer, a much maligned species who in the past has, out of timidity or for fear of being accused of bias, stayed out of the debate. In fact, there has never been any harm in the licensing officer making positive recommendations, in the same way as planning officers do in planning applications: indeed the entire system of local government is founded on professional officers giving advice to lay members, and there is no reason for licensing to be any different. Sometimes the officer in his report will do no more than point out the relevant parts of the policy. Sometimes he will explain to the sub-committee that if they find a particular concern justified (which is a matter for them) then their solutions

---

[16]   See further *Luminar Leisure Ltd v Wakefield Magistrates' Court* [2008] LLR 505.

would be to take particular steps, which may include the imposition of conditions. Sometimes, the officer will be emboldened to make specific recommendations, which may be of a technical nature and so will be of great assistance to the sub-committee. Indeed, the officer's expertise in his field may be an essential component of the democratic debate. Any residual concern that the licensing officer should not enter the fray, though misguided, is now cured by the status of the licensing authority as a responsible authority introduced by the Police Reform and Social Responsibility Act 2011. Now licensing officers, if they feel they have something to contribute to the debate, may join the proceedings as parties and play a full role, using their professional expertise and local licensing knowledge, so as to advance the aims of the licensing policy and promote the licensing objectives locally.

17.45 Third, members themselves should know their own policy, and should be able to bring to the discussion the technique of trying to find the inventive solution, the sensible middle ground, which will enable all parties to leave the chamber with their objectives satisfied. It is not a coincidence that the Act limits the number of councillors on a licensing committee, and through training, reading and the process of policy formulation and decision-making they should develop a culture of competence in this exercise.

17.46 If particular conditions have received particular debate during the hearing, then the sub-committee can be trusted to produce a decision as to whether those conditions should be incorporated or not. If they have not, then it is good practice for the sub-committee to give the parties an opportunity to make representations as to the proposed conditions – both their principle and their wording – before they are imposed. Otherwise, the lack of opportunity to debate the condition will be the first ground of appeal. While there is good authority that this ought to happen in the magistrates' court,[17] there is no equivalent authority in relation to sub-committee hearings, but there is really no reason why the principles, which are rooted in basic fairness, should be any different.

Unilateral action

17.47 A further controversial question is whether authorities can attach conditions which have not been sought by the parties. In one respect, the answer is obvious. If a debate happens in relation to a particular licensing objective, then plainly it is open to the sub-committee to resolve the debate by attaching a condition other than one proposed by the parties, although it ought to give notice of its intention to do so, for the reason just given. But can it go into matters not raised by the parties at all, for the purpose of attaching conditions relating to the topic?

---

[17] R (*Westminster City Council*) v *Metropolitan Stipendiary Magistrate and Merran* [2008] LLR 572.

17.48 The argument against such a power is that if no representations are made, the authority has no discretion but to grant the licence as asked, subject only to the imposition of mandatory conditions. Therefore, if representations are made as to points A and B, the authority has no discretion in relation to point C. Indeed, section 18(3) of the Act requires the authority, where representations have been made, to hold a hearing 'to consider them', and then, having regard to such representations, take the steps which are appropriate for the promotion of the licensing objectives. That does not indicate a discretion to roam over the wide plains of the licensing objectives, but merely to focus on the specific representations with such objectives in mind.

17.49 The counter-argument is that representations trigger the entire discretion, which is to take the steps appropriate for the promotion of the licensing objectives, and were it otherwise important matters of public interest might pass without mitigation or prevention. The absence of discretion where there are no representations does not necessarily narrow the discretion when representations are made. Furthermore, the duty to 'have regard' to representations does not necessarily mean 'have regard only', as Hooper J held in *R (Hestview) v Snaresbrook Crown Court*.[18] Additionally, it would be difficult and impractical to draw a firm dividing line. For example, if residents were concerned at noise from departing customers, would an authority be debarred from considering the crime and disorder implications of this? The better view, it would be argued, is that the authority has full discretion, but in practice will focus primarily on the representations. If it does roam more widely, then plainly it will be important for the applicant to have proper notice of the concern so that he may answer it properly.

17.50 Some support for the latter approach is found in *R (Blackwood) v Birmingham City Council*[19] in which Parker J said:

> 'I remind myself, finally, that, under the Act, the licence authority is obliged to grant the variation unless it receives relevant representations. This indicates that the task of the licensing authority, and, on appeal, the Magistrates, is seen by the legislature as primarily to address the specific points made by interested parties and/or responsible authorities. Consistently with this legislative policy, the Magistrate cannot be expected to take on their own motion points or arguments not put before them, particularly points of the nature that has been suggested in this case.'

17.51 This tends to suggest that while the authority will not usually take novel points, it is not precluded from doing so, subject to ensuring that the applicant has power to deal with them. In the final analysis, the licensing authority is in the business of public protection, not adjudicating at a

---

[18]   [2001] EWHC (Admin) 144.
[19]   [2006] LLR 802.

sporting event. If it becomes plain to the authority that there is a real concern about, say, public safety, it may be a dereliction of duty not to investigate the matter and attach conditions to ameliorate the risk. It is not considered that such protective action is precluded by the language of the statute.[20]

Reasons

17.52 Where there have been relevant representations, the authority is obliged to give reasons for its decision.[21] Where conditions have been imposed, and particularly where they have been imposed without the agreement of one or other party, it is important that the authority gives reasons relating to the appropriateness of each and every condition. If this does not happen, then on an appeal the court will be left in the dark as to the reasons for imposition of the condition and the lack of justification will weaken the authority's case. As the Court of Appeal made clear in the seminal case of *Hope and Glory*,[22] the weight which a decision receives on appeal depends on a number of circumstances, including the nature and quality of the reasons given by the licensing authority. Where the issue is conditions, blanket, catch-all reasons saying little more than 'we considered the conditions appropriate to promote the licensing objectives' is unlikely to receive much weight at all. Indeed, well-expressed reasons not only stand the authority in better stead on appeal, but may even deter the parties from appealing at all, so it is well worth taking the extra effort to consider and express the individual justification for each condition imposed.

C CONDITIONS AND LICENSING OBJECTIVES

17.53 When the national Guidance pursuant to section 182 was first published, it contained model pools of conditions. Those pools have now been relegated to 'supporting guidance'[23] which is to say that they no longer have statutory status, but they are nevertheless a useful reference point for authorities seeking to develop policies concerning conditions or to understand their options in dealing with particular cases. It is important to reiterate that they are in no way to be regarded as a list of standard conditions to be automatically imposed in all cases. They ought to be applied where appropriate and proportionate in the particular circumstances of any individual premises.

---

[20]   For further discussion of this topic, see Chapter 15 (The Premises Licence), Section D.
[21]   Licensing Act 2003, s 23(2).
[22]   *R (Hope and Glory Public House Ltd) v City of Westminster Magistrates Court* [2011] LLR 105.
[23]   http://www.homeoffice.gov.uk/publications/alcohol-drugs/alcohol/alcohol-supporting-guidance/pools-conditions?view=Binary. These conditions are reproduced in Appendix 10 of this book.

17.54 Further commentary is given as to the promotion of the licensing objectives in Chapter 2 of the Guidance, which acts as a useful reference point for current thinking.

(1) Crime and disorder

Crime and disorder: pool of conditions

- Text/radio pagers
- Door supervision
- Bottle bans
- Plastic containers
- Toughened glass
- CCTV
- Open containers not to be taken from the premises
- Restrictions on drinking areas
- Capacity limits
- Proof of age cards
- Crime prevention notices
- Drinks promotions
- Signage regarding hours and admission of children
- Capacity, table/chair: customer ratio and door supervisors in large capacity venues used primarily for the 'vertical' consumption of alcohol

---

17.55 Plainly, the main source of advice on matters of crime and disorder is the police. This is and always has been spelled out in Guidance.[24] However, the Coalition Government has been anxious to strengthen the hand of the police in licensing hearings, and this policy aim has culminated in the following paragraph in Guidance:

'9.12 In their role as a responsible authority, the police are an essential source of advice and information on the impact and potential impact of licensable activities, particularly on the crime and disorder objective. The police have a key role in managing the night-time economy and should have good working relationships with those operating in their local area. The police should be the licensing authority's main source of advice on matters relating to the promotion of the crime and disorder licensing objective, but may also be able to make relevant representations with regards to the other licensing objectives if they have evidence to support such representations. The licensing authority should accept all reasonable and proportionate representations made by the police unless

---

[24] Para 2.1.

the authority has evidence that to do so would not be appropriate for the promotion of the licensing objectives. However, it remains incumbent on the police to ensure that their representations can withstand the scrutiny to which they would be subject at a hearing.'

17.56 It is fair to say that not many front-line police officers want their representations to be given some kind of special status at licensing hearings. Further, the text appears to achieve very little other than confusion, in that one cannot know whether a representation is reasonable and proportionate until one has heard the other side, and so the Guidance appears to be saying little more than that the police are an important source of advice whose representations need to be taken seriously. If that is all it means it is unobjectionable. If it means that a representation which would otherwise, on objective consideration, be rejected ought to be accepted because it comes from the police, it is difficult to justify and is unlikely to be paid more than lip service by experienced councillors used to weighing representations in the balance and coming to sensible conclusions.

(2) *Public safety*

Pool of conditions
- Safety checks
- Escape routes
- Disabled people
- Lighting
- Capacity limits
- Access for emergency vehicles
- First aid
- Temporary electrical installations
- Indoor sports equipment
- Alterations to premises
- Special effects

17.57 The Guidance[25] is at pains to explain that this objective concerns safety and not health, and so matters such as cleanliness and hygiene are not appropriately covered by conditions. It also points out that there is considerable overlap concerning crime and disorder and safety. It sets out its own checklist of issues which a licensing authority may consider[26]:

- Fire safety;
- Ensuring appropriate access for emergency services such as ambulances;

[25] Para 2.8.
[26] Para 2.9.

- Good communication with local authorities and emergency services, for example communications networks with the police and signing up for local incident alerts;
- Ensuring the presence of trained first aiders on the premises and appropriate first aid kits;
- Ensuring the safety of people when leaving the premises (for example, through the provision of information on late-night transportation);
- Ensuring appropriate and frequent waste disposal, particularly of glass bottles;
- Ensuring appropriate limits on the maximum capacity of the premises; and
- Considering the use of CCTV in and around the premises.

17.58 The first item on this list is hard to rationalise since, as the supporting guidance points out, from 1 October 2006 the Regulatory Reform (Fire Safety) Order 2005 has provided that any conditions imposed by the authority that relate to matters of fire safety and which could be imposed by the Order have no effect.

17.59 Obviously, matters of public safety are paramount at licensed premises, particularly where large crowds of people are involved, and the supporting guidance sensibly points to a number of publications which those planning large events should be using when preparing their operating schedules, and which should be points of reference for responsible authorities in making relevant representations:

- 'Model National and Standard Conditions for Places of Public Entertainment and Associated Guidance'. Produced jointly by the Association of British Theatre Technicians, the District Surveyors Association and the Local Government Licensing Forum (now Institute of Licensing). This Guide has been recommended for use by a series of industry and regulatory bodies. Although the guide contains a large bible of conditions, the authors emphasise that individual conditions should be dispensed with or modified where inapplicable to the instant case, presaging the advice later given in Guidance. The Guide provides detailed advice as to the form of conditions across a range of technical areas, and its usefulness as a reference will clearly survive the implementation of the new legislation.
- 'The Event Safety Guide – A guide to health, safety and welfare at music and similar events' (HSE 1999). 'The Purple Book', produced by the Health and Safety Executive in conjunction with a large range of expert bodies, is an essential reference work for those planning or regulating the larger scale music or other events. It was written to cover the many types of music events taking place at a variety of venues such as purpose-built arenas, sites not designed for public entertainment, open air stadia, parks and greenfield sites. It was not primarily intended to be applicable to nightclubs and discotheques. The guide is a

substantial work, based on the principles of health and safety management and risk assessment. It promotes partnership working through the full range of regulatory agencies and event planners, and offers a model for such working which is now the hallmark of modern licensing. It is now available on-line.[27]

- 'Managing Crowds Safely' (HSE 2000)
- '5 Steps to Risk Assessment: Case Studies' (HSE 1998). This is considered in Chapter 29 (Public Safety), Section C (Risk Assessment).
- 'The Guide to Safety at Sports Grounds' (The Stationery Office, 5th ed, 2008) ('The Green Guide')
- 'Safety Guidance for Street Arts, Carnival, Processions and Large Scale Performances' (Independent Street Arts Network).
- 'Technical Standards for Places of Public Entertainment'. This guide, produced by the Association of British Theatre Technicians and the District Surveyors Association sets out the physical standards for buildings and their equipment, for example concerning means of escape, structure of buildings and permanent or temporary structures within, fire safety, services, hygiene, fire and emergency systems, communications and special installations and effects. While of course the guide does not amount to a recommended list of conditions, applicants and their designers should be aware of its contents when designing the premises and preparing risk assessments and operating schedules.

(3) Public nuisance

Pool of conditions
- Hours
- Noise and vibration
- Noxious smells
- Light pollution

17.60 As is described in Chapter 9, nuisance covers a wide range of harms, both in terms and type and extent – from low level harms affecting a few to major upheavals affecting whole communities, and authorities have at their disposal the ability to impose conditions to tailor the mitigation to the proposed activities in their local context.

17.61 While there are already statutory powers to respond to nuisance, contained in the Environmental Protection Act 1990, the Noise Act 1996 and section 161 of the 2003 Act itself (which affords closure powers to the police based on nuisance), the benefit of conditions is that they act to prevent nuisance before it occurs rather than reacting to it once it is in train. It is

[27]   http://www.qub.ac.uk/safety-reps/sr_webpages/safety_downloads/event_safety_guide.pdf.

frequently felt, not without justification, that the *ex post facto* mechanisms that exist for tackling noise disturbance will not suffice and that prevention is better than cure. This would certainly be the case where it is clear that without safeguards in place nuisance would be likely to occur, for example in the case of a nightclub operating near dwellings without any form of sound insulation. Furthermore, the concept of 'statutory nuisance' under section 79 of the Environmental Protection Act arguably carries a higher threshold than the more flexible 'public nuisance' under the Licensing Act 2003. Thus, licensing authorities may take a more protective stance towards neighbouring occupiers than would be permitted to the environmental health authority.

17.62 In the context of light pollution, conditions will usually require careful thought on the basis that bright lighting may be considered necessary to prevent crime and disorder but could result in light pollution for neighbours. The authority will have to balance such issues with care.

(4) Protection of children from harm

Pool of conditions
- Access for children to licensed premises
- Age restrictions (including at cinemas and theatres)
- Performances especially for children
- Children in performances
- The Portman Group Code of Practice on the Naming, Packaging and Promotion of Alcoholic Drinks
- Proof of Age cards

17.63 The Guidance makes clear that the protection of children from harm includes the protection of children from moral, psychological and physical harm. This includes not only protecting children from the harms associated with alcohol but also wider harms such as exposure to strong language and sexual expletives (for example, in the context of exposure to certain films or adult entertainment).[28] Therefore, conditions may be directed at ameliorating all of these types of harm.

17.64 However, care still must be take in imposing conditions not to hinder the development of family-friendly environments in pubs, restaurants, cafes, bars and hotels through the imposition of conditions liable to exclude children from leisure environments. Sensibly, however, the Guidance makes it clear that conditions restricting access should be strongly considered in the following circumstances:

- where adult entertainment is provided;

---

[28]   Para 2.25.

- where a member or members of the current management have been convicted for serving alcohol to minors or have a reputation for allowing underage drinking (other than in the context of the exemption in the 2003 Act relating to 16 and 17 year olds consuming beer, wine and cider when accompanied by an adult during a table meal);
- where it is known that unaccompanied children have been allowed access;
- where there is a known association with drug taking or dealing; or
- where in some cases, the premises are used exclusively or primarily for the sale of alcohol for consumption on the premises.

17.65 In other cases, it may well be adequate to impose conditions which do not exclude access but control it, eg through proof of age conditions such as Challenge 25, limitations on hours of access, requirements to be accompanied by adults, or exclusion from particular parts of premises, as appropriate in individual cases.

D MANDATORY CONDITIONS

17.66 The Act originally contained a limited number of mandatory conditions for premises licences[29] Sections 19–21 impose certain mandatory conditions in respect of premises licences[30] and club premises certificates.[31] This was then augmented by the Licensing Act 2003 (Mandatory Licensing Conditions) Order 2010[32] which provides for a mandatory code or, to more accurately describe its effect, a further list of mandatory conditions, applying principally though not exclusively to on-licences and club premises certificates. It was, however, relaxed by the Legislative Reform (Supervision of Alcohol Sales in Church and Village Halls) Order 2009,[33] which, by adding a new section 25A to the Act, enabled management committees of community premises to apply to take the place of the designated premises supervisor. This increasingly patch-worked picture is described in tabular form below.

17.67 Being mandatory, there is no general discretion to disapply the conditions. However, authorities should be advised in every case that before they consider attaching conditions additional to those proposed in the operating schedule, they ought to take into account that a number of mandatory conditions already apply, and ask themselves whether yet further individual conditions are genuinely appropriate and proportionate.

---

[29] Licensing Act 2003, ss 19–21.
[30] See generally paras 10.24 et seq of the Guidance.
[31] Licensing Act 2003, ss 73–74.
[32] SI 2010/860. The power of the Secretary of State to impose a mandatory code derives from the Licensing Act 2003, s 19A.
[33] SI 2009/1724.

Condition	On-licences	Community premises with alternative licence condition	Off-licences	Club premises
Mandatory conditions				
No supply of alcohol where no DPS, or where DPS does not hold personal licence	✔	✘	✔	✘
Every supply of alcohol to be made or authorised by personal licensee	✔	✘	✔	✘
Restriction of children's admission to film in accordance with recommenda- tion by BBFC or licensing authority	✔	✔	N/a	✔
Door supervisors to be licensed by SIA	✔ Except theatres, cinemas, bingo halls and casinos	✔	✔	✘
Supply of alcohol must be made when the club premises is open for the purposes of consumption by members on the premises	N/a	N/a	N/a	✔
Off-sales to be in a sealed container	✘	✘	✘	✔
Off-sales must be to a club member in person	N/a	N/a	N/a	✔
Mandatory code				
Ban on irresponsible alcohol promotions	✔	✔	✘	✔

Ban on dispensing alcohol directly into customer's mouth	✔	✔	✘	✔
Free tap water on request to customers	✔	✔	✘	✔
Age verification policy to apply	✔	✔	✔	✔
Availability of smaller measures	✔	✔	✘	✔

Figure 1: Mandatory conditions

Mandatory conditions

17.68 The first mandatory condition for premises licences relates to the need for designated premises supervisors (DPS) at alcohol-licensed premises,[34] other than community premises which have successfully applied for the alternative licence condition to be applied.

17.69 The best definition that can be given of the DPS is that s/he is the person designated to supervise the premises. That is a somewhat fuller definition than that helpfully supplied by the Parliamentary draftsman, which is 'the individual for the time being specified in the licence as the premises supervisor.'[35] While that is undoubtedly true, indeed true by definition, it tells one nothing about the role, function or attributes of the post.

17.70 The Guidance fills in the gap, explaining that:

'The designated premises supervisor is the key person who will usually be responsible for the day to day management of the premises by the premises licence holder, including the prevention of disorder.'[36]

17.71 Not only is the DPS the person who has been put in charge, s/he is an important point of contact for the emergency services when things go wrong. According to the Guidance:

'The Government considers it essential that police officers, fire officers or officers of the licensing authority can identify immediately the DPS so that any problems can be dealt with swiftly.'[37]

[34] Licensing Act 2003, s 19(2).
[35] Licensing Act 2003, s 15(1).
[36] Para 2.6.
[37] Para 4.19.

17.72   Their specialist role is reflected in the fact that only the police may object to their inclusion on the licence, and then only where, in the exceptional circumstances of the case, they are satisfied that the designation of the particular individual would undermine the crime prevention objective.[38]

17.73   The police might object to a particular individual, even though s/he has considerable experience in the industry, if s/he is unsuited to the management of the particular venue. For example, a person who has years of experience of managing an off-licence may simply lack the leadership skills to manage a large, town-centre nightclub.

17.74   Much debate has been occasioned on the question of whether the DPS needs to work full-time at the premises. The answer is that s/he does not. A DPS may act in that capacity for a number of off-licences, say, in a particular town. There is no legal bar on this happening. But if the police consider that the dilution of management control might impinge deleteriously on the crime and disorder objective, they may object to that person as the DPS.

17.75   A related question is whether a DPS needs to be on site all the time. Of course, even with the best will in the world, s/he may not be. S/he may be absent on leave or through sickness, or the hours of trade may far exceed his/her working week. None of this, of course, disqualifies someone from being a DPS. There is only one DPS per premises and it is impossible that they will be on site every minute of the day. The system caters for this in part by requiring that all sales of alcohol be made or authorised by a personal licensee, so that there will still be a chain of command in place. If, however, the police find that the DPS is not genuinely in supervisory control, and never seems to be there, they would be justified in bring the premises in for review to remove the DPS.

17.76   The second mandatory condition for premises licences is the need for alcohol sales to be made or authorised by personal licensees.[39] Larger premises may employ a number of personal licensees; any one of them can make or authorise the sale. Others may have a single person with the triple hat of premises licensee, DPS and personal licensee. In either case, it is not the law that only personal licensees may make the sale: they simply have to authorise the sale. Nor does the personal licensee need to be present when the sale is made. However, if sales are made in breach of conditions on the licence, then anybody who can be characterised as carrying on the activities in question or who knowingly allows them to be carried on stands to be prosecuted under section 136. Therefore, a responsible licensee will take great care about how and to whom authorisations are given.

---

[38]   Licensing Act 2003, s 18(9).
[39]   Licensing Act 2003, s 19(3).

17.77 The Guidance gives some clear messages as to how authorisations ought to be conferred:

> '10.30 "Authorisation" does not imply direct supervision by a personal licence holder of each sale of alcohol. The question arises as to how sales can be authorised. Ultimately, whether an authorisation has been given is a question of fact that would have to be decided by the courts on the evidence before it in the course of a criminal prosecution.
>
> 10.31 The following factors should be relevant in considering whether or not an authorisation has been given:
> - the person(s) authorised to sell alcohol at any particular premises should be clearly identified;
> - the authorisation should have specified the acts which may be carried out by the person who is authorised to supply alcohol;
> - there should be an overt act of authorisation, for example, a specific written statement given to the individual who is authorised to supply alcohol; and
> - there should be in place sensible arrangements for the personal licence holder to monitor the activity that they have authorised on a reasonably regular basis.
>
> 10.32 It is strongly recommended that personal licence holders give specific written authorisations to individuals whom they are authorising to retail alcohol. A single written authorisation would be sufficient to cover multiple sales over an unlimited period. This would assist personal licence holders in demonstrating due diligence should issues arise with enforcement authorities; and would protect employees if they themselves are challenged in respect of their authority to sell alcohol.'

Community premises

17.78 The provisions requiring a DPS and personal licensees for premises licences can be disapplied by the licensing authority under section 25A of the 2003 Act. This power arises for community premises which are defined as premises which are or form part of a church hall, chapel hall, village hall, parish hall, community hall or other similar building. For such premises, the management committee may apply for the 'alternative licence condition' to be applied, which is a condition that every supply of alcohol under the licence must be made or authorised by the management committee.[40] In such a case, where the authority is satisfied that the management arrangements are sufficient to ensure adequate supervision of the supply of alcohol, and any representations which are made as to the identity of the supervisor are not upheld, then the alternative licence condition is applied. This

---

[40] Licensing Act 2003, s 25A(2).

obviously relieves the premises from the burden of employing a DPS, but the members of the management committee should be made aware that this is not necessarily a soft option – they effectively assume potential criminal liabilities under the legislation.[41]

17.79 The third mandatory condition, which applies to premises licences and club premises, is that where films are shown the admission of children must be restricted in accordance with any recommendation by the film classification body. Where the film classification body is not specified in the licence or where the authority has notified the licence or certificate holder that the authority's recommendation is to take precedence, then admission of children will be restricted in accordance with any recommendation made by the authority.[42]

17.80 The fourth mandatory condition relates to door supervision and states that where a premises licence includes a condition that at specified times one or more individuals must be at the premises to carry out a security activity, the licence must include a condition that each individual must by licensed by the Security Industry Authority.[43] See further Chapter 35 (Door Supervision).

The mandatory code

17.81 The mandatory code suffers from an initial misnomer, in that it is not a code at all, but a set of licensing conditions enforceable by the criminal law in exactly the same way as any other condition. The code is described in greater detail by the Guidance.[44] However, it is fair to say that its impact has been severely limited, and there have been few if any prosecutions arising from breach. Its effect may, to some extent, be persuasive, in that operators may endeavour to stay a little bit clearer of the boundaries for fear of a review based on breach of the code.

However, as a tool for the creation of criminal liabilities it is deficient, in that the drafting leaves questions as to its legality, practicality and workability.

17.82 The mandatory code grafts five new conditions onto premises licences and club premises certificates, as set out above. In relation to off-licences, only the fourth condition is attached.

The conditions are as follows.

17.83 First, the code bans irresponsible promotions which are particular defined activities or substantially similar activities, carried on for the purpose

---

[41] For Guidance on the operation of these provisions, see Guidance paras 4.33–4.48.
[42] Licensing Act 2003, s 20 for premises licences, s 74 for clubs.
[43] Licensing Act 2003, s 21(1). Section 21(2) sets out certain exceptions to the general rule imposing such a condition.
[44] Paras 10.38–10.53.

of encouraging the sale or supply of alcohol for consumption on the premises in a manner which carries a significant risk of leading or contributing to crime and disorder, prejudice to public safety, public nuisance, or harm to children. The defined activities are:

(a) games or other activities which require or encourage, or are designed to require or encourage, individuals to:
   (i) drink a quantity of alcohol within a time limit (other than to drink alcohol sold or supplied on the premises before the cessation of the period in which the responsible person is authorised to sell or supply alcohol), or
   (ii) drink as much alcohol as possible (whether within a time limit or otherwise);

(b) provision of unlimited or unspecified quantities of alcohol free or for a fixed or discounted fee to the public or to a group defined by a particular characteristic (other than any promotion or discount available to an individual in respect of alcohol for consumption at a table meal, as defined in section 159);

(c) provision of free or discounted alcohol or any other thing as a prize to encourage or reward the purchase and consumption of alcohol over a period of 24 hours or less;

(d) provision of free or discounted alcohol in relation to the viewing on the premises of a sporting event, where that provision is dependent on:
   (i) the outcome of a race, competition or other event or process, or
   (ii) the likelihood of anything occurring or not occurring;

(e) selling or supplying alcohol in association with promotional posters or flyers on, or in the vicinity of, the premises which can reasonably be considered to condone, encourage or glamorise anti-social behaviour or to refer to the effects of drunkenness in any favourable manner.

17.84 The second condition bans the 'dentist's chair' whereby alcohol is dispensed directly by one person into the mouth of another, unless that person is disabled so that they cannot drink without assistance.

17.85 The third condition requires the provision of free tap water on request to customers where it is reasonably available.

17.86 The fourth condition requires an age verification policy in relation to the sale or supply of alcohol, which requires those appearing to be under 18 to be challenged to produce photographic identification. This is the only condition applying to supermarkets, but it is generally exceeded by retailers: certainly the national chains operate Challenge 25 policies.

17.87 The fifth condition requires beer or cider to be available in half pint measures, gin, rum, vodka or whisky to be available in 25 ml or 35 ml measures and still wine to be available in 125 ml measures. It is not a ban on 'up-selling' but at least gives the opportunity for a smaller purchase.

17.88   The main problem with the mandatory code is that rather than simply applying the conditions to the licence in a form such as 'free tap water shall be made available on request', it attempts to cast duties directly on 'the responsible person' by using the formula 'the responsible person shall ... ' The sole exception is the fourth condition which casts the duty on the premises licence holder or club premises certificate holder.

17.89   'Responsible person' is then defined by reference to section 153 of the Licensing Act 2003, which is a sub-optimal solution, because that section deals with unsupervised sales of alcohol by children. So 'responsible person' means, in relation to premises licences, the holder of the licence, the DPS and any individual aged 18 or over who is authorised 'for the purposes of the section by such a holder or supervisor'. The last part of the definition is irrelevant and unhelpful when applied to licensed activities in general. In respect of club premises, 'responsible person' is defined as any member or officer of the club present on the premises in a capacity which enables him to prevent the supply in question, which is acceptable in the context of section 153 but meaningless in the context of the mandatory code. In summary, the basic definition in the mandatory code is derivative and ill thought out.

17.90   This in turn gives rise to a fundamental set of difficulties. While the code purports to cast legal duties on this vaguely defined and shifting set of individuals, there is no clear legal mechanism available for it to do so. Breach of the code is only punishable under section 136, the main offence-creating provision in the legislation. Section 136 does not cast a duty on the responsible person at all. It directs its fire at persons who carry on or attempt to carry on a licensable activity otherwise than in accordance with the licence, and persons who knowingly allow such an activity to be carried on. The effect of this section was demonstrated in *Hall & Woodhouse v Poole Borough Council*,[45] where the Administrative Court quashed the conviction of a brewery which held the premises licences but was not actually carrying on the licensable activities being performed in breach of the licence by its tenant.

17.91   The already uneasy relationship between section 136 and the realities of licensing would strew all manner of difficulties in the way of any prosecutor seeking to enforce this code. For example, is a DPS not on the premises carrying on the activities? If not, then he may not be prosecuted. Is a premises licence holder automatically responsible for any default by a responsible person? Again, arguably not, because the code attempts to cast responsibility directly on the defaulting responsible person, not to imbue the premises licence holder with ministerial responsibility for the acts of others.

---

[45]   [2009] LLR 436.

17.92 The multiplicity of persons taking the mantel of 'responsible person' may itself cause difficulties. For example, what if one responsible person is behaving responsibly and the other not? Is the one the keeper of the other? Since the duty is cast as 'the responsible person shall ensure' it looks as though he may be. Conceivably, if his colleague defaults, then he as the innocent party might raise a due diligence defence, but it seems doubtful that Parliament understood that it was casting a criminal liability on a person with absolutely no responsibility for the state of affairs complained of.

17.93 Regarding the substantive content of the code, the main difficulty is the first condition relating to irresponsible promotions, which is convoluted to the point of unworkability. The condition strikes at six activities. Taking just the first of these, to secure a conviction, the prosecution would need to prove each of the following beyond reasonable doubt: that (1) a responsible person was (2) carrying on licensable activities (3) without having taken all reasonable steps to ensure that staff (4) do not carry out, arrange or participate in (5) games or other activities (6) which require or encourage, or are designed to encourage, individuals (7) to drink a quantity of alcohol within a time limit, (8) other than to drink alcohol before the bar is required to close, (9) and the games or other activities were carried on for the purpose of encouraging the sale or supply of alcohol for consumption on the premises (10) in a manner which carries a significant risk of leading to or contributing to crime and disorder, prejudice to public safety, public nuisance or harm to children.

17.94 The excessive amount of language apart, vague concepts such as 'significant risk of contributing to public nuisance' risk breaching the human rights requirement of certainty in the context of criminal offences. However, it is the sheer number of things which would have to be satisfied to secure a conviction which would deter even the doughtiest authority from using the provision to prosecute, thus rendering the code a dead letter in that regard. And, in the example just given, the express ability to sidestep the code by simply inviting people to play games which involve drinking before closing time rather than within a time limit means that the code will fail to deter the irresponsible, remembering that the responsible don't need to be deterred.

17.95 There is much more that might be said about this from a legal point of view. However, perhaps it should merely be said that when local partnership is working as it ought to, police and licensing authorities recognise irresponsible promotions and head them off at the pass long before it is necessary to prosecute. Where licensees run irresponsible promotions, it is far more sensible for licensing authorities to review the licence and place targeted conditions upon it. The mandatory code, if needed at all, needs to be far clearer, cleaner and simply expressed than this code, which amounts to a linguistic and conceptual quagmire.

E PROHIBITED, SUSPENDED AND DELETED CONDITIONS

17.96 The Act interferes with the ability of authorities to add effective conditions for a number of reasons, set out in the table below.

Nature of condition	Nature of effect
Control on nature of play or manner of performance.	The condition is prohibited, unless for public safety.
Control on sale of alcohol to associate member or guest of a member of a club.	The condition is prohibited, where the club allows such sale.
Control on provision or regulated entertainment to associate member or guest of a member of a club.	The condition is prohibited, where the club rules allow such provision.
Condition imposed in relation to fire where a prohibition or requirement could be applied under the Regulatory Reform (Fire Safety) Order 2005.	The condition has no effect.
Condition relating to musical entertainment in small, alcohol-led premises or unamplified live music before midnight.	The condition has no effect.
Condition relating to unamplified live music or amplified live music before small audiences in alcohol-licensed premises between 8 am and 11 pm	The condition has no effect.
Condition which relates exclusively to sexual entertainment or is inconsistent with and less onerous than a condition in a sexual entertainment venue licence.	The condition is treated as deleted.

Prohibited conditions

17.97 In respect of a premises licence which authorises the performance of plays, no conditions may be attached to the licence as to the nature of the plays which may be performed, or to the manner of performing the plays under the licence.[46] However the authority is not prevented from imposing any condition it considers necessary on the grounds of public safety.[47] Section 76 deals in similar terms with plays and club premises certificates.

17.98 These provisions carry into the new legislation the effect of section 1 of the Theatres Act 1968, which abolished the powers of the Lord Chamberlain to censor plays. The Lord Chamberlain's powers dated back to the Licensing Act 1737, introduced by Prime Minister Sir Robert Walpole to ban pieces such as Gay's *Beggars Opera*, which contained satire of the court of George II, the government and Walpole himself. The Act provided that anyone performing any interlude, tragedy, comedy, opera, play, farce, or other entertainment of the stage, prologue or epilogue without the Chamberlain's fiat was to be termed a rogue and a vagabond and dealt with accordingly. On the day following the commencement of the 1968 Act, *Hair* opened on the West End stage: its cocktail of nudity and anti-Vietnam War sentiment heralded the new censorship-free era now perpetuated in the 2003 Act.

17.99 There is a further prohibited condition in respect of a club premises certificate in that no condition can be imposed preventing the sale of alcohol to any member or associate guest of the club where the rules of the club provide for such provision.[48] Similarly where the rules of a club provide for regulated entertainment to an associate member or their guest, no condition can be attached to a certificate preventing such provision of regulated entertainment to such an associate member or guest.[49]

Conditions having no effect

17.100 The effect of article 43 of the Regulatory Reform (Fire Safety) Order 2005[50] is that conditions imposed in relation to fire have no effect. Thus it is not unlawful to impose such conditions, but they are ineffective to create liabilities under the Licensing Act 2003. Nevertheless, if the need for such conditions has been appreciated, then this may be enforced through the Order itself.

17.101 Under the former legislation, no licence was needed for up to two musicians to play in a bar, the loss of which under this legislation caused an outcry by musicians and their representatives, and caused Parliament to try to find some equivalent exemption.

---

[46] Licensing Act 2003, s 22.
[47] Licensing Act 2003, s 22(2).
[48] Licensing Act 2003, s 75(1).
[49] Licensing Act 2003, s 75(2).
[50] SI 2005/1541.

17.102   The first attempt came in section 177, an almost impossibly contrived provision, which disapplies the effect of a condition relating to musical entertainment in certain circumstances.

17.103   First, the licence concerned must relate to on-sales of alcohol and the provision of music entertainment. Second, the supply of alcohol must be the primary use. Third, the permitted capacity (and it must be permitted capacity and not merely the capacity) must be no more than 200 persons. Fourth, the premises must be open for the purposes of supply of alcohol for consumption on the premises, so presumably the provision does not apply during drinking up time. Fifth, the licence must not specify that the authority considered the condition appropriate for the prevention of crime and disorder or for public safety, whether that specification was added on grant or review.

17.104   A different possibility arising under section 177 is that the venue is being used between 8 am and midnight for unamplified live music. In that case, the condition is disapplied unless a specification that it should apply has been added to the licence on the grounds of prevention of crime and disorder, or public safety.

17.105   More recently, Parliament passed the Live Music Act 2012, which created further exemptions for live music[51] and deregulated the provision of facilities for entertainment. Section 1 of the Act adds a new section 177A to the Licensing Act 2003. It operates to treat certain conditions as having no effect.[52] In order to gain this boon, the premises must be open for consumption on the premises, the live music must be unamplified or take place in the presence of an audience not exceeding 200, and the performance must be between 8 am and 11 pm.[53] However, should the venue blot its copybook, the licence may be called in for review and the condition expressly reactivated.[54] Further, even if the live music is exempt under the Live Music Act, on the review of a premises licence the authority may add a condition relating to live music as though the live music were regulated entertainment and the licence or certificate authorised it, and then add conditions which will govern the activity. This control appears to be 'one way' in the sense that once the premises has crossed that particular Rubicon there would appear to be no way to regain the exemption other than by applying for a new licence or certificate.

17.106   It should be remembered that the section 177A exemption only applies between 8 am and 11 pm, so if the condition operates at all times, it 'kicks in' at 11 pm so that the licensee will need to be vigilant to operate the condition from that hour.

---

[51]   See Chapter 8 (Licensable Activities).
[52]   Licensing Act 2003, s 177A(1).
[53]   Or any hours specified in a special occasions order under s 172.
[54]   Licensing Act 2003, s 177A(4).

17.107 Whether these highly convoluted provisions were necessary is certainly open to debate. The great majority of pubs benefit from regulated entertainment on their licence in any event, and where controls are needed they are easy to apply in the individual circumstances. Be that as it may, this further set of exemptions needs to be understood and applied by licensing authorities.

Conditions treated as deleted

17.108 Sexual entertainment was principally governed under the Licensing Act 2003, the Guidance to which took a somewhat permissive approach to lap dancing and stripping, characterising it as a species of entertainment which ought not to be censored, but which was adequately governed by the law of obscenity. The Policing and Crime Act 2009 rebranded it as a branch of the commercial sex industry and gave authorities the same power to regulate it as it had for sex shops and cinemas under the Local Government (Miscellaneous Provisions) Act 1982. But what to do with the conditions on premises licences governing such activity? The answer was provided by the transitional provisions,[55] which are to the effect that where licences or certificates formerly governed sexual entertainment, but such entertainment then become governed by a sexual entertainment venue licence, then any conditions in the original licence or certificate which relate expressly and exclusively to the regulation of relevant entertainment at the premises, or are inconsistent with, and less onerous than, the conditions in the licence granted under Schedule 3 to the 1982 Act are treated as deleted.[56]

F DUPLICATING OTHER CONTROLS

17.109 The Act is silent on the question of the interface between licensing and the other forms of statutory control that operate in respect of premises and the activities that may be conducted therein. The only requirement in the Act is that the imposition of the condition should be appropriate for the promotion of the licensing objectives. The question is whether it is necessary to impose a licence condition when the obligation arises, or might arise, under a different regime.

Substantive obligation under other legislation

17.110 Where an operator has a substantive statutory obligation under other legislation, it is hard to imagine that a licensing authority would ever

---

[55] The Policing and Crime Act 2009 (Commencement No 1 and Transitional and Savings Provisions) (England) Order 2010 (SI 2010/722); The Policing and Crime Act 2009 (Transitional and Saving Provisions) (Wales) Order 2010 (SI 2010/1395 W 124).
[56] Article 12 of the English Order, art 11 of the Welsh Order.

consider it necessary to impose the self-same obligation as a condition of the licence. For example, a licensing authority ought not simply to replicate in a condition an express statutory obligation arising under building, health and safety or fire safety legislation.

Supplementing substantive obligations

17.111 A substantive statutory obligation might set out a base minimum requirement only, or the circumstances of the particular case before the licensing authority might require that a higher standard is required. In such a case, the licensing authority would be entitled to consider whether it is necessary to impose a higher standard, tailored to the individual circumstances.

Other systems of control

17.112 The above matters are unlikely to be contentious. The difficulty really arises where there is a separate system of control which may or may not already have dealt with the protective measure in question. The classic example of this is planning, in which the planning authority may have already given detailed consideration to the question of the hours of operation, noise control, traffic management and the like. Is the duty of the licensing authority to re-trace the planning authority's steps, with conceivably different results? Or is it to abjure encroaching on that territory, now marked out by a separate regulatory body? A line of case law has developed concerning the interface between planning and other systems of control, including licensing, which sheds light on this matter. The courts, in short, eschew a doctrinaire approach, preferring the principle that it is for the authority itself to consider whether it is necessary to impose controls on the individual facts of the case, and it is not for the courts to draw a line in what are bound to be shifting sands.

17.113 As Mr Jeremy Sullivan QC (sitting as a Deputy Judge of the Queen's Bench Division), said in *Gateshead Metropolitan Borough Council v Secretary of State for the Environment*[57] (a case in which the issue was the extent to which a planning decision could/should properly concern itself with environmental factors, namely emissions from a clinical waste incinerator, which were controllable under the Environmental Protection Act 1990):

> 'Where two statutory controls overlap, it is not helpful, in my view, to try to define where one control ends and another begins in terms of some abstract principle. If one does so, there is a very real danger that one loses sight of the obligation to consider each case on its individual merits. At one extreme there will be cases where the evidence at the

[57] [1993] 3 PLR 100.

planning stage demonstrates that potential pollution problems have been substantially overcome, so that any reasonable person will accept that the remaining details can sensibly be left to the 1990 Act authorisation process.

At the other extreme, there may be cases where the evidence of environmental problems is so damning at the planning stage that any reasonable person would refuse planning permission, saying, in effect, there is no point trying to resolve these very grave problems through the 1990 Act process. Between those two extremes there will be a whole spectrum of cases disclosing pollution problems of different types and differing degrees of complexity and gravity. Reasonable people might well differ as to whether the proper course in a particular case would be to refuse planning permission, or whether it would be to grant planning permission on the basis that one could be satisfied that the problems could and would be resolved by the 1990 Act process. But that decision is for the Secretary of State to take as a matter of planning judgment, subject, of course, to challenge on normal Wednesbury principles.'

17.114 That judgment was accepted as correct by the Court of Appeal[58] and subsequently followed by Mr George Bartlett QC (sitting as a Deputy Judge of the Queen's Bench Division) in *Robert Lethem v Secretary of State for the Environment.*[59] In that case, the planning inspector had refused permission on appeal for a café bar because of its impacts on residents and town centre uses, in the face of a submission by the appellant that these were matters which could be dealt with by the licensing authority. The subsequent appeal to the High Court was dismissed, the learned Deputy Judge holding:

'20. The essential point, in my judgment, is that a consideration that, in the absence of some other statutory control, would be a material consideration under section 70 is not rendered immaterial by the existence of that other statutory control. The extent to which, on application for planning permission, matters that would arise for consideration in the exercise of some other control regime should be treated by the planning authority in determining the application as ones exclusively for that other regime must depend on the circumstances.'

17.115 In Scotland, the Court of Session considered the planning/licensing interface in *Di Ciacca v The Scottish Ministers.*[60] There, the streetscape was of ground floor commercial premises with flats on upper floors. A wine bar was subject to a planning condition regarding terminal hours, and an application to vary those hours failed at first instance and on appeal, on residential amenity grounds. The applicant appealed further, contending that the condition was not 'necessary' since the question of trading hours could be controlled through planning.

---

58   [1994] 1 PLR 79 at 96H–97A.
59   [2002] LLR 462.
60   2003 Scot CS 95.

17.116   Rejecting that argument, Lord Reed made observations of direct relevance here:

'29. In considering the legal relationship between planning and other statutory controls, such as licensing, it may be helpful to begin by reminding oneself briefly of some fundamental principles of administrative law. First, a discretionary power must, in general, be exercised by the authority in which it is vested: that authority cannot divest itself of its power, or transfer its power to a third party. So, for example, in *Ellis* v *Dubowkski* [1921] 3 K.B. 621 a condition imposed by the licensing committee of a county council, that it would not allow films to be shown unless certified for public exhibition by the Board of Film Censors, was held invalid as involving a delegation of its power to the latter. Secondly, a discretionary power must not be used for an improper purpose: so a condition attached to the grant of planning permission must fairly and reasonably relate to the permitted development (*Pyx Granite Co. Ltd* v *Ministry of Housing and Local Government* [1958] 1 Q.B. 554 at page 572 *per* Lord Denning M.R.). Thirdly, a decision will be *ultra vires* if it is based upon irrelevant considerations or if relevant considerations are not taken into account. This principle overlaps with the second: some situations could be dealt with under either principle. Fourthly, a decision will be *ultra vires* if it was one which no reasonable decision-maker could reach.

30. It follows from these general principles that the planning authority (or the Scottish Ministers) must exercise their powers themselves: they cannot take a decision which has the effect of delegating their function to some other body. On the other hand, planning powers must not be used to regulate matters which are not the proper concern of planning but are dealt with under other statutory regimes. Thirdly, the exercise of planning powers must be based solely upon considerations which are relevant to planning, and must have regard to all such relevant considerations. Fourthly, the decision must fall within the range of options open to a reasonable planning authority.'

17.117   Applying those general principles led Lord Reid to conclude that:

'In such circumstances, it follows that a consideration which would be a material planning consideration in the absence of the other regulatory regime is not rendered immaterial by the existence of that regime. At the same time, the existence of the other regime may nevertheless be relevant to the exercise of planning powers. The relationship between two particular regimes will however depend upon their specific circumstances.'[61]

---

[61]   Para 34. For a similar conclusion, see *Ladbrokes (Rentals) Limited v SSE* [1981] JPL 427, 428.

17.118   The matter has been looked at under the Licensing Act 2003, in the case of *R (Blackwood) v Birmingham Magistrates*.[62] Applying earlier case law, Kenneth Parker QC held that the dividing line between planning and licensing is not always easy to draw in practice, although operational matters such as licensing hours are intended primarily for regulation by licensing, although each case has to be considered on its own individual merits.

17.119   In the light of the above, it cannot be so that the mere existence of a separate regime would itself persuade a licensing authority to refrain from imposing a condition which it would otherwise consider necessary to impose. Where, however, a requirement had in fact already been imposed under a separate regime, the licensing authority would certainly wish to consider whether it is necessary to impose an identical control. So, for example, if a regimen of noise control had been imposed as a condition of a planning permission, the licensing authority may hesitate before duplicating the control. But the fact that, for example, a health and safety authority could serve an improvement notice under section 21 of the Health and Safety at Work Act 1974, or that the local authority could serve an abatement notice under section 80 of the Environmental Protection Act 1990 in the case of statutory nuisance could not preclude the licensing authority from attaching conditions as prevention rather than cure.

Indeed, if the mere existence of the enforcement power by other agencies were all that is required, it is hard to see that any conditions would ever be attached to a licence to protect public safety and prevent nuisance. In fact, the enforcement power would not even need to be by another agency. Given that the police have closure powers and the licensing authority has review powers in the event of harm to the prevention of nuisance and public safety objectives, it could be argued that there is no need for the licensing authority to add conditions at the point of granting of licence at all. It seems, however, clear both on the basis of authority and logic that the licensing authority is not trammelled in the exercise of its discretion by the existence of other regimes, but simply needs to consider whether controls imposed or which may be imposed under those other regimes are sufficient to render it unnecessary for it to impose a condition of its own. To do less would be an abdication of its own statutory responsibility.

Controls by applicant

17.120   If the above is true of controls imposed by other agencies, the same must apply even more to controls imposed by the applicant himself. Those controls may be obligatory under statute or simply incidents of good management.

---

[62]   [2006] LLR 802.

17.121   Regulation 3 of the Management of Health and Safety at Work Regulations 1999 (SI 1999/3242) provides:

> '(1)   Every employer shall make a suitable and sufficient assessment of—
>   (a) the risks to the health and safety of his employees to which they are exposed whilst they are at work; and
>   (b) the risks to the health and safety of persons not in his employment arising out of or in connection with the conduct by him of his undertaking, for the purpose of identifying the measures he needs to take to comply with the requirements and prohibitions imposed upon him by or under the relevant statutory provisions.'

17.122   The Regulations then require the employer to put in place measures to implement the measures he has identified. Does this process preclude the imposition of licensing conditions? It is submitted not, for the following reasons:

(1)   The employer is under a duty to review the risk assessment in certain circumstances,[63] and so there is no guarantee that protective measures in the risk assessment at the time of consideration of the licensing application will remain there for the future. Meanwhile, the licensing authority will have no means of ascertaining subsequently that the measures have changed.

(2)   There may be a simple non-compliance with the risk assessment measures, in those cases where the risk assessment has been treated by the employer as a paper exercise without practical effect. Where matters of public safety are at issue, this is not something which should be contemplated by the licensing authority.

(3)   To adapt a point made earlier, it cannot be said that the mere fact of a risk assessment precludes the licensing authority from imposing a condition relating to public safety; otherwise no conditions would ever come to be imposed. The incompetent risk assessment would be a matter for the health and safety authority and the competent risk assessment would shut out any form of licensing control. This is not what the legislature contemplated when giving power to the licensing authority to impose necessary licensing conditions in the interests of public safety.

(4)   The case law cited above, and in particular *Gateshead*, *Lethem* and *Di Ciacca*,[64] show that a preclusive approach is inapposite: it is a matter for consideration in the individual case.

(5)   Therefore, where there have been relevant representations, it is for the licensing authority to consider whether, notwithstanding the risk assessment, conditions need to be imposed.

---

[63]   Management of Health and Safety at Work Regulations 1999, reg 3(3).
[64]   Paras 17.113–17.115 above.

17.123 A related question of real importance then arises: is it necessary for the applicant to include the conclusions of his risk assessment in his operating schedule? If he does so, he is consigned to seeing the protective measures replicated as licence conditions. If he does not, there may be objection by the health and safety authority resulting in a hearing.

17.124 This is a different question from whether it is necessary for the applicant to <u>show</u> his risk assessment to the health and safety and licensing authority, so that the former authority may consider whether to make a relevant representation and the latter authority may consider whether it is necessary to impose a condition covering health and safety.

17.125 Again, this is a matter to be considered on a case by case basis. In a large operation which reviews its risk assessments frequently, it may be very inconvenient to have the risk assessment provisions incorporated into the licence, for each review of the risk assessment would need to be accompanied by an application to vary the licence. On the other hand, in order to procure a licence quickly it is certainly much simpler to include the results of the risk assessment in the operating schedule, since that is less likely to result in representations being made that the measures proposed in the schedule are inadequate.

17.126 The applicant who submits an operating schedule without health and safety measures and without showing the risk assessment to the health and safety or licensing authorities cannot expect the matter to pass without relevant representations being made. In fact, for a licence to be granted in such circumstances may amount to a dereliction of duty on the part of at least one of the authorities concerned. If a major accident were then to happen, scant sympathy would be meted out to the authorities who said 'the applicant told us he had risk-assessed the operation and so we inquired no further.'

17.127 The solution in this situation is for the applicant to attach a schedule to the operating schedule explaining the measures which the applicant already takes, but making it clear that they are not offered as licence conditions. If an authority remains concerned by the matter, it could always take a half-way house approach and require the applicant as a condition to deposit the risk assessment and any subsequent changes with the health and safety authority.

17.128 The last situation to be considered is where control measures are not the subject of any particular regime, but there is a simple assurance that, as a component of good management, the applicant will be implementing the measure. It is possible that an applicant could submit that his track record is such that it is not necessary or proportionate to attach the relevant condition to the licence, with all the criminal consequences that entails.

17.129 The difficulty with that approach is that it involves ceding the regulation of the relevant activity from the licensing authority to the operator himself. If it is wrong for the licensing authority to delegate its duties of controlling the operation in the public interest to other statutory agencies, it must be wrong to delegate it to the operator himself. First, lines of management within licensed premises change, and the quality of management is not guaranteed to be maintained through the life of the operation. Second, for incoming management it is helpful to see the relevant requirements set out in the licence itself, so that the responsibilities are made clear. Third, licensing conditions are essentially protective: it would be a rare case in which, having decided that a particular form of protection is appropriate in order to protect the public interest as represented by the licensing objectives, the licensing authority would simply neglect to put the protection in place because the applicant says he will do it anyway. It is equivalent to not locking the stable door on the horse's assurance that he will not bolt. Fourth, an applicant who did not wish to have any conditions on his licence would simply state that he intended to do anything asked of him to promote the licensing objectives.

17.130 To take an analogy of planning practice, the planning authority – and the inspectorate on appeal – consider what conditions are necessary and then apply them to the consent. It is never an argument that the condition is unnecessary because of the willingness of the developer to comply with it. The analogy is not exact because of course the licensing authority retains its power to add the omitted condition on subsequent review. By contrast, the powers of subsequent modification of the permission in planning[65] are rarely exercised, and costly (for the planning authority itself). But it does underline that the question of appropriateness in the Licensing Act 2003 is to be objectively considered, and a measure does not necessarily cease to be appropriate by virtue of the professed willingness of the applicant to institute the measures voluntarily. Thus, while an assurance by a competent, experienced operator that a matter is safely left to its discretion is a material consideration for the licensing authority, it is unlikely to be treated as of overriding weight if the protective measure involved is an important one.

G CONCLUSION

17.131 The previous regime was divided between the licensing justices, who rarely imposed conditions at all on justices on-licences, and the local authority, who regularly imposed tomes of conditions on public entertainment licences. Under the new regime, some conditions come to be applied to licences without contention, either because they are mandatory or because they are offered. Others may not be applied or are treated as null. Between those extremes, there are conditions sought by an objector but opposed by an

---

[65] Town and Country Planning Act 1990, s 97.

applicant. In such cases, an *a priori* position is to be avoided: the question of what conditions to be attached is a matter which must be considered on the individual merits of the case.

Personal licences

The keeper of an inn or tavern, who is never master of his own house, and who is exposed to the brutality of every drunkard, exercises neither a very agreeable nor a very creditable business. But there is scarce any common trade in which a small stock yields so great a profit.

Wealth of Nations
Adam Smith

A INTRODUCTION

18.01 A split system of licensing was proposed by the White Paper 'Time for Reform: Proposals for the Modernisation of our Licensing Laws'.[1] A premises licence applying to the premises and a personal licence authorising an individual to supply alcohol. The supply of alcohol cannot take place without both there being a premises licence in force for the premises where the supply takes place and there being an individual authorising that supply from the same place. If the premises licence only permits the provision of late night refreshment and/or the provision of regulated entertainment then there is no requirement for such activities to be authorised by a personal licence holder. The reason given in the Guidance is that the sale and supply of alcohol carries with it a greater responsibility than the provision of regulated entertainment and late night refreshment because of the impact on the wider community and on crime and anti-social behaviour.[2]

18.02 Where the supply of alcohol takes place then a personal licence holder who can authorise the supply of alcohol must be named on the premises licence as the designated premises supervisor (DPS).

[1]   April 2000.
[2]   Guidance para 4.2

However, there has been very little enforcement action taken against personal licence holders as individuals by the courts and their very existence could be said to only add to the administrative burden on premises licence holders. councils have very limited powers to revoke a personal licence and no power at all to suspend them.

18.03   Either personal licence holders are very well behaved, the courts are unaware of their powers or personal licence holders appearing before courts manage to forget to inform the courts of the existence of their personal licence. Consequently there have been very few instances of the courts taking action against personal licences.

18.04   The Labour Government had supported the idea for a national database of personal licence holders but with the variety of software used by licensing authorities, this has not come to fruition. There is therefore no prospect of keeping track on where personal licence holders have been named as designated premises supervisors. A premises licence holder may have been the DPS at a number of premises where reviews have been brought but, unless they were brought within the same licensing authority, this is unlikely to come to light.

18.05   There is no requirement to have any individual named as the DPS for premises which hold a club premises certificate, nor for premises which hold an alternative licence condition as community premises.[3] Presumably, the dispensation of the requirement to have a personal licence holder both for a premises holding a club premises certificate and for certain community premises such as church and village halls is because such premises have, in the words of the Guidance,[4] very little impact on the wider community and on crime and anti-social behaviour. However, the experience under the Licensing Act 2003 is that the personal licensing system serves little positive purpose to justify the bureaucratic burden it imposes.

18.06   To ease the 'red tape burden', would it not simply be easier to require premises licence holders, by a mandatory condition, to have a minimum number of persons who hold a relevant qualification[5] to be employed at the premises and for those trading beyond, say, midnight, that one such person has to be present on the premises at all times alcohol is being sold? Having obtained the qualification, what further value is afforded by a person applying for a personal licence other than affording the police an opportunity to object should they have been convicted of a relevant offence?[6] For those individuals who have committed a relevant offence and know they won't get a personal licence, it is very easy in any case to either simply hide behind a personal licence holder they employ to work at the premises as the DPS or to

---

3   See Chapter 15 (The Premises Licence).
4   Guidance para 4.2
5   Licensing Act 2003, s 120(2).
6   Licensing Act 2003, s 120(2).

name a DPS who is never at the premises but meets the requirement to have a person named as the DPS. The legislation could just as easily empower courts to order that a convicted person should be disqualified from working in a licensed premises for a given period of time.

B APPLICATION FOR THE GRANT OF A PERSONAL LICENCE

18.07 Any individual can apply for the grant of a personal licence provided they are aged 18 or over at the date the application is considered by the licensing authority. There is no requirement for the applicant to be 18 at the time the application is submitted.

18.08 The application is submitted to the licensing authority where the applicant is 'ordinarily resident'.[7] In most cases, it will be obvious where a person is ordinarily resident. There may be questions over managers of premises who work away during most of the week and only return back to the family home after four or five nights away. In such cases, the individual would still be ordinarily resident at the family home.

The phrase 'ordinarily resident' was considered by the House of Lords in a case when a local authority was under a duty to bestow awards to students who were 'ordinarily resident' within its area.[8] Lord Scarman stated:[9]

'... I unhesitating subscribe to the view that "ordinarily resident" refers to a man's abode in the particular place or country which he has adopted voluntarily and for settled purposes as part of the regular order of his life for the time being, whether of short or long duration'.

18.09 It could therefore be argued that simply because an individual has decided to register as a voter for the sake of convenience in one area, it does not mean they are ordinarily resident in that area. For most purposes, the acid test is which place the applicant treats as their home.

18.10 Where an applicant does not live in England or Wales the application can be made to a licensing authority of their choice.[10] This is of particular relevance to people who live in Scotland who will normally choose to apply to the licensing authority which is closest to the border, in case there should be any need for them to attend the offices of the licensing authority. Having submitted the application to the licensing authority that licensing authority then becomes the 'relevant licensing authority'[11] for that individual throughout the duration of their personal licence and on any renewal of that licence.

---

[7] Licensing Act 2003, s 117(2)(a)
[8] *R v Barnet LBC ex p Shah* [1983] 2 AC 309.
[9] *R v Barnet LBC ex p Shah*, p 343.
[10] Licensing Act 2003, s 117(2)(b).
[11] Licensing Act 2003, s 112.

The application for the personal licence must also be accompanied by a form which requires the applicant to list any 'relevant or foreign offences', or alternatively sign the declaration that they have not been convicted of any such offences.

18.11 'Relevant offences' are defined by reference to a list in Schedule 4 to the Licensing Act 2003.[12] The Secretary of State may by section 113(2) amend the list to add, modify or omit offences, and the range of offences has been extended by Statutory Instrument to include certain sexual and violent offences[13] and by primary legislation to include certain gambling offences,[14] attempts and conspiracies to commit relevant offences,[15] and conspiracies to defraud.[16]

18.12 A 'foreign offence' is any offence (other than a relevant offence) committed under the law of any place outside England and Wales.[17] There is an interesting difference between offences committed outside and inside England and Wales since all the former will need to be disclosed by an applicant whereas in the case of the latter only those listed in Schedule 4 have to be disclosed as relevant offences.

18.13 There appears to be a difference between the categories of offences that need to be listed on the Disclosure of Convictions and Declaration form, and the definition of a relevant offence or foreign offence contained within section 113.

18.14 The Disclosure of Convictions and Declaration form does not specifically state that any spent convictions should not be listed, although it does refer to the definition of a foreign offence being dealt with in section 113 of the Licensing Act 2003, but states that relevant offences are 'offences listed in Schedule 4 to the Licensing Act 2003'. An applicant should therefore be expected to list all relevant offences committed in England and Wales on this form, whether or not they are spent, and indeed the same could be said for foreign offences.

18.15 But Section 114 states that any conviction for a relevant offence or a foreign offence has to be disregarded if it is spent for the purposes of the Rehabilitation of Offenders Act 1974. That being so, is it necessary for any such conviction to be disclosed? In the view of the authors it is not.

---

[12] Licensing Act 2003, s 113(1).
[13] The Licensing Act 2003 (Personal licence: relevant offences) (Amendment) Order 2005 (SI 2005/2366).
[14] Gambling Act 2005, Sch 16(2) para 20(4).
[15] Police Reform and Social Responsibility Act 2011, s 123(4).
[16] Police Reform and Social Responsibility Act 2011, s 123(5).
[17] Licensing Act 2003, s 113(3).

18.16 However, what happens if spent convictions are disclosed notwithstanding section 114? The licensing officer must determine whether or not he should give the chief officer of police notice that an individual has been convicted of a 'relevant offence or any foreign offence'.[18] At this point spent convictions, for the purposes of the Rehabilitation of Offenders Act 1974, should exercise the mind of the licensing officer before they give notice to the chief officer of police. Should the licensing officer simply ignore all relevant offences or foreign offences which are spent for the purposes of the Rehabilitation of Offenders Act 1974? Taking the Licensing Act 2003 literally then any such offences should be disregarded.

18.17 However, whether or not a conviction should be treated as spent under the Rehabilitation of Offenders Act 1974, section 7(3) of that Act has a proviso that in any proceedings before a 'judicial authority' the authority can admit or require evidence as to a person's spent conviction if it is satisfied that justice cannot otherwise be done than by admitting it. Arguably, therefore, there may be instances under the Rehabilitation of Offenders Act 1974 where spent convictions should be admitted where justice cannot be done without them being considered. This approach has been adopted in two cases in Scotland considered by the Sheriff's Court, one involving an application for an off licence, *Kelly v City of Glasgow Licensing Board and Chief Constable of Strathclyde Police*,[19] and one involving an application for a taxi licence, *Irvine v Dundee City Council*.[20]

18.18 The approach taken by licensing authorities to date has normally been to disregard such spent convictions. The judgment in *Hope and Glory*[21] made it clear that in the view of the Court of Appeal a licensing authority is not a 'judicial authority'. The preferred view would therefore be that such spent convictions should not be referred on to the chief officer of police but rather treated as spent for the purposes of that application. This accords with the approach in the Guidance.[22]

FAQ

Q   Can a person who has been declared bankrupt hold a personal licence?

A   There is nothing in the Licensing Act 2003 which stops a person who has been declared bankrupt and/or who remains an undischarged bankrupt from holding a personal licence.

---

[18]   Licensing Act 2003, s 120(4).
[19]   [2004] LLR 232, SHCT.
[20]   [2005] LLR 637, SC.
[21]   *R (on the Application of Hope and Glory Public House Ltd) v City of Westminster Magistrates Court and Others* [2011] EWCA Civ 31.
[22]   Para 4.6.

18.19 The application forms themselves are relatively straightforward. However, difficulties over the format of the photograph can often delay applications.

The Licensing Act 2003 (Personal Licence) Regulations[23] require two photographs to accompany the application and the Regulations specify, in detail, the format photographs must take.

18.20 There are two common difficulties with photographs which are provided by applicants. Firstly, passports from certain countries require a side image as opposed to a full face image to be taken. Whilst this does not accord with the requirements of regulation 7 of these Regulations, some licensing authorities do accept such photographs. Secondly, licensing authorities are taking issue with the maker of endorsements on the reverse of the photographs verifying the photograph to be to be a true likeness of the individual. The maker must be a 'person of standing in the community',[24] which can include bank or building society officials, police officers, civil servants or a minister of religion. Some licensing authorities take the view that unless such a person holds a qualification then they will not do. Some licensing authorities are even going as far as to say that they need the person verifying the photographs to hold a degree. Whilst the person does indeed have to be someone of standing within the community, requiring a degree is a step too far.

18.21 There is no requirement for the photographs to be taken in colour, but some licensing authorities do incorrectly reject them for not being in colour.

18.22 The application form and photographs also need to be accompanied by the fee and either:

(1) A Criminal Conviction Certificate issued under section 112 of the Police Act 1997;
(2) A Criminal Records Certificate issued under section 113A of the Police Act 1997; or
(3) The results of a subject access search under the Data Protection Act 1998 of the Police National Computer by the National Identification Service;[25]

any of which have to be issued no later than one calendar month before the application has been given to the relevant licensing authority.[26]

18.23 'Given' means it is not sufficient for the certificate or results to be less than a month old when the application is made by the applicant, rather it

23 SI 2005/41.
24 Licensing Act 2003 (Personal Licence) Regulations 2005, reg 7(1)(a)(v).
25 Licensing Act 2003 (Personal Licence) Regulations 2005, reg 7(1)(b).
26 Licensing Act 2003 (Personal Licence) Regulations 2005, reg 7(1)(b).

has to be less than a month old when the application is received by the licensing authority.

18.24 The most common form of disclosure in England and Wales is a Criminal Records Certificate from 'Disclosure Scotland' by use of the relevant form. However, the form itself is confusing in that some mandatory fields are highlighted in yellow but others are not, notably the requirement to specify the last five years' residence. This commonly leads to forms being returned.

18.25 The final piece of the jigsaw is to include evidence that the individual has a 'licensing qualification' defined by section 120(8) of the Licensing Act 2003.

18.26 Such a qualification is a qualification which is both accredited by the Secretary of State and provided by a body which likewise is accredited by the Secretary of State.

The most common form of accreditation is the Award for Personal Licence Holders (APLH). Any qualification obtained either in Scotland, Northern Ireland or in an EEA State (other than the United Kingdom) which is equivalent to such a qualification would also suffice. However, it is difficult to imagine many (if any) instances where such a qualification will be equivalent, other than were there to be a high demand for a qualification acceptable in England and Wales from people within a single foreign nation looking to work within the hospitality industry here.

18.27 When taking the qualification, candidates commonly use a name they like to be referred to, or a nickname which is different from their full name on the application form. Most licensing authorities will reject applications accompanied by a qualification certificate in a different name to that on the application form, and request a replacement certificate in the individual's full name.

By virtue of section 120(2) of the 2003 Act a licensing authority <u>must</u> grant an individual a personal licence if it appears to the authority that:

(a) The applicant is aged 18 or over;
(b) He possesses a licensing qualification or is a person of a prescribed description;
(c) No personal licence held by him has been forfeited in the period of five years ending with the day the application was made; and
(d) He has not been convicted of any relevant offence or foreign offence.

18.28 The licensing authority must reject the application if any of the first three paragraphs above do not apply. It has no discretion to do otherwise.

18.29 The absence of any national database of personal licence holders means that an applicant can with almost certain impunity tick the box saying they have had no personal licence forfeited in the last five years, even when this is not the case. However, knowingly or recklessly making a false statement on the personal licence application form is an offence.[27]

18.30   There would also be nothing to stop an unscrupulous applicant with relevant or foreign offences making multiple applications to a number of licensing authorities where they have evidence that they reside for part of their time, in the hope that one licensing authority may be more lenient that another.

Where an individual has been convicted of any relevant offence or any foreign offence then, subject to the earlier comments on spent convictions, the licensing authority must give the chief officer of police a notice to that effect.[28]

18.31   Some licensing authorities notify the police of any applications which are made for a personal licence whether or not the applicant has any relevant or foreign offences. The reason given by such licensing authorities is it lets the police know who is trying to obtain a personal licence. However, the police have no formal powers in relation to the application unless there is a relevant or foreign offence.

18.32   Having received notice of the relevant or foreign offence from the licensing authority, the chief officer of police must then decide whether or not to object to the application on the grounds that any conviction for a relevant offence, or for a foreign offence which the chief officer of police considers to be comparable to a relevant offence, would undermine the crime prevention objective.[29]

18.33   It is interesting to note that the requirement to disclose only a specified list of 'relevant offences' listed in Schedule 4 of the Licensing Act 2003 contrasts with the requirement to disclose all foreign offences. Presumably this is because it will be for the chief officer of police to determine whether or not the relevant foreign offence is equivalent to a relevant offence listed in Schedule 4.

18.34   The chief officer of police has 14 days from receipt of the notice from the licensing authority to object to the application for the personal licence where satisfied that the granting of the licence would undermine the crime prevention objective. If no such notice of objection is given, then the licensing authority must grant the application. There is no discretion to extend the period.[30]

---

[27]   Licensing Act 2003, s 158(1)(d).
[28]   Licensing Act 2003, s 120(4).
[29]   Licensing Act 2003, s 120(5).
[30]   *Corporation of the Hall of Arts and Sciences v Albert Court Residents Association and Others*

18.35 Upon receipt of the notice of objection the licensing authority must hold a hearing to consider the objection unless the applicant, the chief officer of police and the authority agree it is unnecessary,[31] which is highly unlikely. The hearing must be commenced within 20 working days of the end of the period during which the chief officer of police can object.[32] The procedural requirements of the Licensing Act 2003 (Hearings) Regulations 2005 then apply to any such hearing.

18.36 Other than the requirement to be 18 at the time the application is made, to have a 'licensing qualification' and not to have had a personal licence forfeited in the last five years, there are no other absolute restrictions to holding a personal licence. No conviction excludes by law an individual from holding a personal licence, and at any hearing the sub-committee will need, in the words of Nigel Pleming QC in *Secretary of State for Transport Local Government and The Regions v Snowdon*,[33] to consider a person's conduct 'in context and in the round'.

18.37 The statutory test to be applied by the licensing sub-committee is to ask itself whether, having regard to the police notice, it is appropriate for the promotion of the crime prevention objective to reject the application. Otherwise, it must be granted.[34]

18.38 The Guidance formerly indicated that where any such objection is made by the chief officer of police then the licensing authority 'should normally refuse' the application 'unless there are exceptional and compelling circumstances which justify granting it'. This was very strong language and perhaps explained why so few personal licence applications got as far as a hearing before the licensing authority. The reading of the Guidance however was considered in the case of *R (on application of South Northamptonshire Council) v Towcester Magistrates Court*.[35] In this case, an application for a personal licence had been granted at a hearing despite an objection from the Chief Constable of Northamptonshire Police. The applicant had two recent convictions for drink driving.

18.39 The magistrates court on hearing an appeal from the Chief Constable overturned the grant on the basis of the Guidance.

18.40 On hearing the appeal from the magistrates' court, the High Court held that the magistrates' court had adopted the wording of the Guidance when determining the application, which is much stronger than the wording

---

[2010] EWHC 393 (Admin). See also the Court of Appeal judgment, which dealt with different grounds, at [2011] EWCA Civ 430.

[31] Licensing Act 2003, s 120(7).

[32] Licensing Act 2003 (Hearings) Regulations 2005, reg 4 and Sch 1.

[33] [2002] EWHC 2394 (Admin)

[34] Licensing Act 2003, s 120(7)(b).

[35] [2008] EWHC 381 (Admin).

contained within section 120(7) of the Licensing Act 2003. That section stated that having received the notice of objection the licensing authority must hold a hearing to consider the objection and must reject the application for the personal licence if it considers it 'necessary[36] for the promotion of the crime prevention objective'.[37]

18.41 The High Court found that the magistrates' court had expressed their views in the context of the words of the Guidance as opposed to the statute and as such had erred in law in failing to address the statutory test. The application for judicial review was granted and the case remitted back to the magistrates' court. Although the court did not hold that the Guidance was wrong, what was 'necessary' for the promotion of the crime prevention objective was not the same as rejecting an application unless there were 'exceptional and compelling circumstances' which justified the grant of the application. In any event, the offending element of the Guidance has now been abandoned. The effect is to make it clear that it is for the police to demonstrate why, having regard to the applicant's criminal history, it is appropriate for the promotion of the licensing objectives to refuse the personal licence application.

18.42 The most common forms of argument before the licensing authority are over (a) the circumstances behind any relevant offences; (b) the explanation for such offences; (c) the amount of time that has elapsed since; (d) the applicant's behaviour and attitude during that period;(e) the impact of these offences on the applicant's ability and willingness to promote the crime prevention objective, and (f) the authority's trust in the applicant.

18.43 Upon the grant of <u>any</u> application for a personal licence, the chief officer of police and the applicant must be notified of the grant. This is the case whether or not there has been any objection by the chief officer of police.[38] Presumably, this is simply so that the police are aware of any holders of personal licences within the area of their force.

18.44 If the chief officer of police has objected to the application and it is granted then the notice of the grant must explain the reasons behind the grant of the application.[39]

Where a licensing authority has rejected an application at a hearing, the applicant and the chief officer of police must be notified and the notice must contain a statement of the reasons for rejecting the application.[40]

---

[36] Since the commencement of the Police Reform and Social Responsibility Act 2011 the test is now 'appropriate' rather than 'necessary'.
[37] Licensing Act 2003, s 120(7)(b).
[38] Licensing Act 2003, s 122(1)(a).
[39] Licensing Act 2003, s 122(1)(b).
[40] Licensing Act 2003, s 122(2).

The applicant or the chief officer of police has the right to appeal the refusal or grant (as relevant) to the magistrates' court within 21 days of receiving the notice of the determination in writing from the licensing authority.[41]

C PERIOD OF VALIDITY AND RENEWAL OF PERSONAL LICENCE

18.45 A personal licence has effect for ten years beginning on the date on which it is granted and then may be renewed for further periods of ten years at a time.

A personal licence will continue in force unless it is either surrendered under section 116, forfeited or suspended by a court of law upon the conviction of a relevant offence under section 129, or revoked under section 124 of the 2003 Act.

Any such order or forfeiture or suspension takes effect immediately,[42] although the court can order the suspension of their order pending an appeal against its decision,[43] as may the court to which an appeal is made.[44]

18.46 It is difficult to envisage circumstances where a personal licence would be surrendered by the holder except where the holder is facing conviction for a relevant offence and may be fearful that the personal licence will be forfeited. To avoid being unable to apply for a personal licence for a further five years, the holder of a personal licence could instead surrender the personal licence prior to their conviction and there would then be no personal licence for the court to either suspend or forfeit, thus meaning that they would be eligible to apply for a personal licence within the five year period when they would otherwise be prevented from doing so under section 120(3).

Renewals

18.47 The first renewals will fall due in 2015.

18.48 The application for the renewal is made to the licensing authority which issued the personal licence in the first place. Some licensing authorities will have become unitary authorities by the time the renewal process starts. For example, an applicant who would have submitted their application to West Wiltshire will now apply to Wiltshire Council as the unitary authority.

---

[41] Licensing Act 2003, Sch 5 para 17.
[42] Licensing Act 2003, s 129(5).
[43] Licensing Act 2003, s 129(4).
[44] Licensing Act 2003, s 130.

18.49   The application for renewal is submitted on a prescribed form[45] and will need to be accompanied by two passport sized photographs in the prescribed form[46], and as on an application for a personal licence it also needs to be accompanied by one of the following:

(1)   A Criminal Conviction Certificate issued under section 112 of the Police Act 1997; or

(2)   A Criminal Records Certificate issued under section 113A of the Police Act 1997; or

(3)   The result of a subject access search under the Data Protection Act 1998 of the Police National Computer by the National Identification Service.

18.50   Again, the results of any such certificate or search result must be issued no earlier than one calendar month before the giving of the application to the relevant licensing authority. This means no more than one month before the time the renewal application is received by the licensing authority as opposed to one month before the application is made to the licensing authority.[47]

18.51   The difference between the grant and the renewal is that, on the renewal, there is no requirement to submit evidence of any licensing qualification. There is a requirement to send the original personal licence back with the application or, if that is not practicable, a statement of the reasons for the failure to send the personal licence must be provided.[48]

18.52   The difficulty faced by every applicant for the renewal of their personal licence is that the application for renewal must be made between one and three months before the date the personal licence expires.[49] For example, a personal licence expiring on 1 May 2015 would mean that the earliest any application could be made would be 1 February 2015 and the last day any application could be made would be 31 March 2015. When placed alongside the limited shelf life of the disclosure certificate, this may well cause serious problems of timing, as mentioned below.

18.53   There is a noticeable difference in the wording of section 117(6) of the 2003 Act in that the time period during which a personal licence renewal application can be submitted refers to the time when the application is actually 'made', as opposed to 'given'. Therefore, provided the application is actually submitted within those dates, it will suffice for the purposes of section 117(6).

---

[45]   Licensing Act 2003 (Personal Licence) Regulations 2005, reg 6 and Sch 2.
[46]   Licensing Act 2003 (Personal Licence) Regulations 2005, reg 7.
[47]   Licensing Act 2003 (Personal Licence) Regulations 2005, reg 7(1)(b).
[48]   Licensing Act 2003, s 117(4).
[49]   Licensing Act 2003, s 117(6).

18.54 Under the provisions of section 119(1), provided an application for renewal is made between one and three months before that personal licence expires, and if the application has not been determined before the time the licence would have expired, then the personal licence continues to have effect from the date of expiry until the date the personal licence renewal application is either determined or withdrawn. This continuation is subject to the power of a court to forfeit or suspend a personal licence and the right of any individual to surrender their personal licence.

18.55 There will be a glut of renewal applications in 2015, particularly between February and August. Consequently there are likely to be considerable delays at 'Disclosure Scotland' through whom most applicants request their Criminal Records Certificate. The Criminal Records Certificate or subject access search results can be no more than one month old at the time the application is received by the licensing authority and therefore there is no flexibility in the system for applicants for the renewal of their personal licence to request their certificates earlier in preparation for submitting their application. It remains to be seen whether the government will address this logjam in the making by deregulating the requirements attaching to renewal.

FAQ

Q   Will councils be obliged to notify personal licence holders that their personal licence is due to expire shortly?

A   Unless there is any change made to the legislation then there is no such duty. Indeed, those licensing authorities who try to make the effort to do so will write to personal licence holders at their last known address, which could be out of date if the licensing authority has not been notified of any change.

18.56 It will be very important that applicants submit the applications for the renewal of their personal licence both accurately and with all relevant accompanying documents. Any failure to do so will mean that a licensing authority will reject an application. The application will then have to be resubmitted, and if the certificate or search result is more than one month old then a further request will need to be made for the certificate or results. Consequently, the deadline for submitting the application one month prior to the expiry of the personal licence may be missed.

18.57 Should the deadline be missed that person will cease to be a personal licence holder, will no longer be permitted by law to be the designated premises supervisor named on any premises licence and will have to start the whole application process afresh for a new personal licence. This will mean the individual will need to retake the licensing qualification and submit an application for a new personal licence to the licensing authority where they now live.

18.58   The consequences therefore of getting the application form wrong or missing the deadline are considerable for any individual. Indeed, if they are the designated premises supervisor of a licensed premises, the premises will have to close pending appointment of a new DPS and an application for the appointment to have interim effect.[50]

18.59   Upon receipt of an application for the renewal of a personal licence, the licensing authority must give notice to the chief officer of police if the applicant has been convicted of any relevant offence or any foreign offence since the date the personal licence was originally granted.[51] This would be the case even if the court had notified the licensing authority of a conviction, or an applicant for a personal licence had been convicted of a relevant offence whilst their application was pending and the chief officer of police had given an objection notice which had then been considered at a hearing.

18.60   Upon receipt of a notice from the licensing authority that an applicant for the renewal of their personal licence has been convicted of any relevant offence or foreign offence since the date the personal licence was originally granted, the chief officer of police has a period of 14 days, beginning with the day he received the notice from the licensing authority, to object to the renewal. The chief officer of police can have regard to any conviction of the applicant for a relevant offence or any foreign offence which the chief officer of police considers to be comparable to a relevant offence.[52] The conviction for the relevant offence or foreign offence does not need to have been after the date of the original grant of the personal licence, but could have been prior to the original grant of the personal licence. This could mean that where a personal licence application had originally not been objected to by the police, the police could subsequently object to a renewal of a personal licence, taking into account a conviction for a relevant or foreign offence the applicant had when they had originally applied for the personal licence, when no objection had been raised by the police. Presumably this is because the chief officer of police could determine that this conviction did not undermine the crime prevention objection when the application was first made for a personal licence, but does now undermine the crime prevention objective in light of subsequent convictions for relevant or foreign offences of the individual applicant for the renewal of the personal licence. However, it is considered that the permissiveness of this provision is tempered by section 114 which requires spent convictions to be disregarded.

18.61   The requirement for the chief officer of police to give the licensing authority a notice of objection is strict, and failure to ensure that the notice arrives with the licensing authority within the 14 days will mean that any such notice has not been validly given and the application for the renewal

---

[50]   Licensing Act 2003, s 38.
[51]   Licensing Act 2003, s 121(2).
[52]   Licensing Act 2003, s 121(4).

must be granted.[53] Where any objection notice has been given, the licensing authority must hold a hearing in accordance with the Licensing Act 2003 (Hearings) Regulations 2005.

18.62 The procedure for hearing the determination of an application for the renewal of a personal licence is the same as that for the hearing procedure for the determination of the application for the grant of a personal licence.

18.63 At the hearing, the licensing authority must reject the application if it considers it appropriate for the promotion of the crime prevention objective to do so, otherwise the licensing authority should grant the application.[54]

18.64 The licensing authority must notify the chief officer of police of any grant of a renewal application, whether or not the chief officer of police had given an objection notice to such application.[55]

Where the chief officer of police has given an objection notice, and the licensing authority has subsequently considered the application, then the licensing authority must provide a statement of the licensing authority's reasons for either granting or rejecting the application to the chief officer of police and the applicant.[56] Either the applicant or the chief officer of police has the right to appeal the refusal or grant of the renewal (as relevant) to the magistrates court within 21 days of receiving the notice of the determination from the licensing authority.[57]

D DUTIES OF A PERSONAL LICENCE HOLDER

18.65 A holder of a personal licence is under a duty to notify the licensing authority which issued the personal licence, as soon as reasonably practicable, upon the holder either changing their name or address which is stated on the personal licence.[58]

Any such notice must be accompanied by the original personal licence or, if that is not practicable, a statement of the reasons for the failure to provide the original licence, together with the appropriate fee.[59]

18.66 Any failure to do so, without reasonable excuse, is a criminal offence and the holder of the personal licence can be fined on summary conviction

---

53   *Corporation of the Hall of Arts and Sciences v Albert Court Residents Association and Others* [2010] EWHC 393 (Admin).
54   Licensing Act 2003, s 121(6).
55   Licensing Act 2003, s 122(1).
56   Licensing Act 2003, s 122(1)–(2).
57   Licensing Act 2003, Sch 5 para 17.
58   Licensing Act 2003, s 127.
59   Licensing Act 2003, s 127(3).

up to level 2 on the standard scale.[60] Where applications are made to vary the premises licence by changing the designated premises supervisor, some licensing authorities will check the address of the applicant with the licensing authority which issued the personal licence.

18.67   There have been instances where the address of the applicant to become the DPS on the consent form does not match the address on their personal licence. In some cases the licensing authority has refused to process the application until the personal licence holder has changed their address with the authority which issued their personal licence. It is questionable whether or not there is any statutory ground to refuse to process such an application when no false statement has been made by the applicant and the application is in all other ways complete.

18.68   Where the holder of a personal licence is charged with a relevant offence, they must, no later than their first appearance in the magistrates' court, produce to the magistrates' court their personal licence, or notify the court of the existence of the personal licence, the identity of the relevant licensing authority and the reasons why they cannot produce the licence.[61]

18.69   Should a person be granted a personal licence after their first appearance in the magistrates' court then they are under a duty to make the same notification to the relevant court upon their next appearance.[62]

18.70   Where a personal licence holder has so notified the court and subsequently an application is made or withdrawn for the renewal of the licence, or they surrender their personal licence or the personal licence is revoked by the licensing authority under section 124 of the Licensing Act 2003, then again the personal licence holder must notify the court at their next appearance of such an event.[63]

18.71   Any failure to notify the court means that the personal licence holder is guilty of an offence and is liable on summary conviction to a fine not exceeding level 2 on the standard scale.[64]

18.72   Following conviction for a relevant offence, the scheme of the Act is that the court should consider whether to order the forfeiture or suspension of the licence.[65] The court should then as soon as reasonably practicable send notice of the conviction and sentence to the licensing authority, with a copy to the defendant.[66] Where, however, the defendant has failed to notify

---

[60]   Licensing Act 2003, s 127(4).
[61]   Licensing Act 2003, s 128(1).
[62]   Licensing Act 2003, s 128(2).
[63]   Licensing Act 2003, s 128(4).
[64]   Licensing Act 2003, s 124(6)–(7).
[65]   Licensing Act 2003, s 129.
[66]   Licensing Act 2003, s 131.

the court of the existence of his personal licence and the court remains unaware of it, then the holder must, as soon as reasonably practicable after the conviction, give the licensing authority which issued their personal licence a notice containing the details of the nature and date of the conviction and any sentence imposed upon it.[67] Likewise, as soon as reasonably practicable after the determination of any appeal against any conviction or sentence, they must give to the licensing authority a notice containing details of that determination.[68] The notice must be accompanied by the personal licence or, if that is not practicable, a statement of the reasons for the failure to provide the personal licence. Any failure to notify the licensing authority of the relevant details as soon as reasonably practicable after the conviction or determination renders the holder of the personal licence liable upon conviction to a fine not exceeding level 2 on the standard scale.[69]

18.73 The same applies where any holder of a personal licence is convicted of a foreign offence. As soon as reasonably practicable after the conviction or determination of the appeal, full details need to be given to the licensing authority.[70]

18.74 Standing back from these provisions for a moment, it can be seen that the holder of a personal licence who has failed to tell the court that they hold a personal licence must notify the licensing authority themselves of such a conviction. But by doing so they are acknowledging that they have failed to notify the court in accordance with section 128 and have therefore committed an offence under section 128 (6). The holder of the personal licence is then liable to a prosecution for that offence.

18.75 When on premises in order to make or authorise the supply of alcohol, where the supply is authorised by a premises licence or by a temporary event notice, the holder of a personal licence must produce it to any police constable or authorised officer[71] upon request. The holder of the personal licence may request the constable or authorised officer to produce evidence of their authority to exercise the power.[72] Section 135 of the Licensing Act 2003 does not make it clear whether or not there is a requirement for the personal licence holder to produce both parts of their personal licence, or simply the part bearing their photograph. Since regulation 5 of the Licensing Act 2003 (Personal Licence) Regulations 2005 specifies that a personal licence is in two parts, it should be assumed that, upon request, the holder of a personal licence would need to produce both parts of their personal licence. Any failure to do so, without a reasonable

---

[67]   Licensing Act 2003, s 132(2).
[68]   Licensing Act 2003, s 132(2)(b).
[69]   Licensing Act 2003, s 132(4)–(5).
[70]   Licensing Act 2003, s 132(1)(b).
[71]   As defined by the Licensing Act 2003, s 135(6).
[72]   Licensing Act 2003, s 135(3).

excuse, is an offence and the holder of the personal licence is liable on a summary conviction to a fine not exceeding level 2 on the standard scale.[73] Leaving a personal licence at home would not be a reasonable excuse. However, the fact that a personal licence had not yet been issued following the grant or renewal of an application would be a reasonable excuse, as would the absence of any personal licence whilst it is being amended by the licensing authority following the change of name or address of the personal licence holder.

E POWERS AND DUTIES OF THE COURTS

18.76 As stated above, where the holder of a personal licence is convicted of a relevant offence in England and Wales, the court can either order the forfeiture of the personal licence or order its suspension for a period not exceeding six months.[74] Any appeal against such forfeiture or suspension would need to be made to the Crown Court.

18.77 On such an appeal, the Crown Court or other appellate court can suspend any such order itself upon such terms as the court thinks fit.[75] Should a court suspend the decision to either forfeit or suspend the personal licence then it must give notice of that suspension of the decision to the relevant licensing authority.[76] For clarity, the Act states that any suspension of an order to forfeit the licence means that the personal licence is reinstated for the period that the court has suspended that decision.[77]

18.78 Where a personal licence holder is convicted of any relevant offence before a court in England and Wales, and that person has either given notice to the court that they hold a personal licence, or the court has become aware for any other reason of its existence, the clerk of the magistrates' court or the appropriate officer at the Crown Court must, as soon as reasonably practicable, notify the licensing authority of the conviction.[78] The court is under a duty to send the licensing authority a notice specifying the name and address of the person who has been convicted, the nature and date of their conviction and any sentence that has been passed, including any order made by the court to either suspend or forfeit the personal licence.[79] A copy of that notice has to be sent to the personal licence holder.[80]

18.79 On determination of an appeal against the conviction for the relevant offence or the sentence imposed, the court (as opposed to any individual at

---

[73] Licensing Act 2003, s 135(4)–(5).
[74] Licensing Act 2003, s 129.
[75] Licensing Act 2003, s 130(3), (7).
[76] Licensing Act 2003, s 130(8).
[77] Licensing Act 2003, s 130(9).
[78] Licensing Act 2003, s 131.
[79] Licensing Act 2003, s 131(2).
[80] Licensing Act 2003, s 131(2)(b).

the court) must, as soon as reasonably practicable, arrange for a notice of the quashing of any conviction or the substituting of any sentence, to be sent to the licensing authority and the personal licence holder.[81]

It is unclear as to what sanction may be taken against the court if a court fails to notify the licensing authority as soon as reasonably practicable. Presumably there is none.

F POWERS OF THE LICENSING AUTHORITY

18.80 Once a personal licence has been granted or renewed, a licensing authority has very little jurisdiction over the personal licence.

18.81 This should be contrasted with the situation in Scotland where a licensing board can revoke, suspend for six months or endorse a personal licence where a person is either convicted of a relevant offence during the application period or, being a personal licence holder, is convicted of such an offence.[82]

The only time that a licensing authority, having granted or renewed a personal licence, is able to hold a hearing to consider the continued existence of the licence is where it becomes aware that the holder of the personal licence was convicted of a relevant offence or a foreign offence during the period beginning when the application for the grant or the renewal was made, but prior to the time the grant or renewal was determined.[83]

18.82 Upon the licensing authority becoming aware of this, it must give notice of such fact to the chief officer of police for its area. The chief officer of police has a period of 14 days, beginning with the day he received the notice from the licensing authority, to give to the licensing authority a notice stating that the continuation of the personal licence would undermine the crime prevention objective.[84] This is a strict time limit and again any failure to meet the statutory deadline will be rejected as an invalid notice.[85] When considering whether or not to issue such a notice, the chief officer of police is able to have regard not only to the conviction which has given rise to the notification to him by the licensing authority, but also to any conviction of the applicant for a relevant or foreign offence.

18.83 Where an objection notice has been given by the chief officer of police within the 14 day period, the licensing authority must hold a hearing

---

81 Licensing Act 2003, s 131(3).
82 Licensing (Scotland) Act 2005, s 58(3)(a).
83 Licensing Act 2003, s 124.
84 Licensing Act 2003, s 124(3).
85 *Corporation of the Hall of Arts and Sciences v Albert Court Residents Association and Others* [2010] EWHC 393 (Admin).

to consider the objection notice and must revoke the personal licence if it considers it 'appropriate for the promotion of the crime prevention object-ive'.[86]

18.84 Inevitably, the holder of a personal licence in this position will be in a more precarious position than an applicant who had notified the authority of his conviction at the appropriate time, since the personal licence holder had been under a duty under section 123(1) of the 2003 Act to notify the licensing authority of the conviction of which the licensing authority has now become aware. Any licensing authority is therefore likely to view such a situation very seriously and personal licence holders ought not to be surprised if their personal licences are revoked in these circumstances. Whatever determination the licensing authority makes, it must notify both the personal licence holder and the chief officer of police of the decision and its reasons for making it.[87]

18.85 There is a right of appeal for both the personal licence holder, should the personal licence be revoked, or for the chief officer of police should the personal licence not be revoked.[88] Again, any appeal is made to the local magistrates' court and has to be made within a period of 21 days beginning with the day on which the appellant or the chief officer of police were notified of the decision in writing.

18.86 Any decision to revoke the personal licence does not have effect until the end of the period during which the personal licence holder could appeal its revocation.[89] In other words, the revocation of the personal licence will not take effect for 21 days after the decision has been notified in writing to the personal licence holder. If so appealed, the decision will then only take effect once the appeal has been disposed of.[90]

18.87 Other than the power to revoke a personal licence in such circum-stances where the conviction during the application period of a premises licence holder has come to light, there is no other power for the licensing authority to take any action against a personal licence once it has been granted or renewed.

18.88 There is one licensing authority which runs a 'points system' for personal licences. It issues points in the event of any conviction of which it becomes aware. Such action may serve to inform overt and covert inspections of premises where the personal licensee works. It may lead to a review if a responsible authority, including the licensing authority, takes the view that the involvement of the miscreant is such that there is a risk to the promotion

---

[86] Licensing Act 2003, s 124(4).
[87] Licensing Act 2003, s 124(5).
[88] Licensing Act 2003, Sch 5 para 17.
[89] Licensing Act 2003, s 124(6).
[90] Licensing Act 2003, s 124(6).

of the licensing objectives. However, the addition of points to a licence in and of itself has no statutory effect.

G THE PERSONAL LICENCE

18.89 The personal licence comes in two parts, a paper copy and a card bearing the personal licence holder's photograph. In this respect it is very similar to the new style driving licence. Many licensing authorities are now extremely quick in issuing personal licences, often within 24 hours of the application. Even the slowest of licensing authorities will normally issue a personal licence within a month.

18.90 Many licensing authorities adopt good practice in that they will issue an applicant with a personal licence number whilst the licensing authority processes the physical licence. Licensing authorities will do this particularly where the applicant for the personal licence wishes to become the designated premises supervisor named upon a premises licence.

18.91 Should a personal licence holder lose their personal licence or have it stolen, or should it be damaged or destroyed, the personal licence holder can apply to the relevant licensing authority for a copy of it to be reissued to them.[91] The licensing authority may charge a fee for providing an additional personal licence. The authority is under a duty to issue the personal licence holder with a further copy of their licence, certified by the authority as a true copy, but only if it is satisfied that the licence has been lost, stolen, damaged or destroyed and, where it has been lost or stolen, that the holder of the personal licence has reported the loss or theft to the police.[92]

18.92 The purpose of this seemingly unnecessary exercise is presumably to encourage applicants to look for their licences before seeking replacements, and enabling police to reunite licensees with licences in the event that they are found. However, many licensing authorities take little or no notice of the requirement for the theft or loss to be reported to the police.

The same provisions apply should the licence subsequently be again stolen, lost, damaged or destroyed.[93]

18.93 The licensing authority is under a duty to update any personal licence documentation where it either refuses or grants the renewal of a personal licence, where it revokes a personal licence, or where it receives a

---

[91] Licensing Act 2003, s 126.
[92] Licensing Act 2003, s 126(3).
[93] Licensing Act 2003, s 126(5).

relevant notification from a court that the personal licence has been suspended or forfeited.[94]

18.94   Where it receives notification of a court order suspending or forfeiting the personal licence, the licensing authority must make an endorsement on the licence stating the terms of the court order.[95] Any endorsement would have to be cancelled should the suspension or forfeiture be quashed on an appeal.[96]

18.95   If the licensing authority is not in possession of a personal licence then it may, for the purposes of putting the endorsement onto the personal licence, require the holder of the licence to produce it to the authority within 14 days, beginning with the day on which the personal licence holder is notified of the requirement by the licensing authority.[97] Any failure to produce the personal licence within the 14 days is an offence, and the personal licence holder would be liable to a fine on a summary conviction, not exceeding level 2 on the standard scale.[98]

[94]   Licensing Act 2003, s 134(1).
[95]   Licensing Act 2003, s 134(2).
[96]   Licensing Act 2003, s 134(3).
[97]   Licensing Act 2003, s 134(4).
[98]   Licensing Act 2003, s 134(5).

19

Temporary events

Whoe'er has traveled life's dull round,
Where'er his stages may have been,
May sigh to think he still has found
The warmest welcome at an inn.

William Shenstone, *Written at an Inn in Henley*

A INTRODUCTION

19.01 Part 5 of the Licensing Act 2003 covers permitted temporary activities which are regulated by 'temporary event notices', now universally known as 'TENs'. These notices regulate the temporary carrying on of licensable activities. They are, along with premises licences and club premises certificates, one of the three forms of authorisation under the Act.

The need for a TEN may arise because either:

(a) no premises licence or club premises certificate has been granted in relation to the premises, or
(b) the activities proposed are not authorised by an existing premises or club premises certificate for the premises in question, because they do not fall within the 'licensable activities' so authorised or are restricted by a condition, for example in relation to hours.

19.02 In other words, TENs may operate in relation to virgin sites, ungoverned by any other form of authorisation, or they may operate to 'top up' the entitlements arising under a licence or certificate for a limited period of time.

19.03 The Government's aim in relation to temporary events was summarised by the Department for Culture Media and Sport Minister Lord McIntosh of Haringey on 16 January 2003 as follows:

'We are trying to identify those applicants and events that are so rare or modest as not to be licensable activities. Many events will benefit because they are licensable already, and therefore the requirement to provide a temporary notice is a good deal lighter than what happens now. That is the intention of the Bill. The "light touch" system is to benefit those who do not generally engage in the business of carrying on licensable activities – by allowing them, for example, to hold a fundraising event in a hall without a premises licence.'[1]

19.04 In the event, however, the system of TENs has gone further. It is as much apt to permit a pub with a midnight terminal hour to hold a one-off 21st party until 2 am as it may be used to permit an annual concert in an unlicensed building.

19.05 Experience under the Act demonstrated that in certain respects the system under-regulated, and in others it over-regulated. For example, as originally enacted only the police could object to a TEN, and then only on crime prevention grounds, so that nuisance was not controllable under the TEN procedure. Conversely, a village fete with a TEN which was rained off could not be made the subject of another TEN the following week, due to the time limits for service of a TEN. These and other wrinkles were ironed out through the Police Reform and Social Responsibility Act 2011.

19.06 As a result, there is now a bilateral system of 'standard' TENs, as originally enacted, and late TENs, which came late to the licensing party in 2011. The following table shows the limits now applicable to standard and late TENs.

Maximum	Number
TENs per calendar year – personal licence holder	Up to 10 late TENs[2] Up to 50 standard TENs, less one for each late TEN in the calendar year
TENs per calendar year – other people	Up to 2 late TENs Up to 5 standard TENs, less one for each late TEN in the calendar year[3]
TENs per calendar year per premises	12

---

[1] Hansard. HL Debate, vol 643, col 385.

[2] It is arguable that where ten late TENs have been given then no standard TEN may be given even if the limit of 50 TENs has not been reached; see Licensing Act 2003, s 107(2)(b).

[3] It is arguable that where two late TENs havee been given then no standard TENs may be given even if the limit of five TENs has not been reached; see Licensing Act 2003, s 107(3)(b).

Hours temporary event may last	168
Days per calendar year per premises	21
Time between event periods	24 hours
People attending at any one time	499

Figure 1: Limits

19.07 It will therefore be seen that where there are anticipated to be more than 499 people attending at any one time, the TEN procedure may not be used at all. This figure includes facility staff such as bar staff, waiters and entertainers. Instead, there will need to be a premises licence or club premises certificate. However, it is possible to have events at which there are more than 499 people without falling foul of the provision. A beer tent at a fair may hold fewer than 499 people. If the TEN is applied for just in respect of the beer tent, it does not matter that more than 499 people are simultaneously visiting the fair. What, it is believed, is not permitted is to artificially divide premises and give multiple TENs so as to multiply the capacity entitlement.

19.08 A further means of achieving flexibility is sometimes used by licence applicants. An applicant for a premises licence may include in their operating schedule the ability to hold up to 12 events per calendar year (the precise dates of which will be notified in advance to the licensing authority and the police), for which a later terminal hour is proposed. Provided that this passes without objection, or any objection is overridden, this entitlement arises as a result of the licence, and leaves the licence holder free to augment its events with the full quota of temporary event notices.

B STANDARD TEMPORARY EVENTS NOTICES

19.09 The standard TEN procedure originates with an individual over the age of 18 giving the licensing authority a TEN.[4] It should be noted that, unlike premises licences, which are given by the authority to the individual, TENs are given vice versa. As will be seen, if there are no objections to the notice, then it is the notice itself which constitutes the authorisation for the activity.

19.10 The TEN must be in a prescribed form[5] and contain a raft of information, including the licensable activities concerned, the start and end time of the event, the times during the event when the licensable activities will take place, the maximum number of persons proposed to be on the premises at the same time, and whether alcohol sales are on-sales and/or

---

4   Licensing Act 2003, s 100(1)–(3).
5   The form is prescribed by the Licensing Act 2003 (Permitted Temporary Activities) (Notices) Regulations 2005 (SI 2005/2918).

off-sales.[6] Where alcohol is involved, the notice must include a condition that the person giving the notice is the one who will be supplying or authorising the supply of the alcohol.[7]

19.11 The notice must be given, with the fee,[8] no later than ten working days before the day on which the event begins.[9] If it is not given electronically then it must also be given to each relevant person,[10] namely the police and the environmental health authority.[11] If it is given electronically, then it falls to the licensing authority to forward it to the relevant persons no later than the end of the first working day after the notice was given.[12] In giving notices, care should be taken to ensure that these deadlines are met. For example, some authorities refuse to treat the notice as duly given until the fee has been paid. If it is paid late, the event cannot proceed.

19.12 Parliament wished to ensure that there was some gap between temporary events. Therefore, a notice which does not end at least 24 hours before the event period specified in another extant notice given by the same person, or which begins less than 24 hours after the event period specified in any other notice, is void.[13]

19.13 The licensing authority must acknowledge the notice. If it is received on a working day, it must be acknowledged on that day or the next working day. If it is received on a non-working day, then it must be acknowledged within two working days.[14] A dispensation is given if within that time there has already been a counter-notice under section 107 stating that the permitted limits have been exceeded, since the counter-notice effectively acts as acknowledgment.

19.14 In essence, if a counter-notice is served under section 107, the subsequent procedure is aborted, and so it is important for authorities to decide promptly whether such a notice is warranted, on the basis that the limits set out in Figure 1 above have been exceeded. This would occur in the following situations:

- where the relevant premises user has exhausted his personal entitlement to give temporary event notices;[15]

---

6   Licensing Act 2003, s 100(5).
7   Licensing Act 2003, s 100(6).
8   Licensing Act 2003, s 100(7). The amount of the fee is prescribed by the Licensing Act 2003 (Fees) Regulations 2005 (SI 2005/79), reg 8 and Sch 6.
9   Licensing Act 2003, s 100A(1)–(2).
10   Licensing Act 2003, s 100A(2).
11   Licensing Act 2003, s 99A.
12   Licensing Act 2003, s 100A(4).
13   Licensing Act 2003, s 101.
14   Licensing Act 2003, s 102(1).
15   This includes notices given by his 'associate' or business colleague: Licensing Act 2003, s 107(10). For meaning of 'associate' see s 107(13) and s 101(3)–(4).

- where the full quota of temporary event notices has been given for the premises in question;
- where the full quota of days has been exhausted or will have been exhausted if the event proposed runs its course.[16]

Where a counter-notice is warranted, it must be served in the prescribed form[17] at least 24 hours before the beginning of the event period[18] upon the premises user[19] and each relevant person.[20]

19.15 Assuming that the notice does not fail at the first hurdle by dint of exceeding the basic limits of the scheme, the procedure unfurls. The police and environmental health authorities, or 'relevant persons' as they are known for these purposes, may object to the notice. If they wish to do so, they must do so before the end of the third working day following the day on which they themselves are given the notice.[21] This represents a considerable improvement on the Act as originally drafted, which only gave 48 hours to object, leading to a surfeit of notices served on Friday evenings leaving it too late to object when licensing sergeants returned to their desks on Monday mornings.

19.16 Relevant persons may only object if they are satisfied that allowing the premises to be used in accordance with the notice would undermine one of the licensing objectives.[22] It may seem strange that these authorities are given power to object on grounds with which they are not normally involved, such as public safety. However, were every responsible authority to be able to object, the system would become overly bureaucratic.

19.17 On receipt of the objection notice, the authority must hold a hearing to consider it, unless the authority, the premises user and the relevant person who objected agree that a hearing is unnecessary.[23] If a counter-notice has been given under section 107 because the permitted limits have been exceeded, then the requirement for a hearing is dispensed with.[24]

19.18 Following the hearing, the authority must give the premises user a counter-notice if it considers it appropriate for the promotion of the licensing objectives to do so.[25] The counter-notice acts as a form of refusal for the event to proceed.

[16]   Licensing Act 2003, s 107(2)–(4).
[17]   For the prescribed form see Licensing Act 2003 (Permitted Temporary Activities) (Notices) Regulations 2005 (SI 2005/2918).
[18]   Licensing Act 2003, s 107(8).
[19]   Licensing Act 2003, s 107(7).
[20]   Licensing Act 2003, s 107(11). For meaning of 'relevant person', see below.
[21]   Licensing Act 2003, s 104(3).
[22]   Licensing Act 2003, s 104(2).
[23]   Licensing Act 2003, s 105(2).
[24]   Licensing Act 2003, s 105(6).
[25]   Licensing Act 2003, s 105(2)(b).

19.19   Until the passage of the Police Reform and Social Responsibility Act 2011, the options were black or white – to grant or refuse or, rather to issue or not to issue a counter-notice. However, a more sensitive third way was facilitated by the 2011 legislation,[26] namely for the notice to survive subject to conditions.

19.20   The ability to add conditions is constrained in this way. For conditions to be added, there must have been an objection to the notice. The licensing authority needs to consider the conditions appropriate for the promotion of the licensing objectives. Further, they need also to be imposed on a premises licence or club premises certificate that has effect in respect of part or all of same premises as those covered by the notice. Finally, the conditions must not be inconsistent with the carrying out of the licensable activities under the notice.[27]

19.21   The benefit of this scheme is clear. To take one example, a pub may have a licence allowing it to sell alcohol until midnight, but with a condition requiring there to be a door supervisor on duty after 9 pm. The pub might wish for an extension to 2 am to accommodate a party. Formerly, an authority might have been inclined to permit the temporary event to proceed but, concerned that it could not extend the door supervision might have felt constrained to serve a counter-notice. Now it can allow the event to proceed by extending the existing condition. The reason that the authority is not given carte blanche to add new conditions is that this is intended to be a relatively straightforward procedure completed in a short space of time.

19.22   The effect of this is that already licensed premises are more likely to get their TENs through the system than virgin sites whose promoters will not be able to add conditions. While this is a moderate disappointment for owners of unlicensed sites, it makes sense that it should be easier for promoters to procure authorisations on already licensed, regulated and managed sites. In fact, it might be argued that this competitive advantage is a benefit to the licensed sector, whether this was the legislative intent or not.

19.23   It is perhaps difficult to discern the reason why conditions can only be added after an objection. It would have been more in keeping with the spirit of partnership had premises users been able to agree conditions with the police and environmental health authority prior to submitting an agreed temporary event notices. Indeed, were this course to have been adopted by Parliament, there would be no need to confine the conditions to those already on the premises licence or club premises certificate. Be that as it may, these possibilities do not arise under the currently adopted legislative scheme. However, if the conditions are agreed following objection, then it is

[26]   Section 113(3).
[27]   Licensing Act 2003, s 106A.

always open to the parties to agree that a hearing is unnecessary, so saving the administrative cost of attendance before the sub-committee.

FAQ

Q   Can the decision to impose a condition be made by an officer?

A   The power to add conditions does not lie with the relevant person but with the licensing authority. Because there has been an objection notice, there has to be a hearing unless all parties agree it is unnecessary under section 105(2)(a). However, particularly where the objection notice has resulted in agreed conditions, the hearing could be dispensed with under section 105(2)(a) and the conditions placed before the licensing sub-committee meeting in private (ie not at a public hearing) for the purpose of rubber stamping them. Under section 10(4)(a)(ix) of the Act an officer cannot determine to issue a counter-notice. But subject to proper delegation, there seems to be no impediment to an officer deciding to impose conditions on a TEN under section 106(a) provided that he has delegated authority to do so. This would seem to be much more convenient than trying to convene a sub-committee at short notice where matters have been agreed. The effect of this is that the conditions can be added by the licensing sub-committee at a hearing, or at a meeting if the parties agree to dispense with the hearing, or by a licensing officer provided that the officer has been given delegated authority to do so. The latter would seem sensible where conditions have been agreed by all parties.

19.24 The licensing authority's decision must be made and communicated at least 24 hours before the start of the event period.[28] The communication must be to the premises user and each relevant person. Where the authority decides not to serve a counter-notice, it needs only to give notice of the decision. Where it does decide to serve a counter-notice, it must give the premises user and each relevant person the counter-notice, stating the reasons for its decision.[29]

19.25 There is a right of appeal, although this is in many cases illusory. Where a counter-notice is served under section 105 the premises user may appeal, as may a relevant person where a counter-notice is not served. The appeal period is 21 days from the date of notification of the decision. However, no appeal may be brought later than five working days before the

---

[28]   Licensing Act 2003, s 105(4).
[29]   Licensing Act 2003, s 105(3).

beginning of the event period.[30] Therefore, unless the temporary event notice has been served long before the event, by the time the decision is notified it may be too late to appeal it. Premises users, therefore, who foresee that their application may not be enthusiastically received would do well to put in their temporary event notice very early, to give them elbow room to appeal, and to have their appeal heard, in time to organise the event.

C LATE TEMPORARY EVENTS NOTICES

19.26   The late TEN procedure was devised to provide greater flexibility for premises users. The advantage is that they can give their notices later than the deadline for standard notices. The disadvantage is that any objection from the police or the environmental health authority acts as a veto, from which there is no appeal. Further, as indicated in Figure 1, the limits for late TENs are considerably lower. In many respects, the procedures are similar to those for standard notices. In this section, we concentrate on the variances.

19.27   Late TENs may be given electronically to the licensing authority between five and nine working days before the beginning of the event period, or non-electronically to the licensing authority and each relevant person no later than five working days before that day, provided in the latter case that one of the relevant persons receives notice no earlier than nine working days before that day.[31] When given electronically, the authority has a duty to forward the notice to the relevant persons in the same manner as for standard notices.

19.28   The provisions for acknowledgment of the TEN and section 107 counter-notices is identical to that appertaining for a standard TEN, as is the period for and manner of objection by the relevant persons. The twist is that where an objection notice is given, the authority must give a counter-notice,[32] thus aborting the event, with no possibility of making the notice good by adding conditions, and no right of appeal. Thus, a party relying on the late notice procedure takes a substantial risk that his event will be summarily stopped by dint of a written notice of the police or environmental health authority. For this reason, it is considered that the late notice procedure, while a great blow for flexibility, is a tool of last resort for the event promoter.

D THE EVENT

19.29   While the temporary event notice procedure is an important means of running events without needing to apply for a premises licence or club

---

30   Licensing Act 2003, Sch 5 para 16.
31   Licensing Act 2003, s 100A(3).
32   Licensing Act 2003, s 104A.

premises certificate, it should not be seen as an authorisation devoid of responsibility.

19.30 If the stated capacity or terminal hour is exceeded, or if a condition imposed on the notice is breached, any person carrying on the activity, or who knowingly allows the activity to be carried on, will be guilty of an offence pursuant to section 136 of the Act. These obligations are no less stringent than those pertaining to licences or club premises certificates and need to be closely observed.

19.31 A police constable or an officer of the licensing authority may at any reasonable time enter premises to which a temporary event notice relates, to assess the impact of the notice on the promotion of the crime prevention objective.[33] Police closure powers under section 161 apply equally to temporary event notices, if there is the requisite degree of disorder or nuisance.[34]

19.32 An offence is committed if a person intentionally obstructs a constable or an officer of the licensing authority from exercising the power of entry. The offence is subject to a maximum fine not exceeding level 2 on the standard scale[35].

19.33 When premises are being used for a purpose specified in a temporary event notice, the premises user must:

(a) display a copy of the notice at the premises, together with a copy of any statement of added conditions; or

(b) ensure that the notice and statement of conditions are kept at the premises in his custody or in the custody of a person he has nominated and who is present and working at the premises. In this situation, notice specifying that the temporary event notice and statement of conditions are in the custody of the nominated person and the position held at the premises by that person must be prominently displayed at the premises.[36]

If the premises user does not comply with the said notice display requirements without reasonable excuse, s/he commits an offence.[37]

19.34 Where the notice display requirements in accordance with section 109 of the Act are not complied with, a constable or officer of the licensing authority may require the premises user to produce the temporary

---

[33] Licensing Act 2003, s 108(1).
[34] See Licensing Act 2003, s 161(8) and Chapter 43.
[35] Licensing Act 2003, s 108(3)–(4).
[36] Licensing Act 2003, s 109(2)–(3).
[37] Licensing Act 2003, s 109(4).

event notice for examination[38]. An offence is committed if, on request, the premises user fails to produce the notice without reasonable excuse.[39]

19.35   In practical terms, it is advisable to ensure that a copy of the temporary event notice and a statement of conditions, if any, is prominently displayed at the entrance to premises where a temporary event is taking place.

---

[38]   Licensing Act 2003, s 109(5).
[39]   Licensing Act 2003, s 109(8)–(9).

Challenging licensing decisions

Let us have wine and women, mirth and laughter,
Sermons and soda-water the day after.
Man, being reasonable, must get drunk;
The best of life is but intoxication:
Glory, the grape, love, gold, in these are sunk
The hopes of all men, and of every nation;
Without their sap, how branchless were the trunk
Of life's strange tree, so fruitful on occasion:
But to return,—Get very drunk; and when
You wake with headache, you shall see what then.

Don Juan
Lord Byron

Challenging licensing decisions

A bumper of good liquor
Will end a contest quicker
Than justice, judge or vicar.

Richard Brinsley Sheridan

A INTRODUCTION

20.01 If one wishes to challenge a decision of a licensing authority there are three main options to consider. These are:

(a) appeal to the magistrates' court,
(b) judicial review, and
(c) complaint to the Local Government Ombudsman.

20.02 This chapter deals with appeals to the magistrates' court from decisions of the licensing authority, and available routes of appeal from decisions of that court. The chapter concludes with an examination of alternative means of challenging the decisions of licensing authorities, namely, through judicial review and complaint to the Local Government Ombudsman.

B APPEAL TO MAGISTRATES' COURT

20.03 By far the most common way to challenge a decision of the licensing authority is to appeal to the magistrates' court. The provisions relating to appeals under the Licensing Act 2003 are set out in section 178 and Schedule 5.

On an appeal, a magistrates' court may:

(a)   dismiss the appeal;
(b)   substitute for the decision appealed against another decision which could have been made by the licensing authority; or
(c)   remit the case to the licensing authority to dispose of it in accordance with the direction of the court;

and may make such order as to costs as it thinks fit.[1]

Who can appeal?

20.04   The persons given a right of appeal fall broadly into two categories: those who have made an application and those that have made representations on an application.

The applicant

20.05   An applicant whose application is rejected generally has a right of appeal. This applies to the following applications:

● an application for the grant, variation, or transfer of a premises licence
● an application for the grant or variation of a club premises certificate
● an application for the grant or renewal of a personal licence.

20.06   An applicant whose application is granted may also have a right of appeal. For example, the applicant may wish to complain of conditions that have been imposed, or the exclusion of a licensable activity or a refusal to specify a person as a premises supervisor. An appeal lies from:

● the grant or variation of a premises licence
● the issue of a provisional statement
● the grant or variation of a club premises certificate.

Persons making relevant representations

20.07   A person making relevant representations is also given rights of appeal. There is the additional qualification that the representations made must not have been considered to be frivolous or vexatious.

A person who made relevant representations may appeal:

---

1   Licensing Act 2003, s 178(2).

- against the grant or variation of a premises licence
- against the grant or variation of a club premises certificate
- against the issue of a provisional statement
- against a decision on a review of a club premises certificate or a review or summary review of a premises licence
- against a decision taken on a review of a premises licence following a closure order.

The chief officer of police

20.08 The chief officer of police is given special rights of appeal where he is given a right to object. These are:

- on the grant of an application to change the person specified on a premises licence as the premises supervisor
- on the grant of an application to transfer a premises licence
- on the licensing authority deciding not to cancel an interim authority
- where a temporary event notice is given and the licensing authority decides not to give a counter-notice
- on the grant of a personal licence
- on the grant of an application for the conversion of a club premises certificate under the transitional provisions
- where convictions of a personal licence holder come to light after the grant or renewal of a personal licence and the licensing authority decides not to revoke the licence.

These rights of appeal only arise when the chief officer of police has given notice of his objection prior to the relevant decision. Note that he may also qualify for other rights of appeals as a person who has made relevant representations. Importantly he also has the right to appeal against a decision on a summary review (as the only person entitled to apply for such a review).

Other appellants

20.09 There are other persons entitled to appeal not listed above. These are:

- The holder of a premises licence that has been the subject of a review under section 52 or a review following a closure order or a summary review
- A premises user who has given a temporary event notice and has received a counter-notice from the licensing authority
- A club whose club premises certificate has been the subject of a review, or has been withdrawn
- A person who gives an interim authority notice may appeal against the decision to cancel the notice
- An applicant for a review of a premises licence or club premises certificate.

Appeal against closure order

20.10 Any person aggrieved by the decision of a magistrates' court on a closure order under section 164 may appeal.[2] Since this is an appeal against a decision of the magistrates' court rather than the licensing authority, appeal is to the Crown Court.

20.11 From the above it may seem there is no one who cannot appeal. But there are notable exceptions: those that do not make relevant representations in time, or whose representations are judged to be frivolous or vexatious. For these people, the only remedy may be to seek judicial review (see below).

C PROCEDURE ON APPEAL

Time for appealing

20.12 An appeal must be commenced within 21 days beginning with the day on which the appellant was notified by the licensing authority of the decision.[3] If notification was given on Monday 1 May, the last day for commencing the appeal would therefore be Monday 21 May.

There does not appear to be any power to extend the time for appealing.

20.13 Time runs from the date of notification by the licensing authority. The Act provides that each party that has a right of appeal is to be given 'a notice' forthwith. The Premises Licences Regulations make clear that the notice has to be in writing[4]. A document that is to be given to any person may be given by delivering it to him, or by leaving it at his proper address or by sending it by post to him at that address[5] Where the decision is taken following a hearing the Regulations require the notice is given in writing 'forthwith'[6] and accompanied by information regarding the right of a party to appeal against the decision.

Notification may be sent by electronic means, provided the receiving party has agreed in advance and the same is also sent or given in paper form at the same time. Where these requirements are met then notification is treated as being achieved from the date of transmission.

---

[2]   Licensing Act 2003, s 165.
[3]   Licensing Act 2003, Sch 5, paras 9(2), 15(2), 16(5), 17(7), 18(5).
[4]   Licensing Act 2003 (Premises Licences and Club Premises Certificates) 2005 (SI 2005/42), reg 21.
[5]   Licensing Act 2003, s 184(3).
[6]   Licensing Act 2003 (Hearings) Regulations 2005 (SI 2005/44), regs 28–30.

20.14 There is an additional time restriction in the case of a temporary event notice: no appeal may be brought later than five working days before the day on which the event is due to begin.[7]

Where to appeal?

20.15 The appeal can be made to any magistrates' court, but it is expected that it should be the local court for either the appellant or the premises.[8] In the case of a personal licence, the appeal should be made to a magistrates' court for the local justice area in which the licensing authority's area or any part of it is situated. Assistance with identifying the correct area can be obtained from the magistrates' court.

The respondents

20.16 The licensing authority will be a respondent to every appeal.[9] In addition, the following must be joined as additional respondents where applicable:[10]

- the holder of the licence concerned, where they are not the appellant
- the person who gave a temporary event notice, where the appeal is made by the chief officer of police against the decision not to serve a counter notice
- the person who gave the interim authority notice, where the appeal is by the chief officer of police against a decision not to cancel the notice.

20.17 The court has power to join additional respondents. In *R Chief Constable of Nottinghamshire v Nottingham Magistrates' Court*[11] the police successfully argued that the court has an implied power to join an additional respondent in the furtherance of its statutory objectives. The court refused to give wider guidance on when this should be done leaving decisions to be made on a case by case basis. In the *Nottingham* case this allowed the police to present their own arguments and evidence themselves rather than rely on the way the licensing authority chose to conduct the case.

---

7   Licensing Act 2003, Sch 5, para 16(6).
8   See Guidance, para 12.2. The exception is an appeal against a closure order, which must be brought in the local court for the premises.
9   Licensing Act 2003, Sch 5, para 9.
10 Licensing Act 2003, Sch 5, para 9.
11 [2009] EWHC 3182 (Admin).

Notice of appeal

20.18 An appeal is by way of a complaint for an order.[12] No form is prescribed for commencing the appeal. It is suggested that as a minimum it should contain:

- The name and address of the appellant
- The name and address of all respondents
- The decision appealed against
- The standing of the appellant (whether applicant, person making a relevant representation, a licence holder etc)
- The grounds of appeal.

20.19 Given that the appeal is not a review of the council's decision but a rehearing, there is nothing unlawful about a notice which briefly states that the decision was wrong, perhaps supplemented by time-honoured catch-all phrases such as that the council erred in that it failed to give any or adequate weight to the representations of the applicant, or that its decision was disproportionate in all the circumstances of the case.

It is not suggested that notices of appeal should be a skeleton argument or an essay as to the rights and wrongs of the case. Nevertheless, where specific points are to be made, such as that a particular condition was unlawful, or that a particular element of the decision was unreasoned or disproportionate, it is useful for the notice to state this, so that attention can be focussed by all parties and the court at an early stage. Where the notice is insufficiently specific, it is open to the court at the directions stage to order detailed grounds to be filed.

The position pending the appeal

20.20 In certain specific cases there is a limited power given to the magistrates to protect an appellant's position pending the hearing of an appeal. These exceptions relate to the cancellation of an interim authority notice and a review following a closure order under section 166. The court has power to reinstate the licence pending the hearing of the appeal on such terms as it thinks fit.[13] In effect this allows the licence holder to continue trading until the appeal is heard.

20.21 On a review, summary review or the revocation of a personal licence, the decision does not take effect until the time for appealing has expired, and if an appeal is pursued, until the appeal is concluded. In all other cases the Act is silent on the position pending appeal, the clear inference being that the decision takes effect notwithstanding any appeal. The magistrates' court has no power to grant interim relief.

[12]   Magistrates' Courts Rules 1981, r 34.
[13]   Licensing Act 2003, Sch 5, para 18(3)–(4).

20.22   A running controversy has been whether upon final determination of a summary review, any interim steps ordered continue to have effect pending an appeal. Government guidance was originally to the effect that they did. However, in *Chief Constable of Cheshire v Gary Oates*[14] a District Judge in Halton magistrates' court held to the contrary.

20.23   In this case, interim steps of suspension had been imposed. However, acting on counsel's advice that the Guidance was wrong, the licensee re-opened the premises following the final determination. The police, disagreeing with the licensee's advice, issued three closure notices under section 19 of the Criminal Justice and Police Act 2001 and then applied for a closure order, alleging that the premises were being used for the unauthorised sale of alcohol. The licensee defended the proceedings on the grounds inter alia that there had not been unauthorised sale of alcohol within the meaning of section 21 of the 2001 Act. This meant that the court had to determine whether the interim step of suspension survives the final determination.

20.24   The Chief Constable argued that where, as here, an order for suspension had been made three times, the statute clearly contemplated that the suspension should endure through to the end of the appeal proceedings; otherwise the purpose of the summary review provisions would be defeated. The District Judge rejected that argument, holding that the interim steps had ceased to be effective once the final determination had been made. Section 53B is expressly entitled 'interim steps pending review', while section 53B(1) makes it clear that interim steps are steps pending the determination of the review applied for. The only provision that could possibly prolong the life of such steps is section 53C(2)(c). However, the learned District Judge held that this was an appallingly drafted provision which did not clearly achieve that effect. She accepted the licensee's argument that both the common law principle against doubtful penalisation and section 3 of the Human Rights Act 1998 entailed that the statute should not be taken to remove the rights of the licensee to trade unless such deprivation was clearly expressed, and that any ambiguity should be resolved in favour of the licensee. She also held that the fact that no right of appeal had been conferred by Parliament against the imposition of interim steps reinforced the interpretation that such steps were taken to be short-lived, interim arrangements pending the more mature consideration of the overall position at the final hearing.

20.25   Following that decision, the Guidance was withdrawn and when it reappeared under the authorship of the Home Office,[15] the advice as to the continued effect of interim steps pending appeal had gone. While the District Judge's decision is of persuasive authority only in the magistrates' court, it is

---

[14]   19 December 2011.
[15]   'Section 53A Licensing Act 2003: Summary Review Guidance' (Home Office, 2012).

considered to be right, although of course only the High Court or above may rule definitively on the matter.

Case management

20.26 Magistrates' courts usually hold a case management hearing, at which directions are made regarding disclosure, service of witness statements, rebuttal evidence and skeleton arguments, and also for the agreement of a trial bundle and the lodging of that bundle at court.

20.27 It is strongly recommended that further case management directions are made so as to identify the issues arising and make provision to deal with them expeditiously. For example, if a party has failed to state precisely which part of the decision is being appealed, they ought to do so. There is no reason why orders cannot be made for the preparation of schedules of agreed and non-agreed conditions, so that the court can focus on the true issues at trial. The court might order parties to enter into mediation. The court may order that evidence in witness statements shall stand as evidence in chief and that no further questions in chief shall be asked unless they arise out of new matters which could not have been included in the statement. Parties may also be ordered to notify the other of whether particular witnesses are needed at court or whether their statement can be read.

20.28 At a further stage, in substantial appeals, the court may even timetable witnesses, limiting the time allowed for cross-examination, so as to complete the appeal within an allotted time span.

While these ideas may be considered somewhat radical, in fact they would merely permit licensing to catch up with good practice which takes place in practically every other sort of tribunal.

20.29 Practitioners would do well to note the provisions of rule 3A of the Magistrates Courts Rules 1981, which provide:

'(1) The court must actively manage the case. That includes—
  (a) the early identification of the real issues;
  (b) the early identification of the needs of witnesses;
  (c) achieving certainty as to what must be done, by whom and when, in particular by the early setting of a timetable for the progress of the case;
  (d) monitoring the progress of the case and compliance with directions;
  (e) ensuring that evidence, whether disputed or not, is presented in the shortest and clearest way;
  (f) discouraging delay, dealing with as many aspects of the case as possible on the same occasion and avoiding unnecessary hearings;

    (g) encouraging the participants to co-operate in the progression
        of the case; and
    (h) making use of technology.
(2)   The court must actively manage the case by giving any direction
      appropriate to the needs of that case as early as possible.
(3)   Each party must—
    (a) actively assist the court in managing the case without, or if
        necessary with, a direction; and
    (b) apply for a direction if needed to assist with the management
        of the case.'

20.30 In *R (Drinkwater) v Solihull Magistrates' Court*[16] the President of the Queen's Bench Division Sir John Thomas made some trenchant observations which, although directed at summary criminal trials, directly cross-apply and merit reproduction in full:

'49. ... it is clear that in any case in the Magistrates' Court where a trial is likely to be other than a short one, it should be the ordinary practice for a timetable for the conduct of a trial to be set at the time the trial date is fixed and the estimate made.

50. In setting the timetable, the court should scrutinise the reasons why it is said a witness is necessary and the time examination and cross-examination would take. It is also important in setting a timetable to have regard to the nature of the issues and the fact that the trial is a summary trial; any estimate of more than a day in the Magistrates' Courts should be scrutinised with the utmost rigour. Parties must realise that a summary trial requires a proportionate approach. If a timetable for the trial is not set, it is difficult to have any real confidence that the estimate is accurate.

51. At the commencement of the trial, the Magistrates' Court should check with the parties that the timetable and the estimates remain valid. If there is any variation which lengthens the estimate, the court should make every effort to see if the trial can still be accommodated that day by sitting late or otherwise.

52. Once the trial has started, the court must actively manage the trial, keeping an eye on progress in relation to the timetable. It is essential in a Magistrates' Court, just as the Crown Court, that the court has in mind the observations of Judge LJ, as he then was, made as long ago as 2004 in Jisl [2004] EWCA Crim 696 at paragraphs 114–115:

"The starting point is simple. Justice must be done. The defendant is entitled to a fair trial: and, which is sometimes overlooked, the prosecution is equally entitled to a reasonable opportunity to present the evidence against the defendant. It is not however a concomitant of the entitlement to a fair trial that either or both

---

[16]   [2012] EWHC 765 (Admin).

sides are further entitled to take as much time as they like, or for that matter, as long as counsel and solicitors or the defendants themselves think appropriate. Resources are limited. The funding for courts and judges, for prosecuting and the vast majority of defence lawyers is dependent on public money, for which there are many competing demands. Time itself is a resource. Every day unnecessarily used, while the trial meanders sluggishly to its eventual conclusion, represents another day's stressful waiting for the remaining witnesses and the jurors in that particular trial, and no less important, continuing and increasing tension and worry for another defendant or defendants, some of whom are remanded in custody, and the witnesses in trials which are waiting their turn to be listed. It follows that the sensible use of time requires judicial management and control."

Almost exactly a year ago in R v Chaaban [2003] EWCA Crim. 1012 this Court endeavoured to explain the principle:

...

37. ... nowadays, as part of his responsibility for managing the trial, the judge is expected to control the timetable and to manage the available time. Time is not unlimited. No one should assume that trials can continue to take as long or use up as much time as either or both sides may wish, or think, or assert, they need. The entitlement to a fair trial is not inconsistent with proper judicial control over the use of time. At the risk of stating the obvious, every trial which takes longer than it reasonably should is wasteful of limited resources. It also results in delays to justice in cases still waiting to be tried, adding to the tension and distress of victims, defendants, particularly those in custody awaiting trial, and witnesses. Most important of all it does nothing to assist the jury to reach a true verdict on the evidence.

38. In principle, the trial judge should exercise firm control over the timetable, where necessary, making clear in advance and throughout the trial that the timetable will be subject to appropriate constraints. With such necessary even-handedness and flexibility as the interests of the justice require as the case unfolds, the judge is entitled to direct that the trial is expected to conclude by a specific date and to exercise his powers to see that it does."

...

54. The consequences of the failure of setting a timetable and actively managing a case in the Magistrates' Courts can be much more serious in a particular case than in the Crown Court. In the Crown Court if a trial does not conclude within the estimate, the case will continue on the following day, although this undoubtedly has a serious impact on other cases as was pointed out in Jisl. In the Magistrates' Court, it is often not possible for a case to continue the following day. Although,

where a case does not conclude within the estimate, every effort must be made to see if the trial can continue the following day, there are obvious practical difficulties, particularly given the commitments of the Magistrates and other business that has been scheduled for succeeding days. The practice has thus developed of adjourning a case that has not concluded for a period of two to three weeks, as we are told that that is the sort of time which is needed to find a time at which the availability of a courtroom, staff and, more importantly, the Magistrates, can be secured. A delay in the middle of a case for a period of two to three weeks is plainly inimical to the principles of speedy and summary justice. It is for these reasons and those given in Jisl essential that the closest attention is paid to timetabling, that the case is actively managed and concluded within the estimate.'

20.31 In Northern Ireland, the nettle has been firmly grasped in licensing cases. In *Re Sainsburys*,[17] Gillen J stated:

'[19] In order to meet the overriding objective, in future licensing cases, firm case management prior to the hearing should be invoked and the following steps considered:

- Expert reports, at least so far as they contain factual assertions including for example measurements, distances, surveys etc., should be exchanged not later than 14 days prior to the hearing. I am of course conscious that in an adversarial system an objector is entitled to be wary lest by his industry he unwittingly helps to make a case for the applicant. He remains entitled to put the applicant to proof of his case without assistance from the objector's expert evidence.Nonetheless this is a common problem in almost all litigation to a varying degree and the greater part of expert reports is usually confined to factual assertions which will emerge in cross-examination. At least those aspects must in future be exchanged in advance of trial to speed up litigation.
- Experts should convene meetings by telephonic communication or otherwise in order to narrow issues and draw up a Scott schedule of matters in agreement/matters in dispute.
- At least two weeks prior to trial experts should exchange any literature or statistics being relied on.
- The bundle of documents prepared for the court hearing should include the expert reports so that the court has an opportunity to read the papers in advance of the hearing and thus accelerate the court process.
- Maps, plans, statistics and drawings to be relied on should be exchanged prior to the hearing and contained in the bundle of documents presented to the court.
- Prior to the hearing the parties should exchange correspondence

---

[17]   [2012] NIQB 45.

outlining whether or not there is any issue as to certain of the statutory proofs wherever possible eg. on the validity of the subsisting licence to be surrendered, on planning permission granted, is the objector within the vicinity, have the requirements of service, advertisements and notices been complied with etc. Whilst of course it remains necessary for the applicant to present a number of fundamental proofs at such hearings in order to satisfy the court, nonetheless the process can be speeded up without injustice at least at the appeal stage if it is clear that there is no issue that required proofs exist and are in order.

[20] In short litigation by ambush is a relic of the past. The cards up approach to modern litigation must now find its way into licensing cases to ensure that justice is done and cases are dealt with in a timely, efficient and proportionate manner'.

20.32   As stated above, it is considered that the salutary practices now adopted in criminal trials in this country and in licensing in Northern Ireland ought to govern the process of appeal in licensing matters. Appeals are prohibitively expensive both for licensees and licensing authorities, and what ought to be a relatively expeditious check and balance on the exercise of power by the licensing authority ought not to be allowed to transmogrify into a state trial. Particularly where a large number of incidents is relied upon, the temptation is to treat each and every incident as though it requires proof beyond reasonable doubt, rather than simply reaching an overview of the extent of issues at the premises. Where proper control is not exercised, then trials can run out control. It is the responsibility of the court and the parties to ensure that this does not happen.

20.33   There is no doubt that where the Court has made directions it can enforce them firmly. In *Almada v City of Westminster*[18] a direction had been made that the evidence in chief of any witness called in person shall be by consideration of the witness statement unless the leave of the court is given. An appellant had failed to serve witness statements and at the appeal hearing was debarred by the District Judge from giving evidence. His application for judicial review of the decision was dismissed, and his challenge failed in the Court of Appeal. There, Dyson LJ stated that the fact that licensing proceedings may have been conducted informally in the past was immaterial. The District Judge had been entitled to take the view that he did, and his judgment was upheld. This decision serves to underline the point, that licensing appeals are not a unique case ungoverned by the structures now governing every other type of litigation. Rather, courts have powers to make directions for their expeditious determination, to expect the directions to be adhered to, and to take draconian action where they are not.

---

[18]   [2010] EWCA Civ 386.

Compromise

20.34 An issue sometimes arises as to whether it is open to a licensing authority to compromise an appeal. This may arise, for example, because the applicant is prepared to accept a revised terminal hour, or proffers some conditions to overcome a harm perceived by the authority. Sometimes the magistrates themselves, particularly District Judges, express a view which brings it home to the parties that a compromise is in order. The officers and legal representatives responsible for the conduct of the case rarely have authority to compromise a case. Further, the licensing committee is *functus officio* and cannot simply re-make its decision. Furthermore, since licensing is public interest litigation the parties cannot simply hand up a consent order and expect it to be rubber-stamped by the magistrates.

To overcome these difficulties, a practice has arisen whereby the council officers will take a report back to the committee asking for its approval to place a suggested order before the court. The report is considered under Part II of the committee agenda, so that it is not disclosed to the appellant. If the committee agrees the suggested course, the officers reach a non-binding agreement with the appellant on those terms. The court is then asked to exercise its discretion to make an order in those terms.

Before embarking on that course, the parties should bear two further considerations in mind. First, it is sometimes extremely annoying to local objectors who have supported the council's position to be told that the appeal has been compromised without their being heard. The answer that they are not parties to the litigation is true but not always very satisfactory. It is sometimes better to consult them before returning to committee. Second, if the committee rejects the proposal, a great deal of time and cost may have been wasted. Therefore, while this procedure can be a very useful way of resolving more complex licensing litigation, it should only be used where it is genuinely likely to save time and costs, and not as a substitute for a proper airing of the issues. An objector dissatisfied with the proposed compromise might apply at this stage to be joined as a respondent to defend the appeal in order to block the compromise.

D   The appeal hearing

20.35 The appeal is a re-hearing of the decision.[19] Accordingly the strict rules of evidence do not apply and hearsay evidence is admissible.[20] The burden is on the appellant to show that the decision of the licensing authority is wrong.[21]

---

[19]   *Sagnata Investments Ltd v Norwich Corporation* [1971] 2 QB 614.

[20]   *Kavanagh v Chief Constable of Devon & Cornwall* [1974] 1 QB 624; *Westminster City Council v Zestfair Ltd* (1989) 88 LGR 288.

[21]   See *R (Hope and Glory Public House Ltd) v Westminster Magistrates' Court* [2011] 3 All ER 579.

20.36 The procedure is by way of complaint for an order. The rules provide for the complainant (the appellant) to open the case and call his evidence first.[22] This is a somewhat unwieldy procedure, since it often means that the court hears why the authority made the wrong decision, before it hears what that decision was. For this reason, the magistrates have historically asked the respondent to present its evidence first. This approach has been disapproved in *Hope and Glory* (above) where it was emphasised that the burden lies with the appellant to show that the decision below is wrong, and there it is proper that he should go first. Any difficulties arising from the order of proceedings should be averted by the cases of the parties being set out in written evidence and skeleton arguments, together with the ability for the appellant to call rebuttal evidence.

20.37 Since it is a re-hearing, it is open to either party to bring forward information that has come to light since the initial decision.[23] Where the appeal is against the grant of a licence for example, there may well be evidence presented of problems that have arisen or not arisen recently. Similarly, in a case concerning the duties of a planning inspector on appeal from the decision of a planning authority, it was held that where Circular guidance from the Secretary of State comes into being after the public inquiry but before a decision has been made, the inspector is bound to take the Circular into account.[24] The same rule should apply to new licensing policies or guidance issuing from the licensing authority or the Secretary of State after the original licensing decision but before the decision on the appeal.[25]

20.38 This rule has been re-affirmed in *Khan v Coventry Magistrates Court*,[26] which also answers a point which has caused some confusion: given the procedural restrictions on who may be heard and what they may say in licensing applications at first instance, is it open season in the magistrates' court? Can the court hear whatever evidence is presented to it, even if such evidence does not come from responsible authorities and could not have been presented to the licensing authority? The answer to both questions is yes. Moore-Bick LJ said:

'12. In my view section 182(2)(b) does not have the restrictive effect for which Mr. de Mello contended. It makes it clear that the magistrates have the power to make any order of the kind that the licensing authority could have made, but it does not say anything about the grounds on which such an order might be made. That will depend on the evidence before the court. Indeed, the fact that the magistrates can make any order that the licensing authority could have made itself tends

---

[22] Magistrates' Courts Rules 1981, r 14.
[23] *Rushmoor Borough Council v Richards* (1996) 160 LG Rev 460.
[24] *London Borough of Newham v Secretary of State for the Environment* (1986) 53 P & CR 98.
[25] See further Chapter 9, Section D.
[26] [2011] EWCA Civ 751.

to support the conclusion that they are indeed considering the matter completely afresh. The magistrates' function is to consider the application by reference to the statutory licensing objectives untrammelled by any of the regulations that govern the procedure for a review under section 51. They are therefore entitled to consider evidence of events occurring before the application to the licensing authority as well as evidence of events occurring since its decision.'

Policy

20.39 What should the magistrates' court's approach be to the policy adopted by the licensing authority, ie its licensing statement? This question was dealt with in *R v Middlesex Crown Court ex p Westminster City Council & Chorion plc*[27], a case concerning an application for a public entertainment licence to Westminster City Council. Scott Baker J said this:

'In my view it **[the appeal court] must accept the policy and apply it as if it was standing in the shoes of the council** considering the application. Neither the Magistrates' Court nor the Crown Court is the right place to challenge the policy. The remedy, if it is alleged that a policy has been unlawfully established, is an application to the Administrative Court for judicial review.' (emphasis added)

20.40 It might be thought that this seems eminently sensible and in accordance with the approach adopted in other areas of administrative law, for example planning. However it was not always accepted to be the case in licensing matters, where appeal courts occasionally treated policies with rather less respect.

20.41 Scott Baker J's remarks apply all the more strongly to a policy contained in a licensing statement, since these policies have statutory force. The point of having a policy is so that there can be consistency and fairness in decision making. This would obviously be undermined if the policy could be side-stepped on appeal.

20.42 A recent example of the application of this principle arose in *R (Portsmouth City Council v 3D Entertainment Group (CRC) Ltd*,[28] in which a cumulative policy created a reverse burden on the applicant to demonstrate that there would be no negative cumulative impact. Supperstone J held that the magistrates adopted an approach that was not consistent with the policy and, in particular, the reverse burden, in that they required the police and the council to adduce evidence that there would be a negative cumulative impact. This amounted to an error of law.

---

[27]   [2002] EWHC 1104 (Admin).
[28]   [2011] EWHC 507 (Admin).

20.43   This is one of the few areas of the appeal procedure where the Guidance offers some assistance. It provides:

> '12.8   In hearing an appeal against any decision made by a licensing authority, the magistrates' court will have regard to that licensing authority's statement of licensing policy and this Guidance. However the court would be entitled to depart from either the statement of licensing policy or this Guidance if it considered it was justified to do so because of the individual circumstances of any case. In other words, while the court will normally consider the matter as if it was "standing in the shoes" of the licensing authority, it would be entitled to find that the licensing authority should have departed from its own policy or the Guidance because the particular circumstances would have justified such a decision.'[29]

In this the government appears to be seeking to follow the law as set out in *Chorion*. However, the Guidance goes on:

> '12.9   In addition the appellate court is entitled to disregard any part of a licensing policy statement or this Guidance that it holds to be ultra vires the 2003 Act and therefore unlawful. The normal course for challenging a statement of licensing policy or this Guidance should be by way of judicial review, but where it is submitted to an appellate court that a statement of policy is itself ultra vires the 2003 Act and this has a direct bearing on the case before it, it would be inappropriate for the court, on accepting such a submission, to compound the original error by relying on that part of the statement of licensing policy affected.'[30]

20.44   In this the Guidance appears to open the door for challenges to policy in the magistrates' court. This would include challenges brought to established policies that would not succeed by way of judicial review because they were outside the strict time limits for applications in the Administrative Court.

20.45   If this part of the Guidance is followed, it is likely to lead to licensing authorities having to defend and justify their policies repeatedly on appeal, with consequent time and cost spent in the magistrates' court. Were this to be permitted, challenges could be on any ground, for example that the policy was perverse in that no reasonable authority could have come to the view it did on a material policy, or that a consultation response or some other relevant matter was not taken into account, or that an irrelevant matter was taken into account, or that the consultation exercise itself was deficient.

---

29   Guidance para 12.8.
30   Guidance para 12.9.

20.46 Furthermore, the benefits of rules on judicial review are that challenges are brought promptly, thus producing certainty not only for the parties but for other parties affected by the policy. For example, were a magistrates' court to elect to ignore a certain part of the policy on the basis that it was unlawful, what would the effect be on the decisions (which may be legion) already taken in reliance on the policy? What if different magistrates' courts came to different views as to the lawfulness of the policy? Finally, while the Administrative Court can elect in its discretion to uphold an otherwise unlawful policy where no substantial injustice has been caused by refusing to grant relief, there is no provision for a similar exercise of discretion by the magistrates' court.

20.47 As the Guidance itself observes, nothing in it is intended to override the law.[31] Nor could it do so. The law of licensing policy is clearly laid down by Scott Baker J in *Chorion*. The Guidance does not accurately state the legal position and is legally wrong. In any case, it is thought most unlikely that Parliament intended lay magistrates to exercise such a supervisory jurisdiction over the statutory policy-making of licensing authorities. Nevertheless this passage has remained in the Guidance through repeated updates, although it is fair to say that appellate advocates have not been brave enough to hold that it should hold sway over the judgment of the High Court and therefore it has not been subject to specific challenge.

The relevance of the council's decision

20.48 Does the licensing authority's decision count for anything on appeal? Lord Goddard CJ certainly thought so. He said:

'That does not mean to say that the court of appeal, in this case the metropolitan magistrate, ought not to pay great attention to the fact the duly constituted and elected local authority have come to an opinion on the matter, and it ought not lightly to reverse their opinion. It is constantly said (although I am not sure that it is always sufficiently remembered) that the function of a court of appeal is to exercise its powers when it is satisfied that the judgment below was wrong, not merely because it is not satisfied that the judgment was right'.[32]

This approach has been endorsed by the Court of Appeal in *R (Hope and Glory Public House Ltd) v Westminster Magistrates' Court*[33]. Toulson LJ emphasised that decisions by licensing authorities involve an element of judgment. He said:

'45. ... It is right in all cases that the magistrates' court should pay careful attention to the reasons given by the licensing authority for

[31] Para 1.10.
[32] *Stepney Borough Council v Joffe* [1949] 1 KB 599, 602–3.
[33] [2011] 3 All ER 579

arriving at the decision under appeal, bearing in mind that Parliament has chosen to place responsibility for making such decisions on local authorities. The weight which the magistrates should ultimately attach to those reasons must be a matter for their judgment in all the circumstances, taking into account the fullness and clarity of the reasons, the nature of the issues and the evidence given on the appeal.'

20.49 While there is a lesson for magistrates' courts in that passage, there is a still greater lesson for licensing authorities. If they write a decision containing full and proper reasons for their decision, it is likely to be accorded far greater respect and weight by the court than a decision which simply sets out the result without proper reasons. If the court cannot understand why the licensing authority has reached its views, it is hardly likely to pay much attention to it.

20.50 The next question, however, is the extent of task facing an appellant. At one extreme, does he start with a blank page, so that his burden is simply to show that on balance his case should succeed? Or at the other extreme can he only succeed if he can show that the decision below was *Wednesbury* unreasonable? The Court of Appeal upheld the judgment of Burton J who had placed the task between these two extremes.

> '43. I conclude that the words of Lord Goddard approved by Edmund Davies LJ are very carefully chosen.[34] What the appellate court will have to do is to be satisfied that the judgment below "is wrong", that is to reach its conclusion on the basis of the evidence put before it and then to conclude that the judgment below is wrong, even if it was not wrong at the time. That is what this district judge was prepared to do by allowing fresh evidence in, on both sides.
>
> 44. The onus still remains on the claimant, hence the correct decision that the claimant should start, one that cannot be challenged as I have indicated.
>
> 45. At the end of the day, the decision before the district judge is whether the decision of the licensing committee is wrong. Mr Glen has submitted that the word "wrong" is difficult to understand, or, at any rate, insufficiently clarified. What does it mean? It is plainly not " Wednesbury unreasonable" because this is not a question of judicial review. It means that the task of the district judge – having heard the evidence which is now before him, and specifically addressing the decision of the court below – is to give a decision whether, because he disagrees with the decision below in the light of the evidence before him, it is therefore wrong.'

---

[34] See passage from *Joffe*, para 20.48 above.

20.51 In *R (Townlink Ltd) v Thames Magistrates Court*[35] the court interpreted this as entailing that the magistrates should reach their own conclusion on the appeal, and compare it with the decision below, and if they were different, the appeal should be allowed. However it is hard to see that this gives the respect to the authority's decision suggested in the passages cited above. Indeed, at first instance in *Hope and Glory*[36] Burton J used heightened language to describe the importance of the approach which permits the overturning of a decision only when it is considered to be wrong: he described it as a 'wagging finger'[37] and 'this caveat, this stricture, this limitation'.[38] That is clearly not reflected by an approach which concludes that the previous decision is wrong just because the appellate court would take a different view. In *Townlink* only one side was represented and therefore the decision cannot be cited in court, under the Practice Direction on Citation of Authorities.[39] The decision in *Hope and Glory*, on the other hand, is clearly to be followed. It is fair to add that the Judge in *Townlink* clearly did not believe that he was expressing a rule which differed from that expressed in *Hope and Glory*, which therefore remains the leading authority on the topic.

Use of local knowledge

20.52 It frequently happens that local magistrates have knowledge of the area. When dealing with the night time economy, they may themselves be users of that economy, and witnesses both to its benefits and consequences. They may also, sitting in their criminal jurisdiction, have formed clear views as to the state of the town centre, for better or worse. To what extent may they bring that knowledge to bear in their decision-making? It would seem absurd to have a system of local justices of the peace and then prevent them drawing on their collective experience in making judgments about local priorities. But on the other hand it may be unfair to one or other of the parties that they should lose a case for reasons unconnected to the evidence. A body of principles has emerged in order to ensure that local knowledge can be used, but in a manner that is fair to both parties. The principles may be stated as follows:

(1)   Judges of all kinds sit as laymen and not as experts, and verdicts of all kinds must be given according to the evidence.[40]

(2)   However, Justices may use their local knowledge.[41]

---

35   [2011] EWHC 898 (Admin).
36   [2009]EWHC 1996 (Admin).
37   *Hope and Glory*, para 38.
38   *Hope and Glory*, para 40.
39   'Practice Direction (Citation of Authorities)' [2001] 1 WLR 1001.
40   *Hill v Baxter* [1958] 1 QB 277, 285.
41   *Ingram v Percival* [1969] 1 QB 548, 555.

(3)   Such knowledge must be the common knowledge of persons in the district and not specialised knowledge arising from other cases.[42]

(4)   Justices must measure their views against the evidence presented to them.[43] It is not open to Justices to substitute their own local knowledge for the evidence given in the case, particularly where the evidence is uncontested.[44]

(5)   Before acting on local knowledge, the Justices should notify the parties so that they may comment or call evidence upon the matter if necessary.[45]

Reasons

20.53   In *R (Tofik) v Immigration Appeal Tribunal*[46], Sedley LJ stated that there was now a 'general obligation of judicial and administrative decision-makers to explain, however succinctly, why they are deciding as they are.'

20.54   That there is a duty on justices in hearing appeals from licensing authorities to state the reasons for their decision is beyond doubt. The only issue is as to the extent of such reasons. In *South Bucks District Council v Porter*[47], Lord Brown dealt with the obligation of a planning inspector to give reasons on appeals from the decisions of the local planning authority. In his speech, with which all their Lordships agreed, he stated:

> 'The reasons for a decision must be intelligible and they must be adequate. They must enable the reader to understand why the matter was decided as it was and what conclusions were reached on the "principal important controversial issues", disclosing how any issue of law or fact was resolved. Reasons can be briefly stated, the degree of particularity required depending entirely on the nature of the issues falling for decision. The reasoning must not give rise to a substantial doubt as to whether the decision-maker erred in law, for example by misunderstanding some relevant policy or some other important matter or by failing to reach a rational decision on relevant grounds. But such adverse inference will not readily be drawn. The reasons need refer only to the main issues in the dispute, not to every material consideration. They should enable disappointed developers to assess their prospects of obtaining some alternative development permission, or, as the case may be, their unsuccessful opponents to understand how the policy or approach underlying the grant of permission may impact upon future

---

[42]   *Reynolds v Llanelly Associated Tinplate Co Ltd* [1948] 1 All ER 140, 141–142; *Borthwick v Vickers* [1973] Crim LR 317.

[43]   *R (Daniel Thwaites plc) v Wirral Borough Magistrates' Court*, at para [55].

[44]   *Wetherall v Harrison* [1976] QB 773, 778. For example see *Church v Church* (1933) 97 JP 91, 94; *Thomas v Thomas* [1961] 1 WLR 1, 8.

[45]   *Bowman v DPP* [1991] RTR 263.

[46]   [2003] EWCA Civ 1138.

[47]   [2004] UKHL 33.

such applications. Decision letters must be read in a straightforward manner, recognising that they are addressed to parties well aware of the issues involved and the arguments advanced. A reasons challenge will only succeed if the party aggrieved can satisfy the court that he has genuinely been substantially prejudiced by the failure to provide an adequately reasoned decision.'

Planning appeals tend to be dealt with in considerably more detail than licensing appeals, and often turn on a level of technical detail far beyond that with which mere licensing lawyers would dream of grappling. Nevertheless, the core tenets of that dictum hold true for licensing.

20.55 In *R (Hestview) v Snaresbrook Crown Court*,[48] a betting licensing case, Hooper J applied to licensing the following dictum of Griffiths LJ in *Eagil Trust v Piggott-Brown*:[49]

'... the judge should set out his reasons, but the particularity with which he is required to set them out must depend on the circumstances of the case before him and the nature of the decision he is giving. They need not be elaborate. I cannot stress too strongly that there is no duty on a judge, in giving his reasons, to deal with every argument presented by counsel in support of his case. It is sufficient if what he says shows the parties and, if need be, the Court of Appeal the basis on which he has acted, and if it be that the judge has not dealt with some particular argument but it can be seen that there are grounds on which he would have been entitled to reject it, this court should assume that he acted on those grounds unless the appellant can point to convincing reasons leading to a contrary conclusion (see Sachs LJ in *Knight v Clifton* [1971] 2 All ER 378 at 392–393, [1971] Ch 700 at 721).'

20.56 It is certainly arguable that the reasons given by justices on appeal from licensing authorities ought to be somewhat fuller than previously, since there is no further appeal to the Crown Court, and there is therefore a special interest for the losing party to understand the grounds of their defeat. Nevertheless, cogency and succinctness are often good bedfellows and brief reasons may be perfectly adequate to let a party know why he has lost. In *Stefan v General Medical Council*[50] Lord Clyde stated: 'What will suffice to constitute the reasons is a matter distinct from the duty to give reasons, and there can clearly be circumstances where a quite minimal explanation will legitimately suffice.' That might, for example, be so where a court simply believed one witness over the other.

---

[48] 2001 LLR 214.
[49] [1985] 3 All ER 119,122. *In English v Emery Reimbold & Strick Ltd* [2002] 1 WLR 2409, the Court of Appeal held that the ruling in *Eagil Trust* applied to judgments of all descriptions.
[50] [1999] 1 WLR 1293, 1301.

20.57   It is submitted that in particular where there is a departure from policy or Guidance, the court should state the basis upon which it has departed. But conversely, where an appellant submits unsuccessfully that there should be a departure from policy because, for example, the proposal meets the objectives of the policy if not its strict wording, he is entitled to know why the argument has been rejected.

20.58   Finally, where reasons are inadequate, the principle is now developing that a party that is dissatisfied by a lack of reasons should seek amplification from the court before going to the Administrative Court to complain. The Court of Appeal first marked and encouraged the practice in *English v Emery Reimbold & Strick Limited.*[51] Then, in *Re T (Contact: Alienation: Permission to Appeal)*[52], Arden LJ stated:

> 'In a complex case, it might well be prudent, and certainly not out of place, for a judge, having handed down or delivered judgment, to ask the advocates whether there are matters which he has not covered. Even if he does not do this, an advocate ought immediately, as a matter of courtesy at least, to draw the judge's attention to any material omission of which he is then aware or then believes exists ... It would be unsatisfactory to use an omission by a judge to deal with a point in a judgment as grounds for an application for appeal if the matter has not been brought to the judge's attention when there was a ready opportunity to do so.'

20.59   In *Re B*[53] Thorpe LJ, referring to that dictum, said: 'It may well be that this significant development in the inter-relationship between the process of trial and appeal has yet to be fully appreciated by advocates and judges.'

20.60   It is by no means suggested that the procedure should become over-used, particularly since it may become oppressive to lay justices to have a usually ex tempore decision placed under further scrutiny in this way. As stated by Schiemann LJ in *R v Brent Borough Council ex parte Baruwa:*[54] 'That said, the law gives decision makers a certain latitude in how they express themselves and will recognise that not all those taking decisions find it easy in the time available to express themselves with judicial exactitude.'

20.61   However, where it is plain that reasons are inadequate, there are clear advantages in terms of time and cost to asking the justices to elaborate on their reasons which, on the advice of their clerk, they may be prepared to do. It is noteworthy that in *Hestview* itself[55] brief reasons were given by the Crown Court and then elaborated upon, following request by the respondent to the appeal. More recently, Sales J held that it was in order for a licensing

---

51   *Stefan v General Medical Council,* para 26.
52   [2003] 1 FLR 531 para 41.
53   [2003] 2 FLR 1035, 1038.
54   (1997) 29 HLR 915, 929.
55   See para 20.55 above.

authority to elucidate, but not to modify, its reasons in response to a prospective challenge.[56]

E COSTS ON APPEAL

20.62 On the conclusion of an appeal the magistrates may award costs as they think fit.[57] No further guidance is given within the Act. The leading authority on costs in licensing appeals is *R (Perinpanathan) v City of Westminster Magistrates Court*[58]. The Court of Appeal endorsed the principles previously set out in *Bradford City Council v Booth* for use in licensing cases.[59] The principles are as follows:

- The magistrates' court has a discretion as to costs and that applies to quantum and as to which party, if any, should pay.
- What the court thinks just and reasonable will depend on the relevant facts and circumstances of the case and they may or may not follow the event.
- Where a complainant successfully challenges an administrative decision and where a local authority had acted honestly, reasonably and properly on grounds which reasonably appeared to be sound, the court was to consider in addition to all the relevant facts: (i) any financial prejudice to the claimant in the particular circumstances if an order for costs was not made in his favour; and (ii) the need for a local authority to make honest, sound and reasonable administrative decisions without the fear of undue financial prejudice if its decisions were successfully challenged.

20.63 The Court in *Perinpanathan* said that where the public authority has lost the starting point and default position should be that no order for costs should be made. It also emphasised that if financial prejudice is to be used as a reason to depart from the default position it must be something more than that usually suffered by a losing party in litigation who has to bear his own costs.

---

[56] *R (KVP Ent) Limited v South Bucks District Council* [2013] EWHC 926 (Admin).
[57] Licensing Act 2003, s 181(2).
[58] [2010] 1 WLR 1508.
[59] [2000] COD 338, [2001] LLR 151. It is sometimes argued that the case may not be cited since it was attended by one party only and so fell foul of the Practice Direction (Citation of Authorities) 2001 1 WLR 1001. However, the case clearly purported to resolve issues of costs in licensing appeals, and in any event was followed in *R (Telford and Wrekin) v Shrewsbury Crown Court* 2003 LLR 991. See further *R v Totnes Licensing Justices ex p Chief Constable of Devon & Cornwall* (1990) 156 JP 587; *Chief Constable of Derbyshire v Goodman and Newton* [2001] LLR 127; *Crawley Borough Council v Attenborough* [2006] EWHC 1278 (Admin); *R (Cambridge City Council) v Alex Nestling Ltd* [2006] EWHC 1374 (Admin).

20.64   Nor does success on appeal necessarily presage an order for costs in one's favour. In *Prasannan v Royal Borough of Kensington and Chelsea*[60] the court approved a District Judge's decision to award £20,000 costs against a successful appellant, where she had brought revocation proceedings on herself by her conduct.

F FURTHER APPEALS FROM MAGISTRATES

20.65   There is no provision for a further appeal from the magistrates to the Crown Court[61]. Any further challenge must be made to the Administrative Court. There are two available procedures: appeal by way of case stated, and judicial review. In many cases either option will be available to a party. There are some differences that bear consideration.

20.66   An appeal by way of case stated lies against a decision that was 'wrong in law, or in excess of jurisdiction'.[62] In a case-stated appeal, the lower court provides a summary of the evidence placed before it and its findings of fact, and then poses a number of questions for the consideration of the higher court. This may be very helpful where the facts are complicated or in dispute.[63] Where the challenge to the magistrates' decision is based upon an allegation that their interpretation of the law was incorrect, or that their findings were reached upon inadequate factual basis, then case stated is the better procedure.

20.67   Judicial review[64] is generally available to challenge a decision of a public authority on the grounds of 'illegality, irrationality or procedural impropriety'. Judicial review should not be used where there is a right of appeal or some other alternative remedy,[65] which tends to suggest that a case-stated appeal should be considered first. Judicial review may be commenced without the assistance of the magistrates' court. This will be the only option in urgent cases, or where interim relief is required. This will also be the appropriate course where there is no decision of the magistrates, for example where they have wrongly declined jurisdiction to hear an appeal. Judicial review is the correct method to challenge rulings made by the magistrates in the course of proceedings, rather than those that form part of the conclusion of the hearing.

---

60   [2010] EWHC 319 (Admin).
61   Note that there is a right of appeal to the Crown Court against a decision that was originally made by the magistrates' court: see Licensing Act 2003, s 165. For an appeal from a decision of the magistrates on a closure order, see Chapter 44 on closure notices.
62   Magistrates' Courts Act 1980, s 111.
63   *R v Ipswich Crown Court, ex parte Baldwin* [1981] 1 All ER 596.
64   See further de Smith, Woolf, Jowell, *Judicial Review of Administrative Action* (Sweet & Maxwell, 5th ed, 2005).
65   *Re: Preston* [1985] AC 835; *R. v Secretary of State, ex p. Swati* [1986] 1 WLR 477, CA.

20.68 Where it is alleged that there has been a procedural irregularity or breach of natural justice, for example an allegation of bias, then judicial review rather than case stated is to be preferred.[66]

Case-stated procedure

20.69 The right of appeal derives from section 111 of the Magistrates' Courts Act 1980 which states:

> 'Any person who was a party to any proceeding before a Magistrates' Court or is aggrieved by the conviction order, determination or other proceeding of the court may question the proceeding on the ground that it is wrong in law or is in excess of jurisdiction by applying to the justices composing the court to state a case for the opinion of the High Court on the question of law or jurisdiction involved.'

20.70 The time limit for making the request is 21 days from the date of the decision to be challenged. There is no power for the High Court to extend this time limit.[67]

20.71 The procedure for preparing a case-stated by the magistrates' court is set out in rules 76 to 81 of the Magistrates' Courts Rules 1981. The case should contain the facts found by the magistrates and the question or questions of law or jurisdiction on which the opinion of the High Court is sought.

20.72 The case should not contain a statement of evidence unless one of the issues on the appeal is that there was no evidence on which the magistrates could have come to their decision. Where this is alleged, the case stated must identify the particular finding of fact which it is said cannot be supported by the evidence.

20.73 Once the stated case has been prepared, the procedure in the High Court is governed by Part 52 of the Civil Procedure Rules. Permission to appeal is not required.[68] The appellant should file an appellant's notice (form N161) at the High Court within ten days of receiving the case. A copy can be found on the Court Service website.[69] At the same time the appellant must lodge a bundle of documents including any witness statements he wishes to rely upon.[70] This should incorporate:

(a) the case stated by the magistrates;
(b) a copy of the decision of the magistrates' court;

---

66   *R v Hereford Magistrates' Court ex p. Rowlands* [1998] QB 110.
67   *Chief Constable of Cleveland v Vaughan* [2009] EWHC 2831 (Admin).
68   'Practice Direction to Part 52', para 18.3.
69   www.courtservice.gov.uk.
70   CPR PD 52, para 5.6.

(c) a copy of the original decision of the licensing authority.[71]

A respondent need not serve an acknowledgment of service, but should serve a respondent's notice where he wishes to uphold the decision of the lower court for reasons different from those given by the court. Skeleton arguments are compulsory for any party wishing to present arguments to the court. The appellant has 14 days from the date of filing his appellant's notice. The respondent(s) should file theirs 21 days after receiving the appellant's.

20.74 Although there is no requirement to obtain permission to appeal, the court does have power to strike out an appellant's notice where there is a compelling reason for doing so.[72]

20.75 If successful, the High Court will allow the appeal where it is satisfied the magistrates' decision was wrong or unjust because of a serious procedural or other irregularity in the proceedings.[73] The High Court may exercise any of the powers of the court below: it may affirm the decision, set aside, vary, or remit it for decision either by the magistrates or the licensing authority. It may also make an order for costs.

20.76 There is no appeal from the decision of the High Court on appeal to it by way of case stated from a magistrates' court under section 111 of the Magistrates' Courts Act 1980 on a non-criminal matter.[74] One possible way around this is to apply for judicial review of the magistrates' court. The judge considering the application for permission for judicial review might refuse permission on the grounds that it was an abuse of process. However this suggestion comes from no lesser authority than the Lord Chief Justice.[75]

G JUDICIAL REVIEW OF THE LICENSING AUTHORITY

20.77 Judicial review[76] is the mechanism by which the High Court exercises a supervisory jurisdiction over administrative decisions. It involves an examination of the way in which a decision was reached, rather than the merits of

---

[71] CPR PD52, para 18.5.

[72] CPR, Rule 52.9

[73] CPR, Rule 52.11.

[74] Senior Courts Act 1981, s 28A(4); *Horseferry Road Justices & Anor v Lord Mayor and the Citizens of the City of Westminster* [2003] EWCA Civ 1007; *Maile v Manchester City Council* [1998] COD 19; *Fleury v Westminster City Council* [2003] LLR 456.

[75] *Horseferry Road Justices & Anor v Lord Mayor and the Citizens of the City of Westminster,* above.

[76] See further de Smith, Woolf, Jowell, *Judicial Review of Administrative Action* (Sweet & Maxwell, 6th revised ed, 2006).

the decision. According to the classic definition,[77] there are three principal grounds for basing a challenge. These are illegality, that is that the decision maker has failed to understand the law regulating his decision and apply it correctly; irrationality, meaning 'Wednesbury unreasonableness',[78] a decision so outrageous that no sensible person who had applied his mind to the question to be decided could have arrived at it; and 'procedural impropriety', meaning the failure to follow an express procedural requirement or a breach of the principles of natural justice.

20.78 There is a pre-action protocol that applies to claims for judicial review. Its aim is to prevent proceedings where possible, through encouraging potential litigants to exchange information and documentation. A prospective claimant should send to the defendant a letter (in standard form) identifying the issues in dispute. The defendant should normally reply within 14 days. The protocol recognises that it is not appropriate in every case: it will not apply where the defendant does not have the legal power to change its decision. This will be true of most magistrates' courts decisions. Further, where the case is urgent it may not be appropriate.

There is a special procedure set out in the practice direction for urgent cases, eg if interim relief is requested. The claimant should file a Request for Urgent Consideration. Reference should be made to the Practice Directions to Part 54 and the Administrative Court Guidance.[79]

Alternative remedy

20.79 Judicial review is not intended to be used where there is an alternative remedy available: it will not be appropriate therefore where the claimant can obtain what he seeks by appealing to the magistrates' court. It will be the only option to reverse a decision of the licensing authority where there is no right of appeal. This is the method to use where the applicant seeks to challenge the licensing statement adopted under section 5 of the 2003 Act; where representations on an application were received late so that the objector has no right of appeal, and where a representation on an application has been ignored because it has unreasonably been ruled frivolous or vexatious.

20.80 The mere fact that an alternative remedy exists does not preclude an application for judicial review. The remedy must be adequate, effective and suitable. In *R (JD Wetherspoon plc) v Guildford Borough Council* [2006] EWHC

---

[77] *Council of Civil Service Unions v Minster for the Civil Service* [1985] AC 374 – although the ambit is now arguably broader given the impact of the Human Rights Act 1998, see Chapter 12.

[78] *Associated Provincial Picture Houses Ltd v Wednesbury Corporation* [1948] 1 KB 223. Also embraced within Wednesbury is the concept that a decision maker must bring all material matters into account and leave all extraneous matters out of account.

[79] http://www.justice.gov.uk/downloads/courts/administrative-court/judicial-review.pdf.

815 (Admin) the claimant appealed a decision of a licensing authority to refuse a variation of its licence, but then abandoned the appeal and started judicial review proceedings instead, contending that the case raised general issues as to the interpretation and application of cumulative impact policies. While the challenge failed, the court went on to consider whether relief should also be refused on the grounds of alternative remedy. It decided that it should not. Beatson J held:

> '91. I turn to the adequacy of the remedy in the magistrates court. I accept the defendant's submission that licensing applications are primarily a matter to be dealt with at local level first by local licensing authorities and then by local Magistrates Courts. The claimant's actions showed that initially it also considered that the appropriate remedy was an appeal to the Magistrates. In the present case, however, the issue is not the primarily factual one of whether in the circumstances of this particular case the claimant in fact rebutted the presumption created by the cumulative impact policy. That issue might well have been best resolved by the statutory appeal. The issue here is whether the defendant was entitled to regard an application to extend the hours when the sale of alcohol is permitted in respect of premises within an area subject to a cumulative impact policy as a "material variation" for the purposes of the policy. In general a deliberate decision to abandon an appeal in order to challenge by judicial review that which should have been challenged by way of an appeal may well constitute an abuse of process. In the present case, however, the issue raised is one on which there is a need for uniformity in the understanding of licensing authorities as to the scope of their cumulative impact policies in the light of the Secretary of State's guidance. In this sense as Sir Richard submitted the issue affects the exercise of licensing functions by licensing authorities throughout the country: R v Huntingdon District Council, ex p Cowan [1984] 1 All ER 58 at 63. Accordingly, had the claimant succeeded on the substantive ground, I would not have denied it a remedy on this ground.'

Procedure

20.81   The procedure for bringing any claim for judicial review is governed by Part 54 of the Civil Procedure Rules. Proceedings are begun by filing a claim form (Form N461). Proceedings must be brought promptly, and in any event within three months of the decision complained of.[80] It is likely that time will run from the date of refusal, or grant of the licence, rather than any earlier decision, by analogy with planning law. There was debate as to whether time should start to run from the date the planning committee

---

[80]   It is important to stress that the three months is an outer time limit. An application may be refused earlier if, for example, in the intervening period money has been spent in reliance upon the decision under challenge.

resolved to grant planning permission, or the date of the issue of the planning permission itself. The House of Lords in *Burkett*[81] held it should be the latter, in order to promote certainty and simplicity. This decision also cast some doubt on the whether the requirement to act 'promptly' was sufficiently certain to comply with the European Convention on Human Rights. This has led to the courts paying greater attention to the requirement to act within three months than the requirement to act promptly. Nevertheless, the requirement remains, and if a would-be challenger delays his claim, he does so at his own peril.

20.82 In *R(on the application of Gavin) v The London Borough of Haringey & Wolseley Centres Limited*[82] the court refused to quash a planning permission that it had declared to be invalid because the challenge had been brought after undue delay (of more than two years). The prejudice to the developer was held to outweigh other considerations, not least of which was that the claimant was not to blame for the delay.

20.83 On the other hand, the court does have power to extend time for bringing judicial review proceedings under section 31(6) of the Senior Courts Act 1981. It did so in *R (British Beer and Pub Association) v Canterbury City Council*[83] so as to extend time for judicially reviewing a licensing policy. However, the same section permits the court to refuse relief where there has been undue delay, a power that was used in that case to decline to quash the policy.

20.84 An applicant must be able to show that he has a sufficient interest in proceedings. This should not usually prove difficult for a person who made representations to the licensing authority, or who is likely to be directly affected by the decision. The claim form should include the name and address of all interested parties; that is, persons directly affected by the decision. This will include the holder of a premises licence, but may also include objectors who made representations in the magistrates' court. Any person served with the claim form should file an acknowledgement of service within 21 days, setting out a summary of the grounds for contesting the claim.

20.85 Following service of the claim form, the defendant has 21 days to file summary grounds of opposition to the claim. The court will then consider whether to grant permission for the case to proceed to a full hearing. This is often first considered on the papers, ie without a hearing. If it is refused on the papers, the applicant may apply to renew his application at a hearing. The test for granting permission is arguability; the question is whether there

---

[81] *R v Hammersmith & Fulham London Borough Council, Ex p (1) Robert Burkett (2) Sonia Burkett* [2002] 1 WLR 1593
[82] [2003] EWHC 2591 (Admin); [2004] JPL 784.
[83] [1005] EWHC 1318 (Admin).

is a point fit for further investigation at a substantive hearing.[84] If permission is granted, the defendant is permitted to file detailed grounds of opposition to the claim and written evidence.

20.86 There is provision for the filing of skeleton arguments: the claimant must file his 21 working days before the substantive hearing, the respondent seven working days later.

20.87 If the claim succeeds, the court has power to quash a decision, remit it to the decision maker and direct it to make a decision in accordance with its judgment.

Compromising judicial reviews

20.88 It can sometimes happen that, during the period before the judicial review of the magistrates' decision comes to be heard, the position on the ground moves on so that the parties are able to reach agreement as to the disposal of the case. How should such agreement be carried into a court order? In *R (Festiva Ltd) v Highbury Corner Magistrates' Court*,[85] Timothy Straker QC held that it was not open to the Administrative Court to substitute its own decision for the one made below. He therefore held that the proper course was for the Administrative Court to quash the decision and remit the matter to the District Judge to reach a decision in accordance with the judgment given by the Administrative Court. That judgment, of course, would incorporate the agreement of the parties.

H THE OMBUDSMAN

20.89 A complaint to the ombudsman is another possibility that may be considered where other remedies are not appropriate. The Local Government Ombudsmen is appointed by the Commission for Local Administration in England to investigate complaints of injustice arising from maladministration by local authorities. The objective of the ombudsmen is to secure, where appropriate, satisfactory redress for complainants and better administration for the authorities. There are three Local Government Ombudsmen in England and they each deal with complaints from different parts of the country. There is a separate ombudsman for Wales.

20.90 The service is free, impartial and private: only the council concerned will be informed of the complaint. The ombudsman will investigate a complaint, and if he finds that maladministration has occurred, will issue a report. He may recommend a payment of compensation.

---

[84]   *R v Secretary of State for the Home Department ex p Begum* [1990] COD 107.
[85]   [2011] EWHC 3043 (Admin).

Maladministration

20.91 Maladministration is not defined, but is accepted to include 'bias, neglect, inattention, delay, incompetence, ineptitude, perversity, turpitude and so on.'[86] Injustice is also not defined. It is left to the ombudsman to decide whether injustice has occurred in any particular case.

Who may complain

20.92 There are three principal restrictions on bringing a complaint.

20.93 The complaint must be brought in time; that is, within 12 months of the date the complainant first became aware of the circumstances giving rise to the complaint.

20.94 The authority must have had an opportunity to deal with the complaint. Following the authority's complaints procedure is the best way of satisfying this requirement. If the complainant is not satisfied with the response, or does not receive a response within a reasonable time, then they may proceed to the ombudsman.

20.95 There must not be an alternative remedy. The ombudsman may not entertain a complaint where the person aggrieved has or had a right of appeal or remedy by way of proceedings in any court of law. However, the ombudsman retains a discretion to investigate in cases where it would not be reasonable to expect the complainant to take this course.

Comparison with judicial review

20.96 Since the ombudsman was created in 1974 the scope and intensity of judicial review has widened to the point that there is considerable overlap with the jurisdiction of the ombudsman. Most if not all matters that are investigated by the ombudsman today could also be the subject of judicial review. What then does this leave for the ombudsman to investigate? This question was addressed by the Court of Appeal in *R v Commissioner for Local Administration ex parte Liverpool City Council.*[87]

Lord Justice Henry said at paragraph 28 that:

'In my judgment this was a clear case for the application of the proviso [i.e. the exercise of the discretion to investigate despite the availability

---

[86] From Wade, *Administrative Law* (Clarendon Press, 4th ed, 1977), adopted by Lord Denning MR in *R v Local Commissioner for Administration for the North and North East area of England, ex parte Bradford Metropolitan City Council* [1979] QB 287 at 311H.

[87] The Times, 3 March 2000, (2000) LGR 571, [2001] 1 All ER 462.

of judicial review]. Serious allegations of maladministration had been made. Such allegations could best be investigated by the resources and powers of the Commissioner, with her powers to compel both dis- closure of documents, and the giving of assistance to the investigation. The Commissioner was in a position to get to the bottom of a prima facie case of maladministration, and the ratepayers would be unlikely to have reached that goal, having regard to the weakness of the coercive fact finding potential of judicial review. As she found, it would be very difficult, if not impossible, for the complainants to obtain the necessary evidence in judicial review proceedings. Additionally, the complainants were a group in modest housing, unlikely to have the means to pursue the remedy. The Commissioner was clearly right to use the proviso to continue her investigation. This case is a good example of a case where the Commissioner's investigation and report can provide the just remedy when judicial review might fail to; and can reach facts which might not emerge under the judicial review process.'

20.97 There will be many cases where judicial review will be the better course: the ombudsman cannot resolve disputes on interpretation of the law; he cannot quash a decision and does not have power to grant interim relief while his investigation is progressing. If a legally binding decision is required, then the ombudsman is not appropriate. If a matter is urgent, then judicial review is the only recourse.

20.98 In other cases, the ombudsman may provide a remedy that would not be possible on judicial review. Where a person is seeking to find out what went wrong and perhaps receive an apology, the ombudsman will be better able to pursue this. Where there has been a failure in an administrative system that requires a detailed investigation, the ombudsman may be better positioned to uncover this than the High Court. Further, and importantly, the ombudsman does not have power to award costs. The threat of a costs order made against them if a claim is not made out can be a great deterrent against judicial review proceedings.

The ombudsman's powers

20.99 The principal strength of the ombudsman lies in his powers to investigate. He may require the attendance of any witness or the production of any document to the same extent as the High Court. Failure to cooperate can be punished as a contempt of court. Often this permits a far more thorough investigation than is possible for an ordinary citizen.

20.100 The investigation is inquisitorial rather than adversarial. The ombudsman may decide the procedure to be adopted for the investigation. He may decide which complaints to investigate, how they are to be investi- gated, and when to stop investigating. There is no appeal from the decision of the ombudsman, but it is susceptible to challenge by judicial review. Successful challenges are rare.

20.101 The ombudsman's report may make recommendations to the council to remedy the situation. The aim is to place the complainant as far as possible in the position he would have been in but for the maladministration. This can include a recommendation of financial compensation. Recommendations are not strictly binding, but they are almost always accepted by local authorities.

20.102 More information including details of how to make a complaint is available on the ombudsman's website: www.lgo.org.uk. The Public Services Ombudsman for Wales can be reached at www.ombudsman-wales.org.uk.

Licensing Act 2003: standards of excellence for licensing authorities

Sober or blotto, this is your motto: keep muddling through.

PG Wodehouse, *A Damsel In Distress*

21

Best practice in licensing hearings

Ale, man, ale's the stuff to drink,
for fellows whom it hurts to think.

A E Housman, *A Shropshire Lad*

A INTRODUCTION

21.01 A key plank in the architecture of this book is that the transfer of licensing jurisdiction from the magistrates' court to local authorities was a good thing. This is chiefly because local authorities already exercise powers in so many spheres which are relevant to licensing such as health and safety, environmental health and planning, so the opportunity to integrate strategies was plain for all to see. A further important reason is that licensing is an administrative function guided by published policy and Guidance, which is within the skill-set, arguably even the DNA, of local authorities. Finally, while magistrates are used to dealing with adversarial contests where the views are polarised, modern licensing is more about finding the sensitive balance which meets the needs of all parties to the hearing.

21.02 Much licensing happens behind closed doors. Where there is no relevant representation, there is no debate and no hearing. So licensing processes are really only publicly on show when there has been a representation and the matter is resolved by the licensing sub-committee in a public forum. The credibility of the licensing authority therefore stands and falls on its handling of these processes. If it reaches poor decisions, or expresses them badly, the decision is liable to be overturned in the magistrates' court, which is costly and demoralising for the licensing authority, and is likely to weaken its stance in future cases, particularly if the argument in court concerns a painstakingly prepared licensing policy. Even if the ultimate decision is defensible, if the process is conducted in such a way as to leave one of the parties feeling that they have not been listened to properly or have not had a fair crack of the whip, again the standing of the authority is damaged.

21.03 This chapter, therefore, sets out to do a little more than reproduce the rules of licensing hearings as expressed in Regulations. It tries to give some good practice pointers for the benefit of licensing authorities, which it is hoped will be of some use to those coming to licensing for the first time and those who want to appraise the quality of their own processes.

B PRINCIPLES OF GOOD PRACTICE

Principle (1): the sub-committee sets the procedure

21.04   Hearings under the Licensing Act 2003 operate under the Licensing Act 2003 (Hearings) Regulations 2005.[1] While there is a fair degree of rigidity inherent in the Regulations, they contain the important concession that subject to the provisions of the Regulations, it is for the licensing authority to determine the procedure to be followed at the hearing.[2] Therefore, the authority is enabled to create rules of procedure. which are perfectly lawful provided that they also incorporate or at least do not contradict the rules set out in the Regulations.

21.05   In creating its procedures, the licensing authority should remember that it is a committee hearing, not a court of law. The room may be full of lawyers trying to argue with each other, but this does not require the authority to adopt court-room procedures. In fact, precisely the contrary is recommended. The most important thing is that whatever procedure it adopts should be fair and offer an equal opportunity to all parties to present their case.

Principle (2): remember the point of the procedure

21.06   The fundamental purpose of the procedure is to enable those with a right to appear to advance their own point of view and to test the case of other parties, in order to assist the sub-committee to gather the relevant evidence and understand the relevant issues.

21.07   If procedural issues arise, that basic purpose should be kept in mind. It is extremely unlikely that a sub-committee would ever be criticised for admitting something which was relevant, but it might well be criticised for refusing to admit it.

21.08   Most people attending licensing hearings are not lawyers and will be intimidated by excessive formality. Therefore, within the boundaries of fairness, needless formality should be eschewed. Some formality is necessary. Parties should not interrupt each other. They should not conduct side

---

[1]   SI 2005/44.
[2]   Regulation 21.

conversations. They should in general address the person chairing the meeting. But there is a difference between the kind of formality which helps a meeting proceed in an orderly manner and the kind of pomp and circumstance that places barriers between parties, particularly lay parties, and sub-committees.

Principle (3): establish the ground rules

21.09 It is extremely important to set out the ground rule for the meeting at the beginning. This avoids later conflict, facilitates the smooth running of the hearing and informs parties what to expect. If during the hearing a party is pulled up for something they have done, this may appear arbitrary and unfair to them, but if the chair person has made the ground rule plain right at the outset, then they are more likely to understand and accept the intervention.

21.10 So, for example, the ground rules might include the order of presentation and closing submissions, the way the sub-committee proposes to deal with conditions proposed by the parties and the maximum time for presentation.

21.11 The chair person should also indicate that members have read the papers and understand the issues, and therefore that points will not require repetition. Where there are multiple parties, they may be encouraged to appoint a spokesperson to avoid repetition, although this will not prevent those who have made representations speaking during the meeting.

21.12 It need hardly be said that it is of cardinal importance that members have actually read the papers. This makes for shorter meetings and more focussed debate. It also builds the confidence of participants in the process if they can see that their point has already been ingested.

Principle (4): the meeting proceeds as a discussion

21.13 The Regulations provide that the hearing shall take the form of a discussion.[3] The difference between a discussion and a trial is that in a discussion parties cannot expect to hold the floor throughout – rather there will be a dialogue with the chair person keeping order.

21.14 Consistent with that, the Regulations control the ability for parties to question or cross examine each other. Questions occur with the permission of the sub-committee.[4] Cross-examination, on the other hand, is disallowed unless the sub-committee considers that this is required for it to consider the

---

[3]   Licensing Act 2003 (Hearings) Regulations 2005, reg 23.
[4]   Licensing Act 2003 (Hearings) Regulations 2005, reg 16.

representations, application or notice as the case may require.[5] What is the difference? A question is designed to inquire about something or elicit an answer. Cross-examination is usually designed to discredit what a witness is saying, secure a concession or make a point. While all cross-examination consists of questions, not all questions are cross-examination.

21.15 The distinction is not always easy to draw in practice. But if something is asked in the spirit of inquiry it is a question. If the question starts: 'Are you seriously asking the sub-committee to believe' then it is cross-examination. Similarly, pursuing a witness on a point by repeat questioning would normally be treated as cross-examination.

21.16 It is not easy to reconcile the rule that the hearing proceeds as a discussion with the rule that the authority must allow the parties an equal maximum time to exercise their rights provided for in regulation 16. Those rights are to address the authority, question other parties (with permission) and give further information where this has been requested by an authority in the notice of hearing. How should one compute the time when a party is engaged in discussion? If a witness refuses to answer a question which wastes time, is that time counted against him or against the questioner? If cross-examination is permitted, does this stand outside the rule altogether or is it counted against the questioner? In practice, the only way of making sense of the rule is to allow the parties the same time for an initial address and a closing address, but to count everything in between as the sub-committee's investigation of the case.

Principle (5): the sub-committee may accept hearsay evidence

21.17 Hearsay evidence is evidence of something that the witness neither saw nor heard, but merely heard or read about.

21.18 A witness may say that they saw the club allowing people in after the terminal hour. That is direct evidence. If they say that they did not see it but their friend did, that is hearsay evidence. If they say that their friend wrote to them about what they saw and produce the friend's letter then that is still hearsay evidence. If they say that their friend wrote to them about what their neighbour saw, that is double hearsay. All of this is admissible, although the weight which it receives may vary given that the sub-committee is not hearing about the event directly from the mouth of the person who witnessed it and that person is not available to be questioned. On the other hand, it may still attract very great weight, particularly if it is not contested or is corroborated by other evidence in the case.

21.19 For this reason, the sub-committee is entitled to accept a petition, which amounts to the hearsay written views of the signatories, subject to the

---

[5]   Licensing Act 2003 (Hearings) Regulations 2005, reg 23.

proviso that only limited weight can be attached to it because the individual views will not have been tested before it.

Principle (6): the committee may take into account anything which is relevant and helpful to them

21.20 In Chapter 5 of this book, it was demonstrated that licensing authorities are entitled to use their common sense to make inferences about potential harm and what means are appropriate to avoid it. Indeed, the very definition of a relevant representation is that it is about the likely effect of the premises licence on the promotion of the licensing objectives.[6] The authority does not need to wait for harm to occur before being satisfied that there is a risk of occurrence. If a large nightclub proposes to open until 5 am in the middle of a residential area, those are all the primary facts (or 'evidence') an authority needs in order to draw the inference that there is a risk of public nuisance. Whether that leads to a refusal, the imposition of further conditions or the acceptance of those that are offered in the operating schedule is a matter of what is proportionate in the individual circumstances. The point is that the authority is entitled to use its wisdom, judgment and common sense to draw the inference that, unless proper steps are taken to limit the noise of departing customers, then people may well be woken up.

21.21 In exercising its judgment, the sub-committee may draw upon any material before it, which it finds to be useful and relevant. That does not need to be 'evidence' in the strict sense that courts would understand that term. For the same reason, it may take account of its local knowledge, although it must always be willing to test that knowledge against the other evidence presented to it in the case.

Principle (7): late objections are inadmissible

21.22 The law precludes accepting representations from those whose representations were not made in time.[7] However, nothing precludes a party whose representations were made in time from calling the late objector as one of their witnesses.

Principle (8): the sub-committee should ensure fair treatment of witnesses

21.23 The proceedings should be a discussion, not an ordeal. A sub-committee which permits witnesses to be interrupted or berated risks not

---

[6] Licensing Act 2003, s 18(6)(a).
[7] *R (Albert Court Residents Association) v Westminster City Council* [2010] EWHC 393 (Admin).

hearing what a witness wants to say and therefore risks getting to an unjust result. It also risks the witness leaving the chamber feeling demeaned and frustrated, and over time will leave communities feeling that it is not worth participating in the system at all. It is essential that none of this is allowed to happen, and that a firm line is taken with any advocate or party who seeks to silence the voice of the other.

21.24 The corollary of that is that it is acceptable to require the witness to answer the actual question being put and to prevent them from straying from the point. If not, this creates unfairness to the other side.

Principle (9): the sub-committee should ensure a level playing field

21.25 In court, this is not difficult to achieve. Each party presents its case. Each party's witnesses are cross-examined by the other. Each party makes closing submissions. In the hurly-burly of a discussion this is potentially more difficult to achieve.

21.26 However, there are a number of things which the sub-committee may do to follow this principle. Having set maximum times for the presentation of the case by each party, it can enforce them rigorously. It can ensure that each party gets a proper opportunity to reply to any submission made by the opposite party. It can make sure that if it questions a witness, then other parties are entitled to ask any questions arising. If it seeks help on a given point such as the enforceability of a condition, it can go round the room and make sure that each party has the opportunity to make submissions about it. With an experienced sub-committee, this will happen by instinct. In other cases, it is the role of the legal adviser to make sure that the principle of equal treatment is observed.

Principle (10): the sub-committee may oil the wheels

21.27 Unlike a jury, which is obliged to sit passively and absorb whatever is presented to it, the sub-committee may take a much more forensic, incisive and directed approach to the proceedings. It can remind a witness that it has read the papers and does not require representations to be read out to it. It can explain that it has heard and understood the point and ask whether there is anything to add to the point. It can tell a witness that another witness has already made a particular point, and merely invite additions to that point. It can also ask the parties whether particular facts are really in contest and whether they may be taken as read. It can deal with an in principle objection to grant by asking whether a condition would not deal with the issue and if so what condition the parties might be prepared to accept. In other words, the sub-committee may drive the proceedings so as to facilitate a just result with the minimum of repetitious or pointless debate.

Principle (11): the sub-committee may ask questions

21.28 The regulations specifically state that the sub-committee may ask questions of any party or any other person appearing at the hearing.[8] In *R (Murco Petroleum Limited) v Bristol City Council*[9] it was held that it may therefore demand answers. If an answer is not forthcoming, the sub-committee may adjourn a hearing to a specified date under regulation 13(1)(a) in order for the answer to be given. It is not suggested that this would be a frequent occurrence. In some cases a refusal to answer a question may simply weaken a party's case. In others, a party may hope for an adjournment if they are seeking to delay the grant of a licence or a review decision. But the power exists if the sub-committee wishes to get to the bottom of a matter and does not have the information it needs to make a fully-informed decision.

Principle (12): new information or documents are not admissible without the consent of all parties

21.29 Regulation 18 is drafted quite rigidly. It says that the authority may take into account documentary or other information produced by a party in support of their application, representations or notice either before the hearing or, with the consent of all parties, at the hearing. Put the other way on, it means that a party may not produce documentary or other information at the hearing without the consent of all parties, which in frankness may well not be forthcoming.

21.30 How may this rule be operated in practice to ensure that parties are not (a) prevented from presenting their cases or, on the other hand, (b) taken by surprise?

21.31 Regulation 6 requires the authority to send out a notice of hearing. The contents of the notice of hearing are provided for in regulation 7. The notice of hearing must (among other things) set out the procedure to be followed at the hearing and state any points on which the authority considers that it will want clarification at the hearing from a party. This rule is egregiously underused by authorities, which send out pro forma notices which do little to engage with the issues in the case, and which therefore fail to take the opportunity to bring the case to a state of preparation to help the sub-committee to reach a just decision.

21.32 As a matter of good practice, the licensing officer should consider the application and representations, and ascertain where the issues lie. He should then draft a notice to set out what kind of information and material the sub-committee is likely to need in order to reach a decision. For example, he

---

8   Regulation 17.
9   [2010] EWHC 1992 (Admin).

may consider that the sub-committee needs photographs of the premises, or a plan of the area, or details of the construction of the premises, or a copy of the risk assessment, or the premises' dispersal policies. Or he might think that it is not clear whether a party would be prepared to withdraw their objection in principle if suitable and sufficient conditions were attached to the licence, and if so what conditions might be necessary. All of this, and more, may be required in the notice of hearing.

21.33 The officer may also set out in the notice by which date such information should be provided, in order for it to be included in the sub-committee's agenda papers and referred to in the officer's report.

21.34 If these principles are observed, then the chances of a party being debarred from producing information or being taken by surprise by last minute material produced by the opposition are correspondingly reduced, and the task of the sub-committee will be considerably lightened.

Principle (13): the sub-committee should be proactive with conditions

21.35 Frequently, applicants will not try to resolve outstanding issues by offering conditions because conditions cost money. Objectors may refrain from proposing conditions either because they lack the expertise or because they think that talking about conditions will weaken their in-principle objection to the grant. The sub-committee may then refuse the licence, when the licence could feasibly have been granted, creating investment, jobs and leisure diversity, if only effective conditions had been considered and attached. The matter then goes to appeal at great expense to the public and private purse, and is then resolved – whether by the parties or by the court – by attaching conditions which should have been considered at a far earlier stage.

21.36 It is certainly suggested that officers – whether they are advising the sub-committee or appearing as responsible authorities – should bring forth conditions. This might be done on one of three bases. Either the officers might say that the licence ought to be refused, but if the sub-committee is minded to grant then the following conditions should be considered. Or the officers might say that the sub-committee will need to determine some primary matters, such as whether there is a danger to public safety, and if it considers there is then it may wish to go on and consider the following conditions. Or the officers may simply say that the licence ought to be granted on the basis of particular conditions.

21.37 Whether or not officers perform that essential professional role, the sub-committee should consider conditions, because it can never be justified to refuse a licence or even revoke a licence before the less draconian step of attaching conditions has been properly considered.

21.38   In planning appeals, the planning inspector asks for, and invariably gets, a list of draft conditions for use if he decides to grant permission. He makes it clear that the list is without prejudice, and does not imply that he has made his mind up or that the parties are somehow conceding their case. This list is then subject to informal discussion in the course of the inquiry, and parties are enabled to say whether their issue is over the principle of the condition or the wording or both. There is no reason why a similar practice cannot be followed in the sub-committee hearing, provided that it is made clear that this is to save time and narrow the issues, and that there has been no pre-judgment of the outcome.

21.39   So, to take a basic example, a pub wants to have late night entertainment. The neighbour objects. The sub-committee invites the parties to sit down and discuss what conditions they may be prepared to accept and to come forth with a list. The sub-committee goes through the list. The first item is a self-closing device on the exit door, which the pub is happy to accept. The neighbour Mr Smith, while reminding the sub-committee that he does not want late night entertainment at all, agrees that if the licence is granted then the self-closing device is a good idea and should be incorporated as a condition.

21.40   The second condition is a sound limiter. Mr Smith thinks this a good idea. The pub objects to the principle of the device, because it says that the self-closing device is sufficient protection, there never having been a complaint of noise outbreak before, so that the cost of the sound limiter is disproportionate. The sub-committee now has the wording of the condition and simply needs to make a decision whether the requirement is disproportionate.

21.41   The third condition is that excessive noise shall not be generated outside the premises. Mr Smith agrees this, but the pub says while it sympathises with the objective, the wording is too vague to be enforceable. The sub-committee can then work with its legal adviser on a better form of wording.

21.42   If the sub-committee originates the thinking on a particular condition it should not announce the condition for the first time in its decision. It will be subject to the complaint on appeal that it never gave the parties an opportunity to comment upon it. Rather, it should inform the parties that it is minded to impose a particular condition and hear their representations about it before reaching its conclusion.

21.43   Finally, before refusing (or indeed revoking) a licence, the sub-committee should always consider whether its concerns may be overcome by the addition of conditions. To deprive a person of their business (or prospective business) is by definition disproportionate if conditions would meet the exigencies of the case.

Principle (14): the sub-committee should not express its views about the merits before giving its decision

21.44   It is inevitable that during the hearing, or even before the hearing, the councillors will begin to form some preliminary views about the case. They are only human. But if they make up their mind conclusively, or appear to have done so, they risk the decision being challenged on the grounds of predetermination or apparent bias. Therefore the sub-committee should take conspicuous care not to fall into this trap.

21.45   It is perfectly acceptable for the sub-committee to put questions which ask the applicant to explain their case or how they reached a particular conclusion. It is not acceptable for a sub-committee to express incredulity or hostility towards the case being advanced. It is not acceptable both because it risks legal challenge and/or censure on appeal and also because it is contrary to the exercise of good-spirited inquiry and debate which should characterise these hearings.

21.46   Members who find a case to be without the remotest merit will have all the opportunity they need to say so in their written decision. Until then, their job is to listen, control the debate and ask relevant questions.

21.47   For much the same reason, it is unacceptable for councillors who are going to sit on the sub-committee to talk to the press about the case before the hearing. In order to avoid challenge or loss of confidence in the impartiality of the authority, they should observe the same stricture after the hearing.

Principle (15): the sub-committee should rely on its legal adviser as to matters of law

21.48   The legal adviser has a number of jobs at a hearing:

- Advising the sub-committee as to interpretation of the Licensing Act 2003.
- Ensuring compliance with the procedural rules in the Regulations.
- Advising the sub-committee as to other statutory provisions creating legal duties, such as section 17 of the Crime and Disorder Act 1998 (duty on the authority to do all it reasonably can to prevent crime and disorder) and the Human Rights Act 1998.
- Advising on the admissibility of evidence.
- Assisting with the drafting of the reasons for the decision, including any conditions. Of course, the reasons must be the sub-committee's; the role of the adviser is only to assist with drafting.

21.49 Where advice is sought by the sub-committee in closed session, the advice given should be repeated in open session so that the parties have the opportunity, if they wish, to make submissions upon it.

21.50 While it is acceptable for the legal adviser to retire with the sub-committee, it is inadvisable for a licensing officer to retire with the sub-committee, lest an appearance of bias be given.

Principle (16): the sub-committee should draft thorough reasons for its decision

21.51 It is true but trite to point out that the law requires the provision of reasons.[10] The rationale for thorough reasons is three-fold. First, parties have a right to know why they have won or lost. Second, because parties will be less inclined to appeal if the reasons for the decision are rational and thorough. Third, the weight the decision receives on appeal will be governed in part by the quality of the reasons. In short, properly drafted reasons should be given because the authority cannot afford not to.

21.52 For that reason, while there is always a temptation to give decisions shortly after the conclusion of the hearing, this temptation should be resisted. Reasons should be given only when the authority is good and ready to give them.[11] A half-way house is often adopted – the decision is announced with reasons to follow. However, this is not considered best practice – it can be taken to imply that the sub-committee has rushed to judgment, and may even preclude a slightly more nuanced decision or set of conditions which would arise after lengthier debate.

21.53 What does a good set of reasons look like?

- It should refer to every relevant representation.
- It should state what evidence and submissions have been accepted and rejected, and why.
- It should refer to the parts of policy and Guidance which have been taken into account.
- When a decision is made in accordance with policy or Guidance, it should explain that consideration has been given to whether there should be a departure, and if not why not.
- If a decision is made to depart from the policy or Guidance, proper reasons should be given for the departure.
- If a decision is taken to attach conditions, it should be explained why each and every condition is appropriate and proportionate.

[10] See eg Licensing Act 2003, s 23.
[11] In very limited circumstances, set out in Regulation 26, the authority must make its determination at the conclusion of the hearing.

- If a draconian decision is taken, eg revocation or refusal, the sub-committee should explain why that decision is proportionate and why lesser steps do not suffice.
- It should explain what parallel requirements, such as those arising under the Provision of Services Regulations 2009 or the Human Rights Act 1998, have been taken into account.

C CONCLUSION

21.54 There is no doubt that chairing, and even sitting on, a sub-committee is a skill and not a talent. Maintaining the correct balance of friendliness and authority, listening and directing, requires good people skills. It is a somewhat unfortunate fact that the Licensing Act 2003 did not provide for qualifications for members of licensing sub-committees, and national funding was not made available for training. Nevertheless, the best authorities do train their members, and the standard of decision-making, not to mention its defensibility, can only improve as a result.

22

Licensing officers

The bar of the Six Jolly Fellowship Porters was a bar to soften the human breast. The available space in it was not much larger than a hackney-coach; but no one could have wished the bar bigger, that space was so girt in by corpulent little casks, and by cordial-bottles radiant with fictitious grapes in bunches, and by lemons in nets, and by biscuits in baskets, and by the polite beer-pulls that made low bows when customers were served with beer, and by the cheese in a snug corner, and by the landlady's own small table in a snugger corner near the fire, with the cloth everlastingly laid.

Charles Dickens, *Our Mutual Friend*

A INTRODUCTION

22.01 The licensing authority has many roles. It must devise strategies for the promotion of a sustainable leisure economy. It must ensure liaison with other regulatory departments, the industry and the public so that the efforts of all sectors are properly integrated. It must publish an enlightened licensing policy which sets the pattern for licensing in the area and the standards which are expected of local businesses. It must run a licensing department with administrative competence and budgetary prudence. It must be prepared to ensure that there is compliance with standards and to take enforcement action where necessary, as well as participating as appropriate in enforcement action taken by others. It must prepare for and conduct hearings so as to arrive at defensible and proportionate decisions. And it must be prepared to defend its decisions on appeal and, not least, put itself in a position to maximise its prospects of recovering the costs of the exercise.

22.02 For nearly all of these functions, it is the licensing officers who are responsible for the proper operation of the system. It was long the lament that licensing was the Cinderella function in local government; necessary, but undervalued and disregarded. Now that is not so. Licensing is centre-stage in our towns and cities, both because of the political dimension that alcohol has assumed in our society and because it is upon the success of its work that the civilised development of our leisure environments depends. Whether the next generation inherits a sustainable, diverse, enjoyable and safe town centre or a drab, threatening monoculture is the true litmus test of the man or woman at the heart of the system – the licensing officer. As such, the role offers great scope for professionalism, innovation and creative thinking. It is a career choice, and over the next generation the job of licensing officer can be expected to continue to develop into a key local government position.

22.03   In this short chapter, the opportunity is taken to set down some thoughts as to the attributes of the role, both for those who occupy it or hope to do so, and for those looking in so as to get a clearer understanding of what the job entails.

B   EDUCATION

22.04   Sadly, there are no qualifications currently being offered for licensing officers, although there have been vocational qualifications offered in the past at Birmingham (latterly Warwick) University and also Westminster University.

However, the opportunities for education are far greater now than a decade ago.

22.05   Perhaps the most important source of professional development is the Institute of Licensing. Membership buys one a regular Journal of Licensing, frequent bulletins with legal developments and news stories, the opportunity for professional learning and networking at regional events, and an annual national training event, which is addressed by leading speakers from the public and private sector. The Institute is a broad church, and has done much to promote mutual understanding from the different stakeholders involved in the field. A serious practitioner cannot afford not to be a member.

22.06   There are a number of web-sources which are valuable stores of information on licensing. Pre-eminent is the Local Government Lawyer web-site,[1] which carries a licensing section containing bulletins and articles. There is also a very valuable forum named Licensing Guru[2] which contains discussions on contentious points and is a good way of finding out the opposing views on various licensing topics. The trade journal the Public

---

[1]   www.localgovernmentlawyer.co.uk.
[2]   www.licensingguru.co.uk.

Morning Advertiser[3] is a useful window on the industry perspective, containing journalism on matters of business, law and regulation. Finally, the licensing solicitors Poppleston Allen[4] produce an electronic publication Licensed Trade News which, being written from the perspective of lawyers who are at the sharp end of legal developments, is worth reading.

22.07 There are also many licensing books, of which the main ones are *Paterson's Licensing Acts*, which contains annotated licensing statutes, and Colin Manchester's *Alcohol and Entertainment Licensing Law*, which amounts to a detailed legal reference work.

22.08 Finally, of course, national Guidance itself is a highly useful guide to licensing legislation and the authority's duties under it.

22.09 It is strongly recommended that officers engage in the same discipline of continuing professional development as is now required by most professions. The above sources are all useful means of gaining rapid expertise in the field.

C STRATEGY AND POLICY

22.10 Licensing officers ought to work with councillors to achieve a ten year vision for their leisure economies in their towns and cities, to be developed in tandem with their planning and regeneration colleagues, and to be articulated through the local development framework and the licensing policy. This is unlikely to be a single, once for all, exercise, but rather an ongoing process of review and development, to ensure that the area is well-placed to attract inward investment of the right sort.

22.11 Officers ought also to work with councillors on the development of operational standards to be expressed in licensing policy. They should bring to the party knowledge of what standards are being operated by the best businesses locally and nationally, and what the opportunities are for improvement, eg standards for CCTV, door staff, search and identification methods, glass substitutes, responsible alcohol service, dispersal policies and so forth. Officers should regard it as their job to be on top of such developments so that they can inform members and recommend inclusion in licensing policy.

22.12 They ought to be liaising with police and other regulatory colleagues to ascertain whether policies ought to contain restraint elements, eg regarding cumulative impact, zoning or terminal hours. They ought also to be considering whether there is an argument for an early morning restriction order or a late night levy. Of course, they should be finding methods of gauging the success of past policies to see whether it is time to take a more or

3   www.morningadvertiser.co.uk.
4   www.popall.co.uk.

less liberal, more or less interventionist approach, eg investigating whether alcohol-related crime or people's feelings of safety in the town centre at night are waxing or waning. Otherwise, they will be allowing their authority to make policy in the dark. No successful business or charity operates without key performance indicators. Why should a licensing department be different?

22.13 In terms of consultation on policy and strategy, officers should judge the success of their past consultation exercises and help to devise more effective means of consultation. Are they getting to hard to reach groups? What is the ethnic, gender and age profile of respondents? Are all parts of the district responding or just the wealthier suburbs? What are the most effective means of reaching an audience? Web or telephone surveys? Public meetings? Street surveys? Licensing is a democratic exercise, and if large quantities of money are spent printing consultation forms which nobody completes, there will be an economic and democratic deficit. In contrast, a consultation which yields high degrees of response also yields ownership of the town centre by the local population.

D OPERATING THE SYSTEM

22.14 In licensing, issues cost money. Every time there is a representation, there is likely to be a hearing which involves a large administrative effort. Similarly, where reviews are brought, licensing, legal and democratic services staff have to work together to bring the matter to hearings in a short space of time.

It is therefore in the interests of an efficiently run department to ensure that there are as few issues as possible.

22.15 Licensing involves four questions: what, when, where and how? A policy which directs investors to the right places, encourages the right sort of investment, operating to hours likely to be found acceptable, and to standards which represent best practice locally, will reduce the likelihood of future objections, reviews and appeals. Applications are more likely to conform to the policy and courts are more likely to uphold decisions which follow the policy. Operators will be less likely to push at the boundary, recognising the level playing field which a well-crafted policy presents, and so the system will largely come to run itself.

22.16 The fact that the licensing authority is a responsible authority in its own right colours the relationship between licensing officers and premises managers. Previously, the primary regulatory relationship for the pub manager was with the police. There is no reason why this should still be so. The licensing officer holds the balance between the premises and all the stakeholders, whether these be neighbours or other responsible authorities. An officer may use his time and expertise to nudge premises into compliance through informal conversations. Sometimes more formal action will be necessary, but even this may be headed off by a clear warning letter, an agreed action plan or an agreement to apply for a minor variation to tweak a management condition. Thus on a day to day basis the officer can deal equitably with licensed premises so as to promote a culture of compliance. Fairness, authority and good communication skills are therefore key attributes of the job in the modern era.

22.17 Inevitably, however, there are cases which reach the sub-committee. Two questions arise. First, when should officers join in licence applications and reviews? Second, whether they do or don't, what is the role of the licensing officer at a licensing hearing?

22.18 When should officers join in licence applications and reviews? It is considered that there are three main situations. First, licensing officers are the main guardians of licensing policy. If an application is made contrary to a policy, it is pre-eminently the role of the licensing officer to make representations upon it so as to bring the matter to the attention of the licensing sub-committee. Second, licensing officers will be undertaking compliance visits to premises: how often such visits occur will turn on a priority-based risk assessment of the premises concerned. Where issues are discerned which are either serious or have not yielded to prompting, the licensing officers themselves should bring reviews so that the sub-committee can decide what remedial steps may be necessary. Third, where it is plain that there will be a battle over hours and other conditions, licensing officers may elect to join in the proceedings so as to be able to enter the debate about conditions and give their neutral, expert views to the sub-committee.

22.19 Of course, if officers do join in the process, they will need to ensure that there is proper separation between their role and the role of any licensing officer preparing the report or advising the sub-committee. Once the officer has joined as a party, he is no different to any other party and so must not seek or obtain any preferential access to the decision-making machinery of the authority.[5]

22.20 There is frequently debate as to the role of the licensing officer in writing the report and advising the sub-committee, that is to say when the licensing authority has not joined the proceedings as a responsible authority. One strand of thinking is that that officer must maintain a strictly neutral line and that if he deviates by an inch towards advice which supports or opposes the application, then the whole process is tainted by bias. If that were right then practically every single planning decision made by committee in the United Kingdom would have been unlawful, for in planning the committee is heavily dependent on the expert advice of its planning officers both as to the

---

[5]   See further Guidance paragraphs 9.17–9.19.

principle of the grant and the detailed conditions. The view of the Institute of Licensing is set out below and is advocated as a proper statement of the position:

'Role of the licensing officer in relation to contested hearings

The licensing officer is a professional servant of the licensing authority. S/he brings to the appraisal of the issues his/her own professional expertise and experience, including expertise relating to national guidance, local policy and good practice, together with a familiarity with the proposal, the site and its locational context. The officer is neither an interested party nor a responsible authority in his/her own right, and nor does s/he make relevant representations, but is there to assist the licensing sub-committee to come to a fair, balanced and well-informed decision based on the merits of the application, having regard both to national guidance and local policy.

The Licensing Act 2003 (Hearings) Regulations 2005 (SI 2004/44) make it clear that, subject to the provisions of the Regulations themselves, it is for the licensing authority to determine its own procedure.

The Institute of Licensing recommends that in all contested cases, the licensing officer should produce a report to the licensing sub-committee which should be available at the council offices at least three clear working days before the hearing. This will facilitate an efficient and fair hearing, by ensuring that the same basic material is available to all parties. The sub-committee should be invited to read the report before the hearing, so that the relevant issues are understood by all parties and the sub-committee before the hearing starts.

While the format of the report is a presentational matter for the licensing officer, a suggested format is as follows:

Section 1: The application.

In this section, the application may be summarized. The application form itself should be appended.

Section 2: The representations.

In this section, the relevant representations should be summarized. The representations themselves should be appended, except when they are voluminous, in which case they may be lodged for perusal beforehand in the Members' room.

Section 3: Licensing Policy.

In this section, relevant parts of the statement of licensing policy should be summarized, It may be helpful to append the relevant parts of the policy, or to have copies to hand for perusal during the hearing.

Section 4: Secretary of State's Guidance

In this section, relevant parts of the Secretary of State's Guidance should be summarized. It may be helpful to append the relevant parts of the Guidance, including any potentially relevant model conditions. Alternatively, copies should be available at the hearing.

Section 5: Observations/recommendations.

The officer should state the possible outcomes of the application provided for by the Licensing Act 2003. For example, where the hearing concerns a new premises licence, the officer should state that the authority may take such of the steps mentioned in subsection (4) (if any) as it considers necessary for the promotion of the licensing objectives. Those steps should be specified. The report should also state that if none of the steps is necessary the application should be granted.

The officer should advise the authority that findings on any issues of fact should be on the balance of probability.

The officer may also advise the authority that in arriving at its decision it must have regard to relevant provisions of national guidance and the licensing policy statement and that reasons should be given for any departure.

The officer should also advise that the decision should be based on the individual merits of the application.

The officer is entitled to make a recommendation to the licensing sub-committee. In doing so, the officer should bear in mind that the sub-committee will be hearing evidence or submissions on disputed issues of fact. Therefore the officer should make it clear that any recommendation is contingent upon the factual findings made. Therefore, for example, the officer may advise that if the sub-committee finds that a public nuisance is likely, its options would include attaching conditions to prevent the nuisance or, where conditions would not be an adequate response, refusing the licence, but that if no nuisance is likely the licence should be granted.

In advising upon conditions, the officer should bring their own experience and professional knowledge regarding good practice to the attention of the licensing sub-committee. The sub-committee is entitled to seek the officer's advice during the hearing. Any advice must be given in open session, and the parties shall be entitled to make submissions about such advice.'

22.21 When there is an appeal against a licensing decision, licensing officers sometimes take the view that they ought not to participate in the appeal other than to present the report which they presented to the sub-committee, produce the minutes and the decision and prove that the decision was duly taken. This is seriously misguided. When an appeal is made, the licensing authority is the defendant. It is a party to the appeal. It must marshal its resources to ensure that it is in a position to defend it. If it calls environmental health officers and residents, it will be open to the criticism that not a single witness from the authority itself saw fit to give substantive evidence.

22.22   On the other hand, an officer who can say that they have ten years experience of supervising the management of the town centre and making policies for the safety of the public, and that in their judgment the sub-committee, which applied the statutory policy, got the balance precisely right is likely to find their opinion accorded very great weight by the magistrates' court. If their participation helps to uphold the decision made by their members, they will have performed an important public function, assisted in the recovery of costs which is crucial, particularly in times of budgetary restraint, and augmented the authority's credibility with its local court, which will assist in the next case. Furthermore, the experience of authorities which consistently win appeals is that there are fewer appeals. Operators begin to see that it is not worth the candle, and so success breeds peace. Therefore, the business of preparation of a thorough, helpful, well-ordered witness statement and its presentation in court is a key aspect of the job.

E VOLUNTARY SCHEMES

22.23   Regulation is one way of making safer venues. Another is through good partnership working. Purple Flag, Business Improvement Districts, Best Bar None, Pubwatch and Community Alcohol Partnerships, to name but five dealt with elsewhere in this book, are all excellent schemes for making safe, attractive, diverse and accessible leisure economies, welcoming in a wider mix of customers, improving natural guardianship, creating safer environments and reducing alcohol-related harms.

22.24   In each case, licensing officers can play a key role in providing stimulus to make these schemes happen and then to keep them on the road after the initial rush of enthusiasm. The best authorities have realised that it not a question of whether they can afford to be involved but whether they can afford not to. If the ultimate aim is to make the system run itself, anything which can bring operators voluntarily to the table to take responsibility for the quality of their operating environment merits support. In that officers sit at the heart of the system, with good communications with all statutory and non-statutory stakeholders, and given also that they have enforcement powers if harms are not remedied, they are ideally placed to sound the bugle call to voluntary action.

22.25   Furthermore, partnerships are good news stories which serve to counter-balance the often negative press about our town and city centres. If a wider mix of people can be induced to visit our centres at night, a virtuous circle of natural guardianship, reduced problems and greater investment can arise.

22.26 In short, management of the night time economy involves many actions, of which regulatory action is but one component, which acts as a safety valve when other measures have failed. If a licensing officer can play his part in reducing the need for regulatory proceedings, he will have performed a valuable role in promoting sustainable partnerships, improving the quality of venues and mix of visitors, and saving public sector funds. From a professional point of view, he will derive the satisfaction which comes from playing a creative role in improving the area, for the benefit of local people.

F CONCLUSION

22.27 This chapter has set out to demonstrate that the days when the officer's role was to manually churn out licences have gone. Performed well, the officer can drive the development of our town and city centres as places of delight, attractive and safe for all, occupied by businesses confident that if they work to promote the licensing objectives then so will their competitors, collectively producing a centre used by a wide geographic and demographic catchment, to their mutual benefit. Given that we are here dealing with our hard-earned leisure time and the quality of the environment in which we spend it, the role of licensing officer is one of the most exacting, creative and attractive in local government.

23

Councillors

Then our age was in its prime,
Free from rage, and free from crime,
A very merry, dancing, drinking,
Laughing, quaffing, and unthinking time.

John Dryden, *The Secular Masque*

A INTRODUCTION

23.01 Part of the purpose of transferring licensing functions from magistrates' courts to licensing authorities was to ensure that local licensing was conducted by a body which is accountable to the electorate. By this, of course, one means elected councillors.

23.02 Councillors could elect to play precious little attention to the licensed economy. They could take their place on the licensing committee and make decisions when contentious applications come before them, and they could pass licensing policy on the nod when it is placed before the full council.

23.03 Such an approach would be complacent and misguided. This is because councillors have at their fingertips all the tools they need to leave behind a better town centre than the one they found when they were elected. They have the powers and, just as importantly, the political clout to bring parties together to get the job done.

23.04 Very occasionally councillors talk about 'my residents' as though that is where their duty lies. But even this is seriously miscued. Residents have the need to sleep at night and feel safe when using the streets. That need would be met by shutting the town centre down at night. But they also have needs as users of the night time economy, and licensing is fundamentally about creating a pattern and disposition of business at night to satisfy both needs.

In so far as the expression 'my residents' (who vote) is used to contradistin-guish 'businesses' (who don't), that reflects a lack of profundity of thought. Business owners vote. So do all the people to whom they give employment and who use their earnings to pay for local goods and services. So do their customers who prefer to visit their local high street rather than travel further afield for their entertainment.

23.05   Indeed, a large part of our economy is bound up with the night time economy. A report for Business in Sport and Leisure shows that the UK leisure industry employs 2.6 million people, or 9% of the total UK work-force, and 730,000 16–25 year olds, or 21% of jobs for that age group (in both cases more than manufacturing or financial services); generates over £200 billion of revenue; and is a major generator of small and medium enterprises, with 66% of all leisure industry businesses falling into that category.

23.06   To see leisure businesses, therefore, as one might view an incoming virus is to ignore the crucial social and economic role they perform. Undoubtedly, there are badly run businesses, and they need to be firmly regulated to bring them into regulatory compliance or, as a last resort, to euthanase them. But this is to judge the health of the nation solely in terms of the number of surgical operations. The wider job is to promote a vibrant leisure economy and to make our town and city centres places of delight for all, regardless of the depth of their pocket, their age, gender, race or ethnicity, and whatever their proclivities. Here, councillors come in.

B POLICIES

23.07   Councillors sitting on a licensing committee can work with their officers to devise a long term strategy for their town centres, which balances the needs of investment, employment and public protection. Much of this work will be done in tandem with other arms of the council such as planning, regeneration, culture and tourism. It is at this point that the frequent exhortation in national Guidance to 'integration' plays through into mean-ingful policies.

23.08   Councillors may check that, as their licensing policy develops, proper consideration has been given to the main facets of successful policies, viz:

- A strategic vision for the leisure economy locally.
- Management standards.
- Restraint policies, such as cumulative impact, terminal hours and zoning.
- Enforcement policies.

23.09   Councillors, whether or not they are on the licensing committee, can and should play a full role in the policy formulation process. They can also encourage local groups to become involved through the consultation process, and work to ensure that their constituents play a full role in policy formulation.

C APPLICATIONS AND REVIEWS

23.10 Councillors can play a number of different roles in relation to licence applications.

Disseminating information

23.12 Councillors should have e-mail lists of local associations and groups, and should insist that the licensing department sends all councillors regular bulletins of licence applications so that they can send them on to their constituents.

Making representations

23.13 Councillors can decide to make representations on applications and reviews in their own right. When is it worth their doing so? The most important situation is where they have direct knowledge and information which would not otherwise get in front of the sub-committee. Another might be where they consider there is a serious problem and they wish to add their 'clout' to the representations upon it.

23.14 Before they take this step, however, councillors may wish to consider a wider picture. If nobody else has sought to become involved, this may indicate that there is not really a problem. If a large number of people have become involved, this may indicate that the councillor is not needed. So they should not get involved unless (a) there is something to say and (b) they can add something to the debate.

23.15 In the case of reviews, councillors ought to exercise still greater circumspection before actually initiating a review, for a number of reasons. First, reviews are just one way of achieving regulatory goals. Others include the myriad enforcement powers and voluntary schemes discussed in this book. Therefore, they should ask themselves whether reviews are the best means of achieving the desired outcome. Second, the review may have the undesired effect of frustrating a police operation. For example, if the police are investigating drug dealing at premises, a review brought on the basis of a suspicion may scupper the operation. Third, if a poor review is brought, eg on the grounds of low level nuisance, it will effectively rule out nuisance as an effective ground of review for some time to come because of the rule against repetitious reviews.¹ Fourth, a review which is unsupported by others may itself carry little weight. Therefore, before a councillor considers review proceedings, he or she would be well-advised to discuss the matter with officers to ascertain whether there are other means of resolving the concern, and whether review proceedings would be well-advised at this moment in time.

23.16   If a councillor does decide to make a representation and so become a party to the hearing, the following steps should be considered:

- The representation should:
  - address the four questions of licensing: what, where, when and how? It should explain why this operation, in this place at this time and managed in this way is inimical to the licensing objectives. If the objection is only as to the management of the venue as opposed to the venue itself (for example) the representation should say so. Councillors can be expected to be more and not less objective than other parties.
  - be linked to specific licensing objectives: 'These hours will fail to promote the public nuisance licensing objective because … .'
  - refer specifically to any parts of the licensing policy which bear on the application.
  - explain whether the objection would be met were the proposal to be revised and if so how.
  - contain relevant factual information.
- Councillors are as bound as other parties by the rule that information cannot be given or documents introduced for the first time at the hearing. Therefore, they should compile any necessary information (maps, photographs, petitions, statements, letters etc) and submit them in advance.
- They should ascertain which witnesses they wish to call, make sure they are coming and have transport and notify their names and their proposed topics to the authority in accordance with any directions in the notice of hearing.
- They should come to the hearing prepared to put their points succinctly, to be fair to the other side, to discuss the matter, and to put the argument in the context of authority's powers. Eg the authority has power on review to remove the DPS. Why would that be an insufficient exercise of powers?

Other actions

23.17   Alternative means of becoming involved are to represent local residents before the licensing sub-committee, or simply to advise local groups as

---

¹   Licensing Act 2003, s 51(4)(b)(ii).

to how they should themselves become involved, whether by making representations or applying for reviews.

Appeal

23.18   While a councillor has the same right of appeal as any other person making representations, it is strongly recommended that he does not do so. There is a personal costs risk attached to appealing. Furthermore, if no other party considers the decision worth appealing, an appeal by a single councillor would stand negligible prospects of success and is unlikely to be worth bringing.

Sitting on licensing sub-committees

23.19   Clearly this is an important role for councillors since it involves adjudicating on applications where some controversy has arisen. It is strongly recommended that councillors are trained for the role, since although it is not a judicial but an administrative function, it does involve consideration of the actual evidence in the case in the context of legal tests, which is best approached after some learning on the topic. As part of this, but conceptually distinct, is the role of Chair, who can work to ensure that the hearing takes place in an amicable but efficient manner, that all cases are put, all points of view explored and sensible, defensible decisions reached. Good practice for licensing hearings is set out in Chapter 21.

D CROSS-CUTTING

23.20   It takes many mountains to make a range, but there are some mountains which are sufficiently high to give a vantage point over the whole landscape. The same goes for organisations. Much discourse in recent years has been the structuring of organisations to avoid working 'in silos', that is to say head down and without regard to the wider significance of one's work or the other parallel workers who influence outcomes. In this situation measures fall between stools and all the advantages of synergy and the creativity which comes from bringing disciplines and resources together around a common aim are lost.

23.21   The most successful councils in terms of well-regulated, diverse leisure economies have councillors whose titles may vary but who essentially occupy the role of night time economy champion. Their job is to bring different departments and agencies together to share their vision and their tools for achieving it, to lever in resources and use their influence and advocacy to press for shared initiatives whether voluntary or regulatory. And they act as a beacon for the positive development of their town centres and the dilution of the bad news stories often so well beloved of local press, which serve to perpetuate the negative perspectives they peddle.

23.22   In short, they have the height, the vision and the perspective to see the whole regulatory and non-regulatory landscape, and make it their business to leave their centres in a better state than formerly, for the health, enjoyment and employment of their constituents. For a local politician, this is a key role.

24

Legal advisers

It was my Uncle George who discovered that alcohol was a food well in advance of modern medical thought.

P G Wodehouse, *The Inimitable Jeeves*

A INTRODUCTION

24.01 Within local authority legal departments, licensing is sometimes covered by lawyers who roam the plains of regulatory activity. In truth, however, licensing is an increasingly specialist activity, in which it is necessary to have a grasp not only of licensing law, practice and policy, but also allied statutes which impinge on licensing decision making and public law generally.

B POLICY

24.02 The role of the legal adviser at this stage is to ensure that the basic rules of consultation have been obeyed – that the consultation should occur before the council's mind has been made up, that sufficient time and information are given for effective responses and that the responses are fairly and properly summarised for the decision of the council.

24.03 The adviser should have a hand in checking the legality of the policy. Is it so prescriptive that it does not operate as a policy at all but as an immutable rule? Does it properly represent the law? Does it take account of national Guidance and give reasons for any departure from it? It is comprehensible and internally consistent?

Decision making

24.04   Part of the legal adviser's role is to ensure that decisions are taken by bodies with delegated authority to make them.[1] Furthermore, they should be in a position to advise whether in the circumstances the decision of the sub-committee may be tainted by bias or predetermination because of a councillor's conduct before or even during the hearing.

24.05   The adviser is there also to ensure that proceedings unfold in accordance with the Regulations, with which the adviser must be familiar. They must also accord with natural justice, particularly in that parties should not be taken by surprise by material and all should have an equal claim on the sub-committee's time and attention and the opportunity to answer the case of the other parties.

24.06   When the sub-committee retires, the adviser will frequently accompany them. The adviser's job at this point is to ensure that the decision is taken in accordance with the Licensing Act 2003 and any other legislation relevant to the decision, which may for example include the Crime and Disorder Act 1998, the Human Rights Act 1998, the Regulatory Enforcement and Sanctions Act 2008 and the Provision of Services Regulations 2009. He will also ensure that the sub-committee is taking into account relevant parts of the Guidance and the local policy.

24.07   Of course, if the adviser does give legal advice, it is important that the advice is repeated in open session so that participants have the opportunity to make submissions upon it.

24.08   The adviser has a crucial role in drafting the reasons for the decision. It is important to remember that these are not his reasons but the sub-committee's, but his job goes further than merely couching the reasons in legal language. If he cannot follow the reason which he is being asked to draft he should say so. If it is plain that the sub-committee is proposing (say) to refuse a licence before asking itself whether conditions would not resolve its concern, he should remind them of the diktats of proportionality. If the decision amounts to a departure from policy or Guidance he should ask the sub-committee what its reasons are for the departure. If the sub-committee has been asked to depart but has decided not to do so, he should ask the members to explain why they have decided not to depart.

24.09   The sub-committee may sometimes be tempted to get a decision out within a short period after retiring. It is the job of the legal adviser to point out that rushed decisions are much harder to defend on appeal, and that the

---

[1]   For an argument about delegation, albeit unsuccessful, see *Raphael (t/a Orleans) v Highbury Corner Magistrates' Court* [2011] EWCA Civ 462.

job is not to decide quickly but properly and to produce reasons which fully explain the reasoning of the authority. In the long run, good decisions save money.

24.10 It is definitively not the job of the adviser to advise the sub-committee about the prospects of appeal if the sub-committee takes a particular course. Should the sub-committee ask, the correct answer is that the sub-committee needs to take what it considers to be the appropriate course. If the decision is appealed, then the merits of the appeal will be considered and advice given at that stage.

24.11 Legal advisers should also check through the minutes of the meeting to ensure that they are accurate, since they may be produced and scrutinised on appeal.

C APPEALS

24.12 The moment an appeal is lodged the local authority lawyer ceases to be the clerk to the adjudication authority and instantly converts into a litigation lawyer.

24.13 The frequent mistake is to assume that all that needs to be done is to arrange for the material which was before the sub-committee to be placed before the court. This is a fundamental error. The question for the court is not whether the decision was wrong but whether it is wrong, which is to be judged on the current evidence. It can be assumed that the appellant will not just try to re-present the evidence previously adduced, and nor should the authority.

24.14 Nor should it be assumed that the chief protagonists, such as the police, will devote considerable resources to the appeal; some will and some won't. Some take the view that it is up to the authority to run the appeal, not them. Therefore, it is up to the lawyer to marshal the troops – be they police, environmental health authority, licensing department, councillors or residents – to provide evidence for the appeal. The objective is not simply to re-run the application but to make the most compelling case that the steps which the sub-committee took are the right (strictly, not the wrong) steps to take.

24.15 Finally, of course, the authority must have an eye to costs. On the assumption that the authority will win, the adviser must produce a detailed schedule of costs, which may include the costs of lawyers, officers,[2] disbursements and counsel.

---

[2]   *R v Associated Octel* [1997] 1 Cr App R (S) 435.

24.16 On the assumption that the authority may lose, the adviser must come armed with *Bradford City Council v Booth*[3] and be prepared to argue why the decision made was honest, reasonable and sound. In most cases, that will be sufficient to answer an application for costs even by a successful appellant.

24.17 However, although a decision made at the time may have looked perfectly reasonable, the merits of the case may shift during the appeal process, eg because the police consider that the premises has pulled its socks up. It is open to an appellant to argue that the authority should have taken a different view once this became apparent. Sometimes, appellants will strengthen their position by writing a letter 'without prejudice save as to costs', for production if and when they win the appeal. If the authority does not periodically review the merits of its position pending appeal, or give proper consideration to an offer letter from the appellant, then this alone may result in an order of costs against them, regardless of the merits at the time the decision was made. The adviser needs to be aware of this, and to maintain a proper liaison with the licensing committee, usually through the chairperson, while the appeal proceedings are current.

D CONCLUSION

24.18 Legal advisers in licensing play an important role in ensuring that the licensing process runs efficiently, with fairness to all parties and in accordance with the law. Sub-committees in particular look to the legal adviser to ensure that justice is not only done but is seen to be done, and the legal adviser sits at the heart of the procedure to enable all of the actors on the stage – applicant, objectors, sub-committee, etc – to act out their parts in accordance with the rules.

24.19 In this chapter we have pointed out some of the key functions of the role. Where it is performed properly, all parties gain confidence in the integrity of the system, the scope for successful appeals is reduced and the licensing arms of local authorities run efficiently and to budget.

---

[3]   [2000] COD 338, [2001] LLR 151.

Public sector duties of licensing authorities

A cold rain began to fall, and the blurred street-lamps looked ghastly in the dripping mist. The public-houses were just closing, and dim men and women were clustering in broken groups round their doors. From some of the bars came the sound of horrible laughter. In others, drunkards brawled and screamed.

Oscar Wilde, *Picture of Dorian Gray*

Crime and Disorder Act 1998

A dusty thudding in his head made the scene before him beat like a pulse. His mouth had been used as a latrine by some small creature of the night, and then as its mausoleum. During the night, too, he'd somehow been on a cross-country run and then been expertly beaten up by secret police. He felt bad.

Kingsley Amis, *Lucky Jim*

A INTRODUCTION

25.01 The main statute governing licensing decision-making is obviously the Licensing Act 2003.

25.02 However, orbiting the world of licensing are a number of other statutes which exercise gravitational influence over the process. Authorities ignore these satellites at their peril, for whether they are formulating licensing policy or making decisions on licensing applications, it is vital that account be taken of the wider legal framework within which they are exercising their functions. If they do not, then their exercise of power is potentially susceptible to legal challenge by way of judicial review.

25.03 In this Chapter we consider section 17 of the Crime and Disorder Act 1998, which puts crime and disorder prevention at the forefront of much decision-making within local authorities.

25.04 Section 17 provides as follows:

'(1) Without prejudice to any other obligation imposed on it, it shall be the duty of each authority to which this section applies to exercise its various functions with due regard to the likely effect of the exercise of those functions on, and the need to do all that it reasonably can to prevent –

(a) crime and disorder in its area (including anti-social and other behaviour adversely affecting the local environment); and

(b) the misuse of drugs, alcohol and other substances in its area; and

(c) re-offending in its area.'

B THE PROBLEM OF CRIME AND DISORDER

25.05 Since the early 1990s, many town centres and cities across the United Kingdom have seen a burgeoning night time economy. While this has undoubtedly been positive for the national bar and pub chains which have enjoyed substantial growth, it has also brought challenges for local authorities and other agencies in managing their town centres and in keeping control of crime and disorder.

25.06 Alcohol related crime and disorder is a stubborn problem, not only on the high street but generally. The British Crime Survey in 2009/10 reported that 50% of victims of violent crime believed that the offender was under the influence of alcohol.[1] The figure was still high at 48% in 2001/2 and had increased to 51% in 2003/4.[2] While the present Government has attempted to use the former statistic in making a case for rebalancing the Licensing Act,[3] it appears to ignore the latter. Alcohol Concern has concluded 'there is no evidence for an increase in the proportion of offenders believed to be under the influence of alcohol since the introduction of the Licensing Act.'[4]

25.07 No matter the view one takes of the statistics, it is undeniable that the potential for crime and disorder as a result of a thriving night time economy is significant. It is widely accepted that the practice of drinking at home or in a public place prior to attending town centre drinking establishments ('pre-loading') is widespread. A research paper[5] in 2008 reported on the outcome of a survey among 18–35 year olds in a large city in the North West of England. It found that those who reported pre-loading also reported significantly higher total alcohol consumption over a night out than those

---

[1] 'Crime in England and Wales 2009/10', para 3.11, http://rds.homeoffice.gov.uk/rds/pdfs10/hosb1210.pdf.

[2] http://www.alcoholconcern.org.uk/assets/files/Publications/Night-time-Economy-factsheet.pdf.

[3] http://www.homeoffice.gov.uk/publications/consultations/cons-2010-licensing-act/responses-licensing-consult?view=Binary.

[4] http://www.alcoholconcern.org.uk/assets/files/Publications/Night-time-Economy-factsheet.pdf.

[5] K Hughes, Z Anderson, M Morleo, M Bellis, 'Alcohol, nightlife and violence: the relative contributions of drinking before and during nights out to negative health and criminal justice outcomes', Addiction, Vol 103 (January 2008), pp 60–65.

who waited to drink until reaching the bars and nightclubs. The pre-loaders were also twice as likely to have been involved in a fight in the city's night life.

25.08 The report concluded that measures to reduce drunkenness and alcohol-related violence consequent upon the night time economy should not be restricted to premises such as bars and nightclubs but should also tackle disparities in pricing between on- and off-licensed premises.[6]

25.09 In a report by the Institute of Alcohol Studies[7] it was noted that other features of the night-time economy have also been identified as causes of excessive levels of alcohol consumption. In particular, youth-orientated 'vertical drinking' establishments are seen as particularly problematic. These are establishments where drinking is an end in itself rather than an accompaniment to other activities such as having a meal. Particular factors have been linked to a higher likelihood of aggression in public drinking settings. Individually or cumulatively, these can contribute to higher levels of crime and disorder and local authorities should have regard to these problems both when framing policy and, where appropriate, imposing necessary and proportionate conditions. They are:

- Crowding
- Poor bar layout and traffic flow
- Inadequate seating or inconvenient bar access
- Dim lighting, noise, poor ventilation or unclean condition
- Discount drinks and promotions that encourage heavy drinking (eg 'happy hours')
- Lack of availability of food
- A 'permissive' environment that fails to enforce anti-social behaviour
- Bar workers who do not practice responsible serving

The question which arises is whether and to what extent must local authorities have regard to these issues when exercising their functions under the Licensing Act 2003.

C THE LEGAL DUTY

25.10 As stated above, section 17(1) of the Crime and Disorder Act 1998 places a duty on certain key authorities, including local authorities, to have due regard to the likely effect of the exercise of those functions on, and the need to do all that it reasonably can to prevent, three things, these being (a) crime and disorder in its area (including anti-social behaviour adversely affecting the local environment); (b) the misuse of drugs, alcohol and other substances in its area; and (c) re-offending in its area.

---

[6] At the time of writing, the government is consulting on a minimum unit price for alcohol: 'A consultation on delivering the Government's policies to cut alcohol fuelled crime and anti-social behaviour' (November 2012).

[7] http://www.ias.org.uk/resources/factsheets/crime_premises.pdf.

25.11   The first thing to note about the obligation is that it is specifically without regard to other obligations placed upon the authority. Therefore, this duty sits alongside other duties. It does not suffocate them but stands shoulder to shoulder with them. So, for example, if there is a requirement of proportionality in other legislation, the section 17 duty does not require the decision-maker to abandon the constraints which proportionality imposes: see *Manchester City Council v Pinnock*.[8]

25.12   The second observation is that it is not a free-standing duty. It only arises when an authority is exercising some other function, in this case licensing functions.

25.13   Thirdly, it is not a duty to prevent crime and disorder etc, or to do all it reasonably can to prevent crime and disorder. It is a duty to have due regard to the likely effect of the exercise of its functions on, and the need to do all it reasonably can to prevent crime and disorder etc. The difference is crucial. An authority which wanted to stop alcohol-related crime could shut every bar in town. Section 17 does not require that.

25.14   What, however, does 'have due regard' actually mean? In *Pinnock* Lord Neuberger, giving the judgment of the court, said:[9]

> 'This section imposes no obligation on the authority to do everything to reduce crime and disorder, irrespective of other person's rights or of its own other duties – and it would be very surprising if it did.'

25.15   Lord Neuburger went on to state that the job of the authority was to take account of its section 17 duty alongside other duties upon it, including the convention rights of the parties. This reminds us that while section 17 is cast in broad terms, it does not operate as an absolute obligation but requires 'due regard' to be had when exercising their functions. It would seem that 'due regard' can be equated with 'having such regard as is appropriate in all the circumstances'.

25.16   The concept of 'due regard' in the context of a local authority's obligation to have due regard to the need to eliminate disability discrimination was explored by Aikens LJ in *R (Brown) v Secretary of State for Work and Pensions*[10] at paras 90–96, where six general principles were tentatively advanced. They are equally applicable to the obligation imposed by section 17. They have been suitably adapted for present purposes.

(i)   Those in a local authority exercising relevant functions must be made aware of their obligation to have 'due regard' to the likely effect on crime and disorder in its area and on the need to prevent it;

---

8   [2011] 2 AC 104, at para [91].
9   [2011] 2 AC 104, at para [92].
10   [2008] EWHC 3158 (Admin).

(ii) The 'due regard' duty must be fulfilled before and at the time that a particular policy that will or might affect crime and disorder is being considered by the local authority;

(iii) The duty must be exercised in substance, with rigour and with an open mind. However, the fact that a local authority has not mentioned the duty specifically where it is exercising a function which is likely to have an effect on crime and disorder is not determinative of whether the duty under the statute has been performed;

(iv) The duty imposed on public authorities that are subject to the duty is non-delegable. The duty will always remain on the public authority charged with it;

(v) The duty is a continuing one;

(vi) It is good practice for those exercising public functions in public authorities to keep an adequate record showing that they had actually considered their duty to have due regard to the likely effect on crime and disorder and the need to prevent it and pondered relevant questions. If records are not kept it may make it more difficult, evidentially, for a public authority to persuade a court that it has fulfilled its duty under section 17.

25.17 Therefore, while having due regard reflects the approach and the mental state accompanying it rather than a positive duty to eliminate crime and disorder, the duty is strongly expressed as one to have regard to the need to do all that reasonably can be done to prevent crime etc. When coupled with the test underlying most functions under the Licensing Act 2003 – appropriateness, which is a rather neutral benchmark – it can be seen that the section 17 duty assumes real significance in tilting the authority's mindset when it comes to exercise its functions. Other important objectives – such as the prevention of public nuisance – are not separately underpinned by a specific statutory duty in the same way. So, an authority must have regard to the objective of preventing nuisance and must do what is appropriate to prevent it, but is not subject to a duty to have regard to the need to do all it reasonably can to prevent it.

D THE DUTY IN PRACTICE

25.18 The duty essentially arises when the authority is formulating its policy and making other strategic choices, and when making decisions in individual cases.

25.19 At the former stage, licensing authorities can benefit from the work done by the local authority in formulating and implementing their crime and disorder strategy. Sections 5–7 of the Crime and Disorder Act 1998 place a duty on local authorities to formulate and implement a crime and disorder strategy through community safety partnerships (CSPs). CSPs are obliged to formulate and implement a strategy to reduce crime and disorder and combat substance misuse.

25.20   The strategy group of the CSP is to prepare a strategic assessment and a partnership plan in accordance with the requirements set out in the Crime and Disorder (Formulation and Implementation of Strategy) Regulations 2007.[11] The strategic assessment is an analysis of the levels and patterns of crime and disorder in the area as well as the priorities that should be adopted in tackling these matters. The partnership plan sets out a strategy for meeting those priorities and how that strategy should be implemented by the CSPs.

25.21   The national Guidance issued by the Secretary of State pursuant to section 182 of the Licensing Act 2003 states at paragraph 2.1 that the government believes that licensing authorities should involve the CSP but should 'look to the police' as their principal source of advice on how best to prevent crime and disorder in relation to licensed premises.

25.22   Both the intelligence provided by the police and any research undertaken by the CSP are likely to be invaluable to licensing authorities when, in formulating their policy, they are complying with their duties to have due regard to the need to reduce crime and disorder. The crime and disorder analysis undertaken by the CSP should identify patterns of disorder and crime which are likely to be associated with particular locations, premises or events. That knowledge should inform licensing policy, for example, on whether the existing cumulative effect of licensed premises in a given location is such that further licences should be restricted as a matter of policy, or whether tighter conditions should be suggested in policy.

25.23   In similar vein, this kind of work may assist when the authority deliberates as to whether it should consult on an early morning restriction order. In making that decision, it needs to consider whether the order is appropriate for the promotion of the licensing objectives.[12] Thus, the test is neutrally phrased, which provides something of a blank page on which section 17 may play to orient the thinking towards the order as a crime reduction measure, particularly if it is shown that a disproportionate amount of alcohol-related crime and disorder is occurring in the proposed area of the order and during the hours that it would seek to restrict. In the same way, the CSP work may underpin the imposition of a late night levy, where, having regard to its duty to do all it reasonably can to reduce crime and disorder, the authority may consider it desirable[13] to raise revenue to combat it.

25.24   When making individual licensing decisions, the test under the Licensing Act 2003 is no real constraint at all: it is a duty to take the steps which are considered appropriate for the promotion of the licensing objectives. In that authorities would be unlikely to take steps which they considered

---

[11]   SI 2007/1830.
[12]   Licensing Act 2003, s 172A(1).
[13]   'Desirability' is the test under the Police Reform and Social Responsibility Act 2011, s 125(3)(b).

inappropriate for the promotion of the licensing objectives, the test really only prevents regulatory intervention for reasons other than the licensing objectives.

25.25 The role of section 17 at this stage is to require particular attention to be paid to the crime and disorder consequences of the decision and the need to reduce crime and disorder. The licensee may argue that the duty should be exercised proportionately, and the effect on his business should therefore be properly considered, which exerts a particular pull on the appropriateness test, which is otherwise somewhat neutral. But section 17 ensures that the pull towards proportionality does not happen without tension, for in the opposite direction is an impulsion to reduce crime and disorder. Which wins the day is a matter of what the authority considers to be the appropriate course to take in order to promote the licensing objectives, taking account of all of these valid arguments. So section 17 is not a trump card, but it is a powerful consideration.

E CONCLUSION

25.26 The section 17 duty does not require an authority to do anything in particular. Nor does it tell authorities how to do it. It does however require them to pay attention to a particular factor in the balance and acts as an important reminder that crime and disorder can blight our leisure economies. Authorities must have in mind the need to do all they reasonably can to prevent crime and disorder when making their decisions.

The Equality Act 2010

She's a big lass and a bonny lass and she likes her beer
And they call her Cushie Butterfield and I wish she was here.

George Ridley, *Cushie Butterfield*

A   Introduction 26.01
B   Public sector equality duties 26.03
C   The duty in practice 26.08
D   Conclusion 26.18

A INTRODUCTION

26.01 The Equality Act 2010 was created, in part, to bring together in a single statutory scheme those characteristics in respect of which it is unlawful to discriminate, and to establish a single approach to discrimination. The statute consolidates nine separate pieces of legislation, simplifying and strengthening the law on discrimination and inequality. Most of the legislation took effect from 1 October 2010 and the public sector equality duty, which concerns licensing authorities, was in force from 5 April 2011.

26.02 There are particular 'protected characteristics' under section 4 of the Act, against which it is unlawful to discriminate directly or indirectly. Public bodies are also required[1] to have 'due regard' to the need to advance equality of opportunity and foster good relations between those who share a relevant characteristic and those who do not. These characteristics are:

  (i) Age
 (ii) Disability
(iii) Gender
 (iv) Marriage and Civil Partnership
  (v) Race
 (vi) Religion or belief
(vii) Sex

---

[1]   Equality Act 2010, s 149(2)–(3).

(viii) Sexual orientation
 (ix) Pregnancy and maternity

B   PUBLIC SECTOR EQUALITY DUTIES

26.03   Section 149 of the Equality Act 2010 require public sector bodies, in the exercise of their functions, to have due regard to the need to:

   (i)   eliminate discrimination, harassment, victimisation and any other con-
         duct that is prohibited by or under this Act;
  (ii)   advance equality of opportunity between persons who share a relevant
         protected characteristic and persons who do not share it;
 (iii)   foster good relations between persons who share a relevant protected
         characteristic and persons who do not share it.

26.04   The duty is expressed in deliberately broad terms and applies whenever the public body is exercising any of its *functions*. In the licensing context, this covers a wide range of licensing authority functions from formulating licensing policy to determining individual applications for premises licences and the adjudication of reviews. However, as with the obligation to have 'due regard' to the need to reduce crime and disorder pursuant to section 17(1) of the Crime and Disorder Act 1998, which was canvassed in the previous chapter, the obligation is one not to achieve an outcome but to have such regard as is appropriate in all the circumstances. It will be noted that this duty arises whether or not the question of equality is drawn to the authority's attention, although the practical action required by the duty will obviously be more defined if the relevant factors have expressly been drawn to the authority's attention.

26.05   The nature and extent of the duty have been the subject of judicial scrutiny in a number of cases,[2] from which the following principles may be culled:

 (1)   The decision-maker must be made aware of duty to have 'due regard'.
 (2)   The regard must be had to the need to achieve the goals involved.
 (3)   The duty must be fulfilled before and at the time that the decision
       which might affect those protected by the Act is being taken. It is not a
       rearguard action following a concluded decision. It is an integral part of
       the formation of a proposed policy, not justification for its adoption.
 (4)   The duty involves a 'conscious approach and a state of mind'.
 (5)   Therefore, attempts to justify a decision as being consistent with the
       exercise of the duty when it was not, in fact, considered before the
       decision are not enough to discharge the duty.
 (6)   The duty must be exercised in substance, with rigour and with an open

---

[2]   See in particular *R (JM and NT) v Isle of Wight Council* [2008] EWHC 2911 (Admin) and
      R (Brown) v Secretary of State for Work and Pensions [2008] EWHC 3158 (Admin).

mind. It is not a question of ticking boxes. Nor is general awareness of the duty enough.

(7) However, the fact that a duty is not mentioned is not determinative of whether it has been performed. But it is good practice to make reference to it, because in this way the authority is more likely to ensure that relevant factors have been taken into account.

(8) The duty is non-delegable.

(9) The duty is a continuing one.

(10) It is good practice to keep a record to show that (and how) the duty has been performed.

26.06 A powerful example arose in the planning context in order to illustrate the nature of the 'due regard' duty. In *R (on the application of Harris) v Haringey LBC*[3] it was held that the local authority failed to have due regard to the need to promote equality of opportunity between persons of different racial groups. That case concerned the demolition of existing buildings and erection of new ones in an area with business units and homes predominantly occupied by members of the black and ethnic minority communities. The council had before it a number of representations and consultation responses which referred, in specific terms, to the detrimental impact on ethnic minority residents of the proposed development. However, there was no evidence of any analysis of that material or consideration of how the proposals impacted upon those residents in accordance with the local authority's public sector equality duty. The Court of Appeal quashed the planning permission. Pill LJ stated:

> '40. Not only is there no reference to section 71 in the report to committee, or in the deliberations of the committee, but the required "due regard" for the need to "promote equality of opportunity and good relations between persons of different racial groups" is not demon-strated in the decision-making process. "Due regard" does not require the promotion of equality of opportunity, but on the material available to the council in this case it did require an analysis of that material with specific statutory considerations in mind. It does not, of course, follow that considerations raised by section 71(1) will be decisive in a particular case. The weight to be given to the requirements of the section is for the decision maker but it is necessary to have due regard to the needs specified in section 71(1). There was no analysis of the material before the council in the context of the duty.'

26.07 It is vital that licensing authorities have processes in place to ensure that 'due regard' is had to any relevant material which bears upon its public sector equality duty. This could take the form of ensuring that an 'equality impact assessment' is undertaken in relation to relevant proposals, although an actual assessment is not necessary.

---

3   [2010] EWCA Civ 703.

C THE DUTY IN PRACTICE

26.08   National Guidance gives little assistance as to how the equality duty may play out in the licensing context. It does however state that:

> '13.58 Public authorities are required to publish information at least annually to demonstrate their compliance with the Equality Duty. The statement of licensing policy should refer to this legislation, and explain how the Equality Duty has been complied with. Further guidance is available from Government Equalities Office and the Equality and Human Rights Commission.'

26.09   The practical ramification for authorities is that they have to understand the effect of their policies and decisions on persons with different protected characteristics, in order to ascertain whether the effect will be discriminatory. How they go about doing this is a matter for them, but they must do it nonetheless. In order to carry out their duty, they need to have good information about such effects and good analysis of what the effects are likely to be, when they come to make any decision which may engage the duty. The findings they make should then be incorporated in their policy development and decision-making processes.

26.10   A clear and obvious exercise of the equality duty is in establishing practices and procedures for those with protected characteristics to participate in the licensing process. This may include Braille copies of consultation documents, informal consultation of children and means for those with physical disabilities to attend licensing hearings.

26.11   To require a licensing authority to carry out its equality duty is not to require it to reach any particular result. For example, a particular decision may have a negative equality impact, but if it is considered appropriate to promote the licensing objectives, it is unlikely to hold sway. However, if there are two possible courses and one has a negative equality impact and the other a positive one, it may be irrational not to take the latter course.

26.12   Even then, however, certain policies and decisions may pull in equal and opposite directions in terms of the gender equality duty. A policy to restrict lap dancing venues may gain the support of women who fear to use the pavement outside such venues and who are thus discriminated against. But it may detrimentally affect female performers who may have no other place in the area to earn a living. A policy to promote nightclubs may particularly benefit young people who visit and work in such venues. But it may also increase violent crime in the area, most of the victims of which are young people. It is for the licensing authority to evaluate these differential impacts in the light of full information.

26.13 In some instances the equality duty may be decisive. Imagine a lesbian bar asking for 30 minutes extra trading time at night. The bar says that it needs the extra time to get its customers away by taxi safely. The licensing authority has a policy against extra hours in this particular location, but it cannot show any real harm on the facts of the individual case. In that case, the gender equality duty may be sufficient to amount to an exceptional circumstance justifying departure from the policy.

26.14 Or, imagine that consultation showed that gay or old people feared using city centre bars, which are strongly populated by young, mostly male drinkers. They want an exception made to the policy for bars catering for a different demographic, but there is a cumulative impact policy in place. The authority may decide to relax the policy for bars catering to that demo-graphic, or it may decide to designate a different area for the cultivation of this kind of leisure environment. Either would be a performance of the equality duty, and the need for action would have arisen from the consult-ation exercise, which would itself have set out to investigate the different effects of policy on those with protected characteristics.

26.15 The kinds of impacts which may arise will not always be evident, and may be unexpected. When formulating policy, it is good practice for authorities specifically to investigate the equality considerations which may be in play in licensing policy, and make transparent decisions as to how such considerations will influence the drafting of the policy.

26.16 Similarly, in making decisions, the equality considerations may be buried in a mass of other information. Those affected may be shy to bring the consideration into the open. They may not appreciate that it is even a relevant consideration. Therefore, an enlightened authority, conscious of its duty, will not wait for the issue to be 'pleaded' expressly by the parties before giving it due consideration.

26.17 The limitation on the duty is that it cannot be used to refuse that which would otherwise be granted. But it can be used to weigh choices, either of which would be appropriate for the promotion of the licensing objectives. It may be sufficient to justify a departure from a restraint policy. Furthermore, it may operate in judging overall proportionality in deciding whether, even though regulatory intervention may be justified, there are grounds for taking a more lenient stance. So, to take the lesbian bar example, while a short extension of time may marginally harm the licensing objectives, thus justifying a refusal, the benefit of the proposal in terms of gender equality may yet permit the authority to say that refusal is not appropriate for the promotion of the licensing objectives. All of these approaches are theoretically possible, but it is still emphasised that the steps the authority takes once it has identified the gender equality impacts is a matter for its determination, in relation to the legal test underpinning its discretion, the factual matrix and the strength of the equality considerations in play.

D CONCLUSION

26.18   Where there are open discretions, legislation such as the Equality Act 2010 is easy to apply because it provides a clear orientation for the decision-maker. Where there is already a duty to achieve certain objectives it is not as easy to reconcile that duty with positive duties in relation to equalities. However, once it is recognised that the duty, while a strong one, does not require particular action, the two duties meld in a complementary manner, the first being to pursue the licensing objectives, the second being to do so in a way which, if it can be helped, does not discriminate against those with protected characteristics.

Human rights

'I cannot see the Speaker, Hal, can you?'
'What? Cannot see the Speaker. I see two!'

Morning Chronicle report of drunken conversation in the House of
Commons between Pitt the Younger and Henry Dundas.

A INTRODUCTION

27.01 The Human Rights Act 1998 ('HRA') was introduced in order to incorporate the rights described in the European Convention on Human Rights into domestic law such that they can be enforced in domestic courts as well as in the European Court of Human Rights.[1]

27.02 The HRA provides no pot of gold for licensing operators or objectors. But it can provide useful material for both to use to their advantage if deployed effectively. It ensures that authorities consciously approach their decision-making with rights in mind leading, hopefully, to fairer decision-making.

27.03 Below is a brief consideration of the impact of the HRA 1998 in the field of licensing. It is not intended to be a full guide to the relevant provisions of the Convention or the Human Rights Act 1998.[2]

---

[1]   Subsequent to the HRA coming into force, before the 2nd reading of any new Bill a Minister of the Crown must make a statement that the provisions of the Bill are compatible with the Convention rights – HRA, s 19.

[2]   For further guidance, see Lester and Pannick, *Human Rights Law and Practice* (LexisNexis,

27.04   A useful and simple starting point is to note that incorporation is effected in large part by two important provisions of the HRA.

The first, section 3, requires legislation to be interpreted so as to be compatible with the Convention.

The second, section 6, prohibits public authorities from acting in a way which is incompatible with a Convention right. Thus all local authorities and, on appeal, the magistrates' and High Courts have to apply it.

These two provisions form the basic structure upon which the remainder of the Act hangs.

27.05   On a practical level, it is necessary to consider what effect proportionality will have in three areas: the licensing authority's policy, its decisions on individual applications, and enforcement action, each of which is perused below. But first it is necessary to consider the concept of proportionality, which underpins much of the law on this topic.

B PROPORTIONALITY

27.06   One of the main effects of the HRA has been the spotlight it has placed upon the requirement for public bodies to act 'proportionately'. There is no specific requirement within the Convention to act as such, but it is a guiding principle of the Convention and its effect is all-pervasive. It is interesting to note that the Guidance refers only in passing to the HRA[3] but repeated reference is made to the need to act proportionately or for actions not to be disproportionate.[4]

27.07   Proportionality was arguably becoming a self-standing domestic law principle of administrative law generally, irrespective of the Convention, but the advent of the HRA has pushed it to the forefront of judicial thinking.[5]

27.08   There are three relevant criteria to be examined when considering the question of proportionality:

- whether the objective justifying the interference with a right is sufficiently important to justify the right's limitation (is the aim legitimate?);
- whether the measures designed to meet the objective are rationally connected to it (is the response suitable for achieving that aim?); and
- whether the means used to impair the right are no more than necessary to accomplish the objective (is it necessary to achieve that aim?).

2009); Clayton and Tomlinson, *The Law of Human Rights* (OUP, 2009), and Butterworth's *Human Rights and Judicial Review, Case Studies in Context*.

[3]   Para 1.10.

[4]   Eg at paras 1.16, 1.17.

[5]   See *R (Daly) v Secretary of State for the Home Department* [2001] UKHL 26, [2001] 2 AC 532, per Lord Slynn at para 51.

27.09 The approach by Dyson LJ in *R (Samaroo) v Home Secretary*[6] provides useful practical guidance. He suggests proportionality needs to be considered in two stages:

(i) Can the objective of the measure (eg a restrictive condition upon a licence) be achieved by means which are less interfering with an individual's rights (no condition or a less onerous one)?

(ii) Does the measure have an excessive or disproportionate effect on the interest of the affected individual (ie might it secure very little for the neighbourhood but have a disproportionate effect on an operator's business)?

27.10 When addressing the second issue, the task for the decision maker (eg the licensing authority) is to strike a fair balance between the legitimate aim in question and the individual's Convention rights. Amongst the matters for consideration are the nature of the right in question and the extent to which the issue requires consideration of social, economic and political matters – eg where the balance should be struck between an uninterrupted night's sleep and running an effective business.

27.11 However, the approach in *Samaroo* should not be regarded as a straitjacket. It may need to be adapted to the circumstances, particularly where the decision maker has to balance competing rights. For example, the stage 1 question in *Samaroo* does not require an applicant for a licence to show that there were no other alternative locations for his proposed activities.[7] This is because the stage 1 question 'does not take account of the right, recognised in the Convention, of a landowner to make use of his land, a right which is, however, to be weighed against the rights of others affected by the use of land and of the community in general.'[8] The process in *Samaroo*, 'while appropriate where there is direct interference with Article 8 rights by a public body, cannot be applied without adaptation in a situation where the essential conflict is between two or more groups of public interests.'[9]

27.12 The influence of proportionality on decision-making under the Act is canvassed further in Chapter 12 (The Appropriateness Test).

C POLICY

27.13 Before adopting policy, the responsible licensing authority will wish to balance the rights and freedoms of residential and commercial occupiers. A policy which is too liberal may, if applied, have the effect of impinging on the rights of the former, and if too restrictive may ultimately unreasonably

---

[6] [2001] UKHRR 1150.

[7] *Lough (David) & Ors v First Secretary of State & Bankside Developments Ltd (Interested Party)* [2004] EWCA Civ 905.

[8] *Lough (David) & Ors* per Pill LJ, para 50.

[9] *Lough (David) & Ors* per Keene LJ, para 55

restrict the freedom of trade of the latter. The balancing exercise is similar to the principle of proportionality in that it involves weighing competing interests. However, as shown below, the adoption of a policy alone engages no human rights, and so judicial review will not lie for an alleged breach of those rights stemming from the failure properly or at all to employ the principle of proportionality in arriving at the policy.

D   DECISION MAKING

27.14   The concept of proportionality arises both in deciding whether to grant or refuse a licence and in the imposition of conditions. Its influence can be seen repeatedly in the Secretary of State's Guidance both generally in relation to determinations and specifically in relation to conditions.[10] The requirement of proportionality may temper the width of the discretion afforded by the Licensing Act 2003.

27.15   Until the implementation of the Police Reform and Social Responsibility Act 2011 the test for regulatory intervention of any type under the Licensing Act 2003 was necessity, so that to that extent proportionality was woven into the fabric of decision-making. However, now that the test is 'appropriateness', the concept of proportionality takes on extra importance. Imagine that the authority is faced with a significant decision, such as whether to close a nightclub because of a series of small to middling misdemeanours. It does not think it necessary in the sense that no lesser step would suffice to meet its concerns, but does think it an appropriate exercise of discretion because it will promote the licensing objectives. In such a case, revocation may be justified as an 'appropriate' measure, but the requirement of proportionality may well operate to remove revocation from the menu.

27.16   Fundamentally, what the concept of proportionality does is to ask the authority to focus on two considerations other than merely whether the measure will promote the licensing objectives. First, it asks authorities to review the possible means of achieving its objective and consider whether other equally effective but less economically damaging methods might not achieve much the same effect. Second, it asks authorities to consider what the effects will be on the operator. Third, it asks the authority to draw a balance where the importance and necessity of the measure is weighed against its effect on the operator with a view to considering whether the measure amounts to a proportionate or disproportionate response.

27.17   In some cases, the requirements of proportionality may add very little. For example, in *Belfast City Council v Miss Behavin' Ltd* [2007] UKHL 19 the local authority resolved, pursuant to article 4 of the Local Government (Miscellaneous Provisions) (Northern Ireland) Order 1985, that the system for the licensing of sex establishments contained in Schedule 2 should

---

[10]   See paras 1.7, 1.16, 1.17, 2.20, 9.5, 9.6, 9.39, 10.10, 11.20 and 11.23.

apply to its district. The respondent company applied for a licence to use the premises as a sex shop, and the council refused the application on the ground that, under paragraph 12(3)(c) of the Order, the appropriate number of sex shops in the relevant locality was nil. Before arriving at its decision, the local authority took into account representations made members of the public after the expiry of the 28 day period prescribed by the 1985 Order. The respondent sought judicial review of the local authority's decision arguing, amongst other things, that the council had not sufficiently taken into account the company's right to freedom of expression under article 10 of the ECHR.

27.18 The Court of Appeal held that the council, in exercising its statutory powers, had failed sufficiently to take into account the company's right to freedom of expression. However, the House of Lords held that the Court of Appeal's approach was erroneous. The obligation on the Court was not to consider whether the relevant right had properly been taken into account but to assess whether it had actually been breached. Lord Hoffman at paragraph 14 of the judgment referred to Lord Bingham's judgment in *R (SB) v Governors of Denbigh High School* ([2007] 1 AC 100) where he held:

'... the focus at Strasbourg is not and never has been on whether a challenged decision or action is the product of a defective decision making process, but on whether, in the case under consideration, the applicant's Convention rights have been violated ... The unlawfulness proscribed by section 6(1) is acting in a way which is incompatible with a Convention right, not relying on a defective process of reasoning ...'

It was held that there was no unlawful interference with the company's article 10 right to vend pornography or associated items and that, in any event, such a right was engaged at a very low level.

27.19 The *Miss Behavin'* case is of relevance in the licensing context generally as it shows how restraint policies can be lawful, and may be lawfully applied even if there is no evidence that the right has explicitly been taken into account, although of course there is much less likely to be judicial interference with the outcome if the authority can show that the right was taken into account, and how. In all cases, however, whether there is in fact a breach of a convention right is to be judged on the evidence. In *Miss Behavin'*, Lord Neuberger held at paragraph 92:

'One can imagine circumstances where, for instance, the demand is so great, the level of objections is so low, the articles proposed to be sold are relatively inoffensive to any but the most prudish, and a nil determination is issued for every local authority in the whole city or district, that article 10 considerations in a particular case could outweigh the effect of the nil determination.'

E   ENFORCEMENT

27.20   Here, proportionality should influence both what type of action is necessary and what, if any, sanction should result. The criminal courts are no stranger to the idea of the penalty being proportionate to the crime, but the HRA gives greater emphasis to this approach. Similar considerations are in play when the issue is civil in nature, e g arising out of reviews and closures under the Licensing Act 2003 and other legislation.

F   RELEVANT CONVENTION RIGHTS

27.21   In terms of the Licensing Act 2003, only three rights are likely to be of any particular importance. Two are substantive (article 8 and article 1 of the First Protocol) whilst one is procedural (article 6). Article 10, guaranteeing freedom of expression, is unlikely to be engaged frequently although the Licensing Act does extend to plays and films.

27.22   As to the substantive rights, it is important to note that neither of these two provide absolute protection. Both are qualified rights. In this respect they may be contrasted, for instance, with article 2 – right to life. Since the rights are qualified, the state is entitled to interfere with them in accordance with the exceptions set out within the articles themselves. The rights should be broadly construed, the exceptions to narrowly so.[11]

Article 8 – right to respect for private and family life

27.23   This article provides:

1.   Everyone has the right to respect for his private and family life, his home and his correspondence.
2.   There shall be no interference by a public authority with the exercise of this right except such as is in accordance with the law and is necessary in a democratic society in the interests of national security, public safety or the economic well-being of the country, for the prevention of disorder or crime, for the protection of health or morals, or for the protection of the rights and freedoms of others.

27.24   Article 8 has been interpreted broadly[12] but, in the context of Licensing Act 2003, it is in the context of respect for 'home' that it will be most relevant. It is most likely to be raised in the context of nuisance both

---

[11]   See *Reyes v The Queen* [2002] 2 AC 235 at para 26 in particular per Lord Bingham that a generous and purposive approach is to be given to the HRA, and contrast the approach to exceptions taken in *R v Hughes* [2002] 2 AC 259, para 35.

[12]   Eg it covers subjects as diverse as surveillance, sexual identity and extradition. It is not thought likely that it will become relevant to matters of film classification or similar but if the approach of a licensing authority comes close to censorship then it might become so.

from persons going to and from licensed premises, as well as noise etc emanating from such premises.

27.25 There are a number of steps that can be identified in the consideration of article 8.

Has there been interference?

27.26 First, if the quality of an objector's private life and the scope for enjoying the amenities of his home[13] have been adversely affected by the noise or other impact of licensable activities, article 8 will potentially be engaged, ie there will be an arguable 'interference' with the objector's article 8 rights. It is to be noted that it is at least arguable there must be significant detriment or impact[14] in order to engage article 8. The mere formulation of policy is most unlikely to engage article 8(1) as the formulation of policy alone has no impact by itself.

27.27 Well-known examples are the applications to the European Court concerning nuisance suffered by noise pollution from night flying of aircraft to and from both Gatwick and Heathrow airports.[15] The debate in such circumstances was not as to whether article 8 is relevant, it being accepted that it was, but whether the interference has been justified. The noise from a late night venue in a previously sleepy residential area might well give rise to the need to debate similar considerations, albeit over a much more limited area.

27.28 However, it should not be assumed though that any level of nuisance would be enough to engage article 8. It may in particular be difficult for an objector to demonstrate that he is a victim prior to the opening of a premises. The European Court, upon an admissibility decision,[16] set a high onus on an objector in asserting a prospective breach of article 8 rights.

27.29 It is only in wholly exceptional circumstances that the risk of future violation may nevertheless confer the status of 'victim' on an individual applicant, and only then if he or she produces reasonable and convincing evidence of the probability of the occurrence of a violation concerning him or her personally: mere suspicions or conjectures are not enough in that respect.

---

[13] Most cases in the UK have concentrated upon purely residential properties, but there is at least scope for seeking to widen the boundaries to include certain work and/or leisure places.

[14] See eg Simor and Emmerson, *Human Rights Practice* at para 8.016.

[15] See *Powell and Rayner v UK* (1990) 12 EHRR 355 and the decision of the Grand Chamber of the European Court in *Hatton v UK* (2003) 37 EHRR 611, 8 July 2003.

[16] *Asselbourg v Luxembourg* Unreported Application 29121/95.

27.30 The requirement of exceptional circumstances should not, though, be overstated. Certainly, generalised environmental concerns will not do.[17] However, it is clearly arguable from several planning law cases[18] that the decision maker should take into account the impact of decisions upon individuals' homes, whether they be applicant or objector, if there are likely to be serious impacts upon them. An instance of such serious impact occurred in connection with low flying RAF aircraft when the High Court awarded damages under the HRA for their impact upon home and property.[19] Whilst it is no doubt a matter of fact and degree, some licensed premises could cause a serious impact in respect of enjoyment of a home.

27.31 This approach has been adopted by the High Court in *Bushell & Ors (R on the application of) v (1) Newcastle Licensing Justices (2) Ultimate Leisure & (1) Rinberg Holding Co Ltd (2) Newcastle City Council (Interested Parties)*,[20] see the judgment of Owen J at paragraphs 40 and 41.

> 'I do not accept that the Claimants' case is based on mere suspicion of conjecture. It is reasonable to infer from the evidence as to the behaviour of those resorting to licensed premises in the Osborne Road, that the grant of a full on-licence to the Gresham will result in some increase of such unacceptable behaviour both in and in the immediate vicinity of the Claimants' properties; hence the strong objection to the applications for a licence from the police. Secondly the Claimants plainly do have a generalised concern as to the loutish and drunken behaviour in and about Osborne Road. But their concern goes beyond that. Their evidence demonstrates the direct effect of such behaviour on their enjoyment of their own properties.'

> 'In those circumstances I am satisfied that on the evidence advanced by the Claimants, the special removal of the Mims licence to the Gresham is capable of resulting in an infringement of the Claimants' convention rights.'

27.32 Of interest in this regard is a preliminary decision of Collins J[21] in respect of claim arising from additional noise caused by a road traffic regulation order. He found that a 1dbB(A) increase in traffic noise may well breach article 8(1) and that the mere existence of a scheme for road traffic orders does not mean that it will necessarily be justified under article 8(2). He therefore refused to strike out the claim for damages, which then

---

[17]   See comments of Sullivan J in *R (Vetterlein) v Hampshire County Council* [2002] Env LR, paras 60–61, and Maurice Kay J in *R (Westminster City Council) v Mayor of London* [2002] EWHC 2440 (Admin) – albeit a permission hearing a full judgment was given, see in particular paragraphs 111–5.

[18]   Eg *Vetterlein and Malster v Ipswich BC* [2002] PLCR 14, in the latter case the court assumed a possible infringement by overshadowing.

[19]   *Dennis v MOD* [2003] EWHC 793 (QB).

[20]   [2003] EWHC 1937 (Admin).

[21]   *Andrews v Reading Borough Council* [2004] EWHC 970 (Admin).

proceeded to trial, with damages being awarded to the claimant on full evidence as to the extent of the interference.'[22]

Is the interference justifiable?

27.33 Second, if there is an interference, the next question is whether that interference is justifiable in the terms of the article itself. To answer that question positively (1) the interference must be lawful (which it will be if carried out pursuant to a licence) and (2) it must represent a fair balance that has to be struck between the competing interests of the individual and the community as a whole in permitting that interference to continue. Thus, the mere fact that a negative repercussion of a proposal can be demonstrated does not necessarily result in a breach of article 8. A breach will only result if, having carried out the balancing exercise, the result is not fair or proportionate.

27.34 The difficulty of demonstrating a breach of article 8 where competing interests are at stake, and the margin of discretion afforded to the determining authority, was amply demonstrated by Pill LJ's conclusions on the issue in *Lough (David) & Ors v First Secretary of State & Bankside Developments Ltd (Interested Party)*,[23] which merit recitation:

'43. It emerges from the authorities:

(a) Article 8 is concerned to prevent intrusions into a person's private life and home and, in particular. arbitrary intrusions and that is the background against which alleged breaches are to be considered.

(b) Respect for the home has an environmental dimension in that the law must offer protection to the environment of the home.

(c) Not every loss of amenity involves a breach of Article 8(1). The degree of seriousness required to trigger lack of respect for the home will depend on the circumstances but it must be substantial.

(d) The contents of Article 8(2) throw light on the extent of the right in Article 8(1) but infringement of Article 8(1) does not necessarily arise upon a loss of amenity and the reasonableness and appropriateness of measures taken by the public authority are relevant in considering whether the respect required by Article 8(1) has been accorded.

(e) It is also open to the public authority to justify an interference in accordance with Article8(2) but the principles to be applied are broadly similar in the context of the two parts of the Article.

(f) When balances are struck, the competing interests of the individual, other individuals, and the community as a whole must be considered.

---

22   [2005] EWHC 256 (QB).
23   [2004] EWCA Civ 905.

(g)   The public authority concerned is granted a certain margin of appreciation in determining the steps to be taken to ensure compliance with Article 8.

(h)   The margin of appreciation may be wide when the implementation of planning policies is to be considered.'

27.35   There have been relatively few cases which have been successful even before the European Court relying upon article 8 in the context of nuisance.[24] Therefore, it will probably be a most exceptional case in which the grant of a licence under the Act could be refused by a licensing authority or struck down by a court solely at the behest of an objector upon the basis of the Convention. However, most objectors will not need to rely upon article 8 rights in order to make an objection. The concept of public nuisance under the Licensing Act 2003 sets a lower threshold than the concept of statutory nuisance under the Environmental Protection Act 1990 or indeed the level needed to establish an article 8 breach. Therefore, it will rarely if ever be necessary for an objector to lay great stress on their rights under the Convention and this issue is unlikely to detain a licensing authority or a court for long.

27.36   On the other hand, the mere existence of the HRA and article 8 will serve to emphasise the importance placed upon 'home' and the weight to be attached to interference with it, and in taking account of any conditions which may be attached to a licence – eg hours of opening, deliveries or the nature or extent of any noise reduction scheme. In particular, the requirement that any interference should not be disproportionate, as to which see above, will add to the effectiveness of arguments founded upon the impact on residential amenity.

Article 1 of the First Protocol – protection of property

27.37   This article, which was added by way of the first amendment to the Convention, provides:

'Every natural or legal person is entitled to the peaceful enjoyment of his possessions. No one shall be deprived of his possessions except in the public interest and subject to the conditions provided for by law and by the general principles of international law.

The preceding provisions shall not, however, in any way impair the right of a State to enforce such laws as it deems necessary to control the use of property in accordance with the general interest or to secure the payment of taxes or other contributions or penalties.'

---

[24]   The two best known examples are *Lopez Ostra v Spain* (1995) 20 EHRR 277, ECtHR (air pollution leading to evacuation of local residents from their homes) and *Guerra v Italy* (1998) 26 EHRR 357, ECtHR (toxic pollution leading to arsenic poisoning).

This article will be of primary concern to the operator, particularly since corporate operators are embraced in the expression 'legal person'.

27.38 It is unlikely that third party objectors will find benefit in this article. It was suggested in some planning cases that an adverse effect on value of a neighbouring property of the granting of a planning permission engages article 1 of the First Protocol and, therefore, any decision which does not consider that interference and, more importantly, consider whether compensation should be paid with regard to it, is flawed. However, the Court of Appeal has determined that diminution of value in itself is not a loss contemplated by the articles in the planning context.[25] The same is likely to be true in a licensing context.

27.39 A licence (together with the property to which it is attached) is a possession within the meaning of the article and so generally within the scope of protection afforded by the article.[26] But the article may not be of any particular assistance to an applicant seeking the grant of a new licence as the possession has not then been acquired, its acquisition not being a matter of right but of the exercise of discretion. In *Runa Begum v Tower Hamlets London Borough Council*, Lord Walker reviewed European authorities and held that they 'indicate that article 6(1) is likely to be engaged when the applicant has public law rights which are of a personal and economic nature and do not involve any large measure of official discretion: see *Masson v The Netherlands* (1995) 22 EHRR 491, 511, para 51.'[27]

27.40 Similar conclusions have been arrived at in Scottish cases concerning planning[28] and licensing.[29]

27.41 The article will certainly come into play if an existing licence is revoked or otherwise restricted. However, it is unlikely that revocation of a licence will result in actual breach of this article – although it could do so in an extreme case.

27.42 Firstly, revocation of a licence would not be considered a deprivation of a possession within the second sentence of the first paragraph of the article provided the premises associated with it have retained some economic value (and it would be extremely surprising if they did not). The removal of a licence is, though, a measure of control of the use of the property, and so

---

25 *Lough (David) & Ors v First Secretary of State & Bankside Developments Ltd (Interested Party)* [2004] EWCA Civ 905.
26 *Tre Traktorer v Sweden* (1989) 13 EHRR 309, EctHR, para 53 (a case concerning the withdrawal of an alcohol licence from a restaurant); *Pine Valley Developments Ltd v Ireland* (1991) 14 EHRR 319, para 65; and see *Catscratch Ltd and Lettuce Holdings Ltd v City of Glasgow Licensing Board* [2001] LLR 610, [2001] UKHRR 610.
27 [2003] 2 AC 430, para 114.
28 *Di Ciacca v The Scottish Ministers* [2003] Scot CS 95, para 53.
29 *Mecca Limited Re Petition for Judicial Review* [2004] Scot CS 136, para 43.

falls within the protection afforded by the second paragraph of the article.[30] It is easier to justify a measure of control than total deprivation and so the protection afforded by the second paragraph will be less effective than the first.

27.43 Secondly, a licensing authority is unlikely to revoke or devalue a licence and be upheld on appeal in so doing without following proper procedures or without adequate justification. Although the availability of compensation is a factor which the courts will consider in determining whether there is a breach of the article, in terms of the statutory scheme enacted in the Licensing Act 2003 (which does not provide for compensation) its absence is most unlikely to be decisive.

27.44 Again like article 8, where the impact of article 1 of the First Protocol will be felt is in the extra attention that should be paid to the question of imposition of restrictions or revocation and the justification for it. The punishment of revocation, for example, may be too severe, and/or greater attention will need to be paid to alternative methods of dealing with the problem. For example, in respect of noisy premises earlier closure may be 'in accordance with the general interest' rather than revocation.

27.45 It is instructive to consider the case of *Crompton t/a David Crompton Haulage v Department of Transport North Western Traffic Area* [2003] EWCA Civ 64 [2003] RTR 34. In that case, Mr Crompton carried on a haulage business and his brother had been convicted of tachograph offences. Mr Crompton was found to be complicit and his haulage operator's license had been revoked by the deputy traffic commissioner. That decision was overturned on appeal. At the conclusion of the hearing before the deputy traffic commissioner, the licensee and his brother were involved in an incident where they were abusive and threatening towards to the clerk to the inquiry, a traffic examiner and a journalist. After Mr Crompton's successful appeal, the traffic commissioner decided to hold an inquiry to consider whether his license should be revoked on the basis that he was now not of good repute and not a fit person to hold a licence.

27.46 On appeal, it was held that the traffic commissioner had not interpreted the legislation giving her the power to revoke a licence compatibly with the applicant's convention rights. The operator's licence was a possession for the purposes of article 1 of the First Protocol, and, though it could be revoked lawfully in pursuit of a legitimate aim, the action had to be proportionate. When considering alleged loss of good repute, the traffic commissioner should focus attention on matters relevant to the individual's fitness to hold a licence, bearing in mind that an existing licence was a possession safeguarded by article 1 of the First Protocol. The inevitable consequence of a finding of loss of repute was revocation and there had to be

---

[30]   See *Tre Traktorer*, footnote 25 above.

a relationship of proportionality between the finding and the sanction. Although the traffic commissioner asked herself whether the appellant's behaviour related to his fitness to hold a licence, she was more concerned with the unacceptability of his behaviour and failed to give mature consideration to the question of whether that behaviour demonstrated loss of good repute (the test under the statute), bearing in mind the inevitable consequences of such a finding and the need for proportionality.

27.47 The case is a cautionary tale for local authorities to focus their minds on the statutory test that has to be applied under the Act and to act in a proportionate manner in light of the evidence before them. They should not be influenced by improper behaviour before the tribunal, no matter how objectionable, if it is not relevant to the test that has to be applied.

Article 6 – right to a fair trial

27.48 This article provides:

'In the determination of his civil rights and obligations or of any criminal charge against him, everyone is entitled to a fair and public hearing within a reasonable time by an independent and impartial tribunal established by law. Judgment shall be pronounced publicly but the press and public may be excluded [in certain limited circumstances].'

27.49 Articles 6(2) and (3) make specific further provision for criminal trials. Albeit that they will be relevant to anyone charged with one of the multitude of offences created by the Licensing Act 2003, they are beyond the ambit of this chapter.

27.50 Article 6(1) only affords protection when there has been a determination of substantive civil rights. For example, in *Wilson v First County Trust Limited (No. 2)*[31] the House of Lords held that article 6 of the Convention did not create substantive civil rights, but only guaranteed the procedural right to have a claim in respect of existing civil rights and obligations adjudicated by an independent tribunal.

27.51 So far as operators are concerned, there is no substantive right to the grant of a licence – the matter instead turns on the exercise of discretion by the licensing authority. The absence of such substantive right, but only a procedural right to a determination by the licensing authority arguably precludes the engagement of article 6. See in particular the Scottish cases of *Di Ciacca* and *Mecca* at paragraph 27.40 above. However, it is arguable that those decisions failed properly to give effect to the decision of the House of Lords in *R (Alconbury Developments Ltd and others) v Secretary of State for the*

---

[31]   [2004] 1 AC 816.

Environment, Transport and the Regions[32] where it was clearly held that the decision to grant planning permission may be a determination of civil rights, namely the freedom to develop one's own land. While the matter remains in some doubt, it is submitted that in licensing in this country, the decision in *Alconbury* is likely to be followed.

27.52 Article 6(1) may also be engaged in respect of third party objections depending upon whether they are materially affected by the determination.[33]

27.53 However, the formulation of a policy to be applied to licensing applications, as required by the Licensing Act 2003, is unlikely to engage article 6(1) as the mere formulation of policy will not be directly decisive of any relevant rights. The analogy with planning is reasonably strong and the High Court has held that formulation of development plan policies does not engage article 6(1), notwithstanding that such policies may directly affect the value of land as such change in value did not constitute a determination of the claimant's civil rights.[34]

27.54 The most important matter to understand about the application of article 6(1) is that its application is considered against the procedure as a whole, which includes any appeal or right of appeal.

27.55 The licensing authority may well not be independent or impartial, as local planning authorities are not. This is primarily because they are both decision-makers and policy-makers. However, because nearly every decision of the licensing authority which is likely to engage article 6(1) can be appealed to a magistrates' court, which is (or should now be) both independent and impartial, and the appeal will be a re-hearing the provisions of article 6 are likely to be satisfied whatever the deficiencies of the procedures before the licensing authority. Moreover, the current trend would appear to be that the High Court would expect a right of appeal to the magistrates' court to be exercised before it would consider a complaint in, for example, judicial review proceedings based upon the Human Rights Act 1998.

27.56 Even in respect of those decisions under the Act in respect of which there may be no right of appeal (eg because no right of appeal is available to a third party objector who did not make relevant representations to the licensing authority), there will be a right to challenge by way of judicial review. Provided the objector could bring himself within the protection of article 6(1), which should not be taken for granted, then the High Court would have to consider whether the availability of judicial review was

---

[32]   2003 2 AC 295.

[33]   If a person's use and enjoyment of property is affected by the proposal his rights may be engaged, see *R (Friends Provident) v Environment Secretary* [2002] 1 WLR 1450.

[34]   *R (on the application of Aggregate Industries UK Ltd) v English Nature* [2002] EWHC 908 (Admin), [2003] Env LR 3 and *Bovis Homes Ltd & Anor v New Forest DC* [2002] EWHC 483 (Admin).

sufficient to save the process as a whole before it would strike down the decision as being made by a body that was neither independent or impartial. It remains to be seen whether such a challenge would succeed, but at first sight its chances of success would seem slim. Such challenges have been brought in the context of both the housing and planning systems and have failed. The question will be whether, consistently with the rule of law and constitutional propriety, the relevant decision making powers could be entrusted to administrators with only a right of appeal on a point of law. In these other contexts, the House of Lords has ruled that it can.[35]

27.57 A good example of a failure to ensure such a fair hearing, is, however, provided by a liquor licensing case.[36] The Divisional Court held that it was incompatible with article 6(1) to have licensing justices sitting on appeal in the Crown Court adjudicating upon a decision of licensing justices from the same petty sessional area as those licensing justices. The court made a declaration that, in this respect, rule 3(2) of the Crown Court Rules 1982 was unlawful as it violated article 6. (It is not thought that such reasoning would apply to justices sitting on appeal in the Crown Court from a decision of justices who were themselves hearing the matter as an appeal. In the *Gosling* situation, the problem was that licensing justices do not sit as normal justices but actively promote their own licensing policy and act in a quasi-administrative manner, and are at least potentially parties to the Crown Court appeal.)

27.58 Notwithstanding the relatively safety of licensing authorities from article 6 challenges, given the duty, to be considered below, to act compatibly with a Convention right, a licensing authority should as far as possible seek to ensure any applicant or objector receives a fair trial. The fairer the initial hearing, the greater weight an appeal court is likely to place upon the licensing authority's decision. The less satisfactory the hearing, the less weight the appeal court is likely to attach to its outcome.

27.59 In this regard, it is to be noted that, unlike planning law,[37] the Licensing Act 2003 makes specific provision for oral hearings[38] if requested. Further, of course, proper reasons need to be given for decisions in contested cases.[39]

---

[35] *Begum v London Borough of Tower Hamlets* [2003] UKHL 5 at paragraph 59 in particular.
[36] *R (on the application of the Chief Constable of Lancashire) v Preston Crown Court* and *Gosling, R (on the application of Smith) v Lincoln Crown Court* [2001] EWHC 98 (Admin), [2002] LLR 14, [2002] 1 WLR 1332.
[37] *R (Adlard & Others) v SOSETR* [2002] 1 WLR 2515.
[38] Section 18.
[39] Section 23.

G HUMAN RIGHTS ACT, SECTION 6

27.60 Section 6(1) of the Human Rights Act 1998 provides that it is unlawful for any public authority to act or fail to act in a way which is incompatible with a Convention right.

27.61 The licensing authority is not surprisingly a public authority and so bound by section 6.[40]

27.62 Of equal importance is the fact that courts are also public authorities. This means, at least in theory, that they should take Convention points even if parties do not raise them themselves. This is particularly the case if one party is not represented.

27.63 Section 6(2) provides that section 6(1) does not apply if the licensing authority (or court) could not have acted differently by reason of primary legislation (and that legislation cannot be interpreted so as to ensure compatibility – see section 3). This reaffirms the sovereignty of Parliament.

27.64 More problematically, however, section 6(1) still applies even if secondary legislation appears to require a different result, see section 6(2) again. A licensing authority or court is obliged to ignore secondary legislation which it considers is inconsistent with the Convention unless that incompatibility is a necessary consequence of the primary legislation. That interpretation of section 6(2) is not, perhaps, immediately obvious. Section 6(2) may appear to provide a defence to public authorities faced with incompatible secondary legislation but the High Court has determined that is not so.[41]

27.65 Section 6(2) therefore does not protect an authority in relation to subordinate legislation that is incompatible, but not inevitably so: ie in a case where the enabling provision is in broad general terms and does not require adoption of incompatible regulations it will provide no protection. Many of the regulation making powers under the Licensing Act 2003 fall into this 'broad' category. Indeed, one of the complaints during the introduction of the Act was that much of the necessary flesh to the bones of the new system was to be contained in as yet unpublished regulations about which little was known and even less could be assumed. It should not therefore be assumed that Regulations made under powers contained in the Licensing Act 2003 are HRA compliant.

---

[40] Although there is provision, s 6(5), that private acts are not covered by s 6(1) notwithstanding that the functions are of a public nature, in relation to the ambit of this book it would be most unlikely that any relevant actions of the licensing authority would not be considered public acts.

[41] *R (on the application of Bono) v Harlow DC* [2002] EWHC 423 Admin, [2002] 1 WLR 2475.

27.66 No clear answer has yet been given as to how a public authority should act if the procedure laid down in a regulation is held to be incompatible.[42] It will be left to devise a system that retains as much of the scheme as possible but is not incompatible with the Convention.

27.67 If there is legislation which cannot be ignored but which is incompatible, as stated above, the High Court can make a declaration of incompatibility. Such a declaration may result in a change of the law, eventually, but is not going to get the complainant any substantive remedy in English or Welsh courts. A declaration is not an option open to the magistrates' court although that court is subject to sections 3 and 6 as is any other public body.

27.68 A failure to comply with the duty under section 6(1) can, under section 7(1), lead to proceedings being brought against a public authority to quash its decision and/or for damages.[43] Further, such a failure can afford a person a defence to proceedings brought by a public authority. However a person needs to be a victim[44] before he can avail himself of either the sword or the shield.

27.69 The occurrence of such cases, given in particular the right of appeal, in licensing cases may be rare. However, a clear breach of the duty which leads to delay in granting a licence might give rise to a claim for damages in circumstances where it might not otherwise have done so.

27.70 It is not possible to obtain damages in respect of judicial acts unless done in bad faith.[45] That is going to be most unlikely in licensing cases.

27.71 Akin to other comments made above, the greatest impact of section 6(1) is more likely to be felt in the approach that is adopted to decisions that concern Convention rights. Section 6(1) brings with it a requirement to act proportionately – a concept that has already been dealt with above.

H CONCLUSION

27.72 The Human Rights Act has not caused any severe constriction in the exercise of powers under the Licensing Act 2003. That is in part because much of the thinking underpinning HRA, in particular concerning the

---

42 For an example, see discussion in *Begum v London Borough of Tower Hamlets* [2003] UKHL 5 with reference to the case of *Adan* [2002] 1 WLR 2120.
43 As to the approach to damages under the HRA, see *Anufrijeva v LB Southwark* [2004] 1 All ER 833.
44 A victim is someone who is directly (and adversely) affected by the decision or act in question. The test is stricter than the 'sufficient interest' test in judicial review. Section 7(7) of the Human Rights Act provides that only those people who are eligible by article 34 of the Convention to bring a case before the European Court can be victims for the purposes of the Act. However, article 34 does not define victim, and the area is governed by case law.
45 HRA 1998, s 9(3).

balance of public v private and private v private interests, and concepts of natural justice, already underlay our own common law. Further, the Licensing Act 2003 itself, with its emphasis on gathering all relevant stakeholders together in public meetings to ascertain where the correct balance lies, is itself HRA compliant.

27.73 What the HRA does, in practical terms, is to formalise that which has been innate, to ask public authorities to take cognisance of the rights of the players in the drama upon which it is seeking to adjudicate fairly, to name those rights and ensure that they are fully accounted for in the licensing balance. While it is not merely a tick box exercise, authorities which conscientiously discharge that duty are safe from criticism on the basis of the Human Rights Act 1998.

The Provision of Services Regulations 2009

Be jovial first, and drink, and dance, and drink.

Ben Johnson, *The New Inn*

A INTRODUCTION

28.01   The Provision of Services Regulations 2009[1] implement the Services Directive.[2] The purpose of the Directive was to promote the service economy by restriction and removal of entry barriers and excessive bureaucracy attached to authorisation procedures.

B THE REGULATIONS

28.02   Regulation 14 compels national authorities to ask whether, in respect of any particular service activity, there should be an authorisation scheme at all. Authorities should not have such a scheme unless it is non-discriminatory, justified by an overriding reason relating to the public interest and having an objective that cannot be attained by means of a less restrictive measure. This underlines the fact that schemes such as the Licensing Act survive precisely because they meet those criteria.

28.03   Furthermore, regulation 15 provides that even where there is a justified authorisation scheme, it must be based on criteria which preclude the authority concerned from exercising its power of assessment in an arbitrary manner. The criteria must be non-discriminatory, justified by an overriding reason relating to the public interest, proportionate to that public interest objective, clear, unambiguous, objective, made public in advance and transparent and accessible.

---

[1]   SI 2009/2999.
[2]   2006/123/EC.

28.04 There is some doubt whether the 'appropriateness' test which now underlies much of the Licensing Act 2003 genuinely meets those criteria. If an authority were to refuse a licence on the grounds that it was inappropriate to grant it, without really considering whether refusal was proportionate, it may find itself running foul of this provision. Put another way, in order to render the Licensing Act 2003 lawful, the 'appropriateness' test must arguably be read subject to the requirements in regulation 15 so that licences are not (for example) refused unless the refusal is both proportionate and justified by an overriding reason relating to the public interest.

28.05 Regulation 18 requires that authorisation procedures and formalities must be clear, made public in advance, and secure that applications for authorisation are dealt with objectively and impartially. Nor must such procedures and formalities be dissuasive or unduly complicate or delay the provision of the service. The procedural regulations under the Licensing Act 2003, coupled with authorities' own internal procedures, secure compliance with these requirements.

28.06 Similarly, regulation 19 requires that authorisation procedures and formalities secure that applications are processed as quickly as possible and in any event within a reasonable period running from the time when all documentation has been submitted, which period must be fixed and made public in advance. These requirements are met by the Licensing Act 2003 and the procedural requirements thereunder, although the absence of long-stop dates for determination in the Act may run foul of the requirement in regulation 19(3) that there can only be one extension. No complaint has yet been made about that lacuna in the Act.

28.07 Finally, regulation 18(4) deals with fees, and states that any charges which applicants may incur under an authorisation scheme must be reasonable and proportionate to the cost of the procedures and formalities under the scheme and must not exceed the cost of those procedures and formalities. This is clearly intended as a restraint on application fees, and is dealt with in Chapter 61 (The Fees Regime).

C CONCLUSION

28.08 In conclusion, in most respects, the requirements of the Regulations are woven into the Licensing Act 2003 and its subordinate regulations.

28.09 However, litigation regarding the meaning and effect of regulation 15 lurks in waiting for an authority which takes draconian action based on a low threshold of appropriateness and without clearly considering the proportionality of its response. Further, the latitude to determine fees under the fees regime is tempered by regulation 18, in a manner canvassed further in Chapter 61.

The Legislative and Regulatory Reform Act 2006

In short, to sum up all in one word, a man who is inebriated, or tending to inebriation, is, and feels that he is, in a condition which calls up into supremacy the merely human, too often the brutal part of his nature; but the opium-eater (I speak of him who is not suffering from any disease or other remote effects of opium) feels that the divines part of his nature is paramount; that is, the moral affections are in a state of cloudless serenity, and over all is the great light of the majestic intellect.

Thomas de Quincey, *Confessions of an English Opium-Eater*

A INTRODUCTION

29.01 The Licensing Act 2003 appears to give authorities untrammelled powers in relation to enforcement, just as it appears to give such powers in relation to grant: in both cases the bar which must be surmounted is that of 'appropriateness'. However, the Legislative and Regulatory Reform Act 2006, which applies to licensing,[1] imposes primary legislative restraints upon regulatory action in general and enforcement action in particular.

29.02 These restraints are two-fold. First, authorities must have regard to the principles set out in section 21. Second, authorities must have regard to any code of practice issued under section 22.

29.03 These restraints are considered in turn.

B SECTION 21

29.04 Section 21 provides that any person exercising a regulatory function to which the section applies must have regard to the principles set out in

---

[1]   See s 24 and The Legislative and Regulatory Reform (Regulatory Functions) Order 2007 (SI 2007/3544), art 2.

section 21(2). Here, 'regulatory functions' includes the imposition of requirements, restrictions or conditions and the securing of compliance with, or the enforcement of, requirements, restrictions or conditions. Therefore, these obligations encompass both the setting of conditions and their enforcement. They also plainly encompass all of the enforcement mechanisms under the Licensing Act 2003.

29.05   The section 21(2) principles are themselves two-fold:

(a)   Regulatory activities should be carried out in a way which is transparent, accountable, proportionate and consistent.
(b)   Regulatory activities should be targeted only at cases in which action is needed.

29.06   As to the first principle, the key requirement is obviously that of proportionality. This gives legislative embodiment to the spirit repeatedly conjured in national Guidance.[2] To take but one example, paragraph 9.39 says:

'The authority's determination should be evidence-based, justified as being appropriate for the promotion of the licensing objectives and proportionate to what it is intended to achieve.'

29.07   While, because of section 4 of the Act, the authority needs to have regard to the Guidance, the test under the Act remains appropriateness. Section 21 does not purport to repeal or modify that test, but applying it faithfully does mean that a response will not be appropriate unless it is also proportionate. Thus section 21 is of great importance in tempering the very wide discretion apparently afforded under the Licensing Act 2003.

29.08   The second principle concerns choice of those to be targeted with regulatory activities. Authorities who target their enforcement work at the worst performing premises or those giving rise to the greatest risk are in compliance with this section. In an era of diminishing resources in the public sector, this is an economic as well as a regulatory necessity.

C SECTION 22

29.09   Section 22 enables a Minister to publish a code of practice in relation to the exercise of regulatory functions. The code has statutory force in that any person exercising a regulatory function to which the section applies – which includes licensing functions under the Licensing Act 2003 – must have regard to the code in determining any general policy or principles by reference to which the person exercises the function.

---

[2]   See paragraphs 1.7, 1.16, 1.17, 2.20, 9.39, 10.10, 11.20 and 11.23.

29.10   It is important to note that the duty to have regard to the code does not apply when the regulatory function itself is exercised, only when the policy or principles for exercise of the function are being determined.

29.11   The origins of this section lie in the publication 'Reducing administrative burdens: effective inspection and enforcement', known for short as the Hampton Report.[3] Following the Act, the Government published the 'Regulators' Compliance Code: Statutory Code of Practice for Regulators'.[4]

29.12   The Code's purpose is to promote efficient and effective approaches to regulatory inspection and enforcement which improve regulatory outcomes without imposing unnecessary burdens on those being regulated.[5] Importantly, the Code stresses the need for a positive and proactive approach towards ensuring compliance by helping and encouraging regulated entities to understand and meet regulatory requirements more easily, and also by responding proportionately to regulatory breaches. The first element of this requires emphasis. Good regulation is not just about good enforcement. It is also about helping operators into compliance in the first instance. This is very much in accord with the theme of partnership working which lies at the heart of this book.

Among the specific obligations of the Code are the following:

29.13

'Regulators should recognise that a key element of their activity will be to allow, or even encourage, economic progress and only to intervene where there is a clear case for protection.'

In Chapters 4 and 5, we saw how important it is for policies to set out what they favour as well as what they oppose. Consistent with that, the Code affirms that it is a part of regulatory activity to promote economic progress.

29.14

'Regulators ... should use comprehensive risk assessment to concentrate resources in the areas that need them most.'

The Code exhorts a risk assessment approach based on collection of data, inspection programmes, advice and support programmes and enforcement and sanctions. In assessing risk, authorities should consider the likelihood of non-compliance and the measure of harm which would arise. In judging the likelihood of non-compliance, regulators are to consider past compliance records, the operator's risk management systems, evidence of external accreditations and the operator's competence and willingness to comply.

[3]   HM Treasury (2005).
[4]   BERR (2007).
[5]   Paragraph 1.2.

29.15

'Regulators should provide authoritative, accessible advice easily and cheaply'.

This principle speaks for itself. The Code adds that information, advice and guidance should be given to make it easier for operators to understand and meet their regulatory obligations.

29.16

'No inspection should take place without a reason'.

This principle is a corollary of the risk assessment principle. It means that inspections only occur in accordance with a risk assessment methodology, unless the visit has been requested by the operator or arises from intelligence. Random inspections to test the methodology should only amount to a small element of overall inspection programmes.

29.17

'Operators who persistently break regulations should be identified quickly and face proportionate and meaningful sanctions'.

The Code indicates that while the compliant should be rewarded with lighter inspection and reporting requirements, meaningful action needs to be taken against the non-compliant. Sanctions and penalty policies should be consistent with the principles set out in the Macrory Review[6], in that they should:

- aim to change the offender's behaviour;
- aim to eliminate financial gain or benefit from non-compliance;
- be responsive and consider what is appropriate to the offender and the offence;
- be proportionate to the nature of the offence and the harm caused;
- aim to restore the harm caused by regulatory non-compliance, where appropriate;
- aim to deter future non-compliance.

29.18 The Code also requires regulators to publish enforcement policies, measures outcomes and not just outputs, and be prepared both to enforce and justify their decisions in a transparent manner.

D CONCLUSION

29.19 The Legislative and Regulatory Reform Act 2006 performs an important role in requiring regulators to act according to principles which are proportionate and transparent. It provides a salutary check and balance on

---

[6]   'Regulatory Justice: Making Sanctions Effective' (Better Regulation Executive, 2006).

the regulatory powers in the Licensing Act 2003 which are based on the low threshold of appropriateness, and thus should be borne strongly in mind by licensing authorities.

30

RIPA

Harper: If any of the Ladies choose Ginn, I hope they will be so free to call for it.

Jenny: You look as if you meant me. Wine is strong enough for me. Indeed, Sir, I never drink Strong-Waters, but when I have the Cholic.

Macheath: Just the Excuse of the fine Ladies! Why, a Lady of Quality is never without the Cholic.

The Beggar's Opera
John Gay

A INTRODUCTION

30.01 The Regulation of Investigatory Powers Act 2000 ('RIPA') is intended to place a check and balance on the ability of organs of the state to carry out covert surveillance. Local authorities are bound by the provisions in the Act. The Coalition Government has been concerned to restrict the powers of local authorities to conduct surveillance still further, and has done so through the Protection of Freedoms Act 2012[1] and the Regulation of Investigatory Powers (Directed Surveillance and Covert Human Intelligence Sources) (Amendment) Order 2012.[2]

30.02 Be that as it may, the question addressed by this Chapter is whether the Act is engaged at all by the sort of routine surveillance carried out for the purposes of licensing: CCTV, exterior surveillance and covert surveillance of licensed premises, and test purchasing. The conclusion will be reached that it is not.

---

[1]   Section 38.
[2]   SI 2012/1500.

B HOW RIPA WORKS

Starting point

30.03 RIPA is a means of insulating public authorities from claims under article 8 of the European Convention on Human Rights ('ECHR'). However, surveillance by public authorities is not in itself unlawful and nor does it necessarily engage article 8 of the ECHR. For example, general observations of members of the public by the police in the course of carrying out routine public duties to detect crime and enforce the law is lawful, because it does not interfere with individual citizens in a way which requires specific justification.[3] The starting point is therefore article 8 itself:

> '1. Everyone has the right to respect for his private and family life, his home and his correspondence.
>
> 2. There shall be no interference by a public authority with the exercise of this right except such as is in accordance with the law and is necessary in a democratic society in the interests of national security, public safety or the economic well-being of the country, for the prevention of disorder or crime, for the protection of health or morals, or for the protection of the rights and freedoms of others.'

30.04 If there is no interference with an article 8 right, there is no need for any kind of authorisation. So, where surveillance would not result in the obtaining of private information about a person, no article 8 rights are engaged and so no article 8 rights are breached. Plainly, in that situation, authorisation under RIPA is not needed.[4]

30.05 However, if there is interference, the authorisations under RIPA provide the justification for interference and establish the tests for proportionality. Where there is an authorisation <u>and</u> conduct is in accordance with the authorisation, it is lawful <u>for all purposes</u>.[5] Therefore, using RIPA procedures gives assurance that an authority could not be challenged for any breach of article 8 when carrying out investigations.

30.06 Although RIPA provides a framework for obtaining internal authorisation of certain surveillance, it does not prohibit surveillance without RIPA authorisation. RIPA does not <u>require</u> prior authorisation to be obtained by a public authority to carry out surveillance. Lack of authorisation does not necessarily mean that the carrying out of surveillance is unlawful.[6] This is reinforced by section 80 of RIPA, which specifically provides that the Act does not render unlawful otherwise lawful conduct. RIPA authorisation

---

[3]   *C v The Police*, IPT/03/32/H at para [42].
[4]   See 'Covert Surveillance and Property Interference, Revised Code of Practice', para 1.14.
[5]   RIPA s 27(1).
[6]   *C v The Police* (above) at para [62].

simply provides one means of ensuring that conduct is lawful, so protecting the public authority concerned.[7]

30.07 Therefore, in short, RIPA authorisation is not always required for covert surveillance, but if obtained it insulates the authority from legal complaint based on Article 8. For that reason, some authorities do seek RIPA authorisation as a matter of course for their surveillance work.

RIPA conduct

30.08 The conduct concerned is:

(a) directed surveillance
(b) intrusive surveillance
(c) conduct or use of covert human intelligence sources.[8]

30.09 Only the first and third of these are likely to be relevant to licensing authorities.

Directed surveillance

30.10 For surveillance to be directed, it must be:

(a) Surveillance
(b) Covert (but not intrusive)
(c) For the purpose of a specific investigation or operation
(d) Undertaken in such a manner as is likely to result in the obtaining of private information about a person (including any organisation or association or combination of persons)[9]
(e) Otherwise than by way of immediate response to events.[10]

30.11 Surveillance is not fully defined. But:

(a) Subject to (b) below, it includes:
    (i) monitoring, observing or listening to persons, their movements, their conversations or their other activities or communication;
    (ii) recording anything monitored, observed or listened to in the course of surveillance;
    (iii) surveillance by or with the assistance of a surveillance device.[11]
(b) It does not include:
    (i) any conduct of a covert human intelligence source for obtaining or recording (whether or not using a surveillance device) any information which is disclosed in the presence of the source;

---

[7]   *C v The Police* at para [64].
[8]   RIPA, s 26(1).
[9]   RIPA, s 81(1).
[10] RIPA, s 26(2).
[11] RIPA, s 48(2).

> (ii) the use of a covert human intelligence source for so obtaining or recording information; or
>
> (iii) any such entry or interference with property or wireless telegraphy as would be unlawful unless authorised under the Intelligence Services Act 1994 or the Police Act 1997.[12]

(c) It also includes certain communications interceptions.[13]

30.12 General observations by enforcement officials, even with equipment to reinforce normal sensory perceptions, such as binoculars or cameras, are not surveillance where they do not involve systematic surveillance of an individual. So covert observations of or visits to a shop to verify the supply of goods and services is not surveillance.[14] However, the Office of Surveillance Commissioners advises that processing of data on an individual, e g taking a photograph to put on record, is an invasion of privacy and potentially amounts to directed surveillance.[15]

30.13 Surveillance is covert only if it is carried out in such a manner that it is calculated to ensure that persons subject to the surveillance are unaware it is taking place.[16]

30.14 Private information includes information as to a person's private or family life.[17] This extends to an individual's private or personal relationship with others.[18] It can include conduct in private, e g recording the activities of individuals or their conversations for subsequent consideration or analysis[19] where the target has a reasonable expectation of privacy.[20] The concept of 'private information' is to be read in the light of article 8 so that it includes not only personal information but also relationships with others, and how the target runs business affairs.[21]

How is authorisation for directed surveillance obtained?

30.15 For authorities in general, a designated person must grant the authorisation, but shall not do so unless s/he believes that:

---

[12] RIPA, s 48(3).
[13] RIPA, s 48(4).
[14] 'Code of Practice on Covert Surveillance', para 1.3.
[15] 'Office of Surveillance Commissioners Procedures and Guidance' (December 2008), para 268.
[16] RIPA, s 26(9).
[17] RIPA, s 26 (10).
[18] 'Code of Practice on Covert Surveillance', para 4.3.
[19] 'Office of Surveillance Commissioners Procedures and Guidance' (December 2008), para 149.
[20] 'Revised Code of Practice on Covert Surveillance and Property Interference', para 2.5.
[21] 'Revised Code of Practice on Covert Surveillance and Property Interference', para 150.

(a)   It is necessary on grounds including prevention or detection of crime and disorder, public safety, public health or other purpose specified by order made by Secretary of State;

(b)   The authorised surveillance is proportionate to what is sought to be achieved by carrying it out.[22]

30.16   Proportionality involves balancing the intrusiveness of the activity on the target and others affected against the need for the activity. It is disproportionate where the action is excessive or the information could reasonably be obtained by less intrusive means.[23] Further, more detailed guidance is given by the Office of Surveillance Commissioners.[24]

30.17   However, for local authorities in particular, a further constraint was introduced by article 2(4) of The Regulation of Investigatory Powers (Directed Surveillance and Covert Human Intelligence Sources) (Amendment) Order 2012.[25] This provides that authorisation may only be given if the following two conditions are satisfied. The first condition is, briefly, that the authorisation under section 28 is for the purpose of preventing or detecting conduct which is a criminal offence. The second is that the offence carries at least 6 months imprisonment or relates to section 146 of the Licensing Act 2003 (sale of alcohol to children), section 147 of the Licensing Act 2003 (allowing the sale of alcohol to children), section 147A of the Licensing Act 2003 (persistently selling alcohol to children), or section 7 of the Children and Young Persons Act 1933 (sale of tobacco, etc, to persons under eighteen).

30.18   This new constraint does not of course mean that all local authority observations are directed surveillance. But it does mean that if in a particular case the observation does qualify on the facts as directed surveillance then it cannot be done at all under RIPA unless the proportionality test is satisfied and it relates to conduct which is a criminal offence carrying a maximum of six months imprisonment, or is one of the offences of selling alcohol or tobacco to children. This would rule out directed surveillance for the purpose of defending an appeal against a review decision which related to nuisance but not to crime.

30.19   A yet further constraint was imposed by section 38 of the Protection of Freedoms Act 2012, which added a new section 32A to RIPA. The effect of this is that any authorisation granted under section 28 does not take effect until it has been approved by a single magistrate. Guidance on the procedure is given by the Home Office.[26]

22   RIPA, s 28(2)–(3).
23   'Revised Code of Practice on Covert Surveillance and Property Interference', para 3.5.
24   'Office of Surveillance Commissioners Procedures and Guidance' (December 2008), para 103.
25   SI 2012/1500.
26   'Protection of Freedoms Act 2012 – changes to provisions under the Regulation of

Covert human intelligence sources

30.20 A person is a covert human intelligence source ('CHIS') if:

(a) He establishes or maintains a personal or other relationship with a person for the covert purpose of facilitating the doing of anything falling within (b) or (c).

(b) He covertly uses such a relationship to obtain information or to provide access to any information to another person.

(c) He covertly discloses information obtained by the use of such a relationship etc.[27]

30.21 A purpose is covert where the relationship is conducted in such a manner that it is calculated to ensure that the other party is unaware of the purpose. Similarly, a relationship is used covertly where the other party is unaware of the use.[28]

30.22 In *R v Brett*[29] the Court of Appeal assumed without argument that a police officer with a concealed camera attending a suspect's home purporting to sell stolen goods was a covert human intelligence source.

30.23 LACORS[30] advised that the use of a young person in test purchasing is unlikely to be a covert human intelligence source as the young person does not establish or maintain any relationship with the seller.[31] This view was shared by the Home Office.[32] However, the Office of Surveillance Commissioners appears to have taken a different view where covert technical equipment is worn by the test purchaser or an adult is observing the test purchase: in such a situation the advice is that directed surveillance has occurred.[33]

30.24 Home Office guidance[34] now gives two examples. In the first, a straightforward test purchase operation is conducted. This is not thought to require a CHIS authorisation. The guidance continues, however: '... if the test purchaser is wearing recording equipment but is not authorised as a CHIS, consideration should be given to granting a directed surveillance authorisation.' In the second, sales are made from a back room, but only

---

Investigatory Powers Act 2000 (RIPA): Home Office guidance to local authorities in England and Wales on the judicial process for RIPA and the crime threshold for directed surveillance' (Home Office, October 2012).

27   RIPA, s 26(8).
28   RIPA, s 26(9).
29   [2005] EWCA Crim 983.
30   The now defunct Local Authorities Co-ordinators of Regulatory Services.
31   'Guide to Test Purchasing', para 4.2.
32   Home Office letters to LACORS and Police, 14 December 2004.
33   'Office of Surveillance Commissioners Procedures and Guidance' (December 2008), para 253.
34   'Covert Human Intelligence Sources: Code of Practice'.

once the shopkeeper has come to know and trust the buyers. Therefore, an operative is employed for the purpose to gain the shopkeeper's trust before buying alcohol. In this situation, there is a relationship established and maintained for a covert purpose, so a CHIS authorisation is needed.

How is authorisation obtained?

30.25 A designated person must grant the authorisation, but shall not do so unless s/he believes that:

(a) It is necessary on grounds including prevention or detection of crime and disorder, public safety, public health or other purpose specified by order made by Secretary of State;

(b) It is proportionate to what is sought to be achieved by carrying it out;

(c) The arrangements for the source's case satisfy various requirements regarding oversight of the conduct.[35]

30.26 Proportionality involves balancing the intrusiveness of the activity on the target and others affected against the need for the activity. It is disproportionate where the action is excessive or the information could reasonably be obtained by less intrusive means.[36]

30.27 Onto that scheme has been grafted, by the same means as for directed surveillance, the need for judicial approval of the CHIS authorisation.

C RIPA AND LICENSING

30.28 In licensing, the questions as to use of RIPA most commonly arise in relation to town centre CCTV, the ability of officers to monitor premises for noise and crime and disorder, and test purchasing. These are taken in turn.

CCTV

30.29 Home Office guidance[37] makes it clear that overt CCTV does not normally require an authorisation under the 2000 Act. Members of the public will be aware that such systems are in use, and their operation is covered by the Data Protection Act 1998 and the CCTV Code of Practice 2008, issued by the Information Commissioner's Office. In most cases, of course, the CCTV system is used to gather information retrospectively, for

---

[35]   RIPA, s 29(2)–(3),(5).
[36]   'Covert Human Intelligence Sources: Code of Practice'.
[37]   'Covert Surveillance and Property Interference: Revised Code of Practice', paras 2.27 et seq.

example to identify offenders. Such use does not amount to covert surveil-lance as the equipment was overt and not subject to any covert targeting. Use in these circumstances would not require a directed surveillance authorisa-tion. The guidance goes on to say that where overt CCTV cameras are used in a covert and pre-planned manner as part of a specific investigation or operation, for the surveillance of a specific person or group of people, a directed surveillance authorisation should be considered, since such covert surveillance is likely to result in the obtaining of private information about a person (namely, a record of their movements and activities) and therefore falls properly within the definition of directed surveillance. The use of the CCTV or automatic number plate recognition systems in these circum-stances goes beyond their intended use for the general prevention or detection of crime and protection of the public.

30.30 While that advice is considered to be correct, it is very unlikely that CCTV would be used in such a manner by licensing authorities. For most if not all of the purposes for which CCTV would ever be used by licensing authorities, therefore, no authorisation is required.

Monitoring of premises

30.31 Covert monitoring might happen in two ways. First, an authority might simply watch the premises in order to gain information as to hours of departure, whether departing patrons are intoxicated, whether they are creating a noise etc. In some cases, it might carry out formal noise monitoring to take readings, for example regarding noise breakout. Second, an authority might send in an officer to the premises at night simply to watch how the premises is managed, whether alcohol is being served responsibly, whether conditions are being observed and so forth.

30.32 In none of these cases is it considered that directed surveillance arises. First, it does not meet the definition of surveillance set out above. Second, it is not undertaken in such a manner as is likely to result in the obtaining of private information regarding a person. The situation may be different if particular individuals were being monitored, particular conversa-tions noted or photographs of individuals were being taken. But merely watching premises, whether from the inside or the outside, is not in and of itself directed surveillance.

Test purchasing

30.33 For the same reason as that just given, test purchasing is not directed surveillance. Further, as described above, ordinary test purchasing opera-tions do not require CHIS authorisations.

D CONCLUSION

30.34 There is considerable complexity attached to RIPA authorisations, and it is clear that not all public authorities, let alone practitioners, have held the same views. However, it must be remembered that fundamentally RIPA is concerned with operations that may elicit information on individuals which would breach their article 8 rights. If the town centre in general or premises in particular are simply being monitored for their effect on the licensing objectives, or if test purchasing operations are being conducted in an ordinary manner and without recording equipment, it is not considered that article 8 rights are engaged at all, and so further authorisation is not needed.

30.35 However, given the complexity of the field, any licensing team contemplating any kind of surveillance should take advice to ensure that its *modus operandi* keeps it on the right side of the law.

Parallel consent schemes

All things must change
To something new, to something strange

Henry Wadsworth Longfellow

Planning and other strategies

However beautiful the strategy, you should occasionally look at the results

Winston Churchill

A	Introduction 31.01
B	Local authority plans and strategies 31.03
C	The planning system 31.20
D	The interplay between licensing and planning 31.36
E	Integrating plans and strategies 31.42
F	Conclusion 31.44

A INTRODUCTION

31.01 Local authorities perform a multitude of functions. In this book they are, most importantly, licensing authorities, but they have a range of other responsibilities[1] such as for planning control under the Town and Country Planning Act 1990, the abatement of statutory nuisances under the Environmental Protection Act 1990, the enforcement of requirements for the health and safety of employees and others under the Health and Safety etc Act 1974 and food safety under the Food Safety Act 1990. In addition to these relatively focused areas of regulatory activity local authorities are also expected to perform a broader 'leadership' role, drawing on their various powers to promote the interests of the inhabitants of their areas.

31.02 A common feature of modern local government legislation is the obligation placed on local authorities to prepare a plan, policy or strategy to guide the exercise of administrative power. The scope and content of these documents will vary, depending very much on context: some will provide little more than a check-list of matters to be taken into account, others may seek to identify local needs and aspirations and set out how they are to be met. Reflecting this legislative trend, the Licensing Act 2003 requires

---

[1] The responsibilities referred to are not shared by the Common Council of the City of London, the Sub-Treasurer of the Inner Temple or the Under-Treasurer of the Middle Temple.

licensing authorities to determine and publish a statement of licensing policy every five years.[2] The purpose of the licensing policy is to inform and steer the exercise of a local authority's licensing functions, providing an important element of consistency and coherence. It is, however, only one policy among many others, some of which will also impinge on the licensing regime. This chapter seeks to place licensing in its local government context, by drawing attention to other local authority functions, plans, policies and strategies that have a bearing on the licensing regime. Of particular importance is the interplay between licensing and planning functions, and this is given extended consideration.

B LOCAL AUTHORITY PLANS AND STRATEGIES

31.03 National Guidance encourages authorities to integrate their strategies, although it fights shy of explaining in any great detail how this might be done. It states:

> '13.54 It is recommended that statements of licensing policy should provide clear indications of how the licensing authority will secure the proper integration of its licensing policy with local crime prevention, planning, transport, tourism, equality schemes, cultural strategies and any other plans introduced for the management of town centres and the night-time economy. Many of these strategies are not directly related to the promotion of the licensing objectives, but, indirectly, impact upon them. Co-ordination and integration of such policies, strategies and initiatives are therefore important.'

In this section, we consider some of the strategies relevant to the leisure economy.

Sustainable community strategies in England

31.04 Of all the various strategic documents an English local authority is required to produce, the broadest at present[3] is the 'sustainable community strategy', setting out how the local authority will promote or improve the economic, social and environmental well-being of its area and contribute to the achievement of sustainable development[4] in the United Kingdom.[5] In

---

2   Licensing Act 2003, s 5.
3   In 'Best Value Statutory Guidance' (DCLG, September 2011) the Government has stated that it intends to repeal the duty to prepare sustainable community strategies.
4   The term 'sustainable development' is used increasingly in legislation, but invariably without a definition. According to 'Creating Strong, Safe and Prosperous Communities: Statutory Guidance' (DCLG, July 2008; revoked in 2011), para 3.8: 'The goal of

short, it is the overarching plan for promoting and improving the well-being of an authority's area.[6]

31.05 A sustainable community strategy should contain the following elements: 'a long-term vision based firmly on local needs – this will be underpinned by a shared evidence base informed by community aspirations'; and 'key priorities for the local area, based upon this vision which may realistically be achieved in the medium term – these will inform the strategy's delivery agreement – the Local Area Agreement (LAA)'.[7]

31.06 In assessing whether a priority or policy is sustainable, statutory guidance directs attention to the following desiderata: living within environmental limits; a strong, healthy and just society; achieving a sustainable economy; promoting good governance; using sound science responsibly.[8] Although these aims are wider and more abstract than the statutory licensing objectives, there is unlikely to be significant conflict between the demands of sustainability and the underlying rationale of the licensing objectives – to prevent licensable activities causing harm. Indeed, the licensing objectives can be seen as constituent elements of 'a strong, healthy and just society'.

31.07 In preparing or modifying its sustainable community strategy a county council, London borough council or unitary district council must consult with a wide range of 'partner authorities', including the local policing body or chief officer of police.[9] Other local authorities preparing sustainable community strategies must consult such persons as they consider appropriate.[10] Representatives of local persons[11] may also be involved in the process,[12] potentially including groups supportive of or opposed to licensable activities. Consultation is intended to ensure that the chosen strategy is both soundly based and representative (so far as possible) of the shared views of the partner authorities and other consultees. A local authority preparing its sustainable community strategy will need to give due consideration to the views expressed by consultees, but need not accept them.

sustainable development is to enable all people throughout the world to satisfy their basic needs and enjoy a better quality of life, without compromising the quality of life of future generations.'

5   See Local Government Act 2000, s 4.
6   'Creating Strong, Safe and Prosperous Communities: Statutory Guidance', para 3.11.
7   'Creating Strong, Safe and Prosperous Communities: Statutory Guidance', para 3.2.
8   'Creating Strong, Safe and Prosperous Communities: Statutory Guidance', para 3.9.
9   Local Government Act 2000 s 4(3),(6); Local Government and Public Involvement in Health Act 2007, ss 103–104.
10 Local Government Act 2000, s 4(3),(6); Local Government and Public Involvement in Health Act 2007, s 103.
11 For this purpose, 'local person' means in relation to a function of a local authority, a person who is likely to be affected by, or interested in, the exercise of the function: Local Government Act 1999, s 3A(6).
12 Pursuant to Local Government Act 1999, s 3A.

31.08 It was plainly the government's intention that sustainable community strategies should influence, and in turn be influenced by, other statutory plans and policies, including local authority licensing and planning policies.[13]

Community strategies in Wales

31.09 In Wales the position is largely the same. County councils and county borough councils must initiate, maintain, facilitate and participate in 'community planning', which is the process by which a local authority and its 'community planning partners' identify long term objectives for improving the social, economic and environmental well-being of its area and (in relation to its area) for contributing to the achievement of sustainable development in the United Kingdom.[14] The community planning partners for an area will include the police authority and chief constable of any overlapping police area.[15] Once a sufficient degree of consensus has been reached amongst the community planning partners and the local authority, the authority must produce a 'community strategy', containing a description of the community strategy objectives which the authority considers it appropriate to set having regard to the consensus reached and a description of the actions to be performed and functions to be exercised for the purpose of achieving those objectives.[16] The community strategy is to be the overarching strategy for a local authority's area.[17]

31.10 Local authorities and their community planning partners must ensure that arrangements are made so that, amongst others, residents and business representatives have the opportunity to express their views and have them taken into account in community planning and the production and review of the community strategy.[18] Again, this may allow groups interested in licensable activities to seek to influence the broad strategic environment within which more detailed licensing policies are to be formulated.

Crime and disorder strategies

31.11 The licensing objectives are the prevention of crime and disorder; public safety; the prevention of public nuisance; and the protection of

---

[13] 'Creating Strong, Safe and Prosperous Communities: Statutory Guidance', para 3.22 and Figure 2; 'Amended Guidance Issued Under Section 182 of the Licensing Act 2003' (Home Office, October 2012), para 13.54; Planning and Compulsory Purchase Act 2004, s 19(2)(f)–(g).
[14] Local Government (Wales) Measure 2009, s 37(1)–(2).
[15] Local Government (Wales) Measure 2009, s 38(1).
[16] Local Government (Wales) Measure 2009, s 39(1)–(3).
[17] 'Collaborative Community Planning Part 2: Community Strategies and Planning' (WAG, June 2010), paras 2.3, 4.36.
[18] Local Government (Wales) Measure 2009, s 44(1)–(2).

children from harm.[19] Of particular relevance to all these objective will be the strategy formulated by 'community safety partnerships',[20] pursuant to the Crime and Disorder Act 1998, for the reduction of crime and disorder (including anti-social and other behaviour adversely affecting the local environment), combating the misuse of drugs, alcohol and other substances, and the reduction of re-offending in the area.[21]

31.12 For each local government area, the community safety partnership (involving the local authority, the police and other relevant bodies) is required to prepare a partnership plan, usually called a community safety partnership plan, setting out the following matters (among others): the strategy for the reduction of re-offending, crime and disorder, and for combating substance misuse in the area; identified priorities; the steps to be taken to implement the strategy and meet those priorities; and how resources are to be allocated and deployed.[22] The partnership plan must be reviewed annually, and to this end each community safety partnership is required to carry out an annual strategic assessment of the levels and patterns of re-offending, crime and disorder, substance misuse, and of related matters.

31.13 Underpinning the strategy set out in the partnership plan is the obligation on local authorities, including licensing authorities, under section 17 of the Crime and Disorder Act 1998 to exercise their functions with due regard to the likely effect of the exercise of those functions on, and the need to do all that they reasonably can to prevent, crime and disorder (including anti-social and other behaviour adversely affecting the local environment), the misuse of drugs, alcohol and other substances, and re-offending in their areas.[23] To a great extent this obligation overlaps with, and adds little to, the general duty on licensing authorities to promote the licensing objectives, but the two duties are not entirely coextensive. For instance, alcohol misuse need not involve criminal or anti-social behaviour, or threaten public safety or the well-being of children, and the duty under section 17 can to that extent be said to supplement the duty to promote the licensing objectives. Furthermore, in licensing cases the section 17 duty adds emphasis to the duty to promote the crime prevention objective. This matter is canvassed further in Chapter 25 (The Crime and Disorder Act 1998).

---

[19]   S 4(2), the Licensing Act 2003, s 4(2).
[20]   In England, formerly known as crime and disorder reduction partnerships. Community safety partnerships are made up of the responsible authorities specified in s 5 of the Crime and Disorder Act 1998, including local authorities, chief officers of police, police authorities, primary care trusts in England and local health boards in Wales.
[21]   See the Crime and Disorder Act 1998, ss 5–6.
[22]   Crime and Disorder (Formulation and Implementation of Strategy) Regulations 2007, regs 10–11; Crime and Disorder (Formulation and Implementation Strategy) (Wales) Regulations 2007, regs 8–9; Substance Misuse (Formulation and Implementation of Strategy) (Wales) Regulations 2007, regs 8–9.
[23]   Crime and Disorder Act 1998, s 17(1).

31.14   It is obviously desirable that the licensing policies determined by licensing authorities and the decisions taken in response to licence applications should be consistent with the broader crime and disorder and drugs misuse strategies prepared by community safety partnerships. Accordingly, the advice to licensing authorities is to involve community safety partnerships in decision-making.[24] In particular, where a licensing authority is considering whether to include a special policy on cumulative impact, the assessments carried out by the community safety partnership are likely to be an important source of information.

Local transport plans

31.15   Under the Transport Act 2000 each 'local transport authority'[25] is required to develop and implement policies for the promotion and encouragement of safe, integrated, efficient and economic transport to, from and within its area,[26] and to produce a transport plan containing those policies and other specified matters.[27] Local transport plans must be kept under review.[28]

31.16   In London the Mayor of London is required to prepare and publish a 'transport strategy',[29] and each London borough council must in turn prepare a 'local implementation plan' containing its proposals for the implementation of the transport strategy in its area.[30] In exercising any function a London borough council is required to have regard to the Mayor's transport strategy and to any guidance issued by the Mayor about the implementation of the transport strategy.[31]

31.17   As to the incorporation of transport policy within a licensing authority's statement of licensing policy, until 2012 national Guidance stated, at para 13.61:

> 'A statement should describe any protocols agreed between the local police and other licensing enforcement officers and indicate that arrangements will be made for them to report to local authority transport committees so that those committees may have regard to the need to disperse people from town and city centres swiftly and safely when developing their policies. When developing the statement licensing authorities should have regard to the existing policies and strategies

---

24   Guidance, para 2.1.
25   In England, 'local transport authority' means a county council, a non-metropolitan unitary district council, an integrated transport authority or a combined authority; in Wales, it means a county council or county borough council: Transport Act 2000, s 108(4).
26   Transport Act 2000, s 108(1).
27   Transport Act 2000, s 108(3)–(3A).
28   Transport Act 2000, ss 109, 109B.
29   Greater London Authority Act 1999, s 142.
30   Greater London Authority Act 1999, s 145.
31   Greater London Authority Act 1999, s 144(1)–(3).

of the relevant local transport authority, as set out in their Local Transport Plan. They may also wish to consult licensees who are likely to have a good knowledge of customer expectation and behavioural patterns in relation to transport options.'

The excision of this paragraph from the Guidance appears to be borne of a drive to succinctness than a change in government policy.

Cultural strategies

31.18 Save for the Mayor of London, who is required to prepare and publish a cultural strategy,[32] local government bodies do not have a formal strategic role in the provision or promotion of the arts, entertainment or other cultural experiences.[33] Nonetheless, the general power of competence conferred on local authorities by section 1 of the Localism Act 2011 (and the well-being power retained by Welsh local authorities under section 2 of the Local Government Act 2000) permits local authorities to assume such a role, and a number of local authorities have done so, formulating cultural strategies as expressions of local aspiration. In recognition of these strategies and the effect that the licensing regime may have on cultural events, until 2012 national Guidance advised, at para 13.57:

'In connection with cultural strategies, licensing policy statements should include clearly worded statements indicating that they will monitor the impact of licensing on the provision of regulated entertainment, and particularly live music and dancing, for example, by considering whether premises that provide live music or culture are represented on licensing stakeholder forums, and ensuring that local cultural officers are regularly consulted about the impact on local culture Where appropriate, town centre managers have an important role in coordinating live music events in town centres and can be an important source of information.'

31.19 Promotion of the licensing objectives is plainly in the public interest, insofar as it serves to protect the public from harm. The public interest is, however, multi-faceted (or polycentric in the language of academic commentators) and protection from harm is only one of its faces, albeit an important one. That members of the public should be able to socialize over a drink, see plays and films, listen to music, watch sporting events and so on at establishments of their choosing is also in the public interest. A balance must therefore be struck, otherwise an unduly restrictive licensing policy could

---

[32] Greater London Authority Act 1999, s 376(2).
[33] Local authorities have long had specific powers relating to services and facilities of a cultural nature: see, eg, Local Government Act 1972, s 145 (provision of entertainment); Local Government (Miscellaneous Provisions) Act 1976, s 19 (provision of recreational facilities).

needlessly suppress valued cultural activities. In striking that balance it is important that statements of licensing policy and individual licensing decisions do not go further than is necessary to promote the licensing objective. Thus national Guidance states, at para 2.20:

> '... Any conditions appropriate to promote the prevention of public nuisance should be tailored to the type, nature and characteristics of the specific premises. Licensing authorities should be aware of the need to avoid inappropriate or disproportionate measures that could deter events that are valuable to the community, such as live music.'

It might be added that the replacement by the Police Reform and Social Responsibility Act 2011 of 'necessary' by 'appropriate' as the decision-making threshold in the Licensing Act 2003 may potentially affect the balance between the promotion of leisure and the protection of the community. The effect of the change is discussed in Chapter 12 (The Appropriateness Test).

C THE PLANNING SYSTEM

31.20 In order to understand the significance of planning to licensing in England and Wales it is necessary to trace the outlines of the main elements of the planning system.

Development control

31.21 The planning system regulates the development of land in the public interest. In the view of the government, the purpose of the planning system is to contribute to the achievement of sustainable development.[34]

31.22 The planning system is founded on the concept of 'development'. Under the principal planning Act, the Town and Country Planning Act 1990, development is defined as:

> 'the carrying out of building, engineering, mining or other operations in, on, over or under land, or the making of any material change in the use of any buildings or other land'.[35]

Thus the planning system is concerned with both physical changes to land and changes in the way land is used. The terms 'operational development' and 'material change of use' are often employed as shorthand for these two elements. Sometimes development will involve one or other of these elements alone, at other times both will be present. For example, the construction of a

---

[34] See the 'National Planning Policy Framework' (March 2012), para 6; 'Planning Policy Wales' (5th ed, November 2012), para 1.2.1.
[35] Town and Country Planning Act 1990, s 55(1).

new public house on open land would amount to operational development and a material change of use, but the external alteration of an existing public house, although operational development, might involve no change of use at all.

31.23 In general, planning permission must be obtained from the local planning authority (usually the district or borough council in England; the county or county borough council in Wales) before development can be carried out,[36] although there are exceptions to this. In order to maintain a degree of flexibility and proportionality in the system, certain changes in use and works of operational development are either deemed not to constitute development or automatically granted planning permission. This is achieved by two statutory instruments: in the former case the Town and Country Planning (Use Classes) Order 1987 ('the Use Classes Order') and in the latter case the Town and Country Planning (General Permitted Development) Order 1995 ('the GPDO').

31.24 The Use Classes Order specifies a number of 'use classes' – categories of uses having similar characteristics – and provides that changes of use *within* each use class shall not be taken to involve development.[37] In England, the specified use classes include:

- use class A3, 'Restaurants and cafes': use for the sale of food and drink for consumption on the premises;
- use class A4, 'Drinking establishments': use as a public house, wine-bar or other drinking establishment;
- use class A5, 'Hot food takeaways': use for the sale of hot food for consumption off the premises;
- use class C1, 'Hotels and hostels': use as a hotel or as a boarding or guest house where, in each case, no significant element of care is provided;
- use class D2, 'Assembly and leisure': use as a cinema, concert hall, bingo hall, dance hall, swimming bath, skating rink, gymnasium or area for other indoor or outdoor sports or recreations, not involving motorised vehicles or firearms.

For Wales similar, but not identical, use classes are specified:

- use class A3, 'Food and drink': use for the sale of food or drink for consumption on the premises or of hot food for consumption off the premises;
- use class C1, 'Hotels and hostels': use as a hotel or as a boarding or guest house where, in each case, no significant element of care is provided;
- use class D2, 'Assembly and leisure': use as a cinema, concert hall, bingo hall, casino, dance hall, swimming bath, skating rink, gymnasium

---

[36]   See the Town and Country Planning Act 1990, s 57.
[37]   Town and Country Planning (Use Classes) Order 1987, art 3(1).

or area for other indoor or outdoor sports or recreations, not involving motorised vehicles or firearms.

As an example, the change of use from a restaurant to a café (both within English use class A3) would be deemed not to constitute development, but a change of use from a restaurant (use class A3) to a hotel (use class C1), or a theatre (which is outside any of the specified use classes[38]) would involve development requiring planning permission.

31.25 Under the GPDO planning permission is granted for the classes of development specified in Schedule 2 to the Order.[39] One such class of permitted development is Class B, Part 4 of Schedule 2, which concerns the use of land for any purpose for not more than 28 days in total in any calendar year, and the provision on the land of moveable structures for the purposes of the permitted use.[40] In principle, this would permit a field to be used to host a series of open air concerts, plays or other events, provided the 28-day limit was not exceeded.

31.26 The GPDO also grants permission for certain changes of use between use classes.[41] For present purposes the only relevant change permitted in England is from use class A4 (drinking establishments) to use class A3 (restaurants and cafés), but not the reverse. There is no need for this provision in Wales, where use class A3 embraces drinking establishments as well as restaurants and cafes, so changes between these uses (in any direction) are deemed not to amount to development.

31.27 In the case of development proposals that must be the subject of a planning application to the local planning authority, the decision whether or not to grant permission will be guided by planning policy formulated at the local level[42] and by national policy. In granting planning permission local planning authorities have a broad power to impose conditions.[43]

31.28 If planning permission is refused by the local planning authority (or if it fails to determine a planning application within the prescribed period) the applicant may appeal to the Secretary of State. Most planning appeals are in fact determined by a planning inspector appointed by the Secretary of State.

---

[38] Article 3(6) lists a number of *sui generis* uses that are outside any of the prescribed use classes. These include use as a theatre, amusement arcade or funfair, and in England also include use as a night-club or casino.

[39] GPDO, art 3(1).

[40] Development is not permitted if, inter alia, the land is a building or within the curtilage of a building: see para B1 of Class B, Part 4 of Schedule 2 to the GPDO.

[41] As specified in Part 3 of Schedule 2 to the GPDO.

[42] At present there is also a regional tier of planning policy, which is being revoked by orders made under the Localism Act 2011, s 109.

[43] See the Town and Country Planning Act 1990, ss 70(1), 72(1).

Planning policy

31.29 In determining planning applications local planning authorities are required to have regard to the 'development plan'[44] and to any other material (ie relevant) consideration.[45] Moreover, they must determine planning applications in accordance with the development plan unless material considerations indicate otherwise.[46] The importance given to the development plan in the statutory planning framework has inspired the description 'a plan-led system', in which local development documents (local development plans in Wales) set out a range of policies that seek to meet the community's land-use needs. The statutory presumption is that those policies will determine whether or not planning permission is granted for development. In this way a degree of coherence and predictability is given to planning decisions.

31.30 An innovation introduced in England by the Localism Act 2011[47] is the 'neighbourhood development plan',[48] which is a document setting out planning policies at the neighbourhood level. In areas where there is local concern at the concentration (or lack) of licensed premises, the neighbourhood development plan could prove a decisive influence on development proposals for such premises.

31.31 Local development documents and plans must be prepared having regard to national policy. In England most national planning policy emanates from the Department for Communities and Local Government ('DCLG'), which in March 2012 published the National Planning Policy Framework ('NPPF'). The NPPF sets out the government's main planning policies for England and how they are expected to be applied. At its heart is a presumption in favour of 'sustainable development', which broadly speaking means development that meets the needs of the present without compromising the ability of future generations to meet their own needs.[49] For local authorities preparing development plan policies concerning licensed premises, and for applicants seeking planning permission for development involving licensable activities, there are a number of significant expressions of policy in the NPPF. Paragraph 9 states that pursuing sustainable development involves seeking positive improvements in the quality of the built, natural and historic environment, as well as in people's quality of life,

---

[44] For the meaning of 'development plan' in England and Wales see the Planning and Compulsory Purchase Act 2004, s 38. In London the development plan includes the spatial development strategy, currently the London Plan (July 2011). Policies in the London Plan of particular relevance to licensable activities include policies 2.15, 4.6 and 4.7.

[45] Town and Country Planning Act 1990, s 70(2).

[46] Planning and Compulsory Purchase Act 2004, s 38(6).

[47] By way of amendments to the Town and Country Planning Act 1990 and the Planning and Compulsory Purchase Act 2004.

[48] See the Planning and Compulsory Purchase Act 2004, ss 38(2)(c),(3)(c), 38A–C.

[49] See the text preceding para 6 in the NPPF.

including among other things improving the conditions in which people take leisure. Under the heading 'Ensuring the vitality of town centres' the NPPF states:

- Local planning authorities should 'allocate a range of suitable sites to meet the scale and type of retail, leisure, commercial, office, tourism, cultural, community and residential development needed in town centres. It is important that needs for retail, leisure, office and other main town centre uses[50] are met in full and are not compromised by limited site availability. Local planning authorities should therefore undertake an assessment of the need to expand town centres to ensure a sufficient supply of suitable sites' (paragraph 23).
- Local planning authorities should apply a sequential test to planning applications for main town centre uses that are not in an existing centre and are not in accordance with an up-to-date local plan.[51] They should require applications for main town centre uses to be located in town centres, then in edge of centre locations and only if suitable sites are not available should out of centre sites be considered. When considering edge of centre and out of centre proposals, preference should be given to accessible sites that are well connected to the town centre. Applicants and local planning authorities should demonstrate flexibility on issues such as format and scale (paragraph 24).
- This sequential approach should not be applied to applications for small scale rural offices or other small scale rural development (paragraph 25).
- When assessing applications for retail, leisure and office development outside of town centres, which are not in accordance with an up-to-date local plan, local planning authorities should require an impact assessment if the development is over a proportionate, locally set floorspace threshold (if there is no locally set threshold, the default threshold is 2,500 square metres). This should include assessment of:
  - the impact of the proposal on existing, committed and planned public and private investment in a centre or centres in the catchment area of the proposal; and
  - the impact of the proposal on town centre vitality and viability, including local consumer choice and trade in the town centre and wider area, up to five years from the time the application is made. For major schemes where the full impact will not be realised in five

---

[50] The main town centre uses are defined in Annex 2 to the NPPF as: 'Retail development (including warehouse clubs and factory outlet centres); leisure, entertainment facilities the more intensive sport and recreation uses (including cinemas, restaurants, drive-through restaurants, bars and pubs, night-clubs, casinos, health and fitness centres, indoor bowling centres, and bingo halls); offices; and arts, culture and tourism development (including theatres, museums, galleries and concert halls, hotels and conference facilities).'

[51] In the NPPF the term 'Local Plan' is used in place of the various documents that make up the statutory development plan at the local level.

years, the impact should also be assessed up to ten years from the
time the application is made (paragraph 26).
- Where an application fails to satisfy the sequential test or is likely to
have significant adverse impact on one or more of the above factors, it
should be refused (paragraph 27).

31.32 In seeking to support a prosperous rural economy, the NPPF states
that local and neighbourhood plans should, among other things, 'support
sustainable rural tourism and leisure developments that benefit businesses in
rural areas, communities and visitors, and which respect the character of the
countryside. This should include supporting the provision and expansion of
tourist and visitor facilities in appropriate locations where identified needs
are not met by existing facilities in rural service centres; and promote the
retention and development of local services and community facilities in
villages, such as local shops, meeting places, sports venues, cultural buildings, public houses and places of worship'.

31.33 The NPPF recognises that the planning system can play an important role in facilitating social interaction and creating healthy, inclusive
communities (paragraph 69). It advises local planning authorities to create a
shared vision with communities of the residential environment and facilities
they wish to see. It goes on to say that planning policies and decisions should
plan positively for the provision and use of shared space, community facilities
(including sports venues, cultural buildings and public houses), and should
ensure that established shops, facilities and services are able to develop and
modernise in a way that is sustainable, and retained for the benefit of the
community (paragraph 70).

31.34 The 'Good Practice Guide on Planning for Tourism' (DCLG, 2006)
will also be relevant to the formulation of development plan policies that
cater for, or are likely to have an effect on, tourism, and may also be relevant
to individual planning applications. Where proposed development is likely to
generate a significant level of noise, paragraph 123 of the NPPF and the
'Noise Policy Statement for England' (Department for the Environment,
Food and Rural Affairs, March 2010) will be material.

31.35 In Wales national planning policy is the responsibility of the Welsh
Ministers, who have issued 'Planning Policy Wales' (5th ed) ('PPW'), the
national planning policy framework. This is supplemented by technical
advice notes. Policy of potential relevance to licensable activities can be
found in chapters 7 (Economic Development), 10 (Planning for Retail and
Town Centres) and 11 (Tourism, Sport and Recreation) of PPW, which in
this context is similar to policy in England (particularly in its attempt to
usher leisure development into town centres) and, in relation to noise, in
'Technical Advice Note 11: Noise' (1997).

D THE INTERPLAY BETWEEN LICENSING AND PLANNING

31.36 In essence, a local authority's licensing functions are to be exercised with the aim of preventing harm. They are intended to act as a check on potentially harmful licensable activities, not as an encouragement to the sale or supply of alcohol or the provision of entertainment or late night refreshment. The question of whether there is a need for licensed premises in an area is not one that the Licensing Act 2003 requires licensing authorities to consider.[52] That inquiry is primarily for the planning system and can arise at the level of planning policy formulation and in the determination of individual planning applications.

31.37 The overlap between local authority licensing and planning functions was considered by Kenneth Parker QC (now Mr Justice Parker) in *R (Blackwood) v Birmingham Magistrates* [2006] EWHC 1800 (Admin)[53] at paragraphs 54 to 58 of his judgment:

> '54. In my view, there is plainly an overlap between the objectives of licensing and planning. Other than the protection of children from harm, which is not of itself a land use planning consideration, each of the licensing objectives is also a land use planning objective.
>
> 55. Similar considerations to those that arise on licensing apply to a local planning authority in deciding upon the appropriate planning policy framework for licensed premises applications and in determining planning applications. The planning authority is likely to be concerned about the public impact of the use, direct and indirect, particularly the impact of unsociable hours. Planning authorities must consider the design of any proposed development for leisure use and what conditions should be attached to any permission, if the use might have a detrimental impact on local residents. Local development plans may well adopt policies which direct licensable activities to certain parts of a town centre, and the planning authority may have regard to such policies in determining individual planning applications.
>
> 56. However licensing authorities, in pursuing the licensing objectives, may also have to have regard to locational factors, especially where exceptional circumstances have justified the adoption by the licensing authority of a "cumulative effect" policy of restriction (see the Amended Guidance, paragraphs 315 to 319[54]), but also where the express grant of planning permission is not required for a licensable activity because, for example, there is a change of use of the premises and the existing and the proposed uses are within the same use class.

---

[52]   See the Guidance, para 13.18.
[53]   Also reported at (2006) 170 JP 613.
[54]   See now the Guidance paras 13.19–13.39.

57. As I have earlier explained, the statement of licensing policy should indicate that (paragraph 3.51 of the Guidance):

"planning, building control and licensing regimes will be properly separated to avoid duplication and inefficiency."[55]

58. It is relatively easy to state this as a target, but it is much harder to formulate any general principle that would assist in demarcating the respective competences of planning and licensing authorities. It does seem to me, however, that the framework and substance of the Act, and its underlying rationale, would strongly suggest that operational matters are intended primarily for regulation by the licensing authorities.'

31.38 This judgment recognises that the prevention of harm to the public, be it by way of crime or disorder, prejudice to public safety or public nuisance, is as much a concern for local planning authorities as it is for licensing authorities. The preparation of planning policy and the determination of planning applications may therefore require consideration of the same issues as arise in the licensing sphere.

31.39 In what appears to be an attempt to demarcate the boundary between licensing and planning considerations, national Guidance states at para 13.55:

'The statement of licensing policy should indicate that planning permission, building control approval and licensing regimes will be properly separated to avoid duplication and inefficiency. The planning and licensing regimes involve consideration of different (albeit related) matters. Licensing committees are not bound by decisions made by a planning committee, and vice versa.'

31.40 It is not in fact accurate to say that the planning and licensing regimes are concerned with different matters. In many respects, eg in their consideration of crime and disorder and nuisance, they are the same.[56] The true position is that in determining a planning application a local planning authority is required by statute to have regard to any consideration that is material to the determination of the application. In general, that means any consideration which relates to the use and development of the land in question.[57] This could include public fear of crime[58] or the risk of harm to

---

[55]   See now the Guidance, para 13.55.

[56]   In *Hunter v Canary Wharf Ltd* [1997] AC 655, at 710B–C, Lord Hoffman observed: 'The power of the planning authority to grant or refuse permission, subject to such conditions as it thinks fit, provides a mechanism for control of the unrestricted right to build which can be used for the protection of people living in the vicinity of a development. In a case such as this, where the development is likely to have an impact upon many people over a large area, the planning system is, I think, a far more appropriate form of control, from the point of view of both the developer and the public, than enlarging the right to bring actions for nuisance at common law.'

[57]   See *Stringer v Minister of Housing and Local Government* [1970] 1 WLR 1281, at 1294.

public safety or amenity. Furthermore, by virtue of section 17 of the Crime and Disorder Act 1998 (see paras 31.11–31.14 above) local authorities are required in any event to have regard to crime and disorder and the misuse of drugs and alcohol in the exercise of their planning functions. Where, therefore, a planning application raises considerations that would also be relevant to the licensing regime, it is no answer to assert that duplication should be avoided. The two statutory regimes require proper consideration to be given to applications made under them: if development proposals require both planning permission and authorisation under the Licensing Act 2003, it will be necessary to satisfy both the local planning authority and licensing authority of the acceptability of the proposals.

31.41   That is not to say, however, that in exercising its planning functions a local authority is required to ignore the controls conferred on licensing authorities by the 2003 Act. On the contrary, it is well settled that a local planning authority may take into account the existence of another scheme of control, and may in appropriate circumstances grant planning permission on the assumption that the other scheme of control will be effective.[59] Consistently with this approach, Department of the Environment Circular 11/95 (Welsh Office Circular 35/95): 'The Use of Conditions in Planning Permissions' states at paragraph 22:

> 'Other matters are subject to control under separate legislation, yet also of concern to the planning system. A condition which duplicates the effect of other controls will normally be unnecessary'.

The extent to which planning and licensing conditions may properly overlap is considered in more detail in Chapter 17 (Conditions).

E INTEGRATING PLANS AND STRATEGIES

31.42   As stated above, the Secretary of State recommends that statements of policy should provide clear indications of how the licensing authority will secure the proper integration of its licensing policy with local crime prevention, planning, transport, tourism, race equality schemes, and cultural strategies and any other plans introduced for the management of town centres and the night-time economy.[60]

31.43   How a local authority is to integrate its licensing policy with other plans and strategies – each of which will have been prepared or revised according to its own procedure and timetable – raises practical rather than

---

[58]   *West Midlands Probation Committee v SSE and Walsall MBC* [1997] JPL 323.
[59]   See *Gateshead Metropolitan Borough Council v Secretary of State for the Environment* (1996) 71 P&CR 350; *R (Blackwood) v Birmingham Magistrates* [2006] EWHC 800 (Admin), (2006) 170 JP 613.
[60]   Guidance, para 13.54.

legal issues, issues which the national Guidance leaves to local authorities to resolve. Nonetheless, it is possible to suggest a number of measures that might assist: raising awareness within departments of relevant plans and strategies for which the authority as a whole is responsible; ensuring timely communication between departments when plans or strategies are changed; giving express responsibility to an officer or group of officers to co-ordinate policies; and allocating portfolios to members of an authority's executive so as to accommodate overlapping functions. These are by no means the only steps that could be taken and in the age of localism innovation by local authorities is to be welcomed. However it is done, the proper integration of strategies is essential if the holy grail of town centre leisure development is to be reached. This is discussed further in Chapters 2, 3 and 4.

F CONCLUSION

31.44 In many fields of regulation local authorities are required to take a strategic view: to consider how the interests of those living and working in their areas can best be protected and advanced, and to plan accordingly. Licensing is an important element in the mix of local government responsibilities, yet it has traditionally involved far less of a strategic overview. It is no longer possible, however, and still less desirable, to divorce licensing from the strategies that increasingly influence the work that local authorities do.

31.45 The overlap between licensing and planning in particular means that each must have regard to the other. To an extent, planning sets the broad framework within which individual licensing decisions are taken. High level issues such as the size and shape of settlements, the appropriate location for new housing, retail and employment uses, infrastructure provision, town centre planning, the protection of the countryside and heritage assets are routinely the subject of planning policy, often broadly expressed. Licensing is more concerned with the detail of the use of specific buildings for particular purposes, be they pubs, nightclubs, cafés or theatres, and the internal management conditions needed to protect visitors and neighbours. Individual planning decisions may also descend to this level of detail, but only where 'development' is involved.

31.46 Recognising the importance of the right mix of uses in town centres, it is plain that these two regimes cannot properly be separated by a bright line. Furthermore, the potential for strategic-level thinking in licensing through statements of licensing policy (including general policies dealing with cumulative impact, leisure zoning and terminal hours) and early morning restriction orders means that licensing operates more and more on a strategic level. Yet further, of course, planning authorities are responsible authorities in the licensing regime, and so inevitably bring their perspective to bear on the formulation of policy and the determination of applications. Indeed, to operate a system in which planning officers think of planning and licensing officers think of licensing, and never the twain shall meet, is the kind of silo approach which has long been castigated as wasteful of resources, self-defeating and apt to stifle innovation and partnership.

31.47 In this book, much has been said about the importance of planning and licensing departments working hand in glove over the development of thriving town centre leisure environments. When applications are made, while there needs to be recognition of the spheres of planning and licensing, and the inevitability of substantial overlap from case to case, as a very general proposition planning remains concerned with the principle of the use of land and licensing with the detailed operating conditions. Finally, when matters of enforcement arise, it is always wise to consider whether a breach of a licence also amounts to breach of planning control, in order to allow joint working on enforcement where this is appropriate.

31.48 If planning and licensing officers work together to plan their future strategy and use their respective levers of power to implement the same, more sustainable and diverse leisure economies are likely to follow.

Gambling

The King and Court were never in the world so bad as they are now for gaming, swearing, whoring and drinking and the most abominable vices that ever were in the world – so that all must come to nought.

The Diaries of Samuel Pepys

A INTRODUCTION

32.01 Gambling premises are an integral part of town centre leisure economies. Nationally, gambling provides employment for 109,000 people and generates a gross 'win' (or gross profit) of £5.8 billion,[1] which funds national and local tax regimes, pays for local staff (who in turn spend money on goods and services locally) and generates investment in local premises. It is right to say that gambling premises generate precious little crime and disorder or nuisance.

32.02 The main negative effect of gambling is not on town centres at all, but is problem gambling. In practice, the issue of problem gambling is intractable both because of co-morbidity – problem gamblers frequently have other personal difficulties too – and because problem gamblers gamble across multiple platforms, both terrestrial and remote.

32.03 The role of the Gambling Act 2005 is not to prevent gambling – indeed the key section of the Act, section 153, which governs premises licensing sets out an aim to permit gambling. Rather, the Gambling Act and its subordinate regulations and codes create a hierarchy of gambling facilities and a commensurate hierarchy of controls to promote the gambling licensing objectives.

---

[1]   Gambling Commission, Industry Statistics 2009–2012.

32.04 In this chapter, a brief overview is given of gambling regulation and the rules for gambling in premises such as pubs and members' clubs where gambling is not the primary use.[2]

B FRAMEWORK

32.05 At the heart of the Gambling Act 2005 are the licensing objectives. These are:

(a) preventing gambling from being a source of crime or disorder, being associated with crime or disorder or being used to support crime;

(b) ensuring that gambling is conducted in a fair and open way; and

(c) protecting children and other vulnerable persons from being harmed or exploited by gambling.[3]

32.06 It will immediately be noted that these are different from the licensing objectives under the Licensing Act 2003. In particular, the Gambling Act is not concerned with public nuisance or public safety.

32.07 The main protectors of these objectives are the Gambling Commission and the licensing authority.

32.08 The Commission is responsible for granting operating licences and for publishing the licence conditions and codes of practice which govern them. Operating licences are not premises-specific. They are granted to businesses which wish to provide gambling facilities, and are concerned with the solvency, integrity and corporate systems of the operator. This again may be contrasted with the Licensing Act 2003, which does not licence the corporate excellence of operators.

32.09 All those who wish to provide gambling facilities are required to hold an operating licence, although there is a wide list of exemptions, which includes: those who wish to run low stake and prize arcades operating under family entertainment centre gaming machine permits; permits for members' clubs including club gaming permits and club machine permit; and exemptions and permits operating in pubs such as exempt equal chance gaming, automatic entitlements for up to two gaming machines and licensed premises gaming machine permits. In practice, operating licences are chiefly needed to run casinos, betting offices, bingo clubs, higher order arcades known as adult gaming centres and also family entertainment centres with premises licences, to supply and service gaming machines and to run larger lotteries.[4]

---

2 For a more detailed treatment, see Kolvin, *Gambling for Local Authorities: Licensing, Planning and Regeneration* (Institute of Licensing, 2nd ed, 2010).

3 Gambling Act 2005, s 1.

4 Gambling Act 2005, s 33.

32.10 Parliament was not content with just regulating corporate entities. It also provides for personal licences to be held so as to impose positive obligations on individuals to deliver the requirements of the operating licence.[5] To lose one's personal licence is effectively to lose one's place in the gambling industry.

32.11 The effect of the operating licence regime is to give confidence to licensing authorities that those who apply for premises licences have or will have an operating licence from the national regulator, warranting their fitness to run a gambling business, and personal licensees to manage the business effectively. Thus, for higher order gambling there is effectively a three-fold system of control, with the operating licence giving blessing to the operator, personal licences to the operator's senior staff and the premises licence to the premises. This is a more rigorous form of triple-lock than is applicable under the Licensing Act 2003.

32.12 A premises licence is needed to offer facilities for gambling in premises. A list of exemptions applies, which is much the same as the list of exemptions from operating licences. In practice, as for operating licences, premises licences are needed by casinos, bingo clubs, betting offices and higher order amusement arcades. The application processes are not dissimilar to those under the Licensing Act 2003. There is provision for objection by responsible authorities, which is similar to the list of responsible authorities under the Licensing Act 2003, but also includes the Gambling Commission[6] and 'interested parties', who live sufficiently close to the premises to be likely to be affected by the authorised activities, or have business interests that might be affected by the authorised activities, or representatives of either.[7] In practice, objections are few and far between, because it is uncommon for neighbours to be affected by gambling activities, and if they are affected at all this is likely to be by nuisance which is not a gambling licensing objective.

32.13 Unlike under the Licensing Act 2003, the licensing authority has a discretion whether or not there has been a representation. However, the general orientation required by the Act is to grant, for the authority is required to aim to permit the application where the application coheres with the Commission's guidance and codes of practice, the licensing objectives and the authority's gambling policy. In practice, refusals rarely occur and if they occur are upheld on appeal more rarely still.

---

[5]   Gambling Act 2005, s 127.
[6]   Gambling Act 2005, s 157.
[7]   Gambling Act 2005, s 158.

32.14   If a premises licence is granted, mandatory licence conditions bite.[8] These prevent alcohol being consumed in adult gaming centres, family entertainment centres with premises licences and betting offices.[9]

C INTEGRATING STRATEGIES

32.15   There is no doubt that in regeneration terms, gambling premises can contribute to the economic development of an area. As such, there is scope for gambling to be among the range of leisure catered for in local development frameworks. This is an area in which joint working between the planning and licensing authority is desirable.[10]

32.16   Recognition may be given in licensing policies that gambling premises tend to cause much fewer alcohol-related crime and disorder problems than, say, pubs and nightclubs. For example, Westminster City Council, which has more licensed premises and casinos than any other area in the United Kingdom, has cumulative impact policies which apply to pubs and bars, but casinos are governed by their bespoke policies which more neutrally concern the impact of alcohol and entertainment on the licensing objectives.

32.17   What the Gambling Act does not do is to control the quantum of gambling premises. In some areas (principally in London) there has been concern at the clustering of betting offices. The number of betting offices is in fact growing only marginally, from 8,862 to 9,128 over the period 2009 to 2012,[11] a rise of 3%. However, betting offices have consolidated over the past ten years, tending to move from relatively unnoticed secondary positions to primary positions on the high street in order to compete for business in those high footfall areas. They have generally been enabled to do so because the income from fixed odds betting terminals (see below) enables them to pay high street rents. The perceived increase in concentration in some areas has been noticed by many and elevated by some into a national crisis. However, any causative link between clustering and problem gambling is to date unproven, not least because the opportunities to gamble terrestrially and virtually are legion, so that the addition of one further facility is liable to have a marginal, if any, impact.

32.18   There are also concerns that men gather outside such premises to smoke, which is controllable through good partnership working between the premises management and the police and also through licence conditions. It is impossible to add a condition preventing people from gathering on the

---

[8]   Gambling Act 2005 (Mandatory and Default Conditions) (England and Wales) Regulations 2007 (SI 2007/1409).

[9]   Gambling Act 2005 (Mandatory and Default Conditions) (England and Wales) Regulations 2007, Schs 3–5.

[10]   For further discussion, see Kolvin, *Gambling for Local Authorities: Licensing, Planning and Regeneration* (Institute of Licensing, 2nd ed, 2010).

[11]   Gambling Commission, Industry Statistics 2009–2012.

pavement. But a condition could be imposed requiring the premises to ban customers who persistently drink outside. These matters are also controllable through designated public places orders (or controlled drinking zones): see Chapter 37.

32.19 More strategically, the future growth of betting in town centres may be controlled through development plans controlling change of use to betting offices. Perhaps the biggest driver of betting offices currently, however, is the fixed odds betting terminal, a virtual roulette machine four of which are allowed in betting offices,[12] which now generate £1.4 billion of gaming profit for bookmakers, over 50% of the profit from betting offices.[13] Should there be any government interference with numbers, stakes or prizes of such machines, it is likely that investment in new and refurbished betting offices will fall significantly.

D GAMBLING IN LICENSED PREMISES

32.20 The Gambling Act 2005 aims to usher high stake gaming into dedicated gambling facilities such as casinos and betting offices. However, in recognition of the fact that low level gambling is an age-old and generally harmless pastime, it creates a series of exemptions and permissions for gambling in pubs and members' clubs, which are considered briefly in this section.

(1) Pubs

32.21 Under the Gambling Act 2005 low stake and prize equal chance gaming (ie where players play against each other rather than against a bank) and the provision of gaming machines are permitted in alcohol licensed premises as an exemption, that is to say without a licence or permit.[14]

32.22 To benefit premises must have a premises licence under Part 3 of the Licensing Act 2003 which authorises the supply of alcohol for consumption on the licensed premises. The premises must contain a bar at which alcohol is served for consumption on the premises (without a requirement that alcohol is served only with food). Finally, the gaming can only take place at a time when alcohol may be supplied in reliance on the licence.

Exempt low stake and prize gaming

32.23 Gaming in alcohol licensed premises must be equal chance. Equal chance gaming includes poker, bingo, bridge, whist, cribbage and dominoes

---

[12]   These 'category B2' machines currently have maximum stakes of £100 and maximum prizes of £500.

[13]   Gambling Commission, Industry Statistics 2009–2012.

[14]   See Gambling Act 2005, ss 277–284; Gambling Act 2005 (Exempt Gaming in Alcohol-Licensed Premises) Regulations 2007 (SI 2007/1940).

but not pontoon or roulette. No amount can be deducted or levied from the sums staked or won and there can be no participation fee charged. Therefore all the money staked must go back to the players and operator of the premises cannot profit from the gaming. Under 18s must not be permitted to play. A game played on one set of premises cannot be linked with a game played on another set of premises.

All gaming is expected to be 'low level'[15] although this is not defined. There are limits on stakes and prizes. The limits on stakes are:

- Cribbage and dominoes – no limit.
- All gaming – maximum £5 stake per person per game.
- Poker – maximum aggregate stakes £100 per premises per day.
- Bingo – maximum aggregate stakes of £2,000 per week, although see below for high turnover bingo.

Limits on prizes are as follows:

- Poker – £100 per game.
- Bingo – maximum £2,000 per week in prizes, although see below on high turnover bingo.
- All other gaming – no limit.

32.24 The licensing authority can make an order disapplying the exemption allowing low stake equal chance gaming. The order can be made if the provision of the gaming is not reasonably consistent with the licensing objectives, if gaming has taken place on the premises in breach of a condition, if the premises are mainly used or to be used for gaming, or if an offence under the Gambling Act 2005 has been committed on the premises.

Code of Practice for equal chance gaming in premises with an alcohol licence

32.25 The Gambling Commission has published a 'Code of Practice for equal chance gaming in clubs and premises with an alcohol licence'.[16] The Code of Practice could be considered as best practice advice by the Gambling Commission. Breaches of the Code of Practice could be used in evidence in a prosecution or in regulatory action.

32.26 Compliance with the Code of Practice is the responsibility of the designated premises supervisor. Their responsibilities include ensuring adherence to the limits on stakes and prizes, that the gaming is supervised and that effective procedures designed to prevent underage gambling are in place. It would of course be an offence to exceed the limits or permit under 18s to participate. The Code suggests that all payments in respect of the

[15] See Code of Practice, below, para 1.3.
[16] Gambling Commission, December 2009.

gaming should be made in cash before the commencement of the game and that no credit may be offered to customers. It also recommends that the equipment be provided by the premises, secured when not in use, and that for organised games the rules of the games being played be displayed or made available to all the players. Interestingly the designated person should ensure a pleasant atmosphere and deny participation to customers who cheat or collude with other players or employees, threaten other players or employees, create a disturbance or damage equipment.

32.27 There are specific provisions for poker which include advice that cash games should not be permitted, and if they are allowed that the pot should be kept in sight so that it can be viewed at all times. The designated person should also take all reasonable steps to ensure that individuals' stakes limits are not exceeded through side bets, additional raises, re-buys or other ways of increasing the pot.

High turnover bingo

32.28 Total stakes or prizes for bingo played in a seven day period can exceed £2,000. This is called high turnover bingo. The 12 months following a seven day period of high turnover bingo are referred to as a high turnover period. An offence is committed if there is a further seven day period of high turnover bingo within a high turnover period and the business does not benefit from a bingo operating licence.

32.29 The designated person is required to contact the Commission if there is high turnover bingo, when the total stakes or prizes played in a seven day period exceeds £2,000.

Gaming machines

32.30 Alcohol licensed premises have an automatic right to make one or two low stake and prize gaming machines of category C or D[17] available for use on the premises. To benefit from this right, the premises licence holder must send written notice of their intention to make the machines available with a fee to the licensing authority which granted the premises licence.

32.31 The licensing authority can make an order disapplying the automatic entitlement to gaming machines. The order can be made if the provision of the machines is not reasonably consistent the licensing objectives, gaming has taken place on the premises in breach of a condition, the premises are mainly used or to be used for gaming, or an offence under the Gambling Act 2005 has been committed on the premises.

---

[17]   For maximum stakes and prizes, see the Categories of Gaming Machine Regulations 2007 (SI 2007/2158).

32.32 Those alcohol licence holders who wish to make available three or more category C or D gaming machines must apply to their licensing authority for a licensed premises gaming machine permit.

32.33 Schedule 13 of the Gambling Act 2005 legislates for licensed premises gaming machine permits. A licensing authority to whom an application is made shall consider it having regard to the licensing objectives, any relevant guidance issued by the Commission and such other matters as they think relevant. The authority can grant, refuse or grant an application for a smaller number of machines than applied for; but they cannot add conditions to a permit.

32.34 The permit must be kept at the premises and an annual fee must be paid. The permit will cease to have effect if the alcohol licence ceases to have effect with respect to the premises to which it relates, if the permit holder ceases to be the holder of an on-premises alcohol licence, if the holder surrenders the permit, if the permit is cancelled by the authority or a court forfeits the permit.

32.35 The authority can cancel the permit if the provision of the machines is not reasonably consistent with the licensing objectives, gaming has taken place on the premises in breach of a condition, the premises are mainly used or to be used for gaming or making gaming machines available for use, or an offence under the Gambling Act 2005 has been committed on the premises. Before cancelling a permit the authority must give the holder at least 21 days' notice of their intent to cancel, and the opportunity to make representations, either in writing, or at a hearing if a hearing is requested by the holder. The holder has a right of appeal, following a cancellation of a permit, to the magistrates' court. A permit shall be cancelled by the authority if the annual fee is not paid, although this requirement can be misapplied if the non-payment is due to an administrative error.

32.36 A court can forfeit the permit if the holder or an officer of a permit holder is convicted of a relevant offence under the Gambling Act.

Permits can be transferred with the transfer of the alcohol premises licence.

Code of Practice on gaming machine permits and permissions

32.37 The Gambling Commission has published a 'Code of Practice for gaming machines in clubs and premises with an alcohol licence'.[18]

32.38 The Code places two conditions on the automatic entitlement to gaming machines and on licensed premises gaming machine permits. These are:

---

[18]   Gambling Commission, March 2012.

1   All gaming machines situated on the premises must be located in a place within the premises so that their use can be supervised, either by staff whose duties include such supervision (including bar or floor staff) or by other means.

Permit holders must have in place arrangements for such supervision.

2   All gaming machines situated on the premises shall be located in a place that requires a customer who wishes to use any ATM made available on the premises to cease gambling at the gaming machine in order to do so. 'ATM' means a machine located on the premises, which enables a person using it to obtain cash by use of a credit or debit card.

(2) Members' clubs

32.39 Gaming in clubs is governed by the Gambling Act 2005.[19] Gaming is permitted in clubs which benefit from a club premises certificate under the Licensing Act 2003 as either:

• low stake and prize exempt gaming,
• under a club machine permit,
• under a club gaming permit.

Exempt gaming

32.40 The Gambling Act 2005 defines three types of clubs: members clubs, miners' welfare institutes and commercial clubs. Each can benefit from exempt gaming. To benefit the gaming must be equal chance, no amount can be deducted or levied from the sum staked or won and games played on one set of premises cannot be linked with a game played on another set of premises. Participants must be either members of the club or institute and have been a member for at least 48 hours, or a guest of a member who is entitled to play. All participants must be over 18.

32.41 There are limits on the participation fees, and on stakes and prizes.

Maximum participation fee per person per game:

• Bridge and/or whist (on a day when no other facilities for gaming are provided) – £18.
• Other gaming – £1.
• If a commercial club benefits from a club machine permit, the maximum participation fee per person per day is £3 or, in a members club or miners welfare institute, £1.

[19]   See Gambling Act 2005, ss 266–276; Gambling Act 2005 (Gaming in Clubs) Regulations 2007 (SI 2007/1942); Gambling Act 2005 (Exempt Gaming in Clubs) Regulations 2007 (SI 2007/1944).

The limits on stakes are as follows:

- Poker:
  - Maximum aggregate stakes for the club per week – £1,000.
  - Maximum aggregate stakes per day – £250.
  - Maximum stake per person per game – £10.
- Other gaming – no limit on stake.

Limits on prizes:

- Poker – £250 per game.
- Other gaming – no limit.

High turnover bingo

32.42   High turnover bingo is treated in the same way in clubs as in licensed premises, as to which see paragraph 32.28 above.

Code of Practice for equal chance gaming in clubs

32.43   As stated above, the Gambling Commission has published a 'Code of Practice for equal chance gaming in clubs and premises with an alcohol licence'. The Code of Practice could be considered as best practice advice by the Gambling Commission. Breaches of the Code of Practice could be used in evidence in a prosecution or in regulatory action.

32.44   In clubs which benefit from a club premises certificate, compliance with the Code of Practice is the responsibility of the gaming supervisor who is appointed by the club. Their responsibilities include ensuring adherence to the limits on stakes and prizes, that the gaming is supervised and that effective procedures designed to prevent underage gambling are in place. It would of course be an offence to exceed the limits or permit under 18s to participate. The Code suggests that all payments in respect of the gaming should be made in cash before the commencement of the game and that no credit may be offered to customers. It also recommends that the equipment be provided by the club, and secured when not in use, and that for organised games the rules of the games being played be displayed or made available to all the players. Interestingly the gaming supervisor should ensure a pleasant atmosphere and deny participation to customers who cheat or collude with other players or employees, threaten other players or employees, create a disturbance or damage equipment.

32.45   There are specific provisions for poker which includes advice that cash games should not be permitted, and that if they are allowed the pot should be kept in sight so that it can be viewed at all times. The gaming supervisor should also take all reasonable steps to ensure that individuals' stakes limits are not exceeded through side bets, additional raises, re-buys or other ways of increasing the pot.

32.46 The Code recommends that appropriate membership records are completed for each member, including a record of subscriptions paid, and that records of daily participation fees are kept.

Club gaming permits

32.47 Members clubs or miners' welfare institutes (which will include those clubs who benefit from a club premises certificate) can apply to their local authority for a club gaming permit.

32.48 A club gaming permit allows a club to provide three gaming machines of category B4, C or D.[20] They can also provide facilities for gaming.

32.49 Equal chance gaming is permitted as well as pontoon or chemin de fer, but no other bankers or unequal chance gaming. The public and under 18s must be excluded from any area of the club or institute where the gaming is taking place and cannot participate.

32.50 Under a club gaming permit there is no limit on stakes and no limit on prizes. The maximum participation fee is £3 per day or £20 for bridge or whist.

32.51 The lack of limitation on stakes and prizes has caused operators to push at the boundaries, seeking to cash in on the rise in popularity of tournament poker by trying to establish poker clubs under the aegis of club premises certificates. This is not permitted because section 266 of the Gambling Act restricts the latitude given to members' clubs to those clubs which are established and conducted wholly or mainly for purposes other than the provision of facilities for gaming,[21] which are established and conducted for the benefit of its members, and which are not otherwise established or conducted as a commercial enterprise. Those who flout these rules can expect strict enforcement by licensing authorities in tandem with the Gambling Commission.

Club machine permits

32.52 Members clubs or miners' welfare institutes (which will include those clubs who benefit from a club premises certificate) and commercial clubs can apply to their local authority for a club machine permit.

---

[20] For maximum stake and prize, see para 32.53 below.
[21] The only exceptions to this are bridge and whist clubs.

32.53 A club machine permit only allows up to three category B4[22], C[23] or D[24] machines to be made available for use on the club premises.

32.54 Under 18s are not permitted to play on a category B4 or C gaming machine and the club must comply with the Code of Practice in the location and operation of machines.

32.55 Schedule 12 of the Gambling Act 2005 legislates for club gaming permits and club machine permits. Applications must be copied to the Gambling Commission and chief officer of the police for the area in which the premises are situated. A fee must be paid to the licensing authority for the application.

32.56 A licensing authority may refuse an application for a permit only on one or more of the following grounds:

(a) that the applicant is not:
   (i) in the case of an application for a club gaming permit, a members' club or a miners' welfare institute, or
   (ii) in the case of an application for a club machine permit, a members' club, a commercial club or a miners' welfare institute;
(b) that the premises on which the applicant conducts its activities are used wholly or mainly by children, by young persons or by both,
(c) that an offence, or a breach of a condition of a permit, has been committed in the course of gaming activities carried on by the applicant;
(d) that a permit held by the applicant has been cancelled during the period of ten years ending with the date of the application; or
(e) that an objection to the application has been made by the police or Gambling Commission.

32.57 If a licensing authority are satisfied in relation to an application for a permit of the matters specified in (a) or (b), they shall refuse the application.

32.58 There is a fast track procedure for clubs which benefit from a club premises certificate which removes the requirement to send copies of the application to the police and Gambling Commission and removes the grounds for refusal. Instead the authority shall grant the application unless they think:

(a) that the applicant is established or conducted wholly or mainly for the purposes of the provision of facilities for gaming, other than gaming of a prescribed kind;

---

[22] Maximum stake £1, maximum prize £250.
[23] Maximum stake £1, maximum prize £70.
[24] Maximum stake 10p–£1 depending on precise type of machine, maximum prize £5–£50 depending on type of machine and type of prize.

(b)   that the applicant is established or conducted wholly or mainly for the purposes of the provision of facilities for gaming of a prescribed kind and also provides facilities for gaming of another kind; or

(c)   that a club gaming permit or club machine permit issued to the applicant has been cancelled during the period of ten years ending with the date of the application.

32.59   Before refusing an application for a permit a licensing authority must hold a hearing to consider the application and any objection made by the police or Gambling Commission. There is a right of appeal to the magistrates' court.

32.60   The permit must be kept at the premises and an annual fee must be paid. Permits must be varied if information contained in them ceases to be accurate.

32.61   The permit will cease to have effect after ten years, unless renewed, or if the permit is surrendered.

32.62   If the holder of a permit ceases to be a members' club, a commercial club or a miners' welfare institute, the permit shall lapse.

32.63   The authority can cancel a permit if the authority think the premises on which the holder of the permit conducts its activities are used wholly or mainly by children, by young persons or by both, or that an offence, or a breach of a condition of a permit, has been committed in the course of gaming activities carried on by the holder of the permit.

32.64   Before cancelling a permit the authority must give the holder at least 21 days' notice of their intent to cancel, and the opportunity to make representations, either in writing or at a hearing, if one is requested by the holder. The holder has a right of appeal, following a cancellation of a permit, to the magistrate's court. A permit shall be cancelled by the authority if the annual fee is not paid, although this requirement can be disapplied if the none payment is due to an administrative error.

32.65   A court can forfeit the permit if the holder or an officer of a permit holder is convicted of an offence under the Gambling Act.

Code of Practice on gaming machine permits and permissions

32.66   As stated above, the Gambling Commission has published a 'Code of Practice on gaming machine permits and permissions in clubs and premises with an alcohol licence'.[25] The Code places two conditions on club gaming permits and club machine permits. These are:

---

[25]   Gambling Commission, March 2012.

(1) All gaming machines situated on the premises must be located in a place within the premises so that their use can be supervised, either by staff whose duties include such supervision (including bar or floor staff) or by other means.

Permit holders must have in place arrangements for such supervision.

(2) All gaming machines situated on the premises shall be located in a place that requires a customer who wishes to use any ATM made available on the premises to cease gambling at the gaming machine in order to do so. 'ATM' means a machine located on the premises, which enables a person using it to obtain cash by use of a credit or debit card.

E CONCLUSION

32.67 The location and operation of gambling premises, including the sale of alcohol, is governed collectively by the planning, gambling licensing and alcohol-licensing regimes.

32.68 As components of the attraction of town centres, they ought to be catered for in strategic terms by the local development plan. The system of gambling licensing affords little discretion to control the whereabouts of licences. That is principally dealt with through the planning system.

32.69 On the whole, gambling premises operate below the regulatory radar of local authorities. The main concerns have tended to relate to clustering of betting offices and gathering outside such premises. The problem has in truth been limited to a small number of locations. It can be dealt with through concerted work by planning and licensing authorities, as well as laws dealing with exterior drinking.

32.70 The wider issue regarding gambling is the question of problem gambling, which is a national question of direct concern to the national regulator, rather than one which local licensing is really equipped to control.

Sex licensing

It goes without saying that sex is not confined to Greater London. It is to be found in most parts of the country.

> Michael Neubert MP, House of Commons, 25 November 1981

Sexual intercourse began
In nineteen sixty-three
(which was rather late for me) -
Between the end of the 'Chatterley' ban
And the Beatles' first LP.

> Philip Larkin, *Annus Mirabilis*

A INTRODUCTION

33.01 The licensing of sex shops and sex cinemas, known as 'sex establishments', was left unscathed by the Licensing Act 2003, and remained governed by the Local Government (Miscellaneous Provisions) Act 1982 ('LGMPA'). That legislation calls for judgments to be made about the character of the area, which, in modern legislative thinking, are the province of planning rather than licensing. It also calls for social, possibly even 'moral' (albeit not voiced in that term), judgments to be made as to the 'appropriateness' of sex establishments within particular localities, considerations which are now absent from the licensing objectives under the Licensing Act 2003. Furthermore, the kinds of considerations to which the licensing objectives are directed rarely arise where sex establishments are concerned. The law as to sex establishments was therefore, at least arguably, out of step with current thinking as to the role of licensing.

33.02 One of the peculiarities of the Licensing Act 2003 was that it did govern one branch of the commercial sex industry – lap dancing clubs, which burgeoned under the 2003 regime. Something had to give – either lap dancing clubs had to become governed by the same considerations as governed sex cinemas and sex shops, or sex establishments needed to be deregulated, in recognition of the advent of the online, post-censorship era. In fact, due to the voice of the equality movement, the former prevailed.

33.03 During 2008 there was a campaign rooted in a concern, which was recognised by government, that the Licensing Act 2003 created a loop-hole which allowed what many considered to be a significant sector of the sex industry, namely lap-dancing and strip clubs, to proliferate virtually without regulation.

33.04 Thus, following consultation with local authorities, operators and other interested parties, amendments to the LGMPA were included in the Policing and Crime Act 2009, which, since 6 April 2010 in England and 8 May 2010 in Wales, and where adopted by the local authority, brings a venue which has 'any live performance or any live display of nudity ... for the purpose of sexually stimulating any member of the audience ...' into a new category of sex establishment called a 'sexual entertainment venue' and thereby requires it to be licensed under the LGMPA.

33.05 Thus, those premises which hold such entertainment by virtue of a licence granted under the Licensing Act 2003 find that, where the changes to the legislation are adopted by the local authority, they will have to apply for a sexual entertainment venue licence and renew that licence on an annual basis and, consequently, face objections from local residents as to whether they should be permitted to continue with that form of entertainment in that locality.

33.06 Given that the same local authority licensing committees tend to be the decision-makers under both sets of legislation, and given also that sexual entertainment venues tend to situate themselves in town centres in the heart of the drinking economy, inclusion of sex establishment licensing in this book is warranted. This also gives an opportunity to compare the two regimes where it is relevant to do so.

Background to LGMPA

33.07 Philip Larkin's experience (above) was not atypical. The liberalisation in attitudes to sex was accompanied by a steady growth in the number of sex shops, sex cinemas and peep shows throughout the course of the 1960s and 1970s. By 1981, there were 165 sex industry premises operating in the square mile of Soho.[1] Nor was the increase confined to London, as Michael Neubert MP's startling revelation to the House of Commons,[2] also quoted at the outset of this Chapter, demonstrates. The United Kingdom's involvement in the boom in the sex industry and the steady growth of the number of premises appearing in high streets led to a growing strength of feeling against such premises by local residents and shop keepers who feared a degradation not only in the value of their homes, but also in their level of business.

33.08 Prior to the LGMPA there was no direct regulatory control[3] of sex establishments. The planning legislation was not able to deal with such premises as planning permission was not required for the change of use from a shop to a sex shop; such change falling within the same planning use class (A1) of the Use Classes Order 1972.[4] Thus a baker's shop could change into a sex shop without having to make any application to the local authority for planning permission authorising such change of use. The late 1970s and early 1980s saw calls for the planning legislation to be amended,[5] with consideration being given to the possibility of a new 'use class' or similar vehicle being created to ensure that planning permission was required prior to a change of use of a premises into a premises selling sex articles or showing sex films. However, this was considered to be an ineffective approach as, when considering planning applications, the planning authority are not able to take into consideration the character of the applicant as opposed to the nature of the land use proposed, whereas the character of an applicant involved in the management of a sex establishment may be a highly germane consideration.

33.09 A controlling regime was first proposed in the Greater London Council (General Powers) (No 2) Bill for premises within the Greater London area and, following much debate, these provisions were included within the LGMPA, creating a regime applicable throughout England and Wales, providing local authorities with the power to control sex establishments within their area through a system of licensing should they choose to adopt the legislation.

---

1   Colin Manchester, *Entertainment Licensing, Law and Practice* (Butterworths, 2nd ed, 1999).
2   Hansard HC Debs 25 November 1981, Vol 13 col 923.
3   Save for controls under the Obscene Publications Acts 1959 and 1964, and subsequently the Indecent Displays (Control) Act 1981.
4   SI 1972/1385, now contained in the Town and Country Planning (Use Classes) Order 1987 (SI 1987/764), as amended.
5   Parliamentary Questions (Written Answers), 10th November 1981.

The philosophy of the legislation

33.10 The amendment of the Local Government (Miscellaneous Provisions) Bill, which was initially concerned only with the licensing of public entertainment and refreshment premises, to include the licensing of sex establishments came with cross-party support. The Minister of State introduced the amendment, stating:

'The number of establishments has significantly increased over the past 18 months or so. That has understandably caused a great deal of concern and resentment among local communities. That has been especially true where the establishments have opened in particularly unsuitable locations – near a school or ... a church.'[6]

33.11 The purpose appears to be to control and, as a corollary, limit their number and prevent their potential spread into areas where residents (and local councillors) may not wish to see them develop:

'The object being to prevent the blighting of a district and the creation of an affront to neighbours and passers-by through an unchecked spread of disagreeable establishment.'[7]

33.12 Nevertheless, societal attitudes had progressed sufficiently that a ban on such premises was not seriously contemplated, though there was a pragmatic element in this: to ban would be to drive them underground. As Lord Bridge put it:

'The social background against which the legislation providing for the licensing of sex establishments must be considered is the product of a revolution in public attitudes to every aspect of sexual morality. This is nowhere more marked than in relation to nudity. Newspapers and magazines which in varying degrees overtly exploit nudity for the purposes of titillating the sexual appetite, and many of which, in the first half of this century, would certainly have led to prosecution of the publisher, are now on sale in any newsagent's shop. So also in films, on television and on the stage varying degrees of nudity have come to be accepted as commonplace.'[8]

33.13 Hence, the Local Government (Miscellaneous Provisions) Act 1982 came to be adopted. The political backdrop was well-described by Lord Hoffman in *Belfast City Council v Miss Behavin' Ltd*:[9]

'1. My Lords, the end of the *Chatterley* ban and the Beatles' first LP marked a sudden loss of confidence in traditional British prudishness

---

6   Hansard HC Debs 3 February 1982, Vol 17 col 333.
7   *Lambeth London Borough Council v Grewal* (1986) 82 Cr App R 301, 307 per Mustill LJ.
8   *McMonagle v Westminster City Council* [1990] 2 AC 716.
9   [2007] 1 WLR 1420.

by legislators and jurors which made the law against obscene publications very difficult to enforce. As a result, the distribution of all but the most hard core pornography became, at least in practice, a lawful trade. This gave rise to unexpected social and environmental problems. It was unacceptable for vendors of pornography to flaunt their wares before the public at large. Ordinary newsagents who sold soft porn avoided outraging sensitive customers by putting it on high shelves. Shops which specialised in pornographic publications and videos, together with sex aids and other such articles, tended to have opaque windows, as much to protect the privacy of customers as the sensibilities of passers-by. They congregated in run-down areas of large towns, usually near the railway station, clustering together on the same principle that people carrying on similar businesses have always traded in close proximity to each other. But the other inhabitants of the locality, both commercial and residential, often objected to the proliferation of sex shops on a mixture of environmental, social, aesthetic, moral and religious grounds: fears about the kind of people who ran them and the customers they attracted; distaste or moral or religious objection to what was going on inside; concern that they lowered the tone of the neighbourhood and attracted other even less desirable trades such as prostitution and organised crime.'

33.14 Sexual entertainment, however, had been classified as entertainment, which had so recently been deregulated with the abolition of the office of Lord Chamberlain as a national arbiter of taste and the passage of the Theatres Act 1968. If adults wished to pay for striptease in a local bar or a revue bar, so be it. What caused attitudes to change was the import from the USA at the turn of the millennium of lap dancing clubs. Here, the dancers came off the stage and for £10 or £20 would strip for three minutes or so expressly for the titillation of individual customers, often in private booths and always at close quarters. The economics of this activity are completely different from a strip club, since men will pay more for an intimate, near-sex experience than they will to stand in an audience and watch stripping on a stage. Hence the rise of the lap-dancing club, which could afford to jostle with coffee shops, betting offices and nightclubs on the high street as part of the new leisure economy, but which did not only arouse male customers, but also aroused local sensibilities as to issues such as equality, exploitation, character of the locality and incompatibility of uses. As it was, the Licensing Act 2003 was powerless to halt the rise in these establishments, which actually cause precious little harm in terms of the licensing objectives. These arguments all led to the passage of the Policing and Crime Act 2009, which put sexual entertainment venues on the same footing as sex shops and sex cinemas, thus uniting the form of control over commercial sex on the high street, whether its medium was celluloid, paper or flesh.

B LGMPA AND ITS ADOPTION

33.15 Section 2 LGMPA provides for the adoption of the provisions contained in Schedule 3 of the Act ('the Schedule'), thereby allowing 'appropriate authorities'[10] to control, by way of a licensing regime, sex establishments and sexual entertainment venues in their area, and specifies the procedure to be followed for a successful adoption.

33.16 The procedure is as follows:

- The local authority must pass a resolution adopting Schedule 3 and specifying the day the provisions are to come into effect (which must be no earlier than one month after the date of the resolution).
- The local authority must then publish a notice in a local newspaper in two consecutive weeks stating that they have passed such a resolution and its general effect, with the first notice appearing no later than 28 days before the date the provisions are to come into force.

33.17 A failure to comply strictly with these requirements has been held to be fatal to the adoption: *R v Swansea City Council ex parte Quietlynn Limited*[11]; *R v Birmingham City Council ex parte Quietlynn Limited,*[12] although were the matter to be considered in the light of modern regulatory principles it is conceivable that a less stringent approach would be taken.[13]

33.18 European Court challenges to local authority decisions to adopt the LGMPA provisions on the grounds that a restriction on the sale of imported sex articles breached article 30 of the EEC Treaty (prohibiting quantitative restrictions on imports) were dismissed by the European Court of Justice[14]. No decisions to adopt the legislation have been successfully challenged on this basis.

C WHAT NEEDS TO BE LICENSED?

33.19 Once adopted, the LGMPA prohibits anyone from using any premises, vehicle, vessel or stall as a 'sex establishment' unless they have been granted a licence.[15] A sex establishment means:

---

[10] Defined in paragraph 5 of the Schedule as the local authority who passed the resolution.
[11] Times, 19 October 1983.
[12] (1985) 83 LGR 461.
[13] *R v Secretary of State for the Home Department ex parte Jeyeanthan* [2000] 1 WLR 354.
[14] *Quietlynn Ltd v Southend BC* [1991] 2 WLR 611; *Sheptonhurst v Newham BC* [1991] ECR I-2387.
[15] LGMPA, Sch 3 para 6.

- A sex cinema.[16]
- A sex shop.[17]
- In a London borough, where the council have so resolved, a sex encounter establishment.[18]
- A sexual entertainment venue.

Exemptions and waivers

33.20 A licence is not required for the sale or supply or demonstration of articles which are manufactured for use primarily for the purposes of birth control or primarily relate to birth control.[19] Furthermore, the licensing authority may waive the requirement of a licence in any case where they consider that to require a licence would be unreasonable or inappropriate.[20] This is most likely to apply to temporary events, or where the licence is required for a short period, whether due to an imminent move or cessation of the business. Having said that, the annual Erotica Exhibition that takes place over three days at Earls Court & Olympia (and more recently in the Manchester G-Mex Centre) is licensed, but this is based upon the number of attendees and scale of the event rather than its duration.

33.21 So far as sexual entertainment venues are concerned, a licence is not required where the 'relevant entertainment' (for example, lap-dancing) has not occurred on more than eleven occasions in the last twelve months, no such occasion has begun within the period of one month beginning with the end of any previous occasion and no such occasion lasted longer than 24 hours.

33.22 This exemption will allow premises licensed under the 2003 Act to have 'gentlemen's nights' or 'ladies' nights' without requiring a sexual entertainment venue licence.

Definition of sex cinema

33.23 'Sex cinema' is defined in Schedule 3 paragraph 3 as any premises, vehicle, vessel or stall used to a significant degree for the exhibition of moving pictures which are concerned primarily with the portrayal of, or

---

[16] LGMPA, Sch 3 para 3. See definition in para 33.24 below.

[17] LGMPA, Sch 3 para 2. See definition in para 33.26 below.

[18] Greater London Council (General Powers) Act 1986, s 12. This Act enabled London authorities to resolve to licence sex encounter establishments. Where they have adopted that regime, they may continue to use it, but Art 2 of the Policing and Crime Act (Consequential Provisions) (England) Order 2010 (SI 2010/723) now prevents authorities from adopting the regime. If they wish to licence strip clubs, they must adopt the sexual entertainment venue regime. See further para 33.41 below.

[19] LGMPA, Sch 3 para 6(2).

[20] LGMPA, Sch 3 para 7(4).

primarily deal with or relate to, or are intended to stimulate or encourage, sexual activity, acts of force or restraint which are associated with sexual activity, or are concerned primarily with the portrayal of, or primarily deal with or relate to, genital organs or urinary or excretory functions.

33.24 There are exemptions from this definition for cinemas which are licensed and being used for the exhibition of a film under the Licensing Act 2003.

Definition of sex shop

33.25 The undertaking of a 'sex shop'[21] is defined in Schedule 3 paragraph 4 as any premises, vehicle, vessel or stall used for a business which consists to a significant degree of selling, hiring, exchanging, lending, displaying or demonstrating 'sex articles' or other things intended for use in connection with or for the purpose of stimulating or encouraging sexual activity or acts of force or restraint which are associated with sexual activity.

'Sex article'

33.26 'Sex article' is defined[22] as anything made for use in connection with, or for the purposes of stimulating or encouraging sexual activity or acts of force or restraint which are associated with sexual activity, and is said to include books or magazines, anything that can reproduce or manufacture any sex article and any recording of vision or sound which is concerned primarily with the portrayal of, or primarily deals with or relates to, or is intended to stimulate or encourage, sexual activity or acts of force or restraint which are associated with sexual activity, or is concerned primarily with the portrayal of, or primarily deals with or relates to, genital organs or urinary or excretory functions.

33.27 The inclusion within the definition of articles made for use in connection with or for the purpose of stimulating or encouraging sexual activity gives rise to difficulties. This is clearly broad enough to include all types of exotic lingerie and fetish-wear, yet it could not have been the intention of Parliament to require lingerie shops, or even fetish-wear shops, to be licensed. But where is the line to be drawn? After all, a shop selling riding crops may be an unexciting (or at least unerotic) place to visit for a

---

[21]   The question of exhibition halls with stalls was considered in *R v Newcastle Upon Tyne City Council ex p The Christian Institute* [2001] BLGR 165, QBD, where it was held that only the hall needs to be licensed, not the individual stalls.

[22]   LGMPA, Sch 3 para 4(3)–(4).

horseman, but to a sado-masochist it would provide titillation beyond measure. Who is to decide what is the 'norm'?[23]

33.28 It would appear that most local authorities are taking a common sense approach to this issue and where shops are selling clothing only or articles that have a 'normal' use, they are considered to be outside of the regime. It is only where the intended use is predominantly sexual that the attention of the Act is drawn. But the potential for a local authority taking a very broad view of the definition should not be understated and it would be wise for any potential proprietor to seek the advice of an officer of the local authority within whose district the premises will lie.

33.29 It is worth mentioning here that videos and DVD's portraying sexual activity and which have been rated R18 by the BBFC are 'sex articles' and can only be supplied in licensed sex shops to adults of not less than 18 years.

'Significant degree'

33.30 In order to fall within the definition of a sex cinema or sex shop, it is a requirement that the various premises must be providing their service to a 'significant degree'. This has caused local authorities, the proprietors of premises and the courts a great deal of consternation.

33.31 For example, it is clear that a copy of Playboy or some other 'man's mag' would fall within the definition of a sexual article, and a newsagent stocking 10 or 20 such magazines amongst more general titles and other provisions would not be selling to a significant degree. But what would the situation be if he suddenly started to stock 200 such magazines? Would that then be significant? Similarly, if a cinema began to show certificated 'sex films' every weekday evening after 9 pm, would that be significant?

33.32 In one case[24] it was stated that:

'The word "significant" has more than one meaning. It is capable, in some contexts, of meaning "more than trifling". It does not have this meaning in the present context. A higher standard is set; how much higher cannot be prescribed by any rule of thumb. The ratio between the sexual and other aspects of the business will always be material. So also will be the absolute quantity of sales ... It would be wrong to say that in law any single factor is decisive. It is up to the court of trial to decide which considerations are material to the individual case and what weight is to be attached to them.'

---

[23]   In *R v Westminster City Council ex parte Rezovali* (unreported, 7 June 1999), the High Court (David Pannick QC) summarily dismissed an argument that videos showing corporal punishment were not capable of being sex articles.

[24]   *Lambeth London Borough Council v Grewal* (1986) 82 Cr App R 301, 307 per Mustill LJ.

33.33 That case concerned a newsagent selling men's magazines to the value of between £2000–2500 per annum, representing some 1–1.5% of the premises annual turnover. The court found, as a matter of fact, that the level of sex articles was not significant in the circumstances existing on the premises, and went on to suggest that the following factors would be appropriate considerations in determining whether the sales/display equated to a 'significant degree':

● the character of the remainder of the business;
● the nature of the display; and
● the nature of the articles themselves.

33.34 The court expressly dissociated itself from the following dictum given earlier in the same year by the Divisional Court in *Watford Borough Council v Private Alternative Birth Control Information and Education Centres Limited*:[25]

'... 'significant' must mean something which signifies, something which is not insignificant, perhaps something which cannot be dismissed under the de minimis rule.'

33.35 The judgment in *Grewal* has led to a number of local authorities determining (either expressly or implicitly) a percentage figure for sexual articles within a premises which, if exceeded, would lead to a conclusion that the premises falls within the definition of a 'sex establishment'.[26]

33.36 In a Scottish case[27] the proprietor of a premises was convicted for operating a sex shop without a licence, and one of the grounds of appeal was that, as no evidence had been led on the stocks and sales of sex articles compared to non-sex articles, there was no evidence that the shop was indeed a sex shop. The High Court of Justiciary (Appeal) stated that the Crown did not have to show that the majority of goods sold were sex articles and the Sheriff had been entitled to infer that they formed a significant degree of business from evidence of the value of the goods and the total sales for the shop as recorded on the till roll.

33.37 The lack of clarity surrounding the definition of significant degree has led to many sex shop proprietors carrying large stocks of non-sex items in an attempt to dissuade local authorities from the view that the premises require a licence under the LGMPA.

33.38 Such an avoidance scheme is effective where the local authority officers are concerned only with the extent of the display rather than the other factors referred to in the *Grewal* case. It does, however, have a major drawback, in that only a licensed sex shop is able to deal in R18 certificated

---

[25]   [1985] Crim LR 594 per May LJ.
[26]   One local authority takes no action where the level of displayed items is less than 5% of the total level of displayed items.
[27]   *Rees v Lees* 1997 SLT 872.

videos and if they supply or offer to supply such video recordings without such a licence they will be committing an offence under the Video Recordings Act 1984,[28] and be liable to imprisonment for a term not exceeding six months or a fine not exceeding £5000 or both.

Definition of sexual entertainment venues and sex encounter establishments

33.39 Sexual entertainment venues are defined in LGMPA Schedule 3 paragraph 2A as:

'(1) ... any premises at which relevant entertainment is provided before a live audience for the financial gain of the organiser or the entertainer.

(2) In this paragraph "relevant entertainment" means—
(a) any live performance; or
(b) any live display of nudity;

which is of such a nature that, ignoring financial gain, it must reasonably be assumed to be provided solely or principally for the purpose of sexually stimulating any member of the audience (whether by verbal or other means).'

33.40 Sex encounter establishments are confined to London. They are defined within Schedule 3, paragraph 3A (as inserted by the Greater London Council (General Powers) Act 1986, s 12) which brings peep shows and other such 'entertainment' within the licensing regime. The definition includes performances for the sexual stimulation of customers, services or entertainment involving exposure of private parts, and premises other than sex cinemas displaying images stimulating sexual activity[29]. There are exclusions for premises licensed and used for regulated entertainment or late night refreshment under the Licensing Act 2003. They are largely superseded by the new regime of sexual entertainment venues. Upon a London Borough adopting the new provisions of the 2009 Act, any existing sex encounter venue will be treated as though the licence was granted under the new regime and will continue under its existing conditions. If the new regime is not adopted by the London Borough, the existing regime will continue.

---

[28]   Video Recordings Act 1984, s 12.
[29]   It is not necessary to prove that anyone is actually stimulated by the performance: *Smakowski v Westminster City Council* (1989) 154 JP 345, a pragmatic decision, given the difficulties of proof this might entail. Further, it is not necessary for sexual organs to be displayed. Where dancers in bikinis in a lap-dancing venue had (for example) touched an undercover officer with her breasts, put his tie down her g-string and rubbed her genital area with it, the Divisional Court held that it would have been borderline perverse to hold that this was *not* a 'performance which wholly or mainly comprises the sexual stimulation of persons' within Local Government Act 1982 Sch 3 para 3A(a): *Blenheim Leisure (Restaurants) Ltd v Westminster City Council* [2004] LLR 431, 437.

33.41   In both cases, the question of where the line is to be drawn between performance on the one hand and sex encounter/performance on the other. In one case[30] a coin-operated peep show displayed women gyrating and caressing themselves to music, with larger sums of money producing more explicit action. The Court of Appeal held that this was not 'public dancing or music or other entertainment of the like kind', because the operation involved lewd sexual displays. The difference, held the court, was one of fact and degree, with the Folies Bergère at one end of the spectrum, where the dance is enhanced by the titillation of some nudity, and voyeurism from 'lonely dark cubicles' at the other. In the middle is striptease where 'the exotic is beginning to shade into the erotic.'[31] Plainly, there is room for considerable dispute in the middle of the spectrum. The cusp is usually represented by burlesque shows which are intended to be shocking, funny and titillating but not necessarily overtly sexual. Which side of the line such entertainment falls is fact-sensitive and there is certainly room for adjacent licensing authorities to differ in their conclusions regarding the same type of performance. Perhaps as attitudes to nudity and sexual conduct in performance become more liberated, there is less need to find that particular performances fall under the rubric of sex establishments rather than merely entertainment. If that is right, then the controls over such performances will be governed by the licensing objectives in the Licensing Act 2003 rather than the moral judgment underpinning the 1982 legislation.

D   WHO CAN APPLY FOR THE LICENCE?

33.42   Having determined that a licence is required for premises, the next issue that must be addressed by the potential proprietor is who is entitled to apply for that licence.

33.43   Paragraph 10 of the Schedule provides that an application may be made by an individual, a body corporate or an unincorporated body, with the following provisos contained in paragraph 12 (the mandatory grounds for refusal):

- An individual must be aged 18 or over, have not within the last 12 months have held a sex establishment licence which has been revoked, be and have been resident in an EEA State for the period of six months immediately preceding the date when the application was made and, within the period of 12 months preceding the date of the application, not have been refused the grant or renewal of such a licence, unless such refusal was reversed on appeal.
- If the application is made by a body corporate, it must be incorporated in an EEA State, not have held a sex establishment licence in the area of the appropriate authority which has been revoked within the last 12

---

[30]   *Willowcell v Westminster* CC (1995) 94 LGR 83.
[31]   Per Ward LJ, page 94.

months, and not within the 12 months immediately preceding the date of the application have been refused a grant or renewal of such a licence unless that refusal has been reversed on appeal.

- For an unincorporated body, it must not within the previous 12 months have had a sex establishment licence revoked in the area of the appropriate authority nor had an application for the grant or renewal of a licence refused unless the refusal has been reversed on appeal.

E APPLICATION PROCEDURE

33.44   Paragraph 10 of Schedule 3 details the procedure to be followed for grants, renewals and transfers, and provides that the application must be in writing and, where the application is made by an individual, include that individual's full name, permanent address and age. Where an application is made by a limited company or an unincorporated company, the application must include the full name of the body, the address of its registered or principal office and the full names and private addresses of the directors or other persons responsible for its management.

33.45   In all cases the application must contain the full address of the premises to be licensed and, where it relates to a vehicle, vessel or store, where such vehicle, vessel or stall is to be used.

33.46   In addition to these specified statutory requirements, paragraph 10 allows local authorities to request such other information as they may reasonably require. In most cases this will include the days and hours of operation, whether any other person has an interest in the ownership or management of the business and whether the applicant has any previous convictions.

33.47   Having submitted the application to the local authority the applicant must, within seven days of the date of the application, place a notice in a local newspaper identifying the premises and detailing the application and send a copy of the application to the local police authority. The applicant must also, where the application is in respect of premises, display a notice detailing the application on or near the premises where it can be read by the public for a period of 21 days beginning with the date of the application. The local authority is entitled to prescribe the format of the notice and, invariably, this includes a paragraph inviting objections to the application to be directed to them.

Fees

33.48   There is a requirement under paragraph 19 for the applicant to pay the local authority a fee for the licence. This fee is not prescribed and paragraph 19 allows the authority to determine what that fee should be subject to the proviso that it is 'reasonable'. This has led to a wide variation in the fees sought by local authorities throughout England and Wales.

33.49 The issue of what is reasonable has been considered on a number of occasions by the court and it would appear that the following general principles can be determined:

- It is not wrong for a council to be guided by a policy that the ratepayers should be relieved of the burden of paying the cost of administering the licensing of sex establishments, and so long as it does not exceed that cost the court should not interfere.[32]
- Applying that principle, it is acceptable for the authority to carry deficits over from one year in calculating the fee for the next.[33]

  (It should similarly carry forward surpluses.[34])

- The court has no duty or power to decide what is a reasonable fee and as long as the council has not acted perversely the court will not interfere.[35]
- The local authority should not use licence fees as a way to raise revenue and a proposition that a council had a fiduciary duty to maximise its revenue was rejected.[36]

A further key question is whether an authority may use the fee to fund enforcement work. This is canvassed in Chapter 61 (The Fees Regime).

F CONSIDERATION OF THE APPLICATION

33.50 Once the applicant has submitted the application and the fee, it is then for the local authority to determine whether a licence should be granted. By reason of the Local Government Act 1972[37], local authorities can determine applications made to them by delegation to a committee, sub-committee or an officer, and in the case of sex establishment licensing they invariably do. Those hearing the application must have received the appropriate delegated powers, failing which any decision they make will be unlawful.

33.51 While a wide discretion is conferred, local authorities are subject to the supervisory jurisdiction of the High Court – see Chapter 20 (Challenging Licensing Decisions). While in theory the application may engage human

---

[32] *R v Greater London Council, ex p Rank Organisation*, 19 February 1982, Times; *R v Westminster City Council ex parte Hutton* (1985) 83 LGR 461.

[33] *R v Westminster City Council ex parte Hutton* (1985) 83 LGR 461, p 519.

[34] *R (Hemming t/a Simply Pleasure Limited) v Westminster City Council* [2012] EWHC 1260 (Admin).

[35] *R v Westminster City Council ex parte Hutton* (1985) 83 LGR 461.

[36] *R v Manchester City Council ex parte King* (1991) 89 LGR 696.

[37] Section 99.

rights, including article 10 (freedom of expression) and article 1 of the First Protocol (protection of property), these rights operate at a very low level, and are in any event qualified rights. As Lord Hoffman said *in Miss Behavin'*:[38]

> 'If article 10 and article 1 of the First Protocol are engaged at all, they operate at a very low level. The right to vend pornography is not the most important right of free expression in a democratic society and the licensing system does not prohibit anyone from exercising it. It only prevents him from using unlicensed premises for that purpose. Even if the council considered that it was not appropriate to have a sex shop anywhere in Belfast, that would only have put its citizens in the same position as most of the rest of the country, in having to satisfy their demand for such products by internet or mail order or going to more liberally governed districts like Soho. This is an area of social control in which the Strasbourg court has always accorded a wide margin of appreciation to member states, which in terms of the domestic constitution translates into the broad power of judgment entrusted to local authorities by the legislature. If the local authority exercises that power rationally and in accordance with the purposes of the statute, it would require very unusual facts for it to amount to a disproportionate restriction on Convention rights.'

The hearing

33.52 Paragraph 10(19) of Schedule 3 provides that the applicant for the grant, renewal or transfer of a sex establishment licence is entitled to appear before and make representations to the committee of the authority before a decision is made refusing to grant, renew or transfer such a licence.

33.53 The implication of this sub-paragraph is that, where no relevant objections have been received and the committee are content to grant the application, there need be no attendance at a hearing.

33.54 Where relevant objections have been received then, clearly, there is the potential for the application to be refused and, hence, a hearing should be listed and the applicant invited to attend to make representations.

33.55 Paragraph 10(18) provides that the authority, when considering the application, must have regard to any observations or objections submitted to them by the chief officer of police and any objections submitted to them by others within the 28 day period allowed under paragraph 10(15), and such objections must be provided to the applicant to enable a response to be given to them. However, it is not necessary for the applicant to have the full details of the objection provided they are given the substance or 'general terms'[39] of it.

---

[38] [2007] 1 WLR 1420, para 16.
[39] Paragraph 10(16).

33.56 It had been generally assumed that the wording of paragraph 10(15) prevented objections lodged later than 28 days after the date of the application from being considered.[40] However, this view was laid to rest in *Quietlynn Limited v Plymouth City Council and others*.[41] Here, the local authority considered a number of objections that it had received outside of the 28 day period, including some received on the morning of the hearing. The High Court found that, whilst the authority was obliged to consider objections made within the 28 day period, it had a discretion whether or not to take into consideration objections made thereafter, and if it intended to take those later objections into account the applicant should be informed as to those objections and notice given to him 'as is sufficient to ensure that the hearing of his application is fair'. This approach was endorsed by the House of Lords in *Miss Behavin'*.[42]

33.57 This potentially places the applicant in a difficult position, in that it does not prevent objectors attending the hearing in vast numbers to object to an application on the day of the hearing and, if the licensing committee decide to consider those persons' objections, the applicant will be expected to answer objections as they are placed before him or to apply for an adjournment of the hearing to consider the objections in his own time. However, where the application is for the grant of a licence, this latter course of action would lead to the delay of the opening of the premises (and thus affect the business' profitability). In relation to all types of application it would not prevent further objectors attending the subsequent hearing date, again possibly leading to a further adjournment, although it is to be hoped that the licensing committee would use their discretion not to hear those objections on that date.

33.58 It is worth noting that objections pre-dating the submission of a licence application can be taken into consideration by the committee.[43]

Human rights?

33.59 A local authority is prohibited from providing the objector's name and address to the applicant unless the objector consents,[44] and this, in practice, leads to letters of objection being provided to the applicant with names and addresses deleted.

33.60 Article 6 of the European Convention on Human Rights may have an impact on this requirement on the basis that the applicant should be entitled to know who is making allegations against him. In most cases, the identity of

---

[40] *R v Birmingham City Council and others, ex parte Quietlynn Limited* (1985) 83 LGR 461.
[41] [1987] 3 WLR 189.
[42] [2007] 1 WLR 1420.
[43] *R v Preston Borough Council and others ex parte Quietlynn Limited* (1985) 83 LGR 308.
[44] LGMPA, Sch 3 para 10(17).

the objector is irrelevant. However, it must be right that should objections come from outside of the local area, the applicant should be able to comment on that fact. This may be solved by the local authority providing the applicant with details of the distance the objectors live/work from the premises; although even this could readily identify the objector. More difficult is the situation where the objector is a trade objector, a matter upon which the applicant would wish to comment in relation to weight and credibility. It is submitted that, in keeping with the Convention's fairness requirements, a local authority should read the paragraph as requiring disclosure of the maximum relevant detail about the objector short of disclosure of the actual name and address.

What should the members take into consideration?

33.61 The local authority, when considering applications, do not have an unfettered discretion as to whether to refuse an application for a grant or renewal. There are mandatory grounds for refusal contained in paragraph 12(1), which has been dealt with above.[45] Paragraph 12(3) sets out discretionary grounds. These are:

- that the applicant is unsuitable to hold the licence by reason of having been convicted of an offence or for any other reason;
- that if the licence were to be granted, renewed or transferred the business to which it relates would be managed by or carried on for the benefit of a person, other than the applicant, who would be refused the grant, renewal or transfer of such a licence if he made the application himself;
- that the number of sex establishments in the relevant locality at the time the application is made is equal to or exceeds the number which the authority consider is appropriate for that locality;
- that the grant or renewal of the licence would be inappropriate, having regard:
  - to the character of the relevant locality;
  - to the use to which any premises in the vicinity are put; or
  - to the layout, character or condition of the premises, vehicle, vessel or stall in respect of which the application is made.

These are now considered in turn.

The unsuitability of the applicant

33.62 As with all licensed premises, local authorities will wish to ensure that the person managing it is, in general licensing parlance, 'fit and proper', and applicants with convictions must be considered very carefully before granting them a licence.

---

[45]   Para 33.44 above.

33.63 However, not only can unspent convictions be taken into consideration under this ground, but so can spent convictions:

> 'Once some or all of the spent convictions are admitted in evidence, either before the local authority committee or before justices, the applicant is then entitled naturally to be heard, not by way of suggesting that the convictions were incorrectly arrived at but in order to persuade the judicial authority that they are either, in truth, irrelevant or such, by reason of their age, circumstances or lack of seriousness, that they should not jeopardise his application. All of that is simple natural justice. The judicial authority must then come to its own dispassionate conclusion, having in mind not only the interests of the applicant as a person with spent convictions but also the public in whose interests these exceptional powers are being exercised.'[46]

33.64 This ground for refusal is not limited to convictions (spent or otherwise), and the committee can make a determination as to suitability based upon 'any other reason'. For example, if the committee believe that the applicant has any intention of carrying on the business in a way which would in itself breach any law or cause problems in the area, it appears that they are entitled to conclude that he would not be a fit and proper person and refuse the licence:

> 'It is no doubt right to regard an applicant as fit and proper if adequate evidence of good character and record is adduced and there is no reason to question or doubt it ... They [the local authority] may fail to be satisfied because adequate information of character and record is not forthcoming ... or they might fail to be satisfied for any other good reason. It is in my view impossible to be prescriptive as to what might amount to a good reason. What will be (or may be) a good reason will vary from case to case and vary according to the context in which those words appear. The decision maker may take account of hearsay, provided it is hearsay which is not unreasonably thought to be worthy of credence, and such evidence need not be evidence which will withstand scrutiny according to the formal rules of a court of law. It is not a good reason if a local authority or justices rely on prejudice or assertions shown to be ill-founded or gossip or rumour or any other matter which a reasonable and fair-minded decision maker acting in good faith and with proper regard to the interests both of the public and the applicant would not think it right to rely on. But it is appropriate for the local authority or justices to regard as a good reason anything which a reasonable and fair-minded decision maker, acting in good faith and with proper regard to the interests both of the public and the applicant, could properly think it right to rely on.'[47]

---

[46] *Admanson v Waveney District Council* [1997] 2 All ER 898, 904–5 per Sedley J.
[47] *McCool v Rushcliffe Borough Council* [1998] 3 All ER 889, 896, per Lord Bingham CJ, followed in *Leeds City Council v Hussain* (2002) LTL 23/5/2002.

33.65 The power is not to be exercised on a suspicion of unsuitability, even if reasonably entertained. The local authority would need to make a positive, factual, finding of unsuitability. Furthermore, the unsuitability would need to be related to the holding of a licence – a general finding of disrepute will not suffice. It is submitted that the local authority would, in practice, need to be satisfied that the applicant cannot be trusted to run the premises within the law or without unnecessary harm to his customers, staff or the general public, such that it would be right to refuse him a licence.

The business would be managed or carried on for the benefit of some other person who would have been refused had they applied themselves

33.66 This ground is principally an attempt to stop 'undesirables' using front men to pursue applications on their behalf, and to stop persons who fall within the mandatory grounds for refusal using 'innocents' as the applicant. It also applies to situations where the applicant is unimpeachable, but their manager is not. It is rare for such an objection to be made, let alone proved.

There are already sufficient sex establishments in the relevant locality

33.67 This ground requires the local authority to make a judgment as to the number of premises appropriate in the relevant locality.[48] The 'relevant locality' is defined at paragraph 12(5) as meaning the locality where the premises subject to the application is situated and, in relation to a vehicle, vessel or stall, where it is intended to be used. This clearly does not take the matter much further.

33.68 The question of locality was considered in *R v Peterbrorough City Council ex parte Quietlynn*.[49] The Court of Appeal held that what was the relevant locality was a question of fact to be decided on the facts of the individual application. The local authority had to look at the area in which the prospective licensed premises would lie and then decide either the appropriate number of sex establishments, or determine that the character of the area was such that it was inappropriate to grant a licence at all. The expression 'locality' did not mean a pre-defined area, and it was not necessary to be able to show the boundaries on a map. However, an entire town, or the whole of the authority's administrative area, was too large to be the relevant locality within the meaning of the Act.

33.69 Some localities are by their very nature less suitable as sites for sex establishments than others; for example because of the presence of schools,

---

[48] *R v Bournemouth BC ex p Continental Books Ltd* (1994) TLR 19/5/94, held that the time for determining how many licences would be granted for an area was the close of the hearing of all eligible applications.

[49] (1987) 85 LGR 249.

churches or other sensitive premises[50]; even a family pub[51] may be sufficient to justify a refusal.

33.70 The next question is how the correct number is to be assessed. It is important to note that for the purposes of para 12(3)(c), nil may be an appropriate number (para 12(4)). In the *Peterborough* decision, Sir John Donaldson MR considered the correct question to be 'what is the character of the locality in which the proposed shop is situated and what is the appropriate number of sex establishments for that locality?' If the correct question is asked, there is no reason why, in appropriate circumstances, the answer should not be nil.

Character of relevant locality etc

33.71 This ground complements the last in that it focuses on the character of the relevant locality and the use to which premises in the vicinity are put. The vicinity is presumably a smaller area than the 'locality'. It also makes relevant the lay-out, character and condition of the application premises. This would prevent, for example, dilapidated premises being used as sex establishments, so as to preserve standards of health, safety and convenience for customers. It must be said that the modern sex industry has moved away from the somewhat seedy image of the past and proprietors are now more likely to spend money on renovating a premises they see as having potential, rather than finding a less expensive premises which is not attractive to customers.

The nature of the discretion

33.72 These grounds for refusal under paragraph 12(3) confer a wide discretion and will not easily be shown to be unreasonable. The 'locality' grounds under paragraph 12(3)(c) and (d) are particularly wide. In *R v Westminster City Council ex parte Felway*[52] the Court of Appeal held that para 12(3)(c) and (d):

'relate to planning matters, which are matters for the local authority and the local authority alone. Their sole eminence in this position is made clear by the effect that no appeal to the magistrates lies in relation to an adverse finding on either of those. Those matters are entirely a matter of judgment for the local authority.'

---

[50] *R v Birmingham City Council ex parte Quietlynn Limited* (1985) 83 LGR 461.
[51] *R v Bournemouth District Council ex parte Liam McCann* (unreported, 16 November 1998).
[52] Unreported, 18 October 2000.

Policy

33.73 In *R v Birmingham City Council ex parte Quietlynn Ltd*[53] the Court of Appeal expressly assented to the proposition that the local authority might adopt a policy for the determination of applications, provided of course that such policy does not preclude the individual consideration of applications. The policy may specify areas where applications are more or less likely to succeed and/or establish location criteria, a suggested form of wording for which follows:

(a) the premises must not be sited in or near a residential area;
(b) the premises must not be sited in a primary retail area;
(c) the premises must not be sited near shops used by or directed at families or children, or on frontages frequently passed by the same;
(d) the premises must not be sited near properties which are sensitive for religious purposes such as churches; and
(e) the premises must not be sited near premises or areas which are sensitive because they are frequented by children or families, including but not limited to educational establishments, leisure facilities such as parks, libraries or swimming pools, markets and covered markets.

Moral grounds

33.74 However, what cannot be used as a ground for refusal, but which still has the potential to raise its head as an unspoken consideration, is the moral case against such premises. This notion was firmly scotched by Collins J in *R v Newcastle upon Tyne City Council ex parte The Christian Institute*[54], where the Institute had taken objection on moral grounds to a sex exhibition. The Learned Judge's judgment on the point is worth citing in full:

'Mr Holland has suggested that the provisions of paragraph 12(3)(c) and (d), do enable the authority and the Court to take account of what he has called the "moral case against the activities" but, in my judgment, it does no such thing. What it entitles the local authority to do is to have regard to the character of the relevant locality and, no doubt, to take into account, if it be the case, that there is a strong body of feeling in the locality which objects to the existence of a sex shop in that locality. Equally, paragraph (d) makes plain that, in addition to the character of the relevant locality, the use to which any premises in the vicinity are put is also a relevant consideration. Thus, for example, it might be perfectly reasonable to refuse a licence for a sex shop which is in the vicinity of a school or some religious building. That is a recognition that sex shops may attract a particular clientele whose presence may not be considered desirable in some areas and that is something again which can be taken into account, but it has nothing to

[53] (1986) 85 LGR 249.
[54] [2001] LGR 165.

do with the morality of sex shops as such. It is the effect on the locality and on those living nearby which has to be taken into account and that is the distinction which is drawn. Thus, straightforward objections on the ground that sex shops should not be allowed to exist have no part to play in my or a local authority's consideration of the case. Whether I approve or disapprove is nothing to the point. Whether the local authority approves or disapproves is equally nothing to the point, except insofar as the provisions of paragraph 12 are applicable.'

Therefore, while the authority is not itself to make moral judgments, it may react to local sensibilities, which in truth may well be based precisely on moral condemnation of the activity in question.

33.75 The issue of morality was also visited in *R v Bridgnorth District Council ex parte Prime Time Promotions Limited*[55] in which a licence had been refused for a mail order facility under para 12(3)(d), on grounds that the location was inappropriate, having regard to closeness to a child care facility, closeness to areas where children congregated, and to residential dwellings and family shops and food outlets. There were no relevant objections, but the council refused, taking account of its local knowledge, which the court held was open to it to do. A councillor swore an affidavit to say that the objection was not based on moral grounds.

33.76 Nevertheless, the decision was quashed. Dyson J held that the council had overlooked the trading history of the premises, which had had no effect on the locality whatsoever, given that there were no retail sales at the premises and therefore no visits there by members of the public, and had also overlooked the absence of objections either from the child care facility or anyone else. It was held that the question the council should have asked itself was whether the minor extension of activities (which in turn required the whole premises to be licensed) would make any material difference to the locality. Dyson J said that there was no indication from the minutes of the meeting or the council's affidavit evidence that the committee gave consideration to the effect of the proposed extension of the uses for which the applicant was seeking the licence. It was held that no reasonable council, asking itself that question, could have refused the licence.

33.77 The case of *Interfact Ltd v Liverpool City Council* [2005] EWHC 995 (Admin) has clarified the law regarding mail order sales, in so far as where R18 videos are supplied from a licensed sex shop and sent to an address, an offence under section 12 of the Video Recordings Act 1984 of supplying R18 videos other than to a person in a licensed sex shop is made out. However, it is unlikely that the fact that the premises also engages in mail order sales would affect the discretion whether to grant a sex shop licence, and if its only

---

[55]   *R v Bridgnorth DC, ex p Prime Time Promotions Ltd* [1999] COD 265, [1999] EHLR Dig 455, QBD.

activity is to engage in such sales and it does so without a 'shop window', it is hard to see on what ground a licence would be refused.

Duration of the licence

33.78 A licence may be granted for a maximum period of twelve months, giving the authority the power to grant it for a shorter period, providing them with the opportunity to issue a licence subject to what is in effect a probation period to monitor the effect of the premises on the local area.

G CONDITIONS

33.79 Having determined to grant or renew the licence, the authority is able to impose conditions with which the licence holder must comply.

33.80 These can be either standard conditions, contained within regulations made by the authority by virtue of paragraph 13 of Schedule 3 and which are applicable to all sex establishments, or additional, specific conditions tailored to suit the particular application being considered.[56]

Paragraph 13(3) provides examples of typical standard conditions including conditions regulating:

- the hours of opening and closing of sex establishments;
- displays or advertisements on or in such establishments;
- the visibility of the interior of sex establishments to passers-by; and
- any change of a sex cinema to a sex shop or a sex shop to a sex cinema.

Unless expressly excluded or varied, all licences granted, renewed or transferred are taken subject to the authority's standard conditions.[57]

There is a wide discretion to attach conditions to licences. However, some limitations apply.[58]

The boundaries of reasonableness

33.81 It is submitted that any condition must have a purpose relevant to licensing, fairly and reasonably relate to the licensed premises, and be otherwise reasonable and proportionate. Certainly a condition should not be

[56] LGMPA, Sch 3 para 8.
[57] LGMPA, Sch 3 para 13(4).
[58] *Pyx Granite Company Limited v Minister of Housing and Local Government* [1958] 1 QB 554.

imposed for some ulterior purpose, however desirable it might appear in the public interest.[59]

Conditions that are invalid may not be severable

33.82   In most cases, a condition that is found to be invalid can simply be cut out, or excised, from the licence. But should the removal of the condition alter the character of the licence, the licence may simply fall, leaving the applicant with nothing.

33.83   *R v North Hertfordshire District Council ex parte Cobbold*[60] concerned the granting of a public entertainment licence with a condition requiring the licence holders to meet all of the reasonable expenses incurred by two local authorities in providing public services at an event in Knebworth Park, to include the expenses in relation to policing. The applicants were successful in arguing that the imposition of such a condition was outside of the purpose of the enabling legislation and should, therefore, be excised from the licence.

The authority argued that if the offending words were excised, the licence would be fundamentally different and thus the condition was not excisable.

33.84   Mann J adopted principles of planning law, holding that the condition could be excised only if it was discrete and severable without altering the character or substance of what remained. Applying that principle he stated:

> 'I think that a licence with this provision removed would then be a licence totally silent on policing. I regard policing as fundamental. To remove the requirement as to policing would alter the character of the document. It follows that this clause, failing as it does, brings down with it the whole of the licence'.[61]

33.85   The proper test as to whether a condition is excisable would appear to be whether removing it would affect the essential character of the licence.[62]

H   RENEWAL OF THE LICENCE

33.86   The procedure for applying for renewal of the licence is identical to that applying to an initial grant, as are the provisions for fees and the grounds for refusal. Where before the licence has expired an application is lodged for

---

[59]   *Pyx Granite Company Limited v Minister of Housing and Local Government*, p 572.
[60]   [1985] 3 All ER 486.
[61]   *R v North Hertfordshire District Council ex parte* Cobbold, p 492.
[62]   *R v Inner London Crown Court ex parte Sitki* (1993) 157 JP 523.

its renewal, the licence remains in force until that application (or any subsequent appeal) has been determined.[63]

Is renewal guaranteed?

33.87 An application for the renewal of a licence is treated in exactly the same way as an application for the grant of a licence, and the fact that the premises currently holds a licence, although a relevant factor, is not a determining factor in its renewal. The renewal can be refused even where there have been no changes in the character of the 'relevant locality' or in the use of other premises in the vicinity.

33.88 In *R v Birmingham City Council ex parte Sheptonhurst Limited*,[64] the Court of Appeal heard a number of linked appeals following refusals to renew licences where there had been no change in circumstances. It was submitted on behalf of the appellant owners that it was inherently wrong for the renewal process to be subject to 'the vagaries of local opinion' and that the holder of a licence had a legitimate expectation that it would be renewed where there was no change in the relevant circumstances and no matter of public concern had arisen. O'Connor LJ in his judgment had a rather different view:

> '... where Parliament, having expressly limited the grounds on which a licence may be refused, has drawn no distinction between grant and renewal of the licence and provided that a licence shall not last for more than a year, then it seems to me that to accede to the submission of counsel for the appellants would be to introduce a fetter on the discretion of the local authority in cases of renewal, which Parliament has not done.'[65]

Having said that he continued by expressly stating that the existence of a licence is a factor local authorities must take into consideration:

> 'However, although the discretion is unfettered, there is a difference between an application for grant and an application for renewal and that distinction, as the cases have pointed out, is that when considering an application for renewal the local authority has to give due weight to the fact that a licence was granted in the previous year and indeed for however many years before that. It is of particular importance that the licensing authority should give due weight to this fact in this field, for I do not doubt that there is opposition to sex shops on grounds outside the limits imposed by para 12 of Sch 3.'[66]

[63] LGMPA, Sch 3 para 11.
[64] [1990] 1 All ER 1026.
[65] *Sheptonhurst*, p 1035.
[66] *Sheptonhurst*, p 1035.

He concluded:

> 'I have come to the conclusion that the licensing authority were entitled
> to have a fresh look at the matter as the chairman of the sub-committee
> states in his affidavit, which I have set out earlier in this judgment. In a
> case where there has been no change of circumstances, if the licensing
> authority refuses to renew on the ground that it would be inappropriate
> having regard to the character of the relevant locality, it must give its
> reasons for refusal: see para 10(20) of Sch 3. If the reasons given are
> rational, that is to say properly relevant to the ground for refusal, then
> the court cannot interfere.'[67]

33.89 This principle reached its zenith (or nadir depending on your view
point) in the case of *R v London Borough of Wandsworth ex parte Darker
Enterprises Limited.*[68] In this case, Darker Enterprises Limited judicially
reviewed the decision of the London Borough of Wandsworth licensing
sub-committee, following the refusal to renew the sex establishment licence
for one of its premises.

33.90 The grounds for refusal submitted by the council related to a change
in the character of the relevant locality, and the challenge by the company
was based upon the fact that not only had it held the licence for a period of
some ten years, it had also been granted planning permission by the council
for the installation of a new shop front and refurbishment of the premises
and had received a grant towards the cost of that refurbishment. This
improvement proved, however, to be the premises' downfall as, the council
argued, by improving the premises the company had assisted in the general
improvement of the area which led to the council finding that the premises
was no longer appropriate for that locality.

33.91 The company argued that by permitting the improvements and
paying a grant towards them, the council's sub-committee had made the
premises an integral part of the improvements scheme and, therefore, it was
irrational and unjust to then state that the premises was inappropriate.

Turner J, finding in favour of the council, stated:

> '... the Act of 1982 expressly contemplates the possibility that the
> circumstances in which a licence had been granted or renewed might
> change; hence the provisions of paragraph 12 of the Third Schedule,
> which apply not just in respect of the grant but, more importantly, also
> on the renewal of a licence. Thus the proposition that an existing
> licence holder can expect that he will be granted a licence in perpetuity
> for any given set of premises is plainly wrong.'[69]

He went on:

---

[67]   *Sheptonhurst,* pp 1035–6.
[68]   (1999) 1 LGLR 601.
[69]   *Darker Enterprises,* para 46.

'... the respondents were fully entitled to endeavour to improve the area in the manner in which they did. Their efforts might, or might not, have been successful. On the occasion of the previous renewal, it would not have been open to them to have refused the application on the grounds now being considered, because the process of improvement in the area was, at that time, incomplete. The respondents could not have refused to grant permission to the applicants for alterations to their premises given that it was the respondents' objective to bring about a significant improvement to the area which such consents were intended to assist.'[70]

33.92 The notion that an authority might refuse to grant a renewal of a licence because of the licensee's improvement of the area is unique to sex establishment licensing, and might be thought to provide a disincentive to proprietors to invest in their shops' appearance.

I VARIATION, TRANSFER AND TRANSMISSION

Variation

33.93 The holder of a licence is able, at any time during its term (including upon a renewal application being made), to apply for a variation of the terms, conditions or restrictions to which it is subject. The authority not only have the power to approve or refuse the requested variation; they also have the power to 'make such variations as they think fit'.[71] Thus, from the applicant's point of view, it is safer to approach the authority informally to seek the officers' views on the sought variation and the likelihood of it raising problems before submitting a formal variation application which may result in additional conditions being imposed.

33.94 So far as fees are concerned, it is notable that the Schedule did not provide for a fee to be paid for the variation of a licence[72] outside of the London Boroughs. Within London Boroughs, the Schedule had been amended to include fees for variation applications.[73] The Policing and Crime Act 2009 has addressed this lacuna by amending the Schedule to include fees for variations throughout England and Wales.

---

[70]   *Darker Enterprises*, para 48.
[71]   LGMPA, Sch 3, para 18.
[72]   LGMPA, Sch 3, para 19.
[73]   Greater London Council (General Powers) Act 1986, s 12.

Transfer

33.95 Provision is made for the transfer of a sex establishment licence,[74] which follows the same procedure as for an application for a grant or renewal,[75] and is subject to a 'reasonable fee'.[76]

The grounds for refusal of a transfer relate solely to the suitability of the applicant. A transfer may not be refused on any of the grounds relating to the premises or their locality.[77] Provision is made for continuation of the licence pending the decision on the application.[78]

Transmission

33.96 Should a licence holder die during the period of the licence, it is deemed to pass to the licence holder's personal representatives, and will remain in force for a period of three months from the death.[79] This allows the personal representatives to arrange for the transfer of the licence or its cancellation.[80]

33.97 The three month period can be extended by the authority where it is necessary for the winding-up of the estate or where other circumstances exist which do not 'make it undesirable'[81] to so extend.

33.98 There is no such period of grace where the licence holder is a company entering administration, and it will be necessary for a transfer application to be made should the administrators wish to sell the premises on with the benefit of the licence following the company ceasing to exist.

J REVOCATION

33.99 Prosecution is not the only enforcement option available to the authority. A further option is the ability of the authority to revoke the sex establishment licence during its term rather than waiting for any problems or issues to be dealt with at the annual renewal application. The circumstances in which a licence can be revoked are:[82]

---

[74] LGMPA, Sch 3 para 9(2).
[75] LGMPA, Sch 3 para 10(1).
[76] LGMPA, Sch 3 para 19.
[77] LGMPA, Sch 3 para 12(2)(b).
[78] LGMPA, Sch 3 para 11(2).
[79] LGMPA, Sch 3 para 15.
[80] LGMPA, Sch 3 para 16.
[81] LGMPA, Sch 3 para 15.
[82] LGMPA, Sch 3 para 17.

- where any of the mandatory grounds for refusal exist;[83]
- where the licence holder is unsuitable to hold a licence by reason of a criminal conviction or for any other reason;[84] and
- where the business is being managed or carried on for the benefit of a person who would be refused a licence.[85]

33.100 The licence must not be revoked without affording the licence holder the opportunity of a hearing.[86] The authority must, within seven days of a request to do so, but interestingly not otherwise, provide the licence holder with a written statement detailing the reasons for the revocation. The licence holder has 21 days to appeal against the revocation (subject to an appeal against a revocation based upon the mandatory grounds being limited to the appellant proving that the ground does not apply to him) with the licence remaining in force until the time for bringing the appeal has expired or, where an appeal has been lodged, the determination or abandonment of the appeal.[87]

33.101 The holder of a licence that has been revoked is thereafter disqualified for a period of 12 months from holding such a licence 'in the area of the appropriate authority'.[88] Whilst this would not prevent that person from applying in another authority's area, the disqualification would, no doubt, be taken into consideration under the discretionary ground for refusal under paragraph 12(3)(a) as 'any other reason'.

K APPEALS

33.102 Where an application for grant, renewal or transfer is refused,[89] or a licence revoked,[90] the local authority must, if requested, give written reasons for the decision. This will enable the applicant to consider the merits of an appeal. It has been held that reasons for refusal must be 'proper, sufficient and intelligible': if not, then that alone is a ground of challenge.[91]

33.103 Should the application for the grant, renewal, transfer or variation be refused, or any term, condition or restriction placed on the licence be objected to by the applicant, or a licence be revoked, then the applicant or

---

[83] LGMPA, Sch 3 para 12(1). See para 33.44 above.
[84] LGMPA, Sch 3 para 12(3)(a). See para 33.62 above.
[85] LGMPA, Sch 3 para 12(3)(b). See para 33.62 above.
[86] LGMPA, Sch 3 para 17(1).
[87] LGMPA, Sch 3 para 27(10).
[88] LGMPA, Sch 3 para 17(3).
[89] LGMPA, Sch 3 para 12.
[90] LGMPA, Sch 3 para 17(2).
[91] *R v Westminster City Council ex parte Cameron* (unreported, 12 May 2000). See also *R v Birmingham City Council ex parte Quietlynn Ltd* (1985) LGR 461, 490: giving reasons involves more than giving the mere grounds for the decision. See further Chapter 20 (Challenging Licensing Decisions), Section D (The appeal hearing).

licence holder (as applicable) may, within 21 days from the date of notification of the decision, appeal to the magistrates' court.[92]

33.104 This right of appeal is subject however to the proviso that, where the grant, renewal or revocation is based upon the applicant falling within the mandatory grounds for refusal contained with paragraph 12(1)(a)–(e), there is no right of appeal, unless the applicant can show that the particular ground did not apply to him.[93]

33.105 More importantly, there is no right of appeal where the refusal of the grant or renewal was based upon a finding that the number of sex establishments in the relevant locality was already equal to or exceeded the appropriate number for that locality[94] or that the grant or renewal would have been inappropriate having regard to the character of the locality, the use to which premises in the vicinity were put, or to the layout, character or condition of the premises in respect of which the application was made.[95] It is on these grounds that the most refusals occur. In these circumstances, the only manner of challenging the decision of the authority is by way of judicial review in the High Court.

33.106 Importantly, the 2009 Act amends Schedule 3 by adding a new paragraph, 27(10A), which provides that where a refusal to renew is based upon the grounds stated in paragraph 12(3)(c) or (d), namely that the number of sex establishments in the locality is equal to or exceeds the number considered by the local authority to be appropriate, or that the renewal would be inappropriate having regard to the character of the locality or the use to which other premises in the vicinity are put, the licence is <u>not</u> deemed to remain in force pending any appeal.

Appeals to the magistrates' court

33.107 An appeal to the magistrates' court is by way of complaint made by either the applicant on the grant, renewal, transfer, or variation of the licence, or by the licence holder where the appeal relates to the revocation of the licence or objection to any term therein (in practice, they are likely to be the same person).

33.108 Where the appeal relates to the revocation of or failure to renew a licence,[96] or concerns the imposition of an unwanted condition, the licence is deemed to remain in force and, in relation to an unwanted condition, free of

---

92 LGMPA, Sch 3 para 27(1). Care is needed when a decision is given orally after a hearing; it is strongly arguable that in such a case time runs from that moment, rather than any subsequent written notification.
93 LGMPA, Sch 3 para 27(2).
94 LGMPA, Sch 3 para 12(3)(c).
95 LGMPA, Sch 3 para 12(3)(d).
96 An exception arises in the circumstances specified in LGMPA, Sch 12 para 27(10A).

such condition, until the time for bringing the appeal has expired or upon determination or abandonment of a lodged appeal.[97]

33.109 The appeal itself is by way of rehearing, and the magistrates are entitled to make such order as they think fit.[98] They hear the matter on the same basis as the licensing committee and are thus able to consider what would otherwise be hearsay evidence.[99]

33.110 There is a further appeal against the decision of the magistrates' court to the Crown Court, but the decision of the Crown Court is final.[100]

33.111 Should the magistrates' court find against the authority, the authority need not give effect to the magistrates' order until the time for bringing an appeal to the Crown Court has expired and, where such an appeal is brought, until the determination or abandonment of that appeal.

The High Court

33.112 Where there is no right of appeal to the magistrates' court (see above) the only avenue of appeal is by way of judicial review in the High Court.

33.113 The application in such cases is not limited to those who applied for the licence, but may also be made by other parties who can show that they have a sufficient interest in the proceedings to be heard.[101] This could include objectors to the application who have been unsuccessful in preventing a licence being granted, renewed or varied; in many cases, however the cost of such an application is likely to be prohibitive. The grounds upon which such an application may be brought are limited to errors of law and procedural impropriety.

33.114 In addition to these direct applications to the High Court from the decision of the authority, both the applicant and authority have a right to appeal to the High Court on a point of law by way of case stated from both the magistrates'[102] and Crown Courts[103]. See Chapter 20 (Challenging Licensing Decisions).

---

[97]   LGMPA, Sch 3 para 27(10)–(12).
[98]   LGMPA, Sch 3 para 27(7).
[99]   *Kavanagh v Chief Constable of Devon and Cornwall* (1974) QB 624 and *Westminster City Council v Zestfair* (1989) 88 LGR 288.
[100]   LGMPA, Sch 3 para 27(6).
[101]   Senior Courts Act 1981, s 31.
[102]   Magistrates' Courts Act 1980, s 111.
[103]   Senior Courts Act 1981, s 28; Crown Court Rules 1982, r 26.

L ENFORCEMENT

Powers of enforcement officers

33.115 Having granted a licence to the proprietor of a sex establishment, it is clearly essential for the authority to ensure that such premises are run properly and comply with the conditions imposed by the licence.

33.116 A police constable and/or an authorised officer of the authority is able to enter and inspect, at any reasonable time, a licensed sex establishment to determine whether the conditions on the licence are being complied with, to ensure that no disqualified person is employed at the establishment, to ensure there is no person under the age of 18 in the establishment and also to ensure that no person under that age is employed in the business.[104]

33.117 However, neither a constable nor an authorised officer of the authority is able to enter and inspect a sex establishment without a warrant where the purpose of the entry and inspection is based upon a suspicion that an offence under paragraphs 20, 21 or 23 has been, is being or is about to be committed.

33.118 What this means in practice is that where it is believed a premises is being run as a sex establishment without being licensed, neither a constable nor an authorised officer of the authority is able to enter that premises to determine whether it requires a licence without first obtaining a warrant from a Justice of the Peace.

33.119 However, it would appear that where entry without a warrant is made and evidence of breaches is obtained, such evidence would be admissible where the proprietor consented to the entry.[105]

33.120 Any person on the premises who refuses to allow a constable or an authorised officer of the authority to exercise any power of entry or inspection without reasonable excuse will be committing an offence and be liable on summary conviction to a fine not exceeding level 5 on the standard scale.[106]

33.121 An omission from the Schedule as originally enacted did have the capacity to make enforcement more difficult than it needed to be. That omission was the failure to include a power allowing a constable or an authorised officer to seize goods on the premises that gave rise to an offence. For example, a constable or an officer who obtained a warrant and entered

---

[104] LGMPA, Sch 3 para 25(1)–(3).
[105] *Tunbridge Wells Borough Council and Others v Quietlynn Limited and Others* (1985) Crim LR 594.
[106] LGMPA, Sch 3 para 25(6). Level 5 is currently £5,000: Criminal Justice Act 1982, s 37, as amended.

an unlicensed premises that was selling sex articles to a significant degree had no power to remove the goods to prevent the breach continuing. There may have been other powers available to seize goods,[107] but where such powers did not exist the articles could not be removed.

33.122   However, this deficiency has been addressed in the 2009 Act which inserts a new paragraph into Schedule 3 providing police officers and local authority officers with the power to seize and remove anything found on the premises which could later be forfeited before the court.[108]

33.123   This gap in the legislation had previously been filled so far as the London Boroughs were concerned by section 12 of The Greater London Council (General Powers) Act 1986, which amended paragraph 25 of Schedule 3 to the LGMPA 1982, by adding a power to seize and remove 'any apparatus or equipment or other thing whatsoever found on the premises' which it is believed related to the offence. Such equipment and goods can then be forfeited following a successful conviction arising from the initial breach.

33.124   Local legislation may also assist in the enforcement process. For example, the City of Westminster Act 1996 provides that where the council is satisfied that a premises within its area is being used as an unlicensed sex establishment, a closure notice may be served, leading to an application to a Justice of the Peace for a closure order and the subsequent closure of the premises or the discontinuance of that business from that premises.[109]

M   OFFENCES

33.125   Schedule 3 provides for the following main offences:

- Knowingly using or knowingly causing or permitting the use of any premises, vehicle, vessel or stall as a sex establishment without a licence.[110]
- Being the holder of a sex establishment licence, employing any person known to the licence holder to be disqualified from holding such a licence.[111]

---

[107]   For example under the Video Recordings Act 1984 where the videos being displayed are uncertificated or within a category of obscene materials that may be seized by the police.

[108]   LGMPA, Sch 3 para 25(7).

[109]   City of Westminster Act 1996, ss 3 and 4.

[110]   LGMPA, Sch 3 para 20(1)(a). The prosecution must prove knowledge both that the premises were being used as a sex establishment and also that they were being so used without a licence: *Westminster City Council v Croyalgrange Ltd* [1986] 2 All ER 353.

[111]   LGMPA, Sch 3 para 20(1)(b).

- Being the holder of a licence, without reasonable excuse, knowingly contravening or knowingly permitting the contravention of any term, condition or restriction on the licence.[112]
- Being the servant or agent (which would include employees) of the licence holder, without reasonable excuse, knowingly contravening or knowingly permitting the contravention of any term, condition or restriction.[113]
- Making a false statement which is known to be false in a material respect or which it is not believed to be true when making an application for the grant, renewal or transfer of a licence.[114]
- Being the holder of a licence knowingly permitting a person under the age of 18 years of age to enter the establishment without reasonable excuse or employing such a person knowing that person to be under the age of 18 years of age[115].

The penalty for such offences is a maximum fine on summary conviction of £20,000.

33.126 There is a further offence under paragraph 14 which may be committed by the licence holder of failing to exhibit in a suitable place (as specified in the licence) a copy of that licence and the regulations to which it is subject, without reasonable excuse. The penalty for this offence on summary conviction is a fine not exceeding level 3 on the standard scale.[116] Finally, there are penalties for obstruction of constables and authorised officers in execution of their enforcement duties.[117]

Offences by corporate bodies

33.127 As sex establishment licences can be held by companies, it is necessary to ensure that those making the decisions within the company cannot hide behind the 'corporate veil' and avoid prosecution for breaches committed by them through the company. To ensure this does not occur, the Schedule has adopted the approach of health and safety and other public protection legislation by allowing enforcement against individuals within a corporate body that has committed an offence, where it can be proved that the offence was committed with their consent, connivance or through their neglect.[118]

---

[112]   LGMPA, Sch 3 para 20(1)(c).
[113]   LGMPA, Sch 3 para 20(1)(d).
[114]   LGMPA, Sch 3 para 21.
[115]   LGMPA, Sch 3 para 23.
[116]   Currently £1,000: Criminal Justice Act 1982, s 37, as amended.
[117]   See para 33.117 above.
[118]   LGMPA, Sch 3 para 26(1).

33.128 Indeed, the Schedule goes so far as to include 'members' (that is shareholders) of the corporate body as potential defendants, where such members are involved in the corporate body's management.[119]

N INTEGRATING STRATEGIES

33.129 Although sex establishments stir passions, it is undeniable that they are part of the leisure economy and can add to the attraction and tourist potential of towns and cities. Most larger towns and cities acknowledge this and set out to use their powers under the LGMPA to limit numbers of premises, direct them to certain areas of the city and promote standards.

33.130 Apart from objectors whose fundamental objection is to the activity, most objections relate to the impact on the character of the town centre. These are controllable to a greater or lesser extent by conditions which limit exterior signage, or even ban it during day-time hours, and also ban leafleting, billboard advertising and limousine advertising. Once this impact is acceptably contained, then authorities can ensure that strategies for sex establishments cohere with and support strategies for the night time economy, expressed in planning and licensing policy.

33.131 Finally, sexual entertainment venues all have bars and therefore need alcohol licences. Authorities have the power to create policies which might reflect their presence in cumulative impact areas on the one hand, or which might recognise that intoxication is a far lesser problem in lap dancing clubs than alcohol-led premises, due to the diversion of funds from sins of the grape to sins of the flesh. Whether this is a good thing is left for moralists to ponder.

O CONCLUSION

33.132 The rise of the sexual entertainment venue on the high street has led to a satisfactory outcome, which is that the premises are governed under the LGMPA, which offers planning-type powers to control location, exterior impact and operation. Coupled with the fact that these premises also need alcohol licences, this means that the full arsenal of local authority powers is available to control them. There is undoubtedly a demand, albeit limited and male-dominated, for these premises, and authorities have the power to permit them to take their place as part of a diverse mix of entertainment premises in the town centre, safe in the knowledge that they will have to operate where, when and to what standards the authority thinks apt.

33.133 Sex shops and sex cinemas are not significant numerically in most parts of the United Kingdom, and with the rise of internet sales and

---

[119] LGMPA, Sch 3 para 26(2).

streaming are unlikely to grow in future. However, if the licensing authority considers that they present a seedy aspect or that the quality of the locality has outgrown the quality of the premises, it has all the power it needs to shut the premises down.

Tables and chairs

I followed his gaze and saw that we had paused just before reaching a café where, under an awning, several tables and chairs were disposed upon the pavement. The windows were open behind; half a dozen plants in tubs were ranged beside the door; the pavement was sprinkled with clean bran. It was a dear little quiet old-world café ...

Four Meetings
Henry James

A INTRODUCTION

34.01 Tony Blair was not the first to dream of the café society. In 1956 the Labour politician Anthony Crosland published *The Future of Socialism*. In it, he wrote:

'We need not only higher exports and old-age pensions, but more open-air cafes, brighter and gayer streets at night, later closing hours for public houses, more local repertory theatres, better and more hospitable hoteliers and restaurateurs, brighter and cleaner eating houses, more riverside cafes, more pleasure gardens on the Battersea model, more murals and pictures in public places, better designs for furniture and pottery and women's clothes, statues in the centre of new housing estates, better-designed new street lamps and telephone kiosks and so on ad infinitum.'

34.02 Perhaps nothing conjures up the image of the café society as much as the jumble of tables and chairs outside a café on a town square. Such images, and the characters who populate them, are the stuff of cinema, art and literature. If, in the United Kingdom, the Labour Government of 1997–2010 failed to bring about a café society, this was perhaps because it placed an over-reliance on a single bullet – extended licensing hours – and not on the patient building of partnerships in planning, licensing, regeneration and even street cleaning, which coalesce to make this happen.

34.03 Nonetheless, while politics failed, more inexorable, gradual forces are succeeding. While alcohol consumption outside the home is falling, consumption of coffee outside the home goes from strength to strength. The coffee shop market has grown ten-fold since 1997, and by 2012 there were over 15,700 coffee shops in the UK.[1] This is at the same time as an ongoing net fall in the number of public houses of 18 per week.[2] This phenomenon is due to the quality of marketing of coffee, social trends relating to alcohol, more attractive public spaces encouraging investment, the rise of the patio heater to accompany the gradually warming climes in the UK, and the need of venues to maximise their incomes.

34.04 The effect, of course, is salutary. As more of the consumer's money is diverted into coffee, less is diverted into alcohol, with benefits in relation to health and crime and disorder. The presence of peaceful exterior uses on the street itself attracts in a more diverse range of visitors, and promotes natural guardianship, so reducing crime and increasing perceptions of safety still further.

34.05 Therefore, the question of tables and chairs licences, while ostensibly a minor part of this book, represents an important trend: the rise of the pavement café. Of course, not only cafes take advantage of the table and chairs licence: they are much sought after by public houses too. But the ability of the licensing authority to control hours of operation is apt to ensure that no harm comes of the exercise.

B THE HIGHWAYS ACT 1980

34.06 Section 115E of the Highways Act 1980 allows a council to grant a person permission to place objects or structures in the highway for a purpose which will result in the provision of income.[3]

34.07 Some exterior areas are not in fact highway land, but are part of the premises concerned. They will not need tables and chairs licences. They may, however, still need planning consent.

34.08 If, however, highway land is involved, then a licence will be needed. In practice, many authorities turn a blind eye to certain objects, such as posts and ropes to contain smokers, while others take a much stricter approach.

---

[1] Allegra Strategies, Project Café 2012 report.
[2] CGA Strategies.
[3] In the City of Westminster, the City of Westminster Act 1999 results in the need for a street trading licence: see 'Guidelines for the Placing of Tables and Chairs on the Highway' (WCC, 2005).

34.09 If the premises in front of which the objects are to be placed belong to someone else, then they must consent – their lack of consent operates as a veto,[4] subject to a right of arbitration accorded by section 115J of the Highways Act.

34.10 Before the council grants any licence, it must publish a notice of the application at or near the application site, and serve a copy on the owner and occupier of any premises appearing to be likely to be materially affected.[5] The notice must give details of the proposal and specify a period of at least 28 days during which representations may be made. The council must obviously take into consideration any representations received during that period.[6] The council must also consult any authority other than itself which is the highway authority, as well as the planning authority.[7]

34.11 The Act does not require there to be a hearing. In practice, some councils provide for hearings before their licensing committees where there has been an objection. Where this is so, specific delegation has to be made for the purpose.

34.12 In deciding whether to grant a licence, the authority will remind itself that this is a highway power. Therefore, the following questions will usually be asked:

- Is there room for the use proposed?
- Is the immediate environment suited for the use proposed? Eg is traffic pollution prohibitive in this place?
- What other footway uses and users, including disabled users, need to be considered?
- Will the use impede emergency services?
- How will the use affect neighbouring properties?
- Is the layout such as to enhance or downgrade the street scene?
- Is the layout acceptable for disabled, including wheelchair, users?

34.13 The council is empowered to grant a table and chairs licence upon such conditions as they see fit.[8] Typically, these will include conditions relating to the extent of the area to be licensed, type of equipment, hours, use of external amplification systems, numbers of users, supervision and cleaning up. Conditions may also be imposed requiring the payment to the council of such reasonable charges as they may determine.[9] Despite the apparent width of that discretion, the charging regime may not be used to make a profit: see

---

4   Highways Act 1980, s 115E(2).
5   Highways Act 1980, s 115G.
6   Highways Act 1980, s 115G.
7   Highways Act 1980, s 115H.
8   Highways Act 1980, s 115F(1).
9   Highways Act 1980, s 115F(1).

Chapter 61 (The Fees Regime). Licences are normally granted for a limited period, typically 12 months.

34.14   No appeal is permitted against a refusal of a licence. Any challenge would have to be brought by way of judicial review. See further Chapter 20 (Challenging Licensing Decisions).

34.15   If the holder of a tables and chairs licence breaches any terms of the licence, the authority may serve a notice upon him requiring him to take such steps as are required to remedy the breach within the period specified in the notice. In default, the authority may take the steps itself and charge the licensee the expenses of doing so, with interest.[10]

C OTHER NECESSARY CONSENTS

34.16   Planning permission will normally be required for tables and chairs on the highway, because it involves a change of use of the highway into a pavement café and/or because it may involve change of use of the premises from an A1 to an A3 planning use.[11] With very marginal encroachments, planning authorities may waive the need for permission. If tables and chairs are placed on a private forecourt, this will not, however, normally need planning permission. Planning permission may be granted subject to conditions such as hours of use, although the need for conditions may be obviated by any conditions on a tables and chairs licence.

34.17   Finally, if licensable activities are to be conducted in the licensed area, then the red line on the premises licence plan may need to be extended through a variation application, in order to legitimise the activity.

D CONCLUSION

34.18   The extension of leisure activities in the street ought to be seen as a good thing, even encouraged in licensing policy. Activities here are easier for regulatory authorities to monitor and control. They are frequently not alcohol-led and so lessen problems of alcohol consumption in town centres. They add colour and vibrancy to the town centre. They attract a more diverse age and gender mix than some other premises. And they add to the tourist draw of the town. They are, in short, a civilising influence.

34.19   On the other hand, they may increase the potential for nuisance, impede movement along the footway, are harder for premises operators to supervise, and may even cause public safety issues. However, all of these downsides can be mediated away by proper conditions as to layout, supervision and hours.

---

[10]   Highways Act 1980, s 115K.
[11]   See further Chapter 31 (Planning and Other Strategies).

34.20 In the pursuit of the Holy Grail of the Café Society, therefore, an enlightened and positive policy towards tables and chairs licences, with correlative encouragement in licensing, planning and regeneration policies, is to be applauded where it occurs.

35

Door supervision

Begbie	For ****'s sake.
Man	Sorry, mate, I'll get you another.
Begbie	All down my ****ing front, you ****ing idiot.
Man	Look, I'm sorry, I didn't mean it.
Begbie	Sorry's no going to dry me off, you ****.
Renton	Cool down, Franco. The guy's sorry.
Begbie	Not sorry enough for being a fat ****.
Man	**** you. If you can't hold a pint, you shouldn't be in the pub mate. Now **** off.

Trainspotting (the movie.)

A INTRODUCTION

35.01 This chapter examines the changes made to the private security industry and their effect on door supervision. In short, the Private Security and Industry Act 2001 (PSIA) created a new regulatory body, the Security Industry Authority (SIA), which is responsible for issuing licences to all those wishing to work as door supervisors. At the end of 2012, no fewer than 360,000 such licences were in existence.

35.02 The institution of the SIA marries with three themes running through this book. The first is the ongoing professionalisation of the leisure industry, as exemplified by the Licensing Act 2003, which requires alcohol to be served under the auspices of a trained personal licensee aware of the wider social responsibilities of his role, and the introduction of a designated premises supervisor in alcohol-licensed premises to ensure, amongst other things, compliance with licence conditions and licensing and general criminal law. The second is the promotion and development of a consistent set of standards throughout the industry, promoted through a variety of channels including government guidance and industry codes. The third is a pro-active, risk prevention approach to potential impacts of licensed premises, rather than a reactive approach once such impacts have occurred.

35.03 Variously described in the past as a 'thug in a dicky bow', or a 'gorilla in a suit',[1] excoriatingly immortalised in popular culture,[2] the door supervisor should now be seen as an integral part of the system of holistic management of the night time economy.[3] His/her role extends far beyond that of gatekeeper and ejector of the unruly element, to more general protection of customers and staff alike, and keeping the peace in the immediate environment of the premises, in partnership with other staff, management of the venue and the police. The modern door supervisor should be both trained and licensed to handle the extended role, and supported in his professional development by the SIA.

35.04 In this chapter we consider the history of the door supervision industry, the need for and structure of the PSIA, and finally the nature of the job itself and the part it plays in the overall advancement of the licensing objectives.

B HISTORY OF DOOR SUPERVISION REGULATION

35.05 Door supervision emerged as a wholly unregulated industry, whose subsequent regulation has proceeded in three stages, through voluntary local schemes, local regulation and finally a national registration scheme, the Private Security Industry Act 2001.

Voluntary schemes

35.06 In the late 1980s and the early 1990s various forward-thinking local authorities and police areas initiated door supervisor registration schemes which enabled them to vet, train and monitor the activities of their local pub and nightclub door supervisors. The reasons for the initiation of such programmes were highlighted in a survey conducted by the Home Office in 1991, when some of the earliest schemes in England and Wales were examined to assess how and why they had been started, who ran them, how they worked and whether they were viewed as a success or not. The most common reasons for starting the schemes included: dissatisfaction, usually based on customer complaints, with the attitude and behaviour of some door

---

[1] Abigail Sleat, 'Safety on the Door: An Evaluation of local authority administered registration schemes for door supervisors' (University of West of England, 1998). The industry's self-image was somewhat different; in one survey, only 3% of doormen described themselves as bouncers, other self-descriptions including 'ejection technician' and 'behavioural therapists': Walker, 'The Safer Doors Project' (Home Office, 1999).

[2] Eg John Godber's play 'Bouncers'; Hale and Pace's satirical tuxedo clad heavies, the Two Rons; and Emerson Lake and Palmer's lyrics: 'Benny was the bouncer at the Palais de Danse. He'd slash your granny's face up given half a chance. He'd sell you back the pieces, all for less than half a quid.'

[3] This passage was cited with approval by Kenneth Parker QC in *R* (*Nicholds*) *v Security Industry Authority* [2007] 1 WLR 2067.

supervisors, including assaults and drug dealing; a desire to bring the system into some sort of control; a wish to enhance the quality of door staff through vetting and training, to make them more accountable, and to promote better relations between door staff and police; to improve customer safety and reassure the public; to reduce the problems of agency cartels, intimidation of licensees and inter-agency violence; and to respond to the difficulty that door supervisors refused registration in one area would simply move into registration-free zones.

35.07 When publishing the results of the survey, the Home Office said at the time that 'around 60% of police areas or more had experienced problems of sufficient magnitude with door supervisors to have prompted them to have set up local regulatory schemes or to plan to set up such schemes. The serious problems included incidents of violence, intimidation and, in about 20% of cases, drug dealing'.

35.08 Whilst recognising the obvious success of such schemes, the Home Office concluded that they were not at the time persuaded that it would be appropriate to require the introduction of door supervisor registration schemes nation-wide. This, it said, was because problems with door supervisors were not experienced in every part of the country, and different areas had their own distinct difficulties. It suggested that it might, therefore, be more effective and less bureaucratic to allow each area to select the method of regulation, if any, which suited its particular needs.

35.09 In areas where door supervisor registration schemes were in operation, persons wishing to work within the security function at licensed premises were required to apply to either the local authority or the local police for a 'licence' to do so. They were required to fill out an application form detailing certain information so that a decision could be made as to their suitability for the position, at the same time giving permission for a check to be made with regards to any previous convictions that may have been held against them. A decision was then made as to whether they were suitable for the job, and if so they were normally given provisional status so that they could start work as a door supervisor in that area. Along with the completed application forms, applicants were usually required to submit passport-sized photographs of themselves, and the appropriate registration fee.[4]

35.10 On most schemes the applicants remained on provisional status until they had attended and passed the local training course, after which they received full registration status. Once fully registered, door supervisors were allowed to work at any licensed premises within that area, and were normally required to wear their registration badges conspicuously whenever they were

---

[4]   This paragraph, and the two which follow, were cited with approval by Kenneth Parker QC in *R (Nicholds) v Security Industry Authority* [2007] 1 WLR 2067.

working in that capacity. They were also usually required to abide by a code of conduct. Registration could be revoked upon conviction of a criminal offence deemed to justify such a sanction. Most schemes incorporated some form of appeals procedure for applicants who felt that registration had been unfairly refused or revoked.

35.11   Some local authorities attached conditions to public entertainment licenses to enforce the registration schemes, and some licensing justices even started attaching similar conditions to on-licences when they came up for renewal. Other areas initiated voluntary schemes that required none of the above, relying on the goodwill and common sense of licensees and managers to co-operate with the scheme.

35.12   The success of these early schemes was undoubted, particularly in achieving a significant reduction in incidents involving door staff reported to police. For example, Westminster, Luton, Plymouth and Ealing reported reductions in relevant offences of 60%, 75%, 50% and 35% respectively, while Newcastle upon Tyne reported a 75% reduction in violent and drug-related offences, and Hereford a 70% reduction in drink-related arrests.[5] The success of these schemes naturally caused the propagation of others.

35.13   But why were local door supervisor registration schemes so effective? Research showed that there were four main reasons, which are still instructive for the modern scheme of door supervisor registration:

- The vetting system weeded out many of the habitual criminals;
- The training taught the supervisors how to carry out their work within the constraints of the law;
- The visible registration badges meant that supervisors who did misbehave could be more easily identified than in the past;
- Supervisors did not want to lose their registration and authority to work the doors, and so adjusted their behaviour accordingly.

35.14   However, it eventually came to be recognised that a more structured and consistent system was needed. In December 1995 the Home Office issued circular number 60/1995 entitled 'Registration Schemes for Door Supervisors' to all local authorities and police forces to offer best practice guidance to those wishing to set up their own door supervisor registration schemes. While the circular recognised that door supervisor registration schemes were normally set up as a local response to specific local problems, it drew together common features, or aspects which appeared to work most effectively. The circular covered the setting up of registration committees, the processing of applicants, appeals procedures, types and costs of registration, vetting procedures, training, badges, and the transferability of registration. It also gave example forms for use in the registration process.

---

[5]   Walker, 'The Safer Doors Project' (Home Office, 1999).

35.15 This circular, although welcomed at the time as a guide to best practice on the subject, soon became out of date. Several problems emerged as the result of the vague and non-specific way in which it was written, particularly with respect to the vetting and training procedures. Although many local authorities and police forces took the Home Office circular advice on board, the vagueness of the guidance was reflected in myriad interpretations locally. This meant that systems for vetting, training and registration still varied widely between different local authorities, and sometimes even between different police divisions within the same force area.

35.16 This in turn caused a number of problems, the most frustrating for the door supervisors being that they were often unable to work in areas other than the one in which they were registered, requiring them to re-register and sometimes even re-train in several different areas to be able to do the same job. This was obviously far from ideal, and could be very expensive for those concerned, the practice as to registration fees varying widely between authorities. There were further variations in the enforceability of the schemes, some being regulated through licence conditions and some being purely voluntary, producing unevenness in standards.

35.17 However, the increasing need for regulation reduced the ad hoc nature of the business of recruitment and training, so that by 1999, 79% of door supervisors had been so working for over a year, and 62% were employed by a private security company,[6] with training by a variety of providers, including the police, local authority and door supervision companies, being thought useful by 87% of trainees. Notwithstanding the problems of the local schemes, there was strong grassroots support for the principle: a full 71% of supervisors considered registration schemes a good idea, with a further 23% believing them to be a necessary inconvenience. The patchwork nature of the local schemes, though, led a full 90% of door supervisors to adjudge a national registration scheme important.

35.18 The obituary to local, non-statutory schemes of registration was in fact posted by the Court of Appeal in 2001 in *R v Liverpool City Council ex parte Barry*.[7] In that case the court held that it was lawful for a public entertainment licensing authority to impose a condition requiring licensees and their appointed managers to ensure that no person was employed, engaged or present as an attendant/security person in or about the premises unless they had been registered for such purpose by the local authority prior to the commencement of their duties. But the sting in the tail was that it was unlawful for the authority to charge a fee for registration. The court stated that it would be possible to recover the costs of the scheme through the licensing scheme generally, but this of course works unfairly because the

---

6   Walker, 'The Safer Doors Project (Home Office, 1999).
7   2001 LLR 310.

costs of those with door supervisors are borne partly from the pockets of those with none.

London Local Authorities Act 1995

35.19   This Act was the legislative forerunner to the national legislation of 2001. It applied to on-licensed premises, and prevented employment of door supervisors[8] who were not registered with participating councils.[9] The council was entitled to attach conditions, including those relating to: the wearing of identification; an obligation to notify the council of any arrest or prosecution of the door supervisor for violence or dishonesty; and training.[10] Where the door supervisor was already registered with one council, restrictions were placed on fees chargeable by a second.

The push for national legislation

35.20   Probably the first call for the regulation of the private security industry generally was by MP Norman Fowler in 1972 who introduced the first ten minute rule Bill on the subject, though this was not successful. In 1977, the cudgels were taken up by Labour MP for Walsall South, Bruce George, who wished to see regulation of an industry which was 'totally unregulated, unaccountable, part-criminal, low wage, low esteem, and grossly inefficient.' He introduced five Private Members' Bills on the subject, all unsuccessful.[11]

35.21   However, the call was taken up at institutional level, by the Association of Chief Police Officers (ACPO), the Police Federation, the British insurance industry and the British Security Industry Association (BSIA). The process was accelerated by the intervention of industry groups.

35.22   The now defunct British Entertainment and Discotheque Association (BEDA), the trade association for the late night entertainment industry, had long been the lead voice for the nightclub industry in discussions on door supervisors, and was involved with the drafting of Home Office circular 60/1995 and the new British Standard for those who used or supply door supervisors.[12] In one of its reports to the Home Office, BEDA explained:

> '... voluntary (registration) schemes will never adequately address the fundamental problems surrounding drugs and nightclubs. The guidance notes circulated by the Home Office (60/1995) have not been

---

[8]   Defined as persons employed 'at or near the entrance to licensed premises to ascertain or satisfy himself as to the suitability of customers to be allowed entry on those premises or to maintain order on those premises': s. 29.

[9]   Section 31.

[10]   Section 32.

[11]   A similar fate befell Dr Phyllis Starkey's ten minute rule Bill in 1998.

[12]   'Door Supervisors/Stewards – Code of Practice' (BS 7960: 1999).

implemented by dozens of councils around the country. Indeed many councils appear unaware that they exist. Even where councils have taken up the scheme there is no guarantee that all clubs will comply. Furthermore, action needs to be taken on a national basis in order to prevent those renegade supervisors who find themselves precluded in one area simply relocating. Due to the transient nature of many of those people who work in this area, and the fact that many have historically been involved in illegal activities, problem supervisors regularly migrate around the country. A national scheme would stop the export of crime and violence from areas currently running registration schemes to the rest of the country'.

35.23 BEDA was joined in its crusade by the (now similarly defunct) National Association of Registered Door Supervisors and Security Personnel, which pointed to the lack of training, regulation, registration, supervision or accountability. The drive for a national scheme was given assistance and publicity by a courageous private campaigner, June Steel, whose son Paul had sustained serious brain damage at the hands of an unregistered door supervisor with a string of previous convictions. When the Local Government Association itself joined the fray, the Home Office was persuaded, publishing a White Paper in 1999[13] followed in due course by the Act itself.

In the foreword to the White Paper, the then Home Secretary Jack Straw MP wrote:

'The private security industry is a thriving, diverse industry covering a range of services from manned guarding to alarm systems and from cash-in-transit to wheel clamping. The industry has grown rapidly over recent years as people have taken greater steps to protect themselves and their property ... Despite the importance of the activities which the private industry carries out there is no regulation to control those who work in the industry and no standards to which companies have to adhere. We have discovered examples of firms owned by and run by people with serious criminal records. Research has shown that, in some areas, door supervisors and criminal gangs which control them are responsible for drug dealing in clubs. Reputable companies enforce effective standards and self-regulation but less scrupulous companies are able to undermine their best efforts. Voluntary regulation cannot touch this situation and it leaves the police powerless to protect the public. If the private security industry is to take a greater role in our society then the public have a right to be protected from the rogues who exploit the current unenforceable system and to expect certain standards from the companies they choose to provide the services with which they come into contact ...'

---

[13] The 'Government's Proposals for Regulation of the Private Security Industry in England and Wales' (Cm 4254, 1999).

35.24   The White Paper had the following to say on the subject of door supervisors:

> '5.8. There are widespread concerns about criminality among door staff. Assaults are common and as The Police Research Group Paper 86 "Clubs, Drugs and Doormen" showed, door staff can be involved either directly or indirectly in drug dealing in clubs. At present door supervisors are dealt with at a local level through registration schemes. In January 1996, a Home Office Circular (HO 60/95) was issued to all local authorities and police forces offering best practice guidance on setting up such schemes for door staff working at night-clubs and other establishments with a license for public music and dancing. Applicants for registration usually have to be vetted and successfully complete a training course, which is likely to include core elements of legal issues relevant to licensing and powers, social skills, first aid, drugs recognition and fire safety. The circular was drawn up in consultation with representatives of The Association of Chief Police Officers, the local authority associations and the entertainment industry. There are over 100 schemes in operation around the country covering approximately 20,000 door supervisors.

> 5.9. Registration schemes are not mandatory and not all local authorities operate them. The Government considers that all door supervisors should be licensed to prevent infiltration or intimidation by criminal gangs and to weed out those whose criminal background suggests that they are not suitable for this work.'

C THE PRIVATE SECURITY INDUSTRY ACT 2001

35.25   The PSIA represented, after the long history described above, the first attempt at national regulation of an industry employing up to 500,000 operatives, of whom approximately 95,000 worked as door supervisors.[14] The scheme was introduced on a phased regional basis, with the final region, London, coming under control during 2005.

The Security Industry Authority

35.26   The Act created the Security Industry Authority (SIA) as a uniform regulatory body for, amongst others, door supervisors. As a regulatory body it is obliged to keep the security industry as a whole under review, monitor its activities and effectiveness, carry out inspections, set or approve standards of conduct, training and supervision and make recommendations for maintenance or improvements of standards.[15] In carrying out its functions the

---

[14]   HC Debs 16 June 2004, col 885.
[15]   PSIA, s 1.

Authority is bound to comply with any directions given to it in writing by the Secretary of State, who must consult the Authority before making directions.[16]

35.27 The government's expectations of its creation were set out by the Minister for Crime Reduction, Policing and Community Safety, Hazel Blears:

'The aims of the SIA are: to increase public trust and confidence in the industry; to increase professionalism and standards; to encourage businesses to improve their standards by creating a framework for developing and promoting best practice across the industry; to create a security industry centre of knowledge and expertise, so that the best people in the industry can lead the development of the rest; and to try to strengthen the extended police family, which we hope to develop.'[17]

The licensing requirement

35.28 Section 3 makes it 'an offence for a person to engage in any licensable conduct except under and in accordance with a licence'. Door supervision is explicitly included in the definition of licensable conduct by virtue of Schedule 2 paragraphs 7(1) and 8(1) which brings into regulation as additional controls[18] 'activities of a security operative' which are carried out (a) in relation to licensed premises, and (b) at or in relation to times when those premises are open to the public.

35.29 Activities of a security operative are defined in paragraph 2 of Schedule 2 as:

'(a) guarding premises against unauthorised access or occupation, against outbreaks of disorder or against damage;

(b) guarding property against destruction or damage, against being stolen or against being otherwise dishonestly taken or obtained;

(c) guarding one or more individuals against assault or against injuries that might be suffered in consequence of the unlawful conduct of others.'

35.30 The obligation extends to premises in respect of which premises licences and temporary event notices have effect to authorise consumption of alcohol on the premises or regulated entertainment. Exemptions are granted for: theatres and cinemas; premises being under the aegis of a club premises certificate; premises used for plays and films under a temporary event notice;

---

[16] PSIA, s 2.
[17] HC Debs 16 June 2004, col 885.
[18] See s 3(5) and Sch 2 part 2.

and premises licensed and used as casinos or bingo clubs under the Gambling Act 2005.[19]

35.31   It is important to note that the licensing requirement does not only apply to the door supervisors themselves. By virtue of section 3(2), the requirement is extended to ten categories of individuals, including employers, managers, supervisors, and directors of security companies. Parliament, having been galvanised into action by a unanimous voice, has determined therefore to regulate to the top of the managerial tree.

35.32   The regulatory framework set up by PSIA is directly linked with the provisions in the Licensing Act 2003. By virtue of section 21 of the Licensing Act 2003, if a premises licence is granted with a condition that there must be security staff present, then the staff must be licensed by the SIA.[20]

Obtaining a licence

35.33   Section 7 of PSIA obliges the SIA to publish its criteria for the grant of a licence, which must include criteria to ensure that applicants are 'fit and proper persons to engage in [licensable] conduct' and that they have the 'training and skills necessary to engage in the conduct for which they are licensed.'[21]

35.34   Reflecting that, the SIA has adopted two principal criteria, namely: (i) a criminality check, and (ii) completion of training required by the SIA.

Criminality check

35.35   The SIA states that it will not automatically refuse a licence for those with a criminal record. It will decide according to whether the offences are included in its list of offences, the classification of the seriousness of offences on that list, the actual sentence for the offence and how recent the offences were. However, there will be automatic refusal if less than 12 months has elapsed from the formal end of a custodial sentence (even if the offender was released earlier), and five years in more serious cases. In *R (Nicholds) v Security Industry Authority*[22] it was argued that this blanket rule amounted to an unlawful fetter on the discretion of the SIA. The challenge failed, the court holding that the elimination of criminality among those working as door supervisors was one of the fundamental aims of the Private Security

---

[19]   PSIA, Sch 2 para 8, as amended by the Licensing Act 2003, Sch 6 para 118.
[20]   With exemptions mirroring those in PSIA Sch 2 para 8.
[21]   Section 7(3). The criteria must be approved by the Secretary of State (s 7(5)) and may be revised from time to time (s 7(2)). The current criteria are set out in the SIA publication 'Get Licensed' (February 2012): http://www.sia.homeoffice.gov.uk/Documents/licensing/sia_get_licensed.pdf.
[22]   [2007] 1 WLR 2067.

Industry Act 2001, and, therefore, at the very minimum the commission of certain offences of extreme violence for which a person had received a very substantial term of imprisonment should automatically debar that person for a significant period from being a door supervisor; and that a rule that conviction for certain criminal offences should automatically debar an applicant from obtaining a licence as a door supervisor for a significant period was wholly within the purpose and scope of section 7 of the Act.

35.36 The same conclusion was reached in *Security Industry Authority v Stewart*,[23] where the court emphasised section 8(3) of the Private Security Industry Act 2001 which states: 'In determining whether or not to grant a licence the Authority shall apply the criteria for the time being applicable under section 7.' That, said the court, left the SIA with no discretion in cases where the criteria provided for an automatic refusal. Equally, the magistrates or the Crown Court on appeal from a refusal of a licence are equally bound to apply the criteria;[24] in this they have no more latitude than the SIA does itself.

Approved training

35.37 The second criterion for obtaining a licence is to obtain a qualification from one of the awarding bodies endorsed by the SIA. At present, there are five awarding bodies: the British Institute of Innkeeping, EDI, National Open College Network, Edexcel and City & Guilds. The qualification, which is a Level 2 Award in Door Supervision, must be obtained prior to applying for a licence.

35.38 It is worth setting out the course syllabus, to ensure proper appreciation of the range of responsibilities placed on the shoulders of the modern door supervisor:

Core Learning for Common Security Industry Knowledge

- Session 1: Awareness of the Law in the Private Security Industry
- Session 2: Health and Safety for the Private Security Operative
- Session 3: Fire Safety Awareness
- Session 4: Emergency Procedures
- Session 5: The Private Security Industry
- Session 6: Communication Skills and Customer Care

Door Supervisor Specialist Module

- Session 1: Behavioural Standards
- Session 2: Civil and Criminal Law
- Session 3: Fire Safety Awareness

---

23 [2009] 1 WLR 466.
24 PSIA, s 11(5).

- Session 4: Arrest
- Session 5: Drugs Awareness
- Session 6: Recording Incidents and Crime Preservation
- Session 7: Licensing Law
- Session 8: Emergency Procedures

Conflict Management Module

- Session 1: Avoiding Conflict and Reducing Personal Risk
- Session 2: Defusing Conflict
- Session 3: Resolving and Learning from Conflict
- Session 4: Emergency Procedures
- Session 4b: Application of Communication Skills and Conflict Management for Door Supervisors

Physical Interventions Skills Module

- Session 1: Introduction to Physical Skills
- Session 2: Disengagement Techniques (non-pain related)
- Session 3: Escorting Techniques (non-pain related)

35.39 It will therefore be seen that the expectations upon door supervisors under the new regime are a very far cry from the traditional, and not entirely undeserved, image of a door supervisor, which occasioned the need for this legislation.

The licence

35.40 The licence granted by the SIA may relate to one or more categories of licensable conduct. It must be subject to conditions prescribed by the Secretary of State, which may include: ongoing training, registration and insurances; requirements as to the manner in which activities are carried out; obligations to produce and display the licence; and obligations to provide information to the SIA from time to time.[25] The SIA is given power to make special conditions, such as are 'appropriate in relation to the licence in question.'[26]

35.41 The SIA adds the following standard conditions to 'front line' licences for door supervisors:

- Wear the licence where it can be seen at all times when engaging in designated licensable activity (unless you have reported it lost or stolen, or it is in our possession)★
- Tell us and the police as soon as practical if your licence is lost or stolen
- Tell us as soon as practical of any convictions, cautions or warnings, or charges for relevant offences whether committed in the UK or abroad

---

[25]   PSIA, s 9.
[26]   PSIA, s 11(6).

- Tell us of any changes to your name or address as soon as practical
- Do not deface or change the licence in any way. (Should your licence become damaged, you should advise us and request a replacement)
- Do not wear a licence that has been defaced or altered in any way
- Produce the licence for inspection on the request of any constable, or other person so authorised by the SIA
- Return the licence to us as soon as practical if you are asked to do so
- Tell us as soon as practical of any change to your right to remain or work in the UK.

Revocation

35.42 The SIA is given the right peremptorily to modify or revoke the licence, applying the section 7 criteria. Modification includes suspending the licence for such period as the SIA may determine.[27] It will be noted that this power appears to be exercisable without a hearing, subject to appeal, and the mere existence of the power, with the serious financial consequences of its exercise, can by itself be expected to exert a powerful disciplinary effect on members of the industry. For example, should a company employ unlicensed operatives, the SIA could simply revoke the licence of all the directors, supervisors and managers, leaving the corporate body without a brain or limbs.

Appeals

35.43 Section 11 of the PSIA provides for an automatic right of appeal to the magistrates' court within 21 days from the day on which the decision is notified to the appellant. A further right of appeal can be brought either by the individual or by the SIA in the Crown Court.[28]

35.44 An appeal can be brought against: (i) refusal to grant a licence; (ii) grant of licence subject to conditions; or (iii) modification or revocation of a licence.[29]

35.45 An appeal in both the magistrates' and the Crown Court is a hearing de novo. The appeal in both courts is to be determined in accordance with the current SIA criteria for granting licences.[30]

---

[27] PSIA, s 10.
[28] PSIA, s 11(4).
[29] PSIA, s 11(1).
[30] PSIA, s 11(5).

Registers

35.46   The PSIA contains provisions for mandatory and voluntary registers. The mandatory register is of every licensee under the Act, which is open to inspection on payment of a fee.[31] This register performs the important function of enabling employers (whether of individual door supervisors or of businesses) to check the licensing status of those with whom they are contracting.

35.47   A key element of the Act is to provide for the establishment of a voluntary register of approved contractors.[32] The scheme enables contractors, who satisfactorily meet prescribed standards, to obtain registration[33] and advertise themselves as such. The scheme achieves the quadruple benefit of giving incentives for the achievement of excellence, raising standards throughout the industry, providing assurance to consumers as to the quality of the services provided and promoting the business of those registered. An appeal to the magistrates lies against a refusal to register, and thence by either the contractor or the SIA to the Crown Court.[34]

At the end of 2012, 211 companies had achieved approved contractor status. For licensing authorities, it gives great confidence in the quality of the operation that the door team are employed by an approved contractor. Indeed, in some cases, the requirement for door staff to be employed by an approved contractor has been added as a premises licence condition.

35.48   The Secretary of State has power by regulation under section 17 to prohibit contractors of particular descriptions from providing security services unless they are approved under section 15 by the SIA. This would convert the voluntary approved suppliers scheme into a compulsory one and is thus of great significance to those in the industry. At the time of writing this power has not been exercised.

Powers of entry

35.49   While rewarding the virtuous, the Act further signals the government's desire to exercise full control over the security industry by giving powers of entry to any person authorised by the SIA to enter any premises owned or occupied by any person who appears by him to be a regulated person.[35] 'Regulated person' is extremely widely defined to include not only those licensed under section 8 or approved under section 15 but also those

---

[31]   PSIA, s 12.
[32]   PSIA, ss 14–18.
[33]   Subject to conditions: PSIA s 15(3)–(6).
[34]   PSIA, s 18.
[35]   PSIA, s 19.

who engage in licensable conduct unlicensed.[36] Indeed, the search power applies not only to those persons but to those who merely <u>appear</u> to the authorised person to be a regulated person. The single exception to the power relates to premises occupied exclusively as private dwellings.

Whether or not he gains entry, the authorised person may require production of any documents or other information relating to any matter connected with: licensable conduct which the apparently regulated person may have been engaged in; the provision by that person of security industry services; or matters in respect of which conditions have been imposed on section 8 licences or section 15 approvals.

The SIA has issued guidance as to the exercise of these powers.[37]

Offences

35.50   The PSIA creates a number of offences in relation to door supervision.

Engaging in licensable conduct without a licence

35.51   Section 3(1) makes it an offence to work as a door supervisor without the appropriate SIA licence. It is a summary only offence punishable by imprisonment for a term not exceeding six months or a fine not exceeding level 5 on the standard scale or both.[38] The offence is one of strict liability. No knowledge, or any mental element, need be shown.

Using an unlicensed security operative

35.52   Section 5(1) of the Act fixes criminal liability on a person who provides any security industry services to another through the medium of an unlicensed security operative who engages in licensable conduct. This offence is triable either way, carrying six months imprisonment and the statutory maximum fine before the magistrates and five years imprisonment and an unlimited fine before the Crown Court. The offence is subject to a defence either:

> '(a)   that he did not know, and had no reasonable grounds for suspecting, at the time when the activities were carried out, that the individual in question was not the holder of a licence in respect of those activities; or

---

[36]   PSIA, s 19(8).
[37]   'Enforcement: what to expect from the SIA' (2011): http://www.sia.homeoffice.gov.uk/Documents/enforcement/sia-enforcement.pdf.
[38]   PSIA, s 3(6).

(b)   that he took all reasonable steps, in relation to the services in question, for securing that that individual would not engage in licensable conduct in respect of which he was not the holder of a licence.'

35.53 It is noteworthy that the offence is partly co-extensive with offences under section 3(1), for example of being the employer of a person carrying out relevant activities without a licence.[39] However, where an employer was systematically setting out to abuse the law, one would expect the more serious charge under section 5 to be brought, conceivably with a charge under section 3 added in the alternative.

Right to use approved status

35.54 Section 16 makes it a triable either way offence, punishable by the statutory maximum fine in the magistrates' court and an unlimited fine in the Crown Court, for a provider of security industry services to hold himself out as an approved provider when he does not have such approval or to hold himself out as approved in terms which the SIA has not approved.

Imposition of requirements for approval

35.55 Section 17 makes it an offence to breach any prohibition imposed by any regulations under that section. The offence is one of strict liability and no provision is made for any defence. The offence is triable either way and punishable by an unlimited fine in the Crown Court and by the statutory maximum fine in the magistrates' court.

Entry and inspection

35.56 Section 19(5) creates a cluster of offences to support the powers of entry and inspection. The subject of the search or disclosure requirement commits an offence if he intentionally obstructs the entry of the authorised person, or if he fails without reasonable excuse to comply with a disclosure requirement. Meanwhile the authorised person himself commits an offence if he makes an unauthorised disclosure of any information obtained. These offences are summary only and carry a six month term of imprisonment and the statutory maximum fine.

False information

35.57 Finally, section 22 makes it an offence knowingly or recklessly to make a false statement to the SIA, on pain of summary trial and imprisonment for six months or a fine at level 5.

---

[39]   PSIA, s 3(2)(g).

Criminal liability of directors

35.58 To complete the criminal picture, it is important to note that the effect of any offence under the PSIA is extended to any director, manager, secretary, similar officer, or other person purporting so to act, who consents to, connives in or neglects to prevent its occurrence.[40]

D THE MODERN DOOR SUPERVISOR

35.59 The modern door supervisor should be no hired thug, but a central part of the machinery of management of the premises, working in partnership with other staff, management, the local authority and the police, guided and mentored by the standards evolved by the SIA. The notion of partnership was emphasised in the House of Commons by Hazel Blears, who said:

'It is vital for the SIA to press ahead with its approach as a modern regulator working with the local authority, the police, training providers, the door supervisors and the industry. Time and again we see that what works in these circumstances is a good partnership approach ...'[41]

35.60 The use of door supervisors is a weapon built into the Licensing Act 2003 through the provisions of section 21 of that Act, and is clearly recognised in national Guidance. Paragraph 2.2 of the Guidance in particular recognises the important role of the national regulator and the role of conditions requiring door supervision:

'2.2 In the exercise of their functions, licensing authorities should seek to co-operate with the Security Industry Authority ("SIA") as far as possible and consider adding relevant conditions to licences where appropriate. The SIA also plays an important role in preventing crime and disorder by ensuring that door supervisors are properly licensed and, in partnership with police and other agencies, that security companies are not being used as fronts for serious and organised criminal activity. This may include making specific enquiries or visiting premises through intelligence led operations in conjunction with the police, local authorities and other partner agencies. Similarly, the provision of requirements for door supervision may be appropriate to ensure that people who are drunk, drug dealers or people carrying firearms do not enter the premises and ensuring that the police are kept informed.'

35.61 Today's door supervisors are the eyes and ears of the licensee, and as such are expected to become involved in the many different aspects of running premises designed for entertainment purposes. They are expected to properly welcome customers onto the premises, whilst enforcing the venue's

---

[40] PSIA, s 23.
[41] HC Debs 16 June 2004, col 890.

entry conditions in a firm but fair manner. Once the customers are on the premises the door staff are expected to ensure that the evening runs according to everyone's expectations, whilst maintaining order and preventing breaches of the criminal law, licensing laws and house rules. If any of those laws or rules are breached they need to act within the guidelines of the law and company policy to resolve the situation. Occasionally, and as a part of the customer service aspects of the job, door supervisors may be required to administer first aid to anyone who becomes ill or injured on the premises, before proper medical help arrives. They are also required to patrol the premises and to look out for fire hazards or suspicious packages, and need to be able to carry out basic emergency procedures if problems occur. They have to be aware of basic health and safety rules, and must help the licensee to ensure that the venue is safe enough to be open to the public. They are basically 'policing' the licensed premises for the management.[42]

35.62   The extent of this modern role is underlined by the syllabus to be undertaken to gain registration under the new Act, set out in the previous section.[43]

35.63   There is a strong legal reason for the leisure operator to choose his door staff with care, exemplified by the case of *Mattis v Pollock*[44] in which a door supervisor, known (indeed employed for) his aggressive tendencies carried on an argument started in the nightclub by going back to his flat to fetch a knife and then stabbing the claimant in the street away from the nightclub. The High Court found that the defendant employer was neither personally nor vicariously liable[45] but the Court of Appeal held that he was both, Judge LJ stating:

'Mr Pollock chose to employ Cranston, knowing and approving of his aggressive tendencies, which he encouraged rather than curbed, and the assault on Mr Martin represented the culmination of an incident which began in Mr Pollock's premises and involved his customers, in which his employee behaved in the violent and aggressive manner which Mr Pollock expected of him.'[46]

35.64   While this decision turned on its own facts, having regard to established legal principles,[47] it provides a cautionary tale both for operators

---

[42]   This paragraph was cited with approval by Kenneth Parker QC in *R (Nicholds) v Security Industry Authority* [2007] 1 WLR 2067.

[43]   More detailed consideration of the role of the door supervisor can be found in Chapter 23 (The Operation of the Premises), Sections E (Social Aspects of the Drinking Environment) and F (Operational Controls within Licensed Premises) within the first edition of this book.

[44]   2003 LLR 887.

[45]   2003 LLR 41.

[46]   Pages 728–729.

[47]   See in particular *Lister v Hesley Hall Ltd* [2002] 1 AC 215 and *Dubai Aluminium Co Ltd v Salaam* [2002] 3 WLR 1913.

and their insurers. Even where the door supervisor is not an employee of the licensee but an independent contractor, the operator is still under a duty to take reasonable steps to ensure that he is hiring a competent contractor so as to protect the safety of his customers.[48] This alone is likely to give rise to an enhanced demand for the services of contractors approved under section 15 of the PSIA, since anyone supplied by such a contractor is likely to carry the imprimatur of competence.

35.65 But more than this: good door staff are not just good security and good law, but good business. The last word is left to Martin Baird:

'... Some of the most important people in your venue are the door staff. They are the first and last impression of the venue for the punter. These impressions are lasting ones for Joe Public, so it's essential your door team are made of the right stuff.'[49]

---

[48] *Naylor (t/a Mainstreet) v Payling* 2003 LLR 503, although he is under no duty to ensure that the contractor is insured.

[49] Baird, *Back to Basics: A Guide to Nightclub Operation* (Mondiale Publishing, 2003).

Statutory remedies in the night time economy

When lyart leaves bestrow the yird,
Or wavering like the bauckie-bird,
Bedim cauld Boreas' blast;
When hailstanes drive wi bitter skyte,
And infant frosts begin to bite,
In hoary cranreuch drest;
Ae night at e'en a merry core
O randie, gangrel bodies,
In Poosie-Nansie's held the splore,
To drink their orra duddies;
Wi quaffing an laughing,
They ranted an they sang,
Wi jumping an thumping,
The vera girdle rang,

Robert Burns, *The Jolly Beggars: A Cantata*

Introduction

> What say you, good masters, to a squab pigeon pasty, some collops of
> venison, a saddle of veal, widgeon with crisp hog's bacon, a boar's head
> with pistachios, a bason of jolly custard, a medlar tansy and a flagon of
> old Rhenish?
>
> James Joyce, *Ulysses*

36.01 It might be said with only little exaggeration that when a yet further
remedy for the 'blight of alcohol' is announced, politicians preen, journalists
salivate and practitioners groan. This is because there are already more
remedies for alcohol-related issues than can be found for bodily conditions
on the shelves of the most dedicated homeopath.

36.02 The important thing for local authorities, working with their statutory partners, is to understand the remedies at their disposal, formulate
effective policies as to when to use them based on evidence and not
guesswork, and target them in a way that will make a difference, and which
represents an effective use of their limited resources.

36.03 Part E of this book is deliberately divided into sections so as
encourage some systematic thinking:

- Places.
- Premises.
- People.
- Prosecutions.

36.04 A very large amount of work has gone into enforcement against
licensed premises. Many premises no doubt deserve it. Others are the
unwilling and innocent recipients of poor behaviour by town centre users,
many of whom are alcohol-dependent and hazardous drinkers. Others are
unlucky enough to find themselves in places with real social problems
regarding alcohol. In such instances, the effective response may well be to
target the individuals or the places rather than the premises, without whose
business there would be a less diverse, interesting, economically productive
town centre.

36.05 Another important point is that there is an array of agencies which
might take enforcement action – licensing authorities, police, environmental

health departments, planning authorities, health and safety authorities and trading standards authorities to name the most important. It may immediately be seen how important it is that those agencies work together in partnership.

36.06 The most effective licensing authorities often have police officers sitting together with licensing enforcement officers, to ensure that they work together jointly, share resources and intelligence and avoid their efforts falling between two stools. It is similarly important that they work in partnership with other agencies. A recurrent noise nuisance might be a case for licensing, for police, for planning or environmental health and might be dealt with through reviews, closure powers, planning enforcement or noise abatement. That can only be worked out on a partnership basis, according to clear policies and protocols.

36.07 Further thinking about partnership came as a result of the Local Better Regulation Office's Retail Enforcement Pilot, which concluded that the following elements need to be exhibited by successful joint enforcement schemes:

- Working in partnership
- Sharing information
- Using technology and other tools
- Focusing resources and influencing culture.

36.08 In LBRO's own words, the following lessons were learned from the Pilot:[1]

'Partnerships:

- Create an organisation structure and make it clear who is responsible for each element of the project. (Communications, Finance Control, Steering Group, Project Management etc.,)
- Involve ICT colleagues from all the partnerships as early as possible in the planning of the project.
- Involve cabinet members, local and business communities and enforcement officers. They all need to be involved in the "journey".
- Communicate why this approach is being taken, what are the desired outcomes of the project, the cost implications/savings and explain the need for change and the impact on regulatory services and the business community.
- Anticipate the impact your approach will have on your delivery against National Regulators targets and agree any changes with your SRO/Steering Group.

---

[1]   March   2010.   http://www.bis.gov.uk/assets/brdo/docs/publications-2010/10–1407-rep-lessons-learned.pdf.

Share Information:

- Key message from the previous pilots, the biggest challenge, both in time and resource, is the creation of a functional, accessible, clean and fully integrated database of premises. With the merging of several databases you may find one premise identified in several ways. Agree an approach to purge the systems, remove duplications and agree on a process to maintain the integrity of the data. Give yourself realistic timescales to carry out this task.
- Identify what information needs to be shared. If you are using an alert system to notify colleagues of the results of an inspection, agree what information needs to be sent and how it will be communicated. (Involve ICT colleagues in the decision process.)

Tools:

- Set up a SMART project. Identify how you will measure success.
- Agree on the ways of working, identify who will be the lead regulatory service on each inspection and develop service plans for the duration of the intervention cycles, not just for 12 months.
- Organise training sessions on any new technology and any changes to the ways of working. Have officers explain to other officers the reasoning behind the need to gather intelligence in specific areas.
- Consider the need to incorporate the training as part of the induction modules for new starters.
- Look to introduce realistic timescales in the planning of the project and agree ownership for each task.

Resource and Culture:

- Involve officers in the development of the process, this will enable you to identify "champions" and encourage wider ownership for the approach.
- Explain why a change is being introduced, involve officers from each of the disciplines to formulate the type and content of the intelligence being gathered and use them to "sell" the concept.
- Provide the opportunity for officers to give feedback, listen and respond to all comments.'

36.09 Whenever enforcement is necessary, it is not only important to consider what the problem is, but also to determine the level of intervention. A regulator which always reaches for the gun is not acting proportionately and is therefore in breach of its responsibilities under the Legislative and Regulatory Reform Act 2006 – see Chapter 29.

36.10 In its fact sheet 'A Stepped Approach to Achieving Compliance', produced in concert with the Institute of Licensing, the Home Office reminds regulators that they need to adopt the principles of better regulation and take a stepped approach to securing compliance. The principles set out are that compliance work needs to be:

- proportionate;
- accountable, in that premises inspections are carried out on a risk assessment basis, with the lowest risk premises left to run themselves;
- consistent, in that like premises are treated alike;
- transparent, in that premises know what is expected of them and what inspections have revealed.

36.11 'A Stepped Approach' advises that authorities should respond to difficulties using the minimum interference necessary to address the problem, which might include dialogue, mediation or warning before formal enforcement action is contemplated.

36.12 It reminds authorities that a stepped approach might mean self-regulation first, before progressing through dialogue, monitoring and test visits, request for review and only finally the ultimate steps of summary review, closure orders or prosecution. While clearly there will be emergencies where all the steps cannot be followed religiously, it is plainly right that authorities should not routinely reach for enforcement unless less interventionist means have failed.

36.13 Finally, it is necessary to put all of the remedies in this Part alongside the positive, voluntary schemes set out in Part F (Good Practice in the Night Time Economy). Such schemes may help to change the nature, dynamic and perception of the night time economy and themselves produce beneficial consequence in terms of the licensing objectives. They are not to be considered as a 'nice to have', gestural adjunct to the serious business of enforcement but as collaborative, community-based endeavours which may produce more than enforcement can, remembering that enforcement is always reactive whereas voluntary schemes are ongoing exercises in making better places. Enforcement is necessary, but it should not be thought of as the only means of achieving the deeply serious objective of making our towns and cities places of delight for all.

Places

Then it's drink, my brave boys, as I've told you before,
Come drink, my brave boys, till you cannot drink no more,
For those French dogs they may boast but their brags are all my eye,
They say that they will drink old England dry.
Aye dry, aye dry my boys, aye dry,
They say that they will come and drink old England dry.

Traditional

37

Designated public place orders

When a man in easy circumstances gets drunk at a public house and staggers along the streets; he is seen by everybody, and is inconsiderately taken as a fair example of his class; and thus, through the occasional drunkard, or the drunken vagabond, the whole body are stigmatized and condemned as drunkards when in fact the number of those which are really drunkards is, when compared with the whole body, a very small number.

Improvement of the Working People: Drunkenness – Education
(1834)
Francis Place

A INTRODUCTION

37.01 The Criminal Justice and Police Act 2001[1] made provision for designated public place orders (DPPOs). These enable local authorities to designate areas (called in the legislation 'designated public places') where limits on public drinking apply, and give powers to the police to enforce those orders. Guidance on DPPOs for local authorities is provided by the Home Office.[2]

B OBTAINING A DPPO

37.02 A local authority may make somewhere a 'designated public place' where they are satisfied that:

---

[1] ('CJPA 2001'), ss 12–16, see also Violent Crime Reduction Act 2006, s 26.
[2] 'Guidance on Designated Public Place Orders for Local Authorities in England and Wales' (Home Office, December 2008). http://www.crp-news.com/secure/assets/n20081228.144013_4957640df10c.pdf.

(a) nuisance or annoyance to members of the public or a section of the public; or
(b) disorder;

has been associated with the consumption of alcohol in that place.[3]

37.03 For these purposes public place means any place to which the public or any section of the public has access, on payment or otherwise, as of right or by virtue of express or implied permission.[4]

37.04 Before making a DPPO the local authority must consult[5] the following in relation to the proposed area:[6]

- The chief officer of police for the area, and for any nearby area which the local authority consider may be affected by the designation.
- The parish or community council, and that for any nearby area which the local authority consider may be affected by the designation.
- The licence holder of any premises likely to be affected by the designation which holds a premises licence, club premises certificate or for which a temporary event notice has been given.

37.05 The authority must also take reasonable steps to consult the owners or occupiers of any land which will be included in the order.[7]

37.06 Additionally the local authority must publish a notice in a newspaper identifying the area to be designated, explaining the effect of the designation and inviting representations about whether an order should be made.[8]

A local authority must consider all representations received as a result of the above.[9]

The Home Office guidance on DPPOs recommends that the decision to promote a DPPO should be evidence-based. It states:

> 'The evidence you will require for a DPPO is that there is an alcohol related nuisance or annoyance to the public in the proposed area/s. You should make an assessment as to the likelihood that the problem will

[3] CJPA 2001 s 12(2).
[4] CJPA 2001 s 16(1).
[5] Consultation requirements are set out at Local Authorities (Alcohol Consumption in Designated Public Places) Regulations 2007, reg 3(3).
[6] Local Authorities (Alcohol Consumption in Designated Public Places) Regulations 2007,, reg 3(1).
[7] Local Authorities (Alcohol Consumption in Designated Public Places) Regulations 2007,, reg 3(2).
[8] Local Authorities (Alcohol Consumption in Designated Public Places) Regulations 2007, reg 5.
[9] Local Authorities (Alcohol Consumption in Designated Public Places) Regulations 2007, reg 4.

continue unless these powers are adopted. In addition, you must have a belief that the problem could be remedied by the use of these powers. Evidence should be based not just on information you have obtained, but also from the police and members of the local community who have reported incidents of alcohol-related anti-social behaviour or disorder. Evidence of alcohol-related nuisance could for example include litter related to the consumption of alcohol (e.g. bottles and cans) as well as police information and residents' complaints.'

37.07 Although there is no statutory requirement to consult residents and local businesses, the guidance on DPPOs recommends that this be done, stating:

'Where residential areas are proposed to be included in the DPPO area, you should endeavour to consult with residents of those areas. Some councils have notified the local residents by means of a leaflet drop. You may also wish to consider holding residents' meetings. Some have carried out surveys of their residents and businesses to gauge their opinion on the proposal to introduce a DPPO and to identify any experience of alcohol related anti-social behaviour or disorder.'

37.08 For further discussion regarding methods of consultation, see Chapter 11 (Licensing Policy Consultation).

37.09 A DPPO cannot be made until at least 28 days after the publication of the notice in the newspaper,[10] although obviously that is a minimum not a target. The guidance advises that it is good practice in addition to place the notice in any council publication circulating in the area, although this supplements rather than replaces the newspaper notice. It suggests that 4–6 weeks is a sufficient period for consultation.

37.10 In considering the overall situation the guidance on DPPOs advises that the effect of the order might be to displace harmful drinking into neighbouring areas, so that the authority should ensure that those areas are also assessed and their inhabitants consulted. If displacement is likely to occur, then the order area might be enlarged accordingly. However borough-wide DPPOs are discouraged since, in order for the order to be proportionate, there would have to be evidence of alcohol-related anti-social behaviour in each and every part of the borough.

37.11 Once a DPPO has been made, before it takes effect a local authority must publish a further notice identifying where the order will effect, identifying the effect of the order and indicating when the order will take

---

[10] Local Authorities (Alcohol Consumption in Designated Public Places) Regulations 2007, reg 6.

effect.[11] It must further erect signs in the place affected by the order sufficient to draw attention to members of the public to the effect of the order.[12] The guidance states that signs must not give the impression that drinking itself is a criminal offence in the areas, and suggests that a picture of a bottle with a line through it is avoided for this reason. A model sign is produced at Annex A of the guidance.

37.12   A copy of the order must additionally be sent to the Secretary of State as soon as reasonably practicable after it is made.[13]

C AREAS EXCLUDED FROM DPPOS

37.13   The following are specifically stated in the legislation not to be a 'designated public place' or part of such a place:[14]

- Premises which hold a premises licence[15] authorising the sale or supply of alcohol, or anywhere within the curtilage of such a premises.
- Premises which hold a club premises certificate[16] authorising the sale or supply of alcohol, or anywhere within the curtilage of such a premises.
- An area where a temporary event notice permits the sale of alcohol or has done so in the last 30 minutes.
- A place where facilities or activities relating to the sale or consumption of alcohol are permitted under section 115E of the Highway Act 1980.[17]

37.14   In relation to exceptions relating to the holding of premises licences, if the premises licence is held by the local authority or the premises are occupied by a local authority or managed by or on behalf of a local authority, then the exception only applies at times when the premises is actually being used for the sale or supply of alcohol or within 30 minutes after the end of such a period.[18] This is, as explained in the guidance, to enable local authorities to apply for premises licences for public spaces for community events such as carnivals, without undermining their ability to tackle anti-social behaviour in those places when events are not taking place.

---

[11]   Local Authorities (Alcohol Consumption in Designated Public Places) Regulations 2007, reg 7.
[12]   Local Authorities (Alcohol Consumption in Designated Public Places) Regulations 2007, reg 8.
[13]   Local Authorities (Alcohol Consumption in Designated Public Places) Regulations 2007, reg 9.
[14]   CJPA 2001, s 14.
[15]   As defined in the Licensing Act 2003, s 1.
[16]   As defined in the Licensing Act 2003, s 60.
[17]   Ie under a table and chairs licence. See further Chapter 34 (Tables and Chairs).
[18]   CJPA 2001, s 12(1A)–(1B).

D EFFECT OF A DPPO

37.15 Where an area is, by virtue of a DPPO, a 'designated public place', if a constable reasonably believes someone is or has been consuming alcohol[19] in that place[20] they may require them either not to consume anything which the constable reasonably believes is alcohol in that place or to surrender to him anything he reasonably believes to be alcohol.[21] A constable is empowered to dispose of anything surrendered to him as he thinks fit.[22] The constable must inform the subject that failure to comply with such an instruction is an offence.[23] If the subject fails without reasonable excuse to comply they commit an offence which is triable summarily only, and subject to a fine up to level 2 on the standard scale.[24] Alternatively a £50 penalty notice for disorder can be issued. In the past the government has indicated that they would raise the maximum fine to £2,500, but this has not been done yet.

37.16 Although nothing in the legislation requires that the person is acting in an anti-social manner in order to commit an offence under the legislation, in some instances local authorities have agreed protocols with the police that individuals would only be approached and asked to stop drinking in specified circumstances.

The matter is put aptly in the guidance on DPPOs:

> 'These powers are not intended to disrupt peaceful activities, for example families having a picnic in a park or on the beach with a glass of wine. While police officers have the discretion to require an individual to refrain from drinking regardless of behaviour, our advice is that it is not appropriate to challenge an individual consuming alcohol where that individual is not causing a problem. Bodies responsible for introducing and enforcing DPPOs must keep in mind section 13 of the Criminal Justice and Police Act 2001 which makes it clear that this power is to be used explicitly for addressing nuisance or annoyance associated with the consumption of alcohol in a public place.'

37.17 When a DPPO is brought into force, any by-law in place affecting the area covered by the DPPO which makes the consumption of alcohol a criminal offence or makes incidental supplementary or consequential provision ceases to have effect in relation to the area covered by the DPPO (or if

---

[19] Alcohol carries the same definition as in s 191 of the Licensing Act 2003, by virtue of CJPA 2001, s 16(1).
[20] CJPA 2001, s 12(1).
[21] CJPA 2001, s 12(2).
[22] CJPA 2001, s 12(3).
[23] CJPA 2001, s 12(5).
[24] CJPA 2001, s 12(4).

made following the DPPO will not have effect in relation to the area covered by the DPPO).[25]

37.18   Further and in any event, any by-laws prohibiting the consumption in a public place of alcohol, or making incidental supplementary or consequential provision ceased to have effect on 1 September 2006.[26]

E   USE OF DPPOS

37.19   Home Office statistics show that there are over 800 DPPOs currently in operation,[27] so it is a widely used tool.

37.20   A DPPO is a valuable tool where the police require extra power to prevent drinking in their area which is proving harmful in terms of disorder and nuisance. It is a dead letter if the police do not have the interest or the resources to enforce it. The guidance on DPPOs states:

> 'As with any decision to introduce a particular power to tackle anti-social behaviour in a local area, it is essential that you work with the relevant agencies within the Crime & Disorder Reduction Partnership (CDRP) – such as the police – from the start of the DPPO process. In particular, this is to ensure that when the order comes into force, the DPPO is monitored and the police have the resources to be able to enforce it.'

37.21   A DPPO which is made and then not enforced is likely to raise and then dash expectations, divert resources from more cost effective methods of tacking social harms, and reduce the credibility of both the licensing authority and the police. It is not therefore a panacea, but a useful tool in the armoury of responses, to be used where proper analysis and assessment indicates that it is likely to be used and effective.

37.22   The DPPO, while beneficial in certain circumstances, remains an encroachment on the liberty of the citizen, and so should be kept under review. The guidance recommends reviews at least every two years, in order to find out whether the DPPO has stopped or helped to reduce alcohol-related anti-social behaviour. If it has, then the further question should be asked whether the DPPO is still required, and whether its coverage needs to be reviewed. Conversely, if there has been no change in anti-social behaviour, then there may need to be analysis as to whether this is because of displacement (in which case the order might need to be extended), or because of a lack of enforcement, which may itself need to be remedied.

---

[25]   CJPA 2001, s 15(1)–(2).
[26]   CJPA 2001, s 15(3) provides for this to occur five years after commencement of the section, which was 1 September 2001.
[27]   http://www.homeoffice.gov.uk/about-us/freedom-of-information/released-information1/foi-archive-crime/19441-place-order-confiscate-alc/19441-place-order-confiscate-alc?view=Binary.

37.23 The guidance also recommends that a dataset be maintained by the police, so that progress against the benchmark can be reviewed. This is not only good advice for DPPOs but good advice for town centres in general, and is canvassed further in Chapters 2–4. If town centre management tools are to be more than gestural guesswork but are to be effective surgical interventions, then it is crucial that a baseline position be taken and their success measured.

38

Dispersal orders

The rain it poor'd aw the day an' myed the groons quite muddy,
Coffy Johnny had a white hat on – they war shootin' "Whe stole the cuddy."
There wes spice stalls an' munkey shows an' aud wives selling ciders,
An' a chep wiv a hapenny roond aboot, shootin' "Noo, me boys, for riders."

Geordie Ridley, *Blaydon Races*

> A   Introduction 38.01
> B   When can a dispersal order be made? 38.02
> C   Effect of a dispersal order 38.06
> D   Use of dispersal orders 38.12

A INTRODUCTION

38.01 Part 4 of the Anti-Social Behaviour Act ('ASBA') 2003 provides for ordering groups of people to disperse. Such directions have been judicially described as a 'significant restriction on the liberty of persons'[1] and a 'novel form of criminalisation'.[2] Yet they have come to be seen by some police forces as an important tool for dealing with acute problems of disorder, including alcohol related disorder in town centres.

B WHEN CAN A DISPERSAL ORDER BE MADE?

38.02 A dispersal order can be made by a police officer of or above the rank of superintendent,[3] where he has reasonable grounds for believing:

[1]   *Kieron Carter v Crown Prosecution Service* [2009] EWHC 2197 (Admin), para 3.
[2]   *Carter* at para 16.
[3]   ASBA 2003, s 36.

(a)   that any members of the public have been intimidated, harassed, alarmed or distressed as a result of the presence or behaviour[4] of groups of two or more persons in public places in any locality in his police area[5] (the 'relevant locality'), and

(b)   that anti-social behaviour is a significant and persistent problem in the relevant locality.[6]

38.03   Within this part of the ASBA 'public places' means any highway and any place to which at the material time the public or any section of the public has access, on payment or otherwise, as of right or by virtue of express or implied permission.[7]

In deciding whether to make such an order the officer must have regard to any code of practice in force under section 34 of the ASBA 2003.

Such an order (referred to in the legislation as an 'authorisation') must be in writing, signed by the officer giving it and specify where it applies to, the grounds on which it is given and the period for which it lasts.[8] The grounds on which the authorisation is given must be specified.[9]

The authorisation is a public document and must not be marked, for example, as restricted. It was recommended in *Carter* that the authorisation should be a single document including map and prohibitions, and should be drafted in the language of the vernacular.

The authorisation must not be made without the consent of the local authority(s) whose area it covers.[10]

38.04   Before an order comes into force[11] it must be publicised by placing a notice either or both in a newspaper circulating in the relevant locality or in conspicuous places within the relevant locality,[12] which states that the order has been made, the place to which it relates and its period of applicability. The court in *Carter* was not impressed with publicity that comprised a non-statutory document explaining the effect of the order being placed in the window of a single local shop.

---

[4]   Including the presence or behaviour of one or more members of the group: ASBA 2003, s 30(7).

[5]   An officer of the British Transport Police has the same power in relation to the area which forms part of property in relation to which he has all the powers and privileges of a constable by virtue of the Railways and Transport Safety Act 2003, s 31(1)(a)–(f).

[6]   ASBA 2003, s 30(1).

[7]   ASBA 2003, s 36.

[8]   ASBA 2003, s 31(1).

[9]   *Sierny v DPP* [2006] EWHC 716 (Admin).

[10]   ASBA 2003, s 31 (2).

[11]   ASBA 2003, s 31 (5).

[12]   ASBA 2003, s 31 (3)–(4).

38.05   Following consultation with the relevant local authority/authorities the order may be withdrawn by the officer who made it or any other officer of the same or higher rank whose area includes that covered by the order.[13] This does not affect the exercise of any power which took place prior to its withdrawal, or prevent making a further order in respect of the same area or part of the same area.[14]

C   EFFECT OF A DISPERSAL ORDER

38.06   A dispersal order can be made for up to six months.[15] During that time if a constable in uniform[16] has reasonable grounds for believing the presence[17] of a group of two or more persons in a public place in the area to which the order applies has resulted or is likely to result in any member of the public being intimidated, harassed, alarmed or distressed they may direct one or more of the following things:[18]

- That the group disperse (immediately or by a specified time) in any way he specifies.
- That those people who do not live in the area covered by the order leave the area, or leave a particular part of it.
- That those people who do not live in the area covered by the order do not return to the area for 24 hours.

38.07   In *Marc Bucknell v DPP*[19] the court considered what constituted reasonable grounds for believing the presence of the group has resulted in, or would be likely to result in, the relevant consequences. The defendant had been hanging around outside the station, on his way home from school. The court said:

'8. There is no evidence that any member of the public in the present case was harassed, intimidated, alarmed or distressed. In my view, unless there are exceptional circumstances not present in this case, a reasonable belief for the purpose of section 30(3) must normally depend, in part at least, on some behaviour of the group which indicates in some way or other harassment, intimidation, the cause of alarm or the cause of distress. If this were not so, there would, in my judgment, in a case such as this be an illegitimate intrusion into the rights of people to go where they please in public. In particular, as this case illustrates, it would intrude into the legitimate activities of young people going home from school by a reasonable route, behaving

---

[13]   ASBA 2003, s 31 (6)–(7).
[14]   ASBA 2003, s 31(8)–(10).
[15]   ASBA 2003, s 30(2).
[16]   Or community support officer – see ASBA 2003, s 33.
[17]   Including the presence of one or more members of the group: ASBA 2003, s 30(7).
[18]   ASBA 2003, s 30(4).
[19]   [2006] EWHC 1888 (Admin).

properly as they do so. Objectively, in my judgment, it was not on the facts a proportionate response within the terms of the legislation for PC McNally to act as he did. I have some sympathy with the Constable because he was put in the position of having to operate what, at the margins, is difficult legislation, but in my judgment the apparent characteristics of these groups alone, at 5 o'clock in the afternoon of an early summer day, was not capable, objectively, of giving rise to the necessary reasonable belief.'

In deciding whether to exercise this power the officer must have regard to any code of practice in force under section 34 of the ASBA 2003.

38.08 The anti-social behaviour giving rise to the direction to leave does not have to be the same anti-social behaviour which gave rise to the original order. In *R (Singh) v Chief Constable of the West Midlands*,[20] an authorisation had been given due to concerns about anti-social behaviour by revellers in the lead up to Christmas. Mr Singh and a number of other people were protesting within the area about a play they considered offensive to Sikhs and a direction was made for them to move. The court held that section 30 dispersals could be made when there was a public protest (subject to consideration of the proportionality of those actions). That the authorisation was made on different grounds did not prevent a dispersal order being made.

38.09 A direction can be made orally and can be made to one or more of the group of people. It can be withdrawn or varied by the person who gave it.[21] Anyone who knowingly contravenes the direction commits a summary only offence and can be punished by a fine up to level 4 on the standard scale or imprisonment for up to three months.[22]

Such a direction cannot apply to certain trade union activity[23] or a public procession.[24]

38.10 Additionally, if a constable in uniform finds someone they have reasonable grounds for believing is under 16 and not under the effective control of a parent or responsible person aged 18 or over in the area covered by the order between the hours of 9 am and 6 pm, then they can remove them to where they live unless they have reasonable grounds for believing that if removed to where they live they would be likely to suffer significant harm.[25] In removing such a young person the police may use reasonable

---

[20]   [2006] EWCA Civ 1118.
[21]   ASBA 2003, s 32(1).
[22]   ASBA 2003, s 32(2).
[23]   Conduct which is lawful under s 220 of the Trade Union and Labour Relations (Consolidation) Act 1992
[24]   In accordance with s 11(1) of the Public Order Act 1986.
[25]   ASBA 2003, s 30(6).

force if necessary.[26] The power to remove should not be exercised arbitrarily to remove anyone between the hours of 9 am and 6 pm, and can only act for the purposes for which the power was conferred, which are generally to protect those under 16 from the effects of other people's anti social behaviour and to prevent them behaving in an anti-social manner themselves.

If the constable takes such a step any local authority whose area the order covers must be notified.[27]

In deciding whether to exercise this power the officer must have regard to any code of practice in force under section 34 of the ASBA 2003.

38.11 In prosecuting for breach of a direction made under a dispersal order it is essential to understand at an early stage whether the defence are taking a point as to whether the authorisation is properly made and publicised. This point must be raised at a pre-trial review. If the point is being taken, the prosecution must be in a position to demonstrate that the making of the actual authorisation and its publicity complied with the requirements of the act[28]. In *Carter* the court suggested strongly that a 'pack' of information should be sent to the courts in the area when an authorisation was made so that a defence advocate could satisfy themselves that there was an authorisation properly in place.

D USE OF DISPERSAL ORDERS

38.12 Provided that they are properly resourced and enforced, dispersal orders provide an acute response to problems of place-related anti-social behaviour. If they are not properly resourced or enforced, they are counterproductive in wasting the time and energy of the community with an initiative which carries few practical consequences.

38.13 Even if made, the order needs to be enforced with very great care. They run the danger of driving a wedge between the police and the people whose conduct it is sought to improve, particularly young people. There is a danger that enforcement might occur in a way which is offensive to some sectors of the community, including particular ethnic groups. Section 30(4) allows the constable to direct dispersal merely on the grounds that the 'presence' of a group is likely to result in members of the public being intimidated, harassed, alarmed or distressed. Strictly applied, that might result in an invasion of liberty of group A merely because group B feels distressed by them.

---

[26]   *R (W) v Metropolitan* Police *Commissioner* [2006] EWCA Civ 458.
[27]   ASBA 2003, s 32(4).
[28]   *Carter* at paras 14, 20, 21 and 22.

38.14 The matter was well put in a report to the Joseph Rowntree Foundation:[29]

'Dispersal orders, where well planned, can offer short-term respite to ASB and trigger longer-term problem-solving strategies in conjunction with key local partners. Symbolically, they can serve as a wake-up call to focus attention and galvanise energies to local troubles that have a significant impact on community well-being and the use of public spaces:

"I think it gave people breathing space and disrupted the habits of some young people, but it is only a sticking plaster." (Resident)

"The reason why they're out on the streets is they've got to go somewhere, and kids will be kids. And I think that is the basic line. Kids will be kids, and they will be noisy, and they will show off, and they will damage things, because that's what they do. And what we're doing is just sticking plasters over this." (Middle-ranking officer, Metropolitan Police)

A theme to emerge from this research is that the introduction of dispersal orders was prompted by, and justified in terms of, requests by the police for additional tools to assist them in managing ASB. Yet it is police officers who offer some of the most critical and reflective insights into the shortcomings of the powers and the challenges they entail.

Through practice police have come to appreciate both the limitations and the unintended consequences of such sweeping and highly discretionary powers. There is a growing realisation among knowledgeable practitioners of the need to retain exceptional powers for focused, short-term and well-evidenced use.

Police officers felt that the powers to disperse were useful as tools of last resort, but many were also aware of the dangers to relations, with young people particularly, regarding overuse and inconsistent implementation. More often than not, the powers provided a framework for negotiation about the conditions of orderly behaviour. Police were also acutely aware of the dangers of falsely raising public expectations about the level of police patrols during the period of the dispersal order and the capacity of an enforcement strategy to solve problems of local disorder and insecurity.'

38.15 Similar conclusions were reached by a study in Scotland:[30]

'10.1 Dispersal powers were seen by the police and residents of dispersal areas to have had mainly positively effects. At a minimum they

---

[29] Adam Crawford and Stuart Lister, 'The use and impact of dispersal orders: Sticking plasters and wake-up calls' (2007).

[30] 'A Review of Dispersal Powers' (Scottish Government, 2007), http://www.scotland.gov.uk/Resource/Doc/201001/0053723.pdf.

provided a period of respite for local communities. This was greatly appreciated by residents of dispersal areas. In many of the locations this reduction in antisocial behaviour continued for a significant period after the dispersal period ended. The gains were achieved mainly through the additional focus given to the problem area by the police but also through the way in which dispersal powers allowed police to intervene in situations that they would not have been able to with existing powers.

10.2 There were however, reservations expressed with regard to the extension in police powers, the use of discretion and the severity of penalties for breach of directions to disperse. There was also an expressed desire to see continuing efforts dedicated to other possible solutions through community involvement in problem-solving approaches. The most commonly mentioned of these other methods included restricting the provision of alcohol, the re-design of problem areas and the provision of mutually acceptable services and activities for perceived perpetrator groups.'

38.16 As with many of the remedies canvassed in this Part, dispersal orders are potentially beneficial in particular circumstances and in certain respects, but their potential benefits have to be weighed against their detrimental effects. These may go further than failing to achieve the benefits intended but may include unintended consequences, such as a rupturing of relations between the police and the problem groups whom it is sought to control. Properly handled, though, the evidence has suggested that dispersal orders are a useful short term intervention while longer term strategies for handling disorderly behaviour are developed.

39

Direction to leave

Avaunt! and quit my sight! let the earth hide thee!

William Shakespeare, *Macbeth*

A INTRODUCTION

39.01 The direction to leave procedure was instituted by the Violent Crime Reduction Act ('VCRA') 2006, amongst a package of measures which reflected a turning back from the deregulatory bent of the Licensing Act 2003, including drink banning orders, alcohol disorder zones and summary reviews. The idea of the direction to leave is that it amounts to an early intervention tool to banish potential trouble-makers from a place for up to 48 hours, before they have had the chance to create problems for the authorities or other people. It also allows police to take young persons home or to a place of safety if they are issued with a direction to leave. Properly used, it can be an effective preventive measure.

The power is contained in a single section of the VCRA – section 27 – but guidance on use of the power is contained in a much longer Home Office publication.[1]

B THE POWER

39.02 The provision for making a direction to leave is set out in section 27 of the Violent Crime Reduction Act 2006. Such a direction may be given to someone aged 10 or over where a constable in uniform is satisfied that:

---

[1] 'Giving Directions to Individuals to Leave a Locality. (Section 27 of the Violent Crime Reduction Act 2006). Practical Advice' (Home Office, 2nd ed, January 2010). http://library.npia.police.uk/docs/hocrimereduc/crimereduction053a.pdf.

'(a)   … the presence of the individual in that locality is likely, in all the circumstances, to cause or to contribute to the occurrence of alcohol related crime or disorder in that locality, or to cause or to contribute to a repetition or continuance there of such crime or disorder; and

(b)   … the giving of a direction under this section to that individual is necessary for the purpose of removing or reducing the likelihood of there being such crime or disorder in that locality during the period for which the direction has effect or of there being a repetition or continuance in that locality during that period of such crime or disorder.'[2]

39.03   A direction may only be given where the individual in question is in a public place. For the purpose of the subsection 'public place' means a highway or any place (including a place on a means of transport) to which at the material time the public or any section of the public has access, on payment or otherwise, as of right or by virtue of express or implied permission.[3]

The direction must be given in writing. It may be withdrawn or varied, but not so as to apply for a period of more than 48 hours.[4]

39.04   The effect of the direction is to require the individual to leave the locality and prohibit them from returning within a period of up to 48 hours.[5] The constable can require the individual to leave the area immediately or within an identified time period. The written direction must make it clear both what the locality the individual must leave is, and the time period within which the individual is prevented from returning to the locality. It may include requirements as to how the individual is to leave the locality (for example by reference to a particular route).[6]

39.05   A record must be made of the terms of the direction, the individual to whom it is given, the time at which it is given and the period during which the individual is required not to return to the locality.[7]

39.06   If it is reasonably suspected that the individual is under 16 the constable may remove them to where they reside or a place of safety.[8]

39.07   A direction must not be given where it prevents the individual directed from:

2   VCRA 2006, s 27(2).
3   VCRA 2006, s 27(8).
4   VCRA 2006, s 27(3)(a),(f).
5   VCRA 2006, s 27(1).
6   VCRA 2006, s 27(3)(b)–(e).
7   VCRA 2006, s 27(5).
8   VCRA 2006, s 27(4A).

- having access to where he lives.
- going anywhere he is required to go for his employment or of any contract of services to which he is a party.
- going anywhere he is expected to attend for the purposes of education training or receiving medical treatment.
- or attending any place he is required to attend by an obligation imposed on him by an Act or by order of a court or tribunal.[9]

39.08 Failure to comply with the leave area direction is a criminal offence, triable summarily only, and subject to a maximum sentence of a fine not exceeding level 4 on the standard scale[10].

C USE OF THE POWER

39.09 As the Home Office guidance on direction to leave powers recognises:

'This power isn't necessarily needed to be used every evening of the week, but should be part of focused multi-agency activity on tackling and preventing alcohol-related crime or disorder. In considering if it is appropriate to use this power it is important that the risk of displacing the potential problem, for example to a neighbourhood area or transport facility, is taken into account.'

The guidance gives helpful examples of when directions to leave may be appropriate, which are respectfully reproduced here.

- Where an individual – or group of individuals – is in a public place and is causing a nuisance by being loud or troublesome. While no criminal activity or disorder may have taken place, the likelihood is that their continued presence is likely to lead to the occurrence of alcohol-related crime or disorder. A Direction to Leave may therefore be necessary for the purpose of removing or reducing the likelihood of such crime or disorder from taking place.
- Where an individual – or group of individuals – in a public space who have been drinking alcohol are compliant but it is likely they will insist on continuing to drink and will become drunk. While no criminal activity has taken place, the likelihood of the behaviour of the individual(s) causing or contributing to the occurrence of alcohol-related crime or disorder is present. A Direction to Leave, provided the individual is able to understand its terms, may therefore be necessary for the purpose of removing or reducing the likelihood of such crime or disorder from taking place. For young people this may link in to the new offence of

---

[9] VCRA 2006, s 27(4).
[10] VCRA 2006, s 27(6).

persistent possession and the Direction to Leave may be given alongside the police officer confiscating the alcohol under stage 1 of the new approach.

- There may be situations where a constable is asked to help expel disorderly individual(s) from a licensed premises, or to prevent individual(s) from entering such premises. In such circumstances, it may mean the likelihood of the behaviour of the individual(s) causing or contributing to the occurrence of alcohol-related crime or disorder. A Direction to Leave may therefore be necessary for the purpose of removing or reducing the likelihood of such crime or disorder from taking place.

- Where an individual, aged 16 years and over, is given a Penalty Notice for Disorder (PND) for an offence and the police officer is satisfied there is a likelihood of the individual's ongoing behaviour causing or contributing to the occurrence, repetition or continuance of alcohol-related crime or disorder, a direction to leave may also be appropriate. A Direction to Leave might therefore be given in parallel with, but separate from, the PND where it may be necessary for the purpose of removing or reducing the likelihood of any repetition or continuance of the alcohol-related crime or disorder from taking place.

- Where a group of individuals represent a likelihood of alcohol-related crime or disorder taking place. The behaviour of the lead individual(s) in the group may necessitate them being arrested or justify a PND. This may not apply to the others in the group but, as their behaviour represents a likelihood of causing or contributing to the occurrence, repetition or continuance of the alcohol-related crime or disorder, a Direction to Leave may be necessary for these other group members for the purpose of removing or reducing the likelihood of such crime or disorder taking place.'

39.10 The guidance also asks constables to take particular care in issuing directions to vulnerable people (eg drug addicts or rough sleepers), and to consider the unintended consequence of displacement of the problem to other places. It emphasises that the local licensees can play a role in ensuring that those issued with directions do not seek to enter licensed premises, which implies a proper partnership between police and local operators.

39.11 The direction to leave is a powerful tool. It involves no court order, no taking of evidence and no fiat by a senior officer. It involves a forecast by a constable of what an individual, who may not have caused or be causing any problems, is likely to do, an assessment of the prospective effect of such behaviour and a judgment that the direction is necessary to avert that effect. When engaging in that exercise, the constable will need to consider whether a step short of a brief exile (eg a warning) is likely to achieve the same effect, for if it is the direction may well not be necessary. He will also need to assess whether the direction may put the person themselves in danger, and whether the problem may simply be displaced elsewhere. He will need to co-opt the partnership of local operators to help ensure that directions are obeyed.

39.12 From this, it will be seen that it is not a power to be exercised lightly. However, experienced constables with knowledge of their neighbourhood and the personalities who populate it, particularly at night, will recognise the circumstances in which a direction should be made. While it is a strong power, it is not a punishment or a custodial sentence. It is a breathing space and a cooling off period. The problems in town centres at night are caused by a minority of those who visit them, and frequently these are repeat offenders.

39.13 Given that this is a recurrent issue, it makes sense that law enforcement officers, operating on diminishing resources, should not have to wait for trouble to occur before stepping in. First, by that time, the harm may be caused. Second, to have to make arrests takes the officers off the streets at the precise moment they need to be on it. Third, waiting for harm to be caused frequently results in reviews of premises licences whose holders are entitled to be aggrieved that their management has been acceptable but the offence has been caused by a known trouble maker who should have been taken off the streets long before they caused trouble.

39.14 Therefore, the direction to leave is a useful tool in the armoury of front line police officers, provided that it is exercised judiciously and only in circumstances where deployment is clearly merited.

40

Early morning restriction orders

Solemnly, mournfully,
Dealing its dole,
The Curfew Bell
Is beginning to toll.

Cover the embers,
And put out the light;
Toil comes with the morning,
And rest with the night.

Dark grow the windows,
And quenched is the fire;
Sound fades into silence,–
All footsteps retire.

No voice in the chambers,
No sound in the hall!
Sleep and oblivion
Reign over all!

Henry Wadsworth Longfellow, Curfew

A INTRODUCTION

40.01 The early morning restriction order ('EMRO') was not presaged in the manifestos of the Conservatives or Liberal Democrats prior to the 2010 general election, or in the Coalition Agreement.[1] However, the measure was a Labour beast whose DNA had been designed in the Crime and Security Act 2010,[2] albeit to be only effective from 3 am and dependent on satisfaction of a test of necessity, but which had not yet been given life through a commencement order before the Coalition came to power.

40.02   Yet, within three months of the election, the Government had issued an extensive consultation, which included EMROs, stating broadly:

> 'For too long town centres up and down the country have been blighted by crime and disorder driven by irresponsible binge drinking. Local communities have not had a strong enough voice in determining which pubs and clubs should be open in their area and for how long they should trade. Local authorities have had their hands tied by an overly bureaucratic licensing regime meaning they have not been able to adequately respond to local concerns ...

> The Government believes that the Licensing Act is due an overhaul and that through this the power to make licensing decisions needs to be rebalanced in favour of local communities ... [A] new licensing regime needs to be established with local authorities and the police better able to respond to local residents' concerns. If local communities don't want nightclubs open until six in the morning then the local authority should be able to respond flexibly to this concern.'

40.03   Following a brief consultation, the Police Reform and Social Responsibility Act 2011 was ushered through Parliament with very little opposition on its alcohol measures in general or EMROs in particular – unsurprisingly since its architects sat opposite. Notwithstanding that, the early enthusiasm of local authorities for the measure has been less than thunderous, many seeing it as a bureaucratic imbroglio, apt to drive down the economic base of the town centre and create as many crime and disorder problems as it solves. In this chapter, we shall consider when and how the measure may be usefully employed, as well as pointing out its practical difficulties and downsides, which number more than a few.

EMROs were loosed upon the world by the Licensing Act 2003 (Early Morning Restriction Orders) Regulations 2012. In this chapter, they shall simply be termed 'the Regulations'.

B   WHAT DOES AN EMRO DO?

40.04   An EMRO is only concerned with the sale and supply of alcohol. It does not purport to control any other activity. What it does is to prevent the

---

[1]   'The Coalition: our programme for government' (HM Government, 2010).
[2]   Section 55.

sale (in licensed premises or under temporary event notices) or supply (in premises governed by club premises certificates) of alcohol within the area covered by the EMRO during the 'witching hours'. The area of the EMRO and the witching hours are a matter for the authority, although the hours must not be earlier than midnight or after 6 am.

40.05 The EMRO does not involve tampering with anybody's licence or club premises certificate. The position is simply that, once the EMRO is made, the licence or certificate is ineffective to permit the sale or supply of alcohol during the witching hours. The EMRO trumps everything, and it does not matter whether the licence or certificate concerned precedes or post-dates the making of the EMRO. Breaching an EMRO may result in a prosecution under section 136 of the Act for carrying out unauthorised licensable activities, or indeed a review.

40.06 The EMRO can be used surgically. It may apply to the whole or part of the authority's area. It can provide for different hours on different days of the week. It can be for an open-ended or a limited period. Therefore, in theory, it allows the authority to react in a very directed way to the precise source of its concern.

Here are some examples of how the EMRO might be used:

- Midnight to 6 am on Sunday to Thursday nights (to allow people to get to sleep on work/school nights but to let their hair down at weekends).
- Midnight to 6 am on Sunday to Thursday nights except in August (because many people are on holiday during that period).
- Midnight to 6 am on Sunday to Thursday nights in August (because alcohol related problems seem to increase over the summer holidays).
- Midnight to 6 am outside the town centre, 3 am to 6 am in the town centre (making allowance for later hours in the leisure zone).
- 2 am to 6 am in the town centre for 12 months (on an experimental basis, to see whether the EMRO does reduce alcohol-related crime and disorder).

40.07 The area may be irregularly shaped. But it must be one area. If two different areas are proposed, they must be the subject of two EMROs. There is nothing precluding this in the Act. In theory the authority may have as many EMROs as it likes.

C EXCEPTIONS FROM EMROS

40.08 The exceptions from EMROs are very limited.[3]

---

[3] The Licensing Act 2003 (Early Morning Alcohol Restriction Orders) Regulations 2012 (SI 2012/2551), reg 15.

40.09 The first is premises which are a hotel or comparable premises (defined as a guest house, lodging house or hostel), at which the supply of alcohol between midnight and 6 am on any day may only be made to a person who is staying there for consumption only in the room in which they are staying. As to this exception, a number of observations are required:

(1)   It is not enough if the hotel observes those strictures. It must observe them because they are a condition on its licence.

(2)   The hours restriction needs to be a condition even if the witching hours under the EMRO are shorter. So if the EMRO only operates from 4 am, the hotel is not exempt unless a licence condition precludes sale after midnight except to a person in their room.

(3)   The consumption, however, need not only be by the person to whom the alcohol was supplied. Provided that the condition limits supply to the guest, the consumption may be by them and/or their friend(s).

40.10   The second exception is premises which are authorised to sell alcohol for consumption on the premises between midnight and 6 am only on 1 January. This, it should be observed, is not a general dispensation from EMROs on New Year's Eve. It is a general dispensation for those premises whose authorisation permits such supply on New Year's Eve but which 'are not so authorised at those times on any other day in the year'. It seems very unlikely that this was intended – why should all alcohol suppliers in the EMRO area have to close when those whose post-midnight trade is confined to that one day be able to open? But that is what the Regulations say and it would be a brave operator who defied them. Rather, the solution is for those affected to argue against there being an EMRO at all (relying in part on the absurdity which the Regulations create) and, as a fallback, to argue that they should not be in it.

D   THE TEST FOR AN EMRO

40.11   Section 172A(1) of the Licensing Act 2003 gives the discretion to make an EMRO 'if a licensing authority considers it appropriate for the promotion of the licensing objectives.'

The meaning of the test

40.12   This test gives an apparently open discretion. It does not depend on there having been any past harm to the licensing objectives. Far less does there need to be proof of such harm. Rather, it is a question of whether the authority considers the order appropriate in order to avert harm. Given that such consideration is to be used effectively to curfew a town centre and override legal authorisations to trade, then even judged as an early intervention power it is very draconian in nature.

The question inevitably therefore becomes whether it is tempered by any other legal considerations.

40.13 The correct interpretation and application of the 'appropriateness' test, which underpins nearly all of the Licensing Act 2003 powers, is dealt with in Chapter 12 (The Appropriateness Test). There it was concluded that the requirement of proportionality operates to temper the test, and that when making an important regulatory decision it is unlikely that an authority would consider a step appropriate unless it is necessary. The same applies in this instance.

The Guidance touches tangentially on this issue. It states in paragraph 16.38:

'... As set out in paragraphs 9.38–9.40 of this Guidance, when determining whether a step is appropriate to promote the licensing objectives, a licensing authority is not required to decide that no lesser step will achieve the aim, but should consider the potential burden that would be imposed on premises licence holders as well as the potential benefits in terms of promoting the licensing objectives.'

40.14 It is correct to say that the authority is not required to decide that no lesser step would achieve the aim of the EMRO. But stating what the test is not is not the same as stating what it is. As stated above, it is considered that 'appropriateness' does not simply mean that the authority thinks the EMRO is the right thing to do. It is most unlikely that it would introduce the order if it thought this the wrong thing to do. Rather, it must be the proportionate thing to do, which does certainly involve consideration of what the authority seeks to achieve and whether other measures would produce a similar effect, together with the burdens and other unintended consequence to which it would give rise.

It is considered that the regulatory impact assessment accompanying the implementing Regulations[4] is correct to say:

'EMROs are not a blanket regulation. They are a focussed tool for licensing authorities. Where an EMRO is used, it will be fully justified in the context of the promotion of the licensing objectives in an area.'

E THE EVIDENCE FOR AN EMRO

40.15 Is evidence required for the making of an EMRO? The regulatory impact assessment suggests it is. It says:

'7. The Early Morning Restriction Order will allow licensing authorities to react to problems resulting from the supply of alcohol in specific areas, at specific late night times, and on specific days. The imposition of an EMRO must be appropriate for the promotion of the licensing objectives. A licensing authority must provide

---

[4] 'Dealing with the problems of late night drinking – implementation of secondary legislation' (9 May 2012).

evidence to support its decision. Premises will then be able to make representations to prove that they do not, in fact, undermine the licensing objectives. As such, it would be reasonable to assume that those premises that eventually fall within an EMRO are partially responsible for alcohol-related crime, public nuisance or disorder in that area.'

40.16   While the notion of evidence-based policy making is commendable, the Act does not require there to be actual evidence of alcohol-related harm, and certainly not evidence which would pass muster in a criminal court. It must be remembered that this is, at root, an administrative decision which can be based on any material which the decision-maker considers probative in the individual circumstances of the case. The question of the need for hard evidence in licensing matters, and the specious legal arguments which the debate has engendered, is dealt with in Chapter 5 (Evidence and Inference), and is not rehearsed here. In summary, while the test in practice provides a higher threshold than merely 'appropriate', the material which satisfies the test can be of any nature, and from any source and does not need to comprise 'evidence' in the strict sense of the word.

What factors are material?

40.17   Clearly, a directly material factor is whether the step is appropriate for the promotion of the licensing objectives. Ie will it achieve the desired effect? But that does not exhaust the list. It might be said with quite a bit of confidence that shutting a major town centre at midnight would produce a reduction in alcohol-related crime and disorder there. But that does not necessarily make it the right thing to do.

40.18   The Guidance correctly acknowledges that an authority ought to go into the exercise with its eyes open as the extent of the problem to be solved, and any underlying trends. At paragraph 16.7 it suggests that in establishing its evidence base it may wish to consider the approach set out in paragraphs 13.23 to 13.26 of the Guidance for the establishment of cumulative impact policies. These are reproduced here, for convenience:

'13.23 There should be an evidential basis for the decision to include a special policy within the statement of licensing policy. Local Community Safety Partnerships and responsible authorities, such as the police and the local authority exercising environmental health functions, may hold relevant information which would inform licensing authorities when establishing the evidence base for introducing a special policy relating to cumulative impact into their licensing policy statement. Information which licensing authorities may be able to draw on to evidence the cumulative impact of licensed premises on the promotion of the licensing objectives includes:

- local crime and disorder statistics, including statistics on specific types of crime and crime hotspots;
- statistics on local anti-social behaviour offences;
- health-related statistics such as alcohol-related emergency attendances and hospital admissions;
- environmental health complaints, particularly in relation to litter and noise;
- complaints recorded by the local authority, which may include complaints raised by local residents or residents' associations;
- residents' questionnaires;
- evidence from local councillors; and
- evidence obtained through local consultation.

13.24 The licensing authority may consider this evidence, alongside its own evidence as to the impact of licensable activities within its area, and consider in particular the times at which licensable activities are carried on. Information which may inform consideration of these issues includes:

- trends in licence applications, particularly trends in applications by types of premises and terminal hours;
- changes in terminal hours of premises;
- premises' capacities at different times of night and the expected concentrations of drinkers who will be expected to be leaving premises at different times.

13.25 Where existing information is insufficient or not readily available, but the licensing authority believes there are problems in its area resulting from the cumulative impact of licensed premises, it can consider conducting or commissioning a specific study to assess the position. This may involve conducting observations of the night-time economy to assess the extent of incidents relating to the promotion of the licensing objectives, such as incidences of criminal activity and anti-social behaviour, examples of public nuisance, specific issues such as underage drinking and the key times and locations at which these problems are occurring.

13.26 In order to identify the areas in which problems are occurring, information about specific incidents can be mapped and, where possible, a time analysis undertaken to identify the key areas and times at which there are specific issues.'

40.19 This may appear to be a significant piece of work for licensing authorities, and in fairness it is. However, it is justified. A cumulative impact policy sets out to prevent new things happening as a matter of policy. An EMRO makes lawful activities unlawful. It should be underpinned by at least the same amount of justification as supports a cumulative impact policy.

40.20 The Guidance accepts that the authority ought to consider whether other measures might achieve the same result. It states:

'16.8 An EMRO is a powerful tool which will prevent licensed premises in the area to which the EMRO relates from supplying alcohol during the times at which the EMRO applies. The licensing authority should consider whether other measures may address the problems that they have identified as the basis for introducing an EMRO. As set out in paragraphs 9.38–9.40 of this Guidance, when determining whether a step is appropriate to promote the licensing objectives, a licensing authority is not required to decide that no lesser step will achieve the aim, but should consider the potential burden that would be imposed on premises licence holders as well as the potential benefits in terms of promoting the licensing objectives. Other measures that could be taken instead of making an EMRO might include:

- introducing a CIP;
- reviewing licences of specific problem premises;
- encouraging the creation of business-led best practice schemes in the area; and
- using other mechanisms such as those set out in paragraph 13.39 of this Guidance.'

40.21   As to the last point, the measures referred to in paragraph 13.39 of the Guidance are:

'- planning controls;
- positive measures to create a safe and clean town centre environment in partnership with local businesses, transport operators and other departments of the local authority;
- the provision of CCTV surveillance in town centres, taxi ranks, provision of public conveniences open late at night, street cleaning and litter patrols;
- powers of local authorities to designate parts of the local authority area as places where alcohol may not be consumed publicly;
- the confiscation of alcohol from adults and children in designated areas;
- police enforcement of the general law concerning disorder and anti-social behaviour, including the issuing of fixed penalty notices;
- prosecution for the offence of selling alcohol to a person who is drunk (or allowing such a sale);
- police powers to close down instantly for up to 24 hours (extendable to 48 hours) any licensed premises in respect of which a TEN has effect on grounds of disorder, the likelihood of disorder, or noise emanating from the premises causing a nuisance;
- the power of the police, other responsible authorities or other persons to seek a review of a licence or certificate; and
- Early Morning Alcohol Restriction Orders (EMROs).'

40.22 In other words, EMROs are not to be considered in isolation, but their appropriateness is to be judged in relation and comparison to the whole panoply of measures available by way of planning, licensing and police powers to create better town centre environments and leisure economies. Given that the EMRO is the only power which actually involves shutting down that economy, while the authority is not required to conclude that no lesser measure will suffice it ought to consider whether other measures may be more proportionate and prudent in all the circumstances.

40.23 The concept of proportionality has been mentioned above. One of the key components of a proportionality analysis is the effect which a measure will have on the person to be regulated. This is recognised by the Guidance, when in paragraph 16.8 it enjoins authorities to 'consider the potential burden that would be imposed on premises licence holders'. Authorities will need to look closely at that matter once material is placed before them by such operators who, after all, have licences allowing them to do precisely that which the EMRO now seeks to stop them doing. Presumably, had they been under-performing in regulatory terms they would have been subject to enforcement measures. So, in most cases, the starting point in the proportionality equation is that all of the businesses affected have a lawful authorisation, none of them merits individual enforcement, but all are to be subject to early closure for the common good. It may be imagined that drawing the balance in such circumstances will be a delicate task.

40.24 Further than this, however, the question arises of whether general socio-economic considerations may be brought into account when the proportionality scales are in play. The general view of the Home Office is that such circumstances are not relevant, and there is no room for such considerations to be entered on the prescribed form published under the Regulations.[5] On the other hand, neither is there room on the form to deal with burdens on operators, which the Guidance also says should be brought into account. The forms have boxes which refer only to the licensing objectives. More fundamentally, it is clearly right that, as the Guidance recognises, burdens on operators are part of the proportionality equation. That being so, it is impossible to conclude that the consequences for the town as a whole – be it in terms of economy, employment, tourism, regeneration or culture – are to be ignored. What is a town but a concatenation of economic activity? It is, with respect, impossible to separate out effects on operators and effects on the town, and logically, practically, ethically and legally wrong to do so. For these reasons, it is strongly advanced that the authority is not only entitled but obliged to consider the wider social consequences of the EMRO, assuming that these are raised before it.

---

[5] The Licensing Act 2003 (Early Morning Alcohol Restriction Orders) Regulations 2012 (SI 2012/2551), reg 5; Sch 2.

F   THE PROCEDURE FOR AN EMRO

40.25   The procedure will be considered in a number of stages.

(1) Who decides?

40.26   Like the making of policy, the making, varying or revoking an EMRO is not a licensing committee function.[6]

40.27   Ostensibly, therefore, the function will fall to the full council or a committee with delegated authority. The Guidance assumes that there will be no delegation.[7] In theory there could be, but in practice, due to the highly significant nature of the decision (politically, legally, economically, reputationally), it ought to be made by the full council.

40.28   However, the Licensing Act 2003 also provides for hearings. Plainly, such hearings cannot be conducted by the full council. The Regulations[8] and the Guidance[9] assume that the hearing will be before the licensing committee, but nothing in the Act or Regulations actually creates the delegation. Therefore, acting prudently, the council will itself expressly delegate the task of holding the hearing and making recommendations to the full council.

(2) The decision to consult

40.29   The Act contemplates that there will be proper consultation before an EMRO is made. In theory the decision to consult could be made by officers, who could also devise the form of the consultation. In practice this would be most unwise. Not only are there significant ramifications to the making of an EMRO, and much to consider, but the final EMRO must be in essentially the same form as that consulted upon, including the area of the EMRO, the hours, days and longevity. Therefore, in practical terms, it is essential that the green light for consultation and its terms comes from the full council itself.

40.30   The full council ought to consider the full evidence base, and arguments for and against the EMRO, as canvassed above. It will need to receive a report from officers for that purpose, which fairly and squarely sets out the case for and against.

40.31   In short, while the Act does not require the process to be 'bookended' by full council decisions at the beginning and end, in practical terms this is considered prudent if not essential.

---

6   Licensing Act 2003, s 7(2)(aa).
7   Para 16.20.
8   The Licensing Act 2003 (Early Morning Alcohol Restriction Orders) Regulations 2012 (SI 2012/2551), reg 6.
9   Para 16.16.

(3) Advertisement

40.32 The authority must advertise the proposed EMRO[10] for at least 42 days by publishing a notice of the proposal on its web-site and by displaying a notice in the EMRO area in a manner which is likely to bring the proposal to the attention of persons who have an interest in it. It must also, once during that period, publish notice of the proposal in a local newspaper (or, if there is none, a local newsletter, circular or similar document circulating in its area) and must send a notice to all affected persons.[11] Affected persons are the holders of relevant licences, club premises certificates and TENs, and applicants for such authorisations.[12]

40.33 There is no prescription as to the contents of the notice, but it should at least set out the area concerned, the days, hours and lifespan of the proposed EMRO, and give the time period for making representations about it.

(4) Relevant representations

40.34 The Regulations[13] allow a responsible authority or any other person making representations to do so within a period of 42 days starting the day after the day on which the proposal to make the EMRO is advertised. It is not clear whether 'advertised' means 'first advertised'. If it does, then if on day 1 am EMRO is advertised on a web-site and on day 42 it is advertised in a newspaper, then time for representations runs out on day 43. This does not appear just. Authorities would therefore be well-advised to advertise by all the stated means on the same date.

40.35 The representations have to be in writing and in the form prescribed in Schedule 2 of the Regulations.[14]

40.36 The Regulations do not use the term 'relevant representations' but the prescribed form at Schedule 2 of the Regulations does. Moreover, the form attempts to circumscribe the matters of debate thus:

> 'Please state clearly, in the relevant box below, the evidence on which you intend to rely in support of your representations and what the likely effect of the proposal to make the order will have on the promotion of the licensing objectives. A relevant representation must be about the

---

10 Licensing Act 2003, s 172B(1)(a).
11 The Licensing Act 2003 (Early Morning Alcohol Restriction Orders) Regulations 2012, reg 4.
12 Licensing Act 2003, s 172B(3).
13 The Licensing Act 2003 (Early Morning Alcohol Restriction Orders) Regulations 2012, reg 5.
14 The Licensing Act 2003 (Early Morning Alcohol Restriction Orders) Regulations 2012, reg 5.

likely effect of the making of the order on the promotion of the licensing objectives. Those making representations may provide evidence in relation to one or more of the licensing objectives.'

40.37 This might be thought to derive some support from the definition of 'relevant representations' in the Act, which means representations which 'are about the likely effect of the making of the proposed order on the promotion of the licensing objectives',[15] are made by an affected person, a responsible authority[16] or any other person, are made in the prescribed form and manner in the prescribed time and are not (except for responsible authorities) frivolous or vexatious.

40.38 However, if representations were genuinely confined to the licensing objectives then a licensee who stood to be put out of business by an EMRO could not make a representation about anything other than crime and disorder etc. This is not what is contemplated in the Guidance.

40.39 While the Act, the Regulations and the Guidance read together appear to create confusion, there is a solution. The solution challenges the notions that:

- Representations cannot be taken into account unless they relate to the licensing objectives.
- Representations which are made late cannot be taken into account.

40.40 The narrow view is, put simply, that the discretion to make an EMRO is only exercisable when the authority considers it appropriate for the promotion of the licensing objectives, that relevant representations are defined in terms of the licensing objectives, and that therefore this is all that the hearing concerns. Moreover, where a time limit is given for representations, it is to be applied strictly.

40.41 The wide view is that the fact that an authority considers it appropriate for the promotion of the licensing objectives is the minimum prerequisite for making an order: it does not exhaust all relevant factors, eg those mentioned in Guidance. While the authority is bound to listen to representations which are relevant, it is not precluded from taking account of other representations. A 'human rights compliant' reading of the legislation would allow for these wider views, which may be socio-economic and concerning the impact on the operator, to be taken into account.

40.42 There is precedent for such an approach. In *R (TC Projects Limited) v Newcastle Licensing Justices*[17] the Court of Appeal was concerned with Schedule 2 of the Gaming Act 1968, which gave a discretion to refuse a

---

15   Licensing Act 2003, s 172B(2).
16   As defined in the Licensing Act 2003, s 172B(4).
17   [2008] EWCA Civ 428.

casino licence in the absence of proof of substantial demand. Did this allow other considerations to be taken into account?

40.43 Richards LJ relied on dicta of Lord Widgery in *R v Manchester Crown Court ex parte Cambos Enterprises Ltd*[18] in which Lord Widgery said:

'Obviously Parliament intended that there should be an opportunity for considerations other than the existence of a demand to be taken into account, and I think what is really contemplated here is that in the absence of proof of a substantial demand, the licensing committee may in its wisdom and with its knowledge of the area, still think it right to grant a second bingo licence for the district, and I think it would be perfectly entitled if it thought it right, to be influenced in favour of granting further facilities to a competitor, by the fact that the competitor was prepared to supply the gaming facilities in question on a more lavish scale, with greater comfort, and in circumstances which the patrons would find more attractive than the existing establishment. That in my judgment, is the kind of legitimate consideration which might move the committee to make its decision in favour of the applicants even though no existing substantial demand had been proved.'

40.44 Richards LJ also relied on a further judgment of Lord Widgery in *R v Licensing Justices of the Brighton Crown Court, ex parte Sergeant Yorke Casino Limited*[19] in which Lord Widgery held that the question of whether competition was desirable was relevant, and also held that:

'[t]hese are powers intended to go to local men, to consider local solutions to local problems, and we should not interfere unless it is quite clear that a wrong principle has been applied or some element of law has been overlooked'.

Richards LJ held:

'39. A reason in favour of the grant of a licence may lie in the competition created by additional facilities, provided that it is shown that competition might be expected to have beneficial effects rather than being harmful or merely neutral in its impact. Thus Lord Widgery said in *Cambos* that the licensing justices were entitled to be influenced in favour of granting a licence for further facilities to a competitor by the fact that the competitor was prepared to supply them "on a more lavish scale, with greater comfort, and in circumstances which the patrons would find more attractive than the existing establishment"; and he made clear in *Sergeant Yorke* that the question whether competition was desirable was amongst the many matters that the licensing justices might have to consider. As appears strongly in the authorities,

---

[18] Unreported, 2 March 1973.
[19] Unreported, 19 June 1979.

such matters have to be assessed not as a matter of abstract principle but by reference to the particular circumstances in the locality, by licensing justices using their local knowledge.

40. It is for the licensing justices to decide what weight to attach to the various factors against or for the application and to decide where the overall balance lies. This is not a mathematical exercise but a matter of judgment, to be exercised in the light of all the material considerations. The justices must take all such considerations into account and reach a rational decision whether to refuse or grant a licence. The same, of course, applies to the Crown Court rehearing the matter on an appeal.'

The width of the discretion, notwithstanding the apparently narrow terms of the legislative discretion, was confirmed by Clarke MR, who stated at paragraph 52:

'... the authority must have regard to all relevant circumstances in the local area, whether they point one way or another and decide where the overall balance lies. As I see it, this is a broad discretion to be decided in the circumstances as they are today ...'

40.45   In conclusion, it is strongly contended that the Act, when asking whether an order is appropriate for the promotion of the licensing objectives, does not rule out consideration of anything except the promotion of the licensing objectives. If the order will not further the licensing objectives, it should not be made. If it may or will, then all the factors for and against the order stand to be considered. These include the burden on operators, as acknowledged by the Guidance, and the burdens on the town, which are not mentioned in Guidance at all.

40.46   It is right to say that if the representation has nothing to say on the question of the licensing objectives then it is not a relevant representation within the meaning of the Act. However, this is not the same as saying that it may not be considered. Section 172B(1)(b) of the Act states that the authority must hold a hearing to consider the relevant representations. It does not state that it may not hear anything else. Thus, while there is an obligation to hear the relevant representations, there is a discretion to hear anything else. If the representation goes to the advantages or disadvantages of the EMRO and has been made in sufficient time for it to be considered, it is not easy to imagine why it would or should be excluded. Further support for this discretionary approach is considered immediately below.

Late representations

40.47   While the Act and Regulations prescribe the time within which a representation must be made to be relevant, can a late representation be admitted? The answer in the case of premises licence applications is no.[20] However, the logic does not carry across. The reason for the decision in *Albert Court* is that where there are no relevant representations then there must be a grant.[21] However, that is not the case with EMROs. The correct analogy here is Schedule 3 paragraph 8 of the Local Government (Miscellaneous Provisions) Act 1982 which provides 28 days for objections to sex establishment licences and obliges authorities to take such representations into account. However, in *Belfast City Council v Miss Behavin' Limited*[22] the House of Lords held that there was a discretion to accept late objections, that this should not be treated as an 'exceptional' course but should instead be decided on ordinary administrative principles, including prejudice to other parties and disruption to council business.

40.48 Therefore, it is concluded that representations do not have to concern promotion of the licensing objectives and can be made late. In either case, the authority is not obliged to consider them at a hearing but has a discretion to do so.

40.49 Finally, it would be wrong to assume that all representations will be anti-EMRO. Many may be expected to be supportive. They are entitled to be taken into account and considered at the hearing.

(5) The hearing

40.50 Section 172B(1)(b) of the Act requires a hearing to consider relevant representations, unless the authority and all those making representations agree that such a hearing is unnecessary. Frivolous and vexatious representations may be ruled out and are not characterised as relevant,[23] so presumably their makers are not invited to the hearing.

40.51 The procedure is governed by the Licensing Act 2003 (Hearings) Regulations 2005 as amended by The Licensing Act 2003 (Early Morning Alcohol Restriction Orders) Regulations 2012. The hearing must commence within 30 days of the end of the period for representations, and can be held on days which are not consecutive if the authority considers this necessary for its considerations of the representations and in the public interest.[24]

40.52 Notice of the hearing has to be given to those who have made relevant representations,[25] with copies of the representations going to

---

20   *R (Albert Court Residents Association) v Westminster City Council* [2010] EWHC 393 (Admin).
21   See para [43].
22   [2007] 1 WLR 1420.
23   Licensing Act 2003, s 172B(2)(e), (5).
24   Licensing Act 2003 (Hearings) Regulations 2005, reg 5.
25   See Licensing Act 2003 (Hearings) Regulations 2005, Schedule 2.

affected persons who have made relevant representations.[26] If, for the sake of argument, 1,000 people make relevant representations, this appears to entail that all 1,000 relevant representations have to go to all 1,000 of them. The bureaucratic exercise involved may prove overwhelming. It is hard to imagine that much thought was given to this when the Regulations were framed.

40.53 In relation to the procedure at the hearing, there is some question as to whose case it is. The procedure will fail if there is nobody to make the case for the EMRO, and nobody of whom to ask questions. Therefore, it is strongly recommended that the case for the EMRO be presented by the licensing service, which can and should be represented. To square the procedural circle, the licensing service should make a representation during the prescribed period, which will give them rights of appearance in a capacity independent of that of the adjudicating committee.

40.54 A further difficulty, however, is how to handle a multiplicity of opponents to the scheme. In most licensing hearings, it is possible to persuade objectors to unite and speak with one voice. This is not likely to be the situation in relation to EMROs. Some operators may support the EMRO. Others may support it but for a different area or different hours. Others may consider that the EMRO should have a 'hole' in it to exclude them. Others may say that the whole problem is caused by a particular bar which should therefore be dealt with individually, to prevent collective suffering. The authority has no power to corral them into single representation and to do so would in any event be unproductive. The authority will therefore have to consider whether to try to hear everybody at once, or to list different parts of the area, or different issues, or different operators, in separate sessions. This will take some considerable organisation to ensure that all view points are heard in an efficient manner.

Doughnutting and emmentaling

40.55 May a party submit that the EMRO should exclude their individual premises? Or are they restricted to saying that the EMRO is entirely inappropriate and so should not be progressed?

40.56 The answer to the question turns on whether an area with a gap in its midst is still an area. It is submitted that it is. Just as the Vatican City is not part of Rome but Rome is still an area, so an EMRO area with premises excised is still an area. It would be absurd if premises on the edge of an area could be excised to make a smaller area but premises in the midst could not.

The Home Office appears to agree. In its Guidance it states:

---

[26] See Licensing Act 2003 (Hearings) Regulations 2005, Schedule 3.

'16.4 An EMRO can apply to the whole or part of the licensing authority's area. The area may, for example, comprise a single floor of a shopping complex or exclude premises which have clearly demonstrated to the licensing authority that the licensable activities carried on there do not contribute to the problems which form the basis for the proposed EMRO.'

40.57 This can be viewed in a different way with similar results. Imagine the EMRO comprises only two venues. One of them wishes to come to the hearing to say that it creates no problems whatsoever and all the problems stream from the competitor venue, which should be reviewed before the blunt instrument of an EMRO is used to destroy the trade of compliant premises. Undoubtedly it is entitled to say that. If that can be said where there are only two proposed venues, why should it not be said when there are 200?

40.58 This approach is also supported by the extract from the regulatory impact assessment cited at para 40.15 above. This plainly contemplates that innocent premises can plead for exclusion in a 'doughnutting' manoeuvre.

40.59 If it is right that one premises may be excluded, then it must follow that more than one premises may be excluded, so that an EMRO is 'Emmentaled'.

40.60 While this process was not debated in Parliament, it is a logical corollary of the power to designate areas. The Act does not require that the innocent shall be swept up with the guilty. There is power to define the EMRO area, and there is no reason why it should not exclude the innocent. Indeed, by retaining a small number of well-performing premises, the authority may avoid problems of mass exodus at fixed terminal hours which so preoccupied the Labour Government when the Licensing Act 2003 was being conceived.

40.61 Therefore, the committee hearing can and should receive evidence that individual premises should be excluded from the EMRO.

(6) Decision-making

40.62 Following the hearing, the committee must consider whether it is appropriate to make the EMRO. However, section 172C prevents the making of an EMRO which is not for the area (or for the days or for periods) specified in the proposed order which was advertised. Therefore, if it is not satisfied, for example, that the EMRO area should include a particular wine bar or cinema bar, then there should not be an EMRO. The logic of section 172C is easy to discern. If the EMRO is permitted to grow over the consultation draft EMRO, people will be affected who have not been able to make representations. If it is allowed to shrink then those happy with it as proposed will not be allowed to voice their objections at its shrinking. Therefore the EMRO must proceed as advertised or not at all.

40.63   As the Guidance states,[27] in the event that the authority considers that there should be a different EMRO to that advertised, it should start the whole procedure again.

40.64   However all of this, of course, is not the decision of the licensing committee. The committee only hears the representations. It will be recalled that the actual decision has to be made by the full council. This poses certain challenges.

40.65   First, regulation 26 of the Hearings Regulations provide that the authority must make its determination within the period of ten working days beginning with the day or the last day on which the hearing was held. This is not understood correctly in the Guidance, which supposes that this means that the licensing committee has to come to its decision in that time, and that the committee's 'determination must be put to the full council for its final decision.'[28] This is not so. The licensing committee does not make a determination but a recommendation. The only party able to make a decision is the full council. Plainly, it will pose a serious challenge to authorities to finesse their procedures to enable the full council to meet and make a decision within ten days of the last day of the hearing.

40.66   Second, in order for this to occur, the licensing committee will need to come to its view and then will need to express that view in a report which will have to be published in time as part of the full council's agenda papers. In cases where one local authority committee is making recommendations to another, it is essential that a full and fair report is given of all of the points which have been made: *R v Birmingham City Council ex parte Quietlynn*.[29] Given the plethora of potentially relevant matters, the licensing committee will need to allocate time to think, conclude and produce a report in a very short space of time.

40.67   The options open to the full council are as stated above. It may allow the EMRO to proceed. It may decide that it should not proceed. Or it may decide that a modified EMRO should be published and the procedure should start again.

(7) Publication of EMRO

40.68   Section 172C of the Act requires the EMRO to be published in the prescribed form and manner. This is particularised in regulation 14 of the

27   Para 16.19.
28   Para 16.20.
29   (1985) 83 LGR 461, 491.

Regulations which requires the authority within seven days of making the EMRO to send notice of it to all affected persons to publish it on its website and to display it in its area for 28 days.[30]

G APPEAL AGAINST AN EMRO

40.69 There is no appeal against an EMRO. Any challenge would have to be brought by way of judicial review, for which see Chapter 20 (Challenging Licensing Decisions).

40.70 There would obviously be a great incentive for commercial operators, banding together, to challenge EMROs, with some of the procedural and substantive issues canvassed in this chapter being candidates for debate.

H VARIATION AND REVOCATION OF EMROS

40.71 The Guidance[31] advises monitoring the effectiveness of an EMRO to ensure that it continues to be appropriate for the promotion of the licensing objectives. It also recommends setting out the policy in relation to reviewing EMROs in its statement of licensing policy.

40.72 The variation or revocation of an EMRO requires the same process as is required for making the EMRO in the first place.[32] An authority should bear that in mind in deciding whether to embark on the process at all. An alternative would be for the authority to make an EMRO for a limited period so that at the end of its shelf life it simply dies. The authority might prefer to take this course where it wishes to treat the EMRO as a limited-life intervention or an experiment rather than a long term palliative.

I USING EMROS

40.73 As the Guidance correctly observes, an EMRO is a powerful tool.[33]

40.74 On the plus side, it may be an effective tool for dealing with localised issues, such as cumulative impact, particularly bearing in mind that cumulative impact is not a proper ground for review of licences.[34] It may also provide protection to residential communities where they are juxtaposed with night time leisure environments. It is, unlike the levy (for example), a

---

[30] The Licensing Act 2003 (Early Morning Alcohol Restriction Orders) Regulations 2012, reg 14.
[31] Para 16.23.
[32] Licensing Act 2003, s 172D.
[33] Para 16.8.
[34] Guidance para 13.36.

targeted remedy in that it can be focused on the most problematic times and areas. Certain options are set out in section B above.

40.75   On the minus side, EMROs risk a serious cluster of effects. First, they may well drive the largest venues, which tend to be nightclubs operating to late hours, to the wall. Second, if they do so, they will produce knock-on effects for all the economic activity which feeds from or is parasitic upon that late night activity, including, for example, bars, restaurants, cinemas, door supervisors, bar staff, the taxi trade and so forth. The potential is that by excising the late night venues, the town centre is sent into a spiral of decline.

40.76   Third, the EMRO has the potential to drive trade into local high streets abutting residential suburbs or, worse still, into neighbouring boroughs, thus driving investment from the borough. Fourth, it could produce a situation whereby all venues in the town centre close simultaneously, creating problems for the emergency services and transport providers in dealing with them, precisely the situation which the Licensing Act 2003 was designed to resolve.

40.77   Fifth, the bureaucracy involved in EMROs is substantial, and certainly far beyond anything that was contemplated in the Government's consultation of 2010.

40.78   Sixth, the potential for legal challenge, particularly from large operators who stand to lose very large investments, even being locked into leases for premises they are unable to operate economically, is significant.

J   CONCLUSION: A LOCAL RESPONSIBILITY DEAL

40.79   The careful reader will have discerned certain misgivings in this chapter as to the utility of the EMRO. To place a curfew on a town centre, or indeed any part of it, is not a measure to be taken lightly, and to do so carries a large number of risks, costs and detrimental consequences, not all of which will be possible to foresee or control. As such, it is concluded that an authority ought to embark on the EMRO process only with the very greatest of care and with its eyes wide open.

40.80   An alternative which is commended is this. In areas where the licensing objectives are not being achieved, the authority may summon the relevant operators to the table. They may be asked to agree what the problems are, and also what the baseline data are, eg in terms of alcohol-related crime and disorder. They may be told that they may work together and with the full support of the authorities for a given period of time in order to reduce the problems to an agreed level. If they do not succeed in doing so, then the 'nuclear' options of EMROs and late night levies will be taken. This might be termed a local responsibility deal, which places a strong onus on the industry locally to respond to local concerns. Where this is warranted, it is considered to be a better option than reaching for the nuclear trigger in the first instance.

41

Area closure orders

If you do not put that knife this instant in your pocket, I promise, upon my honour, you shall hang at the next assizes.

Conversation in the Admiral Benbow
Robert Louis Stevenson: *Treasure Island*

A INTRODUCTION

41.01 Part 8 of the Licensing Act 2003 contains two separate powers under which licensed premises can be closed temporarily. Under section 160 a magistrates' court, acting on the application of the police, can make an order requiring all licensed premises situated at or near a place of disorder (or expected disorder) to close for up to 24 hours. This is a magistrates' closure order for premises in an identified area, and is the subject of this chapter.

41.02 In addition, under section 161, the police can make an order requiring a particular licensed premises to close for up to 24 hours on the ground that there is (or is likely imminently to be) disorder on the premises, or in the vicinity of and related to them. Alternatively, the premises can be closed on the ground that a public nuisance is being caused by noise coming from the premises. This is a police closure order for identified premises, which is dealt with in Chapter 43 (Licensing Act Closures).

41.03 It would be wrong to see these powers as the sole weapons for police to deal with anti-social behaviour, actual or prospective. They are among a wide range of powers canvassed in this book, and many that are not, including the power to deal with myriad crimes associated with violence, disorder and drunkenness.

41.04 Within that context, the powers of closure detailed in Part 8 of the Act can be read, to a certain extent, as supplemental to those powers already in place. They enable the police to clamp down on alcohol-related disorder before it occurs. The powers are specific, in that they are targeted at the licensing trade, and seek to bring the trade within the scope of police powers to combat the anti-social behaviour which can result from its operation. Whilst the powers should not be used to exact punishment on poorly run licensed premises,[1] the necessary direct effect of the exercise of those powers is that licensed premises, and not the people involved in the disorder, will incur a tangible loss.

B AREA CLOSURE ORDERS

41.05 It is worth noting that magistrates have had the power to close down public houses in the event of major public disorder for many years. For example, in a Home Office circular dated 17 August 1911,[2] police authorities were reminded of the power then contained in section 63 of the Licensing (Consolidation) Act 1910 enabling:

> 'any two Justices of the Peace acting for any county or place where any riot or tumult happens, or is expected to happen, to order every holder of a justices' licence in or near the place where the riot or tumult happens, or is expected to happen, to close his premises during any time which the Justices may order'.

41.06 If the police were of the opinion that the closure of licensed premises would be useful in those circumstances, they were encouraged to notify the Justices and ask them to consider using their powers. More recently, section 188 of the Licensing Act 1964 contained a more formal version of the same power. The power under section 160 of the 2003 Act is the modernised version of this provision, operating in a similar way but with some modifications.

41.07 Under section 160, an application can only be made by a police officer of the rank of superintendent or above, and it is only when that application is made that the magistrates' power of closure is engaged.[3] In order for the closure order to be made, the magistrates must be satisfied that such an order is necessary to prevent disorder.[4] The burden of proof plainly lies with the police, and it is tempting to read this part as requiring a standard of proof on the balance of probabilities. However, it may be that the consideration does not involve a standard of proof at all, but requires the exercise of judgment or evaluation by the magistrates.

41.08 Although it is envisaged that the power under section 160 will most commonly be used when there is 'expected to be' disorder, ie at a point in

---

1   Guidance, para.11.15
2   75 JPN 402.
3   Section 160(2).
4   Section 160(3).

the future; subsection (1) also allows an order to be made when the disorder is actually occurring. In anticipation of this, constables can use 'such force as may be necessary' to close premises ordered to be closed.[5] The order itself will have an effect on all premises for which a premises licence and temporary event notice is in place.[6]

41.09 The order is limited in two ways. It is limited geographically to those premises situated 'at or near' the place of the disorder or expected disorder, and limited temporally in that the premises can only be closed for a period up to 24 hours.

41.10 Compliance with the order is ensured by the creation of an offence of knowingly keeping (or allowing to be kept) open any premises to which an order relates, during the period of the order.[7] The offence can only be committed by managers of premises, premises licence holders, designated premises supervisors and, where a temporary event notice is in place, the premises user, as appropriate.[8]

41.11 There is no appeal against an area closure order.

C USE OF AREA CLOSURE ORDERS

41.12 The area closure order is a very limited intervention – requiring closure for 24 hours at most, to be used in serious cases where disorder is expected. The evidence of such prospective disorder may well be intelligence-based, and the disorder itself, or even the expected protagonists, may not yet have materialised. There is no necessity that the licensed premises themselves are considered to be the potential source or even place of disorder. But there must be at least a reason why the disorder is less likely, or is more likely to be managed, if the order is made. For example, the police may fear that disorder may be fuelled by the ready availability of alcohol.

41.13 The kind of events which might occasion such an order are football matches and political marches or demonstrations. The police would obviously be sensitive to the issues which may arise from a mass closure of premises, and ensure that the order is genuinely necessary.

41.14 A number of practical points arise:

• First, it is not clear how the area will be defined, and in that light the wording of the Act seems ambiguous. On the one hand, the heading to

---

[5] Section 160(7).
[6] Premises with club premises certificates remain unaffected by any order because of the rigorous criteria for qualification and restricted access to members of the public (as guests of members only).
[7] Licensing Act 2003, s 160(4).
[8] Licensing Act 2003, s 160(5).

the section reads 'Closure of premises in an *identified area*' (emphasis added), but the section itself allows for premises to be closed which are 'at or near' the place of the disorder and does not require the police to define an area. Where a football fixture is the source of the disorder, the area might be defined by marking a half-mile radius from the stadium. However, it is submitted that a more accurate way to define the area would be to designate the roads or places involved and even include a list of the licensed premises affected. The provision is designed to cover those premises 'at or near the place of the disorder', and the place of disorder might also cover the local transport station (and so the licensed premises there) although some distance from the stadium.

- Second, unlike section 161, there is no equivalent express provision for the cancellation of the order where the basis for it is removed. As such, even more emphasis is placed on the application, the evidence on which it is based, and the real necessity for the order to prevent disorder. In the circumstances, it is submitted that it would be very rare for the need for an order to vanish after it has been made such that the police would be content for the order to be withdrawn.

- Third, the previous point raises the question of timing. It is clear from the above that the application should be made only when the police are confident that they have good evidence, and this may mean that the application is delayed. On the other hand, all of the licensed premises affected by any order will have to be informed that an order has been obtained, and an early notification may save them some financial loss.

- Fourth, whenever possible, the police should initially seek voluntary agreement to closure. This may meet the point on timing. As soon as the intelligence is received, the police should inform licensees of their intentions. It is only if voluntary closure is not achieved that the police should consider making the application. As soon as practicable after the application is granted, the licensees should be informed of the existence of the order.[9]

D CONCLUSION

41.15 Much of the successful work around the alcohol economy depends on partnership between police and local operators. In that context, the use of area closure orders is likely as a matter of practice to be a weapon of last resort. For when use of the power is justified, which will not be often, one would expect venue operators to close their doors willingly at the behest of the police. Where, however, its use is needed, it is an important tool for the protection of communities.

---

[9]   Thereby laying the foundation for the mental element of the offence under s 160(4) to be proved.

Premises

When you have lost your inns, drown your empty selves, for you will have lost the last of England

Hillaire Belloc, *The Four Men*

Reviews

Just at the crowded hour one night, the door opened and a man entered
with the quiet blue uniform and peaked cap of the mine police ... 'A
straight whiskey; for the night is bitter,' said the police officer. 'I don't
think we have met before, Councillor.'

Sherlock Holmes: *The Valley of Fear*
Sir Arthur Conan Doyle

A   Introduction 42.01
B   Ordinary review 42.06
C   Summary review 42.29
D   Use of reviews 42.52

A INTRODUCTION

42.01   As the Guidance states,[1] the procedures contained in sections 51–53
of the Licensing Act 2003 to allow a premises licence to be reviewed
represent a key protection to the community where problems associated with
the licensing objectives are occurring. The Act permits responsible authorities[2] or other persons, wherever they happen to live or work, to apply for
review of the premises licence, which could ultimately lead to the revocation
of the premises licence. Equivalent provisions for clubs are set out in
sections 87–89 of the Act, to which reference may be made. In this chapter,
the focus is on premises licences, which are the subject of the overwhelming
majority of reviews. Home Office statistics indicate that only 1% of reviews
concern club premises certificates.

42.02   Further, the Violent Crime Reduction Act 2006 inserted into the
2003 Act a power for the police to apply for a summary review of premises
licences, an expedited process which also carries with it a power to request
that interim steps (including closure of the premises) be imposed pending the
determination of that review.

---

[1]   Para 11.1.
[2]   Section 13(4).

42.03   The wide-ranging power to review a premises licence was at the heart of the aspiration that the 2003 Act would provide for 'light-touch bureaucracy'[3] with a presumption that applications for new licences would be granted (or varied) unless it could be shown that to do so would prejudice the licensing objectives. A power to review the licence if it transpired that the objectives were being prejudiced by the operation of the premises was seen as a central safeguard built in to that new approach.

42.04   It was also at the heart of the aspiration that the Act would usher in a new era of better community engagement. Introducing the Licensing Bill during the second reading debate in the House of Lords, Baroness Blackstone, the Minister of State DCMS, drew attention to the proposal that local residents should better influence the licensing process. She said:

> 'Our plans to enable local residents to make representations about any applications for new or varied licences will give them a greater say than ever before in licensing decisions. We have gone further still. Local residents and businesses, as well as expert bodies, will have the power to request that the licensing authority review existing licences where problems arise. Such a review could result in the modification of the licence, its suspension, or, ultimately, its revocation.'[4]

42.05   This was a departure from the previous regime whereby the only opportunity to determine whether a licence should continue in force (or with modifications) arose on renewal unless, in the case of a justices licence, application was made for revocation, which was described in the White Paper preceding the publication of the Licensing Bill as 'the final deterrent'. It was, however, like the final nuclear deterrent, much vaunted but practically never used. This 'all or nothing' approach was to be replaced with a more flexible, responsive suite of powers that better allowed participation in the conversation about the operation of a licence by those people most affected by it.

B   ORDINARY REVIEW

42.06   Where a premises licence has effect, a responsible authority[5] or any other person may apply to the relevant licensing authority for a review of the licence, where they have concerns relating to any of the licensing objectives.

42.07   The application must be made in writing and in the prescribed form, but there is no prescribed fee. The form requires the applicant to give grounds for requesting the review and any supporting information. It also requires the applicant to mention any previous representations he may have made in relation to the premises in question.

---

3   Original (July 2004) Guidance issued pursuant to s 182 of the Licensing Act 2003, para 5.99.
4   Hansard, HL Debate, 26 November 2002, col 642.
5   Licensing Act 2003, s 13(4).

42.08 The grounds for review must be relevant to one or more of the licensing objectives; and the licensing authority may reject any ground if it is satisfied that it is not relevant. Further, in the case of an application for review made other than by a responsible authority, any ground that is 'frivolous' or 'vexatious' may be rejected.

42.09 Further, if a ground for review made other than by a responsible authority is considered to be 'repetitious' (ie identical or substantially similar to a ground for review or a representation previously made and considered in relation to applications concerning the same premises licence, unless a reasonable time has elapsed since that previous representation was made) then it too may be rejected by the licensing authority.

42.10 The Act does not give any further indication of what a reasonable time may be. However, the Guidance states:

> '11.13 Licensing authorities are expected to be aware of the need to prevent attempts to review licences merely as a further means of challenging the grant of the licence following the failure of representations to persuade the licensing authority on an earlier occasion. It is for licensing authorities themselves to judge what should be regarded as a reasonable interval in these circumstances. However, it is recommended that more than one review originating from a person other than a responsible authority in relation to a particular premises should not be permitted within a 12 month period on similar grounds save in compelling circumstances or here it arises following a closure order.'

42.11 The Guidance is understandable so far as it goes. However, it does not deal with a review brought on the same grounds as a representation opposing the original grant of a premises licence. If a local resident unsuccessfully opposes a licence on grounds of prospective nuisance but, as soon as the premises opens, their fears prove justified, it would be a harsh exercise of the discretion which ruled out their representation on the grounds that a reasonable interval had not elapsed. To take a more extreme example, what if the licensee, permitted to provide regulated entertainment, did so without any control on the noise output of the instruments and with the windows wide open? Would it then be said that a neighbour had to wait 12 months before bringing a review? The answer is plainly no. What is reasonable must always be judged in the circumstances of the case.

42.12 So far as reviews by responsible authorities are concerned, the Guidance advises that reviews are best brought after early warnings that the premises are heading towards a review unless their promotion of the licensing objectives improves. It states:

> '11.10 Where authorised persons and responsible authorities have concerns about problems identified at premises, it is good

practice for them to give licence holders early warning of their concerns and the need for improvement, and where possible they should advise the licence or certificate holder of the steps they need to take to address those concerns. A failure by the holder to respond to such warnings is expected to lead to a decision to apply for a review. Co-operation at a local level in promoting the licensing objectives should be encouraged and reviews should not be used to undermine this co-operation.'

42.13 In *R (Harpers Leisure International Limited) v Chief Constable of Surrey*,[6] the licensee claimed that the police had brought the review precipitately and in breach of its own policies, and that therefore the licensing authority should have stayed the review as an abuse of process. The High Court held that as a matter of construction of the Act, the authority had no such implied power, and that if there was to be a challenge to the decision to bring the review, then it should be brought against the police in the High Court. Charles J also pointed to the informal nature of the review proceedings, which is intended to eschew legal arguments of this nature:

'28. Further, and to my mind of importance, is that, albeit that the process put in place has a number of formal aspects, at heart, as demonstrated by the provision that the proceedings should take place by reference to a discussion promoted by the sub-committee, and as argued on behalf of the second defendant, the process is intended to be one which has significant areas of informality, an investigatory aspect, and one in which the position of the licence holders is protected by the provisions relating to an appeal and a stay which would fall to be governed by the process adopted in the Magistrates' Court and a stay pending the appeal.'

42.14 In keeping with the scheme of the legislation, and the central importance ascribed to providing the opportunity for participation in the licensing process, the Act (and accompanying Regulations) set out a detailed framework for advertising the application. The applicant for review must give notice of his application to each responsible authority and to the holder of the premises licence in question, which requirement is satisfied by giving them a copy of the application together with any supporting documentation on the same day as the application is given to the licensing authority. The licensing authority must then advertise the review by displaying prominently a notice in the prescribed format[7] or near the site of the premises where the public can conveniently read it from the exterior of the premises. Further provisions apply where the premises concerned covers an area of more than 50 metres square. A notice of the review must also be displayed at the offices of the licensing authority, and on the website of that authority (if the

6   [2009] EWHC 2160 (Admin).
7   The detailed requirements of the prescribed form are contained the Licensing Act 2003 (Premises Licences and Club Premises Certificates) Regulations 2005, reg 38.

authority has a website). The notices must be displayed for at least 28 consecutive days starting on the day after the day on which the application was given to the authority. In certain magistrates' courts dealing with appeals, failures to advertise the original application for review strictly in accordance with the requirements are being treated as fatal, given that section 52, which provides for determination of the application, is apparently only triggered where there has been full compliance.[8]

42.15   The notice must state the address of the premises, the dates between which representations may be made in respect of the application by interested parties and responsible authorities, the grounds of the application for review, the place where the register of the licensing authority is kept and where the grounds for the review may be inspected (including the website address if applicable), and a warning that it is an offence knowingly to make a false statement in connection with an application, and the maximum fine applicable for such an offence.

42.16   The right to make representations (which must be relevant to one or more of the licensing objectives) in response to or in relation to the application for review is extended to interested parties, responsible authorities and the holder of the premises licence. Any such representations must be made in writing (which includes by e-mail) to the licensing authority at any point during the 28-day period beginning with the day on which the application was first advertised.

42.17   Any determination by the licensing authority that any representation is frivolous, vexatious or repetitious must be notified to the maker of that representation, with reasons. There is no avenue of appeal provided in the Act against such a determination; judicial review is likely to be the only available route.

42.18   The review is to be determined by the holding of a hearing to consider the application and any relevant representations. Unlike the provisions relating to applications for new premises licences or variations, there is no provision permitting the review to be determined without a hearing where all parties agree. The wording of section 52 is mandatory and apparently clear: a hearing must be held even if the parties to the review agree on the appropriate outcome.

42.19   Otherwise the procedural rules in respect of the conduct of hearings[9] apply. Reference may be made to Chapter 21 (Best Practice in Licensing Hearings).

---

[8]   See Licensing Act 2003, s 52(1).

[9]   The Licensing Act 2003 (Hearings) Regulations 2005 and the Licensing Act 2003 (Hearings) (Amendment) Regulations 2005.

42.20 In particular, the focus of the hearing (and the sub-committee's approach) should be to consider in the light of the evidence before it whether it is appropriate to take steps to ensure that the licensing objectives are promoted. Because reviews are often the result of incidents where it is alleged (at least) that something has gone wrong, the focus on the future is important: what steps should be taken to ensure that the licensing objectives will not be prejudiced (again) in the future?

42.21 To that end, although the role of the authority on review is not to impose a punishment, in cases concerning crime and disorder it is appropriate to consider, as a part of the raft of factors to be taken into account, the deterrent effect of any steps imposed – see *R (Bassetlaw District Council) v Worksop Magistrates' Court.*[10] Where the alleged events leading to the review include criminal behaviour to which criminal proceedings are directed, it will rarely be appropriate to adjourn the review pending the resolution of those proceedings.[11] The Guidance suggests that in certain categories of case, where the premises have been used to further crime, revocation might be seriously considered, even in the first instance.[12]

42.22 The authority may, at the conclusion of the hearing, take any of the following steps as it considers appropriate for the promotion of the licensing objectives:

(1)   modify the conditions of the licence (including the hours permitted);
(2)   exclude a licensable activity from the scope of the licence;
(3)   remove the designated premises supervisor;
(4)   suspend the licence for a period not exceeding three months; and/or
(5)   revoke the licence.

42.23 Any modification of the conditions of the licence (1 above) or exclusion of one or more licensable activities from the scope of the licence (2 above) may be imposed for a fixed period, so long as that period does not exceed three months.

42.24 It is important to recall that the authority is not obliged to take any steps at all. If it does not consider any steps appropriate, then no steps should be taken. Obviously, no steps should be taken if the case is simply not made out, or proves to be have been trivial or a one-off lapse in management. But there will be other cases in which no steps need to be taken. One of the benefits of the review procedure is that it gives clear notice to premises licence holders of the community's and the responsible authorities' concerns. A well-advised licensee will do all it can to rectify these matters before the case reaches the licensing sub-committee. Where it has done so, and it is not

---

[10]   [2008] WLR(D) 350. Deterrence is also mentioned in Guidance at para 11.23.
[11]   See Guidance, para 11.25. See also *R v Derby Licensing Justices, ex parte Black* (15 December 1995, unreported).
[12]   Paragraphs 11.27–11.28.

considered proportionate to lock in those improvements by condition, then the authority may choose to deal with matters through a simple warning. The Guidance acknowledges that this may be a suitable quietus:

> '11.17 The licensing authority may decide that the review does not require it to take any further steps appropriate to promote the licensing objectives. In addition, there is nothing to prevent a licensing authority issuing an informal warning to the licence holder and/or to recommend improvement within a particular period of time. It is expected that licensing authorities will regard such informal warnings as an important mechanism for ensuring that the licensing objectives are effectively promoted and that warnings should be issued in writing to the licence holder.'

42.25 A decision on the review must be reached within five working days of the hearing, and must be notified forthwith to the applicant for review, the holder of the premises licence, any person who made relevant representations and the chief officer of police for the relevant area. The notification of the determination must include reasons for the decision, and a statement of the right of appeal to a magistrates' court against the determination.

42.26 The importance of giving comprehensive reasons cannot be over-stated. In *R (on the application of Hope and Glory Public House Ltd) v City of Westminster Magistrates' Court*[13] the Court of Appeal upheld the principle arising from a previous case[14] to the effect that on appeal, the decision of the licensing authority on a review should not be lightly reversed, and should only be reversed where the appellate court is satisfied that the decision of the licensing authority was wrong. In assessing whether that decision was 'wrong', the appellate court will wish to consider carefully the reasons given for the decision. The authority that does not fully reason its conclusions will find itself seriously disadvantaged on appeal. Where draconian steps are taken, the authority will be well advised to explain why lesser steps are not considered appropriate.

42.27 The authority should also have regard to the wider legislative context arising from section 17 of the Crime and Disorder Act 1998 and the need to do all it reasonably can to reduce crime and disorder[15] and the proportionality requirements in the Human Rights Act 1998[16] and the Legislative and Regulatory Reform Act 2006.[17]

[13] [2011] EWCA Civ 31.
[14] *Stepney BC v Joffe* [1949] 1 KB 599.
[15] See further Chapter 25 (The Crime and Disorder Act 1998).
[16] See further Chapter 27 (Human rights).
[17] See further Chapter 29 (The legislative and regulatory reform act 2006).

42.28 The determination does not have effect until 21 days after the notification of the decision has been given; or, where an appeal against the decision is lodged, until the final disposal of that appeal.

C SUMMARY REVIEW

42.29 By the Violent Crime Reduction Act 2006, and with effect from 1 October 2007, a new power to seek 'summary review' of a premises licence was inserted into the Act as section 53A. It only applies to premises licenses which authorise the sale of alcohol, and is a power only available to the police. It is a regime designed to provide an urgent and 'quick' process in circumstances of serious crime, serious disorder or both. It should be recognised that it provides for draconian powers which can have a heavy impact on operators in the licensed trade.

42.30 The provisions are supported by non-statutory guidance published by the Home Office.[18] This expresses the purpose of this regime as allowing:

> '... a quick process for attaching interim conditions to a licence and a fast track licence review when the police consider that the premises concerned is associated with serious crime or serious disorder (or both).'

42.31 Where a senior member (of the rank of superintendent or higher) of the police force considers that a licensed premises (authorised to sell alcohol) is associated with serious crime, disorder or both, he may issue a certificate to that effect. In such circumstances the chief officer of police for the local area may apply to the licensing authority for a summary review of the licence.

42.32 Serious crime is given the same meaning as in section 81 of the Regulation of Investigatory Powers Act 2000. Essentially, the conduct involved must be such that a person who is at least 21 and of good character could expect to be sentenced to at least three years in prison, or it must involve the use of violence, result in substantial financial gain or be conduct by a large number of persons in pursuit of a common purpose. The effect of this is that any single act of violence could trigger summary review, even if it does not even merit a custodial sentence, let alone one of three years for a person of good character. Serious disorder is not defined, and there is clearly an element of subjectivity in the definition. It is to be hoped that these provisions are applied judiciously so that summary reviews are not brought except in serious, urgent cases.

42.33 Further, even where there has been serious criminal conduct, this does not automatically mean that summary review, as opposed to an ordinary review, or no review at all, should be brought. It should, it is submitted, only

---

[18]   'Section 53A Licensing Act 2003, Summary Review Guidance' (2012).

be brought where the police consider that there is a reason why expedition and interim steps are genuinely necessary in this case, eg because of a risk of repetition.

42.34 The section 53A guidance supports the judicious approach. It states:

'2.4 In deciding whether to sign a certificate, the senior officer will want to consider the following (as applicable):
- The track record of the licensed premises concerned and whether the police have previously had cause to give advice about serious criminal or disorderly conduct (or the likelihood of such conduct) attributable to activities taking place on the premises – it is not expected that this power will be used as a first response to a problem.
- The nature of the likely crime and/or disorder – is the potential incident sufficiently serious to warrant using this power?
- Should an alternative power be deployed? Is the incident sufficiently serious to warrant use of the powers in sections 161 to 165 of the 2003 Act to close the premises? Or could the police trigger a standard licence review to address the problem? Alternatively, could expedited reviews be used in conjunction with other powers (for example, modifying licence conditions following the use of a closure power).
- What added value will use of the expedited process bring? How would any interim steps that the licensing authority might take effectively address the problem?

2.5 It is recommended that these points are addressed in the chief officer's application to the licensing authority. In particular, it is important to explain why other powers or actions are not considered to be appropriate. It is up to the police to decide whether to include this information in the certificate or in section 4 of the application for summary review. The police will also have an opportunity later to make representations in relation to the full review.'

42.35 Upon receipt of an application, the licensing authority must do a number of things in a short time. Firstly, it must arrange for a hearing of the application to be held within 28 days of the receipt of the application. It must, on the day after the day on which the application is received, advertise the summary review and invite representations upon it, and do so for seven consecutive days, by notice and on the authority's website. The notice must set out that any representations should be received within ten working days of the advertisement appearing. Within 48 hours (not to include non-working days) of receiving the application the authority must also give a copy of it to premises licence holder and to each responsible authority.

42.36   Also within 48 hours (not including non-working days) of receiving the application, the authority must consider whether it is necessary to take interim steps pending determination of the review of the premises licence. The steps available are to:

(1)   modify the conditions on the licence;
(2)   exclude the sale by retail of alcohol (or other licensable activities) from the licence;
(3)   remove the designated premises supervisor; and/or
(4)   suspend the licence.

42.37   The authority is not required to give the premises licence holder concerned an opportunity to make representations about interim steps prior to any decision to impose them, and there is no requirement that a hearing be held before such an imposition.[19] In practice, some authorities do put the licensee on notice and permit him to attend. This may sometimes have the salutary effect of obviating the need for further interim hearings, and in any event in the interests of justice there is no good reason for excluding the licensee if he can get there in time, with or without his representatives.

42.38   If the authority decides to impose one or more of the above interim steps pending the review of the licence, the decision takes effect immediately (or, in practical reality, as soon as the decision is notified to the premises licence holder). It must give immediate notice of any such decision both to the premises licence holder and also to the chief officer of police.

42.39   The premises licence holder, although not entitled to make representations or be heard prior to the imposition of interim steps, may make representations to the authority against those steps. There is no time limit to do so but the fact that the steps are imposed pending the 'full' review after 28 days means that early representations are likely to be the only effective approach. Upon receiving such representations, the authority must hold a hearing within 48 hours (not including non-working days) of such receipt to consider them. 'Advance notice' of the hearing must be given to the premises licence holder and the chief officer of police. At the hearing the authority must consider, in the light of the representations and the certificate issued by the police, whether to withdraw or modify the interim steps imposed.

42.40   There is no right of appeal to a magistrates' court against the outcome of such a hearing. As such, a party aggrieved by the decision will either have to wait until the full review after 28 days, or in more urgent cases apply for judicial review of the decision.

---

[19]   Licensing Act 2003, s 53B.

42.41 Any interim steps imposed (and not withdrawn following a hearing) on the licence will continue to apply 'pending the determination of the summary review'.[20]

42.42 Within 28 days of the application for review, and regardless of whether interim steps are imposed, the authority must hold a hearing to consider the application for a summary review of the licence. The procedural requirements at the hearing mirror those in respect of 'ordinary' reviews. The authority may take such of the following steps as it considers appropriate for the promotion of the licensing objectives:

(1) modify the conditions of the premises licence;
(2) exclude the sale of alcohol (or other licensable activities) from the scope of the licence;
(3) remove the designated premises supervisor;
(4) suspend the licence for a period up to three months; and/or
(5) revoke the licence.

42.43 There is a right of appeal against the decision of a licensing authority on a summary review. Any decision imposed by the authority does not take effect until the expiry of 21 days from notification of the decision; or, if an appeal is lodged against the decision, until that appeal is finally determined.

42.44 The question of whether interim steps continue to have effect pending determination of the appeal has proved controversial. However, in the case of *Chief Constable of Cheshire v Gary Oates*[21] District Judge Knight held that, contrary to what was then said in government guidance, they did not. Interim steps are what they say they are in section 53B: 'Interim steps pending review.' There is no other express provision giving them wider effect, and the fact that they cannot be appealed does not favour a construction which allows them to continue to have effect for many months, regardless of what the final review decision is. Following her judgment, the then Guidance was withdrawn, with the new Guidance omitting all reference to the matter. The District Judge's decision, while of persuasive force only, has not been contradicted by any other judicial dicta and is respectfully submitted to be right.

42.45 Proponents of the opposite view rely on section 53C(2)(c), which provides that the licensing authority must on a summary review 'secure' that from the coming into effect of the decision made on the determination of the review, 'any' interim steps having effect pending that determination cease to have effect. It is not clear in what circumstances any interim steps might have effect pending the coming into effect of that decision (ie between the

---

[20] Licensing Act 2003, s 53B(1).
[21] See Local Government Lawyer, 'Government Guidance on fate of interim steps is wrong, says District Judge' (4 January 2012).

notification of the decision on summary review, and the coming into effect of that decision, for example after an appeal).

42.46   In fact, the section is not easy to understand, and indeed in the *Oates* case the learned District Judge considered that it defied understanding. It is respectfully submitted that such a provision does nothing to displace the prima facie position that interim steps are intended to be just that: interim steps pending determination of the summary review.

42.47   Any other interpretation is liable to produce obviously absurd results. For example, take the case where a suspension is imposed by way of interim steps, but on summary review the authority decides not to impose any further suspension but instead imposes additional conditions. If the premises licence holder appeals against the imposition of those additional conditions, the suspension imposed as an interim step would endure until the determination of the appeal – some months later – despite the considered view of the authority, after a summary review hearing, that no further suspension is necessary. Indeed, in such a situation it might even be an appeal by the police (aggrieved by the failure to impose a further suspension, or insufficiently stringent conditions) that triggered the requirement to remain closed pending their appeal.

42.48   It is acknowledged that an equal and opposite case can be made – ie if a more serious sanction is applied at the full review hearing and then appealed, the licensee may avoid any kind of control until the hearing of the appeal. However, that is arguably inherent in the system. Parliament has similarly provided that, in the case of 'ordinary' reviews, any decision of the authority upon review does not take effect until final determination of any appeal, including, for example, where the decision upon review was to revoke the licence (because to do so was appropriate for the promotion of the licensing objectives). If Parliament had intended a different effect in respect of summary reviews, it can be expected that it would have made express provision to that effect. Even if it had done so, it is likely that it would have been the effect of the final determination on summary review that had immediate effect, not interim steps imposed 'pending' that review.

42.49   Given that a premises licence is a property right, and the imposition of interim steps has the effect of interfering with (or depriving) that property right, both the doctrine of doubtful penalisation[22] and section 3 of the Human Rights Act 1998 (read with article 1 of the First Protocol of the ECHR) require that where there is ambiguity in a provision that deprives a party of a property right or interferes with such a right, the ambiguity should be resolved in favour of the holder of that property right.

---

[22]   See *Methuen-Campbell v Walters* [1979] QB 525 and *Hartnell v Minister of Housing and Local Government* [1965] AC 1134.

42.50 For all of these reasons, the position is submitted to be that interim steps do not have effect pending appeal, but lapse once the summary review is determined; and any steps imposed by the outcome of the summary review have effect once any appeal is finally determined (or when appeal rights expire). This does mean that in some cases, during the period between determination of the summary review and the final determination of an appeal against that outcome, a premises would be entitled to trade without complying either with the interim steps imposed, or the conditions or restrictions imposed as the outcome of the summary review. It must be assumed that Parliament could have legislated to remove this effect had it so wished.

42.51 The solution to this debate is in fact for Parliament to legislate to allow authorities to stipulate that their decision upon review – whether ordinary or summary – has immediate effect, and for courts on appeal to make interim orders varying those steps pending appeal. There is no sign that such legislation is imminent.

D USE OF REVIEWS

42.52 There is no doubt that reviews have been a successful check and balance on the relatively liberal regime introduced by the Licensing Act 2003. They allow everything from the most minor to the most serious matters to be brought to the attention of the licensing authority and for the authority to calibrate its response as appropriate in the individual case. They also have the effect of bringing the relevant stakeholders together in one room so that the most appropriate means of promoting the licensing objectives can be discussed.

42.53 The availability of review is no doubt in and of itself a deterrent or inducement (depending on one's perspective) for some licensees, and the warning of a review by responsible authorities may achieve as much as the actual review itself. Many authorities will meet with licensees to formulate agreed action plans which, if they are not adhered to or do not produce desired effects, will lead on to review proceedings. An action planning approach now has a respectable pedigree, and in many cases will result in effective joint working to eliminate the source of the problem. It also helps focus attention at a senior level in the company.

42.54 The action planning approach is sometimes accompanied by a 'top ten' strategy, whereby all the licensed premises in the area are analysed for their crime and disorder record, which are then called in for the formulation of action plans. The top ten approach is consistent with good regulation, which demands that priority is given to the premises which are most in need of attention.

42.55   However, a sensitive approach is needed to the statistics. If only crude figures are taken, there may be undue focus on premises whose statistics (perhaps because of the wealth of their clientele) are mostly bound up with mobile phone thefts and insufficient focus on those where alcohol-related crime and disorder is a genuine problem. Further, premises with high levels of police call-outs may indicate good management wanting to work with the police rather than a poor premises seeking to bury its mistakes. There is a clear danger that licensees who become aware that every report will be taken down and used in evidence against them will become reluctant to report, which drives a wedge between them and the police, harms partnership working and may endanger the public. Further, a high level of crime and disorder may simply indicate larger premises trading longer hours on seven nights a week. Before premises are castigated for their record, it is always important to compare apples with apples.

42.56   The action planning approach does enable the responsible authority concerned to say that it has tried alternative means before bringing the review, which is more likely to yield a satisfactory result from its perspective, since it denudes the licensee of the argument 'but we never knew'. The practice described is properly in accordance with the Home Office and Institute of Licensing factsheet, 'A Stepped Approach to Achieving Compliance'.[23] However, reviews are not inevitable even when an action plan has failed to produce improvement in outcomes. A series of questions might be asked first, including:

* Why has the action plan failed? Is a better action plan needed?
* Is the management improving/responsive aware of problems.
* Are incidents properly logged/reported/acted upon?
* Is the DPS/management present/contactable/responsive/aware?
* Are the premises members of Pub Watch?
* Is there a culture of compliance?

42.57   Furthermore, a review may also be prevented if the licensee is willing or can be persuaded to accept further conditions on its licence. Where this is the case, an agreement may be reached that the licence will not be reviewed if the licensee applies to incorporate such conditions by way of minor variation.

42.58   If a review does become necessary, it should be brought promptly. Stale evidence is poor evidence, and dilatory conduct may indicate a lack of urgency.

42.59   Licensing sub-committees attach considerable weight, as they ought, to the views of the responsible authorities. Therefore, there is a heavy professional onus on such authorities to put the matter fairly, and to give proper consideration to the remedies which they seek. Such remedies should be directed at the harms to the licensing objectives relied upon, and should

---

[23]   See further Chapter 36 (Introduction).

never be more than a proportionate response. For example, this means focusing on management measures which may reduce harm to the licensing objectives before striking at the business itself through shorter hours or removal of licensable activities. If the response is misjudged, it risks alienating the sub-committee, making its job harder rather than easier, harming relations with the licensee and risking a poor decision and therefore an appeal.

42.60 While reviews are used, they are not over-used by all accounts. For 2011/2012, the Home Office reports[24] that 1100 reviews were completed, with 85% being ordinary reviews and 13% expedited. In 18% of cases, there was revocation, 13% led to suspension, 6% led to no action and the remainder – 63% – led to some kind of intermediate action. This kind of bell curve distribution demonstrates that authorities are using their powers relatively judiciously so as to moderate the activities or the conditions, rather than reaching for the extreme response of revocation in the first instance.

42.61 Provided that authorities and others use their ability to apply for review with some discretion and after due warning, and authorities take care to impose only proportionate steps on licensees, reviews will continue their status as the safety valve of the licensing system.

---

[24] 'Review, Hearings and Appeal, Home Office Statistics' (2012).

43

Licensing Act closures

Shall I not take mine ease in mine inn but I shall have my pocket picked?

Falstaff
King Henry IV Part 1
William Shakespeare

A	Introduction 43.01
B	The procedure 43.04
C	Use of power 43.34

A INTRODUCTION

43.01   Police closure orders were first introduced onto the statute books by section 17 of the Criminal Justice and Police Act 2001, which created the power to close certain licensed premises due to disorder and disturbance. The provisions in section 161 of the Licensing Act 2003 can be seen as replacing and extending[1] those powers.

43.02   Non-statutory guidance to the police on the exercise of the power was published by the Department of Culture, Media and Sport (DCMS) in June 2007[2] and has been carried over to the Home Office website. It remains useful today.

43.03   The police power to close premises immediately is intended as an acute intervention where the circumstances warrant immediate action. In reality, most closures are voluntary rather than statutory, either because the police secure the co-operation of the DPS in closing premises in which there is ongoing disorder, or because the DPS, seeing the writing on the wall, closes them in any event.

---

[1]   The s 17 power included all on-licensed premises under the 1964 Act, thereby excluding off-licences, occasional licences, and registered members clubs from the provisions. The s 161 power covers all premises licences, as well as temporary event notices, and only stops short of club premises certificates.

[2]   'Police Powers to Close Premises under the Licensing Act 2003'.

B THE PROCEDURE

43.04 The procedure for closure consists of a number of steps, which are taken in turn.

Step 1: police order

43.05 The procedure under section 161 may be initiated by a police officer of at least the rank of inspector.[3] While it is good practice for the inspector to attend to make the assessment whether closure is necessary, he does not have to do so, although where he cannot it is important that the full picture is conveyed to him, both because closure is a serious step and because he remains accountable for the decision.[4] Whilst the order must be made by the senior police officer, it may be served by a constable under section 161(5).

43.06 There are, broadly speaking, two situations in which the closure order can be made, and the officer must reasonably believe that one or other exists before acting.[5] The first situation relates to public disorder and the second to public nuisance.

Public disorder

43.07 Under the first situation, the officer must reasonably believe that a number of circumstances exist, namely that:

(1)   there is (or is likely imminently to be) disorder on the premises; or
(2)   there is (or is likely imminently to be) disorder in the vicinity of and related to the premises;

AND (if either (1) or (2) exists)
(3)   the closure of the premises is necessary in the interests of public safety.

43.08 The wording of the provision clearly implies that there should be at least near contemporaneity between the decision to act and the occurrence of disorder or its likely imminence, and this reading also supports the view that the police closure order is a measure to be used in an emergency.

43.09 The way in which the second, alternative, circumstance is framed makes an important point about the principle behind the section. The officer must reasonably believe not just that there is disorder in the vicinity of the premises but that the disorder is related to those premises. That is, there must exist a causal connection between any disorder and the licensed premises. The closure of the premises will therefore be expected directly to

---

[3]   Section 161(8).
[4]   'Police Powers to Close Premises under the Licensing Act 2003' at paras 39–40.
[5]   Section 161(1).

impact on the danger to the public being caused by the disorder. The rationale behind this requirement is presumably that whilst licensees cannot be held accountable for the actions of customers once they are beyond their immediate control, where a causal connection can be shown, licensed premises can be closed as a means of ensuring public safety.

43.10 To the extent that the closure hinges on the occurrence of 'disorder', a word encompassing a broad range of statutory offences, the basis on which an officer can act is quite a broad one. However, the breadth of the term is limited by two important circumstances. The first, as the DCMS guidance points out, is that decisions to close premises will almost always have a seriously damaging commercial impact, and so it is essential that orders are sought only where they are necessary to prevent disorder.[6] The second is that the closure has to be necessary in the interests of public safety. In other words, the Act is contemplating a significant outbreak of disorder before it would be right to exercise discretion to close premises, and a well-founded belief that closure will diminish the disorder or its likelihood.[7]

43.11 This last point assumes some importance in real-life situations. There may be cases where disorder is occurring in large premises but is being contained by door staff and police. An order then to close the premises may result in a large number of disgruntled people who having paid an admission charge and being mid-drink find themselves being put out onto the street. If there are insufficient police and door staff to handle this exceptional situation, the effect of the closure order may be to cause more disorder than it cures. This should be taken into account by the police when deciding whether to make a closure order, as should the question of whether police reinforcements are needed before the order is made.

Public nuisance

43.12 Under the second situation, the officer must reasonably believe that the following, more specific circumstances exist, namely that:

(1) a public nuisance is being caused, and
(2) it is being caused by noise, and
(3) the noise is coming from the premises, and
(4) the closure of the premises is necessary to prevent that nuisance.

43.13 It is of note that (probably for reasons of practicality, and the likely impossibility of being able to know that a noise nuisance was imminent) under this second situation the public nuisance must actually be occurring for the officer to be able to take action. The requirement that the noise is *coming from* the premises provides the causal connection between the

---

6   'Police Powers to Close Premises under the Licensing Act 2003', para 9.
7   'Police Powers to Close Premises under the Licensing Act 2003', para 26.

nuisance and the premises, such that the issuing of the closure order would have a direct impact.

43.14   In both the first and second situations, in determining whether to make the order, the officer is also obliged to have regard to the conduct of the appropriate person[8] in relation to the disorder or disturbance.[9] The police are not, under the section, obliged to take into account the good reputation of a licensee or the fact that premises are well run generally; it is the conduct in relation to the disorder or nuisance that is principally relevant.[10] However, the fact that the manager is known and can be trusted to handle matters may well be a relevant circumstance, albeit not articulated in the Act itself.

43.15   It should be noted that the officer is only required to *have regard to* that conduct, and the fact that a licence holder has acted responsibly does not necessarily mean that the officer must refrain from using the power. Closure, after all, is not a punishment: the overriding question is whether closure is necessary, not whether the licensee has behaved or not.

43.16   The conduct which is of most direct relevance to the decision to make a closure order is, of course, voluntary action by the licensee. The DCMS guidance advises that if there are signs of problems brewing, the police should give early warnings to licensees, including reminding them of the police closure powers. Where they form the view that closure is necessary, there should be an opportunity for voluntary closure before the Sword of Damocles falls. It should, however, be said that even voluntary closure does not make it impossible for the police to serve a closure order, and certainly does not prevent a subsequent application for review.[11]

43.17   Once it is determined that a closure order should be made, the order must be given by a constable to the appropriate person.[12] The order must specify the premises, the period of the closure, the grounds on which it is made and the effect of sections 161–168 of the Act.[13]

---

[8]   That is, the premises licence holder, the designated premises supervisor, the premises user (for temporary event notices), or the manager of the premises as appropriate: Licensing Act 2003, s 171(5).

[9]   Licensing Act 2003, s 161(3) and paras 15–17 of the DCMS guidance.

[10]   'Police Powers to Close Premises under the Licensing Act 2003', para 15.

[11]   'Police Powers to Close Premises under the Licensing Act 2003', paras 18–22.

[12]   Within the meaning of Licensing Act 2003, s 171(5).

[13]   Section 161(4).

43.18 The order will come into force as soon as a constable[14] gives notice of it to the appropriate person[15]. A constable may use 'such force as may be necessary' to close the premises in compliance with the order.[16]

43.19 Although a closure order can last up to 24 hours[17] it can be made for a shorter period. It would not be uncommon for an order to be made up until the normal closing time of the premises, as the DCMS guidance contemplates.[18]

43.20 A person who permits relevant premises to be open in contravention of the order commits an offence.[19] Given that the closure order will have been issued on a single, identified premises the offence is one of strict liability, subject to the defence of reasonable excuse.[20] The burden will be on him to prove the excuse and its reasonableness. The standard of proof is the balance of probabilities.

Step 2: application to magistrates' court

43.21 The making of a closure order sets in train a series of further procedural steps. Following the coming into force of a closure order, the responsible senior police officer must as soon as reasonably practicable apply to the magistrates' court for it to consider the order and any extension of it.[21] The local licensing authority must also be notified of the order, its contents and any application to the magistrates' court. The court must as soon as reasonably practicable after receiving such an application, hold a hearing to consider whether to exercise its powers in relation to the closure order. This part of the procedure is considered further below.

Step 3: extension of police order (optional)

43.22 It should be noted that the senior police officer can extend the closure period for a further period of up to 24 hours where he reasonably believes that the magistrates' court will not have determined whether to exercise its powers in respect of the order by the end of the initial closure

---

14 See para 39 of the DCMS guidance: the senior police officer does not have to be present to authorise service.
15 Licensing Act 2003, s 161(5).
16 Licensing Act 2003, s 169.
17 Licensing Act 2003, s 161(2).
18 Paras 36–37.
19 Licensing Act 2003, s 161(6). For interpretation on the word 'permit', see Chapter 51 Section C (Elements of the offences).
20 The penalties available are also much greater, the maximum fine being £20,000: Licensing Act 2003, s 161(7).
21 Licensing Act 2003, s 164(1).

period[22] – for example over a weekend or bank holiday when courts are not open. The conditions which must be satisfied for the extension to be made are similar to those which must be met for the initial closure order.[23] For the extension to come into force, notice of it must be given before the end of the previous closure period.[24] Apparently, there is no limit to the number of extensions, provided that these requirements are satisfied for each extension.[25]

Step 4: cancellation of order (optional)

43.23   A significant consequential power under section 163 of the Act allows the officer who made the closure order, at any time after the making of the order but before the magistrates' court has determined whether to exercise its own powers (see below), to cancel the closure order at his own discretion.[26] Further, if there comes a time (prior to the magistrates' court hearing) when the officer no longer reasonably believes either that the order is necessary in the interests of public safety (section 161(1)(a)) or that the order is necessary to ensure that no public nuisance is caused (section 161(1)(b)), the officer is obliged to cancel the closure order.[27]

43.24   The existence of this power to cancel the closure order before the magistrates' court gets involved allows the whole review process to be bypassed in certain circumstances. For example, where the disorder about to be caused is a pub brawl, but an isolated incident, it would be open to the police to issue a closure order until the pub closed on that night, and then cancel the order under section 163 when it was no longer necessary, thereby avoiding the necessity for the magistrates' court and licensing authority to consider the matter. It is clearly right that the order should be cancelled as soon as possible when it is no longer needed, and that must be the reasoning behind the power. However, the use of this power may well give rise to the question of whether the order was necessary in the first place. The notion that the power to cancel the order has been used to avoid the involvement and scrutiny of the courts on an order which was unnecessary in the first place will be dispelled by a rigorous application of the necessity test under section 161(1), underpinned by cogent evidence. An officer who makes the order unnecessarily, or leaves it in place longer than necessary, will be abusing his power.

---

[22]   Licensing Act 2003, s 162(1).
[23]   Licensing Act 2003, s 162(2).
[24]   Licensing Act 2003, s 162(4). The notice is given in the same way as the initial closure order (s 162(3)).
[25]   Licensing Act 2003, s 162(1).
[26]   Licensing Act 2003, s 163(1).
[27]   Licensing Act 2003, s 163(2).

Step 5: magistrates' hearing

43.25 As stated above, as soon as reasonably practicable after a closure order comes into force, the officer who made it is obliged both to apply to the magistrates' court for it to consider the order, and to notify the relevant licensing authority of the order.[28] The magistrates' first duty after receiving the application is to determine whether to exercise any of their powers, and they must hold a hearing to consider whether it is appropriate to do so.[29]

43.26 Their powers are to:

(a) revoke the closure order;

(a) order that the premises be closed (or remain closed) until the licensing authority has made its determination on review;

(c) order that the premises be closed (or remain closed) until the licensing authority's determination on review, subject to such exceptions as are specified in the order (for example, remaining open on all nights save for Fridays and Saturdays); or

(d) order that the premises be closed (or remain closed) until the licensing authority's determination on review, subject to such conditions as are specified in the order (for example, only open where two SIA-accredited door supervisors are deployed).

43.27 Where the magistrates are considering the continued closure of the premises, their guiding principles are the same as those for the police: they are required to consider whether closure is necessary in the interests of public safety or to ensure that no public nuisance is caused by noise, respectively.[30]

43.28 There is an express right of appeal from the magistrates' court to the Crown Court for any person aggrieved by the decision.[31] This is rarely if ever exercised.

43.29 A person who permits premises to be open in breach of the magistrates' order without reasonable excuse commits an offence.[32]

Step 6: review

43.30 Once the magistrates' determination has been received, the licensing authority is required to review the premises licence and to reach a determination within 28 days.[33] The provisions for review are identical to those for

---

[28] Licensing Act 2003, s 164.
[29] Licensing Act 2003, s 165.
[30] Licensing Act 2003, s 165(3).
[31] Licensing Act 2003, s 166(1).
[32] Licensing Act 2003, s 165(7). The offence carries a fine of £20,000: s 165(8).
[33] Licensing Act 2003, s 167(1),(2), (3)

review of a premises licence under Part 3 of the Act[34] and reference should be made to Chapter 42 (Reviews). In essence, however, section 167 requires notice to be given to the premises licence holder, and provides for the advertisement of the review. Responsible authorities and other persons may make relevant representations and the authority must hold a hearing to consider the closure order.

43.31 A range of sanctions is available and the authority can:

(a)   modify the conditions of the premises licence;
(b)   exclude a licensable activity from the scope of the licence;
(c)   remove the designated premises supervisor from the licence;
(d)   suspend the licence for a period not exceeding three months; or
(e)   revoke the licence.

43.32 Finally, section 168 makes provision about when the determination takes effect. In general, this will be when the period for appealing against the decision has expired (or when any appeal has been finally determined)[35] – called the 'relevant time'.[36] However, where a premises has been closed (by order of the magistrates' court) pending review by the licensing authority, and upon review the licensing authority decides to take a step short of revocation, the determination takes effect as soon as it is notified.[37] The reasoning behind this exception is relatively clear: where upon review it is considered that it is no longer necessary for the premises to be closed, it would be unjust to require its continued closure pending an appeal against the review (which appeals can take months to determine finally). However, the licensing authority has the power to suspend the effect of its decision in such circumstances, on such terms as it sees fit, until the end of the 'relevant time'.[38] In addition, the magistrates' court has power to suspend the licensing authority's decision (if the licensing authority has not done so) on such terms as it thinks fit, or to cancel or alter the terms of a suspension granted by the licensing authority.[39] The statute does not specify a procedure for such consideration. Presumably, an appellant wishing to have the magistrates consider exercising this power would have to make an application to be heard on it at short notice. The licensing authority, automatically a respondent to the appeal, will be entitled to appear at any such hearing.

43.33 Where the licensing authority decides to revoke the licence upon review following a closure by the magistrates' court, the position is different. The basic position is that in such circumstances the premises must remain closed until the end of the 'relevant time'. But paragraph 18(4) of Schedule 5

---

34   Licensing Act 2003, ss 51–53.
35   Licensing Act 2003, s 168(1).
36   Licensing Act 2003, s 168(2).
37   Licensing Act 2003, s 168(4).
38   Licensing Act 2003, s 168(5).
39   Licensing Act 2003, Sch 5 para 18(3).

provides that in such circumstances, where an appeal against the decision to revoke is made, the magistrates' court may order that the premises may re-open pending the hearing of the appeal, on such conditions as it sees fit.

C USE OF POWER

43.34   As the DCMS guidance indicates,[40] the closure power is only for use where it is genuinely necessary to prevent disorder, and even then it will only normally be necessary if police advice to close voluntarily is rejected.[41] There is sometimes complaint that the premises management feel compelled to close, for if they do not a closure order will be made and it will be said at the subsequent review that the management refused to co-operate. The safe-guard is, and can only be, that officers must use the closure power with real circumspection.

43.35   The guidance also advises that these powers should not be used to drive a wedge between the police and local management, particularly if the latter become reluctant to call the police to deal with incidents for fear of closure. The decision to close the premises should therefore be pre-warned if possible, and the police and management should work hand in hand over the exercise, whether the closure is voluntary or coercive. This advice is very much in step with the good practice set out in 'A Stepped Approach to Achieving Compliance',[42] and is to be commended.

43.36   Home Office statistics show that formal closure is a rarely used option. Only 1% of reviews in 2011/2012 arose as a result of police closures.[43] Clearly this does not account for voluntary closures, but equally it does not suggest that the use of these powers is anything other than moderate.

---

[40]   Para 9.
[41]   Para 20.
[42]   See Chapter 36 (Introduction).
[43]   'Reviews, Hearings and Appeals' (Home Office, 2012).

44

Closure notices

A dark medal of blood had formed itself near the man's head on the tessellated floor. The manager, alarmed by the grey pallor of the man's face, sent for a policeman ... The manager asked repeatedly did no one know who the injured man was or where had his friends gone. The door of the bar opened and an immense constable entered ... The manager at once began to narrate what he knew. The constable, a young man with thick immobile features, listened. He moved his head slowly to right and left and from the manager to the person on the floor, as if he feared to be the victim some delusion. Then he drew off his glove, produced a small book from his waist, licked the lead of his pencil and made ready to indite.

James Joyce, *Grace*

A INTRODUCTION

44.01 The closure notice procedure introduced by the Criminal Justice and Police Act 2001 ('CJPA') gives the police and local authorities power to deal rapidly with premises selling alcohol without licences or in breach of their licences. It does not replace the use of other powers, including review or prosecution, and so may be used alone or as an adjunct to those powers, giving the enforcement agencies a relatively simple extra string to their bow. It has however been misused in recent times, and the purpose of this chapter, as well as setting out the basic principles, is to discuss how and when it is proper to use the power.

B THE POWER

Step 1: service of notice

44.02 The power to serve a closure notice arises where there is or has within the previous 24 hours been:

- unauthorised sale of alcohol
- for consumption on or in the vicinity of the premises.[1]

44.03 'Unauthorised sale' means any supply of alcohol which is made either without an authorisation under the Licensing Act 2003 or in breach of any condition of an authorisation.[2] So the Act bites on criminal operators selling without a licence at all as well as those accused of minor breaches of licence conditions.

44.04 The requirement that the sale be for consumption on or in the vicinity of the premises obviously captures all on-licences. It would capture few if any off-licences, since it is not enough to show that the alcohol was being consumed in the vicinity: it must be shown that the sale was for consumption in the vicinity. It would not suffice that that is the purpose of the consumer: it would have to be the purpose of the seller.

44.05 Where a constable or local authority is satisfied that this has occurred or is occurring then a notice may be served on a person having control of, or responsibility for, the activities carried on at the premises.[3] Provision is also made for service on other occupiers of the building,[4] others having control or responsibility and any person who has an interest in the premises.[5]

The notice served must do three things:

(1) It must specify the alleged use and the grounds for the belief that the conditions for exercise of the power, as set out above, are met.
(2) It must state the effect of section 20, ie that if the unauthorised use does not cease then court proceedings may follow.
(3) It must specify what steps may be taken to ensure that the alleged use ceases or (as the case may be) does not recur.[6]

44.06 In most cases, that will be that. The person served with the notice will bring himself into compliance and there will be no need for the process to continue. In that event, the police or local authority concerned will serve a notice of cancellation on all those originally served, and it has effect when it is served on the first of those recipients.[7] In such cases, the process serves as a written warning that compliance is required.

44.07 Importantly, the notice is just that: a notice. It is not a closure order and certainly does not require the premises to close. Of course, the fact that a notice is served at all means that the police or local authority believes that

---

[1]   CJPA, s 19(1)–(2).
[2]   CJPA, s 28.
[3]   CJPA, s 19(3).
[4]   CJPA, s 19(4).
[5]   CJPA, s 19(5).
[6]   CJPA, s 19(6).
[7]   CJPA, s 19(7)–(9).

an offence is being committed. Once it is served it is hard to see how the recipient could ever claim that they were not aware of the alleged breach, which may go to whether they knowingly allowed the offence to occur,[8] and whether they can run a due diligence defence[9] and it may also affect culpability and therefore sentence. However, all that is the operator's risk. The simple fact is that the notice does not make it obligatory to close.

Step 2: application for closure order

44.08   After waiting seven days (and less than six months) the constable or local authority may apply to a justice of the peace for a closure order.[10] In most cases they will do so because the unauthorised use is still continuing. Interestingly, however, the fact that the use has ceased does not preclude the exercise of the power. The power is only precluded where the constable or local authority is satisfied both that the use has ceased and there is no reasonable likelihood of that it will recur in the future.[11]

44.09   The procedure is that a complaint is made for an order in accordance with the Magistrates' Courts Act 1980, which is followed by a summons directed to all those on whom the closure notice was served who had control of or responsibility for the activities carried on at the premises.

44.10   In order for the court to have any discretion to issue a closure order, then two requirements must be satisfied:

(1)   the notice must have been properly served; and
(2)   the premises have to be continued to be used as complained of, or there must be a reasonable likelihood of such use in the future.

44.11   If those matters are satisfied then the court gains a discretion to make such order as it considers appropriate.[12] Its powers are threefold:

(1)   It may order the premises to be closed immediately and to remain closed until the constable or local authority certify that the need for the order has ceased.
(2)   It may order the use of the premises for the unauthorised activity to cease.
(3)   It may order the defendant to pay a sum of money into court, not to be released until the other requirements of the order are met.

44.12   So, it will be seen that the court is not confined to ordering the use to cease. It can actually order the premises to close. Furthermore, it can

---

8   See Licensing Act 2003, s 136.
9   Licensing Act 2003, s 139.
10   CJPA, s 20.
11   CJPA, s 20(3).
12   CJPA, s 21(1).

support those orders by requiring the payment into court of a sum of money to be held pending compliance.

44.13 If the order is for premises to close, then the court may make dispensation in the order for admission of persons onto premises or for access between the premises and other parts of the building.[13] This would be important, say, if there were a flat above the premises to which access is gained through the premises.

Step 3: notice of the order

44.14 A copy of the order is then to be affixed conspicuously to the premises concerned.[14]

Step 4: appeal

44.15 There is an appeal against an order to the Crown Court but, interestingly, no appeal against a refusal to make the order.[15] The appeal does not suspend the operation of the order.

Step 5: enforcement

44.16 The order can be enforced by a constable or a person authorised by a local authority for the purpose. Enforcement consists of entering the premises and doing anything reasonably necessary for the purpose of securing compliance. Reasonable force may be used in the operation.[16] Offences are committed by those who intentionally obstruct the operation and those who without reasonable excuse permit premises to be open in contravention of an order or fail to comply with or do an act in contravention of an order.[17]

Step 6: termination

44.17 Once the order has been made, it can be terminated in two ways.

[13] CJPA, s 21(3).
[14] CJPA, s 21(4).
[15] CJPA, s 24.
[16] CJPA, s 25.
[17] CJPA, s 25(3)–(5).

44.18 First, the constable or local authority can certify that the need for the order has ceased. Upon certification, the order ceases to have effect[18] and any money paid into court is returned.[19]

44.19 Second, the court can discharge its order on the complaint of anyone served with the closure notice or anyone else with an interest in the premises, provided that it is satisfied that the need for the order has ceased.[20] The procedure is the same as that for complaints under the Magistrates' Courts Act 1980, the summons being served on the police or local authority concerned.

C USE OF POWER

44.20 The closure notice procedure is a fairly straightforward way to bring to the licensee's attention that they are breaching their licence and that they have to put it right or face court proceedings. In fact, it is hard to see how a licensee who, faced with a constable demanding that they comply with their licence, could resist the demand. If they do, they can hardly complain that they are served with a notice asking them to comply with the criminal law.

44.21 The procedure, however, came to be over-used. In its publication, 'The Practical Guide for Preventing and Dealing with Alcohol-related Problems: What You Need to Know',[21] the Home Office stated the following:

'Q.   What is the effect of a closure notice?
A.   As soon as the closure notice has been issued all licensable activity must cease immediately (ie no sales of alcohol, no regulated entertainment).
Q.   What can I do if the premises continues to sell alcohol after I have issued it with a s.19 closure notice?
A.   Anyone who sells alcohol after a closure notice has been issued and is in effect can be arrested or summonsed for the criminal offence under s.136 of unlicensed activity.'

44.22 This advice was wrong. As shown above, it is not the case that all licensable activity must cease immediately just because a notice has been served. For example, the licensee may remedy the matter of non-compliance immediately in which case there can be no objection to his continuing to trade. Further, it was misleading to say that anyone who sells alcohol after the notice has been issued can be arrested or summoned. If they remedy the breach of condition, there would be nothing to summon them for. Furthermore, the power of arrest is circumscribed by section 24 of the Police and

---

[18]   CJPA, s 22(2).
[19]   CJPA, s 22(3).
[20]   CJPA, s 23.
[21]   Home Office, 3rd ed, November 2010, Appendix W.

Criminal Evidence Act 1984, and it is extremely unlikely that it would arise to enable a known designated premises supervisor to be arrested for breach of a licence condition.

44.23 However, in reliance on the advice, and encouraged by the Home Office, police in certain locations began to use the closure notice in that way, by requiring premises to close immediately on service, threatening arrest for those who did not comply.

44.24 This practise ceased when a bar owner in Wakefield, which had been repeatedly closed, judicially reviewed both the police and the Home Office, claiming damages for breach of human rights, arising from the loss of profits of the bar not only on the nights of closure but also on subsequent nights due to the bad publicity arising from those nights.[22] The claim was conceded. Damages were paid to the bar owner, and a consent order was made recording that:

> 'The service of a Closure Notice pursuant to section 19 of the Criminal Justice Police Act 2001 does not:
>
> (a) require the premises to close or cease selling alcohol immediately; or
> (b) entitle the Police to require it to do so; or
> (c) entitle the Police to arrest a person on the sole ground of non-compliance with the Notice.'

44.25 In consequence of the claim, the Home Office withdrew the 'Practical Guide', so that to that extent the guide, which is still in circulation on the internet, should not be relied upon.

44.26 The police and local authorities have many powers to deal with problems in the night-time economy. The closure notice power is a highly targeted and very simple procedure which can be used where there are particular matters which need to be put right. The use of the power does not obviate the use of reviews or prosecutions if the closure notice procedure is not achieving its desired effect. Therefore, the closure notice procedure can be seen as an 'entry level' mode of enforcement the use of which, where appropriate, can be commended. It is, however, as the Home Office now accepts, a nutcracker and not a sledgehammer.

---

[22] *R (The Bar (Wakefield) Limited) v Secretary of State for Home Department and Chief Constable of West Yorkshire Police)* (unreported).

45

Persistent sale closure notices

Assisting Oliver to rise, the young gentleman took him to a near by grocery store, where he bought a supply of ready-dressed ham and a half-quartern loaf, or, as he himself expressed it, 'a fourpenny bran!' Taking the bread under his arm, the young gentleman turned into a small public-house, and led the way to a tap-room in the rear of the premises. Here a pot of beer was brought in by direction of the mysterious youth; and Oliver, falling to at his new friend's bidding, made a long and hearty meal, during which the strange boy eyed him from time to time with great attention

Charles Dickens, *Oliver Twist*

A INTRODUCTION

45.01   This power, set out in section 169A of the Licensing Act 2003, was introduced by the Violent Crime Reduction Act 2006. It exists to provide a rapid alternative for licensed premises, enabling them to accept a closure rather than face prosecution for persistent sale of alcohol to children. With the passage of time, both the meaning of 'persistent sale' and the length of closure have changed, to give the power more teeth.

B THE POWER

45.02   Section 146 of the Licensing Act 2003 makes it an offence for any person to sell alcohol to an individual aged under 18. Section 147 of the Act makes it an offence to knowingly sell alcohol to children on relevant premises, meaning those with licences, certificates or temporary event notices.

45.03   Section 147A makes it a further offence if on two different occasions within 3 consecutive months alcohol is sold to someone under 18 and the seller either believed the purchaser to be under 18 or did not have reasonable grounds for believing otherwise. Reasonable grounds arise only if he actually asked for evidence of age and the individual concerned produced evidence that would have convinced a reasonable person or nobody could have suspected from the individual's appearance that he was under 18.[1] This then places a heavy onus on the seller to ask for identification. If the seller fails to do so, then if anybody could have thought the buyer to be under 18, the seller is guilty of an offence. However, this offence applies only to premises with licences and TENs.[2]

45.04 The defendant to this charge is the person holding the licence or the premises user under the TEN. In the case of a supermarket, say, the sale may be by a cashier, but it is the licensee who is guilty of the offence of persistent sale under section 147A. The convicting court may then suspend the licence for up to three months.[3]

45.05 The number of occasions was reduced from three to two by the Policing and Crime Act 2009 and the maximum penalty was ratcheted up from £10,000 to £20,000 by the Police Reform and Social Responsibility Act 2011, so the measures demonstrates a seriousness of intent by Government to stamp out underage sales.

45.06 Section 169A applies only to premises licences. What it does is to give the licensee a Hobson's choice at the instance of a police officer of the rank of superintendent or above or a trading standards officer.[4]

45.07 The relevant officer may serve a notice setting out the facts of the persistent sale, and proposing a prohibition for up to 336 hours (or 14 days in common parlance) upon the sale of alcohol on the premises, which acts to discharge all criminal liability if accepted.[5] The starting date must be specified, and must begin at least 14 days after service of the notice.

45.08 Provision is made in the Act for the contents of the notice, the beginning of the prohibition period, service of the notice and the date of its service.[6]

45.09 The licensee may, at any time before the prohibition is to commence, accept the prohibition and cease selling alcohol in accordance with the notice. That is, they are not actually obliged to close, so that the title of section 169A (closure notices) is a misnomer. But they must cease selling alcohol. If they do, then their criminal liability is cleared. If they do not, then

1   Licensing Act 2003, s 147A(2)–(3).
2   Licensing Act 2003, s 147A(1).
3   Licensing Act 2003, s 147B(1).
4   Licensing Act 2003, s 169A(11).
5   Licensing Act 2003, s 169A(2).
6   Licensing Act 2003, s 169A.

all the forces of the law may be rained down on their heads, by way of prosecution under sections 146, 147 or 147A, with the possibility of a three month suspension arising under section 147B.

C USE OF POWER

45.10 The power may be viewed two ways. Some licensees, particularly those who are served with closure notices, see it as a draconian and commercially damaging intrusion, when they take reasonable steps to avoid underage sales and they are being punished for the actions of staff whom they have taken great care to train. The period of prohibition, which was lengthened from 48 hours to 336 hours by the Police Reform and Social Responsibility Act 2011, is seen as a significant penalty. Authorities, however, see it as a good solution for themselves (avoiding the bureaucracy of prosecution) and a light touch solution for the licensee who would otherwise acquire a criminal record, a hefty fine and possibly a three month suspension.

45.11 It is fair to say that the off-trade has made great strides in dealing with underage sales, through implementation of Challenge 21 policies and then Challenge 25 policies, the use of till prompts and refusals books, and regular training and refresher training of staff. Working collectively, the industry has introduced community alcohol partnerships which address the issue of underage sales at community level: see Chapter 57 (Community Alcohol Partnerships).

45.12 Against this background, it might be argued that authorities should not use the section 169A power where prosecution is not necessary at all. Authorities should ask themselves, in accordance with their own enforcement policy, whether, in the light (eg) of the culpability of the operator on the occasions in question, the number of incidents arising, the quality of its systems, its track record of compliance and the steps it has taken to remedy its faults, a formal warning would be an adequate means of dealing with the incidents in question. The authorities ought also to ask themselves what the purpose is of the notice. It is not a criminal sanction, and so should presumably be used as deterrence, so the question might be asked whether deterrence is necessary in the individual circumstance of the case.

45.13 As to the period, the authorities ought to have regard to the economic effect on an operator of closure, and fix the period accordingly. A 14 day suspension over Christmas might put a small off-licence out of business, which is presumably not the intention of the provisions. Given that there is no appeal against the length of prohibition in the notice, authorities may also wish to err on the side of shorter orders.

45.14 Home Office guidance[7] on these provisions sets out aggravating and mitigating factors relevant to the length of the closure as follows:

'*Aggravating factors*

These may include: the age of the purchaser (the gravity of the offence increases if sales were made to a younger purchaser); following an offence, a failure to take appropriate steps, such as refresher training, to prevent further underage sales; the quantity of alcohol sold to the underage purchaser; whether previous offences have been committed by the premises licence holder; absenteeism of the Designated Premises Supervisor ("DPS") or premises licence holder at the time of the offence; a failure to follow an action plan agreed with police to tackle the sale of alcohol to children; and a failure to comply with relevant conditions, among others.

Mitigating factors

These may include situations where: a negligent staff member had not followed the premises stringent standard practice/age verification scheme despite good and established training schemes; the sale of alcohol forms a large part of the business and a longer closure period would cause financial hardship or threaten the survival of the business; and if the premises licence holder is willing to make a minor variation/ accept conditions on his licence.'

45.15 Finally, while acceptance of a period of closure may stave off prosecutions, licensees ought not to assume that they will be out of the woods so far as review is concerned: in fact quite the contrary. The Guidance under section 182 states:

'11.30 Where persistent sales of alcohol to children have occurred at premises, responsible authorities should consider applying for a review of the licence, whether there has been a prosecution for the offence under section 147A or a closure notice has been given under section 169A of the 2003 Act. In determining the review, the licensing authority should consider revoking the licence if it considers this outcome is appropriate. Responsible authorities should consider taking steps to ensure that a review of the licence is routine in these circumstances.'

45.16 With all of those caveats aside, the closure notice procedure is a useful summary intervention to be used where operators are not doing enough to ensure that the serious offence of selling to underage people is not being committed, to remind them that the matter is taken seriously, and to attach some further bite to the warning by way of a deterrent sanction.

---

7   'Guidance: persistently selling alcohol to children. Revised guidance following amend-
     ments introduced through the Police Reform and Social Responsibility Act 2011' (Home
     Office, 2012).

ASBO Act closures

Benny was the bouncer at the palais de dance
He'd slash your granny's face up given half a chance.
He'd sell you back the pieces, all for less than half a quid
He thought he was the meanest-
Until he met with Savage Sid.

Emerson Lake and Palmer, *Benny the Bouncer*

A INTRODUCTION

46.01 The Anti-Social Behaviour Act ('ASBA') 2003 provides three separate powers, which may be directed at licensed premises which are failing to promote the licensing objectives in different ways. The purpose of this chapter is to describe these powers in brief terms. In Section B, we shall look at premises where drugs are used unlawfully, dealt with in Part 1 of the Act. In Section C, we shall consider Part 1A, which deals with premises associated with persistent disorder or nuisance. In Section D, we shall consider Part 6, which provides for closure of noisy premises.

B DRUGS

46.02 Section 1 enables a police officer inhabiting the rank of superintendent or above to authorise the issue of a closure notice where the following conditions are satisfied;

(1) he has reasonable grounds for believing that within the previous three months the premises have been used for the unlawful use, production or supply of Class A drugs;
(2) he has reasonable grounds for believing that the use of the premises is associated with the occurrence of disorder or serious nuisance to members of the public;

(3)   he is satisfied that the local authority has been consulted; and

(4)   he is satisfied that reasonable steps have been taken to establish the identity of any person who lives there, or has responsibility for an interest in the premises.[1]

46.03   The notice can be given in writing or orally and then confirmed in writing as soon as practicable.[2] The notice is then affixed to the premises and served on those with responsibility for the premises.[3]

46.04   An application must then be made to the magistrates' court for a closure order, which must then be heard within 48 hours. The court may make the order if satisfied that the premises have been used as alleged, that the use of the premises is associated with disorder or serious nuisance, and that the order is necessary to prevent its occurrence.[4]

46.05   The order requires the premises to close for up to three months,[5] although this can be extended on further complaint.[6] It may be enforced by a constable or a person authorised by the local authority, who may enter and do anything reasonably necessary to secure the premises against entry by others.[7] It is an offence to remain on the premises in breach of a closure order or to obstruct enforcement.[8]

46.06   The order may also be appealed to the Crown Court. Anyone served with the closure notice or anyone else with an interest in the premises may appeal against the order, and the constable or local authority may appeal against a refusal to make an order, whereupon the Crown Court may make such an order as it thinks appropriate.[9]

46.07   The power to make an order under these provisions is highly constrained by the statutory provisions themselves. Any operator of licensed premises where Class A drugs are being dealt and where disorder or serious nuisance is occurring ought not to be surprised to find such powers being exercised against it.

[1]   ASBA 2003, s 1.
[2]   ASBA 2003, s 1(3).
[3]   ASBA 2003, s 1(6),(7).
[4]   ASBA 2003, s 2(3).
[5]   ASBA 2003, s 2(4).
[6]   ASBA 2003, s 5.
[7]   ASBA 2003, s 3.
[8]   ASBA 2003, s 4.
[9]   ASBA 2003, s 6.

C PERSISTENT DISORDER OR NUISANCE

46.08 Section 11A gives further powers to a police officer of the rank of superintendent or above or a local authority to authorise the issue of a closure notice where the following conditions are satisfied:

(1) he has reasonable grounds for believing that within the previous three months a person has engaged in anti-social behaviour on the premises;

(2) he has reasonable grounds for believing that the use of the premises is associated with significant and persistent disorder or persistent serious nuisance to members of the public;

(3) he is satisfied that the local authority (or, if the authorisation is by the local authority, the chief police officer) has been consulted; and

(4) he is satisfied that reasonable steps have been taken to establish the identity of any person who lives there, or has responsibility for an interest in the premises.[10]

46.09 The notice can be given in writing or orally and then confirmed in writing as soon as practicable.[11] The notice is then affixed to the premises and served on those with responsibility for the premises.[12]

46.10 An application must then be made to the magistrates' court for a closure order, which must then be heard within 48 hours. The court may make the order if satisfied that the premises have been used as alleged, that the use of the premises is associated with significant and persistent disorder or serious nuisance, and that the order is necessary to prevent its occurrence.[13]

46.11 The order requires the premises to close for up to three months,[14] although this can be extended on further complaint.[15] It may be enforced by a constable or a person authorised by the local authority, who may enter and do anything reasonably necessary to secure the premises against entry by others.[16] It is an offence to remain on the premises in breach of a closure order or to obstruct enforcement.[17]

46.12 The order may also be appealed to the Crown Court. Anyone served with the closure notice or anyone else with an interest in the premises may appeal against the order, and the constable or local authority may appeal

---

[10] ASBA 2003, s 11A.
[11] ASBA 2003, s 11A(4).
[12] ASBA 2003, s 11A(6)–(8).
[13] ASBA 2003, s 11B(4).
[14] ASBA 2003, s 11B(5).
[15] ASBA 2003, s 11E.
[16] ASBA 2003, s 11C.
[17] ASBA 2003, s 11D.

against a refusal to make an order, whereupon the Crown Court may make such an order as it thinks appropriate.[18]

46.13   The power to make an order under these provisions is again constrained by the statutory provisions themselves, and can be expected to be used only very rarely in relation to licensed premises. In cases where there is serious disorder and nuisance persistently emanating from premises due to anti-social behaviour it is more likely that summary reviews will be used to control the issue and bring the premises into compliance.

D   NOISY PREMISES

46.14   This power, contained in sections 40–41 of ASBA 2003, belongs solely to the chief executive of the local authority, who may delegate it to an environmental health officer.[19]

46.15   The power is specifically directed to premises with premises licences or temporary event notices.[20] It is exercisable where the chief executive reasonably believes that a public nuisance is being caused by noise coming from the premises.[21]

46.16   In such a case, the chief executive may serve a closure order for up to 24 hours which begins when a manager receives written notice of the order and requires the entire premises to be kept closed. Breach of the order is an offence carrying serious penalties – up to three months' imprisonment and a £20,000 fine.

46.17   There is no appeal against an order under these provisions. While in theory an order is judicially reviewable, in practice the order is live for such a short period that this is not achievable.

46.18   This then, is an emergency intervention when rapid action is needed to prevent public nuisance on account of noise coming from the premises. It is right to say that public nuisance covers a multitude of sins from major disturbances to the community to relatively low level disturbance affecting a smaller number of neighbours.[22] The dual facts that the order cannot be appealed and the serious consequences that the order may have on the premises concerned means that the power should be used with some circumspection and where the disturbance is at the higher end of the spectrum.

---

[18]   ASBA 2003, s 11F.
[19]   ASBA 2003, s 41.
[20]   ASBA 2003, s 40(2).
[21]   For meaning of public nuisance see Chapter 9 (The General Duties of Licensing Authorities). For general commentary on the power, see N Parpworth, 'The Anti-social Behaviour Act 2003: the provisions relating to noise', [2004] JPL 541.
[22]   See Chapter 9 (The General Duties of Licensing Authorities).

46.19 Given that the premises one is dealing with are by definition authorised under the Licensing Act 2003, it ought to be possible for an environmental health officer to persuade the management to abate the nuisance, thus obviating need for an order. Where, however, persuasion has not been effective, and serious disturbance is occurring due to noise breakout, no manager of licensed premises could claim to be unjustly treated if the local authority serves an order requiring it to stop.

47

Other statutory remedies

When the drunkard is seated on the ale-bench he presently becommeth a reproover of Magistrates, a controller of the State a murmerer and repiner against the best established government.

John Downame, *Foure Treatise, Tending to Dissuade all Christians from foure no lesse heinous than common sinnes namely the abuses of Swearing, Drunkennesse, Whoredome, and Bribery* (1613)

A INTRODUCTION

47.01 At the heart of the Licensing Act 2003 was a recognition that the management of the night time economy is a cross-disciplinary exercise involving authorities across the local authority domain and outside. When these authorities manage to work together in a strategic and coherent way, allying their efforts with genuine partnerships with the entities to be regulated, and directed at creating a safe, diverse leisure economy, the results are palpable and mark out the successful from the unsuccessful economies.

47.02 In this chapter we consider a number of powers vesting in responsible and other authorities, all of which are relevant to the management of the night time economy, but each of which would merit a book in their own right. Here, we set down these powers but briefly, so that they can be recognised for the role they play. Plainly, the question of whether enforcement should occur under these statutory schemes or under the licensing regime, or indeed both, is always fact-dependent but should also be decided in the light of the local authority's own enforcement protocols and policies.

B NOISE

47.03 In other chapters of the book, we have considered a series of powers to control noise. These include review powers in respect of nuisance

(Chapter 42), Licensing Act closures (Chapter 43) and ASBO Act closures (Chapter 46). Environmental legislation also gives the environmental health authority express powers to control noise nuisance.

Statutory nuisance

47.04 Where an authority is satisfied that a statutory nuisance exists, or is likely to occur or recur it shall serve an abatement notice requiring the abatement of the nuisance or prohibiting or restricting its recurrence or requiring the execution of such works and the taking of any steps necessary to achieve these purposes.[1] The matter most likely to constitute a statutory nuisance in respect of licensed premises is noise. By virtue of section 79(1)(g) of the Environmental Protection Act 1990, noise (including vibration) emitted from premises so as to be prejudicial to health or a nuisance is a statutory nuisance. It is the duty of every local authority to cause its area to be inspected from time to time to detect statutory nuisances which require action and to investigate complaints made to the extent that it is reasonably practicable.

47.05 An abatement notice must be served on the person responsible for the nuisance where that person can be found and, if not, on the occupier, unless the nuisance arises from a defect of a structural character (which may well be the case in relation to noise and vibration), in which case the owner of the premises must be served.[2] There is a right of appeal against an abatement notice to the magistrates' court within 21 days of the date of service.[3] It is an offence to contravene or fail to comply with the requirements or a prohibition of any notice without reasonable excuse, although in the case of noise nuisance on trade or business premises it is a defence to prove that the best practicable means ('BPM') were used to prevent or counteract the effects of the nuisance.[4] What is 'practicable' is judged by reference to local conditions and circumstances, to the current state of technical knowledge and to financial implications. The 'means' include the design, installation, maintenance, manner and periods of operation of plant and machinery and the design, construction and maintenance of buildings and structures.[5] The BPM defence is, therefore, an exacting defence to make out for any defendant and particularly exacting in the context of noise nuisances, which can usually be abated by either turning the volume down, by regulating the hours of operation or by acoustic alterations to buildings. The question of BPM has been considered in two cases relating to public houses.

---

1   Environmental Protection Act 1990, s 80(1),
2   Environmental Protection Act 1990, s 80(2).
3   Environmental Protection Act 1990, s 80(3).
4   Environmental Protection Act 1990, s 80(4) and (7).
5   Environmental Protection Act 1990, s 79(9).

47.06 In the first, *St Albans District Council v Patel*,[6] the issue was noise from a pub garden. The magistrates found that the licensee had taken steps to reduce the noise, including closing one area of the garden and restricting the number of people allowed there. While an environmental health officer had advised that the garden be closed, the implications of doing so, from a financial perspective, would not be practicable. Appealing against the acquittal, the local authority submitted that the magistrates had failed to apply the proper test of BPM under section 80(7) of the 1990 Act. It argued that the magistrates had considered only the practicability of one option, namely to close the garden altogether, but that they had not considered lesser measures such as further reducing the area of the garden used by customers or by restricting the hours of use. However, the High Court held that the magistrates were aware of the contention that there were lesser measures that could have been taken and had properly applied the BPM test, including the question of whether the measures demanded by the authority were practicable in a financial sense. In this case, while the prosecution failed, given that there was in fact a public nuisance a review might have been a better option to pursue.

47.07 On the other hand in *R (South Kesteven District Council) v Grantham Magistrates' Court*,[7] the BPM defence failed and the defendant was convicted for breach of an abatement notice in relation to noise from a party in a pub marquee. The defendant said that he had used the same means as he had applied on a previous occasion when there had been no nuisance, which the magistrates accepted as a proper defence. However, the environmental health officer gave evidence that there were better practicable means which in this case would have involved bringing the music indoors or turning it down. The High Court agreed, and remitted the matter for reconsideration.

47.08 The test for BPM was formulated by Forbes J in the *Patel* case and applied by Wyn Williams J in the *Grantham* case, and can be considered authoritative:

> '14. Mr Reed submitted, uncontroversially, that the expression "best practical means" must be construed having regard to the factors set out in section 79(9) of the 1990 Act but requires, ultimately, that a decision be reached that the person relying on that defence has established that he used the best practicable means on the balance of probabilities. Mr Reed contended that if the means undertaken are not established to be the best then the defence has not been made out. I agree with those submissions which, as I have indicated, are essentially uncontroversial and not in dispute.
>
> 15. It was Mr Reed's submission that, in order to be satisfied that the statutory defence under section 80(7) has been established, the court

---

6   [2008] EWHC 2767 (Admin).
7   [2010] EWHC 1419 (Admin).

must reach the conclusion that the means employed were the best practicable to prevent or counteract the effects of the nuisance in question when compared with any other means or methods which are before the court for its consideration and which, on their face, are practicable and have the ability to prevent or counteract the effects of the nuisance more effectively than has been achieved by the defendant. Mr Reed submitted that, in short, the defendant must establish why all other obvious or, on the face of it, practicable means are not practicable, otherwise it has not been established that the best practicable means have been used. Again, I agree with those submissions which were, in effect, uncontroversial.'

Noise Act 1996

47.09 The Noise Act 1996 provided a summary means for authorities to take action in relation to noise at night. The powers were extended to enable authorities to deal with licensed premises and premises with TENs by the Clean Neighbourhoods and Environment Act 2005.

47.10 If an officer of the authority is satisfied that noise is being emitted from the premises during night hours (11 pm – 7 am[8]) which may exceed the permitted level[9] he may serve a warning notice under section 3 of the Noise Act. The effect of the notice is that any person responsible for noise thereafter in excess of the permitted level is guilty of an offence, subject to a defence of reasonable excuse.[10] The penalty is a fine not exceeding level 3 on the standard scale. The matter may also be dealt with by a fixed penalty notice.[11]

47.11 Further, once the authority has served a notice which has been breached, it has powers to enter the offending premises and seize and remove any equipment which it appears is being or has been used in the emission of the noise.[12] This, then, is a powerful weapon against the commission of noise nuisance from licensed premises.

47.12 Guidance on the use of these powers may be found in 'The Noise Act 1996 as amended by Anti-Social Behaviour Act 2003 and the Clean Neighbourhoods and Environment Act 2005: Guidance to Local Authorities in England'.[13]

---

[8] Noise Act 1996, s 2(6).
[9] The permitted level is (a) 34 dB where the underlying level of noise does not exceed 24 dB, and (b) otherwise, 10 dB in excess of the underlying level of noise: the Permitted Level of Noise (England) Directions 2008, para 3.
[10] Noise Act 1996, s 4.
[11] Noise Act 1996, s 8.
[12] Noise Act 1996, s 10.
[13] DEFRA, 2008.

C PLANNING

47.13   A general account of the planning system is given in Chapter 31 (Planning and Other Strategies), to which reference should be made.

47.14   In licensing, the most commonly arising issues are premises operating outside their lawful planning use or in breach of their conditions. The former may arise where premises with a lawful planning use as a restaurant (use class A3) turn into a bar (use class A4). The latter may arise if hours conditions on a planning permission are flouted, the existence of longer hours on a licence being of no relevance in this regard.

47.15   Where there has been a material change of use, the planning authority has the power to serve an enforcement notice,[14] setting out the breach of control and what steps the authority requires to be taken, or what activities are required to cease, to remedy the breach. The options open to the landowner are then to comply with the notice or appeal against it to the Secretary of State.[15] The grounds of appeal include that planning permission ought to be granted for the offending activity, so that in effect the Secretary of State (or in fact his inspector) stands in the shoes of the planning authority.

47.16   If there is no appeal, or if the appeal fails, then failure to comply with an enforcement notice is an offence[16] carrying a £20,000 fine on summary trial and an unlimited fine in the Crown Court.

47.17   A summary method of dealing with breaches of conditions of a planning permission is provided by the breach of condition notice.[17] Here, the notice, which sets out the breach and the steps which are now required to comply with the permission, is not subject to an appeal, and breach may be visited with prosecution carrying a fine not exceeding level 4 on the standard scale.[18]

D HEALTH AND SAFETY

47.18   The purpose of the Health and Safety at Work Act (HSWA) 1974 is contained in section 1 of that Act. Its aims are to protect the health, safety and welfare of people at work and to safeguard others, mainly the public, against risks to health or safety from the way work is carried out.

---

[14]   Town and Country Planning Act 1990, s 172.
[15]   Town and Country Planning Act 1990, s 174.
[16]   Town and Country Planning Act 1990, s 179.
[17]   Town and Country Planning Act 1990, s 187A.
[18]   Level 3 in Wales.

47.19   The HSWA sets out a number of general duties upon employers in relation to the way they run their undertakings, ie business. Breach of these duties does not give rise to civil liability but may amount to a criminal offence.

47.20   The general duties relevant to employers in relation to licensed premises are contained in sections 2, 3 and 4 of the HSWA.

47.21   The Act requires employers to ensure 'so far as is reasonably practicable' that employees (section 2), and non-employees (section 3) are not exposed to risks to their health and safety from the employer's undertaking (ie business).

47.22   Section 4 imposes duties with respect to non-employees and the use of non-domestic premises made available to them as a place of work or 'as a place where they may use plant or substances provided for their use.' This may, for example, extend to the use by spectators at a music event of a temporary stand. The duty is upon anyone having, to any extent, 'control' over the premises. Thus, if several contractors, an event organiser and a premises licensee have any degree of control over the premises, they all have a potential liability under the section. The duty is to take such measures as it is reasonable for a person in that position to take to ensure, 'so far as is reasonably practicable', that the premises are safe for the purpose for which the visitors are expected to use them.

47.23   The test for what is reasonably practicable was set out in the case of *Edwards v National Coal Board*.[19] This case established that the risk must be balanced against the 'sacrifice', whether in money, time or trouble, needed to avert or mitigate the risk. By carrying out this exercise the employer can determine what measures are reasonable to take.

47.24   The function of enforcement of health and safety falls on the Health and Safety Executive and local authorities, with the respective roles provided for by section 18 of the HSWA and the Health and Safety (Enforcing Authority) Regulations 1998.[20] Under Schedule 1 of the Regulations, local authorities are allocated particular responsibilities for premises where the main activity is 'the practice of presentation of the arts, sports, games, entertainment or other cultural or recreational activities ... '.[21] Thus, it will be for licensing authorities to take the enforcement role for premises whose main activity is the provision of regulated entertainment.

47.25   Local authority inspectors can issue an improvement notice (section 21 of the HSWA) when they consider health and safety legislation is

[19]   [1949] 1 AER 743.
[20]   SI 1998/494
[21]   Regulation 3 and Sch 1, para 9.

being contravened. The notice can be issued whether the legislation being breached is the HSWA or some other health and safety statutory provision.

47.26 The notice must specify the legal requirements that the inspector thinks are being broken and give reasons. The time allowed to put matters right cannot be less than 21 days (as this is the time limit to submit an appeal to the employment tribunal). How long is allowed is in the discretion of the inspector. It will depend on factors such as the seriousness of the matters involved and the ease with which action necessary to comply with the notice can be taken. In the notice the inspector can also set out what s/he requires to be done to put matters in order.

47.27 An inspector may issue a prohibition notice pursuant to section 22 of the HSWA when s/he thinks that there is a risk of serious personal injury. The notice prohibits the carrying on of the work activity that the inspector believes is creating the risk of injury. If the inspector considers the risk is of imminent danger, the notice must take immediate effect and the work activity be stopped at once. If not, the notice can be deferred, stating that the work activity must be stopped within a certain time.

47.28 Someone served with a notice may appeal to an employment tribunal (section 24 of the HSWA). The appeal may challenge the inspector's views about whether the law has been broken or about the risk of serious personal injury, the time limit in the notice or, if applicable, the measures specified for remedying matters.

47.29 An appeal should be made in writing to an employment tribunal within 21 days (unless extended) of the service of the notice. The procedure for appeals is contained in Schedule 5 of the Employment Tribunals (Constitution and Rules of Procedure) Regulations 2004.[22]

47.30 Contravention of an improvement or prohibition notice is an offence under section 33(g) of the Act, carrying a £20,000 fine on summary trial and an unlimited fine in the Crown Court, together with custodial sentences (HSWA, Schedule 3A).

47.31 The prohibition and improvement notice routes thus provide quick and effective remedies where there is a danger to public safety caused by licensable activities.

E LITTER

47.32 A recurring complaint in relation to licensable activities is the problem of litter left behind by customers or those who have attended events, particularly temporary events. Frequently this is worst immediately outside

---

[22] SI 2004/1861.

the premises, but litter travels efficiently over considerable distances whether carried or blown. Local authorities in England and Wales are 'principal litter authorities',[23] and litter in the highway is the responsibility of district councils/unitary authorities or London boroughs in London. It is the duty of litter authorities to keep the highway clear of litter and refuse and clean as far as is practicable.[24]

47.33   The Environmental Protection Act 1990 was amended by the Clean Neighbourhoods and Environment Act 2005 to enable principal litter authorities to serve litter clearing notices in relation to any land[25] which is open to the air.[26] The notice requires the person on whom it is served to clear the land of litter or refuse within a period specified in the notice. Provision is made for appeal against notices to the magistrates' court.[27] Breach of a notice carries a level 4 fine.[28]

47.34   A different but useful and underused tool is the street litter control notice ('SLCN'). These help to prevent litter build up and also to transfer the burden of controlling litter onto occupiers of premises responsible for significant accumulations of litter. Where a litter authority is satisfied that relevant premises have a street frontage and that there is recurrent defacement by litter or refuse of the street or open land adjacent to the street and within the vicinity of the premises it can serve an SLCN.[29] In addition, where the activities on the premises are such that the quantities of litter are likely to cause defacement of the street or adjacent open land in the vicinity of the premises then an SLCN may be served on the occupier of the premises. Relevant premises are defined by Regulations[30] and include premises used wholly or partly for the sale of food or drink for consumption off the premises or consumption on part of the premises which forms open land adjacent to the street (eg a forecourt) as well as premises used wholly or partly as a cinema, theatre, concert hall, bingo hall, casino or dance hall. The notice must state the grounds upon which it is issued, specify the open land which adjoins it or is in the vicinity of the frontage of the premises and specify reasonable requirements to be complied with. Those requirements may include the clearance of litter from the frontage of the premises at specified times and over a specified area together with the provision of or emptying of litter bins. Open land which may be specified in a SLCN includes land within up to 100 metres of relevant premises. A litter authority

---

23   Environmental Protection Act 1990, s 86.
24   Environmental Protection Act 1990, s 89.
25   Certain land is exempt, as set out in the Environmental Protection Act 1990, s 92A(11), including highways maintainable at the public expense. In such cases, a review on the grounds of litter-related nuisance may be more appropriate to secure a condition requiring clean-up after the premises close or a street litter control notice (see below).
26   Environmental Protection Act 1990, s 92A.
27   Environmental Protection Act 1990, s 92B.
28   Environmental Protection Act 1990, s 92C.
29   Environmental Protection Act 1990, s 93.
30   Street Litter Control Notices Order 1991.

proposing to serve a notice must allow the person on whom it intends to serve a notice 21 days to make representations about the notice and take those representations into account in making their decision. There is a right of appeal to the magistrates' court who may quash, vary or add to any requirement imposed by the notice. If the person served fails to comply with the requirements of the litter control notice, the litter authority may apply to a magistrates' court for an order requiring compliance within such time as may be specified in the order. It is an offence for a person to fail to comply with an order without reasonable excuse.[31] The offence carries a level 4 fine.

47.35 Neither of these powers necessarily provides adequate litter control in respect of clubs, institutes, sports arenas or stadia to require the clean up of streets within a prescribed area of the premises after special events. This is a matter which should be addressed by the licensing authority when considering the conditions to be attached to the licence for such events, assuming that there have been relevant representations. More generally, in the absence of a thematic environmental strategy, the integration of litter control with the licensing function is best addressed through the community strategy and liaison with those responsible for street cleansing within the authority. The significance of this issue is demonstrated by the fact that litter is frequently a key concern in community responses to consultations under-taken by local authorities in their areas.

---

[31] Environmental Protection Act 1990, s 94(9).

People

UNDERSHAFT. My dear Barbara: alcohol is a very necessary article. It heals the sick–

BARBARA. It does nothing of the sort.

UNDERSHAFT. Well, it assists the doctor: that is perhaps a less questionable way of putting it. It makes life bearable to millions of people who could not endure their existence if they were quite sober. It enables Parliament to do things at eleven at night that no sane person would do at eleven in the morning. Is it Bodger's fault that this inestimable gift is deplorably abused by less than one per cent of the poor?

Major Barbara
George Bernard Shaw

48

Drink banning orders

He drank the spirits and impatiently bade us go; terminating his command with a sequel of horrid imprecations too bad to repeat or remember.

'It's a pity he cannot kill himself with drink,' observed Heathcliff, muttering an echo of curses back when the door was shut. 'He's doing his very utmost; but his constitution defies him. Mr Kenneth says he would wager his mare that he'll outlive any man on this side Gimmerton, and go to the grave a hoary sinner; unless some happy chance out of the common course befall him.'

Emily Bronte, *Wuthering Heights*

A INTRODUCTION

48.01 A drink banning order ('DBO') is an order which prohibits an individual from doing certain acts, and is designed to:

'address an individual's alcohol misuse behaviour, and protect others and their property from such behaviour'.[1]

48.02 DBOs are governed by sections 1 to 14 of the Violent Crime Reduction Act ('VCRA') 2006. Guidance is provided by the Crown Prosecution Service (CPS)[2] and the Home Office.[3]

---

[1]   CPS guidance on DBOs (see footnote 2), section headed 'Principles'.
[2]   http://www.cps.gov.uk/legal/d_to_g/drinking_banning_orders/#an01.
[3]   'Guidance for Local Authorities, Police Forces, Magistrates and Course Providers',

48.03 Although the legislation has not been judicially considered, in many ways it is similar to the provisions dealing with applications for anti-social behaviour orders. Cases on ASBOs are likely to provide assistance in how courts will interpret the DBO legislation, and are referred to in a number of instances below.

B WHEN CAN A DBO BE OBTAINED?

48.04 A DBO is available when a court is satisfied that since 31 August 2009[4] an individual aged over 16[5] has engaged in criminal or disorderly conduct while under the influence of alcohol, and such an order is necessary to protect other persons from further conduct by him of that kind while he is under the influence of alcohol.[6]

48.05 It is to be assumed that criminal conduct will be considered as conduct contrary to the criminal law. In terms of 'disorderly' in the context of the offence of being 'drunk and disorderly' the court has held that 'disorderly' bears its ordinary and natural meaning,[7] and it is likely that the same approach would prevail under the VCRA.

48.06 Although applications for DBOs are civil proceedings and there is no guidance in the legislation on the applicable standard of proof, it is highly likely that the courts will follow *R (McCann & Ors) v Crown Court at Manchester*[8] in holding that the applicant must prove that the defendant (a) has engaged in criminal or disorderly conduct (b) under the influence of alcohol to the 'heightened civil standard' (in practical terms the criminal standard).Hearsay evidence is admissible as in all civil proceedings, subject to complying with Part 33 of the Civil Procedure Rules in the county court. However, as for ASBOs the question of burden/standard of proof has no applicability in the second part of the test, namely whether a DBO is 'necessary to protect other persons from further conduct by him of that kind while he is under the influence of alcohol'.[9]

48.07 There are three ways of making an application for a DBO:

(1) on complaint to a magistrates' court:
(2) in existing county court proceedings: and
(3) on conviction.

---

available at: http://www.homeoffice.gov.uk/publications/alcohol-drugs/alcohol/guidance-drinking-banning-order?view=Binary.
4   VCRA 2006, s 3(2).
5   VCRA 2006, s 3(1).
6   VCRA 2006, s 3(2).
7   *Andrew Carroll v The Director of Public Prosecutions* [2009] EWHC 554 (Admin).
8   [2003] 1 AC 787.
9   See Lord Steyn in *McCann* at para [37].

Complaint

48.08 An application can be made on complaint[10] to a magistrates' court[11] by a local authority,[12] chief officer of police, or the Chief Constable of the British Transport Police (collectively known in the Act as a 'relevant authority'). Before making an application, the applicant must consult the chief officers of police for the area where the conduct to which the application relates occurred and where the person the subject of the application normally resides, every local authority in whose area the place where the individual normally resides is situated and the Chief Constable of the British Transport Police Force[13] (a group known in the Act as the 'appropriate persons'). In the context of ASBOs it has been held that Chief Constables of Police may delegate their powers of bringing applications and replying to consultations: there is no reason why the same would not apply here.[14]

48.09 The requirement is for consultation, not consent from the appropriate persons. All that is required to provide to the court is a letter showing proof of consultation.[15]

48.10 The section is expressly stated to be subject to section 127 of the Magistrates' Courts Act 1980. Therefore the complaint must be made within six months of the time when the 'matter of complaint arose'. The Home Office guidance on DBOs states that the effect of this is that at least one incident must have occurred within the last six months, although provided that this is the case earlier behaviour may be taken into account.[16]

48.11 Provided they are satisfied the conditions are met the magistrates' court *may* make an order,[17] wording which plainly gives the court a discretion.

County court

48.12 An application can also be made by a relevant authority where there are existing proceedings in the county court. This can arise either where both the relevant authority and potential subject of the order are parties in the

---

[10] This must be on the form provided at Sch 1 of the Magistrates Court (Drink Banning Orders) Rules 2009, by virtue of para 2 of those Rules.
[11] VCRA 2006, s 14.
[12] Defined in VCRA 2006, s 14.
[13] VCRA 2006, ss 3(5) and 14(1).
[14] *The Chief Constable of West Midlands Police v Birmingham Justices* [2002] EWHC 1087 (Admin).
[15] Home Office guidance on DBOs, p 18.
[16] Home Office guidance on DBOs, p 17.
[17] VCRA 2006, s 3(5).

proceedings,[18] where the subject is a party to the proceedings and the relevant authority applies to be joined[19] or where the relevant authority is party to proceedings and considers it would be appropriate to join the subject (provided the conduct complained of is material to the proceedings in question).[20] Again the relevant authority must consult the appropriate persons before making an application.

48.13 The Home Office guidance on DBOs suggests that they do not expect many applications to be made in existing county court proceedings.[21]

48.14 Section VI, Part 65 of the Civil Procedure Rules provided procedural guidance on applications for DBOs in county court proceedings. Where the applicant is a party to the main proceedings they should make their application in the claim form, or by application form filed with the defence. If they only later become aware of the basis for making an order they should apply as soon as possible. Otherwise an application to join a party to the proceedings for the purposes of making an order is made in accordance with Part 19 of the Civil Procedure Rules.

48.15 A county court may make a DBO against someone if the criteria set out at the beginning of this section are satisfied and the criminal or disorderly conduct is material to the proceedings.

Conviction

48.16 The final way in which a DBO can be granted is on conviction. At present this only applies in relation to specified areas of the country,[22] and where DBOs on conviction are available detailed guidance on the procedure to be followed is to be found at Part 50 of the Criminal Procedure Rules. Where an individual aged 16 or over commits an offence at a time when he was under the influence of alcohol, the court must consider making a DBO.[23] If it considers the conditions above are satisfied in relation to the offender it may make an order.[24] The court retains a discretion whether to make an order but if it does not do so it must give reasons in open court either why the DBO conditions are not satisfied or why they do not propose to make an order in this case.[25]

---

[18]   VCRA 2006, s 4(2).
[19]   VCRA 2006, s 4(3).
[20]   VCRA 2006, s 4(4).
[21]   Home Office guidance on DBOs, p 21.
[22]   Those specified under the Violent Crime Reduction Act 2006 (Commencement No 8) Order 2010 (SI 2010/469), Sch 1, and the Violent Crime Reduction Act 2006 (Commencement No 9) Order 2010 (SI 2010/2541), Sch 1.
[23]   VCRA 2006, s 6(2).
[24]   VCRA 2006, s 6(3).
[25]   VCRA 2006, s 6(4) and (5).

48.17 The court must not make an order unless the person to whom it is directed has had an opportunity to consider the order being proposed and why, and to make representations at a hearing.[26] In deciding whether to make an order on conviction the court may take into account evidence provided by both the defence and prosecution, regardless of whether that would have been admissible in the proceedings under which the offender has been convicted.[27] This would allow evidence such as hearsay evidence to be led, and also evidence of matters not relevant to the specific offence (such as of a pattern of offending while under the influence of alcohol). If any party wishes to rely on hearsay evidence for this purpose they must give notice and the other party may apply to cross-examine the maker of the hearsay statement.[28] Another party must give notice if they propose to question the credibility and consistency of the maker of a hearsay statement.[29] The Home Office guidance on DBOs suggests that the provisions of the Magistrates' Courts (Hearsay Evidence in Civil Proceedings) Rule 1999 should also be complied with. Where a court indicates it is considering making an order on conviction a party who wants the court to take account of any particular evidence must serve notice in writing as soon as possible on the court and any other party.[30] In order to decide whether to make a DBO the court can adjourn (even after sentencing),[31] and if the offender does not appear at the adjourned hearing the court may issue a warrant if the offender had notice of the adjourned hearing.[32]

48.18 DBOs on conviction can only be made additionally to a sentence or a discharge,[33] which suggests that they should not be used as an alternative to a sentence. If the offender has been sentenced to custody the DBO takes effect on the day they are released, otherwise it takes effect on the day it is made. In the context of ASBOs it appears to be relatively settled law that, where a lengthy prison sentence is conferred, it is not possible to say an ASBO (or presumably by extension a DBO) would be necessary in the future because custody combined with the deterrence of a return to custody for breach of a licence is likely to be sufficient.[34]

---

[26] Criminal Procedure Rules, r 50.2.
[27] VCRA, s 7(1) to (2).
[28] Criminal Procedure Rules, rr 50.6 and 50.7.
[29] Criminal Procedure Rules, r 50.8.
[30] Criminal Procedure Rules, r 50.4.
[31] VCRA 2006, s 7(4).
[32] VCRA 2006, s 7(5) and (6).
[33] VCRA 2006, s 7(3).
[34] *R v P* [2004] EWCA Crim 287.

48.19   Where a DBO is made against anyone under 18[35] the normal reporting restrictions do not apply,[36] but the court retains a power to prohibit publication of certain matters.[37]

48.20   There is plainly a discretion whether to grant a DBO, and both the Home Office and the CPS guidance recognises a number of situations in which a DBO may not be appropriate:

- where a ban of more than two years is needed;
- where behaviour is related to attendance at a football match;
- where the individual is subject to proceedings related to domestic violence or to non-molestation proceedings;
- where an individual is vulnerable and suffering from drug or alcohol dependency, or mental health problems; or
- where an individual's offending behaviour is solely related to drug use.

48.21   In respect of an individual suffering from mental health problems the Divisional Court considered the correct approach in the context of ASBOs in *The Queen on the Application of Jamie Cooke v Director of Public Prosecutions*[38]. The court said:

> '[10] ... if the justices had concluded that the appellant's mental state was such that he was truly incapable of complying with the conditions of any ASBO that they were minded to make, they would have been wrong in law to make the order ... however
>
> [12] ... The justices should not refuse to make an ASBO on such grounds unless the defendant does not have the mental capacity to understand the meaning of the order, or to comply with it. Such an incapacity being a medical matter, evidence should normally be given by a psychiatrist and not by a psychologist or a psychiatric nurse ...
>
> [13] A defendant who suffers from a personality disorder may on that account be liable to disobey an ASBO. In my judgment, however, that is not a sufficient reason for holding that an order, which is otherwise necessary to protect the public from a defendant's anti-social behaviour, is not necessary for that purpose, or that the court should not exercise its discretion to make an order.'

48.22   The Home Office guidance on DBOs also suggests that where someone is vulnerable or suffering from an alcohol dependency this should be identified in the early stages of DBO consultation and support should be

---

[35]   See definition of 'young person' in VCRA, s 14, incorporating the definition at s 107(1) of the Children and Young Persons Act 1933.

[36]   Those under the Children and Young Persons Act 1933, s 49.

[37]   Children and Young Persons Act 1933, s 39.

[38]   [2008] EWHC 2703 (Admin).

provided, rather than seeking a DBO.[39] However, as the Guidance points out, there is no legislative bar on seeking a DBO against someone who is vulnerable.

48.23 A DBO is more likely to be appropriate where other early interventions have not worked,[40] although there is no obligation in the legislation to try other interventions prior to seeking a DBO.

C INTERIM DBO

48.24 On any of the methods of application[41] set out above, the court may make an interim DBO if they consider 'it is just to do so'.[42] It is expressly provided that this power arises before the court has determined whether the DBO conditions are satisfied[43] so they plainly do not have to make detailed factual findings in relation to the defendant's behaviour or its causes before making an order.

48.25 Other than in the case of an application for a DBO on conviction, an application for an interim DBO may be made without notice to the subject and in the absence of the defendant with the permission of the court[44] or the proper officer,[45] who must be satisfied it is necessary for the application to be made without notice and in the absence of the individual.[46] An interim order made on application in the magistrates' court does not take effect until served on the individual, and if not served on the individual within seven days ceases to have effect.[47] A similar regime in the context of ASBOs has been held to be compatible with Article 6 of the ECHR.[48]

48.26 An interim DBO can contain any provision which may be contained in a full DBO.[49]

48.27 Interim DBOs can be made for any period up to four weeks,[50] and may be renewed a number of times but never for more than four weeks.[51]

---

[39]   Home Office guidance on DBOs, p 8.
[40]   Home Office guidance on DBOs, p 7.
[41]   In relation to an application to a magistrates' court (not on conviction) this must be on the form provided at Sch 2 of the Magistrates Court (Drink Banning Orders) Rules 2009, by virtue of r 2 of those Rules.
[42]   VCRA 2006, s 9(3).
[43]   VCRA 2006, s 9(2).
[44]   In the case of applications to county courts, see VCRA 2006, s 9(3) and (4)(a).
[45]   In the case of applications to magistrates' courts, see VCRA 2006, s 9(3) and (4)(b).
[46]   VCRA 2006, s 9(5).
[47]   Magistrates Court (Drink Banning Orders) Rules 2009, r 3.
[48]   *R (M) v Secretary State for Constitutional Affairs Lord Chancellor & Anr* [2004] 2 All ER 531.
[49]   VCRA 2006, s 9(6)(a).
[50]   VCRA 2006, s 9(6)(b).
[51]   VCRA 2006, s 9(7)(a) .

Interim orders come to an end on the hearing of the application for the full order, or may be varied or discharged on application in the same way as full orders.[52]

D PROHIBITIONS CONTAINED WITHIN DBOS

48.28   A DBO can include any prohibition:

'necessary for the purpose of protecting other persons from criminal or disorderly conduct by the subject while he is under the influence of alcohol.'[53]

48.29   It must include such prohibitions as the court considers necessary on the defendant entering:

(a)   premises in respect of which there is a premises licence[54] authorising the use of the premises for the sale of alcohol by retail;[55] and

(b)   premises in respect of which there is a club premises certificate[56] authorising the use of the premises for the supply of alcohol to members or guests.[57]

It must not include prohibitions which prevent the subject:

(a)   from having access to a place where he resides;

(b)   from attending at any place which he is required to attend for the purposes of any employment of his or of any contract of services to which he is a party;

(c)   from attending at any place which he is expected to attend during the period for which the order has effect for the purposes of education or training or for the purpose of receiving medical treatment; or

(d)   from attending at any place which he is required to attend by any obligation imposed on him by or under an enactment or by the order of a court or tribunal.[58]

48.30   The Home Office guidance on DBOs considers that the prohibitions should:

● cover the range of criminal and disorderly conduct committed by the defendant while under the influence of alcohol;

● be necessary for protecting other persons from the defendant's criminal conduct (or property from unlawful loss or damage by the defendant) while they are under the influence of alcohol;

---

52   VCRA 2006, s 9(7)(b) and (8).
53   VCRA 2006, s 1(2).
54   As defined in the Licensing Act 2003, s 1.
55   As defined in the Licensing Act 2003, s 192.
56   As defined in the Licensing Act 2003, s 60.
57   VCRA 2006, s 1(3).
58   VCRA 2006, s 1(6).

- be reasonable and proportionate, realistic and practical, clear concise and easy to understand;
- be specific when referring to a named set of premises with a premises licence or club premises certificate in a given street (or streets) or within a defined geographical area;
- be specific when referring to matters of time if, for example, prohibiting the subject from being in a set of licenced premises at certain times; and
- be specific when referring to exclusion from a geographic area, including street names and clear boundaries (a map with identifiable street names could be provided).

48.31 Of particular importance will be ensuring that those premises from which the defendant is banned by the DBO are aware of this. Licensees should be encouraged to play their part in upholding DBOs, and, if a defendant enters the premises in breach of the ban, should not serve them but should contact the police. This is plainly a situation in which an effective Pub Watch scheme comes into its own: see Chapter 54 (Pub Watch).

48.32 More generally, authorities can use publicity to support the enforcement of a DBO, but in deciding whether to do so (and what form the publicity should take) they must take into account the human rights of the defendant. The Home Office makes clear that the guidance must be consistent with the characteristics of a DBO as a civil order.[59]

48.33 The CPS guidance on DBOs gives the following examples of suggested provisions:

- exclusion from an individual set of licensed premises or a number of licensed premises;
- exclusion from consuming alcohol in public places. What 'public places' means will need to be carefully explained in the DBO. For example, it could be any place to which the public has access (whether as of right or by express or implied permission). It could also include places to which the person gains unlawful access;
- exclusion from all licensed premises in a geographically defined area such as a street or town centre; and
- exclusion from purchasing alcohol in a particular set of licensed premises or a number of licensed premises or any licensed premises in England and Wales.

48.34 Both the CPS and Home Office guidance on DBOs refer to the need to have particular care when banning an individual from premises that sell alcohol, because, as many supermarkets and fuel outlets sell alcohol, this could prevent the defendant from being able to purchase food or fuel.

---

[59] Home Office guidance on DBOs, p 32.

48.35 A DBO can be imposed for any period between two months and two years.[60] Provided no term is shorter or longer than that, different provisions of the order may last for different periods of time.[61]

48.36 A DBO may provide for termination of the order on completion of a specified approved course.[62] However, the termination date must not be before half of the period of the order has elapsed or before the course has been completed.[63] If the court is going to impose provisions in relation to an approved course they must satisfy themselves that the course will be available to the subject and that he has consented to inclusion of the course in the DBO.[64] They should also satisfy themselves that it is appropriate to include the course (for example that the defendant has not already failed it).[65] The subject must be told in ordinary language the effect of including provision in relation to the course, what attendance on the course will require, what fees will be required for the course and when he will have to pay those fees.[66]

48.37 If the court is not going to make an order in relation to an approved course they must give reasons in open court for not doing so.[67]

48.38 A subject will only be considered to have completed a course satisfactorily if the course provider issues a certificate to that effect[68] and the certificate is received by the proper officer of the court making the order.[69] A certificate must be issued unless the subject has failed to pay the fees, attend the course in accordance with the reasonable instructions of the provider or comply with other reasonable instructions of the provider.[70] If the course provider refuses to provide a certificate they must provide a notice giving reasons why.[71] On receipt of a notice giving reasons, or following a failure to provide such a notice, the subject may seek a declaration that none of the above grounds for refusing the certificate applied.[72]

---

[60]   VCRA 2006, s 2(1).
[61]   VCRA 2006, s 2(2).
[62]   VCRA 2006, s 2(3).
[63]   VCRA 2006, s 2(4)–(5).
[64]   VCRA 2006, s 2(6).
[65]   Home Office guidance on DBOs, p 12.
[66]   VCRA 2006, s 2(7).
[67]   VCRA 2006, s 2(8).
[68]   Which must be in the form provided at Sch 1 of the Violent Crime Reduction Act 2006 (Drinking Banning Orders) (Approved Courses) Regulations 2009 (SI 2009/1839).
[69]   VCRA 2006, s 13(1).
[70]   VCRA 2006, s 13(3).
[71]   In the form provided at Sch 2 of the Violent Crime Reduction Act 2006 (Drinking Banning Orders) (Approved Courses) Regulations 2009, and in accordance with reg 11 of those Regulations.
[72]   VCRA 2006, s 13(5); the application is made in accordance with the Magistrates' Courts (Drinking Banning Orders) Rules 2009, r 7.

48.39 If a course provider wishes to get their course approved for these purposes, they should make an application to the Secretary of State.[73] Detailed guidance on the approval of courses is set out in section 12 of the VCRA and the Violent Crime Reduction Act 2006 (Drinking Banning Orders) (Approved Courses) Regulations 2009.

E VARIATION, DISCHARGE, APPEAL

48.40 An order made on complaint to the magistrates' court[74] or in county court proceedings may be varied or discharged on application by the subject or the relevant authority.[75] It may not be varied so as to extend it for more than two years[76] or to discharge it earlier than half way through its original period unless the original applicant consents to its earlier discharge.[77]

48.41 A DBO on conviction can be varied or discharged on application by the subject, relevant authority or the Director of Public Prosecutions.[78] The same limitations on variation set out above are applicable.[79] Anyone applying to vary an order on conviction[80] must apply in writing explaining what material circumstances have changed since the making of the order. Any additional evidence the applicant wishes to rely on must be identified. The applicant must have an opportunity to make representations at a hearing, but everyone must be given 14 days to consider their representations prior to the hearing.

48.42 A DBO made in the magistrates' court (whether on conviction or on application) may be appealed to the Crown Court.[81] Although there is no specific provision for appeal in relation to an order made in the county court, it would appear the normal civil rules would apply in relation to appeal.

F BREACH OF A DBO

48.43 The power of DBOs lies in the fact that breaches of them are a criminal offence:

---

[73] VCRA 2006, s 12(1).
[74] This is done by way of complaint and must specify the reasons why it should be discharged: Magistrates Court (Drink Banning Orders) Rules 2009, r 4.
[75] VCRA 2006, s 5(1)–(2).
[76] VCRA 2006, s 5(5).
[77] VCRA 2006, s 5(6).
[78] VCRA 2006, s 8(1).
[79] VCRA 2006, s 8(5) or (6).
[80] Civil Procedure Rules, 50.5.
[81] VCRA 2006, s 10.

'If the subject of a drinking banning order or of an interim order does, without reasonable excuse, anything that he is prohibited from doing by the order, he is guilty of an offence.'[82]

48.44 The offence is triable summarily only and the maximum penalty is a fine not exceeding level 4 on the standard scale.[83] A court cannot make a conditional discharge on conviction of the offence.[84]

48.45 In the case of breach of ASBOs, the Court of Appeal has held that a 'reasonable excuse' could include a claim that the defendant has misunderstood or forgotten the terms of the order. Although this could be used to frustrate the effective application of the law this was a matter for the jury (or magistrates) to deal with in the circumstances of a particular case.[85] The burden of proof in ASBOs (and again there is no reason why the DBO regime should be treated differently) is on the prosecution to show that the defendant acted without reasonable excuse.[86]

48.46 A prosecution for the offence may be brought by either a local authority or persons specified by order by the Secretary of State.[87] The guidance states that it will be the responsibility of the CPS to prosecute breaches of DBOs (although the relevant order of the Secretary of State is not cited).[88]

G USE OF DBOS

48.47 Many people who cause trouble in town centres do not live there. If they misbehave there, they may be ejected from a bar, be spoken to by a police officer, or even (rarely) spend a night in a police cell. But their night out may carry very few other consequences for them. They may return to their place of residence, school or workplace and carry on life as normal before repeating the exercise on their next visit.

48.48 The DBO confronts the individual with their behaviour, and has the effect of banning them from the place where their misbehaviour is occurring. They will not be able to participate in the next big night out. Their identity will have been noted by Pub Watch participants who will be minded to ban them from their premises. They will have entered the justice system, and received a genuine shock, but without acquiring a criminal record which could blight their future career.

---

[82]   VCRA 2006, s 11(1).
[83]   VCRA 2006, s 11(2).
[84]   VCRA 2006, s 11(3).
[85]   *Regina v Nicholson* [2006] EWCA Crim 1518.
[86]   *R v Charles* [2009] EWCA Crim 1570.
[87]   VCRA 2006, s 11(4) and (5).
[88]   Home Office guidance on DBOs, p 15.

48.49 The DBO is therefore a worthwhile remedy, which focuses on the minority of people who are causing the alcohol-related disorder, rather than punishing the bars where they have elected to misbehave. The remedy is underused, and it will take a concerted effort by local authorities, local police and the CPS to get the system up and running properly. If they manage to do so, the payback will be official identification of the actual troublemakers in our night-time economy environments, to allow them the opportunity to mend their ways or find themselves airbrushed from the scene.

Confiscation of alcohol

What is the good of a man and he
Alone and alone with a speckled shin
I would that I drank with my love on my knee
Between two barrels at the inn

William Butler Yeats, *Two Songs Rewritten for the Tune's Sake*

A	The power 49.01
B	Use of the power 49.06

A THE POWER

49.01 The Confiscation of Alcohol (Young Persons) Act ('CA(YP)A') 1997 makes provision for the confiscation of alcohol from those under the age of 18.

49.02 This Act applies to any public place other than a licensed premises and any place other than a public place to which the person has unlawfully gained access. For these purposes, public place means a place to which the public or any section of the public has access, on payment or otherwise, as of right or by virtue of express or implied permission.[1]

49.03 The Act is applicable where a constable reasonably suspects a person is in possession of alcohol[2] and that he is either:

- under 18;
- intends the alcohol to be consumed by someone under 18; or
- he is with or has recently been with someone under 18 who has recently consumed alcohol.[3]

49.04 In such circumstances the constable may require the individual to surrender anything in his possession which he reasonably believes to be

---

[1]   CA(YP)A 1997, s 1(6).
[2]   Alcohol carries the same definition as in s 191 of the Licensing Act 2003, by virtue of CA(YP)A 1997, s 1(7).
[3]   CA(YP)A 1997, s 1(1).

alcohol or a container for alcohol.[4] The constable can then dispose of that surrendered to him as he sees fit.[5] If a constable does confiscate anything under this power he must require the person to give their name and address,[6] and may, if he reasonably suspects they are under 16, remove them to their home or a place of safety.[7]

49.05   Failure to comply with a requirement to surrender an item or to give a name and address is a criminal offence, triable summarily only and punishable by a fine not exceeding level 2 on the standard scale. When a constable imposes a requirement he must inform the subject of his suspicion and warn them that failure to comply with the requirement is a criminal offence.[8]

B   USE OF THE POWER

49.06   The power is a useful means of removing the immediate problem, where young people are drinking in public places. Their use may be considered at the same time as other powers canvassed in this book at Chapters 37 (DPPOs), 38 (Dispersal Orders) and 39 (Directions to Leave). Alone or compendiously they are all weapons in the armoury. All of these might be considered as part of community alcohol partnerships, dealt with at Chapter 56.

49.07   For more persistent problems, section 30 of the Policing and Crime Act 2009 may be utilised. This new offence, of persistently possessing alcohol in a public place, is again directed at those under 18. It is committed where a person, without reasonable excuse, is in possession of alcohol in any relevant place[9] on three or more occasions within a period of 12 consecutive months. Ultimately, bringing the drinker into the criminal justice system may be inevitable but it is considered that all other measures should be considered first, including diversionary programmes such as the alcohol arrest referral scheme considered in the next chapter.

---

4   CA(YP)A 1997, s 1(1).
5   CA(YP)A 1997, s 1(2).
6   CA(YP)A 1997, s 1AA.
7   CA(YP)A 1997, s 1AB.
8   CA(YP)A 1997, s 1(4).
9   As defined in the Policing and Crime Act 2009, s 30(2).

Alcohol arrest referral schemes

Cuando yo me muera tengo ya dispuesto
en el testamento que me han de enterrar
en una bodega, dentro de una cuba
con un grano de uva en el paladar

Spanish drinking song, popular

A	Alcohol arrest referral schemes 50.01
B	Use of schemes 50.16

A ALCOHOL ARREST REFERRAL SCHEMES

50.01 Alcohol arrest referral schemes are not the product of a legislative intervention. They arose out of referral schemes for substance misuse that have been operating in some parts of England since the 1980s.[1] In June 2007, the Department of Health issued a paper entitled 'Safe. Sensible. Social. The next steps in the National Alcohol Strategy',[2] following on from the 'Alcohol Harm Reduction Strategy for England', a cross-governmental publication of March 2004.[3] The 2004 strategy had identified arrest diversion schemes as a potentially fruitful way of reducing re-offending.

50.02 The 2007 paper identified one of the 'next steps' as follows:

'Sharpened criminal justice for drunken behaviour – The criminal justice system will be used to bear down on those committing crime and antisocial behaviour when drunk. Points of intervention will be introduced following arrest, through conditional caution and through disposal. Offenders will be given the facts about unsafe drinking and its link to criminal behaviour. They will be offered advice, support and treatment where appropriate. And we will explore ways to make them pay for these interventions.'

[1] Home Office guidance on alcohol arrest referral schemes (see footnote 4), page 3.
[2] http://www.dh.gov.uk/prod_consum_dh/groups/dh_digitalassets/@dh/@en/documents/digitalasset/dh_075219.pdf.
[3] http://webarchive.nationalarchives.gov.uk/+/http://www.cabinetoffice.gov.uk/media/cabinetoffice/strategy/assets/caboffce%20alcoholhar.pdf.

50.03   The paper committed to assessing the contribution of the existing arrest referral pilot projects and initiatives, and establishing a number of alcohol referral schemes. In particular the objective was to establish whether brief alcohol interventions reduce re-offending among those arrested for alcohol related offences, investigate how referral schemes can be established to provide effective and appropriate interventions in a cost efficient manner and increase the number of conditional cautions that have alcohol referral attendance as a condition.

50.04   The Home Office has now produced detailed guidance on setting up alcohol arrest referral schemes[4]. The guidance points out that there are no fixed criteria for establishing such a scheme, but that they are a response to local circumstances.[5] The aims of such a scheme need to be clearly defined, but are likely to include a reduction in crime and the fear of crime, a reduction in reoffending and safer communities. Although the primary aim of such a scheme is likely to be preventing reoffending the guidance also says it is appropriate for such schemes to prevent damage to an individual's health.

50.05   There is no single model for how to set up an alcohol arrest referral scheme. However there are a number of factors which are common to the schemes:

- Identification of an alcohol related offender (usually by custody staff although the guidance notes that some areas are using different routes including pub watch, solicitors, domestic violence units and the court).
- A system in place to pass the arrestee between criminal justice and alcohol services. The most common practices include: (a) police/custody staff provide information to, refer to or make an appointment with an alcohol service; (b) dedicated alcohol or generic drug/alcohol custody based arrest referral staff identify/screen, refer or give a brief intervention in custody, or (c) off-site dedicated alcohol or generic drug/alcohol workers who are allowed access into the custody suite and carry out the actions above.

50.06   Getting clients to attend appointments can be either voluntary or compulsory (for example as a condition of bail or a conditional caution), or theoretically a scheme could have both voluntary and compulsory elements. The guidance reports that, unsurprisingly, coercive schemes report a better take up from the point of referral to attendance at first interview.

50.07   There are three main ways of adding a coercive element into the scheme:

---

4   http://www.drugscope.org.uk/Resources/Drugscope/Documents/PDF/Good%20Practice/alcoholarrest.pdf.

5   Home Office guidance on alcohol arrest referral schemes, p 6.

- Making attending an appointment a condition of a conditional caution.
- Making attending an appointment a bail condition.
- Agreeing to withdraw a fixed penalty notice on completion of the course.

50.08 A conditional caution is a caution given to someone aged over 18 containing conditions seeking to do one or more of the following:

(a) facilitating the rehabilitation of the offender;
(b) ensuring that the offender makes reparation for the offence;
(c) punishing the offender.[6]

Plainly a conditional caution within an alcohol arrest referral scheme would be directed at the first of those provisions.

50.09 A conditional caution can be given on any summary only offence except for those under the Road Traffic Act 1988 and the Road Traffic Offenders Act 1988, plus a number of either way offences. Most usefully for these purposes that includes offences such as common assault, assaulting a police officer, section 4 and 4A Public Order Act offences, and being drunk and disorderly. They are available where there is sufficient evidence to charge for an offence, and suitable conditions may provide reparation to the victim or community, be effective in modifying offending behaviour or provide an appropriate penalty, and a Crown Prosecutor considers it is appropriate in all the circumstances of the case.

50.10 Alternatively the intervention can be made a condition of bail. If a custody officer releases a suspect on bail after charge under section 38 of the Police and Criminal Evidence Act 1984, this is deemed by virtue of section 47 of that Act to be a release on bail 'in accordance with sections 3, 3A, 5 and 5A of the Bail Act 1976'. By virtue of section 3(6) of the Bail Act 1976 the suspect may be required to comply with such requirements as appear to be necessary to ensure that (inter alia) he 'does not commit an offence while on bail'. It is suggested in the guidance that this could encompass a condition requiring attendance at a referral scheme interview.

50.11 Others have piloted schemes whereby a penalty notice is given for disorder and the fine is waived if a brief intervention is attended. From the examples given it seems as if these systems work by essentially suspending the fine and, it appears, not requiring it to be paid on completion of the course. There is specific provision within the statutory scheme[7] for this to happen, although the limited detail provided in the guidance about how a fixed penalty notice scheme works makes it difficult to analyse the legality of this approach.

---

[6] Criminal Justice Act 2003, s 22(3).
[7] The statutory scheme for fixed penalty notices is found at ss 1–2 of the Criminal Justice and Police Act 2001.

50.12   Although most schemes only take people aged over 18, some schemes have been specifically designed for young people (in Blackpool, East Sussex, Lincolnshire, Liverpool, Newcastle and Staffordshire).

50.13   As there is no overarching legislation, there is no list of trigger offences for intervention. However, in drawing up a scheme it is likely to be sensible if the local agencies agree a list of such offences amongst themselves.

50.14   Once the individual is in the brief intervention, the idea is that the intervention takes the form of a 'structured motivational conversation'. The Home Office guidance on arrest schemes identifies that it works in two ways:

- By getting people to think differently about their alcohol use so that they begin to think about or make changes in their alcohol consumption.
- By providing those who choose to drink with insight into skills that allow them to consume alcoholic beverages in a safer way with the aim of reducing reoffending.

50.15   Screening is often undertaken using the AUDIT methodology.[8] The individual's drinking is then classified and either a simple brief intervention or an extended intervention can be offered. Where moderate or severe dependency is identified there is a possibility of referring people on for specialist treatment services.

B USE OF SCHEMES

50.16   The Home Office commissioned two major pilot alcohol arrest referral schemes, the first in 2007 in four areas and the second in 2008 in eight.

50.17   In the first study, 2,177 people participated in the schemes and were diverted to alcohol workers. Most referrals were voluntary, from the custody suite. Three of the schemes found an overall reduction in alcohol consumption, but in the absence of a control group it was not possible to say whether this was due to the intervention or the prior arrest. However, no statistically significant reduction in re-arrest rates could be discerned when compared with a retrospective matched control group. It was not possible for the researchers to conclude that the schemes represented value for money when comparing the cost of the schemes with the amount saved by reduced offending.[9]

50.18   In the second study, 4,739 arrestees were subjected to a brief intervention. The study showed that the intervention did not reduce

---

8   http://whqlibdoc.who.int/hq/2001/who_msd_msb_01.6a.pdf.
9   'Evaluation of Alcohol Arrest Referral Pilot Schemes (Phase 1)' (Home Office, Occasional Paper 101, March 2012).

re-offending as compared with a matched comparison group, but there was some evidence of reduced alcohol consumption. It was concluded that the schemes may be more beneficial for health purposes than criminal justice ones, and the study pointed to the importance of screening in custody for alcohol needs and referral for appropriate support.[10]

50.19 Perhaps the most striking statistics from these studies is the high proportion of people arrested for alcohol-related matters who are assessed as problem drinkers. In the first study, 38% were dependent drinkers and a further 35% hazardous drinkers. In the second study, 37% were assessed as being alcohol-dependent and a further 36% were hazardous drinkers. The great majority of those in the scheme had been picked up for offences typically associated with the leisure economy – violence, disorder and drunkenness. This demonstrates with great clarity that much greater focus needs to be placed on those who are actually causing the disorder which affects town centre leisure economies, making them no-go areas for some. Licensing authorities and the police should put in place programmes to keep such offenders away from the town centre (eg drink banning orders) and develop means to ensure that they confront their own drinking behaviour.

50.20 The pilot studies demonstrated the great importance of developing alcohol policy from a standpoint of evidence and not politics or guesswork, or both. Rigorous studies were conducted of what appeared to be a good idea, and demonstrated that the schemes did not succeed in reducing offending. While it would be too early to conclude that diversionary interventions cannot reduce offending, in their current form that appears to be an inescapable conclusion.

---

[10]   'Evaluation of Alcohol Arrest Referral Pilot Schemes (Phase 2)' (Home Office, Occasional Paper 102, March 2012).

Prosecution

There are likewise another sort of men, of whom we have heard much, and are sufficiently ashamed, who spend their time in taverns, tipling houses and debauches, giving no other evidence of their affection to us but in drinking our health, and inveighing against all others who are not of their own dissolute temper, and who, in truth, have more discredited our cause by the license of their manners and lives, than they could ever advance it by their affection or courage. We hope that … they will cordially renounce all that licentiousness, profaneness and impiety with which they have been corrupted, and endeavour to corrupt others, and that they will hereafter become examples of sobriety and virtue, and make it appear that what is past was rather the vice of the time than of the persons, and so the fitter to be forgotten together.

Charles II
Proclamation against vicious, debauched and prophane persons,
30 May 1660

Prosecution

The Committee of the Imperial Commission of Liquor Control is directed to draw your attention to the fact that you have disregarded the Committee's communications under the Act for the Regulation of Places of Public Entertainment; and that you are now under section 47C of the Act amending the Act for the Regulation of Places of Public Entertainment aforesaid. The charges on which prosecution will be founded are as follows.

The Flying Inn, GK Chesterton.

A INTRODUCTION

51.01 As much as the Licensing Act 2003 offers greater choice and flexibility to the licensing trade, various concepts within the Act are clearly designed to rein in its liberalising elements and provide safeguards. At the application stage, for example, this is the intention behind the licensing objectives,[1] the pivotal role of the designated premises supervisor,[2] and the provision for local stakeholders to make representations on applications for premises licences in their area.[3] Once a premises licence has been granted, however, a different set of provisions exists to provide the safeguards.

---

[1] Licensing Act 2003, s 4(2).
[2] Licensing Act 2003, s 1; Guidance, para 10.25.
[3] Licensing Act 2003, ss 13(3) and 18(7).

51.02 The procedure for review of a licence, together with the many other powers set out in this Part, provide a medley of remedies in the night time economy, directed at areas, premises and persons. At the end of the line, however, is the remedy of prosecution, which this chapter covers. This chapter does not deal with every conceivable offence in the night time economy. There are many offences which cover drunkenness, disorder and violence. Here, we are concerned with the offences arising under the Act.

51.03 The offences in Part 7 of the Act directly promote the licensing objectives[4] of the prevention of crime and disorder and the protection of children from harm. The offences also indirectly engage the objectives of public safety and the prevention of public nuisance. The very existence of the offences, as well as the proper and effective prosecution of individuals and individual businesses for committing them, should help to encourage responsible management, ensure the public's safety, and prevent nuisance to the public.

51.04 The offences are set out under six headings:

- unauthorised licensable activities (sections 136–139);
- drunkenness and disorderly conduct (sections 140–143);
- smuggled goods (section 144);
- children and alcohol (sections 145–155);
- vehicles and trains (sections 156–157); and
- false statements relating to licensing (section 158).

It should be noted that Part 7 does not contain all of the offences under the Act. There are a large number of other offences, many of which seek to underpin the administrative scheme of the Act by criminalising non-compliance with its procedural requirements. Instead, this chapter concentrates on the Part 7 offences, which are at the nub of the scheme. The offences under the six headings are considered below.[5]

The prosecuting authority

51.05 Although the police are regarded as key enforcers of licensing law,[6] proceedings for offences under Part 7 of the Act can be instituted by the licensing authority as well as the Director of Public Prosecutions on behalf of the police.[7] In relation to the offences of selling alcohol to a person under the age of 18 and knowingly allowing the sale of alcohol to a person under the age of 18,[8] there is a duty placed on every local weights and measures

---

4   See footnote 1 above.
5   See Sections D–I below.
6   Guidance para 1.8.
7   Section 186(2)(a)–(b).
8   Section G below.

authority under section 154 of the Act to enforce those provisions and where appropriate bring proceedings[9] (through trading standards officers).

Choosing an offence to prosecute

51.06 Two of the more difficult issues which a prosecuting authority will face when considering the offences under Part 7 of the Act will be in choosing which offence to prosecute and then deciding whether to prosecute that offence.

51.07 The issues can be illustrated by way of an example. Upon the grant of a premises licence for a typical city centre public house, a number of steps will be taken and safeguards put in place, all with a view to protecting the public from crime and disorder:

• The name of the designated premises supervisor will have been supplied prior to the grant of the licence, and his criminal record will have been checked. He will possess a licensing qualification.[10]

• Conditions may require door supervisors to be at the premises. They will possess licences issued by the Security Industry Authority.[11]

• Conditions will also set the parameters within which the licensable activity can take place.[12] For example, the licensed capacity and the last entry time will be specified as conditions on the licence and be enforced as such.

51.08 The measures set out above can be regarded as the licensing scheme within which the premises will operate. In that context, the commission of certain offences may occur after and as a result of that licensing scheme breaking down in some way.

51.09 So, where a group of young men who are known to the local licensing trade as troublemakers are allowed to enter, consume alcohol, and later cause a fight in the premises, the operation of the scheme may have broken down in a number of ways:

• There may have been fewer door supervisors on the door than was required by condition, thus allowing intoxicated persons to enter.

• The admission may have occurred in breach of a last entry condition.

• They may have been served while intoxicated.

• The designated premises supervisor may have failed to seek a rapid response to the situation in breach of a condition requiring police call-outs for significant incidents, thereby allowing the incident to escalate.

---

9   Section 186(2)(c), as defined in s 69 of the Weights and Measures Act 1985.
10 Licensing Act 2003, s 120(2)(b)–(d).
11 Licensing Act 2003, s 21(1).
12 Licensing Act 2003, s 18(2).

51.10 In the scenario provided above, the prosecuting authority will have a number of options to choose from.[13] Firstly, a review of the licence could be initiated under the Act.[14] A modification of the conditions on the licence could be sought as a preventative measure. Equally, removal of the designated premises supervisor from the licence could be sought as a more proactive measure, depending on the view taken of his actions in response to the incident. Secondly, those involved with the pub could be prosecuted under Part 7 of the Act. The designated premises supervisor could be prosecuted under section 136 for knowingly allowing the sale of alcohol in breach of the condition as to the maximum number of people allowed on the premises.[15] The bar staff could be prosecuted for selling to intoxicated people. The corporate licence holder could be prosecuted for the offences too, and its directors for knowingly allowing the conduct or conniving in the offences.[16] Finally, the police could seek to prosecute the group of men who caused the fight under conventional criminal offences such as assault, wounding, violent disorder or affray. In theory, nothing would prevent all these approaches being taken.

51.11 In such situations, prosecuting authorities benefit from having an enforcement protocol to guide the prosecution decision. Such an agreement could set out the enforcement options available to the authorities, the degree of overlap between the authorities' powers of prosecution, and also establish a prioritised scheme for enforcement action. At the very least, the choice of enforcement action and prosecution should be made after consideration of all of the various options available, and a decision-making process which involves consideration of the views of both the licensing authority and the police would be sensible. The use of an enforcement protocol is in line with the partnership approach to licensing functions advocated in the Guidance, which states:

> '13.16 The Government recommends that licensing authorities should establish and set out joint-enforcement protocols with the local police and the other authorities and describe them in their statement of policy. This will clarify the division of responsibilities for licence holders and applicants, and assists enforcement and other authorities to deploy resources more efficiently.
>
> 13.17 In particular, these protocols should also provide for the targeting of agreed problem and high-risk premises which require greater attention, while providing a lighter touch for low risk premises or those that are well run ... '

---

[13] Only the options available after the disorder has occurred are considered here. In attending the premises when the incident is actually occurring, the police may consider that the disorder is such that closure of the premises is necessary in the interests of public safety. If so, they may decide to serve a closure order on the premises under s 161 of the Act (see Chapter 42: Licensing Act Closures).

[14] Sections 51–53.

[15] See Section D below.

[16] See Section E below.

Regulator's Compliance Code and Enforcement Concordat

51.12 In Chapter 29 (The Legislative and Regulatory Reform Act 2006), we pointed out the importance of adherence to better regulation principles. In addition to that, many authorities are voluntary adherents to the Enforcement Concordat in exercising their enforcement functions.[17] Adoption of the Concordat commits the local authority to good enforcement policies and procedures, which may be supplemented by additional statements of enforcement policy. Reference should be made to the text of the Concordat and the Good Practice Guide accompanying it.[18] Key commitments contained within the Concordat include the following:

- In consultation with businesses etc, clear standards will be drawn up setting out the level of service and performance the public and business people can expect to receive.
- Information and advice on the rules that are applied will be provided and disseminated as widely as possible.
- The exercise of enforcement functions involves actively working with businesses to advise on and assist with compliance.
- Well publicised, effective and timely complaints procedures which are easily accessible will be provided.
- Any action which is required will be proportionate to the risks. As far as the law allows, the circumstances of the case and the attitude of the operator will be taken into account when considering action.
- Unless immediate action is required, an opportunity to discuss the circumstances of the case and, if possible, resolve points of difference will be provided before enforcement action is taken.
- Where immediate action is necessary, an explanation of why action is required will be provided at the time and confirmed in writing in all cases within ten working days.
- Where there are rights of appeal against action, advice on the appeal mechanism will be clearly set out in writing at the time the action is taken.

51.13 The Concordat will be of particular relevance where enforcement principles are not covered by the 2006 legislation, the Guidance or any enforcement protocol.

Decision to prosecute

51.14 The decision to prosecute forms an important part of the enforcement process. The Code for Crown Prosecutors provides guidance on the

[17] The Enforcement Concordat was signed on 5 March 1998. Although adoption is voluntary, to date over 96% of all central and local government organisations with an enforcement function have adopted the Concordat.
[18] Both of which can be found by following the links on the Cabinet Office website: http://webarchive.nationalarchives.gov.uk/+/http://www.berr.gov.uk/files/file10150.pdf.

general principles to be applied in determining whether proceedings for an offence should be instituted or discontinued. The guidance in the Code must of course be followed by the Crown Prosecution Service whenever they consider prosecuting for an offence,[19] and offences under the 2003 Act are no exception. The Code should also be followed by licensing authorities and local weights and measures authorities in deciding whether to institute prosecutions under the Act.

51.15   Reference should be made to the full text of the Code.[20] However, in summary, the Code provides general principles applicable to the way in which the prosecutor must approach every case. These include the principle that the prosecutor must act in a way which is fair, independent, objective, and must not be affected by improper or undue pressure from any source.[21]

51.16   Thereafter, there is a two-stage test to the decision to prosecute.[22] Firstly, the prosecution must pass the evidential test,[23] namely that when viewed objectively there is enough evidence to provide a realistic prospect of conviction. As part of that test, the prosecutor must consider whether the evidence can be used and is reliable. If the evidential test is not passed, the case must not go ahead, however serious. If the prosecution meets the evidential test, the prosecutor must then decide if the prosecution meets the public interest test.[24]

51.17   In essence, in applying the public interest test the prosecutor is required to balance the factors for and against the prosecution carefully.[25] A prosecution will usually take place unless there are public interest factors tending against prosecution which clearly outweigh those tending in favour.[26] This stage of the test is likely to be of particular relevance to the decision to prosecute for the procedural offences under the Act.

51.18   The Code states that prosecutors should consider the alternatives to prosecution in deciding whether a case should be prosecuted in the courts, and the availability of a police caution is one of those alternatives.[27] In the licensing context, the availability of the review procedure is also a possible alternative to prosecution.[28]

---

[19]   Prosecution of Offences Act 1985, s 10.
[20]   www.cps.gov.uk/publications/docs/code2013english_v2.pdf.
[21]   Code, para 2.4.
[22]   Code, para 4.1.
[23]   Code, para 4.5 et seq.
[24]   Code, para 4.10 et seq.
[25]   Code, para 4.13. Common public interest factors both for and against prosecution are set out at paras 4.16 and 4.17 of the Code.
[26]   Code, para 4.12.
[27]   Code, para 4.12.
[28]   Licensing Act 2003, ss 51–53. The Code also covers the selection of charges, the acceptance of guilty pleas, and the restarting of a prosecution.

In addition, it is imperative that prosecution decisions are made having regard to the prosecuting authority's own enforcement policy. In *R v Adaway*,[29] a defendant appealed to the Crown Court against his conviction for trade description offences on the grounds that the prosecution was not justified, having regard to the prosecuting council's public protection enforcement policy. The Crown Court judge said that the policy gave him the right to stop a prosecution: that was the prerogative of the prosecutor. The Court of Appeal disagreed, holding it oppressive to proceed with a prosecution in clear breach of the terms of the policy. The coda to the judgment has particular resonance for strict liability offences under the Licensing Act 2003:

> 'We cannot emphasise too strongly that before criminal proceedings are instituted by a local authority, acting in relation to strict liability offences created by the Trade Descriptions Act 1968, they must consider with care the terms of their own prosecuting policy. If they fail to do so, or if they reach a conclusion which is wholly unsupported, as the conclusion to prosecute in this case was, by material establishing the criteria for prosecution, it is unlikely that the courts will be sympathetic, in the face of other demands upon their time at Crown Court and appellate level, to attempts to justify such prosecutions.'

B PROCEDURE

51.19 All of the offences under Part 7 are summary only. With the exception of the offences involving unauthorised licensable activities under section 136,[30] the offence of exposing alcohol for unauthorised sale under section 137,[31] and the offences involving vehicles and trains under sections 156 and 157,[32] the Act lays down financial penalties for commission of the offences. Perhaps as a concession to licensing authorities and the administrative burdens they face under the Act, the time limit within which an information must be laid for any offence under the Act is extended from six to twelve months.[33]

51.20 Where a prosecution is taken against an individual, proceedings may be taken at any place where he is for the time being.[34] Companies and partnerships can be prosecuted under the Act as well as their officers, members, or other partners respectively, where the offence is shown to have been committed with their consent or connivance, or is attributable to any

---

[29] [2005] LLR 142.
[30] Section D below.
[31] Section D below.
[32] Section H below.
[33] Section 186(3), by reference to s 127(1) of the Magistrates' Courts Act 1980.
[34] Section 188(5)(b).

neglect on their part.[35] A number of procedural rules are established where unincorporated associations are prosecuted.[36] These are as follows:

- Any fines imposed must be paid out of the funds of the association.
- Proceedings for the offence must be brought in the name of the association and not in the name of any of its members.
- The rules of court in relation to service of documents upon, and the rules of procedure in relation to, a body corporate[37] are to apply to unincorporated associations.
- Proceedings can be taken at any place at which it has a place of business.[38]

Rights of entry

51.21 Constables and authorised persons,[39] including officers from the licensing authority, have rights of entry to premises where they have reason to believe that the premises are (or are about to be) used for a licensable activity.[40] The purpose for entering must be to see whether the activity is being (or is to be) carried out under or in accordance with a licence. If requested, the authorised person must produce evidence of his authority to exercise the power of entry.[41] If necessary, reasonable force may be used in exercising the power.[42] A broad interpretation of this subsection suggests that, subject to the requirement of necessity being met, the use of reasonable force is not limited to gaining entry to the premises, but could be used in exercising the power of seeing whether the activity is being carried out under and in accordance with a licence.[43]

51.22 It should be noted that the rights of entry do not extend to premises licensed as club premises.[44] The fact that applicants must meet a stringent set of criteria to obtain a club premises certificate, that public access is restricted to such premises, and that alcohol is supplied other than for profit

---

[35]   Section 187.

[36]   Section 188.

[37]   Criminal Justice Act 1925, s 33, and Magistrates' Courts Act 1980, Sch 3.

[38]   Licensing Act 2003, s 188(1)–(5)(a).

[39]   Defined under Licensing Act 2003, s 13(2). These include officers of the licensing authority, fire inspectors, health and safety inspectors, environmental health officers, etc.

[40]   Licensing Act 2003, s 179.

[41]   Licensing Act 2003, s 179(2).

[42]   Licensing Act 2003, s 179(3).

[43]   Under Licensing Act 2003, s 179(4) it is an offence carrying a level 3 fine for a person intentionally to obstruct an authorised person exercising a power under the section. Under the Police Act 1996, a similar offence would be committed if a constable were obstructed.

[44]   Licensing Act 2003, s 179(7). However, the restriction only applies where a club premises certificate is the only authorisation attaching to the premises. Where, for example, a temporary event notice is also being operated at the same premises, there is a right of entry.

on them explains why the right of entry is restricted. Club premises are considered private and not generally open to the public.[45]

51.23 There is no such restriction for constables entering and searching premises where they have reason to believe that an offence under the Act has been (or is about to be) committed.[46] Constables may, if necessary, use reasonable force in exercising that power.[47] On the other hand this power of entry cannot be exercised by officers of the licensing authority, despite the fact that it is open to the licensing authority to prosecute for any offences committed under the Act.[48] A joined up approach to enforcement which involves the exchange of information and intelligence would overcome this restriction.[49]

Police and Criminal Evidence Act 1984

51.24 Where the offences involve a mental element, the investigation will normally include an interview with the suspect. Police investigations may also involve the search of premises and the seizure of property found on those premises. The police will be well familiar with the Codes of Practice provided for under section 66 of the Police and Criminal Evidence Act 1984. However, it should be noted that local authority enforcement officers charged with the duty of investigating offences must also have regard to any relevant provisions of those codes in the discharge of their duty.[50] As such, Code C on the questioning of persons and Code E on the tape recording of interviews with suspects will be most relevant to investigations by enforcement officers.[51]

51.25 Where a confession has been obtained, the court has the power not to allow the confession to be given in evidence where, for example, it is represented that it may have been obtained as a result of something said or done which was likely to render it unreliable and the prosecution cannot prove otherwise.[52] More broadly, the court has a discretion to refuse to allow evidence if it considers that the admission of it would have such an adverse

---

45   Guidance, para 6.2.
46   Section 180(1).
47   Section 180(2).
48   See para 51.05 above.
49   Guidance, para 13.16, see para 51.11 above.
50   Police and Criminal Evidence Act ('PACE') 1984, s 67(9). However, reference should be made to *R (Beale) v South East Wiltshire Magistrates' Court* [2002] EWHC 2961 (Admin) where it was held that the obligation imposed by statute to inform a person of his rights to legal advice is restricted to persons under arrest at a police station or in police detention. The relevant provisions of PACE Code C were not intended to cover interviews by Trading Standards Officers because the interviewee was not in police detention.
51   Code C: The detention, treatment and questioning of persons by police officers. Code E: Tape recording of interviews with suspects.
52   PACE 1984, s 76(2)(b).

effect on the fairness of the proceedings that it ought not to admit it.[53] Breaches of the Codes of Practice will expose the prosecution to the risk that crucial parts of the evidence will be excluded under those powers.

Test purchasing

51.26 For the purposes of enforcing the law against underage alcohol sales, weights and measures inspectors are given express powers of test purchasing. Either by themselves, or by authorising others, they may make such purchases of goods as appear expedient to see whether the provisions of sections 146 and 147 are being complied with.[54]

51.27 The involvement of children in the enforcement of this legislation raises a number of issues: consent of the child; the welfare of the child involved; the use of the evidence of the child in any prosecution; the potential for interference with the right to respect for private life;[55] and the use of covert intelligence. In order to negotiate this legal minefield, licensing authorities must familiarise themselves with the Better Regulation Delivery Office's 'Code of Practice on Age Restricted Products'.[56] The Code is endorsed by the Department for Business, Innovation and Skills and provides detailed guidance on test purchase exercises involving children, particularly by reference to the Regulation of Investigatory Powers Act 2000. It must be the starting point for any officer considering the use of test purchasing involving children.

51.28 A table of relevant offences relating to the sale and supply of alcohol to children is contained at paragraph 2.35 of the Guidance. The Guidance also encourages licensing authorities to maintain close contact with the police, young offenders' teams and trading standards officers about the extent of unlawful sales and consumption of alcohol by minors. Licensing authorities are also expected to be involved in the development of any strategies to control or prevent such unlawful activities and to pursue prosecutions.

Disclosure

51.29 Once the decision to prosecute has been taken, proper adherence to the disclosure rules will ensure the smooth running of the prosecution at court. The statutory scheme for disclosure comprises the Criminal Procedure and Investigations Act 1996 (as amended by the Criminal Justice Act 2003 and the Criminal Justice and Immigration Act 2008) supplemented

---

[53] PACE 1984, s 78(1).
[54] Section 154.
[55] Under Art 8(1) of the ECHR.
[56] http://www.bis.gov.uk/assets/brdo/docs/publications-2013/13–537-code-of-practice-age-restricted-products.pdf.

by the Code of Practice issued under Part II of that Act and the Criminal Procedure Rules 2010, Part 22. The Attorney General's Guidelines on Disclosure of Information in Criminal Proceedings and the Protocol for the Provision of Advance Information, Prosecution Evidence and Disclosure of Unused Material in the Magistrates' Courts should also be consulted.

51.30 In essence, where proceedings for a summary offence are concerned, the following rules and principles apply:

(1) The investigator is responsible for ensuring that any information which may be relevant to the investigation is recorded and retained. Where it is considered that the defendant is likely to plead not guilty, the disclosure officer must ensure that a schedule of unused material is prepared.[57]

(2) The Attorney General's Guidelines advise that the prosecutor should provide to the defence all evidence on which it proposes to rely, allowing the accused and his legal advisers sufficient time properly to consider the evidence before it is called.[58] Standard directions in the magistrates' court usually require disclosure in any event.

(3) If the defendant pleads not guilty and the court proceeds to summary trial, the prosecution's duty of disclosure will be engaged.[59]

(4) However, there is no requirement that the defendant provide a defence statement in the magistrates' court. Once the prosecutor has complied (or purported to comply), the defendant has a discretion to provide a defence statement.[60]

(5) There is a continuing duty to review questions of disclosure after the initial disclosure. If a defence statement is provided, then the investigator must look again at the unused material and draw to the prosecutor's attention any material which might reasonably be considered capable of undermining the prosecution case or of assisting the defence case is it were to be disclosed.[61]

Costs

51.31 The general rules on costs in criminal proceedings apply to prosecutions under the Act. The main provisions are contained in the Prosecution of Offences Act 1985, sections 16–21, and the Costs in Criminal Cases (General) Regulations 1986.[62] Reference should also be made to the Practice

---

[57] Code of Practice, paras 5.1 and 6.6.
[58] A-G's Guidelines, para 57.
[59] Criminal Procedure and Investigations Act 1996, ss 1(a) and 3(1).
[60] CPIA 1996, s 6(2)(a).
[61] CPIA 1996, s 7A; A-G's Guidelines, para 51.
[62] SI 1986/1335.

Direction on Costs in Criminal Proceedings which came into force on 18 May 2004.[63]

Prosecution costs

51.32   Where a conviction has been secured, or the defendant has appealed to the Crown Court and the appeal has been dismissed, the court has a discretionary power to order the defendant to pay such costs as it considers just and reasonable.[64] The court must specify the amount of costs in the order.[65] Further, the court itself must determine the amount which the accused should pay, and this cannot be delegated to the clerk of the court.[66]

51.33   The principle that the time of an investigating officer can properly be claimed in the costs was confirmed in *Neville v Gardner Merchant Ltd.*[67] In that case, the defendant company had been prosecuted under the Food Hygiene (General) Regulations 1970 and had pleaded guilty to the charges. In awarding costs, the magistrates disallowed the eight hours of time spent by the Environmental Health Officer in connection with the offences. They did so on the basis that the officer was doing no more than her job and because she was under a duty to make such investigations in any event. It was held that the magistrates had misdirected themselves in concluding that they had no discretion to award those costs. Not only did the magistrates have a discretion to award those costs, but prima facie, costs of that kind should be awarded. In reviewing the case law, it was noted that the fact that a person is salaried makes no difference to the power to award costs in respect of his time, and regard should be had to the overhead and other administrative costs of the organisation in question. If it were found that all the time and trouble of the investigating officer had been due to the offences committed by the defendant, then it would be right to award the whole of those costs.[68]

51.34   *Neville* was followed by the Court of Appeal in *R v Associated Octel Ltd*[69] and the principles were applied to the award of costs under section 18(1) of the Prosecution of Offences Act 1985. Thus it was held that the costs of the prosecution might include the costs of the prosecuting authority in carrying out the investigations with a view to the prosecution of the defendant. The fact that the prosecution had eventually modified its case was not a reason for denying or reducing costs which had been incurred. The court suggested the following procedure on costs:

---

[63]   [2004] 2 All ER 107.
[64]   Prosecution of Offences Act ('POOA') 1985, s 18(1). There are two exceptions to this rule contained in s 18(4) and (5).
[65]   POOA 1985, s 18(3).
[66]   *Bunston v Rawlings* [1982] 1 WLR 473.
[67]   (1983) 5 Cr App R (S) at 349.
[68]   351–353 per Kerr LJ.
[69]   [1997] Crim LR 144.

(1) Full details of costs should be served on the defence at the earliest time, so as to give the defence a proper opportunity to consider them and make representations, if appropriate.

(2) If the defendant wished to dispute the whole or any part of the schedule, proper notice should be given to the prosecution of the objections. It should at least be made clear to the court what the objections were. In exceptional circumstances, a full hearing might need to be held for the objections to be resolved.[70]

51.35 The principle which underlies the exercise of the discretion to award costs is that an order should be made where the court is satisfied that the defendant has the means and the ability to pay.[71] Factors such as a plea of guilty, the conduct of the parties, and apportionment between co-defendants may also be taken into account. The guidelines set out by the Divisional Court in *R (Dove) v Northallerton Magistrates Court*[72] should also be considered.

Defendant's costs

51.36 Where an information is not proceeded with, the defendant is acquitted after summary trial or the defendant pursues a successful appeal to the Crown Court,[73] the court may make a defendant's costs order in favour of the defendant.[74] In essence, this means that the defence costs are paid out of central funds. The only way in which the prosecution could be asked to pay the defendant's costs is where they are ordered to pay costs thrown away as a result of an unnecessary or improper act or omission.[75]

C ELEMENTS OF THE OFFENCES

51.37 There are certain elements of the offences which appear several times throughout Part 7 of the Act, and it is convenient to consider them here.

Strict liability offences

51.38 There are several strict liability offences contained within Part 7 of the Act. These are offences which do not depend upon proof of actual

---

[70] At 146.
[71] Practice Direction, VI.1.4.
[72] [1999] Crim LR 760.
[73] This includes where the appeal is against sentence only and the defendant is awarded a less severe punishment.
[74] POOA 1985, s 16.
[75] POOA 1985, s 19(1) and Costs in Criminal Cases (General) Regulations 1986 (SI 1986/1335).

negligence or intent to harm by the accused. In other words, no mental element need be present for the offence to be committed.

51.39   In the licensing context, it has been noted that the principles which are engaged under a strict liability offence are quite independent of the doctrine of delegation in offences involving knowledge or intent. In *R v Winson*,[76] Lord Parker stated:

> 'When an absolute offence has been created by Parliament, then the person on whom a duty is thrown is responsible, whether he has delegated or whether he has acted through a servant; he is absolutely liable regardless of any intent or knowledge or mens rea.'[77]

Knowingly

51.40   In the vast majority of cases where a mental element is included as an element in the offence, the prosecution is required to prove that something has been done knowingly. It has been observed that the word 'knowingly' has long been associated with the Licensing Acts, and it seems that the Act is no exception.

51.41   Of course, where the offence requires it, actual knowledge on the part of a defendant should normally be established as a fact in order for the offence to be proved. However, the courts have created an additional method by which knowledge can be proved in the context of licensing offences, namely by the doctrine of delegation: in the absence of proof of actual knowledge, a licensee or owner may be held liable if it can be shown that he effectively delegated his proprietary or managerial functions, and the person to whom the function was delegated committed the offence with knowledge.

51.42   The doctrine was first considered by the House of Lords in *Vane v Yiannopoullos*.[78] In that case, the holder of a restaurant licence was prosecuted for knowingly supplying alcohol to persons to whom he was not permitted by the conditions of the licence.[79] A condition on the licence limited the supply of alcohol only to persons taking table meals in the restaurant. On the day in question, the licence holder was generally supervising the conduct of his staff at the restaurant. However, whilst he was in another part of the restaurant (and unknown to him), one of the waitresses sold alcohol to two customers who had not ordered a meal. There was thus no actual knowledge on the part of the licence holder as to the sale of alcohol to the customers. In fact, the waitress had been instructed by the licence holder that she should only serve alcohol to customers ordering a meal.

---

[76]   [1968] 1 All ER 197.
[77]   202E.
[78]   [1964] 3 All ER 820.
[79]   Contrary to s 22(1)(a) of the Licensing Act 1961.

51.43 The licence holder argued that he had not known that the drink had been supplied in that he did not know that the waitress had supplied it. The prosecution argued that the waitress' knowledge could be imputed to the licence holder under the doctrine of delegation.

51.44 The case was decided on the basis of the construction of the section in its context within the Act, and it was held that the word 'knowingly' in this section predicated knowledge in the licence holder, not in his servant. Knowledge in the licence holder had not been established and so he was not guilty.[80]

51.45 However, their Lordships were divided in their approach to the doctrine of delegation. Lords Reid and Evershed both considered that, whether or not the doctrine was justified when originally created, it was by that time so long-standing a practice that it was impossible to reject it. They applied the doctrine to the offence under this section. However, on the facts of this case, they held that there was no sufficient evidence of delegation to render the licence holder liable under the doctrine.[81]

51.46 On the other hand, Lords Morris and Donovan did not find it necessary to express a view on the doctrine. The case could be decided on the language of the section alone which did not need elucidation by reference to case law.[82]

51.47 Finally, Lord Hodson agreed that even if the doctrine of delegation was to remain undisturbed, there was no justification for enlarging the ambit of the section so as to embrace the activities of any servant as here.[83]

51.48 In light of the decision in *Vane*, the defence in *Ross v Moss and Others*[84] submitted that the doctrine of delegation had no application to the same offence. Lord Parker CJ highlighted the uncertainty as to the applicability of the doctrine which had resulted from the separate decisions of their Lordships in *Vane*. However, having decided the case on the facts, which Lord Parker considered stuck out a mile,[85] the court found it unnecessary to

---

[80] 822I per Lord Reid.
[81] 823F, 827G, and 829A.
[82] 830D and 832H.
[83] 832C.
[84] [1965] 3 All ER 145.
[85] The defendant was the holder of a licence for club premises under which intoxicating liquor could only be sold to elected members and their guests. The rules of the club provided that candidates for membership should be proposed and seconded, their names should be posted for 48 hours, annual subscriptions should be paid, and that guests should sign the visitors' book. The magistrates found that the practice at the club was for non-members simply to fill out an application form and pay a small fee. They were then allowed to enter and enjoy the full facilities of the club. Further, there was no system of checking whether a person was a member. The defendant was in charge of the premises and ran this system. However, when the offences were committed the defendant was away

state the true position on the application of the doctrine to the section. The prospect of the court holding that the doctrine applied to the offence was kept open.[86]

51.49 Lord Parker CJ, sitting in the Court of Appeal, finally resolved the issue in *R v Winson*.[87] The director of a company was the holder of a justices' on-licence for club premises. A condition on the licence stated that intoxicating liquor should not be sold to a person who had been a member of the club for less than 48 hours. Two police officers were admitted to the club and served with alcohol in breach of that condition. At the time of the offences, the club was being run by a manager who had been appointed by a managing director, who in turn was a member of the board of the company of which the defendant was director. The defendant confirmed that he had delegated his responsibility as licence holder to the manager. The defendant took little interest in ensuring compliance with the conditions on the licence, and his defence was that he did not knowingly sell the alcohol to the police officers. The prosecution relied on the doctrine of delegation.

51.50 The question therefore was whether the doctrine of delegation had any application to section 161(1) of the Licensing Act 1964, and the parties relied on the speeches in *Vane* as appropriate. Whilst Lord Parker noted the very powerful and persuasive authority of the speeches of Lord Morris and Lord Donovan that the doctrine of delegation could not apply to the section, he also noted that Lord Reid and Lord Evershed were quite clearly saying that if on the facts there had been delegation, the doctrine would apply to that section.[88] Having reviewed the case law leading to the inception of the

---

from the premises on holiday and had delegated the management of the club to his father. It was held that in going away the defendant was not merely shutting his eyes to what was going on, but intending that that system should continue. The word 'knowingly' in the section covered the cases of actual knowledge, shutting one's eyes to what is going on, but also where someone intended what occurs to go on, but deliberately looked the other way. It made no difference if instead of being on the premises and turning his head the other way, the defendant was in fact away on holiday, but had every intention that the system should continue to operate in his absence (148D–H).

[86] It should be noted that the factual scenario in *Ross v Moss* was distinguished from that in *Buxton v Chief Constable of Northumbria* (1984) 148 JP Rep 9. The joint licensee of a Mecca centre had been convicted, inter alia, of knowingly allowing a person to sell intoxicating liquor to a named person being under the age of 18 years, contrary to s 169(1) of the Licensing Act 1964. The prosecution had alleged that the defendant had turned a blind eye to what was going on. However, on the facts, Lord Goff took a different view. Far from deliberately closing his eyes or turning his head away in order to avoid knowing the relevant facts, he found that the defendant was doing his best to enforce a system where the circumstances were such that it was extremely difficult to enforce it. It seems that *Ross v Moss* was the only authority cited to the court in that case. Further, it appears that the case is in part a decision on due diligence under s 169(10) of the 1964 Act. It is suggested that *Buxton* should be limited to its facts.

[87] [1968] 1 All ER 197.

[88] 202D.

doctrine, Lord Parker stated that the doctrine was well established, and that it applied to the section under consideration:

'Parliament must be taken, when this section was originally introduced in 1961 and continued in 1964, to know that the doctrine of delegation had been applied in a number of licensing cases, and that the principle of those cases was that a man cannot get out of the responsibilities and duties attached to a licence by absenting himself. The position of course is quite different if he remains in control. It would be only right that he should not be liable if a servant behind his back did something which contravened the terms of the licence. If, however, he wholly absents himself leaving somebody else in control, he cannot claim that what has happened has happened without his knowledge if the delegate has knowingly carried on in contravention of the licence.'[89]

51.51 Having recognised and applied the doctrine in *Winson*, Lord Parker refused to extend it in *Duncan v Hart and Another*[90] where the defendant, a licence holder, had been summarily dismissed prior to the offences being committed.[91] It was held that since he could not sell, and nor could anyone sell on his authority, to find him guilty would be an unwarranted extension of the doctrine.[92]

51.52 The application of the doctrine was stretched to its limit in *Howker v Robinson*,[93] where intoxicating liquor had knowingly been sold to a person under the age of 18. The court was bound by the findings of the magistrates and decided that the defendant, who was the holder of the licence and present on the premises, had been rightly convicted after his barman had knowingly sold alcohol to a person who was not quite 15 years of age. The findings were that the barman had complete control over the sale of intoxicating liquor in the lounge, and that the responsibility of ensuring that persons under 18 years of age were not sold intoxicating liquor had been delegated to him by the defendant.[94] The principle in *Winson* was applied: although the defendant was present in another bar on the premises, was not present in the lounge where the sale had taken place, and had no knowledge of what took place, he had effectively delegated his managerial functions and responsibilities in respect of the lounge bar to the barman; he was therefore liable. Thus, delegation could apply to part of a premises, even though the licence holder remained in another part of the premises.

---

[89] 204F–H.
[90] (1967) 111 SJ 887.
[91] The defendant was a hotel manager, who was the holder of a restaurant licence. He was charged with, inter alia, knowingly selling intoxicating liquor to non-members contrary to s 161(1), and knowingly permitting intoxicating liquor to be consumed on the premises by persons not taking a table meal contrary to s 161(2) of the Licensing Act 1964.
[92] At 888.
[93] [1972] 2 All ER 786.
[94] 792A–D per Bristow J.

51.53 More recently, the doctrine of delegation was considered by the Divisional Court in *LB Southwark v Allied Domecq Leisure Ltd.*[95] In that case, a public house owned by the respondent company was used for the provision of public entertainment without a licence. Under the doctrine of delegation, knowledge was imputed to the area manager who was charged and convicted of an offence of being a person concerned in the organisation or management of that entertainment contrary to paragraph 10(1)(a) of Schedule 12 to the London Government Act 1963. A separate information alleged that the respondent company had allowed the premises to be used for the purposes of the entertainment 'knowing or having reasonable cause to suspect' that such entertainment would be provided at the premises contrary to paragraph 10(1)(b) of the same schedule. This information was based on the same facts, but the magistrate refused to impute knowledge to the company and acquitted it. The prosecutor appealed to the High Court.

51.54 Mitchell J summarised the doctrine of delegation from the case law and made two points. Firstly, he stated that for the doctrine to apply, the delegator's offence must be the same offence as is actually committed by the person to whom the responsibility has been delegated. Secondly, he noted that none of the delegation cases involved the prosecution of someone to whom the licensee had not delegated his responsibility. For the company to be liable, it would have to be shown that it had delegated its responsibility to the co-licensees, and that would be an extension of the doctrine. Even if that could be shown, the offence committed would be under paragraph 10(1)(a), not 10(1)(b). He therefore held that the magistrate was correct to acquit the company.

Allow or permit

51.55 The starting point when considering an offence which requires proof that the defendant 'allowed' something to be done is that there must be some direct, or indirect, sanction of it.[96] Thus a distinction can be made between 'allowing' something to be done and 'suffering' things to happen.

51.56 The case of *Crabtree v Fern Spinning Co Ltd*[97] is often cited for the principle that a man cannot 'allow' that of which he is unaware. That case involved a prosecution under the Factory and Workshop Act 1895. A boy had been ordered to do some cleaning of a machine, and in order to do so, he was obliged to be in the space between the fixed and traversing portions of it. Whilst the boy was still in this space, the defendant's employee, thinking the boy was clear of the space, started the machine. The boy was injured and later died. The company was charged with an offence contrary to section 9 of

---

[95] 1998 162 JP 1010.
[96] Greenberg, *Stroud's Judicial Dictionary of Words and Phrases* (Sweet & Maxwell, 7th ed), Vol 1 p 111.
[97] 112 LT 107.

that Act, whereby a factory employee shall not be allowed to be in such a space unless the machine is stopped. The court held that the justices were right to dismiss the information on the ground that the defendant's employee, believing at the time he started the machine that the boy was clear of the space, did not 'allow' the boy to be in the space in question when the machine was started.

51.57 When considering an offence which involves proof that the defendant 'permitted' something, *Test Valley Investments Ltd v Tanner*[98] is useful as authority for the proposition that a person might be said to 'permit' something not only if they gave express permission but also if they failed to take reasonable steps to prevent it. Thus, a failure to take unreasonable steps would not amount to 'permitting'.

51.58 The case involved an unauthorised gypsy encampment. The owners of the land were charged with permitting their land to be used as a caravan site without a licence,[99] and with allowing land to be used for camping purposes on more than 42 consecutive days without a licence.[100] The owners had taken injunctive proceedings in the county court against those on the land, but given that the population on the site was floating, it was recognised by all parties that it was impossible to take effective steps in the county court. The correspondence between the council and the owners made clear that the council expected the owners to take the law into their own hands and physically to evict the gypsies.

51.59 In giving the leading judgment, Lord Parker stated that 'a man may be said to permit something, not merely if he gives express permission but if he fails to take what in the cases have sometimes been called proper steps, and in other cases adequate steps, to prevent that which it is said he is permitting.'[101] However, he considered that that did not include steps which in all the circumstances were unreasonable. It was held that to expect the owners physically to eject the gypsies was wholly unreasonable in all the circumstances of the case; there were perhaps 30 gypsies with their caravans, rough shelters, tents and the like. Thus the owners were not liable to be prosecuted for the period when they took action. It should be noted that Lord Parker considered 'allowing' and 'permitting' under the different sections as synonymous.[102]

51.60 In most of the offences under Part 7, the prosecution will have to prove not only that the defendant allowed something but that he knowingly allowed it. To that extent reference should be made to the above section on interpretation of the word 'knowingly'. An example of judicial interpretation

[98]   (1964) 15 P&CR 279.
[99]   Contrary to s 1 of the Caravan Sites and Control of Development Act 1960.
[100] Contrary to s 269 of the Public Health Act 1936.
[101] At 281.
[102] At 282.

of the phrase 'knowingly allow' can be found in *Buxton v Chief Constable of Northumbria*.[103] On the facts of that case, it was held that the joint licensee had not deliberately closed his eyes or turned his head away to avoid knowing that persons under the age of 18 were being admitted and served alcohol. He was in fact doing his best to enforce a system despite the fact that the circumstances made enforcement extremely difficult and it was inevitable that some persons under the age of 18 would be served alcohol. He had therefore not 'knowingly allowed' a person to sell alcohol to a named person under the age of 18 years.

Corporate liability

51.61 Under section 187 of the Act, a statutory scheme is established under which key management figures within corporate bodies, unincorporated associations, and partnerships can, in certain circumstances, be prosecuted in addition to the company or partnership to which they belong for any offence[104] under the Act.

51.62 Section 187(1) states that where an offence has been committed by a corporate body, and was committed with the consent or connivance of an officer or was attributable to any neglect on his part, then the officer is guilty of the offence in addition to the corporate body. The provision extends beyond formally appointed officers. The net is cast sufficiently widely to include members where the company is managed by members.[105] It also includes persons purporting to act in the capacity of one of the company officers or an individual who is the controller of the body.[106] The latter fixes liability on someone with no day-to-day involvement but who is in *de facto* control of the whole.

51.63 In the case of partnerships the liability extends to consenting, conniving or neglectful partners and purported partners.[107] Similarly, for unincorporated associations, it extends to officers of the association and members of its governing body.[108]

51.64 The requirements of consent, connivance and causative neglect are the same as those set out in section 37 of the Health and Safety at Work Act 1974 and reference should be made to the case law under that section.

---

[103] (1984) 148 JP Rep 9. See footnote 85 above.
[104] Section 187(8).
[105] Section 187(2).
[106] Section 187(3).
[107] Section 187(4), (5).
[108] Section 187(6).

51.65 The word 'connivance' means a 'willingness to secretly allow or be involved in an illegal act',[109] and its meaning can be considered as similar to 'wilful blindness'. Thus, the presence of this word allows for liability to be established where something less than consent is shown. As one commentator has noted, there is no direct authority on the construction of the term (in the context of safety legislation).[110]

51.66 In *Wotherspoon v HM Advocate*,[111] the High Court of Justiciary considered[112] whether a jury had been misdirected by the failure to give a proper direction as to the meaning of the words 'attributable to any neglect' in section 37(1) of the Health and Safety at Work Act 1974. In holding that the judge had said 'just enough' to satisfy the requirements of the law, the Lord-Justice General interpreted the words 'neglect' and 'attributable to', making the following observations:

- The word 'neglect' in its natural meaning presupposes the existence of some obligation or duty on the part of the person charged with neglect.
- When read as a whole, section 37 is concerned primarily to provide a penal sanction against those persons charged with functions of management who can be shown to have been responsible for the commission of a relevant offence by an artificial persona, a body corporate.
- Thus, where an officer is charged, there must be a search to discover whether he has failed to take steps to prevent the commission of the offence by the corporation, if the taking of those steps either expressly falls or should be held to fall within the scope of his functions as an officer.
- The functions of the officer will therefore be a highly relevant consideration for the court.
- The question of whether there was a failure to take a step which could and should have been taken must be answered in the light of all the circumstances of the case, including his state of knowledge of the need for action, or the existence of a situation requiring action to be taken of which he ought to have been aware.
- The words 'attributable to' are also well understood in ordinary speech.
- Any degree of attributality will suffice.[113]

---

[109] See the *Oxford English Dictionary*.

[110] Ford, *Redgrave's Health and Safety* (LexisNexis, 7th ed), at 2.58: 'It is submitted that it connotes a specific mental state not amounting to actual consent to the commission of the offence in question, concomitant with a failure to take any step to prevent or discourage the commission of that offence.'

[111] 1978 JC 74.

[112] As a Scottish case, and one where the court was considering an application for leave to appeal, it is of persuasive force only.

[113] In *Regina v E* [2007] EWCA Crim 1937, the Court of Appeal held that the judge had given a misdirection at a preparatory hearing on the issue of neglect and set the burden on the prosecution too high. Parliament had chosen quite plainly that there should be a distinction between consent, connivance, and neglect. The court applied the judgement in *Wotherspoon* and reiterated that the correct question in terms of neglect, where there was no actual

Thus, the commission of a relevant offence by a body corporate may well be found to be attributable to failure on the part of a number of directors, managers or other officers to take steps which each could and should have taken in the discharge of the particular functions of their office.

51.67   It is clear from the wording of the section that the scheme is intended to be far reaching; the inclusion of a residual category of officer, defined as any 'similar officer of the body', in addition to those specified for corporate bodies, is one indication of this. Of more significance is the further category of person who can be caught, namely persons 'purporting to act' in the capacity of a director, etc in corporate bodies, and those 'purporting to act' as a partner in the case of partnerships.[114] This potentially exposes to criminal liability all sorts of people who operate at the coalface of the company or partnership.

51.68   When considered against the background of the doctrine of delegation[115] and the potential for companies to attract criminal liability, the scheme under section 187 of the Act reinforces the view that no company or part of a company will be immune from prosecution under the Act.[116]

Due diligence

51.69   There are two categories of due diligence defence contained within Part 7 of the Act. The first category is the due diligence defence set out in section 139 of the Act. This applies only to the offences of carrying on or attempting to carry on a licensable activity without authorisation, exposing alcohol for unauthorised sale, and keeping alcohol on premises for unauthorised sale.[117] It contains two elements. The first is as follows:

'**Defence of due diligence**

(1)   In proceedings against a person for a [specified] offence ... it is a defence that –
his act was due to a mistake or to reliance on information given to him, or to an act or omission by another person, or to some other cause beyond his control, and

---

knowledge of a state of facts, was whether the officer in question should have, by reason of the surrounding circumstances, been put on enquiry so as to require him to have taken steps to determine whether or not the appropriate safety procedures were in place (paras 12–13).

[114]   Licensing Act 2003, s 187(3)(a) and (5).

[115]   See para 51.41 et seq above.

[116]   Under s 187(7), the Secretary of State is also empowered to issue regulations providing for the application of any provision of the section to bodies corporate and partnerships formed or recognised under foreign law.

[117]   Licensing Act 2003, ss 136(1)(a), 137 and 138.

he took all reasonable precautions and exercised all due diligence to avoid committing the offence.'[118]

51.70 A defence in exactly the same terms is included for the offence of prohibiting the sale of alcohol on moving vehicles.[119] It is unusual for a due diligence defence to contain both of the above elements, and it is clear that both must be in place for the defence to be effective.[120] This is clearly a specialised version of the due diligence defence which is perhaps intended to be more difficult to establish in light of the relative seriousness of the offences to which it attaches.

51.71 The second category of due diligence defence is a simpler version. A due diligence offence is included for certain offences concerning children: the prohibition of unaccompanied children from certain premises; the sale of alcohol to children; and the sale of liqueur confectionery to children under 16.[121] Given the limited application of the section 139 defence, these defences are presumably to be interpreted quite separately. There is no further explanation of the words 'due diligence' either in the Act or the Guidance.[122] It is suggested that, in effect, the defence will be interpreted in line with the second limb of the section 139 defence.

Reverse burden and criminal offences

51.72 It is well established that, as a general rule, the onus of proving a defence is on the defendant, and where he does so the standard of proof is on the balance of probabilities.[123] As such, these defences can be said to involve what is known as a reverse burden. With the incorporation of the European Convention on Human Rights into UK law, the courts have on a number of occasions been asked to consider the extent to which such provisions are compatible with the presumption of innocence guaranteed by Article 6(2) of the Convention.[124] In other words, it has been argued that clauses requiring a defendant to prove a defence to avoid criminal liability are at odds with the

---

[118] Licensing Act 2003, s 139(1).

[119] Licensing Act 2003, s 156(3).

[120] Guidance, para 14.14.

[121] Licensing Act 2003, ss 145(8), 146(6), and 148(5).

[122] One example is provided in relation to the offence of selling alcohol to children (Guidance, para 12.9). Where a barman made the sale after being told by his manager that he knew that the purchaser was 18 or over, the barman may be able to rely on the defence, if he can show that, in addition, he exercised all due diligence to avoid committing the offence.

[123] *R v Carr-Briant* [1943] 2 All ER 156. The Court of Appeal considered the offence of corruptly making a gift or loan to an employee of the War department, under which consideration was deemed to be given corruptly 'unless the contrary was proved'.

[124] Article 6(2) of the Convention provides: 'Everyone charged with a criminal offence shall be presumed innocent until proved guilty according to the law.' The Convention was incorporated by the Human Rights Act 1998, s 3(1) of which provides: 'So far as is possible to do so, primary legislation ... must be read and given effect in a way which is compatible with Convention rights'.

fundamental right to the presumption of innocence under Article 6(2) of the Convention.

51.73   There is no question that the defences under the Licensing Act 2003 impose a legal burden on the defendant. That is, if he fails to prove his defence on balance of probabilities, he will be convicted. It is not for the prosecution to disprove the defence, but for the defendant to prove it. When a legal burden is imposed on the defendant the approach of the courts is to consider whether the imposition of the burden is disproportionate. Where it is, the courts will 'read down' the legal burden so as to treat it as an evidential burden. The effect of that is to impose on the defendant a burden merely to raise the issue by evidence. If he discharges that relatively light burden, it then becomes incumbent on the prosecution to disprove the defence according to the usual standard – beyond reasonable doubt.

51.74   The principles upon which the court should make the determination of whether to 'read down' the defence have been developed over a large number of appellate cases, of which the most important have been the House of Lords decisions in *R v Director of Public Prosecutions ex parte Kebilene*[125] and *R v Johnstone*,[126] the Court of Appeal's decision in *Attorney General's Reference (No 1 of 2004)*[127] and, finally, the decision of the House of Lords in *Attorney General's Reference (No 4 of 2002)*.[128] These warrant some detailed exposition.

R v Johnstone

51.75   In this case, the House of Lords considered the foregoing authorities, including *Kebilene*. Lord Nicholls of Birkenhead, with whom the other members of the committee agreed, held that reverse burdens derogated from the presumption of innocence, and therefore imposed on the state an obligation to justify the derogation and demonstrate that a reasonable balance had been struck. He did not believe that identifying the requirements of a reasonable balance was easy, but did believe that the reasons in favour of the derogation would need to be strong ones:

> '... all that can be said is that for a reverse burden of proof to be acceptable there must be a compelling reason why it is fair and reasonable to deny the accused person the protection normally guaranteed to everyone by the presumption of innocence.'[129]

51.76   Notwithstanding the requirement that the reasons for derogation be compelling ones, Lord Nicholls considered that the court's role was one of

---

[125]   [2000] 2 AC 326.
[126]   [2003] 1 WLR 1736.
[127]   [2004] 1 WLR 2111.
[128]   [2004] UKHL 43.
[129]   Para 49.

review only, and that it was for Parliament, and not the court, to carry the primary responsibility of deciding, as a matter of policy, what should be the constituent elements of a criminal offence. The court would only reach a different conclusion from the legislature 'when it is apparent the legislature has attached insufficient importance to the fundamental right of an individual to be presumed innocent until proved guilty.'[130]

51.77 Lord Nicholls pointed out that a legal burden on the accused permits a conviction in spite of the court having a reasonable doubt as to his guilt. Conversely, of course, a mere evidential burden leaves the onus on the prosecution to prove the case beyond reasonable doubt. Lord Nicholls felt that the consequences of a reverse burden on the accused should colour the approach of the court when considering whether the burden should be legal or evidential. The court should ask itself whether the public interest would genuinely be prejudiced by a mere evidential burden to such an extent that a legal burden on the accused is justified. In considering the question of justification, Lord Nicholls referred to the following factors as potentially relevant:

(a) The more serious the penalty, the more compelling must be the reason for the legal burden on the accused.
(b) The extent and nature of the factual matters to be proved by the accused.
(c) The importance of those factual matters relative to the matters to be proved by the prosecution.
(d) The extent to which those matters may be readily proved by the accused from his own knowledge or relate to facts to which he has ready access.[131]

Attorney General's Reference (No 1 of 2004)

51.78 In this case, a five judge Court of Appeal reviewed all of the relevant authorities and set out principles for the benefit of the lower courts. Whilst it was acknowledged that the principles would not be applicable in every single instance, Lord Woolf CJ made it clear that courts 'should be robust and not allow extensive argument.' Lord Woolf CJ, speaking for the court, hoped that if the lower courts bore in mind the principles they would not go far wrong:[132]

> '(A) Courts should strongly discourage the citation of authority to them other than the decision of the House of Lords in Johnstone and this guidance. Johnstone is at present the latest word on the subject.

130 Para 51.
131 Para 50.
132 2134A.

(B)   The common law (the golden thread) and the language of Article 6(2) have the same effect. Both permit legal reverse burdens of proof or presumptions in the appropriate circumstances.

(C)   Reverse legal burdens are probably justified if the overall burden of proof is on the prosecution i.e., the prosecution has to prove the essential ingredients of the offence, but there is a situation where there are significant reasons why it is fair and reasonable to deny the accused the general protection normally guaranteed by the presumption of innocence.

(D)   Where the exception goes no further than is reasonably necessary to achieve the objective of the reverse burden (i.e. it is proportionate), it is sufficient if the exception is reasonably necessary in all the circumstances. The assumption should be that Parliament would not have made an exception without good reason. While the judge must make his own decision as to whether there is a contravention of Article 6, the task of a judge is to "review" Parliament's approach, as Lord Nicholls indicates in Johnstone.

(E)   If only an evidential burden is placed on the defendant there will be no risk of contravention of Article 6(2).

(F)   When ascertaining whether an exception is justified, the court must construe the provision to ascertain what will be the realistic effects of the reverse burden. In doing this the courts should be more concerned with substance than form. If the proper interpretation is that the statutory provision creates an offence plus an exception that will in itself be a strong indication that there is no contravention of Article 6(2).

(G)   The easier it is for the accused to discharge the burden the more likely it is that the reverse burden is justified. This will be the case where the facts are within the defendant's own knowledge. How difficult it would be for the prosecution to establish the facts is also indicative of whether a reverse legal burden is justified.

(H)   The ultimate question is: would the exception prevent a fair trial? If it would, it must either be read down if this is possible; otherwise it should be declared incompatible.

(I)   Caution must be exercised when considering the seriousness of the offence and the power of punishment. The need for a reverse burden is not necessarily reflected by the gravity of the offence, though, from a defendant's point of view, the more serious the offence, the more important it is that there is no interference with the presumption of innocence.

(J)   If guidance is needed as to the approach of the European Court of Human Rights, that is provided by the *Salabiaku*[133] case at para 28 of the judgment where it is stated that "Article 6(2) does not therefore regard presumptions of fact or of law provided for in

---

[133]   (1991) 13 EHRR 379, 388.

the criminal law with indifference. It requires states to confine them within reasonable limits which take into account the importance of what is at stake and maintains the rights of the defence".'[134]

Attorney General's Reference (No 4 of 2002)

51.79 In this case, the House of Lords echoed what had been said in *R v Johnstone*, but sounded a cautionary note that the task of the court is not to decide for itself whether a reverse burden is justified but to assess whether a burden enacted by Parliament unjustifiably infringes the presumption of innocence.[135] In other words, the power is one of review, not one of drawing the balance without reference to what Parliament itself has decided. Drawing on European authorities, Lord Bingham reiterated the overriding concern that the trial should be fair, and held up the presumption of innocence as a fundamental right directed to that end. For him, the relevant principles in the review were:

(a)   the opportunity given to the accused to rebut the presumption;
(b)   maintenance of the rights of the defence;
(c)   flexibility in application of the presumption;
(d)   retention by the court of a power to assess the evidence;
(e)   the importance of what is at stake; and
(f)   the difficulty for the prosecutor in the absence of a reverse burden.[136]

51.80 Lord Bingham sounded a cautionary note that the judgment of the Court of Appeal in *Attorney General's Reference No 1 of 2004* was subordinate to the leading House of Lords cases, and that its guidance was not to be endorsed save to the extent that it was consistent with those leading domestic authorities.[137]

Application of principles to licensing

51.81 Applying the above principles to the due diligence defence in section 139 of the Act, it is suggested that the courts will leave undisturbed the legal burden on the defendant, for the following reasons:

(1)   The prosecution retains the burden of proving the acts constituting the offence, for example that a concert was held without a licence, or that a licensing condition as to the capacity of the premises was breached.
(2)   The burden then passes to the defendant to prove why he did what he did, eg that his act was due to reliance on information given to him by

---

[134]   Pages 2134B–2135A.
[135]   Para 31 per Lord Bingham.
[136]   Para 21.
[137]   Para 32.

---

another person, and that he took reasonable precautions and exercised diligence to avoid the commission of the offence.

(3) In most cases, the defendant will have the relevant facts at his fingertips, and could readily discharge the defence if it applies to him, but the prosecution would not even know what facts to look for when investigating the offence.

(4) All of the offences to which the defence applies are summary only, and punishable according to the jurisdiction of the magistrates only.

51.82 To take an example, the defendant licensee may have employed sufficient competent door supervisors, had them all sign contracts as to manning the door, ensured they all had mechanical counters, instituted a system to ensure they were doing their job correctly and so on. However if, just after leaving the premises on a busy night, a door supervisor, as an aberration, decided to let in a busload of his friends, it would be invidious to convict the defendant of the offence. In those circumstances, the prosecution would establish that the offence had been committed through its investigations. The burden would then pass to the defendant to give evidence and show what steps he had taken to ensure the non-commission of the offence. If he succeeded on balance of probabilities, he would be acquitted.

51.83 It should be said that this conclusion is reached with some diffidence. There are no reported cases relating to the offences under the Licensing Act 2003 in which the issue has been considered.[138] In the Attorney General's Reference itself, Lord Woolf CJ stated that the same section of an Act could impose a legal burden when applied to one offence in the Act, and an evidential burden – having been read-down – when applied to another.[139] Thus, individual consideration would need to be given to each offence as the occasion arises. Given the risk that the prosecution will be held to have a legal burden of disproving the defence, extra care will have to be taken to investigate the matter fully and properly during the investigation. In almost all cases, an interview with the suspect will have to be conducted to find out what they knew at the time, and why they did what they did.

51.84 It is now appropriate to turn to the section 139 defence itself which, as stated above, has two limbs.

---

[138] Although it should be noted that in the Scottish case of *McLean v Carnegie* 2006 SLT 40, the High Court rejected the argument that the due diligence defence contained in s 71 of the Licensing (Scotland) Act 1976 should be read down. The court held that there was nothing either unfair or incompatible with the Convention if a legal (as opposed to evidential) burden rested on the defendant to make out the defence. The due diligence defence contained in s 71 required the defendant to prove (as relevant) that he used due diligence to prevent the occurrence of the offence of selling alcohol to a person under the age of 18. This provides limited persuasive authority for the view set out above.

[139] 2133C.

First limb

51.85 In one sense, the first limb can be said to be restrictive, in that it provides four specific categories into which the defendant's reason for acting must fall. On the other hand, there is nothing in the Act or the Guidance which explains what acts these categories might cover. In light of that fact, it is suggested that they are not to be construed as legal terms of art. It will be open to the courts to interpret them in accordance with their plain everyday usage, and as such they may be viewed as broad categories.

Second limb

51.86 Prima facie, the second limb would appear to fall into two parts. That is, the defendant must prove firstly that he took 'all reasonable precautions', and secondly that he 'exercised all due diligence' to avoid committing the offence. This interpretation is perhaps reinforced by the absence of the 'reasonable precautions' part of the defence in the simple due diligence offences contained elsewhere in Part 7 of the Act.[140] But that begs the question as to what difference there is, if any, between a person who takes all reasonable precautions and a person who exercises all due diligence.

51.87 In practice, the notion of taking all reasonable precautions could perhaps be considered as a subset of the exercise of all due diligence. However, the express inclusion of this phrase appears to provide a heightened test for the defendant to pass under the second limb of the defence. Where in any given case a finite number of reasonable precautions can be discerned, the defendant will only establish this part of the defence if he can show that he took all of them. Thus, although it can be suggested that there is some overlap between the two parts, each part must be given its full meaning.

51.88 Drawing on related case law and experience, the following points can be made on the legal and evidential approach to the defence:

(1) In *Tesco Ltd v Nattrass*,[141] the House of Lords considered the due diligence defence under section 24(1) of the Trade Descriptions Act 1968, which is framed in almost identical terms to the second limb of the defence under section 139 of the 2003 Act. Full reference should be made to that case. Two points were established. The first was that a shop manager was capable of being 'another person' for the purposes of the equivalent first limb of that defence such that the company could properly seek to blame him and rely on the due diligence defence.[142] The second point was that the House took the opportunity to wipe the

---

[140] See, for example, s 145(8) whereby in certain circumstances it is a defence simply that the accused exercised all due diligence to avoid committing the offence.

[141] [1972] AC 153.

[142] 169A per Lord Reid.

slate clean of a body of case law which had provided a restricted meaning for the due diligence test.[143]

Following that case law the lower court had held that the word 'he' in 'he took all reasonable precautions' meant the accused and all his servants who were acting in a managerial or supervisory capacity. Thus where it had been established that the shop manager was responsible for seeing that proper packs were on sale, but had failed to see to this,[144] the defendant company could not defend on the basis that it had taken all reasonable steps. Having reviewed the case law, the House of Lords held that there were no grounds for reading that part of the defence in that way. By enacting the defence, Parliament plainly intended to make a just and reasonable distinction between the corporate employer who is wholly blameless and ought to be acquitted and the employer who was in some way at fault.[145]

The House required scrutiny of the 'directing mind and will'[146] or the 'brain area'[147] of the corporate employer in the discharge of its responsibilities. A system had to be created which could rationally be said to be so designed that the commission of offences would be avoided.[148] The principle is that where a system is so designed and properly scrutinised to ensure compliance, a slip by someone down the food chain is not sufficient to displace the defence. It was held that the manager of the store was not part of the directing will of the defendant company, and his failure to exercise proper supervision over his subordinates did not demonstrate a want of due diligence on the part of the company.

(2)   Given that the offences are summary only, there is no requirement for the defence to provide a defence statement.[149] This could potentially lead to a situation where the prosecution becomes aware that a due diligence defence is to be relied upon at a very late stage in the proceedings.[150] In theory, it would be open to the prosecution in those circumstances to apply for an adjournment in order to verify and further investigate the defence and any evidence on which it is based. In practice, it is suggested that that should rarely happen.[151] There is a greater burden on the prosecution to carry out its initial investigation more fully and thoroughly where the defence of due diligence is

---

[143]   170B per Lord Reid.
[144]   Thereby giving rise to the offence under s 11(2) of the 2003 Act.
[145]   174D per Lord Reid.
[146]   Page 180F, per Lord Morris of Borth-y-Gest.
[147]   181A.
[148]   180F.
[149]   Criminal Procedure and Investigations Act 1996, s 6(2)(a). See para 51.30 above.
[150]   It should be noted that the Act does not contain a provision requiring notice to be given to the prosecutor if the accused is blaming another person (cf s 24(2) of the Trade Descriptions Act 1968).
[151]   Quite aside from the question of costs.

concerned. If the investigation has been carried out properly, the prosecution should not be caught unawares by such a defence.

(3) Non-compliance with industry and other approved guidance will make it very difficult to establish the second limb of the defence. On the other hand, total compliance will go a long way towards helping to establishing it. Evidence of the existence and use of the following procedures will also assist:

- regular auditing;
- spot checks;
- immediate disciplinary action where any breaches are found;
- regular supervision;
- training and refresher courses;
- automatic reminder documentation notifying staff that retraining is required;
- a system to suspend staff if they do not attend for training at the required time; and
- random drug and alcohol testing of employees (where relevant).

(4) In order to discharge the burden of proving due diligence, all procedures should be carefully and clearly documented. The procedures should also be fully understood by all staff. The existence of lengthy operational guidance on, for example, the prevention of alcohol being exposed for unauthorised sale, will carry little weight as evidence if no one is required to read it, or if the staff have read it but not fully understood its contents.[152]

(5) The approach of the courts when considering the due diligence defence in health and safety prosecutions has increasingly been to focus on organisational failings. As a consequence, it is becoming more and more difficult for a company simply to blame operators or employees. It is suggested that the courts may well approach offences involving the due diligence defence under the 2003 Act in the same way.

(6) The current approach is reflected in recognised health and safety guidance. The health and safety guidance document 'Reducing Error and Influencing Behaviour'[153] provides (p 6):

> '... many accidents are blamed on the actions or omissions of an individual who was directly involved in operational or maintenance work. This typical but short sighted response ignores the fundamental failures which led to the accident. These are typically rooted deeper in the organisations' design, management and decision making functions.'

---

[152] Where employees use English as a second language, the use of certified translations should be considered.

[153] HSE HSG 48 'Reducing error and influencing behaviour' (Norwich HMSO, 1999).

51.89 With regard to risk assessing human contributions the document encourages employers to address human functions in four ways:

- during risk assessments;
- when analysing incidents, accidents and omissions;
- in design and procurement; and
- in aspects of day to day health and safety.

Directors' responsibility

51.90 There is currently a hostile climate for directors who fail to take their general duties on public safety seriously. In 2007 the HSC issued guidelines for board members in the public and private sectors entitled 'Leading Health and Safety at Work'.[154]

51.91 The guidance sets out a four-point agenda for embedding the essential health and safety principles including the need for the board to establish a health and safety policy that is much more than a document – it should be an intergral part of the organisation's culture, of its values and performance standards. The policy should set out the board's own role and that of individual board members in leading the health and safety of its organisation.[155]

51.92 There is also an ever-increasing number of prosecutions of directors and managers for breaches of health and safety and manslaughter. The HSE's Enforcement Policy Statement[156] advises that when enforcing authorities prosecute they should ensure that a senior officer of the dutyholder concerned, at board level, is also notified. Enforcing authorities should also consider the management chain and the role played by individual directors and managers, and should take action against them where the investigation reveals that the offence was committed with their consent or connivance or to have been attributable to neglect on their part and where it would be appropriate to do so in accordance with the policy. In that context, it is also noteworthy that there has been an increasing use of directors' disqualification powers by the courts in sentencing for health and safety offences.

51.93 It should be noted that the issue of directors' responsibility is a highly political one in the health and safety sphere. Where prosecutions are brought against directors for licensing offences involving health and safety issues, there is a real possibility that the courts, whether directly or indirectly, will draw on the principles contained in health and safety guidance on directors' responsibility.

---

[154] INDG417, http://www.hse.gov.uk/pubns/indg451.pdf.
[155] At the time the first edition of this book was published, the HSC Chairman was quoted as saying 'Health and Safety is a boardroom issue. Good Health and Safety reflects strong leadership from the top.'
[156] HSE (2009). http://www.hse.gov.uk/pubns/hse41.pdf.

D UNAUTHORISED LICENSABLE ACTIVITIES

51.94 There are two offences contained within section 136 of the Act. The first is a strict liability offence, and is committed by a person who carries on (or attempts to carry on) a licensable activity on or from any premises otherwise than under and in accordance with an authorisation.[157] The second includes a mental element, and is committed by a person who knowingly allows a licensable activity to be carried on in the way described under the first offence.[158]

51.95 A person found guilty of either offence can be sentenced to imprisonment for up to six months and/or to a fine not exceeding £20,000.[159]

51.96 The following issues are relevant in considering the offences.

(1) Who is a 'person' for the purposes of the offence?

51.97 'Person' is not defined within the Act, but where the licensable activity is the provision of regulated entertainment, certain persons involved in the provision of regulated entertainment are exempted from liability. They are people who:

- perform in a play;
- participate as a sportsman in an indoor sporting event;
- box or wrestle in a boxing or wrestling entertainment;
- perform live music;
- play recorded music;
- perform dance; or
- provide entertainment of a similar description to performing live music, playing recorded music, or performing dance.[160]

Thus, where the entertainment is the performance of a play, the actors whose only involvement in the play has been to perform in it cannot commit an offence under the section. On the other hand, if an actor has also helped to organise the event, his involvement will not have been limited to performance and he may be liable.

51.98 Unlike with other offences under Part 7 of the Act where the word 'person' is applied to limited categories of people,[161] in theory any 'person' could commit the offences under section 136.

---

[157] Section 136(1)(a).
[158] Section 136(1)(b).
[159] Section 136(4).
[160] Section 136(2)(a)–(g).
[161] Eg s 140(2).

(2) Has the person 'carried on or attempted to carry on' a licensable activity?

51.99 No guidance is provided on the question of what would constitute the carrying on of a licensable activity for the purposes of the offence and, at first blush, the concept would appear to be a nebulous one. Outside of the licensing context, the expression 'carrying on' has been interpreted as implying 'a repetition of acts' but excluding 'one particular act' which is not repeated,[162] and that interpretation is perhaps a useful starting point here. On the other hand, within the broader context of the section, the distinction between one act and a series of acts would appear to be irrelevant. Any 'attempt to carry on' a licensable activity is also caught by the section and so one particular act would appear to be covered.[163] A broad interpretation of the phrase is consistent with the interpretation of the offence as wide in its scope.

51.100 This part of the section now has to be read in light of the decision in *Hall & Woodhouse Ltd v The Borough and County of the Town of Poole*.[164] In that case, the appellant owned a large number of public houses in the south of England. The prosecution related to one of them which the appellant had let to tenants. The council had successfully prosecuted the appellant when the conditions on the premises licence had been breached. The appellant had argued that although it owned the freehold of the premises and held the premises licence, it had not itself carried on a licensable activity on the premises so as to come within section 136(1)(a), and it was accepted that it had no knowledge and so could not come within section 136(1)(b). Having reviewed the statutory context, the court allowed the appeal and held that section 136(1)(a) is directed at persons who, as a matter of fact, actually carry on or attempt to carry on a licensable activity on or from premises and that that was the natural meaning of the language used. The court stated:

> 'Section 136(1)(a) is not directed at holders of premises licences as such. An offence may be committed by carrying on a licensable activity when no premises licence exists at all. Where there is a premises licence but a licensable activity is carried on outside the scope of that licence or in breach of the conditions of the licence, it must, in my view, be a question of fact whether it is carried on by the holder of the licence. The mere fact that he is the holder of a licence does not make him

---

[162] *Smith v Anderson* (1879) 15 Ch D 247 per Brett LJ at 277. Although the court in that case was considering whether an investment trust was, amongst other things, formed for the purpose of 'carrying on' a business within s 4 of the Companies Act 1862 such that it had to be registered, the interpretation is perhaps one of broader application (See *Stroud's Judicial Dictionary of Words and Phrases* (7th ed), Vol 1, p 373).

[163] Under s 1(1) of the Criminal Attempts Act 1981, an attempt is defined as an act which is 'more than merely preparatory' to the offence attempted. The distinction between attempts and mere preparatory acts has caused difficulties and is essentially a matter of degree.

[164] [2009] EWHC 1587 (Admin)

automatically liable in respect of the carrying [on] of a licensable activity on or from the premises to which the licence relates.'[165]

(3) Is the activity a 'licensable activity'?

51.101 The licensable activities are set out in section 1 of the Act.[166] In addition, reference should be made to sections 173–175 of the Act under which activities in certain locations, activities on certain premises certified on grounds of national security, and certain other specified activities are all excluded from the definition of licensable activity under the Act.[167]

(4) Is the licensable activity carried on either 'on or from premises'?

51.102 It would seem that the scope of the offence is not significantly limited by the requirement that the activity takes place on or from premises. Under section 193, 'premises' means 'any place and includes a vehicle, vessel or moveable structure'.

(5) Is the licensable activity carried on 'otherwise than under and in accordance with an authorisation'?

51.103 Under section 136(5) of the Act an authorisation means, as appropriate, a premises licence, club premises certificate, or temporary event notice. That is, all of the authorisations which can be obtained and operated from premises under the Act are covered by the offence under this section.

The licensable activity must have been carried on 'otherwise than under and in accordance with an authorisation', and this element of the offence underlines its wide scope. Three scenarios are covered by it. Firstly, where the premises are entirely unlicensed, such as in the case of a drinking den, the licensable activity will be carried out without authorisation. Secondly, where premises are licensed for one activity, such as the sale of alcohol, but not for another, such as the provision of regulated entertainment, the latter licensable activity will be carried out without authorisation. Thirdly, where a premises has the benefit of a premises licence granted under the Act, but the conditions of that licence are being breached in some way, for example by the terminal hour being exceeded, then a licensable activity will not have been carried out in accordance with the authorisation.

(6) Does the defence of due diligence apply?

51.104 Under section 139(2)(a) of the Act, the defence of due diligence applies to the section 136(1)(a) offence only.

---

[165] Para [18], per Richards LJ.
[166] See Chapter 4 (Licensable Activities).
[167] For example, raffles and tombolas where the prizes include alcohol are exempt by virtue of s 175 of the Act.

(7)   Where the section 136(1)(b) offence is contemplated, did the person 'knowingly allow' the licensable activity to take place?

51.105   See Section C above for definition of 'knowingly allow.'

51.106   The Act creates licensable activities which are required to be the subject of authorisations granted under it. In that context, the offences under section 136 play a central role in criminalising licensable activities which take place without those authorisations being in place. However, its broad scope also allows for offences to be committed where, after grant of the authorisation, the terms and conditions have been breached. The Explanatory Notes rightly refer to this section as 'central to the enforcement of the licensing regime introduced by the Act'.[168] The type of offences which could be committed under this section are potentially serious and the penalties reflect this. However, the section covers a very wide spectrum of acts or omissions some of which will be considerably less serious, presumably with a sentence to match.

Exposing alcohol for unauthorised sale

51.107   Section 137 of the Act creates a strict liability offence. It is an offence for a person, on any premises, to expose for sale by retail any alcohol in circumstances where the sale of that alcohol would be unauthorised.

51.108   A person found guilty of this offence can be sentenced to imprisonment for up to six months and/or to a fine not exceeding £20,000.[169] In addition, the sentencing court can order the alcohol, and any container for it, to be forfeited.[170]

51.109   This section focuses on sales by retail of alcohol.[171] The offence covers the situation where the exposure occurs when no licence is in place, as well as where there is a licence but its terms and conditions have been breached in some way by the exposure[172].

51.110   The technical definition of 'alcohol' for the purposes of the Act is set out in section 191 of the Act. Reference should also be made to the definition of 'sale by retail' under section 192 of the Act. In essence, business-to-business sales, such as a sale to a premises licence holder for the purpose of making sales under that licence, are not caught by the section.

51.111   Given that the sale by retail of alcohol is a licensable activity, and given that under section 136 of the Act it is an offence to carry on a

---

[168]   Para 219.
[169]   Licensing Act 2003, s 137(3).
[170]   Licensing Act 2003, s 137(4).
[171]   For discussion of this expression, see Chapter 8 (Licensable Activities).
[172]   Licensing Act 2003, s 137(2).

licensable activity on premises otherwise than under or in accordance with a licence,[173] the circumstances in which the section 137 offence is committed could clearly be covered by a broad interpretation of the section 136 offence. The key difference between the two sections is the specific requirement that alcohol be 'exposed' for sale by retail under section 137. The offence under section 137 therefore provides a specific offence which can be committed in a case where no sale or attempted sale is actually made.[174]

51.112　Rather unhelpfully, the word 'expose' is not defined anywhere in the Act. However, its meaning has been considered by the courts under food legislation. Under section 1(3)(a) of the Food Safety Act 1990 a 'commercial operation' in relation to any food includes the exposing of food for sale.[175] Two of the cases often cited when considering exposure for sale in the food context are of some use here.

51.113　In *Keating v Horwood*,[176] the question before the court was whether a baker was exposing loaves for sale when, after completing his round delivering bread from an open car, a baker was stopped on his way back to the bakehouse by an inspector who found a weight deficiency in the remaining loaves. It was held that there was an exposure for sale of the bread left in the car.[177] The loaves were taken for the purpose of being sold if customers wanted them, and at the start of the journey it would have been uncertain which of them would remain.

51.114　In *McNair v Terroni*,[178] the question was whether milk on a counter in an eating-house, which was not to be sold as milk alone, but only to add to cups of tea, was exposed to sale. An inspector had applied to the manager of the eating-house to purchase a glass of milk for the purpose of analysis, but the manager had refused to sell the milk on the counter on the basis that it was not for sale as milk alone. It was held that although the milk was only intended to be sold to add to cups of tea, it had nevertheless been exposed to sale and was on sale by retail. The manager was therefore liable to pay a penalty for refusing to sell the milk to the inspector.

51.115　Two points can be made. The first is that, historically speaking at least, the courts have been prepared to interpret the phrase broadly for the purposes of enforcing food legislation. Secondly, it is submitted that in the licensing context the modern practice of providing clear signs and coverings

---

[173]　See above.
[174]　It is unclear whether a person who exposes alcohol without a sale taking place could be said to have attempted to carry on a licensable activity under s 136 of the Act. Exposure may be considered a mere preparatory act and so not within the scope of an attempt.
[175]　Under s 1(1) of the same Act, the word 'food' includes drink.
[176]　(1926) 90 JP 141.
[177]　The bread did not weigh one pound or an even number of pounds, so by exposing it for sale, an offence had been committed.
[178]　[1915] 1 KB 526.

for items not intended to be sold may well have helped to avoid liability in each of the above cases.

51.116 Consider a modern day mini-market which, following the Act, operates under a premises licence authorising the sale of alcohol for consumption off the premises until midnight, but then is allowed to remain open for the sale of convenience goods until 2 am. The most effective way for the designated premises supervisor to ensure that no alcohol is exposed for sale by retail after midnight is to provide screens to be pulled down to cover the alcohol at midnight, ideally with signs indicating that the alcohol section of the store is closed. The proper use of such screens would provide an effective means of avoiding exposure of the alcohol under section 137, and also might help to relieve the pressure on staff requested by customers to sell alcohol after midnight.

51.117 The defence of due diligence applies to this offence.[179]

Keeping alcohol on premises for unauthorised sale

51.118 Two offences are contained in section 138 of the Act. Under the first, a person who intends to sell by retail alcohol in his possession or under his control, in circumstances where that sale would be unauthorised by virtue of being otherwise than under and in accordance with an authorisation, commits an offence.[180] In essence, the second offence is the first offence translated into the context of club premises certificates. That is, the alcohol is supplied rather than sold, by or on behalf of a club to, or to the order of, a member of the club.[181]

51.119 Commission of either offence can give rise to a fine not exceeding level 2 on the standard scale.[182] In addition, the sentencing court can order the alcohol, and any container for it, to be forfeited.[183]

51.120 This offence can be read as complementing the offence under section 137: where there is any ambiguity as to whether alcohol has actually been exposed for sale by retail, it might be shown that the alcohol was in the defendant's possession and that he intended to sell it by retail. The offences are therefore apt to be used as alternative offences on an information. However, the fact that the section 138 offence is liable to be used as a default offence, does not necessarily make it easier to prove. It must be shown that the person intends to sell the alcohol by retail.

---

[179] See para 51.69 et seq above.
[180] Licensing Act 2003, s 138(1).
[181] Licensing Act 2003, s 138(1) and (3).
[182] Licensing Act 2003, s 138(4).
[183] Licensing Act 2003, s 138(5).

51.121 It is noticeable that although the heading to the section refers to the keeping of alcohol 'on premises', the word 'premises' is not mentioned in the section. Its absence theoretically allows the offence to be committed by any person intending to sell alcohol which he is carrying on his person. It should be noted that the inclusion of the words 'under his control' makes ownership of the alcohol irrelevant for the purposes of the offence, and indeed for forfeiture.

51.122 The penalties for committing this offence are markedly less serious than those laid down for the offences under sections 136 and 137. This perhaps reflects the fact that the actual harm to the public caused by commission of the offence is more limited. The alcohol will not yet have been exposed for sale, let alone purchased by any member of the public.

E DRUNKENNESS AND DISORDERLY CONDUCT

Allowing disorderly conduct on licensed premises

51.123 Section 140 creates an offence of knowingly allowing disorderly conduct on relevant premises.[184]

51.124 A person found guilty of the offence can be fined up to level 3 on the standard scale.[185]

51.125 For the first time under Part 7, section 140(2) sets out the categories of person who can commit the offence. They are, where appropriate:

(1) any person who works at the premises in a capacity (whether paid or unpaid) which authorises him to prevent the conduct;[186]

(2) the premises licence holder in respect of the premises;[187].

(3) the designated premises supervisor under a premises licence;[188]

(4) any member or officer of a club (which holds a club premises certificate) who, at the time of the conduct, is present in a capacity which enables him to prevent it;[189] and

---

[184] The offence essentially re-enacts part of the offences in ss 172(1) and 172A(1) of the Licensing Act 1964.

[185] Licensing Act 2003, s 140(3).

[186] Door supervisors and bar staff are clearly covered by this category.

[187] He may be liable under the doctrine of delegation. See Section C above.

[188] The designated premises supervisor must surely be the most likely person to be prosecuted under this section. It is his job to be in charge of the day to day running of the premises where alcohol is concerned, and he plays a pivotal role as a point of contact for the police if any disorder breaks out.

[189] This category is equivalent to (1) but in the context of a club premises certificate. It should be noted that members are only liable to be prosecuted if they are present in some sort of administrative or supervisory capacity, and so in a position to prevent the disorder.

(5) the premises user where a permitted temporary activity has been authorised.[190]

51.126 At the heart of this offence is the concept of 'disorderly conduct'; a concept which is not defined anywhere in the 2003 Act, despite its inclusion in one of the licensing objectives.[191] The absence of a definition of disorder within the Act is not only unhelpful, but potentially problematic for the effective prosecution of the offence. Defences may well be raised on the basis that the particular conduct did not amount to disorder, and in the absence of a clear and precise definition, the benefit of the doubt may be given to the defendant. Ultimately, the principle of legal certainty may be offended. The problem of defining 'disorder' in the context of the crime prevention objective is discussed in Chapter 9 (The General Duties of Licensing Authorities), Section B (The Licensing Objectives).

51.127 The incorporation of the European Convention of Human Rights has underlined this problem by effectively prescribing that a criminal offence must be clearly defined in law. The issue was foreshadowed by Brooke LJ in *Westminster City Council v Blenheim Leisure (Restaurants) Ltd.*[192] In that case, licensees had been charged with failing to 'maintain good order' contrary to the Council's rules of management for places of public entertainment, in that they had allowed prostitutes to offer sexual services for money. The learned Judge felt that the language of the provision should be tightened up if it was to be used to cover such activities after incorporation of the Convention. Citing the principle that a criminal offence must be clearly defined in law, he did not accept that it was impossible to define the conduct with greater precision, or that it was satisfactory to leave it to magistrates to decide where a finding of a breach of good order would render the licensees liable to criminal penalties.

51.128 Although the most obvious form of disorder contemplated under the section must be alcohol related, the offence applies equally to premises where other licensable activities are taking place. There, a perhaps greater problem arises. Who is to say at a rock concert, for example, at what point boisterousness tips into disorder? That which a court might retrospectively view as unacceptable in the cold light of day may have been part of the 'buzz' of a large entertainment event. Further, a licensee may find himself in some difficulty, risking prosecution by allowing the behaviour to continue or risking still greater disruption by trying to break it up. It is hoped that licensing authorities would exercise considerable circumspection before prosecuting licence holders under this provision. Amongst the main considerations, it is suggested, would be the extent to which the behaviour was

---

[190] This category is equivalent to (2) and (3) above but in the context of a temporary event notice.
[191] The prevention of crime and disorder under s 4(2)(a).
[192] (1999) 163 JP 401.

endangering or intimidating others, and whether the licensee was monitoring the behaviour or ignoring it.

51.129 However, one aspect of the offence which is clear is the requirement that the disorder is occurring on the premises. This is in line with the view that licence holders cannot properly be held responsible for anti-social acts caused by customers once they have left their premises and are beyond their control.

It should also be noted that the offence is only committed by a person who knowingly allows the disorderly conduct. The outbreak of disorder may not give rise to this offence. It is the failure to address the problem either through direct action or calling the police that is likely to give rise to the offence.

51.130 Given its direct relevance to the crime prevention objective, it is unsurprising that the offence was described in the first version of the Guidance as an extremely important offence which is central to the management of premises where alcohol is sold for consumption on those premises. Licensing authorities were encouraged to draw the offence to the attention of the relevant applicant when granting a licence, as well as the readiness of the authority to prosecute for it.

Sale of alcohol to a person who is drunk

51.131 Two offences are contained in section 141 of the Act. Specified categories of people[193] commit an offence if, on relevant premises, they either knowingly sell or attempt to sell alcohol to a person who is drunk.[194] The same categories of people also commit an offence if they knowingly allow alcohol to be sold to such a person.[195] The offence is also made to apply to club premises by substituting the word 'supply' for 'sell' in the offence.[196] Conviction can lead to a fine not exceeding level 3 on the standard scale.[197]

51.132 Although on first reading it might appear that the mental element of the offences applies to each of their elements (so that, for example, in the case of the first offence the person must know that the person he is selling to is drunk), the better view is that it applies only to the first element of each respective offence. It would be extremely difficult for the prosecution to prove that the defendant knew that the person he was selling to was drunk.

---

[193] Section 141(2). These are the same categories, mutatis mutandis, as apply to section 140.
[194] Section 141(1)(a).
[195] Section 141(1)(b).
[196] These offences effectively re-enact the offences in ss 172(3) and 172A(3) of the Licensing Act 1964 with the addition of the adverb 'knowingly.'
[197] Section 141(4).

Thus the person must knowingly sell to a person who is, in fact, drunk.[198] There is no definition of the word 'drunk' in the Act. The case law under the offence of being found drunk in public[199] is helpful here. In *Neale v RMJE (A Minor)*,[200] the Divisional Court considered the meaning of the word 'drunk' under that section. It held that the natural and ordinary meaning of the word 'drunk', in ordinary common speech, coincided with the primary meaning in the Shorter Oxford Dictionary, namely 'that has drunk intoxicating liquor to an extent which affects steady self-control'. In *Lanham v Rickwood*,[201] Goff LJ followed the decision in *Neale*.[202] He went on to consider the legislative background to the section, as well as that of the offence of being drunk and disorderly,[203] and held that the definition provided was reinforced by it.[204]

51.133   The interpretation above presumably allows for a subjective assessment in the evidence. An officer's evidence supporting a prosecution may well include evidence of the number of alcoholic drinks consumed by the individual over a specified period, as well as the individual's behaviour prior to being served by the defendant.

51.134   There is clearly a benefit in the effective prosecution of these offences as a strong deterrent to such sales. The sale of alcohol to people who are already drunk might well result in anti-social behaviour by those people once they have left the premises and are beyond the control of the licensee. Equally, the proper control of such sales should prevent offences under section 140 of the Act from being committed.

Obtaining alcohol for a person who is drunk

51.135   Under section 142, an offence is committed by any person who knowingly obtains (or attempts[205] to obtain) alcohol for consumption on those premises by a person who is drunk.[206]

51.136   A person found guilty of the offence is liable to a fine not exceeding level 3 on the standard scale.[207]

---

[198]   See further the commentary to ss 144 and 147 at paras 51.144 et seq and 51.159 et seq below.
[199]   Section 12 of the Licensing Act 1872.
[200]   (1985) 80 Cr App R 20.
[201]   (1984) 148 JP 737.
[202]   At 739, iv.
[203]   Section 91(1) of the Criminal Justice Act 1967.
[204]   At 740, i.
[205]   Under s 1(1) of the Criminal Attempts Act 1981 an attempt is defined as an act which is 'more than merely preparatory' to the offence attempted. The distinction between attempts and mere preparatory acts has caused difficulties and is essentially a matter of degree.
[206]   The section effectively re-enacts the offence under s 173(1) of the Licensing Act 1964.
[207]   Licensing Act 2003, s 142(2).

51.137 The inclusion of this offence in the Act is clearly intended to avoid the loophole whereby people who are already drunk covertly obtain alcohol by asking others to buy drinks for them. It should be noted that the offence is limited to the obtaining of alcohol 'for consumption on [the] premises'.[208] Where the consumption takes place off the premises, no offence is committed.

Failure to leave licensed premises

51.138 There are two strict liability offences contained within section 143 of the Act. The first offence is committed by a person who is drunk or disorderly and who, without reasonable excuse, fails to leave relevant premises when requested to do so by a constable or a person in a specified category.[209] The second offence is also committed by a person who is drunk or disorderly but who, without reasonable excuse, enters or attempts[210] to enter relevant premises after a constable or a person in a specified category has requested him not to enter.[211]

51.139 The penalty is a low one, with conviction leading to a maximum fine not exceeding level 1 on the standard scale.[212] Constables are under a duty when requested to help to expel the person who is drunk from the premises or help to prevent them from entering as appropriate.[213]

51.140 The phrase 'drunk or disorderly' must be read disjunctively. In theory at least, a person may commit an offence under the section whilst not being disorderly. The two concepts have been considered above.

51.141 It is suggested that requests made of the person should be accompanied by a reference to the offence which can be committed under the Act. In light of the likely state of the person being requested to leave or not to enter, it is advisable to obtain evidence corroborating the fact that the request has been made.

51.142 Where a person is disabled or injured, this might provide 'a reasonable excuse' for not leaving under the section.[214] However, the categories are not closed. Consider the situation where a fight takes place just outside licensed premises. It is submitted that a person might be held to have

---

[208] Licensing Act 2003, s 142(1).
[209] Licensing Act 2003, s 143(1)(a) and s 143(2). The specified category replicates that for s 140, for which see above.
[210] Under s 1(1) of the Criminal Attempts Act 1981 an attempt is defined as an act which is 'more than merely preparatory' to the offence attempted. The distinction between attempts and mere preparatory acts has caused difficulties and is essentially a matter of degree.
[211] Licensing Act 2003, s 143(1)(b). The section re-enacts certain provisions in s 174 of the Licensing Act 1964.
[212] Licensing Act 2003, s 143(3).
[213] Licensing Act 2003, s 143(4).
[214] These examples are taken from the Explanatory Notes to the section (para 227).

a reasonable excuse in attempting to enter the premises so as to avoid meeting his foe, even though he has been requested not to enter on the basis that he is drunk. It is conceivable that defences will be raised on the basis that the person was too drunk to understand or comply with the request. While the court may not be sympathetic to such a plea, given that by definition the accused may have been drunk at the time, there does not seem to be any reason in principle why such a defence should not be raised.

51.143 This offence clearly provides support for those dealing with drunk or disorderly people. The issue of a request under section143, might well act as a mitigating factor for any person prosecuted under sections 140 and 141. If the request is made but not complied with, the choice of prosecution will be a difficult one. In *Semple v DPP*,[215] the Divisional Court held that a constable, when requested to assist a licence holder in expelling a person from licensed premises or preventing a person from entering the same premises under this section (section 143(4)), had the power to use reasonable force.

F SMUGGLED GOODS

Keeping of smuggled goods

51.144 Under section 144 of the Act, a person in a specified category[216] commits an offence if he knowingly keeps or allows to be kept, on any relevant premises, any goods which have been imported without payment of duty, or which have otherwise been unlawfully imported.

51.145 A person found guilty of the offence can be fined up to level 3 on the standard scale.[217] The convicting court can also order the goods in question, and any container for them, to be forfeited.[218]

51.146 When compared to the offence under section 138 of keeping alcohol on premises for unauthorised sale, it is noticeable that the word 'keep' is not defined in the Act, and is not glossed as it is in the previous section, as 'having in [one's] possession or under [one's] control'. Nevertheless, it is submitted that the word 'keep' in section 144 has no special meaning, and in effect can be interpreted in the same way as it has been in section 138. That is, ownership of the particular goods will be irrelevant to the commission of the offence.

51.147 The mental element in the offence should be interpreted as applying to the first element only, and not to the others. That is, in order for the

---

[215] [2009] EWHC 3241 (Admin).
[216] Section 144(2). These are the same categories, mutatis mutandis, as apply to s 140.
[217] Section 144(3).
[218] Section 144(4).

offence to be committed, the defendant must knowingly keep goods on the premises which are in fact smuggled; he need not know that they are smuggled. The interpretation of drugs offences is of some use here: for the offence of possession of a controlled drug to be made out,[219] the person must know that he is in possession of something which is, in fact, a controlled drug.[220] It would be extremely difficult for the prosecution to prove knowledge that the goods were smuggled.[221] As for the goods, it is clear that the importation of contraband cigarettes and alcohol is targeted by the offence. The possibility that such goods could contain dangerous ingredients justifies the fact that the penalty is more serious for this offence than the one under section 138, despite the fact that no intention to sell is required to be proved.

51.148 In fact, the lack of a requirement that there be an intention to sell the goods on the premises illustrates the broad scope of the offence. Premises which are used for hoarding smuggled goods before they are moved on elsewhere will also be caught by the section. Moreover, there is no requirement that the types of goods be linked in any way to the type of licensed premises under the Act. The existence of this offence should encourage all those involved in the operation of licensed premises to be vigilant to prevent contraband cigarettes and alcohol passing through their business.

G CHILDREN AND ALCOHOL

Unaccompanied children prohibited from certain premises

51.149 The two offences contained within section 145 of the Act seek to protect 'unaccompanied children': children under the age of 16 who are not in the company of someone aged 18 or over.[222] To commit the first offence, a person in a specified category[223] must first know that the premises are exclusively or primarily used for the supply of alcohol for consumption on the premises.[224] If such knowledge is present, the offence is committed by allowing an unaccompanied child to be on the premises when they are open for that purpose.[225] The second offence is one of strict liability and is committed by a person in the same category who allows an unaccompanied child to be on any licensed premises or club premises[226] between midnight and 5 am when the premises are open for the same purpose.[227] It should be noted that where the unaccompanied minor is on the premises solely for the

---

[219] Contrary to s 5 of the Misuse of Drugs Act 1971.
[220] See *Warner v Metropolitan Police Commissioner* [1969] 2 AC 256.
[221] It should also be noted that the section could, but does not say 'any goods which *he knows* have been imported without payment of duty ... '
[222] Section 145(2).
[223] These are the same categories, mutatis mutandis, as apply to s 140.
[224] Section 145(4)(a).
[225] Section 145(1)(a).
[226] See definition of 'relevant premises' in s 159.
[227] Section 145(1)(b).

purpose of passing to or from some other place, and there is no other convenient means of accessing or egressing from that place, no offence is committed.[228]

51.150   The penalty for both offences is a fine not exceeding level 3 on the standard scale.[229]

51.151   The creation of these offences on the prohibition of unaccompanied children from certain premises in certain circumstances does not provide a right for children to be present in other circumstances. For example, a restaurant whose main business activity is the consumption of both food and drink might not commit an offence in admitting unaccompanied children before midnight. But that does not mean that children should automatically be admitted to such premises. The discretion of the management to admit is paramount, and the fact that the law does not bar children at a particular time does not require the management to admit them.

51.152   The offence is qualified by two defences. The first defence applies if the defendant can show:

(1)   that he believed that the unaccompanied child was aged 16, OR that the individual accompanying him was 18 or over; AND
(2)   that he had taken all reasonable steps to establish the individual's age, OR nobody could reasonably have suspected from the individual's appearance that he was aged under 16 or 18 as relevant.[230]

51.153   A person is deemed to have taken all reasonable steps if he asked the individual for evidence of his age, and the evidence would have convinced a reasonable man.[231] Thus if the prosecution can prove that a proof of age card provided as evidence was an obvious forgery, they could rebut the defence by arguing that no reasonable man would have been convinced by it. The defence clearly also covers the situation where a person looks exceptionally old for their age.

51.154   The second defence is one of due diligence.[232] The test suggests that good licensing practice and indeed the powers of discernment of licensees have advanced considerably over the last century. When, in 1872, Parliament was debating whether the legal age for purchasing alcohol should be 14 or 16, one MP stated:

‘nothing could be more absurd than to expect that a licensed victualler should be a judge of whether a child was under 14 or under 16 years of age. Children of the same age differ very much in their apparent age;

---

[228]   Section 145(5).
[229]   Section 145(9).
[230]   Licensing Act 2003, s 145(6).
[231]   Licensing Act 2003, s 145(7).
[232]   See 'due diligence' at para 51.69 et seq above.

and it is well known that young Spanish ladies of 14 are more advanced than English ladies of 16. How, then, could a person in trade be expected to know that a child was under 14 or under 16 years of age?'[233]

Clearly, proof of age cards, asking questions and erring strongly on the side of caution were not current practice in 1872.

Sale of alcohol to children

51.155 On its face, the offence under section 146 of the Act is very broad in its scope. It is a strict liability offence. Any person who sells alcohol to an individual who is under 18 years of age commits an offence. The offence can be committed by any person[234] and can be committed anywhere; it is not limited to members of the licensing trade and their actions on licensed premises. The scope of the offence is also widened so as to catch clubs and their employees who supply members or their guests who are under 18.

51.156 A person found guilty of this offence is liable to fine up to level 5 on the standard scale.[235]

51.157 Despite its broad scope, in considering whether to institute proceedings for this offence, under the original Guidance, licensing authorities were encouraged to focus on sales at establishments with premises licences, temporary event notices, or club premises certificates.

51.158 The same defences as for the section 145 offence apply.[236]

Allowing the sale of alcohol to children

51.159 Under section 147 of the Act, a specified category of person commits an offence if they knowingly allow the sale of alcohol to an individual under the age of 18 on relevant premises.[237] The people who can commit the offence are those who work at the premises in a capacity, whether

---

[233] HC Debs 23 July 1872 Col 1679.
[234] This includes the employer of the person selling, see *R v Winson* [1968] 1 All ER 197, 202E, cited above. This is further made plain by s 146(6) which indicates that the offence can be committed 'by reason of the act ... of another.' *London Borough of Haringey v Marks & Spencer* [2004] LLR 479 turned on the legislative history of the former provision in s 169A of the Licensing Act 1964.
[235] Section 146(7).
[236] See para 51.152 above.
[237] The mental element applies only to the allowance of the sale; the prosecution does not need to prove that the defendant knew that the individual was under 18, simply that the individual was under 18 as a matter of fact (see discussion and footnotes to ss 141 and 144 above).

paid or unpaid, which authorises them to prevent the sale. The same offence is created for the supply of alcohol on club premises.[238] That offence can be committed by employees of clubs as well as their members who are present in a capacity which enables them to prevent the supply.

51.160 The penalty for the offence is a fine not exceeding level 5 on the standard scale.[239]

51.161 It is worth noting that the category of person who can commit the offence is more limited. This contrasts with the categories of people specified in other offences. Indeed the wording of the category here is in substantially the same terms as the first of the categories under the offences in sections 140–144.[240] Yet the other categories of people included in those offences are not included here. In particular, there is no express reference to the holder of the premises licence or the designated premises supervisor as persons who can commit this offence.

51.162 In that context, one properly arguable interpretation of the section is that Parliament did not intend the offence to be committed by licence holders or designated premises supervisors. If it had intended them to be caught, it would have expressly included them as a category as it did in other offences under Part 7 of the Act. If that is right, the doctrine of delegation[241] would appear to have been heavily restricted by Parliament in this offence.

51.163 On the other hand, on a plain reading of the category, a designated premises supervisor clearly would be a person who works at the premises in a capacity which would authorise him to prevent the sale. Further, certain licence holders would work at the premises in that capacity. Interpreted in that way, it could be argued that the wording of the section in effect only excludes certain licence holders such as an area manager within a pub chain who has no direct involvement in the pub where the offence is committed, and others further up the chain of management, including the company itself. The doctrine of delegation would therefore apply to the other persons as before, and would only fall short of certain licence holders and other line managers. Ultimately, whatever the vocational position of the person, they only commit the offence if they knowingly allow the sale.

51.164 There are no statutory defences to the offence.

Persistent selling of alcohol to children

51.165 By section 23(1) of the Violent Crime Reduction Act 2006, a new offence was added to the array of offences relating to the sale of alcohol and

---

[238]   Licensing Act 2003, s 147(3).
[239]   Licensing Act 2003, s 147(5).
[240]   See ss 140(2)(a), 141(2)(a), 143(2)(a), and 144(2)(a) respectively.
[241]   See Section C above.

children under the Act. Under section 147A of the 2003 Act, a person is guilty of an offence if, on two or more occasions within a consecutive period of three months, alcohol is unlawfully sold on the same premises to an individual under the age of 18.[242]

51.166 The offence is focussed in two respects. Firstly, it is tied to a single premises which are either licensed premises or authorised by a temporary event notice.[243] This indicates the intention to target problem premises by the offence. Secondly, the offence can only be committed by a person who was a responsible person (ie a premises licence holder, or a premises user in respect of a temporary event notice).[244] This indicates the intention to target those at the highest end of the management chain with regard to licensed premises and temporary events.

51.167 The provisions are also prescriptive as to what an unlawful sale means. This will only occur where the person making the sale believed the individual to be under 18 or the person did not have reasonable grounds for believing an individual to be 18 or over.[245] What constitutes reasonable grounds for the belief that someone is over 18 years of age is then also prescribed.[246] Convictions, cautions, and fixed penalty notices are admissible as evidence of an unlawful sale.[247]

51.168 The court's powers where an offence is made out are also relatively broad ranging. By amendment under section 118(2) of the Police Reform and Social Responsibility Act 2011, the court has the power to impose a fine of up to a maximum of £20,000 for the offence. Alternatively, under section 147B of the Licensing Act 2003 the court has the power to suspend the part of the licence authorising the sale by retail of alcohol for a period up to three months. The court can specify when the suspension is to come into force and also has the discretion whether or not to suspend its suspension pending an appeal.[248] The power not to suspend pending the outcome of an appeal is in marked contrast to the general position on appeals from decisions of licensing authorities on review, where the lodging of an appeal has the effect of suspending the licensing authority's decision pending the outcome of the appeal. It has been common practice amongst enforcing authorities to seek to review a premises licence where a number of underage sales have taken place. In real terms, the relatively extensive powers contained in sections 147A and 147B of the 2003 Act could make prosecution an effective alternative to seeking such a review where the offence can be made out. The

---

[242] Licensing Act 2003, s 147A(1)(a).
[243] Licensing Act 2003, s 147A(1)(a).
[244] Licensing Act 2003, s 147A(4).
[245] Licensing Act 2003, s 147A(2).
[246] Licensing Act 2003, s 147A(3).
[247] Licensing Act 2003, s 147A(7).
[248] Licensing Act 2003, s 147B(3)–(4).

power to issue a closure notice for persistent sale of alcohol to children is dealt with in Chapter 44.

Sale of liqueur confectionery to children under 16

51.169 Under section 148 of the Act, it is an offence for any person to sell liqueur confectionery to an individual under the age of 16.[249] A similar offence is also created under the section whereby clubs and their employees commit an offence by supplying such confectionery to members or their guests who are under 16.[250]

51.170 A person found guilty of the offence can be fined up to level 2 on the standard scale.[251]

51.171 The definition of 'liqueur confectionery' is contained in section 191(2) of the Act.[252] The same two defences as appear in section 145 apply to this offence (with the age 16 replacing 18).[253]

Purchase of alcohol by or on behalf of children

51.172 Sections 149 and 150 of the Act complement sections 146 and 147 in that they criminalise the acts of the children in buying and consuming alcohol. In fact there are three types of offence contained within section 149.

51.173 It is an offence for an individual aged under 18 to buy or attempt to buy alcohol.[254] It should be noted that the offence is not location specific, and can be committed anywhere. A similar offence is created whereby an individual who is aged under 18 and a member of a club is supplied with alcohol (or attempts to have alcohol supplied) to his order or as a result of his act or default.[255]

51.174 The second category of offence within section 149 simply makes it an offence for a person to act as an agent for a person under 18 in purchasing or attempting to purchase alcohol, or as a member of a club in arranging (or attempting to arrange) for alcohol to be supplied to that person.[256] The provisions in effect mirror those of the basic offence. A typical example of this offence is where a child pays an adult to buy alcohol for him from an off-licence.

---

[249] Licensing Act 2003, s 148(1)(a).
[250] Licensing Act 2003, s 148(1)(b).
[251] Licensing Act 2003, s 148(6).
[252] It is defined by reference to proportion and strength of alcohol, and weight.
[253] See para 51.154 above.
[254] Licensing Act 2003, s 149(1)(a).
[255] Licensing Act 2003, s 149(1)(b).
[256] Licensing Act 2003, s 149(3).

51.175 The third category of offence is really a more specific version of the second offence, in that it involves buying or attempting to buy alcohol for a person aged under 18 where the alcohol is for consumption on the premises.[257] The equivalent offence is created for club premises.[258] The example given in the original version of the Guidance for this offence was where a father bought alcohol for his 17 year old son in a pub. In both the second and third offences, the requirement is that the alcohol must be purchased 'on behalf of' the person under 18. Although at first sight it might be thought that this phrase suggests that the purchase must be instigated by the person under 18, the example under the third offence indicates that that need not be the case; the alcohol need only be bought for a person under 18 for the offence to be committed.

51.176 A specific exemption is created for the third category of offence where the person who buys the drink is 18 or over, the person under 18 is aged either 16 or 17, the alcohol is beer wine or cider, the purchase or supply is for consumption at a table meal, and the 16 or 17 year old is being accompanied at the meal by someone aged 18 or over.[259] This detailed, specific exemption should be interpreted narrowly: the exemption only applies while the table meal is being consumed; bar snacks will not amount to a table meal.

51.177 Where a person charged with a second or third category offence can prove that he had no reason to suspect that the individual was aged under 18, he will have a defence.[260] It should be noted that the defence is a simplified one and appears to require an assessment of all the circumstances. If the prosecution can show that there was a reason to suspect, which the defendant cannot rebut on balance of probability[261] (the onus being on him), the defence will fail.

51.178 The first category of offence carries a penalty of a fine not exceeding level 3 on the standard scale. The others carry penalties of a fine not exceeding level 5 on the same scale.[262]

Consumption of alcohol by children

51.179 Under section 150, it is an offence for a person aged under 18 knowingly to consume alcohol on relevant premises.[263] Specified categories of person can also commit an offence of knowingly allowing the consumption

---

257 Licensing Act 2003, s 149(4)(a).
258 Licensing Act 2003, s 149(4)(b).
259 Licensing Act 2003, s 149(5).
260 Licensing Act 2003, s 149(6).
261 *R v Carr-Briant* [1943] 2 All ER 156.
262 Licensing Act 2003, s 149(7).
263 Licensing Act 2003, s 150(1).

of alcohol on such premises by a person aged under 18.[264] The categories of person who can commit this latter offence are persons who work at the premises in a capacity (whether paid or unpaid), which authorises them to prevent the consumption, and any member or officer of a club who is present at club premises at the time in a similar capacity.[265]

51.180 A specific exemption for accompanied 16- or 17-years-olds who are having a table meal with beer, wine, or cider is contained within the section.[266]

51.181 The person aged under 18 who commits the first offence is liable to a fine not exceeding level 3 on the standard scale. The person committing the latter offence is liable to a fine not exceeding level 5 on the same scale.[267]

Delivering alcohol to children

51.182 Under section 151 of the 2003 Act, offences are created under which the delivery of alcohol to persons under the age of 18 is criminalised. A person who works on relevant premises commits an offence if he knowingly delivers alcohol sold on the premises, or supplied on club premises, to a person aged under 18.[268] An offence of knowingly allowing someone else to deliver the alcohol is also created, together with its equivalent offence in relation to club premises.[269]

51.183 Exemptions are made where:

(1) The alcohol is delivered to a place where the buyer or person supplied lives or works.

(2) The person under the age of 18 works on the premises in a capacity which involves the delivery of alcohol.

(3) The alcohol is sold or supplied for consumption on the relevant premises.[270]

51.184 Commission of the offence can lead to a fine not exceeding level 5 on the standard scale.[271]

---

[264] Licensing Act 2003, s 150(2).
[265] Licensing Act 2003, s 150(3).
[266] Licensing Act 2003, s 150(4).
[267] Licensing Act 2003, s 150(5).
[268] Licensing Act 2003, s 151(1).
[269] Licensing Act 2003, s 151(2) and (4).
[270] Licensing Act 2003, s 151(6).
[271] Licensing Act 2003, s 151(7).

Sending a child to obtain alcohol

51.185 Under section 152, it is an offence knowingly to send a person aged under 18 to obtain alcohol sold or to be sold on relevant premises for consumption off those premises.[272] The equivalent offence is created for club premises.[273]

51.186 A person found guilty of this offence is liable to a fine not exceeding level 5 on the standard scale.[274]

51.187 A typical example of this offence would be where a parent sends their child to collect alcohol from an off-licence where the alcohol has been bought over the telephone. The place of the collection is immaterial.[275] A specific exemption is created where the person aged under 18 works on the premises in a capacity which involves the delivery of alcohol.[276]

Prohibition of unsupervised sales by children

51.188 Section 153 of the Act is targeted at the scenario where a person under the age of 18 is employed on any relevant premises in a capacity which allows him to sell or supply alcohol. Where that is the case, the Act requires each sale or supply to be specifically approved by a responsible person. That requirement is both created and enforced by the offence under the section: a responsible person who knowingly allows a person aged under 18 to make a sale or supply on relevant premises commits an offence unless the supply has been specifically approved.[277]

51.189 The offence carries a penalty of a fine not exceeding level 1 on the standard scale.[278]

51.190 The responsible people in relation to licensed premises, club premises and temporary event notices are specified.[279] A specific exemption is made where the sale or supply is for consumption with a table meal, on premises (or a part of the premises) which are being used for that purpose.[280] Thus, a person under the age of 18 who is working as a waiter in a restaurant can serve alcohol lawfully there.

---

[272] Licensing Act 2003, s 152(1)(a).
[273] Licensing Act 2003, s 152(1)(b).
[274] Licensing Act 2003, s 152(5).
[275] Licensing Act 2003, s 152(2).
[276] Licensing Act 2003, s 152(3).
[277] Licensing Act 2003, s 153(1).
[278] Licensing Act 2003, s 153(3).
[279] Licensing Act 2003, s 153(4).
[280] Licensing Act 2003, s 153(2).

H VEHICLES AND TRAINS

Prohibition on sale of alcohol on moving vehicles

51.191 Under section 156 of the Act, a person commits an offence if he sells by retail[281] alcohol on or from a vehicle at a time when the vehicle is not permanently or temporarily parked.[282] The offence is one of strict liability.

51.192 A person who is found guilty of the offence is liable to imprisonment for up to three months or to a fine not exceeding £20,000, or to both penalties.[283]

51.193 The word 'vehicle' means a vehicle intended or adapted for use on roads.[284] The original version of the Guidance made clear that the offence does not prohibit the consumption of alcohol on coach trips; what is prohibited is the sale of alcohol by retail when the vehicle is moving. Given that the sale by retail of alcohol is a licensable activity,[285] and premises for the purposes of the Act includes a vehicle,[286] it is clear that this offence is targeted at a limited type of commercial venture: companies operating intercity and football coach services are prohibited from selling alcohol during the journey.

51.194 A due diligence defence is provided, under which a person has a defence if he can show that the sale was due to a mistake, or reliance on information given to him, or an act or omission of another person, or some other cause beyond his control, and that he took all reasonable precautions and exercised all due diligence.[287] Where the person mistakenly believed that the drinks they were serving were non-alcoholic, he might have a defence.[288]

Power to prohibit sale of alcohol on trains

51.195 A power is established under section 157(1) of the Act under which the sale of alcohol on trains can be prohibited. Non-compliance offences are then created where sales of alcohol take place in contravention of the prohibition.

---

[281] See Licensing Act 2003, s 192.
[282] Licensing Act 2003, s 156(1).
[283] Licensing Act 2003, s 156(2).
[284] Licensing Act 2003, s 193.
[285] Licensing Act 2003, s 1(1)(a).
[286] Licensing Act 2003, s 193.
[287] Licensing Act 2003, s 156(3).
[288] Explanatory Notes, para 245.

51.196 In essence, a senior police officer can apply to a magistrates' court[289] for an order prohibiting the sale of alcohol for a specified period, on any railway vehicle at specified railway stations or travelling between such stations.[290] The basis for the application must be to prevent disorder and the magistrates' court must not make an order unless satisfied that it is necessary to prevent such disorder.[291] The provisions require a copy of the order to be served on the relevant train operators immediately after the order is made.[292]

51.197 The requirement that the application must be made to a magistrates' court indicates that the power is to be exercised by the police in line with contingency planning and as a pre-emptive measure. The power should be read in conjunction with that to close premises in an identified area under section 160 of the Act,[293] and in one sense this power can be read as a measure complementing that power. Where, for example, the police apply to close licensed premises in an area before a football match with a history of alcohol related violence, the police can include the buffet cars on trains coming into the area by this section. To that extent, the application process and the test which the magistrates must apply are the same.[294]

51.198 It is an offence, knowingly to sell or attempt to sell alcohol in contravention of the order, or knowingly to allow the sale of alcohol in contravention of the order.[295] The foundation for the commission of the offence will only be in place once a copy of the order has been served on the train operator. Given that the application can be made at any time, a system which ensures that the relevant employees are notified immediately will be essential.

51.199 The offence carries a penalty of imprisonment for a term not exceeding three months, or a fine not exceeding £20,000, or both penalties.[296]

---

[289] Licensing Act 2003, s 157(2).
[290] Licensing Act 2003, s 157(1).
[291] Licensing Act 2003, s 157(3).
[292] Licensing Act 2003, s 157(4).
[293] See Chapter 42 (Licensing Act Closures).
[294] One difference between the two provisions is the absence of a maximum time period for an order under this section. Under s 160(1), the closure order is for a maximum of 24 hours. Given that the powers are likely to be exercised together, and the existence of the requirement for the order to be necessary, it is submitted that the order will rarely exceed 24 hours in any event.
[295] Licensing Act 2003, s 157(5).
[296] Licensing Act 2003, s 157(6).

I FALSE STATEMENT RELATING TO LICENSING

False statements made for the purposes of the Act

51.200 Section 158(1) of the Act contains an offence of knowingly or recklessly making a false statement in or in connection with the various applications for licences under the Act.

51.201 A person who is found guilty of the offence can be fined up to level 5 on the standard scale.[297]

51.202 It is clear that the offence is broad in its scope. Firstly, the offence can be committed if the false statement is made 'recklessly', thereby relieving the burden on the prosecution of showing that the statement was made knowingly in every case.[298] Secondly, the statement need only be made 'in connection with' the application for the offence to be committed.[299] Thus the prosecution is not limited to statements made on the application papers. Finally, the prosecution can be based on any document containing a false statement which is produced, furnished, signed, or otherwise made use of by the person.[300]

51.203 In essence, this offence underpins the administrative requirements of the various applications under the Act, ensuring that the licences are not obtained through the use of false statements. Applicants at all levels should be made aware of the terms of this offence at the start of the application process.

J SENTENCING

51.204 Reference should be made to criminal practitioner textbooks for the general principles of sentencing. However, certain observations particular to licensing may be made.

51.205 Where public safety has been endangered, then principles regarding sentence for health and safety breaches are engaged, with the caveat that the most serious health and safety offences carry no maximum financial penalty. In *R v Howe & Son (Engineers) Ltd*,[301] Scott Baker J said that the law requires employers to do what good management and common sense require them to do anyway, ie look at what the risks are and take sensible measures to tackle

---

[297] Licensing Act 2003, s 158(3).
[298] Licensing Act 2003, s 158(1).
[299] Licensing Act 2003, s 158(1).
[300] Licensing Act 2003, s 158(2).
[301] [1999] 2 All ER 249.

them. He pointed out that failure to fulfil these general duties is particularly serious as they are the foundations for protecting health and safety. He went on to say:

> 'The objective for health and safety offences in the workplace is to achieve a safe environment for those who work there and for other members of the public who may be affected. A fine needs to be large enough to bring that message home where the defendant is a company not only to those who manage it but also to its shareholders.'

Scott Baker J also made it clear that the standard of care imposed by the health and safety legislation is the same regardless of the size of the defendant company.

51.206   The Court of Appeal said the following factors should be taken into account.

General factors

(1)   The gravity of the offence – how far short of the appropriate standard the defendant fell in failing to take reasonably practicable steps to ensure health and safety.

(2)   The degree of risk and the extent of the danger created by the offence.

(3)   The extent of the breach or breaches: for example, whether it was an isolated incident or continued over a period.

(4)   An important factor is the defendant's resources and the effect of the fine on its business.

Aggravating features

(1)   A failure to heed warnings.

(2)   Deliberately profiting financially from failure to take necessary health and safety steps or specifically running the risk to save money.
It was said: 'A deliberate breach of health and safety legislation with a view to profit seriously aggravates the offence'.

(3)   The breach has resulted in death.
The penalty 'should reflect the public disquiet at the unnecessary loss of life'.

Mitigating factors

(1)   Prompt admission of responsibility and a timely plea of guilty.

(2)   Steps to remedy deficiencies after they are drawn to the defendant's attention.

(3)   A good safety record.

51.207 The Court of Appeal said that any fine should reflect not only the gravity of the offence but also the means of the offender, and that this applies just as much as to corporate defendants as any other.

51.208 It went on to say:[302]

> 'Difficulty is sometime found in obtaining timely and accurate information about a corporate defendant's means.
>
> The starting point is its annual accounts.
>
> If a defendant company wishes to make a submission to the court about its ability to pay a fine it should supply copies of its accounts and any other financial information on which it intends to rely in good time before the hearing both to the court and to the prosecution.
>
> This will give the prosecution the opportunity to assist the court should the court wish it.
>
> Usually accounts need to be considered with some care to avoid reaching a superficial and perhaps erroneous conclusion.
>
> Where accounts or other financial information are deliberately not supplied the court will be entitled to conclude that the company is in a position to pay any financial penalty it is minded to impose.
>
> Where the relevant information is provided late it may be desirable for sentence to be adjourned, if necessary at the defendant's expense, so as to avoid the risk of the court taking what it is told at face value and imposing an inadequate penalty.'

It should be noted, as was pointed out by counsel for the defendant in this case, neither the fines nor the costs imposed upon an employer are deductible against tax and therefore the full burden falls upon the company.

51.209 The Court of Appeal also stated that, in its judgment, magistrates should always think carefully before accepting jurisdiction in health and safety at work cases where it is arguable that the fine may exceed the limit of their jurisdiction or where death or serious injury has resulted from the offence. The trend now appears for more cases to be heard in the Crown Court.

51.210 In the case of *R v Friskies Petcare Ltd*,[303] the Court of Appeal recommended that where there is a plea of guilty, the prosecution and defences should set out in advance the aggravating and mitigating features in the case. In practice the prosecution is required to serve a schedule setting out the aggravating and mitigating features of the case for agreement. This has become known as a 'Friskies Schedule'.

---

[302] *R v F Howe & Son (Engineers) Ltd* [1999] 2 All ER 249 at 254.
[303] [2000] 2 Cr App R(S) 401.

The Court of Appeal said in this case if it is possible to place an agreed basis of plea before the court that should be done. If there is a 'disagreement of substance', the presiding judge can determine whether a Newton hearing is required.[304]

51.211 Finally in *R v Rollco Screw and Rivet Co*,[305] the Court of Appeal said the question was not only the level of penalty merited by the offence, but also the level the defendants could reasonably be expected to meet. In relation to the latter it was relevant to consider the issue of time over which the penalty should be payable.

51.212 It is good practice for a licensing authority to consider in each case whether offending behaviour should be charged under licensing legislation or health and safety legislation or both. Where the offence is a serious one, the matter should always be charged under health and safety provisions, because of the larger penalties available to meet the gravity of the offence. However, there is merit in adding offences under licensing legislation, particularly for breach of condition, as an alternative, because the defence of due diligence[306] imposes a higher standard on the defendant than the reasonable practicability test under section 40 of the Health and Safety at Work Act 1974. It is also imperative for licensing authorities to have regard to the aggravating and mitigating circumstances set out in *Howe* when investigating an offence, so that it may give the court full information on these matters, and ensure that the matter is sentenced in the light of full knowledge. The prosecution should also, through company searches and general inquiry and observation, be able to tell the court what it knows about the defendant's means.

51.213 Where offences cause harm to the licensing objective of preventing public nuisance, some analogy may be drawn with environmental sentencing guidelines, making allowance for the fact that in environmental cases serious harm may be done to the natural environmental and natural resources. The general principles may be seen from *SOSE v Yorkshire Water Services Ltd*,[307] where the Court of Appeal held that the *Howe* guidelines cross-applied to environmental offences and articulated some of its own, all of which will be relevant in licensing cases:

'(1) The degree of culpability involved in the commission of what is in effect an offence of relatively strict though not absolute liability (where relevant).

---

[304] A Newton hearing is where the defendant admits his guilt but does not accept the facts presented by the prosecution as the basis of his guilt: *R v Newton* [1983] Crim LR 198. Evidence is then called at the hearing in order to determine the facts.
[305] [1999] IRLR 439.
[306] Licensing Act 2003, s 139, see para 51.69 above.
[307] [2002] 2 Cr App R (S) 13.

(2) The damage done. This will include the spatial and temporal ambit of the effect of the offence, together with ill effects both physical and economical. ... It seems to us that the above two are the most important, but also

(3) The defendant's previous record, including any failure to heed specific warnings or recommendations will also be material.

(4) A balance may have to be struck between a fitting expression of censure, designed not only to punish but to stimulate improved performance on the one hand, and the counter-productive effect of imposing too great a financial penalty on an already underfunded organisation on the other.

(5) The defendant's attitude and performance after the events, including their pleas ...

(6) Finally it must be correct to determine what the penalty for any one incident should be rather than tot up the various manifestations of that incident as reflected in the counts in the indictment. ... Having determined the overall penalty, as a matter virtually of formality it is then divided among the separate counts. ... the number of complainants named should not be used as a multiplier since that is the result of an arbitrary decision of the prosecution.'[308]

K CONCLUSION

51.214 Parliament has enacted a stringent criminal code within its licensing legislation. The net of potential defendants is cast wide, the thresholds for statutory defences are set high and the penalties are relatively severe. The leitmotif of the licensing system is risk prevention and management rather than merely punishment. However, where the checks and balances written into the system have failed, and offences have been committed, Parliament has provided all the necessary tools to deter further offending, and to encourage others to stay in compliance with their obligations.

---

[308] Per Rougier J, para 51.

Good practice in the night time economy

I have an affection for a great city. I feel safe in the neighborhood of man, and enjoy the sweet security of the streets.

Henry Wadsworth Longfellow

Introduction

In the morning the city
Spreads its wings
Making a song
In stone that sings.
In the evening the city
Goes to bed
Hanging lights
About its head.

Langston Hughes

52.01 In this part of the book, best practice in the management of the night time economy is examined.

52.02 The first five chapters, dealing with Purple Flag, Pub Watch, Best Bar None, Business Improvement Districts and Community Alcohol Partnerships, exemplify the exhortation in this book towards creative development of sustainable leisure environments.

52.03 It is worth taking a moment to spell out what this means, and why they are different from regulation.

REGULATION	VOLUNTARY SCHEMES
Coercive	Voluntary
Enforcement of minimum standards	Promotion of best standards
Focussed on a small number of non-compliant operators	Focussed on every operator
Operates through system of punishments	Operates through system of rewards
Based on deterrents	Based on incentivisation
Directed at performance of individual premises	Works through partnership
Designed to avoid failure	Designed to promote success
Roots out the worst operators in the night time economy using regulatory tools	Promotes better night time economies with no limitation in available tools

52.04 The fundamental distinction is that regulation is an effective tool for ensuring that premises obey minimum standards in their operation. But even with that necessary but limited ambition, the tools are rarely likely to be sufficient in and of themselves. Moreover, they are not a substitute for the patient work of building alliances to make town and city centres places of delight for all. That is where partnership comes in.

52.05 The chapters on the voluntary schemes should be read in conjunction with Appendix 2, which sets out good practice examples from across the land. These are not intended to be blueprints so much as examples to whet the appetite, lubricate the imagination and refute the naysayers. Good practice works, and is worth it. Indeed, some authorities take the view that, in an age of recession, voluntary schemes are an essential part of their work, without which they could not afford to regulate the night time economy with their existing level of resources.

52.06 In Chapter 58, we look at another form of partnership, a regulatory partnership, where different enforcement authorities come together to ensure that the licensing objectives are being promoted. The example used is Hammersmith & Fulham.

52.07 Finally, in Chapter 59, consideration is given to the question of designing for the night-time economy, so as to produce safer and better town centres.

53

Purple Flag – better town centres at night

Today the words night-time economy provoke salivation among gutter journalists and documentary makers who cannot find anything enlightening to report.

Philip Kolvin QC

A INTRODUCTION: WHAT IS PURPLE FLAG?

53.01 Purple Flag was launched in October 2009 by the Association of Town Centre Management, after nearly eight years of research, market testing, pilot projects and pathfinder initiatives. The following January, six pathfinders received their flags at the first accreditation ceremony held in the Banqueting Suite of Birmingham's Council House – appropriately bathed in purple light for the occasion! Three years later, no fewer than 35 centres ranging from the biggest to the smallest in the United Kingdom have received Purple Flags.

Town Centres awarded Purple Flags

ABERYSTWYTH	IPSWICH
AYLESBURY	KINGSTON UPON THAMES
BANGOR	LEICESTER SQUARE,
BATH	WESTMINSTER
BELFAST	LINCOLN
BIRMINGHAM	LIVERPOOL
BOURNEMOUTH	MANCHESTER
BRISTOL	NOTTINGHAM
CAMDEN TOWN, LONDON	OXFORD
CANTERBURY	PRESTON
CLERKENWELL, ISLINGTON,	SALISBURY
LONDON	SHEFFIELD
COVENT GARDEN,	SOUTHEND
WESTMINSTER	STOCKTON HEATH –
DERRY-LONDONDERRY	WARRINGTON
ENNISKILLEN	TORQUAY
GANTS HILL	VICTORIA – WESTMINSTER
HALIFAX	WATFORD
HIGH WYCOMBE	WINCHESTER
HULL	

53.02   Purple Flag is an accreditation scheme for town centres at night. Its mission is to raise the standard and broaden the appeal. Very simply, those centres that reach the standards can fly the flag. It is therefore a golden opportunity to celebrate success in the face of the negative publicity that has plagued town centres after hours. But Purple Flag is more than just a competition with a prize. Purple Flag can help to alter negative perceptions, drive up standards, increase choice and attract new customers. It offers a sound basis for partnership and for the management of the night time economy.

B THE 24 HOUR ECONOMY

53.03   The story began in 2002 at the former Civic Trust and with members' concerns about government proposals for the 2003 Licensing Act. These largely revolved around the fear that 24 hour licensing would 'open the floodgates' and that the voices of local people would be marginalised. Looking back, it is clear that this marked a turning point in national policy. Until then the tide of government policy had been running in favour of liberalisation and deregulation – seen as appealing to the electorate and beneficial to the economy. However a backlash was gathering momentum, fuelled by a sense of public outrage at the reality of life on the streets at night and the impact of alcohol abuse on the health of the nation.

53.04   The Act's tight focus on the management of individual licensed premises left a policy vacuum for others, like the Civic Trust, to try and fill.

In particular there appeared to be an absence of concern for the local context, wider interests, more varied attractions, the range of services needed to keep places clean, safe and convivial at night – in short the building blocks of a successful neighbourhood and destination. At the time the national debate was heavily polarised between the key interests and the mood was overwhelmingly negative. The Trust had a track record in town centres and urban regeneration and saw the need for a more positive vision of what the future could hold.

C BETTER TOWN CENTRES AT NIGHT

53.05 The three year research project that followed deliberately sought to piece together the perspectives of a wide range of stakeholders: regulators, landlords, local authorities, policy-makers, business people, those who went out and those who didn't – either because they were afraid to, or because they felt town centres at night had little to offer them. The findings were published in 2006 ('NightVision: Town Centres for All'). The Trust found:

- There were sparks of excellence and imagination all around the country, but there was no way of collecting and sharing this good practice.
- Individual specialists were working within their topics and in fact there was a 'new front line' of people dedicated to keeping centres running safely at night. But there was insufficient cohesion. The night time economy is the quintessential cross-cutting theme and a collaborative and corporate approach is essential.
- Town centres were still run largely for the daytime. Commercial attractions were open at night, but the infrastructure of town centres was still being managed for 9 am to 5 pm.
- Commercial pressures had squeezed out diversity. The government, local authorities, many consumers and others sought variety, diversity and choice, but large sections of industry had placed an overwhelming emphasis on youth-oriented and alcohol-based entertainment to the exclusion of other interests.
- There was a 'missing market' of those who would go out at night if things were better. They wanted more visible policing, adequate public transport home, more choice and variety in venues and things to do that were free or affordable for families.
- Little improvement seemed likely without action and intervention. The rather disheartening consensus amongst experts the Trust interviewed was that in ten years' time without further action town centres might be a little bit better, but otherwise would be much the same.
- The Trust's market analysis pointed to areas of potential, such as the growth in dining out, the importance of a good food offer for pubs, the trend towards catering to a slightly older clientele, increased flexibility in shop closing times and the contribution made by arts and cultural

attractions. These and other trends could lead to a better mix of clientele and a different atmosphere on the streets.

D   TOWN CENTRES FOR ALL

53.06   This last conclusion became a central idea. Almost everyone the Trust spoke to in the course of its research agreed that part of the recipe for future success lay in attracting a more diverse clientele to a more varied choice of attractions. As Commander Simon O'Brien (then ACPO Licensing Lead) later put it: 'If you get the right mix of people out on the streets at night town centres will police themselves.' The NightVision pilot projects that followed the research became 'test beds' for the ideas.

53.07   The idea for a new accreditation scheme was one of several to emerge from the research. Initially in 2006 it got the 'thumbs down' from consultees, but a year later it was understood more clearly and the mood had changed. In particular, there was growing interest from local authorities and partnerships searching for new and better ways of doing things. It seemed the right moment to press on. The arrival of Philip Kolvin as Chair of the Civic Trust prompted a burst of energy leading to the eventual launch of Purple Flag two years later. During this time the concept was tried, tested and developed into a credible national programme.

E   PURPLE FLAG – A FRESH APPROACH

53.08   Given the range of topics, the expertise of professionals and the concerns of key interests, Purple Flag could not afford to be shallow or superficial. It would have received little respect. The scheme therefore has considerable complexity, but its essence can be conveyed fairly simply in three diagrams: the Core Agenda, Six Steps to Success and the Assessment Pyramid. The aim is to explain the fundamentals of Purple Flag in an accessible and memorable way.

Purple Flag Core Agenda

53.09   This is the framework of standards and values used by entrants and assessors for the evaluation of centres at night. It has five key themes and 30 attributes. It emerged from the research, NightVision Pilot projects and a review of international good practice. It is designed to capture the quality and the rounded experience that people expect from their town centres – whoever they are and whatever the type and size of centre. The Trust's research showed that managing town centres at night suffered from 'not seeing the wood for the trees'! There was some excellent good practice, but a coherent overview was missing. The topics are not new. The Core Agenda just brings them together in one place. As Steve Jobs said 'Innovation is about joining up the dots'.

PURPLE FLAG CORE AGENDA

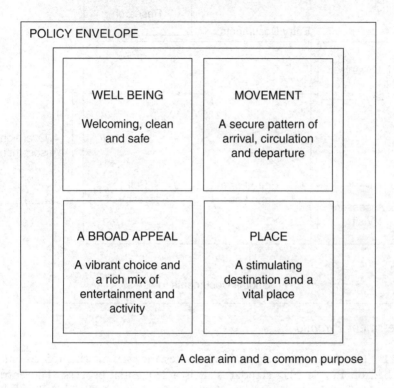

POLICY ENVELOPE

WELL BEING	MOVEMENT
Welcoming, clean and safe	A secure pattern of arrival, circulation and departure

A BROAD APPEAL	PLACE
A vibrant choice and a rich mix of entertainment and activity	A stimulating destination and a vital place

A clear aim and a common purpose

Six Steps to Success

53.10 This sequence is followed by entrants in preparing their submissions. They are asked to form a partnership, appoint a coordinator and develop their own conclusions on how well their centre performs at night. They pool their knowledge of policy and data, guided by the Purple Flag Entrants Resource Pack, and undertake their own overnight assessment. Their shared conclusions are a key input to the assessment process. The Six Steps process is unique to Purple Flag and is based on a solid rationale. The best people to understand how a town centre works at night are those who operate, manage, visit and live in it. Any external opinion needs to be based on solid evidence if it is to be credible. The Six Steps are intended to provide this solid evidence. It may be challenging for some, but experience has shown that it need not be onerous if the right people are gathered around the table from the outset. Moreover the benefits to entrants can be great, including a greater shared understanding, a stronger partnership and a clearer vision for the future.

THE ENTRY PROCESS

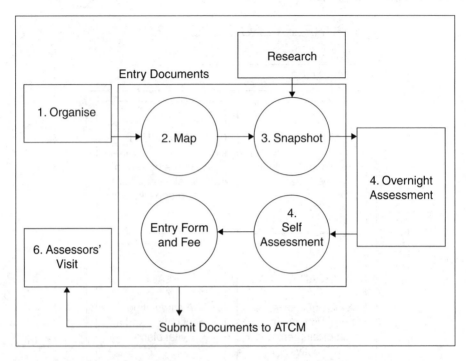

Assessment Pyramid

53.11 The Assessment Pyramid illustrates the way in which decisions are reached on Purple Flag standards. It is a sequential process. The entrants create the foundation by making their own assessment. Trained Purple Flag assessors take this as the starting point for their own assessment. They may agree or not, but at least the entrants know their own judgement counts. The Purple Flag Accreditation Panel looks at both assessments and considers a recommendation from the assessors on whether a flag should be awarded. At every stage participants are asked to choose between five standards for each of the five themes and 30 attributes in the Core Agenda. There is a right of appeal to the Purple Flag Policy and Standards Committee, whose decision is final. The ethos of the scheme is not that of 'success' and 'failure' – rather whether a centre is ready for Purple Flag or not. The aim is to help as many centres reach the standards as possible, even if it takes more than one attempt to get there. At each stage therefore Purple Flag officers, assessors and panellists offer practical advice; giving credit where it is due and indicating areas for improvement where necessary. The process is transparent: points of agreement and divergence are itemised in a Purple Flag Feedback Report.

DECISION PYRAMID

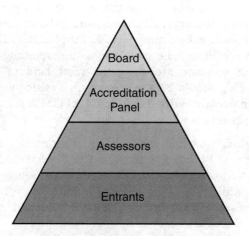

Spreading the message

53.12   Purple Flag holders are justifiably proud of their success. There are good stories to be told. For example:

- In Kingston upon Thames a new theatre, the Rose, has added new clientele and has strengthened fine dining in the vicinity.
- In Birmingham the Broad Street BID has turned this 'party street' into a place to enjoy rather than avoid.
- Covent Garden and Leicester Square show that a trip to the West End is no longer a 'walk on the wild side' as one journalist put it. Services there run through the night.
- In Manchester the early evening economy is a particular strength with more shoppers at this time than in the morning.
- In Bath there is a track record of innovation. Taxi marshals were pioneered here.
- In Kingston upon Thames hackney carriage operators and private hire operators work well together. There are three marshalled private hire pick-up points around the centre to speed revellers homewards.

What are the benefits to participants? Feedback gathered for ATCM by the Spirit Marketing Group in early 2011 showed that Purple Flag holders believed that 'Purple Flag has galvanised the night time economy in their areas, increased partnership working and improved performance on safety, crime reduction and cleanliness.'

F PURPLE FLAG FOR TODAY

53.13   After many years of research, testing and development Purple Flag is now a reality. But it was conceived at the height of the last economic boom, when the challenge was to try and control a runaway sector. Today the reality is very different: the young have less money in their pockets, night time activity has shrunk to a couple of nights a week in most places, more people are drinking at home and enjoying their leisure at home, pubs and clubs are closing, the public sector is cutting back. Is Purple Flag still relevant today? Even more so, we believe. The conclusions underpinning Purple Flag are very much about securing growth – the right kind of growth. Ideally, attaining Purple Flag should be about more than raising a flag. It should be part of a local renaissance. With this in mind ATCM is responding to harder times with stronger services:

- **Adding value.** New benefits to Purple Flag participants (and others) now include a Branding Guide, a PR Toolkit and a Purple Flag Exchange Network. The first Good Practice Source Book has been published, whilst the Purple Flag website (www.purpleflag.org.uk) contains research, good practice, guidance, tools and templates – free of charge for all to use as they wish.
- **Training and motivation.** ATCM reaches out to potential entrants through Purple Flag Kickstart Workshops. It supports and develops the specialist skills needed through training programmes for assessors and the Night Time Economy Managers Network.
- **The Purple Flag Development Programme** uses the knowledge gained from the research and accreditation scheme to help aspiring partnerships reach Purple Flag standards, attract the 'missing market', strengthen and recruit new businesses.
- **Plugging the knowledge gap.** Despite the endless debate and publicity, it is surprising how little hard data exists on the night time economy. It is therefore difficult to track its performance and progress, and managers and policy makers are 'flying blind'. ATCM has developed a 'Data Dashboard' of seven key metrics to fill this gap. Purple Flag holders will use the Dashboard to demonstrate continuing success year by year. ATCM will use it to spread the message to a national and international audience that Purple Flag places really are better than the rest.
- **New wave of pathfinders.** The range and application of Purple Flag is being extended through a new wave of pathfinder initiatives: in Northern Ireland, the Irish Republic, Europe and also in university campuses – each an opportunity to learn more and develop good practice.

G ... AND TOMORROW?

53.14 Until recently the night time economy was seen as a cause of distress rather than an opportunity. New research (NightMix[1] and Milestone[2]) reveals that it is an integral part of town centre economies and deserves to be taken seriously. Those centres with successful night time economies appear

[1]   http://www.tbr.co.uk/pages/tbr-observatory/night-time-economy.php.
[2]   http://www.atcm.org/suppliers/info.php?refnum=137.

to be outperforming the rest. Coming full circle, the future brings us back to the 24 hour economy and how to make it work. Purple Flag teaches us that town and city centres are too important to be abandoned to market forces and to a narrow consumer interest. There is strength and endurance in diversity, in a closer understanding of consumer preference and aspiration, in partnership and in the specialist application of urban management skills. More than ever before we need to believe that a better future is possible and practically attainable.

H A CASE STUDY: LIVERPOOL

53.15 In 2010 Liverpool was awarded a Purple Flag, which it has retained on re-assessment. The following text, which describes the City's achievements,[3] is taken from the City's self-assessment, and is a good example of the harmony of regulatory and non-regulatory tools to shape a place in transition from a post-industrial town centre to an international tourist draw and regional hub.

The centre

The Liverpool Purple Flag area covers the city centre, which is a significantly important area of the city (both economically and culturally) and brings together a wide range of unique quarters and districts including major retail areas (The City Central Business Improvement District and the hugely successful new Liverpool ONE development), along with the more historic Waterfront, the Commercial District, the Cultural Quarter, Ropewalks, the Cavern Quarter, the Knowledge Quarter and the Creative Quarter. The area is also home to four residential neighbourhoods, as the quality and variety of city centre living accommodation continues to grow and expand, and also incorporates parts of two political ward boundaries, Central and Riverside.

Liverpool is built on its river and received the accolade of UNESCO World Heritage Status in 2004 as a supreme example of its mercantile and maritime past. It is a stylish and vibrant city centre, which is steeped in history and rooted in a rich cultural heritage. The city is a major destination for tourism and welcomes over 20 million visitors per year, with a further 15 million extra visitors during its European Capital of Culture year in 2008. Liverpool is therefore seen internationally as a centre of cultural excellence and is home to a collection of museums and galleries with national status. In addition, the city is somewhat unique in that it has two cathedrals, some of the country's finest architecture, a diverse range of entertainment venues, excellent restaurants, theatres, cafes and bars and one of the UK's most modern retail and leisure centres in Liverpool ONE which was completed during the 2008

---

[3] By kind permission of Mike Cockburn, Area Manager, City Centre and South Liverpool.

cultural celebrations and which operates successfully between 5 and 8 pm, six nights a week.

By day the city centre is primarily a thriving retail, business and tourism hub; during the evening and night, the area is utilised for its wide array of entertainment activities, restaurants, clubs, bars, theatres and cinemas.

The partnership

A Purple Flag Accreditation Working Group was established, led by Liverpool City Council, bringing together a wide range of partners: Merseyside Police, Citysafe, British Transport Police, Merseyside Fire & Rescue Service, Merseytravel, Liverpool ONE, Liverpool City Central BID, Liverpool Echo Arena & BT Convention Centre (ACC), Liverpool Arts Regeneration Consortium (LARC), Hotels Association, and ENGAGE (leaseholders group). In addition, a number of specific City Council services were directly involved in the working group including: City Centre Management, Destination Liverpool, Emergency Planning Unit, Licensing, Highways & Transportation, Liverpool Asset Management Project, Policy & Evaluation and City Watch.

The programme

Liverpool City Council itself works in partnership with a number of agencies including Merseyside Police, Merseyside Fire & Rescue Service, NHS Primary Care Trust, various different service areas within the local authority and city centre stakeholders to drive forward a cleaner, safer, more inclusive night time offer.

The city centre benefits from an established and well-developed crime and disorder reduction partnership (city centre arm of the Citysafe CDRP) which includes all the main agencies. The partnership works together to identify the crime and disorder priorities which allow innovative and effective arrangements to address such concerns, particularly in the night time economy.

The city centre has many initiatives that are focussed on creating a safe, clean and inclusive experience for the visitor and resident alike. These include:

City Plan Policing Operation

This operation is implemented each weekend to ensure that sufficient resources are in the appropriate locations. This operation is supported by the Proactive Licensing Team.

Gold Zone Police

Liverpool City Council funds police officers who patrol the city centre named The Gold Zone Police Team. They work closely with the City Council and its partners on a range of initiatives. Successful operations include:

- tackling aggressive begging,
- enforcing touting bylaws,
- traffic regulation enforcement,
- community safety campaigns,
- dealing with issues in the night time economy.

Design out Crime Research

This was a major research project analysing the city centre night time economy and in particular how the environment impacts on crime and fear of crime.

City Centre Licensing Enforcement

The Licensing Unit licences a range of premises, vehicles and persons to ensure public safety, public protection and comfort. The unit has responsibility for taxis, premises for sale/supply of alcohol and/or regulated entertainment and gambling, street trading, animal health and welfare.

Safer Night Time Economy Support Officer and Safer Alcohol Retail Officer

These officers are responsible for organising strategic and operational support to all the activities that form part of the night time economy

CCTV coverage

The city centre is comprehensively covered by high quality CCTV cameras which are shared by the police, Liverpool ONE and the City Council – one of the most advanced sharing agreements in the UK. The city centre is covered by 145 high quality CCTV cameras plus five cameras funded by City Central BID, covering footfall flows in Bold Street, the Cavern Quarter and key pedestrianised areas. Liverpool ONE has an additional 600 cameras.

Help Points

Help points are strategically placed around areas of the city centre to provide the public with a direct means of contact to the CCTV control room

Licensees Watch

Liverpool City Centre Licensees Watch supersedes the former Pub Watch to take in off licence and shop sales of alcohol. It is fully supported by

Merseyside Police, Liverpool City Council, Trading Standards, the Primary Care Trust and National Pub Companies. Licensees Watch has brought about a number of significant improvements including:

1. Banning problematic and prolific offenders from all members' premises
2. Radio communication sharing information from premises to premises
3. Distribution of photographs and details of offenders and criminal activity
4. Advice on crime reduction (CCTV/Security)
5. Social responsibility issues and due diligence
6. Advice to the trade/coordination of events
7. Arbitrator for the trade and the agencies
8. Working with off sales to ensure best practice.

PsssT Campaign

Citysafe – Liverpool's Crime and Disorder Reduction Partnership – works with all the strategic partners: Liverpool City Council, Liverpool Primary Care Trust, Merseyside Police and Merseyside Fire and Rescue Service to devise an overarching alcohol brand to unify all alcohol consumption related campaign work. From the concerted efforts of all partners, the *Pssst! Be Alcohol Aware* identity is now established and is used long term to address the three primary areas of health, law enforcement/crime reduction and community safety. This campaign is also targeting excessive drinking through social marketing initiatives, such as Drink Drive initiative cards printed in five different languages.

Hospital Police Access

Merseyside Police have a dedicated access point situated in the A&E department at the Royal Liverpool Teaching Hospital, staffed by a police officer to offer advice and support to patients and staff.

Taxi Rank Marshals

This initiative was designed to provide reassurance and support for visitors enjoying a night out in the city centre.

Radio Network

This system is utilised by licensed premises, which enables staff to share information about potential offenders and to quickly notify police about emerging incidents.

Banning orders

Used by police and licensees to ban any person involved in violence inside or outside of premises

Drink drive banning orders

All drivers breathalysed inside the city centre boundary and found to be over the legal alcohol limit are nominated to be banned from premises in the Licensee Watch scheme.

Zero tolerance ambulance initiative

A zero tolerance approach to offences against ambulance crews.

Metal detection mitts

Metal detection mitts have been issued to door staff at premises that could potentially attract an inappropriate clientele. These have been funded by the City Centre Joint Agency Group (JAG) to discourage the carrying of knives. These mitts are supportive of the 'Search or Refuse' campaign and act as a deterrent and detection tool.

Bluetooth message technology

Health and safety messages going out in areas of high night time footfall.

Identification armbands for SIA door staff

In order to identify SIA door supervisors and provide professionalism, funding was secured to provide high visibility arm band holders. These are worn by door staff to ensure easy identification in a crowd.

Conflict resolution training

A joint initiative between the Chamber of Commerce and Merseyside Police to provide training for bar managers and staff to recognise and deal more effectively with drunk and aggressive customers and people under age.

Polycarbonate glasses at venues

A high profile campaign reducing glass related injuries and offences.

Search or Refuse

Supported by Licensees Watch and is intended to reinforce the discretionary policy of searching random customers as a condition of entry to the premises.

Alcohol Free Zone

Joint work involving Liverpool City Council, Citysafe and Merseyside Police. A designation order for the city centre was obtained under powers contained in sections 12–14 of the Criminal Justice Act 2001 to prevent alcohol consumption in public places.

Night buses

Merseytravel run night buses taking customers north, south and east and across the river to the Wirral Peninsula.

Whitechapel Centre

Working with the third sector to provide help, information and assertive outreach work for people in need including rough sleepers and street drinkers.

ENGAGE Leaseholders

Liverpool City Council and partners have helped establish an innovative and unique engagement mechanism for city centre residents known as Engage. Engage is effectively in partnership with Liverpool City Council, city centre resident associations and Plus Dane (local registered social landlord) to provide city centre residents with a representative body and opportunities for interaction with main agencies and each other. Engage have a constituted board and organise a range of events and conferences for city centre residents. Through Engage, which represents all city centre residents, the City Council and its partners can consult with residents about planning future service provision. In turn, residents can utilise Engage to raise concerns such as noise and anti-social behaviour to the appropriate agency.

Your Community Matters (YCM)

Led by Liverpool City Council and fully supported by Liverpool Charity & Voluntary Services (LCVS) The YCM events give an opportunity for residents and community groups to meet with the police, City Council officers and other agents to raise issues involved in the night time economy. YCM events are run three times per year within each ward area.

NHS Walk In Centre

This centre is open until 10 pm with no appointment necessary. The centre treats minor illness and injuries and is open 365 days a year

24 hour British Transport Police Station located at Lime Street mainline rail station

British Transport Police have ensured a year on year incremental reduction in crime on the rail network, and have a proven history of dealing with safe mass transit events such as European Capital of Culture year, Grand National and the Mathew Street Music Festival.

Noise Abatement

Working in partnership with local businesses, police, Environmental Health, Licensing Enforcement and residents. It is coordinated through the City Centre JAG Environmental Enforcement Sub Group.

Public Toilets

Provision of public toilets has been significantly enhanced through the establishment of the high quality, award winning toilets at Liverpool ONE. These are accessible in the night time economy.

Street Cleansing

Core cleansing operations of city centre between 04.15 am and 23.45 pm. Enhanced cleansing services provided by City Central Business Improvement District between 09.00 am and 18.00 pm and 20.00 pm on Thursdays.

City Centre Evacuation Plan

Liverpool City Council's Emergency Planning Unit and other partner agencies have prepared a city centre zoning map for use in an emergency situation. The city centre is divided into zones that can be used for a full or partial evacuation of the city centre if necessary.

Project Griffin

This project has been formed to advise and familiarise managers, security officers and employees of large public and private sector organisations across the city centre on security, counter-terrorism and crime prevention issues.

Operation Bond

Funded by the City Centre JAG and utilising sniffer dogs from the prison service to detect drug crime in the evening economy areas.

As well as the initiatives above:

- The city centre has received multi million pound public and private investments in the public realm including several new public squares. This has encouraged new business to participate in café culture.
- Bespoke initiatives through the City Centre Joint Agency Groups and other stakeholder/steering groups to maintain levels of all recorded crime at a ten year low.
- Introduction of an additional floating taxi marshalling rank on a needs basis.
- Night time Environmental Enforcement Operations to tackle low level environmental crime including: touting, glass waste and trade waste.
- Introduction of amended Traffic Regulation Orders.
- Introduction of a Student Survival Guide, a 'one stop' resource which covers important issues such as health, wellbeing and safety as well as acting as a welcome guide to the city centre and its vibrant night life. 35,000 copies were produced and distributed at halls of residence, popular student venues and student fairs.

Recent initiatives for safer and better movement were:

- Environmental and pedestrian improvements to The Strand to ensure better links to the waterfront
- Lime Street Gateway includes measures to improve pedestrian connectivity to the rest of the city centre
- A significant upgrade to signing on the strategic road network including Variable Message Signing (VMS) on car parking availability and other issues affecting the road system including real time traffic information for major events
- Pedestrianisation of the Victoria Street area to enhance its role in the night time economy and made safer for users
- Installation of wayfinders, finger posts and information boards
- New street lighting in areas of high night time footfall
- New curtain lights installed in the Cavern Quarter
- Taxi Marshalling Service
- Introduction of new wooden bollards in the Ropewalks area to ensure pedestrian safety
- Introduction of automatic bollard system into the Victoria Street area, complementing the existing automatic bollards in the main pedestrian zone
- City centre map available from various sites including tourist outlets, hotels, bus and train stations.

The public and private sectors in Liverpool run a large number of festivals and other events to complement the array of entertainment opportunities available in the city, and to maintain its reputation as a vibrant and dynamic centre. For example:

- Liverpool Music Week featuring international acts alongside up-and-coming local talent. As well as numerous live acts, the festival features a series of music cinema screenings and a programme of the best of Liverpool's under-18 musical talent.
- Mathew Street Music Festival. The two day August Bank Holiday music extravaganza. The largest of its type in Europe, it features live music on six outdoor stages.
- RAIN young persons music event which provides an activity for considerable numbers of young people. RAIN is now a weekly event and attracts upwards of 300 young people to the events at which young musicians and bands play. RAIN is held at the night time venue 'The Zanzibar' with a dry bar. Since the event became established, levels of anti-social behaviour in the city centre at weekends have reduced.
- Hope Street Feast. A family friendly Sunday street party packed with music, theatre, dance, great food, drink and produce.
- Liverpool Comedy Festival, which is one of the UK's best comedy events. The festival takes place in venues all over Liverpool including the city centre. Each year there are about 100 shows in approximately 40 different venues around the city.
- Liverpool Biennial, which is a British International Festival of Contemporary Art held in Liverpool. The festival comprises the International Exhibition, the John Moores Painting Prize, the Bloomberg New Contemporaries Exhibition and the Independents Biennial also Long Night and Light Night events.
- Annual Christmas Markets. The city centre plays host to a variety of speciality markets each year. Traders come to the city from across the world, and each market brings with it a unique atmosphere and shopping experience.
- Winters Trail. Liverpool City Council together with the City Central Business Improvement District and cultural partners bought a season of festive events to the city centre for five Thursday evenings in the run up to Christmas, enhancing the footfall. The city centre was transformed into a glittering winter spectacle.
- Homotopia Festival, a bold and ambitious festival celebrating gay culture, featuring a variety of events including theatre, film, art, performance, photography, heritage and storytelling.
- Pride Festival, which in 2012 attracted 52,000 people and was supported by Liverpool Football Club.

The management of the City Centre environment activities has been improved through:

- A bespoke City Centre Management Team.
- Development of a five year management strategy.
- Destination Liverpool has been created to pull together the huge variety of public and private sector bodies with an interest in the marketing and management of the city as a place to live, work, study and invest.
- Communities of Interest Engagement. The City Centre Management

Team has worked with LCVS to engage and consult with the city's 'communities of interest' about provision in the city centre. Groups and representatives that are consulted include the following: Lesbian Gay Bisexual and Transgender (LGBT) Network, Black and Racial Minority (BRM) Forum, Chinese Community, Chinese Business Association, Corporate (Disabled) Access Forum, Student Safety and Welfare Joint Agency Group and The Alternative Youth Project. Members of the City Centre Management Team meet representatives to discuss issues such as access and specific requirements. Team members are also in contact with groups representing older members of the community and provision for this user group is extensive in the city centre.

The activity has achieved excellent results. The most recent annual City Centre Perceptions Survey carried out in June 2011 achieved the best set of collective results since the survey began nine years ago. Feelings of safety at night have improved; people believe the city centre is clean and offers a better provision than peer competitors. Police data shows that violent crime and injury violence associated with the city centre's night time economy continue to reduce. Levels have halved during the past five years to 2012 and both have reduced by over 20% from the previous year. Trip Advisor announced that Liverpool is the UK's 'top night time destination' as voted by their participants, beating London and all other cities.

Perhaps most importantly, the programme of partnership has produced a vigorous, committed network of regulatory agencies, business operators and community organisations to make Liverpool City Centre one of the best places to visit, work in and invest in the United Kingdom, and has instilled a huge sense of civic pride in its achievements.

54

Pub Watch

'... as for you, Joseph, who do your wicked deeds in such confoundedly holy ways, you are as drunk as you can stand.'

'No, Shepherd Oak, no! Listen to reason, shepherd. All that's the matter with me is the affliction called a multiplying eye, and that's how it is I look double to you – I mean, you look double to me.'

'A multiplying eye is a very bad thing,' said Mark Clark.

'It always comes on when I have been in a public-house a little time,' said Joseph Poorgrass, meekly.

Thomas Hardy, *Far From the Madding Crowd*

A. INTRODUCTION: WHAT IS A PUB WATCH SCHEME?

54.01 Pub Watch is often quoted as being the pub trade's equivalent to Neighbourhood Watch, but in fact it's a much more hands on initiative. Pub Watch schemes are not a new phenomenon, having been operating in some areas as far back as the 1960s. In its simplest form it is a group of licensees who have identified a local crime problem in their area – usually violent crime or drugs – and who decide that they need to take action to combat the issue. The members agree their own aims and objectives, which in most cases will involve the setting out a common standard of behaviour that will be expected from anyone using their premises, and they will enforce that good behaviour by using sanctions against anyone conducting themselves in a violent or anti-social way.

54.02 It is the collective use of a licensee's long held right to ban an individual under common law that makes a Pub Watch scheme unique and has captured the public imagination. The term 'banned from one – banned from all' has proved to be a powerful message to anyone who has a propensity for anti-social behaviour, as they know that whatever the outcome of a police investigation the matter will not end there and that the Pub Watch members may restrict their right to socialise and drink in every pub and club in the scheme.

54.03 It sounds a harsh lesson for a moment's madness; but licensees have a duty to consider the safety of their staff and customers when deciding who they will allow into their pubs, and of course a disruptive customer can damage not only the business's reputation but also its profitability.

54.04 As with Neighbourhood Watch, a Pub Watch scheme will seek to foster a good working relationship with the police. The attendance of a police liaison officer at Pub Watch meetings ensures a two-way flow of information and the identification of common areas of interest. It is important that the police are made aware of any decision to ban an individual from a scheme because they may be called upon to assist a licensee if the person refuses to quit licensed premises.

54.05 The scheme will also usually benefit from the sharing of police photographs to aid identification. This is a long established process and is deemed justifiable for the purpose of prevention and detection of crime: *Hellewell v Chief Constable of Derbyshire*.[1] The provision of such photographs will be subject of a local information-sharing protocol between the scheme and police. Many police forces will also be willing to locate and either serve an individual with a Pub Watch issued banning notice or inform them of the decision in order to reduce the likelihood of a future confrontation if the person attempts to gain access to a member's premises.

54.06 If a Pub Watch scheme stores or circulates its own data, which could include photographs and CCTV footage, they should register their activity with the Information Commissioner's Office to comply with the Data Protection Act 1998.

B WHY SHOULD THE LICENSING TRADE SUPPORT PUB WATCH?

54.07 First, it should be acknowledged that Pub Watch is a voluntary licensing trade response to violent crime and has been active for many years. Violent crime can have a devastating affect on a business and Pub Watch provides a low cost and effective means of protecting the individual business and at the same time enhancing safety in other local pubs and the wider community. In fact due to their positive efforts many schemes have been able

---

[1]   [1995] 1 WLR 804.

to show remarkable reductions in police recorded crime levels and an increase in customer satisfaction.

54.08 Individual licensees would therefore appear to have a vested interest in joining an existing scheme or forming a scheme if there isn't already one in their neighbourhood. Alcohol and its association with anti-social behaviour are an uncomfortable truth but it must also be recognised that most people would prefer to see alcohol sold and consumed in a well regulated and safely managed premises.

54.09 It could be argued that a licensee who never knowingly experiences crime in their own premises will have no need for membership of such a scheme. Unfortunately it is the nature of the licensing trade that anyone can walk off the street and into a pub or club. If that person has a propensity towards violent behaviour or other forms of criminality it can be difficult to identify and neutralise the threat. Good management and staff training will of course help to reduce or defuse a difficult situation; but if that person has already demonstrated that they have a track record of bad behaviour and other pubs and clubs have excluded them from their premises why would a publican not want to be given prior warning about the potential danger and in turn warn other licensees about the problem?

54.10 Experienced licensees may also feel that they can handle any potential problem without recourse to outside intervention. That may be true but the licensee also has a duty of care to their staff and customers and preventing an incident preserves not only the reputation of that pub but the whole business community. If the public perceives a town to be unsafe then many will avoid the area, reducing social control as only the young or those who are not risk averse will venture into its pubs and clubs.

54.11 The police service and Home Office have consistently recognised the effectiveness of Pub Watch schemes. In fact, membership of a scheme is a route to a reduction in the late night levy: see Chapter 62 (Late Night Levy).

C RECENT CHALLENGES TO THE PUB WATCH MOVEMENT

54.12 The police have long promoted the advantages of Pub Watch as a successful crime prevention initiative and its success has led people in some quarters to question its voluntary nature and put forward the idea that compulsory membership should be a prerequisite for obtaining a premises licence. Such thinking fails to grasp the reason that licensees come together to form a Pub Watch scheme or what motivates them to play a full part in its activities. There are also real practical difficulties in ensuring attendance at meetings; let alone compliance with agreed Pub Watch decisions from licensees whose participation is achieved under duress.

54.13 Following the introduction of the Licensing Act 2003, some police and council licensing authorities sought to encourage licensees in their area to commit to joining the local Pub Watch scheme as part of their licensing conditions. It is unclear as to whether those licensing authorities fully understood the voluntary nature of Pub Watch other than that it was seen as best practice. Many applicants may also have voluntarily entered into the agreement without fully understanding what would be expected of them. At present, however, there are no publicised cases of any premises licence being suspended or revoked for the sole reason of the operator failing to participate in a Pub Watch scheme.

54.14 Perhaps inevitably, Pub Watch schemes have also been placed under scrutiny by the courts as a result of individuals seeking to challenge the right to ban them from members' premises. Pub Watch members will be all too familiar with banned people stating that refusal to allow them to socialise in pubs and clubs in some way infringes their human rights. There have been two recent cases where the individual concerned has sought to overturn the Pub Watch ban through judicial review.

54.15 The most recent challenge took place in the High Court in 2009 when the claimant Francis Boyle brought an application for judicial review against the Haverhill Pub Watch scheme.[2] The claimant sought to prove that the scheme was exercising 'functions of a public nature', and was thus a public authority within the meaning of section 6(3)(b) of the Human Rights Act 1998 and therefore amenable to judicial review. If the claim had been successful it could have had far-reaching implications for the licensing trade. In particular it would have meant that it would no longer be acceptable for a banning decision to be made simply on the basis of information provided by an individual licensee or the police without first giving the person affected the opportunity to make representations and conducting the decision making process on a much more formal footing.

54.16 The High Court decision in this case shows that his Honour Judge Mackie QC was unconvinced by the claimants' arguments as to the degree of involvement of the public authority and the police. In relation to the licensing authority he stated:

> 'The imposition of a requirement upon some of the member premises to become a member of Pub Watch (albeit only to a proportion of the members of Pub Watch) does not contribute to the conversion of a private function into a public one. These public bodies rightly encourage and support a scheme which is run by the licensees who alone take the decisions of the kind for which Mr Boyle seeks redress'.

---

[2] *R (Boyle) v Haverhill Pub Watch* [2009] EWHC 2441 (Admin). See also *R (Proud) v Buckingham Pubwatch Scheme* [2008] EWHC 2224 (Admin).

54.17 He also commented that the public no longer accept that the involvement of the police should start only after a crime has been committed. He said:

> 'Legitimate schemes run by sections of the public to discourage crime should not have to run the risk of their decisions being subject to the threat of judicial review simply because their work receives assistance and support from the police and other public agencies'.

54.18 The judge stated that individual licensees have an unrestricted right to exclude anyone, particularly those whom they see as troublemakers from their premises. Similarly, individual licensees have the right to exclude those whom others have found to be troublemakers. Furthermore licensees are entitled to form groups or associations to pool information and discuss matters of common interest and make the exclusion of potential troublemakers more organised and systematic.

54.19 He concluded that the only basis for an argument that such banning decisions are amenable to judicial review lies in the degree of involvement of the public authority and the police. In considering what level of involvement would nevertheless keep the operation within the private sphere, he noted that he would not expect that the operations of a particular Pub Watch scheme would be open to judicial review if the role of the police and other public bodies was limited to that of advice and support, as recommended by the 'Good Practice Guide' issued by National Pub Watch.

D   SUPPORT FOR LOCAL PUB WATCH SCHEMES

54.20 Pub Watch relies on committed individuals from the pub trade who are willing to take on the role of administrating or coordinating their local schemes. This is not necessarily an onerous task, particularly in a small town centre scheme, but it does require a commitment to liaise with members, arrange meetings and deal with correspondence as well as having a familiarity with and knowledge of process. Unfortunately the pub trade does suffer from a certain amount of 'churn' in that key individuals will often move out of the area, either to further their career or as a result of commercial necessity. The loss of such people can cause disruption even to the most successful scheme.

54.21 National Pub Watch was set up in 1997 to provide help and guidance to people wishing to launch new schemes or support to existing schemes. In keeping with the low cost ethos of Pub Watch it is not a membership-based organisation and its committee provides its services free of charge, as it is wholly funded by the licensing trade.

54.22 The National Pub Watch Committee has considerable breadth and depth of experience and its volunteer members are drawn from a number of professions such as the law, press, police and the licensing trade. The organisation's website www.nationalPubWatch.org.uk provides a gateway to a number of services including a frequently asked questions page and also access to its Good Practice Guide and newsletters. Small start-up packs containing window stickers and posters can be posted to members of a local scheme and a number of publications can be downloaded direct from the site.

54.23 The scheme's regional representatives offer a personal contact point for Pub Watch members who may need to discuss local issues or have someone support their activities; for example attending and speaking at a start-up meeting.

54.24 National Pub Watch is not a trade body but regularly speaks to the police and Home Office on issues directly affecting the operational integrity and effectiveness of the Pub Watch movement. Its annual conference seeks to bring together representatives from the police, licensing trade and other interested parties to discuss areas of mutual interest and promote partnership working.

E CASE STUDY – READING PUB WATCH

54.25 Reading Pub Watch is a voluntary partnership arrangement, which brings together seven autonomous groups, representing a variety of licensed premises, spread over a wide geographic area. This includes the town centre scheme which draws its members from the vibrant bars, clubs and restaurants in the busy town centre, to the more sedate Tilehurst scheme with its range of traditional pubs and off-licences and the Student Watch which covers student promotions and the bars at the local university campus. The individual groups are represented on a Pub Watch council which coordinates the strategic direction of the scheme. Police and council licensing officers regularly attend meetings in a liaison capacity.

54.26 Reading Pub Watch was the winner of the Pub Watch Award at the 2007 Responsible Drinks Retailing Awards where they demonstrated that over a two year period they had achieved an impressive 33% reduction in police-recorded wounding. It has a formal banning and appeals policy, but its approach to crime reduction is much more sophisticated. The scheme is represented on a number of partnership bodies which have a direct responsibility for the reduction of crime and disorder and cleaner and safer streets. For example it supported the successful application for the renewal of a second term of the Business Improvement District (BID) and its members represent the licensing community on the BID committee.

54.27 Perhaps more importantly, the scheme has demonstrated that it actively takes a leading role in improving the operating standards of licensed premises. It promotes and administers its own Safer Bars Awards Scheme, including an annual dinner dance and awards ceremony. Safer Bars is associated with the nationally recognised Best Bar None Scheme. It also organises a number of training events and conferences throughout the year to keep its members informed of changes in law and local and national trends; such as its annual conference in association with the National Counter Terrorism Security Office, to prevent terrorism and improve major incident handling in licensed premises.

55

Best Bar None

You won't have seen the new bar maid in the Rovers will you? First time I saw her I thought it were a juke box. (Hilda Ogden, of Bet Lynch)

They've not barred anyone since Dick Turpin's time and then it was only his horse. (Bet Lynch, of the Flying Horse)

Drinking's a serious business. You gotta keep at it – like training for a football match. (Stan Ogden)

Coronation Street

A   Introduction 55.01
B   How the scheme works 55.04
C   Conclusion 55.14

A INTRODUCTION

55.01   Best Bar None was conceived in Manchester by the City Centre Safe team as a multi-agency safety award scheme that sets a benchmark of good practice through the licensed trade. An annual awards ceremony recognises and celebrates the achievement of premises in reaching the set standard of evidenced good practice in their management and an active customer care programme, thereby providing a safer drinking environment. The hard-earned plaques are then displayed inside and outside premises as a badge of honour, a marketing tool and an assurance to customers. To apply, premises must complete a comprehensive application form that covers a wide range of issues. The premises are visited by trained, independent external assessors who inspect the premises with the form and the scheme standards in mind. The first award ceremony was held in March 2003, since when the scheme has been rolled out nationally under the stewardship of the British Institute of Innkeeping. The scheme is not a coercive arrangement but is a voluntary scheme which incentivises bar owners and staff to place safety at the heart of what they do. It has been highly successful in its work, with approximately 100 local schemes and 3,000 bars now participating. Recently, the scheme has been adopted in Edmonton, Alberta.

55.02   The mission statement of the scheme is as follows:

'To promote and maintain an inclusive national awards scheme for all licensed premises across England, Wales, Scotland and Northern Ireland, building on good practice and leading to an enhanced customer experience.

Best Bar None raises standards and rewards excellence for those venues that attain the award standard. This is delivered at a local level by active partnerships between the industry, local authorities and police.

The awards are based on core national standards with local flexibility to ensure they address local needs.

Assessment of licensed premises will be carried out by trained, impartial assessors, who will ensure consistency of approach. The assessment criteria will be clear and straightforward, with a minimum of bureaucracy with constructive feedback provided to all entrants.'

55.03 At the end of 2012 the following areas had Best Bar None schemes:

- Altrincham
- Aylesbury Vale
- Banbury
- Barnsley
- Bedford
- Birmingham
- Bishop Auckland
- Bournemouth
- Bradford
- Brent
- Bromley
- Carlisle & Eden
- Ceredigion – covering Aberystwyth, Cardigan, Lampeter, Aberaeron, Llandysul, Tregaron
- Cheltenham
- Chester-le-Street
- City of York & Selby District
- Consett
- Conwy and Denbighshire
- Cornwall
- Croydon
- Darlington
- Derby City Centre
- Doncaster
- Durham City Centre
- East Lindsey
- East Riding including Bridlington, Beverley, Driffield, Hornsea, Coltingham, Hessle, Goole, Howden & Pocklington
- Filey
- Harrogate
- High Wycombe
- Hull
- Ipswich
- Isle of Wight
- Islington
- Kensington & Chelsea
- Kingston
- Kingston Upon Hull
- Leicester
- Lincoln
- Luton
- Manchester
- Middlesbrough
- National Union of Students – nationwide.
- Newcastle upon Tyne City Centre
- Newcastle under Lyme
- Newport, South Wales
- Northamptonshire
- Norwich
- Nottingham

- Oldham
- Plymouth
- Poole
- Reading
- Redbridge
- Rochdale
- Rhondda Cynon Taff
- Sefton
- Scarborough
- Sheffield
- Shropshire
- Stafford

- Stockport
- Sunderland
- Sutton
- Swindon
- Thames Valley Area – covering Newbury
- Walsall
- Watford
- Whitby
- Wigan
- Woking

B HOW THE SCHEME WORKS

55.04 Best Bar None is run at national level by the British Institute of Innkeeping through the medium of a not for profit company which employs two staff members, and a national board drawn from the industry and regulators. It is supported nationally by Diageo, Molson Coors, Heineken and Bacardi Brown-Forman. The board is responsible for the strategic direction of the scheme, its marketing, development and, crucially, local support where necessary in setting up and maintaining schemes and the provision of helpful materials and toolkits.

55.05 However, the beating heart of the scheme is at local level. Each local area is responsible for setting its own standards, making its own assessment and deciding who is worthy to receive a Best Bar None award. The very process of applying for an award encourages an improvement in standards and rigorous self-analysis by the bars concerned. The imprimatur of a Best Bar None award is intended to do two crucial things. First, it is a badge of achievement which signals to the bar staff concerned that they have excelled in making their venue safe, motivates them to continue to improve, and gives them bragging rights in their town. Second, it signals to customers that this is a safe place in which to drink, so marrying safety, reputation and profit. Best Bar None bars therefore report lower crime and higher profit – a win-win for them, the regulatory authorities and the community.

55.06 The stakeholders involved in Best Bar None schemes are wide-ranging, including, of course, the bars themselves, crime and disorder partnerships, local strategic partnerships, police, licensing officers, health professionals, fire officers and town centre managers. There is typically a steering group drawn from this spectrum.

55.07 There is also a voluntary Best Bar None manager who runs the scheme locally on top of his or her day job. In a small number of areas, the scheme employs a full time manager. The main job of the manager is:

- To liaise with all stakeholders to promote and sustain the Best Bar None scheme as part of the town centre's overall vision, aims and objectives.
- To develop and maintain operational, marketing and promotional plans.
- To encourage active participation in the Best Bar None initiative and secure external funding and sponsorship funds/assistance to ensure that the scheme becomes self-sufficient.
- To prepare and present progress reports and ensure assessments and general operations are equitable and transparent.
- To liaise with all stakeholders (including licensed retail managers).
- To arrange dates, times and venues for meetings, the launch event, the annual dinner, feedback and evaluation.
- To liaise with assessors and ensure training and objectives of Best Bar None are up to date.
- To bid for funds internally.
- To manage fees for the Best Bar None application and awards dinner.
- To arrange press releases and media participation.[1]

55.08 The scheme works by the submission of a form of application annually by the bar concerned, having regard to the standards set down locally contained in a scoring booklet and assessors' guide. The bar is then assessed by trained assessors and marks accorded. A judging panel then meets and winning venues are chosen.

55.09 This leads to an awards night in which bars receive their awards and overall winners are announced. There may be different categories of awards, eg best pub, best nightclub, best hotel bar, best student bar, best suburban bar, etc. These are all different ways of recognising and publicly rewarding achievement. Some description of the winners and their qualities is usually given to explain the reasons why they won and to provide yet further incentives for the following year. The awards night is a central part of the Best Bar None cycle, and at the heart of what the scheme is about. To take one example, Birmingham attracts over 400 people to a black tie dinner in recognition of the standards which its local bars have achieved. This is not only important to Best Bar None but also to Birmingham, because it means that a significant proportion of its bars are striving for even greater achievements in the way they promote the licensing objectives, and not just in the way they market alcohol.

55.10 For successful bars, the Best Bar None award is a way of achieving free advertising for their premises, in the form of press releases, promotional materials and websites. The awards night is usually covered by local press, entailing good publicity for the scheme and the smiling winners. Licensees

---

[1]   Alexandra J Kenyon, *Introduction to the Best Bar None Scheme and Its Benefits* (Leeds Metropolitan University).

appreciate being recognised and rewarded by people in authority such as the Chief Constable or the chair of the licensing committee. It also means that bars, rather than merely competing with each other, begin to share a common agenda, and work together to ensure that *their* town is safe. The sharing of best practice is obviously a fundamental aspect of the scheme. Local winners may also be nominated for a national Best Bar None award which is then delivered at an annual Parliamentary reception, so incentivising excellence still further.

55.11 Best Bar None award winners report better income and lower crime. They also find that they are that they are charged lower insurance premiums, and become part of a professional network promoting excellence.

55.12 From the point of view of regulators, the scheme is important in that it provides a voluntary framework for the improvement of standards across the town, paints a positive picture of the town to counteract the sometimes negative press around the night time economy, encourages different demographics to access the town, and helps to make places safer, better managed and more civilised.

55.13 The work at local level is supported by the following:

- A Best Bar None Assessors' Scoring Booklet.
- An Assessors' Guide which sets out standards against each of the licensing objectives.
- Tool kits to assist new and existing schemes with their work, eg regarding self-assessment of performance indicators, management, publicity and website development.
- A 'Buddy' system has been established for new and existing schemes.
- Best Bar None Scheme Helpline.
- A quarterly newsletter to share ideas and best practice and to celebrate successful schemes.
- Best Bar None marketing materials.

C CONCLUSION

55.14 Best Bar None can be seen as a grassroots movement rather than a national organisation, because the work which really matters is done by local schemes across the nation, bound to each other not by constitution or contract but by the values which they hold. At the heart of a Best Bar None venue is a commitment to its community that the bar will do all in its power to ensure that its customers will be safe if they choose to spend their valuable time and hard earned cash there.

55.15 The scheme exists and thrives on the dedication of volunteers from the public and private sector and is a good example of how partnerships can arise to share expertise outside of the regulatory sphere, creating a more lucid and productive dialogue than sometimes arises in a sanction-oriented setting between the regulator and the regulated.

55.16 It has proved to be popular both with participating bars and with local regulators and can be seen as an effective part of a partnership approach to the promotion of a sustainable, diverse night time economy.

56

Community Alcohol Partnerships

Many people are good at talking about what they are doing, but in fact do little. Others do a lot but don't talk about it; they are the ones who make a community live.

Jean Vanier, *Community and Growth*

A INTRODUCTION

56.01 Community Alcohol Partnerships are local projects developed within individual communities to tackle underage drinking and related anti-social behaviour. Operated nationally by Community Alcohol Partnerships CIC, the individual partnerships are developed to suit local needs and, depending on the nature and extent of the problem, adopt different methods of best practice in order to best tackle the particular issues they face.

Origin

56.02 Community Alcohol Partnerships were developed out of the Retail of Alcohol Standards Group (RASG) in 2007. RASG was formed at the end of 2005 following poor performances of the supermarkets during the government's AMEC test purchasing programme. The results showed a high level of test purchasing failures and retailers were called to a meeting with the then Home Secretary and urged to find solutions. The group formed consisted of all major retailers of alcohol in the UK who agreed to work together to examine ways they could co-operate to reduce the incidence of alcohol sales to minors.

56.03 RASG initially conducted research into underage sale and found there were a number of key issues which prevented them from enforcing their proof of age policies more effectively. This included the difficulty staff had of judging people's exact age, managing the time pressure of a busy checkout, and wanting to avoid potentially difficult confrontations. In response to this RASG developed the Challenge 21 initiative.

56.04 Challenge 21 is a retailing strategy that encourages anyone who is over 18 but looks under 21 to carry acceptable ID (a card bearing the PASS hologram, a photographic driving licence or a passport) if they wish to buy alcohol. Anyone appearing under 21 will be challenged to prove their age or face refusal of service.

56.05 RASG supported the launch and has developed a suite of designs, from posters to shelf markers and badges, to reinforce the message throughout the store. The new signage in red and black added a fresh and striking look and made it clear that under 21s must expect to be challenged to prove their age. It also spelled out the heavy fines which could follow for those caught breaking the law.

56.06 The signage was rolled out in RASG member stores across the UK in 2009. The uniform RASG look ensured recognition and awareness by consumers up and down the country and the variety of formats reinforced the message throughout the store.

56.07 Challenge 21 proved an effective tool to tackle underage purchase; research demonstrated that 90% of 18–24 year olds were aware of the Challenge 21 scheme. However, with levels of sales to minors still not low enough and the personal consequences of illegal sales for the member of shop staff more severe, retailer employees requested a programme which gives them a greater backing and a higher margin of error in challenging customers for proof of age.

56.08 In 2009 retailers increased the threshold by raising the age at which consumers were challenged to 25 and launched a rebranded Challenge 25 policy.

56.09 While Challenge 21/25 had a significant impact on underage sales, with a reduction in supermarkets from 50% to 19% failure rate, underage drinking and, one of its causes, proxy purchasing, continued to be an issue. RASG then looked to develop a partnership programme over and above Challenge 25, working with the local authority and retailers in order to tackle underage sales and the wider issues of alcohol related anti-social behaviour.

B PILOT SCHEMES

Cambridgeshire Community Alcohol Partnership

56.10 The first Community Alcohol Partnership launched in June 2007 in St Neots, Cambridgeshire and established a partnership between the RASG, local authority, police and the local media.

56.11 St Neots is a typical English market town. Situated to the West of Cambridgeshire on the Bedfordshire border, it lies on the banks of the river Great Ouse. St Neots has a number of parks and recreation grounds. The Riverside Park has a car park, café, skateboard park and children's play area where young people like to gather. There are 20 different off-licence premises in the town ranging from a national superstore on the outskirts to several small independent retailers.

56.12 There was a perception amongst the community, police and local authority that there was a problem with anti-social behaviour (ASB) and youth related disorder – much of which could be associated with underage alcohol consumption. Adding to this the negative effects on the health of young people participating in underage drinking, it was clear that something needed to be done.

56.13 The project included the training of local independent retailers, introduction of Challenge 21, high profile joint police and youth outreach patrols in hotspot areas, notification to parents of young people found in possession of alcohol and highlighting the dangers of proxy purchasing. Information on responsible drinking for both young people and adults was also provided.

56.14 In the last four months of the pilot, incidents of ASB dropped by 2% and by 45.8% in one of the main hotspot areas. Reports of alcohol related litter also fell dramatically. At the end of the pilot, far fewer young people were caught with alcohol and the local Member of Parliament commented that he received fewer complaint letters in respect of ASB in the hotspot areas.

56.15 The importance of the CAP was the cultural change that was brought about in the way the partners worked together. The pilot improved their relationships, which had a positive knock-on effect for other, non-related, projects. Attitudes changed, with the police for example now focusing on working with retailers, rather than just looking to prosecute for under-age sales.

56.16 In addition, concerns about vulnerable young people identified through the pilot were fed back into the wider multi-agency team so that, if needed, the root causes of the under-age drinking such as problems at home could also be addressed.

56.17   The project developed a number of initiatives and established the three CAP principles of education, enforcement and public perception.

County Scheme Development – Kent

56.18   Following publication of the St Neots results, Kent County Council, supported by the Chief Constable, approached RASG to develop a county-wide scheme. The KCAP project was funded by the county council, to allow sufficient resources to be allocated and to cover the cost of an independent evaluation by Kent University. The principles of CAP – education, enforcement and public perception – remained the same but in addition funds were allocated to provide youth outreach and diversionary activities.

56.19   Three different and distinct areas were chosen: Edenbridge, a small market town environment with a strong local community ethos; Canterbury, a student-based town centre; and Thanet, an area with other social problems in addition to alcohol. This project was the first to include the on-trade and in addition roll out the new RASG Challenge 25 programme.

56.20   During the KCAP period between March and September 2009, the KCAP pilot areas saw a decline in offences of criminal damage some 6% greater than in non-pilot areas. Drinking by minors is frequently associated with various acts of criminal damage and this was a key issue upon which KCAP sought to make an impact. There were substantial falls in recorded crime in both Thanet and Edenbridge, with the latter reducing violent crime by almost a third.

56.21   The figures for Canterbury, whilst good, did not show a significant improvement over the non pilot areas. Canterbury's focus was aimed at a different group of young people, mainly students in the city centre, and signalled the need to better involve the late night economy in any future project. This was thought to reflect the differences between pilot areas and those young people they focused on. Another difference between the pilot areas was that in Edenbridge the focus was very much on minors drinking in public places, whereas in Thanet the KCAP team was also particularly concerned to address proxy sales, seen as a particular problem in the area.

56.22   Public perception surveys overall showed an improvement twice that of the non-pilot areas: 4% compared with 2%. The issue of teenagers hanging around in public places is one that many members of the public wanted addressed especially if the young people are drinking.

56.23 Kent Police's survey of members of the public indicated that, during the life of the KCAP pilot, concerns about teenagers fell by 4% compared with a fall of 1% in non-pilot areas.

56.24 On the question of people drunk or rowdy in public, the pilot areas had a 3% reduction compared with 1% for non-pilot areas. This may have had a positive effect on the overall feelings of safety, reflected in the improved public perception figures.

56.25 Following the results of the pilot, KCAP developed plans to roll out the CAP model across the county and where appropriate link the initiative with the night time economy.

56.26 Kent University's full report can be found online.[1]

C CAP MODEL

56.27 The experience of the Cambridgeshire and Kent Community Alcohol Partnerships enabled CAP officers to develop a more consistent model for delivery, which formed the basis for new projects. While they continued to respond to local needs, the 'CAP Toolkit' was developed to support the development as the number of CAP schemes increased across the UK.

Model

56.28 Community Alcohol Partnerships' principal aim is to tackle under-age drinking and associated alcohol related problems in partnership with local stakeholders. CAP cannot solve non-alcohol related anti-social behaviour and drug related problems; however it can be set up as a work stream within a larger project aimed at dealing with these issues.

56.29 Partnerships normally consist of the following representatives:

- Trading Standards
- Drug & alcohol team
- Youth service
- Community safety
- Police
- Local health authority
- Local schools or education authority
- District council

---

[1] 'An Evaluation of the Kent Community Alcohol Partnership, April – September 2009' (University of Kent), http://www.communityalcoholpartnerships.co.uk/images/stories/KCAP%20Evaluation.pdf.

- Retail of Alcohol Standards Group
- On-licence trade groups

56.30   CAP aims to address both the demand and supply side of under-age drinking through three key elements – education, enforcement and public perception.

Setting up a CAP

56.31   Following initial contact with a local authority keen on establishing a CAP, meetings will be arranged between the CAP Officer, trading standards, police, and other local authority representatives.

The first piece of work to be undertaken is to clearly define the problem. The primary headings under which a CAP will operate are:

- Under-age drinking
- 18–24 drinking
- Street drinking
- Proxy purchasing.

It is important to identify and agree the main problem headings right at the start, as these will be the basis for the development of the project's objectives. On occasion these meetings can identify that the problem does not require a CAP solution.

Area of focus

56.32   For CAP to work well there needs to be an identifiable community and preferably a small or compact area for a pilot scheme where the partnership can gain knowledge and experience before tackling more problematic areas.

56.33   The secret of any CAP is a balance between the ideal area and available resources. If the geographical area is too large or resources limited, the project will be broken down into constituent parts, and rolled out progressively. Ultimately, the size of the CAP area will always be determined by geography and availability of resources.

Mapping the area

56.34   Mapping the proposed area is also an important first stage. The map will show licensed premises, problem hot spots and other locations where young people associate such as schools, youth clubs, etc.

This activity helps identify vulnerable areas or outside influences. Once complete the map will also help identify patterns and clusters and assist in targeting resources.

56.35 An ideal map will show:

- The CAP area defined by line or natural boundary
- Licensed premises
- Parks and hotspot incident areas
- Schools, youth clubs etc
- External influences, eg bus or train stations.

56.36 The second stage of mapping is to list the existing alcohol-related activities, services and diversionary activities already operating in the area.

Once this work has been completed, the project is ready for its first partners meeting.

Partners meeting

56.37 The first meeting is crucial and is held primarily to explain the project and to discuss the partnership role. The partners at this first meeting would normally consist of the key decision makers from the local authority and police. The CAP officer will attend to explain how CAP works and present results of other schemes operating around the country.

56.38 The outcome of this meeting will be to agree that a CAP should be formed, who should be represented on the working group, and who should take the lead.

A partner activity document is circulated so that partners are aware of their potential role and contribution to the project. Partners are encouraged to contribute to and/or amend the activity document so that it accurately reflects their roles and responsibilities.

Management structure

56.39 Experience has shown that the governance of CAP is crucial. A two tier structure is usually best, consisting of a management group and a working group. A management group which has the ability to control and manage resources at a senior or strategic level within the local authority is crucial to the success of a CAP scheme. It is now common for CAP to be controlled via the Community Safety Partnership or similar strategic body.

56.40 The working group will generally represent those involved in carrying out the CAP action plan on a day-to-day basis, eg PCSOs, trading standards, detached youth worker, trade representatives, licensing officers, etc.

Terms of reference

56.41 A formal contract between partners such as terms of reference and service level agreements together with a draft protocol for retailers and trading standards helps ensure that the relevant relationships are maintained and expectations are clear.

Project summary

56.42 Once all the above groundwork has been completed, a project summary is then produced. This document sets out the aims and objectives of the CAP together with a summary of the area and its problems, desired outcomes and the strategic approach. The document will have an attached action plan together with clear objectives and agreed measurements. This ensures that all partners are aware of their contribution and that the project stays on track.

Action plan

56.43 As stated above, CAP is based upon the three main principles of education, enforcement and public perception. The working group will develop an action plan that reflects the objectives stated in the project summary and which will enable them to manage the progress of each work stream. The plan is updated at regular progress meetings.

Communication

56.44 Once the project summary and objectives have been agreed, RASG and trading standards write a joint letter to all alcohol traders in the CAP area. These are normally hand-delivered allowing trading standards officers and PCSOs to meet store mangers/owners and have an initial discussion about problems and working together on solutions. The CAP officer will facilitate contacts with other CAP projects to develop ideas and learning from other areas.

Traders meeting

56.45 Before activities and plans are finalised, a meeting of the alcohol retailers in the area will be called to inform them of the CAP and outline what is expected from both sides. This is an important step in building the new partnership and developing relationships.

The draft action plan will be presented to gain feedback/buy in to the project. Feedback is essential and allows local issues that are important to traders to be reflected in the plan thus creating better ownership.

56.46 Presentations would normally be given by the CAP Officer, trading standards and police and the agenda constructed to achieve the following:

- Inform and review
- Gather intelligence
- Deal with issues
- Offer support
- Gain buy in
- Agree communications
- Share the protocol for retailers and trading standards
- Agree method of communication between traders and CAP partners.

Launch event

56.47 This is the first opportunity to generate public awareness of the CAP and must not be undertaken until all the building blocks are in place. There should not be a gap between the launch event and commencement of activity. All partners attend the event, together with local politicians and trade representatives. The event format will very much depend upon local conditions but will be designed to achieve local interest and publicity.

D CAP IN ACTION

56.48 As stated above, CAP activity falls under one of three headings – education, enforcement and public perception.

Education

56.49 Whilst enforcement bodies are partners in the CAP, education is the most important place to start. Education is key to raising knowledge and awareness about the law relating to young people and alcohol and the impacts they together have on health and society.

Education is delivered to three target groups: retailers, young people and adults.

Retailers

56.50 The RASG supermarket lead will deliver training to local retailers in the area. All retailers will be invited. The training will centre on alcohol and young people but can also include all other age-restricted sales products such as tobacco, knives and solvents. Training materials such as staff training documents and point of sale posters, leaflets and stickers will be provided to educate the public and show that the retailer is working in partnership to create a safer community. Premises are encouraged to 'challenge 25' and the point of sale material will clearly show this.

56.51   Retailers, after receiving training and agreeing to be part of CAP, then sign up to the partnership agreement. This is an agreement between all partners, helping to facilitate the smooth running of the scheme.

Young people

56.52   CAPs support teaching resources for schools through the funding of PHSE education either through the Alcohol Education Trust or through 'In Tuition' sponsored by Drinkaware. They also support work in youth clubs around the short and long term effects on health, the legalities of purchasing and consuming alcohol and the enforcement work of the CAP.

Posters and leaflets are distributed and young people are encouraged to pass on intelligence to help with the partnership work. CAPs also try to work closely with local schools on these activities, as they can often provide the best communication route to young people.

Diversionary activity for young people is an important element and CAPs look to help fund extra provision where possible.

Adults

56.53   CAP recognises the fact that work within the community and enforcement will mean that only a small proportion of young people will be buying the alcohol themselves. Proxy purchasing is therefore targeted by gathering intelligence from adults, retailers and young people. Proxy purchasing is an ever increasing problem reported to enforcement bodies and is very difficult to detect.

56.54   Information in relation to the law surrounding proxy purchasing is provided through posters and leaflets which include the Crimestoppers telephone number so that all intelligence is pooled and distributed to the correct agencies. Youth outreach, neighbourhood management teams, environmental rangers, etc provide signposting information to services which may assist young displaced people and adult street drinkers.

Enforcement

Trade

56.55   Following the education stage, a non-punitive Challenge 25 test purchasing event takes place to test the robustness of licensees' systems. Further advice and guidance is then offered should there be any failures. Should premises within the CAP area be found to be breaking the law subsequently then usual enforcement policies will apply.

Young people

56.56 Police and other agencies make regular patrols of the pilot area looking for under 18s drinking in public. Where such persons are found, alcohol is confiscated and the parents informed. Police warning letters about anti-social behaviour, called section 30 letters, are sent to advise parents about individuals being found with alcohol. Advisory information can be offered to both the young person and parents/guardians on services and CAP.

56.57 Where a young person is found intoxicated, the guardian will be called to collect them or they will be taken home in a police vehicle. Cases are reported to children's services where deemed appropriate and necessary. An alcohol workshop has been developed in some areas attended by young people found with alcohol and their parents/guardians.

56.58 In some areas environmental rangers can issue fixed penalty notices for littering and waste offences. Such action on young people is only taken after verbal/written warnings. This approach would not normally be taken against persons under 16 years of age.

Proxy purchasers

56.59 Intelligence from retailers and the public will often identify the places where adults are buying alcohol on behalf of young people. Adults found to be purchasing alcohol for or on behalf of under 18s are issued with an £80 fixed penalty notice or, if deemed appropriate, prosecuted. A central telephone number is often provided for retailers on patrol operations to facilitate the swift action required when proxy purchasers are identified.

Public perception

56.60 Two-way communication with the local community is very important. A key measurement of CAP success comes through local community reporting. Concerns around people being drunk, anti-social behaviour and groups of youths hanging around are all measures of how people view their local community. There is also a responsibility for local people to ensure that they play their part in the partnership by ensuring young people are not given alcohol either directly or via proxy, and that parents are aware of where their children are and what they are doing. This message is supported by leaflets, posters and local media coverage.

Evaluation

56.61 The CAP agreement insists that the project work is evaluated. This is normally an internal evaluation using the agreed objectives and measures set out in the project summary. Occasionally, where funds permit, CAPs engage external consultants such as a local university to carry out an independent evaluation. In these cases, CAPs also look to evaluate the management and operational process.

56.62   Most local authorities set a six month review period on the project, which can make it difficult to establish the full extent of the impact the CAP unless good quality year on year data has been made available.

56.63   A typical evaluation will review data to ascertain if there has been a change in the number of intelligence referrals relating to young people drinking as well as police incident reports etc. This work would normally include:

(1)   Residents' questionnaire to determine public perception before and after the CAP launch
(2)   Young persons' questionnaire
(3)   Ascertaining whether police intelligence reflects anti-social behaviour related to alcohol misuse in young people has reduced
(4)   Police reports of anti-social behaviour hot spots
(5)   Crime reports
(6)   Statistics regarding the reports of sales of alcohol to minors.

A key measure of any CAP is of course the desire by partners to roll out into more areas.

E   DEVELOPMENT OF COMMUNITY ALCOHOL PARTNERSHIPS COMMUNITY INTEREST COMPANY

56.64   The initial Community Alcohol Partnerships were funded by RASG retailers who contributed to the employment of the Community Alcohol Partnerships project officer and supported one-off projects that formed part of the different schemes. The Wine and Spirit Trade Association also provided the secretariat support for the schemes.

56.65   Due to the nature of the partnership, which focuses on using existing resources available to local communities, CAPs are relatively low cost, with the centrally funded officers making up the majority of the expense of each scheme. However, in addition to central funding, local stores and partners offer in kind services such as the use of facilities and the sharing training programmes. Further funding is also received from local authorities and partners, in order to fund one-off projects or evaluations which complement the schemes.

56.66   In June 2011 a new three-year funding agreement was agreed with RASG retailers and, for the first time, producers, including Bacardi Brown-Forman, Beverage Brands, Diageo, Heineken and Molson Coors, to support the operation of CAPs. This equated to nearly £1m over three years and sought to support Community Alcohol Partnership's development into a Community Interest Company and the expansion of the number of operational partnerships.

56.67 Government adviser and community campaigner Baroness Helen Newlove was appointed as chair of the new CIC and an advisory board made up of retailers and stakeholders from the police, voluntary, charity and trading standards was appointed to oversee the running of the scheme.

56.68 The commitment to Community Alcohol Partnerships by alcohol retailers and producers was further formalised as part of the government's Public Health Responsibility Deal. The individual pledge, monitored by the Wine and Spirit Trade Association, confirmed the commitment to the scheme for three years and funding support to expand the number of schemes across the UK. The full terms of the deal in relation to CAPs is set out in Annex 2 to this chapter.

F CURRENT SCHEMES

56.69 As at December 2012, there are 50 schemes that are active or in advanced stages of development. These are:

County	Area	
Bath	1.	Midsumer Norton
Bedfordshire	2.	Sharnbrook
	3.	Caversham
Berkshire	4.	Tilehurst
	5.	Slough
Birmingham	6.	Sutton Coldfield
	7.	City
	8.	East Cambs – Ely & Soham
Cambridge	9.	South Cambs
	10.	Huntingdonshire – St Neots
	11.	Huntingdonshire – Chatteris
	12.	Fenlands – Wisbech
Cheshire East	13.	Crewe
Devon	14.	Tiverton, Crediton, Cullompton
Durham	15.	Stanley
East Sussex	16.	Hastings
Edinburgh	17.	Edinburgh City
Fife	18.	Rosyth

Gateshead	19.	Birtley
Gloucestershire	20.	Gloucester
Hampshire	21.	Havant
	22.	Gosport
Kent	23.	Ashford Town Centre
	24.	Canterbury
	25.	Edenbridge
	26.	Gravesham
	27.	Headcorn, Marden and Staplehurst
	28.	Maidstone
	29.	Snodland
	30.	Swanley
	31.	Thanet
	32.	Whitstable, Margate, Cliftonville.
London	33.	Islington
Medway	34.	Rainham
Norfolk	35.	Great Yarmouth
North Yorkshire	36.	Bedale, Northallerton, Ripon, Thirsk, Pickering, Malton & Ripon
Northern Ireland	37.	Derry/Londonderry
Powys	38.	Brecon
Reading	39.	Caversham
	40.	Tilehurst
Rotherham	41.	Dinnington, East Herringthorpe
Shropshire	42.	Bridgnorth
	43.	Ludlow
	44.	Oswestry
	45.	Whitchurch
South Yorkshire	46.	Barnsley – Dearne
	47.	Barnsley – Peniston
	48.	Barnsley – Grimethorpe
	49.	Barnsley – Kendray & Worsbrough
Wirral	50.	East Wallesley

G IMPACT AND EVALUATIONS

Mid-Devon

56.70 In February 2010, Devon County Council Trading Standards Service proposed a pilot project for Tiverton, Crediton and Cullumpton. These areas were selected based on a range of factors including data on young people's use of alcohol, anti-social behaviour, concerns about usage of fake or fraudulent identification and problems relating to under-age sales.

56.71 The aim was to follow the principles of the Community Alcohol Partnership model using the Community Alcohol Partnership toolkit, but modifying it to suit the needs of the chosen pilot area.

The partnership's key objectives were to:

(1) give retailers more confidence in dealing with under age purchase attempts;
(2) make young people more aware of the potential harms of alcohol; and
(3) improve the perception of Mid-Devon as a safer place to go out at night.

56.72 The CAP used partner resources where possible, including the community survey which was commissioned through the consultation department of Mid Devon District Council.

Resources were committed to the pilot for a one year minimum period, to enable an effective estimate of benefits to be recorded. There were to be no significant increases in enforcement costs.

56.73 A non-punitive test purchase programme was undertaken to establish a benchmark. Failing premises were followed up by trading standards/ licensing officers where they received support and guidance to enable their staff to refuse the sale of alcohol with confidence. Each licensee received a copy of the trading standards CD Rom 'No Proof of Age, No Sale' toolkit. A survey was also used to record their views on the issue of preventing underage sales.

56.74 The partnership developed a training programme for all Mid-Devon licensees, focused on understanding the law and adopting practical strategies for avoiding illegal sales. The training also promoted acceptance of only three forms of proof of age: A driving licence, passport or PASS approved card.

56.75 The project trained 170 Mid-Devon licensees and their staff, including those selling alcohol from village halls, pubs, clubs, shops and supermarkets. Use of the 'No Proof of Age, No Sale' toolkit was also a key component of this process.

56.76   Under the CAP, an ID 'bailment' pilot scheme was introduced in the Tiverton area specifically to address an area of concern for the local retail trade and door staff – the use of fake or 'borrowed' forms of identification. As part of the scheme, door staff, if presented with proof of age they felt was not genuine, could retain it, provide the holder with a receipt and then pass it to the police. The owner was then required to visit the police station to retrieve the document, during which time it could be checked and verified.

Twenty-nine suspect IDs were seized by door staff in Mid-Devon under this scheme, including one stolen passport. Perhaps unsurprisingly, none were reclaimed from the police.

56.77   In November 2010, CAP organised an alcohol retailers meeting, which was attended by large retailers and local independents. There was interest in further progressing the CAP objectives within Mid-Devon. This, combined with the retailer training, has developed a firm and effective working partnership between agencies and local businesses, producing benefits which include increased levels of local intelligence.

56.78   Mid-Devon District Council has published a report highlighting the scheme as an excellent example of communities and businesses working together to produce improvements to the area. The work undertaken has resulted in a significant drop in the number of test purchase failures from 34% to 14% off-sales and 48% to 13% in pubs and clubs.[2]

Barnsley

56.79   Barnsley CAP was launched in two areas, Penistone and Dearne, in February 2011. Unlike other projects, this was led by the police. The CAP working group was chaired by the Chief Inspector with responsibility for carrying out the local programme through the safer neighbourhood team sergeants. CAP majored on engagement with both on- and off-trade through a series of training events organised and run by Tesco. This established a firm foundation for responsible retailing and a consistent approach to Challenge 25.

56.80   The Pub Watch groups in both Dearne and Penistone were very strong supporters of the CAP with the Penistone group incorporating both on- and off-trade members.

56.81   The Barnsley team also developed a unique alcohol workshop, where young people found with alcohol were 'requested' to attend with their parents. The workshops were run by the youth team supported by the police. Youth diversionary activities were also organised with CAP funding to provide access to local sports facilities.

2   The Mid-Devon Community Alcohol Partnership, 'First Year Activity Report' (December 2011), http://www.devon.gov.uk/cap_report_first_year_81211.pdf.

56.82 The CAP achieved significant reductions in street drinking and ASB in both areas. In Dearne, the reductions were matched by improvements in residents' perceptions of the issue, which were over and above that seen in other areas. They were by far the best reductions of any Barnsley SNT. The sports initiatives in Dearne and Penistone were very important. One of the main aims of the CAP was to increase awareness of the problems that can result from alcohol abuse and to show young people that there were activities available to occupy their time other than drinking. There were large reductions in ASB, and alcohol was harder to purchase. In summary, the CAP was seen to have a positive impact on the Dearne and Penistone safer neighbourhood teams.

56.83 The increased patrols and awareness campaign have visibly shown the police are tackling the issue of underage drinking. Training for staff selling alcohol has lowered the amount available to young people and the interventions/sports initiative has potentially reduced the number of youths drinking on the streets.

Derry, Northern Ireland

56.84 Launched in January 2011, the Challenging Underage Drinking Initiative involves the statutory, community and business sectors, and is led by Derry City Council's Civic Alcohol Forum.

The project involved a range of measures, including high visibility patrols, engagement with young people and visits to local retailers to discuss proxy buying. The initiative proved successful, and there was no evidence that the problems moved to another part of the city.

56.85 Since the pilot scheme was put in place there has been a downward trend in the amount of alcohol litter found in the hot spot areas. Statistics show that there was also a marked reduction in referrals to youth diversion officers during the summer period of 2011 (114 for the April–September period in 2010, as compared to 40 for the same period in 2011). Neighbourhood police report that the initiative has improved the quality of life for local residents.

56.86 At the time of writing, the Derry project is not yet complete but extracts from the interim evaluation of the scheme published in December 2011 are set out here.

56.87 Detailed information on type and amount of alcohol litter found at 13 'hot-spots' within the project area has been collected monthly since October 2010. Analysis of the statistics has shown that there has been a general downward trend in the amount of litter found which is more marked in some areas (Creggan Burn open space) than others (Zig Zag steps at Lower Nassau Street). The statistics will be used to assist in targeting more resources to problem areas.

56.88 The police have provided a number of statistics in relation to alcohol related crime and disorder showing dramatic reductions during the project to date.

Youths causing annoyance	down 50%
Rowdy behaviour and nuisance	down 31%
Vehicle related nuisance	down 64%

56.89 Feedback in relation to the project has been positive, although formal evaluation has not yet been completed. Community police officers, youth intervention officers and community safety wardens have noticed a significant reduction in alcohol related disorder in the area and anecdotal feedback from local residents shows that they have noticed a difference.

56.90 The Derry CAP team will be continuing to target areas that have not shown significant improvements to date. Further work has been planned within schools relating to awareness of the project and the effect that underage drinking has on local communities.

56.91 A programme of training courses for parents; 'talking about tough issues' to give them skills in how to discuss alcohol use with their teenagers will be rolled out through local schools and community centres. The group will also be producing a DVD about the project which will be used to publicise CAP and highlight good practice.

ANNEX I MEMBERS OF THE RETAIL OF ALCOHOL STANDARDS GROUP

56.92 Association of Convenience Stores

Aldi Stores Ltd
Asda Stores Ltd
Bargain Booze Limited
Booker Premier
British Retail Consortium
BP
Co-operative Group Ltd
Lidl
Marks & Spencer plc
Mills Group
Musgrave Budgens Londis
Wm Morrison Supermarkets plc
Nisa-Today's
One Stop Stores Limited
Sainsbury's Supermarkets Ltd

Snax 24
Tesco Stores Ltd
Total
Spar
Waitrose Ltd
Winemark

Supporting Partners
Bacardi
Heineken
Diageo
Molson Coors
Beverage Brands

ANNEX 2 EXTRACT FROM PUBLIC HEALTH RESPONSIBILITY DEAL

56.93 In support of the collective alcohol pledge on Community Actions to Tackle Alcohol Harms (A7), Community Alcohol Partnerships Ltd[3] commits to the individual pledge set out below.

Individual pledge: new funding to expand Community Alcohol Partnerships

We will expand the reach of Community Alcohol Partnerships (CAPs) in the UK through an investment of at least £800,000 by alcohol retailers and producers[4] over the next three years.[5] This will allow us to significantly increase the number of CAP schemes in local communities and extend the remit of CAPs beyond tackling under-age sales to wider alcohol-related harm and in particular. We will seek to:

- Reduce young people's demand for alcohol through prevention, infor-mation and diversionary activities.
- Improve the delivery, consistency and quality of alcohol education for all age groups – education,[6] promotion of knowledge and safer drinking concepts; and
- Promote key health initiatives – unit information and sensible drinking messages in store.

How this pledge will work

- CAP supporters will commit at least £800,000 in CAP funding over the next three years.

---

[3] Community Alcohol Partnerships Ltd is a wholly owned subsidiary of the Wine & Spirit Trade Association.
[4] For a full list of current funders and supporters, see Annex 1.
[5] Financial Years July 2011–June 2014.
[6] Schools education projects will be delivered by recognised third-parties without direct industry involvement.

- There are currently 30 CAPs operating around the UK and these new resources will allow there to be a significant increase in the number of CAPs, in local areas that wish to use them.
- A CAP Advisory Board will be established to lead the further roll-out of CAPs, supported by two full-time members of staff.
- The new Advisory Board will be made up of a new Independent Chairman, senior representatives of the Police service, Trading Standards, Public Health and Education Community alongside nominated industry representatives.
- CAPs allow alcohol retailers to work with local partners including the police, trading standards, and local government to address alcohol-related issues. There will be an assessment of local need in consultation with these partners before any new CAP projects are developed.
- CAPs can be tailored to address a range of alcohol-related misuse, disorder and health and education issues, depending on the needs of each area.
- The goals of each CAP and how success against these will be measured, will be agreed by local partners at the start of each project and when appropriate independent evaluation will also be agreed with partner organisations.
- A CAP report will be published annually.

The overall objectives set out in the CAP 3-year business plan include:

- Achieving reductions in actual and perceived alcohol-related disorder in all CAP areas;
- Proving CAP methodology as a way to tackle local alcohol misuse issues;
- Proving CAP methodology as a working alternative to enforcement and prosecution;
- Communicating CAP methodology to all relevant communities;
- Creating a brand and reputation for high quality community intervention;
- Developing new funding streams for CAP initiatives;
- Creating a common cause between local communities, local business and local regulatory authorities; and
- Developing consistent national standards for community alcohol engagement.

The public health benefit we expect to follow in partnership areas

As each project is different with different objectives there will be an agreement on the goals with local partners. Examples of different outcomes might be:

- Reduction of actual and perceived alcohol related disorder in CAP areas;
- Fall in number of convictions for under-age selling in CAP areas;

- Reduction in the number of under-age purchases and a reduction in the percentage of under 15 year olds drinking alcohol obtained outside of the home in CAP areas;
- If the data is available and applicable for the project area locally, reduction in 'Ambulance pickups for under-age related incidents' and/or reduction in 'A&E attendances for U18s'.

How partners will demonstrate that they have acted as pledged

A CAP report will be published annually that will include:

- Company accounts;
- Details of all funding and supporting partners;
- Update on all existing and all new CAPs;
- Details of all evaluated projects.

How the public health benefit could be evaluated

- CAP will publish the goals and purpose of each CAP and how success will be measured.
- Each area will set baseline and identifiable goals as part of the scheme.
- Updates on results achieved will be published locally and included within the CAP annual report.

This will be used to produce a more in-depth evaluation to the value of at least £10k on the benefit of CAPs overall by an independent organisation and will also eventually feed through into national surveys of alcohol related issues.

Business Improvement Districts

What is the city but the people?

William Shakespeare, *Coriolanus*

A INTRODUCTION

57.01 Business Improvement Districts (BIDs) originated in Canada, and have been used in other countries including the USA, South Africa, New Zealand and Germany. They are a development of great practical and philosophical importance because they exemplify how businesses can work together as corporate citizens to improve their environments, rather than merely taking care of their internal domain in a way which keeps them below the radar of the regulator.

The essence of the BID scheme is that business ratepayers within a self-determined, delineated zone vote to pay an additional rate to be applied for the purposes of the BID.

B HOW BIDS WORK

57.02 BIDS are governed by Part 4 of the Local Government Act 2003 and the Business Improvement Districts (England) Regulations 2004.[1]

57.03 The BID starts its life with a ballot of the ratepayers in the defined area, in which a vote is taken whether there should be a BID or not. A positive result[2] enables the local authority to levy a further rate for the projects specified in the BID arrangements to be carried out for the benefit of

---

[1]   SI 2004/2443. Similar provision is made for Wales and Scotland.
[2]   The Local Government Act 2003 requires that the BID is voted for by a majority of those

the BID area. It is, therefore, a collectively self-imposed charge for the benefit of the area. The Local Government Act provides for the keeping of a BID revenue account,[3] and for debits to the account to be made only in accordance with the BID arrangements. The BID arrangements must be for no longer than five years.[4] It is then of course open to the local businesses to conduct a further ballot.

57.04 There is no constraint on the area of the BID. It is, however, ideally suited to town centre economies, including night time economies, particularly where extra services are desired over and above those which the public sector is able to provide.

57.05 As the national advisory service for BIDs, UKBIDs, puts it:

'Improvements may include extra safety/security, cleaning and environmental measures, improved promotion of the area, improved events, and greater advocacy on key issues ... '.[5]

57.06 BIDs were piloted in 22 locations in England and Wales during 2002–2005, co-ordinated by the Association of Town Centre Management, with the first successful ballots held in Kingston at the end of 2004. There are now over 170 BIDs operating across the UK.

57.07 Typically, the BID levy is 1% of rateable value, although in some towns and cities a higher amount is levied following the BID proposals in the ballot. The 2011 British BIDs survey found that the average levy income exceeds £500,000.[6]

57.08 The local authority plays a crucial role in the development of the BID, both at the time of formulation (eg in providing rating list information and costing services) and in the joint working to advance the aims of the BID, eg through improvements in safety, cleanliness and marketing of an area.[7]

57.09 BIDs are supported by the Coalition Government. In 2011, the Department for Communities and Local Government (DCLG) observed

voting and that sum of the rateable values of the hereditaments voting in favour of the proposal exceeds the sum of those voting against: s 50.

3   Section 47.
4   Section 54.
5   UKBIDs, 'Fast facts for BID Partners'.
6   Business Improvement Districts, Standard Note, 7 November 2012, House of Commons Library.
7   See 'Local Authority Guide to Business Improvement Districts', London BIDs and Association of London Government. http://www.ukbids.org/files/files/LA-BIDs.pdf.

that BIDs gave 'local authorities powerful opportunities to work with businesses to agree priorities for investment and growth in their area.'[8]

C NOTTINGHAM: A CASE STUDY[9]

57.10 'A city of shootings, intimidation and drugs'. That was the headline of an article about Nottingham in the *Daily Telegraph* on 15 March 2005.

Two days earlier the *Sunday Telegraph* contained an article which mentioned that: 'The rocketing of the murder rate, fuelled by a raging drugs turf war, has been nothing short of astronomical, giving rise to Nottingham's nick-name of "Assassination City".'

57.11 All of this followed an interview with the Chief Constable of Nottinghamshire, in which Steve Green was quoted as saying: 'We are reeling with the murders. We are in a longstanding crisis situation with major crime and it won't go away overnight'.

57.12 At a subsequent meeting in the council house attended by licensees, retailers, hoteliers and representatives of both universities reference was made to the negative public perception of Nottingham and the declining number of applications for places at the universities.

57.13 The Violent Crime Reduction Act of 2006 contained a provision which permitted local authorities (with the consent of the police) to designate areas where there were problems with alcohol-related nuisance, crime and disorder as alcohol disorder zones. In order to pay for additional policing and other enforcement activities they could impose charges on premises and clubs within the alcohol disorder zone that sold or supplied alcohol. Nottingham, however, along with every other town and city in the country, was not enthused by the self-imposed moniker of alcohol disorder zone, but did want to take steps to reduce crime and disorder and improve the public perception of the city.

57.14 It was in this context that the city council and leisure operators combined to establish the Leisure Business Improvement District at the end of 2007. There are 243 levy payers in the Leisure Business Improvement District, with contributions ranging from a minimum of £150 to a maximum of £5,000, and providing a total levy of approximately £250,000.

57.15 The vision of the Nottingham Leisure Business Improvement District was to drive thorough a series of business-led initiatives that significantly

---

8 DCLG, 'Local Government Resources Review: Proposals for Business Rates Retention Consultation' (July 2011).
9 The text for this section was supplied by David Lucas, the Chairman of the Nottingham BID.

improve the attraction and appeal of Nottingham city centre to investors, workers, residents and visitors, thereby raising the profitability of those businesses participating in the Business Improvement District.

The Nottingham Leisure Business Improvement District was established for the maximum period of five years.

57.16 The BID first of all established a Board which was drawn from a cross-section of leisure operators within the city.

The Board then had the task of delivering projects across four areas:

- Marketing
- Safety
- Access
- Business services

The following are some of the main activities undertaken.

Marketing

57.17

- Light Night – an annual event to highlight the attractions of the city at night and to attract in a wider demographic who might not otherwise view the city as the place to be at night.
- The Food and Drink Festival – high profile annual events involving a range of different leisure operators.
- Street ambassadors – recently introduced as a joint initiative between the Leisure and Retail Business Improvement Districts. They provide a warm and friendly welcome to visitors, providing on-street information and advice. They report graffiti and other on-street issues and ensure that these are dealt with quickly, to ensure that the city looks its best at all times. They also act as a liaison between BID businesses and the BID office, to enable the office to respond quickly to concerns.
- Website and social media – providing promotional marketing opportunities for leisure operators.
- Positive media coverage – in the national and local broadcast and print media, so as to enhance tourism and other visitation, business and therefore greater natural guardianship in the streets.

Safety

57.18

- Taxi marshals – initially a joint initiative between the Leisure Business Improvement District and Nottingham City Council but latterly funded totally by the Leisure Business Improvement District. The BID provides six taxi marshals at peak weekend times to manage queues and help reduce disorder at the ranks.

- Street pastors and the Safe Place – independently operated but provided with support from the Leisure Business Improvement District. Street pastors are volunteers who provide support to the night time economy and its visitors at weekends. This ranges from simple practical help such as providing a pair of flip flops to those who are having problems with their heels, to giving water to help people rehydrate at the end of the night. Most of all, the pastors provide a reassuring and caring presence in the city. The pastors have also established a 'Safe Place', where assistance can be sought and given, eg if first aid is needed or a person has become separated from their friends.
- Night time co-ordinator – supplied by the Leisure Business Improvement District to provide liaison between leisure venues in the city and the authorities. The co-ordinator visits all late night premises at weekends to share intelligence between the premises, police and other partners working in the night time economy.
- Street lighting – the Leisure Business Improvement District has worked with Nottingham City Council to improve lighting in particular areas of the city centre.
- Door staff procedures – the Leisure Business Improvement District has worked with the authorities to implement a procedure at closing time.

Access

57.19

- Coaches from Trent Bridge – provided by the Leisure Business Improvement District to transport spectators into the city.
- Taxis and late night bus services – the Leisure Business Improvement District has been influential in improving transport services.
- Parking – the Leisure Business Improvement District continues to influence the improved provision of parking facilities and reduction of charges in the city centre.

Business services

57.20

- Purple Flag – the Leisure Business Improvement District played an important part in the city securing Purple Flag status.
- Best Bar None – the Leisure Business Improvement District is solely responsible for implementing the scheme in the city, in which over 40 premises participate.
- Training – the Leisure Business Improvement District provides free or reduced cost training for leisure businesses.

- Lobbying – representatives of the Leisure Business Improvement District have met with members of both Houses of Parliament, Home Office officials, senior industry figures, trade associations, senior police officers and local councillors to make representations on behalf of leisure operators within the city.

57.21 In 2011, a Retail Business Improvement District was established in Nottingham. There has already been a very effective partnership established between the two Business Improvement Districts. That liaison assisted in introducing street ambassadors as a new project. There are obviously benefits in other joint initiatives involving events such as Christmas and combined marketing campaigns.

57.22 In September 2012, the Nottingham Retail and Leisure Business Improvement Districts (BID) were merged into a single entity – Nottingham BID – creating one of the largest BIDs in the country. The new BID has around 770 levy payers comprised of retail businesses and licensed premises in the city centre and a combined levy income of over £850,000. The move brings a number of significant benefits to the current BIDs as well as to the city centre as a whole, creating an operation that is more customer focused, produces a more cohesive approach and creates costs savings arising from economies of scale and elimination of duplication.

D CONCLUSION

57.23 There can be no doubt that BIDs are a highly effective method of improving town centre environments in an era of austerity, particularly where the ability of local authorities to provide non-statutory services is severely circumscribed.

57.24 A BID also carries three further benefits of great significance. It allows the businesses themselves to dictate how their money is spent for their common benefit, in effect a system of hypothecated taxation denied to other taxpayers. It produces exemplary joint working between businesses themselves in which best practice is shared and mutual goals attained. Finally, it creates a productive dialogue – or partnership – between the public and private sectors which stands outside conventional models of regulation and helps to create better town centres for all.

58

Regulatory partnership

> Society is indeed a contract. It is a partnership in all science; a
> partnership in all art; a partnership in every virtue, and in all perfection.
> As the ends of such a partnership cannot be obtained in many
> generations, it becomes a partnership not only between those who are
> living, but between those who are living, those who are dead, and those
> who are to be born.
>
> Edmund Burke, *Reflections on the Revolution in France*

A INTRODUCTION: THE LICENSING ACTION GROUP

58.01 This chapter is written by the Licensing Action Group in Hammersmith & Fulham, to demonstrate a real-life example of partnership working at borough level. While it does not represent the formal policy of the council, it is hoped that some of the practices described will be found valuable in other areas.

58.02 In Hammersmith & Fulham, the Licensing Action Group (LAG) was inaugurated as a group of key partners who could work together to tackle licensing issues. The group consists of officers from the licensing team, trading standards, environmental health, planning, the Metropolitan Police, the London Fire Brigade (LFB), Drug and Alcohol Action Team (DAAT) and community safety. As a result of the formation of the LAG, a memorandum of understanding (MoU) and joint enforcement protocol was signed by all partners to agree consistency in approach and a commitment to working together effectively so as to assist with the promotion of the four licensing objectives.

58.03 LAG members meet on a fortnightly basis to discuss licence applications, licensing issues and joint enforcement/action. The group shares best practice, exchanges information and has adopted a problem solving and collaborative way of working within the borough. This chapter illustrates the holistic approach that has been taken at Hammersmith & Fulham and talks about the roles and responsibilities of some key LAG members.

58.04   Local authorities are set up in many different ways. In Hammersmith & Fulham, licensing officers have the benefit of working in the same building as many key partners, such as environmental health, trading standards and the planning enforcement team. This in itself makes it easier to communicate, meet regularly through the LAG and also share information. In short, everyone has a role to play, as we shall see in this chapter.

58.05   One key matter for the LAG to consider at its meetings is whether to expend the resources involved in joint enforcement actions. The following factors have been used as a trigger for such actions:

- More than one complaint from local residents, businesses or any other party over a two month period.
- Issues that have been raised by more than one responsible authority.
- More than one breach of condition in a three month period.
- Serious assault(s) at the premises, eg ABH, knife/gun crime.
- Premises considered as a crime generator, eg drugs.

B LICENSING OFFICERS

58.06   It is appropriate to start with the role of a licensing officer, as the hub and catalyst for a joined-up enforcement approach.

Venue inspections

58.07   The inspection of licensed premises is one of the key tools the licensing authority has in promoting the four licensing objectives and detecting non-compliance.

Whilst the duration and frequency of such inspections may vary, the purpose and intent of them is quite clear. The licensing authority will carry out a venue inspection to establish if a licence holder is adhering to the conditions of their premises licence. This would include the mandatory conditions which are automatically attached to every relevant premises licence in addition to any legally enforceable conditions attached to a premises licence.

58.08   Whilst licensing officers thoroughly check each individual condition as a matter of routine, they may pay particular attention to conditions recently added to the licence, by way of a licence review hearing for example, or any conditions which are particularly significant in the local area, for example conditions relating to beer and cider strength in an area where street drinking is prevalent.

58.09 The decision to carry out a venue inspection at licensed premises is a result of several factors. Firstly, many local authorities set service standards to inspect all premises within the borough within a certain time frame. Naturally this would depend on the size of the local authority and indeed the ratio of licensed premises to licensing authority officers. Many authorities determine the frequency of these inspections by the risk that any premises potentially poses. This is imperative to promote better standards of regulation.

58.10 Once a risk rating has been established, a local authority can pursue a line of no inspection without a reason. Risk rating is a tool whereby a number of factors are used to calculate the relative risk of individual premises. These factors may include the capacity, terminal hour, previous non-compliance and incidents of crime and disorder at the premises. Those premises with a higher risk rating will naturally receive visits from their local licensing officer on a more regular basis. Risk ratings are constantly changeable and can go up or down with each inspection or intermittent incident at the premises.

58.11 Understandably, another common trigger for venue inspections is complaints made to the local authority about a particular premises. The complaint could relate to a number of issues ranging from the most serious kinds of disorderly behaviour and criminal activity to unpleasant odours from the premises. It is a real possibility that a complaint relating to the premises in question was not even made to the licensing authority in the first instance.

58.12 Different services in a local authority talk to each other. Some local authorities may have measures in place to secure that this is done more effectively than others. At Hammersmith & Fulham the LAG has been found to be very effective in this respect. In general a complaint relating to particular licensed premises will reach the ears of a licensing officer at some point. Indeed, other teams, some of which are responsible authorities in their own right, may complain to the licensing authority directly following one of their own venue inspections.

58.13 For example it is not unheard of for an environmental health officer (EHO) carrying out a food hygiene inspection at a fast food takeaway to notice that the trading hours advertised on their menus exceed those allowed for a business without a premises licence for late night refreshment. The EHO sends an email to the licensing officer who knows full well that the pizza takeaway premises was refused an application for late night refreshment last year and promptly arranges a test purchase every night at the premises after 11 pm to verify whether or not an offence is taking place.

58.14 It is not only complaints that could lead to venue inspections. Another common trigger for an inspection is the pursuit of outstanding debts for annual maintenance fees. The non-payment of the annual licensing maintenance fee causes substantial losses for licensing authorities across the country. The Police Reform and Social Responsibility Act 2011 now obliges the local authority to suspend a licence for non-payment of the annual fee in certain circumstances (see further Chapter 61 on fees) but prior to this the only recourse for the local authority was civil debt recovery. However, just because a licence now falls to be suspended, this does not mean that suspension will be the end of the matter. The local authority may still send officers to the premises to pursue the debt. Whilst carrying out such a visit the licensing officer may choose to inspect the premises.

58.15 In the past licensing officers have found that a premises licence holder who has not paid their licence fee on time has also breached other conditions of their premises licence. It is therefore very possible that non-payment of a debt can lead to the detection of much more serious offences. This has become a reality in the London Borough of Hammersmith & Fulham, where a simple visit and subsequent inspection has led to one of the largest prosecution cases brought by the licensing authority for a multitude of licensing and trading standards related offences. It is simple to see how a premises that has avoided detection for a considerable amount of time can suddenly be on the licensing authority's radar without a single complaint.

58.16 Whilst the vast majority of complaints about licensed premises are made by local residents, they can come from a whole host of people including MPs, councillors, residents' associations and local businesses. A licensing authority has a duty to act on complaints and the likelihood is that when a complaint is made, an inspection will follow. Details of what licence holders can expect from a venue inspection will follow, as will details of possible legal action open to the licensing authority should the licence holder be unfortunate enough to be found to be non-compliant.

Preparation

58.17 But first, it is beneficial to understand the preparation that goes into a venue inspection. It would be unwise to think that licensing officers will carry out a venue inspection without prior research and fact gathering. This is not just to establish whether certain officer safety precautions should be taken due to the high risk nature of the premises, although these concerns are undoubtedly of paramount importance. But at an absolute minimum a licensing officer will check the history of the premises before a visit as follows:

- Have there been any non-compliance issues previously?
- How often has the designated premises supervisor (DPS) changed in recent years?
- Have there been any complaints?
- Is there a history of the premises committing repeat offences?

58.18 These are all questions to which the licensing officer will need the answers before they even leave the office. A more prudent licensing officer would then expand their research to include data from partners both within the council and externally. For example they may check with environmental health to establish if there have been any noise complaints, if trading standards have recently prosecuted the licence holder for selling counterfeit wine or if the police have ongoing issues with bag thefts from the premises. This comprehensive picture of a premises results in a fully prepared licensing officer anticipating and preparing for a variety of circumstances prior to even setting foot in the premises.

58.19 Furthermore, the licensing officer can utilise the data that they have collected to decide that the premises may be suited to a multi-agency visit. The multi-agency visit is, in its simplest terms, a visit by the licensing officer and one or more responsible authorities at the same time to carry out a comprehensive venue inspection covering several areas of the business at once.

58.20 A premises could find itself in a situation where officers from the licensing authority, trading standards, environmental health, the planning authority, the fire brigade and the police turn up at the peak trading hour to inspect everything from door security to the cleanliness of the toilets. Understandably such visits are not carried out as a matter of routine, but for problem premises they are highly effective at killing several birds with one stone.

58.21 Of course, it is usual practice to arrange for some undercover officers to enter the premises prior to the multi-agency visit to minimise the risk of certain issues being quickly swept under the carpet when a van full of enforcement officers arrives.

58.22 Most licence holders will know that a venue inspection will normally commence with the licensing officer asking to see the premises licence and the summary so that they can go through all of the conditions attached and make sure they are being complied with. However, this is purely to establish if the premises are complying with the legal requirement to display the summary and keep the licence on the premises.

58.23 The prudent licensing officer will already know the conditions attached to the premises and they will have printed off a copy of the licence prior to the inspection to take along with them, just in case a situation should arise where the licence holder has misplaced their original copy. The preparation for a successful venue inspection is absolutely crucial and it is important for licence holders to appreciate that licensing officers will carry out venue inspections thoroughly.

Full licensing inspection

58.24 For visits to larger licensed premises or when late night inspections are carried out it is highly recommended that two officers take part in the licensing inspection.

58.25 When entering a licensed premises officers should ask to speak with the DPS (where relevant) or the person responsible for the management of the premises. It should be explained that a full licensing inspection may take some time and may require additional staff cover whilst the inspection takes place.

58.26 The current full premises licence should be the focus of any licensing inspection. Although the officers should have a copy of the most up to date full licence with them, a copy of the full premises licence is required to be kept on the premises and this should be asked for. A check should be made to ensure that both licences match and that both the officers and the manager are referring to the same document. The full premises licence is often kept away from the shop floor or bar area in a back room or office. Reviewing the licence away from a public area will give the first officer an opportunity to concentrate on their inspection and fully check all of the conditions attached to the licence.

58.27 Questions should initially be asked about the DPS. If the DPS is unavailable the first officer should seek to establish if the individual named on the premises licence is still employed at the premises. Premises history checks before the inspection was carried out should have indicated if there were any pending DPS variations. Where a DPS has left and has not been replaced this is a serious offence and likely to result in immediate action. Enforcement options for this eventuality are dealt with later on in this chapter.

58.28 The first officer should then methodically work through the premises licence with the manager. Evidence of compliance with certain conditions may be required, such as a complaints book, minutes of Pub Watch meetings, storage of CCTV footage for a set period, etc. This information should be asked for as the inspection begins to save time later on.

58.29 Any breaches of conditions or other issues noticed during the inspection should be noted on the premises inspection sheet. A minor variation application should be recommended for any conditions which are irrelevant or unenforceable. Many of these conditions may have originated from old public entertainment licences or special hours certificates, such as obtaining permission from the local police licensing sergeant before putting up Christmas decorations.

58.30 Apart from conditions which are specific to the premises, questions should also be asked about:

- The mandatory conditions which are attached to the licence (irresponsible drinks promotions, proof of age schemes, the availability of free drinking water, alcohol being available in smaller measures).
- The attendance at pub-watch meetings (where appropriate).
- Responsible retailer schemes such as Best Bar None or Purple Flag which may be operational in the area.
- Any other complaints or comments which may have been received about the premises or which may have been highlighted in the premises history check before the inspection took place.

58.31 Whilst the first officer is reviewing the licence it is a good opportunity for the second officer to check other areas of the premises (with the manager's consent). A check should be made initially for the summary premises licence which should be prominently displayed (all pages of the summary licence should be on display). Details of any drinks promotions (for on-licensed premises) which may be irresponsible should also be noted. Challenge 21 or Challenge 25 notices or any other notices which may be required by the premises licence should also be checked for. The officer may also wish to carry out checks for basic health and safety/fire safety requirements such as blockages to fire exits, fire extinguishers and fire blankets.

58.32 The second officer should look to engage with other members of staff at the premises (if available). Staff who are involved with the sale of alcohol should be asked questions about their training, the licensing objectives and generally about their role at the premises. Certain conditions require staff participation, such as CCTV conditions which ask that all staff are familiar with the operation of CCTV systems or conditions which require members of staff to conduct litter patrols on a daily basis. Often questions of this type, directed to staff members, can reveal more about the true operation of a premises than discussions with a manager who may confidently confirm that they comply with all the conditions attached to their licence.

58.33 If the premises has door supervisors on duty, the officer should also record the registration numbers of these individuals. Depending on the time available to officers, the registration numbers can be checked online at www.sia.homeoffice.gov.uk or they can be recorded and checked at a later date. Door supervisors should also be asked what time they arrive on duty and what time they leave as certain licences place requirements on door supervisor attendance.

58.34 If the second officer has drug wipes available these should also be used. The officer should ask the manager if they object to a wipe being used in one of their toilet cubicles. An explanation should be given as to how the wipe will react if the presence of drugs is detected. Most wipes only detect one type of drug. The wipe should be used on any flat surface within the toilet area. Most likely this will be in a toilet cubicle but traces of drugs have been found outside of cubicles where cisterns and toilet roll holders have been enclosed.

58.35   The officer will need to make an assessment of the toilet space when they enter and decide on the most likely place that drugs would be taken. Once the wipe has been used it should be immediately bought back to the manager or DPS to show them the results. If the wipe has reacted to the presence of a drug this should be explained. On some occasions certain drugs can visibly be seen on cistern tops or other flat surfaces without the use of a wipe. This should be highlighted to the manger. There are a number of enforcement options that are available following the use of drug wipes, as detailed later on in this chapter.

58.36   At the end of the second officer's duties they should return to the first officer to exchange information on their findings. There may be inconsistencies with the information supplied by the manager and the information obtained from the staff and the overall inspection of the premises. The first officer will need to decide how to address these issues (if any) with the manager. Some issues may be dealt with immediately without further action, such as removing a poster/notice which obscures a Challenge 21 notice or requesting that a member of staff receives some additional training on how to use the CCTV system. Other issues may require a warning letter or further action.

58.37   Finally, the officer should talk to the manager about the general operation of the premises. Any local pub watch scheme should be promoted where it is not a requirement of the licence. Any changes in policy which may affect the premises (a review of licensing policy or new cumulative impact policy) should also be raised. Upcoming temporary event notices should also be discussed to deal with issues relating to the four licensing objectives or the maximum limit for temporary event notices (TENs) for the premises.

58.38   Any other issues which the manager has should be recorded on the premises inspection sheet and clearly distinguish what is required by law and what is good practice. The first licensing officer and the manager should both sign the inspection form. The top copy should be left at the premises.

Enforcement

58.39   When deciding whether to take enforcement action the licensing authority must have regard to their licensing policy, their enforcement policy and the Enforcement Concordat. Having regard to these publications is essential in ensuring that action taken is proportionate, necessary and fair. The officer undertaking such enforcement action must be designated to carry out duties under the provision of the relevant legislation. Without such formal delegation any formal action, which the licensing authority may consider as overwhelmingly justified, may be dismissed in a court of law.

58.40 Licensing authorities have a wide range of enforcement options, ranging from providing advice to pursuing legal action. Legal action is not always necessary; a soft touch approach in certain circumstances can have the same effect as more formal action. In any instance, formal action such as prosecution should only be taken if it is in the public interest and is likely to succeed, eg if the matter is serious or there is a continuous chain of offences. For a minor breach or first offence, advice would normally be given and followed up in writing to the DPS and licence holder. Enforcement action should be seen as a mechanism to bring the premises into compliance and to ensure the promotion of the four licensing objectives, which lie at the heart of the Licensing Act 2003.

58.41 During any inspection officers have a plethora of powers to deal with the range of issues they may uncover. The most common offences are failing to have the summary licence displayed or a breach of condition. There are no definitive answers as to which powers to exercise when breaches are found.

58.42 The London Borough of Hammersmith & Fulham have prosecuted a number of defendants for a range of offences under the Licensing Act 2003, including section 136 (unauthorised sale of alcohol), section 137 (exposing alcohol for unauthorised sale), section 138 (storing alcohol for unauthorised sale) and section 141 (sale of alcohol to a person who is drunk).

58.43 How officers deal with a section 136 contravention will depend on a number of factors, such as the history of the operator, the history of contraventions as well as the type of condition breached. In all instances an officer will need to consider the potential impact the breach may have on the licensing objectives and the immediate risk to safety of those attending or working in the premises.

58.44 Take a premises licence inspection, for example, for a late night town centre venue. A common scenario is for officers to witness a number of minor breaches. These may include windows being open whilst regulated entertainment is taking place or the summary licence not being displayed. However, apart from these minor breaches, the premises is well operated, there is no history of crime and disorder or previous breaches of the licence and officers have confidence in the management to operate a busy venue in a high risk area. In this instance, officers may consider giving advice to the management of the premises and writing to the licence holder and DPS, stipulating the offences and what action is required. If, during a follow up visit, the premises are found to be in compliance, then no further action is required.

58.45 A second and more concerning scenario, for a premises inspected in the same high risk geographical location, would be breaches in relation to the CCTV system not being operational, the stated number of door supervisors not being on duty, the manager in charge being unaware of who the DPS is and whether he/she still works for the operator. Further concern would arise if the premises were busy, had a history of breaches and recent violent disorder and the officers had a lack of confidence in the management. If the officer believes that due to the lack of CCTV and security there was the potential for disorder or risk to a person's safety, immediate action which could be considered is the serving of a section 19 closure notice under the Criminal Justice and Police Act 2001.

58.46 A section 19 closure notice can be issued where a police officer or an authorised officer for the local authority is satisfied that any premises are being, or within the last 24 hours have been used for the unlicensed sale of alcohol, including breaches of licence conditions which relate to the sale of alcohol. The notice can be served on the person responsible for the premises at the time of the inspection or up to 24 hours after the offence. Once the premises is in compliance with the terms stated on the notice a termination notice can be issued. If the premises fail to comply with the notice the officer may apply to the magistrates' court for a closure order. Issuing a section 19 closure notice does not hinder any further action, such as prosecution.[1]

58.47 This type of action has an immediate effect, and for a premises that provides goods and/or services other than alcohol, it does not require the premises to close. The notice advises that any further sales of alcohol will be an offence until the operator is in compliance. If the notice is breached and the sale of alcohol continues, the officer may apply to the magistrates' court after seven days for a closure order.

58.48 As with all action, there is no definitive guide as to when a section 19 notice should be served. Careful consideration should be given before proceeding. In all instances where the premises is busy, the police authority for that area should be consulted and a risk assessment undertaken. If the police support the serving of a section 19 notice, either the local authority officer or the police officer can serve the notice on the person responsible for the premises. Once the premises are in compliance, the officer must issue a termination notice.

58.49 If offences are observed, the officer may decide to caution the person responsible at the premises, under the Police and Criminal Evidence Act (PACE) 1984, and carry out an on the spot PACE interview by asking strategic questions relating to the offences. Any additional evidence should then be obtained, such as photographs, video footage, till receipts and details of witnesses including employees of the premises.

---

[1] Section 19 notices are dealt with in further detail in Chapter 44 (Closure Notices).

58.50 It is a common occurrence that, when confronted with issues at particular premises, the focus remains on 'what action to take'. It is vital for officers to remember to acquire key evidence, which will be fundamental in any formal action.

58.51 Successful enforcement action is often undertaken after officers have considered all the factors, and where necessary discussed with partners at forums such as the LAG on the most effective way to proceed to bring the premises back into compliance. An investigation, if necessary, can then be instigated.

58.52 A PACE interview (either undertaken at the premises at the time of the offence or subsequently at a later date) is a vital element of any investigation if prosecution is being contemplated.

58.53 Licensing authorities may wish to undertake their own assessment to determine which power to exercise. The assessment should consider factors such as: the enforcement policy; the seriousness of the alleged offences; whether there are multiple offences; whether previous advice been given and ignored; whether there was a deliberate disregard for the law; the likelihood of re-offending; the willingness of witnesses to co-operate; the public perception of offences; whether vulnerable groups have been affected, and whether there was significant economic advantage obtained by the defendant. By adopting a systematic approach, officers should ensure that any action is proportionate, fair and necessary.

58.54 An effective course of action if the defendant submits an admission of guilt is to issue a simple caution. A simple caution can be offered as an alternative to prosecution. The simple caution states the offences, times, dates and any relevant additional information. A caution is kept on record and used as evidence if further offences occur. Signing the caution is itself an admission of guilt. If the defendant refuses to sign a simple caution, the matter would normally be referred for prosecution. It is of paramount importance that cautions are only offered as an alternative to prosecution, not due to lack of evidence to place the case before the magistrates.

58.55 Prior to pursuing legal action, it is useful for the licensing authority to discuss the matter at a forum such as the LAG. If a partner authority is prosecuting the same defendant, consideration should be given to carrying out a joint PACE interview and instigating a joint prosecution for all offences. Offences across multiple statutes can only reinforce that the premises is problematic and in any case are more cost effective for the authority.

58.56 Robust cases are often multiple offences on multiple dates. To take one example from Hammersmith & Fulham, a particular premises was reported for apparently selling alcohol without a licence in effect, operating until the early hours and disturbing local residents. Inspections were under-taken and advice was provided and issued in writing. The defendant ignored the advice and continued to sell alcohol. Subsequently a warning letter was issued, to warn that if further offences were committed then formal action may be taken. The offences still continued. Due to the nature of the premises a test purchase was not appropriate. Therefore licensing officers and police officers inspected the premises; statements were obtained from customers who admitted purchasing the alcohol, photographs were taken of the alcohol on display and the alcohol being stored, receipts in the till and orders showing alcohol sales were seized. The person responsible for the premises was cautioned and questioned at the premises. Additionally a section 19 closure notice was issued at the time. The defendant was invited to attend a PACE interview but failed to attend. Informations were laid for offences under sections 136, 137 and 138 of the Licensing Act 2003. After consider-ing the evidence the magistrates found the defendant guilty and they were ordered to pay a fine for each offence and full costs. The overwhelming evidence obtained at the final inspection was key in proving alcohol was being sold and securing a successful conviction.

58.57   The most frustrating inspections are often those where the premises is badly managed (often resulting in the premises and its clientele having a detrimental impact on the local area) and the premises licence lacks sufficient conditions to deal with the problems. A useful tool in the licensing author-ity's armoury for tackling these problematic premises are action plans. Usually, if the premises are problematic for licensing, then partner author-ities will also have concerns. In the first instance problematic premises should be discussed with other responsible authorities.

58.58   An action plan can be used by one or more of the responsible authorities. The action plan document should stipulate the issue and then the proposed action. For instance, if there has been an increase in crime and disorder related to the premises and one of the authorities believes that this could be reduced by extra security at the premises, the measure imposed could be for the premises to have door security at peak times. An action plan must be specific to the problems and clearly state what is required by the licence holder. The plan should be seen as a step to work with the premises to resolve the issues.

58.59   It is essential that the plan is agreed and signed by all parties including senior management of the premises. A time limit for the plan to be in effect will need to be decided and reviewed; each case will need to be assessed separately. Action plans are not legally enforceable. However, if they are breached and the premises remains problematic, then a review can be submitted by the relevant responsible authority. Action plans are, therefore, a very useful tool for ensuring that the premises are promoting the four licensing objectives and are an effective way of partnership working to deal with problematic premises.

58.60 An area of concern for licensing authorities and the police authority is drugs in licensed premises. As part of a licensing inspection, drug detection wipes are used to identify premises which have a significant problem with patron drug use. If positive traces are detected, a notice can be served on the person responsible. It is vital that the information obtained by officers relating to drug use is reported to the police. In Hammersmith & Fulham, information on such matters is also passed on to the local authority Drug and Alcohol Action Team (DAAT). Further inspections are then scheduled to ensure improvement.

C POLICE OFFICERS

58.61 Throughout this chapter, there are several references to working with the police. The role of the police in licensing matters should not be underestimated. At Hammersmith & Fulham, officers have found that a little bit of knowledge can go a long way and have invested a great deal of time and effort in providing dedicated licensing training to local police officers and safer neighbourhood teams (SNTs) in conjunction with the police licensing sergeant and the Home Office.

58.62 In any licensing authority, it is advantageous to have a good working relationship with the local police licensing sergeant. Officers have found that by working together and meeting regularly through the LAG, local police support can be 'proactive' rather than 'reactive'.

58.63 The evidence to back up the fact that there is a clear relationship between crime in the borough and certain licensed premises has meant that the borough can now take a more strategic approach to tackling local issues, as part of any alcohol or licensing strategies.

58.64 Whilst any police officer could be assimilated into a police licensing sergeant role and fulfil the basic functions of a responsible authority, it takes gumption and experience fully to realise the potential of the role to benefit the local community and promote the licensing objectives.

Police powers

58.65 Police officers have powers to enter premises to investigate licensable activities, which they share with licensing officers under section 179 of the Licensing Act 2003 and have their own powers of entry to investigate offences under section 180. Police officers generally have more powers which allow them to ask for identification from members of staff, eg cashiers, bar staff, etc, and are able to confirm the details and carry out background checks, carry out SIA checks and seize CCTV footage. They can also make arrests, if necessary.

58.66   Police powers following the visit are also greater. If serious issues are discovered, then officers can call premises in for summary review the next day or can issue a closure order on the night.[2] Licensing officers are limited to standard reviews, section 19 closure notices or prosecution.

58.67   The culmination of both sets of powers provides flexibility and regulatory teeth to choose the most appropriate sanction, in order to achieve compliance.

Policing the borough

58.68   Police officers, including SNTs, work unsociable hours and are, therefore, better placed to visit late night premises at short notice. Test purchases are often carried out to establish whether premises are trading after their licensed hours, breaching a specific licence condition or carrying out licensable activities without the correct authorisation.

58.69   Officers regularly work in partnership with trading standards to carry out test purchases for underage sales of alcohol. Police cadets are often used and where sales are made officers can choose to issue fixed penalties to the seller as an immediate sanction.

58.70   Venue inspections play an important part of the police officer's role. Many authorities may have limited police licensing resources, and therefore use the knowledge, skills and experience of specifically trained SNT officers. In one instance, during two joint operations led by the police and supported by the licensing authority and other responsible authorities/partners, over 900 premises were visited over the course of two weekends. The operations dealt with a number of issues including, amongst other things, breaches of licence conditions and the sale of alcohol to underage children. This is just one example to illustrate what can be achieved when partners work together.

58.71   Having SNTs on board allows incidents at licensed premises to be dealt with promptly and the information can be passed on to the licensing authority for further action, if necessary, rather than disappear into a 'black hole', with no links to the licensing regime whatsoever, due to the different means used to record/report crime and other information.

58.72   Multi-agency venue inspections are carried out more frequently at licensed premises which have been found very effective. Although licensing officers also carry out evening visits in pairs, by themselves, having a police officer available helps to prevent a breach of the peace, assists in the identification of individuals working at the premises and means that more serious matters which require a closure order, for example, can be dealt with expeditiously.

---

[2]   See Chapter 43 (Licensing Act Closures).

58.73 When carrying out venue inspections, multi-agency or otherwise, officer safety is paramount. There may be certain premises where it is deemed not be safe for council officers to visit without the police. Police officers are trained to conduct a risk assessment before entering premises and will normally lead during a multi-agency operation on advising whether they consider a certain situation to be unsafe. Police officers and SNTs, in particular, also have the added advantage of being more familiar with people in the local community and can advise about potentially dangerous individuals.

58.74 Sometimes, the decision is made to carry out separate visits even when working a shift together with licensing officers. All premises are assessed on their own characteristics. If it is felt that a police presence is not appropriate then licensing officers will carry out the inspection alone. This also works in reverse if officers feel that it is not appropriate for licensing officers to enter the premises.

58.75 The presence of uniformed police may create an uneasy atmosphere, just by the nature of police work, which can potentially cause more problems than it solves. This is usually overcome by having plain clothes officers as opposed to uniformed police.

58.76 On the other hand some people tend to respond more cooperatively to uniformed police and may well view the police more seriously than they would a council officer. It is likely that they will be more forthcoming with information and do so in a more polite manner. Perhaps the fact that they could potentially be arrested and end up with a criminal record makes the police more of a threat. The point is that officers have the flexibility to react according to each situation.

58.77 Hammersmith & Fulham is unique in that it has three major football league clubs, which attract a large number of supporters to the borough, over many weekends and evenings, throughout the year. The proactive stance of the police has meant that following inspections to individual licensed premises, many licensees within the vicinity of any of the football clubs have either requested a variation or had their licence reviewed to ensure that the licence conditions are robust enough to effectively manage any crime and disorder issues. These conditions may relate to the serving of alcohol on match days, the use of plastic glasses, CCTV, outside areas and accredited door staff. Many of these conditions have been suggested by the police as a result of their observations during venue inspections, and now form part of the local authority's statement of licensing policy.

58.78 Of course, the policing of the borough can also take place back at the office. On a day to day basis, a key part of a police licensing sergeant's role as a responsible authority is to monitor and comment on applications. Only the police and EHOs can object to TENs and only the police can object to variations of the Designated Premises Supervisor and personal licence applications. The importance of this role cannot be over-stressed, as a failure to pick up on issues during the consultation period could result in having to deal with problematic, irresponsibly run, premises later on.

Working with licence holders

58.79   In terms of visits by the police alone, without a licensing officer, officers have found that visits to premises applying for a licence are always helpful to identify any conditions which may be appropriate. For example, advice may be given on appropriate hours for licensable activities to save making a formal representation to an application.

58.80   There are also issues such as theft, violence or crime and disorder at established licensed premises. As crime and disorder is a licensing objective, the police are best placed to visit and offer advice. Using crime data the police can identify premises which are crime generators. These premises can then be targeted for test purchasing or advice visits where appropriate.

58.81   As alluded to earlier in the chapter, where there are problematic premises, there is always the option of starting an action plan to proactively work with the premises to try to address and reduce crime. Police officers are able to give expert crime prevention advice and proactively discuss local crime trends with licence holders.

58.82   Police officers can ask licence holders to take part in an action plan to tackle a range of issues linked to crime and disorder; such measures could include extra door supervisors at certain times, extra CCTV coverage or an improved dispersal policy for customers. Compliance with the action plan over a specified period could stop the police having to ask for the review of a licence.

D ENVIRONMENTAL HEALTH OFFICERS: NUISANCE

58.83   The Environmental Protection department at Hammersmith and Fulham has a mixture of EHOs and other officers who deal with noise and nuisance issues who fulfil the function of the responsible authority for public nuisance.

58.84   When environmental protection receive an application, officers assess for the potential impacts the application may have. The assessment is not a desk top exercise and both the premises and the locality must be visited to consider the following aspects:

- Any noise from licensable activities, such as amplified music.
- The use of outdoor areas.

- The proposed hours of operation.
- Any noise and disturbance from customers leaving premises or re-entering.
- The location of premises and proximity to residential properties.
- Any noise from activities such as deliveries and collections
- Any noise from plant such as kitchen ventilation extract systems.
- The prevention of nuisance from odour.
- The prevention of nuisance from artificial lighting.

Noise from licensable activities

58.85 The main concern is the transmission of airborne or structure-borne sound from the licensed premises to any neighbouring residential properties.

58.86 The question of structure-borne sound and vibration is significant where the premises physically adjoin others. When visiting the premises officers note any areas likely to allow noise breakout, such as glazed areas (especially windows which can be opened), lightweight roof structures, and doors from noisy areas that open directly to the outside. It is good practice to discuss with the applicant specific noise control measures such as the location of speakers, the necessity for acoustic double doors and fixed or acoustic double glazing with attenuated mechanical ventilation. If any of these aspects is of particular concern then that concern can be highlighted in the representation and made the subject of a specific condition. Officers check for any history of noise and if there are any complaints this information is included in any representation.

The use of outdoor areas

58.87 The use of outdoor areas such as beer gardens, alfresco dining areas and for outdoor seating in close proximity to residential premises is likely to give rise to disturbance from conversation alone.

58.88 Officers consider the size and assess whether there are any noise sensitive premises adjoining or overlooking the outside areas. There are likely to be fewer complaints if the use of the area finishes at a reasonable time, if there is a limit to the number of people that can use it and if no music is played outdoors.

The proposed hours of operation

58.89 Often, the later a premises remains open the more likely it is to give rise to disturbance, particularly when the premises is near a residential area. It depends on a range of factors, such as (but not limited to) the nature and size of the premises, the type of clientele likely to be attracted, the location (in the town centre/residential area/station), the transportation links, the provision of any regulated entertainment and any controls offered by the applicant in their operating schedule.

58.90   Officers have to make a judgement about the likelihood of nuisance in all the circumstances, based on the individual merits of the application, and whether the premises is in an area with a local cumulative impact policy (CIP). If nuisance is likely, the officer considers recommending refusal of the application in their representation or, alternatively, suggesting more appropriate hours of operation that are less likely to give rise to nuisance.

58.91   At the time of writing, two CIPs are in operation in Hammersmith & Fulham. The council made a decision to implement these policies as a result of evidence gathered by the licensing authority (which included public consultation results, residents' complaints, crime data, accident and emergency data, observational studies, street cleansing reports and the views of licensees, residents, responsible authorities and other interested parties). It was determined that the defined areas were saturated with licensed premises. As a result, if the licensing authority receives new or variation applications for premises licences in the defined area and objections are received, the presumption is that the application will be refused.

Customers leaving premises or re-entering

58.92   The issues of concern are the routes that customers leaving the premises will take to public transport or where cars are parked, as the level of noise during dispersal can be disturbing to local residents. By having a condition that prohibits re-entry after a certain time, it helps to prevent customers congregating outside or people going from one licensed premises to another late in the evening.

The location of premises

58.93   This is an important factor in assessing impact through public nuisance – it may be appropriate that licensed premises in dense residential areas, particularly pubs, close earlier than those in town centre locations. Each premises would have to be assessed on its own merits and consideration given to any CIP.

Deliveries and collections

58.94   These are often a source of noise and disturbance to residential premises, particularly in the case of premises where alcohol is sold. If the officer considers that this aspect is likely to cause disturbance then a condition with appropriate times is recommended. Matters such as the emptying of waste receptors and disposal of empty containers are considered and if necessary, appropriate conditions are recommended.

Noise from plant

58.95 Noise sources of concern include kitchen extract ventilation, air conditioning plant and compressors serving freezer and chiller cabinets, which in many cases will already be in place. The officer tries to assess the noise impact of such plant and makes appropriate representations if necessary. It may also be necessary to check planning conditions, although colleagues in the planning enforcement team would normally carry out such checks, as detailed later in this chapter.

Prevention of odour nuisance

58.96 This aspect relates to the cooking of food, which will necessitate an effective extract ventilation system.

Prevention of nuisance from artificial lighting

58.97 Officers consider fascia lights, security lights, car park floodlights, and lights which illuminate the premises.

Assessing the overall impact of the licence application

58.98 All of the above aspects, where relevant, are considered, alongside the premises history, when assessing the likely impact of the granting of a premises licence, and in particular in relation to the prevention of public nuisance.

58.99 Most commonly, the likelihood of disturbance through noise from the premises and the hours of operation are the two key factors. The EHO has to decide whether:

- the potential impact is such that the application can be granted on the basis of the proposed operating schedule (ie no change of hours nor type of licensable activity), *but* with conditions attached regarding the transmission of noise, etc; or
- the potential impact is such that the application can be granted *but* not for the hours requested because it is felt that an earlier terminal hour is appropriate; or
- the potential impact is such that the application should be refused, because it is felt that the proposed use is inappropriate for the location or that it is not possible to overcome the impacts that the licensed use would create.

Dealing with complaints about licensed premises

58.100   When a complaint is received, it is good practice for officers to check the complaints database for details of the premises' history of previous complaints. Basic checks would include the premises licence for the name of the DPS, the telephone number for the premises and any licence conditions relevant to the complaint, eg: 'No noise shall be audible outside', or: 'There shall be no use of the outside area after 10 pm', etc.

58.101   Where at all possible, it is useful to contact the complainant and arrange to visit them. If visiting a complainant, the officer should provide a clear statement if a statutory nuisance has been witnessed. The statement should include a brief description of what was observed and the relevant grounds for the nuisance.

Visiting the premises

58.102   If the complainant declines a personal visit for any reason, a visit to the licensed premises to address the issues witnessed should be considered. This visit may either be undercover as part of surveillance during any monitoring period or announced at the premises.

58.103   The visit will require a degree of professional judgement by the EHO, particularly of any potential personal safety risks that may be encountered, for example, visiting a busy public house where drunkenness and/or hostility to 'officials' may be encountered. The same can rarely be said of a restaurant, an off-licence or private members club, but the individual risks of any visit should be assessed and decided upon.

58.104   The EHO will visit the premises to establish the type of premises, area and distance from the complainant's property, whether any suitable observations can be made from outside or if there are any matters that may still be actionable even in the absence of having witnessed these from a complainant's property, eg breaches of conditions.

58.105   When carrying out a visit to substantiate or investigate the complaint, comprehensive notes are made, which may include the following details:

- any breaches of licence conditions;
- the level of the noise witnessed, eg 'just audible when standing outside the premises' or 'audible on the other side of the road between/over passing traffic' or 'audible all the way down the street';
- an indication of whether public nuisance would be likely or not, eg if the premises are in close proximity to residential properties;
- whether there were any windows open (licensed premises and/or resident's home);

- if there is music, whether it was disturbing, eg 'the music volume was very high' or 'the music had a lot of bass';
- if customers are outside, whether the outside area is particularly rowdy;
- an estimate of the number of customers on the premises;
- whether there were any cars/taxis dropping/picking up customers;
- the weather conditions, eg warm, wet, windy;
- the number of door staff on duty;
- whether the doors were open or closed;
- whether there is a smoking area;
- whether there were any queues and, if so, how these are controlled/managed.

58.106 During any announced visit to the premises, the EHO will ask to speak to the DPS (by title, *not name*) or duty manager/person in charge. On arrival of this person the officer should confirm their status, eg DPS or duty manager, etc and their name. If introduced as the duty manager the officer should ask for the DPS's name for reference. If this name, or if the person has advised that they are the DPS their name, does not match the name of the DPS recorded on the premises licence then the officer should question the whereabouts/status of that person, eg 'Has Joe Bloggs left then?' and, if so, when. This is critical information, as mentioned earlier on in this chapter, because if the DPS named on the premises licence has left then every sale of alcohol since their departure is a breach of the premises licence. This is not a matter that the environmental protection team would normally be expected to deal with or enforce at the time of a visit, but instead the information obtained would be passed on to the licensing team.

Follow up action from the visit

58.107 Having checked the premises history and premises licence the EHO will be able to decide on the most appropriate course of action. The options available include:

- a letter about the offence;
- a formal legal notice;
- a fixed penalty notice (FPN);
- a formal PACE interview;
- simple caution;
- prosecution;
- a review application.

This decision will hinge on a number of factors, including but not limited to:

- Any noise witnessed from within a complainant's property or merely outside in the street.
- If inside a complainant's property, whether a statutory nuisance is witnessed.
- If outside in the street, whether there are any conditions on the

premises licence regarding noise not being audible outside or at the boundary of the nearest residential premises.

• If outside and there are no any relevant noise or nuisance conditions on the premises licence, whether the noise witnessed is likely to cause a nuisance.

• The location, whether it is in a town centre or near residential properties.

• The hours of operation.

Monitoring

58.108 Should there be regular complaints about any premises which licensing officers have not been able to witness, or where they require further evidence to take enforcement action, programmed monitoring is normally considered by officers in the environment protection team, as they work late at night and at weekends, as a matter of routine. Best evidence would require access to the complainant's premises, but if this is not possible then monitoring should occur externally from a suitable location. The nature of the complaint, relevant licence conditions, day of the week, time of night and duration are normally confirmed before any monitoring takes place.

However it may be necessary to carry out monitoring without the complainant knowing so as to establish whether the complaints are justified or malicious, although from experience the latter is very unlikely.

Monitoring may be requested by colleagues from other teams such as licensing, health and safety or planning.

58.109 There should be follow up action to the monitoring. This can be in the form of writing to the premises making them aware of the findings, arranging a meeting with them to discuss the findings, and/or letting the complainant know of the findings.

58.110 In all monitoring, the time of year, special events such as sports competitions and festivals, and busy seasons such as Christmas and Halloween should be taken into account.

58.111 All in all, EHOs have a crucial role to play in the licensing regime, particularly in light of the new powers that they have been granted to be able to object to TENs.

E ENVIRONMENTAL HEALTH OFFICERS: HEALTH AND SAFETY

58.112 It is useful to also consider the health and safety role of an EHO, as a responsible authority, when reviewing licence applications and carrying out venue inspections.

58.113 An assessment of a new premises licence, variation or provisional statement application allows the responsible authority the opportunity to ascertain whether the public safety licensing objective has been satisfactorily addressed by the applicant.

The assessment should determine whether the applicant has satisfactorily assessed and developed management controls to promote public safety in accordance with the council's own licensing policy.

58.114 This is primarily determined by reviewing the application and operating schedule in order to determine whether it properly addresses public safety issues relevant to the premises, its usage and licensable activities sought and any foreseeable public safety risks. This may include determining:

- whether a safe capacity has properly been assessed;
- whether there is a safe means of access and egress;
- what maintenance arrangements are in place;
- the efficacy of crowd control arrangements;
- the nature of evacuation management arrangements; and
- the suitability of the premises in terms of layout and internal arrangements from a public safety perspective.

58.115 Attention should also be paid to the applicant's awareness and application of health and safety legislation. Where the assessment of the suitability of the application and operating schedule shows deficiencies the responsible authority may consider it necessary to carry out a full health and safety inspection of the premises. If the concerns of the authority cannot be satisfied, it is also likely that representations will be made with recommendations for public safety licence conditions to be applied.

58.116 The responsible authority may also take the opportunity with a new application to offer advice and information about other environmental health related legal requirements outside the Licensing Act remit. The rationale for this is that early engagement with a commercial business to educate, offer advice and ultimately to seek legal compliance in relation to food safety, health and safety, public nuisance and smoking legislation, etc is always beneficial.

58.117 Ordinarily, it would be advisable to carry out an inspection of premises where a new licence has been applied for. It may well be that the premises is unknown to the responsible authority or is under new ownership and therefore would normally necessitate (where applicable) a food safety or health and safety inspection and risk rating. A bar in a basement, for example, would raise more safety concerns than one at street level in terms of ensuring that patrons can exit quickly and safely in the event of an emergency.

58.118 Any inspection from a public safety perspective would assess the size and space available, physical condition of the premises (floors, walls and ceilings), adequacy of lighting, staircases, corridors, means of escape, emergency lighting, condition of electrical equipment, wiring and gas installations and whether current inspections and testing have been carried out by a competent person.

58.119 As well as the physical inspection of the premises, the officer will have an opportunity to review safety management documentation including health and safety risk assessments, safety management operational arrangements, staff training records, accident book, test and inspection certification, housekeeping arrangements, first aid provision, etc.

F TRADING STANDARDS OFFICERS

58.120 The days of verifying the integrity of coinage are long gone, but trading standards still check weights and measures. They also check that consumers pay no more than they should and get what they have paid for. Fake or watered down spirits, overcharging and short measure could all result in a prosecution. Being criminal offences they could also prompt a review of a premises licence. The same applies to underage sales, which relate not only to the licensing objective of preventing crime, but also to the objective of protecting children.

58.121 The profession focuses on outcomes. Consumers and traders should be confident of a fair and safe trading environment. Those who do not sell fake wine should not be undercut by those who do; nor should customers be exposed to the dangers of a drink produced in sheds where the safety of the product was not even a consideration.

58.122 In this context, prosecution is simply a tool available to trading standards, and not an end in itself. Advice remains the most commonly used tool: for example a shopkeeper is unlikely to be prosecuted simply because of the absence of a notice warning that tobacco will not be sold to under 18s, or one stating the quantity in which spirits or wine are served: advice is the obvious response. However, if advice is ignored, or the absence is just one part of an irresponsible approach to doing business, more assertive enforcement is more likely to follow.

58.123 When advice seems inadequate, and it comes to formal action, other authorities with which the business may have dealings have various options, such as serving formal legal notices. When advice proves inadequate, trading standards usually have the tools of review, simple caution and prosecution. The Licensing Act 2003 is unique in providing the option to seek to have a practice incorporated within the operating conditions of the business, enforceable by the criminal law, thus ensuring that good practice becomes an obligation rather than an option. Once again this is simply a tool to achieve the right outcome. If a representation is made, or a review requested, discussions between the licensee and trading standards will focus on what solutions need to be put in place in order to achieve the desired outcome.

Advice

58.124 Trading standards officers must distinguish between legal requirements and good practice when advising businesses. However, good practice may have legal implications because of the due diligence defence, which is explained below.

58.125 In some circumstances statutes create this defence, which enables a business that has committed what is, on the face of it, an offence to defend themselves. They can do this by demonstrating that they diligently took the precautions that any well-run business of their type would take to avoid the offence.[3] Trading standards deal with a wide variety of businesses and come across practices which tend to work in ensuring adherence to the law. Thus advice about good practice, though it does not set out what must be done, may also be of legal significance, as it may be relevant to establishing such a defence. The following, which relates to underage sales,[4] illustrates the distinctions.

58.126 Trading standards are advising about a legal requirement if they state that the licensee must ensure that a scheme is in force that requires those who appear to be under 18 to prove that they are old enough to buy alcohol.

58.127 Trading standards are going beyond advice about legal obligations if they recommend that, although the legal age for selling alcohol remains at 18 years, anyone who does not appear to be at least 21 is asked to prove that they are 18 or over by providing photographic proof of age (bearing a hologram). This may be desirable and good practice, because of the difficulties in assessing a customer's age: it is effectively building in room for error and standardising what amounts to acceptable proof of age. However, the advice is not without legal significance, because if such a policy is not followed there is the risk that a court might think that the business had not taken adequate precautions, and the due diligence defence[5] might not succeed.

58.128 Additionally the service may advise that a business could keep a 'refusals register', where employees record when they refuse to sell age-restricted goods to young people. This may help managers to see if some

---

[3]   See eg Licensing Act 2003, s 139.
[4]   See Licensing Act 2003, s 146.
[5]   See Licensing Act 2003, s 146(6).

employees do not appear to refuse such sales as often as others, or that refusals are not as numerous as they would expect from their own experience. Such a gap may reflect that staff simply do not record such incidents, rather than reflect that they sell to under 18s; but even this allows managers to emphasise the importance of this legislation, and require a practice that reflects its importance. Many retailers that scan goods before selling ensure that there is a till-prompt for staff to remind them of the need to be sure of the customer's age. Once again both measures are good policy, but they may also enable a business to show that it is doing all that can be reasonably expected of it.

58.129 Other factors such as training of staff and correct supervision will help a business to comply with the law, and not just the law relating to age restrictions. The extent to which such actions should be documented depends on the size of the business. One that consists of three family members is not expected to have the sort of documentation that a corporate giant may have. This reflects that it is easier for those in charge of such small enterprises to know what is going on. However, it is a common mistake in such family businesses to assume that everyone knows what is required; training and supervision are still required, both in terms of good practice and being able to demonstrate diligence, and it is highly desirable to be able to demonstrate that staff have been trained.

Conditions

58.130 As mentioned previously the Licensing Act 2003 provides a unique tool. That is to seek, by compulsion or by agreement, to have good practices included in an operating schedule, thus making them an obligation for the licensee.

58.131 An example would be requiring a business to use the Challenge 21 policy described above. Thus what has been identified above as desirable practice, which may also help establish a defence, can become a legal obligation. The same may apply if the business is required to perform regular stock audits where the nature of spirits are also checked.

58.132 Such additional requirements should not be added to licences as a matter of course. There should be grounds to justify them for those specific premises. The example mentioned above relating to stock-taking illustrates how this may be justified.

58.133 To take an example, a business was prosecuted for selling watered down spirits. The explanation it offered was that it had been done by an employee leaving the business who had arranged a party, and instead of paying for the drinks had topped up the bottles with water. Though the company stock-take compared recorded sales with the amount of spirits they had supplied to the premises, no check was made of the quality of the spirits on sale. When an area manager explained that he was confident that the departing manager had done this because he had come across the problem before, the court concluded that a basic check for watered down or substituted spirits could have been undertaken, without undue burden, during those stock takes and that the business had not done what could have reasonably been expected of it to avoid the offence. This example relates to establishing a due diligence defence, and is something that would not normally form part of the conditions of the licence. However, if there was such a sale, and the practice was not followed, it is now an option for trading standards to ask a licensing committee to incorporate such practice in a condition in the operating schedule by means of an application for review.

58.134 Trading standards has the option of seeking the incorporation of conditions when making representations in an application for review. However, once again, if the licence holder believes that the condition is unnecessary or overly burdensome, it will be advantageous in any negotiation with trading standards if they can show they will adopt an alternative, and equally effective measure to ensure the desired outcome. It is also possible that during discussion with an authority it will be agreed that the licensee requests a variation incorporating the terms into the operating schedule, rather than go through a review.

58.135 An area which may potentially become more problematic is the increasing number of premises supplying alcohol directly from a warehouse to the homes of consumers. The mandatory condition that the licensee operates a scheme using photographic proof of age to avoid underage sales remains. This requires the licensee to ensure, not just that the policy exists, but that it is followed. When delivery of alcohol is made by employees, such control is not easy, and is even more difficult when delivery is made by another company, such as a courier. In the latter case, the business should negotiate with the couriers to enable the licensee to verify that the policy is followed, and that if challenged they can show how they can be confident that it is.

Closure

58.136 There is a separate offence, which can attract a fine of up to £20,000 under section 147A of the Licensing Act 2003, of persistently selling alcohol to children. This applies if sales are made from the same premises twice within three months. If this occurs it is possible for trading standards (or the police) to seek an order which will close the premises for up to three months.[6] If trading standards have advised a business about a previous unlawful sale, and advice has not been followed, it may be difficult to dissuade an authority from pursuing such a closure.

---

[6]   Licensing Act 2003, s 147B.

Prosecution, simple caution and fixed penalty notices

58.137 When deciding whether or not to prosecute, a trading standards department will have regard to an enforcement policy, which will be publicly available. The decision to prosecute usually requires that conviction is likely and that such a prosecution is in the public interest. The latter may be influenced by the harm done by the breach, by the need to ensure that those who break the law are aware that it is taken seriously, by the extent to which it is a problem in the area and many other factors. Previous behaviour, including response to advice, will also be relevant.

58.138 Zero tolerance is not technically a policy option. However, it is often used loosely to reflect that certain offences are regarded as so serious that if conviction is likely, it is very likely that prosecution will follow. The area of underage sales is one which may be regarded this way in some councils.

58.139 Sales of goods which breach the Trade Marks Act 1994 are also serious offences, as the fine is unlimited and a ten year sentence can be imposed. Though these penalties are most likely to be applied to those behind a counterfeiting business, and do not indicate the fines likely to be faced by a retailer, they do indicate the seriousness with which such an offence is regarded.

58.140 Any investigation should follow rules which oblige trading standards officers to obtain and keep evidence relevant to the defence as well as the prosecution, and will usually involve an attempt to interview the alleged offender under caution, where it is made clear to the accused that what is said may be used in court, and the interviewee is informed of his or her rights.

58.141 It is necessary to distinguish between two different uses of the word caution. The caution (under the Police and Criminal Evidence Act 1984) referred to in the previous paragraph is a warning about the significance of any such interview: a warning about the defendant's rights, and how what is said may be used in evidence. This should not be confused with a simple caution, which is issued where the accused admits guilt, for a minor or first offence. If this simple caution is accepted by the accused, he or she will not be tried before a court or fined, but if a similar offence is repeated, and a conviction follows, the caution may be presented to the court as if it was a previous offence. The admission may also be revealed to potential future employers.

58.142 In the case of underage sales, one other option that may be available to trading standards, but is more usually employed by the police, is the issuing of a fixed penalty notice (FPN). This notifies that, in the opinion of the authority issuing it, an offence has been committed, but it allows the recipient to discharge their liability by paying a fine. It does not result in a criminal record for committing an offence, though it may be disclosed by the Criminal Records Bureau. If the notice is ignored a prosecution may follow.

Other interaction

58.143 Contact may be prompted by receipt of a complaint or by routine inspection, but it may also be offered as part of support mechanisms. One example from Hammersmith & Fulham is Pub Watch, where those enforcing the law, such as the police and a range of local authority services, share a forum with managers of licensed premises to pool information and knowledge. Central to this is the co-ordination between different agencies so that publicans can receive a broad range of advice, and can share problems and solutions. It also enables publicans to provide feedback about the reality of their circumstances, and for all partners to identify achievements in promoting the licensing objectives.

58.144 A common form of contact for businesses which operate at locations in a number of authorities is through a relationship known as home authority. This recognises that an element of opinion affects both how laws are construed or interpreted, and what is, or is not, regarded as good practice. It is possible, or even likely, that a business operating in more than one area could come across variations in the advice it receives from trading standards. To avoid that problem trading standards developed and encouraged relationships between the business and the local authority where those running the business are based. A recently introduced variation of this principle is that of Primary Authority under Part 2 of the Regulatory Enforcement and Sanctions Act 2008. However, the number of businesses involved in this remains relatively small.

58.145 Of course one to one interaction through inspection of premises remains a major source of advice, which has the value of being tailored to the needs of the individual premises. It is also a means of ensuring that businesses are properly run. Mail shots and publications which include advice from other parts of the council are also ways in which trading standards communicates with the licensed trade. Additionally advice and information will be made available on council websites. The latter approaches are economically efficient and effective in reaching a large number of businesses, with minimal burden on them, but tend to involve a 'broad brush' approach. The advantage of advice on a website is that the licensee can access the information when they need it.

58.146 In summary, other than the licence application process, the main issues for which someone in the licensed trade is most likely to have dealings with trading standards are as follows:

- Adulterated drink, substituted or counterfeit products or mis-described food, eg rump steak described as sirloin steak.

- Not displaying required information, such as the quantities in which drink is supplied, the prices charged or a notice regarding restrictions on sales of tobacco.
- Overcharging.
- Making cigarette vending machines available to the public or selling tobacco or alcohol to under 18s.
- Selling short measure alcohol, or using unapproved measures or quantities.
- Failing to adhere to a licence condition relevant to the above.

58.147 The main tools available to trading standards include:

- Co-operative working, advice or warning.
- Simple caution or prosecution.
- Request for suspension of licence for multiple underage sales.
- Representations regarding an application.
- Request for review of a licence.
- PNDs for under-age sales of alcohol.

G PLANNING OFFICERS

58.148 Over the years, understanding about the role of planning as a responsible authority across different local authorities has been varied. This is not at all surprising. On the one hand the planning authority is given the same responsibility and power to make representations on applications and to apply for reviews. On the other hand, the absence of planning permission cannot be used as an excuse to refuse a licence. This has caused some planning authorities to limit their involvement in the licensing system.

Planning background

58.149 In Hammersmith & Fulham, the local planning authority exercises its powers to control opening times of all new establishments seeking planning permission, where harm would otherwise arise. With this in mind the licensing objectives are paramount in any representations that planning have provided to the licensing authority.

58.150 The council's planning policies are currently set out in its unitary development plan (UDP) and subsequently in the local development framework, supplemented by additional guidance on: A3 use of restaurants and cafés, A4 use of public houses, and A5 use for take-aways.

58.151 The strength of these policies is that there is an obligation, both on the council as the local planning authority and the decision maker on any appeal, to give considerable weight to them, to ensure consistency in the decision making process. The council's policy urges applicants to obtain planning permission, including relating to hours, before applying for a licence. The absence of such permission, if relevant representations are made, may well carry considerable weight in the licensing process.

The licence application

58.152 It is important to re-emphasise that licensing applications cannot be a re-run of the planning application. However, the granting by the licensing committee of any variation of a licence, which involves a material alteration to a building, would not relieve the applicant of the need to apply for planning permission or building regulation control, where appropriate.

58.153 In many cases where an application is made for a new licence or variation, the town planning use will already be authorised by a previous planning permission or because the premises has a long-standing lawful use. Therefore, a new application for planning permission is often not required.

58.154 However, the existing planning permission might, and if recently granted is very likely to, have conditions restricting the use of the premises in some way, eg the hours of operation. In such cases, applicants seeking a licence to operate beyond those hours are advised to seek and obtain a revised planning permission or a variation or removal of the relevant planning condition.

58.155 All premises licence applicants are encouraged to obtain the correct planning permission. In order for applications to be carefully considered applicants are advised to include a description of the current use of the premises and whether there will be a change of use, eg: 'It is currently being used as a take-away and will be changing to a restaurant.' Additionally, applicants are reminded that operating a licence without the relevant planning permission could be a breach of planning control and could leave them vulnerable to planning enforcement action.

Making a representation

58.156 The planning team are likely to object if the licence application is clearly in breach of the planning permission.

58.157 The licensing sub-committee has been assisted where a representation from the planning team clearly sets out the current planning status, as illustrated below:

> 'The licence application is for the use of the premises as a take-away, for the purchase of food for consumption off the premises.

> A take-away falls within Use Class A5 of the Town and Country Planning Act (Use Classes) Order; planning permission would therefore be required for the proposed change of use from Class A3 to Class A5.'

58.158   Other factors to consider and include in a representation, as a result of a venue inspection, would be:

- where the premises are located;
- whether they have a retail frontage;
- whether they are on the ground floor or in the basement;
- whether the premises have residential accommodation above;
- whether the road is a busy and well-used route with day and night bus services; and
- whether there is a significant level of pedestrian and other activity in the location during the day and how this would change during the hours requested when the background noise levels may be relatively lower, eg at night.

58.159   When considering a premises licence application, the council's policies, as previously mentioned above, will always be a factor. For example, where planning policy advises that in town centres, food and drink establishments shall not be open to customers later than midnight, it is useful to clarify whether or not the subject premises is located within a town centre.

58.160   The council's planning policy in respect of environmental nuisance requires that all developments (including changes of use) shall ensure that there is no undue detriment to the general amenities at present enjoyed by existing surrounding occupiers of their properties, particularly where commercial and service activities are close to residential properties.

58.161   An inspection of the licensed premises, will allow the officer to provide a description of the area, eg:

> 'The general area comprises retail shops on both sides of the street; the shops trade generally between 9.00 am and 5:00 pm. After the shops close, whilst it is true that the premises may be situated on a main bus route, the ambient noise levels would be considerably lower.'

58.162   Where planning policy seeks to ensure that no adverse impact arises from Class A food and drink uses in terms of traffic and environmental conditions, it is helpful to advise about where the nearest residential premises are situated, the nature of any adjacent buildings and whether they are set back from the pavement. The application for the extension of hours must be considered in the light of whether the land use at different times during both day and night would be acceptable in the public interest.

58.163   In some circumstances council policy may lay down the criteria, which have to be met in order to allow extended opening hours whilst limiting the impact on local residents. Although it may be the case that many of the patrons would not cause noise disturbance, it only needs a small group of people to create noise, nuisance and disturbance to result in problems in the early morning.

58.164 A hot food take away outlet is by its very nature more likely to generate an increase in activity in and around the premises, as opposed to a restaurant, which primarily provides for the consumption of food on the premises where customers may enjoy a sit down meal with beverages and table service. The target audience for restaurants is generally smaller groups, ie families, couples, etc, where the diners tend to arrive at different times in smaller numbers, spend a number of hours on the premises and, most importantly, do not leave all at once at closing time. Diners also generally do not loiter outside the premises after vacating the restaurant.

58.165 By contrast, hot food take-away outlets provide fast food and are more likely to attract a different target audience. They often serve large groups, including younger people who may have been drinking. This could give rise to anti-social behaviour, including increased litter and general noise and disturbance. The main issues relate to whether the use of premises as a hot food take-away operating late would adversely affect the amenity of the area in terms of environmental nuisance, noise and disturbance and traffic generation in the area. A typical observation may be:

'A take-away premises with a closing time beyond 1:00 am would inevitably attract customers leaving the nearby drinking establishments. This would further increase the potential for anti-social behaviour since there would be a high level of activity with people entering and leaving the premises. Patrons are also more likely to congregate outside on the pavement resulting in a public nuisance due to noise and disturbance especially in the early morning hours when ambient noise levels are generally much lower.

This could manifest itself and be obvious to local residents since it would occur at a time when it would be reasonable to expect a good degree of peace and quiet. As well as noise, the issue of disturbance from fumes and smells is also a relevant consideration.

In conclusion it is considered that the licensing application fails to meet the licensing objectives in terms of crime and disorder and the prevention of public nuisance; and for the reasons previously stated I would object to the application for the extension to the hours of operation.

It is the opinion of the planning authority that a more reasonable hour would be 24:00 hrs in line with Town Centre Policy.'

58.166 Finally, planning officers may include a paragraph about reserving the right to exercise powers of enforcement under the Town and Country Planning Act 1990 in the event that by reason of the change of use, the extended hours gave rise to noise and disturbance to neighbouring occupiers.

Other activities

58.167   The role of the planning authority as a responsible authority is not limited to making representations and calling for reviews. As a regular attendee at the authority's LAG meetings, officers are able to use their local knowledge and expertise to provide their perspective and advice on matters such as cumulative impact policies. In coming to any decision regarding the adoption of cumulative impact policies the licensing authority will have regard to other mechanisms outside of the licensing regime, such as planning controls (where development or change of use is involved, or where trading hours are limited by planning conditions). The planning authority is likely to assist with evidence and information in relation to such matters.

58.168   In addition, the Licensing Act 2003[7] states that any authorisation for the supply of alcohol will have no effect if the premise is used primarily as a garage. It is for the licensing authority to decide in the light of the facts whether or not any premises is used primarily as a garage. The licensing authority will usually establish primary use based on an examination of the intensity of use by customers of the premises and any representation from the planning team.

58.169   In summary, whilst the planning authority may not be the first to call for a review, they can certainly play their part. The LAG at Hammersmith & Fulham has been a refreshing approach to dealing with licensing issues, across the authority, allowing planning officers to become more engaged and contribute their experience and expertise in the licensing process.

---

[7]   Section 176.

Design of the night time economy

Work stops at sunset. Darkness falls over the building site. The sky is filled with stars. 'There is the blueprint,' they say.

Italo Calvino, *Invisible Cities*

A INTRODUCTION

59.01 To date, there has been a huge disconnect in the UK between licensing and planning (and other disciplines) in the design of well-considered, sustainable and diverse urban places after dark. This chapter outlines why such a lack of strategic thinking about design for the 'night time economy' has often led to a range of short-term problems in town centres and neighbourhoods; problems which planners, licensing officers, the police, town centre managers, councillors and residents then end up 'fire-fighting'.

59.02 This chapter also argues that licensing cannot simply operate as a reactive 'process-based' public service, prioritising its independence and impartiality (though of course it must enact the law). The licensed economy has a huge (and often unheralded) impact on job and wealth creation as well as on quality of place and quality of life for residents (both good and bad). Therefore, as a discipline, licensing needs to work more imaginatively and proactively with a wide range of partners in a process of what could increasingly be called 'designing for the night'. Therefore, for the purposes of this chapter 'design' is taken in its broadest sense: not simply the architecture and construction of buildings, but more strategically about how cities, town centres and neighbourhoods are made and function 'after dark'.

59.03 This chapter is also intended as a 'call to arms' for licensing and planning professionals, but also highways engineers, town centre managers and those with a remit for what is increasingly known as 'place-making' to consider how we may better re-design our cherished urban places after dark. It also highlights some of the tools that can be deployed and examples of good practice (and where things have gone wrong). As such it is not an exhaustive list of issues and techniques, for which there are other useful sources,[1] but is instead a brief portrait of the challenges and good practice solutions. It is divided into three sections based on geographical scale.

59.04   The first is the **town/city-scale** and addresses how the planning design process, with the input of key partners such as licensing, can set out a vision and delivery mechanism for truly sustainable places after dark. 'Sustainable' is about creating a diverse range of healthy activities and experiences that are accessible to all, characteristics that so many towns and cities in the UK currently lack after 6 pm.

59.05   The second level is the **neighbourhood scale**. Here we examine the design of new neighbourhoods, urban masterplans and how getting the 'balance right at night' can create distinct and appealing urban quarters which do not end up being 'young people's drinking ghettoes'.

59.06   The third and final level, and one which has been tremendously underplayed in the development of towns at night, is the **micro-scale**. Design at street-level can make a huge impact on reducing incidents of violence or accidents at night where intoxication means usual levels of restraint, awareness and care are suspended.

59.07   This chapter concentrates on the design of towns, cities and neighbourhoods after 6 pm, and even though the management of urban places should be integrated over 24 hours, there are a number of reasons why a night time focus is defensible.

59.08   Firstly, design for the night has been profoundly under-researched. Secondly, the licensed economy, while operational during the day, would not exist in its current form (or anything like it) if it were not for its main period of operation after 6 pm. This is crucial: unlike weekdays during office hours when the majority of people in town centres are there to earn a living, people's use of the city in the evening and at night is, in the main, discretionary. If we are not designing and managing safe, accessible and attractive after dark destinations that have a 'wow' factor (for all potential user groups, not just 18 to 25 year olds), then what reason is there for people to visit? Mary Portas' recent review[2] of the UK high street noted that town centres faced unprecedented challenges, and while the report regrettably ignored the post-6 pm period, the review's general point was clear: town centres must adapt or die.

---

[1]   Eg M Roberts and A Eldridge, *Planning the Night time City* (2009).
[2]   Department of Business Innovation and Skills/Mary Portas 'The Portas Review: An Independent Review into The Future of Our High Streets' (2011).

59.09 Those involved in licensing, planning, developing and managing town centres need to start thinking less like bureaucrats in silos and more like leisure-retail providers such as Westfield or Grosvenor, working together to design night time economies that are 'destinations', 'experiences' and 'inspirations'. As an industry, in 2011 the night time economy employed over a million people and was estimated to be worth at least £60 billion or 5% of UK plc.[3] This is more than twice the revenue of the property or telecoms industries, three times the UK fashion industry, and six times the car industry or publishing. And, while footfall in UK town centres has fallen during the recession, figures for the post-6 pm period have held up better than the daytime.[4] Indeed, the after dark economy, along with the likes of some financial services, green industries and telecoms, has outperformed most other sectors of the UK during the recession. Yet the night time economy is rarely accorded the same level of importance in economic policy debate or service delivery as these other industries.

59.10 This links to this introduction's crucial final point: nearly all town and city centres were 'designed' for a bygone era of post-6 pm socialising practices, perhaps as far back as the Edwardian lifestyle and if not that long ago, then certainly the safe and predictable 1950s. The rise of the 'night time economy' in such a short space of time (and in reality the majority of expansion has come in the past 20 years) has meant that spaces and thoroughfares that were once designed for workers during the week, shoppers on a Saturday and churchgoers on a Sunday are often overrun by high flows of users after dark. Estimates of visitor numbers in night time economies range from up to 3,000 to 5,000 in a small location like Oldham or York to 100,000 on a busy night in Manchester city centre. At the extreme, up to half a million people pass through Leicester Square in London's West End on a Saturday night,[5] with seasonal flows higher still.

59.11 Sydney has produced data[6] that shows pedestrian flows at night through some of its general city centre thoroughfares (not even its dedicated night time circuits) can be twice what they are during the day. And, within the city's busiest night time hubs, key junctions are crossed by up to 3,000 people between midnight and 1 am. Put in context, this is 50 (often intoxicated) people per minute or nearly one per second using a single crossing. This is the oft talked about transformation from the industrial nation into the post-industrial leisure society made very, *very* real.

59.12 Such places were never built for these numbers, and the resulting strains on pavements, junctions, transport and toilets (where they remain) is often overwhelming – and it is taking too long for the infrastructure to catch

---

3   TBR & MAKE Associates, 'Night Mix Index 2009' (2010).
4   Milestone, 'Night Time Footfall Figures' (2011).
5   Heart of London BID, 'West End Footfall Figures' (2011).
6   City of Sydney Council/Parsons Brinckerhoff, 'Late Night Management Area Research Project' (2011).

up. However, while this gives us shorter-term 'growing pains', it also presents an opportunity – to use what has already been learnt in those locations at the forefront of after dark design development to avoid making the same mistakes, as we look to remodel and redesign our town centres and neighbourhoods so they are fit for 21st century purpose, around the clock.

B THE CITY-SCALE

59.13 At the forefront of designing the city at night on the town centre level or even metropolitan scale is the spatial planning process. In the UK,[7] town planning can be proactive as well as reactive and regulatory, whereas licensing, due to its statutory limitations, remains *mainly* reactive and process based (although see 'Cumulative Impact' from para 59.35 below). However, while they have distinct jurisdictions, both planning and licensing could and should operate a lot more effectively together than they do at present. This section sets out how various licensing and planning tools can be used to enable positive and joined-up change for town centres and neighbourhoods at night.

Planning policy

59.14 The planning system in England has recently changed with the coalition government's introduction of its National Planning Policy Framework.[8] The current system is based on each location having a 'local development framework' or LDF. The LDF is a suite of, typically, 20 or 30 documents such as 'area action plans' for particularly important local town centres or neighbourhoods and 'supplementary planning documents' (SPDs). These SPDs deal with local specifics (anything from transport to noise to the night time economy itself). The LDF is to be replaced by a single 'Local Plan', prepared to be consistent with the National Planning Policy Framework.

59.15 While this new system does create more upheaval, for those of us trying to design better cities after dark it offers the chance for planners to atone for the past omission of the night time economy from their plans in an informed and substantive way. For far too long local planning documents have ignored the challenges and opportunities of urban places after dark, inadvertently leaving licensing to deal with the 'design' and experience of town centres in the evening and at night, something that could only ever be done in a limited, ad hoc and retrospective sense. Frequently it's been a case

---

[7]   England and Wales share a planning regime, Scotland has a similar system with a Scottish Planning Policy (SPP) due to go live in 2013 setting out the principles to which plans from the National Planning Framework down to local Development Plans must fit.

[8]   Department of Communities and Local Government, 'The National Planning Policy Framework' (2012).

of trying (and often failing) to put the genie back in the bottle, when thoughtful planning at the city scale would have been much a more efficient and effective way of avoiding large clusters of alcohol-led licensed venues.

59.16 This failing is partly because planners appear to have very little understanding of how cities work after 6 pm. This is where licensing officers and licensees groups as consultees on local planning documents could do much more to inform the night time planning process, and reduce the numbers of problems that end up on their *own* desks five or ten years down the line.

59.17 An example of a location that has attempted to use the planning process to influence the development of the city after dark is Sunderland, where the council created a specific evening economy supplementary planning document ('SPD').[9] Working closely with all stakeholders it was able to set out the various 'quarters' of the city and what type of 'after dark offer' each location would ideally have, for example, large format 'vertical drinking' would not be permitted in the Cultural Quarter. By formally adopting this SPD as part of the local development framework it becomes a 'material consideration' in planning decisions, and unlike licensing can address issues of 'need' for new/larger/later licensed premises. Sunderland's SPD has had some success in setting an agenda for a more balanced night time city centre.

Use classes order

59.18 A key factor in Sunderland's night time SPD, but one which has generally been underused and misunderstood, was the change in 2005 in England and Wales of the 'Use Classes Order'; the use classes being the typology of land use that allows planners to control the quantity and location of land use across a borough. For example, A1 is retail, A2 financial and professional services, B2 industrial, C1 hotels, etc.[10] Prior to this change, pubs, bars, restaurants and takeaways were all contained within one category: A3. This meant that restaurants could be turned into pubs or bars without the need to obtain planning permission. Indeed, this is what frequently happened and there was little that a council, even if it was aware of the potential negative impacts of growing clusters of alcohol-led venues, could do about it.

59.19 The change in use classes in 2005 meant that A3 was restricted to food-led businesses (cafes and restaurants), A4 alcohol-led (pubs and bars), and take-aways were given their own new A5 category. Nightclubs, which were often presumed to be a D2 (assembly and leisure) use are now specified as a 'sui generis' ('of its own kind') category, which means they are treated

---

[9]   Sunderland City Council, 'Sunderland City Centre Evening Economy: Supplementary Planning Document' (2006).
[10] See further Chapter 31.

on a case-by-case basis. This new structuring, though not perfect, does allow a more nuanced approach to designing for the night on both the city and neighbourhood scales, most importantly because it prevents food-led premises metamorphosing into drink-led venues without planning permission.

59.20 However, the benefits of this legal change in shaping the night time economy are blunted, at least to some extent, because planners have so little understanding of the night time economy and possess very little evidence of its impacts (positive or negative). Often councillors are worried about giving off negative signs to investors and have themselves been guilty of accepting any kind of investment, particularly in less affluent areas.

59.21 To be fair to planners, the planning process (due to its complexity, and its democratic and consultative nature) is very slow and the development of the night time economy has been incredibly fast, in reality creating a two-speed system. Nevertheless the poverty of ambition amongst planners to limit (not by any means ban) alcohol-led venues for the collective health of communities, the reduction of crime and city reputation has been very limited. This must change under the new local plans that will emerge over the next few years. However, because the new National Planning Policy Framework creates a presumption in favour of sustainable development (as broadly defined in the Framework[11]), councils and communities will therefore need to be proactive in setting out and evidencing what is sustainable in terms of the scale, density and location of after dark activity for their locations.

Premises density

59.22 One crucial area where planning (through the tools above) and licensing (through 'cumulative impact policies' – see below), can do more to design healthy, safe and successful towns and cities after dark is in controlling (in particular alcohol-led) premises density.

59.23 There are a number of problems that occur when excessive densities of such premises are created, including on-street congestion and 'pinch points' where intoxicated people bump into each other, falling alcohol prices due to excessive competition, flashpoints caused by competition for scarce resources (transport, fast food, etc) and people having been ejected by door supervisors creating problems with other users in the street outside.[12]

59.24 Alcohol-led licensed premises density and its impact on crime and disorder levels is increasingly an area of study by academics analysing the

---

[11] Para 7.
[12] A Barton and K Husk, 'Controlling Pre-Loaders: Alcohol Related Violence in an English Night Time Economy' (University of Plymouth Research Paper, 2012).

dynamics of violence after dark. Research from Melbourne[13] shows that as the density of such premises increases within a demarcated urban area, a 'tipping point' is reached at which stage alcohol-related crime and disorder problems rise disproportionately sharply for each new alcohol-led premises added.

59.25 Further research from Sydney[14] suggests that this relationship (at least in town and city centres) then stabilises (as opposed to levels out), with each further alcohol-led premises adding a fairly predictable number of additional public space assaults. The evidence also clearly shows that problems linked to these alcohol-led licensed premises do not occur in the same numbers in the immediate vicinity of alternative forms of land use or at randomly chosen locations.

59.26 What this research from Sydney did for the first time, and this is one of the most crucial points in this chapter, is demonstrate that the old argument that operators sometimes make to obtain licences or planning permissions ('We are a good operator with a great record, we will look after our clientele and ensure no problems on our premises,') won't wash as a 'rubber stamp' for a new venue or later licence any more. This is because the Sydney research shows very clearly that no matter how well individual alcohol-led premises are managed, it is once outside that the majority of problems take place: beyond the control of operators.

59.27 The work in Sydney showed that of those assaults reported at night in the city centre (and we must remember that there will be substantial underreporting), twice as many took place outside as inside the premises. This blows the 'good management' argument out of the water once and for all (not that good management is to be sniffed at). Once those customers are outside mixing with others on the street, they are more likely to be either a perpetrator or, as is often forgotten, a victim of crime.

59.28 Night time economy specialists MAKE Associates and Merseyside Police in Liverpool did the first repeat of this research in the UK in 2012. It showed that while not quite as extreme as Sydney, the picture is the same – most after dark crime and disorder incidents occur away from licensed premises, but in their immediate vicinity. As a result Liverpool has introduced a cumulative impact policy (see below) and in addition to the usual data (crime mapping, noise complaints, CCTV statistics and A&E admissions) it now has evidence that adding more alcohol-led premises to an

---

[13] M Livingston, 'A longitudinal analysis of alcohol outlet density and assault', Alcoholism: Clinical and Experimental Research 32 (6)(2008).

[14] M Burgess and S Moffatt, 'The Association Between Alcohol Outlet Density and Assaults On and Around Licensed Premises' (New South Wales Bureau of Crime and Statistics Research – Research Paper 147, 2011). (NB: It is important to note the authors specifically state that this relationship is likely to be both context dependent and on the type of alcohol-led venue and clientele.)

already volatile mix is almost certain to increase levels of crime, disorder and nuisance in the public spaces around key licensed premises hotspots, no matter how well run they are inside.

59.29   This growing body of evidence on the problems of excessive premises density contravenes what police, licensing and planning officers have often thought: that the coalescence of alcohol-led young persons' venues helped them contain alcohol-related problems and maximise limited police resources. This approach (at least in terms of limiting crime and disorder) has been shown to be a self-fulfilling prophecy and views amongst many senior police officers are now changing to one of challenging clustering and supporting the dispersal and mixing of premises types.

59.30   Evidence also clearly shows that high densities of alcohol-led licensed premises are off-putting to other groups in society, outside of their core 18–30 year old target market. For example, research in Wales[15] found there were only two areas of one major city where many residents of all ages weren't comfortable walking through at night. One was the pedestrianised shopping area where there was no evening usage and which as a result felt 'eerie', and the other was in the main night time strip where they felt threatened by the loud, alcohol-driven street experience.

59.31   This research has been reinforced by more recent work in Liverpool, which showed that people avoided specific parts of the Ropewalks area (the largest night time economy circuit in the city) because the congestion, drunkenness and threatening behaviour raised their fear of becoming a victim of crime. Indeed, the city's own research clearly showed that public 'drunkenness' (not fear of crime) was the main factor affecting city centre visitors' feelings of safety.[16]

59.32   So what can be done? A good example of where licensing and planning has worked effectively together to de-intensify a night time hotspot cluster has been in York. York traditionally managed to keep its alcohol-led young person venue economy 'corralled' into one 600m street – Micklegate, on the periphery of the city centre. The outcome of this was the 'Micklegate Run', a popular challenge in the 1980s and 1990s in which young people attempted to drink a pint of beer in each of its then 15 or so pubs and clubs. The result was the city's only hotspot for alcohol-related crime and disorder. One of the unintended consequences of this planning policy was that more aspirational operators did not invest in York despite the wealthy demographic because they weren't permitted to open venues in the city centre away from Micklegate, where they were not prepared to put their brands.

---

[15]   Bromley R et al, 'Exploring safety concerns in the night time city: revitalising the evening economy', Town Planning Review 71(1) (2000).
[16]   Cited in MAKE Associates, 'Design out Crime: An After Dark Strategy for Liverpool' (2010).

59.33 However, over time the city has take a strategic decision to allow carefully considered licensed economy development within its highly protected historic core, with strong conditions regarding hours, type of noise insulation and so on. Most of the new venues were more upmarket and offered a range of options that differed from those on Micklegate. While this has created some noise issues, it has generally worked, with a more sophisticated offering centrally. Micklegate, while still the prime night time hotspot (both in user numbers and crime and disorder), has seen reduced problems, a welcome decrease in the number of young persons' alcohol-led venues and new operations based on food, music and real ale opening to diversify the street.

59.34 Licensing and planning committees need to wise up and ensure that they have solid evidence like that in Sydney and Liverpool if they want to have greater control and confidence in turning down applications for more alcohol-led premises in areas where there are known problems. Such evidence can be used to resist particular applications but also, crucially, to formulate policy.

Cumulative impact

59.35 While the legal and technical elements of cumulative impact (as set out by the Licensing Act 2003's accompanying Guidance) is dealt with elsewhere in this volume, it is worth noting here the potential of such a policy to help 'design' the urban form after dark. It is the one area of policy where licensing is genuinely afforded some power to influence *proactively* rather than *reactively* the shape of the night time economy.

59.36 Specifically, there is some emerging evidence suggesting that a cumulative impact policy may not only limit the expansion of licensed premises in a given area, but that it may shift the balance of venue type from alcohol to food-led (if the policy is so set out). The only research so far is for Westminster, where analysis showed that in the West End Stress Area, between 2006 and 2009, the number of alcohol-led venues (such as pubs, bars and clubs, which are subject to a cumulative impact policy) fell slightly, while the number of food-led operations, which are outside the policy, rose.[17] Although the change is quite small and may be explicable by market trends, it is at least arguable that, given demand by alcohol-led operators for a presence in the West End, there would have been a much larger increase in this venue type had these restrictions not been in place.

59.37 Westminster's cumulative impact (stress area) policy is the most controversial of its kind, with even some of Westminster's own councillors believing it is stifles innovation and the quality of offer in the West End.

---

[17] MAKE & TBR 'Analysis of Licensed Premises in Westminster West End Stress Area' (2011).

There is also anecdotal evidence that such polices have also had the unintended consequences of protecting poor operators who are attracting a problematic clientele against competition that could change the after dark economy positively and improve the clientele of an area.[18]

59.38   While there is little doubt that potentially positive developments get caught up in a cumulative impact policy, there appear to be some benefits over and above simply preventing more venues from opening. A good example of this is Richmond upon Thames,[19] where crime and disorder in and around a problem venue in the town fell when its owners changed it from a young person's alcohol-led bar into a 'gastropub'. They made this change because they were unable to secure a licence for a later operation and to increase its capacity. There were no other changes in the area that might have led to such a fall in problems (eg no additional police, street pastors, etc). As such there is a degree of certainty that the change of operational style at this venue was the direct result of the borough's cumulative impact policy and that in turn the policy has helped reduce crime in that area.

C THE NEIGHBOURHOOD SCALE

59.39   While town- and city-wide policies can make a real difference to where the licensed economy can grow and develop, the night time economy is best understood at the neighbourhood scale or 'quarter' level. While a typical market town has perhaps enough venues that might form, in the industry's terms, a 'circuit' (though more often than not they are 'strips'), by the time we get to a location the size of say Ipswich, Swansea or Sunderland there may be three or four distinct circuits, attracting different types of client and operating at different times. Cities the size of Nottingham, Liverpool or Manchester may have five to eight circuits and London probably has over 50.

59.40   The planning system, through documents such as area action plans and masterplans, have the ability to design and shape (at least to some extent) how neighbourhoods and quarters can develop while still allowing for innovation, creativity and surprise.

Neighbourhood planning

59.41   Sitting beneath the main local plan, 'area action plans' and master-plans have become key ways to set out a vision and delivery mechanism for the design and development of new neighbourhoods, quarters and large strategic sites.

---

[18]   Poppleston Allen 'The Impact of Cumulative Impact Policies' (2012), available at www.popall.co.uk.
[19]   MAKE 'Cumulative Impact: A Study into Crime and Disorder in Richmond and Twickenham Town Centres' (2011).

59.42 However, these documents rarely attend to how places work after 6 pm, and while in the case of town and city centre sites this omission is likely to have the largest impact, it is still a problem for local neighbourhood planning where a mix of uses that attract people out in the evening can add to the viability of a specific high street or district centre. Likewise, failure to establish a round the clock vision for diversity can also cause problems with over-concentration of licensed premises. For example, Didsbury in Manchester, Headingley in Leeds, Upper Street in Islington and Clapham High Street have all had major problems at times from the creeping development of a night time economy much more suited to a city centre than an urban village setting.

59.43 So why, when considerable research effort is put into understanding what type of retail offer is required from a site (even down to the names of retailers), what the commercial (ie office) provision should be and what the residential mix should provide, is the evening and night time economy almost always neglected? How is it possible to create a sustainable community/ economy if a neighbourhood is designed mainly to operate between 9 am and 5 pm?

59.44 So often the licensed economy is seen as an area for regulation, enforcement and restriction; and of course there is a time for this. But there is a (much) bigger picture: the creation of exciting, visually stimulating, well-lit and walkable destinations and neighbourhoods that are the kinds of places that research shows many people want to visit, live and (often overlooked) invest in.

59.45 A good example of where licensing working more effectively with planning would have created a more sustainable new urban neighbourhood is in the vision and masterplan for Liverpool's Ropewalks – one of the UK's most historic quarters. The 2005 supplementary planning document for Ropewalks, an old warehouse district in the city centre, set out an exciting mix of uses: culture, retail, leisure, community facilities and residential. It was in many ways a well thought through document, winning a Royal Town Planning Institute award for best masterplan.

59.46 The general concept was to place residential and smaller bars and restaurants around the periphery, allowing for larger format restaurants, bars and clubs to open in the centre around a new piazza – Concert Square. This was done primarily to allow residents in the new developments a reasonable night's sleep. Yet partly because of the speed at which the market changed (from café and food-oriented offers to alcohol-led), the number of licences and planning consents approved (with no joined up-reviewing) and the lateness of licences after the Licensing Act 2003, Ropewalks (and particularly Concert Square) went quickly from 'café society' in 2005 to a 'boozed up

Faliraki-style binge pit'[20] by 2008.[21] By 2010 there were over 70 venues, some with 24 hour licences and planning terminal hours as late as 6 or 7 am, which were associated with high levels of violence, frequently becoming more extreme the later the operation.

59.47 As a result the city commissioned the UK's most comprehensive night time economy strategy that took in all of Liverpool city centre but with a focus on Ropewalks. It suggested a long-term plan for changing this culture with quick wins around removing posters advertising cheap alcohol, enhanced cleansing and some lighting improvements. It also advised a CIP area and the possibility of introducing early morning restriction orders if a new partnership led by local businesses could not deliver positive change. Longer term plans were outlined for the redesign of night time hotspots for better round the clock pedestrian flows and user experiences.

59.48 The council has taken the strategy's implementation seriously, perhaps more so than any other area in the UK, and crime has continued to fall despite the council having to terminate its funding of ten additional city centre police officers on Friday and Saturday nights. It is not too late for Ropewalks, which remains a unique and exciting quarter, but it will take a long time to put right the toxic combination of incoherent regulation, one simple mistake in a planning and design document and the tidal wave of late night investment that poured in after 2005.

Mixed-use development

59.49 A complex set of social, planning and technological processes that took place during the 20th century effectively 'designed' out the traditional European urban living model that had typified most of the UK's towns.[22]

59.50 However, these epochal changes created what planners call the 'doughnut effect' – the exodus of (often mixed) communities from the inner cities to live in suburban rings around the urban cores, only for the centres to be replaced with retail, offices and leisure (as well as brownfield sites as heavier industry left). This has brought both positive and negative outcomes, something that is reflected after dark. A mixed community helps create

[20]   MAKE Associates 'Design out Crime: An After Dark Strategy for Liverpool' (2010).
[21]   Faliraki is a resort on the island of Rhodes, similar to Majorca's Magaluf, Ibiza's San Antonio and Ayia Napa in Cyprus: destinations where young Brits (and other nationalities) go to let their hair down on summer holidays, involving large quantities of alcohol and in some cases drugs. Over time, these much more permissive environments (where the rules of home are suspended) have been brought back to the UK, with some venue operators keen to recreate a similar atmosphere by using touts to drag people into bars, leaving windows and doors open with music pumping out and with deep discounted drinks offers etc (albeit minus the sun!)
[22]   There are exceptions to this with a small handful of heritage cities, eg Bath, Bristol, York and Edinburgh as well as London, where the Georgian urban forms, streets and buildings continued to prove desirable as residential neighbourhoods.

purchasers for goods and services for the night time city such as food shopping and gyms, as well as local customers for the licensed economy. In addition, it creates vital natural surveillance, and a community that has an interest in the effective planning and management of the town centre, not just during the day, but also around the clock. The great urban thinker Jane Jacobs[23] believed that such natural surveillance and community engagement were the building blocks of safe and cohesive places. The doughnut effect removes these natural advantages.

59.51 An example of this doughnut effect impacting negatively on the after dark life of a town or city is in Oldham, the subject of an infamous BBC Panorama programme in 2009 supposedly addressing the ills of the Licensing Act 2003. In reality it dwelled on some of the more eccentric measures proposed by the borough council to try and get a grip on binge drinking and late night disorder that had apparently resulted from the more relaxed licensing environment.

59.52 Yet what had happened in Oldham was that in those shops and other premises left empty from the recession of the early 1990s, planning permission was given to pretty much any user prepared to take a lease, in order to avoid leaving empty windows.[24] In Oldham's case this was overwhelmingly young persons' alcohol-led venues. Therefore by 2008, and for the best part of the prior ten years, the town had become a law unto itself, with nobody but a small population of 18–35 year olds using it after dark. It was at the point where the town's incredibly popular repertory theatre (easily packing out its capacity of 500) couldn't open on Friday and Saturday nights because patrons weren't prepared to brave the 'carnage' on the town's main night time strip off which the theatre was situated. Here there were 20 late night venues within 200m of each other, yet in a town centre with only around 30 licensed venues, of which only two were food-led!

59.53 If Oldham town centre and its periphery had an established residential community of even modest size, alarm bells would have been rung years earlier about the impacts of the homogenous alcohol-led binge culture that was growing. But most of the borough's citizens were tucked up in bed well away from the centre as it grew out of control. Since 2008 the town has done some good work to improve the situation and the journey away from an alcohol-driven monoculture is slowly underway. There is even now an example of urban living with the town's first 50 or so residents now resident just off the main strip.

59.54 Oldham, although a rather extreme example, it is not alone. Across the UK, considerable progress has been made over the past two decades in reintroducing residential uses into the urban core, a trend given impetus by

---

[23]   Jane Jacobs, *The Death and Life of Great American Cities* (1961).
[24]   MAKE Associates, 'A Night-time Strategy for Oldham' (2010).

Lord Rogers' Urban Renaissance Report in 1997. For example, Manchester city centre's population grew from fewer than 3,000 residents in 1991 to over 23,000 by 2011. This trend has added a real sense of 'renaissance', creativity and round the clock dynamism to locations such as Manchester, Liverpool, Leeds and Newcastle. Even smaller towns and cities have benefited.

59.55 However, while there are numerous benefits to a growing urban population, it can bring very real frictions, particularly conflict between town centre residential uses and the licensed economy. A useful example is Kingston-upon-Thames, where the riverside was developed in the late 1990s into an upmarket mix of retail, residential, licensed premises and public space. While the development has generally been a great success, its early days were fraught with tension between the owners and incoming residents, who were on the receiving end of noise issues from the café-bars located on the ground floor. However, because the owners were able to limit the opening hours and eventually change some of the tenants, these issues have dissolved.

59.56 This micro-management by property owners is not possible in most locations. This is seen most vividly in the UK's most high profile battle between the night time economy and an urban residential development to date. At the time of writing, the council's planning decision to reject the development has been 'called in' for decision by the Mayor of London, only the fourth time a mayor has ever done so. The proposed development is for a 40 storey tower in London's Elephant & Castle in the Borough of Southwark. But why is it so controversial?

59.57 On one side of the road is the Ministry of Sound, the world's most famous nightclub, Europe's largest independent record label and a major international business employing 180 people. On the other is Oakmayne, a major property developer looking to turn an eyesore into a major asset to this deprived part of the capital. The problem is that the 40 storeys of residents would be located 10m across the road from the Ministry. It is the club's contention that it will only take one complaint to shut the club, which has operated in this location (often until 9 am the next morning) for 20 years with no complaints and which has a constructive, professional relationship with the council and police.

59.58 The outcome will be crucial indicator of how seriously the night time economy is taken as an economic and culturally valid part of the life of our cities. And, because there is a need for 1.5 million further housing units on brownfield land in England over the next two decades, this type of conflict can only grow. To deliver this accommodation while maintaining good night time business and jobs, there needs to be a closer relationship between planning and licensing as well as the development of more organisations such as Liverpool's groundbreaking Engage residents' federation in order to ensure that residential amenity is balanced with growth.[25]

D THE MICRO SCALE

59.59 Street-level or micro-scale design, such as lighting, pedestrian crossings and junctions, 'shared space', surface texture, tactile pavements (for the blind and visually impaired), street furniture and so on, is increasingly an area of focus for planners, urban designers and traffic engineers. However, understanding of how the micro-scale works at night and of how to ensure designs work 24/7 remains limited. All too frequently public spaces are designed for daytime vehicular traffic and office or shopper-based pedestrian flows, the result of which can feel uninviting or even intimidating at night. This final section sets out how designing for the night requires that additional considerations are taken into account.

Lighting

59.60 Traditionally, much urban lighting has focused on meeting street lighting standards in terms of number of 'lumens' (ie levels of brightness), with highway engineers specifying schemes based primarily on the need to minimise accidents (pedestrian fatalities are three to seven times more likely in the dark compared to daylight[26]).

59.61 While there is a need to address sustainability in terms of power consumption and ensure that a place is not 'overlit', the use of LED lighting has hugely reduced the energy consumed by public realm and architectural lighting and in many cities the replacement of the orange sodium lamps with white light has delivered further improvements in pedestrian safety (via a reduction in vehicle accidents) and enhanced crime prevention (white light allows enhanced facial recognition by CCTV). Less certain but often suggested is that brighter and clearer lighting may attract new users into a town centre and therefore play its part in making neighbourhoods and town centres more 'sustainable' in the most holistic sense.

59.62 However, important though highway lighting is, increasingly there has been a realisation that lighting can be used much more creatively, and that an imaginatively lit public realm may be an important part of the package of attractors that will bring in those groups to our town centres who are looking for more than simply an opportunity to get drunk.[27]

---

[25] www.engageliverpool.com.
[26] Rea et al, 'Review of the Safety Benefits and Other Effects of Roadway Lighting' (2009).
[27] Civic Trust 'Night Vision' (2006).

59.63   There are numerous ways that lighting can be designed into the contemporary urban realm beyond highways; indeed, we are really only just scratching the surface.

59.64   Firstly, the most established technique is the architectural lighting of buildings, and this approach remains extremely valuable. It is often the first step for residents and councillors to realise how lighting can transform a town centre or neighbourhood, build local pride and allow people to see their place afresh after dark (which is what we must do with the night time economy if we are to change those negative perceptions).

59.65   Secondly, and more recently, there has been a surge of exciting public realm lighting schemes that go further than simply augmenting what is already there. These range from simple and relatively low cost projects such as Liverpool's Lucy in the Sky with Diamonds canopy in its musical Cavern Quarter through to Brighton's New Road redevelopment. In the latter, some of the world's best landscape architects were brought together to turn a previously traffic dominated street into a pedestrian priority boulevard.

59.66   New Road is an important exemplar because, unusually, Brighton and Hove Council paid particular attention to the way it works at night. Street furniture has lights built in to it and the physical space was specifically designed to work seamlessly as a daytime and evening destination (and also not just a thoroughfare, as it had been before). Here users can sit outside in cafes or on public seating people watching, but it also enhances its former thoroughfare role by creating a pleasant conduit between areas of the city's day and night time economy. Most importantly New Road demonstrates a council and a city genuinely committed to enhancing both the safety and the quality of its visitor experience after dark, particularly through design and animation.

59.67   A third source of lighting techniques that can be used to create a better after dark experience is through temporary light events, lighting installations and night time festivals. The most famous of these is Lyon's Fête des Lumières that takes place each December, when the world's leading light designers take over the city and its residents place candles in their windows each night creating a magical effect. In addition to the economic impact of the 4 million visitors who arrive at the start of December each year to see the fête, there has been a knock on from this to improved year round lighting in the city which shows how a major industrial city can reinvent itself after dark.

59.68   This concept was picked up and broadened by both Paris's Nuit Blanche and Como in northern Italy's Notte Bianca (white nights) festivals.[28]

---

[28]   The literal translation of these is 'white nights'; however the actual meaning is nearer to 'night of restless dreams and awakenings'.

Both events bring together lighting projects, art installations, performances and the opening of galleries and museums until late. In the UK the Association of Town Centre Management has supported a network of 'light nights' in cities like Liverpool, Nottingham and Leeds, the latter being the original. Visitor numbers often double on light nights and critically they introduce new audiences, including families, to the pleasure of cities after dark. There has been no evidence produced that shows if these events – which accentuate the design of the buildings and public realm – actually change attitudes towards the evening economy amongst these new visitors (or increase future propensity to visit), but we do know that most of the visitors are not regular users of their city's after-dark offer.

59.69 Lighting (other than the statutory duty to provide street lighting) falls between a range of different organisations and departments and therefore the more creative possibilities are often lost. This is best prevented by a lighting strategy that links lighting to various other strategies including planning, community safety, tourism and economic development and which may or may not be adopted as part of the local development framework/local plan.

Lines of sight and public safety

59.70 There is some evidence that 'fear of crime' in the night time economy is a deterrent to more users taking advantage of it, although not as much as the media appear to make of it. Rather there are other reasons and research showing that a 'lack of things to do' and 'lack of public transport' (outside London) are more likely to put people off using their city or town in the evening and at night, with worries about personal safety coming third.[29]

59.71 It is not just lighting that makes people feel safer, but also the physical design of space. Design of the public realm that allows users to be seen by others and also to anticipate and avoid any potential encounter with a criminal can play its part in reducing crime and the fear of crime. Therefore, recessed doorways, dead ends, invasive public planting, etc can all contribute to negative feelings, particularly for the individual walking through a relatively unpopulated part of a city or neighbourhood late at night.

59.72 Gender also plays a major part in how safe people feel in the city at night. Famously some years ago John Prescott, when he was Deputy Prime Minster, made a statement about cutting back thickets in order to prevent men 'jumping out' on women. While this was rather a crude way of putting the problem, the principle stands: certain groups are more or less likely to feel safe in a town centre at night depending on how it has been designed. The UN's safer cities programme has issued guidance on how using

---

[29] Civic Trust, 'Night Vision' (2006).

female-led public space audits can produce critical information for policy-makers and designers to act upon in creating more reassuring and enjoyable spaces for everybody.[30]

59.73 Yet the design of public space – not just individual buildings or public spaces, but how the whole town centre or city quarter actually feels and flows when it is dark – is one of the least implemented areas of design and needs considerably more coherence between police, development agencies, planners, highways engineers, transport agencies and business improvement districts.

Design of public space

59.74 Licensing of public space by councils has been one of the unsung outcomes of the Licensing Act 2003. By using existing public realm assets, from parks to town squares, market places to riversides for events that attract people both during the day and in the evening councils can earn revenue from hire fees and animate public spaces. However, there is still some way to go in terms of the design of public spaces for multi-purpose, round the clock use. In addition to Brighton's New Road mentioned previously, one of the other highest profile new spaces is the regenerated Old Market Square in Nottingham, which is a jewel in the crown of the city centre.

59.75 The square was the result of a collaborative design process, with focus groups including input from older people giving advice on how it could meet their needs. The range of events it is now able to hold year round is staggering, with some of them running on after dark, including its now famous 'urban beach' in summer and the council's collaboration with the BBC: Nottingham's Big Night Out. This is an event with entertainment for all the family but is particularly focused on activities for senior citizens, who are often absent from the city centre after dark. The (new) Old Market Square has also produced a regular income stream for the council, which helps to offset its maintenance costs.

59.76 What the Old Market Square does well and what many new public space developments still fail to design in is an 'event infrastructure', eg concealed electricity, drainage and water points built into the structure, as well as toilets open into the evening. The absence of these facilities limits the use of even the most aesthetically pleasing new spaces and is something that designers, planners and highways engineers need to make the norm if we are to truly animate our town and city centres after dark.

---

[30] United Nations Human Settlements Programme, 'Women's Safety Audits for a Safer Urban Design' (2007).

Pedestrianisation

59.77 With the best of intentions, planners have tended to 'design out' traffic from the heart of many town centres. In most cases there are considerable benefits – greater pedestrian/cycle safety, more pleasant and unpolluted squares and piazzas and increased footfall during the day, leading to more successful shops and businesses. Yet there are a number of occasions where the benefits of pedestrianisation during the day do not continue at night. This is because the whole dynamic of a town or neighbourhood can change after dark.

59.78 A telling example of this is Bexley in southeast London. Here a study by the Civic Trust[31] showed that the town centre is split into two distinct zones, a lower mixed use area based on a two way 'high street' with smaller shops and the main night time economy, and an upper area where the main retail facilities are located and which is pedestrianised. This pedestrianised area thrives during the day, particularly at the weekend, but in the evening once the shops shut and at night it is 'tumbleweed alley' due to its mono-cultural retail use. This is also accentuated because vehicles are not allowed through at night. A strategy for the town centre suggested that by opening up the space at night and carefully changing the planning restrictions to diversify from pure retail (which is increasingly under pressure) this could create a genuinely mixed-use precinct and multifunctional space that works around the clock.

59.79 Another parallel study undertaken in Bexley[32] demonstrated that by investing in the public realm the quality and range of leisure and food operators wanting to invest in the area could be increased. The research showed that although the 'travel-to-leisure' catchment and affluence of its demographic, as well as footfall, are top investment priorities for quality restaurants and café-bars (which most towns want to attract more of), the quality of the public realm also sits relatively high on their list. Therefore, a space that is clean, attractively landscaped and well-lit, with outdoor options for table service in better weather, provides a strong motivator for investors to consider towns and even specific streets as a genuine investment possibility.

Café culture and outside seating

59.80 Nobody, not even the Daily Mail (which can be assumed to have tried very hard), has ever found the statement in which a government minister actually claimed that the Licensing Act 2003 would directly create a 'European café style society'. However, the media reported it anyway, and it

---

[31] Civic Trust et al, 'Bexley: Night Vision' (2007).
[32] MAKE Associates, 'Evening and Night Time Audit of Bexley – Getting the Mix Right' (2007).

is fair to say that at one time the 'Holy Grail' of changing British relation-ships with alcohol and 'civilising' the night time economy was to try and emulate Italy's mature relationship with alcohol and town centre socialising.

59.81 This was based on little more than a few commentators and policymakers having been there on holiday and seen that, yes, it was a lot more civilised than most of the UK on a Friday night out. Having argued strongly for the last 15 years against trying to import this seductive but culturally distant vision, I have tried to offer an alternative hypothesis: that we need our own outdoor socialising culture based on what Britain does best: pubs, ale, cool bars, live music. If we combine this with what we like to think we do well (and could) but currently don't – food, coffee, customer service – and then mix in much more outside table service (and the UK population will sit out under a heater most of the year) then it is possible we would have our own world-class public socialising life.

59.82 There are other barriers to this – often the police will object to an alcohol-led venue gaining outside seating, even if it's for table service only, because it potentially causes unhealthy, UK-style interaction between intoxi-cated patrons of one establishment and those moving around the drinking circuit. There are also other issues around outside seating, such as the blocking of pavements ('clutter creep') and reducing the ability for disabled people in particular to safely navigate town centres.

59.83 To address this, outside seating policy should be drawn up by planning and licensing in conjunction with other stakeholders. A good example is Weymouth, which didn't have such a policy until 2011 which, given its seaside location and status as host venue of the 2012 Olympic sailing, seems strange at first, although it was certainly not alone in this regard. The town's policy is positive about the role of outside seating and the benefits it can bring, but also sets out what is desirable and what is unacceptable. Such policies are enforceable through the system of premises licensing under the Licensing Act 2003 and table and chairs licensing under the Highways Act 1980 (for which see Chapter 34).

Traffic management

59.84 Barriers and railings are a favourite device of traffic engineers, who historically have put safety first, second, and third, often creating both cluttered and visually unappealing spaces, but ones that they would claim create safer pedestrian environments.

59.85 However, while barriers can improve safety by reducing the number and severity of pedestrian-vehicular accidents, at night they can perform the impromptu function of 'kettling' large flows of unpredictable and often-intoxicated people, creating potential hotspots for violence.

59.86 A typical example of this is Richmond Station in southwest London, opposite which the town's largest and (once most problematic) venue was sited (it has now changed its operation). At its 2 am closing time, this venue disgorged 500 people onto a pavement 1.5m wide (often physically 'assisted' by door supervisors). But because there was a stretch of around 30m of railing this meant that those partygoers, who often take time to disperse once outside premises, were compressed into a space of 45 square metres.

59.87 Using typical fire capacity recommendations for <u>inside</u> licensed premises (of 0.5 square metres per person), this translates into this space safety holding around 90 people, yet it regularly held 200 to 400 during those 15 minutes after closure. Observational evidence clearly showed that this artificial 'cocktail' of accelerated venue dispersal, high levels of intoxication and a rigidly enclosed space contributed to the creation of a public nuisance and violence hot spot.

59.88 The increasing development of 'shared space' and the targeted removal of excessive street clutter means that dispersal from licensed premises where barriers once stood and night time flows around towns are likely to be made easier. However, highway engineers still need to consider how traffic itself might be moderated to reduce the need for railings and barriers by reducing volumes and speeds, and via traffic mitigation methods.

Road closures

59.89 Traffic management orders have become increasingly popular tools in managing the night time economy. However, they have to be treated with caution: the main reason that they have been used in the UK is to reduce pedestrian-vehicle impacts. Like SoS buses or street pastors, they are a very useful short-term intervention, but it is important to question their longer-term benefit. Should we really be closing streets simply to avoid people being hit by traffic because they are too intoxicated to look after themselves? Surely this is addressing the symptoms and not the problem? It also suggests that the density of premises in those streets is so great that we have over-concentrated alcohol and fast food land uses in one hotspot and that a longer-term process of de-intensification and diversification is required.

59.90 There are also negative signals that some methods of blocking roads in the evening and at night can give off. For example, in some towns the process has been to park a police van at either end of the main drinking circuit and then to divert traffic manually. This remains both a terrible signifier of what town centre users are about to enter (or an effective signifier to 'stay out') and at the same time a crushing waste of resources.

59.91 If there is a genuine benefit in closing the street, eg to create a more vibrant atmosphere or a new temporary destination (rather than as a mitigation technique), then pop-up bollards are the most appropriate resource. In Liverpool's Stanley Street gay quarter, for example, a strategy to turn the roads into a connected series of temporary spaces to hold events, to facilitate outdoor seating and to prevent drive-by homophobic harassment (which was an occasional problem) was implemented by installing a series of pop-up bollards.[33] It has been a major success.

Parking

59.92 The impact on the night time economy of parking provision is surprisingly overlooked, yet may be crucial in enhancing diversity after dark. While there is no empirical evidence that a lack of safe, accessible and affordable parking deters families and older people (exactly the type of visitors that policymakers want to attract into town centres in the evening), there is substantial anecdotal evidence that the presence of safe quality parking facilities is a crucial motivator to them. The success of out-of-town 'leisure' parks is testament to this.

59.93 Fortunately, despite the difficult balance to be struck by city-makers between climate change and town centre vibrancy and accessibility, there has been a rise in the number of quality parking developments and Park Mark accredited schemes in town and city centres over the past twenty years. The Light centre in Leeds is a good example of a secure and safe and well-lit location that gives direct access to restaurant, bars and cinema as well as the rest of the city centre. Likewise, innovations like Westfield's developments in London's Shepherds Bush and Stratford where users type in their registration and get exact directions back to their vehicle are also enhancing the 'customer experience'.

59.94 Research in Liverpool showed that women's fashion for high heels combined with minimal 'going out' clothing meant that where previous generations would have walked from a railway or bus station into the city centre, this is now augmented by large volumes of socialisers using cabs to get as close as possible to the main night life circuits. In many instances this does not pose a problem, but in historic areas with narrow roads it can cause huge challenges around congestion and making emergency service access impossible. It also leads to impromptu taxi ranks with cabs 'kerb-bumping' (ie half on and half off pavements) which causes substantial and costly damage to pavements as well as constricting available pedestrian space.

Bus shelters

59.95 Well-lit and clean bus shelters with access to real-time information are important to any city throughout the day but are essential to the success

---

[33] MAKE Associates, 'Design out Crime: An After Dark Strategy for Liverpool' (2010).

of the after dark economy. Late-night services are absolutely vital where there is no rail, tram or underground system, which even when they do exist often cease around midnight.

59.96 However, bus shelters themselves can become a problem because they create bottlenecks on pavements (as the space is very narrow) or, since the smoking ban, because they have made surprisingly useful impromptu smoking shelters. Again these do offer flashpoints for violence and planners and transport providers need to think carefully about their location late at night. It is no longer enough simply to place a bus shelter in the right place for shoppers and office workers. Shelter location is also important because anecdotal evidence shows that some town centre users will walk much further to other bus stops in the evening if the most convenient stop has become besieged by intoxicated and sometimes volatile individuals from busy licensed premises, in order to avoid contact with such individuals.

Taxi ranks

59.97 While taxi marshals are increasingly being deployed to reduce 'frustration violence' at taxi ranks, the secondary benefit is in creating a more orderly and civilised way of getting home. Marshals, by placing a number of passengers with different but similar destinations in one cab, are able to make more efficient use of often scarce resources, reducing both flashpoints and waiting times.

59.98 However useful though taxi marshals are, the number and location of ranks is something that needs careful consideration after dark. This is because locations often need to change completely from what works during the day. Therefore designing and switching to 'after dark ranks' post-7 or 8 pm is one way of tackling this issue. Creating temporary ranks in loading bays can be another.

59.99 A good example of the challenge was in Morpeth, a market town north of Newcastle upon Tyne with a surprisingly large after-dark economy. Here the town's main taxi rank was located next to its busy market place, but at the opposite side of the road to the main nightclub and bars. As the road was also the main thoroughfare and vehicle speeds were high, having a rank which means people have to cross a road in an intoxicated state was inviting an accident to happen. This was redesigned to allow pick ups from the opposite side of the road after 6 pm.[34]

59.100 One area where design for the night time economy has not yet been fully thought through is how to enhance the user experience of waiting for a taxi at night in the rain. Queuing in the rain does not create a positive customer experience and is particularly likely to deter those older people who

---

[34] MAKE Associates, 'Morpeth Night Time Economy Audit' (2007).

are less prepared to wait around, so some form of shelter or covered space, which doesn't unnecessarily add to street clutter, would be a beneficial way of enhancing the customer night out.

Building frontages and active streets

59.101 While this chapter does not deal with the internal design of premises, the street frontages of buildings do have two impacts on the quality and attractiveness of the night time economy.

59.102 The first of these is the impact of daytime businesses on the feeling of the public realm at night. While it is understandable that businesses, particularly retailers, want to protect their premises and stock, the type of roller shutter used makes a massive difference to how 'hard' a street feels. A street full of solid shutters, particularly if covered in graffiti, creates an inherently hostile environment, not just to look at but because it prevents light from casting on to the street, and also prevents pedestrians viewing the goods in the windows. While planners in a few supplementary planning documents have insisted on quality open or semi-open grills, there has been nothing like enough effort made to promote these, and it is an area that can make a huge difference to the enjoyment of town and cities after dark; one only has to think of Paris with its unqiue and ubiquitous art deco shutter design.

59.103 Secondly, more needs to be done to influence large-scale town centre retail developers to better animate the streets surrounding their developments during the evening and at night. For example, developers and mall operators like to close their premises at night, which can create long pedestrian 'walkarounds'. This can reduce the ease of navigation around a town centre and degrade the user experience. Fortunately planners have increasingly resisted this, but a new challenge has arrived from shopping centre developers in the form of the 'leisure terrace', where the evening offer of food, bars, cinema, bowling and gyms are situated two or even three storeys off the street. This is reasonably enough done for rental yield reasons.

59.104 So, while the likes of Westfield in Derby, Grosvenor's Liverpool ONE and Hammerson's Cabot Circus in Bristol have all brought the retail and leisure-retail offer into the 21st century and are to be generally welcomed, their design is flawed from a public realm perspective because there is little or no animation at ground level, creating a tumbleweed feeling later in the evening. Liverpool ONE does avoid the closed and covered mall problem by providing a well-lit 24 hour open pseudo-public space which provides a way forward for the design of these developments in the future.

Waste management

59.105 While seemingly prosaic, the design of trade waste bin stores and the good management of bins and dumpsters are critical to the licensed economy and the wider quality of the public realm in two ways.

59.106 Firstly, licensed premises have increasingly ended up using their bin stores (which are often required as part of their planning conditions) as storage space for beverages, crates, bottles and barrels, etc as the licensed economy and their trade has expanded. As a result dumpsters and bins are often found on the street outside premises leading to an aesthetic degradation and public order obstructions as well as posing potential fire hazards. Bin bags are still common on the street in areas such as Westminster and are frequently kicked around by intoxicated individuals with contents such as food, bottles and tins spilling out onto the pavement creating numerous potential hazards. Councils can avoid these issues to some extent by enforcing conditions that ensure bins are only put out when collection is due and ensuring via inspections that bin storage is only being used for its original purpose.

59.107 Secondly, the presence of bottles (in crates, bags or boxes) directly outside or in the vicinity licensed premises can lead to their use as weapons in the night time economy. After a number of serious incidents involving bottles, Greater Manchester Police commissioned the design of new street bins that meant bottles were impossible to retrieve once disposed of. However, the bins do not reduce the possibility of problems where venues themselves have left large volumes of bottles outside.

59.108 A good example of a solution to the issues of waste management in the night time economy has been pioneered in Dublin's Temple Bar. With its historic streets and buildings, waste management was a major logistical problem for the world famous tourist area. Increasingly, with the privatisation of waste services and a multiplicity of providers, a chaotic street scene was developing, with some venues' refuse and recycling seemingly left out on the street for days. The local police, environmental health and refuse providers, with the support from the local business organisation – Temple Bar Traders Association – developed a code of conduct and a schedule for collections with two hour windows. Any bins left out after that resulted in an enforcement notice and fine. Designs for new premises were to include ample space for both bin and beverage storage. The problem stopped almost immediately.

CCTV

59.109 In the UK, CCTV has grown inordinately over the past two decades, both inside and outside licensed venues. Even in an era of reduced public spending the appetite for maintaining and even expanding CCTV networks remains. The effectiveness of CCTV is very context dependent and there are concerns around its use in some quarters, although these are not debates that need to be rehearsed here. However, from a design perspective, the overarching concern of CCTV control room managers is the presence of trees, particularly when in full leaf during the spring and summer. Often a typical system with 80 or 100 cameras may lose the full surveillance range in as many as ten of these during the summer months. While this is certainly not an argument for cutting trees down, there is a case for improving the siting of cameras when new CCTV systems are installed and of thinking through street planting and landscaping impacts on existing CCTV systems, as well as regular tree surgery of existing specimens to ensure that, where realistic, views remain as unobstructed as possible.

Toilets

59.110 Finally, an absolute 'no brainer' for the design and successful operation of the public realm after dark is the provision of appropriate public toilets. However, councils have consistently removed or downgraded their public toilet provision over the second half of the 20th century and continue to do so, particularly in an era of austerity. None of us would find it acceptable to go to a theme park, a holiday resort or a shopping mall and find the owners hadn't provided any communal toilets, saying instead: 'You need the toilet but didn't go in the café or shop? Well don't worry, just urinate against the rollercoaster/on the beach/against the escalator'. So why is it, particularly at night when people need the toilet most, that we believe it is acceptable not to provide toilet options?

59.111 Unless we view the evening and night time economy as a crucial part of our social, cultural and economic experience of urban living and invest in the facilities needed to support it, then is it any surprise that the media has a limitless supply of negative stories about the behaviour of some of its users? Yes, there will be those that will urinate in public spaces, even when there is a toilet close to hand, but observational research shows that most people just want to use a convenient convenience!

59.112 Solutions to the problem are varied. Community toilet schemes (where venue owners are paid an annual fee to permit the public use of their toilets) are potentially useful, but unproven in terms of its efficacy in preventing street urination. Pissoirs or pop-up toilets are another solution, though only for men, and ones that have potential impacts on other users of the public realm after dark – it's not the nicest thing to see a man in the middle of a pavement urinating, even if it's into an officially sanctioned urinal. A key role here could be business improvement districts with a night time element providing staffed public toilets as part of their mandate.

59.113 However, ultimately, with an industry worth over £60 billion a year, is it really so hard to envision providing it with the proper infrastructure, including public toilets to enhance the consumer experience for all?

E CONCLUSION

59.114 In some ways, the provision of public toilets is a barometer for how seriously we are prepared to take the design for the night time economy and the urban after dark experience more generally. Do we see the night time economy as an arena that is reactive/regulatory/enforceable or a space of vision/investment/proactivity/celebration? Of course the answer is that we need both. But the tragic irony is that for one of the UK's most important and successful industries, we are blinded by the limited returns of the former to the huge possibilities of the latter.

59.115 It is clear that the after dark design of the town or city, its neighbourhoods and even individual buildings, public spaces and street furniture is crucial to the safety and attractiveness of a destination. It is for planners and urban designers to lead on after dark design, but a whole range of other specialties and interested parties must also be engaged in that process.

59.116 This means bringing developers, licensing officers, transport planners, lighting engineers, disability and minority groups and health professionals, as well as the community and visitors, into the design processes. As a practice, 'after dark design' remains far too ad hoc; organisations such as the Royal Town Planning Institute, the Royal Institute of British Architecture and the Landscape Institute need to be working much more closely with licensing, property and town centre management bodies to define and spread best practice in the area of design for the night.

59.117 Crucially those 'designing' our cities (in the broadest sense) need to understand a thousand fold better the challenges and opportunities presented by the night time economy in creating vibrant, socially and economically successful places. The agenda is radical but not revolutionary – upon it depends whether we leave to our children civilising places of delight, an aim to which anyone who has read this far in this book should aspire.

Financing the management of the night time economy

There is no such thing as a good tax

Winston Churchill

Introduction

In the obscure parlour of a low public house, in the filthiest part of Little Saffron Hill; a dark and gloomy den, where a flaring gas-light burnt all day in the winter-time; and where no ray of sun ever shone in the summer: there sat, brooding over a little pewter measure and a small glass, strongly impregnated with the smell of liquor, a man in a velveteen coat, drab shorts, half boots, and stockings, who even by that dim light no experienced agent of the police would have hesitated for one instant to recognise as Mr. William Sikes.

Oliver Twist, Charles Dickens

60.01 In this Part, we turn our attention to financing the management of the night time economy. This comprises administration of the licensing system itself, its enforcement and the general upkeep and development of the public realm. In an era in which private funds are tight, investment limited and public coffers diminishing, the subject is of utmost importance. This is not the place to debate government policy, but as the state shrinks it is important to open channels of contribution from the private sector. Much recent legislation has been drafted with that end in view.

Funding sources:
Fees
Late night levy
Community Infrastructure Levy
Planning obligations
Business Improvement Districts

60.02 Chapter 61 will cover the new fees regime introduced by the Police Reform and Social Responsibility Act 2011. This is intended to enable authorities to recover a greater level of fees from licensees to fund the administration of the licensing system. Whether it succeeds in this aspiration will be considered.

60.03 Chapter 62 deals with the late night levy, a new taxation regime also introduced by the 2011 legislation, which entitles authorities to recover from those with the right to trade in alcohol after midnight a levy to be split between the authority and the police and to be used principally for the prevention of crime and disorder.

60.04   Chapter 63 contains an explanation of the Community Infrastructure Levy, another tax which may be applied to those developing land in the area of the authority so as to take a share of the uplift in value of the land and apply it to the common good.

60.05   Chapter 64 deals with planning obligations, which are agreements or unilateral obligations entered into by those seeking planning permission, which can contain promises to pay capital or period sums, and which can again be used for the common good.

60.06   In addition, Chapter 57 has already covered Business Improvement Districts, or BIDs. This scheme enables businesses within a defined area to vote to pay an extra sum, to be collected as part of non-domestic rates, to fund particular initiatives. The advantage of the scheme is that use of the funds is in the hands of the BID company itself, so that payers obtain a high degree of control over how the sums are to be spent for their benefit.

60.07   Far-sighted authorities ought to consider these schemes in the round to ensure that they are raising sufficient funds from the private sector, but without risking driving local businesses into penury or, just as bad, deterring investors altogether. But the public sector is not, and may never again be, a cash cow. Thus, the role of the public authority must become that of fund-raiser and conductor, and judicious use of these powers is liable over time to foster better leisure economies for all.

Chapter 61

The fees regime

If you like to be a jitterbug,
first thing you must do is get a jug
put whisky wine and gin within and shake it all up,
and then begin

Cab Calloway

A INTRODUCTION

61.01 The Licensing Act 2003 gave power to the Secretary of State to prescribe fees for the different types of application under the Act. Licensing authorities enjoyed no discretion in the matter – the fees they charged were those set by the Secretary of State.

61.02 The Police Reform and Social Responsibility Act 2011 enabled the Secretary of State to give licensing authorities autonomy over fees, so that they could set their own fees on the basis of full cost recovery. Those authorities, therefore, whose costs were higher, perhaps by dint of local wage rates, a greater degree of staff activity per application or higher costs generally, might be entitled to charge more rather than being constrained by the mean rates inherent in regulations.

61.03 However, Parliament left out of account the effect of the Provision of Services Regulations 2009[1] which implement the European Services Directive 2006[2] and which significantly constrain the ability of licensing authorities to charge fees going beyond the cost of the authorisation procedure themselves.

---

[1]   SI 2009/2999.
[2]   2006/123/EC.

61.04   This all came to light in the case of *R (Hemming) v Westminster City Council*, in which the decision of Keith J[3] was upheld in a landmark judgment by the Court of Appeal.[4] There is no question but that the judgment will prevent the implementation of the Police Reform and Social Responsibility Act 2011 fees provisions in their current form. The extent of its actual impact will be considered below. However the effect of the judgment, or rather the effect of the Directive and Regulations as determined by the Court of Appeal, may well be to have rendered unlawful even the existing fees regulations.

61.05   The conclusion will be that the government does not have a secure foothold with the current fees regulations, or an alternative foothold in the 2011 Act. It is likely to have no alternative but to legislate in such a way as to bring fees under the Licensing Act 2003 into conformity with the Services Directive and its implementing Regulations. If that is right, then this chapter comes to be written at a transformative point in the funding of licensing in particular and, indeed, of regulation in general. It is too early to state how the government is likely to resolve the situation, but when it does its solution will be described in a supplement to this edition.

B   THE COMMON LAW OF LICENSING FEES

61.06   Where a statute leaves the licensing authority to fix a fee, or requires it to fix a reasonable fee, the amount of the fee is governed by the common law.

61.07   In setting out the common law principles, the starting point must be the judgment of Forbes J in *R v Westminster City Council ex parte Hutton*.[5] This concerned the determination of licensing fees for sex shops under the Local Government (Miscellaneous Provisions) Act 1982, which required an applicant for the grant or renewal of a licence to pay a reasonable fee determined by the licensing authority.[6]

61.08   Forbes J decided, first of all, that this gave a wide discretion to the authority in setting the fee. He said:

> 'I regard it as virtually axiomatic in this field that this court has no duty, or power, in such circumstances to decide what in the court's view is a reasonable fee. The determination of the amount lies in the sphere of policy with which the court will not interfere except on the well-known principles, summarised by Lord Greene MR in *Associated Provincial*

3   [2012] EWHC 1260 (Admin).
4   [2013] EWCA Civ 591.
5   (1985) 83 LGR 461.
6   Schedule 3, para 19.

Picture Houses v Wednesbury Corporation[7] ... Of those the two relevant here are that the committee should not take into account irrelevant material and that it should not act perversely.'[8]

61.09 Second of all, counsel conceded, but the court would no doubt have so found had he not, that it is permissible for the authority, when considering the level of fees, to be 'guided by a policy that the ratepayers should, so far as is reasonable, be relieved of the burden of paying the cost of administering the provisions for the control of sex establishments in the city.'[9]

61.10 Third, Forbes J made it clear that such costs included third party enforcement. He was untroubled by the administrative machinery operated by the council, which:

'... provided ... not only for processing licence applications but also for inspecting premises after the grant of licences and for what might be called vigilant policing of establishments within the city in order to detect and prosecute those who operated sex establishments without licences.'[10]

61.11 Fourth, Forbes J dealt with the question of what should happen if an authority incurs a deficit in a particular year. Does it have to swallow it, so that the deficit is effectively paid from its reserves or met by the general ratepayer? Or can it bring the deficit forward so that it is met by licensees in the following year through the medium of an increased licensing fee? Forbes J had no difficulty with the latter proposition. He was unpersuaded by the argument that this might mean that a higher burden falls on licensees who might not have been licensed in the previous year, so that they are effectively being penalised for the failure of the authority to recoup a sufficient sum in the previous year. This, he said was inherent in a system of local government finance which sets out to balance the books. In a system in which the true costs are not verifiable until the year end, there is always a danger that there will be a current year deficit, so 'the only sensible way to fix the level of the charge is to take one year with another.'

61.12 Similar conclusions were reached by the Divisional Court in *R v Manchester City Council ex parte King*[11] which dealt with another part of the Local Government (Miscellaneous Provisions) Act 1982, this time Schedule 4, which concerns street trading. Schedule 4, paragraph 9 permitted a council to charge such fees as they considered reasonable for the grant or renewal of a street trading licence or a street trading consent. In this case, the council decided to increase fees by a factor of ten, apparently to reflect what

---

7 [1948] 1 KB 223.
8 (1985) 83 LGR 461, p 518.
9 *R v Westminster City Council ex parte Hutton*, p 516.
10 *R v Westminster City Council ex parte Hutton*, p 517.
11 (1991) 89 LGR 696.

it considered to be a commercial charge for the authorisations. Its decision was struck down. Roch J held that:

> 'The fees charged ... must be related to the street trading scheme operated by the district council and the costs of operating that scheme. The district council may charge such fees as they reasonably consider will cover the total cost of operating the street trading scheme or such lesser part of the cost of operating the street trading scheme as they consider reasonable.'[12]

61.13 Further, he stated that the authority was not confined to the cost of issuing licences. Instead, he said:

> 'They may take into account the costs which they will incur in operating the street trading scheme, including the prosecution of those who trade in the streets without licences.'[13]

61.14 Nolan LJ described as a fallacy the notion that the fee-creating power 'authorises the council to use their licensing powers as an income-producing asset.' The Act, he stated, was not a fiscal measure.[14]

61.15 Nothing which followed those authorities cast any doubt on their correctness. Indeed, King was cited by the Home Office in its Circular No 13/2000: 'Public Entertainment Licensing – Fees and Conditions'. Authorities were particularly enjoined to bear in mind the following consideration, amongst others:

> 'Cost recovery: this relates to reasonable charges to cover administration, inspection and enforcement in respect of public entertainment licensing only. Anything over and above that which is included in the calculation of the public entertainment licence fees would be *ultra vires.*'

The effect of Hemming on the common law

61.16 The case of *Hemming* was brought to the Administrative Court by seven operators of thirteen Soho sex shops. None of them had previously been the subject of enforcement action. The service they derived from their licensing authority, Westminster City Council, was an administrative annual renewal and one or two short licensing inspections each year. For this, they paid an annual renewal fee of £29,102, which had been set by the council's licensing applications sub-committee for the licensing year 2005/06 pursuant

---

12   *R v Manchester City Council ex parte King*, p 709.
13   *R v Manchester City Council ex parte King*, p 710.
14   *R v Manchester City Council ex parte King*, p 712. Nolan LJ noted that his conclusions aligned with those of the Divisional Court, albeit without argument, in *R v Greater London Council ex parte The Rank Organisation Ltd*, The Times, 19 February 1982.

to the powers in Schedule 3, paragraph 19 of the Local Government (Miscellaneous Provisions) Act 1982. Of that fee, £2,667 was ostensibly for the administration of the application and £26,435 for the management of the licensing regime, in effect the pursuit and prosecution of illegal, unlicensed third party operators. The legality of charging the latter sum to lawful, licensed operators is considered below. What is of relevance here is that, after 2005/06, the fee was not determined by the licensing applications sub-committee or any other body with delegated authority to do so until finally the council determined fees for 2012/13, but even then without taking into account any surpluses or deficits from previous years.

61.17 In so far as it dealt with common law principles, *Hemming* raised two points. The first was whether surpluses need to be carried forward from year to year, or only deficits. The second is what happens when the fee has not been duly determined.

61.18 As to the first point, Keith J held:

'26. ... It does not necessarily follow that just because a local authority acts lawfully in carrying forward a deficit from one year to the next; it acts unlawfully when it declines to carry forward a surplus. But if the justification for carrying forward a deficit from one year to the next is because it is not known in the current year what the expenditure on administering and enforcing the system will be, that reasoning should apply to a surplus just as much. If a local authority were to be treated as acting lawfully if it failed to carry forward a surplus from one year to the next, the making of profits would become legitimized.

27. It follows that the Council has to determine the annual licence fee for sex establishments by adjusting what would otherwise have been the appropriate fee to reflect any previous deficit or surplus.'

61.19 As to the second point, Keith J held that where a fee is demanded which has not been properly determined, the licensee is entitled to restitution of the fee. However, the licensee should not be entitled to all of his money back. The council has only been unjustly enriched to the extent that the fees paid exceed the fees which would have been determined. Therefore, the restitutionary entitlement is merely to the excess of the fees paid over the sum which should have been determined.[15]

These elements of the judgment of Keith J were not appealed by Westminster City Council and so may be regarded as authoritative.

61.20 A further matter considered by Keith J was whether a licensing authority with discretion to determine licence fees is obliged to do so annually. The plain answer was that it is not. It can determine for one, two or

---

[15] The principle of restitution of the excess derived from the judgment of the Privy Council in *Waikato Regional Airport Ltd v AG* [2003] UKPC 50.

more years ahead. Or it can determine the licence fee indefinitely,[16] ie on a rolling basis, provided of course that when it comes to redetermine the fee it brings into account past deficits and surpluses accruing since the fee was last determined.

61.21   The principles established in this line of cases may therefore be summarised as follows:

(1)   A licensing authority given power to determine licence fees has a wide discretion to be exercised on ordinary administrative principles.

(2)   The fee must be determined by a body with delegated authority to do so.

(3)   An authority may determine the fees for a fixed period or on a rolling basis.

(4)   If the fee for any year is not determined by a body with delegated authority to do so, or is not determined at all, then any demand for payment of the fees is *ultra vires* and subject to restitution, less the amount of the reasonable fee for the year(s) concerned.

(5)   In determining fees, both previous deficits and surpluses must be brought into account.

(6)   The authority may not use the licensing regime to make a profit.

(7)   To the extent that the licensing authority is entitled to recover particular categories of costs, it may operate on the basis of full cost recovery, so as to ensure that licensees pick up all of those costs and none of them fall on the general rate payers in the area.

61.22   All of those principles apply and survive the Services Directive, the Provision of Services Regulations 2009 and the Court of Appeal judgment in *Hemming*. The principle which is upturned by that trio of documents concerns which costs may actually be recovered as part of the licensing system. Until *Hemming*, it was thought that, in line with Hutton and King, all of the costs of administering the system were recoverable as part of the licence fee, including the cost of prosecution of illegal third party operators. That thinking has been shown to be fallacious, at least since the commencement of the Provision of Services Regulations 2009 on 28 December of that year. It is, therefore, to those Regulations and their European parentage that we must now turn.

C THE SERVICES DIRECTIVE

61.23   The underpinning philosophy of the Directive is neatly expressed in the first of its Recitals:

---

[16]   *Hemming* [2012] EWHC 1260 (Admin), para 21.

'The elimination of barriers to the development of service activities between Member States is essential in order to strengthen the integration of the peoples of Europe and to promote balanced and sustainable economic and social progress.'

61.24 The Directive sought to do this in many ways, which are outwith the scope of this chapter. However, the objective of administrative simplification in order to promote the service economy was summarised in the 49th recital, which stated that its modernising action was:

'... intended to eliminate the delays, costs and dissuasive effects which arise, for example, from unnecessary or excessively complex and burdensome procedures, the duplication of procedures, the "red tape" involved in submitting documents, the arbitrary use of powers by the competent authorities, indeterminate or excessively long periods before a response is given, the limited duration of validity of authorisations granted and disproportionate fees and penalties.'

61.25 It was this penultimate aim, to remove disproportionate fees, which was at play in *Hemming*. For Article 13.2 states:

'Authorisation procedures and formalities shall not be dissuasive and shall not unduly complicate or delay the provision of the service. They shall be easily accessible and any charges which the applicant may incur from their application shall be reasonable and proportionate to the cost of the authorisation procedures and shall not exceed the cost of the procedures.'

It will immediately be seen that it is not enough that the fees are reasonable and proportionate to the cost of the authorisation procedures. That is only one thrust of the sword. The killer blow is that the licence fee shall not exceed the cost of the authorisation procedures.

61.26 The Directive was transposed into UK law by the Provision of Services Regulations 2009, regulation 18(4) of which provides:

'Any charges provided for by a competent authority which applicants may incur under an authorisation scheme must be reasonable and proportionate to the cost of the procedures and formalities under the scheme and must not exceed the cost of those procedures and formalities.'

61.27 The main question in *Hemming* was whether these procedures and formalities comprised merely authorisation procedures on grant and renewal of licences, including of course the costs of investigating compliance with licences as part of the renewal process. Or did they include the wider costs of the enforcement of the licensing regime, including against unlicensed operators? Keith J unhesitatingly decided that they merely included the former costs. He put the matter in this way:

'36. ... The relevant costs are the costs of the procedures and formalities under the *authorisation* scheme, and those costs are, on the face of it, the costs involved in the process by which those who are to be, or are no longer to be, licensees under the scheme are determined.'

61.28 Westminster City Council appealed to the Court of Appeal, complaining that Keith J's interpretation would critically undermine not only its licensing regime, but many other authorisation regimes including those relating to solicitors and the Bar. It argued that the Directive, which should be construed purposively, was not intended to undo rational principles of licence fee determination which had operated in member states for many years. And it advanced the theory that the Directive was only intended to limit that element of the fee which reflected the actual costs of the authorisation process, and not further fees which really represented the cost of belonging to the scheme rather than applying to join it, and which could include the costs of enforcement. All of its arguments were unanimously rejected by the Court of Appeal.

61.29 Beatson LJ, with whose judgment the other members of the court agreed, pointed out that to permit states which had previously based licence fees on enforcement costs to continue to do so would create a distinction between such states which had and had not done so. This would be inimical to the removal of barriers to entry to the internal market and may undermine the unity and effectiveness of Community law.[17]

61.30 As for the characterisation of the larger part of the council's licence fee as a kind of membership fee outwith the scope of the Directive, this argument was also rejected, for a reason which is resonant in the present context, as will appear below. He said:

'106. ... But the regime of the Services Directive and the 2009 Regulations applies not only to schemes requiring authorisation in order to have "access" to a service activity, but also to schemes that require authorisation "to exercise" that service activity.[18] The relevant proportion of the £26,435 appears to be payable to enable, i.e. to authorise, an operator "to exercise" the activity.'

61.31 The remaining question answered by *Hemming* is what costs can be characterised as the cost of the authorisation procedures in question. This was dealt with by Keith J, who stated at paragraph 41:

'Those procedures are the steps which an applicant for a licence has to take if he wishes to be granted a licence or to have his licence renewed. And when you talk about the cost of those procedures, you are talking about the administrative costs involved, and the costs of vetting applicants (in the case of applications for a licence) and the costs of

---

[17] *Hemming* [2013] EWCA Civ 591, para 100.
[18] See European Services Directive 2006, Art 4.6.

investigating their compliance with the terms of their licence (in the case of applications for the renewal of their licence). There is simply no room for the costs of the "authorisation procedures" to include costs which are significantly in excess of those costs.'

61.32 In *Hemming*, the facts before the court were quite stark. The costs at issue were in essence the costs of prosecuting illegal, unlicensed operators and not the costs of enforcement against licensees themselves. The dividing line between legitimate and illegitimate costs was, however, investigated further by the Court of Appeal although what it had to say on the subject was arguably *obiter dictum*. The proper interpretation of its judgment is submitted to be that costs of compliance monitoring of licensees fall on the right side of the line but costs of enforcement against licensees, eg through reviews and prosecution, are not authorisation procedures and so fall on the wrong side of it.

61.33 As shown above, Keith J held the line to be one which separates compliance from enforcement. The Court of Appeal did not attempt to move the line, although some of Beatson LJ's language, which includes the phrase 'compliance and enforcement' in the same breath, needs to be understood in the context of the judgment which he was considering, which the court approved and which drew the distinction between compliance and enforcement. That this was the Court of Appeal's intention is apparent from paragraph 103 of Beatson LJ's judgment, in which he stated:

'It is clear and undisputed that costs incurred in investigating the suitability of an applicant for a licence can be reflected in the fee. In the case of an application to renew a licence, I consider that the costs of monitoring the applicant's continued suitability can include the costs of monitoring compliance with the terms of their licences in the past.'

61.34 It is right to say that on this point, the judgment of the Court of Appeal leaves some room for interpretation. For example, Beatson LJ appeared to contemplate that the system of disciplining of barristers may be an authorisation procedure, when it is to all intents and purposes a review procedure. However, a reading of the judgment against the judgment of Keith J, and the terms of the Directive and Regulations themselves, leads to the conclusion that, on balance the line is properly drawn between compliance and enforcement procedures in the case of licensees.

D APPLICATION TO THE LICENSING ACT 2003

61.35 The application of the Directive and the Regulations (as applied in *Hemming*) to the system of fees under the Licensing Act 2003 needs to be considered in two parts. First, there is the question of how it applies to the current system, which involves the Secretary of State prescribing fees for different types of application under the Act. Second, there is the question of how it applies to the changes wrought by the Police Reform and Social Responsibility Act 2011, which if implemented would permit authorities to determine their own fees.

The current system

61.36 First, the current system. Sections 55, 92, 100 and 133 of the Licensing Act 2003 provide for the payment of prescribed fees in relation to applications in respect of premises licences, club premises certificates, temporary events notices and personal licences respectively. The fees were prescribed by the Licensing Act 2003 (Fees) Regulations 2005.[19] There is nothing inherently wrong with central prescription of licensing fees, even if it proceeds on a formulaic basis, provided that it is designed to achieve cost recovery and no more.[20]

61.37 However, the difficulty with the 2005 Regulations is that the prescribed fees were calculated in part on the costs of enforcement of the regime, now outlawed by the Court of Appeal in *Hemming*. The Explanatory Memorandum to the Regulations stated:

'7.1 The Government intends that the new regime in relation to the use of premises for licensable activities should achieve the recovery of the full costs of administration, inspection and enforcement from the payment of fees made by those wishing to use premises and using premises for such activities.'

61.38 Moreover, as Beatson LJ expressly observed in *Hemming*:

'68. An example of encouraging fees to reflect enforcement costs is the Regulatory Impact Assessment for the Licensing Act 2003 (Transitional conversions fees) Order 2005 SI 2005 No. 80 and the Licensing Act 2003 (Fees) Regulations 2005 SI 2005 No. 79. The Impact Statement states that "the objective of the Regulations and Order is to set the level of these fees, so far as possible, at a level that would achieve full recovery of the administrative, inspection and enforcement costs falling on licensing authorities' associated with their licensing under the 2003 Act" (paragraph 2(i)) and "the Government has consistently expressed the aim of ensuring that the costs of local authorities administration, inspection and enforcement associated with the new regime should not fall on the central or local taxpayer, but on those choosing to engage in licensable activities" (paragraph 2(ii)).'

61.39 That this was the policy aim of the Government in setting fees under the Licensing Act 2003 was made explicit by the Parliamentary Under-Secretary of State at the Department for Culture, Media and Sport

---

[19]   SI 2005/79.
[20]   See e g *Re Shopping Centres Licensing: European Commission v Spain*, Case C-400/08, [2011] 2 CMLR 50, considered by Beatson LJ in *Hemming* at paras 80–84 and 103.

(Lord McIntosh of Haringey), who, speaking for the Government on the fees regulations, said:

> 'So the focus of this debate on fees must be on the recovery of the full costs associated with the administration, inspection and enforcement required to deliver the new legislation in operational terms in respect of those premises.'[21]

61.40 That the objective of the fees regime was in part to recover enforcement costs was confirmed by Sir Les Elton's Report of the Independent Fees Review Panel,[22] which stated:

> '2.2 The objective of the Regulations is to set the level of these fees so far as possible to allow licensing authorities full recovery of their legitimate administration, inspection and enforcement costs of the new regime, while at the same time achieve arrangements which are fair to businesses of differing sizes and to non commercial organisations and other individuals seeking licences.'

61.41 All of this passed muster at the time. It was wholly consonant with the tenets of the common law that a licensing authority could set fees calculated to recover the full costs of its regime, including enforcement costs, from licensees. If a licensing authority could do so directly, then the Secretary of State could do so with the same end in view. However, as soon as the Provision of Services Regulations 2009 came into force on 28 December 2009, this became unlawful.

61.42 Thus, it is submitted that fees under the Fees Regulations have to be recalculated so as to remove the element of enforcement from their calculation.

The Police Reform and Social Responsibility Act 2011

61.43 Section 121 of this Act inserted new sections 197A and 197B into the Licensing Act 2003, principally to permit licensing authorities to set their own fees and to make explicit that they must seek to recover the broader costs of the system in so doing. At the date of writing, no commencement order has been made in relation to these provisions.

Granted, the Secretary of State may continue to set fees, and in so doing have regard to the costs of any licensing authority to whom the fee is to be payable which are referable to the discharge of the function to which the fee relates and the general costs of any such licensing authority.[23]

---

[21] HL Deb, 24 February 2005, Col 1387.
[22] December 2006.
[23] Licensing Act 2003, s 197A(2).

However the beating heart of these new provisions was to enable the Secretary of State to provide that authorities should determine their own fees.[24]

61.44 The new provisions go on to specify with some particularity how the authority will calculate and set out to recover its costs, which are divided for these purposes into 'direct' costs (although that expression is not actually used) and general costs. Section 197A(7) provides:

'In determining the amount of the fee, the licensing authority must seek to secure that the income from fees of that kind will equate, as nearly as possible, to the aggregate of –

(a) the licensing authority's costs referable to the discharge of the function to which the fee relates, and

(b) a reasonable share of the licensing authority's general costs ... '

61.45 As to the costs set out in section 197A(7)(a), the direct costs, flesh is put on the bones of that term by section 197B(2), which defines them as:

'(a) administrative costs of the licensing authority so far as they are referable to the discharge of the function, and

(b) costs in connection with the discharge of the function which are incurred by the licensing authority acting –
(i) under this Act, but
(ii) in a capacity other than that of licensing authority (whether that of local authority, local planning authority or any other authority).'

61.46 As to the general costs set out in section 197A(7)(b), these are given further definition in section 197B(3) as:

'... costs of the authority so far as they are referable to the discharge of functions under this Act in respect of which no fee is otherwise chargeable and include, in particular –

(a) costs referable to the authority's functions under section 5;[25]

(b) costs of or incurred in connection with the monitoring and enforcement of Parts 7[26] and 8[27] of this Act;

(c) costs incurred in exercising functions conferred by section 197A.'

While some part of those costs is clearly within the bounds of the Services Directive, other parts stand clearly outside, in particular costs incurred in relation to enforcement of the criminal provisions of the Act and powers of closure. As such, it would, it is submitted, be unlawful for the Secretary of

---

[24] Licensing Act 2003, s 197A(3).
[25] The determination and publication of licensing policy.
[26] The main offences under the Act.
[27] Closure of premises.

State to promulgate regulations which permit the collection of such fees, or to prescribe fees based on such costs.

61.47   One remaining matter is whether the strictures just described apply to renewal fees in the same way as they apply to application fees. It is submitted that they do, essentially for three reasons. The first is that described by Beatson LJ in *Hemming* when rejecting the council's argument that the Directive only applies to application fees and not subsequent fees, which are properly characterised as fees for being in rather than being authorised to join the scheme. He held that the Directive does not just apply to gaining access to a service activity but to the exercise of the activity itself. Second, further force is given to Beatson LJ's approach by sections 55A and 92A of the Licensing Act 2003, which require suspension for non-payment of annual fees for premises licences and club premises certificate fees respectively. This underlines that these fees are very much for the exercise of the service activity: in default of payment the right to exercise the activity is suspended. Third, were any other interpretation to be given to the Directive, the provisions would lack all efficacy: a member state could simply detach the bulk of the application fee and characterise it as a membership fee, leaving in place a nominal application fee, and so sidestep the entire object of Article 13.2. Given that a purposive approach is to be taken to the interpretation of EU provisions[28] it seems highly unlikely that a differential approach would be taken by the European Court of Justice to year 1 application fees and year 2 renewal fees.

61.48   It remains to be seen how the Secretary of State will react to the judgment in *Hemming*. However, it is submitted that to accord with the judgment it will be necessary to pass regulations which either prescribe fees reflecting only the costs of authorisation procedures and nothing more, or which allow licensing authorities to set fees on that restricted basis.

E   SUSPENSION

61.49   One of the problems with the Licensing Act 2003 was that it gave licensing authorities no effective recourse for non-payment of fees. A fee was treated as a civil debt, enforceable by claim in the county court, which was rarely economic to pursue. Section 55A now requires the licensing authority to suspend the premises licence if the licensee has not paid the annual fee.

61.50   The authority may not suspend during a grace period of 21 days, provided that during that period the failure to pay was due to an administrative error or, before or at the time the fee became due, the holder notified the authority in writing that the holder disputed liability. These provisions create some difficulty for licensing authorities. How are they to know that there has been an administrative error? If there has been such an error then any

---

[28]   *Litster v Forth Dry Dock Engineering Co Ltd* [1990] 1 AC 546.

suspension would be unlawful. It is therefore strongly recommended that prior to serving a notice of suspension, the authority ascertains from the licensee precisely why the fee has not been paid. If, however, the authority determines to suspend the licence, it must give two working days notice of the suspension. Then, the licensee may either prevent the suspension taking effect or (as the case may be) cause it to come to an end by paying the requisite fee.

61.51 Similar provisions apply to club premises certificates under section 92A.

F CONCLUSION

61.52 In an age of austerity, there was no doubt attraction, and not a little nod to localism, in provisions allowing authorities to set their own fees and in so doing to bring in all of the costs of the system, including enforcement. However, this attempt to shift the costs of the licensing system onto licensees and away from the general public has fallen foul of a still higher objective – that those wishing to ply their services in Europe should not have administrative barriers strewn in their way. Just as it is in general for the state to enforce the criminal law, and just as many functions of local authorities – health and safety and environmental health to name but two – are funded by the general ratepayer, so the effect of the Directive is that those who wish to provide services should only be paying the marginal costs of the authorisation procedures for the privilege of doing so. How the UK government will bring itself into compliance remains to be seen, and will be covered in a supplement to this book.

62

Late night levy

And that is called paying the Dane-geld; but we've proved it again and again, that if once you have paid him the Dane-geld you never get rid of the Dane.

Rudyard Kipling

A INTRODUCTION

62.01 The principle underlying the late night levy is that the polluter pays. It was foreshadowed in the Conservative Manifesto of 2010, which proclaimed: 'Under Labour's lax licensing regime, drink-fuelled violence and disorder are a blight on many communities', and which went on to state that a Conservative government would 'permit local councils to charge more for late night licences to pay for additional policing.' This nascent proposal evolved into the levy brought onto the statute book by the Police Reform and Social Responsibility Act ('PRSRA') 2011.

62.02 The levy is a form of tax, which a licensing authority may choose to impose on those with a licence to supply alcohol on any night of the year between hours which it specifies, which must be no earlier than midnight and no later than 6 am. The authority may grant exemptions and reductions for certain categories of premises specified in regulations. Having collected the levy, the authority must give at least 70% of the net receipts to the police, and may itself spend the balance for purposes set out in regulations.

62.03 The levy is a blunt measure. It has to be imposed across the whole area of the authority or not at all. It applies however often a licence to supply during the specified hours is used, or even if it is not used at all. These factors, together with the bureaucratic nature of the scheme, the proportion of receipts which must be given to the police and the relatively small sums therefore left for use by the licensing authority itself, are likely to conspire to render the late night levy a rarely spotted beast.

B THE LEVY

Who pays?

A person who holds a premises licence or a club premises certificate

Which authorises the supply of alcohol

At a time or times during the late night supply period

On one or more days

In the related payment year[1]

Who is not exempt.[2]

62.04   Each of the elements set out in the box above is worthy of comment.

62.05   Premises licence or club premises certificate. The first point to note is that the levy is payable only by those who hold premises licences and club premises certificates. It does not apply to those who trade under the auspices of temporary event notices. Thus, for operators who wish only to trade occasionally during the late night supply period, an obvious solution to avoid the levy is to vary their licences so as to draw back their licensed hours, and then use their temporary event notice entitlement for their late night trade.

62.06   Supply of alcohol. Second, those caught are only those authorised to sell alcohol. The levy does not apply to those whose business is late night refreshment or regulated entertainment. This may be considered surprising, given that a late night takeaway can sometimes cause as many problems as a bar, but clearly the government's fire was here directed only at the alcohol industry.

62.07   It might also be noted that the operative term is 'authorises the supply of alcohol' rather than 'consumes alcohol'. Therefore, provided that

[1]   PRSRA 2011, s 126.
[2]   PRSRA 2011, s 135.

the authorisation in question does not permit the supply of alcohol during the late night supply period, it does not matter that consumption occurs during that period. The levy is a tax on the right to supply, not consume. Whether this gives rise to a temptation to bars to diminish their hours for supply while leaving intact their closing hours remains to be seen.

62.08 During the late night supply period. So far as the late night supply period is concerned, this is to be determined by the licensing authority, but it must be within the tramlines of midnight to 6 am.[3] For example, it might be 1 am to 5 am or 2 am to 6 am. Authorities might select those hours according to when the key crime and disorder problems arise, or how many premises they wish to catch with their drag-net, or conceivably how many premises they wish to deter from trading late. They may even be influenced by police evidence as to shift patterns. For example if the police showed that bars trading past 3 am caused them to incur the expenses of a whole new shift, the late night supply period might be set at 3 am to cover the cost.

62.09 Whatever hours the authority chooses, they must be the same hours on every night of the year.[4] It is not open to an authority to reflect varying pressures on policing on different days of the week or different weeks of the year by varying the late night supply period. This is another respect in which the levy acts as a blunt instrument.

62.10 On one or more days. It is important to note that the levy does not bite on those who actually supply alcohol during the late night supply period. It is wider than that. It affects those who are <u>authorised</u> to do so. Furthermore, they only need to be authorised to do so on one night during the related payment year. So, for example, a restaurant whose licence gives it extended hours for the sale of alcohol during the late night supply period on Valentine's Day might find itself subject to a levy. From a tax collection point of view, this is of central importance. It means that collection of the levy does not ride on finding premises trading late on a given night in the year. It is simply a desk exercise of identifying those licences and club premises certificate which grant authorisation to do so.

62.11 From a payer's point of view, it may be seen as unfair that a venue which trades late on a few nights, or even one night, a year would be liable to the same levy as a venue which trades late on every night of the year. To some extent this is mitigated by the availability of exemptions, which are discussed below, and also by the ability of premises to vary their authorisations to remove themselves from the levy and trade late under TENS. However, the somewhat crude way in which the levy operates remains worthy of note.

---

[3] PRSRA 2011, s 126(4).
[4] PRSRA 2011, s 126(5).

62.12   In the related payment year. It might have been thought that the obvious means of assessment would be to levy payment on all of those whose authorisations permit the sale of alcohol during the relevant hours on any night in a calendar year, or failing that a defined 365 day period common to all. Instead, the draftsman chose a much more complicated route.

62.13   Here, it is necessary to introduce the concept of the 'levy year'. The first levy year is the year commencing with the date specified by the authority for the introduction of the levy.[5] The second levy year, obviously, is the following year and so on.

62.14   The payment year is, sadly, not always the same as the levy year. If a person holds a relevant late night authorisation at the start of the levy year, then the payment year and the levy year coincide.[6] If, however, a person is granted a late night authorisation during the levy year, then the payment year runs from the date of the grant.[7] Due to an oddity of drafting, it is arguable that in the latter case the second payment year coincides with the levy year. However, to make sense of the regulations it is considered that the better interpretation is that once the payment year is set it continues unaltered until the levy is abolished or the payer ceases to be liable to pay it. In any event, what is for sure is that in any given authority area there will be a variety of different payment years.

62.15   Exemptions. The authority may choose to exempt certain types of premises. However, they may not define their own exemption categories. They can only choose from the list supplied in the relevant regulations. The question of exemptions and reductions is dealt with below.

C   AMOUNT OF LEVY

62.16   The amount of the levy depends upon the rateable value of the premises and, in the case of rateable bands D and E, whether they are used exclusively or primarily for the sale of alcohol for consumption on the premises, in which cases multipliers of two and (just shy of) three apply respectively.[8]

---

5   PRSRA 2011, s 132(1)(a).
6   The Late Night Levy (Application and Administration) Regulations 2012 (SI 2012/2730), reg 3(1).
7   The Late Night Levy (Application and Administration) Regulations 2012, reg 3(2).
8   The Late Night Levy (Application and Administration) Regulations 2012, reg 5, Schs 1 and 2.

Rateable value (£)	Band	Amount (£)
0 – 4,300	A	299
4,301 – 33,000	B	768
33,001 – 87,000	C	1,259
87,001 – 125,000	D	1,365
87,001 – 125,000 Exclusively or primarily alcohol	D	2,730
125,001 +	E	1,493
125,001 + Exclusively or primarily alcohol	E	4,440

Provision is made where the premises form only part of the rateable hereditament and where the premises comprises two or more hereditaments. In the former case, the rateable value of the whole is taken and in the latter the highest value is taken, so there is no wriggle room for licensees when drawing the red lines on their licence application plans.[9]

D EXEMPTIONS AND REDUCTIONS

62.17 Exemptions and reductions are provided for in the Late Night Levy (Expenses, Exemptions and Reductions) Regulations 2012.[10]

Exemptions

Permitted exemptions

Premises with overnight accommodation

Theatres

Cinemas

Bingo halls licensed under Gambling Act 2005 and bingo is the primary activity

Community Amateur Sports Clubs (CASCs)

Community premises

---

9   The Late Night Levy (Application and Administration) Regulations 2012, reg 4.
10   SI 2012/2550.

| Country village pubs |
| Business Improvement Districts (BIDs) |
| New Year's Eve |

62.18 In most authority areas, there will be geographical pockets experiencing higher levels of late night crime and disorder, and some might be characterised as violent crime 'hotspots'. The levy provisions do not allow authorities to levy only premises trading in such places. Rather, the levy applies across the whole area of the authority. This led many to make representations to the government that the levy would amount to an unfair tax on their activity. To take one example, rural pubs, which may not spot a uniformed police officer from year to year, and which have suffered in the recession, objected to paying a levy whose proceeds were likely to be directed principally at town centre crime reduction.

62.19 In consequence, the government specified a number of 'permitted exemption categories' in regulation 4 of the Late Night Levy (Expenses, Exemptions and Reductions) Regulations 2012. These are listed in the table above, with brief commentary set out below. It is important to stress that these exemptions are not automatic. It is for the authority to decide which if any of these exemptions are to apply in its area. In so deciding, it will no doubt take account of economic considerations, and also ask itself whether the particular categories of premises do contribute in any material way to late night crime and disorder.

62.20 Premises with overnight accommodation. This exemption applies to hotels, guest houses, lodging houses or hostels at which the supply of alcohol between midnight and 6 am on any day may only be made to a person who is staying there and for consumption on the premises. The phraseology of this exemption is such that it is not enough that the hotel does not supply except to guests from midnight to 6 am. It must be prevented by a condition from doing so. Moreover, the condition must prevent supply from midnight to 6 am, even if the late night supply period is narrower. This appears to be legislative oversight – certainly it is hard to find a principled reason for it. On the other hand, the supply may be to a resident in the hotel bar – it does not have to be confined to the bedroom by way of room service or a mini bar. Furthermore, it seems that the resident may entertain non-resident friends at the hotel without loss of the exemption; for so long as the supply is made to the resident it does not seem to matter who thereafter consumes the alcohol.

62.21 Theatres. Theatres are potentially exempt where, between midnight and 6 am alcohol may only be supplied for consumption on the premises to ticket holders, guests at private events and those concerned in the performance, organisation or management of the relevant production. Again, this would need to be specified by condition for the exemption to apply. This enables theatres to supply alcohol in their green room as well as their theatre bars and at private or corporate parties, without attracting the levy, provided of course that the authority decides that the exemption should apply.

62.22 Cinemas. A similar exemption potentially applies to cinemas, save that, for obvious reasons, there is no exemption in respect of those concerned in the performance, organisation or management of the venue. In other words, it is only applies to ticket holders and those attending private events which attract the exemption.

62.23 Bingo halls. The bingo halls attracting the exemption are those where there is both an operating and premises licence under the Gambling Act 2005 authorising the playing of bingo at the premises and where the playing of bingo is also the primary activity. So, it is not sufficient if bingo is an activity at the premises and is carried on under an exemption conferred upon pubs and clubs for low stakes bingo under the Gambling Act 2005.[11] The draftsman had in mind traditional bingo clubs, which equally traditionally are not associated with crime and disorder.

62.24 Community Amateur Sports Clubs (CASCs). This exemption extends to CASCs registered for relief from business rates under section 658 of the Corporation Tax Act 2010.

62.25 Community premises. These are premises in which the premises licence contains the alternative licence condition under section 25A of the Licensing Act 2003, releasing it from the obligation of having a designated premises supervisor and a personal licensee, and instead permitting all alcohol supplies to be made or authorised by a management committee.[12] Again, the thinking is that such venues are unlikely to be associated with significant crime and disorder, and were they to be so they would have been unlikely to have been permitted to trade under the more emollient alternative licence condition.

62.26 Country village pubs. This exemption applies to public houses in rural settlements designated for rural rate relief in Part III of the Local Government Finance Act 1988. This exemption was drafted to attempt to meet the concerns of rural pubs that they would be mulcted of the levy without enjoying its fruits. If they are fortunate enough to be sited in a relevant rural settlement, then it lies within the gift of their licensing authority to exempt them.

62.27 Business Improvement Districts (BIDs). BIDS are dealt with in Chapter 56. Their essence is that premises vote for an increment to their

---

[11] Gambling Act 2005, Parts 12 and 13.
[12] See further Chapter 15 (The Premises Licence).

rates bill to defray the cost of activities conducted for their mutual benefit. Where the BID premises are making a financial contribution towards initiatives that tackle alcohol-related crime and disorder between midnight and 6 am the licensing authority has a discretion to exempt them from the levy. Regulation 2 constrains the discretion somewhat, in that the BID arrangements have to be established *inter alia* for purposes which 'result in, or are likely to result in, the reduction or prevention of crime and disorder in connection with the supply of alcohol between midnight and 6 am at premises in relation to which a relevant late night authorisation has effect.' It seems, therefore that the licensing authority would have to make a judgment that the BID purposes are at least likely to result in the reduction of crime and disorder before any discretion even arises.

62.28   NewYear's Eve. The final potential exemption is a very narrow one. It applies only to premises whose <u>only</u> entitlement to supply alcohol for consumption on the premises is between midnight and 6 am on New Year's Eve. If they are entitled to supply alcohol during those hours on any other night of the year, the exemption does not apply. The exemption works in a strange, in fact unjust, way. Take an authority which wishes to adopt the hours 2 am to 6 am as its late night supply period because the late night crime about which it is concerned occurs after 2 am. The Dog and Duck has a licence entitling it to trade until 1 am on seven nights per week, but throughout the night on New Year's Eve. Logic dictates that it should be entitled to an exemption. The Regulations dictate otherwise. The fact that it can trade beyond midnight on more than one night a year disentitles it to an exemption, even though the only night it can trade during levy hours is New Year's Eve. Whether or not this was intended, it is the law.

Permitted reductions

Permitted reductions
Relevant arrangements
Low rateable value

62.29   The government decided that there should be a discretion to grant reductions in the levy to two categories of premises, set out in the table above. The amount of the reduction is 30%, whether the premises falls within one or both categories, and regardless of how many 'relevant arrangements' the premises participates in. The reduction categories are contained in regulation 5.

62.30   Relevant arrangements. This reduction is intended to benefit members of schemes such as Purple Flag, Best Bar None and Pub Watch.

However, the phraseology of the regulation is such that it is likely, in most cases, to be self-defeating.

62.31 First, the definition of 'relevant arrangement' is that the arrangement must be an arrangement which is established for purposes which 'result in, or are likely to result in, the reduction or prevention of crime and disorder in connection with the supply of alcohol between midnight and 6 am at premises in relation to which a relevant late night authorisation has effect.'[13] Therefore, the authority will need to come to a view as to whether the likelihood test is satisfied.

62.32 Second, the arrangement must have members. While membership may plausibly be claimed for Best Bar None[14] and Pub Watch[15] participants, this is less easy to argue for public realm-based schemes such as Purple Flag.[16]

62.33 Third, the arrangement must 'require' members to take steps to promote the relevant purposes. This represents something of a misunderstanding of how voluntary schemes work. They are, on the whole, intended to be aspirational and voluntary rather than coercive: carrots and not sticks.

62.34 Fourth, the arrangement must contain provision for the cessation of membership of the member who has failed to take steps to promote the relevant purpose. Mercifully, it does not actually require the scheme to expel non-conforming members, but even the provision for expulsion runs counter to the ethos of most voluntary schemes, in which peer pressure, cajoling and mutual support are the order of the day.

62.35 The structure of the permitted reduction category is to require the mutual co-operation on which such schemes are based to be replaced by behaviour as quasi-licensing authorities. This is not a mantle which those running the schemes want or believe would work in any case, all to achieve a 30% reduction in the amount of the levy.

62.36 While, therefore, the reduction category exists, it remains very much to be seen whether it will be given life beyond the arid print of the statutory instrument.

62.37 To complete the view of the author,[17] it is highly regrettable that the opportunity was not taken, both in the interests of localism and in order to promote worthwhile voluntary schemes, to permit full exemptions for such schemes, but merely to permit reductions It is still harder to rationalise the

---

[13] See Late Night Levy (Application and Administration) Regulations 2012, reg 2.
[14] See Chapter 55.
[15] See Chapter 54.
[16] See Chapter 53.
[17] Who declares an interest as the current Chairman of both Best Bar None and Purple Flag.

highly restrictive terms in which qualification for the reduction is drafted. It is hoped that this is a topic to which the Secretary of State will return swiftly.

62.38   Low rateable value. A potential reduction is conferred where the ratepayer may sell alcohol for consumption on the premises only, and the rateable value does not exceed £12,000.

Other matters

62.39   It will have been discerned from the above account that the phraseology of the exemption and reduction categories is not entirely straightforward. A decision to include (or not to include) a category is challengeable only by way of judicial review. What may be more problematic is, having included a category, ascertaining whether particular premises fall within it. It is highly to be recommended that the authority seek to clarify this with individual premises before the start of the first levy year, to avoid payment disputes during the currency of the levy year particularly since, as will be seen, the penalty for non-payment is suspension.

E   THE TEST

62.40   The licensing authority is given the sole discretion to decide that the late night levy is to apply in its area.[18] As stated above, it cannot decide that the levy is to apply in part only of its area.[19]

The Act provides that in making its decision as to levy:

'... a licensing authority must consider–

(a)   the costs of policing and other arrangements for the reduction or prevention of crime and disorder, in connection with the supply of alcohol between midnight and 6 am, and

(b)   having regard to those costs, the desirability of raising revenue to be applied in accordance with section 131.'[20]

62.41   Section 131, which prescribes how the levy receipts may be used, is dealt with below. In essence, section 131 and its accompanying regulations dictate that at least 70% of the net levy receipts must be given to the police.

62.42   A crucial question is whether section 125(3) is exhaustive, in that it sets out a complete list of relevant factors for the authority to consider. Or,

---

[18]   PRSRA 2011, s 125(2).
[19]   PRSRA 2011, s 125(4).
[20]   PRSRA 2011, s 125(3).

alternatively, does it merely set out the factors which an authority <u>must</u> consider, while leaving it open to the authority to decide what other factors it <u>may</u> consider?

62.43 The narrow view of the Act is that section 125(3) is exhaustive so that an authority acts unlawfully if it takes account of any other matters. The wide view is that, while the Act sets out matters which an authority must take into account, it does not prohibit it from taking account of other matters.

62.44 A narrow view is found in the Regulatory Impact Assessment underpinning the regulations:[21]

'It is a local tax-raising power for local authorities (acting in their capacity as a licensing authority). The licensing authority will, having regard to the costs of policing late night alcohol-related crime and disorder, consider the desirability of raising revenue in their area through a levy. We recognise that many authorities may not consider it desirable in their area. For example, they may consider that enforcement costs are not sufficiently high, or that potential net receipts would be too low in their area (for example, because few premises are open after midnight, or because they would have particularly high administrative costs, which would be incurred by the licensing authority but then recouped from income, thereby lowering net receipts).'

62.45 However, it is considered that the wide view is clearly to be preferred, for the following reasons.

62.46 First, the Act states what the authority must consider. It does not state that those considerations are exclusive, or preclude any others.

62.47 Second, the Act even envisages that other considerations may be made compulsory. Section 134(4) permits the Secretary of State to make regulations specifying matters of which the authority must be satisfied before adopting the levy. This is on its face inconsistent with an argument that nothing else is relevant.

62.48 Third, in other licensing spheres, where material factors have been set out, the higher courts have not hesitated to find that all material considerations have to be taken into account.[22]

62.49 Fourth, there are many considerations which seem plainly material to whether it is appropriate to adopt a new local taxation regime not mentioned in the Act but which it seems difficult to imagine that Parliament considered immaterial:

---

[21] 'Impact Assessment: Dealing with the problems of late night drinking – implementation of secondary legislation' (9 May 2012).

[22] See eg *R (Hestview) v Snaresbrook Crown Court* [2001] EWHC Admin 144; *R (TC Projects) v Newcastle Licensing Justices* [2008] EWCA Civ 428.

- whether there are alternative means of reducing crime and disorder;
- the economic effects of the levy on operators;
- the existence of voluntary schemes for the reduction of crime and disorder, the cost of those schemes for operators, their success in reducing crime and disorder and the effect of the levy upon such schemes;
- the fairness of passing the burden to operators rather than their being borne by the community at large;
- the police's own capacity to fund crime prevention;
- the fairness of non-town centre operators funding town centre policing.

62.50   All of these factors are potentially material and, while it would be for the authority to decide what weight they receive, it would, it is submitted, be illogical and wrong for the authority to discount them as a matter of law.

F PROCESS

62.51   In strict theory, an authority, acting through its licensing officers, could carry out a minimal consultation exercise before placing the outcome before councillors to decide whether to introduce the levy. In practice, that would be an unwise course for three reasons.

62.52   First, while there is some constraint as to how authorities may spend their share of the levy there is no constraint on how the police do so. In areas in which the boundaries of the licensing authority and the police authority are not contiguous, this may mean that money raised from businesses in Area A is actually spent in Area B, which may be viewed dimly by ratepayers and electors alike. Therefore, there ought to be some early dialogue between officers and the police as to how any prospective levy would be spent.

62.53   The second reason is principally political. The introduction of a taxation regime is an emotive topic which is liable to occasion significant local debate. Before embarking on the issue, officers would be well-advised to take a steer from their members. In particular, members are likely to want to know what the prospective economic benefits from the levy are before deciding whether they subscribe to the idea even as a matter of broad principle.

62.54   The third reason is practical and important. There are five key topics that have to be consulted upon, as set out below. It is crucial that members approve the terms of the consultation because it will not be open to them to vary those parameters when subsequently deciding to introduce the levy in response to the consultation.

62.55   Therefore, a well-advised authority will take the following measures before introducing the levy.

62.56 Discussions with police. Officers ought to conduct preliminary discussions with police, with two ends in view. The first will be to agree the scope of the material which the Council is likely to require to proceed to a public consultation on the levy. This may, for example, include crime and disorder statistics and trends and the costs of policing the night time economy during particular hours between midnight and 6 am. The second will be for the police to agree how they would use their share of the levy. This may even be reduced to a proposed service level agreement, setting out particular obligations on the police, for example to provide specified levels of personnel at particular times of night.

62.57 Presentation to members. This is not a statutory stage, and therefore the presentation could in theory be to any configuration of members, including the licensing committee. However, since it is likely to be the full council which decides to introduce the levy, and given the import-ance of the ultimate decision, it is recommended that the presentation is to the full council.

62.58 The presentation should include, as a minimum:

(1) the material relied upon by the police and licensing officers to support the introduction of the levy;
(2) the rationale;
(3) the test;
(4) the process;
(5) budgetary considerations;
(6) the costs of policing and other arrangements for the reduction or prevention of crime and disorder, in connection with the supply of alcohol between midnight and 6 am;
(7) the desirability of raising revenue by means of the levy;
(8) other material considerations;
(9) the likely net proceeds;
(10) the proposed use of the specified and non-specified proportions;
(11) the process;
(12) the need for the ultimate decision on the levy, the date of implemen-tation, the late night supply period, the permitted exemption and reduction categories and the specified proportion;
(13) explanation of the reasons why the late night supply period, the permitted exemption and reduction categories and the specified pro-portion have been selected for consultation;
(14) financial implications (costs and benefits);
(15) legal risks;
(16) equality considerations; and
(17) human rights considerations.

Most of the above matters speak for themselves, but it is necessary to focus here on two of them.

62.59   First of all, the members need to be asked to decide the five matters which need to be consulted upon: the date of implementation; the late night supply period; the permitted exemption categories; the permitted reduction categories, and the specified proportion. The specified proportion is the proportion of the net levy receipts paid to the police, which must be at least 70%.[23]

62.60   Second of all, the members will want some clear advice as to how much the exercise is likely to raise for the benefit of the authority and the police. This is a somewhat complex projection, whose elements are as follows:

(1)   Make assumption as to the late night supply period.

(2)   Identify the premises whose licences permit trade within the late night supply period.

(3)   Estimate those (or the numbers and rateable bands of those) likely to vary their licences/certificates to fall outside the late night supply period.

(4)   Make assumption as to the likely exemption categories and those premises (or the numbers and rateable bands of those) likely to achieve full exemption.

(5)   Assess the numbers of remaining premises, their rateable bands and, in respect of Bands D and E, whether they are exclusively or primarily for the sale of alcohol on the premises.

(6)   Make assumption as to the likely reduction categories and which of the likely non-exempt premises are within them.

(7)   Project the gross income from those premises likely to be fully or partially liable for the levy.

(8)   Deduct the likely expenses which are deductible according to the Regulations.

(9)   Make assumption as to the specified proportion, which is to be paid to the police.

(10) 'Deduct from the remaining sum the authority's expenses which are not deductible according to the Regulations.

(11) The balance is the net income to the authority.

62.61   While the projection is a complicated one, it is essential that it is undertaken at an early stage in the procedure, for if it is not the authority may discover that it has sanctioned a bureaucratic and politically sensitive process for a relatively slight economic return, which may itself cause unnecessary controversy and act as a distraction from other attempts to promote the licensing objectives.

62.62   The outcome of this preliminary appraisal is that officers should have a clear steer on what they are to consult upon, and members should

---

[23]   PRSRA 2011, s 131(4).

understand the likely returns should they ultimately decide to proceed with the scheme.

62.63 Consultation. The Late Night Levy (Application and Administration) Regulations 2012 envisage a slimmed down consultation. The only persons who are required to be consulted are the relevant local policing body, the relevant chief officer of police and the holders of relevant late night authorisations,[24] which means those who would be leviable if the levy is introduced in the terms of the consultation.[25]

62.64 In addition, the authority must publish notice of its proposal on its web-site and in a local newspaper or, if there is none, in a local newsletter, circular or similar document circulating in the authority's area. The notice must also be sent to the holders of relevant late night authorisations, the relevant local policing body and the relevant Chief Officer of Police.[26] The web-site notice must contain the five main building blocks of the levy:

- the date on which the levy requirement is first to apply;
- the late night supply period;
- the permitted exemption categories;
- the permitted reduction categories;
- the specified proportion.[27]

62.65 Of course, nothing prevents a wider consultation than that. Given that the ultimate payers of the levy are likely to be local drinkers, the authority may consider it prudent to consult on a wider basis, but it is not bound to do so.

62.66 The Regulations are silent on the period for consultation. Nor do they expressly require the authority to give any information other than that set out above. However, it is considered that ordinary principles as to consultation still apply.[28] Consultees ought to have enough time to reply to the consultation. They ought also to have sufficient information on which to respond. For example, the Regulations do not even require the authority to set out the costs of policing and other arrangements for the reduction or prevention of crime and disorder at the material times, which amount to a fundamental determinant of their decision. It is hard to see how a consultation which fails to give (or direct the reader to) such central information could pass muster in the Administrative Court. This is a further reason why the preliminary steps set out above are so important to fill in the gaps in the skeletal process set out in the Regulations.

---

[24] The Late Night Levy (Application and Administration) Regulations 2012, reg 9.
[25] PRSRA 2011, s 134(5).
[26] The Late Night Levy (Application and Administration) Regulations 2012, reg 9.
[27] The Late Night Levy (Application and Administration) Regulations 2012, reg 9.
[28] See Chapter 11.

62.67   As a matter of good practice, it is suggested that the consultation should do more than ask whether the proposal is supported. It should ask directed questions as to whether each element (the late night supply period, the specified proportion, etc) is supported.

62.68   The decision. It is imperative that officers report fully and fairly on the response to the consultation. It is likely that the report format will follow that set out above, only now armed with the public response to the consultation.

62.69   While the Act does not specify this, it is probable that the decision will be made by the full council.[29] In theory, the full council could delegate the decision to a subordinate committee. In practice, the decision is too important to delegate.

62.70   Since the decision is not governed by the Licensing Act 2003 but by the Local Government Act 1972, there does not have to be a hearing. Some authorities will have provisions for deputations and other speeches at council meetings, and there seems to be no reason why these procedures cannot be used to permit public participation.

62.71   A potentially controversial matter is whether the authority may decide to adopt a scheme other than that upon which it has consulted. Neither the Act nor the Regulations appear to contemplate such an eventuality, and it is considered that the better view is that it cannot be done. If the authority proposes a scheme different from that upon which it has consulted, eg because it wants a different late night supply period, it should re-consult, remembering that the consultation obligation is not a particularly onerous one, and so it is better to get it right than to face legal challenge for tolerating lacunae.

62.72   From decision to implementation. Having decided to implement the scheme, the authority must publish notice of its decision in the same manner as notice of its proposal described above.

62.73   The Regulations do not state that bills must be sent out, so that if nothing more is done many licensees will be completely in the dark as to how their levy is to be assessed. Even if they happen to know that the levy is assessed on rateable bands and which band they fall within, they may not know what the levy is for each rateable band, whether they are considered to be in the business primarily or exclusively of supplying alcohol for consumption on the premises and therefore liable to pay a multiplier if they are in

---

[29]   The Local Authorities (Functions and Responsibilities) (England) Regulations 2000 (SI 2000/2853) (Sch 1 Part B para 14A) says that 'functions relating to licensing' are not the responsibility of the executive. It is considered that setting a levy is a function relating to licensing. Therefore, the function goes to the full council.

Bands D or E, or whether they are considered to fall within an exemption or reduction category. This amounts to a striking omission from the Regulations.

62.74 For these reasons, it is considered that an authority ought: (a) to bill each premises setting out how the levy is calculated, and (b) plan the implementation date sufficiently far in advance to iron out any disputes prior to that date. This latter point is particularly important because there is a mandatory suspension of the licence for non-payment of the levy[30] and it would be unfortunate to say the least were licences suspended when there is genuine doubt as to whether a levy is payable at all, or the amount of the due payment.

62.75 **Variation and abolition.** The authority is given power to vary or abolish its levy scheme, eg by adding or removing exemption categories or changing the late night supply period.[31] However, any changes may take place only at the end of the levy year and following the same consultation process as applies to the introduction of the levy in the first place.

62.76 **Challenging the levy.** There is no provision for appeal against a decision to introduce, vary or abolish the levy. Challenges may only be made by way of judicial review and on conventional public law principles.[32]

G ADMINISTRATION OF THE SCHEME

62.77 A number of detailed duties and other considerations arise, which are dealt with briefly in this section.

62.78 **Free variation.** The Act[33] and the Late Night Levy (Application and Administration) Regulations[34] both make provision for holders of relevant late night authorisations to apply without paying a fee for variations or minor variations so that the authorisations cease to be relevant late night authorisations before the beginning of the levy year. Some may term it a get out of jail free card. So, for example, if the chosen late night supply period is 2 am to 6 am, a licensee may apply to vary their licence so that they cease to be entitled to supply alcohol at 1.45 am. It is important that an authority leaves enough time between the decision to implement the levy and the first levy year to enable all variation procedures to be completed, failing which licensees who have no desire to trade during the levy period will end up being liable for the levy by default.

---

30   PRSRA 2011, s 129(6).
31   PRSRA 2011, s 133.
32   See Chapter 20.
33   PRSRA 2011, s 134(2)(c).
34   The Late Night Levy (Application and Administration) Regulations 2012, reg 9(5).

62.79 Some licensees may be concerned that if they do reduce their trading hours in this way then they may not recover their hours if the levy is subsequently abolished, particularly if they are in a cumulative impact area. The solution to this would be for them to apply by minor variation to add a condition stating: 'Alcohol shall not be supplied during any late night supply period under a current late night levy scheme in the area of the authority.' Then, if the scheme is abolished, the condition would simply become redundant.

62.80 Budget. Prior to the start of each levy year, the authority has to publish a statement of its estimate of the amount of deductions which it is permitted to make.[35] Those expenses are specified in regulation 3 of the Late Night Levy (Expenses, Exemptions and Reductions) Regulations 2012 as being the expenses incurred in connection with or in consequence of the statutory procedure for adoption, the collection of payments, the enforcement of the levy requirement, the application of the net amount of the levy payments and the publication of statements. Any other expenses will still fall on the authority but they cannot be brought into account when determining how much is to be paid to the police. Nor can they be used to reduce the amount spent by the authority for permitted purposes: they would need to be defrayed from the authority's general fund.

62.81 Payment. Liability to pay falls on the holder of the relevant late night authorisation.[36] Although regulation 6 is somewhat opaque, it is thought that the effect is that those holding authorisations in advance of the first levy year must pay the levy on the date upon which their annual licence or club premises certificate fee is due. Those who are granted authorisations after the start of the first levy year must pay the levy 14 days after the grant and annually thereafter. As stated above, the penalty for non-payment is suspension. Payment is also recoverable as a debt.[37]

62.82 Lapse. Provision is made where during the payment year a relevant late night authorisation lapses under section 27 of the Act (eg because of the death of the licensee) or when supply during the late night supply period is rendered unlawful due to a supervening early morning restriction order.

62.83 In such cases, the levy is reduced *pro rata* and any overpayments are to be refunded. For instance, if an EMRO is introduced after 73 days in the payment year then 80% of any payment falls to be refunded.

62.84 Other events. No provision is made in the Regulations for a host of other circumstances which might otherwise have justified reduction or repayment of the levy. Eg if a licence is granted for hours including the late night supply period but the grant is reversed on appeal; if premises fall into

---

[35] PRSRA 2011, s 130(5).
[36] The Late Night Levy (Application and Administration) Regulations 2012, reg 6.
[37] PRSRA 2011, s 129(5).

an exemption category during the payment year; if a licence is varied during the payment year so as to fall outside the late night supply period, or if a licence is revoked, suspended or made subject to a closure order during the payment year. In all of these circumstances it is considered that, unfortunately, the licensee has no recourse. The liability crystallises at the beginning of the payment year and any changes in the licensee's favour during the year do not fall to be reflected until the following year. While one may wish to argue for an implied discretion to the licensing authority to make an 'extra statutory concession', given that they are mainly collecting a fund for the benefit of a third party, the police, and may be thought to have quasi-fiduciary duties in that regard, it is not considered that such a discretion genuinely arises. This, then, is a further respect in which the levy operates in a less than surgical manner.

62.85 Payment. As set out above, there are certain expenses which the authority is entitled to bring into account. Deducting those expenses from the aggregate amount of payments to the authority in respect of the levy year produces what is known as the 'net amount of levy payments.'[38] The authority must pay the specified proportion of that amount to the relevant local policing body within 28 days of the last day of the levy year to which it relates.[39] It should perhaps be noted that by that date the authority may not have succeeded in collecting all payments which are due, so a further matter for agreement between the authority and the police, not provided for in the regulations, might be the ability to adjust for accounting differences arising after the end of the levy year.

62.86 Police use of funds. Unless constrained by a service level agreement with the authority, the police have carte blanche as to when, where and how they spend their portion of the levy receipts. However, the Regulatory Impact Assessment makes a number of eminently sensible suggestions as to the application of funds:

- Multi-agency education and information programmes – to increase the understanding of risk to children and young persons, targeted at parents and teachers for the under 16s.
- Multi-agency education programmes targeting bar staff in the night-time economy – to increase awareness of risks, vulnerability and consequences and their personal responsibility.
- Financial support for projects to expand the use of volunteers in the night-time economy – with an emphasis on safeguarding vulnerable people and promoting the perception of safety.
- High profile policing initiatives – to tackle violent or disorderly behaviour.

---

[38] PRSRA 2011, s 130(1).
[39] The Late Night Levy (Application and Administration) Regulations 2012, reg 8.

- Operations to tackle a range of alcohol-related offences or other offences connected to the late night economy, such as offences relating to drugs, public order or violence against the person.
- Enhanced partnership working between licensing authorities and the police, with the two bodies working better together to tackle the negative effects of the sale of alcohol late at night.

62.87   Application of non-specified proportion. The non-specified proportion is what is left to the licensing authority after deduction of the permitted expenses and the specified proportion. This, according to regulation 8(2) of the Late Night Levy (Application and Administration) Regulations 2012, may be spent on the reduction or prevention of crime and disorder, the promotion of public safety, the reduction or prevention of public nuisance and the cleaning of any relevant highway or other open land to which the public is entitled or permitted to have access. This last category of expenditure is difficult to reconcile with the main test for imposition of the levy discussed above. On the one hand, the levy is imposed for reasons to do with the cost of reducing crime and disorder. On the other hand, proceeds may be used for street cleaning. It is considered doubtful at best whether the regulations are *intra vires* the Act, but it is unlikely that a wise authority would expose itself to challenge by applying its (relatively meagre) net proceeds in this way, so the matter is unlikely to be tested in the near future.

62.88   Again, the Regulatory Impact Assessment makes helpful suggestions as to how the authority may use the non-specified proportion:

- Late night street wardens – to provide a visible presence on the street, alert the police to incidents, and assist door staff with problem customers.
- Late night taxi marshals – to help people disperse safely and speedily.
- Late night CCTV – to deter crime and help the police identify offenders.

62.89   There is also no reason why the authority should not use its share of the receipts to promote voluntary schemes, such as Pubwatch, Best Bar None or Purple Flag, so long as it considers such schemes to be apt to promote the purposes set out in the Regulations.

62.90   Statement. Following the end of the levy year, the authority must publish, in such manner as it thinks fit, a statement of the net amount of levy payments for the year, showing in particular the aggregate payments in and the aggregate deductible expenses.[40] There is no timescale for such a statement, but presumably the authority will wish to ensure that all income and expenses are finalised so as to be able to publish a conclusive statement of the position.

---

[40]   PRSRA 2011, s 130(5)(b).

H CONCLUSION

62.91 On the credit side of the balance sheet, the provisions recognise that there are public costs associated with policing the late night economy and so require payment by those trading into the night.

62.92 On the debit side is that, as the above description shows, this is a highly bureaucratic system which is likely, in most areas, to raise only modest sums of money. Worse, it applies in ways which are recognisably unjust. For example, unlike the early morning restriction order it cannot be applied to part only of an administrative area. Particularly in rural authorities, this may mean that outlying pubs, which cause no problems whatsoever, end up paying for the policing of the town centre. Where there is a Business Improvement District in the town centre and the authority elects to create an exemption for BIDs, the outcome may be that the only late night premises which don't pay the levy are those whose operations are causing the crime and disorder.

62.93 Arguably, a broader perspective is required. Late-trading town centre bars are likely already to have a higher rates commitment. Because of their rateable band they may pay higher licence fees. They may generate greater sales and so pay greater duty and VAT. They may employ and pay more staff and therefore pay more national insurance and PAYE etc. Therefore, while the 'polluter pays' rationale for the levy is superficially attractive, it does not always hit the polluter and the polluter may be paying already.

62.94 A further important consideration is that, in contrast to the levy, the new fees provisions will enable regulatory costs, including costs of compliance monitoring, to be apportioned among the entire body of fee payers including, for example, late night refreshment providers. In most areas, very modest fee increases will raise much more for authorities than the late night levy, albeit that for the reasons discussed in Chapter 61 (the Fees Regime) enforcement costs are not recoverable as part of the licence fee.

62.95 The conclusion, therefore, is an unequivocal one. In most cases, the introduction of the levy will be an unnecessary, unfair, unprofitable and disproportionate bureaucratic intervention. There is little that the levy can achieve which is not attainable by more effective and economic means.

Community Infrastructure Levy

Breakfast – a chine of beef, a loaf, a gallon of ale.
Luncheon – bread and a gallon of ale.
Dinner – a piece of boiled beef, a slice of roast meat, a gallon of ale.
Supper – porridge, mutton, a loaf and a gallon of ale.

Henry VIII's allowance to Lady Lucy, a maid of honour.
Lord Askwith, *British Taverns, Their History and Laws*

A INTRODUCTION

63.01 Community Infrastructure Levy ('CIL'), which was introduced by
the Planning Act 2008, is a means for the state to take a share in the uplift in
the value of land arising from development without having to wait for the
land to be sold and Capital Gains Tax to be paid. Planning authorities may
introduce the levy in their area, according to a charging schedule, and use the
proceeds to fund infrastructure works for the benefit of the community.

63.02 Infrastructure contemplated by the Act includes roads and other
transport facilities, sporting and recreational facilities and open spaces.
There is no reason why CIL could not be used to help to fund infrastructure
works needed for the development of a vibrant and safe night time economy,
for example a new town square used for cultural activities and public
gatherings, from which other streets key to the night time economy radiate.

63.03 In this chapter, the underlying tenets of CIL will be briefly described.

B CIL

63.04 As is often the case in modern statutes, the primary legislation sets
out a thin framework for the regime, with the detail fleshed out in regulations. Part 11 of the Planning Act 2008 creates provision for CIL, with

much greater detail provided in the Community Infrastructure Levy Regulations 2010.[1]

63.05   Section 206 states baldly that a charging authority, which is the planning authority, may charge CIL in respect of development of land in its area. The amount of CIL is set out in a charging schedule, setting rates or other criteria by reference to which the amount of CIL chargeable in respect of development is to be determined.[2] In setting its rates or other criteria, the authority has to have regard to a number of matters, including its actual and expected costs of infrastructure, matters specified by CIL regulations relating to the economic viability of development and other actual and expected sources of funding for infrastructure.[3]

63.06   CIL is chargeable on the gross internal floor space of the net additional liable development. Therefore, the schedule will express levy rates in pounds per square metre of development floor space.[4]

63.07   Before approving a charging schedule, the authority must consult on a preliminary draft charging schedule.[5] Provision is then made for publication of the draft charging schedule[6] and for the receipt of representations upon it.[7] The authority must appoint an independent examiner to examine the draft schedule,[8] hear representations upon it,[9] and make recommendations upon the draft.[10] The authority may not approve the schedule if the examiner recommends rejection.[11] If the authority decides to approve the schedule, it must publicise the fact in the manner required by the Regulations.[12]

63.08   CIL is payable on the commencement of chargeable development, which is defined in regulation 9. In the simplest case, where planning permission is granted for development, CIL is payable when the development commences. The charge is *prima facie* payable by those with 'material interests', being the freehold owners or those with leases extending for at

---

[1]   SI 2010/948.
[2]   Planning Act 2008, s 211(1).
[3]   Planning Act 2008, s 211(2); Community Infrastructure Levy Regulations 2010 (SI 2010/948), reg 14.
[4]   See 'Community Infrastructure Levy Guidance' (Department for Communities and Local Government, December 2012).
[5]   Community Infrastructure Levy Regulations 2010, reg 15.
[6]   Community Infrastructure Levy Regulations 2010, reg 16.
[7]   Community Infrastructure Levy Regulations 2010, reg 17.
[8]   Planning Act 2008, s 212(1).
[9]   Community Infrastructure Levy Regulations 2010, reg 21.
[10] Planning Act 2008, s 212(7).
[11] Planning Act 2008, s 213.
[12] Community Infrastructure Levy Regulations 2010, reg 25.

least seven years after the grant of planning consent.[13] However, others such as developers may by notice assume liability for CIL.[14]

63.09 Provision is made for exemptions for minor development,[15] for charities,[16] for social housing[17] and for other exceptional circumstances.[18]

C CONCLUSION

63.10 The process for raising money through CIL involves extensive work on the part of the authority. This is not, however, ground to shun the use of CIL for the funding of infrastructure projects. An authority will, however, have to think carefully about the respective uses of section 106 contributions[19] and CIL to fund infrastructure works. A dividing line is set out in the Regulations.[20] The Community Infrastructure Levy guidance[21] states that the authority should set out at examination a draft list of the projects or types of infrastructure that are to be funded in whole or in part by the levy, and also those known site-specific matters where section 106 contributions may continue to be sought, in order to create certainty and transparency.[22]

63.11 CIL, however, is not a silver bullet, since it is constrained by considerations of viability – set too high it can choke of investment altogether – and also by the timing of development. Nevertheless, it can be used as one income stream to fund development, to bring in wider investment and to raise confidence.

63.12 A relevant example is provided by the improvement of Barkingside High Street in the borough of Redbridge, where the aim is to create a sense of place in Barkingside and improve leisure opportunities and the shopping experience through the delivery of a new town square and associated public realm improvements. Here CIL funding has been used to augment funding of the scheme, which is principally to be underpinned by wider funding initiatives.[23]

63.13 In economically pressed times, funds for regeneration are in short supply. A number of funding streams have to be exploited. CIL is one such

---

[13] Community Infrastructure Levy Regulations 2010, reg 4. Regulation 34 provides for apportionment between material interests.
[14] Community Infrastructure Levy Regulations 2010, reg 31.
[15] Community Infrastructure Levy Regulations 2010, reg 42.
[16] Community Infrastructure Levy Regulations 2010, reg 43.
[17] Community Infrastructure Levy Regulations 2010, reg 49.
[18] Community Infrastructure Levy Regulations 2010, reg 55.
[19] See Chapter 64 (Planning Obligations).
[20] Community Infrastructure Levy Regulations 2010, reg 123. See further Chapter 64.
[21] Department for Communities and Local Government, December 2012.
[22] Community Infrastructure Levy Guidance, para 15.
[23] 'Decisions decisions: governance and spending the CIL' (Local Government Association and Planning Advisory Service).

stream, with the potential to assist in the development of the leisure experience in towns and cities. Authorities have the delicate job of stimulating investor confidence and attracting investors, while asking them to contribute to the pot for infrastructure works. Set sensitively, CIL has an undoubted role to play in the overall exercise, but is unlikely to supplant other funding initiatives.

Planning obligations

... I write this reeling,
Having got drunk exceedingly today,
So that I seem to stand upon the ceiling
I say – the future is a serious matter –
And so – for God's sake – hock and soda water!

I Would to Heaven That I Were So Much Clay
Lord Byron

A INTRODUCTION

64.01 Section 106 of the Town and Country Planning Act 1990 makes provision for those seeking planning permission to offer, whether unilaterally or by agreement, sums of money to the planning authority.

64.02 There is no reason in principle why such sums cannot be earmarked for funds intended for off-site infrastructure needed for the leisure-based regeneration or regulation of an area. This may, for example, be for town centre CCTV, bottle bin provision, new taxi ranks, improved open space or public art.

64.03 The topic of planning obligations is a substantial one, whose detail is beyond the scope of this book.[1] The purpose of this chapter is briefly to set out the money-raising powers within section 106.

B PLANNING OBLIGATIONS

64.04 A planning obligation usually arises by a bilateral agreement known as a section 106 agreement. But where for any reason an agreement is

---

[1]   For further reading, see *Encyclopaedia of Planning Law and Practice* (Sweet and Maxwell).

impossible, then an alternative is a unilateral planning obligation. Planning obligations may serve a number of functions. They may restrict the development or use of the land in a specified way. They may require specified operations or activities to be carried out on the land. They may require the land to be used in a specified way. Or, germane to this chapter, they may require a sum to be paid to the authority, which may be a one-off capital sum or a periodical payment. In the latter case, the payments may be open-ended or for a fixed period.

64.05   The obligation, which must be contained in a deed,[2] is entered into by any person interested in the relevant land.[3] The beauty of the obligation from an authority's point of view is that it is enforceable not only against that person but also against any person deriving title from that person,[4] eg a subsequent purchaser or lessee. It is also registrable as a land charge under the Local Land Charges Act 1975.[5]

64.06   The Community Infrastructure Levy Regulations 2010 set out important limitations on the use of planning obligations.

64.07   First, regulation 122 provides that a planning obligation may only constitute a reason for granting planning permission for development if the obligation is necessary to make the development acceptable in planning terms, is directly related to the development and is fairly and reasonably related in scale and kind to the development. This is to ensure that the obligation does not represent a bribe used to purchase a planning permission which is unacceptable, but is instead designed to cure ills which would otherwise arise.

64.08   Second, there is a need to draw a principled line between Community Infrastructure Levy and planning obligations so as not to duplicate requirements. Regulation 123 provides that a planning obligation may not constitute a reason for granting planning permission to the extent that the obligation provides for the funding of relevant infrastructure. Relevant infrastructure is that which the authority has stated will be the subject of Community Infrastructure Levy or, where it has published no list of such infrastructure, any infrastructure.

C CONCLUSION

64.09   Section 106 obligations represent a means of securing payment from those who seek to develop land in the area of the authority in order to contribute to the common good. In the case of leisure operators, while they

---

2   Town and Country Planning Act 1990, s 106(9).
3   Town and Country Planning Act 1990, s 106(1).
4   Town and Country Planning Act 1990, s 106(3).
5   Local Land Charges Act 1975, s 1.

hope that their interior environment and service will provide attraction enough, experience shows that the creation of attractive public realms is key to drawing in custom. However great the restaurant, no-one wishes to access it through a war zone.

64.10   Section 106 agreements can be used to attract payments from developers, albeit modest taken individually but significant when aggregated, to contribute to public works.

64.11   One particularly good example of use of section 106 moneys was the London Borough of Tower Hamlets 'Paths to Gold', created to coincide with the 2012 Olympic Games. This was a series of walks through the borough, guiding visitors through local historical, cultural, retail and recreational destinations. The routes in question were waymarked and branded. Paths to Gold could also be downloaded as an app for smart phone users. The project aimed to help reduce retail vacancy levels, increase visitation and therefore levels of spending and encourage more businesses into the borough. It demonstrates the potential for facilitation of the night time economy, and the strategic role which public authorities can play in its future direction.

64.12   In short, planning obligations, properly marshalled and directed, make a useful contribution to the creation of attractive, sustainable leisure environments, and can be seen as part of the overall financial mix.

Alcohol and politics

... Drunkennesse is the mother of outrages, the matter of faults, the roote of crimes, the fountaine of vice, the intoxicateor of the head, the quelling of sences, the tempest of the tongue, the storme of the body, the shipwracke of chastitie, losse of time, boluntarie madnesse, an ignominious languor, the filthinesse of manners, the disgrace of life, the corruption of the soule ...

Saint Augustine
Young, *England's Bane*

65

Alcohol politics: assessing the consequences of the Licensing Act 2003

For too long town centres up and down the country have been blighted by crime and disorder driven by irresponsible binge drinking.

Ministerial foreword, Home Office[1]

It is time the Government listened more to the CMO (Chief Medical Officer) and the President of the RCP (Royal College of Physicians) and less to the drinks and retail industry.

House of Commons Health Committee[2]

A INTRODUCTION

65.01 This chapter is essentially about expectations. It is about how expectations are created, managed, and delivered in a policy area where government tries to weigh what are defined as competing interests. More specifically the chapter focuses on the recent politicisation of alcohol in Britain and looks at the extent to which the Licensing Act 2003 has been part of this phenomenon. It also takes stock of the situation at a point in time when a new government, not responsible for the original Act, has taken office.

---

[1]   Home Office, 'Rebalancing the Licensing Act. A consultation on empowering individuals, families and local communities to shape and determine local licensing' (2010), Ministerial foreword, p 2, Available at: http://www.homeoffice.gov.uk/publications/consultations/cons-2010-licensing-act/.

[2]   House of Commons Health Committee, 'Alcohol. First Report of Session 2009–10. Volume 1. Report, together with formal minutes', HC 151-I (HMSO, London, 2010), p 7

65.02   Every citizen of the United Kingdom today has a relationship with alcohol, either directly or indirectly.[3] A majority of the population are quite happy to freely use alcohol within the laws and regulations that govern its sale and availability. Alcohol can blight lives (both temporarily and permanently) but it is also the source of employment – albeit indirectly – for hundreds of thousands, including no doubt many (if not all) reading this chapter. As well as raising significant revenue through taxation, alcohol also generates costs that are borne by individuals and by society as a whole. Recognition of this duality has, however, only recently become a matter for public debate in the UK.

65.03   In 2010 a Home Office document stated that the alcohol industry "contributes around £8.5 billion to the Exchequer through excise duty alone',[4] presumably per annum, though this not stated.[5] In 2009/10 there were 1,057,000 alcohol-related admissions to hospital in England, 12% higher than the 2008/9 figure (945,500) and more than twice as many as in 2002/3 (510,800).[6] A Department of Health study estimated the overall annual cost of alcohol harm to the NHS in England alone to be £2.7 billion in 2006/7 prices, including an estimated 6.6 million alcohol-related attendances at hospital accident and emergency (A&E) per year at a cost of £645 million.[7] In 2009 a total of 6,584 deaths directly related to alcohol were recorded in England, 3% fewer than in 2008, but 20% more than in 2001.[8] The links between alcohol, disorder and crime have been very widely

---

3   Readers should note that this chapter necessarily focuses on England and Wales, where almost 89% of the present 61.8 million UK population lives (around 84% of the UK total live in England).

4   The figure for 2010/11 was £9.3 billion: HM Revenue and Customs Alcohol Bulletin, October 2011.

5   Home Office, 'Rebalancing the Licensing Act. A consultation on empowering individuals, families and local communities to shape and determine local licensing' (2010), pg 4. Available at: http://www.homeoffice.gov.uk/publications/consultations/cons-2010-licensing-act/.

6   National Statistics, 'Statistics on Alcohol: England, 2011' (The Health and Social Care Information Centre, May 2011), p 8. Available online: www.ic.nhs.uk.

   Editor's note:
   Since this chapter was written, figures released in 'Statistics on Alcohol in England 2013' (Health and Social Care Information Centre) show that part of the reason for the recorded increase in alcohol-related hospital admissions is the increase in coding of secondary conditions, including alcohol-related admissions, rather than a rise in such conditions themselves. When adjusted for the change in recording practice, the increase alcohol-related hospital admissions has been from 807,700 in 2002/3 to 1,219,000 in 2008/9 to 1,220,300 in 2011/12. The increase in admissions where alcohol is the primary diagnosis, which is unaffected by coding changes, was from 141,700 in 2002/2 to 185,800 in 2008/9 to 200,900 in 2011/12.

7   Department of Health, 'The cost of alcohol harm to the NHS in England. An update to the Cabinet office (2003) study' (Health Improvement Analytical Team, Department of Health, July 2008).

8   National Statistics, 'Statistics on Alcohol: England, 2011' (The Health and Social Care Information Centre, May 2011), p 8.

debated, and caution is needed when comparing figures.[9] In the 2009/10 British Crime Survey victims believed offender(s) were under the influence of alcohol in half (50%) of all violent incidents, equating to 986,000 incidents of this nature across England and Wales.[10]

65.04 The two quotes at the beginning of this chapter encapsulate two prominent dimensions of how alcohol is manifest in the society and economy of the UK. The first, taken from the Ministerial foreword to a document proposing reform of the Act (under the Coalition Government that was formed in May 2010), projects a notion that alcohol-related crime and disorder is monocausal, arising from individual lack of responsibility. The second quote, however, highlights a quite different tension that is intrinsic to contemporary debate, with government subject to ostensibly countervailing forces – alcohol seen from a public health perspective and from a commercial perspective.

65.05 First, if we are to understand the politics of alcohol and where the Act fits then it is important to revisit the ways that knowledge of the issue has been generated, and how it has informed policy decisions at crucial stages.

B LICENSING REFORM: A CRITICAL LOOK AT USE OF THE EVIDENCE BASE

65.06 What is the process through which policy makers come to follow a particular direction or policy option rather than an alternative? Political steps towards licensing reform came to public prominence in 2000 when, in the first term of the Labour government led by Tony Blair, the 'Time for Reform' White Paper was published.[11] In proposing what was described as a radically new system the White Paper set out what the government saw as the problems with the then current arrangements for licensing the sale of alcohol in England and Wales based on the Licensing Act 1964. One of these problems was described as follows:

'[The 1964 Act] creates public order problems through standard closing hours which mean that large numbers of drinkers come out onto the street late at night at the same time.'[12]

---

[9]   P Hadfield and A Newton, 'Alcohol, Crime and Disorder in the Night-time Economy', Alcohol Concern Factsheet (September 2010), esp 1–3. Available at: http://www.alcoholconcern.org.uk/assets/files/Publications/Night-time-Economy-factsheet.pdf.

[10]   Home Office, 'Crime in England and Wales 2009/10. Findings from the British Crime Survey and police recorded crime' (Edited by: John Flatley, Chris Kershaw, Kevin Smith, Rupert Chaplin and Debbie Moon) (Home Office, London, 2010), p 60.

[11]   Home Office, 'Time for Reform: Proposals for the Modernisation of Our Licensing Laws', Cm 4696 (HMSO, London, 2000).

[12]   Home Office, 'Time for Reform: Proposals for the Modernisation of Our Licensing Laws', p 9.

65.07   Seventeen years earlier, Hope, in a study of drinking and disorder in Newcastle upon Tyne city centre,[13] provided a nuanced account of the causes of such disorder. His analysis found that city centre disorder was both time-specific and location-specific, though its determinants were identified as complex. In proposing a ('by no means exhaustive') list of preventative options, including four on time-specific disorderliness, he cautioned that decisions about the feasibility of any measures would need to take into account their likely efficacy in reducing or controlling drink-related disorder, as well as unintended consequences of such measures. Of the four measures he proposed, option 2(a) proposed altering permitted opening hours – extend, abandon, or selectively stagger pub closing times to avoid a concentration of drinkers inside pubs and on the street – and option 2(b) proposed an increase in the number of late-night premises through permissive licensing – to achieve the same effect as (a) but under somewhat more restrictive controls (ie special hours certificates).[14] He offered the following assessment:

> 'Few measures do not involve at least some difficult choices. To give a few examples: while extending permitted hours (option 2a), or increasing the number of late night premises (option 2b) *might* reduce the closing time bulge of disorder, increasing the availability of alcohol might also increase the overall level of alcohol-related harm.'[15]

65.08   This prescient, thoughtful analysis was nowhere to be seen in the arguments put forward by ministers in 2000. In the White Paper it was claimed without any qualification that 'Longer hours generally should promote a more gradual drift from licensed premises as customers make for home, and end the unnaturally early race to drink as much as possible before closing time, when many are not yet ready to go'.[16] The White Paper then cited a 'recent Home Office study' that, it was claimed, had drawn attention to evidence of the benefits of reducing the rate of drinking and the number of drinkers leaving at the same time.[17] It was then claimed that spreading the period during which customers leave should produce 'five key outcomes', namely:

> '–   a more gradual, and orderly, pattern of dispersal of peak densities between the hours of 11pm – 12 midnight, and 2am and 3am in urban centres
>
> –   significant reductions in reports of drink-related offences and in arrests for such offences
>
> –   reductions in binge drinking and drunkenness on the streets

---

13   T Hope, 'Drinking and disorder in the city centre: a policy analysis', in 'Implementing Crime Prevention Measures', Home Office Research Study No 86 (HMSO, London, 1985).

14   T Hope, 'Drinking and disorder in the city centre: a policy analysis', p 57.

15   T Hope, 'Drinking and disorder in the city centre: a policy analysis', p 58.

16   Home Office, 'Time for Reform: Proposals for the Modernisation of Our Licensing Laws', p 31.

17   Home Office, 'Time for Reform: Proposals for the Modernisation of Our Licensing Laws', p 32.

- increased availability of refreshment and transportation facilities due to more evenly spread demand
- a decrease in reports of nuisance and noise in direct proportion to the lower densities at any given time'[18]

65.09 The sole evidence cited in support of these outcomes was a study produced by consultants to the drinks industry,[19] paid for by the Portman Group, a trade body which speaks on behalf of the major UK alcoholic drinks producers.[20] Hadfield[21] has highlighted the curious narrowness of this reliance, a point further compounded by the fact that the 'recent Home office study' cited in the White Paper[22] had itself relied solely on this same study of questionable independence when discussing the potential effect of staggered closing times.[23] As well as noting the findings of Hope, the Home Office could also have examined the findings of a 1989 study designed and written by the former head of its research and planning unit, Mary Tuck.[24] Like Hope, she also found evidence correlating disorder around pub closing times and offered support in principle to the idea that staggering closing times could reduce this. However, again in common with Hope, she added an important qualification:

'Many would fear that longer opening times would result in more alcohol consumption with accompanying health problems.'[25]

65.10 In its clear, unqualified assertion that standard hours caused public order problems the White Paper established a strong – and politically marketable – characterisation of the nature of the problem at hand. The Institute for Alcohol Studies observed of the White Paper at the time:

'Throughout the White Paper there is an assumption that the problems associated with alcohol [sic] confined to public disorder and nuisance. Many will see the absence of any mention of the health effects of the consumption of alcohol as an omission which weakens the document's impact.'[26]

How then did the government respond to wider concerns around alcohol when preparing legislation?

---

[18] Page 32.
[19] P Marsh and K Fox-Kibby, 'Drinking and Public Disorder. A report of research conducted for The Portman Group by MCM Research'. Available http://www.sirc.org/publik/dandpd.pdf.
[20] See Harkins, 'The Portman Group', BMJ 340 (2010) for a critical account of the Group's lobbying activities.
[21] Hadfield and Newton, 'Alcohol, Crime and Disorder in the Night-time Economy', p 4.
[22] A Deehan, 'Alcohol and Crime: Taking Stock', Crime Reduction Research Series paper 3 (Home Office, London, 1999). Available at: http://library.npia.police.uk/docs/hocrimereduc/crrs3.pdf.
[23] Deehan, 'Alcohol and Crime: Taking Stock', pp 12–14, 16.
[24] M Tuck, 'Drinking and Disorder: A study of Non-Metropolitan violence', Home Office Research Study No 108 (HMSO, London, 1989).
[25] Tuck, 'Drinking and Disorder: A study of Non-Metropolitan violence', p 68.
[26] IAS (Institute of Alcohol Studies), 'Time for Reform', Alcohol Alert 2 (2000), p 4.

C MEASURING THE HARM FROM ALCOHOL

65.11 In the year prior to the publication of the White Paper an explicit call, led by the voluntary sector (and by Alcohol Concern in particular), had been made regarding the pressing need for a national alcohol strategy, citing evidence of a significant increase in consumption of alcohol during the 1990s. In September 2003 the Cabinet Office Strategy Unit published a document entitled 'Alcohol Misuse: how much does it cost?'.[27] This gave a systematic and comprehensive analysis of the various costs attributable to misuse, concluding that the annual cost of alcohol misuse was between £18 billion and £20 billion per annum at that time. This document drew upon an earlier Interim Analytical Report by the Strategy Unit intended to shape a National Alcohol Harm Reduction Strategy.[28]

65.12 The analytical report detailed the costs of alcohol misuse against four categories: (1) health; (2) crime and public disorder; (3) productivity at work; and, (4) family and social networks. It was unable to quantify cost for the latter category but of the remaining three it was the cost of crime and public disorder that was afforded the highest individual figure ('up to £7.3bn'). In the evidence collated against this category only very limited reference was made to temporality, cited in connection with the location of alcohol-related violence, wherein over half of such violence was defined as occurring in or around pubs, clubs and discos, of which 70% took place on weekend evenings.[29]

65.13 Given that the five key outcomes claimed in the White Paper for staggered closing were so central to the notion of reducing crime and disorder, it seems surprising that no evidence on its temporal distribution or cause and effect links to the night-time economy could be provided. However, as the next section illustrates, by this time the idea that staggered closing was a 'solution' had essentially become an accepted 'fact' among policy makers.

65.14 After the 2001 general election, responsibility for licensing was passed from the Home Office to the Department of Culture, Media and Sport (DCMS) as the government moved to enact new legislation. The Licensing Bill was first introduced in the House of Lords in November 2002, accompanied by a press release from DCMS, in which Hazel Blears MP (a Home Office Minister, but designated 'sponsor' of the alcohol harm reduction strategy) stated:

---

[27] Cabinet Office, 'Alcohol Misuse: how much does it cost?' (Prime Minister's Strategy Unit, 2003). Available at: http://sia.dfc.unifi.it/costi%20uk.pdf.

[28] Cabinet Office, 'Interim Analytical Report' (Prime Minister's Strategy Unit, 2003). Available at: http://webarchive.nationalarchives.gov.uk/+/http://www.number10.gov.uk/files/pdf/SU%20interim_report2.pdf.

[29] Cabinet Office, 'Interim Analytical Report', pp 50–69.

'I believe that the Licensing Bill will complement the government's drive to reduce the harm caused by alcohol misuse, the goal of our National Alcohol Harm Reduction Strategy.

We believe that fixed closing times can encourage binge-drinking as people rush to beat "last orders". There is also evidence that fixed closing times can drive up crime and disorder in town centres, as large numbers of people leave pubs at the same time. The Government believes that a relaxation of permitted hours will help us to combat both binge drinking and crime.'[30]

65.15 Again, evidence was cited as if it was beyond question, coupled with a belief that licensing reform and alcohol harm reduction were complementary. Tessa Jowell MP, then Culture Secretary, wrote in the DCMS Departmental Report claiming that the Act:

'Reforms archaic licensing laws, strengthens competition and increases choice and flexibility for consumers. It introduces tough new measures to tackle alcohol-related crime and disorder and encourage a more civilised café–style culture in pubs and bars.'[31]

65.16 The aforementioned Cabinet Office research papers were precursors to the publication of the 'National Alcohol Harm Reduction Strategy for England'.[32] This strategy emerged some six years after government had first given indications of a commitment to produce a new public health strategy on alcohol. The 2004 strategy defined four 'key ways' for government to reduce alcohol-related harms:

'–   improved, and better-targeted, education and communication;
–   better identification and treatment of alcohol problems;
–   better co-ordination and enforcement of existing powers against crime and disorder; and
–   encouraging the industry to continue promoting responsible drinking and to continue to take a role in reducing alcohol-related harm.'[33]

65.17 In his foreword to the Strategy the then Prime Minister Tony Blair made reference to what he described as a 'small minority' causing:

'two major, and largely distinct, problems: on one hand crime and antisocial behaviour in town and city centres, and on the other harm to health as a result of binge- and chronic drinking'.[34]

[30]   'Licensing Bill launched', DCMS Press Release 200/02 (15 November 2002).
[31]   House of Commons Health Committee, 'Alcohol. First Report of Session 2009–10. Volume 1. Report, together with formal minutes', p 82.
[32]   Cabinet Office, 'Alcohol Harm Reduction Strategy for England' (Prime Minister's Strategy Unit, March 2004).
[33]   Cabinet Office, 'Alcohol Harm Reduction Strategy for England', p 17.
[34]   Cabinet Office, 'Alcohol Harm Reduction Strategy for England', p 2.

The strategy acknowledged that government had previously failed to take a strategic approach to addressing alcohol issues, listing eleven government departments involved in various aspects of alcohol policy.[35] The strategy allocated joint responsibility for coordination and delivery to the Department of Health and the Home Office as 'the key harms in terms of cost and numbers lie in health and crime'. Chapter 6 of the strategy considered alcohol-related crime and disorder, claiming that they 'are fuelled by three main factors' (viz individual reactions, the supply of alcohol, and the surrounding infrastructure).[36] Against the third of these factors reference was made to 'scarce infrastructure' at night, such as food outlets and transport leading to fights and disputes, and suggested that 'these problems are worse where premises all close at the same time and there is no supervision from authority figures. The Licensing Act 2003 has been designed to tackle this'.[37]

65.18   The notion of shared responsibility between individuals, the alcoholic drinks industry, and statutory authorities in managing problems generated by the night-time economy was then raised. The drinks industry 'needs to take more responsibility for preventing and tackling the harmful effects of alcohol misuse not only inside but outside premises'.[38] The strategy went on to suggest that the government would consult with the industry on a voluntary social responsibility scheme that would also seek a financial contribution from the industry towards harms caused by what it termed 'excessive drinking' (without providing a definition). Despite making explicit a causal link between the industry and alcohol misuse the strategy failed in any way to acknowledge the fact that the Act would potentially extend opening hours with the obvious potential to raise alcohol consumption (and thereby harm) for individuals through excessive drinking.

65.19   To a certain extent the strategy appeared to address the issues raised by Alcohol Concern about the licensing reform White Paper but in other respects, including the Prime Minister's depiction of a small minority, it continued to indicate a government treating crime and disorder and health as functionally distinct areas in relation to alcohol. The Act, making legislative progress in the background, was positioned as a critical vehicle to achieve progress in reducing crime and disorder harms, but its potential connection to health harms was effectively disassociated. In contrast, the devolved administration in Scotland had introduced a plan of action on alcohol problems in 2002 and protection and improvement of public health was set as one of the objectives of the parallel process of licensing reform which culminated in the Licensing (Scotland) Act 2005. [39]

---

[35]   Cabinet Office, 'Alcohol Harm Reduction Strategy for England', p 73.
[36]   Cabinet Office, 'Alcohol Harm Reduction Strategy for England', pp 46–47.
[37]   Cabinet Office, 'Alcohol Harm Reduction Strategy for England', p 46.
[38]   Cabinet Office, 'Alcohol Harm Reduction Strategy for England', p 47.
[39]   For an account of this process and its consequences see Elvins, 'Alcohol politics: the impact of the Licensing Act 2003' (2009).

65.20 The government did introduce a set of voluntary Social Responsibility Standards for the alcohol industry in 2005, taking the form of a code aimed mainly at avoiding actions that encouraged or condoned excessive alcohol consumption (eg via marketing). The government saw the Act, the National Alcohol Strategy, and the Social Responsibility Standards as collectively offering a way of reducing the four categories of cost emanating from the UK relationship with alcohol. The Act came into force in November 2005 amid the full glare of public and media attention, accompanied by a clear set of expectations created by the government.

D REVIEWING PROGRESS ON REDUCING ALCOHOL HARMS

65.21 Policy development is underpinned by knowledge held and gleaned by civil servants over time and communicated to governments in office. It has become increasingly common for policy documents to build in progress review, and the Alcohol Strategy was a case in point. In 2007 the Department of Health and the Home Office jointly published 'Safe. Sensible. Social. The next steps in the Government's Alcohol Strategy'.[40] According to this document, published around 20 months after the Act had come into force, 'significant progress has been made ... levels of violent crime have fallen and levels of alcohol consumption are no longer rising'.[41] In a section of the document reviewing overall progress called 'What's working: building on successes so far', reference to progress as a result of the Act (and its augmentation in the form of powers under the Violent Crime Reduction Act 2006[42]) was devoid of any substantive evidence, providing only very brief, generalised case studies from Liverpool and Sheffield.[43] Neither case study made reference to changes that had occurred in patterns of closing times of licensed premises in each respective city, hence this was not identified as a factor in the claimed progress. No mention was thus made of the primary effect that it had been claimed would emerge from reform. In any case, the government was unable to offer convincing evidence of tangible progress in any meaningful sense in relation to crime and disorder as a result of the first 20 months of the Act.

---

[40] HM Government (Department of Health, Home Office, Department for Education and Skills and Department for Culture, Media and Sport, 2007).

[41] Page 10.

[42] The Violent Crime Reduction Act 2006, which had only entered force in February 2007 (four months prior to the document) focused on measures to control 'irresponsible' licensed premises and individuals, and introduced the principle that 'as a last resort' police and local authorities could charge some licensed premises for the cost of additional enforcement activity through designating an area as an 'alcohol disorder zone' (ADZ) (HM Government, 2007: 40). ADZ regulations entered force in 2008 but none were ever established before the provisions were repealed by the Police Reform and Social Responsibility Act 2011.

[43] Pages 39–43.

65.22 On this basis the emergence of what was a new, revised political narrative around alcohol in 'Safe. Sensible. Social.' is perhaps unsurprising. The executive summary opening the document claimed that the revised alcohol strategy would deliver three things. The first of these, rather than something to deliver, actually appeared to be an admission or implication of failure effectively to utilise the control measures provided for in the Act:

'First, we need to ensure that the laws and licensing powers we have introduced to tackle alcohol-fuelled crime and disorder, protect young people and bear down on irresponsibly managed premises are being used widely and effectively.'[44]

This line of argument allowed the government to avoid questions of whether the Act was flawed and looked to other parties – that is, local administration, police and industry – for reasons why the policy had not worked in ways it was claimed it would. A separate review of the voluntary Social Responsibility Standards introduced in 2005 found 'no evidence of any direct causal link between the impact of the standards and a reduction in alcohol-related harm'.[45]

65.23 In March 2008 DCMS published an 'Evaluation of the impact of the Licensing Act 2003'.[46] Embedded in this document (as an appendix) was a Home Office evaluation of the impact of the Act on levels of crime and disorder. This study concluded that the Act had not resulted in chaos, as predicted by some, but added 'neither is there clear evidence that positive benefits have accrued from staggered and better managed closing times'.[47] The report found that most premises had extended their opening hours, but the number of extra hours applied for was low (generally one or two extra hours of trading), few on-licensed premises had requested 24 hour licences, and that extra hours were not routinely used (generally only at weekends).[48] In relation to crime and disorder the study drew on a separate study by Babb,[49] which used data from 30 of the 43 police forces in England and Wales. This study found that a basket of violent and other offences fell overall by 1%in the 12 months after implementation of the Act but rose by 22% in the 3 am to 6 am period. The author reflected on this:

'The rise from 3 am and up to 6 am is likely to partly reflect the change to opening hours of licensed premises and the increased numbers of

---

44   Page 6.
45   2008 KPMG report cited in House of Commons Health Committee, 'Alcohol. First Report of Session 2009–10. Volume 1. Report, together with formal minutes', p 85.
46   'Evaluation of the Impact of the Licensing Act 2003' (Department for Culture, Media and Sport, March 2008).
47   M Hough, G Hunter, J Jacobson, and S Cossalter, 'Report: The impact of the Licensing Act 2003 on levels of crime and disorder: an evaluation', Home Office Research Report 04 (Home Office, London, March 2008), p 18.
48   Page 5.
49   P Babb, 'Violent crime, disorder and criminal damage since the introduction of the Licensing Act 2003', Home Office Online Report 16/07 (Home Office, 2nd edition, London, 2007). Available at: http://www.ias.org.uk/resources/nighttime/policy/homeoffice-report1607.pdf.

people in a public place at these times, including the police, with greater resources being placed on the streets to deal with disorder.'[50]

No evidence in support of the claim about extra police resources was provided. As well as containing the questionable inference that more police present in the night-time economy causes more offences to occur (as opposed, for example, to more offences being recorded), the analysis also highlighted an additional cost to public resources arising directly from the Act. The statistical tables supporting the report show data from a subset of 18 forces where only offences in city centres and near licensed premises were compared (a more valid comparison, one might argue). This indicated, over the 12 month period, a 154% increase in cases of assault with no injury and a 179% increase in cases of harassment.[51] Despite arguably providing a better reflection of the impact arising from the concentrated nature of night-time economies, these data did not merit mention in the relevant section of the main report.[52]

65.24 In their study of the implementation of the Act, Humphreys and Eisner[53] highlight a critical issue, namely that the mere issuing of statutory guidance by DCMS under section 182 of the Act does not guarantee that the desired outcome of staggered closing times will actually occur. In fact, the original guidance was at pains to explain that fixing licence extensions or staggered closing hours was against the ethos of the Act – that market forces should determine the pattern rather than the hand of local licensing authorities.[54]

65.25 The 2008 DCMS report presented data analysis of closing hours of on-licensed premises, finding an overall picture it described as evolution not revolution, reaching the following conclusion:

'This data suggests that there has been a modest change to actual opening hours, with a spreading out of closing times between 11pm and midnight, reducing the 11pm peak.'[55]

Home Office findings on the impact of the Act in relation to the prevention of crime and disorder were largely inconclusive, finding no clear signs that the abolition of standard closing time had significantly reduced problems of

[50] Babb, 'Violent crime, disorder and criminal damage since the introduction of the Licensing Act 2003', p i.
[51] Babb, 'Violent crime, disorder and criminal damage since the introduction of the Licensing Act 2003', pp 18–19.
[52] Hough, Hunter, Jacobson, and Cossalter, 'Report: The impact of the Licensing Act 2003 on levels of crime and disorder: an evaluation', p 9.
[53] D K Humphreys and M P Eisner, 'Evaluating a natural experiment in alcohol policy. The Licensing Act (2003) and the requirement for attention to implementation', Criminology & Public Policy, Vol 9, No 1 (2010), p 45.
[54] 'Guidance issued under section 182 of the Licensing Act 2003' (Department for Culture, Media and Sport, London, 2006), esp at p 111.
[55] 'Evaluation of the Impact of the Licensing Act 2003' (Department for Culture, Media and Sport, March 2008), p 13.

crime and disorder, with overall levels unchanged.[56] On the other hand some evidence of temporal displacement was found 'in that the small proportion of violent crime occurring in the small hours of the morning has grown'.[57] The DCMS also observed:

'The main conclusion to be drawn from the evaluation is that licensing regimes may be one factor in effecting change in the country's drinking culture – and its impact on crime – but they do not appear to be the critical factor. The key issue is how they interact with other factors.'[58]

65.26   It was also noted that research by the University of Westminster[59] supported this conclusion. This recognition of complexity is in marked contrast to the more simplistic notions of cause and effect promulgated without question by ministers when trying to build support for licensing reform. One of the factors examined by Roberts and Eldridge was dispersal from late-night venues. They found that 'in situations of good management staggered hours can even out the peaks, but the peaks remain', noting what they felt was the failure of the Act to consider the subtleties of late night transport infrastructure.[60]

65.27   The DCMS evaluation concluded that there is:

'currently no evidence for fundamental change to the Licensing Act in relation to crime and disorder. However it seems clear that the Act has had much less impact in some areas and there may be scope to better use the legislation, alongside other interventions, as part of a strategic approach'.[61]

In terms of alcohol politics this might all seem perfectly reasonable were it not for the fact that a central claim of the reform process was that it would transform the crime and disorder situation, with the mechanism of staggered hours central to this. The absence of any consideration of this aspect is strikingly myopic.

65.28   In its 2010 report the Health Committee quite correctly pointed out that the effectiveness of legislation relies on enforcement.[62] However, the Committee was 'surprised to discover' that a key facet of the Licensing Act covering sale of alcohol to a person who is drunk (section 141 of the Act) 'is scarcely enforced'. A Commons written answer on 29 November 2010 made

---

[56]   'Evaluation of the Impact of the Licensing Act 2003', p 17.

[57]   'Evaluation of the Impact of the Licensing Act 2003', p 17.

[58]   'Evaluation of the Impact of the Licensing Act 2003', p 17.

[59]   M Roberts and A Eldridge, 'Expecting "Great Things"? The Impact of the Licensing Act 2003 on Democratic Involvement, Dispersal and Drinking Cultures' (University of Westminster for the IAS, 2007). http://www.ias.org.uk/cci/cci-0707.pdf.

[60]   Roberts and Eldridge, 'Expecting "Great Things"? The Impact of the Licensing Act 2003 on Democratic Involvement, Dispersal and Drinking Cultures', p 63.

[61]   'Evaluation of the Impact of the Licensing Act 2003', p 20,

[62]   House of Commons Health Committee, 'Alcohol. First Report of Session 2009–10. Volume 1. Report, together with formal minutes', p 89.

this clear, showing that in England and Wales a total of six cautions, 26 cases where proceedings of some description were brought, and a mere nine prosecutions occurred over the period 2005–2008. Hadfield and Newton[63] provide an account of the reasons for this, highlighting a gap between expectation and reality in the policing of alcohol-related matters.

65.29 The Health Committee reported in what turned out to be the final few months of the Labour government, shortly before what proved to be a political sea-change.

E NEW GOVERNMENT, NEW DIRECTION?

65.30 The formation of a Westminster coalition government (between the Conservative and Liberal Democrat parties) in May 2010 marked a profound shift in the political landscape after 13 years of governments controlled by the Labour party. In July 2010 the government transferred responsibility for the Act to the Home Office, with the exception of regulated entertainment, which remained with DCMS. Shortly afterwards the Home Office issued a public consultation document 'Rebalancing the Licensing Act'.[64] The document expressed the belief of the new government that an overhaul of the Act was required, emphasising a strong preference to raise the power of local residents in the licensing decision process. Did this mark evidence of new thinking on alcohol? The signs were not encouraging. The foreword to the document began with the quote that opened this chapter, placing binge drinking as the key problem that needed to be addressed. The document also strongly suggested that the Act itself had fostered an unwelcome change in drinking behaviour:

'The last 5 years have introduced a new drinking culture in our towns and cities.'[65]

65.31 The message that this 'new culture' was of the negative rather than the café variety was confirmed by an accompanying list of statistics on crime, violence and accident and emergency admissions, inviting the reader to conclude that this state of affairs had stemmed from the Act. Later in the document the phrase '24 hour drinking culture' is also used, alongside the remarkable admission that 'the number of premises open to sell alcohol after midnight or between 3am and 6am is not precisely known [to the government]'.

65.32 The first legislative action of the new government came in the form of the Police Reform and Social Responsibility Bill 2010, which was enacted

---

63   Hadfield and Newton, 'Alcohol, Crime and Disorder in the Night-time Economy',
64   Home Office, 'Rebalancing the Licensing Act. A consultation on empowering individuals, families and local communities to shape and determine local licensing' (2010).
65   Home Office, 'Rebalancing the Licensing Act. A consultation on empowering individuals, families and local communities to shape and determine local licensing' (2010), p 5.

largely as drafted the following the year. With regard to licensing the Act amended and supplemented the Licensing Act with the intention of 'rebalancing' it in favour of local authorities, the police and local communities. The consultation had put forward the possibility that the prevention of health harm could be made a material consideration in the Act. In a document detailing responses the government recorded that 'we want to ensure that this is considered alongside wider work to address the harm of alcohol to health. Accordingly, we do not intend to legislate at this stage but will consider the best way to do so in future'.[66]

65.33 The Government also signalled its intention to encourage licensing authorities to develop strategies based around fixed and staggered closing times (specifically discouraged under the original Guidance as noted above). This runs directly counter to the claim made in the White Paper, and rationalising the Act; that staggered closing times can lead to less crime and disorder by effecting gradual dispersal.[67] The implementation of the power to impose early morning restriction orders carries this to its logical extreme, by enabling licensing authorities to engineer a single terminal hour for late-opening premises.

65.34 Away from licensing reform other aspects of the new government's policy on alcohol have proved controversial. It was reported in March 2011 that eight leading UK health organisations had refused to sign up to a Department of Health-sponsored 'responsibility deal', accusing the Department of 'allowing the drinks industry to dictate policy'.[68] The organisations were also critical of the government for promoting policies lacking evidence of effectiveness.[69]

F CONCLUSIONS

65.35 Alcohol presents one the toughest of all policy challenges for government, arising from the sometimes diametrically opposed interests it has come to embody. However, the Health Committee of the House of Commons did not hold back in this damning assessment of how it has been tackled:

---

[66] Home Office, 'Rebalancing the Licensing Act: Responses to Consultation' (2010), at p 7. Available at: http://www.homeoffice.gov.uk/publications/consultations/cons-2010-licensing-act/responses-licensing-consult. The Government subsequently consulted on a measure to make health a material consideration in the formulation of cumulative impact policies: 'A consultation on delivering the Government's policies to cut alcohol fuelled crime and anti-social behaviour' (Home Office, November 2012).

[67] See further Chapter 1: Challenges.

[68] J Adetunji, 'Too close? The drinks industry's unsteady deal with government', Guardian Professional, 7 April 2011.

[69] IAS, 'Coalition's alcohol policy comes under attack', Alcohol Alert (No 1, 2011), p 2.

'Faced by a mounting problem, the response of successive Governments has ranged from the non-existent to the ineffectual.'[70]

65.36 Regarding the Act, the Committee pulled no punches either when saying that it felt the DCMS had shown 'extraordinary naivety' in believing the Act would bring about 'civilised café culture'.[71] Despite basing his call for a minimum unit price of alcohol on leading clinical studies (for example, from the British Medical Association, and the Nuffield Council on Bioethics) the then Chief Medical Officer, Sir Liam Donaldson, found his proposals loudly rejected by the then Prime Minister Gordon Brown on the basis that they would punish the 'sensible majority' of drinkers.[72] At the date of publication of this edition, the verdict of the Coalition Government on minimum pricing has yet to be pronounced. This places the politics of alcohol into sharp relief. Despite ample evidence on the scale of harms the recent agenda has been politically energised not by harm reduction but by licensing reform. A licensing White Paper emerged in 2000, but an alcohol harm reduction strategy did not emerge until 2004. History was repeated (though whether as tragedy or farce is a moot point) when the Police Reform and Social Responsibility Act 2011 preceded the new national Alcohol Strategy.[73] In any rational system, the strategy would precede the legislation.

65.37 The liberalisation of licensing – shown especially in relation to the development of the night-time economy – predated the Act but it was the Act that created new expectations and hastened the process. This chapter has highlighted the weakness of the evidence underlying the idea that extended hours, staggered or not, would achieve the kind of positive outcomes projected. That ministers failed to understand the ambiguities, gaps and complexities of the available evidence can at least in part be blamed on the civil servants who advised them. In a telling commentary in a national newspaper article, Professor (now Professor Emeritus) Griffith Edwards, a distinguished practitioner in addiction behaviour invited by government to give his expertise regarding alcohol strategy, revealed much about the inner workings of government:

'It didn't matter where we pointed or however we said it, the civil servants were deaf,' Edwards says. 'They were not able to be impartial.

---

[70] House of Commons Health Committee, 'Alcohol. First Report of Session 2009–10. Volume 1. Report, together with formal minutes', p 5.

[71] House of Commons Health Committee, 'Alcohol. First Report of Session 2009–10. Volume 1. Report, together with formal minutes', p 7.

[72] Shortly before retiring Sir Liam described this rejection as his biggest disappointment in his 12-year tenure as CMO ('Gordon Brown's refusal to ban cheap booze is biggest health failing, claims chief doctor', The Daily Telegraph, 14 March 2010). The Coalition Government has subsequently consulted on a minimum unit price of 45p per unit: 'A consultation on delivering the Government's policies to cut alcohol fuelled crime and anti-social behaviour' (Home Office, November 2012).

[73] Cm 83365, March 2012.

It was like being in secret service meetings. All they wanted to do was keep the drinks industry happy and excise levels stable.'[74]

65.38   However, a minister – in this case the 'sponsor' of the government alcohol harm reduction strategy at the time – blithely revealed what may be an even more uncomfortable truth about contemporary decision making. When asked in the same newspaper article why the government had rejected the advice of its scientific advisers in relation to the alcohol strategy the minister, Hazel Blears, observed:

'I respect the scientific view, but it wasn't for us. We needed practical measures.'[75]

65.39   Without offering any sympathy to Ms Blears' position, government is bombarded with analysis, data and opinion about alcohol.[76] So, is it fair to say we should expect more from our policy makers? In the case of the Act, did they allow pragmatism (what is popular with voters, or good for the economy, say) to colour their views on deciding on the need to prioritise something that might be politically unpopular or expensive? In sensible pursuit of reforms to an outdated licensing system the government sold the Act to Parliament – and the voting public – as a cure all for alcohol problems. However, the political focus on closing times came at the expense of marginalising health aspects of the alcohol issue. The now infamous text message sent by the Labour party to young voters on the eve of the 2001 general election, implying that a vote for Labour would see the end of 'last orders', showed the degree to which alcohol was seen to have political currency.

65.40   The motives for a number of government actions regarding alcohol are also open to question. Moving licensing from the Home Office to DCMS in 2001 had, as Room[77] points out, the effect of further fragmenting alcohol matters across government, in his view tending 'to provide the [alcohol] industry with a more reliable governmental ally (alcohol licensing falls under the 'tourism' section of the ministry's portfolio)'.[78] The Health Committee concurred with this view when it observed 'DCMS has been particularly close to the drinks industry. The interests of large pub chains and the promotion of the 'night-time' economy have taken priority'.[79] Evidence that

---

[74]   A Levy and C Scott-Clark, 'Under the influence', The Guardian Weekend, 20 November 2004, at p 22.

[75]   Levy and Scott-Clark, 'Under the influence', The Guardian Weekend, 20 November 2004, p 27.

[76]   The Health Committee report provided a list of 16 'key documents' alone specifically on the impact of alcohol 2000–2009 (at p 33), many by leading clinicians or clinical bodies.

[77]   R Room, 'Disabling the public interest: alcohol strategies and policies for England', Addiction, Vol 99 (2004), pp 1083–99.

[78]   Room, 'Disabling the public interest: alcohol strategies and policies for England', p 1085.

[79]   House of Commons Health Committee, 'Alcohol. First Report of Session 2009–10. Volume 1. Report, together with formal minutes', p 120.

the experience of other countries regarding the extension of licensing hours had been largely negative[80] was, it seems, unlikely to be what DCMS wanted to hear.

65.41 The fact that, in the end, the impact of the Act turned out to be largely neutral should not really be a surprise. As Hadfield has pointed out, in terms of licensed premises the Act was largely responding to the existing reality of opening times in licensed premises. This quote illustrates his point:

> 'With a range of licensing arrangements allowing for the sale of alcohol up to 2 am (3 am in London) and the potential for licensed entertainment until dawn, Britain's night-time high streets were, pre-November 2005, far removed from the 11 pm curfew zones of media mythology.'[81]

65.42 So, what of the future? A new government has taken office and has been critical of the Act, going so far as to suggest that it has created a 'new culture' (albeit without real substantiation of this view). In practical terms legislation has been passed that would see one of the original rationalising principles of the Act cast aside, as local licensing authorities are given liberty to pass policies of restraint, including cumulative impact zones, staggered hours, fixed terminals and zoning. The legislation also permits early morning restriction orders which would enable a common terminal hour to be fixed, precisely the situation which the Licensing Act 2003 was enacted to avoid, creating a perfect circle of alcohol politics in less than a decade.

65.43 With so many perspectives and a mountain of literature and media accounts to draw upon it is not an easy process to make sense of the UK relationship with alcohol – for anyone, policy-makers and analysts included. Whilst this short chapter cannot provide any more than an individual, necessarily selective topographical survey of the course of policy and the choices taken it does attempt to highlight – if nothing else – that volition is in the hands of policy makers, however difficult the policy challenge may be. The only real way to reduce harm – reducing the overall consumption of alcohol – cannot realistically be achieved through licensing change as the main policy; controls on pricing and marketing offer far greater potential. Yet, these arguments were made back in the early part of the century. Licensing will remain an important component of alcohol policy but expectations about reducing harm will depend on political imagination that puts evidence before practicality.

---

[80] Eg E J Plant and M Plant, 'A 'leap in the dark?' Lessons for the United Kingdom from past extensions of bar opening hours', *International Journal of Drug Policy* Vol 16 (2005), pp 363–368.

[81] Hadfield and Newton, 'Alcohol, Crime and Disorder in the Night-time Economy', p 177.

Alcohol control and the public interest: international perspectives

Iago   I learned [the song] in England, where, indeed, they are most potent in potting: your Dane, your German, and your swag-bellied Hollander – Drink, ho! – are nothing to your English.

Cassio Is your Englishman so expert in his drinking?

Iago   Why, he drinks you, with facility, your Dane dead drunk; he sweats not to overthrow your Almain; he gives your Hollander a vomit, ere the next pottle can be filled.

William Shakespeare, *Othello*

A INTRODUCTION

66.01 Alcoholic beverages have been known to humankind for all of recorded history, and even before the European expansion of the last half-millennium fermented beverages were used in all parts of the world except Australia, Oceania, and North America north of Mexico. Distilled spirits, coming to Europe from Arabia in the early Middle Ages, only escaped from the medicine chest into mundane use about 500 years ago, and came into use throughout the world as part of the European expansion. In traditional societies, alcoholic beverages were often relatively expensive to make, in terms of time and resources. With the industrial production of alcohol, in an early stage of the industrial revolution, alcoholic beverages became progressively cheaper in relative terms. In the absence of controls, the result was often an extended societal binge, as in the gin craze in 18th century England.[1]

B CONSEQUENCES OF DRINKING

66.02   Recognition that drinking can bring pain and harm, as well as pleasure, also extends through recorded history. The spectrum of harms from drinking is broad, affecting public health, safety, welfare, and productivity, and affecting others as well as the drinker. Alongside private and informal responses, governments have taken a wide spectrum of measures to reduce the harms from drinking. Such measures have often included laws regulating public drinking places, which can be found already in the Code of Hammurabi 3,800 years ago.[2]

66.03   In public health terminology, regulation of the production and sale of alcohol is often referred to as alcohol control,[3] by which is meant all regulation of the extent and conditions of alcohol availability, including a variety of measures such as excise taxation, licensing of premises and servers, and regulation of circumstances of sale such as permitted opening hours and days. Such regulations have a long and complex history in the UK.[4]

66.04   In the frame of public health and safety, alcohol policymaking starts from a consideration of the extent of, and trends in, problems related to drinking. These include social as well as health problems and acute problems as well as chronic. Considering only the health consequences, and after subtracting out protective effects on the heart, the World Health Organisation's study of the Global Burden of Disease in 2000 found that alcohol is the third most important risk factor for death and disability in developed societies such as the United Kingdom.[5] Various reports have brought together what evidence there is on problems from drinking for the United Kingdom.[6] For instance, it is estimated that alcohol-attributable hospital visits in England have risen in recent years, reaching 945,000 in 2008/9,

1   J Warner, *Craze: Gin and Debauchery in the Age of Reason* (Four Walls Eight Windows, New York, 2002); P G Dillon, *The Much-Lamented Death of Madame Geneva* (Justin, Charles & Co, Boston, 2003).
2   T Babor et al, *Alcohol: No Ordinary Commodity – Research and Public Policy* (Oxford University Press, 2nd ed, 2010). See Appendix 11 of this book for a full list of contributors.
3   R Room, 'Alcohol control and public health', Annual Review of Public Health 5 (1984), pp 293–317. http://www.bks.no/alcocont.pdf.
4   J Nicholls, *The Politics of Alcohol: A History of the Drink Question in England* (Manchester University Press, 2009).
5   M Ezzati, A D Lopez, A Rodgers, S Vander Hoorn, C J L Murray, and the Comparative Risk Assessment Collaborating Group, 'Selected major risk factors and global and regional burden of disease', The Lancet 360 (2002), pp 1347–1360.
6   York Health Economics Consortium, 'The Societal Cost of Alcohol Use in Scotland for 2007' (Scottish Government Social Research, Edinburgh, 2010), at http://www.scotland.gov.uk/Publications/2009/12/29122804/21; P S Meier, 'Polarised

about 7% of total admissions, and that alcohol is involved in up to one third of Accident and Emergency (A&E) visits. About 2.9 million British adults are reckoned to be dependent on alcohol. 47% of victims of violence in the British Crime Survey believed that their attacker was under the influence of alcohol. Between 30% and 60% of child protection cases involve drinking in the family. A study of the social costs in Scotland for 2007 found a mid-point estimate of over £3.5 billion, with 7.5% of the costs in health care expenditures, 6.5% in social work services, 20.4% in crime, and 24.3% in productive capacity. From the limited data available, the levels of harm from drinking were increasing until about 2007, even though consumption levels have been fairly stable. Between 1970 and 2000, for instance, deaths between the ages of 25 and 64 from chronic liver disease, a great majority of which involve heavy drinking, rose by 466%.

C THE RELATION OF DRINKING LEVELS AND PATTERNS TO CONSEQUENCES: THE INDIVIDUAL AND THE POPULATION LEVEL

66.05 Both the level of drinking over time and the pattern of drinking affect the risks for the individual drinker. The contribution of different aspects of drinking varies for different consequences. Thus the risk of problems such as injuries and overdose deaths primarily depends on drinking on a particular occasion. On the other hand, the risk of liver cirrhosis, gastritis or other chronic health consequences of drinking reflects levels of drinking over time. A pattern of relatively frequent light drinking seems to be protective against heart disease for those who are middle-aged or older. Most of this benefit can be gained by drinking as little as one drink every second day. On the other hand, a pattern of recurrent bouts of heavy drinking seems to be bad for the heart.[7]

66.06 In recent years, it has become more clearly recognised that these patterns as described at the individual level are only part of the picture when the effect of alcohol consumption on the population as a whole is considered. First, as discussed further below, many of the problems from drinking do not only affect the drinker.[8] Drink-driving potentially affects other drivers, passengers and pedestrians. Alcohol-fuelled violence may hurt family members, acquaintances or strangers. Time and resources spent out drinking may adversely affect children's upbringing and the quality of family life. Secondly,

drinking patterns and alcohol deregulation: Trends in alcohol consumption, harms and policy, United Kingdom 1990–2010', *Nordic Studies on Alcohol and Drugs* 27 (2010), pp 383–408.

[7]   A Britton, and M McKee, 'Relation between alcohol and cardiovascular disease in Eastern Europe: Explaining the paradox', *Journal of Epidemiology and Community Health* 54 (2000), pp 328–332; J Rehm and R Room, 'A case study in how harmful alcohol consumption can be', *The Lancet* 373 No 9682 (2009), pp 2176–2177.

[8]   R Room, 'Alcohol consumption and social harm: conceptual issues and historical perspectives', *Contemporary Drug Problems* 23 (1996), pp 373–388.

levels of drinking in the population are heavily skewed, with less than 20% of drinkers typically responsible for more than half of overall consumption.[9] Patterns among the heavier drinkers may have a disproportionate influence on consequences. Third, in thinking about the population as a whole there is a need to take into account that drinking is primarily a social behaviour. How I drink today is likely to affect how you drink today or tomorrow. If I buy you a round as part of a group at the pub, my expectation is that you will sooner or later buy one for me – and drink another one for yourself at the same time. If I bring a bottle of wine to your dinner-party, the chances are you will bring one to mine the next time. So there is a tendency for changes in drinking in a population to be linked. The result of these three factors is that the risk levels based on individual-level data are not always a good guide to what will happen in the population as a whole as levels of drinking change.[10]

66.07 For many chronic health consequences of drinking, such as liver cirrhosis, what seems to matter most at the population level, in predicting cirrhosis mortality in a given year, is the level of drinking in the previous few years. For drink driving and violence, the dominant patterns of drinking in a population – how much of the consumption leads to intoxication – affect the rate of harm. But customary drinking patterns in a population change only slowly over time.[11] Thus, while dominant patterns of drinking matter for comparisons of one drinking culture with another, they do not make much difference in comparisons over time within a given population. In a given society, it seems that changes in rates of injuries track quite closely changes in the population's overall level of consumption.[12]

66.08 For the middle-aged or older individual, the protective effect on the heart may be a relevant consideration in choices about drinking. But the effect is apparently not important for alcohol policy and controls. At the levels of drinking which are current in Britain and western Europe, a change in the population's level of drinking does not affect the rate of heart disease mortality.[13] It seems that any gains for those adopting protective drinking patterns are offset by losses for those who change to patterns more risky for the heart.[14]

[9]   T K Greenfield and J D Rogers, 'Who drinks most of the alcohol in the US? The policy implications', Journal of Studies on Alcohol 60 (1999), pp 78–89.
[10] O-J Skog, 'Public health consequences of the J-curve hypothesis of alcohol problems', Addiction 91 (1996), pp 325–337.
[11] J Simpura, 'Trends in alcohol consumption and drinking patterns: Sociological and economic explanations and alcohol policies', Nordisk Alkohol & narkotikatidskrift 18 (English Supplement, 2001), pp 3–13.
[12] T Norström (ed), 'Alcohol in Postwar Europe: Consumption, Drinking Patterns, Consequences and Policy Response in 15 European Countries', (National Institute of Public Health, Stockholm, 2002).
[13] Ö Hemström, 'Per capita alcohol consumption and ischaemic heart disease', Addiction 96 (Supplement 1, 2001), pp 93–112S.
[14] Skog, 'Public health consequences of the J-curve hypothesis of alcohol problems'.

66.09 The conclusion is that, at the population level, both the level of consumption and the dominant patterns of drinking have an effect on problems caused by alcohol. In terms of patterns, an extra litre of pure alcohol per annum per capita will have a greater effect on homicide, for instance, in northern Europe than in southern Europe. But it is difficult to find examples of successful purposive efforts to change a population's overall patterns of drinking,[15] although changes in behaviour around drinking and driving seem to be an exception. On a smaller scale, this generally pessimistic conclusion is supported by the general failure of school education or public information campaigns to show lasting results.[16] This leaves governments with three main effective strategies for reducing the rates of alcohol problems in the population: reducing the level of drinking; reducing or eliminating drinking in specific risk situations, notably in connection with driving; and reducing the risk from drinking in specific situations, for instance by changing the environment of drinking.

D THE WARRANT FOR ALCOHOL CONTROLS

66.10 It may well be asked, what warrant does a government have for acting to reduce rates of alcohol problems in the population? Views differ, for instance, on whether and to what extent it is appropriate for a government to intervene to prevent suicide or other actions impacting primarily on the actor him- or herself. Even for effects which are limited to the actor, however, society at large has an interest in what happens where there are health or welfare costs for society from the actions. Beyond this, many problems from alcohol involve effects on others besides the drinker. In the case of such effects, there is wide social consensus that there is a warrant for action, including, as needed, governmental action. Along with the very serious harms already noted such as homicide, domestic violence and drink-driving casualties, it includes a broader penumbra of personal conflict and infringement and disturbance of the peace. An Australian study found that 28.5% of adults had been negatively affected by the drinking of relatives and others known to them in the last year, that 43.4% reported tangible harm from the drinking of strangers, and that 5.1% reported that other adults' drinking had adversely affected their children. The study found that the costs to others of drinking were about equal to the costs to the drinker and to governments usually measured in economic cost studies.[17]

---

[15]   R Room, 'The impossible dream? Routes to reducing alcohol problems in a temperance culture', Journal of Substance Abuse 4 (1991), pp 91–106. http://www.bks.no/imposs.pdf.

[16]   Babor et al, *Alcohol: No Ordinary Commodity – Research and Public Policy*.

[17]   A-M Laslett et al, *The Range and Magnitude of Alcohol's Harm to Others* (Alcohol Education and Rehabilitation Foundation, Canberra, 2010), http://www.fare.org.au/research-development/alcohols-harm-to-others/. See Appendix 11 for a full list of contributors.

E PREVENTING PROBLEMS FROM DRINKING: THE RESEARCH LITERATURE ON ALCOHOL CONTROL

66.11 The idea of establishing an evidence base for alcohol control is not new. For instance, a pioneer British study during the First World War of the effects of restricting the opening hours of pubs at the factory gates found that there were fewer accidents among men and during the first spell of work on a shift, since drinking before going to work had diminished.[18] But the modern tradition of studies of the effects of alcohol controls is a product of the last 50 years. We here review briefly the evidence on particular strategies relevant to alcohol licensing and control. A more complete review of the literature can be found in Babor et al.[19]

Taxation and price

66.12 As with other commodities, the consumption of alcohol is influenced by both price and income. A substantial economic depression is a very effective way of reducing alcohol consumption, but no-one would argue for this as a deliberate strategy. Taxes on alcohol, which raise the price of alcoholic beverages relative to other choices for the consumer, are an effective strategy for reducing rates of problems from drinking – for instance, drink-driving casualties, cirrhosis and homicides.[20] The tradition of relatively high alcohol taxes in Britain, recently considerably eroded,[21] was not only a source of revenue for the Treasury but also effective in restraining the rates of alcohol-related problems. An alternative strategy for mild discouragement of heavy drinking, recently much discussed in Britain, is through setting a minimum price per unit of pure alcohol, a strategy particularly directed at the bottom of the off-sale market. A Canadian study found that raising the minimum price by 10% reduced overall alcohol consumption by 3.4%.[22] Modelling of data on drinking patterns in subgroups of the British population has shown that the primary effect of requiring a minimum price at the

---

[18] E L Collis, 'Discussion on alcohol as a beverage and its relation to certain social problems: alcohol and industrial efficiency', British Medical Journal 2 (1922), pp 244–248.

[19] Babor et al, *Alcohol: No Ordinary Commodity – Research and Public Policy.*

[20] P J Cook, 'The effect of liquor taxes on drinking, cirrhosis and auto fatalities' in M Moore and D Gerstein (eds), *Alcohol and Public Policy: Beyond the Shadow of Prohibition* (National Academy of Sciences, Washington, DC, 1981), pp 255–285; P J Cook and M J Moore, 'Violence reduction through restrictions on alcohol availability', Alcohol Health and Research World 17 (1993), pp 151–156.

[21] 'Calling Time, The Nation's drinking as a major health issue', Academy of Medical Sciences (2004).

[22] T Stockwell, M C Auld, J Zhao and G Martin, 'Does minimum pricing reduce alcohol consumption? The experience of a Canadian province', Addiction 107(5) (2012), pp 912–920.

levels under consideration by policymakers would be on heavier drinkers, those most at risk of health and other problems from drinking.[23]

Hours and days of sale

66.13 British studies of the effects of extending hours of pub opening on health and drink-driving, which have been few and rather weak in design, have shown mixed results.[24]

66.14 Elsewhere, there are a number of studies which demonstrate that changing either hours or days of alcohol sale at a minimum redistributes when alcohol-related crashes and other violent events related to alcohol take place, which holds implications for rescheduling of police shifts and of public transportation.[25] More recent studies in Western Australia[26] and Iceland[27] have found an overall increase in such problems as injuries and drinking-driving incidents with lengthened hours of sale. Studies of changes in the opposite direction have also found clear effects. A study of reduced off-sales hours in Geneva, Switzerland, with no sales allowed between 9 pm and 7 am, found a reduction of over 25% in hospitalisations for intoxication among adolescents and young adults.[28] A study in the Australian city of Newcastle found a 37% reduction in night assaults when pubs in the central business district were required to close earlier (initially by 3 am and then by 3:30 am).[29]

[23] P S Meier, R Purshouse and A Brennan, 'Policy options for alcohol price regulation: the importance of modelling population heterogeneity', Addiction 105(3) (2010), pp 383–393.

[24] D Raistrick, R Hodgson and B Ritson, *Tackling Alcohol Together: The Evidence Base for a UK Alcohol Policy* (Free Association Books, London and New York, 1999).

[25] Eg D I Smith, 'Effectiveness of restrictions on availability as a means of preventing alcohol-related problems', Contemporary Drug Problems 15 (1988) pp 627–684; S Nordlund, 'Effects of Saturday closing of wine and spirits shops in Norway', Paper presented at the 31st International Institute on the Prevention and Treatment of Alcoholism, Rome, Italy, 2–7 June 1985, SIFA Mimeograph No. 5/85. (National Institute of Alcohol Research, Oslo).

[26] T Chikritzhs and T R Stockwell, 'The Impact of later trading hours for Australian public houses (hotels) on levels of violence', Journal of Studies on Alcohol 63(5) (2002), pp 591–599.

[27] T Ragnarsdottir, A Kjartansdottir and S Davidsdottir, 'Effect of extended alcohol serving-hours in Reykjavik' in R Room (ed) *The Effects of Nordic Alcohol Policies: What Happens to Drinking and Harm when Alcohol Policies Change?*, Publication No 42 (Nordic Council for Alcohol and Drug Research, Helsinki, 2002), pp 145–154.

[28] M Wicki and G Gmel, 'Hospital admission rates for alcohol intoxication after policy changes in the canton of Geneva, Switzerland', Drug and Alcohol Dependence 118(2–3) (2011), pp 209–215.

[29] K Kypri, C Jones, P McElduff and D Barker, 'Effects of restricting pub closing times on night-time assaults in an Australian city'. Addiction 106(2) (2011), pp 303–310.

Concentration and density of alcohol outlets

66.15 Cross-sectional studies suggest that alcohol-related problems, especially motor vehicle crashes, are more likely to occur where drinking places are more densely packed.[30] These results appear to extend to other pedestrian injury collisions[31] and violent assaults.[32]

66.16 Studies of the density of outlets have also found an effect of increased numbers of outlets on alcohol problem rates. A time-series study of changes in the number of on-premise outlets in Norway as a whole in 1960–1995 found a significant relation to changes in the number of crimes of violence which were investigated by the police.[33] The most dramatic change studied was in Finland, and its effects were also dramatic. In 1969, the number of off-premise sales points for beer up to 4.7% increased from 132 to about 17,600, and the number of on-premise sales points from 940 to over 4000.[34] The overall consumption of alcohol increased by 46%. In the following five years, mortality from liver cirrhosis increased by 50%, hospital admissions for alcoholic psychosis by 110% for men and 130% for women, and arrests for drunkenness by 80% for men and 160% for women.[35]

66.17 In general, it is clear that dramatic changes in the number of outlets can have a substantial influence on consumption and problem levels. Recent studies of the effects of marginal changes in outlet density have also found effects on indicators of harm. Thus studies in the metropolitan region of Melbourne, Australia have shown significant effects of changes in the number of on-sales outlets on street assaults in the neighbourhood,[36] and of changes in the number of off-sales outlets on domestic violence incidents and on hospitalisations for chronic alcohol-induced diseases.[37]

---

[30]   R T Jewell and R W Brown, 'Alcohol availability and alcohol-related motor vehicle accidents', Applied Economics 27 (1995), pp 759–765.

[31]   E A LaScala, F Johnson and P J Gruenewald, 'Neighborhood characteristics of alcohol-related pedestrian injury collisions: A geostatistical analysis', Prevention Science 2 (2001), pp 123–134.

[32]   M L Alaniz, R S Cartmill and R N Parker 'Immigrants and violence: the importance of neighborhood context', Hispanic Journal of Behavioral Sciences 20 (1998), pp 155–174; R J Stevenson, B Lind and D Weatherburn, 'Relationship between alcohol sales and assault in New South Wales, Australia', Addiction 94 (1999), pp 397–410.

[33]   T Norström, 'Outlet density and criminal violence in Norway, 1960–1995', Journal of Studies on Alcohol 61 (2000), pp 907–911.

[34]   E Österberg, 'Recorded Consumption of Alcohol in Finland, 1950–1975', report no 125 (Social Research Institute of Alcohol Studies, Helsinki, 1979).

[35]   K Poikolainen, 'Increase in alcohol-related hospitalisations in Finland 1969–1975', British Journal of Addiction 75 (1980), pp 281–291.

[36]   M Livingston, 'A longitudinal analysis of alcohol outlet density and assault', Alcoholism: Clinical and Experimental Research 32(6) (2008), pp 1074–1079.

[37]   M Livingston, 'A longitudinal analysis of alcohol outlet density and domestic violence', Addiction 106(5) (2011), pp 919–925; 'Alcohol outlet density and harm: Comparing the impacts on violence and chronic harms', Drug and Alcohol Review 30(5) (2011), pp 515–523.

Regulation of service

66.18 Responsible Beverage Service (RBS) programs focus on attitudes, knowledge, skills, and practices of persons involved in serving alcoholic beverages on licensed premises.[38] In the absence of institutional support and regulatory oversight, stand-alone training in RBS appears to have few lasting effects. But if supported by actual changes in the serving policies of licensed establishments and reinforced by local police or licensing inspectors, RBS training can reduce heavy consumption and high risk drinking.[39] A Swedish study found that a program combining stricter enforcement of alcohol sales laws and training in responsible beverage service had a significant effect in reducing the rate of violent crimes between 10 pm and 6 am.[40] There are also promising results from a Canadian controlled trial of staff training in reducing pub-related violence.[41]

66.19 In many jurisdictions in the US and Canada, alcohol sellers or suppliers are legally liable for damages caused by patrons they served when already drunk or who are under age ('dram-shop' laws), and such liability has been shown to be effective in reducing drink-driving casualties.[42] It has the further advantage of encouraging effective server training, and of making insurers deeply interested in house policies and practices on unlawful serving. It has been argued that this strategy could also be used as an extension of common law in Britain.[43]

---

[38]   T L Toomey, G R Kilian, J P Gehan, C L Perry, R Jones-Webb, and A C Wagenaar, 'Qualitative assessment of training programs for alcohol servers and establishment managers', Public Health Reports 113 (1998), pp 162–169.

[39]   B Howard-Pitney, M D Johnson, D G Altman, R Hopkins and N Hammond, 'Responsible alcohol service: A study of server, manager, and environmental impact', American Journal of Public Health 81 (1991), pp 197–199; E Lang, T Stockwell, P Rydon and A Beel, 'Can training bar staff in responsible serving practices reduce alcohol-related harm?', Drug and Alcohol Review 17 (1998), pp 39–50.

[40]   E Wallin, T Norström and S Andréasson, 'Alcohol prevention targeting licensed premises: a study of effects on violence', Journal of Studies on Alcohol 64 (2003), pp 270–277.

[41]   K Graham and S Wells, 'Somebody's Gonna Get Their Head Kicked in Tonight!: Aggression Among Young Males in Bars – A Question of Values?', British Journal of Criminology 43 (2003), pp 546–566.

[42]   A C Wagenaar and H D Holder, 'Effects of alcoholic beverage server liability on traffic crash injuries', Alcoholism: Clinical and Experimental Research 15 (1991), pp 942–947.

[43]   J Goodliffe, 'Can the civil law implement alcohol policy?' Alcohol Alert (No 3, 2003), pp 20–22. http://www.ias.org.uk/publications/alert/03issue3/alert0303_p20.html.

Drink-driving countermeasures

66.20 The evidence indicates that setting a low legal BAC (blood-alcohol content) level for drivers significantly reduces alcohol-related driving fatalities.[44] The present UK BAC level, 0.08%, is higher than the 0.05% level which applies in most of Europe. Evaluations have shown that further reducing the level in Sweden to 0.02% further reduced drink-driving fatalities.[45]

66.21 In recent years the greatest emphasis has been placed not on catching and punishing drinking drivers but on deterring drinkers from driving in the first place. The most effective deterrence approach is through random breath testing (RBT),[46] where motorists are stopped at random by police and required to take a preliminary breath test. The evidence shows that highly visible, non-selective testing on a regular basis can have a sustained effect on drinking-driving and the associated crashes, injuries, and deaths.[47]

There are a number of other drink-driving countermeasures which have also been shown to have effects.[48]

F CHANGES IN BRITISH AND IRISH DRINKING

66.22 The new millennium brought increasing reports of widespread problems with alcohol-related public disorder on the streets of British and Irish cities.[49] The focus in news reports has been primarily on the drinking of

[44] R A Shults, R W Elder, D A Sleet et al, 'Reviews of evidence regarding interventions to reduce alcohol-impaired driving', American Journal of Preventive Medicine 21 (2001), pp 66–88.

[45] B Borschos, 'Evaluation of the Swedish drunken driving legislation implemented on February 1, 1994' presented at the 15th International Conference on Alcohol, Drugs and Traffic Safety, Stockholm, Sweden, 22–26 Sept 2000, http://www.vv.se/traf_sak/t2000/508.pdf; T Norström, 'Assessment of the impact of the 0.02% BAC-limit in Sweden'. Studies on Crime and Crime Prevention 6(2) (1997), pp 245–258.

[46] Shults, Elder, Sleet, et al, 'Reviews of evidence regarding interventions to reduce alcohol-impaired driving'; J Henstridge, R Homel and P Mackay, 'The Long-term Effects of Random Breath Testing in Four Australian States: A Time Series Analysis' (Federal Office of Road Safety, Canberra, 1997).

[47] L Stewart and K Conway, 'Community action to reduce rural drink driving crashes: encouraging sustainable efforts in changing environments' in S Casswell, H Holder, M Holmila, S Larsson, R Midford, H M Barnes, P Nygaard and L Stewart (eds), 'Fourth Symposium on Community Action Research and the Prevention of Alcohol and Other Drug Problems: Based upon Kettil Bruun Society Thematic Meeting' (Alcohol and Public Health Research Unit, University of Auckland, NZ), pp 233–246.

[48] Babor et al, *Alcohol: No Ordinary Commodity – Research and Public Policy*.

[49] P Chatterton and R Hollands, *Urban Nightscapes: Youth Cultures, Pleasure Spaces and Corporate Power* (Routledge, 2003); D Hobbs, P Hadfield, S Lister and S Winlow, *Bouncers: Violence and Governance in the Night-time Economy* (Oxford University Press, 2003), available at http://www.oup.co.uk/isbn/0–19–925224–6; Strategic Task Force on Alcohol, 'Interim Report' (Department of Health, May 2002).

young adults, with complaints that the central parts of many cities in Britain have become 'no go' areas on weekends for those wishing to avoid trouble. The focus has tended to divert attention from the fact that the weekly volume of drinking is higher among the middle aged, who are at more risk of chronic health problems.[50]

66.23 Problems with youth drinking are not unique to the British Isles, although the problems are manifested differently in different European cultures. Spanish authorities have complained about and tried to suppress 'el botellón', the custom of teenagers gathering in town squares to drink large amounts of mixed beverages such as cheap wine and cola.[51] A French study of young adults finds that many of them value intoxication, confining their drinking to weekends, and generally rejecting any pattern of regular light consumption, particularly of red wine, as tantamount to alcoholism.[52] While British and Irish 15-year-olds have consistently been near the top among 30 countries in Europe in terms of the proportion drinking five or more drinks on an occasion, the proportion in Ireland dropped a little in the 2011 survey,[53] and there is also some evidence of a reduction in heavy drinking sessions among British teenagers.[54]

66.24 There are also structural elements to the current situation in Britain and Ireland. The problems primarily revolve around public drinking. Although the proportion of drinking which is in pubs and restaurants has been slowly declining, it remains much higher in Britain and Ireland than anywhere else for which there is data.[55] In the following paragraphs, some suggestions are put forward concerning structural elements which seem to be making the situation worse in Britain.

66.25 The British tradition of 'tied houses' (where pubs were often owned by large operators, originally the brewers) has meant that the ownership is not on site, not living in town and not open to informal pressure from neighbours, and can lead to a situation where the lessee is being squeezed to

---

[50] S Dunstan (ed), 'General Lifestyle Survey Overview: A Report on the 2010 General Lifestyle Survey' (Office for National Statistics, Newport, 2012). http://www.ons.gov.uk/ons/rel/ghs/general-lifestyle-survey/2010/index.html.

[51] A Baigorri, R Fernándezand Giesyt, *Botellón: Un Conflicto Postmoderno (Botellón: A postmodern conflict)* (Ed Icaria, Barcelona, 2004).

[52] J Freyssinet-Dominjon and A-C Wagner, *L'alcool en fête — manières de boire de la nouvelle jeunesse étudiante (Party drinking: ways of drinking of the new student youth)* (L'Harmattan, 2003).

[53] B Hibell, B Andersson, S Ahlström, O Balakireva, T Bjarnasson, A Kokkevi, and M Morgan, 'The 1999 ESPAD Report: Alcohol and Other Drug Use among Students in 30 Countries' (CAN, 2000); Freyssinet-Dominjon and Wagner, *L'alcool en fête — manières de boire de la nouvelle jeunesse étudiante (Party drinking: ways of drinking of the new student youth)*.

[54] 'Drinking habits: sobering: the British love affair with the bottle appears to be ending', The Economist, 6 October 2012.

[55] Babor et al, *Alcohol: No Ordinary Commodity – Research and Public Policy*; 'Calling Time: The Nation's Drinking as a Major Health Issue' (Academy of Medical Sciences, London, 2004), http://www.acmedsci.ac.uk/p_callingtime.pdf.

maximise takings. (In the US, for instance, tied houses, where the retail level is owned by the producers or wholesalers of alcoholic beverages, have been forbidden by both federal and state legislation since Repeal of Prohibition in 1934.) The Monopoly Commission's order in the 1980s to remove many of the pubs from brewer ownership means that there is now a new set of actors on the scene: the pub companies ('pubcos'). The 'estates' of hundreds of pubs in common ownership were not broken up, simply commoditised and sold off. Evidence given in parliamentary hearings has depicted the pubcos as often lacking the sense of social responsibility that the brewers had retained from the days when the temperance movement was strong.[56] Allegations of exploitation have been made by leaseholders, but are denied by the pubcos. In the recession after 2008, both the leaseholders and several of the pubcos have been under extreme economic pressure.[57]

66.26 As Hobbs and his colleagues[58] explain, city councils and planners have also contributed to the situation by encouraging the 'night-time economy', seen as a way to resuscitate de-industrialised city centres. However, instead of the lively cultural centre which was hoped for, the result has often been an oversupply of 'enormous city bars'; 'vertical drink factories', as they are described in parliamentary debate.[59] It is much more difficult for servers and other staff to keep track of customers and ensure good order when the drinking area is large and crowded. The situation has been exacerbated by the abolition of the concept of 'need' as a constraint on new pub licences,[60] and the Town and Country Planning (Use Classes) Order 1987,[61] which until April 2005 tied the hands of local planners so that they were been unable to resist changes of use within Class A3 from restaurants and cafes to pubs in central districts.[62]

66.27 The regulatory system has also often become non-functional. The licensing justices system was often co-opted by the trade, and it remains to be seen if this will happen with the new regulators. As elsewhere, licences have become more and more viewed as a property right, well-defended by legal teams. The police tended until fairly recently to regard alcohol trouble as routine and everyday, and not something which could be affected by their policies and priorities. There has in particular been a lack of enforcement of

---

56   See UK House of Commons Trade and Industry Committee, 22 June 2004, 6 July 2004, 20 July 2004, HC 751, i–iii.

57   J Harris, 'Pub giants fall into debt, but publicans feel the pain'. The Guardian, 18 March 2012, http://www.guardian.co.uk/commentisfree/2012/mar/18/pub-debt-publicans-pain-pubcos.

58   Hobbs, Hadfield, Lister and Winlow, *Bouncers: Violence and Governance in the Night-time Economy.*

59   HL Debates 12 May 2004, col 325, 8 June 2004, cols 230, 236.

60   'Justices Clerks Society Good Practice Guide' (1999, amended 2001).

61   SI 1987/764.

62   S Owens, 'Pubs, clubs and restaurants: The impact of the new Licensing Act together with a difficult trading environment and other new legislation on capital and rental values of UK nightclubs', Journal of Retail and Leisure Property 5 (2006), pp 341–353.

the criminal law both regarding drunkenness in licensed premises, and the sale of liquor to people who are drunk. The international experience is that alcohol regulation tends to work better when there are specific alcohol control inspectors (whether civilian or as a police unit) whose job it is to hold down alcohol-related troubles, rather than making enforcement a part of general police work.

66.28 There is no other English-speaking society, and it is difficult to think of any society, where the alcohol industry (the producers and the pubcos, particularly) has more political power than in the UK.[63] The industry's power in UK politics is on the current agenda for further research.[64]

G BRINGING LIQUOR LICENSING AND REGULATION TOGETHER WITH EVIDENCE-BASED PROMOTION OF PUBLIC HEALTH AND SAFETY

66.29 There is an imperfect fit between what those involved in liquor licensing decisions may want to know and what is available in the literature on alcohol controls. The gap between the content of alcohol control legislation and the research literature has been documented in the US[65] and is undoubtedly at least as great in Britain and Ireland. The studies in the research literature are sometimes done because a change was controversial in a particular jurisdiction, and funding an evaluation was a way of defusing the controversy. Other studies have been opportunistic, where a researcher seizes the chance to do a 'natural experiment' study ('natural' here means that the researcher did not have a voice in the circumstances of the change, so that the study's design is often constrained). Often studies have made use of available data, such as per-capita consumption data or mortality registers. Since research is usually a national government responsibility, its topical focus is not necessarily attuned to the concerns of local jurisdictions.

66.30 Nevertheless, the growth of the literature evaluating the effects of alcohol controls has been a substantial achievement involving a number of national traditions, and lessons from it can be applied, with suitable caution, across jurisdictions. For action at the community level, there are some

---

[63] R Room, 'Disabling the public interest: alcohol policies and strategies for England', Addiction 99 (2004), pp 1083–1089; S Bosely, 'Drinks industry grip on alcohol panel criticised', The Guardian, 1 August 2011. http://www.guardian.co.uk/society/2011/aug/01/alcohol-abuse-drinks-representatives.

[64] B Hawkins, C Holden and J McCambridge, 'Alcohol industry influence on UK alcohol policy: A new research agenda for public health', Critical Public Health 22(3) (2012), pp 297–305.

[65] A C Wagenaar, and T L Toomey, 'Alcoholic policy: Gap between legislative action and current research', Contemporary Drug Problems 27 (2000), pp 681–733.

publications reviewing community-level environmental approaches to preventing alcohol problems.[66]

66.31 It is notable how small the contributions from Britain and Ireland have been to this international literature. British social alcohol research was systematically dismantled at the time of the Thatcher government, with the result that until recently there was little tradition in Britain of the kind of research-involved prevention and policy studies on alcohol problems that can be found in Australia, Canada, the US, the Nordic countries, the Netherlands, or Poland. Relevant work is now under way, but it takes time for knowledge to accumulate about what works and (more important) what doesn't.

66.32 The modern British approach to liquor licensing appears to have been to muddle through on the basis of presumptions and good intentions, with little concern about the evidence base for actions, and no investment in monitoring and evaluating what the actual results of a policy or official action are. Sometimes it appears that a deliberate blind eye is turned to the evidence.[67] This is actually a considerable backsliding from the position 70 to 90 years ago, when Britain was a world leader in studies of the effects of alcohol controls.[68] Much can be learned from local experiments and policy changes. This may involve setting up local data-collection systems for collection of data by the licensing authorities, police, A&E services, and health and welfare services. Such data collection may be used for studying the effects of a specific change, but it also potentially becomes a means of reflexive monitoring, by which problems can be identified and responded to as they occur. Studies of the effects of a specific change or action need to be analysed and published, so that other localities can learn from the experience. In this way, a cumulative literature of evaluations of the effects of licensing and alcohol control measures can be built up. As it once before was,[69] evidence-based practice needs to become the watchword for licensing and regulation in Britain and Ireland.

---

[66] P Grover (ed), 'Preventing Problems Related to Alcohol Availability: Environmental Approaches – Reference Guide'. Prevention Enhancement Protocols System No 3. (Substance Abuse and Mental Health Services Administration, Center for Substance Abuse Prevention, Rockville, MD, 1999). DHHS Publication No (SMA)99–3298. Available at http://ncadi.samhsa.gov/govpubs/PHD822/. See also H D Holder, *Alcohol and the Community: A Systems Approach to Prevention* (Cambridge University Press, 1998).

[67] R Room, 'The impotence of reason in the face of greed, moral cowardice, and selfish ambition', Addiction 99 (2004), pp 1092–1093.

[68] Eg H Carter, *The Control of the Drink Trade: A Contribution to National Efficiency 1915–1917* (Longmans, Green & Co, 1918); A Shadwell, *Drink in 1914–1922: A Lesson in Control* (Longmans, Green & Co, 1923); G E G Catlin, *Liquor Control* (Henry Holt & Co, New York and Thornton Butterworth, London, 1931).

[69] R Room, 'Classic texts revisited: George EG Catlin, Liquor Control', Addiction 99 (2004), pp 925–927.

Case summaries

| CAMBRIDGE CITY COUNCIL v ALEX NESTLING LTD | Divisional Court [2006] EWHC 1374 (Admin) [2006] LLR 397 | Facts: On an appeal against a licensing decision the magistrates' court awarded the appellant costs on the basis that it had reached a different conclusion, notwithstanding that the licensing authority had dealt with matters correctly.

Issue: Was the award of costs proper?

Decision: No. The fact that the local authority has acted reasonably and in good faith in the discharge of its public function is a most important factor.

Toulson J:

The decision in *City of Bradford Metropolitan District Council v Booth* [2001] LLR 151 is applicable in all cases where there is a statutory appeal from a decision of the local authority and the court has a broad discretion as to costs.

Although as a matter of strict law the power of the court in such circumstances to award costs is not confined to cases where the local authority acted unreasonably and in bad faith, the fact that the local authority has acted reasonably and in good faith in the discharge of its public function is plainly a most important factor. |
| CARMARTHEN-SHIRE COUNTY COUNCIL v LLANELLI MAGISTRATES | [2009] EWHC 3016 (Admin) [2010] LLR 11 | Facts: A licensing authority revoked a premises licence after failed test purchases. The magistrates' court allowed the licensee's appeal, holding that revocation was not necessary or proportionate, and also ordered the authority to pay costs. The authority appealed against the costs order.

Issue: Was the costs decision proper? Decision: No, because the substantive decision was not proper.

Silber J:

1. The magistrates took the wrong approach by considering whether revocation was necessary and proportionate, which thereby disregarded attaching any weight to the licensing objectives in the 2003 Act.

2. The magistrates erred, as they did not expressly or impliedly consider the licensing objective of 'prevention of children from harm' or the prevention of crime and disorder contained in the 2003 Act and the guidance under it. |

		3. The Section 182 Guidance states that the review provisions represent a key protection for the community and should, in general, allow licensing authorities to apply a light touch bureaucracy to the grant and variation of premises licences by providing a review mechanism when concerns relating to the licensing objectives arise later in respect of individual premises. The Guidance also states that the use of premises for sale to underage persons should be treated particularly seriously, because this impacts on the health, educational attainment, employment prospects and propensity for crime of young people. The magistrates failed to heed this guidance. In *R (Daniel Thwaites plc) v Wirral Borough Magistrates' Court* Black J stressed that the magistrates' court is not entitled to do is simply to *ignore* the Guidance or fail to give it any weight; that when a magistrates' court is entitled to depart from the Guidance and justifiably does so, it must give proper reasons for so doing; and that the magistrates did not need to work slavishly through the Guidance in articulating their decision but they did need to give full reasons for their decision overall and full reasons for departing from the Guidance if they considered it proper so to do. Similarly, in *R (Bassetlaw District Council) v Worksop Magistrates' Court* SladeJ emphasised the need for the magistrates' court to identify why and in what respects it was departing from the guidance. This case is a stronger case, because the magistrates did not merely fail to follow the Guidance: they did not even refer to it at all.
		4. The magistrates also erred in failing to consider the harm caused by the sale of alcohol to these 15-year-old youths. Instead, they concentrated on the absence of any connection between the premises and the commission of a crime in the village. The magistrates had to consider further matters other than the commission of a crime in relation to the effect of selling alcohol to under-age youths, such as the effect on other aspects of their life.
		5. The magistrates also failed properly to consider the representations of the responsible authorities on the issue of revocation. *Daniel Thwaites* makes it clear that weight must be given to their views, and paragraph 2.1 of the Guidance states that the police should be treated as the main source of advice on crime and disorder.
		6. Finally, the reasoning of the magistrates shows that they regarded as definitive in this case the absence of any link between the premises and the commission of crime and disorder, as well as the fact that steps had been taken by the interested party to ensure no sales were made in the future to underage youths. This shows a misunderstanding of the legislative objectives.

CITY OF BRAD-FORD METRO-POLITAN DISTRICT COUN-CIL v BOOTH	Court of Appeal [2001] LLR 151	Facts: Licensing appeal. Magistrates' court ordered licensing authority to pay £750 to successful appellant on 'just and reasonable' basis.

Issues:

(1)   Do costs follow the event in licensing appeals?

(2)   Is it necessary to find that licensing authority acted unreasonably to found an order for costs?

Decision:

(1)   No.

(2)   No.

Lord Bingham CJ:

(1)   Magistrates' court has a discretion on appeal to make such order as to costs as it thinks just and reasonable. That provision applies both to the quantum of the costs (if any) to be paid, but also as to the party (if any) which should pay them.

(2)   What the court will think just and reasonable will depend on all the relevant facts and circumstances of the case before the court. The court may, but is not obliged to, think it just and reasonable that costs should follow the event.

(3)   Where a complainant has successfully challenged before justices an administrative decision made by a police or regulatory authority acting honestly, reasonably, properly and on grounds that reasonably appeared to be sound, in exercise of its public duty, the court should consider, in addition to any other relevant fact or circumstances, both (i) the financial prejudice to the particular complainant in the particular circumstances if an order for costs is not made in his favour; and (ii) the need to encourage public authorities to make and stand by honest, reasonable and apparently sound administrative decisions made in the public interest without fear of exposure to undue financial prejudice if the decision is successfully challenged.

CORPORATION OF THE HALL OF ARTS AND SCIENCES v ALBERT COURT RESIDENTS' ASSOCIATION AND OTHERS.	Court of Appeal [2011] EWCA Civ 430 [2011] LLR 240	Facts: The corporation applied for a variation of its premises licence. The licensing authority had a practice of conducting an extra-statutory consultation of residents within 30 metres of application sites. On this occasion, it failed to do so. Certain residents, having learned of the application, submitted representations out of time, but the licensing authority, in the absence of representations made in time, considered itself bound to grant the variation and did so. The residents judicially reviewed the grant. The High Court held that the residents had a legitimate expectation of consultation and quashed the grant. The authority and the corporation appealed to the Court of Appeal.
		Issues:
		(1) Did the authority have a discretion to accept the representations out of time?
		(2) Was the authority bound to grant the licence?
		Decision:
		(1) No.
		(2) Yes.
		Stanley Burnton LJ:
		In the absence of relevant representations the authority was bound to grant the variation. The authority has no discretion to accept late representations. Even if the residents had a legitimate expectation of consultation, this cannot entitle or require the licensing authority to depart from its statutory duty of granting the licence. If the residents' fears are realised, they have the remedy of review.
CRAWLEY BOROUGH COUNCIL v ATTENBOR- OUGH	Administrative Court [2006] EWHC 1278 (Admin) [2006] LLR 403	Facts: The magistrates' court awarded the appellant their costs on a successful appeal against the hours imposed on a variation of a premises licence, stating that they had ordered costs in accordance with their discretion following consideration of all the circumstances concerning the facts and the history of the case.
		Issues:
		(1) Were the conditions imposed too vague to be enforced?
		(2) Was the award of costs proper?
		Decision:
		(1) The parties agreed that the conditions were too vague to be enforced.
		(2) The award of costs was proper. The discretion under s 181 Licensing Act 2003 is very wide.

		Scott Baker LJ:
		1. It is important that the terms of a premises licence and any conditions attached to it should be clear; not just clear to those having specialised knowledge of licensing, such as the local authority or the manager of the premises, but also to the independent bystander such as neighbours, who may have no knowledge of licensing at all. The terms of a licence and its conditions may of course be the subject of enforcement. Breach carries criminal sanctions. Everyone must know where they stand from the terms of the document. It must be apparent from reading the document what the license and its conditions mean.
		2. As to costs, it is sufficient that the justices have made it clear that they appreciated the principle under which they were operating.
		3. It is highly undesirable that the courts should do anything to encourage satellite litigation on questions such as costs.
		4. The justices have a very wide discretion in what costs order they see fit to make. They will, after all, have heard the appeal, which in this case took something in the region of 2 days.
		5. The Licensing Act does not require licensing authorities to have behaved unreasonably before an award of costs is made against them.
DI CIACCA v SCOTTISH MINISTERS	Court of Session (Outer House) [2003] LLR 426	Facts: Challenge to planning decision refusing to remove terminal hour for wine bar.
		Issues:
		(1) Did the decision maker act unlawfully by failing to take into account the existence of the licensing regime?
		(2) Was there an infringement of the human rights of the applicant pursuant to Article 1 Protocol 1 European Convention on Human Rights?
		Decision:
		(1) No. The decision maker was entitled and obliged to and did consider the effect on residential amenity.
		(2) The Convention protects existing not prospective rights.
		Lord Reed:
		1. Licensing legislation does not restrict the jurisdiction of the planning authority.
		2. The planning authority cannot lawfully fetter its own discretion by deferring to the decision of the licensing board.
		3. The planning authority cannot lawfully disregard a material consideration, such

		as the effect of late night opening of licensed premises upon residential amenity, on the basis that that matter also falls within the scope of licensing legislation.
	4.	However, the principle that a planning authority cannot delegate the exercise of its functions to some other body does not mean that the existence of another body exercising different functions is necessarily irrelevant to the exercise of planning powers: *Gateshead Metropolitan Borough Council v Secretary of State for the Environment* [1994] 1 PLR 85 followed.
	5.	Planning permission is an anticipatory form of control. It cannot be proper for planning permission to be granted which would permit a development contrary to sound planning; and a planning authority cannot therefore grant permission, where it has unresolved concerns, merely on the basis that another raft of legislation exists under which a separate authority has the power thereafter to exercise controls which might address the remaining planning concerns. On the other hand, as the *Gateshead* decision demonstrates, the existence of another statutory regime may, in particular circumstances, resolve the concerns of the planning authority and enable it to be reasonably satisfied that the grant of permission will not have the effect of permitting a development contrary to sound planning. Such circumstances will exist in particular where the other statutory regime can reasonably be relied upon to address the remaining planning concerns satisfactorily: *Lethem v Secretary of State for Local Government and the Regions* [2002] EWHC 1549, [2002] LLR 462 followed.
	6.	Article 1 of Protocol 1 to the Convention protects existing rights: it does not guarantee a right to acquire what one does not already have. Whether a decision taken by a planning authority interferes with a right protected under Art 1 therefore depends upon the circumstances. A refusal of outline planning permission, for example, will not normally engage Art 1 since it will not normally interfere with an existing right to develop the land in question. The refusal to remove a condition attached to an existing grant of planning permission did not encroach upon any existing right of the appellant.

HALL AND WOODHOUSE LTD v POOLE BOROUGH COUNCIL	Administrative Court [2009] EWHC 1587 (Admin) [2009] LLR 436	Facts: A brewery held a premises licence and leased the premises to a third party who exercised control over the premises. The third party breached the premises licence and the council successfully prosecuted the brewery for the breach of conditions under section 136 Licensing Act 2003.
		Issue: Is the premises licence holder automatically liable for breaches of licence conditions?
		Decision: No.
		Richards LJ:
		Section 136(1)(a) is directed at persons who, *as a matter of fact*, actually carry on or attempt to carry on a licensable activity on or from premises. The section is not directed at holders of premises licences as such. Where there is a premises licence but a licensable activity is carried on outside the scope of that licence or in breach of the conditions of the licence, it is a question of fact whether it is carried on by the holder of the licence. The mere fact that he is the holder of a licence does not make him automatically liable in respect of the carrying of a licensable activity on or from the premises to which the licence relates. Had the intention been to make the holder of the premises licence automatically liable, the section could and would have made express provision to that effect. The conviction was therefore quashed.
LETHEM v SECRETARY OF STATE FOR LOCAL GOVERNMENT, TRANSPORT AND THE REGIONS AND WORCESTER CITY COUNCIL	Queen's Bench Division [2002] EWHC 1549 (Admin) [2002] LLR 462	Facts: Appeal against inspector's refusal of planning permission for change of use to a café/bar.
		Issue: Should the inspector have left issues of public nuisance to be controlled by the licensing regime?
		Decision: Appeal dismissed. The extent to which a decision-maker should leave issues to be dealt with under separate regimes is a matter for the decision-maker to decide on the facts of each case, following *Gateshead Metropolitan Borough Council v Secretary of State for the Environment* [1993] 3 PLR 100.
		George Bartlett QC:
		A consideration that, in the absence of some other statutory control, would be a material consideration under s 70 is not rendered immaterial by the existence of that other statutory control. The extent to which, on application for planning permission, matters that would arise for consideration in the exercise of some other control regime should be treated by the planning authority in determining the application as ones exclusively for that other regime must depend on the circumstances.

LUMINAR LEISURE LTD v WAKEFIELD MAGISTRATES' COURT	Administrative Court [2008] EWHC 1002 (Admin) [2008] LLR 505	Facts: The licensing authority allowed an increase in the capacity of Luminar's bar. Trade rivals successfully appealed to the magistrates' court on the basis of anticipated problems occurring away from the premises.
		Issue: Was the District Judge permitted to take into account events occurring away from the premises?
		Decision: Yes.
		Note: The appellant did not ultimately contend that the District Judge had been legally debarred from taking into account such events, but merely contended that he had placed too much reliance on such events. Ouseley J did not consider that that amounted to a valid ground of challenge and unequivocally held that it is open to the District Judge to consider events occurring away from the premises.
MACDONALD v THE WESTERN ISLES LICENSING BOARD	Court of Session (Outer House) [2001] LLR 655	Facts: Judicial review of licensing board decision to refuse extension of hours, based on local knowledge.
		Issue: procedural requirement where board intends to rely on local knowledge
		Decision: The board may rely on local knowledge, but must inform parties of its intention to do so, in order that the parties may respond to the issues raised.
		Lady Paton:
		A board is entitled to apply its local knowledge and experience to material before it. But it is elementary justice that the parties should be told about it, so that they may have the opportunity of meeting or commenting upon it.
McCOOL v RUSHCLIFFE BOROUGH COUNCIL	Queen's Bench Division [1998] EWHC 695 (Admin) [1998] 3 All ER 889	Facts: The council refused to grant a private hire vehicle licence, as did the magistrates' court on appeal. The applicant appealed to the High Court.
		Issue: Were the magistrates entitled to find that the applicant was unfit to hold a licence on the basis of hearsay evidence of criminal offending?
		Decision: Yes.
		Lord Bingham CJ:
		It is common ground that in reaching their decision the justices were entitled to rely on hearsay evidence. That is in my judgment clear from [the relevant legislation] and also from *Kavanagh v Chief Constable of Devon and Cornwall* [1974] QB 624 and the judgment of Pill J in *Westminster City Council v Zestfair* (1989) 88 LGR 288. In reaching their respective decisions, the Borough Council and the justices were entitled to rely on any evidential material which might reasonably and properly influence the making of a responsible judgment in good faith on the question in issue. Some evidence such as gossip, speculation and unsubstantiated innuendo would be rightly disregarded. Other evidence, even if hearsay, might by its source, nature and inherent probability carry a greater degree of credibility. All would depend on the particular facts and circumstances.

PORTSMOUTH CITY COUNCIL v 3D ENTERTAINMENT GROUP (CRC) LTD AND ATMOSPHERE BARS AND CLUBS	Queen's Bench Division [2011] EWHC 507 (Admin) [2011] LLR 271	Facts: A licensee applied to extend its hours of operation, but was refused because the premises lay in a cumulative impact area. The licensee appealed successfully to the magistrates' court. The licensing authority appealed by way of case stated to the High Court. The issues included the following: (1) Were the magistrates correct to require the police and the council to adduce evidence that there would be a negative cumulative impact? (2) Were the magistrates entitled to reject the evidence of the police? (3) Were the magistrates correct to order costs against the licensing authority? Decision: (1) No. (2) No. (3) No. Supperstone J: The police evidence was unequivocal. To arrive at the decision that they did the magistrates must have rejected the police evidence, and yet they gave no reasons for doing so. In *R (Daniel Thwaites plc) v Wirral Borough Magistrates' Court and Others* [2008] EWHC 838 Admin, [2008] LLR 536, this court made it very clear that the views of the police concerning issues of crime and disorder should 'weigh heavily' with magistrates. The magistrates erred in law in concluding that the appellant had to have 'hard evidence' from the police that there would be a cumulative impact. The burden was on the respondent to persuade the appellant that the operating schedule was such that there would be no cumulative impact. Having found the conditions put forward by the respondent on the appeal (one of which they described as 'significant') were sufficient to demonstrate that there would be no negative cumulative impact on any of the licensing objectives, the magistrates were dealing with an application that was different to the one presented at the committee. For this reason, when allowing the appeal, they should not have awarded the respondent their costs of the hearing before the committee.

PRASANNAN v KENSINGTON AND CHELSEA LONDON BOROUGH COUNCIL	Queen's Bench Division [2010] EWHC 319 (Admin) [2010] LLR 465	Facts: Upon a review, the licensing authority revoked a premises licence following failed test purchases. The licensee appealed and even though the District Judge did not accept the licensee's veracity he held that the licensing objectives would be sufficiently promoted by the imposition of conditions. He did, however, hold that the licensee had brought the revocation upon herself and ordered her to pay £20,000 towards the authority's costs.
		Issues:
		(1) Did section 181 permit the court to order a successful appellant to pay costs?
		(2) Was the discretion exercised properly here?
		Decision:
		(1) Yes.
		(2) Yes.
		Belinda Bucknall QC:
		Parliament doubtless had good reason for making it clear that in licensing cases where the permutations of result may frequently be very much more complex than a simple success or failure, the court has an unfettered power in relation to the costs. That being so, the court's discretion is subject only to the usual requirement that in deciding what order is just, it must take into account all relevant matters and must not take into account irrelevant matters. Here, there was no error of law; the District Judge he had a discretion to make a costs order in favour of the respondent and he exercised it on proper grounds.
R (BASSETLAW DISTRICT COUNCIL) v WORKSOP MAGISTRATES' COURT	Administrative Court [2008] EWHC 3530 (Admin) [2010] LLR 366	Facts: Upon a review, the licensing authority suspended a premises licence for one month following a test purchase operation during which alcohol was sold to 14 year old girls. The licensee successfully appealed to the magistrates' court, the District Judge holding that his powers were not to be exercised for punitive purposes, and imposing further conditions instead.
		Issue: Did the District Judge properly take into account the Secretary of State's Guidance?
		Decision: No.
		Slade J:
		The Guidance makes it clear that where premises have been used for criminal purposes, the licensing authority's duty is to take steps with a view to the promotion of the licensing objectives in the interests of the wider community and not those of the individual holder of the premises licence. Where criminal activity is applicable, as here, wider considerations come into play and the furtherance of the licensing objective engaged includes the prevention of crime. In those circumstances, deterrence is an appropriate objective and one contemplated by the guidance issued by the Secretary of State. The District Judge's decision was accordingly quashed.

| R (BLACKPOOL COUNCIL) v HOWITT AND SECRETARY OF STATE FOR CULTURE MEDIA AND SPORT | Administrative Court [2008] EWHC 3300 (Admin) [2008] LLR 572 | Facts: A publican who opposed the smoking ban under the Health Act 2006 was twice convicted for permitting people to smoke in defiance of the ban. His premises licence was reviewed and revoked. His appeal to the magistrates' court was allowed on the basis that smoking was a matter of health, not crime and disorder, and that the absence of police objection was immaterial. The licensing authority judicially reviewed the decision.

Issues:

(1) Was the licensing objective of preventing crime and disorder engaged?

(2) Was the absence of police objection material?

Decision:

(1) Yes

(2) No.

HH Judge Denyer QC:

The commission of a crime does not need to involve disorder for the crime prevention objective to be engaged. The words 'crime and disorder' in section 4 of the Licensing Act 2003 are to be read disjunctively. The decision of the licensing authority was therefore restored. |
| R (BLACKWOOD) v BIRMINGHAM MAGISTRATES, BIRMINGHAM CITY COUNCIL, MITCHELLS & BUTLER LEISURE RETAIL LTD | Administrative Court [2006] EWHC 1800 (Admin) [2006] LLR 802 | Facts: Magistrates dismissed an appeal by residents against a variation in a premises licence permitting an extension in hours. The residents complained that the variation would be in conflict with a planning permission, but the magistrates held that this was not a matter for them.

Issue: Should the magistrates have taken account of planning matters?

Decision: No.

Kenneth Parker QC:

1. There is an overlap between the objectives of licensing and planning.

2. While the Guidance advocates the separation of planning and licensing, the dividing line is not always easy to achieve in practice, although operational matters such as licensing hours are intended primarily for regulation by the licensing authorities, and so the planning authority may decide to leave such matters to the licensing authority.

3. It is not for the magistrates in a licensing appeal under the Act to examine whether a proposed variation requires planning consent or to speculate whether, if it did, such consent would be forthcoming. That would be a planning matter falling exclusively within the competence of the planning authority. |

R (BRISTOL CITY COUNCIL) v BRISTOL MAGISTRATES' COURT AND SOMERFIELD STORES LTD	Administrative Court [2009] EWHC 625 (Admin) [2009] LLR 333	**Facts:** The licensing authority granted a premises licence subject to conditions. On appeal by the licensee, the magistrates removed certain conditions, holding that the subject matter of such conditions was adequately covered by other legislation. The licensing authority sought judicial review of the magistrates' decision.

Issues:

(1) Did the magistrates fail to recognise that the operating schedule submitted with Somerfield's application was deficient so that conditions had to be imposed to deal with that deficiency?

(2) Did the magistrates err in considering that they could not lawfully strengthen other legislation governing the operation of the premises without specific reasons relating to the premises in question?

Decision:

(1) No.

(2) No, but this element of the decision was not integral to the result.

John Howell QC:

The Licensing Act 2003 does not require an applicant to include any particular material in the operating schedule (*R (British Beer & Pub Association et al) v Canterbury City Council* [2005] EWHC 1318 (Admin), [2005] LLR 353 applied) and nor is the licensing authority obliged to include all the contents of the operating schedule into the licence.
Section 18(2) of the Act gives a licensing authority a power to impose conditions consistent with the schedule where this is necessary to promote the licensing objectives. It does not impose a duty to impose conditions that reproduce the effect of the operating schedule. Indeed, if the operating schedule contained matters which would in fact harm the achievement of the licensing objectives, it is hard to conceive that Parliament would have required a licensing authority to impose such a condition.

If the steps in the operating schedule are proposed in language which is general or opaque, the licensing authority may impose a condition describing more specifically and concretely what is proposed if that is necessary to promote the licensing objectives.
A licensing authority has power to impose conditions that are necessary to promote the licensing objectives. Such a condition may be unnecessary if the relevant objective is sufficiently secured by the application of other legislation. That may involve a judgment about what is necessary to promote the licensing objectives in a particular case and what any other relevant legislation provides. Such other legislation may be relevant, but insufficient generally to achieve what is necessary to promote the licensing objectives. Alternatively it may be generally sufficient but, for some reason

		it may be insufficient in a particular case. It may be the case, therefore, that it is unnecessary to show that there are specific reasons relating to the particular premises why any other relevant legislation is insufficient. However, the view which the magistrates' court expressed was not necessary for its decision. The magistrates were entitled to come to the views they did as to the necessity for each of the conditions and the challenge to the decision therefore failed.
R (BRITISH BEER & PUB ASSOCIATION, ASSOCIATION OF LICENSED MULTIPLE RETAILERS AND BRITISH INSTITUTE OF INNKEEPING) v CANTERBURY CITY COUNCIL	Administrative Court [2005] EWHC 1318 (Admin) [2005] LLR 353	Facts: Challenge by trade associations to a licensing policy on grounds that it purported to give power to the licensing authority to reject a licence application even where there had been no relevant representations. Council inserted addendum into policy stating that discretion was engaged only where there had been relevant representations. Issue: Was the policy lawful? Decision: Although the policy in its original form was unlawful, relief refused on basis of adoption of addendum. Richards J: 1. It is permissible, if not essential, for the policy to set out how the council will approach the making of decisions, indicating what the council considers to be important, what control measures it will be looking for, and so forth. For a policy to indicate a decision-maker's general expectations is acceptable in principle and, in this particular context, is also in accordance with the Guidance. It is, of course, vital that the policy does not turn into a rule that is applied inflexibly and fetters the exercise of discretion. There must be a willingness to consider individual applications on their particular merits. 2. If, however, the policy purports to prescribe or dictate the contents of an application and gives the impression that the council will assess, and exercise substantive discretionary powers in relation to, all applications and not just those which have received relevant representations, it is unlawful.
R (CHIEF CONSTABLE OF NOTTINGHAM-SHIRE) v NOTTINGHAM MAGISTRATES' COURT AND TESCO STORES LTD	Queen's Bench Division [2009] EWHC 3182 (Admin) [2010] LLR 112	Facts: The licensing authority imposed conditions on a new premises licence at the instance of the police. The licensee appealed to the magistrates' court. The police applied to be joined as respondents to the appeal.

		Issues:
		(1) Does the Licensing Act 2003 either expressly or impliedly confer the right upon a responsible authority, such as the police, to appear and make representations on the appeal?
		(2) If not, does the magistrates' court have a discretion to allow such participation?
		Decision:
		(1) No.
		(2) Yes.
		Moses LJ:
		Unlike the Licensing Act 1964, the Licensing Act 2003 does not provide the right for objectors to appear at the appeal. The omission appears deliberate.
		Nevertheless, there is an implied power for a tribunal to control and regulate their own procedure, so as to ensure the effective resolution and determination of those functions imposed upon them by a statute:
		R (V) v Asylum and Immigration Tribunal and the Secretary of State for the Home Department [2009] EWHC 1902 (Admin), [2009] All ER (D) 266 (Jul).
		It was up to the magistrates' court to determine how best it could achieve the objectives which it was obliged to pursue and how to reach a fair result. In particular, it had to bear in mind the different considerations in relation to interested parties and responsible authorities. It had to bear in mind that there was a need to protect the applicant from the undue burden of duplication of argument, and also bear in mind that it did have the power to protect a party, such as the applicant in this case, against the unnecessary incurring of costs, should the appeal fail.
		Here, the District Judge had wrongly held that his discretion was constrained against joinder by Schedule 5 of the Act. Accordingly, the decision was remitted to the magistrates' court for redetermination.
R (DANIEL THWAITES PLC) v WIRRAL BOROUGH MAGISTRATES' COURT AND OTHERS	Administrative Court [2008] EWHC 838 (Admin) [2008] LLR 536	Facts: Daniel Thwaites applied for longer hours for a pub. The environmental health authority did not object and a police objection was compromised. Local residents continued to object but their objection was not upheld by the licensing authority. The residents appealed and pending the appeal the pub traded to the varied hours without incident. The magistrates allowed the residents' appeal, stating that they feared migration from other pubs which traded to shorter hours. Daniel Thwaites judicially reviewed the decision.

		Issue:
		(1) Were the magistrates entitled to come to that conclusion?
		(2) Is it open to a licensing authority to impose a condition regarding hours of opening?
		Decision:
		(1) No.
		(2) Yes
		The hours of opening can be regulated as part of the licensing of premises as opposed to merely the hours during which licensable activities take place. Clearly keeping premises open (as opposed to providing entertainment or supplying alcohol there) is not a licensable activity as such. However, the operating schedule which must be supplied with an application for a premises licence must include a statement of the matters set out in s 17(4) and these include not only the times when it is proposed that the licensable activities are to take place but also 'any other times during which it is proposed that the premises are to be open to the public'.
		On a new grant of a premises licence, where there are no representations the licensing authority has to grant the application subject only to such conditions as are consistent with the operating schedule. There is no reason why, if it is necessary to promote the licensing objectives, these conditions should not include a provision requiring the premises to be shut by the time that is specified in the operating schedule. If representations are made and the licensing authority ultimately grants the application, it can depart from the terms set out in the operating schedule when imposing conditions insofar as this is necessary for the promotion of the licensing objectives. It must follow that it can impose an earlier time for the premises to be locked up than the applicant wished and specified in its operating schedule.
R (HOPE AND GLORY PUBLIC HOUSE LTD) v CITY OF WESTMINSTER MAGISTRATES' COURT	Administrative Court [2009] EWHC 1996 (Admin) [2009] LLR 742	Facts: In deciding a licensee's appeal against a decision following an application for review, the District Judge stated that he would approach the appeal on the basis that he would not overturn the licensing authority's decision unless satisfied that it was wrong.
		The District Judge adopted the test for public nuisance set out in the Secretary of State's Guidance, namely:
		'Public nuisance is given a statutory meaning in many pieces of legislation. It is however not narrowly defined in the 2003 Act and retains its broad common law meaning. It is important to remember that the prevention of public nuisance could therefore include low-level risk perhaps affecting a few people living locally as well as major disturbance affecting a whole community. It may also include in appropriate circumstances the reduction of the living and working community and environment,

interested parties ... in the vicinity of licensed premises.'

The licensee challenged both of the District Judge's rulings.

Issues:

(1)   Did the District Judge direct himself correctly as to the test to be applied on appeals from the decision of licensing authorities.

(2)   Did the District Judge err in law in adopting the test for public nuisance in the Secretary of State's Guidance?

Decision:

(1)   Yes.

(2)   No.

Burton J:

The appeal is a *de novo* hearing with fresh evidence allowed on both sides. The test on appeal was decided in *Stepney Borough Council v Joffe* [1949] 1 KB 599 and *Sagnata Investments Limited v Norwich Corporation* [1971] 2 QB 614, which are binding. What the appellate court will have to do is to be satisfied that the judgment below '*is wrong*', that is to reach its conclusion on the basis of the evidence before it and then to conclude that the judgment below *is wrong*, even if it *was not wrong* at the time. The onus still remains on the claimant, hence the correct decision that the claimant should start, one that cannot be challenged. At the end of the day, the decision before the district judge is whether the decision of the licensing committee is wrong. What does this mean? It is plainly not '*Wednesbury* unreasonable' because this is not a question of judicial review. It means that the task for the district judge – having heard the evidence which is now before him, and specifically addressing the decision of the court below – is to give a decision whether, because he disagrees with the decision below in the light of the evidence before him, it is therefore wrong. What he is not doing is either, on the one hand, ignoring the decision below, or, on the other hand, simply paying regard to it. He is addressing whether it is wrong.

As to the meaning of public nuisance under the Licensing Act 2003, the Guidance is correct. Properly understood, case law does not decide that the effect of the public nuisance must be very indiscriminate or very widespread. It simply needs to be sufficiently widespread and sufficiently indiscriminate to amount to something more than private nuisance. (The licensee did not obtain permission to appeal against this part of Burton J's judgment, which therefore remains an authoritative statement of the law.)

R (HOPE AND GLORY PUBLIC HOUSE LTD) v CITY OF WESTMINSTER MAGISTRATES' COURT AND LORD MAYOR AND CITIZENS OF WESTMINSTER CITY	Court of Appeal [2011] EWCA Civ 31 [2011] LLR 105	**Facts:** In deciding a licensee's appeal against a decision following an application for review, the District Judge stated that he would approach the appeal on the basis that he would not overturn the licensing authority's decision unless satisfied that it was wrong. That approach was upheld on an application for permission for judicial review by Burton J. The licensee appealed to the Court of Appeal. **Issues:** (1) How much weight was the district judge entitled to give to the decision of the licensing authority? (2) Was he right to hold that he should only allow the appeal if satisfied that the decision of the licensing authority was wrong? (3) Was the district judge's ruling compliant with Article 6 of the European Convention on Human Rights? **Decision:** (1) It depends on the circumstances. (2) Yes. (3) Yes. Toulson LJ: The weight which a licensing authority's decision receives on appeal depends on a number of circumstances, including the nature of the issue, the nature and quality of the reasons given by the licensing authority and the nature and quality of the evidence on the appeal. The fuller and clearer the authority's reasons, the more weight they are likely to receive on appeal. Nevertheless, the evidence called on appeal may throw a new light on matters. The appellant bears the burden of satisfying the magistrates' court that the licensing authority's decision is wrong. The court agrees with the way Burton J put the matter below. The form of appeal provided by s 182 and Schedule 5 to the 2003 Act amply satisfies the requirements of Article 6. The court doubted that part of the District Judge's ruling in which he stated that he was not concerned with the way in which the decision was approached or the process by which it was made. However, the point was academic in the instant case and the court did not decide it.

R (JD WETHERSPOON PLC) v GUILDFORD BOROUGH COUNCIL	Administrative Court [2006] EWHC 815 (Admin) [2006] LLR 312	Facts: A cumulative impact policy applied to new applications and 'material variations'. The council applied the policy so as to refuse an application for an extension in hours. Issue: Was the application of the policy to variations in hours unlawful as contrary to national guidance which promotes longer hours to reduce the impact on the environment?
		Decision: No.
		Beatson J:
		1. The Licensing Act 2003 does not directly preclude reliance on a cumulative impact policy in the case of an application to extend the permitted hours.
		2. The Act itself neither promotes nor prohibits longer hours.
		3. The Guidance is not to be read as a statute, and a legalistic approach is to be avoided. Resort is needed to elements of value judgment. The guidance recognises that, notwithstanding the general desirability of lengthening licensing hours, the needs of an area in which there is a particular concentration of licensed premises have to be balanced against this. How this tension should be resolved is a matter for the licensing authority.
		4. Where wording of a policy document is properly capable of more than one meaning the question is whether the public body involved, here the licensing subcommittee, has adopted and applied a meaning which it is capable of bearing. If it has, its decision will not be flawed on public law grounds. Here, the interpretation of the words 'material variation' as applying to extensions in licensing hours was not flawed.
R (KHAN) v COVENTRY MAGISTRATES' COURT	Court of Appeal [2011] EWCA CIV 751	Facts: An application for review of an off-licence was brought based on failed test purchases, resulting in revocation of the licence. Upon the licensee's appeal to the magistrates' court, the licensing authority made a further allegation, that the licensee was trading in alcohol upon which duty had not been paid. The appeal was dismissed and the licensee judicially reviewed the magistrates' decision.
		Issue: Were the magistrates entitled to take into account representations different from those relied upon in the review application?
		Decision: Yes.
		Moore-Bick LJ:
		Prior to the Licensing Act 2003 the law was that magistrates were not restricted to receiving evidence about events that had occurred before the decision under appeal. On the contrary, they were bound to consider all the relevant evidence put before them, whether it related to events before or after the decision under appeal: *Rushmoor Borough Council v Richards* (unreported, 30 January 1996). The position was no different now.

		Section 182 of the Licensing Act 2003 makes it clear that the magistrates have the power to make any order of the kind that the licensing authority could have made, but it does not say anything about the grounds on which such an order might be made. That will depend on the evidence before the court. Indeed, the fact that the magistrates can make any order that the licensing authority could have made itself tends to support the conclusion that they are indeed considering the matter completely afresh. The magistrates' function is to consider the application by reference to the statutory licensing objectives untrammeled by any of the regulations that govern the procedure for a review under section 51. They are therefore entitled to consider evidence of events occurring before the application to the licensing authority as well as evidence of events occurring since its decision. A party whose licence is under threat ought to know the nature of the case against him so that he has a fair chance of meeting it. In principle that must be right, but it does not follow that it can be achieved only by limiting the hearing before the magistrates to the allegations that were made before the licensing authority. What is required is that proper procedures be in place in the magistrates' court to ensure that both parties are aware in advance of the hearing of the case they have to meet and the evidence on which it will be based. It should be remembered that the right to call new evidence cuts both ways: it may benefit the licensee if he can show that some or all of the concerns which led the licensing authority to revoke or restrict his licence have been met.
R (MURCO PETROLEUM LTD) v BRISTOL CITY COUNCIL	Administrative Court [2010] EWHC 1992 (Admin) [2010] LLR 683	Facts: A petrol company applied for a premises licence for a shop in a petrol station. Local residents objected. At the hearing, the licensing sub-committee requested the provision of information to demonstrate that the premises were not primarily a garage within the meaning of section 176 of the Licensing Act 2003. The applicant contended that it had the right to decide what, if any, information was provided to the sub-committee and it refused to comply with the request. The licensing sub-committee adjourned the proceedings pending compliance. The applicant appealed to the magistrates' court but the court declined jurisdiction on the basis that there had been no final decision by the sub-committee. The applicant therefore judicially reviewed the authority's refusal to proceed with the hearing. Issues: (1) Was the sub-committee entitled to demand an answer to its question? (2) In default of an answer, was it entitled to adjourn the proceedings?

		Decision: (1) Yes. (2) Yes. Cranston J: Regulation 17 of the Hearings Regulations permits the authority to ask any question of any party. Moreover, s 111 of the Local Government Act 1972 confers an incidental or implied power on the sub-committee to ask a question of a party, where the question is calculated to elicit an answer which will facilitate the function of considering and adjudicating upon a relevant: see *R(Chief Constable of Nottinghamshire) v Nottingham Magistrates' Court and Tesco Stores Ltd* [2009] EWHC 3182 (Admin), [2010] LLR 112, [35]. Once the claimant failed to respond to the question on turnover, the sub-committee was entitled to adjourn the hearing for a satisfactory answer, since regulation 12 confers an express power to adjourn a hearing to a specific date where necessary for the consideration of a representation made by a party. To hold that the authority may not demand an answer to a relevant question would make a mockery of the standing of the council as the licensing authority and its function as the primary decision maker. It would also be inimical to the aim of the legislation to promote the licensing objectives. Perhaps as important it would frustrate the role which local residents have in making representations under the 2003 Act and would downgrade the role of democratically elected decision makers. The claim for judicial review was dismissed.
R (TC PROJECTS LTD) v NEWCASTLE JUSTICES, GROSVENOR CASINOS LTD AND STANLEY CASINOS LTD	Administrative Court [2006] EWHC 1018 (Admin) [2006] LLR 499	Facts: A statutory advertisement of a gaming licence application allegedly gave 13 days notice instead of the 14 days required. Issue: Was this fatal to the application? Decision: No. The requisite period had in fact been given, but even if it had not this was not fatal. Gibbs J: 1. The distinction between mandatory and directory requirements is unhelpful. 2. The important question is what the legislator should be judged to have intended should be the consequence of the non-compliance. This has to be assessed on a consideration of the language of the legislation against the factual circumstances of the non-compliance: *R v Secretary of State for the Home Department ex parte Jeyeanthan; Ravichandran v Secretary of State for the Home Department* [2000] 1 WLR 354 followed. 3. Here, the breach was accidental, minor and unlikely to have prejudiced any objector.

R (UTTLESFORD DISTRICT COUNCIL) V ENGLISH HERITAGE	Queen's Bench Division [2007] EWHC 816 (Admin) 2007 LLR 273	**Facts:** English Heritage appealed against a licence condition relating to the audibility of regulated entertainment. It served a report by a noise expert with a compromise proposal. The council did not accept the proposal or make a counter-proposal. The court awarded costs to English Heritage, taking into account the council's failure to negotiate.
		Issue: Was the costs order reasonable?
		Decision: Yes, although the sum awarded was reduced.
		Pitchford J:
		The whole purpose of Lord Bingham CJ's guidance in *City of Bradford MDC v Booth* was to the draw to the attention of practitioners and justices the public role reposed in certain authorities whose position required careful consideration. On some occasions, depending upon the particular facts of the case, the public nature of the authority's role may be critical in the balancing exercise where the test identified in Lord Bingham CJ's para [3] is met. In others, those considerations may not be critical. It depends upon the particular facts of the case, as considerations of costs almost always do. Here, for example, English Heritage was itself in part a publicly funded body carrying out a quasi-public function.
		There was no tension between the decisions in *Crawley Borough Council v Attenborough and Cambridge City Council v Nestling.* They each turned on their own facts.
R (WESTMINSTER CITY COUNCIL) v METROPOLITAN STIPENDIARY MAGISTRATE AND MERRAN	Administrative Court [2008] EWHC 1202 (Admin) [2008] LLR 572	**Facts:** A District Judge granted an extension of hours of a premises licence on the basis of a list of conditions. The licensing authority judicially reviewed the decision.
		Issues:
		(1) Was the drafting of the conditions such that they were unenforceable and so ineffective or void, so requiring that the licence be quashed.
		(2) Did the District Judge give the council adequate opportunity to address the details of the conditions before she spelt them out.
		Decision:
		(1) While some of the conditions were unenforceable, in the circumstances of the case this did not vitiate the decision: the conditions could be sent back to the District Judge for redrafting.
		(2) No.
		Mitting J:
		Where a district judge or magistrates' court is considering imposing conditions on the grant or variation of a licence it will almost always be good practice for the conditions under consideration to be outlined for debate by the parties. In that way errors of drafting can be

		identified, as can improvements, as can, most important, consideration of the underlying propositions behind the conditions themselves If excision or redrafting of the conditions is fundamental or would alter the substance of the licence, then the decision is to be quashed, otherwise it need not be: *R v Inner London Crown Court ex parte Sitki* (1993) *The Times*, 26 October applied. I turn, therefore, to the individual conditions themselves. The yardstick to be applied is that set out in the judgment of Scott Baker LJ in *Crawley Borough Council v Attenborough and Attenborough* [2006] EWHC 1278 (Admin), [2006] LLR 403, at [7]: 'The terms of a licence and its conditions must be clear from the document itself. The looser test applicable to bye-laws is inapplicable, since breach carries serious criminal sanctions'. Some of the conditions were not sufficiently clear but the variation of hours did not need to be quashed. The matter was remitted to the District Judge for redrafting of the conditions in the light of further submissions by the parties.
R (WESTMINSTER CITY COUNCIL) v MIDDLESEX CROWN COURT AND CHORION PLC	Administrative Court [2002] EWHC 1104 (Admin) [2002] LLR 538	Facts: Council's judicial review of grant by Crown Court of public entertainments licence in the council's stress area, on finding that the premises were well-managed and there had been no previous complaints Issue: Was the Crown Court entitled to depart from the policy in those circumstances? Decision: Yes. The policy was not sufficiently robust to prevent such an exception. Scott Baker J: 1. The council may have a policy. 2. The policy may be so precise that it could well be called a rule. There can be no objection to that, provided the authority is always willing to listen to anyone with something new to say: *British Oxygen Co v Minister of Technology* [1971] AC 610 applied. 3. The magistrates' and Crown Court must accept the policy and apply it as if it was standing in the shoes of the council considering the application. Neither the magistrates' court nor the Crown Court is the right place to challenge the policy. The remedy, if it is alleged that a policy has been unlawfully established, is an application to the Administrative Court for judicial review. 4. Where there is a general policy and an applicant is seeking to persuade a court to make a proper departure from that general policy, then amongst the most important of the matters which the court or the justices must consider is the reasons for the policy and whether, if they were to grant what is sought by way of exception, those reasons would still be

		met: *R v Chester Crown Court ex parte Pascoe and Jones* 151 JP752 applied.
		5. It is for the party seeking to persuade the committee to depart from its policy to show that it can be done without imperilling it or the reasons which underlie it. It is not for the committee to have to justify its decision to apply the policy: *R v Sheffield Crown Court ex parte Consterdine* (1998) 34 Licensing Review 19 applied.
		6. It is both understandable and appropriate for the claimant to have a policy in the light of the problems it has identified in the West End. The policy needs to make it clear that it is not directed at the quality of the operation or the fitness of the licensee but on the global effect of these licences on the area as a whole. If the policy is not to be consistently overridden in individual cases it must be made clear within it that it will only be overridden in exceptional circumstances and that the impeccable credentials of the applicant will not ordinarily be regarded as exceptional circumstances. It should be highlighted that the kind of circumstances that might be regarded as exceptional would be where the underlying policy of restricting any further growth would not be impaired. An example might be where premises in one place would replace those in another.
R v LICENSING JUSTICES OF EAST GWENT EX PARTE CHIEF CONSTABLE OF GWENT	Queen's Bench Division [2001] LLR 693	Facts: Licensing justices refused to admit hearsay evidence advanced by the police on application for renewal of a licence.
		Issue: Were they correct to do so?
		Decision: No. Hearsay evidence is admissible in licensing hearings, following *Kavanagh v Chief Constable of Devon and Cornwall* [1974] 1 QB 624
		Dyson J:
		The obligation of the justices was to act fairly, and that included giving the applicant the opportunity to put his case. How much weight the justices attached to the hearsay statements was, of course, a matter for them. They would take into account the fact that the makers of the statements had not given oral evidence and that it had not been tested by cross-examination. They would also take into account the comments made by the applicant, if any, about those statements and his credibility. But none of those matters could justify refusing to allow the statements to be considered by them at all.

R v MANCHESTER CROWN COURT EX PARTE DRANSFIELD NOVELTY COMPANY LIMITED	Queen's Bench Division [2001] LLR 556	Facts: Judicial review of Crown Court's refusal of a gaming permit. Issues: (1) The relevance of a decision by a planning inspector granting planning permission for the development. (2) The nature of evidence required to found a refusal of a gaming permit. Decision: Application dismissed. Glidewell J: (1) The authorities establish that the Crown Court must have some evidence before it on which it can properly reach its conclusion. It cannot decide on no evidence. It cannot properly guess or simply make assumptions not founded on evidence. But on the other hand, if there is some evidence to support its decision, the weight to be given to any particular piece of evidence is a pure matter of discretion for the Crown Court. (2) The nature of the evidence called and accepted in licensing matters generally is not of the nature of evidence called, for instance, in the criminal courts. Licensing courts and authorities dealing with licensing matters are not bound by the strict rules of evidence, and they can therefore, and properly do, accept hearsay evidence and unproved documents. Again, what weight they attach to such evidence is a matter for them to consider. (3) The Crown Court is entitled to reconsider, and if it thinks right, to differ from the inspector who dealt with the planning issues. However, if an inspector in a matter of this sort has specifically dealt with a particular issue, and expressed his view or conclusion on that issue, it is clear that his view or conclusion must be given great weight by the local authority, and by the Crown Court on an appeal, and there would have to be good reason for rejecting that view or conclusion.
TAYLOR V MANCHESTER CITY COUNCIL	Administrative Court [2012] EWHC 3467 (Admin)	Facts: Following relevant representations on a variation application, the applicant amended its application, and the application was granted with conditions. Issue: Is there a right to amend an application under the Licensing Act? Decision: No. However, the licensing authority could in its discretion grant an application to reflect a proposed amendment by granting less than was originally applied for or attaching conditions. Hickinbottom J:

		'... the applicant could not formally amend his application, once it had been submitted; but the Council, in determining whether it was appropriate to reject the whole or part of the application, or modify the licence conditions to accommodate the proposal, was entitled to take into account the applicant's changed wishes and intentions.'
WESTMINSTER CITY COUNCIL v BLENHEIM LEISURE (RESTAURANTS) LTD AND LANGER AND CURA	Divisional Court [2001] LLR 424	Facts: A licence condition stated: 'The licensee shall maintain good order in the premises'. Issue: Was the licence breached by an offer of prostitution so as to found a prosecution under the London Government Act 1963? Decision. Yes, but the licensee was not guilty of an offence because he lacked *mens rea* which was necessary under the statute. Brooke LJ: The council would do well, in my judgment, to tighten up the language of rule9 if it wishes to be able to use it to prohibit activities like these on licensed premises after the Human Rights Act 1998 comes into force. The extension of the very vague concept of the maintenance of good order to the control of the activities of prostitutes may have passed muster in the days when English common law offences did not receive critical scrutiny from national judicial guardians of a rights-based jurisprudence, but those days will soon be over. English judges will then be applying a Human Rights Convention which has the effect of prescribing that a criminal offence must be clearly defined in law.
WESTMINSTER CITY COUNCIL v MENDOZA	Court of Appeal [2001] EWCA Civ 216 [2001] LLR 578	Facts: The magistrates' court dismissed an application for a closure order because of defective service of a closure notice under Schedule 3 to the Local Government (Miscellaneous Provisions) Act 1982. Issue: Was defective service fatal? Decision: No. Lord Woolf CJ: 'Under the Act it is wrong to look at a requirement of service on others than the principal in the technical manner in which the magistrate did ... I would hope that if the guidance which I sought to give in *R v Immigration Appeal Tribunal, ex parte Jeyeanthan* and *Ravichandran v Secretary of State for the Home Department* [1999] 3 All ER 231 had been available, he would have resisted the inclination to do so. However, that case was decided late in 1999. Nor could he be referred to the decision of the House of Lords in the recent case of Attorney General's Reference No 3 of 1999, which was given on 14 December 2000, when both Lord Steyn and Lord Cooke referred, with approval, to what I had said in *Jeyeanthan* about the approach to contentions that a requirement of a procedural nature was mandatory. In making the comments which I did, I followed the approach of Lord Hailsham of St Marylebone LC in *London and*

		Clydeside Estates Ltd v Aberdeen DC [1980] 1 WLR 182. I sought to emphasise that the fact that a procedural requirement states that something shall be done does not mean that if it is not, that the result is a nullity. It is very important to look at the intention of the legislation in assessing the requirement. It may be an obligation which is clearly set out, but the consequences of not complying with the obligation depend very much upon what is the statutory intent of the legislation as a whole.'

Best practice examples

A	Bournemouth Quality Nights Initiative
B	Operation Santiago, St Helens
C	Designing in safety and vitality, Nottingham
D	Enniskillen at night – an integrated approach
E	The Romford way
F	Making Brixton Better
G	'Descans dels veins' – respecting the peace in Barcelona
H	Cardiff: Traffic Light System (TLS) – targeting problematic licensed premises
I	Above Bar Street, Southampton
J	Stockton Heath, Warrington
K	Leicestershire: county wide alcohol licensing and enforcement initiative

The examples in this Appendix are not blueprints but are used to stimulate the imagination and whet the appetite with ideas for use, as appropriate in other areas. The words are those of the scheme organisers themselves.

A BOURNEMOUTH QUALITY NIGHTS INITIATIVE[1]

The explosion of the licensed trade in the 1990s led to a significant deterioration in the image and perception of Bournemouth. To tackle this issue a strong partnership between public and private sectors was built, and tasked to consider every aspect of the operation of the town at night and its future development. This partnership would establish the direction for new schemes and projects and ensure the continued success of existing ones. Now in its sixth year the partnership has started to reverse the negative perceptions and is building a quality image of the town, with benefits for all stakeholders as a result of a growing and successful night time economy.

The resort of Bournemouth has grown significantly with high visitor numbers:

[1] Courtesy of ATCM.

- Around 5 million visitors per year
- More than £450m in visitor spend
- From the late 1990's the town has also become a prominent night destination:
- Over 50 core town centre bars, pubs and clubs
- Providing over 40,000 licensed capacity

The attraction of high visitor levels and corresponding expansion of night time venues to entertain the party crowd caused a gradual change in the dynamics of the town with potential to harm the excellent reputation built over many years. A strategic group was formed by the key partners to look at the options available and the best way to implement them.

Quality Nights Policy Objectives:

- Reduction of crime and anti social behaviour
- Improving and promoting the image of the town
- Encouraging close partnership working, especially with the trade
- Creating a strong future for the resort

The core strategy was set out in the Bournemouth Quality Nights Initiative plan. Key projects were established to meet the objectives that were agreed by the partnership. These projects included:

- Establishing a sustainable Best Bar None scheme
- Growth and development of the trade association Town Watch
- Participation in the Alcohol Harm Reduction Strategy
- Late night transport alternatives
- Changing the perception of the town at night

Given the range and complexity of projects being considered, it would require more than voluntary contributions from the trade sector. The partners therefore agreed that a new full time position would be created – an innovative and pioneering strategic decision with the funding shared between the trade and the local authority, so that the role of the Night Time Economy (NTE) co-ordinator would be balanced. This was also an opportunity to build the relationship between the private and public sector – regarded as essential for the future success and sustainability of the project.

In 2006 the first ever night time economy co-ordinator was established in Bournemouth as a shared asset between the trade and the local authority with the balance of shared ownership a key factor for delivery of the proposed projects and initiatives.

All marketing and promotion activity has been undertaken with the support of local media and creativity in local promotional campaigns.

All elements of this programme can be adopted by other centres who nurture the relationship of the partnership of all stakeholders in the night time sector.

Results/Outcomes:

In 2012 Bournemouth will be delivering the following key Projects:

- Year 5 of Best Bar None
- Year 3 for Light Night
- The second year under Purple Flag (awarded November 2010)
- Continued Night Bus service 24 hours over Friday and Saturday
- New upgraded Safe Bus with medical practitioner.

Many other projects have been introduced and underway to support the proactive work of Dorset Police in both police led projects and front line policing. The partnership remains committed to this balanced and inclusive approach to delivering positive change to the safe yet vibrant night time offer in Bournemouth. This has realised a real benefit to all stakeholders and users with a significant decrease in violent crime in the town on Friday and Saturday nights between 9 pm and 6 am:

- 2009/10–2010/11 – down 24.7%
- 2010/11–2011/12 – down 19.3% (estimated)

Finance was provided through the shared funding of the council and the trade plus any other funding sourced by the NTE Co-ordinator in cash or kind. The project is now in its sixth year and continues to operate within the original format.

> 'This was a pioneering agreement between the council and the trade to implement projects and strategies effectively and at pace. The initial contract for two years has already become six and we are emphatic about the future success of this scheme.'

Key Partners:

Bournemouth Tourism and Town Centre Management (TCM), together with Bournemouth Town Watch (representing the licensed trade), were the lead partners with TCM responsible for the organisation of the project. The project was fully supported by Bournemouth Safer and Stronger Communities, Dorset Police and Council enforcement agencies and other stakeholders as the success of this project grew.

Contact:

Jon Shipp, Tourist Information Centre, Westover Rd, Bournemouth
01202 456560
Jon.Shipp@Bournemouth.gov.uk

B OPERATION SANTIAGO, ST HELENS[2]

Operation Santiago is a high visibility policing (HVP) initiative in St Helens town centre linking businesses, CCTV and beat officers in conjunction with wider communications and crime prevention strategies. A dedicated team of experienced officers provides a 'neighbourhood policing' style approach to problem solving adjusted to suit town centre issues. Officers patrol hot-spot locations and micro-beats in areas of high footfall to maximise the impact of police presence. The initiative has led to significant reductions in crime in St Helens town centre; specifically there was 428 incidents of all crime recorded from July to December 2010, reduced to 296 incidents for the same period in 2011, a 31% reduction.

Surveys show that residents feel safer, better informed, have more confidence in agencies and see anti-social behaviour as less of a problem than previously. At the heart of its success is a proactive partnership approach using targeted marketing initiatives alongside the high visibility policing patrolling. A dedicated ShopWatch scheme provides an immediate police response through radio link and Santiago officers maintain a strong working relationship with St Helens Council CCTV, the team who won Retail Crimestopper of the Year award in 2010.

In 2009/10, Police in St Helens recorded 108 public order offences, 260 drug related offences, 178 incidents of violence against people and 958 incidents of rowdy inconsiderate behaviour (RIB) in St Helens town centre. The statistics were accompanied by a wide public and partner consensus that the town centre was being damaged by a number of people frequenting the area engaged in criminal activity, street drinking, ASB, drug activity and illegal street trading.

So, Operation Santiago was born with the objective to:

- Send a clear message to offenders that their actions will not be tolerated
- Identify, target and arrest those individuals and groups responsible for nuisance behaviour
- Enhance feelings of safety and reassurance, and the image of the town centre
- Target harden locations and vulnerable people by delivering crime prevention campaigns and messages
- Adopt a 'zero tolerance' policy

Santiago officers hold individual action plans to target improvement in specific areas of business. These include supporting licensees to focus on the risk area of violence; the sale of stolen goods in public houses during the day, and alcohol related offending. Marketing and promotional activities in the town centre have included mobile property marking, issuing purse snatch

[2]   Courtesy of ATCM.

cables and targeting violence in the night time economy through campaigns such as 'One Punch Can Kill' – used to highlight the dangers of alcohol related violence. The team consists of an Inspector, Sergeant and six constables, working alongside the Town Centre Neighbourhood Policing Team. They receive invaluable support from PCSOs and the Special Constabulary. The scheme is funded by Merseyside Police, and although initially piloted for two years it has been so successful that it is now ongoing. Operation Santiago was launched in 2009 with the responsibility of policing the town centre daytime and early evening economy, and in 2010/11 there was a recorded **20% decrease** in rowdy and inconsiderate behaviour, 58 fewer public order offences, a **9% reduction** in drug related offences and a **24% reduction** in the number of violence offences against people in the town centre. Thefts from town centre shops have also reduced, with 323 incidents recorded from July to December 2010 and 175 recorded during the same period in 2011 – a **46% reduction**.

The project continues to evolve to suit the needs of the town centre. The Santiago Team and St Helens Council have introduced the use of wireless CCTV via IPAD. Recently, following an incident of theft from a person in the town centre, CCTV footage showing a man matching the offender's description was circulated to officers on their IPAD, resulting in the offender being located and arrested. This incident resulted in positive media articles in the local press. The wider use of mobile CCTV, implemented alongside a thematic calendar of events and crime reduction initiatives are recommended for other towns.

> 'We are an enthusiastic supporter of Operation Santiago. We work closely with Merseyside Police and St. Helens Council and make sure that the views of the town centre business community are taken into consideration. We employ a Business Crime Reduction Coordinator to work alongside the Police and the retail community and we pay for and manage the Police Radio system enabling Shops and Pubs to instantly contact the Santiago Unit. We liaise with relevant businesses through the St. Helens Retail Forum and Business Watch group, which represents the majority of the relevant town centre businesses. Firms have repeatedly said to us that Santiago has made a tremendous impact and increased business confidence. Businesses believe that this way of working is a vast improvement on the previous town centre policing model and is directly contributing to the regeneration and growth of St. Helens Town Centre.'

> Tracy Mawson, Director of Business Services at St Helens Chamber

There is a strong series of interlocking partnerships working together to reduce crime. Merseyside Police was the lead partner agency working together with members of The St Helens Community Safety Partnership, PubWatch and ShopWatch schemes. The initiative involves St Helens Council CCTV, Trading Standards, Licensing, Safer Communities, Integrated

Offender Management, Children and Young People's services, St Helens Chamber, St Helens Rugby League Club, British Transport Police, Community Payback, Retail Parks and YMCA.

Contact:

Jennifer Kaye, Strategic Communications Team, 3rd Floor Wesley House, Corporation Street, St Helens
Tel: 01744 673120

C DESIGNING IN SAFETY AND VITALITY, NOTTINGHAM[3]

The impact and importance of urban design and maintenance on the safety and vitality of the night time economy was clearly recognised in the Nottingham City Centre Masterplan published in 2005. The Masterplan was completed after many months of hard work by council officers working with stakeholders from across the city. In broad terms a key pillar of the plan is to give pedestrians priority by creating simple uncluttered streets and spaces, promoting the use of the public realm for daytime and evening activity. The Masterplan targeted a number of areas where spaces would be created or improved and linked by pedestrianised streets. The vision in the Masterplan is enshrined within two policy documents: The City Centre Design Guide (2009), and the Streetscape Design Manual. The two policy documents are nationally acclaimed and the method of producing them and implementing the actions can be utilised in other centres.

The City Centre Urban Design Guide promotes the highest standard of urban design and architecture in Nottingham City Centre. Nottingham is a beautiful city that has developed over more than a thousand years and is today an eclectic mix of the ancient and modern. This Design Guide is rooted in a careful analysis of the city centre and the characteristics that make it work and make it special. The Guide sets out a physical framework for the city centre alongside strategic proposals planned for the Eastside and Waterside regeneration areas on the fringes of the city centre. The Guide takes as its starting point these existing plans and develops them into a tool to guide and shape the quality and appearance of development in the city so that it contributes to the implementation of the overall Masterplan vision.

The implementation of the vision requires considerable consultation with user groups. Pedestrianised streets such as Hockley and spaces like the Old Market Square have been nationally acclaimed as examples of good design and practise in engaging partners throughout the design process. These routes and spaces have been complemented by high quality lighting and a

[3]   Courtesy of ATCM.

legible signage strategy directing customers and visitors to key facilities and attractions. This in turn has facilitated iconic attractions such as the Nottingham Contemporary, the implementation of an outdoor seating policy and active building frontages, and facilitates the movement of people during the day and evening adding to the vitality and safety of the city.

One of the key factors to Nottingham receiving the Cleanest City award in 2010 was to ensure that the public realm was designed in close consultation with those responsible for the maintenance regime, facilitating efficient management and cleaning to sustain the improved environment.

Key Partners: Nottingham City Council was lead partner and other stakeholders included designers, operators, users and local businesses, maintenance schedulers, bus operators and taxi services.

Contact:

Paul Tansey, Policy and Research Team, Planning and Transport Strategy Development Department, Nottingham City Council, Loxley House, Station Street

Nottingham Tel: 0115 8763973

D ENNISKILLEN AT NIGHT – AN INTEGRATED APPROACH[4]

Back in 2003 Enniskillen's evening economy was generally considered to be 'a problem' and the town was described as almost being a 'different place' at night. The Police Service Northern Ireland (PSNI) District Commander reported that 70% of all crime in Fermanagh including 62% of assaults and 69% of criminal damage occured in Enniskillen town. These offences were particularly prevalent at weekends when 58% of assaults and 48% of criminal damage occurred. This led one local newspaper to dub Enniskillen 'The Crime Capital of Fermanagh'. There were wider issues too – increased noise and litter, increased pressure on the emergency services and the fear of crime generated by aggressive, drunken behavior.

To address these issues, the Fermanagh District Policing Partnership (DPP) and Fermanagh Community Safety Partnership (CSP) which both have a remit to prevent crime carried out initial work which sought:

- through historical and statistical evidence, to examine some of the elements which contribute to, and impact upon, the problems which arise in the late evening

---

[4]   Courtesy of ATCM.

- to identify those agencies which, in partnership, can address the issues identified
- to facilitate and assist in establishing real and lasting solutions to crime and anti-social behavior in Enniskillen town.

The outcome of this baseline work concluded that 'successful management of night-time leisure will depend on proactive planning by all those involved to develop a leisure culture in which the whole community can participate'. So, it was decided 'to build a partnership approach to ensure that Enniskillen town centre can continue to develop as a vibrant and family orientated area, whilst ensuring visitors and inhabitants feel safe, and that the town is a place where everyone can visit and enjoy themselves'.

The report identified six core areas to be addressed:

1. **Transport** – in 2004/05 two taxi ranks were introduced and taxi registration plates brought in, and the police now closely monitor vehicles that appear to be plying for hire illegally. A late bus service was being explored with private sector providers although some concerns remained about safety at the drop off locations.
2. **Hot Food Outlets** – all 17 agreed to a voluntary reduction of opening hours until 3.00 am (1.5 hours after most licensed premises in the town close) instead of 5 am, and the local authority decided not to grant any further late night street trading permits. All traders, both shop and street, signed up to a voluntary Code of Practice with signs displayed in their premises or vans.
3. **Alcohol** – the use of plastic 'glasses' was introduced. A 'Not on the Street' Campaign ran to inform visitors that in Enniskillen there is a bylaw which prohibits the consumption of alcohol in public places. There was the development of a Pub Watch scheme and a radio network. A pilot scheme for 'wind down' or 'chill out' times was implemented which involved making non-alcoholic drinks available, providing food, increased lighting and light music in licensed premises for the last half hour at the end of the night. Funding was secured for a full-time worker to implement a Street Drinkers programme. Finally, both education and enforcement activities were introduced to reduce under age drinking.
4. **Policing** – there was increased visible presence of police in town, the reintroduction of town beats and the introduction of zero tolerance operations.
5. **CCTV** – in 2004 the local authority funded the capital cost of introducing CCTV in the town centre, and the ongoing running costs are shared between the private sector and the council.
6. **Training/Education** – there was a 'Sensible Serve Programme' which provides training for bar staff, a Door Supervisors Scheme, education programmes such as a 'Youth Against Alcohol & Crime' poster competition, an Anti-Social Behaviour play written and performed by

and for local teenagers (2005), Citizenship and Safety Programme in schools, and Alcohol and Drug education including 'Drug Wiser' seminars.

Following the improvements that this inclusive partnership approach has provided, the next phase of measures being explored includes:

- Provision of safe, secure, well lit and attractive evening public car parks
- Enhancement of street lighting, focusing on key walking routes and 'dark areas'
- Planning Team to work closely with the Police Architectural Liaison officer to ensure that crime is 'designed out' in all future developments in Enniskillen town centre
- Examination of the possible use of taxi rank shelters
- 'Management' of the location of any future new evening venues for fast food outlets, taxi offices, licensed premises, etc.
- Provision of appropriate training for taxi staff.

The Enniskillen experience demonstrates both the importance of partnership working and the ongoing nature of this kind of work. The creation of safe enjoyable town centres at night is a perpetual process of collaboration, lateral thinking, and practical operational management.

Key Partners: Fermanagh District Council, Fermanagh Community Safety Partnership, Fermanagh District Policing Partnership, Northern Ireland Office (Community Safety/CCTV), private sector led by Enniskillen Retailers, PSNI, DRD (Roads Service), evening venue operators in the town centre.

This case study is distilled from a 21 page report. For the full report go to:

http://www.districtpolicing.com/fermanagh/report_-_ekn_at_night_-_an_integrated_approach.pdf

E THE ROMFORD WAY[5]

Romford, in the Borough of Havering, has one of London's largest night time economy sectors including; 41 restaurants, 21 bars and pubs, 4 nightclubs and a cinema. At one time in the 1990's Romford's evening economy had earned the town a reputation for crime and alcohol related disorder. The Town Centre Management Team including the Police and local authority took steps to address the issues, including: a Taxi Marshall Scheme, Street Pastors, The Deeper Lounge (safe haven), Search Arches, Drugs Dogs, Digital Radios, and Dispersal Orders. Weekly Door Supervisor briefings and post weekend feedback meetings with the Police and CCTV

[5] Courtesy of ATCM.

operators were introduced. Following the implementation of these changes most serious crime was down 2.9% with a sanction detection rate of 39.9% in a short time. As a result, in 2009, the Borough of Havering became the only London Borough to achieve Beacon status from central government for managing the local night time economy.

F   MAKING BRIXTON BETTER[6]

The Town Centre Team in Brixton, south London, have taken a business support and partnership approach to bring about positive change in a gritty urban area. They recognised the need to improve the quality, safety, cleanliness and economic sustainability of their town centre and launched a package of initiatives under the 'Making Brixton Better' banner. The initiatives include; working with the ATCM to develop integrated partnership working, an innovative Purple Flag pilot scheme, introduction of Springboard footfall counting cameras, Brixton Explorer Map, Windrush Square gum clear treatment, installation of a pop-up toilet, Brixton Initiative (short listed for LGC Awards), launch of the Brixton Pound, and commissioning Skillsmart Retail to conduct mystery shopping exercises and street surveys. This 'ground up' approach also included the provision of local business support, training and job opportunities for residents and genuine partnership working between licensing, the police and night time businesses. This work is ongoing but the results have already been recognised in a satisfaction survey in which 64% of local people said they now feel safer walking around the town centre at night, and three new national brands have opened up on the high street.

G   'DESCANS DELS VEINS' – RESPECTING THE PEACE IN BARCELONA[7]

The City of Barcelona has already implemented educational campaigns to reduce noise disturbance from outdoor drinking at tables and chairs on the pavement or in squares. Licences in the city appear to be granted on the basis of micro-management, with cafes and bars on narrow streets, where noise disturbance is greater because the sounds reverberate, being required to remove their outdoor tables and chairs at an earlier time than those on wider streets. A typical time for earlier removal might be midnight with the bar itself closing at 1 am or 2 am. The City Council sponsors campaigns aimed at three different groups: customers, bar workers and bar owners. They have used measures such as banners, with signs in Catalan, reminding customers to be quiet. Attractively designed drinks coasters and postcards reinforce the

---

6   Courtesy of ATCM.

7   Taken from 'Good Practice in Managing the Evening and Late Night Economy', Marion Roberts, ODPM, 2004.

same message. Licensees are also encouraged to display notices that set out the clearing away and closing times for their premises. Outdoor seating is licensed on an annual basis and licenses are enforced through inspections and a series of sanctions

H CARDIFF: TRAFFIC LIGHT SYSTEM (TLS) – TARGETING PROBLEMATIC LICENSED PREMISES[8]

Main project objectives

To:

- Reduce crime and disorder
- Reduce harm and suffering
- Support those who would otherwise be fearful of violence and disorder

Organisation name: South Wales Police
Part of a wider programme: Tilley
Partnership agencies contributing to this project:

- Cardiff & Vale NHS Trust
- Cardiff City Council
- South Wales Police
- Cardiff Victim Support
- Cardiff Women's Aid Safety Unit
- Cardiff University

Areas addressed by project:

- Alcohol related crime and disorder

Was Project a hate crime? No
Did the project involve an offender? Yes
Sex of Offender: Both
Type of Offender: Alcohol Abuser, Licensed Premises Licensee
Did the project involve a victim? Yes
Age of the victim? Various
Sex of the victim? Both
Type of victim: local community, visitors to the City Centre's night life
Region where project took place: Wales
Type of area that project took place within: urban
Start and end date: July 2007 – ongoing

Scanning: Cardiff's night time economy attracts over 40,000 persons, with licensed premises capacity in excess of 100,000 in a city with a total population of 360,000. Alcohol-related crime and disorder at licensed

---

[8]   Home Office.

premises – in particular assaults – are one of significant concern. As a consequence of this concentration of licensed premises and related crime and disorder, there was a growing need to address alcohol-related crime and disorder.

Scanning included:

- Data from Police (NPIS) and (NICHE RMS)
- Accident & Emergency (A&E) attendance records
- Intelligence
- Feedback from PACT (Police And Communities Together) Meetings
- Negative Media Coverage

Analysis: There is a long standing data information sharing protocol between South Wales Police (SWP) and the University Hospital of Wales (UHW) which together provides detailed information on the time, place and nature of alcohol related crime and disorder and changes to UK licensing laws. However this information sharing was not exploited. Pubs and clubs in Cardiff City Centre are graded according to their size, location and capacity and are subsequently split into three categories – small, medium and large.

Disorder in licensed premises was due to:

- Severe intoxication
- Lack of control by Designated Premises Supervisor (DPS)
- Wide availability of glass drinking vessels
- Illicit drug use
- Problematic licensed premises were also less likely to have CCTV systems and adequate levels of lighting, making identification more difficult

Response:

- The Traffic Light System (TLS) was developed and validated in corroboration with the City's Licensees Forum to quickly identify problematic premises and facilitate early interventions, preventive measures and continuous premises audit.
- Police and A&E data integrated and A&E attendance classified by crime type – this provides a remarkably precise picture of where and when alcohol related crime and disorder occurs. Each premises-specific offence is classified according to its seriousness.
- Points are allocated on the basis of recorded alcohol related crime and disorder, incidents recorded by the local hospital accident and emergency department, evidence of selling alcohol to individuals under 18 years of age and incidents involving door staff.
- The total number of incidents for each venue places premises into a red (immediate action), amber (monitor closely), or green (no concerns) category.

- Premises in the red category are allocated to a dedicated officer charged with working with the premises managers to agree a SMART action plan. This plan contains measures that would assist the Designated Premises Supervisor (DPS). Close monitoring and reviews are built in to ensure the action plan is executed and lack of compliance could result in enforcement action.
- Action plans can include anything that may help reduce disorder in the premises crime profile.
- In extreme cases where there is no improvement the conditions of the licence are changed, eg have their hour of operation cut, change licensee or revoke the premises license completely.
- A close watch is made of amber premises and if a problem is identified contact is made with a view to putting actions in place to prevent further problems reoccurring.

Evaluation Details:

- The TLS has been independently assessed by Dr Simon Moore, Senior Lecturer at Cardiff University. He found evidence that use of the TLS appeared to have a significant and sustained effect in reducing alcohol related incidents.
- This evaluation was published in Jane's Police Review in December 2006.

Assessment:

- In order to assess the effectiveness of the Traffic Light System analyses focused on those premises classified into the Red category. Looking solely at the difference between the numbers of offences recorded in the month before premises were classified as Red and the month post-intervention with the lowest number of crimes we see a 71% reduction in the average number of offences across all intervention premises.
- Looking at the average number of offences in the preceding four months and comparing this with the average number of offences in the following five months then we see a reduction of 35% in intervention premises.
- The initiative has received positive comments from the media and from the vast majority of licensees at the licensees forum.
- Presentation given at the National AMEC (Alcohol Misuse Enforcement Campaign) Conference in Bournemouth on 23rd November 2006 was well received and has resulted in a substantial number of visits from other community safety groups, local authorities and police constabularies from a wide range of areas to seek further information and best practice methods in relation to the Traffic Light System.
- The TLS has also been identified as one of the best practices with regard to meaningful partnership working in both England and Wales by LACORS (Local Authorities Coordinators of Regulatory Services). This was recently highlighted in the LACORS Handbook which has

had national distribution amongst Licensing Committees thus maximising the profile of this initiative both locally and nationally.

- The National Audit Office (NAO) were particularly impressed with the Traffic Light System and used it as a case example to explore quality assurance and best practice.

Most important lessons:

- The major difficulty encountered was persuading the DPS of the advantages of compliance. This was overcome by working with licensees rather than against them.
- A further problem, not surprisingly, was the reluctance of licensees to report incidents of crime and disorder. This problem was overcome by working with the Chair of the Licensees Forum.
- Positive press coverage and regular presentations at the Licensees Forum, emphasizing that hiding crime and disorder incidents would not be tolerated was also found to be beneficial.

Contact Name: PS Trevor Jones
Email Address: trevor.jones@south-wales.pnn.police.uk
Organisation: South Wales Police

I ABOVE BAR STREET, SOUTHAMPTON[9]

In 2009, Above Bar Street in Southampton was identified as the most violent street in Hampshire. It received negative press coverage, which had an impact on the image of the city and increased the fear of crime for local residents and users of the night-time economy.

Project objectives

A comprehensive package of projects and new ways of working were developed and implemented. These included:

- providing a safe haven for people on a night out who have been injured or are vulnerable, through the introduction of 'ICE' or in case of emergency bus
- street pastors providing support to those in need during peak times
- the development of a yellow card scheme whereby offenders are issued with a yellow card for antisocial behaviour, and upon further warnings, could be excluded from venues for a year
- introduction of taxi marshals, trained security officers, who provide a visible deterrent at taxi ranks

CSP name: Southampton
Programme: Tilleys

---

9   Home Office.

Area type: Rural and urban area
Start date: 2009
End date: 2009

Evaluation

The Project adhered to the SARA methodology. Full details are in the document available to download below.

Lessons learnt

This work has seen huge improvements to safety in the night-time economy including:

- 67 per cent reduction in violent offences linked to the night-time economy (from 439 from April to June 2009 to 142 from January to March 2011)
- 22 per cent reduction in emergency department admissions during peak night times (when compared with 1,300 presentations for assault in 2009 during the hours 18.00 and 09.00)
- 19 per cent increase in people stating they feel safe in the city after dark, up to 57 per cent

J STOCKTON HEATH, WARRINGTON

Stockton Heath is a village community with 35 food and drink venues and an excellent example of what a small settlement can do to improve its night time economy for all. The following text is taken from its successful Purple Flag submission.[10]

Safety and Regulation.

Stockton Heath Village has a specific Police Night-time Economy Strategy. There is an effective and visible Police presence, particularly as the Police station is located within the heart of the village. Up to nine officers cover the centre at peak times between 9 pm and 2 am and there is a minimum presence of two officers at any one time. The local Parish Council Consortium fund nine PCSOs for the area and Stockton Heath has its own designated PCSO.

The *Safer, Stronger Together in Warrington* Local Partnership has published an action plan, which focuses on reducing alcohol-related anti-social behaviour

---

[10] With kind permission of David Watson, Community Safety and Licensing Manager, Warrington Borough Council.

and health inequalities. The Police and Public Protection Services have developed methods of joint working; and the village benefits from a designated Police Licensing Officer. A Stockton Heath Village Early Evening Economy Group has been informed to help manage the centre effectively including, importantly, the connection of (and transition between) early evening and late night economies.

Specific examples of good practice include a Pubwatch Scheme, use of Directions to Leave, and CCTV coverage.

Joint initiatives have included:

- Cigarette littering and health campaigns, including upgrading of litter bins with cigarette stub plates, disposable ashtrays, promotional beer mats and bluetooth messaging.
- Conflict resolution training for door supervisor firms.
- Use of controlled drinking zones.
- Funding for hi vis arm bands.
- Targeted intervention to reduce underage sales.
- Youth project to for 12–17 year olds, providing leisure activities for that age group. Since its introduction, ASB rates have reduced.
- Annual Stockton Heath Festival, involving 35 events over four days.
- Annual winter market.

K LEICESTERSHIRE: COUNTY WIDE ALCOHOL LICENSING AND ENFORCEMENT INITIATIVE[11]

A six month project began in Leicestershire in July 2012 looking at the role the Licensing Act 2003 could play in reducing alcohol harms across Leicester and Leicestershire for the benefit of all of the licensing authorities across the County.

The aim of the project was:

To ensure that adequate, effective and appropriate arrangements are in place across Leicester and Leicestershire to deal with alcohol licensing and enforcement, by:

- Developing clear and enforceable alcohol licensing conditions which utilise the full powers of the Licensing Act 2003.
- Ensuring all licensing decision makers (responsible authorities, licensing officers and elected members) have the right knowledge, skills and behaviours to enable better informed and evidence based licensing decisions.

[11] Text kindly provided by Lee Mansfield, Environmental Health Team Manager, Project Manager.

- Developing a shared vision and refreshed approach to alcohol licensing and enforcement across the seven districts of Leicestershire which brings an improved level of coherence and consistency to delivery and which has the flexibility to respond to changing local priorities and legislation.
- Mapping out alcohol licensing and enforcement process and stake-holder interactions across the districts, so as to identify and understand the customer perspective and areas for improvement.
- Identifying regulatory improvements locally and across the County, supported by mechanisms to identify and share best practice, fully utilise the legislation and new powers, raise awareness of the impacts of licensing decisions across the County and identify the tools and guidance needed to support effective and efficient licensing and enforcement.
- Raising awareness of the Police Reform and Social Responsibility Act, consequent amendments to the Licensing Act 2003 and new powers available to Licensing Authorities.

The following actions were delivered:

Training packages were developed for licensing officers, committee members and each of the responsible authorities. Front line staff and licensing committee members will receive training using the new materials.

A pool of licence conditions has been developed in conjunction with partners and verified by a solicitor. The conditions will be available for use by responsible authorities and committee members.

The temporary event notice, Licensing Act grant/variation and licensing sub-committee hearing procedures have been reviewed. The procedures at each organisation can now be reviewed referencing the template procedures. Once completed, appropriate staff and committee members will be briefed on the new procedures. The procedures will be available to customers of the service, including applicants and responsible authorities.

Local Licensing Forums are now in operation in each locality, providing an opportunity for licensing officers, responsible authorities and police licensing sergeants to discuss alcohol licensing issues.

A terms of reference has been devised for the Leicester, Leicestershire & Rutland Licensing Forum providing more structure and accountability. The forum will devise an annual work plan and will report to the Regulatory Services Partnership. Each organisation will benefit from being able to refer issues such as policy review, technical updates or consistency to the county group for discussion.

A 'Responsible Alcohol Retailer Scheme' has been piloted in two districts of Leicestershire with feedback from businesses being positive. The Home

Office has recently endorsed the draft scheme. Every licensed premises will be assessed with each premises deemed to be broadly compliant with alcohol licensing laws receiving a window sticker branding them as a 'Responsible Alcohol Retailer'. A task and finish group will continue with this work.

A training event was held to mark the close of the project, focusing on 'Using the Licensing Act to reduce the harms from alcohol'. Knowledge gained from the training event will inform the review of licensing policy statements.

Noctis Dispersal Policy[1]

INTRODUCTION

It is clear that the licensed trade has played a major role in regenerating our town and city centres; however, there is a tipping point where the positive benefits give way to problems as a lack of infrastructure creates pressure points which in turn lead to disorder and disturbance.

'The night time economy is helping enable economic regeneration in many deserted and run down traditional urban centres. However, it is in no-one's long-term interest if such economic regeneration leads to social degeneration in the shape of violence, disorder and destruction of private and public property.'

Page 36, Lessons from the 2004 Summer Alcohol Misuse Enforcement Campaign – PSU

It is widely accepted that the vast majority of problems relating to alcohol occur at the end of the evening and in the public realm as customers leave venues and begin to compete for scarce resources. Potential victims and aggressors are to be found side by side at taxi ranks, in the queue for fast food or walking the streets in a bid to hail a cab.

'From the information given to Nitelite it was clear that poor lighting, not enough transport and overcrowding at closing time can pave the way for people feeling unsafe.'

Nitelite Southport

Operators accept that their responsibilities cannot simply end at their front door and that, by contributing to a better managed end of night, they can deliver a safer town or city centre. The most popular venues will attract large numbers of customers and, by their very nature, can be potential sources of nuisance, antisocial behaviour and crime which may create concern for the immediate neighbourhood, its residents and the authorities. Operators are,

---

[1] Although NOCTIS, the trade association for late night operators, has been subsumed into the Association of Licensed Multiple Retailers, this dispersal policy remains a useful tool for promoting a well-regulated process of dispersal.

therefore, eager to develop, in partnership with the police and council, a dispersal policy which will seek to reduce the pressure on the police at the end of trading, ease customers' passage home and minimise the likelihood of local residents being disturbed.

PREPARING A DISPERSAL POLICY

Every venue, be it pub, club or bar, can and should prepare and implement a dispersal policy. Such a policy would set out the steps the venue will take at the end of the trading session to minimise the potential for disorder and disturbance as customers leave the premises. Clearly the contents of the policy would vary widely from one venue to the next based on its size, location and offering.

Prepared in consultation with the licensing officers of the local council and police and, ideally, in place prior to a venue beginning to trade, the policy should be kept under review to address new issues as they arise.

While preparing their policy, operators should consider the local statement of licensing policy and any relevant conditions attached to the premises licence.

ELEMENTS OF A DISPERSAL POLICY

Transport

Probably the biggest single factor triggering disorder and disturbance is a lack of public and private transport at the end of the evening, preventing the swift dispersal of customers away from the venue. There are a number of steps operators can take to reduce transport related problems:

- Promote safety on leaving, for example through operating a concierge service and providing a safe place for customers to wait for taxis (particularly lone females);
- Advertise reliable services by providing free phone numbers for licensed mini-cabs and details of nearby taxi ranks, bus timetables or other local transport networks;
- Agree an operating policy with local private and public hire vehicles, for example banning the sounding of horns after 11 pm;
- Discuss with the council the location of taxi ranks to ensure they are easily accessible without causing bottlenecks outside venues;
- Consider, in discussion with the police and council, the use of stewards to act as marshalls at bus stops and taxi ranks; and
- Work with the local authority and transport providers to agree bus routes, stops and timetables.

Road Safety

Should the venue exit onto a public highway, operators should ensure separation of customers and traffic – if necessary by the installation of permanent or removable barriers.

Car Parking

If appropriate, operators could advise customers of the best car park to use (either through their website or on printed material) so that they leave in a direction with minimum disturbance to local residents. Operators might also be able to negotiate with local car park operators to allow customer usage.

Staffing

During the last half hour of trading, the service points in each bar may be reduced and some staff reallocated to collect glasses or work in the cloakroom. This will assist customer departure and reduces the potential for people to carry glassware out of the premises.

Cloakroom

The cloakroom should be set up in order to assist the swift return of coats with staffing and control systems increased in the period prior to closure.

Music & Lighting (internal)

During the last 20 minutes of trading, the DJ may typically play slower music and reduce the volume of the music played. In addition, lighting levels can be manipulated to encourage the gradual dispersal of patrons during the last part of trading and the drinking up period (see winding down).

Lighting (external)

Operators have found that the use of bright lights at the exit of the venue encourages customers to leave more quietly. Operators should liaise with the local council to establish guidelines on the positioning of these lights which will also prompt customers to leave the area quickly and enhance CCTV coverage.

Minimising Noise on Exit

If possible, a manager should be in the area close to the main exit to oversee the end of night departure period. DJ announcements should be used to remind customers to be considerate on leaving the premises. While highly visible notices can be placed in the foyer requesting exiting customers to leave quietly and to respect neighbours and their properties.

Bottles or glasses

Signage should make clear that customers will not be allowed to leave the premises with bottles or glasses. This policy should be supported by a vigilant door team searching customers where necessary. If appropriate, bins can be provided at exits for use by customers. Operators could also provide advice on any drinking ban in the area.

Litter

Operators should send out a 'Rubbish Patrol' following closure. This patrol will pick up bottles, flyers, food wrappings etc in the immediate vicinity of the premises. As well as clearing rubbish, the patrol acts as another set of eyes and ears identifying potential disorder. Their activity, particularly sweeping the pavement, will also encourage customers to vacate the area outside the premises.

Door staff

The door team play a key role in the implementation of several aspects of any dispersal policy:

- encouraging customers to drink-up and progress to the exit within a venue throughout the latter part of drinking-up time;
- drawing the attention of exiting customers to the notices in the foyer and ask them to be considerate;
- ensuring the removal of all bottles and glasses from departing customers;
- actively encouraging customers not to congregate outside the venue; and
- directing customers to the nearest taxi ranks or other transportation away from the area.

Marshalls

The use of venue security staff as marshalls should always be in negotiation with the police and kept under review. A marshall is a patrolling security officer wearing high visibility clothing, who works close to the venue in a designated area and is in direct communication with the venue management.

Their aim is to create a highly visible presence and to communicate, rather than deal with, potential problems.

Wind down period or 'Chill out hour'

Many aspects of a model dispersal policy can be drawn together into a chill out hour that gently winds down the evening rather than bringing it to an abrupt halt. Operators might find there is a profit to be had from offering a taxi booking service and providing coffee, soft drinks and bar snacks as a way of keeping customers in the premises and thus spreading departures over a longer period of time.

EXAMPLES OF GOOD PRACTICE

Perhaps the most comprehensive example of the steps venues can take to reduce anti-social behaviour comes from Newport where a club has worked with local police to develop a model dispersal policy. Rather than be pushed out on to the street to compete for the all too few taxis operating late at night, customers can book a taxi through the club, wait in comfort, warmth and safety, purchase snacks and coffee while they wait and be escorted to the taxi when it arrives.

In Dursley, a club extended its hours to sell soft drinks and coffee after bar staff stop serving alcohol at 2 am. This chill-out hour allows customers to disperse over a longer time period and reduce the risks of flashpoints in the centre of town. Previously, Dursley had three late night venues all closing at the same time with only one kebab house and one small taxi-rank.

In Edinburgh, one operator details staff to monitor customers on departure identify lone customers (particularly lone females) and hand them a small card which states 'If you are traveling alone and require a CLUBSAFE CAB please speak to a steward or a member of staff'.

A Middlesbrough operator stocks lollipops to be given out free to people leaving late night events in a bid to curb noise. A taxi ordering system is also in operation to prevent people waiting in the street.

Drugs and Pubs: A Guide for Licensees

Produced by the British Beer & Pub Association

It is the duty of all licensees and pub operators to create and maintain a safe, secure and relaxing environment for their customers. Running a well-ordered outlet requires continual vigilance, especially where illegal drugs are concerned.

This leaflet details the tell-tale signs of possible drugs misuse on the premises and offers advice on how to keep to your pub a drug free zone.

A video-based learning package for licensees and their staff entitled Drug and Pubs is available. It gives all the facts, inside information and practical advice necessary to help licensees keep their premises drug-free.

THE PROBLEM

Why be Concerned?

- It is illegal
- Damage to trade and reputation
- Potential for other criminal activity: extortion, violence etc.
- Risk loss of licence and livelihood

The Law

Under the *Misuse of Drugs Act 1971*, heavy penalties can be imposed on those who permit drug-related activities on their premises including producing or supplying a controlled drug and smoking cannabis.

PREVENTION

Standards and Management Style

High standards of cleanliness and service are a powerful deterrent to the drugs trade. They show that you care about your pub and will not tolerate illegal activity.

Low standards indicate the "don't care" management that dealers and users are looking for – dirty ashtrays, uncollected glasses and sloppy service are as good as a written invitation to the drugs trade.

High-profile management – being there, knowing your customers, making your presence felt and staying alert – will discourage the drugs trade from your pub. They are not stupid and will not take unnecessary risks.

Bar staff are your ambassadors. To deter drug dealers and users, they need to maintain your high standard of cleanliness, service and vigilance at all times.

What to Look For

Signs of drug use – Materials

- Torn-up beer mats/cigarettes packets/bits of cardboard left on table or in ashtrays
- Foam stuffing taken from seats/bits of foam left around
- Roaches (home-made filter tips from cannabis cigarettes)
- Small packets made of folded paper, card or foil
- Empty sweet wrappings left in toilets
- Payment with tightly rolled banknotes or notes that have been tightly rolled
- Traces of blood or powder on banknotes
- Drinking straws left in toilets
- Traces of powder on toilet seats or other surfaces in toilets – or obviously wiped-clean surfaces
- Syringes (danger of infection – **do not touch with bare hands**)
- Spoons left in toilets
- Pieces of burned tinfoil

Signs of drug use – Physical

- Very dilated pupils
- Excessive sniffing, dripping nose, watering or red eyes
- Sudden severe cold symptoms following visit to toilet/garden/car park
- White mark/traces of powder around nostrils

Signs of drug use – Behaviour

- Excessive giggling, laughing at nothing, non-stop talking
- Unnaturally dopey, vacant staring, sleepy euphoria
- Non-stop movement, jiggling about, dancing
- Gagging or retching actions
- Excessive consumption of soft drinks or water
- Sudden, inexplicable tearfulness or fright

- Any marked alteration in behaviour following visit to toilet/garden/car park

Signs of dealing

- A person "holding court", with a succession of "visitors" who only stay with him/her a short time
- A person making frequent visits to the toilet, garden or car park followed by a different person/people each time
- People exchanging small packages or cash, often in secretive manner, but may be quite open (to avoid suspicion)
- Furtive, conspiratorial behaviour – huddling in corners and whispering
- Conversation includes frequent references to drugs (slang names)
- Remember: dealers are not identifiable by appearance, they often look highly respectable

Monitoring

- Frequent glass-collecting, emptying ashtrays or wiping tables provides "cover" for surveillance
- Combine careful monitoring with sociability, get to know customers, make sure they know you
- Make regular checks on toilets (ladies as well), car park and garden
- Train staff in unobtrusive monitoring techniques and the signs to look out for
- Ensure that staff inform you immediately, but discreetly, if they see or hear anything suspicious
- Remember: frequent tidying, high-profile presence and alertness act as very powerful deterrents to users and dealers

Working with the Police

- Take the initiative. Ask the police for advice on preventative measures.
- Show that you are making an effort. Attend police briefings, join the local Pubwatch scheme etc. This will also keep you up-to-date on valuable local information.
- Remember that the police will support all efforts to prevent drug use and dealing in pubs, but will take a very hard line with licensees who tolerate, or even **appear** to tolerate, illegal activity

Write your police contact name and number here

Note: Licensees of brewery or other company outlets should keep their company management informed of any incidents or suspicions they have.

CONTROL

Decisions

Never ignore a small problem in the hope that it will go away. It won't. By turning a blind eye you are encouraging further illegal activity.

Use judgement and common sense in deciding when to handle a problem yourself, and when to call the police. Do not expect the police to run your pub, but do not try to be a hero. You, your staff and your customers may be at risk.

Minor problems may be handled by the licensee, but if hard or extensive drug use or dealing are suspected, inform the police.

When calling the police to report suspicions and ask for advice, ring the local station and speak to your usual police contact. Keep a record of all calls, including the time, the date, the person you spoke to and what about.

When calling the police in an emergency (e.g. violence, disorder etc) dial 999. Do not call the local station direct.

Approach

- Stay calm. Avoid provoking anger or aggression.
- Tell minor offenders firmly but politely that such activities are not allowed in your pub
- De-personalise the situation by emphasising your legal obligations. Explain that you could lose your licence for allowing drug-taking or dealing to take place. Give facts, not opinions or moral judgements.
- Always allow offenders the opportunity to "back down" without losing face

Further Information

www.homeoffice.gov.uk/tacklingdrugs

For any enquiries relating to the management of licensed premises please contact the BBPA directly:

Tel: 020 7627 9191
Email: enquiries@beerandpub.com
www.beerandpub.com

Basic Drug Facts

DRUG AND SLANG NAMES	FORM	HOW TAKEN	SIGNS TO LOOK FOR
Ecstasy ('E')	Tablets, capsules or powder	Swallowed	• Excessive energy, dancing, euphoria • Dehydration • Big demand for non-alcoholic drinks
Amphetamines (Speed, sulph, uppers, whiz)	Tablets, capsules or powder	Swallowed	• Rapid speech • Confusion • Enlarged pupils • Effects increased by alcohol
LSD (Acid, tabs)	Paper squares with various designs, gelatine, microdots Less commonly in tablets	Swallowed	• Hallucinations • Erratic and unpredictable behaviour • Incoherence
Cannabis (Dope, hash, pot, weed ganga, tac, bush, tarry, skunk, draw, grass, marijuana)	Resin (brownish lumps) or herbal	Smoked in hand-rolled cigarettes known as joints, reefers, doobies and spliffs. Resin can also be eaten.	• Talkativeness, euphoria, lack of co-ordination, relaxed inhibitions • Dilated pupils, bloodshot eyes • Strong smell of burnt leaves • Torn beer mats or foam upholstery • used to make filters
Cocaine (Coke, snow, charlie, 'C')	White powder	Sniffed ('snorting') More rarely injected	• Euphoria, but sometimes causes anxiety • Runny nose, sniffing • Traces of powder around nostrils • Payment in tightly rolled banknotes

Crack (Stone, base, rock, wash)	Yellowish rocky lumps	Smoked in home-made pipes or heated on foil	• Instant elation-wears off quickly • Violent behaviour • Empty wrappers, scorched foil
Heroin ('H', smack, horse, scag, gear, junk)	Off-white or brownish powder	Injected Can also be heated on foil and inhaled through straw – known as 'Chasing the Dragon'	• Sleepy euphoria. Slow breathing, runny nose and eyes • Needle marks on body • Syringes, needles, blood-stained • cotton wool, scorched tinfoil or spoons

Licensed Property: Noise Control

Effective Management of Noise from Licensed Premises

Produced by the British Beer & Pub Association

The hospitality industry is vibrant, dynamic and constantly changing to meet the aspirations of consumers. Within this, the pub sector is continually updating and modernising to meet consumer demands.

Pub companies and licensees strive to maintain high standards and levels of professionalism in order to run entertaining and well-ordered outlets to enhance enjoyment for all.

Live entertainment is one such enhancement. However, unwanted sound or nuisance noise from licensed premises can cause complaints. **Businesses have a statutory duty to control excess noise and failure to do so can lead to prosecution.** Noise control is an essential part of the business. It is achievable through constructing an environment that controls noise and by increasing staff awareness and training so they can assess potential risks and work towards minimising possible disturbances.

This booklet outlines measures to help reduce or control noise disturbance. No one element is likely to work in isolation and so design, technical and management systems are also considered including physical control methods, operational issues and staff involvement.

Some suggestions can be included in refurbishments. Others may be incorporated without a major overhaul. Many of the design elements will relate to new-builds and should be incorporated at the earliest stages of design. It is not expected that all elements will be used, or are even necessary, since each property is unique and very few will lend themselves to every solution detailed here.

The booklet also offers suggestions for management and operational styles, which could help properties that are not planning refurbishment or structural changes to control potential disturbance to neighbours or in-house residents.

Noise control is good business sense. Not every premise will create problem noise levels and those that do will vary depending on design and location and the type of entertainment. Pubs, hotels, restaurants and other licensed premises range from several centuries to a few weeks old and everything in between, so there are many reasons why problems may or may not arise.

All possible noise sources should be considered at both the design and operational stages. The following are the types of noise source which should be assessed and which are tackled here:

- Amplified and non-amplified music, singing and speech
- Plant and machinery
- Gardens
- Car parks and other outside areas
- Delivery and collection vehicles

Again, it is unlikely that any one property will need to address all these – maybe only one or two are relevant – but careful consideration here is financially wise as it reduces the chances of failed planning or licensing applications. It also helps prevent subsequent problems with in-house and local residents and ultimately, the local authority. By acting to prevent problems and by tackling them positively if they do arise, your business will benefit now and in the future.

NOISE CONTROL MANAGEMENT

This booklet should help licensees to be aware of, and able to prevent, problems that occur from noise disturbance. If, however, complaints do arise then it will help address them and tackle their cause resulting in:

- A move away from confrontational, complaint-based control to pro-active, considerate and neighbour-based control
- Neighbours protected from unacceptable levels of noise

Every business should assess the potential for noise problems in relation to their particular premises and activities. This booklet helps to identify appropriate control measures that, once implemented, should be monitored and reviewed.

Noise assessments should be carried out when necessary e.g:

- On existing un-assessed noise sources
- Prior to launching new entertainment
- When planning alterations
- Before introducing new machinery

Reviews should be undertaken regularly e.g:

- Periodically (e.g. once a year)
- After introducing new sources and/or controls
- Following a complaint
- When monitoring procedures identify that controls are inadequate

Noise control measures and systems for monitoring and reviewing them vary according to what is practical for the size of the business and the nature of the noise source. Assessment can range from simply listening to establish whether a noise is intrusive through to the specialised use of metering equipment. It is important to remember matters such as:

- Nature of noise in or on the property
- Noise heard at the perimeter of the property
- Proximity of noise-sensitive dwellings
- History of any noise complaints from neighbours or local authorities
- All other noise generated in the area from other sources i.e. transport and industry

Companies should consider implementing a noises issues management policy at corporate level. This should include:

- Internal communications, logging and responding to complaints within time limits
- General advice on noise controls with useful details of advisers and suppliers
- Provision of monitoring systems to demonstrate compliance

This system will vary according to what is reasonable given the size of the business and nature of existing or potential problems.

Businesses should ensure appropriate staff training covering:

- Awareness of responsibilities re: logging or responding to complaints
- Internal communication
- Policy relating to liaison with outside agencies
- General advice and instruction relating to the policy and any control measures specific to them.

Possible measures for inclusion in a written noise policy are outlined throughout this booklet.

Sound level meters can help assess if there are noise level problems. However, the person using one must be trained and be able to interpret the results correctly. If trained personnel are unavailable consult the local Environmental Health Officer or an external consultant.

LOCATION

No two licensed premises are the same and location is the most obvious difference. When thinking about a new-build or refurbishment consider the proposed type of operation, the location and its proximity to neighbours to assess which specific problems may arise or have arisen previously.

Consider the aspects detailed on pages 6 to 9 paying special attention to other properties in the area. Are they residential or business? How close are they to your premises? Research your local area by talking to local residents groups or other local licensees? You may wish to use a specialist noise consultant.

This is equally applicable to those proposing to change the type of entertainment. Your neighbours may be happy for you to offer a barbecue and music in your garden once a week but not every night, for example.

If your property is in a noise-sensitive location consider the acoustic suitability of the proposed or existing premises when deciding which type of operation to run.

Also keep in mind the noise during construction and refurbishment. Building contractors should be made aware of their contractual and statutory obligations.

MUSIC, SINGING AND SPEECH

Common causes of complaint. While the type and volume of the music is acceptable to those on the premises it can be very intrusive to the public. Problems may arise because music levels increase as the event progresses, while noise levels in the external environment may fall. Dance and disco music in particular rely on a bass beat, which can create a booming noise in neighbouring premises.

If noise is coming from outside e.g. a garden party, then it is likely to be louder to neighbours than if it were coming from indoors and this might cause more of a disturbance.

Well-managed pubs in built-up areas need not give rise to noise nuisance, but it is more of an issue than if the pub is in an isolated area.

How to control this type of noise

- Be sensitive to the needs of local residents and the views of local residents associations
- Advise them of specific events well in advance
- Invite them to attend

If problems occur with this type of noise from inside a building there are several control methods. The most simple and most effective things to remember are:

- Doors should not be opened unnecessarily
- Windows should be kept closed
- Consider changing the room in which the music is played to one where there are fewer windows or air extractors
- Keep the doors and windows of adjacent rooms, such as toilets and corridors, closed especially if they are next to noise sensitive residential properties
- Ventilate the premises by artificial means if possible
- Bedrooms should be away from areas where structure-borne sound can cause disturbance
- Review the type of music
- Reduce bass content
- Review the location, direction and number of speakers
- Install noise-limiting devices to prevent the volume from going above a certain level
- Inform the DJ/musicians/performers of any problems and controls
- If necessary, get a written agreement on any controls that need to be implemented
- Relocate and/or isolate speakers which are adjacent to wall or ceiling mounted extractors
- Mount speakers on rubber or similar material to reduce transmission into the main building structure

Noise control experts recommend considering:

- Direction, location and quantifying of speakers
- Non-openable, noise-insulated windows
- Acoustic doors
- Ducted mechanical ventilation, including extract and intake grill silencers
- A full air conditioning (AC) system may be necessary but remember these can also create noise
- Attenuated covers to wall extractors
- For new builds or refurbishments, cavity masonry wall construction or additional acoustic dry-lining treatment with no windows should be applied near any stage or performance area

Also consider a volume regulatory device – such as a noise limiter that prevents noise from going above a certain volume – to all permanent music equipment and all available AC mains power sockets. This should be sited away from the entertainers to prevent it from being overridden. It's best to keep it locked away.

N.B. A noise limiter does not always prevent noise problems particularly if the device has to be set so low that a music event is not viable.

For outdoor events:

- Point speakers away from the most noise sensitive premises
- Position stages as far away from noise sensitive premises as possible
- Use the screening provided by existing non-sensitive buildings, barriers and natural features
- Provide an effective acoustic screen to boundaries with noise-sensitive premises getting expert advice on what constitutes 'effective'

PLANT AND MACHINERY

Ventilation and AC allow windows and doors to be kept closed which helps control noise. Chiller units, although necessary, can create noise since they usually have large external units, which may be roof-mounted without any kind of shielding. Often they are fan-driven and the fans may cut in and out at random during the day and night. They may also create noise when they are started up or shut down.

How to control this type of noise

- For a new-build or refurbishment consider the proper attenuation and siting of plant and machinery to emit the minimum noise levels
- Position them so that the building structure provides as much screening as possible to the nearest noise-sensitive premises
- Machinery should be mounted on anti-vibration mounts and/or provided with an acoustic enclosure or additional acoustic screening where necessary
- It may be necessary to seek the advice of a noise expert regarding siting and/or screening
- Ventilation systems should include extract and intake grille silencers
- Timing clocks may be added to plant and machinery
- With a closed cellar it may be possible to switch off the cooler equipment to reduce noise provided temperature levels are not prejudiced
- Arrange regular maintenance contracts to ensure the smooth functioning of ventilation and other equipment

USE OF OUTSIDE AREAS

This noise source, usually shouting or loud voices, is likely to be especially noticeable at night, when noise levels in the external environment are relatively low. In most circumstances people arriving at and leaving the premises will not cause any disturbance, but it does happen and must be acknowledged.

It is not only people that cause a disturbance. Their vehicles can also create noise through stereos, slamming doors, revving engines, the horn or screeching tyres for example.

Noise can also arise from beer gardens and play areas.

How to control this type of noise

- For new-builds and refurbishments consider the positioning of exits from the building and outside areas such as car parks in relation to noise-sensitive premises.
- Where noise-sensitive premises may overlook the frontage of a licensed premise then an alternative exit-route possibly onto a rear or side street may minimise disturbance.
- Post notices close to exit doors advising that there are residential properties nearby and asking patrons to leave quickly and quietly.
- If music has been playing consider reducing the volume and/or playing slower, more mellow music as the evening draws to a close. This often quietens people down before they leave.
- For new-builds access roads, car parks and play areas should be kept as far away as possible from noise sensitive properties.
- Natural screening should be used and, where appropriate, screening provided by the premises should be utilised.
- Screening of outside areas by walling or fully boarded fencing can help to control noise from vehicles.
- Consider introducing monitoring devices such as CCTV to outside areas. (Use of CCTV raises a number of issues which are highlighted in the BBPA publication Licensed Property: Security in Design.)

DELIVERY/COLLECTION VEHICLES

All pubs will have commercial vehicles visiting the premises to deliver goods and remove refuse and that sometimes disturbs neighbours, particularly early in the morning.

How to control this type of noise

- At the design stage of a new-build or refurbishment consider the site layout with particular reference to preventing unnecessary noise from vehicles entering and leaving
- Consider means of attenuating such noise e.g. the collection/delivery area might be covered by a lightweight roof that would help to contain the noise and provide a weatherproof area
- Screening
- If frequent deliveries/collections are necessary consider restricting the delivery times as far as possible to those when disturbance would be minimised

- Attempt to limit the number and/or frequency of such activities
- Alternative methods of delivery/collection/loading/unloading

RESPONDING TO A COMPLAINT

Occasionally premises receive complaints about noise. To show due consideration in residential communities it is suggested that the actions below be followed, where applicable to each individual outlet:

- Staff to log and report any complaints to the manager/duty manager
- Where applicable Unit Managers should inform their Area Managers of any complaint and seek their advice
- Where possible seek advice from Head Office specialists in noise control/law enforcement
- On receipt of a complaint and/or where noise-generating events are held the area around the premises should be monitored at the boundaries of the noise-sensitive premises (if known) by the Unit Manager. Do this as the equipment is set up and tested and on several occasions throughout the event.
- Remember, the hearing of someone who has been inside the building may have been affected by raised noise levels making the noise outside seem quieter
- If a noise problem is established, consider the controls throughout the rest of this booklet that might tackle it
- Seek guidance and suggestions from your Local Authority Environmental Health or Environmental Services section

Further information

For more information on noise control or any other enquiries relating to the management of licensed premises please contact the BBPA directly:

Tel: 020 7627 9191
Email: enquiries@beerandpub.com
www.beerandpub.com

Managing Safety in Bars, Clubs and Pubs

Produced by the British Beer & Pub Association

INTRODUCTION

The on-trade licensed retailing industry is vibrant, dynamic and continually changing to meet the needs and aspirations of its customers. The broad range of outlets, ranging from small traditional pubs, to large pub restaurants, hotels and nightclubs, play a vital role in the hospitality and leisure sector of the UK economy. Most venues trade to different customer requirements and occasions at different times of the week and throughout the day.

The industry operates in a highly regulated environment and through the licensing objectives must ensure the responsible operation of its premises at all times for customers, staff and the local community. A key priority of the industry is to ensure that both customers and staff feel secure, comfortable and relaxed in all licensed premises.

Unfortunately human nature dictates that there is a very small minority of people in some communities who have a propensity to resort to violence in certain situations or act in a way that elicits violence in others, which can occur in, or in the vicinity of, a licensed premise. Violence and aggression can occur for any number of reasons, e.g. an individual could be annoyed or upset by someone, be seeking revenge or even be acting in self-defence. Bar staff and door supervisors might also be targeted whilst enforcing policies on under-age sales, drunkenness, smoking, refusing entry and closing time. The form of violence that might take place could involve pushing and the use of fists or improvised weapons such as bottles, glasses, pool cues and furniture. In extreme cases customers may deliberately carry guns and knives with the deliberate intention to cause injury.

Regrettably incidences of violence do sometimes occur but most disturbances or incidents are diffused quickly and professionally by staff. In order to mitigate the menace of some individuals' behaviour towards staff or other customers, it is important that a full assessment of the risks from intentional violence is undertaken.

This guide seeks to set out the salient factors to be considered and to identify preventative measures that can be taken where appropriate. The risk assessment should be reviewed on a regular basis, particularly in the light of any incidents that do occur, and in any event to ensure that the assessment is kept up to date. The guide may also be used when preparing an operating schedule for a licence application or variation.

August 2007

RISK FACTORS

The following may be significant factors in the occurrence of violent incidents in pubs and other late-night venues:

- Social tension and rivalry (sporting, territorial)
- Romantic rivalry (past and desired relationships)
- Frustration – waiting to get served
- Over-crowding and discomfort – pushing to the bar and lavatories
- Intolerance – bumping on dance floor/busy area, spilled drinks
- Influence of drugs taken before entry
- Smoking restrictions
- Queues at the door and refused entry (ID checks)
- Staff (lack of intervention or too aggressive)
- Refusal to serve those underage or drunk
- Removal of glasses with drinks remaining
- Failure to clear tables

PREVENTATIVE MEASURES

Existing premises should review their operating schedule on a regular basis to ensure the licensing objectives continue to be met. A number of preventative measures can be taken to assist in keeping premises secure and safe:

Design and layout of premises:

Premises should be designed and planned to provide an environment that minimises opportunities for violence and disorder.

(See BBPA Guidance – Security by Design)

Increase staff awareness and training so they can work towards reducing risks:

Staff Training

BIIAB Qualifications:

- Drug Awareness
- Award in Responsible Alcohol Retailing
- Award in Conflict Management
- Physical Intervention: Reducing Risk

Mystery Shopper programmes

Electronic devices
- CCTV cameras in operation and recordings saved
- Radio links to Pubwatch members

Industry guidance and good practice
- BBPA Guidance on Drinks Promotions
- BBPA Drugs in Pubs
- BEDA – dispersal policy

ASSESSING THE RISK

A key factor in assessing the level of risk is the profile of the business. Premises should continue to be assessed on a regular basis:

LEVEL OF RISK

Location	HIGH	MEDIUM	LOW
Town centre			
Urban community			
Rural community			
Destination			
Sports/concert arena near by			
Leisure complex			

Clientele	HIGH	MEDIUM	LOW
Families			
Age profile 18–24			
Students			
Regulars/local			
Out of town visitors			
Predominantly female			
Predominantly male			
Mixed age and sex			

Offering	HIGH	MEDIUM	LOW
Energy levels			
Music			
Dance venue			
Regulars/local			
TV sports/live matches			
Food – mix of trade			
Cocktails/wine			
Traditional ales			
Bottled beers and RTDs			
Theme bar with promotions			

Layout and design	HIGH	MEDIUM	LOW
Proportion of seating			
Density – ratio of customers to space			
Gardens			
Patios/pavements			

Any previous violent incidents
Details of any incidents and subsequent action taken:

INHERENT RISK LEVEL:	HIGH	MEDIUM	LOW

SOLUTIONS

Indicate which of the following measures apply at the premises (√)

If they do not – indicate (*) where these might further enhance safety.

	√/*		√/*
Door Supervisors		Table service	
CCTV		Frequent collection of glasses/bottles	
FIxtures & fitting secured		Bottle banks in consumption areas	

Internal patrols by door supervisors/staff		Toughened glass	
Member of local Pubwatch		Plastic glasses – all areas, some/all hours (deleted as applicable)	
Best Bar None accreditation		Plastic glasses outdoor areas	
Member of Town/City Safe Scheme		Plastic glasses special events	
Business Improvement District		Plastic bottles	
Mandatory licensing conditions		Decant products in glass bottles	
Challenge 21 policy implemented		Refusal buttons	
Search on entry for drugs/other items		Food served until 11pm or beyond	
Sports/concert arena near by		Staffing levels sufficient	
Implement BBPA promotions code		Soft drinks promotions	
Frequent circulation by management		Dress code	
Staff trained in conflict management		Dispersal policy	
Experienced management		Cool down music policy	

Entry by ticket		Other:	
Toilet attendants/ regular checks			
External smoking area			
Zero tolerance notices			
Point of sale material			
ID scanners			
Reduce opening hours (i.e. open later or close earlier)			

SUMMARY

FURTHER RECOMMENDED ACTION (see * above)	
Signed:	Date:
Date of next review:	

Licensed Property: Security in Design

Effective Licensed Property Security Systems

Produced by the British Beer & Pub Association and the Metropolitan Police Service

The hospitality industry is vibrant, dynamic and continually changing to meet the aspirations of contemporary consumers. Nowhere is this truer than in pubs where feeling relaxed and safe is vital to customers and staff.

Security, therefore, is a vital element in any professionally run outlet.

It is achievable through a variety of methods including:

- Designing an environment that minimises opportunities for crime
- Providing hardware and electronic devices, which minimise access to intruders and maximise possibilities for detection of criminal activity
- Increasing staff awareness and training so they can work towards reducing risks

This booklet focuses on design elements. However, no one element can work in isolation so management systems including physical and electronic prevention methods and staff involvement are also considered.

This booklet also offers an outline of aspects for consideration during the design of a new-build, refurbishment or minor alterations. Some suggestions will feature in refurbishments while others may be incorporated into properties without the need of a major overhaul.

Many of the design elements relate to new-builds and refurbishments and should be incorporated at the earliest stages of design. This improves cost effectiveness as incorporating aspects later is always more expensive and often less effective. It is unlikely that all elements will be used since each property is unique and few will lend themselves to every aspect outlined here.

There are also suggestions for management and operational styles to help properties not planning refurbishment or structural changes to become more secure.

Crime prevention makes sense. Risks vary depending on the type and design of premises and should be considered at both the design and operational stages. **In every case a risk assessment should be carried out for each individual property and type of operation.**

Risks to be assessed include:

- Theft, burglary, robbery
- Vandalism
- Personal attack
- Protection rackets
- Drugs
- Terrorism

It is highly unlikely that any one property will be threatened by or vulnerable to all of these. However, tackling one problem-area usually reduces the risk from others, which is a huge advantage now and in the future.

LOCATION

Every public house is different. When considering a new-build or refurbishment review the proposed type of operation and the location to assess which specific problems may exist or have existed. Illegal drugs, for example, are a national issue so consultation with your local crime prevention officer is recommended. There are several ways to research your locality and issues to consider include:

- The local Police Crime Prevention Officer
- The local Police Crime Prevention Design Adviser
- The local Licensing Authority
- Check the local Planning Department's Unitary Development Plan
- Liaise with other outlets in the area
- Consider joining Pubwatch or a similar scheme

Entrances

Design Checkpoints:

- Ensure that entrances are easily visible from the bar
- Consider incorporating a facility for viewing outside such as a spy-hole, particularly out of licensed hours
- Keep entrances to a minimum. One is ideal. However, in family pubs for example, police and licensing authorities often require a separate entrance to the family area.
- Fire Officers and other regulatory bodies will stipulate the number of fire escapes
- Where Door Managers are used ensure that space is available for them to avoid congestion in the doorway
- This area should be covered and well-lit

- Door Managers should be visible from the bar and able to communicate internally with other staff easily
- If there is no door management consider CCTV— please see page 8

Toilets

Design Checkpoints:

TOILET ENTRANCES:

- Should be clearly visible from the bar
- Should be away from main entrances to the pub
- Should be away from other at-risk-areas e.g. accommodation or kitchen entrances

There are three types of toilet entrance:

- separate male and female facilities
- entrances to male and female facilities next to each other
- shared entrance with separate doors to each facility behind the first entrance – this is the most difficult to control
- Consider CCTV for entrances and lobby areas

LIGHTING:

- Use adequate lighting to avoid dimly lit areas

FACILITIES:

- Avoid areas where goods can be hidden e.g. suspended ceilings. Fittings should be flush to avoid tampering. Enclose cisterns, basins, pipe-work etc in tamper-proof casings. If this is not possible, fittings should be tamper-proof.

CONSIDER:

- Graffiti and vandal proof materials i.e. stainless steel, laminates and plastics
- The safety of vending machines
- Cash boxes can be tampered with so consider fitting them with alarms

PROVIDE:

- Hooks or shelves high up on the back of cubicle doors or partitions for bags and coats
- Separate staff toilet and changing facilities

Staff Checkpoints:

- Ensure staff checks of facilities are routine to guarantee cleanliness and security
- Consider notices in toilets so customers know that random checks are carried out regularly

Licensed Areas

Design Checkpoints:

THE BAR/SERVERY AREA:

- Where viable consider raising the floor behind the bar to maximise staff visibility. This also raises staff above customers so they seem more imposing and in control.
- Maximise viewing from the bar by not closing down the space with glass racks, low canopies, screens, pillars etc.
- Keep the counter top as clear as possible
- Make the counter top as high and wide as possible to dissuade people from reaching across it
- Tills should be out of public reach either in the front or back, but front facing tills, while easier to reach, retain staff eye contact with customers and ensure more consistent control
- Keep merchandise and glasses out of public reach
- Ensure charity boxes are in clear view of staff and securely fastened
- Consider a roller shutter to prevent access outside serving times

TELEPHONE:

Ensure:

- The phone cash box is in clear view of bar staff
- That staff has easy access to a phone with a dedicated line for emergency services-this should be behind the bar

SEATING AND SCREENS:

- Avoid areas that are not clearly visible from the bar such as alcoves or separate rooms e.g. games rooms
- If there are alcoves consider having them at 90° angles to the bar to maximise visibility
- If screens are used incorporate transparent areas to improve visibility
- Consider raising areas that are some distance from the bar to improve visibility
- Have a clear policy regarding seating and/or standing of customers e.g. standing can obstruct visibility from bar, but ambience must be

considered and other measures can be taken to improve visibility (raised areas for example)

- Incorporate mirrors into the design to improve visibility of awkward areas
- For separate rooms or mezzanine floors consider CCTV

LIGHTING:

Adequate lighting improves visibility although there must be a balance between practicality and ambience.

- Consider zoned dimmers to increase control of areas from the bar
- Ensure lighting controls are clearly labelled
- High-level house lighting is an important element of control. The following should be considered:
- switches
- alarms
- music

High-level house lighting may be linked to music controls. In an emergency music can be turned off immediately as well as lighting increased. It could also be linked to burglar alarms so that when alarms are triggered so is full lighting.

Licensees should have access to licensed area lights from the accommodation area and vice versa.

MACHINES:

- The licensing authority often regulates positioning and numbers of machines. Think carefully about the practicalities of machine positions before making an application.
- To avoid tampering ensure AWP and other cash machines are clearly visible from the bar
- Ensure machines do not block visibility from the bar to other areas
- Consider having a music policy with volume levels and switch off times etc controlled by staff
- Consider a PA system for security announcements as well as promotions and entertainment

CLOTHING/HANDBAG PROTECTION:

- Create secure areas for staff belongings
- Provide hanging space for coats, which is clearly visible to staff and customers and away from entrances and exits. Decide if this should be supervised.
- Decide if storage is needed for customers' possessions. Hooks or shelf units under the bar front or tables may be provided.

FURNITURE:

- The choice and design of furniture can help minimise the risk of theft:
  - consider benefits/drawbacks of fixed furniture
  - avoid high barstools where customers leave possessions on the floor out of sight and reach
  - avoid furniture that can be used to hide objects in or under

DOORS:

- Panic bolts on fire doors can be easily operated. Try keeping fire doors under watch and alarming them internally so staff are aware of tampering. Consider magnetic locks incorporated into the fire alarm system.
- Fire and other statutory authorities' regulations will affect the design of these

Staff Checklist:

- Produce a clear security policy and ensure staff are aware of it
- Train staff on awareness and operational procedures for problem dealing. This might include drug use awareness, conflict management and operational procedures.
- Operational procedures could include:
  - regular staff checks of areas not visible from the bar
  - regular glass and bottle collections
  - high level house lights
  - emergency telephone
  - locking up
  - CCTV
  - alarm procedures
  - cash control

Outside Areas

Design Checkpoints:

- Maximise visibility from inside areas, particularly the bar – see and be seen
- Site gardens, patios etc as close to the main building as possible
- Assess lighting levels for clear visibility of all areas
- Consider passive sensors for lighting up areas when they are not in use, to deter unwelcome visitors
- Consider securing outdoor furniture etc.
- Provide secure storage areas for outside furniture, beer kegs, etc.
- Consider external landscape design
- Assess the need for CCTV

Staff Checklist:

ENSURE:

- regular staff checks on outside areas
- regular collections of glasses and bottles

Accommodation Areas

Design Checkpoints:

- Consider the different risks inherent in business and accommodation areas. Assess design and operational requirements accordingly
- It is essential to provide secure access to and from private accommodation areas

ASSESS:

- requirements for alarm systems and other security measures
- provision of access from inside and/or outside the building

CONSIDER:

- external access for the manager and family
- internal access from business areas to accommodation areas
- lighting requirements, alarm systems, CCTV, necessary building material requirements etc – see sections on entrances and the building

The office/cashing-up area and storerooms

Design Checkpoints:

- Ideally the office should be separate from family accommodation
- Position the office away from access points and common areas
- Provide appropriate door security. Ensure there is visibility from the office to outside areas. A small one-way window or peephole in the door for example, with the access well lit for visibility from the office
- Design elements to consider include:
  - minimise or remove windows
  - add window burglar bars
  - strengthen ceilings with metal plating for example
  - alarm the office and storeroom
  - consider passive sensors
  - provide an adequate safe ideally with a letter box drop facility

Staff Checklist:

- Have clear policies for key control and lock-up procedures and make sure staff are aware of them

- Count cash away from and out of view of public areas – ideally, in an office
- Regularly "milk" tills to prevent too much cash being available at any one time
- Vary banking routines so nobody can predict your movements and lie in wait for you. Consider going with somebody else or organising a secure service for cash collection

The building

Design Checkpoints:

Careful design is an integral part of improvement. There are many issues to take into account regarding security including:

- Ensure doors and windows are good quality and conform to appropriate British Standards
- Consider the type of materials used in both doors and windows e.g. where risk is high consider laminated glass
- Choose quality locks to British or European Standards – think about the appropriate use of rim locks or deadlocks

CONSIDER:

- Multiple locking
- Window restraints
- Internal beading and screw fixing for windows
- Window location: low level glazing is more vulnerable
- Make doors and windows open outwards as this makes breaking in more difficult
- Make sure that decorative features are well secured

Staff Checklist:

- Have clear policies for control of keys and locking up and ensure staff are regularly reminded of them

CCTV

While CCTV is an effective deterrent it may not workable in every situation and certainly will not be effective unless used alongside a clear policy.

It is essential when considering CCTV to be clear about what you want to achieve. There are several aspects to be considered. The Home Office has produced a comprehensive document *CCTV – Looking Out for You* (see Further Information) which considers the difficult and complex area of CCTV.

If using CCTV ensure the use of competent and reputable suppliers. Most businesses will already by registered for the purposes of Data Protection under the *Data Protection Act 1998*. Where CCTV is installed, businesses will also need to notify the Date Protection Commissioner of the purpose for which CCTV is being used (normally for the prevention or detection of crime).

Check list

Why use CCTV?

It is vital to weigh-up the benefits of using CCTV versus not using it.

CONSIDER:

- crime reduction
- enhanced public safety
- enhanced staff safety
- enhanced residents safety
- tackling unresolved incidents
- increased public confidence
- increased trade
- reduced fear of crime
- reduced insurance premiums
- dealing effectively with complaints
- improved chances of licence applications

Areas of Interest:

- Consider which areas to observe. Each specific area should then have a corresponding checklist as below:
  - entrances (from outside and inside)
  - toilets (entrances/inside)
  - rooms/areas not clearly visible from the bar
  - outside areas (the building/garden/storage areas/car parks)
  - office
  - safe
  - storerooms

Issues:

- Will the cameras be overt or covert? Will there be signage telling people that cameras are in operation?

Problem:

- Which targets are to be observed?

- people
- groups or individuals
- packages/objects (e.g. briefcase)
- vehicles (e.g. in car park)
- is the object still or moving?
- Which activity at each observation target is likely to cause concern?
  - damage to property
  - robbery/burglary
  - changing hands of drugs/money/weapons
  - drug abuse
  - violence
  - handling stolen property
  - theft/pickpocketing
  - bogus collectors/officials
  - car crime
  - anti-social behaviour
- What is the purpose of the observation?

Monitor, detect, recognise, identify

- what picture quality/content factors are needed to achieve success
- clear view of suspect's body language to anticipate problems
- ability to follow the progress of a target
- true colour
- exact time of incident
- clarification of actions (is the suspect using a key/implement etc?)
- pictures showing vehicle/facial details for evidence of identity
- overall view of the scene

Operational Response:

- Desired results of a successful response:
  - restore order
  - dispersal/control of situation
  - prevention/minimisation of injury or damage
  - reduction of crime/disorder
  - improvement of safety
  - identification of suspect
  - exclusion of innocent parties
  - intelligence gathering
  - gathering of evidence
  - area secured
- Who should respond?
  - police
  - private security staff
  - observer
  - management
  - owner

- What time scale is needed for a successful response?
    - ASAP
    - within minutes
    - within hours
    - within days
    - once a video result has been achieved
- When is observation needed?
    - until arrest/curtailment
    - during whole incident initiated by alarm
    - between particular times (e.g. licensing hours)
    - days of the week
    - during/outside trading hours
    - during pre-organised events based on advance information
    - when few/many people are about
    - on demand of manager
    - daylight/darkness
- Conditions needed for the system to be effective:
    - normal/special weather conditions (rain/fog/snow)
    - all likely conditions during applicable times
    - fire
    - flood
    - any combination of the above
    - changing light levels
        - using existing lighting only
        - using enhanced lighting

Observer Role:

- What the observer does when the activity occurs:
    - switch on recorder
    - follow action with camera
    - identify the location of object/activity
    - search for target
    - notify response team
    - investigate personally
    - alert police
    - follow set operational procedures
- How will the observer know when and where to look?
    - direct request
    - response to alarm
    - past experience/training
    - briefing of specific or daily events
    - constant monitoring
    - automatic sequencing of pictures
    - random picture monitoring
- How quickly does the observer need to act?
    - immediately

- within minutes
- within hours
- within days
- dependent on each individual case
- ASAP
- Who makes the observation on which the response is based?
  - private security staff
  - management
  - owner
  - supervisor
  - bar staff
  - casual staff
- Where will the observation take place?
  - in public view
  - away from public view

Miscellaneous:

- Whose views should be taken into account before installing a system?
  - police
  - owner
  - management
  - staff
  - residents on property
  - local residents
  - community groups
  - customers
- Who should know that a system is in place?
  - police
  - other emergency services
  - insurers
  - owner
  - management
  - staff
  - residents on property
  - local residents
  - customers
- What priority should be given to CCTV?
  - essential
  - desirable (high, medium or low)
  - threat-dependent
- What is the likelihood of an activity occurring and how often?
  - very high
  - high
  - medium
  - low
  - very unlikely

Frequency:

- continuous
- hourly
- daily
- monthly
- How effectively does the task have to be done?
  - right first time
  - every time
  - initially effective but becoming less so as time passes
  - standards high enough to meet needs of particular incidents
  - detect x% of incidents

Further information

The following web sites offer comprehensive information on security issues relating to licensed premises.

www.met.police.uk

www.homeoffice.co.uk

From the Home Office, 50 Queen Anne's Gate, London SWIH 9AT:

CCTV – Looking Out for You

Bombs – Protecting People and Property

From the Directorate of Public Affairs and Internal Communications, Metropolitan Police Service, New Scotland Yard, Broadway, London SW1H 0BG:

Communal Door Security

The Garden Strikes Back – A guide to plants that burglars hate

Terrorism – Help us defeat it

From British Beer and Pub Association, Market Towers, 1 Nine Elms Lane, London SW8 5NG

Drugs and Pubs – A guide for licensees

For these and any other enquiries relating to the management of licensed premises please contact the BBPA directly:

Tel: 020 7627 9191

Email: enquiries@beerandpub.com

www.beerandpub.com

Acknowledgements

This booklet was produced by British Beer and Pub Association in conjunction with the Metropolitan Police Service.

Portman Group Code of Practice November 2012

ABOUT THE PORTMAN GROUP

The Portman Group is the responsibility body for drinks producers in the UK.

Our role is:

- To **regulate** the promotion and packaging of alcoholic drinks sold or marketed in the UK through our Code of Practice.
- To **challenge** and encourage the industry to market its products responsibly.
- To show **leadership** on best practice in alcohol social responsibility through the actions of member companies.

The Portman Group is a not-for-profit organisation funded by nine member companies[1] who represent every sector of drinks production and collectively account for more than half the UK alcohol market.

ABOUT THE CODE

The Portman Group Code of Practice was first introduced in April 1996 to regulate alcohol marketing. It applies to all alcoholic drinks sold and marketed in the UK and covers activity which is not subject to regulation through the ASA or Ofcom. Its sole purpose is to ensure that alcohol is marketed in a socially responsible way and only to adults.

The Code is recognised as a gold standard in effective self-regulation at global, EU and UK levels. It is referenced in the Supporting Guidance to the Licensing Act 2003 and endorsed by the Government in its Alcohol Strategy. The Code is upheld and supported throughout the industry, including producers, importers, wholesalers, retailers and trade associations. There are over 140 signatories who are committed to abide by the Code and uphold the

---

[1]   AB InBev; Bacardi Brown-Forman Brands; Carlsberg; C&C Group; Diageo; Heineken; Molson Coors; Pernod Ricard; and SHS Drinks (formerly Beverage Brands).

rulings made by the Independent Complaints Panel. This self-regulatory framework offers significant benefits over statutory alternatives including:

- Speed of action in modifying and enforcing the rules
- Willingness by industry to engage with the spirit of the rules
- Commercially effective sanctions that are voluntarily adopted
- Preventative activity programmes funded by industry.

Since the Code was introduced in 1996 there have been 207 complaints and 134 irresponsible or inappropriate products and promotions have been amended or removed from market. The overriding aim is not to find products in breach but to support the industry in marketing products responsibly in the first place. The Portman Group provides a free and confidential Advisory Service for producers to check their products and promotions before launch. Over 1,000 separate advice requests have been dealt with by the service in the past two years alone. For more information see the Advisory Service section.

REVIEWING THE CODE

We announced a review of the Code in March 2011 as part of our commitment to the Government's Public Health Responsibility Deal. Our aim is to continually strengthen the Code so that it remains at the forefront of good practice and an exemplar of industry self-regulation. We want to ensure there is seamless consistency with the Advertising Standards Authority and Ofcom rules on alcohol marketing and advertising.

The aim is to achieve the right balance between legitimate and creative marketing activity and public protection, especially of young people. We have consulted extensively over the past year including a public consultation, a series of expert workshops and ongoing discussions with all stakeholders from government bodies, health and marketing experts and industry representatives. We have considered views from over one hundred stakeholders in developing the new Code.

The new Code rules will come into effect in May 2013.

This booklet gives a short overview of the main areas where we have tightened up the Code. It also provides details of where to go for more information and how to arrange tailored Code training sessions.

STRENGTHENING THE CODE

In response to the consultation we will strengthen the Code in the following key areas:

Comprehensive regulation – the remit of the Code has been clarified so that it applies to all alcohol marketing that is not otherwise regulated by the ASA or Ofcom – this includes all producer-led as well as joint promotions with retailers (where the producer has given approval or agreed to the promotion and/ or promotional materials). The remit has also been extended to cover public relations activity and digital marketing which is not within the ASA remit.

Clamping down on inappropriate marketing claims – the sexual success rule has been tightened up. The rule will continue to prohibit reference to sexual success and will prohibit any direct or indirect associations with sexual activity. It is also now prohibited for alcohol marketing to make any claims about having therapeutic properties such as being an aid to relaxation.

Protecting under 18s and social media – producers need to take extra care when using images of people who are, or who look as if they are, under 25. They should not be featured in a significant role nor should they be seen drinking alcohol. It is acceptable to use images of under 25s provided they are portrayed in an incidental context only. This rule is entirely consistent with the ASA advertising rules. Most social media activity, including user-generated content which has been solicited or adopted by a producer as part of their own marketing, will be subject to the ASA rules. The PG Code will continue to apply to all non-marketing related brand content on producer-controlled social media platforms that are not subject to the ASA rules.

As marketing on social media platforms is a fast-moving area we will continue to work in partnership with producers, marketing companies, social networking sites and regulators to develop a better technical solution to improved alcohol age verification in the online space.

Promoting lower alcohol alternatives – producers will now be able to draw attention to products which are below the average strength of similar drinks by making the lower strength a dominant theme. This was previously disallowed under the old strength rule. This change will support producers' pledge to remove 1 billion units from the alcohol market by introducing and promoting new lower alcohol ranges.

For more information see the Guidance Note: *Communication of Alcoholic Strength*

NEW SPONSORSHIP CODE

As of next year there will be a new separate Code for sponsorship which will require for producers to include a recognisable commitment to alcohol responsibility – work is ongoing to develop the detail of this Code which is expected to be completed by Spring 2013.

REVISED CODE RULES

The revised rules for the fifth edition of the *Responsible Naming, Packaging and Promotion of Alcoholic Drinks* are shown below with the changes highlighted. These changes are explained in more detail in the following section.

3.1 The alcoholic nature of a drink should be communicated on its packaging with absolute clarity.

3.2 A drink, its packaging and any promotional material or activity should not in any direct or indirect way:

 a. **Give higher alcoholic strength,** or intoxicating effect, undue emphasis. A product's lower alcoholic strength may be emphasised proportionately when it is below the average strength for similar beverages. Factual information about alcoholic strength may be given[2];

 b. suggest any association with bravado, or with violent, aggressive, dangerous or anti-social behaviour (though sponsorship of activities which may be dangerous after alcohol consumption, such as motor racing or yachting, are not in themselves in breach of this clause);

 c. suggest any association with, acceptance of, or allusion to, illicit drugs;

 d. suggest any association with sexual activity or sexual success;

 e. suggest that consumption of the drink can lead to social success or popularity;

 f. encourage illegal, irresponsible or immoderate consumption, such as drink-driving, binge-drinking or drunkenness;

 g. urge the consumer to drink rapidly or to down a product in one;

 h. have a particular appeal to under 18s (in the case of sponsorship, those under 18 years of age should not comprise more than 25% of the participants, audience or spectators);

 i. incorporate images of people who are, or look as if they are, under twenty-five years of age, where there is any suggestion that they are drinking alcohol or they are featured in a significant role. Images may be shown where people appear only in an incidental context; or

 j. suggest that the product has therapeutic qualities, or can enhance mental or physical capabilities.

For more information see the Guidance Notes: *General Interpretation of the Fifth Edition of the Code; Remit of the Fifth Edition of the Portman Group Code*

REMIT OF THE CODE

From May 2013, the Portman Group Code will apply to;

---

[2] Under the UK Food Labelling Regulations 1996, Regulation 42(1) and Schedule 8 Part I, the description 'low alcohol' or any other word or description which implies that the drink being described is 'low' in alcohol shall not be applied to any alcoholic drink unless the drink is no more than 1.2% abv.

'The naming, packaging, marketing and promotional activity under-taken by a drinks producer for an alcoholic drink which is marketed for sale and consumption in the UK, where such activity is primarily UK-targeted, and is not already subject to regulation through the ASA or Ofcom.'

Previously, the remit was defined by identifying the specific areas covered by the Code. In the new Code we have defined the remit as being all producer alcohol marketing which is not otherwise subject to regulation by the Advertising Standards Authority (ASA) or Ofcom's. This will ensure that there are no gaps in the regulation of drinks producers' marketing activity going forward.

Companies are strongly advised to make use of the free Advisory Service when undertaking drinks' marketing to in understanding whether the Code applies and, if so, whether they are likely to comply with the requirements under the Code.

For more information see the Guidance Note: *Remit of the Fifth Edition of the Portman Group Code*

PUBLIC RELATIONS (PR)

The fifth edition of the Code covers *all* public relations (PR) activity. PR includes elements such as the content of press releases, tool kits, media relations activities, blogs, the hosting of events and other media partnership activities. Producers must take extra care to ensure that PR activity does not associate the brands with:

- Irresponsible or excessive consumption
- Sexual or social success
- Images of people under 25.

For more information see the Guidance Notes: *Remit of the Fifth Edition of the Portman Group Code; Guidance on Public Relations (PR) Materials and Activities; Use of images of Under 25s in alcohol marketing*

CO-PROMOTIONAL ACTIVITY

Co-promotional activity is defined as:

Any marketing activity between a producer and retailer or wholesaler that relates to a producer's products and which has taken place with the approval or agreement of a producer, even if that activity is predominantly retailer/wholesaler – led.

This is a new addition to the Code. Promotions with on/off trade retail partners where producers give approval or agree that their brand can be used are now subject to the Code. The guidance advises producers who engage in co-promotional activity with a retailer to take all reasonable steps to discourage retailers from using their brands as the basis for drinks or promotional activity which associates their brands with:

- Strength and/or the intoxicating effect of alcohol (e.g. bombs, slammers)
- Energy claims or energy drinks (brands should not be co-promoted or featured with an energy drink mixers)
- Slimming claims
- Irresponsible or excessive consumption
- Sexual and social success
- A particular appeal to under-18s.

For more information see the Guidance Notes: *Guidance on Co-promotional activity; Remit of the Fifth Edition of the Portman Group Code; General Interpretation of the Fifth Edition of the Code*

SEXUAL IMAGERY

We have tightened up this rule which now prevents alcohol from being associated with any sexual activity and not just sexual success.

This is stricter wording than the fourth edition of the Code which referred only to sexual success. It not only disallows claims which imply a link between alcohol and sexual success but also categorically disallows any reference to types of sexual activity.

Allusions to romance are acceptable under the Code providing there is no suggestion that the alcohol has been the catalyst for the behaviour, is essential to the success of the relationship, and/or has played a role in the outcome of the event.

For more information see the Guidance Note: *General Interpretation of the Fifth Edition of the Code*

THERAPEUTIC PROPERTIES

This is a new addition to rule and is consistent with CAP/BCAP rules. Producers can not suggest that alcohol has therapeutic qualities or can enhance mental or physical capabilities. Producers should avoid:

- Any direct or implied suggestion that consumption of alcohol has helped the consumer relax is likely to be unacceptable under the Code
- Suggesting that alcohol can be a catalyst for change of mood or mental state.

The portrayal of drinking as a legitimate accompaniment to a relaxing setting may be acceptable. However, any claims that directly link consumption with relaxation will be unacceptable.

For more information see the Guidance Note: *General Interpretation of the Fifth Edition of the Code*

PREPARING FOR THE NEW CODE

The new Code rules will not come into effect until May 2013 giving six months for the producers and marketers to prepare. The Portman Group offers the following support materials and advice services:

Guidance Notes

We have developed a detailed set of Guidance Notes which provide further information about the changes and what they mean. These can be downloaded from the Marketing Advice section of the Portman Group's website www.portmangroup.org.uk and include:

- General Interpretation of the Fifth Edition of the Code
- Remit of the Fifth Edition of the Portman Group Code
- Communication of Alcoholic Strength
- Use of images of Under 25s in alcohol marketing
- Guidance on Co-promotional activity

Code Advisory Service

The Code Advisory Service offers fast, free and confidential infomration about all aspects of alchohol marketing. Simply email your request to advice@portmangroup.org.uk and we will get back to you within 48 hours.

You can also write to us at:

Portman Group Code Advisory Service
4th Floor
20 Conduit Street
London
W1S 2XW
t: +44 (0)020 7290 1460
email: advice@portmangroup.org.uk
www.portmangroup.org.uk
Twitter: @portmangroup

IN-HOUSE TRAINING

We can arrange comprehensive tailored in house training for producers through our Code Advisory Service. To arrange a training session email

advice@portmangroup.org.uk or contact Kay Perry or Robyn Dunwoodie on
020 7290 1460

Amended Guidance issued under section 182 of the Licensing Act 2003

October 2012

1. INTRODUCTION

The Licensing Act 2003

1.1 The Licensing Act 2003 (referred to in this Guidance as the 2003 Act), its explanatory notes and any statutory instruments made under it may be viewed online at **www.legislation.gov.uk**. The statutory instruments include regulations setting out the content and format of application forms and notices. The Home Office has responsibility for the 2003 Act. However, the Department for Culture, Media and Sport (DCMS) is responsible for regulated entertainment, for which there is provision in Schedule 1 to the 2003 Act.

Licensing objectives and aims

1.2 The legislation provides a clear focus on the promotion of four statutory objectives which must be addressed when licensing functions are undertaken.

1.3 The licensing objectives are:

- The prevention of crime and disorder;
- Public safety;
- The prevention of public nuisance; and
- The protection of children from harm.

1.4 Each objective is of equal importance. There are no other statutory licensing objectives, so that the promotion of the four objectives is a paramount consideration at all times.

1.5 However, the legislation also supports a number of other key aims and purposes. These are vitally important and should be principal aims for everyone involved in licensing work.

They include:

- Protecting the public and local residents from crime, anti-social behaviour and noise nuisance caused by irresponsible licensed premises;
- Giving the police and licensing authorities the powers they need to effectively manage and police the night-time economy and take action against those premises that are causing problems;
- Recognising the important role which pubs and other licensed premises play in our local communities by minimising the regulatory burden on business, encouraging innovation and supporting responsible premises;
- Providing a regulatory framework for alcohol which reflects the needs of local communities and empowers local authorities to make and enforce decisions about the most appropriate licensing strategies for their local area; and
- Encouraging greater community involvement in licensing decisions and giving local residents the opportunity to have their say regarding licensing decisions that may impact upon them.

The guidance

1.6   Section 182 of the 2003 Act provides that the Secretary of State must issue and, from time to time, may revise guidance to licensing authorities on the discharge of their functions under the 2003 Act. This guidance comes into force as soon as it is laid. Where a licence application was made prior to the coming into force of the revised guidance, it should be processed in accordance with the guidance in force at the time at which the application was made; the revised guidance does not apply retrospectively. However, all applications received by the licensing authority on or after the date the revised guidance came into force should be processed in accordance with the revised guidance.

Purpose

1.7   This Guidance is provided to licensing authorities in relation to the carrying out of their functions under the 2003 Act. It also provides information to magistrates' courts hearing appeals against licensing decisions and has been made widely available for the benefit of those who run licensed premises, their legal advisers and the general public. It is a key medium for promoting best practice, ensuring consistent application of licensing powers across England and Wales and for promoting fairness, equal treatment and proportionality.

1.8   The police remain key enforcers of licensing law. This Guidance does not bind police officers who, within the parameters of their force orders and the law, remain operationally independent. However, this Guidance is provided to support and assist police officers in interpreting and implementing the 2003 Act in the promotion of the four licensing objectives.

Legal status

1.9 Section 4 of the 2003 Act provides that, in carrying out its functions, a licensing authority must 'have regard to' guidance issued by the Secretary of State under section 182. This Guidance is therefore binding on all licensing authorities to that extent. However, this Guidance cannot anticipate every possible scenario or set of circumstances that may arise and, as long as licensing authorities have properly understood this Guidance, they may depart from it if they have good reason to do so and can provide full reasons. Departure from this Guidance could give rise to an appeal or judicial review, and the reasons given will then be a key consideration for the courts when considering the lawfulness and merits of any decision taken.

1.10 Nothing in this Guidance should be taken as indicating that any requirement of licensing law or any other law may be overridden (including the obligations placed on any public authorities under human rights legislation). This Guidance does not in any way replace the statutory provisions of the 2003 Act or add to its scope and licensing authorities should note that interpretation of the 2003 Act is a matter for the courts. Licensing authorities and others using this Guidance must take their own professional and legal advice about its implementation.

Licensing policies

1.11 Section 5 of the 2003 Act requires a licensing authority to determine and publish a statement of its licensing policy at least once every five years. The policy must be published before it carries out any licensing functions under the 2003 Act.

1.12 However, determining and publishing a statement of its policy is a licensing function and as such the authority must have regard to this Guidance when taking this step. A licensing authority may depart from its own policy if the individual circumstances of any case merit such a decision in the interests of the promotion of the licensing objectives. But once again, it is important that it should be able to give full reasons for departing from its published statement of licensing policy. Where revisions to this Guidance are issued by the Secretary of State, there may be a period of time when the licensing policy statement is inconsistent with the Guidance (for example, during any consultation by the licensing authority). In these circumstances, the licensing authority should have regard, and give appropriate weight, to this Guidance and its own existing licensing policy statement.

Licensable activities

1.13 For the purposes of the 2003 Act, the following are licensable activities:

- The sale by retail of alcohol;
- The supply of alcohol by or on behalf of a club to, or to the order of, a member of the club;
- The provision of regulated entertainment; and,
- The provision of late night refreshment.

Further explanation of these terms is provided in Chapter 3.

Authorisations or permissions

1.14 The 2003 Act provides for four different types of authorisation or permission, as follows:

- Premises licence – to use premises for licensable activities.
- Club premises certificate – to allow a qualifying club to engage in qualifying club activities as set out in Section 1 of the Act.
- Temporary event notice – to carry out licensable activities at a temporary event.
- Personal licence – to sell or authorise the sale of alcohol from premises in respect of which there is a premises licence.

General principles

1.15 If an application for a premises licence or club premises certificate has been made lawfully and there have been no representations from responsible authorities or other persons, the licensing authority must grant the application, subject only to conditions that are consistent with the operating schedule and relevant mandatory conditions. It is recommended that licence applicants contact responsible authorities when preparing their operating schedules.

Licence conditions – general principles

1.16 Conditions on a premises licence or club premises certificate are important in setting the parameters within which premises can lawfully operate. The use of wording such as "must", "shall" and "will", is encouraged. Licence conditions:

- must be appropriate for the promotion of the licensing objectives;
- must be precise and enforceable;
- must be unambiguous and clear in what they intend to achieve;
- should not duplicate other statutory requirements or other duties or responsibilities placed on the employer by other legislation;
- must be tailored to the individual type, location and characteristics of the premises and events concerned;

- should not be standardised and may be unlawful when it cannot be demonstrated that they are appropriate for the promotion of the licensing objectives in an individual case;
- should not replicate offences set out in the 2003 Act or other legislation;
- should be proportionate, justifiable and be capable of being met, (for example, whilst beer glasses may be available in toughened glass, wine glasses may not);
- cannot seek to manage the behaviour of customers once they are beyond the direct management of the licence holder and their staff, but may impact on the behaviour of customers in the immediate vicinity of the premises or as they enter or leave; and
- should be written in a prescriptive format.

Each application on its own merits

1.17 Each application must be considered on its own merits and in accordance with the licensing authority's statement of licensing policy; for example, if the application falls within the scope of a cumulative impact policy. Conditions attached to licences and certificates must be tailored to the individual type, location and characteristics of the premises and events concerned. This is essential to avoid the imposition of disproportionate and overly burdensome conditions on premises where there is no need for such conditions. Standardised conditions should be avoided and indeed may be unlawful where they cannot be shown to be appropriate for the promotion of the licensing objectives in an individual case.

Additional guidance

1.18 From time to time, the Home Office may issue additional supporting guidance to licensing authorities and other persons on its website. This supporting guidance is good practice guidance and should be viewed as indicative and subject to change. Such supporting guidance will broadly reflect but will not be part of the statutory guidance issued by the Secretary of State under section 182 of the 2003 Act. Licensing authorities may wish to refer to, but are under no statutory duty to have regard to such supporting guidance issued by the Home Office.

Other relevant legislation

1.19 Whilst licence conditions should not duplicate other statutory provisions, licensing authorities and licensees should be mindful of requirements and responsibilities placed on them by other legislation.

Legislation which may be relevant includes:

- The Gambling Act 2005
- The Environmental Protection Act 1990
- The Noise Act 1996
- The Clean Neighbourhoods and Environmental Act 2005
- The Regulatory Reform (Fire Safety) Order 2005
- Health and Safety (First-Aid) Regulations 1981
- The Equality Act 2010.

2. THE LICENSING OBJECTIVES

Crime and disorder

2.1 Licensing authorities should look to the police as the main source of advice on crime and disorder. They should also seek to involve the local Community Safety Partnership (CSP).

2.2 In the exercise of their functions, licensing authorities should seek to co-operate with the Security Industry Authority ("SIA") as far as possible and consider adding relevant conditions to licences where appropriate. The SIA also plays an important role in preventing crime and disorder by ensuring that door supervisors are properly licensed and, in partnership with police and other agencies, that security companies are not being used as fronts for serious and organised criminal activity. This may include making specific enquiries or visiting premises through intelligence led operations in conjunction with the police, local authorities and other partner agencies. Similarly, the provision of requirements for door supervision may be appropriate to ensure that people who are drunk, drug dealers or people carrying firearms do not enter the premises and ensuring that the police are kept informed.

2.3 Conditions should be targeted on deterrence and preventing crime and disorder. For example, where there is good reason to suppose that disorder may take place, the presence of closed-circuit television (CCTV) cameras both inside and immediately outside the premises can actively deter disorder, nuisance, anti-social behaviour and crime generally. Some licence holders may wish to have cameras on their premises for the prevention of crime directed against the business itself, its staff, or its customers. But any condition may require a broader approach, and it may be appropriate to ensure that the precise location of cameras is set out on plans to ensure that certain areas are properly covered and there is no subsequent dispute over the terms of the condition.

2.4 The inclusion of radio links and ring-round phone systems should be considered an appropriate condition for public houses, bars and nightclubs operating in city and town centre leisure areas with a high density of licensed premises. These systems allow managers of licensed premises to communicate instantly with the police and facilitate a rapid response to any disorder which may be endangering the customers and staff on the premises.

2.5 In the context of crime and disorder and public safety, the preservation of order on premises may give rise to genuine concerns about the ability of the management team with responsibility for the maintenance of order. This may occur, for example, on premises where there are very large numbers of people and alcohol is supplied for consumption, or in premises where there are public order problems.

2.6 Conditions relating to the management competency of designated premises supervisors should not normally be attached to premises licences. The designated premises supervisor is the key person who will usually be responsible for the day to day management of the premises by the premises licence holder, including the prevention of disorder. A condition of this kind may only be justified as appropriate in rare circumstances where it can be demonstrated that, in the circumstances associated with particular premises, poor management competency could give rise to issues of crime and disorder and public safety.

2.7 It will normally be the responsibility of the premises licence holder as an employer, and not the licensing authority, to ensure that the managers appointed at the premises are competent and appropriately trained. However, licensing authorities must ensure that they do not stray outside their powers and duties under the 2003 Act. This is important to ensure the portability of the personal licence and the offences set out in the 2003 Act and to ensure, for example, that the prevention of disorder is in sharp focus for all managers, licence holders and clubs.

Public safety

2.8 Licence holders have a responsibility to ensure the safety of those using their premises, as a part of their duties under the 2003 Act. This concerns the safety of people using the relevant premises rather than public health which is addressed in other legislation. Physical safety includes the prevention of accidents and injuries and other immediate harms that can result from alcohol consumption such as unconsciousness or alcohol poisoning. Conditions relating to public safety may also promote the crime and disorder objective as noted above. There will of course be occasions when a public safety condition could incidentally benefit a person's health more generally, but it should not be the purpose of the condition as this would be outside the licensing authority's powers (be ultra vires) under the 2003 Act. Conditions should not be imposed on a premises licence or club premises certificate which relate to cleanliness or hygiene.

2.9 A number of matters should be considered in relation to public safety. These may include:

- Fire safety;
- Ensuring appropriate access for emergency services such as ambulances;
- Good communication with local authorities and emergency services, for example communications networks with the police and signing up for local incident alerts (see paragraph 2.4 above);
- Ensuring the presence of trained first aiders on the premises and appropriate first aid kits;
- Ensuring the safety of people when leaving the premises (for example, through the provision of information on late-night transportation);
- Ensuring appropriate and frequent waste disposal, particularly of glass bottles;
- Ensuring appropriate limits on the maximum capacity of the premises (see paragraphs 2.13–2.15, and Chapter 10; and
- Considering the use of CCTV in and around the premises (as noted in paragraph 2.3 above, this may also assist with promoting the crime and disorder objective).

2.10 The measures that are appropriate to promote public safety will vary between premises and the matters listed above may not apply in all cases. As set out in Chapter 8 (8.34–8.42), applicants should consider when making their application which steps it is appropriate to take to promote the public safety objective and demonstrate how they achieve that.

Ensuring safe departure of those using the premises

2.11   Licence holders should make provision to ensure that premises users safely leave their premises. Measures that may assist include:

- Providing information on the premises of local taxi companies who can provide safe transportation home; and
- Ensuring adequate lighting outside the premises, particularly on paths leading to and from the premises and in car parks.

Maintenance and repair

2.12 Where there is a requirement in other legislation for premises open to the public or for employers to possess certificates attesting to the safety or satisfactory nature of certain equipment or fixtures on the premises, it would be inappropriate for a licensing condition to require possession of such a certificate. However, it would be permissible to require as a condition of a licence or certificate, if appropriate, checks on this equipment to be conducted at specified intervals and for evidence of these checks to be retained by the premises licence holder or club provided this does not duplicate or gold-plate a requirement in other legislation. Similarly, it would be permissible for licensing authorities, if they receive relevant representations from responsible authorities or any other persons, to attach conditions which require equipment of particular standards to be maintained on the premises. Responsible authorities – such as health and safety authorities – should therefore make their expectations clear in this respect to enable prospective licence holders or clubs to prepare effective operating schedules and club operating schedules.

Safe capacities

2.13 "Safe capacities" should only be imposed where appropriate for the promotion of public safety or the prevention of disorder on the relevant premises. For example, if a capacity has been imposed through other legislation, it would be inappropriate to reproduce it in a premises licence. Indeed, it would also be wrong to lay down conditions which conflict with other legal requirements. However, if no safe capacity has been imposed through other legislation, a responsible authority may consider it appropriate for a new capacity to be attached to the premises which would apply at any material time when the licensable activities are taking place and make representations to that effect. For example, in certain circumstances, capacity limits may be appropriate in preventing disorder, as overcrowded venues can increase the risks of crowds becoming frustrated and hostile.

2.14 It should also be noted in this context that it remains an offence under the 2003 Act to sell or supply alcohol to a person who is drunk. This is particularly important because of the nuisance and anti-social behaviour which can be provoked after leaving licensed premises.

2.15 The special provisions made for dancing in section 177 of the 2003 Act apply only to premises with a "permitted capacity" of not more than 200 persons. In this context, the capacity must be where the fire and rescue authority has made a recommendation on the capacity of the premises under the 2005 Order. For any application for a premises licence or club premises certificate for premises without an existing permitted capacity where the applicant wishes to take advantage of the special provisions set out in section 177 of the 2003 Act, the applicant should conduct their own risk assessment as to the appropriate capacity of the premises. They should send their recommendation to the fire and rescue authority which will consider it and decide what the "permitted capacity" of those premises should be.

2.16 Whilst the Cinematograph (Safety) Regulations 1955 (S.I 1955/1129) – which contained a significant number of regulations in respect of fire safety provision at cinemas – no longer apply, authorisations granted under Schedule 8 to the 2003 Act will have been subject to conditions which re-state those regulations in their new premises licence or club premises certificate. Any holders of a converted licence seeking to remove these conditions and reduce the regulatory burden on them (to the extent to which that can be done while still promoting the licensing objectives), would need to apply to vary their converted licences or certificates. When considering applications for variations, minor variations, and the grant of new licences, licensing authorities and responsible authorities should recognise the need for steps to be taken to assure public safety at these premises in the absence of the 1995 Regulations.

2.17 Public safety includes the safety of performers appearing at any premises.

Public nuisance

2.18 The 2003 Act enables licensing authorities and responsible authorities, through representations, to consider what constitutes public nuisance and what is appropriate to prevent it in terms of conditions attached to specific premises licences and club premises certificates. It is therefore important that in considering the promotion of this licensing objective, licensing authorities and responsible authorities focus on the effect of the licensable activities at the specific premises on persons living and working (including those carrying on business) in the area around the premises which may be disproportionate and unreasonable. The issues will mainly concern noise nuisance, light pollution, noxious smells and litter.

2.19 Public nuisance is given a statutory meaning in many pieces of legislation. It is however not narrowly defined in the 2003 Act and retains its broad common law meaning. It is important to remember that the prevention of public nuisance could therefore include low-level nuisance, perhaps affecting a few people living locally, as well as major disturbance affecting the whole community. It may also include in appropriate circumstances the reduction of the living and working amenity and environment of other persons living and working in the area of the licensed premises. Public nuisance may also arise as a result of the adverse effects of artificial light, dust, odour and insects or where its effect is prejudicial to health.

2.20 Conditions relating to noise nuisance will usually concern steps appropriate to control the levels of noise emanating from premises. This might be achieved by a simple measure such as ensuring that doors and windows are kept closed after a particular time, or more sophisticated measures like the installation of acoustic curtains or rubber speaker mounts. Any conditions appropriate to promote the prevention of public nuisance should be tailored to the type, nature and characteristics of the specific premises. Licensing authorities should be aware of the need to avoid inappropriate or disproportionate measures that could deter events that are valuable to the community, such as live music. Noise limiters, for example, are very expensive to purchase and install and are likely to be a considerable burden for smaller venues.

2.21 As with all conditions, those relating to noise nuisance may not be appropriate in certain circumstances where provisions in other legislation adequately protect those living in the area of the premises. But as stated earlier in this Guidance, the approach of licensing authorities and responsible authorities should be one of prevention and when their powers are engaged, licensing authorities should be aware of the fact that other legislation may not adequately cover concerns raised in relevant representations and additional conditions may be appropriate.

2.22 Where applications have given rise to representations, any appropriate conditions should normally focus on the most sensitive periods. For example, music noise from premises usually occurs from mid-evening until either late-evening or early-morning when residents in adjacent properties may be attempting to go to sleep or are sleeping. In certain circumstances, conditions relating to noise immediately surrounding the premises may also prove appropriate to address any disturbance anticipated as customers enter and leave.

2.23 Measures to control light pollution will also require careful thought. Bright lighting outside premises which is considered appropriate to prevent crime and disorder may itself give rise to light pollution for some neighbours. Applicants, licensing authorities and responsible authorities will need to balance these issues.

2.24 Beyond the immediate area surrounding the premises, these are matters for the personal responsibility of individuals under the law. An individual who engages in anti-social behaviour is accountable in their own right. However, it would be perfectly reasonable for a licensing authority to impose a condition, following relevant representations, that requires the licence holder or club to place signs at the exits from the building encouraging patrons to be quiet until they leave the area and to respect the rights of people living nearby to a peaceful night.

Protection of children from harm

2.25 The protection of children from harm includes the protection of children from moral, psychological and physical harm. This includes not only protecting children from the harms associated with alcohol but also wider harms such as exposure to strong language and sexual expletives (for example, in the context of exposure to certain films or adult entertainment).

2.26 The Government believes that it is completely unacceptable to sell alcohol to children. Conditions relating to the access of children where alcohol is sold and which are appropriate to protect them from harm should be carefully considered. Moreover, conditions restricting the access of children to premises should be strongly considered in circumstances where:

- adult entertainment is provided;
- a member or members of the current management have been convicted for serving alcohol to minors or with a reputation for allowing underage drinking (other than in the context of the exemption in the 2003 Act relating to 16 and 17 year olds consuming beer, wine and cider when accompanied by an adult during a table meal);
- it is known that unaccompanied children have been allowed access;
- there is a known association with drug taking or dealing; or
- in some cases, the premises are used exclusively or primarily for the sale of alcohol for consumption on the premises.

2.27 It is also possible that activities, such as adult entertainment, may take place at certain times on premises but not at other times. For example, premises may operate as a café bar during the day providing meals for families but also provide entertainment with a sexual content after 8.00pm. It is not possible to give an exhaustive list of what amounts to entertainment or services of an adult or sexual nature. Applicants, responsible authorities and licensing authorities will need to consider this point carefully. This would broadly include topless bar staff, striptease, lap-, table- or pole-dancing, performances involving feigned violence or horrific incidents, feigned or actual sexual acts or fetishism, or entertainment involving strong and offensive language.

2.28 Applicants must be clear in their operating schedules about the activities and times at which the events would take place to help determine when it is not appropriate for children to enter the premises. Consideration should also be given to the proximity of premises to schools and youth clubs so that applicants take appropriate steps to ensure that advertising relating to their premises, or relating to events at their premises, is not displayed at a time when children are likely to be near the premises.

2.29 Licensing authorities and responsible authorities should expect applicants, when preparing an operating schedule or club operating schedule, to set out the steps to be taken to protect children from harm when on the premises.

2.30 Conditions, where they are appropriate, should reflect the licensable activities taking place on the premises. In addition to the mandatory condition regarding age verification, other conditions relating to the protection of children from harm can include:

- restrictions on the hours when children may be present;
- restrictions or exclusions on the presence of children under certain ages when particular specified activities are taking place;
- restrictions on the parts of the premises to which children may have access;
- age restrictions (below 18);

- restrictions or exclusions when certain activities are taking place;
- requirements for an accompanying adult (including for example, a combination of requirements which provide that children under a particular age must be accompanied by an adult); and
- full exclusion of people under 18 from the premises when any licensable activities are taking place.

2.31 Please see also Chapter 10 for details about the Licensing Act 2003 (Mandatory Licensing Conditions Order) 2010.

2.32 Licensing authorities should give considerable weight to representations about child protection matters.

2.33 The 2003 Act provides that, where a premises licence or club premises certificate authorises the exhibition of a film, it must include a condition requiring the admission of children to films to be restricted in accordance with recommendations given either by a body designated under section 4 of the Video Recordings Act 1984 specified in the licence (the British Board of Film Classification is currently the only body which has been so designated) or by the licensing authority itself. Further details are given in Chapter 10.

2.34 Theatres may present a range of diverse activities and entertainment including, for example, variety shows incorporating adult entertainment. It is appropriate in these cases for a licensing authority to consider restricting the admission of children in such circumstances. Entertainments may also be presented at theatres specifically for children. It will be appropriate to consider whether a condition should be attached to a premises licence or club premises certificate which requires the presence of a sufficient number of adult staff on the premises to ensure the wellbeing of the children during any emergency.

Offences relating to the sale and supply of alcohol to children

2.35 Licensing authorities are expected to maintain close contact with the police, young offenders' teams and trading standards officers (who can carry out test purchases under section 154 of the 2003 Act) about the extent of unlawful sales and consumption of alcohol by minors and to be involved in the development of any strategies to control or prevent these unlawful activities and to pursue prosecutions. For example, where, as a matter of policy, warnings are given to retailers prior to any decision to prosecute in respect of an offence, it is important that each of the enforcement arms should be aware of the warnings each of them has given.

TABLE OF RELEVANT OFFENCES UNDER THE 2003 ACT

Section	Offence
Section 145	Unaccompanied children prohibited from certain premises
Section 146	Sale of alcohol to children
Section 147	Allowing the sale of alcohol to children
Section 147A	Persistently selling alcohol to children
Section 148[1]	Sale of liqueur confectionery to children under 16
Section 149	Purchase of alcohol by or on behalf of children
Section 150	Consumption of alcohol by children
Section 151	Delivering alcohol to children
Section 152	Sending a child to obtain alcohol
Section 153	Prohibition of unsupervised sales by children

3.   LICENSABLE ACTIVITIES

Summary

3.1   A premises licence authorises the use of any premises (see Chapter 5) for licensable activities. Licensable activities are defined in section 1 of the 2003 Act, and a fuller description of certain activities is set out in Schedules 1 and 2 to the 2003 Act.

3.2   The licensable activities are:

- the sale by retail of alcohol;
- the supply of alcohol by or on behalf of a club to, or to the order of, a member of the club;
- the provision of regulated entertainment; and
- the provision of late night refreshment.

Wholesale of alcohol

3.3   **The sale of alcohol to the general public is licensable under the 2003 Act in accordance with the definition of "sale by retail" in section 192 of the 2003 Act.** This section makes it clear that, to be excluded from the meaning of "sale by retail", a sale must be:

- made from premises owned by the person making the sale, or occupied under a lease with security of tenure; and

---

[1]   Note. The Government has announced its intention to repeal this offence in 2013 at the earliest.

- for consumption off the premises.

3.4 In addition, to be excluded, the sales must be sales which are made to:

- a trader for the purpose of his trade;
- to a club for the purposes of that club;
- to a holder of a premises licence or a personal licence for the purpose of making sales under a premises licence; or
- a premises user who has given a temporary event notice, for the purpose of making sales authorised by that notice.

3.5 If an employee were buying alcohol as an "agent" for their employer and for the purposes of their employer's trade (i.e. selling alcohol), this could be treated as a sale to a trader. If, however, an employee were buying for the employee's own consumption, this would be a retail sale, and would require a licence.

3.6 The same considerations apply in the case of caterers who supply alcohol to their customers. Where a caterer purchases alcohol and then sells this alcohol to its customer, an authorisation will be required at the location where the retail sale of the alcohol is made (likely to be the caterer's own premises). If the customer was proposing to sell the alcohol under an authorisation, it is the customer who would need an authorisation under the 2003 Act. In this case, the exemption under the 2003 Act may apply to the sale made by the caterer.

Mobile, remote, internet and other delivery sales

3.7 The sale by retail of alcohol is a licensable activity and may only be carried out in accordance with an authorisation under the 2003 Act. Therefore, a person cannot sell alcohol from a vehicle or moveable structure at a series of different locations (e.g. house to house), unless there is a premises licence in respect of the vehicle or moveable structure at each location at which a sale of alcohol is made in, on or from it.

3.8 The place where the order for alcohol, or payment for it, takes place may not be the same as the place where the alcohol is appropriated to the contract (i.e. the place where it is identified and specifically set apart for delivery to the purchaser). This position can arise when sales are made online, by telephone, or mail order. Section 190 of the 2003 Act provides that the sale of alcohol is to be treated as taking place where the alcohol is appropriated to the contract. It will be the premises at this location which need to be licensed; for example, a call centre receiving orders for alcohol would not need a licence but the warehouse where the alcohol is stored and specifically selected for, and despatched to, the purchaser would need to be licensed. These licensed premises will, as such, be subject to conditions including the times of day during which alcohol may be sold. The premises licence will also be subject to the mandatory licence conditions.

3.9   Persons who run premises providing 'alcohol delivery services' should notify the relevant licensing authority that they are operating such a service in their operating schedule. This ensures that the licensing authority can properly consider what conditions are appropriate. Premises with an existing premises licence, which choose to operate such a service in addition to their existing licensable activities, should therefore apply to vary their licence to add this activity to their existing licensable activities.

Regulated entertainment

3.10   Schedule 1 to the 2003 Act, sets out what activities are to be treated as the provision of regulated entertainment and those that are not and are therefore exempt from the regulated entertainment aspects of the licensing regime (including incidental music – see paragraphs 15.1 and 15.2 below). Chapter 15 of this Guidance document sets out the types of entertainment regulated by the 2003 Act.

Late night refreshment

3.11   Schedule 2 to the 2003 Act sets out what activities are to be treated as the provision of late night refreshment and those that are not and are therefore exempt from the late night refreshment aspects of the licensing regime.

3.12   Schedule 2 provides a definition of what constitutes the provision of late night refreshment. It involves only the supply of 'hot food and hot drink'. Shops, stores and supermarkets selling cold food and cold drink that is immediately consumable from 11.00pm are not licensable as providing late night refreshment. The 2003 Act affects premises such as night cafés and take away food outlets where people may gather at any time from 11.00pm and until 5.00am. In this case, supply takes place when the hot food or hot drink is given to the customer and not when payment is made. For example, supply takes place when a table meal is served in a restaurant or when a take-away is handed to a customer over the counter.

3.13   Some premises provide hot food or hot drink between 11.00pm and 5.00am by means of vending machines. The supply of hot drink by a vending machine is not a licensable activity and is exempt under the 2003 Act provided the public have access to and can operate the machine without any involvement of the staff.

3.14   However, this exemption does not apply to hot food. Premises supplying hot food for a charge by vending machine are licensable if the food has been heated on the premises, even though no staff on the premises may have been involved in the transaction.

3.15 It is not expected that the provision of late night refreshment as a secondary activity in licensed premises open for other purposes such as public houses, cinemas or nightclubs or casinos should give rise to a need for significant additional conditions. The key licensing objectives in connection with late night refreshment are the prevention of crime and disorder and public nuisance, and it is expected that both will normally have been adequately covered in the conditions relating to the other licensable activities on such premises.

3.16 The supply of hot drink which consists of or contains alcohol is exempt under the 2003 Act as late night refreshment because it is caught by the provisions relating to the sale or supply of alcohol.

3.17 The supply of hot food or hot drink free of charge is not a licensable activity. However, where any charge is made for either admission to the premises or for some other item in order to obtain the hot food or hot drink, this will not be regarded as "free of charge". Supplies by a registered charity or anyone authorised by a registered charity are also exempt. Similarly, supplies made on vehicles – other than when they are permanently or temporarily parked – are also exempt.

3.18 Supplies of hot food or hot drink from 11.00pm are exempt from the provisions of the 2003 Act if there is no admission to the public to the premises involved and they are supplies to:

- a member of a recognised club supplied by the club;
- persons staying overnight in a hotel, guest house, lodging house, hostel, a caravan or camping site or any other premises whose main purpose is providing overnight accommodation;
- an employee supplied by a particular employer (for example, a staff canteen);
- a person who is engaged in a particular profession or who follows a particular vocation (for example, a tradesman carrying out work at particular premises); and
- a guest of any of the above.

Unauthorised activities

3.19 **It is a criminal offence under section 136 of the 2003 Act to carry on any of the licensable activities listed at paragraph 3.2** above other than in accordance with a licence or other authorisation under the 2003 Act. The maximum fine for this offence is £20,000, six months imprisonment or both. Police and local authorities have powers to take action in relation to premises carrying on unauthorised activities.

4. PERSONAL LICENCES

4.1 This chapter provides advice about the framework for personal licences. It also contains guidance for decision-making on applications by those managing community premises (church and village halls etc.) to remove the usual mandatory conditions that relate to personal licences and the requirement for a designated premises supervisor (DPS).

Requirements for a personal licence

4.2 The sale and supply of alcohol, because of its impact on the wider community and on crime and anti-social behaviour, carries with it greater responsibility than the provision of regulated entertainment and late night refreshment. This is why sales of alcohol may not be made under a premises licence unless there is a DPS in respect of the premises (who must hold a personal licence); and every sale must be made or authorised by a personal licence holder. The exception is only for those community premises which have successfully applied to remove the DPS requirement (see paragraph 4.18 below).

4.3 Any premises at which alcohol is sold or supplied where the requirement for a personal licence holder does apply may employ one or more such licence holders. For example, there may be one owner or senior manager and several junior managers holding a personal licence. However, the requirement that every sale of alcohol must at least be authorised by a personal licence holder does not mean that the licence holder has to attend or oversee each sale; it is sufficient that such sales are authorised. It should be noted that there is no requirement to have a DPS in relation to a Temporary Event Notice (TEN) or club premises certificate, and sales or supplies of alcohol authorised by a TEN or club premises certificate do not need to be authorised by a personal licence holder.

Who can apply?

4.4 In the case of an application for a personal licence under Part 6 of the 2003 Act, the requirements are that:

- the applicant must be aged 18 or over;
- the applicant possesses a licensing qualification accredited by the Secretary of State (or one which is certified as if it is such a qualification or is considered equivalent) or is a person as prescribed in regulations[2]).
- the applicant must not have forfeited a personal licence within five years of their application;

---

[2] Currently persons prescribed in regulations are: a member of the company of the Master, Wardens, Freemen and Commonalty of the Mistery of the Vintners of the City of London;

- the applicant has paid the appropriate fee to the licensing authority; and
- in a case in which the applicant has an unspent conviction for a relevant offence or a foreign offence, the police have not objected to the grant of the application on crime prevention grounds or the licensing authority has considered their objection but determined that the grant of the application will not undermine the crime prevention objective.

4.5 Any individual may apply for a personal licence whether or not they are currently employed or have business interests associated with the use of the licence. The issues which arise when the holder of a personal licence becomes associated with particular licensed premises and is specified as the DPS for those premises are dealt with at paragraphs 4.20 to 4.27 below. Licensing authorities may not therefore take these matters into account when considering an application for a personal licence.

CRIMINAL RECORD

4.6 Regulations made under the 2003 Act require that, in order to substantiate whether or not an applicant has a conviction for an unspent relevant offence, an applicant for the grant or renewal of personal licence must include a criminal conviction certificate, a criminal record certificate or the results of a subject access search of the Police National Computer by the National Identification Service to the licensing authority.

4.7 The requirement for an individual to establish whether or not they have unspent convictions for a relevant offence or foreign offence applies whether or not the individual has been living for a length of time in a foreign jurisdiction. It does not follow that such individuals will not have recorded offences in this country. All applicants are also required to make a clear statement as to whether or not they have been convicted outside England and Wales of a relevant offence or an equivalent foreign offence. This applies both to applicants ordinarily resident in England and Wales and any person from a foreign jurisdiction. Details of relevant offences as set out in the 2003 Act should be appended to application forms for the information of applicants, together with a clear warning that making any false statement is a criminal offence liable to prosecution.

4.8 Licensing authorities are required to notify the police when an applicant is found to have an unspent conviction for a relevant offence defined in the 2003 Act or for a foreign offence. The police have no involvement or locus in such applications until notified by the licensing authority.

4.9 Where an applicant has an unspent conviction for a relevant or foreign offence, and the police object to the application on crime prevention

a person operating under a licence granted by the University of Cambridge; or a person operating premises under a licence granted by the Board of the Green Cloth.

grounds, the applicant is entitled to a hearing before the licensing authority. If the police do not issue an objection notice and the application otherwise meets the requirements of the 2003 Act, the licensing authority must grant it.

4.10   A number of relevant offences never become spent. However, where an applicant is able to demonstrate that the offence in question took place so long ago and that the applicant no longer has a propensity to re-offend, a licensing authority may consider that it is appropriate to grant the application on the basis that doing so would not undermine the crime prevention objective.

4.11   If an application is refused, the applicant will be entitled to appeal against the decision they make. Similarly, if the application is granted despite a police objection notice, the chief officer of police is entitled to appeal against the licensing authority's determination. Licensing authorities are therefore expected to record in full the reasons for any decision which they make.

Issuing of personal licences by Welsh licensing authorities

4.12   All application forms in Wales should be bilingual. Proceedings before a court must capable of being conducted in Welsh at the request of the applicant. There is a panel of Welsh speaking magistrates so this can be arranged if necessary. Licensing authorities in Wales should consider issuing personal licences in a bilingual format.

Licensing qualifications

4.13   Details of licensing qualifications accredited by the Secretary of State will be notified to licensing authorities and the details may be viewed on the Home Office website.

Relevant licensing authority

4.14   Personal licences are valid for ten years unless surrendered, suspended, revoked or declared forfeit by the courts. Once granted, the licensing authority which issued the licence remains the "relevant licensing authority" for it and its holder, even though the individual may move out of the area or take employment elsewhere. The personal licence itself will give details of the issuing licensing authority.

Changes in name or address

4.15   The holder of the licence is required by the 2003 Act to notify the licensing authority of any changes of name or address. These changes should be recorded by the licensing authority. The holder is also under a duty to notify any convictions for relevant offences to the licensing authority and the courts are similarly required to inform the licensing authority of such convictions, whether or not they have ordered the suspension or forfeiture of the licence. The holder must also notify the licensing authority of any conviction for a foreign offence. These measures ensure that a single record will be held of the holder's history in terms of licensing matters.

4.16 The 2003 Act authorises the provision and receipt of such personal information to such agencies for the purposes of that Act.

Renewal

4.17 Renewal of the personal licence every ten years provides an opportunity to ensure that the arrangements ensuring that all convictions for relevant and foreign offences have been properly notified to the relevant licensing authority have been effective, and that all convictions have been properly endorsed upon the licence. It also provides an opportunity to ensure that the photograph of the holder on the personal licence is updated to aid identification.

Specification of new designated premises supervisors

4.18 Every premises licence that authorises the sale of alcohol must specify a DPS. This will normally be the person who has been given day to day responsibility for running the premises by the premises licence holder. The only exception is for community premises which have successfully made an application to remove the usual mandatory conditions set out in the 2003 Act. Guidance on such applications is set out in paragraphs 4.33 to 4.46 of this Guidance.

4.19 The Government considers it essential that police officers, fire officers or officers of the licensing authority can identify immediately the DPS so that any problems can be dealt with swiftly. For this reason, the name of the DPS and contact details must be specified on the premises licence and this must be held at the premises and displayed in summary form.

4.20 To specify a DPS, the premises licence holder should normally submit an application to the licensing authority (which may include an application for immediate interim effect) with:

- a form of consent signed by the individual concerned to show that they consent to taking on this responsible role, and
- the relevant part (Part A) of the licence.

4.21 If they are applying in writing, they must also notify the police of the application. If the application is made electronically via GOV.UK or the licensing authority's own electronic facility, the licensing authority must notify the police no later than the first working day after the application is given.

4.22 The premises licence holder must notify the existing DPS (if there is one) of the application on the same day as the application is given to the licensing authority. This requirement applies regardless of whether the application was given by means of an electronic facility, or by some other means.

4.23 The general guidance in Chapter 8 on electronic applications applies in respect of new applications.

4.24 Only one DPS may be specified in a single premises licence, but a DPS may supervise two or more premises as long as the DPS is able to ensure that the licensing objectives are properly promoted and that each premises complies with licensing law and licence conditions.

4.25 Where there are frequent changes of DPS, the premises licence holder may submit the form in advance specifying the date when the new individual will be in post and the change will take effect.

Police objections to new designated premises supervisors

4.26 The police may object to the designation of a new DPS where, in exceptional circumstances, they believe that the appointment would undermine the crime prevention objective. The police can object where, for example, a DPS is first specified in relation to particular premises and the specification of that DPS in relation to the particular premises gives rise to exceptional concerns. For example, where a personal licence holder has been allowed by the courts to retain their licence despite convictions for selling alcohol to children (a relevant offence) and then transfers into premises known for underage drinking.

4.27 Where the police do object, the licensing authority must arrange for a hearing at which the issue can be considered and both parties can put forward their arguments. The 2003 Act provides that the applicant may apply for the individual to take up post as DPS immediately and, in such cases, the issue would be whether the individual should be removed from this post. The licensing authority considering the matter must restrict its consideration to the issue of crime and disorder and give comprehensive reasons for its decision. Either party would be entitled to appeal if their argument is rejected.

4.28 The portability of personal licences between premises is an important concept under the 2003 Act. It is expected that police objections would arise in only genuinely exceptional circumstances. If a licensing authority believes that the police are routinely objecting to the designation of new premises supervisors on grounds which are not exceptional, they should raise the matter with the chief officer of police as a matter of urgency.

Police objections to existing designated premises supervisors

4.29 The 2003 Act also provides for the suspension and forfeiture of personal licences by the courts following convictions for relevant offences, including breaches of licensing law. The police can at any stage after the appointment of a DPS seek a review of a premises licence on any grounds relating to the licensing objectives if problems arise relating to the perform-ance of a DPS. The portability of personal licences is also important to industry because of the frequency with which some businesses move man-agers from premises to premises. It is not expected that licensing authorities or the police should seek to use the power of intervention as a routine mechanism for hindering the portability of a licence or use hearings of this kind as a fishing expedition to test out the individual's background and character. It is expected that such hearings should be rare and genuinely exceptional.

Convictions and liaison with the courts

4.30 Where a personal licence holder is convicted by a court for a relevant offence, the court is under a duty to notify the relevant licensing authority of the conviction and of any decision to order that the personal licence is suspended or declared forfeit. The sentence of the court has immediate effect despite the fact that an appeal may be lodged against conviction or sentence (although the court may suspend the forfeiture or suspension of the licence pending the outcome of any appeal).

4.31 When the licensing authority receives such a notification, it should contact the holder and request the licence so that the necessary action can be taken. The holder must then produce the relevant licence to the authority within 14 days. It is expected that the chief officer of police for the area in which the holder resides would be advised if they do not respond promptly. The licensing authority should record the details of the conviction, endorse them on the licence, together with any period of suspension and then return the licence to the holder. If the licence is declared forfeit, it should be retained by the licensing authority.

Relevant offences

4.32 Relevant offences are set out in Schedule 4 to the 2003 Act.

Disapplication of certain mandatory conditions for community premises

4.33 The 2003 Act was amended in 2009 to allow certain community premises which have, or are applying for, a premises licence that authorises alcohol sales to also apply to include the alternative licence condition in sections 25A(2) and 41D(3) ("the alternative licence condition") of that Act in the licence instead of the usual mandatory conditions in sections 19(2) and 19(3). Such an application may only be made if the licence holder is, or is to be, a committee or board of individuals with responsibility for the management of the premises (the "management committee"). If such an application is successful, the effect of the alternative licence condition will be that the licence holder (i.e. the management committee) is responsible for the supervision and authorisation of all alcohol sales authorised by the licence. All such sales will have to be made or authorised by the licence holder. There will be no requirement for a DPS or for alcohol sales to be authorised by a personal licence holder.

4.34 Community premises are defined as premises that are or form part of a church hall, chapel hall or other similar building; or a village hall, parish hall or community hall or other similar building.

4.35 The process requires the completion of a form which is prescribed in regulations made under the 2003 Act. Where the management committee of a community premises is applying for authorisation for the sale of alcohol for the first time, it should include the form with the new premises licence application or the premises licence variation application. No extra payment is required beyond the existing fee for a new application or a variation.

4.36 Where a community premises already has a premises licence to sell alcohol, but wishes to include the alternative licence condition in place of the usual mandatory conditions in sections 19(2) and 19(3) of the 2003 Act, it should submit the form on its own together with the required fee.

Definition of community premises

4.37 In most instances, it should be self evident whether a premises is, or forms part of a church hall, chapel hall or other similar building; or a village hall, parish hall, community hall or other similar building.

4.38 Licensing authorities may have previously taken a view on how to determine whether a premises meets the definition of community premises for the purpose of the fee exemptions set out in regulation 9(2)(b) of the Licensing Act 2003 (Fees) Regulations 2005 (SI 2005/79). As the criteria are the same, premises that qualify for these fee exemptions for regulated entertainment will also be "community premises" for present purposes.

4.39 Where it is not clear whether premises are "community premises", licensing authorities will need to approach the matter on a case-by-case basis. The main consideration in most cases will be how the premises are predominately used. If they are genuinely made available for community benefit most of the time, and accessible by a broad range of persons and sectors of the local community for purposes which include purposes beneficial to the community as a whole, the premises will be likely to meet the definition.

4.40 Many community premises such as school and private halls are available for private hire by the general public. This fact alone would not be sufficient for such halls to qualify as "community premises". The statutory test is directed at the nature of the premises themselves, as reflected in their predominant use, and not only at the usefulness of the premises for members of the community for private purposes.

4.41 If the general use of the premises is contingent upon membership of a particular organisation or organisations, this would strongly suggest that the premises in question are not a "community premises" within the definition. However, the hire of the premises to individual organisations and users who restrict their activities to their own members and guests would not necessarily conflict with the status of the premises as a "community premises", provided the premises are generally available for use by the community in the sense described above. It is not the intention that qualifying clubs, which are able to apply for a club premises certificate, should instead seek a premises licence with the removal of the usual mandatory conditions in sections 19(2) and 19(3) of the 2003 Act relating to the supply of alcohol.

Management of the premises

4.42 Sections 25A(1) and 41D(1) and (2) of the 2003 Act allow applications by community premises to apply the alternative licence condition rather than the usual mandatory conditions in sections 19(2) and 19(3) of the 2003 Act only where the applicant for the licence is the management committee of the premises in question. In addition, sections 25A(6) and 41D(5) require the licensing authority to be satisfied that the arrangements for the management of the premises by the committee or board are sufficient to ensure the adequate supervision of the supply of alcohol on the premises.

4.43 The reference to a "committee or board of individuals" is intended to cover any formally constituted, transparent and accountable management committee or structure. Such a committee should have the capacity to provide sufficient oversight of the premises to minimise any risk to the licensing objectives that could arise from allowing the responsibility for supervising the sale of alcohol to be transferred from a DPS and personal licence holder or holders. This could include management committees, executive committees and boards of trustees.

4.44 The application form requires applicants to set out how the premises is managed, its committee structure and how the supervision of alcohol sales is to be ensured in different situations (e.g. when the hall is hired to private parties) and how responsibility for this is to be determined in individual cases and discussed within the committee procedure in the event of any issues arising. The application form requires that the community premises submit copies of any constitution or other management documents with their applications and that they provide the names of their key officers. Where the management arrangements are less clear, licensing authorities may wish to ask for further details to confirm that the management board or committee is properly constituted and accountable before taking a decision on whether to grant the application (subject to the views of the police). Community premises may wish to check with the licensing authority before making an application. The management committee is strongly encouraged to notify the licensing authority if there are key changes in the committee's composition and to submit a copy to the chief officer of police. A failure to do so may form the basis of an application to review the premises licence, or be taken into account as part of the consideration of such an application.

4.45 As the premise licence holder, the management committee will collectively be responsible for ensuring compliance with licence conditions and the law (and may remain liable to prosecution for one of the offences in the 2003 Act) although there would not necessarily be any individual member always present at the premises. While overall responsibility will lie with the management committee, where the premises are hired out the hirer may be clearly identified as having responsibility for matters falling within his or her control (e.g. under the contract for hire offered by the licence holder), much in the same way that the event organiser may be responsible for an event held under a Temporary Event Notice. Where hirers are provided with a written summary of their responsibilities under the 2003 Act in relation to the sale of alcohol, the management committee is likely to be treated as having taken adequate steps to avoid liability to prosecution if a licensing offence is committed.

4.46 As indicated above, sections 25A(6) and 41D(5) of the 2003 Act require the licensing authority to consider whether the arrangements for the management of the premises by the committee are sufficient to ensure adequate supervision of the supply of alcohol on the premises. Where private hire for events which include the sale of alcohol is permitted by the licence, it would be necessary to have an effective hiring agreement. Licensing authorities may wish to consider model hiring agreements that have been made available by organisations such as ACRE and Community Matters. Such model agreements can be revised to cater for the circumstances surrounding each hire arrangement; for example to state that the hirer is aware of the licensing objectives and offences in the 2003 Act and will ensure that it will take all appropriate steps to ensure that no offences are committed during the period of the hire.

Police views

4.47 In exceptional circumstances, the chief officer of police for the area in which the community premises is situated can object to a request for inclusion of the alternative licence condition on the grounds of crime and disorder, and any responsible authority or other person can seek reinstatement of the mandatory conditions through a review of the licence (as provided in section 52A of the 2003 Act). The police will want to consider any history of incidents at an establishment in light of the actual or proposed management arrangements, include the use of appropriate hire agreements. If the chief officer of police issues a notice seeking the refusal of the application to include the alternative licence condition, the licensing authority must hold a hearing in order to reach a decision on whether to grant the application.

Appeals

4.48 Where the chief officer of police has made relevant representations against the inclusion of the alternative licence condition, or given a notice under section 41D(6) which was not withdrawn, the chief officer of police can appeal the decision of the licensing authority to allow the inclusion of the alternative licence condition. Similarly, a community premises can appeal a decision by the licensing authority to refuse to include the alternative licence condition following a hearing triggered by relevant representations or by a notice given under section 41D(6). Following a review of the licence in which the mandatory conditions are reinstated, the licence holder may appeal against the decision. If the alternative licence condition is retained on review, the applicant for the review or any person who made relevant representations may appeal against the decision.

5. WHO NEEDS A PREMISES LICENCE?

5.1 A premises licence authorises the use of any premises (which is defined in the 2003 Act as a vehicle, vessel or moveable structure or any place or a part of any premises) for licensable activities defined in section 1 of the 2003 Act.

Relevant parts of Act

5.2 In determining whether any premises should be licensed, the following parts of the 2003 Act are relevant:

Relevant part of Act	Description
Section 1	Outlines the licensable activities.
Part 3	Provisions relating to premises licences.
Part 4	Provisions for qualifying clubs.
Section 173	Activities in certain locations which are not licensable.
Section 174	Premises that may be exempted on grounds of national security.
Section 175	Exemption for incidental non-commercial lottery (e.g. a minor raffle or tombola).
Section 176	Prohibits the sale of alcohol at motorway service areas; and restricts the circumstances in which alcohol may be sold at garages.
Section 189	Special provision in relation to the licensing of vessels, vehicles and moveable structures.
Section 190	Where the place where a contract for the sale of alcohol is made is different from the place where the alcohol is appropriated to the contract, the sale of alcohol is to be treated as taking place where the alcohol is appropriated to the contract.
Section 191	Defines "alcohol" for the purposes of the 2003 Act.
Section 192	Defines the meaning of "sale by retail".
Section 193	Defines among other things "premises", "vehicle", "vessel" and "wine".
Schedules 1 and 2	Provision of regulated entertainment and provision of late night refreshment.

5.3 Section 191 provides the meaning of "alcohol" for the purposes of the 2003 Act. It should be noted that a wide variety of foodstuffs contain alcohol but generally in a highly diluted form when measured against the volume of the product. For the purposes of the 2003 Act, the sale or supply of alcohol which is of a strength not exceeding 0.5 per cent ABV (alcohol by volume) at the time of the sale or supply in question is not a licensable activity. However, where the foodstuff contains alcohol at greater strengths, for example, as with some alcoholic jellies, the sale would be a licensable activity.

Premises licensed for gambling

5.4 Gambling is the subject of separate legislation and licensing authorities should not duplicate any conditions imposed by this legislation when granting, varying or reviewing licences that authorise licensable activities under the 2003 Act. When making a licence application, the applicant may, in detailing the steps to be taken in promoting the licensing objectives, refer to the statutory conditions in respect of their gambling licence (where relevant). In addition, any conditions which are attached to premises licences should not prevent the holder from complying with the requirements of gambling legislation or supporting regulations. Further information about the Gambling Act 2005 can be found on the DCMS website at **www.culture.gov.uk**.

Designated sports grounds, designated sports events and major outdoor sports stadia

5.5 Outdoor sports stadia are regulated by separate legislation and sports events taking place at outdoor stadia do not fall within the definition of the provision of regulated entertainment under the 2003 Act, with the exception of boxing and wrestling matches. Licensing authorities should therefore limit their consideration of applications for premises licences to activities that are licensable under the 2003 Act.

5.6 Major stadia will often have several bars and restaurants, including bars generally open to all spectators as well as bars and restaurants to which members of the public do not have free access. Alcohol may also be supplied in private boxes and viewing areas. A premises licence may make separate arrangements for public and private areas or for restaurant areas on the same premises. It may also designate areas where alcohol may not be consumed at all or at particular times.

5.7 Licensing authorities should be aware that paragraphs 98 and 99(c) of Schedule 6 to the 2003 Act and the repeals of section 2(1A) and section 5A of the Sporting Events (Control of Alcohol etc.) Act 1985 have not been commenced because their effect would have been different from that which Parliament had intended.

Sports stadia with roofs that open and close

5.8 Major sports grounds with roofs that open and close, do not fall within the definition of an "indoor sporting event" under the 2003 Act. As a result, events taking place in these stadia are not 'regulated entertainment' and are not licensable under the 2003 Act.

Vessels

5.9   The 2003 Act applies to vessels (including ships and boats) as if they were premises. A vessel which is not permanently moored or berthed is treated as if it were premises situated in a place where it is usually moored or berthed. The relevant licensing authority for considering an application for a premises licence for a vessel is therefore the licensing authority for the area in which it is usually moored or berthed.

5.10   However, an activity is not a licensable activity if it takes place aboard a vessel engaged on an international journey. An "international journey" means a journey from a place in the United Kingdom to an immediate destination outside the United Kingdom or a journey from outside the United Kingdom to an immediate destination in the United Kingdom.

5.11   If a vessel is not permanently moored and carries more than 12 passengers it is a passenger ship and will be subject to safety regulation by the Maritime and Coastguard Agency (MCA).

5.12   When a licensing authority receives an application for a premises licence in relation to a vessel, it should consider the promotion of the licensing objectives, but should not focus on matters relating to safe navigation or operation of the vessel, the general safety of passengers, or emergency provision; all of which are subject to regulations which must be met before the vessel is issued with its Passenger Certificate and Safety Management Certificate.

5.13   If the MCA is satisfied that the vessel complies with Merchant Shipping standards for a passenger ship, the premises should normally be accepted as meeting the public safety objective. In relation to other public safety aspects of the application, representations made by the MCA on behalf of the Secretary of State should be given particular weight.

5.14   If a vessel, which is not permanently moored and carries no more than 12 passengers, goes to sea, it will be subject to the Code of Practice for the Safety of Small Commercial Sailing Vessels. This code sets the standards for construction, safety equipment and manning for these vessels and MCA will be able to confirm that it has a valid safety certificate.

5.15   If a vessel carries no more than 12 passengers and does not go to sea, it may be regulated or licensed by the competent harbour authority, navigation authority or local authority. The recommended standards for these vessels are set out in the (non-statutory) Inland Waters Small Passenger Boat Code, which provides best practice guidance on the standards for construction, safety equipment and manning. Some authorities may use their own local rules. MCA has no direct responsibility for these vessels and will not normally comment on a premises licence application.

International airports and ports

5.16 Under the 2003 Act, the Secretary of State may 'designate' a port, hoverport or airport with a substantial amount of international traffic so that an activity carried on there is not licensable. The Secretary of State may also preserve existing designations made under earlier legislation.

5.17 Areas at designated ports which are "airside" or "wharfside" are included in the exemption in the 2003 Act from the licensing regime. The non-travelling public does not have access to these areas and they are subject to stringent bye-laws. The exemption allows refreshments to be provided to travellers at all times of the day and night. Other parts of designated ports, hoverports and airports are subject to the normal licensing controls.

Vehicles

5.18 Under the 2003 Act, alcohol may not be sold on a moving vehicle and the vehicle may not be licensed for that purpose. However, licensing authorities may consider applications for the sale of alcohol from a parked or stationary vehicle. For example, mobile bars could sell alcohol at special events as long as they were parked. Any permission granted would relate solely to the place where the vehicle is parked and where sales are to take place.

5.19 The provision of any entertainment or entertainment facilities on premises consisting of or forming part of any vehicle while it is in motion and not permanently or temporarily parked is not regulated entertainment for the purposes of the 2003 Act.

Trains and aircraft

5.20 Railway vehicles and aircraft engaged on journeys are exempted from the requirement to have an authorisation to carry on licensable activities (although a magistrates' court can make an order to prohibit the sale of alcohol on a railway vehicle if this is appropriate to prevent disorder). Licensing authorities should note that some defunct aircraft and railway carriages remain in a fixed position and are used as restaurants and bars. These premises are subject to the provisions of the 2003 Act.

Garages and motorway service areas

5.21 Section 176 of the 2003 Act prohibits the sale or supply of alcohol at motorway service areas (MSAs) and from premises which are used primarily as a garage, or are part of premises used primarily as a garage. Premises are used as a garage if they are used for one or more of the following:

- the retailing of petrol;
- the retailing of derv;
- the sale of motor vehicles; and
- the maintenance of motor vehicles.

5.22 The licensing authority must decide whether or not premises are used primarily as a garage. The accepted approach is based on "intensity of use" to establish "primary use". For example, if a garage shop in any rural area is used more intensely by customers purchasing other products than by customers purchasing the products or services listed above, it may be eligible to seek authority to sell or supply alcohol.

5.23 Where there is insufficient evidence to establish primary use, it is for the licensing authority to decide whether to grant the licence and deal with any issues through enforcement action and it may be able to use its case management powers to enable further evidence to be obtained.

Large scale time-limited events requiring premises licences

5.24 Licensing authorities should note that a premises licence may be sought for a short, discrete period. The 2003 Act provides that a temporary event notice is subject to various limitations (see Chapter 7 of this Guidance). The temporary provision of licensable activities that fall outside these limits will require the authority of a premises licence if the premises are currently unlicensed for the activities involved.

5.25 The procedures for applying for and granting such a licence are identical to those for an unlimited duration premises licence except that it should be stated on the application that the applicant's intention is that the period of the licence should be limited. Licensing authorities should clearly specify on such a licence when it comes into force and when it ceases to have effect. If the sale of alcohol is involved, a personal licence holder must be specified as the designated premises supervisor.

6. CLUB PREMISES CERTIFICATES

6.1 This Chapter covers the administration of the processes for issuing, varying, and reviewing club premises certificates and other associated procedures.

General

6.2 Clubs are organisations where members have joined together for particular social, sporting or political purposes. They may then combine to buy alcohol in bulk as members of the organisation to supply in the club.

6.3 Technically the club only sells alcohol by retail at such premises to guests. Where members purchase alcohol, there is no sale (as the member owns part of the alcohol stock) and the money passing across the bar is merely a mechanism to preserve equity between members where one may consume more than another.

6.4 Only 'qualifying' clubs may hold club premises certificates. In order to be a qualifying club, a club must have at least 25 members and meet the conditions set out below. The grant of a club premises certificate means that a qualifying club is entitled to certain benefits. These include:

- the authority to supply alcohol to members and sell it to guests on the premises to which the certificate relates without the need for any member or employee to hold a personal licence;
- the authority to provide late night refreshment to members of the club without requiring additional authorisation;
- more limited rights of entry for the police and authorised persons because the premises are considered private and not generally open to the public;
- exemption from police powers of instant closure on grounds of disorder and noise nuisance (except when being used under the authority of a temporary event notice or premises licence) because they operate under their codes of discipline and rules; and
- exemption from orders of the magistrates' court for the closure of all licensed premises in an area when disorder is happening or expected.

6.5 Qualifying clubs should not be confused with proprietary clubs, which are clubs run commercially by individuals, partnerships or businesses for profit. These require a premises licence and are not qualifying clubs.

6.6 A qualifying club will be permitted under the terms of a club premises certificate to sell and supply alcohol to its members and their guests only. Instant membership is not permitted and members must wait at least two days between their application and their admission to the club. A qualifying club may choose to apply for a premises licence if it decides that it wishes to offer its facilities commercially for use by the general public, including the sale of alcohol to them. However, an individual on behalf of a club may give temporary event notices. See Chapter 7.

6.7 The 2003 Act does not prevent visitors to a qualifying club being supplied with alcohol as long as they are 'guests' of any member of the club or the club collectively, and nothing in the 2003 Act prevents the admission of such people as guests without prior notice. The 2003 Act does not define "guest" and whether or not somebody is a genuine guest would in all cases be a question of fact.

6.8 There is no mandatory requirement under the 2003 Act for guests to be signed in by a member of the club. However, a point may be reached where a club is providing commercial services to the general public in a way that is contrary to its qualifying club status. It is at this point that the club would no longer be conducted in "good faith" and would no longer meet "general condition 3" for qualifying clubs in section 62 of the 2003 Act. Under the 2003 Act, the licensing authority must decide when a club has ceased to operate in "good faith" and give the club a notice withdrawing the club premises certificate. The club is entitled to appeal against such a decision to a magistrates' court. Unless the appeal is successful, the club would need to apply for a premises licence to authorise licensable activities taking place there.

Qualifying conditions

6.9   Section 62 of the 2003 Act sets out five general conditions which a relevant club must meet to be a qualifying club. Section 63 also sets out specified matters for licensing authorities to enable them to determine whether a club is established and conducted in good faith – the third qualifying condition. Section 64 sets out additional conditions which only need to be met by clubs intending to supply alcohol to members and guests. Section 90 of the 2003 Act gives powers to the licensing authority to issue a notice to a club withdrawing its certificate where it appears that it has ceased to meet the qualifying conditions. There is a right of appeal against such a decision.

Associate members and guests

6.10   As well as their own members and guests, qualifying clubs are also able to admit associate members and their guests (i.e. members and guests from another 'recognised club' as defined by section 193 of the 2003 Act) to the club premises when qualifying club activities are being carried on without compromising the use of their club premises certificate.

Applications for the grant or variation of club premises certificates

6.11   The arrangements for applying for or seeking to vary club premises certificates are extremely similar to those for a premises licence. Clubs may also use the minor variation process to make small changes to their certificates as long as these could have no adverse impact on the licensing objectives. Licensing authorities should refer to Chapter 8 of this Guidance on the handling of such applications.

6.12   In addition to a plan of the premises and a club operating schedule, clubs must also include the rules of the club with their application (as well as making a declaration to the licensing authority in accordance with regulations made under the 2003 Act). On notifying any alteration to these rules to the licensing authority, the club is required to pay a fee set down in regulations. Licensing authorities cannot require any changes to the rules to be made as a condition of receiving a certificate unless relevant representations have been made. However, if a licensing authority is satisfied that the rules of a club indicate that it does not meet the qualifying conditions in the 2003 Act, a club premises certificate should not be granted.

Steps needed to promote the licensing objectives

6.13 Club operating schedules prepared by clubs, must include the steps the club intends to take to promote the licensing objectives. These will be translated into conditions included in the certificate, unless the conditions have been modified by the licensing authority following consideration of relevant representations. Guidance on these conditions is given in Chapter 10 of this Guidance.

7. TEMPORARY EVENT NOTICES (TENS)

7.1 This Chapter covers the arrangements in Part 5 of the 2003 Act for the temporary carrying on of licensable activities which are not authorised by a premises licence or club premises certificate.

General

7.2 The system of permitted temporary activities is intended as a light touch process, and as such, the carrying on of licensable activities does not have to be authorised by the licensing authority on an application. Instead, a person wishing to hold an event at which such activities are proposed to be carried on (the "premises user") gives notice to the licensing authority of the event (a "temporary event notice" or "TEN").

7.3 The TEN must be given to the licensing authority in the form prescribed in regulations made under the 2003 Act. Unless it is sent electronically, it must be sent to the relevant licensing authority, to the police and "local authority exercising environmental health functions" ("EHA") at least ten working days before the event (although a premises user may give a limited number of TENs to the licensing authority less than 10 working days before the event to which they relate). "Working day" under the 2003 Act means any day other than a Sunday, Christmas Day, Good Friday or Bank Holiday. For limited purposes in relation to a TEN, a "day" is defined as a period of 24 hours beginning at midnight.

7.4 If a TEN is sent electronically via GOV.UK or the licensing authority's own facility, the licensing authority must notify the police and EHA as soon as possible and no later than the first working day after the TEN is given.

7.5 The police or "local authority exercising environmental health functions" ("EHA") may intervene to prevent such an event taking place by sending an objection to the licensing authority, which the licensing authority must consider on the basis of the statutory licensing objectives and decide whether the event should go ahead. The police or EHA ("relevant persons" for the purposes of TENs) may also intervene by agreeing a modification of the proposed arrangements directly with the TENs user, (see paragraph 7.31–7.35 below). If a relevant person sends an objection, this may result in the licensing authority imposing conditions on a TEN but only where the venue at which the event is to be held has an existing premises licence or club premises certificate. When giving a TEN, the premises user should consider the promotion of the four licensing objectives. The licensing authority may only otherwise intervene if the statutory permitted limits on TENs would be exceeded.

7.6 A TEN does not relieve the premises user from any requirements under planning law for appropriate planning permission where it is required.

Limitations

7.7 A number of limitations are imposed on the use of TENs by the 2003 Act. The limitations apply to:

- the number of times a premises user may give a TEN (50 times in a calendar year for a personal licence holder and five times in a calendar year for other people);
- the number of times a TEN may be given for any particular premises (12 times in a calendar year);
- the maximum duration of an event authorised by a TEN is 168 hours (seven days);
- the maximum total duration of the events authorised by TENs in relation to individual premises (21 days in a calendar year);
- the maximum number of people attending at any one time (fewer than 500); and
- the minimum period between events authorised under separate TENs in relation to the same premises (not including withdrawn TENs) by the same premises user (24 hours).

7.8 Any associate, relative or business partner of the premises user is considered to be the same premises user in relation to these restrictions. The 2003 Act defines an associate, in relation to the premises user, as being:

- the spouse or civil partner of that person;
- a child, parent, grandchild, grandparent, brother or sister of that person;
- an agent or employee of that person; or
- the spouse or civil partner of a person listed in either of the two preceding bullet points.

7.9 A person living with another person as their husband or wife, is treated for these purposes as their spouse. 'Civil partner' has its meaning in the Civil Partnership Act 2004.

7.10 A TEN that is given and subsequently withdrawn by the TEN user can be included within the limits of the numbers of TENS allowed in a given calendar year. The limits for the number of TENs that may be given include a combination of both "standard" and "late" TENs.

7.11 Proposed activities that exceed these limits will require a premises licence or club premises certificate.

7.12 TENs may be given in respect of premises which already have a premises licence or club premises certificate to cover licensable activities not permitted by the existing authorisation.

7.13 In determining whether the maximum total duration of the periods covered by TENs at any individual premises has exceeded 21 days, an event beginning before midnight and continuing into the next day would count as two days towards the 21-day limitation.

7.14 There is nothing in the 2003 Act to prevent notification of multiple events at the same time, provided the first event is at least ten working days away (or five working days away in the case of a late TEN). For example, an individual personal licence holder wishing to exhibit and sell beer at a series of farmers' markets may wish to give several notices simultaneously. However, this would only be possible where the events are to take place in the same licensing authority (and police area) and the limits are not exceeded in the case of each notice.

Who can give a temporary event notice?

Personal licence holders

7.15 A personal licence holder can give a TEN at any premises on up to 50 occasions in a calendar year. This limit is inclusive of any late TENs given in the same year. The use of each TEN must of course observe the limits described above, including the limit of 12 TENs in respect of each premises in a calendar year.

Non-personal licence holders

7.16 The 2003 Act provides that any individual aged 18 or over may give a TEN whether or not that individual holds a personal licence. Such an individual will not, therefore, have met the requirements that apply to a personal licence holder under Part 6 of the 2003 Act. Where alcohol is not intended to be sold, this should not matter. However, many events will involve a combination of licensable activities. In the absence of a premises user holding a personal licence, the 2003 Act limits the number of notices that may be given by any non-personal licence holder to five occasions in a calendar year (this limit is inclusive of any late TENs in the same year). In every other respect, the Guidance and information set out in the paragraphs above applies.

Standard and late temporary event notices

7.17   There are two types of TEN: a standard TEN and a late TEN. These are subject to different processes: a standard notice is given no later than ten working days before the event to which it relates; and a late notice is given not before nine and not later than five working days before the event.

Standard temporary event notices

7.18   "Ten working days" (and other periods of days which apply to other requirements in relation to TENs) exclude the day the notice is received and the first day of the event. A notice that is given less than ten working days before the event to which it relates, when the premises user has already given the permitted number of late TENs in that calendar year, will be returned as void and the activities described in it will be not be authorised.

7.19   The police and EHA have a period of three working days from when they are given the notice to object to it on the basis of any of the four licensing objectives. Where an objection is given, there is provision under section 106 of the 2003 Act for the police or EHA to agree with the premises user to modify the TEN (see paragraph 7.36 below).

7.20   Although ten clear working days is the minimum possible notice that may be given, licensing authorities should publicise their preferences in terms of advance notice and encourage premises users to provide the earliest possible notice of events planned by them. Licensing authorities should also consider publicising a preferred maximum time in advance of an event by when TENs should ideally be given to them.

Late temporary event notices

7.21

Late TENs are intended to assist premises users who are required for reasons outside their control to, for example, change the venue for an event at short notice. However, late TENs may, of course, be given in any circumstances providing the limits specified at paragraph 7.7 are not exceeded.

7.22 For a standard TEN, the police and EHA have a period of three working days from when they are given the notice to object to it on the basis of any of the four licensing objectives. However, if there is an objection to a late TEN from either the police or EHA, the event will not go ahead. In these circumstances there is no scope for a hearing or the application of any existing conditions. There is no scope under the 2003 Act for the modification of a late TEN as is possible in relation to a standard TEN.

7.23 Late TENs can be given up to five working days but no earlier than nine working days before the event is due to take place and, unless given electronically to the licensing authority, must also be sent by the premises user to the police and EHA. A late TEN given less than five days before the event to which it relates will be returned as void and the activities to which it relates will not be authorised. The number of late TENs that can be given in a calendar year is limited to ten for personal licence holders and two for non-personal licence holders. Late TENs count towards the total number of premitted TENs (for example, the limit of five TENs per year for non-personal licence holders and 50 TENs for personal licence holders). Once these limits have been reached, the licensing authority should issue a counter notice (permitted limits) if any more are given.

Role of the licensing authority

7.24 The licensing authority must check that the limitations set down in Part 5 of the 2003 Act are being observed and intervene if they are not (see paragraph 7.7). For example, a TEN would be void unless there is a minimum of 24 hours between events notified by the same premises user, or an associate, or someone who is in business with the relevant premises user, in respect of the same premises. This is to prevent evasion of the seven-day (or 168 hour) limit on such events and the need to obtain a full premises licence or club premises certificate for more major or permanent events. In addition, for these purposes, a TEN is treated as being from the same premises user if it is given by an associate.

7.25 Where the application is not within the statutory parameters described earlier, the licensing authority will issue a counter notice to the premises user.

7.26 Where the TEN is in order, the relevant fee paid, the event falls within the prescribed limits and there has been no objection from the police or EHA on the basis of any of the four licensing objectives, the licensing authority will record the notice in its register and send an acknowledgement to the premises user (which may be given electronically).

7.27 If the licensing authority receives an objection notice from the police or EHA that is not withdrawn, it must (in the case of a standard TEN only) hold a hearing to consider the objection (unless all parties agree that this is unnecessary). The licensing committee may decide to allow the licensable activities to go ahead as stated in the notice. If the notice is in connection with licensable activities at licensed premises, the licensing authority may also impose one or more of the existing licence conditions on the TEN (insofar as such conditions are not inconsistent with the event) if it considers that this is appropriate for the promotion of the licensing objectives. If the authority decides to impose conditions, it must give notice to the premises user which includes a statement of conditions (a "notice (statement of conditions)") and provide a copy to each relevant party. Alternatively, it can decide that the event would undermine the licensing objectives and should not take place. In this case, the licensing authority must give a counter notice.

7.28 Premises users are not required to be on the premises for the entire duration of the event authorised by the TEN, but they will remain liable to prosecution for certain offences that may be committed at the premises during the period covered by it. These include, for example, the offences of the sale of alcohol to a person who is drunk; persistently selling alcohol to children; and allowing disorderly conduct on licensed premises.

7.29 In the case of an event authorised by a TEN, failure to adhere to the requirements of the 2003 Act, such as the limitation of no more than 499 being present at any one time, would mean that the event was unauthorised. In such circumstances, the premises user would be liable to prosecution.

7.30 Section 8 of the 2003 Act requires licensing authorities to keep a register containing certain matters, including a record of TENs received. There is no requirement to record all the personal information given on a TEN.

Police and environmental health intervention

7.31 The system of permitted temporary activities gives police and EHAs the opportunity to consider whether they should object to a TEN on the basis of any of the licensing objectives.

7.32 Such cases might arise because of concerns about the scale, location, timing of the event or concerns about public nuisance. However, in most cases, where (for example) alcohol is supplied away from licensed premises at a temporary bar under the control of a personal licence holder, (for example, at weddings with a cash bar or small social or sporting events) this should not usually give rise to the use of these powers.

7.33 The police and EHA have the right under sections 109(5) and (6) of the 2003 Act to request the premises user to produce the TEN for examination. If the police do not intervene when a TEN is given, they will still be able to rely on their powers of closure under Part 8 of the 2003 Act should disorder or noise nuisance be expected or arise.

7.34 If the police or EHA believe that allowing the premises to be used in accordance with the TEN will undermine the licensing objectives, they must give the premises user and the licensing authority an objection notice. The objection notice must be given within three working days of their receipt of the TEN.

7.35 Where a standard TEN was given, the licensing authority must consider the objection at a hearing before a counter notice can be issued. At the hearing, the police, EHA and the premises user may make representations to the licensing authority. Following the hearing, the licensing authority may decide to impose conditions where there is an existing premises licence or club premises certificate at the venue or issue a counter notice to prevent the event going ahead. If the police, EHA or both give an objection to a late TEN, the TEN will not be valid.

Modification

7.36 As noted above, the police or EHA (as "relevant persons") may contact the premises user to discuss their objections and try to come to an agreement which will allow the proposed licensable activities to proceed. The TEN can be modified (for example, by changing the details of the parts of the premises that are to be used for the event, the description of the nature of the intended activities or their duration). The other relevant person has to agree.

Applying conditions to a TEN

7.37 2003 Act provides that only the licensing authority can impose conditions (from the existing conditions on the premises licence or club premises certificate) to a TEN. The licensing authority can only do so:

- if the police or the EHA have objected to the TEN;
- if that objection has not been withdrawn;
- if the licensing authority considers it appropriate for the promotion of the licensing objectives to impose one or more conditions.

7.38 This decision is one for the licensing authority alone, regardless of the premises user's views or willingness to accept conditions. The conditions must be notified to the premises user on the form prescribed by regulations.

Hearings to impose conditions

7.39 Section 105 of the 2003 Act is clear that a licensing authority must hold a hearing to consider any objections from the police or EHA unless all the parties agree that a hearing is not necessary. If the parties agree that a hearing is not necessary and the licensing authority decides not to give a counter notice on the basis of the objection, it may impose existing conditions on the TEN.

8. APPLICATIONS FOR PREMISES LICENCES

Relevant licensing authority

8.1 Premises licences are issued by the licensing authority in which the premises are situated or, in the case of premises straddling an area boundary, the licensing authority where the greater part of the premises is situated. Where the premises is located equally in two or more areas, the applicant may choose but, in these rare cases, it is important that each of the licensing authorities involved maintain close contact.

8.2 Section 13 of the 2003 Act defines the parties holding important roles in the context of applications, inspection, monitoring and reviews of premises licences.

Authorised persons

8.3 The first group – "authorised persons" – are bodies empowered by the 2003 Act to carry out inspection and

enforcement roles. The police are not included because they are separately empowered by the 2003 Act to

carry out their duties.

8.4 For all premises, the authorised persons include:

- officers of the licensing authority;
- fire inspectors;
- inspectors with responsibility in the licensing authority's area for the enforcement of the Health and Safety at Work etc Act 1974 etc; and
- officers of the local authority exercising environmental health functions.

8.5 Local authority officers will most commonly have responsibility for the enforcement of health and safety legislation, but the Health and Safety Executive is responsible for certain premises. In relation to vessels, authorised persons also include an inspector or a surveyor of ships appointed under section 256 of the Merchant Shipping Act 1995. These would normally be officers acting on behalf of the Maritime and Coastguard Agency. The Secretary of State may prescribe other authorised persons by means of regulations, but has not currently prescribed any additional bodies. If any are prescribed, details will be made available on the Home Office website.

Responsible authorities

8.6 The second group – "responsible authorities" – are public bodies that must be fully notified of applications and that are entitled to make representations to the licensing authority in relation to the application for the grant, variation or review of a premises licence. These representations must still be considered 'relevant' by the licensing authority and relate to one or more of the licensing objectives. For all premises, responsible authorities include:

- the relevant licensing authority and any other licensing authority in whose area part of the premises is situated;
- the chief officer of police;
- the local fire and rescue authority;
- the local enforcement agency for the Health and Safety at Work etc Act 1974 etc;
- the local authority with responsibility for environmental health;
- the local planning authority;
- a body that represents those who are responsible for, or interested in, matters relating to the protection of children from harm;
- Primary Care Trusts (PCTs)[3] and Local Health Boards (in Wales); and
- the local weights and measures authority (trading standards).

8.7 The licensing authority should indicate in its statement of licensing policy which body it recognises to be competent to advise it on the protection of children from harm. This may be the local authority social services department, the Local Safeguarding Children Board or another competent body. This is important as applications for premises licences have to be copied to the responsible authorities in order for them to make any representations they think are relevant.

8.8 In relation to a vessel, responsible authorities also include navigation authorities within the meaning of section 221(1) of the Water Resources Act 1991 that have statutory functions in relation to the waters where the vessel is usually moored or berthed, or any waters where it is proposed to be navigated when being used for licensable activities; the Environment Agency; the Canal and River Trust; and the Secretary of State (who in practice acts through the Maritime and Coastguard Agency (MCA)). In practice, the Environment Agency and the Canal and River Trust only have responsibility in relation to vessels on waters for which they are the navigation statutory authority.

8.9 The MCA is the lead responsible authority for public safety, including fire safety, affecting passenger ships (those carrying more than 12 passengers) wherever they operate and small commercial vessels (carrying no more than

---

[3] When relevant provisions in the new Health and Social Care Act 2012 are brought into force, PCTs will be replaced as responsible authorities by the primary health function of local authorities.

12 passengers) which go to sea. The safety regime for passenger ships is enforced under the Merchant Shipping Acts by the MCA which operates certification schemes for these vessels. Fire and rescue authorities, the Health and Safety Executive and local authority health and safety inspectors should normally be able to make "nil" returns in relation to such vessels and rely on the MCA to make any appropriate representations in respect of this licensing objective.

8.10   Merchant Shipping legislation does not, however, apply to permanently moored vessels. So, for example, restaurant ships moored on the Thames Embankment, with permanent shore connections should be considered by the other responsible authorities concerned with public safety, including fire safety. Vessels carrying no more than 12 passengers which do not go to sea are not subject to MCA survey and certification, but may be licensed by the local port or navigation authority.

8.11   The Secretary of State may prescribe other responsible authorities by means of regulations. Any such regulations are published on the Government's legislation website: **www.legislation.gov.uk**

Other persons

8.12   As well as responsible authorities, any other person can play a role in a number of licensing processes under the 2003 Act. This includes any individual, body or business entitled to make representations to licensing authorities in relation to applications for the grant, variation, minor variation or review of premises licences and club premises certificates, regardless of their geographic proximity to the premises. In addition, these persons may themselves seek a review of a premises licence. Any representations made by these persons must be 'relevant', in that the representation relates to one or more of the licensing objectives. It must also not be considered by the licensing authority to be frivolous or vexatious. In the case of applications for reviews, there is an additional requirement that the grounds for the review should not be considered by the licensing authority to be repetitious. Chapter 9 of this guidance (paragraphs 9.4 to 9.10) provides more detail on the definition of relevant, frivolous, vexatious and repetitious representations.

8.13   Whilst any of these persons may act in their own right, they may also request that a representative makes the representation to the licensing authority on their behalf. A representative may include a legal representative, a friend, a Member of Parliament, a Member of the Welsh Government, or a local ward or parish councillor who can all act in such a capacity.

The role of local councillors

8.14   Local councillors as noted above, can make representations. Local councillors are subject to the Local Authorities (Model Code of Conduct)

Order 2007. The Code applies to any elected council member whether or not they are a member of the licensing committee. A member of a licensing committee, representing others or acting in their own right, would need to consider carefully at a committee meeting whether they had a prejudicial interest in any matter affecting the licence or certificate of the premises in question which would require them to withdraw from the meeting when that matter is considered (for example, where a councillor has made representations in their capacity as an elected member of the licensing authority). In addition, a member with a prejudicial interest in a matter should not seek to influence improperly a decision on the licence or certificate in any other way.

Who can apply for a premises licence?

8.15 Any person (if an individual aged 18 or over) who is carrying on or who proposes to carry on a business which involves the use of premises (any place including one in the open air) for licensable activities may apply for a premises licence either on a permanent basis or for a time-limited period.

8.16 "A person" in this context includes, for example, a business or a partnership. Licensing authorities should not require the nomination of an individual to hold the licence or determine the identity of the most appropriate person to hold the licence.

8.17 In considering joint applications (which is likely to be a rare occurrence), it must be stressed that under section 16(1)(a) of the 2003 Act each applicant must be carrying on a business which involves the use of the premises for licensable activities. In the case of public houses, this would be easier for a tenant to demonstrate than for a pub owning company that is not itself carrying on licensable activities. Where licences are to be held by businesses, it is desirable that this should be a single business to avoid any lack of clarity in accountability.

8.18 A public house may be owned, or a tenancy held, jointly by a husband and wife, civil partners or other partnerships of a similar nature, and both may be actively involved in carrying on the licensable activities. In these cases, it is entirely possible for the husband and wife or the partners to apply jointly as applicant for the premises licence, even if they are not formally partners in business terms. This is unlikely to lead to the same issues of clouded accountability that could arise where two separate businesses apply jointly for the licence. If the application is granted, the premises licence would identify the holder as comprising both names and any subsequent applications, for example for a variation of the licence, would need to be made jointly.

8.19 A wide range of other individuals and bodies set out in section 16 of the 2003 Act may apply for premises licences. They include, for example, Government Departments, local authorities, hospitals, schools, charities or police forces. In addition to the bodies listed in section 16, the Secretary of State may prescribe by regulations other bodies that may apply and any such regulations are published on the Government's legislation website. There is nothing in the 2003 Act which prevents an application being made for a premises licence at premises where a premises licence is already held.

Application forms

8.20   The Provision of Services Regulations 2009 require local authorities to ensure that all procedures relating to access to, or the exercise of, a service activity may be easily completed, at a distance and by electronic means. Electronic application facilities for premises licences may be found either on GOV.UK or the licensing authority's own website. It remains acceptable to make an application in writing.

Electronic applications

8.21   Applicants may apply using the licence application forms available on GOV.UK, or will be re-directed from GOV.UK to the licensing authority's own electronic facility if one is available. Applicants may also apply directly to the licensing authority's facility without going through GOV.UK.

Electronic applications using forms on GOV.UK

8.22   GOV.UK will send a notification to the licensing authority when a completed application form is available for it to download from GOV.UK. This is the day that the application is taken to be 'given' to the licensing authority, even if it is downloaded at a later stage, and the application must be advertised from the day after that day (as for a written application). The licensing authority must acknowledge the application as quickly as possible, specifying the statutory time period and giving details of the appeal procedure.

8.23   The period of 28 consecutive days during which the application must be advertised on a notice outside the premises is, effectively, the statutory timescale by which the application must be determined (unless representations are made). This will be published on GOV.UK and must also be published on the licensing authority's own electronic facility if one exists. If no representations are made during this period, the licensing authority must notify the applicant as quickly as possible that the licence has been granted. The licensing authority must send the licence to the applicant as soon as possible after this, but the applicant may start the licensed activity as soon as they have been notified that the application is granted. The licence may be supplied in electronic or written format as long as the applicant is aware which document constitutes 'the licence'. If representations are made, the guidance in Chapter 9 applies.

Requirement to copy application to responsible authorities

8.24 The licensing authority must copy electronic applications, made via GOV.UK or its own facility, to responsible authorities no later than the first working day after the application is given. However, if an applicant submits any part of their application in writing, the applicant will remain responsible for copying it to responsible authorities.

Applications via the local authority electronic application facility

8.25 Where applications are made on the licensing authority's own electronic facility, the application will be taken to be 'given' when the applicant has submitted a complete application form and paid the fee. The application is given at the point at which it becomes accessible to the authority by means of the facility. The licensing authority must acknowledge the application as quickly as possible, specifying the statutory time period and giving details of the appeal procedure.

'Holding' and 'deferring' electronic applications

8.26 The Government recommends (as for written applications) that electronic applications should not be returned if they contain obvious and minor errors such as typing mistakes, or small errors that can be rectified with information already in the authority's possession. However, if this is not the case and required information is missing or incorrect, the licensing authority may 'hold' the application until the applicant has supplied all the required information. This effectively resets the 28 day period for determining an application and may be done any number of times until the application form is complete. Licensing authorities must ensure that they notify the applicant as quickly as possible of any missing (or incorrect) information, and explain how this will affect the statutory timescale and advertising requirements.

8.27 If an application has been given at the weekend, the notice advertising the application (where applicable) may already be displayed outside the premises by the time that the licensing authority downloads the application. It is therefore recommended that, if a licensing authority holds an application, it should inform the applicant that the original (or if necessary, amended) notice must be displayed until the end of the revised period. The licensing authority should also advise the applicant that they should not advertise the application in a local newspaper until they have received confirmation from the licensing authority that the application includes all the required information. To ensure clarity for applicants, the Government recommends that licensing authorities include similar advice on their electronic application facilities (where these exist) to ensure that applicants do not incur any unnecessary costs.

8.28 If an applicant persistently fails to supply the required information, the licensing authority may refuse the application and the applicant must submit a new application.

8.29 Licensing authorities may also 'defer' electronic applications once if the application is particularly complicated, for example if representations are received and a hearing is required. This allows the licensing authority to extend the statutory time period for the determination of the application by such time as is necessary, including, if required, arranging and holding a hearing. Licensing authorities must ensure that applicants are informed as quickly as possible of a decision to defer, and the reasons for the deferral, before the original 28 days has expired.

Written applications

8.30 A written application for a premises licence must be made in the prescribed form to the relevant licensing authority and be copied to each of the appropriate responsible authorities. For example, it would not be appropriate to send an application for premises which was not a vessel to the Maritime and Coastguard Agency. The application must be accompanied by:

- the required fee (details of fees may be viewed on the Home Office website);
- an operating schedule (see below);
- a plan of the premises in a prescribed form; and
- if the application involves the supply of alcohol, a form of consent from the individual who is to be specified in the licence as the designated premises supervisor (DPS).

8.31 If the application is being made in respect of a community premises, it may be accompanied by the form of application to apply the alternative licence condition.

8.32 Guidance on completing premises licence, club premises certificate and minor variation forms can be found on the Home Office website. The Licensing Act 2003 (Premises licences and club premises certificates) Regulations 2005 contain provision about the prescribed form of applications, operating schedules and plans and are published on the **legislation.gov.uk** website.

Plans

8.33 Plans, for written and electronic applications, will not be required to be submitted in any particular scale, but they must be in a format which is "clear and legible in all material respects", i.e. they must be accessible and provides sufficient detail for the licensing authority to be able to determine the application, including the relative size of any features relevant to the application. There is no requirement for plans to be professionally drawn as long as they clearly show all the prescribed information.

Steps to promote the licensing objectives

8.34 In completing an operating schedule, applicants are expected to have regard to the statement of licensing policy for their area. They must also be aware of the expectations of the licensing authority and the responsible authorities as to the steps that are appropriate for the promotion of the licensing objectives, and to demonstrate knowledge of their local area when describing the steps they propose to take to promote the licensing objectives. Licensing authorities and responsible authorities are expected to publish information about what is meant by the promotion of the licensing objectives and to ensure that applicants can readily access advice about these matters. However, applicants are also expected to undertake their own enquiries about the area in which the premises are situated to inform the content of the application.

8.35 Applicants are, in particular, expected to obtain sufficient information to enable them to demonstrate, when setting out the steps they propose to take to promote the licensing objectives, that they understand:

- the layout of the local area and physical environment including crime and disorder hotspots, proximity to residential premises and proximity to areas where children may congregate;
- any risk posed to the local area by the applicants' proposed licensable activities; and
- any local initiatives (for example, local crime reduction initiatives or voluntary schemes including local taxi-marshalling schemes, street pastors and other schemes) which may help to mitigate potential risks.

8.36 Applicants are expected to include positive proposals in their application on how they will manage any potential risks. Where specific policies apply in the area (for example, a cumulative impact policy), applicants are also expected to demonstrate an understanding of how the policy impacts on their application; any measures they will take to mitigate the impact; and why they consider the application should be an exception to the policy.

8.37 It is expected that enquiries about the locality will assist applicants when determining the steps that are appropriate for the promotion of the licensing objectives. For example, premises with close proximity to residential premises should consider how this impact upon their smoking, noise management and dispersal policies to ensure the promotion of the public nuisance objective. Applicants must consider all factors which may be relevant to the promotion of the licensing objectives, and where there are no known concerns, acknowledge this in their application.

8.38 The majority of information which applicants will require should be available in the licensing policy statement in the area. Other publicly available sources which may be of use to applicants include:

- the Crime Mapping website;
- Neighbourhood Statistics websites;
- websites or publications by local responsible authorities;
- websites or publications by local voluntary schemes and initiatives; and
- on-line mapping tools.

8.39 Whilst applicants are not required to seek the views of responsible authorities before formally submitting their application, they may find them to be a useful source of expert advice on local issues that should be taken into consideration when making an application. Licensing authorities may wish to encourage co-operation between applicants, responsible authorities and, where relevant, local residents and businesses before applications are submitted in order to minimise the scope for disputes to arise.

8.40 Applicants are expected to provide licensing authorities with sufficient information in this section to determine the extent to which their proposed steps are appropriate to promote the licensing objectives in the local area. Applications must not be based on providing a set of standard conditions to promote the licensing objectives and applicants are expected to make it clear why the steps they are proposing are appropriate for the premises.

8.41 All parties are expected to work together in partnership to ensure that the licensing objectives are promoted collectively. Where there are no disputes, the steps that applicants propose to take to promote the licensing objectives, as set out in the operating schedule, will very often translate directly into conditions that will be attached to premises licences with the minimum of fuss.

8.42 For some premises, it is possible that no measures will be appropriate to promote one or more of the licensing objectives, for example, because they are adequately covered by other existing legislation. It is however important that all operating schedules should be precise and clear about the measures that are proposed to promote each of the licensing objectives.

Variations

Introduction

8.43 Where a premises licence holder wishes to amend the licence, the 2003 Act in most cases permits an application to vary to be made rather than requiring an application for a new premises licence. The process to be followed will depend on the nature of the variation and its potential impact on the licensing objectives. Applications to vary can be made electronically via GOV.UK or by means of the licensing authority's own electronic facility following the procedures set out in Chapter 8 above.

Simplified processes

8.44 There are simplified processes for making applications, or notifying changes, in the following cases:

- a change of the name or address of someone named in the licence (section 33);
- an application to vary the licence to specify a new individual as the designated premises supervisor (DPS) (section 37);
- a request to be removed as the designated premises supervisor (section 41);
- an application by a licence holder in relation to community premises authorised to sell alcohol to remove the usual mandatory conditions set out in sections 19(2) and 19(3) of the 2003 Act concerning the supervision of alcohol sales by a personal licence holder and the need for a DPS who holds a personal licence (sections 25A and 41D); and
- an application for minor variation of a premises licence (sections 41A to 41C) or club premises certificate (sections 86A to 86C).

8.45 If an application to specify a new DPS or to remove the mandatory conditions concerning the supervision of alcohol sales is made electronically via GOV.UK or the licensing authority's own electronic facility, the authority must notify the police no later than the first working day after the application is given.

8.46 Where a simplified process requires the applicant (if they are not also the personal licence holder) to copy the application to the licence holder for information, this will apply regardless of whether the application is made in writing or electronically. Otherwise the general guidance set out above (paragraphs 8.22 to 8.29) on electronic applications applies.

Minor variations process

8.47 Variations to premises licences or club premises certificates that could not impact adversely on the licensing objectives are subject to a simplified 'minor variations' process. Under this process, the applicant is not required to advertise the variation in a newspaper or circular, or copy it to responsible authorities. However, they must display it on a white notice (to distinguish it from the blue notice used for full variations and new applications). The notice must comply with the requirements set out in regulation 26A of the Licensing Act 2003 (Premises licences and club premises certificates) Regulations 2005. In accordance with those regulations, the notice must be displayed for a period of ten working days starting on the working day after the minor variation application was given to the licensing authority.

8.48 On receipt of an application for a minor variation, the licensing authority must consider whether the variation could impact adversely on the licensing objectives. It is recommended that decisions on minor variations should be delegated to licensing officers.

8.49 In considering the application, the licensing authority must consult relevant responsible authorities (whether the application is made in writing or electronically) if there is any doubt about the impact of the variation on the licensing objectives and they need specialist advice, and take their views into account in reaching a decision.

8.50 The licensing authority must also consider any relevant representations received from other persons within the time limit referred to below. As stated earlier in this Guidance, representations are only relevant if they clearly relate to the likely effect of the grant of the variation on the promotion of at least one of the licensing objectives. In the case of minor variations, there is no right to a hearing (as for a full variation or new application), but licensing authorities must take any representations into account in arriving at a decision.

8.51 Other persons have ten working days from the 'initial day', that is to say, the day after the application is received by the licensing authority, to submit representations. The licensing authority must therefore wait until this period has elapsed before determining the application, but must do so at the latest within 15 working days, beginning on the first working day after the authority received the application, with effect either that the minor variation is granted or the application is refused.

8.52 If the licensing authority fails to respond to the applicant within 15 working days (see section 193 of the 2003 Act for the definition of working day), the application will be treated as refused and the authority must return the fee to the applicant forthwith. However, the licensing authority and the applicant may agree instead that the undetermined application should be treated as a new application and that the fee originally submitted will be treated as a fee for the new application.

8.53 Where an application is refused and is then re-submitted through the full variation process, the full 28 day notification period will apply from the date the new application is received and applicants should advertise the application and copy it to all responsible authorities (in accordance with the regulations applicable to full variations).

8.54 Minor variations will generally fall into four categories: minor changes to the structure or layout of premises; small adjustments to licensing hours; the removal of out of date, irrelevant or unenforceable conditions or addition of volunteered conditions; and the addition of certain licensable activities. In all cases the overall test is whether the proposed variation could impact adversely on any of the four licensing objectives.

Changes to structure/layout

8.55 Many small variations to layout will have no adverse impact on the licensing objectives. However, changes to layout should be referred to the full variation process if they could potentially have an adverse impact on the promotion of the licensing objectives, for example by:

- increasing the capacity for drinking on the premises;
- affecting access between the public part of the premises and the rest of the premises or the street or public way, for instance, block emergency exits or routes to emergency exits; or
- impeding the effective operation of a noise reduction measure such as an acoustic lobby.

8.56 Licensing authorities will also need to consider the combined effect of a series of applications for successive small layout changes (for example, as part of a rolling refurbishment of premises) which in themselves may not be significant, but which cumulatively may impact adversely on the licensing objectives. This emphasises the importance of having an up-to-date copy of the premises plan available.

8.57 An application to remove a licensable activity should normally be approved as a minor variation. Variations to add the sale by retail or supply of alcohol to a licence are excluded from the minor variations process and must be treated as full variations in all cases.

8.58 For other licensable activities, licensing authorities will need to consider each application on a case by case basis and in light of any licence conditions put forward by the applicant.

Licensing hours

8.59 Variations to the following are excluded from the minor variations process and must be treated as full variations in all cases:

- to extend licensing hours for the sale or supply of alcohol for consumption on or off the premises between the hours of 23.00 and 07.00; or
- to increase the amount of time on any day during which alcohol may be sold or supplied for consumption on or off the premises.

8.60 Applications to reduce licensing hours for the sale or supply of alcohol or, in some cases, to move(without increasing) the licensed hours between 07.00 and 23.00 will normally be processed as minor variations.

8.61 Applications to vary the time during which other licensable activities take place should be considered on a case by case basis with reference to the likely impact on the licensing objectives.

Licensing conditions

A) IMPOSED CONDITIONS

8.62 Licensing authorities cannot impose their own conditions on the licence through the minor variations process. If the licensing officer considers that the proposed variation would impact adversely on the licensing object-ives unless conditions are imposed, they should refuse it.

B) VOLUNTEERED CONDITIONS

8.63 Applicants may volunteer conditions as part of the minor variation process. These conditions may arise from their own risk assessment of the variation, or from informal discussions with responsible authorities or the licensing authority.

8.64 For instance, there may be circumstances when the licence holder and a responsible authority such as the police or environmental health authority, agree that a new condition should be added to the licence (for example, that a nightclub adds the provision of late night refreshment to its licence to ensure a longer period of dispersal). Such a change would not normally impact adversely on the licensing objectives and could be expected to promote them by preventing crime and disorder or public nuisance. In these circumstances, the minor variation process may provide a less costly and onerous means of amending the licence than a review, with no risk to the licensing objectives. However, this route should only be used where the agreed variations are minor and the licence holder and the responsible authority have come to a genuine agreement. The licensing authority should be alive to any attempts to pressure licence or certificate holders into agreeing to new conditions where there is no evidence of a problem at the premises and, if there is any doubt, should discuss this with the relevant parties.

C) AMENDING OR REMOVING EXISTING CONDITIONS

8.65 However, there may be some circumstances when the minor variation process is appropriate. Premises may change over time and the circumstances that originally led to the condition being attached or volunteered may no longer apply. For example, there may be no need for door supervision if a bar has been converted into a restaurant. Equally some embedded conditions may no longer apply.

8.66 Changes in legislation may invalidate certain conditions. Although the conditions do not have to be removed from the licence, licence holders and licensing authorities may agree that this is desirable to clarify the licence holder's legal obligations. There may also be cases where it is appropriate to revise the wording of a condition that is unclear or unenforceable. This would be acceptable as a minor variation as long as the purpose of the condition and its intended effect remain unchanged. Such a change could be expected to promote the licensing objectives by making it easier for the licence holder to understand and comply with the condition and easier for the licensing authority to enforce it.

Full variations process

8.67 Any other changes to the licence or certificate require an application to vary under sections 34 or 84 of the 2003 Act.

8.68 Licensing authorities may wish to consider whether there is any likely impact on the promotion of the licensing objectives in deciding whether there is a need for an application to vary in relation to features which are not required to be shown on the plan under section 17 of the 2003 Act, but have nevertheless been included, for example, moveable furniture (altering the position of tables and chairs) or beer gardens (installation of a smoking shelter that will not affect the use of exits or escape routes).

8.69 However, it should be noted that a section 34 application cannot be used to vary a licence so as to:

• extend a time limited licence;
• transfer the licence from one holder to another; or
• transfer the licence from one premises to another.

8.70 If an applicant wishes to make these types of changes to the premises licence, the applicant should make a new premises licence application under section 17 of the 2003 Act; or, to transfer the licence to another holder, an application under section 42 of the 2003 Act.

Relaxation of opening hours for local, national and international occasions

8.71 It should normally be possible for applicants for premises licences and club premises certificates to anticipate special occasions which occur regularly each year – such as bank holidays and St. George's or St. Patrick's Day – and to include appropriate opening hours in their operating schedules. Similarly, temporary event notices should be sufficient to cover other events which take place at premises that do not have a premises licence or club certificate.

8.72 However, exceptional events of local, national or international significance may arise which could not have been anticipated when the application
was first made. In these circumstances, the Secretary of State may make a
licensing hours order to allow premises to open for specified, generally
extended, hours on these special occasions. This avoids the need for large
numbers of applications to vary premises licences and club premises certificates. Typical events might include a one-off local festival or a Royal Jubilee.

Advertising applications

8.73 The requirements governing the advertisement of applications for the
grant, variation or review of premises licences and club premises certificates
are contained in the regulations made under the 2003 Act which are
published on the Government's legislation website.

8.74 Applicants are required to:

- publish a notice in a local newspaper or, if there is none, in a local
  newsletter, circular or similar document circulating in the area in which
  the premises are situated; and
- display a brief summary of the application on an A4 size notice
  immediately on or outside the premises.

8.75 As prescribed in regulations, licensing authorities must also place a
notice on their website outlining key details of the application as set out in
regulations, including:

- the name of the applicant or club;
- the postal address of the premises or club premises;
- the postal address and, where applicable, the internet address where the
  relevant licensing authority's register is kept and where and when the
  record of the application may be inspected;
- the date by which representations from responsible authorities or other
  persons should be received and how these representations should be
  made; and
- that it is an offence knowingly or recklessly to make a false statement in
  connection with an application and the maximum fine for which a
  person is liable on summary conviction for the offence.

8.76 The summary of the application should set out matters such as the
proposed licensable activities and the proposed hours of opening and should
be clearly displayed for the period during which representations may be
made, together with information about where the details of the application
may be viewed.

8.77 Licensing authorities in Wales should consider encouraging applicants
to provide details in the alternative language (Welsh or English) to that of the
main advertisement itself where the application may be viewed. Therefore, if

an applicant publishes a notice in English they should be encouraged to provide a statement in Welsh as to where the application may be viewed, and vice versa. This would allow the reader of the notice to make enquiries to the licensing authority and find out the nature of the application.

8.78 Licensing authorities in Wales are also required to publish key information from licence applications in Welsh on their websites.

8.79 In the case of applications for premises licences involving internet or mail order sales, notices should be conspicuously displayed at the place where the alcohol is appropriated to the contract.

8.80 A vessel which is not permanently moored or berthed is treated as if it were a premises situated in a place where it is usually moored or berthed. The newspaper advertisement notice for such a vessel would need to be in relation to this place (where it is usually moored or berthed) and there is no provision requiring such advertising in other areas, for instance, if the vessel journeys through other licensing authority areas.

8.81 Arrangements should be put in place by the licensing authority for other parties to view a record of the application in the licensing register as described in Schedule 3 to the 2003 Act. Charges made for copies of the register should not exceed the cost of preparing such copies. Licensing authorities may wish to conduct random and unannounced visits to premises to confirm that notices have been clearly displayed and include relevant and accurate information.

Applications to change the designated premises supervisors

8.82 Chapter 4 covers designated premises supervisors and applications to vary a premises licence covering sales of alcohol by specifying a new designated premises supervisor. Chapter 4 covers applications by community premises to disapply the usual mandatory conditions in sections 19(2) and 19(3) of the 2003 Act concerning the authorisation of alcohol sales by a personal licence holder and the need for a designated premises supervisor who holds a personal licence.

Provisional statements

8.83 Where premises are being or are about to be constructed, extended or otherwise altered for the purpose of being used for one or more licensable activities, investors may be unwilling to commit funds unless they have some assurance that a premises licence covering the desired licensable activities would be granted for the premises when the building work is completed.

8.84 The 2003 Act does not define the words "otherwise altered", but the alteration must relate to the purpose of being used for one or more licensable activities.

8.85 Any person falling within section 16 of the 2003 Act can apply for a premises licence before new premises are constructed, extended or changed. This would be possible where clear plans of the proposed structure exist and the applicant is in a position to complete an operating schedule including details of:

- the activities to take place there;
- the time at which such activities will take place;
- the proposed hours of opening;
- where the applicant wishes the licence to have effect for a limited period, that period;
- the steps to be taken to promote the licensing objectives; and
- where the sale of alcohol is involved, whether supplies are proposed to be for consumption on or off the premises (or both) and the name of the designated premises supervisor the applicant wishes to specify.

8.86 In such cases, the licensing authority would include in the licence the date upon which it would come into effect. A provisional statement will normally only be required when the information described above is not available.

8.87 The 2003 Act therefore provides for a person, if an individual aged 18 or over, who has an interest in the premises to apply for a "provisional statement". This will not be time limited, but the longer the delay before an application for a premises licence is made, the more likely it is that there will be material changes and that the licensing authority will accept representations. "Person" in this context includes a business.

8.88 When a hearing is held, the licensing authority must decide whether, if the premises were constructed or altered in the way proposed in the schedule of works and if a premises licence was sought for those premises, it would consider it appropriate for the promotion of the licensing objectives to:

- attach conditions to the licence;
- rule out any of the licensable activities applied for;
- refuse to specify the person nominated as premises supervisor; or
- reject the application.

It will then issue the applicant with a provisional statement setting out the details of that decision together with its reasons.

8.89 The licensing authority must copy the provisional statement to each person who made relevant representations, and the chief officer of police for the area in which the premises is situated. The licensing authority should give full and comprehensive reasons for its decision. This is important in anticipation of an appeal by any aggrieved party.

8.90 When a person applies for a premises licence in respect of premises (or part of the premises or premises which are substantially the same) for which a provisional statement has been made, representations by responsible authorities and other persons will be excluded in certain circumstances. These are where:

- the application for a licence is in the same form as the licence described in the provisional statement;
- the work in the schedule of works has been satisfactorily completed; and
- given the information provided in the application for a provisional statement, the responsible authority or other person could have made the same, or substantially the same, representations about the application then but failed to do so without reasonable excuse; and there has been no material change in the circumstances relating either to the premises or to the area in the proximity of those premises since the provisional statement was made.

8.91 Any decision of the licensing authority on an application for a provisional statement will not relieve an applicant of the need to apply for planning permission, building control approval of the building work, or in some cases both planning permission and building control.

8.92 A provisional statement may not be sought or given for a vessel, a vehicle or a moveable structure (see section 189 of the 2003 Act).

Transfers of premises licences

8.93 The 2003 Act provides for any person who may apply for a premises licence, which includes a business, to apply for a premises licence to be transferred to them. Where the application is made in writing, the applicant must give notice of the application to the chief officer of police. Where it is made electronically via GOV.UK or the licensing authority's electronic facility, the licensing authority must notify the police no later than the first working day after the application is given. However, the responsibility to notify the DPS remains with the applicant. Otherwise the general guidance on electronic applications set out in paragraphs 8.22 to 8.29 applies.

8.94 In the vast majority of cases, it is expected that a transfer will be a very simple administrative process. Section 43 of the 2003 Act provides a mechanism which allows the transfer to come into immediate interim effect as soon as the licensing authority receives it, until it is formally determined or withdrawn. This is to ensure that there should be no interruption to normal business at the premises. If the police raise no objection about the application, the licensing authority must transfer the licence in accordance with the application, amend the licence accordingly and return it to the new holder.

8.95 In exceptional circumstances where the chief officer of police believes the transfer may undermine the crime prevention objective, the police may object to the transfer. Such objections are expected to be rare and arise because the police have evidence that the business or individuals seeking to hold the licence or business or individuals linked to such persons are involved in crime (or disorder).

8.96 Such objections (and therefore such hearings) should only arise in truly exceptional circumstances. If the licensing authority believes that the police are using this mechanism to vet transfer applicants routinely and to seek hearings as a fishing expedition to inquire into applicants' backgrounds, it is expected that it would raise the matter immediately with the chief officer of police.

Interim authorities

8.97 The 2003 Act provides special arrangements for the continuation of permissions under a premises licence when the holder of a licence dies suddenly or becomes bankrupt or mentally incapable. In the normal course of events, the licence would lapse in such circumstances. However, there may also be some time before, for example, the deceased person's estate can be dealt with or an administrative receiver appointed. This could have a damaging effect on those with interests in the premises, such as an owner, lessor or employees working at the premises in question; and could bring unnecessary disruption to customers' plans. The 2003 Act therefore provides for the licence to be capable of being reinstated in a discrete period of time in certain circumstances.

8.98 These circumstances arise only where a premises licence has lapsed owing to the death, incapacity or insolvency of the holder. In such circumstances, an "interim authority" notice may be given to the licensing authority within 28 consecutive days beginning the day after the licence lapsed. Where applications are made in writing, the applicant must give notice of the application to the chief officer of police. If an application is made electronically via GOV.UK or the licensing authority's electronic facility, the licensing authority must notify the police no later than the first working day after the notice is given. Otherwise the general guidance on electronic applications set out in at paragraphs 8.22 to 8.29 applies.

8.99 An interim notice may only be given either by a person with a prescribed interest in the premises as set out in the regulations made under the 2003 Act (which may be viewed on the Government's legislation website); or by a person connected to the former holder of the licence (normally a personal representative of the former holder; or a person with power of attorney; or where someone has become insolvent, that person's insolvency practitioner).

8.100 The effect of giving the notice is to reinstate the premises licence as if the person giving the notice is the holder of the licence and thereby allow licensable activities to continue to take place pending a formal application for transfer. The maximum period for which an interim authority notice may have effect is three months.

8.101 The interim authority notice ceases to have effect unless, by the end of the initial period of 28 consecutive days, a copy of the notice has been given to the chief officer of police. Within two working days of receiving the copy, and if satisfied that in the exceptional circumstances of the case failure to cancel the interim authority would undermine the crime prevention objective, the police may give a notice to that effect to the licensing authority. In such circumstances, the licensing authority must hold a hearing to consider the objection notice and cancel the interim authority notice if it decides that it is appropriate to do so for the promotion of the crime prevention objective.

8.102 Licensing authorities should be alert to the need to consider the objection quickly. Under section 50 of the 2003 Act, where the premises licence lapses (because of death, incapacity or insolvency of the holder) or by its surrender, but no interim authority notice has effect, a person who may apply for the grant of a premises licence under section 16(1) may apply within 28 consecutive days of the lapse for the transfer of the licence to them with immediate effect pending the determination of the application. This will result in the licence being reinstated from the point at which the transfer application was received by the licensing authority. Where the application is made in writing, the person applying for the transfer must copy their application to the chief officer of police. If the application is made electronically the licensing authority must copy the application to the police.

Right of freeholders etc to be notified of licensing matters

8.103 A person (which will include a business or company) with a property interest in any premises situated in the licensing authority's area may give notice of their interest to the authority using a prescribed form and on payment of the relevant fee. The application may be made in writing or electronically via GOV.UK or the licensing authority's own facility, in which case the guidance at paragraphs 8.22 to 8.29 applies. Details of fees and forms are available on the Home Office website. It is entirely at the discretion of such persons whether they choose to register or not. It is not a legal requirement. Those who may take advantage of this arrangement include the freeholder or leaseholder, a legal mortgagee in respect of the premises, a person in occupation of the premises or any other person prescribed by the Secretary of State.

8.104   The notice will have effect for 12 months but a new notice can be given every year. Whilst the notice has effect, if any change relating to the premises concerned has been made to the licensing register (which the licensing authority has a duty to keep under section 8 of the 2003 Act), the licensing authority must notify the person who registered an interest of the matter to which the change relates. The person will also be notified of their right under section 8 to request a copy of the information contained in any entry in the register. In cases relating to interim authority notices (see above), it is important that such communications are dealt with promptly.

9.   DETERMINING APPLICATIONS

General

9.1   When a licensing authority receives an application for a new premises licence or an application to vary an existing premises licence, it must determine whether the application has been made in accordance with section 17 of the 2003 Act, and in accordance with regulations made under sections 17(3) to (6), 34, 42, 54 and 55 of the 2003 Act. It must similarly determine applications for the grant of club premises certificates made in accordance with section 71 of the 2003 Act, and in accordance with regulations made under sections 71(4) to (7), 84, 91 and 92 of the 2003 Act. This means that the licensing authority must consider among other things whether the application has been properly advertised in accordance with those regulations.

Where no representations are made

9.2   A hearing is not required where an application has been properly made and no responsible authority or other person has made a relevant representation. In these cases, the licensing authority must grant the application in the terms sought, subject only to conditions which are consistent with the operating schedule and relevant mandatory conditions under the 2003 Act. This should be undertaken as a simple administrative process by the licensing authority's officials who should replicate the proposals contained in the operating schedule to promote the licensing objectives in the form of clear and enforceable licence conditions.

Where representations are made

9.3   Where a representation concerning the licensing objectives is made by a responsible authority about a proposed operating schedule and it is relevant, (see paragraphs 9.4 to 9.10 below) the licensing authority's discretion will be engaged. It will also be engaged if another person makes relevant representations to the licensing authority, which are also not frivolous or vexatious (see paragraphs 9.4 to 9.10 below). Relevant representations can be made in opposition to, or in support of, an application and can be made by any individual, body or business that has grounds to do so.

Relevant, vexatious and frivolous representations

9.4 A representation is "relevant" if it relates to the likely effect of the grant of the licence on the promotion of at least one of the licensing objectives. For example, a representation from a local businessperson about the commercial damage caused by competition from new licensed premises would not be relevant. On the other hand, a representation by a businessperson that nuisance caused by new premises would deter customers from entering the local area, and the steps proposed by the applicant to prevent that nuisance were inadequate, would be relevant. In other words, representations should relate to the impact of licensable activities carried on from premises on the objectives. For representations in relation to variations to be relevant, they should be confined to the subject matter of the variation. There is no requirement for a responsible authority or other person to produce a recorded history of problems at premises to support their representations, and in fact this would not be possible for new premises.

9.5 It is for the licensing authority to determine whether a representation (other than a representation from responsible authority) is frivolous or vexatious on the basis of what might ordinarily be considered to be vexatious or frivolous. A representation may be considered to be vexatious if it appears to be intended to cause aggravation or annoyance, whether to a competitor or other person, without reasonable cause or justification. Vexatious circumstances may arise because of disputes between rival businesses and local knowledge will therefore be invaluable in considering such matters. Licensing authorities can consider the main effect of the representation, and whether any inconvenience or expense caused by it could reasonably be considered to be proportionate.

9.6 Frivolous representations would be essentially categorised by a lack of seriousness. Frivolous representations would concern issues which, at most, are minor and in relation to which no remedial steps would be warranted or proportionate.

9.7 Any person who is aggrieved by a rejection of their representations on either of these grounds may lodge a complaint through the local authority's corporate complaints procedure. A person may also challenge the authority's decision by way of judicial review.

9.8   Licensing authorities should not take decisions about whether representations are frivolous, vexatious or relevant to the licensing objectives on the basis of any political judgement. This may be difficult for councillors who receive complaints from residents within their own wards. If consideration is not to be delegated, contrary to the recommendation in this Guidance, an assessment should be prepared by officials for consideration by the sub-committee before any decision is taken that necessitates a hearing. Any councillor who considers that their own interests are such that they are unable to consider the matter independently should disqualify themselves.

9.9   It is recommended that, in borderline cases, the benefit of the doubt about any aspect of a representation should be given to the person making that representation. The subsequent hearing would then provide an opportunity for the person or body making the representation to amplify and clarify it.

9.10   Licensing authorities should consider providing advice on their websites about how any person can make representations to them.

The role of responsible authorities

9.11   Responsible authorities under the 2003 Act are automatically notified of all new applications. Whilst all responsible authorities may make representations regarding applications for licences and club premises certificates and full variation applications, it is the responsibility of each responsible authority to determine when they have appropriate grounds to do so.

Representations from the police

9.12   In their role as a responsible authority, the police are an essential source of advice and information on the impact and potential impact of licensable activities, particularly on the crime and disorder objective. The police have a key role in managing the night-time economy and should have good working relationships with those operating in their local area.[4] The police should be the licensing authority's main source of advice on matters relating to the promotion of the crime and disorder licensing objective, but may also be able to make relevant representations with regards to the other licensing objectives if they have evidence to support such representations.

---

4   Elections for Police and Crime Commissioners (PCCs) in all police force areas in England and Wales (except in London, where the Mayor of London has taken on the powers of a PCC in relation to the Metropolitan Police) will take place on 15th November 2012. Once appointed, PCCs will be expected to have a central role working in partnership with local authorities, enforcement bodies and other local partners to decide on what action is needed to tackle alcohol-related crime and disorder in their areas. However, the Chief Officer of Police will remain the named responsible authority under the 2003 Act.

The licensing authority should accept all reasonable and proportionate representations made by the police unless the authority has evidence that to do so would not be appropriate for the promotion of the licensing objectives. However, it remains incumbent on the police to ensure that their representations can withstand the scrutiny to which they would be subject at a hearing.

Licensing authorities acting as responsible authorities

9.13 Licensing authorities are included in the list of responsible authorities. A similar framework exists in the Gambling Act 2005. The 2003 Act does not require responsible authorities to make representations about applications for the grant of premises licences or to take any other steps in respect of different licensing processes. It is, therefore, for the licensing authority to determine when it considers it appropriate to act in its capacity as a responsible authority; the licensing authority should make this decision in accordance with its duties under section 4 of the 2003 Act.

9.14 Licensing authorities are not expected to act as responsible authorities on behalf of other parties (for example, local residents, local councillors or community groups) although there are occasions where the authority may decide to do so. Such parties can make relevant representations to the licensing authority in their own right, and it is reasonable for the licensing authority to expect them to make representations themselves where they are reasonably able to do so. However, if these parties have failed to take action and the licensing authority is aware of relevant grounds to make a representation, it may choose to act in its capacity as responsible authority.

9.15 It is also reasonable for licensing authorities to expect that other responsible authorities should intervene where the basis for the intervention falls within the remit of that other responsible authority. For example, the police should make representations where the representations are based on concerns about crime and disorder. Likewise, it is reasonable to expect the local authority exercising environmental health functions to make representations where there are concerns about noise nuisance. Each responsible authority has equal standing under the 2003 Act and may act independently without waiting for representations from any other responsible authority.

9.16 The 2003 Act enables licensing authorities to act as responsible authorities as a means of early intervention; they may do so where they consider it appropriate without having to wait for representations from other responsible authorities. For example, the licensing authority may (in a case where it has applied a cumulative impact policy) consider that granting a new licence application will add to the cumulative impact of licensed premises in its area and therefore decide to make representations to that effect, without waiting for any other person to do so.

9.17 In cases where a licensing authority is also acting as responsible authority in relation to the same process, it is important to achieve a separation of responsibilities within the authority to ensure procedural fairness and eliminate conflicts of interest. In such cases licensing determinations will be made by the licensing committee or sub committee comprising elected members of the authority (although they are advised by a licensing officer). Therefore, a separation is achieved by allocating distinct functions (i.e. those of licensing authority and responsible authority) to different officials within the authority.

9.18 In these cases, licensing authorities should allocate the different responsibilities to different licensing officers or other officers within the local authority to ensure a proper separation of responsibilities. The officer advising the licensing committee (i.e. the authority acting in its capacity as the licensing authority) must be a different person from the officer who is acting for the responsible authority. The officer acting for the responsible authority should not be involved in the licensing decision process and should not discuss the merits of the case with those involved in making the determination by the licensing authority. For example, discussion should not take place between the officer acting as responsible authority and the officer handling the licence application regarding the merits of the case. Communication between these officers in relation to the case should remain professional and consistent with communication with other responsible authorities. Representations, subject to limited exceptions, must be made in writing. It is for the licensing authority to determine how the separate roles are divided to ensure an appropriate separation of responsibilities. This approach may not be appropriate for all licensing authorities and many authorities may already have processes in place to effectively achieve the same outcome.

9.19 For smaller licensing authorities, where such a separation of responsibilities is more difficult, the licensing authority may wish to involve officials from outside the licensing department to ensure a separation of responsibilities. However, these officials should still be officials employed by the authority.

Health bodies acting as responsible authorities

9.20 Where a Primary Care Trust (PCT)[5] or Local Health Board (LHB) (in Wales) acts as a responsible authority, they should have sufficient knowledge of the licensing policy and health issues in order to be able to fulfil this function. If they wish to make representations, the PCT or LHB will need to decide how best to gather and coordinate evidence from other bodies

---

[5] When relevant provisions in the new Health and Social Care Act 2012 are brought into force, PCTs will be replaced as responsible authorities by the primary health function of local authorities.

exercising health functions in the area, such as emergency departments and ambulance services.

9.21 Health bodies may hold information which other responsible authorities do not, but which would assist a licensing authority in exercising its functions. For example, drunkenness can lead to accidents and injuries from violence, resulting in attendances at emergency departments and the use of ambulance services. Some of these incidents will be reported to the police, but many will not. Such information would be relevant to the public safety objective and in some cases the crime and disorder objective. In making representations, PCTs and LHBs will need to consider how to collect anonymised information about incidents that relate to specific premises or premises in a particular area (for example, a cumulative impact zone). Many areas have already developed procedures for local information sharing to tackle violence, which could provide useful evidence to support representations. The College of Emergency Medicine has issued guidelines for information sharing to reduce community violence which recommends that data about assault victims should be collected upon admission to emergency departments, including the date, time and location of the assault – i.e. the name of the pub, club or street where the incident occurred. Sometimes, it may be possible to link ambulance callouts or attendances at emergency departments to irresponsible practices at specific premises, such as serving alcohol to people who are intoxicated or targeting promotions involving unlimited or unspecified quantities of alcohol at particular groups.

Disclosure of personal details of persons making representations

9.22 Where a notice of a hearing is given to an applicant, the licensing authority is required under the Licensing Act 2003 (Hearings) Regulations 2005 to provide the applicant with copies of the relevant representations that have been made.

9.23 In exceptional circumstances, persons making representations to the licensing authority may be reluctant to do so because of fears of intimidation or violence if their personal details, such as name and address, are divulged to the applicant.

9.24 Where licensing authorities consider that the person has a genuine and well-founded fear of intimidation and may be deterred from making a representation on this basis, they may wish to consider alternative approaches.

9.25 For instance, they could advise the persons to provide the relevant responsible authority with details of how they consider that the licensing objectives are being undermined so that the responsible authority can make representations if appropriate and justified.

9.26 The licensing authority may also decide to withhold some or all of the person's personal details from the applicant, giving only minimal details (such as street name or general location within a street). However, withholding such details should only be considered where the circumstances justify such action.

Hearings

9.27 Regulations governing hearings may be found on the **www.legislation.gov.uk** website. If the licensing authority decides that representations are relevant, it must hold a hearing to consider them. The need for a hearing can only be avoided with the agreement of the licensing authority, the applicant and all of the persons who made relevant representations. In cases where only 'positive' representations are received, without qualifications, the licensing authority should consider whether a hearing is required. To this end, it may wish to notify the persons who made representations and give them the opportunity to withdraw those representations. This would need to be done in sufficient time before the hearing to ensure that parties were not put to unnecessary inconvenience.

9.28 Responsible authorities should try to conclude any discussions with the applicant in good time before the hearing. If the application is amended at the last moment, the licensing committee should consider giving other persons time to address the revised application before the hearing commences.

9.29 Regulations made under the 2003 Act require that representations must be withdrawn 24 hours before the first day of any hearing. If they are withdrawn after this time, the hearing must proceed and the representations may be withdrawn orally at that hearing. However, where discussions between an applicant and those making representations are taking place and it is likely that all parties are on the point of reaching agreement, the licensing authority may wish to use the power given within the hearings regulations to extend time limits, if it considers this to be in the public interest.

9.30 Applicants should be encouraged to contact responsible authorities before formulating their applications so that the mediation process may begin before the statutory time limits come into effect after submission of an application. The hearing process must meet the requirements of regulations made under the 2003 Act. Where matters arise which are not covered by the regulations, licensing authorities may make arrangements as they see fit as long as they are lawful.

9.31 There is no requirement in the 2003 Act for responsible authorities that have made representations to attend, but it is generally good practice and assists committees in reaching more informed decisions. Where several responsible authorities within a local authority have made representations on an application, a single local authority officer may represent them at the hearing if the responsible authorities and the licensing authority agree. This local authority officer representing other responsible authorities may be a licensing officer, but only if this licensing officer is acting as a responsible authority on behalf of the licensing authority and has had no role in the licensing determination process. This is to ensure that the responsible authorities are represented by an independent officer separate from the licensing determination process.

9.32 As noted in paragraphs 9.13 to 9.19 above, where the licensing officer is acting as a responsible authority the relevant steps should be followed to ensure that this individual has no role in the decision making process regarding the licensing determination.

9.33 As a matter of practice, licensing authorities should seek to focus the hearing on the steps considered appropriate to promote the particular licensing objective or objectives that have given rise to the specific representation and avoid straying into undisputed areas. A responsible authority or other person may choose to rely on their written representation. They may not add further representations to those disclosed to the applicant prior to the hearing, but they may expand on their existing representation.

9.34 In determining the application with a view to promoting the licensing objectives in the overall interests of the local community, the licensing authority must give appropriate weight to:

• the steps that are appropriate to promote the licensing objectives;
• the representations (including supporting information) presented by all the parties;
• this Guidance;
• its own statement of licensing policy.

9.35 The licensing authority should give its decision within five working days of the conclusion of the hearing (or immediately in certain specified cases) and provide reasons to support it. This will be important if there is an appeal by any of the parties. Notification of a decision must be accompanied by information on the right of the party to appeal. After considering all the relevant issues, the licensing authority may grant the application subject to such conditions that are consistent with the operating schedule. Any conditions imposed must be appropriate for the promotion of the licensing objectives; there is no power for the licensing authority to attach a condition that is merely aspirational. For example, conditions may not be attached which relate solely to the health of customers rather than their direct physical safety.

9.36 Alternatively, the licensing authority may refuse the application on the grounds that this is appropriate for the promotion of the licensing objectives.

It may also refuse to specify a designated premises supervisor and/or only allow certain requested licensable activities in the interests of transparency, the licensing authority should publish hearings procedures in full on its website to ensure that those involved have the most current information.

9.37 In the context of variations or minor variations, which may involve structural alteration to or change of use of a building, the decision of the licensing authority will not exempt an applicant from the need to apply for building control approval, planning permission or both of these where appropriate.

Determining actions that are appropriate for the promotion of the licensing objectives

9.38 Licensing authorities are best placed to determine what actions are appropriate for the promotion of the licensing objectives in their areas. All licensing determinations should be considered on a case by case basis. They should take into account any representations or objections that have been received from responsible authorities or other persons, and representations made by the applicant or premises user as the case may be.

9.39 The authority's determination should be evidence-based, justified as being appropriate for the promotion of the licensing objectives and proportionate to what it is intended to achieve.

9.40 Determination of whether an action or step is appropriate for the promotion of the licensing objectives requires an assessment of what action or step would be suitable to achieve that end. Whilst this does not therefore require a licensing authority to decide that no lesser step will achieve the aim, the authority should aim to consider the potential burden that the condition would impose on the premises licence holder (such as the financial burden due to restrictions on licensable activities) as well as the potential benefit in terms of the promotion of the licensing objectives. However, it is imperative that the authority ensures that the factors which form the basis of its determination are limited to consideration of the promotion of the objectives and nothing outside those parameters. As with the consideration of licence variations, the licensing authority should consider wider issues such as other conditions already in place to mitigate potential negative impact on the promotion of the licensing objectives and the track record of the business. Further advice on determining what is appropriate when imposing conditions on a licence or certificate is provided in Chapter 10. The licensing authority is expected to come to its determination based on an assessment of the evidence on both the risks and benefits either for or against making the determination.

Considering cases where licensing and planning applications are made simultaneously

9.41 Where businesses have indicated, when applying for a licence under the 2003 Act, that they have also applied for planning permission or that they intend to do so, licensing committees and officers should consider discussion with their planning counterparts prior to determination with the aim of agreeing mutually acceptable operating hours and scheme designs.

10. CONDITIONS ATTACHED TO PREMISES LICENCES AND CLUB PREMISES CERTIFICATES

General

10.1 This chapter provides further guidance in relation to conditions attached to premises licences and club premises certificates. General principles on licence conditions are set out in Chapter 1 (paragraphs 1.16).

10.2 Conditions include any limitations or restrictions attached to a licence or certificate and essentially are the steps or actions that the holder of the premises licence or the club premises certificate will be required to take or refrain from taking in relation to the carrying on of licensable activities at the premises in question. Failure to comply with any condition attached to a licence or certificate is a criminal offence, which on conviction is punishable by a fine of up to £20,000 or up to six months imprisonment. The courts have made clear that it is particularly important that conditions which are imprecise or difficult for a licence holder to observe should be avoided.

10.3 There are three types of condition that may be attached to a licence or certificate: proposed, imposed and mandatory. Each of these categories is described in more detail below.

Proposed conditions

10.4 The conditions that are appropriate for the promotion of the licensing objectives should emerge initially from the risk assessment carried out by a prospective licence or certificate holder, which they should carry out before making their application for a premises licence or club premises certificate. This would be translated into the steps recorded in the operating schedule or club operating schedule, which must also set out the proposed hours during which licensable activities will be conducted and any other hours during which the premises will be open to the public.

10.5 It is not acceptable for licensing authorities to simply replicate the wording from an applicant's operating schedule. A condition should be interpreted in accordance with the applicant's intention.

Consistency with steps described in operating schedule

10.6 The 2003 Act provides that where an operating schedule or club operating schedule has been submitted with an application and there have been no relevant representations made by responsible authorities or any other person, the licence or certificate must be granted subject only to such conditions as are consistent with the schedule accompanying the application and any mandatory conditions required under the 2003 Act.

10.7 Consistency means that the effect of the condition should be substantially the same as that intended by the terms of the operating schedule. If conditions are broken, this may lead to a criminal prosecution or an application for a review and it is extremely important therefore that they should be expressed on the licence or certificate in unequivocal and unambiguous terms. The duty imposed by conditions on the licence holder or club must be clear to the licence holder, club, enforcement officers and the courts.

Imposed conditions

10.8 The licensing authority may not impose any conditions unless its discretion has been engaged following receipt of relevant representations and it is satisfied as a result of a hearing (unless all parties agree a hearing is not necessary) that it is appropriate to impose conditions to promote one or more of the four licensing objectives.

10.9 It is possible that, in certain cases, where there are other legislative provisions which are relevant and must be observed by the applicant, no additional conditions are appropriate to promote the licensing objectives.

Proportionality

10.10 The 2003 Act requires that licensing conditions should be tailored to the size, type, location and characteristics and activities taking place at the premises concerned. Conditions should be determined on a case by case basis and standardised conditions which ignore these individual aspects should be avoided. Licensing authorities and other responsible authorities should be alive to the indirect costs that can arise because of conditions. These could be a deterrent to holding events that are valuable to the community or for the funding of good and important causes. Licensing authorities should therefore ensure that any conditions they impose are only those which are appropriate for the promotion of the licensing objectives.

Hours of trading

10.11 The Government acknowledges that different licensing strategies may be appropriate for the promotion of the licensing objectives in different areas. The 2003 Act gives the licensing authority power to make decisions regarding licensed opening hours as part of the implementation of its licensing policy statement and licensing authorities are best placed to make decisions about appropriate opening hours in their areas based on their local knowledge and in consultation with responsible authorities. However, licensing authorities must always consider each application and must not impose predetermined licensed opening hours, without giving individual consideration to the merits of each application.

10.12 Where there are objections to an application to extend the hours during which licensable activities are to be carried on and the licensing authority determines that this would undermine the licensing objectives, it may reject the application or grant it with appropriate conditions and/or different hours from those requested.

10.13 Shops, stores and supermarkets should normally be free to provide sales of alcohol for consumption off the premises at any times when the retail outlet is open for shopping unless there are good reasons, based on the licensing objectives, for restricting those hours.

The performance of plays

10.14 The 2003 Act provides that other than for the purposes of public safety, conditions must not be attached to premises licences or club premises certificates authorising the performance of a play which attempt to censor or modify the content of plays in any way. Any such condition would be ultra vires the 2003 Act.

Censorship

10.15 In general, other than in the context of film classification for film exhibitions, licensing authorities should not use their powers under the 2003 Act to seek to impose conditions which censor the content of any form of regulated entertainment. This is not a proper function of licensing law and cannot be properly related to the licensing objectives. The content of regulated entertainment is a matter which is addressed by existing laws governing indecency and obscenity. Where the concern is about protecting children, their access should be restricted where appropriate. But no other limitation should normally be imposed.

Major art and pop festivals, carnivals, fairs and circuses

10.16 Licensing authorities should publicise the need for the organisers of major festivals and carnivals to approach them at the earliest opportunity to discuss arrangements for licensing activities falling under the 2003 Act. For some events, the organisers may seek a single premises licence to cover a wide range of activities at varied locations within the premises. This would involve the preparation of a substantial operating schedule, and licensing authorities should offer advice and assistance about its preparation.

10.17   For other events, applications for many connected premises licences may be made which in combination will represent a single festival. It is important that licensing authorities should publicise the need for proper co-ordination of such arrangements and will need to ensure that responsible authorities are aware of the connected nature of the individual applications.

10.18   In the case of circuses and fairgrounds, much will depend on the content of any entertainment presented. For example, at fairgrounds, a good deal of the musical entertainment may be incidental to the main attractions and rides at the fair that are not themselves regulated entertainment.

10.19   In addition, in the context of festivals and carnivals, local authorities should bear in mind their ability to seek premises licences from the licensing authority for land or buildings under public ownership within the community in their own name. This could include, for example, village greens, market squares, promenades, community halls, local authority owned art centres and similar public areas where festivals and carnivals might take place. Performers and entertainers would then have no need to obtain a licence or give a temporary event notice themselves to enable them to give performances in these places, although they would need the permission of the local authority to put on the event.

Fixed prices

10.20   Licensing authorities should not attach standardised blanket conditions promoting fixed prices for alcoholic drinks to premises licences or club licences or club premises certificates in an area. This may be unlawful under current law. However, it is important to note that the mandatory conditions made under sections 19A and 73B of the 2003 Act prohibit a number of types of drinks promotions where they give rise to a significant risk to any one of the four licensing objectives.

10.21   Where licensing authorities are asked by the police, other responsible authorities or other persons to impose restrictions on promotions in addition to those restricted by the mandatory conditions, they should consider each application on its individual merits, tailoring any conditions carefully to cover only irresponsible promotions in the particular and individual circumstances of any premises where these are appropriate for the promotion of the licensing objectives. In addition, when considering any relevant representations which demonstrate a clear causal link between sales promotions or price discounting and levels of crime and disorder on or near the premises, it would be appropriate for the licensing authority to consider the imposition of a new condition prohibiting irresponsible sales promotions or the discounting of prices of alcoholic beverages at those premises. However, before pursuing any form of restrictions at all, licensing authorities should take their own legal advice.

Large capacity venues used exclusively or primarily for the "vertical" consumption of alcohol (HVVDS)

10.22 Large capacity "vertical drinking" premises, sometimes called High Volume Vertical Drinking establishments (HVVDs), are premises with exceptionally high capacities, which are used primarily or exclusively for the sale and consumption of alcohol, and have little or no seating for patrons. Previous research has demonstrated that the environment within such establishments can have a significant bearing on the likelihood of crime and disorder.

10.23 Where appropriate, conditions can be attached to premises licences for the promotion of the prevention of crime and disorder at such premises that require the premises to observe:

- a prescribed capacity;
- an appropriate ratio of tables and chairs to customers based on the capacity; and
- a requirement that security staff holding the appropriate SIA licence or exemption are present to control entry for the purpose of compliance with the capacity limit and to deny entry to individuals who appear drunk or disorderly or both.

Mandatory conditions in relation to the supply of alcohol

10.24 The 2003 Act provides for the following mandatory conditions to be included in every licence and/or club premises certificate in the circumstances specified.

Designated Premises Supervisor

10.25 The 2003 Act provides that, where a premises licence authorises the supply of alcohol, it must include a condition that no supply of alcohol may be made at a time when no designated premises supervisor has been specified in the licence or at a time when the designated premises supervisor does not hold a personal licence or the personal licence has been suspended.

10.26 The main purpose of the 'designated premises supervisor' as defined in the 2003 Act is to ensure that there is always one specified individual among these personal licence holders who can be readily identified for the premises where a premises licence is in force. That person will normally have been given day to day responsibility for running the premises by the premises licence holder. The requirements set out in relation to the designated premises supervisor and authorisation of alcohol sales by a personal licence holder do not apply to community premises in respect of which a successful application has been made to disapply the usual mandatory conditions in sections 19(2) and 19(3) of the 2003 Act (see Chapter 4 of this Guidance).

10.27 The 2003 Act does not require a designated premises supervisor or any other personal licence holder to be present on the premises at all times when alcohol is sold. However, the designated premises supervisor and the premises licence holder remain responsible for the premises at all times including compliance with the terms of the 2003 Act and conditions attached to the premises licence to promote the licensing objectives.

Authorisation by personal licence holders

10.28 In addition, every premises licence that authorises the sale of alcohol must require that every supply of alcohol under the premises licence must be made or authorised by a person who holds a personal licence. This in most instances will be the designated premises supervisor who must hold a valid personal licence. Any premises at which alcohol is sold or supplied may employ one or more personal licence holders. This does not mean that the condition should require the presence of the designated premises supervisor or any other personal licence holder on the premises at all times.

10.29 Similarly, the fact that every supply of alcohol must be made under the authority of a personal licence holder does not mean that only personal licence holders can make sales or that they must be personally present at every transaction. A personal licence holder may authorise members of staff to make sales of alcohol but may be absent at times from the premises when a transaction takes place. However, the responsible personal licence holder may not be able to escape responsibility for the actions of anyone authorised to make sales.

10.30 "Authorisation" does not imply direct supervision by a personal licence holder of each sale of alcohol. The question arises as to how sales can be authorised. Ultimately, whether an authorisation has been given is a question of fact that would have to be decided by the courts on the evidence before it in the course of a criminal prosecution.

10.31 The following factors should be relevant in considering whether or not an authorisation has been given:

- the person(s) authorised to sell alcohol at any particular premises should be clearly identified;

- the authorisation should have specified the acts which may be carried out by the person who is authorised to supply alcohol;
- there should be an overt act of authorisation, for example, a specific written statement given to the individual who is authorised to supply alcohol; and
- there should be in place sensible arrangements for the personal licence holder to monitor the activity that they have authorised on a reasonably regular basis.

10.32 It is strongly recommended that personal licence holders give specific written authorisations to individuals whom they are authorising to retail alcohol. A single written authorisation would be sufficient to cover multiple sales over an unlimited period. This would assist personal licence holders in demonstrating due diligence should issues arise with enforcement authorities; and would protect employees if they themselves are challenged in respect of their authority to sell alcohol.

10.33 Written authorisation is not a requirement of the 2003 Act and its absence alone could not give rise to enforcement action.

10.34 It must be remembered that whilst the designated premises supervisor or a personal licence holder may authorise other individuals to sell alcohol in their absence, they are responsible for any sales that may be made. Similarly, the premises licence holder remains responsible for ensuring that licensing law and licence conditions are observed at the premises.

Arrangements for the mandatory licence conditions

10.35 The mandatory conditions made under sections 19A and 73B of the 2003 Act (the conditions governing irresponsible promotions, dispensing alcohol directly into the mouth, provision of free tap water, age verification and small measures) do not have to be physically included in the licence or certificate but nonetheless will apply to every licence and certificate authorising the sale and supply of alcohol for consumption on the premises. The mandatory conditions set out in section 19 of the 2003 Act (the requirement for a DPS and for all sales to be made or authorised by a personal licence holder) do, however, have to be physically included in the licence. The mandatory aspirational licence conditions do not apply to activities (including the supply of alcohol) authorised by a temporary event notice.

10.36 Whereas the initial mandatory conditions in section 19 of the 2003 Act are set out in Annex A of the licence, the additional mandatory conditions made under section 19A of the 2003 Act are treated as if they were included in existing licences and certificates on the date that those conditions came into force.

10.37 Following their commencement, the mandatory conditions overrode any pre-existing conditions already included in a licence or certificate insofar as the mandatory conditions were identical to, or inconsistent with or more onerous than, any pre-existing conditions. It is not necessary to record on the face of existing licences and certificates the impact that the introduction of the mandatory conditions has had on pre-existing conditions.

Irresponsible promotions

10.38 Under this condition, the "responsible person" (defined in the 2003 Act as the holder of a premises licence, designated premises supervisor, a person aged 18 or over who is authorised to allow the sale or supply of alcohol by an under 18 or a member or officer of a club present on the club premises who can oversee the supply of alcohol) should be able to demonstrate that they have taken all reasonable steps to ensure that staff do not carry out, arrange or participate in any irresponsible promotions. An irresponsible promotion is one that fits one of the descriptions below (or is substantially similar), is carried on for the purpose of encouraging the sale or supply of alcohol for consumption on the premises and carries a significant risk of leading or contributing to crime and disorder, prejudice to public safety, public nuisance or harm to children. The aim of the condition is to prohibit or restrict promotions which encourage people to drink more than they might ordinarily do and in a manner which does not promote the licensing objectives.

Drinking games

10.39 Irresponsible promotions can include activities, whether drinking games or not, which may require or encourage individuals to drink a quantity of alcohol within a time limit, or drink as much alcohol as possible within a time limit or otherwise. For example, this may include organised 'drink downing' competitions. This would not prevent the responsible person from requiring all drinks to be consumed or abandoned at, or before, the closing time of the premises. Nor does it necessarily prohibit 'happy hours' as long as these are not designed to encourage individuals to drink excessively or rapidly.

Large quantities of alcohol for free or a fixed price

10.40 Irresponsible promotions can include the provision of unlimited or unspecified quantities of alcohol free or for a fixed or discounted price. This includes alcohol provided to the public or to a group defined by a particular characteristic, for example, a promotion which offers women free drinks before a certain time or "all you can drink for £10". This condition does not apply to a promotion or discount on alcohol for consumption with a table meal. Promotions can be designed with a particular group in mind (for example, over 65s). A common sense approach is encouraged, which may include specifying the quantity of alcohol included in it or not targeting a group which could become more vulnerable or present a greater risk of crime and disorder as a result of excessive alcohol consumption.

Prizes and rewards

10.41 The sale, supply or provision of free or discounted alcohol or any other item as a prize to encourage or reward the purchase and consumption of alcohol can be within the definition of an irresponsible promotion. This may include promotions under which free or discounted alcohol is offered as a part of the sale of alcohol, for example, "Buy one and get two free" and "Buy one cocktail and get a second cocktail for 25p". This includes promotions which involve the provision of free or discounted alcohol within the same 24 hour period.

Sporting events

10.42 Irresponsible promotions can include the provision of alcohol for free or for a discounted price in relation to a sporting event shown on the premises, where the sale, supply or provision of alcohol depends on the outcome of a race, match or other event. For example, this may include offering unlimited drinks based on the outcome of a sporting competition. It also applies to events which are unpredictable, such as offering free double shots for every foul committed in a football match, or heavily reduced drinks for five minutes after a try is scored in a rugby match.

Posters and flyers

10.43 Irresponsible promotions can also include the sale or supply of alcohol in association with promotional materials on display in or around the premises, which can either be reasonably considered to condone, encourage or glamorise anti social behaviour or refer to the effects of drunkenness in any favourable manner.

Dispensing alcohol directly into the mouth

10.44 The responsible person (see paragraph 10.38) must ensure that no alcohol is dispensed directly by one person into the mouth of another person. For example, this may include drinking games such as the 'dentist's chair' where a drink is poured continuously into the mouth of another individual and may also prevent a premises from allowing another body to promote its products by employing someone to dispense alcohol directly into customers' mouths. An exception to this condition would be when an individual is unable to drink without assistance due to a disability.

Free tap water

10.45   The responsible person (see paragraph 10.38) must ensure that free potable tap water is provided on request to customers where it is reasonably available on the premises. What is meant by reasonably available is a question of fact; for example, it would not be reasonable to expect free tap water to be available in premises for which the water supply had temporarily been lost because of a broken mains water supply.

Age verification

10.46   The premises licence holder or club premises certificate holder must ensure that an age verification policy applies to the premises in relation to the sale or supply of alcohol. This must as a minimum require individuals who appear to the responsible person (see paragraph 10.38) to be under the age of 18 years of age to produce on request, before being served alcohol, identification bearing their photograph, date of birth, and a holographic mark.

10.47   It is acceptable, and indeed encouraged, for premises to have an age verification policy which requires individuals who appear to the responsible person to be under an age greater than 18 to produce such identification on request. For example, if premises have a policy that requires any individual that appears to be under the age of 21 to produce identification that meets the criteria listed above, this is perfectly acceptable under the mandatory code.

10.48   Licence holders should consider carefully what steps they are required to take to comply with the age verification requirements under the 2003 Act in relation to sales of alcohol made remotely. These include sales made online, by telephone and mail order sales, and alcohol delivery services. Each of these sales must comply with the requirements of the 2003 Act. The mandatory condition requires that age verification takes place before a person is served alcohol. Where alcohol is sold remotely (for example, online) or through a telephone transaction, the sale is made at this point but the alcohol is not actually served until it is delivered to the customer. Age verification measures (for example, online age verification) should be used to ensure that alcohol is not sold to any person under the age of 18. However, licence holders should also consider carefully what steps are appropriate to ensure that age verification takes place before the alcohol is served (i.e. physically delivered) to the customer to be satisfied that the customer is aged 18 or over. It is, therefore, the responsibility of the person serving or delivering the alcohol to ensure that age verification has taken place and that photo ID has been checked if the person appears to be less than 18 years of age.

10.49 The premises licence holder or club premises certificate holder must ensure that staff (in particular staff who are involved in the supply of alcohol) are made aware of the existence and content of the age verification policy applied by the premises.

Smaller measures

10.50 The responsible person (see paragraph 10.38) shall ensure that the following drinks, if sold or supplied on the premises, are available in the following measures:

- Beer or cider: 1/2 pint
- Gin, rum, vodka or whisky: 25ml or 35ml
- Still wine in a glass: 125ml

10.51 As well as making the drinks available in the above measures, the responsible person must also make customers aware of the availability of these measures – for example, by making their availability clear on menus and price lists, and ensuring that these are displayed in a prominent, conspicuous place in the relevant premises (for example, at the bar).

10.52 This condition does not apply if the drinks in question are sold or supplied having been made up in advance ready for sale or supply in a securely closed container. For example, if beer is only available in pre-sealed bottles the requirement to make it available in 1/2 pints does not apply.

10.53 The premises licence holder or club premises certificate holder must ensure that staff are made aware of the application of this condition.

Exhibition of films

10.54 The 2003 Act provides that where a premises licence or club premises certificate authorises the exhibition of a film, it must include a condition requiring the admission of children to films to be restricted in accordance with recommendations given either by a body designated under section 4 of the Video Recordings Act 1984 specified in the licence (currently only the British Board of Film Classification – BBFC) or by the licensing authority itself.

10.55 The effect of paragraph 5 of Schedule 1 to the Act is to exempt adverts from the definition of regulated entertainment, but not to exempt them from the definition of exhibition of a film. Since the above mandatory condition applies to 'any film' it is therefore applicable to the exhibition of adverts.

Door supervision

10.56   Under section 21 of the 2003 Act, when a condition is included in a premises licence that at specified times an individual must be present at the premises to carry out a security activity (as defined in section 21(3)(a) by reference to the Private Security Industry Act 2001 ("the 2001 Act"), the licence must include a condition requiring that individual to be licensed by the Security Industry Authority ("the SIA") under the 2001 Act, or be entitled to carry out that activity by virtue of section 4 of the 2001 Act.

10.57   A premises licence need not require a person to hold a licence granted by the SIA if that person benefits from an exemption under section 4 of the 2001 Act. For example, certain employees benefit from an exemption when carrying out conduct in connection with a certified sports grounds (section 4(6 to 12)). Furthermore, in certain circumstances persons benefit from an exemption where they operate under the SIA's Approved Contractor Scheme (section 15).

10.58   Conditions under section 21 of the 2003 Act should only relate to individuals carrying out security activities defined by section 21(3)(a) of the 2003 Act. Therefore, they should only relate to an activity to which paragraph 2(1)(a) of Schedule 2 to the 2001 Act applies (certain manned guarding activities) and which is licensable conduct within the meaning of section 3(2) of that Act. The requirement does not relate to individuals performing non-security related activities, and section 21 should not be used in relation to any such activities.

10.59   Section 21 of the 2003 Act continues to ensure that a premises licence need not impose such a requirement in relation to those licensed premises which the 2001 Act treats as unlicensed premises.

Those are:

- premises staging plays or exhibiting films;
- casinos or bingo halls licensed under the Gambling Act 2005;
- premises where a club certificate is in force when activities are being carried on under the authority of that certificate.

See paragraph 8(3) of Schedule 2 to the 2001 Act for full details.

10.60   It should be noted, however, that the 2001 Act will require contractors and a small number of employees (those managing/supervising and those supplied under contract) to be licensed as manned guards (rather than door supervisors) when undertaking licensable conduct on premises to which paragraph 8(3) of Schedule 2 to the 2001 Act applies.

10.61   It is therefore important that if a licensing authority intends that individuals must be present to carry out security activities (as defined by section 21(3)(a) of the 2003 Act) this should be explicit, as should the mandatory condition for those individuals to hold an SIA licence or be entitled to carry out that activity by virtue of section 4 of the 2001 Act. On the other hand, where a licensing authority intends that individuals must be present to carry out other activities (for example, activities related to safety or steward activities to organise, advise and direct members of the public) no mandatory condition should be imposed under section 21 of the 2003 Act. In all cases it is important when determining whether or not a condition is to be imposed under section 21 of the 2003 Act to consider whether the activities of any individual working in licensed premises fall within the definition of security activities in section 21(3)(a) of the 2003 Act.

(Regardless of whether a condition is imposed under section 21 of the 2003 Act, under the 2001 Act the appropriate SIA licence must be held by any individual performing an activity for which they are licensable under that Act).

11. REVIEWS

The review process

11.1 The proceedings set out in the 2003 Act for reviewing premises licences and club premises certificates represent a key protection for the community where problems associated with the licensing objectives occur after the grant or variation of a premises licence or club premises certificate.

11.2 At any stage, following the grant of a premises licence or club premises certificate, a responsible authority, or any other person, may ask the licensing authority to review the licence or certificate because of a matter arising at the premises in connection with any of the four licensing objectives.

11.3 An application for review may be made electronically, provided the licensing authority agrees and the applicant submits a subsequent written application. The licensing authority may also agree in advance that the application need not be given in writing. However, these applications are outside the formal electronic application process and may not be submitted via GOV.UK or the licensing authority's electronic facility.

11.4 In addition, the licensing authority must review a licence if the premises to which it relates was made the subject of a closure order by the police based on nuisance or disorder and the magistrates' court has sent the authority the relevant notice of its determination, or if the police have made an application for summary review on the basis that premises are associated with serious crime and/or disorder.

11.5 Any responsible authority under the 2003 Act may apply for a review of a premises licence or club premises certificate. Therefore, the relevant licensing authority may apply for a review if it is concerned about licensed activities at premises and wants to intervene early without waiting for representations from other persons. However, it is not expected that licensing authorities should normally act as responsible authorities in applying for reviews on behalf of other persons, such as local residents or community groups. These individuals or groups are entitled to apply for a review for a licence or certificate in their own right if they have grounds to do so. It is also reasonable for licensing authorities to expect other responsible authorities to intervene where the basis for the intervention falls within the remit of that other authority. For example, the police should take appropriate steps where the basis for the review is concern about crime and disorder. Likewise, where there are concerns about noise nuisance, it is reasonable to expect the local authority exercising environmental health functions for the area in which the premises are situated to make the application for review.

11.6 Where the relevant licensing authority does act as a responsible authority and applies for a review, it is important that a separation of responsibilities is still achieved in this process to ensure procedural fairness and eliminate conflicts of interest. As outlined previously in Chapter 9 of this Guidance, the distinct functions of acting as licensing authority and responsible authority should be exercised by different officials to ensure a separation of responsibilities. Further information on how licensing authorities should achieve this separation of responsibilities can be found in Chapter 9, paragraphs 9.13 to 9.19 of this Guidance.

11.7 In every case, any application for a review must relate to particular premises in respect of which there is a premises licence or club premises certificate and must be relevant to the promotion of one or more of the licensing objectives. Following the grant or variation of a licence or certificate, a complaint regarding a general issue in the local area relating to the licensing objectives, such as a general (crime and disorder) situation in a town centre, should generally not be regarded as a relevant representation unless it can be positively tied or linked by a causal connection to particular premises, which would allow for a proper review of the licence or certificate. For instance, a geographic cluster of complaints, including along transport routes related to an individual public house and its closing time, could give grounds for a review of an existing licence as well as direct incidents of crime and disorder around a particular public house.

11.8 Where a licensing authority receives a geographic cluster of complaints, the authority may consider whether these issues are the result of the cumulative impact of licensed premises within the area concerned. In such circumstances, the authority may also consider whether it would be appropriate to include a special policy relating to cumulative impact within its licensing policy statement. Further guidance on cumulative impact policies can be found in Chapter 13 of this Guidance.

11.9 Representations must be made in writing and may be amplified at the subsequent hearing or may stand in their own right. Additional representations which do not amount to an amplification of the original representation may not be made at the hearing. Representations may be made electronically, provided the licensing authority agrees and the applicant submits a subsequent written representation. The licensing authority may also agree in advance that the representation need not be given in writing.

11.10 Where authorised persons and responsible authorities have concerns about problems identified at premises, it is good practice for them to give licence holders early warning of their concerns and the need for improvement, and where possible they should advise the licence or certificate holder of the steps they need to take to address those concerns. A failure by the holder to respond to such warnings is expected to lead to a decision to apply for a review. Co-operation at a local level in promoting the licensing objectives should be encouraged and reviews should not be used to undermine this co-operation.

11.11 If the application for a review has been made by a person other than a responsible authority (for example, a local resident, residents' association, local business or trade association), before taking action the licensing authority must first consider whether the complaint being made is relevant, frivolous, vexatious or repetitious. Further guidance on determining whether a representation is frivolous or vexatious can be found in Chapter 9 of this Guidance (paragraphs 9.4 to 9.10).

Repetitious grounds of review

11.12 A repetitious ground is one that is identical or substantially similar to:

- a ground for review specified in an earlier application for review made in relation to the same premises licence or certificate which has already been determined; or
- representations considered by the licensing authority when the premises licence or certificate was granted; or
- representations which would have been made when the application for the premises licence was first made and which were excluded then by reason of the prior issue of a provisional statement; and, in addition to the above grounds, a reasonable interval has not elapsed since that earlier review or grant.

11.13 Licensing authorities are expected to be aware of the need to prevent attempts to review licences merely as a further means of challenging the grant of the licence following the failure of representations to persuade the licensing authority on an earlier occasion. It is for licensing authorities themselves to judge what should be regarded as a reasonable interval in these circumstances. However, it is recommended that more than one review originating from a person other than a responsible authority in relation to a particular premises should not be permitted within a 12 month period on similar grounds save in compelling circumstances or where it arises following a closure order.

11.14 The exclusion of a complaint on the grounds that it is repetitious does not apply to responsible authorities which may make more than one application for a review of a licence or certificate within a 12 month period.

11.15 When a licensing authority receives an application for a review from a responsible authority or any other person, or in accordance with the closure procedures described in Part 8 of the 2003 Act (for example, closure orders), it must arrange a hearing. The arrangements for the hearing must follow the provisions set out in regulations. These regulations are published on the Government's legislation website (**www.legislation.gov.uk**). It is particularly important that the premises licence holder is made fully aware of any representations made in respect of the premises, any evidence supporting the representations and that the holder or the holder's legal representative has therefore been able to prepare a response.

Powers of a licensing authority on the determination of a review

11.16 The 2003 Act provides a range of powers for the licensing authority which it may exercise on determining a review where it considers them appropriate for the promotion of the licensing objectives.

11.17 The licensing authority may decide that the review does not require it to take any further steps appropriate to promote the licensing objectives. In addition, there is nothing to prevent a licensing authority issuing an informal warning to the licence holder and/or to recommend improvement within a particular period of time. It is expected that licensing authorities will regard such informal warnings as an important mechanism for ensuring that the licensing objectives are effectively promoted and that warnings should be issued in writing to the licence holder.

11.18 However, where responsible authorities such as the police or environmental health officers have already issued warnings requiring improvement – either orally or in writing – that have failed as part of their own stepped approach to address concerns, licensing authorities should not merely repeat that approach and should take this into account when considering what further action is appropriate.

11.19 Where the licensing authority considers that action under its statutory powers is appropriate, it may take any of the following steps:

- to modify the conditions of the premises licence (which includes adding new conditions or any alteration or omission of an existing condition), for example, by reducing the hours of opening or by requiring door supervisors at particular times;
- to exclude a licensable activity from the scope of the licence, for example, to exclude the performance of live music or playing of recorded music (where it is not within the incidental live and recorded music exemption);
- to remove the designated premises supervisor, for example, because they consider that the problems are the result of poor management;
- to suspend the licence for a period not exceeding three months;
- to revoke the licence.

11.20 In deciding which of these powers to invoke, it is expected that licensing authorities should so far as possible seek to establish the cause or causes of the concerns that the representations identify. The remedial action taken should generally be directed at these causes and should always be no more than an appropriate and proportionate response.

11.21 For example, licensing authorities should be alive to the possibility that the removal and replacement of the designated premises supervisor may be sufficient to remedy a problem where the cause of the identified problem directly relates to poor management decisions made by that individual.

11.22 Equally, it may emerge that poor management is a direct reflection of poor company practice or policy and the mere removal of the designated premises supervisor may be an inadequate response to the problems presented. Indeed, where subsequent review hearings are generated by representations, it should be rare merely to remove a succession of designated premises supervisors as this would be a clear indication of deeper problems that impact upon the licensing objectives.

11.23 Licensing authorities should also note that modifications of conditions and exclusions of licensable activities may be imposed either permanently or for a temporary period of up to three months. Temporary changes or suspension of the licence for up to three months could impact on the business holding the licence financially and would only be expected to be pursued as an appropriate means of promoting the licensing objectives. So, for instance, a licence could be suspended for a weekend as a means of deterring the holder from allowing the problems that gave rise to the review to happen again. However, it will always be important that any detrimental financial impact that may result from a licensing authority's decision is appropriate and proportionate to the promotion of the licensing objectives. But where premises are found to be trading irresponsibly, the licensing authority should not hesitate, where appropriate to do so, to take tough action to tackle the problems at the premises and, where other measures are deemed insufficient, to revoke the licence.

Reviews arising in connection with crime

11.24 A number of reviews may arise in connection with crime that is not directly connected with licensable activities. For example, reviews may arise because of drugs problems at the premises; money laundering by criminal gangs, the sale of contraband or stolen goods, or the sale of firearms. Licensing authorities do not have the power to judge the criminality or otherwise of any issue. This is a matter for the courts. The licensing authority's role when determining such a review is not therefore to establish the guilt or innocence of any individual but to ensure the promotion of the crime prevention objective.

11.25 Reviews are part of the regulatory process introduced by the 2003 Act and they are not part of criminal law and procedure. There is, therefore, no reason why representations giving rise to a review of a premises licence need be delayed pending the outcome of any criminal proceedings. Some reviews will arise after the conviction in the criminal courts of certain individuals, but not all. In any case, it is for the licensing authority to determine whether the problems associated with the alleged crimes are taking place on the premises and affecting the promotion of the licensing objectives. Where a review follows a conviction, it would also not be for the licensing authority to attempt to go beyond any finding by the courts, which should be treated as a matter of undisputed evidence before them.

11.26 Where the licensing authority is conducting a review on the grounds that the premises have been used for criminal purposes, its role is solely to determine what steps should be taken in connection with the premises licence, for the promotion of the crime prevention objective. It is important to recognise that certain criminal activity or associated problems may be taking place or have taken place despite the best efforts of the licence holder and the staff working at the premises and despite full compliance with the conditions attached to the licence. In such circumstances, the licensing authority is still empowered to take any appropriate steps to remedy the problems. The licensing authority's duty is to take steps with a view to the promotion of the licensing objectives in the interests of the wider community and not those of the individual licence holder.

11.27 There is certain criminal activity that may arise in connection with licensed premises which should be treated particularly seriously. These are the use of the licensed premises:

* for the sale and distribution of Class A drugs and the laundering of the proceeds of drugs crime;
* for the sale and distribution of illegal firearms;
* for the evasion of copyright in respect of pirated or unlicensed films and music, which does considerable damage to the industries affected;

- for the illegal purchase and consumption of alcohol by minors which impacts on the health, educational attainment, employment prospects and propensity for crime of young people;
- for prostitution or the sale of unlawful pornography;
- by organised groups of paedophiles to groom children;
- as the base for the organisation of criminal activity, particularly by gangs;
- for the organisation of racist activity or the promotion of racist attacks;
- for knowingly employing a person who is unlawfully in the UK or who cannot lawfully be employed as a result of a condition on that person's leave to enter;
- for unlawful gambling; and
- for the sale of smuggled tobacco and alcohol.

11.28 It is envisaged that licensing authorities, the police and other law enforcement agencies, which are responsible authorities, will use the review procedures effectively to deter such activities and crime. Where reviews arise and the licensing authority determines that the crime prevention objective is being undermined through the premises being used to further crimes, it is expected that revocation of the licence – even in the first instance – should be seriously considered.

Review of a premises licence following closure order

11.29 Licensing authorities are subject to certain timescales, set out in the legislation, for the review of a premises licence following a closure order. The relevant time periods run concurrently and are as follows:

- when the licensing authority receives notice that a magistrates' court has made a closure order it has 28 days to determine the licence review – the determination must be made before the expiry of the 28th day after the day on which the notice is received;
- the hearing must be held within ten working days, the first of which is the day after the day the notice from the magistrates' court is received;
- notice of the hearing must be given no later than five working days before the first hearing day (there must be five clear working days between the giving of the notice and the start of the hearing).

Review of a premises licence following persistent sales of alcohol to children

11.30 Where persistent sales of alcohol to children have occurred at premises, responsible authorities should consider applying for a review of the licence, whether there has been a prosecution for the offence under section 147A or a closure notice has been given under section 169A of the 2003 Act. In determining the review, the licensing authority should consider revoking the licence if it considers this outcome is appropriate. Responsible authorities should consider taking steps to ensure that a review of the licence is routine in these circumstances.

12. APPEALS

12.1 This chapter provides advice about entitlements to appeal in connection with various decisions made by a licensing authority under the provisions of the 2003 Act. Entitlements to appeal for parties aggrieved by decisions of the licensing authority are set out in Schedule 5 to the 2003 Act.

General

12.2 With the exception of appeals in relation to closure orders, an appeal may be made to any magistrates' court in England or Wales but it is expected that applicants would bring an appeal in a magistrates' court in the area in which they or the premises are situated.

12.3 An appeal has to be commenced by the appellant giving of a notice of appeal to the designated officer for the magistrates' court within a period of 21 days beginning with the day on which the appellant was notified by the licensing authority of the decision which is being appealed.

12.4 The licensing authority will always be a respondent to the appeal, but in cases where a favourable decision has been made for an applicant, licence holder, club or premises user against the representations of a responsible authority or any other person, or the objections of the chief officer of police or local authority exercising environmental health functions, the holder of the premises or personal licence or club premises certificate or the person who gave an interim authority notice or the premises user will also be a respondent to the appeal, and the person who made the relevant representation or gave the objection will be the appellants.

12.5 Where an appeal has been made against a decision of the licensing authority, the licensing authority will in all cases be the respondent to the appeal and may call as a witness a responsible authority or any other person who made representations against the application, if it chooses to do so. For this reason, the licensing authority should consider keeping responsible authorities and others informed of developments in relation to appeals to allow them to consider their position. Provided the court considers it appropriate, the licensing authority may also call as witnesses any individual or body that they feel might assist their response to an appeal.

12.6 The court, on hearing any appeal, may review the merits of the decision on the facts and consider points of law or address both.

12.7 On determining an appeal, the court may:

- dismiss the appeal;
- substitute for the decision appealed against any other decision which could have been made by the licensing authority; or
- remit the case to the licensing authority to dispose of it in accordance with the direction of the court and make such order as to costs as it thinks fit.

Licensing policy statements and Section 182 guidance

12.8 In hearing an appeal against any decision made by a licensing authority, the magistrates' court will have regard to that licensing authority's statement of licensing policy and this Guidance. However, the court would be entitled to depart from either the statement of licensing policy or this Guidance if it considered it was justified to do so because of the individual circumstances of any case. In other words, while the court will normally consider the matter as if it were "standing in the shoes" of the licensing authority, it would be entitled to find that the licensing authority should have departed from its own policy or the Guidance because the particular circumstances would have justified such a decision.

12.9 In addition, the court is entitled to disregard any part of a licensing policy statement or this Guidance that it holds to be ultra vires the 2003 Act and therefore unlawful. The normal course for challenging a statement of licensing policy or this Guidance should be by way of judicial review, but where it is submitted to an appellate court that a statement of policy is itself ultra vires the 2003 Act and this has a direct bearing on the case before it, it would be inappropriate for the court, on accepting such a submission, to compound the original error by relying on that part of the statement of licensing policy affected.

Giving reasons for decisions

12.10 It is important that a licensing authority should give comprehensive reasons for its decisions in anticipation of any appeals. Failure to give adequate reasons could itself give rise to grounds for an appeal. It is particularly important that reasons should also address the extent to which the decision has been made with regard to the licensing authority's statement of policy and this Guidance. Reasons should be promulgated to all the parties of any process which might give rise to an appeal under the terms of the 2003 Act.

Implementing the determination of the magistrates' courts

12.11 As soon as the decision of the magistrates' court has been promulgated, licensing authorities should implement it without delay. Any attempt to delay implementation will only bring the appeal system into disrepute. Standing orders should therefore be in place that on receipt of the decision, appropriate action should be taken immediately unless ordered by the magistrates' court or a higher court to suspend such action (for example, as a result of an on-going judicial review). Except in the case of closure orders, the 2003 Act does not provide for a further appeal against the decision of the magistrates' courts and normal rules of challenging decisions of magistrates' courts will apply.

Provisional statements

12.12 To avoid confusion, it should be noted that a right of appeal only exists in respect of the terms of a provisional statement that is issued rather than one that is refused. This is because the 2003 Act does not empower a licensing authority to refuse to issue a provisional statement. After receiving and considering relevant representations, the licensing authority may only indicate, as part of the statement, that it would consider certain steps to be appropriate for the promotion of the licensing objectives when, and if, an application were made for a premises licence following the issuing of the provisional statement. Accordingly, the applicant or any person who has made relevant representations may appeal against the terms of the statement issued.

13. STATEMENTS OF LICENSING POLICY

Introduction

The Licensing Act 2003

13.1 This chapter provides guidance on the development and preparation of local statements of licensing policy for publication by licensing authorities, the general principles that it is recommended should underpin them, and core content to which licensing authorities are free to add.

General

13.2 Section 5 of the 2003 Act requires a licensing authority to prepare and publish a statement of its licensing policy at least every five years. Such a policy must be published before the authority carries out any function in respect of individual applications and notices made under the terms of the 2003 Act. During the five-year period, the policy must be kept under review and the licensing authority may make any revisions to it as it considers appropriate, for instance in the light of feedback from the local community on whether the licensing objectives are being met. If the licensing authority determines and publishes its policy in this way, a new five-year period commences on the date it is published. Previously, licensing authorities were required to determine their licensing policies for each three-year period. Licensing policies published in respect of the three-year period that began on 7 January 2011 are to be treated as though they apply to a period of five years beginning at that date.

13.3 Where revisions to the section 182 Guidance are made by the Secretary of State, it will be for the licensing authority to determine whether revisions to its own licensing policy statement are appropriate.

Consultation on policies

13.4 Before determining its policy, the licensing authority must consult the persons listed in section 5(3) of the 2003 Act. These are:

- the chief officer of police for the area;
- the fire and rescue authority for the area;
- each Primary Care Trust or Local Health Board for an area any part of which his in the licensing authority's area;
- persons/bodies representative of local premises licence holders;
- persons/bodies representative of local club premises certificate holders;
- persons/bodies representative of local personal licence holders; and
- persons/bodies representative of businesses and residents in its area.

13.5 The views of all these persons or bodies should be given appropriate weight when the policy is determined. It is recognised that in some areas, it may be difficult to identify persons or bodies that represent all parts of industry affected by the provisions of the 2003 Act, but licensing authorities must make reasonable efforts to do so. Licensing authorities should note that the terms of the 2003 Act do not prevent them consulting other bodies or persons.

13.6 Subject to the statutory requirements, it is for each licensing authority to determine the extent of the consultation it should undertake, and whether any particular person or body is representative of the groups described in the 2003 Act. Whilst it is clearly good practice to consult widely, this may not always be necessary or appropriate (for example, where a licensing authority has recently carried out a comprehensive consultation in relation to a revision to its policy made within five years of a full revision to it). As such, it may decide on a simple consultation with those persons listed.

13.7 However, licensing authorities should consider very carefully whether a full consultation is appropriate as a limited consultation may not allow all persons sufficient opportunity to comment on and influence local policy (for example, where an earlier consultation was limited to a particular part of the policy, such as a proposal to introduce a cumulative impact policy).

13.8   When undertaking consultation exercises, licensing authorities should have regard to cost and time. Fee levels are intended to provide full cost recovery of all licensing functions including the preparation and publication of a statement of licensing policy, but this will be based on the statutory requirements. Where licensing authorities exceed these requirements, they will have to absorb those costs themselves.

Fundamental principles

13.9   All statements of policy should begin by stating the four licensing objectives, which the licensing policy should promote. In determining its policy, a licensing authority must have regard to this Guidance and give appropriate weight to the views of consultees.

13.10   While statements of policy may set out a general approach to making licensing decisions, they must not ignore or be inconsistent with provisions in the 2003 Act. For example, a statement of policy must not undermine the right of any person to apply under the terms of the 2003 Act for a variety of permissions and to have any such application considered on its individual merits.

13.11   Similarly, no statement of policy should override the right of any person to make representations on an application or to seek a review of a licence or certificate where provision has been made for them to do so in the 2003 Act.

13.12   Statements of policies should make clear that:

- licensing is about regulating licensable activities on licensed premises, by qualifying clubs and at temporary events within the terms of the 2003 Act; and
- conditions attached to various authorisations will be focused on matters which are within the control of individual licence holders and others with relevant authorisations, i.e. the premises and its vicinity.

13.13   A statement of policy should also make clear that licensing law is not the primary mechanism for the general control of nuisance and anti-social behaviour by individuals once they are away from the licensed premises and, therefore, beyond the direct control of the individual, club or business holding the licence, certificate or authorisation concerned. Nonetheless, it is a key aspect of such control and licensing law will always be part of a holistic approach to the management of the evening and night-time economy in town and city centres.

Licence conditions

13.14   Statements of licensing policy should reflect the general principles regarding licence conditions set out in Chapter 1 of this guidance.

13.15 Statements of licensing policy should include a firm commitment to avoid attaching conditions that duplicate other regulatory regimes as far as possible. Chapter 10 provides further detail on this issue.

Enforcement

13.16 The Government recommends that licensing authorities should establish and set out joint-enforcement protocols with the local police and the other authorities and describe them in their statement of policy. This will clarify the division of responsibilities for licence holders and applicants, and assists enforcement and other authorities to deploy resources more efficiently.

13.17 In particular, these protocols should also provide for the targeting of agreed problem and high-risk premises which require greater attention, while providing a lighter touch for low risk premises or those that are well run. In some local authority areas, the limited validity of public entertainment, theatre, cinema, night café and late night refreshment house licences has in the past led to a culture of annual inspections regardless of whether the assessed risks make such inspections necessary. The 2003 Act does not require inspections to take place save at the discretion of those charged with this role. Principles of risk assessment and targeted inspection (in line with the recommendations of the Hampton review) should prevail and, for example, inspections should not be undertaken routinely but when and if they are judged necessary. This should ensure that resources are used efficiently and for example, are more effectively concentrated on problem premises.

The need for licensed premises

13.18 There can be confusion about the difference between the "need" for premises and the "cumulative impact" of premises on the licensing objectives, for example, on crime and disorder. "Need" concerns the commercial demand for another pub or restaurant or hotel and is a matter for the planning authority and for the market. This is not a matter for a licensing authority in discharging its licensing functions or for its statement of licensing policy.

The cumulative impact of a concentration of licensed premises

What is cumulative impact?

13.19 "Cumulative impact" is not mentioned specifically in the 2003 Act. In this Guidance, it means the potential impact on the promotion of the licensing objectives of a significant number of licensed premises concentrated in one area. The cumulative impact of licensed premises on the promotion of the licensing objectives is a proper matter for a licensing authority to consider in developing its licensing policy statement.

13.20   In some areas, where the number, type or density of premises selling alcohol is high or exceptional, serious problems of nuisance and disorder may be arising or have begun to arise outside or some distance from those premises. Such problems generally occur as a result of large numbers of drinkers being concentrated in an area, for example when leaving premises at peak times or when queuing at fast food outlets or for public transport.

13.21   Queuing in itself may lead to conflict, disorder and anti-social behaviour. Moreover, large concentrations of people may also increase the incidence of other criminal activities such as drug dealing, pick pocketing and street robbery. Local services such as public transport services, public lavatory provision and street cleaning may not be able to meet the demand posed by such concentrations of drinkers leading to issues such as street fouling, littering, traffic and public nuisance caused by concentrations of people who cannot be effectively dispersed quickly.

13.22   Variable licensing hours may facilitate a more gradual dispersal of customers from premises. However, in some cases, the impact on surrounding areas of the behaviour of the customers of all premises taken together will still be greater than the impact of customers of individual premises. These conditions are more likely to arise in town and city centres, but may also arise in other urban centres and the suburbs, for example on smaller high streets with high concentrations of licensed premises.

Evidence of cumulative impact

13.23   There should be an evidential basis for the decision to include a special policy within the statement of licensing policy. Local Community Safety Partnerships and responsible authorities, such as the police and the local authority exercising environmental health functions, may hold relevant information which would inform licensing authorities when establishing the evidence base for introducing a special policy relating to cumulative impact into their licensing policy statement. Information which licensing authorities may be able to draw on to evidence the cumulative impact of licensed premises on the promotion of the licensing objectives includes:

- local crime and disorder statistics, including statistics on specific types of crime and crime hotspots;
- statistics on local anti-social behaviour offences;
- health-related statistics such as alcohol-related emergency attendances and hospital admissions;
- environmental health complaints, particularly in relation to litter and noise;

- complaints recorded by the local authority, which may include complaints raised by local residents or residents' associations;
- residents' questionnaires;
- evidence from local councillors; and
- evidence obtained through local consultation.

13.24 The licensing authority may consider this evidence, alongside its own evidence as to the impact of licensable activities within its area, and consider in particular the times at which licensable activities are carried on. Information which may inform consideration of these issues includes:

- trends in licence applications, particularly trends in applications by types of premises and terminal hours;
- changes in terminal hours of premises;
- premises' capacities at different times of night and the expected concentrations of drinkers who will be expected to be leaving premises at different times.

13.25 Where existing information is insufficient or not readily available, but the licensing authority believes there are problems in its area resulting from the cumulative impact of licensed premises, it can consider conducting or commissioning a specific study to assess the position. This may involve conducting observations of the night-time economy to assess the extent of incidents relating to the promotion of the licensing objectives, such as incidences of criminal activity and anti-social behaviour, examples of public nuisance, specific issues such as underage drinking and the key times and locations at which these problems are occurring.

13.26 In order to identify the areas in which problems are occurring, information about specific incidents can be mapped and, where possible, a time analysis undertaken to identify the key areas and times at which there are specific issues.

13.27 After considering the available evidence and consulting those individuals and organisations listed in section 5(3) of the 2003 Act and any others, a licensing authority may be satisfied that it is appropriate to include an approach to cumulative impact in its licensing policy statement. The special policy should also be considered alongside local planning policy and other factors which may assist in mitigating the cumulative impact of licensed premises, as set out in paragraph 13.39. The licensing authority decides to introduce an approach to cumulative impact, it may decide it is appropriate to indicate in its statement that it is adopting a special policy whereby, when it receives relevant representations, there is a rebuttable presumption that, for example, applications or variation applications which seek to extend the sale or apply of alcohol are refused or subject to certain limitations.

Steps to a special policy

13.28   The steps to be followed in considering whether to adopt a special policy within the statement of licensing policy are summarised below.

- Identify concern about crime and disorder; public safety; public nuisance; or protection of children from harm.
- Consider whether there is good evidence that crime and disorder or nuisance are occurring, or whether there are activities which pose a threat to public safety or the protection of children from harm.
- If such problems are occurring, identify whether these problems are being caused by the customers of licensed premises, or that the risk of cumulative impact is imminent.
- Identify the boundaries of the area where problems are occurring (this can involve mapping where the problems occur and identifying specific streets or localities where such problems arise).
- Consult with those specified in section 5(3) of the 2003 Act, and subject to the outcome of the consultation, include and publish details of the special policy in the licensing policy statement.

Effect of special policies

13.29   The effect of adopting a special policy of this kind is to create a rebuttable presumption that applications for the grant or variation of premises licences or club premises certificates which are likely to add to the existing cumulative impact will normally be refused or subject to certain limitations, following relevant representations, unless the applicant can demonstrate in the operating schedule that there will be no negative cumulative impact on one or more of the licensing objectives. Applicants should give consideration to potential cumulative impact issues when setting out the steps they will take to promote the licensing objectives in their application.

13.30   However, a special policy must stress that this presumption does not relieve responsible authorities (or any other persons) of the need to make a relevant representation, referring to information which had been before the licensing authority when it developed its statement of licensing policy, before a licensing authority may lawfully consider giving effect to its special policy. If there are no representations, the licensing authority must grant the application in terms that are consistent with the operating schedule submitted.

13.31   Once adopted, special policies should be reviewed regularly to assess whether they are needed any longer or if those which are contained in the special policy should be amended.

13.32   The absence of a special policy does not prevent any responsible authority or other person making representations on an application for the grant or variation of a licence on the grounds that the premises will give rise to a negative cumulative impact on one or more of the licensing objectives.

13.33 Special policies may apply to the impact of a concentration of any licensed premises. When establishing its evidence base for introducing a special policy, licensing authorities should be considering the contribution to cumulative impact made by different types of premises within its area, in order to determine the appropriateness of including different types of licensed premises within the special policy.

13.34 It is recommended that licensing authorities should publish contact points in their statements of licensing policy where members of public can obtain advice about whether or not activities should be licensed.

Limitations on special policies relating to cumulative impact

13.35 A special policy should never be absolute. Statements of licensing policy should always allow for the circumstances of each application to be considered properly and for applications that are unlikely to add to the cumulative impact on the licensing objectives to be granted. After receiving relevant representations in relation to a new application for or a variation of a licence or certificate, the licensing authority must consider whether it would be justified in departing from its special policy in the light of the individual circumstances of the case. The impact can be expected to be different for premises with different styles and characteristics. For example, while a large nightclub or high capacity public house might add to problems of cumulative impact, a small restaurant or a theatre may not. If the licensing authority decides that an application should be refused, it will still need to show that the grant of the application would undermine the promotion of one of the licensing objectives and that appropriate conditions would be ineffective in preventing the problems involved.

13.36 Special policies should never be used as a ground for revoking an existing licence or certificate when representations are received about problems with those premises. Where the licensing authority has concerns about the effect of activities at existing premises between midnight and 6am on the promotion of the licensing objectives in a specific area, it may introduce an Early Morning Alcohol Restriction Order (EMRO) if there is sufficient evidence to do so (see chapter 16). The "cumulative impact" on the promotion of the licensing objectives of a concentration of multiple licensed premises should only give rise to a relevant representation when an application for the grant or variation of a licence or certificate is being considered. A review must relate specifically to individual premises, and by its nature, "cumulative impact" relates to the effect of a concentration of many premises. Identifying individual premises in the context of a review would inevitably be arbitrary.

13.37 Special policies can also not be used to justify rejecting applications to vary an existing licence or certificate except where those modifications are directly relevant to the policy (as would be the case with an application to vary a licence with a view to increasing the capacity limits of the premises) and are strictly appropriate for the promotion of the licensing objectives.

13.38 Every application should still be considered individually. Therefore, special policies must not restrict such consideration by imposing quotas – based on either the number of premises or the capacity of those premises. Quotas that indirectly have the effect of predetermining the outcome of any application should not be used because they have no regard to the individual characteristics of the premises concerned.

Other mechanisms for controlling cumulative impact

13.39 Once away from the licensed premises, a minority of consumers will behave badly and unlawfully. To enable the general public to appreciate the breadth of the strategy for addressing these problems, statements of policy should also indicate the other mechanisms both within and outside the licensing regime that are available for addressing such issues. For example:

- planning controls;
- positive measures to create a safe and clean town centre environment in partnership with local businesses, transport operators and other departments of the local authority;
- the provision of CCTV surveillance in town centres, taxi ranks, provision of public conveniences open late at night, street cleaning and litter patrols;
- powers of local authorities to designate parts of the local authority area as places where alcohol may not be consumed publicly;
- the confiscation of alcohol from adults and children in designated areas;
- police enforcement of the general law concerning disorder and anti-social behaviour, including the issuing of fixed penalty notices;
- prosecution for the offence of selling alcohol to a person who is drunk (or allowing such a sale);
- police powers to close down instantly for up to 24 hours (extendable to 48 hours) any licensed premises in respect of which a TEN has effect on grounds of disorder, the likelihood of disorder, or noise emanating from the premises causing a nuisance;
- the power of the police, other responsible authorities or other persons to seek a review of a licence or certificate; and
- Early Morning Alcohol Restriction Orders (EMROs). See Chapter 16.

Designated public places orders

13.40 Where a local authority occupies or manages premises, or where premises are managed on its behalf, and it licences that place for alcohol sales, the Designated Public Place Order (DPPO) will not apply when the licence is being used for alcohol sales (or 30 minutes after), but the place will be subject to the DPPO at all other times[6]. This allows local authorities to promote community events whilst still using DPPOs to tackle the problems of anti-social drinking. Further guidance about DPPOs is available on the Home Office website.

13.41 It should be noted that when one part of a local authority seeks a premises licence of this kind from the licensing authority, the licensing committee and its officers must consider the matter from an entirely neutral standpoint. If relevant representations are made, for example, by local residents or the police, they must be considered fairly by the committee. Anyone making a representation that is genuinely aggrieved by a positive decision in favour of a local authority application by the licensing authority would be entitled to appeal to the magistrates' court and thereby receive an independent review of any decision.

Licensing hours

13.42 With regard to licensing hours, the Government acknowledges that different licensing approaches may be appropriate for the promotion of the licensing objectives in different areas. The 2003 Act gives the licensing authority power to make decisions regarding licensed opening hours as part of the implementation of its licensing policy statement and licensing authorities are best placed to make such decisions based on their local knowledge and in consultation with other responsible authorities. However, licensing authorities must always consider each application and must not impose predetermined licensed opening hours, without giving individual consideration to the merits of each application.

13.43 Statements of licensing policy should set out the licensing authority's approach regarding licensed opening hours and the strategy it considers appropriate for the promotion of the licensing objectives in its area. The statement of licensing policy should emphasise the consideration which will be given to the individual merits of an application. The Government recognises that licensed premises make an important contribution to our local communities, and has given councils a range of tools to effectively manage the different pressures that licensed premises can bring. In determining appropriate strategies around licensed opening hours, licensing authorities cannot seek to restrict the activities of licensed premises where it is not appropriate for the promotion of the licensing objectives to do so.

Children

13.44 It is an offence under the 2003 Act to:

[6]   Licensed premises in general are exempt from the effect of DPPO.

- permit children under the age of 16 who are not accompanied by an adult to be present on premises being used exclusively or primarily for supply of alcohol for consumption on those premises under the authorisation of a premises licence, club premises certificate or where that activity is carried on under the authority of a TEN; and
- to permit the presence of children under 16 who are not accompanied by an adult between midnight and 5am at other premises supplying alcohol for consumption on the premises under the authority of any premises licence, club premises certificate or TEN.

13.45   Outside of these hours, the offence does not prevent the admission of unaccompanied children under 16 to the wide variety of premises where the consumption of alcohol is not the exclusive or primary activity. This does not mean that children should automatically be admitted to such premises and the following paragraphs are therefore of great importance notwithstanding the offences under the 2003 Act. The expression 'exclusively or primarily' should be given its ordinary and natural meaning in the context of the particular circumstances.

13.46   Where it is not clear that the business is predominately for the sale and consumption of alcohol, operators and enforcement agencies should seek to clarify the position before enforcement action is taken. Mixed businesses may be more difficult to classify and in such cases operators and enforcement agencies should consult where appropriate about their respective interpretations of the activities taking place on the premises before any moves are taken which might lead to prosecution.

13.47   The 2003 Act does not automatically permit unaccompanied children under the age of 18 to have free access to premises where the consumption of alcohol is not the exclusive or primary activity or to the same premises even if they are accompanied, or to premises where the consumption of alcohol is not involved. Subject only to the provisions of the 2003 Act and any licence or certificate conditions, admission will always be at the discretion of those managing the premises. The 2003 Act includes no presumption of giving children access but equally, no presumption of preventing their access to licensed premises. Each application and the circumstances of individual premises must be considered on their own merits.

13.48   A statement of licensing policy should not seek to limit the access of children to any premises unless it is appropriate for the prevention of physical, moral or psychological harm to them (please see Chapter 2). It may not be possible for licensing policy statements to anticipate every issue of concern that could arise in respect of children in relation to individual premises and therefore the individual merits of each application should be considered in each case.

13.49 A statement of licensing policy should make clear the range of alternatives which may be considered for limiting the access of children where that is appropriate for the prevention of harm to children. Conditions which may be relevant in this respect are outlined in paragraph 2.30.

13.50 Statements of policy should also make clear that conditions requiring the admission of children to any premises cannot be attached to licences or certificates. Where no licensing restriction is appropriate, this should remain a matter for the discretion of the individual licence holder, club or premises user.

13.51 Venue operators seeking premises licences and club premises certificates should consider including such prohibitions and restrictions in their operating schedules particularly where their own risk assessments have determined that the presence of children is undesirable or inappropriate.

Responsible authority and children

13.52 A statement of licensing policy should indicate which body the licensing authority judges to be competent to act as the responsible authority in relation to the protection of children from harm. This may be the local authority social services department, the Local Safeguarding Children Board or other competent body as agreed locally. It would be practical and useful for statements of licensing policy to include descriptions of the responsible authorities in any area and appropriate contact details.

Children and cinemas

13.53 The statement of policy should make clear that in the case of premises giving film exhibitions, the licensing authority will expect licence holders or clubs to include in their operating schedules arrangements for restricting children from viewing age-restricted films classified according to the recommendations of the British Board of Film Classification or the licensing authority itself (see paragraphs 10.54 to 10.55).

Integrating strategies

13.54 It is recommended that statements of licensing policy should provide clear indications of how the licensing authority will secure the proper integration of its licensing policy with local crime prevention, planning, transport, tourism, equality schemes, cultural strategies and any other plans introduced for the management of town centres and the night-time economy. Many of these strategies are not directly related to the promotion of the licensing objectives, but, indirectly, impact upon them. Co-ordination and integration of such policies, strategies and initiatives are therefore important.

Planning and building control

13.55 The statement of licensing policy should indicate that planning permission, building control approval and licensing regimes will be properly separated to avoid duplication and inefficiency. The planning and licensing regimes involve consideration of different (albeit related) matters. Licensing committees are not bound by decisions made by a planning committee, and vice versa.

13.56 There are circumstances when as a condition of planning permission, a terminal hour has been set for the use of premises for commercial purposes. Where these hours are different to the licensing hours, the applicant must observe the earlier closing time. Premises operating in breach of their planning permission would be liable to prosecution under planning law. Proper integration should be assured by licensing committees, where appropriate, providing regular reports to the planning committee.

Promotion of equality

13.57 A statement of licensing policy should recognise that the Equality Act 2010 places a legal obligation on public authorities to have due regard to the need to eliminate unlawful discrimination, harassment and victimisation; to advance equality of opportunity; and to foster good relations, between persons with different protected characteristics. The protected characteristics are age, disability, gender reassignment, pregnancy and maternity, race, religion or belief, sex, and sexual orientation.

13.58 Public authorities are required to publish information at least annually to demonstrate their compliance with the Equality Duty. The statement of licensing policy should refer to this legislation, and explain how the Equality Duty has been complied with. Further guidance is available from Government Equalities Office and the Equality and Human Rights Commission.

Administration, exercise and delegation of functions

13.59 The 2003 Act provides that the functions of the licensing authority (including its determinations) are to be taken or carried out by its licensing committee (except those relating to the making of a statement of licensing policy or where another of its committees has the matter referred to it). The licensing committee may delegate these functions to sub-committees or in appropriate cases, to officials supporting the licensing authority. Where licensing functions are not automatically transferred to licensing committees, the functions must be carried out by the licensing authority as a whole and not by its executive. Statements of licensing policy should indicate how the licensing authority intends to approach its various functions. Many of the decisions and functions will be purely administrative in nature and statements of licensing policy should underline the principle of delegation in the interests of speed, efficiency and cost-effectiveness.

13.60 The 2003 Act does not prevent the development by a licensing authority of collective working practices with other parts of the local authority or other licensing authorities for work of a purely administrative nature, e.g. mail-outs. In addition, such administrative tasks may be contracted out to private businesses. But any matters regarding licensing decisions must be carried out by the licensing committee, its sub-committees or officers.

13.61 Where, under the provisions of the 2003 Act, there are no relevant representations on an application for the grant of a premises licence or club premises certificate or police objection to an application for a personal licence or to an activity taking place under the authority of a temporary event notice, these matters should be dealt with by officers in order to speed matters through the system. Licensing committees should receive regular reports on decisions made by officers so that they maintain an overview of the general situation. Although essentially a matter for licensing authorities to determine themselves, it is recommended that delegation should be approached in the following way:

Table: Recommended Delegation of Functions

Matters to be dealt with	Full Committee	Sub Committee	Officers
Application for personal licence		If a police objection	If no objection made
Application for personal licence with unspent convictions		All cases	
Application for premises licence/club premises certificate		If a relevant representation made	If no relevant representation made
Application for provisional statement		If a relevant representation made	If no relevant representation made
Application to vary premises licence/ club premises certificate		If a relevant representation	If no relevant representation made
Application to vary designated premises supervisor		If a police objection	All other cases
Request to be removed as designated premises supervisor			All cases

Application for transfer of premises licence		If a police objection	All other cases
Applications for interim authorities		If a police objection	All other cases
Application to review premises licence/ club premises certificate		All cases	
Decision on whether a complaint is irrelevant frivolous vexatious etc			All cases
Decision to object when local authority is a consultee and not the relevant authority considering the application		All cases	
Determination of an objection to a temporary event notice		All cases	
Determination of application to vary premises licence at community premises to include alternative licence condition		If a police objection	All other cases
Decision whether to consult other responsible authorities on minor variation application			All cases
Determination of minor variation application			All cases

14. LICENCE FEES

14.1 The 2003 Act requires a licensing authority to suspend a premises licence or club premises certificate if the annual fee is not paid when it is due. However, this does not apply immediately if the payment was not made before or at the time of the due date because of an administrative error, or because the holder disputed liability for the fee before or at the time of the due date. In either of these cases, there is a grace period of 21 days. This period is intended to allow the licensing authority and the licence or certificate holder an opportunity to resolve the dispute or error. If the dispute or error is not resolved during this 21-day period, the licence will be suspended.

Dispute

14.2 The 2003 Act describes a dispute as one relating to liability to pay the fee at all or relating to its amount. In either case, the licence or certificate holder must notify the licensing authority of the dispute on or before the date on which the fee to which it relates becomes due.

Administrative error

14.3   There is no definition of "administrative error" in the 2003 Act, but it can include an error on the part of the licensing authority, the licence or certificate holder, or any other person. Therefore, "administrative error" will be given its plain, ordinary meaning. An example might be where post has been misdirected.

Suspension

14.4   If a licensing authority suspends a licence or certificate, it must notify the holder in writing and specify the date on which the suspension takes effect; this date must be at least two working days after the day the authority gives the notice. It should be noted that this is the minimum period only, and licensing authorities should consider applying longer periods. The authority may wish to inform the police and other responsible authorities that the licence or certificate has been suspended.

14.5   A suspension ceases to have effect on the day on which the licensing authority receives payment of the outstanding fee from the licence or certificate holder. To enable the licence holder to demonstrate that the licence has been reinstated, the licensing authority is required to give the holder written acknowledgment of receipt as soon as practicable following receipt, and:

a)   If payment was received on a working day, no later than the end of the next working day, or;

b)   If payment was received on a day when the authority is not working, no later than the end of the second working day after the day on which the fee was received.

14.6   Licensing authorities may wish to consider requesting, in the notice of suspension mentioned above, that subsequent payment of the outstanding fee may be made in such manner as would most expeditiously bring it to the attention of the authority. The licensing authority may also wish to inform the police and other responsible authorities that the licence or certificate has been reinstated.

Effects of suspension

14.7   A premises licence or certificate that has been suspended does not have effect to authorise licensable activities. However, it can for example be subject to a hearing or, in the case of a premises licence, an application for transfer. The licence will nevertheless only be reinstated when the outstanding fee has been paid. Formally, the debt is owed by the holder who held the licence at the time it was suspended. However, it may be more likely in practice that the new holder will actually make the payment. The suspension of licences and certificates is only applicable to unpaid annual fees that become due after sections 55A and 92A of the 2003 Act came into force on 25 April 2012. In the case of a licence or certificate where more than one payment year has been missed (since the coming into force of sections 55A and 92A) payment of the outstanding fee in relation to each year will be required to reinstate the licence.

Additional fees for large scale events

14.8   It should be noted that premises licences for large scale events do not automatically attract the higher fee levels set out in the fee regulations made under the 2003 Act, which must be paid in addition to the standard application or variation fees when the premises licence relates to activities attracting the attendance of 5,000 or more. Venues that are permanent or purpose built or structurally altered for the activity are exempt from the additional fee.

14.9   Regulations prescribe that the additional fee for large scale events would not be payable where the premises is a structure which is not a vehicle, vessel or moveable structure, and has been constructed or structurally altered to allow:

- the proposed licensable activities to take place;
- the premises to be modified temporarily, from time to time, if relevant for the proposed licensable activities;
- the proposed number of people on the premises at any one time; and
- the premises to be used in a manner which complies with the operating schedule.

14.10   The full details of where the additional fee is applicable can be found in regulations on the Government's legislation website – **www.legislation-.gov.uk**.

15. REGULATED ENTERTAINMENT

Types of regulated entertainment

15.1   Subject to the conditions, definitions and the exemptions referred to in Schedule 1, the types of entertainment regulated by the 2003 Act are:

- a performance of a play;
- an exhibition of a film;
- an indoor sporting event;
- a boxing or wrestling entertainment (whether indoor or outdoor);
- a performance of live music (but note the changes brought in by the Live Music Act 2012 ("the 2012 Act"), see paragraph 15.10 below);
- any playing of recorded music;
- a performance of dance;
- entertainment of a similar description to a performance of live music, any playing of recorded music or a performance of dance.

15.2 However, these types of entertainment are only regulated where the entertainment takes place in the presence of an audience and is provided, at least partly, to entertain that audience.

Activities that do not constitute "regulated entertainment"

15.3 Licensing authorities should consider whether an activity constitutes the provision of regulated entertainment, taking into account the conditions, definitions and exemptions set out in Schedule 1 to the 2003 Act. This Guidance cannot give examples of every eventuality or possible activity. The following activities, for example, are not regulated entertainment:

- education – teaching students to perform music or to dance;
- activities which involve participation as acts of worship in a religious context;
- activities that take place in places of public religious worship;
- the demonstration of a product – for example, a guitar – in a music shop; or
- the rehearsal of a play or performance of music for a private audience where no charge is made with a view to making a profit (including raising money for charity).

15.4 Of course, anyone involved in the organisation or provision of entertainment activities – whether or not any such activity is licensable – must comply with any applicable duties that may be imposed by other legislation (e.g. crime and disorder, fire, health and safety, noise, nuisance and planning).

Entertainment facilities

15.5 As a result of changes to the 2003 Act made by the 2012 Act, 'entertainment facilities' are no longer licensable. Conditions on a licence that relate solely to entertainment facilities may no longer apply, but note paragraphs 15.18 and 15.19 below.

Private events

15.6 Events that are held in private are not licensable unless those attending are charged for the entertainment with a view to making a profit (including raising money for charity). For example, a party held in a private dwelling for friends featuring amplified live music, where a charge or contribution is made solely to cover the costs of the entertainment would not be regulated entertainment. Similarly, any charge made to the organiser of a private event by musicians, other performers, or their agents does not of itself make that entertainment licensable – it would only do so if the guests attending were themselves charged by the organiser for that entertainment with a view to achieving a profit. The fact that this might inadvertently result in the organiser making a profit would be irrelevant, as long as there had not been an intention to make a profit.

15.7 Schedule 1 to the 2003 Act also makes it clear that before entertainment is regarded as being provided for consideration, a charge has to be:

- made by or on behalf of a person concerned with the organisation or management of the entertainment; and
- paid by or on behalf of some or all of the persons for whom the entertainment is provided.

Pub games

15.8 Games commonly played in pubs and social and youth clubs (such as pool, darts, table tennis and billiards) would only be licensable activities if hosted in the presence of a public audience, to entertain, at least in part, that audience. For example, a darts championship competition is often licensable and could be a licensable activity, but a game of darts played for the enjoyment of the participants is not usually licensable.

Stand up comedy

15.9 Stand-up comedy is not regulated entertainment, and music that is incidental to the main performance would not make it a licensable activity. Licensing authorities should encourage operators to seek their advice, particularly with regard to their policy on enforcement.

Live music

15.10 To encourage more performances of live music, the 2012 Act has amended the 2003 Act by deregulating aspects of the performance of live music so that, in certain circumstances, it is not a licensable activity. However, live music remains licensable:

- where a performance of live music – whether amplified or unamplified – takes place other than between 08:00 and 23:00 on any day;
- where a performance of amplified live music does not take place either on relevant licensed premises, or at a workplace that is not licensed other than for the provision of late night refreshment;
- where a performance of amplified live music takes place at relevant licensed premises, at a time when those premises are not open for the purposes of being used for the supply of alcohol for consumption on the premises;
- where a performance of amplified live music takes place at relevant licensed premises, or workplaces, in the presence of an audience of more than 200 people; or
- where a licensing authority intentionally removes the effect of the deregulation provided for by the 2003 Act (as amended by the 2012 Act) when imposing a condition on a premises licence or certificate as a result of a licence review (see paragraphs 15.23–15.24 below).

15.11 In any of the above circumstances, unless the performance of live music is appropriately authorised by a premises licence, club premises certificate or Temporary Event Notice, allowing it to continue could lead to enforcement action and a review of the alcohol licence or certificate.

Key terms used in the Live Music Act 2012

15.12 Under the 'live music' provisions, 'music' includes vocal or instrumental music or any combination of the two". 'Live music' is a performance of live music in the presence of an audience which it is intended to entertain. While a performance of live music can include the playing of some recorded music, 'live' music requires that the performance does not consist entirely of the playing of recorded music without any additional (substantial and continual) creative contribution being made. So, for example, a drum machine or backing track being used to accompany a vocalist or a band would be part of the performance of amplified live music. A DJ who is merely playing tracks would not be a performance of live music, but might if he or she was performing a set which largely consisted of mixing recorded music to create new sounds. There will inevitably be a degree of judgement as to whether a performance is live music or not and organisers of events should be encouraged to check with their licensing authority if in doubt. In the event of a dispute about whether a performance is live music or not, it will ultimately be for the courts to decide in the individual circumstances of any case.

15.13 A "workplace" is as defined in regulation 2(1) of the Workplace (Health, Safety and Welfare) Regulations 1992 and is anywhere that is made available to any person as a place of work. It is a very wide term which can include outdoor spaces, as well as the means of entry and exit.

15.14 "Audience" – an activity is licensable as regulated entertainment if it falls within one or more of the descriptions of entertainment in paragraph 2 of Schedule 1 to the 2003 Act and takes place in the presence of an audience for whose entertainment (at least in part) it is provided. An audience member need not be, or want to be, entertained: what matters is that an audience is present and that the purpose of the licensable activity is (at least in part) intended to entertain any person present. People may be part of an audience even if they are not located in exactly the same place as the performers, provided they are present within the audible range of the performance. So, for example, if a band is performing in a marquee, people dancing outside that marquee may nevertheless be members of the audience. The audience will not include performers, together with any person who contributes technical skills in substantial support of a performer (for example, a sound engineer or stage technician), during any activities associated with that performance. These activities include setting up before the performance, reasonable breaks (including intervals) between songs and packing up thereafter. Similarly, security staff and bar workers will not form part of the audience while undertaking their duties, which includes reasonable breaks.

15.15 For the purposes of this Chapter only, "relevant licensed premises" refers to premises which are authorised to supply alcohol for consumption on the premises by a premises licence or club premises certificate. Premises cannot benefit from the deregulation introduced by the 2012 Act by virtue of holding an authorisation for the sale of alcohol under a Temporary Event Notice.

15.16 Public performance of live unamplified music that takes place between 08:00 and 23:00 on any day no longer requires a licence in any location. An exception to this is where a specific condition related to live music is included following a review of the premises licence or certificate in respect of relevant licensed premises.

15.17 This amendment to the 2003 Act by the 2012 Act means that section 177 of the 2003 Act now only applies to performances of dance.

Live music – conditions and reviews

15.18 Any existing licence conditions on relevant licensed premises (or conditions added on a determination of a licence application) which relate to live music remain in place but are suspended between the hours of 08:00 and 23:00 on the same day.

15.19 In some instances it will be obvious that a condition relates to live music and will be suspended, for example "during live music all doors and windows must remain closed". In other instances, it might not be so obvious, for example, a condition stating "during Regulated Entertainment all doors and windows must remain closed" would not apply if the only entertainment provided was live music between 08:00 and 23:00 on the same day to an audience of up to 200, but if there was a disco in an adjoining room then the condition would still apply to the room in which the disco was being held.

15.20 However, even where the 2003 Act (as amended by the 2012 Act) has deregulated aspects of the performance of live music, it remains possible to apply for a review of a premises licence or club premises certificate if there are appropriate grounds to do so. On a review of a premises licence or club premises certificate, section 177A(3) of the 2003 Act permits a licensing authority to lift the suspension and give renewed effect to an existing condition relating to live music. Similarly, by section 177A(4), a licensing authority may add a condition relating to live music as if live music were regulated entertainment, and as if that licence or certificate licensed the live music.

15.21 An application for a review in relation to premises can be made by a licensing authority, any responsible authority or any other person. Applications for review must still be relevant to one or more of the licensing objectives and meet a number of further requirements: see Chapter 11 of this guidance for more information about reviews under the 2003 Act.

15.22 More general licensing conditions (e.g. those relating to overall management of potential noise nuisance) that are not specifically related to the provision of entertainment (e.g. signage asking patrons to leave quietly) will remain in place.

Applying conditions to non-licensable activities

15.23 If appropriate for the promotion of the licensing objectives, and there is a link to remaining licensable activities, conditions that relate to non-licensable activities can be added to or altered on that licence or certificate at review following problems occurring at the premises. This has been a feature of licence conditions since the 2003 Act came into force. A relevant example could be the use of conditions relating to large screen broadcasts of certain sporting events which, combined with alcohol consumption, create a genuine risk to the promotion of the licensing objectives. It is also not uncommon for licence conditions relating to the sale of alcohol to restrict access to outside areas, such as unlicensed beer gardens, after a certain time.

15.24 Similarly, while karaoke no longer needs licensing as the provision of entertainment facilities (and will generally be live music – see paragraph 15.12 above) it might, for example, be possible on review to limit the use or volume of a microphone made available for customers, if a problem had occurred because of customers purchasing alcohol for consumption on the premises becoming louder and less aware of causing noise nuisance later in the evening. Another example might be a condition restricting access to a dance floor, where the presence of customers who had been consuming alcohol on the premises had led to serious disorder.

More than one event in the same premises

15.25 The amendments to the 2003 Act made by the 2012 Act do not prevent more than one performance of amplified live music being held concurrently at relevant licensed premises or a workplace, provided that the audience for each such performance is 200 or less. In some circumstances, there will be a clear distinction between performances, for example in separate rooms or on separate floors. However, any person involved in organising or holding these activities must ensure that audiences do not grow or migrate so that more than 200 people are in the audience for any one performance at any time. If uncertain, it might be easier and more flexible to secure an appropriate authorisation for a larger event.

Beer gardens

15.26 Beer gardens are often included on a premises licence. Where a beer garden does not form part of licensed premises and so is not included in plans attached to a premises licence or club premises certificate, it is nevertheless very likely that it will be a workplace. Paragraph 12B of Schedule 1 to the 2003 Act, says that a performance of live music in a workplace that does not have a licence (except to provide late night refreshment) is not regulated entertainment if it takes place between 08:00 and 23:00 on the same day in front of an audience of no more than 200 people.

15.27 However, a licensing authority may, in appropriate circumstances, impose a condition on a licence or certificate that relates to the performance of live music in an unlicensed beer garden using any associated licence or certificate. Provided such a condition is lawfully imposed, it takes effect in accordance with its terms.

15.28 Live amplified music that takes place in a beer garden is exempt from licensing requirements, provided that the beer garden is included in the licence applying to the relevant licensed premises, and the performance takes place between 08:00 and 23:00 on the same day before an audience of 200 or fewer people. Unamplified music that takes place in a beer garden between 08:00 and 23:00 is exempt from licensing requirements, whether or not the beer garden is part of the premises licence.

Morris dancing

15.29 The amendments to the 2003 Act by the 2012 Act extend the exemption relating to music accompanying Morris dancing in paragraph 11 of Schedule 1 to the 2003 Act, so that it applies to the playing of live or recorded music as an integral part of a performance of Morris dancing, or similar activity.

Incidental music

15.30 In addition to provisions introduced by the 2012 Act, the performance of live music and playing of recorded music is not regulated entertainment under the 2003 Act to the extent that it is "incidental" to another activity which is not itself one of the entertainments described in paragraph 2(1) of Schedule 1 to the 2003 Act.

15.31 Whether or not music is "incidental" to another activity will depend on the facts of each case. In considering whether or not music is incidental, one relevant factor will be whether or not, against a background of the other activities already taking place, the addition of music will create the potential to undermine the promotion of one or more of the four licensing objectives of the 2003 Act. Other factors might include some or all of the following:

- Is the music the main, or one of the main, reasons for people attending the premises?
- Is the music advertised as the main attraction?
- Does the volume of the music disrupt or predominate over other activities, or could it be described as 'background' music?

15.32 Conversely, factors which would not normally be relevant in themselves include:

- The number of musicians, e.g. an orchestra providing incidental music at a large exhibition.
- Whether musicians are paid.
- Whether the performance is pre-arranged.
- Whether a charge is made for admission to the premises.

Spontaneous music, singing and dancing

15.33 The spontaneous performance of music, singing or dancing does not amount to the provision of regulated entertainment and is not a licensable activity because the premises at which these spontaneous activities occur would not have been made available to those taking part for that purpose.

16. EARLY MORNING ALCOHOL RESTRICTION ORDERS

General

16.1 This chapter provides guidance to licensing authorities about Early Morning Alcohol Restriction Orders ("EMROs"). The power conferred on licensing authorities to make, vary or revoke an EMRO is set out in sections 172A to 172E of the 2003 Act. This power enables a licensing authority to prohibit the sale of alcohol for a specified time period between the hours of 12am and 6am in the whole or part of its area, if it is satisfied that this would be appropriate for the promotion of the licensing objectives.

16.2 EMROs are designed to address recurring problems such as high levels of alcohol-related crime and disorder in specific areas at specific times; serious public nuisance; and other instances of alcohol-related anti-social behaviour which is not directly attributable to specific premises.

16.3   An EMRO:

- applies to the supply of alcohol authorised by premises licences, club premises certificates and temporary event notices;
- applies for any period beginning at or after 12am and ending at or before 6am. It does not have to apply on every day of the week, and can apply for different time periods on different days of the week;
- applies for a limited or unlimited period (for example, an EMRO could be introduced for a few weeks to apply to a specific event);
- applies to the whole or any part of the licensing authority's area;
- will not apply to any premises on New Year's Eve (defined as 12am to 6am on 1 January every year);
- will not apply to the supply of alcohol to residents by accommodation providers between 12am and 6am, provided the alcohol is sold through mini-bars and/or room service; and
- will not apply to a relaxation of licensing hours by virtue of an order made under section 172 of the 2003 Act.

The EMRO process

16.4   An EMRO can apply to the whole or part of the licensing authority's area. The area may, for example, comprise a single floor of a shopping complex or exclude premises which have clearly demonstrated to the licensing authority that the licensable activities carried on there do not contribute to the problems which form the basis for the proposed EMRO.

16.5   If the licensing authority already has a Cumulative Impact Policy ("CIP") in its Licensing Policy Statement, it should consider the relationship between the CIP and proposed EMRO area, and the potential overall impact on its local licensing policy.

Evidence

16.6   The licensing authority should be satisfied that it has sufficient evidence to demonstrate that its decision is appropriate for the promotion of the licensing objectives. This requirement should be considered in the same manner as other licensing decisions, such as the determination of applications for the grant of premises licences. The licensing authority should consider evidence from partners, including responsible authorities and local Community Safety Partnerships, alongside its own evidence, to determine whether an EMRO would be appropriate for the promotion of the licensing objectives.

16.7 When establishing its evidence base, a licensing authority may wish to consider the approach set out in paragraphs 13.23 to 13.26 of this Guidance which includes indicative types of evidence, although this should not be considered an exhaustive list of the types of evidence which may be relevant.

Introducing an EMRO

16.8 An EMRO is a powerful tool which will prevent licensed premises in the area to which the EMRO relates from supplying alcohol during the times at which the EMRO applies. The licensing authority should consider whether other measures may address the problems that they have identified as the basis for introducing an EMRO. As set out in paragraphs 9.38–9.40 of this Guidance, when determining whether a step is appropriate to promote the licensing objectives, a licensing authority is not required to decide that no lesser step will achieve the aim, but should consider the potential burden that would be imposed on premises licence holders as well as the potential benefits in terms of promoting the licensing objectives. Other measures that could be taken instead of making an EMRO might include:

- introducing a CIP;
- reviewing licences of specific problem premises;
- encouraging the creation of business-led best practice schemes in the area; and
- using other mechanisms such as those set out in paragraph [13.39] of this Guidance.

16.9 If the licensing authority has identified a problem in a specific area attributable to the supply of alcohol at two or more premises in that area, and has sufficient evidence to demonstrate that it is appropriate for the promotion of the licensing objectives, it can propose making an EMRO. The licensing authority should first decide on the matters which must be the subject of the proposal. These are:

- the days (and periods on those days) on which the EMRO would apply;
- the area to which the EMRO would apply;
- the period for which the EMRO would apply (if it is a finite period); and
- the date from which the proposed EMRO would apply.

In relation to the date when it plans to introduce the EMRO, the licensing authority should note that this may change when it is specified in the final order.

Advertising an EMRO

16.10 The proposed EMRO must be advertised. The licensing authority should include a short summary of the evidence and the manner in which representations can be made in the document, as well as the details of the proposed EMRO. The proposal must be advertised for at least 42 days (a reference in this Chapter to a period of "days" means a period made up of any days and not only working days). The licensing authority must publish the proposal on its website and in a local newspaper. If no newspaper exists, it must be published in a local newsletter, circular or similar document. The licensing authority must also send a notice of the proposal to all affected people in its area. They are:

- holders of (and applicants for) premises licences or club premises certificates to which the proposed EMRO would apply;
- premises users in relation to TENs to which the proposed EMRO would apply;
- those who have received a provisional statement in respect of a premises to which the proposed EMRO would apply.

16.11 Licensing authorities must, moreover, display a notice of the proposal in the area to which the EMRO would apply, in a manner which is likely to bring the proposal to the attention of those who may have an interest in it.

16.12 The licensing authority should also inform responsible authorities in its area and neighbouring licensing authorities of its proposal to make an EMRO. It may also like to consider what further steps could be taken, in any particular case, to publicise the proposal in order to draw it to the wider attention of any other persons who are likely to have an interest in it.

Representations

16.13 Those who are affected by a proposed EMRO, responsible authorities or any other person have 42 days (starting on the day after the day on which the proposed EMRO is advertised) to make relevant representations. To be considered a relevant representation, a representation must:

- be about the likely effect of the making of the EMRO on the promotion of the licensing objectives;
- be made in writing in the prescribed form and manner, setting out the EMRO to which it relates and the nature of the representation;
- be received within the deadline; and

- if made by a person other than a responsible authority, not be frivolous or vexatious. Chapter 9 of this Guidance gives further advice on determining whether a representation is frivolous or vexatious.

Representations can be made in relation to any aspect of the proposed EMRO. If a licensing authority decides that a representation is not relevant, it should consider informing the person who has made that representation.

16.14 Responsible authorities may wish to make representations, as may affected persons (as set out in the above paragraph).

16.15 Others may also wish to make representations about the proposed EMRO. These persons could include, but are not limited to:

- residents;
- employees of affected businesses;
- owners and employees of businesses outside the proposed EMRO area; and
- users of the late night economy.

Hearings

16.16 If a relevant representation or representations are received, the licensing authority must hold a hearing to consider them (unless the authority and anyone who has made representations agree that this is unnecessary). The licensing authority should consider, based on the number of relevant representations received by it and any other circumstances it considers appropriate, whether to hold the hearing over several days, which could be arranged to take place other than on consecutive working days.

16.17 Licensing authorities should be familiar with the hearing process as it has similarities with other processes under the 2003 Act. Further guidance on hearings can be found in Chapter 9 of this Guidance (paragraphs 9.27 to 9.37). However, licensing authorities should note the following key points in relation to a hearing about a proposed EMRO:

- the hearing must be commenced within 30 working days, beginning with the day after the end of the period during which representations may be made;
- the hearing do not have to take place on consecutive working days, if an authority considers this to be necessary to enable it to consider any of the representations made by a party or if it considers it to be in the public interest;
- a licensing authority must give its determination within 10 working days of the conclusion of the hearing; and
- the authority is not required to notify those making representations of its determination so that the determination may be put before the full council of the authority to decide whether or not to make the EMRO.

16.18 The licensing authority will determine the manner in which the hearing will be conducted in accordance with the Licensing Act 2003 (Hearings) Regulations 2005. If a licensing authority determines that a representation is frivolous or vexatious, it must notify in writing the person who made the representation.

16.19 As a result of the hearing, the licensing authority has three options:

- to decide that the proposed EMRO is appropriate for promotion of the licensing objectives;
- to decide that the proposed EMRO is not appropriate for the promotion of the objectives and therefore that the process should be ended;
- to decide that the proposed EMRO should be modified. In this case, if the authority proposes that the modified EMRO should differ from the initial proposal in relation to the area specified, any day not in the initial proposal or the period of any day specified, the authority should advertise what is in effect a new proposal to make an EMRO in the manner described above, so that further representations are capable of being made.

Final EMRO

16.20 If the licensing authority is satisfied that the proposed order is appropriate for the promotion of the licensing objectives, its determination must be put to the full council for its final decision.

16.21 The matters set out in the final order must be no different from the matters set out in the proposal to make the order, subject to the caveat described above in paragraph 16.18. The order must be set out in the prescribed form and contain the prescribed content.

16.22 No later than 7 days after the day on which the EMRO is made, the licensing authority must send a notice to all affected persons of the EMRO, and make the order available for at least 28 days on its website and by displaying a notice in the EMRO area. A licensing authority should retain details of the EMRO on its website for as long as the EMRO is in force. It is recommended that the licensing authority advises neighbouring licensing authorities and the Secretary of State that the order has been made, the nature of the order and when (and for how long) it will take effect.

16.23 The licensing authority should monitor the effectiveness of the EMRO to ensure it continues to be appropriate for the promotion of the licensing objectives and periodically review whether it is appropriate to continue to apply it. The licensing authority should consider setting out its policy in relation to reviewing EMROs (if any) in its statement of licensing policy.

16.24 The variation or revocation of an order requires the licensing authority to undertake the same process as that which applied on its introduction; that is after gathering the appropriate evidence, it advertises its new EMRO proposal, following the process set out above so that those affected and anyone else can make representations.

16.25 If an order applies for a finite period, the order will cease to apply on its last day. If the licensing authority wishes to introduce a further (new) EMRO, it must follow the full process for proposing a new EMRO.

16.26 Licensing authorities should update their statement of licensing policy (in accordance with section 5 of the 2003 Act) to include reference to the EMRO as soon as reasonably possible.

Exceptions to an EMRO

16.27 EMROs will not apply on New Year's Eve in recognition of its status as a national celebration. The supply of alcohol to residents through mini-bars and room service in premises with overnight accommodation will also not be subject to an EMRO.

Enforcement of EMROS

16.28 The supply of alcohol in contravention of an EMRO is an 'unauthorised licensable activity' which is an offence under section 136 of the 2003 Act. Moreover, it may result in a closure notice being served on the premises under section 19 of the Criminal Justice and Police Act 2001 as a precursor to an application for a closure order under section 21 of that Act. This may alternatively, result in the licence being reviewed on crime prevention grounds. Further information on reviews can be found in Chapter 11 of this Guidance. 16.29 An EMRO overrides all authorisations to supply alcohol under the 2003 Act (including temporary event notices). It is immaterial whether an authorisation was granted before or after an EMRO was made as there are no authorisations that have the effect of authorising the sale of alcohol during the EMRO period, with the only exception being a licensing hours order made under section 172 of the 2003 Act.

EXPLANATORY MEMORANDUM TO THE AMENDED GUIDANCE ISSUED UNDER SECTION 182 OF THE LICENSING ACT 2003, DATED OCTOBER 2012

1. This explanatory memorandum has been prepared by the Home Office ("the Department") and is laid before Parliament by command of Her Majesty.

2.   **Purpose of the guidance**

    2.1 The Secretary of State is revising the guidance issued under section 182 of the Licensing Act 2003 ("the 2003 Act") to provide advice to licensing authorities in relation to the implementation of new provisions in the 2003 Act as a result of amendments made to that Act by the Police Reform and Social Responsibility Act 2011 ("the 2011 Act") and the Live Music Act 2012 ("the 2012 Act").

3.   **Matters of special interest to the Joint Committee on Statutory Instruments**

    3.1 None.

4.   **Legislative context**

    4.1 The 2003 Act provides a system of authorisation for the following activities (referred to as "licensable activities"), namely: the sale by retail of alcohol; the supply of alcohol by or on behalf of a club to, or to the order of, a member of the club; the provision of regulated entertainment; and the provision of late night refreshment. It is a criminal offence to carry on, or attempt to carry on, a licensable activity on or from premises without an appropriate authorisation under the 2003 Act. Such an authorisation may comprise a premises licence, a club premises certificate or a temporary event notice.

    4.2 The 2003 Act provides a framework within which licensing authorities process and determine applications and exercise other licensing functions. By section 182 of the 2003 Act, the Secretary of State must issue guidance to licensing authorities on the discharge of their functions under the 2003 Act. Licensing authorities must have regard to this guidance but may depart from it if they have good reason to do so, although any departure may give rise to an appeal or judicial review. The Secretary of State may also issue revised guidance from time to time. The introduction of the amendments to the 2003 Act made by the 2011 Act and the 2012 Act makes it necessary to issue the revised guidance to which this memorandum relates.

5.   **Territorial extent and application**

    5.1. This revised guidance applies in England and Wales only.

6.   **European Convention on Human Rights**

    6.1 As the guidance is subject to negative resolution procedure and does not amend primary legislation, no statement is required.

7.   **Policy background**

    • ***What is being done and why***

    Amendments by the 2012 Act

7.1 The 2012 Act began as a Private Member's Bill. This Bill received Government support as it was consistent with the Coalition commitment to remove red tape that prevents live music performances; its aim was to deregulate live music performances in "low risk" scenarios and environments, and was compatible with the Government's drive to promote economic growth and remove unnecessary regulation on businesses

7.2 The 2012 Act amended the 2003 Act so that the following public performances of live music taking place between 8am and 11pm are no longer licensable activities:

- unamplified live music in any location and which in certain circumstances, is not precluded by review conditions;
- amplified music in premises authorised to supply alcohol for consumption on the premises by a premises licence or club premises certificate under the 2003 Act where the live music is performed, at a time when the premises are open for the supply of alcohol for consumption on the premises, to audiences of 200 or less (and is not precluded by review conditions); and
- amplified music in other workplaces which are not licensed under the 2003 Act (or which are licensed only for the provision of late night refreshment), where live music is performed to audiences of 200 or less.

7.3 In addition, the 2012 Act amended Schedule 1 to the 2003 Act to remove the definition of provision of entertainment facilities and extended the exemption relating to music accompanying morris dancing (or similar activities) to apply to the performance of live music (amplified or unamplified) or the playing of recorded music which forms an integral part of that activity.

Early Morning Alcohol Restriction Orders

7.4 As part of the Government's commitment to overhaul alcohol licensing to tackle alcohol-related crime and disorder and resulting harms, a number of relevant measures were introduced or amended by the 2011 Act. These included Early Morning Alcohol Restriction Orders (EMROs).

7.5 EMROs are a tool which licensing authorities can use to address certain, specific problems caused by the late night supply of alcohol in their areas. Licensing authorities will be able to use EMROs to prohibit sales of alcohol in the whole or a part of their areas for any specified period between 12 midnight and 6am, if they have evidence of specific problems and consider that making the EMRO is appropriate for the promotion of the licensing objectives.

Revisions to the guidance

7.6 As a result of the legislative changes described above, the guidance is being revised to provide licensing authorities with advice in relation to their exercise of these new functions. Moreover, the guidance has been subject to a number of additional minor revisions to improve clarity and brevity in some areas.

- **Consolidation**

7.7 Not applicable.

8.   **Consultation outcome**

Live Music Act changes

8.1 The content of the revised guidance on regulated entertainment (chapter 15) has not been the subject of a full public consultation because the revisions are necessary to reflect the changes made by the 2012 Act to the 2003 Act, which were the subject of earlier consultation. A public consultation on the deregulation of live music was undertaken by the Department for Culture, Media and Sport between 31st December 2009 and 26th April 2010. This generated over 900 responses, including views from live music organisations, local authorities and members of the public. Details of the consultation, as well as the responses, are available on the website of the Department for Culture, Media and Sport at http://www.culture.gov.uk/.

8.2 The preparation of this revised Chapter 15 of the guidance is also informed by consultation with a technical advisory group comprising representatives of the licensed trade, licensing law specialists, organisations representing community and resident groups, the police, licensing authorities and local government and a six-week technical consultation between 22nd August and 28th September 2012.

Early Morning Alcohol Restriction Orders

8.3 Early Morning Alcohol Restriction Orders and other measures in the 2011 Act were previously the subject of consultation between July and September 2010. This consultation generated over 1,000 formal responses and over 2,500 campaign responses. Consultation on further detail in relation to Early Morning Alcohol Restriction Orders took place by virtue of the "Dealing with the Problems of Late Night Drinking" consultation between January and April 2012; this generated 631 formal responses. Details of both consultation exercises and the Government's responses are available on the Home Office website at http://www.homeoffice.gov.uk/ The content of the guidance in relation to this new measure has also been informed by consultation with a technical working group.

9.   **Guidance**

9.1 Not applicable.

10. **Impact**

10.1 Chapter 15 of the revised guidance reflects changes made by the 2012 Act to the 2003 Act. A copy of the impact assessment that has been prepared by the Department of Culture, Media and Sport on the introduction of the 2012 Act is available at www.culture.gov.uk.

10.2 Chapter 16 of the revised guidance on Early Morning Alcohol Restriction Orders reflects changes made by the 2011 Act to the 2003 Act. The changes made to or under the 2003 Act were the subject of an impact assessment and this is available on the Home Office website at www.homeoffice.gov.uk.

10.3 An impact assessment has not been prepared for this revised guidance.

11. **Regulating small business**

11.1 This revised guidance applies to small business.

11.2 It is expected that any costs for small businesses arising from the implementation of the 2012 Act will be greatly outweighed by the benefits. The removal of administrative burdens as a result of the 2012 Act is expected to benefit smaller live music events and venues in particular.

11.3 The amended Guidance reflects the introduction of measures on Early Morning Alcohol Restriction Orders which will impact on premises operating in the late night economy, including small businesses. Impact assessments were produced for the legislative measures which amended and introduced these measures. These are available on the Home Office website at www.homeoffice.gov.uk.

12. **Monitoring and review**

12.1 The Government will continue to monitor and review the statutory guidance, including these revisions, as to their impact on licensing authorities and others to whom this guidance is relevant.

13. **Contact**

13.1 Helen Brewis at the Home Office, telephone 0207 035 8716 or e-mail: Helen.Brewis@homeoffice.gsi.gov.uk, can answer queries regarding the instrument. Stuart Roberts, Department for Culture, Media and Sport, on 020 7211 6099 or stuart.roberts@culture.gsi.gov.uk can answer queries regarding the changes introduced as a result of the 2012 Act.

Supporting Guidance – Pools of Conditions

The content of this guidance broadly reflects but is not the statutory guidance (or any part of the statutory guidance) issued by the Secretary of State under section 182 of the Licensing Act 2003. This good practice guidance should be viewed as indicative and may be subject to change. Revised statutory guidance issued under section 182 of the Licensing Act 2003 was laid in Parliament on 25 April 2012 and is available on the Home Office website.

CORE PRINCIPLES

1. Licensing authorities and other responsible authorities (in considering applications) and applicants for premises licences and clubs premises certificates (in preparing their operating schedules) should consider whether the measures set out below are appropriate to promote the licensing objectives.

2. Any risk assessment to identify appropriate measures should consider the individual circumstances of the premises and the nature of the local area, and take into account a range of factors including:

- the nature, type and location of the venue;
- the activities being conducted there and the potential risk which these activities could pose to the local area;
- the location (including the locality in which the premises are situated and knowledge of any local initiatives); and
- the anticipated clientele.

Under no circumstances should licensing authorities regard these conditions as standard conditions to be automatically imposed in all cases.

3. Any individual preparing an operating schedule or club operating schedule is at liberty to volunteer any measure, such as those below, as a step they intend to take to promote the licensing objectives. When measures are incorporated into the licence or certificate, they become enforceable under the law and breach could give rise to prosecution.

4. Licensing authorities should carefully consider conditions to ensure that they are not only appropriate but realistic, practical and achievable, so that they are capable of being met. Failure to comply with conditions attached to a licence or certificate could give rise to a prosecution, in particular, as the provision of unauthorised licensable activities under the 2003 Act, which, on conviction would be punishable by a fine of up to £20,000 or up to six months imprisonment or both. As such, it would be wholly inappropriate to impose conditions outside the control of those responsible for the running of the premises. It is also important that conditions which are imprecise or difficult to enforce must be excluded.

PART I. CONDITIONS RELATING TO THE PREVENTION OF CRIME AND DISORDER

Radio links and telephone communications

Two-way radio links and telephone communications connecting staff of premises and clubs to local police and other premises can enable rapid responses to situations that may endanger the customers and staff on and around licensed premises. It is recommended that radio links or telephone communications systems should be considered for licensed premises in city and town centre leisure areas with a high density of premises selling alcohol. These conditions may also be appropriate in other areas. It is recommended that a condition requiring a radio or telephone link to the police should include the following requirements:

- the equipment is kept in working order (when licensable activities are taking place);
- the link is activated, made available to and monitored by the designated premises super visor or a responsible member of staff at all times that the premises are open to the public;
- relevant police instructions/directions are complied with where possible; and
- instances of crime or disorder are reported via the radio link by the designated premises super visor or a responsible member of staff to an agreed police contact point.

Door supervisors

Conditions relating to the provision of door super visors and security teams may be valuable in relation to:

- keeping out individuals excluded by court bans or by the licence holder;
- searching those suspected of carrying illegal drugs, or carrying offensive weapons;
- assisting in the implementing of the premises' age verification policy; and

- ensuring that queues outside premises and departure of customers from premises do not undermine the licensing objectives.

Where the presence of door supervisors conducting security activities is to be a condition of a licence, which means that they would have to be registered with the Security Industry Authority, it may also be appropriate for conditions to stipulate:

- That a sufficient number of supervisors be available (possibly requiring both male and female supervisors);
- the displaying of name badges;
- the carrying of proof of registration; and
- where, and at what times, they should be in operation.

Door supervisors also have a role to play in ensuring public safety (see Part 2) and the prevention of public nuisance (see Part 4).

Restricting access to glassware

Traditional glassware and bottles may be used as weapons or result in accidents and can cause very serious injuries. Conditions can prevent sales of drinks in glass for consumption on the premises. This should be expressed in clear terms and can include the following elements:

- no glassware, whether open or sealed, shall be given to customers on the premises whether at the bar or by staff service away from the bar; or
- no customers carrying glassware shall be admitted to the premises at any time that the premises are open to the public (note: this needs to be carefully worded where off-sales also take place).

In appropriate circumstances, the condition could include exceptions, for example, as follows:

- but bottles containing wine may be given to customers for consumption with a table meal by customers who are seated in an area set aside from the main bar area for the consumption of food.

The banning of glass may also be a relevant and appropriate measure to promote public safety (see Part 2).

Alternatives to traditional glassware

Where appropriate, consideration should therefore be given to conditions requiring the use of safer alternatives to prevent crime and disorder, and in the interests of public safety. Location and style of the venue and the activities carried on there are particularly important in assessing whether a condition is appropriate. For example, the use of glass containers on the terraces of some outdoor sports grounds may obviously be of concern, and similar concerns may also apply to indoor sports events such as boxing matches. Similarly, the use of alternatives to traditional glassware may be an appropriate condition during the showing of televised live sporting events, such as international football matches, when there may be high states of excitement and emotion.

Open containers not to be taken from the premises

Drinks purchased in licensed premises or clubs may be taken from those premises for consumption elsewhere. This is lawful where premises are licensed for the sale of alcohol for consumption off the premises. However, consideration should be given to a condition preventing customers from taking alcoholic and other drinks from the premises in open containers (e.g. glasses and opened bottles) for example, by requiring the use of bottle bins on the premises. This may again be appropriate to prevent the use of these containers as offensive weapons, or to prevent consumption of alcohol, in surrounding streets after individuals have left the premises. Restrictions on taking open containers from the premises may also be appropriate measures to prevent public nuisance (see Part 4).

CCTV

The presence of CCTV cameras can be an important means of deterring and detecting crime at and immediately outside licensed premises. Conditions should not just consider a requirement to have CCTV on the premises, but also the precise location of each camera, the requirement to maintain cameras in working order, to retain recordings for an appropriate period of time and produce images from the system in a required format immediately to the police and local authority. The police should provide individuals conducting risk assessments as part of preparing their operating schedules with advice on the use of CCTV to prevent crime.

Restrictions on drinking areas

It may be appropriate to restrict the areas of the premises where alcoholic drinks may be consumed after they have been purchased. An example would be at a sports ground where it is appropriate to prevent the consumption of alcohol on the terracing during particular sports events. Conditions should not only specify these areas, but indicate the circumstances and times during which the ban would apply.

Restrictions on drinking areas may also be relevant and appropriate measures to prevent public nuisance (see Part 4).

Capacity limits

Capacity limits are most commonly made a condition of a licence on public safety grounds (see Part 2), but can also be considered for licensed premises or clubs where overcrowding may lead to disorder and violence. If such a condition is appropriate, door supervisors may be required to ensure that the numbers are appropriately controlled (see above).

Proof of age cards

It is unlawful for persons aged under 18 years to buy or attempt to buy alcohol just as it is unlawful to sell or supply alcohol to them. To prevent the commission of these criminal offences, the mandatory conditions require licensed premises to ensure that they have in place an age verification policy. This requires the production of age verification (which must meet defined criteria) before alcohol is served to persons who appear to staff at the premises to be under 18 (or other minimum age set by premises).

Such verification must include the individual's photograph, date of birth and a holographic mark e.g. driving licence, passport, military ID. Given the value and importance of such personal documents, and because not everyone aged 18 years or over necessarily has such documents, the Government endorses the use of ID cards which bear the PASS (Proof of Age Standards Scheme) hologram. PASS is the UK's national proof of age accreditation scheme which sets and maintains minimum criteria for proof of age card issuers to meet. The inclusion of the PASS hologram on accredited cards, together with the verification made by card issuers regarding the personal details of an applicant, gives the retailer the assurance that the holder is of relevant age to buy or be served age-restricted goods. PASS cards are available to people under the age of 18 for other purposes such as access to 15 rated films at cinema theatres so care must be taken to check that the individual is over 18 when attempting to purchase or being served alcohol.

Crime prevention notices

It may be appropriate at some premises for notices to be displayed which warn customers of the prevalence of crime which may target them. Some premises may be reluctant to voluntarily display such notices for commercial reasons. For example, in certain areas, a condition attached to a premises licence or club premises certificate might require the display of notices at the premises which warn customers about the need to be aware of pickpockets or bag snatchers, and to guard their property. Similarly, it may be appropriate for notices to be displayed which advise customers not to leave bags unattended because of concerns about terrorism. Consideration could be given to a condition requiring a notice to display the name of a contact for customers if they wish to report concerns.

Drinks promotions

Licensing authorities should not attach standardised blanket conditions promoting fixed prices for alcoholic drinks to premises licences or club licences or club premises certificates in an area. This may be unlawful under current law. It is also likely to be unlawful for licensing authorities or the police to promote generalised voluntary schemes or codes of practice in relation to price discounts on alcoholic drinks, 'happy hours' or drinks promotions. The mandatory licensing conditions (see chapter 10 of the statutory guidance) ban defined types of behaviour referred to as 'irresponsible promotions'.

Signage

It may be appropriate that the hours at which licensable activities are permitted to take place are displayed on or immediately outside the premises so that it is clear if breaches of these terms are taking place. Similarly, it may be appropriate for any restrictions on the admission of children to be displayed on or immediately outside the premises to deter those who might seek admission in breach of those conditions.

Large capacity venues used exclusively or primarily for the "vertical" consumption of alcohol (HVVDS)

Large capacity "vertical drinking" premises, sometimes called High Volume Vertical Drinking establishments (HVVDs), are premises that have exceptionally high capacities, are used primarily or exclusively for the sale and consumption of alcohol, and provide little or no seating for their customers.

Where appropriate, conditions can be attached to licences for these premises which require adherence to:

- a prescribed capacity;
- an appropriate ratio of tables and chairs to customers based on the capacity; and
- the presence of security staff holding the appropriate SIA licence or exemption (see Chapter 10 to control entry for the purpose of compliance with the capacity limit).

PART 2. CONDITIONS RELATING TO PUBLIC SAFETY

The attachment of conditions to a premises licence or club premises certificate will not relieve employers of their duties to comply with other legislation, including the Health and Safety at Work Act 1974 and associated regulations; and, especially, the requirements under the Management of Health and Safety at Work Regulations 1999 and the Regulatory Reform (Fire Safety) Order 2005 to undertake risk assessments. Employers should assess the risks, including risks from fire, and take measures necessary to avoid and control them. Conditions enforcing these requirements are therefore inappropriate.

From 1 October 2006 the Regulatory Reform (Fire Safety) Order 2005 replaced previous fire safety legislation. Licensing authorities should note that under article 43 of the Regulatory Reform (Fire Safety) Order 2005 any conditions imposed by the licensing authority that relate to any requirements or prohibitions that are or could be imposed by the Order have no effect. This means that licensing authorities should not seek to impose fire safety conditions where the Order applies. See Chapter 2 of the statutory guidance for more detail about the Order or http://www.communities.gov.uk/fire/firesafety/firesafetylaw/

General

Additional matters relating to cinemas and theatres are considered in Part 3. It should also be recognised that special issues may arise in connection with outdoor and large scale events.

In addition, to considering the points made in this Part, those preparing operating schedules or club operating schedules; and licensing authorities and other responsible authorities may consider the following guidance, where relevant:

- Model National and Standard Conditions for Places of Public Entertainment and Associated Guidance ISBN 1 904031 11 0 (Entertainment Technology Press – ABTT Publications)
- The Event Safety Guide – A guide to health, safety and welfare at music and similar events (HSE 1999) ("The Purple Book") ISBN 0 7176 2453 6
- Managing Crowds Safely (HSE 2000) ISBN 0 7176 1834 X
- 5 Steps to Risk Assessment: Case Studies (HSE 1998) ISBN 07176 15804
- The Guide to Safety at Sports Grounds (The Stationery Office, 1997) ("The Green Guide") ISBN 0 11 300095 2
- Safety Guidance for Street Arts, Carnival, Processions and Large Scale Performances published by the Independent Street Arts Network, copies of which may be obtained through: www.streetartsnetwork.org.uk/pages/publications.htm The London District Surveyors Association's "Technical Standards for Places of Public Entertainment" ISBN 0 9531229 2 1

The following British Standards should also be considered:

- BS 5588 Part 6 (regarding places of assembly)
- BS 5588 Part 9 (regarding ventilation and air conditioning systems)
- BS 5588 Part 9 (regarding means of escape for disabled people)
- BS 5839 (fire detection, fire alarm systems and buildings)
- BS 5266 (emergency lighting systems)

In most premises, therefore, relevant legislation will provide adequately for the safety of the public or club members and guests. However, where this is not the case, consideration might be given to the following conditions.

Safety checks

- Safety checks are carried out before the admission of the public.
- Details of such checks are recorded and available to the relevant authorities for inspection.

Escape routes

- Exits are not obstructed (including by curtains, hangings or temporary decorations), and accessible via non-slippery and even surfaces, free of trip hazards and clearly identified.
- Where chairs and tables are provided in restaurants and other premises, internal gangways are kept unobstructed.
- All exits doors are easily opened without the use of a key, card, code or similar means.
- Doors at such exits are regularly checked to ensure that they function satisfactorily and a record of the check kept.
- Any removable security fastenings are removed whenever the premises are open to the public or occupied by staff.
- The edges of the treads of steps and stair ways are maintained so as to be conspicuous.

Disabled people

That adequate arrangements exist to enable the safe evacuation of disabled people in the event of an emergency; and that disabled people on the premises are made aware of those arrangements.

Lighting

- That lighting in areas accessible to the public, members or guests shall be adequate when they are present.
- That emergency lighting functions properly.

- In the event of the failure of normal lighting, where the emergency lighting batter y has a capacity of one hour, arrangements are in place to ensure that the public, members or guests leave the premises within 20 minutes unless within that time normal lighting has been restored and the battery is being re-charged; and, if the emergency lighting batter y has a capacity of three hours, the appropriate period by the end of which the public should have left the premises is one hour.

Capacity limits

- Arrangements are made to ensure that any capacity limit imposed under the premises licence or club premises certificate is not exceeded.
- The licence holder, a club official, manager or designated premises supervisor should be aware of the number of people on the premises and be required to inform any authorised person on request.

Access for emergency vehicles

- Access for emergency vehicles is kept clear and free from obstruction.

First aid

Adequate and appropriate supply of first aid equipment and materials is available on the premises.

If necessary, at least one suitably trained first-aider shall be on duty when the public are present; and if more than one suitably trained first-aider that their respective duties are clearly defined.

Temporary electrical installations

- Temporary electrical wiring and distribution systems are not provided without notification to the licensing authority at least ten days before commencement of the work and/or prior inspection by a suitable qualified electrician.
- Temporary electrical wiring and distribution systems shall comply with the recommendations of BS 7671 or where applicable BS 7909.
- Where they have not been installed by a competent person, temporary electrical wiring and distribution systems are inspected and certified by a competent person before they are put to use.

In relation to the point in the first bullet above, it should be recognised that ten days notice may not be possible where performances are supported by outside technical teams (for example, where temporary electrical installations are made in theatres for television show performances). In such circumstances, the key requirement is that conditions should ensure that temporary electrical installations are only under taken by competent qualified persons (for example, those employed by the television company).

Indoor sports entertainment

- If appropriate, a qualified medical practitioner is present throughout a sports entertainment involving boxing, wrestling, judo, karate or other sports entertainment of a similar nature.
- Any ring is constructed by a competent person and/or inspected by a competent authority.
- At any wrestling or other entertainments of a similar nature members of the public do not occupy any seat within 2.5 metres of the ring.
- At water sports entertainments, staff adequately trained in rescue and life safety procedures are stationed and remain within the vicinity of the water at all material times (see also Managing Health and Safety in Swimming Pools issued jointly by the Health and Safety Executive and Sport England).

Special effects

The use of special effects in venues being used for regulated entertainment can present significant risks. Special effects or mechanical installations should be arranged and stored so as to minimise any risk to the safety of the audience, the per formers and staff. Further details and guidance are given in Part 3.

Alterations to the premises

Premises should not be altered in such a way as to make it impossible to comply with an existing licence condition without first seeking a variation of the premises licence to delete the relevant public safety condition. The applicant will need to propose how they intend to take alternative steps to promote the public safety objective in a new operating schedule reflecting the proposed alteration to the premises.

The application for variation will enable responsible authorities with expertise in safety matters to consider whether the proposal is acceptable.

Other measures

Other measures previously mentioned in relation to the Prevention of Crime and Disorder may also be appropriate to promote public safety. These might include the provision of door supervisors, bottle bans, and requirements to use plastic or toughened glass containers (see Part 1 for further detail).

PART 3. THEATRES, CINEMAS, CONCERT HALLS AND SIMILAR PLACES (PROMOTION OF PUBLIC SAFETY)

In addition to the points in Part 2, there are particular public safety matters which should be considered in connection with theatres and cinemas.

PREMISES USED FOR CLOSELY SEATED AUDIENCES

Attendants

(a) The number of attendants on each floor in a closely seated auditorium should be as set out on the table below:

Number of members of the audience present on a floor	Minimum number of attendants required to be present on that floor
1 – 100	One
101 – 250	Two
251 – 500	Three
501 – 750	Four
751 – 1,000	Five
And one additional attendant for each additional 250 persons (or part thereof)	

(b) Attendants shall not be engaged in duties that would prevent them from promptly discharging their duties in the event of an emergency or require their absence from that floor or auditorium where they are on duty.

(c) Attendants shall be readily identifiable to the audience (but this need not entail the wearing of a uniform).

(d) The premises shall not be used for a closely seated audience except in accordance with seating plan(s), a copy of which is available at the premises and shall be shown to an authorised person on request.

(e) No article shall be attached to the back of any seat which would reduce the clear width of seatways or cause a tripping hazard or obstruction.

(f) A copy of any certificate relating to the design, construction and loading of temporary seating shall be kept available at the premises and shall be shown to an authorised person on request.

Seating

Where the potential audience exceeds 250 all seats in the auditorium should be securely fixed to the floor or battened together in lengths of not fewer than four and not more than twelve.

Standing and sitting in gangways etc

(a) Sitting on floors shall not be permitted except where authorised in the premises licence or club premises certificate.
(b) Waiting or standing shall not be permitted except in areas designated in the premises licence or club premises certificate.
(c) In no circumstances shall anyone be permitted to-
    (i) sit in a gangway;
    (ii) stand or sit in front of an exit; or
    (iii) stand or sit on a staircase, including landings.

Drinks

Except as authorised by the premises licence or club premises certificate, no drinks shall be sold to, or be consumed by, a closely seated audience except in plastic and paper containers.

Balcony fronts

Clothing or other objects shall not be placed over balcony rails or upon balcony fronts.

Special effects

Special effects or mechanical installations should be arranged and stored so as to minimise risk to the safety of the audience, the per formers and staff.

Specials effects include:

- dry ice machines and cryogenic fog;
- smoke machines and fog generators;
- pyrotechnics, including fireworks;
- real flame;
- firearms;
- motor vehicles;
- strobe lighting;
- lasers; and
- explosives and highly flammable substances.

In certain circumstances, it may be appropriate to require that certain special effects are only used with the prior notification of the licensing authority. In these cases, the licensing authority should notify the fire and rescue author-ity, who will exercise their inspection and enforcement powers under the Regulatory Reform (Fire Safety) Order. Further guidance can be found in the following publications:

- HSE Guide 'The radiation safety of lasers used for display purposes' (HS(G)95
- 'Smoke and vapour effects used in entertainment' (HSE Entertainment Sheet No 3);
- 'Special or visual effects involving explosives or pyrotechnics used in film and television production' (HSE Entertainment Sheet No 16);
- 'Electrical safety for entertainers' (HSE INDG 247)
- 'Theatre Essentials' – Guidance booklet produced by the Association of British Theatre Technicians 8

Ceilings

Ceilings in those parts of the premises to which the audience are admitted should be inspected by a suitably qualified person, who will decide when a further inspection is necessary, and a certificate concerning the condition of the ceilings forwarded to the licensing authority.

PREMISES USED FOR FILM EXHIBITIONS

Attendants – premises without a staff altering system

Where the premises are not equipped with a staff alerting system the number of attendants present should be as set out in the table below:

Number of members of the audience present on the premises	Minimum number of attendants required to be on duty
1 – 250	Two
And one additional attendant for each additional 250 members of the audience present (or part thereof)	
Where there are more than 150 members of audience in any auditorium or on any floor	At least one attendant shall be present in any auditorium or on any floor

Attendants – premises with a staff alterting system

(a) Where premises are equipped with a staff alerting system the number of attendants present should be as set out in the table below:

Number of members of the audience present on the premises	Minimum number of attendants required to be on duty	Minimum number of other staff on the premises who are available to assist in the event of an emergency

1 – 500	Two	One
501 – 1,000	Three	Two
1001 – 1,500	Four	Four
1,501 or more	Five plus one for every 500 (or part thereof) persons over 2,000 on the premises	Five plus one for every 500 (or part thereof) persons over 2,000 on the premises

(b) Staff shall not be considered as being available to assist in the event of an emergency if they are:
   (i) the holder of the premises licence or the manager on duty at the premises; or
   (ii) a member of staff whose normal duties or responsibilities are likely to significantly affect or delay their response in an emergency situation; or
   (iii) a member of staff whose usual location when on duty is more than 60 metres from the location to which they are required to go on being alerted to an emergency situation.

(c) Attendants shall as far as reasonably practicable be evenly distributed throughout all parts of the premises to which the public have access and keep under observation all parts of the premises to which the audience have access.

(d) The staff alerting system shall be maintained in working order.

Minimum lighting

The level of lighting in the auditorium should be as great as possible consistent with the effective presentation of the film; and the level of illumination maintained in the auditorium during the showing of films would normally be regarded as satisfactory if it complies with the standards specified in BS CP 1007 (Maintained Lighting for Cinemas).

PART 4. CONDITIONS RELATING TO THE PREVENTION OF PUBLIC NUISANCE

It should be noted that provisions of the Environmental Protection Act 1990, the Noise Act 1996 and the Clean Neighbourhoods and Environment Act 2005 provide some protection to the general public from public nuisance, including noise nuisance. In addition, the provisions in Part 8 of the Licensing Act 2003 enable a senior police officer to close down instantly for up to 24 hours licensed premises and premises carrying on temporary permitted activities that are causing nuisance resulting from noise emanating from the premises. These matters should be considered before deciding whether or not conditions are appropriate for the prevention of public nuisance.

Hours

The hours during which the premises are permitted to be open to the public or to members and their guests can be restricted for the prevention of public nuisance. Licensing authorities are best placed to determine what hours are appropriate. However, the four licensing objectives should be paramount considerations at all times.

Restrictions could be appropriate on the times when certain licensable activities take place even though the premises may be open to the public as such times. For example, the playing of recorded music after a certain time might be prohibited, even though other licensable activities are permitted to continue. Or the playing of recorded music might only be permitted after a certain time where conditions have been attached to the licence or certificate to ensure that any potential nuisance is satisfactorily prevented.

Restrictions might also be appropriate on the parts of premises that might be used for certain licensable activities at certain times. For example, while the provision of regulated entertainment might be permitted while the premises are open to the public or members and their guests, regulated entertainment might not be permitted in garden areas of the premises after a certain time.

In premises where existing legislation does not provide adequately for the prevention of public nuisance, consideration might be given to the following conditions.

Noise and vibration

In determining which conditions are appropriate, licensing authorities should be aware of the need to avoid disproportionate measures that could deter the holding of events that are valuable to the community, such as live music.

Noise limiters, for example, are very expensive to purchase and install and are likely to be a considerable burden for smaller venues. The following conditions may be considered:

Noise or vibration does not emanate from the premises so as to cause a nuisance to nearby proper ties. This might be achieved by one or more of the following conditions:

- a simple requirement to keep doors and windows at the premises closed;
- limiting live music to a particular area of the building;
- moving the location and direction of speakers away from external walls or walls that abut private premises;
- installation of acoustic curtains;
- fitting of rubber seals to doorways;

- installation of rubber speaker mounts;
- requiring the licence holder to take measures to ensure that music will not be audible above background level at the nearest noise sensitive location;
- require licence holder to undertake routine monitoring to ensure external levels of music are not excessive and take action where appropriate;
- noise limiters on amplification equipment used at the premises (if other measures have been unsuccessful);
- prominent, clear and legible notices to be displayed at all exits requesting the public to respect the needs of local residents and to leave the premises and the area quietly;
- the use of explosives, pyrotechnics and fireworks of a similar nature which could cause disturbance in surrounding areas are restricted; and
- the placing of refuse – such as bottles – into receptacles outside the premises to take place at times that will minimise the disturbance to nearby proper ties.

Noxious smells

Noxious smells from the premises are not permitted to cause a nuisance to nearby proper ties; and the premises are properly vented.

Light pollution

Flashing or particularly bright lights at the premises do not cause a nuisance to nearby proper ties. Any such condition needs to be balanced against the benefits to the prevention of crime and disorder of bright lighting in certain places.

Other measures

Other measures previously mentioned in relation to the crime prevention objective may also be relevant as appropriate to prevent public nuisance. These might include the provision of door supervisors, open containers not to be taken from the premises, and restrictions on drinking areas (see Part 1 for further detail).

PART 5. CONDITIONS RELATING TO THE PROTECTION OF CHILDREN FROM HARM

An operating schedule or club operating schedule should indicate any decision for the premises to exclude children completely. This would mean there would be no need to detail in the operating schedule steps that the applicant proposes to take to promote the protection of children from harm. Otherwise, where entry is to be permitted, the operating schedule should outline the steps to be taken to promote the protection of children from harm while on the premises.

Access for children to licensed premises – in general

The 2003 Act prohibits unaccompanied children from premises that are exclusively or primarily used for the supply of alcohol for consumption on the premises. Additional restrictions on the access of children under 18 to premises where licensable activities are being carried on should be made where they are appropriate to protect children from harm. Precise policy and details will be a matter for individual licensing authorities.

It is recommended (unless there are circumstances justifying the contrary) that in relation to:

- premises with known associations (having been presented with evidence) with or likely to give rise to: heavy or binge or underage drinking;
- drugs, significant gambling, or any activity or entertainment (whether regulated entertainment or not) of a clearly adult or sexual nature, there should be a strong presumption against permitting any access at all for children under 18 years;
- premises, not serving alcohol for consumption on the premises, but where the public are allowed on the premises after 11.00pm in the evening, there should be a presumption against the presence of children under the age of 12 unaccompanied by adults after that time.

Applicants wishing to allow access under the above circumstances should, when preparing new operating schedules or club operating schedules or variations of those schedules:

- explain their reasons; and
- outline in detail the steps that they intend to take to protect children from harm on such premises.

In any other case, it is recommended that, subject to the premises licence holder's or club's discretion, the expectation would be for unrestricted access for children, subject to the terms of the 2003 Act.

Age restrictions – specific

Whilst it may be appropriate to allow children unrestricted access at particular times and when certain activities are not taking place, licensing authorities will need to consider:

- The hours in a day during which age restrictions should and should not apply. For example, the fact that adult entertainment may be presented at premises after 8.00pm does not mean that it would be appropriate to impose age restrictions for earlier parts of the day.
- Types of event or activity that are unlikely to require age restrictions, for example:
  – family entertainment; or
  – alcohol free events for young age groups, such as under 18s dances,
- Types of event or activity which give rise to a more acute need for age restrictions than normal, for example: during "Happy Hours" or drinks promotions;

Age restrictions – cinemas

The British Board of Film Classification classifies films in accordance with its published Guidelines, which are based on research into public opinion and professional advice. It is therefore recommended that licensing authorities should not duplicate this effort by choosing to classify films themselves. The classifications recommended by the Board should be those normally applied unless there are very good local reasons for a licensing authority to adopt this role.

Licensing authorities should note that the provisions of the 2003 Act enable them to specify the Board in the licence or certificate and, in relation to individual films, to notify the holder or club that it will make a recommendation for that particular film.

Licensing authorities should be aware that the BBFC currently classifies films in the following way:

- U Universal – suitable for audiences aged four years and over
- PG – Parental Guidance. Some scenes may be unsuitable for young children.
- 12A – Suitable for viewing by persons aged 12 years or older or persons younger than 12 when accompanied by an adult.
- 15 – Suitable for viewing by persons aged 15 years and over.
- 18 – Suitable for viewing by persons aged 18 years and over.
- R18 – To be shown only in specially licensed cinemas, or supplied only in licensed sex shops, and to adults of not less than 18 years.

Licensing authorities should note that these classifications may be subject to occasional change and consult the BBFC's website at www.bbfc.co.uk before applying relevant conditions. In addition to the mandatory condition imposed by section 20, conditions restricting the admission of children to film exhibitions should include that:

- where the licensing authority itself is to make recommendations on the admission of children to films, the cinema or venue operator must submit any film to the authority that it intends to exhibit 28 days before it is proposed to show it. This is to allow the authority time to classify it so that the premises licence holder is able to adhere to any age restrictions then imposed;

- immediately before each exhibition at the premises of a film passed by the British Board of Film Classification there shall be exhibited on screen for at least five seconds in such a manner as to be easily read by all persons in the auditorium a reproduction of the certificate of the Board or, as regards a trailer advertising a film, of the statement approved by the Board indicating the classification of the film;

- when a licensing authority has made a recommendation on the restriction of admission of children to a film, notices are required to be displayed both inside and outside the premises so that persons entering can readily be made aware of the classification attached to any film or trailer.

Such a condition might be expressed in the following terms:

"Where a programme includes a film recommended by the licensing authority as falling into an age restrictive category no person appearing to be under the age specified shall be admitted to any part of the programme; where a programme includes a film recommended by the licensing authority as falling into a category requiring any persons under a specified age to be accompanied by an adult no person appearing to be under the age specified shall be admitted to any part of the programme unaccompanied by an adult, and the licence holder shall display in a conspicuous position a notice clearly stating the relevant age restrictions and requirements. For example:

Persons under the age of [insert Appropriate age] cannot be admitted to any part of the programme

Where films of different categories form part of the same programme, the notice shall refer to the oldest age restriction. This condition does not apply to members of staff under the relevant age while on-duty provided that the prior written consent of the person's parent or legal guardian has first been obtained."

Theatres

The admission of children to theatres, as with other licensed premises, is not expected to be restricted normally unless it is appropriate to promote the protection of children from harm. However, theatres may be the venue for a wide range of activities. The admission of children to the performance of a play should normally be left to the discretion of the licence holder and no condition restricting the access of children to plays should be attached. However, theatres may also present entertainment including, for example, variety shows, incorporating adult entertainment. A condition restricting the admission of children in such circumstances may be appropriate. Entertainment may also be presented at theatres specifically for children (see below). Licensing authorities are also expected to consider whether a condition should be attached to a premises licence which requires the presence of a sufficient number of adult staff on the premises to ensure the wellbeing of children during any emergency (See Part 3).

Performances especially for children

Where performances are presented especially for unaccompanied children in theatres and cinemas, licensing authorities will also wish to consider conditions to specify that:

- an attendant to be stationed in the area(s) occupied by the children, in the vicinity of each exit, provided that on each level occupied by children the minimum number of attendants on duty should be one attendant per 50 children or part thereof.

Licensing authorities should also consider whether or not standing should be allowed. For example, there may be reduced risk for children in the stalls than at other levels or areas in the building.

Children in performances

There are many productions each year that are one-off shows where the cast is made up almost entirely of children. They may be taking part as individuals or as par t of a drama club, stage school or school group. The age of those involved may range from 5 to 18. The Children (Performances) Regulations 1968 as amended prescribe requirements for children per forming in a show. Licensing authorities should familiarise themselves with these Regulations and not duplicate any of these requirements. However, if it is appropriate to consider imposing conditions, in addition to these requirements, for the promotion of the protection of children from harm then the licensing authority should consider the matters outlined below.

- **Venue** – the backstage facilities should be large enough to accommodate safely the number of children taking part in any performance.
- **Special effects** – it may be inappropriate to use certain special effects, including smoke, dry ice, rapid pulsating or flashing lights, which may trigger adverse reactions especially with regard to children.
- **Care of children** – theatres, concert halls and similar places are places of work and may contain a lot of potentially dangerous equipment. It is therefore important that children per forming at such premises are kept under adult supervision at all times including transfer from stage to dressing room and anywhere else on the premises. It is also important that the children can be accounted for at all times in case of an evacuation or emergency.

The Portman Group code of practice on the naming, packaging and promotion of alcoholic drinks

The Portman Group operates, on behalf of the alcohol industry, a Code of Practice on the Naming, Packaging and Promotion of Alcoholic Drinks. The Code seeks to ensure that drinks are packaged and promoted in a socially responsible manner and only to those who are 18 years old or older. Complaints about products under the Code are considered by an Independent Complaints Panel and the Panel's decisions are published on the Portman Group's website, in the trade press and in an annual report. If a product's packaging or point-of-sale advertising is found to be in breach of the Code, the Portman Group may issue a Retailer Alert Bulletin to notify retailers of the decision and ask them not to replenish stocks of any such product or to display such point-of-sale material, until the decision has been complied with. The Code is an important mechanism in protecting children from harm because it addresses the naming, marketing and promotion of alcohol products sold in licensed premises in a manner which may appeal to or attract minors. Consideration can be given to attaching conditions to premises licences and club premises certificates that require compliance with the Portman Group's Retailer Alert Bulletins.

Proof of age cards

Proof of age cards are discussed under Part 1 in connection with the prevention of crime and disorder.

Bibliography

Chapter 1

'Implementation of the Licensing Act 2003: A national survey' (Alcohol Education and Research Council, January 2008)

Lord Askwith, *British Taverns: their history and laws* (Routledge, 1928)

A Barr, *Drink: An Informal Social History* (Bantam Press, 1995)

P Brown, *Man Walks into a Pub: A Sociable History of Beer* (Macmillan, 2003)

'Code of Practice on Consultation' (Department for Business, Enterprise and Regulatory Reform, July 2008)

'Evaluation of the Impact of the Licensing Act 2003' (Department for Culture, Media and Sport, March 2008)

S Earnshaw, *The Pub in Literature* (Manchester University Press, 2000)

G Edwards, *Alcohol: the Ambiguous Molecule* (Penguin 2000)

P Haydon, *Beer and Britannia: An Inebriated History of Britain* (Sutton Publishing, 2003)

'The Public Health Responsibility Deal' (Department of Health, March 2011)

'Health Select Committee report on Alcohol', HC 151-I (2010)

'Fifth Report of Session 2004–2005', HC 80-I (Home Affairs Select Committee, March 2005)

'Rebalancing the Licensing Act – a consultation on empowering individuals, families and local communities to shape and determine local licensing' (Home Office, 2010)

'Responses to Consultation: Rebalancing the Licensing Act' (Home Office, 2010)

'The Government's Alcohol Strategy', Cm 8336 (Home Office, April 2012)

B Kumin and A Tlusty (eds), *The World of the Tavern: Public Houses in Modern Europe* (Ashgate, 2002)

C MacAndrew and R B Edgerton, *Drunken Comportment: A Social Explanation* (Aldine, 1969)

'Statistics on Alcohol: England, 2011' (NHS, Health and Social Care Information Centre)

S Mehigan, J Phillips, *Paterson's Licensing Acts 2003* (Butterworths, 111th ed)

J Paxman, *The English: A Portrait of a People* (Penguin, 1999)

S Schama, *A History of Britain: The British Wars 1603–1776* (BBC, 2001)

A Shadwell, *Drink in 1914–1922: A Lesson in Control* (Longmans, Green & Co, 1923)

Sidney and Beatrice Webb, 'The History of Liquor Licensing in England', English Local Government (1903)

G B Wilson, *Alcohol and the Nation* (Nicholson and Watson, 1940)

Chapter 2

'The Practical Guide for Preventing and Dealing with Alcohol Related Problems: what you need to know' (Home Office, 3rd ed, November 2010)

'Good Practice in Managing the Evening and Late Night Economy: A Literature Review from an Environmental Perspective' (Office of the Deputy Prime Minister, 2004)

Chapter 3

'Reducing Regulation Made Simple' (Better Regulation Executive, 2010)

Berglund et al, 'World Health Organisation Guidelines on Community Noise' (World Health Organisation, 1999)

'Planning for Leisure and Tourism' (Office of the Deputy Prime Minister, 2001)

M Elvins and P Hadfield, 'West End "Stress Area", Night Time Economy Profiling: A Demonstration Project' (2003)

P Hadfield and A Newton, 'Alcohol, Crime and Disorder in the Night Time Economy' Alcohol Concern Factsheet (September 2010)

'Home Office Guidance for Local Partnerships on Alcohol-related Crime and Disorder Data', Home Office Development and Practice Report No 6 (2003)

'A National Evaluation of Community Support Officers' (Home Office, 2006)

'National Population Projections' (Office for National Statistics, 2011)

Tierney and Hobbs, 'Alcohol-related Crime and Disorder Data: Guidance for Local Partnerships' (Home Office, 2003)

'Night Noise Guidelines for Europe' (World Health Organisation, 2009)

Chapter 4

W Bently Capper, *Licensed Houses and Their Management* (Caxton, 4th ed, 1946)

Chapter 5

'The Evening Economy and the Urban Renaissance: Twelfth Report of Session 2002–03', HC 396-I (Office of the Deputy Prime Minister: Housing, Planning, Local Government and the Regions Committee)

'The Government Response to Office of the Deputy Prime Minister Housing, Planning, Local Government and the Regions Committee's Report on the Evening Economy and the Urban Renaissance', Cm 5971 (2003)

Chapter 6

F A R Bennion, *Statutory Interpretation* (Lexis Nexis, 5th ed, 2008)

Chapter 7

S H Bailey (ed), *Cross on Local Government Law* (Sweet & Maxwell)
P Elias and J Goudie, *Butterworths Local Government Law* (Butterworths)
De Smith, Lord Woolf, J Jowell and A Le Sueur, *Judicial Review of Administrative Action* (Sweet & Maxwell, 2006)
H W R Wade and C F Forsyth, *Administrative Law* (Oxford University Press, 10th ed, 2009)

Chapter 9

'Guidance to Local Authorities' (Gambling Commission, 4th ed, 2012)
J Maurici, 'The Meaning of Policy: A Question for the Court', Judicial Review 85 (1998)

Chapter 11

'Code of Recommended Practice on Local Authority Publicity' (Department for Communities and Local Government, 2011)
'Learning to Listen, Core Principles for the Involvement of Children and Young People' (Department for Education and Skills, 2001)
'Local Plans and Unitary Development Plans, Guide to Procedures' (Department of Environment, Transport and the Regions, 2000)
'Building a Culture of Participation, involving children and young people in policy, service planning, delivery and evaluation', (Department for Education and Skills, 2003)
Fajerman et al, 'Children are Service Users Too' (Save the Children, 2004)
'Citizenship: young people's perspectives', Home Office Development and Practice Report 10 (2004)
K Olley, 'The Principles of Proper Consultation', Judicial Review 99 (2001)
Thompson, 'General duties to consult the public: how do you get the public to participate?', Nottingham Law Journal 33 (2002)
'Modern Local Government: In Touch with the People' Cm 4014 (White Paper, 1998)

Chapter 12

'Rebalancing the Licensing Act – a consultation on empowering individuals, families and local communities to shape and determine local licensing' (Home Office, 2010)

Chapter 15

'Rebalancing the Licensing Act – a consultation on empowering individuals, families and local communities to shape and determine local licensing' (Home Office, 2010)

'Responses to Consultation: Rebalancing the Licensing Act' (Home Office, 2010)

'Alcohol and Late Night Refreshment Licensing England and Wales 2011/12' (Home Office, 2012)

'The Government's Alcohol Strategy', Cm 8336 (Home Office, April 2012)

Chapter 16

'Time for Reform – Proposals for the Modernisation of our Licensing Laws' (White Paper, April 2000)

Chapter 17

'Technical Standards for Places of Public Entertainment' (Association of British Theatre Technicians, 2009)

'Model National and Standard Conditions for Places of Public Entertainment and Associated Guidance' (Entertainment Technology Press, 2002)

'5 Steps to Risk Assessment: Case Studies' (Health and Safety Executive, 1998)

'The Event Safety Guide – A guide to health, safety and welfare at music and similar events' ('The Purple Book', HSE, 1999)

'Managing Crowds Safely' (HSE, 2000)

'Safety Guidance for Street Arts, Carnival, Processions and Large Scale Performances' (Independent Street Arts Network, 2004)

'The Guide to Safety at Sports Grounds' ('The Green Guide', 5th ed, The Stationery Office, 2008)

Chapter 18

'Time for Reform: Proposals for the Modernisation of our Licensing Laws' (White Paper, April 2000)

Chapter 20

De Smith, Lord Woolf, J Jowell and A Le Sueur, *Judicial Review of Administrative Action* (Sweet & Maxwell, 2006)

Chapter 22

C Manchester, *Entertainment Licensing, Law and Practice* (Butterworths, 2nd ed, 1999)

S Mehigan, J Phillips, *Paterson's Licensing Acts 2003* (Butterworths, 111th ed)

Chapter 25

K Hughes, Z Anderson, M Morleo, M Bellis, 'Alcohol, nightlife and violence: the relative contributions of drinking before and during nights out to negative health and criminal justice outcomes' Addiction, Vol 103 (January 2008), pp 60–65

'A consultation on delivering the Government's policies to cut alcohol fuelled crime and anti-social behaviour' (Home Office, November 2012)

Chapter 27

R Clayton and H Tomlinson, *The Law of Human Rights* (Oxford University Press, 2009)

I S Goldrein, T Straker and R Bhose, *Human Rights and Judicial Review, Case Studies in Context* (Butterworths)

Lord Lester, Lord Pannick and J Herberg, *Human Rights Law and Practice* (LexisNexis, 2009)

J Simor and B Emmerson, *Human Rights Practice* (Sweet & Maxwell)

Chapter 29

'Regulatory Justice: Making Sanctions Effective' (Better Regulation Executive, 2006)

'Regulators' Compliance Code: Statutory Code of Practice for Regulators' (Department for Business, Enterprise and Regulatory Reform, 2007)

'Reducing administrative burdens: effective inspection and enforcement' ('The Hampton Report', HM Treasury, 2005)

Chapter 30

'Guide to Test Purchasing' (Local Authorities Co-ordinators of Regulatory Services, 2010)

'Revised Code of Practice on Covert Surveillance and Property Interference' (Home Office, 2010)

'Covert Human Intelligence Sources: Code of Practice' (Home Office, 2010)

'Protection of Freedoms Act 2012 – changes to provisions under the Regulation of Investigatory Powers Act 2000 (RIPA): Home Office guidance to local authorities in England and Wales on the judicial process for RIPA and the crime threshold for directed surveillance' (Home Office, October 2012)

'Office of Surveillance Commissioners Procedures and Guidance' (December 2008)

Chapter 31

'Creating Strong, Safe and Prosperous Communities: Statutory Guidance' (Department for Communities and Local Government, July 2008)

'Best Value Statutory Guidance' (DCLG, September 2011)

'National Planning Policy Framework' (DCLG, March 2012)

'Planning Policy Wales' (Welsh Government, 5th ed, November 2012)

Chapter 32

'Code of Practice for equal chance gaming in clubs and premises with an alcohol licence' (Gambling Commission, December 2009)

'Code of Practice for gaming machines in clubs and premises with an alcohol licence' (Gambling Commission, March 2012)

P Kolvin, *Gambling for Local Authorities: Licensing, Planning and Regeneration* (Institute of Licensing, 2nd ed, 2010)

Chapter 33

C Manchester, *Entertainment Licensing, Law and Practice* (Butterworths, 2nd ed, 1999)

Chapter 34

'Guidelines for the Placing of Tables and Chairs on the Highway' (Westminster City Council, 2005)

Chapter 35

M Baird, *Back to Basics: A Guide to Nightclub Operation* (Mondiale Publishing, 2003)

'Door Supervisors/Stewards – Code of Practice', British Standard 7960 (BSI, 1999)

'Enforcement: what to expect from the SIA' (Security Industry Authority, 2011)

'Get Licensed' (SIA, February 2012)

A Sleat, 'Safety on the Door: An Evaluation of local authority administered registration schemes for door supervisors' (University of West of England, 1998)

A Walker, 'The Safer Doors Project' (Home Office, 1999)

'Government's Proposals for Regulation of the Private Security Industry in England and Wales', Cm 4254 (White Paper, 1999)

Chapter 37

'Guidance on Designated Public Place Orders for Local Authorities in England and Wales' (Home Office, December 2008)

Chapter 38

A Crawford and S Lister, 'The use and impact of dispersal orders: Sticking plasters and wake-up calls' (Joseph Rowntree Foundation, 2007)
'A Review of Dispersal Powers' (Scottish Government, 2007)

Chapter 39

'Giving Directions to Individuals to Leave a Locality. (Section 27 of the Violent Crime Reduction Act 2006). Practical Advice' (Home Office, 2nd ed, January 2010)

Chapter 40

'The Coalition: our programme for government' (HM Government, 2010)
'Dealing with the problems of late night drinking – implementation of secondary legislation' (Home Office, May 2012)

Chapter 43

'Police Powers to Close Premises under the Licensing Act 2003' (Department of Culture, Media and Sport, 2007)

Chapter 44

'The Practical Guide for Preventing and Dealing with Alcohol Related Problems: what you need to know' (Home Office, 3rd ed, November 2010)

Chapter 45

'Guidance: persistently selling alcohol to children. Revised guidance following amendments introduced through the Police Reform and Social Responsibility Act 2011' (Home Office, 2012)

Chapter 46

N Parpworth, 'The Anti-social Behaviour Act 2003: the provisions relating to noise', Journal of Planning and Environment Law 541 (2004)

Chapter 48

'Guidance on Drinks Banning Orders on Application for Local Authorities, Police Forces, Magistrates and Course Providers' (Home Office, 2009)

Chapter 50

'Alcohol Harm Reduction Strategy for England' (Cabinet Office, 2004)

'Safe. Sensible. Social. The next steps in the National Alcohol Strategy' (Department of Health, 2007)

'Evaluation of Alcohol Arrest Referral Pilot Schemes (Phase 1)' (Home Office, Occasional Paper 101, March 2012)

'Evaluation of Alcohol Arrest Referral Pilot Schemes (Phase 2)' (Home Office, Occasional Paper 102, March 2012)

Chapter 51

'Code of Practice on Age Restricted Products' (Better Regulation Delivery Office, 2013)

'Code for Crown Prosecutors' (Crown Prosecution Service, 2013)

M Ford and J Clarke, *Redgrave's Health and Safety* (LexisNexis, 7th ed, 2010)

Greenberg, *Stroud's Judicial Dictionary of Words and Phrases* (Sweet & Maxwell, 7th ed)

'Reducing Error and Influencing Behaviour' (Health and Safety Executive, 1999)

'Leading Health and Safety at Work' (HSE, 2007)

'Enforcement Policy Statement' (HSE, 2009)

'Enforcement Concordat Good Practice Guide for England and Wales' (Department for Trade and Industry, 1998)

Chapter 53

Civic Trust, 'NightVision: Town Centres for All' (2006)

Chapter 55

A J Kenyon, 'Introduction to the Best Bar None Scheme and Its Benefits' (Leeds Metropolitan University, 2011)

Chapter 56

The Mid-Devon Community Alcohol Partnership, 'First Year Activity Report' (December 2011)

'An Evaluation of the Kent Community Alcohol Partnership, April – September 2009' (University of Kent)

Chapter 57

'Local Government Resources Review: Proposals for Business Rates Retention Consultation' (Department for Communities and Local Government, July 2011)

'Local Authority Guide to Business Improvement Districts' (London BIDs, 2005)

UKBIDs, 'Fast facts for BID Partners' (2011)

Chapter 59

A Barton and K Husk, 'Controlling Pre-Loaders: Alcohol Related Violence in an English Night Time Economy' (University of Plymouth Research Paper, 2012)

R Bromley et al 'Exploring safety concerns in the night time city: revitalising the evening economy', Town Planning Review 71(1) (2000)

M Burgess and S Moffatt, 'The Association Between Alcohol Outlet Density and Assaults On and Around Licensed Premises' (New South Wales Bureau of Crime and Statistics Research – Research Paper 147, 2011)

Department of Business Innovation and Skills/Mary Portas 'The Portas Review: An Independent Review into The Future of Our High Streets' (2011)

City of Sydney Council/Parsons Brinckerhoff 'Late Night Management Area Research Project' (2011)

Civic Trust, 'NightVision: Town Centres for All' (2006)

Civic Trust et al, 'Bexley: Night Vision' (2007)

'The National Planning Policy Framework' (Department of Communities and Local Government, 2012)

Heart of London BID, 'West End Footfall Figures' (2011)

J Jacobs, *The Death and Life of Great American Cities* (1961)

M Livingston, 'A longitudinal analysis of alcohol outlet density and assault', Alcoholism: Clinical and Experimental Research 32(6) (2008)

MAKE Associates, 'Evening and Night Time Audit of Bexley – Getting the Mix Right' (2007)

MAKE Associates, 'Morpeth Night Time Economy Audit' (2007)

MAKE Associates, 'Design out Crime: An After Dark Strategy for Liverpool' (2010)

MAKE Associates, 'A Night-time Strategy for Oldham' (2010)

MAKE 'Cumulative Impact: A Study into Crime and Disorder in Richmond and Twickenham Town Centres' (2011)

MAKE Associates & TBR, 'Night Mix Index 2009' (2010)

MAKE & TBR, 'Analysis of Licensed Premises in Westminster West End Stress Area' (2011)

Milestone, 'Night Time Footfall Figures' (2011)

M Roberts and A Eldridge, *Planning the Night time City* (2009)

Poppleston Allen 'The Impact of Cumulative Impact Policies' (2012)

M S Rea, J D Bullough, C R Fay, J A Brons, J van Derlofske, E T Donnell, 'Review of the Safety Benefits and Other Effects of Roadway Lighting' (Transportation Research Board, 2009)

Sunderland City Council, 'Sunderland City Centre Evening Economy: Supplementary Planning Document' (2006)

'Women's Safety Audits for a Safer Urban Design' (United Nations Human Settlements Programme, 2007)

Chapter 62

'Dealing with the problems of late night drinking – implementation of secondary legislation' (Home Office, May 2012)

Chapter 63

'Community Infrastructure Levy Guidance' (Department for Communities and Local Government, December 2012)

'Decisions decisions: governance and spending the CIL' (Local Government Association and Planning Advisory Service, April 2013)

Chapter 64

C Lockhart-Mummery, J Harper, D Elvin and M Grant (eds), *Encyclopaedia of Planning Law and Practice* (Sweet & Maxwell)

Chapter 65

'Alcohol Misuse: how much does it cost?' (Cabinet Office, 2003)

'Interim Analytical Report' (Cabinet Office, 2003)

'Alcohol Harm Reduction Strategy for England' (Cabinet Office, 2004)

'Evaluation of the Impact of the Licensing Act 2003' (Department for Culture, Media and Sport, March 2008)

P Babb, 'Violent crime, disorder and criminal damage since the introduction of the Licensing Act 2003', Home Office Online Report 16/07 (Home Office, 2nd edition, London, 2007)

A Deehan, 'Alcohol and Crime: Taking Stock', Crime Reduction Research Series paper 3 (Home Office, London, 1999)

M Elvins, 'Alcohol politics: the impact of the Licensing Act 2003' (2009)

J Flatley, C Kershaw, K Smith, R Chaplin and D Moon (eds), 'Crime in England and Wales 2009/10. Findings from the British Crime Survey and police recorded crime' (Home Office, London, 2010)

P Hadfield and A Newton, 'Alcohol, Crime and Disorder in the Night Time Economy' Alcohol Concern Factsheet (September 2010)

C Harkins, 'The Portman Group', British Medical Journal 340 (2010)

'Safe. Sensible. Social. The next steps in the National Alcohol Strategy' (Department of Health, 2007)

'The cost of alcohol harm to the NHS in England. An update to the Cabinet office (2003) study' (Health Improvement Analytical Team, Department of Health, July 2008)

'Health Select Committee report on Alcohol', HC 151-I (2010)

'Rebalancing the Licensing Act – a consultation on empowering individuals, families and local communities to shape and determine local licensing' (Home Office, 2010)

'Responses to Consultation: Rebalancing the Licensing Act' (Home Office, 2010)

'The Government's Alcohol Strategy', Cm 8336 (Home Office, April 2012)

'A consultation on delivering the Government's policies to cut alcohol fuelled crime and anti-social behaviour' (Home Office, November 2012)

T Hope, 'Drinking and disorder in the city centre: a policy analysis', in 'Implementing Crime Prevention Measures', Home Office Research Study No 86 (HMSO, London, 1985)

M Hough, G Hunter, J Jacobson, and S Cossalter, 'Report: The impact of the Licensing Act 2003 on levels of crime and disorder: an evaluation', Home Office Research Report 04 (Home Office, London, March 2008)

D K Humphreys and M P Eisner, 'Evaluating a natural experiment in alcohol policy: The Licensing Act (2003) and the requirement for attention to implementation', Criminology & Public Policy, Vol 9, No 1 (2010)

IAS (Institute of Alcohol Studies), 'Time for Reform', Alcohol Alert 2 (2000), p 4

IAS, 'Coalition's alcohol policy comes under attack', Alcohol Alert (No 1, 2011), p 2

P Marsh and K Fox-Kibby, 'Drinking and Public Disorder. A report of research conducted for The Portman Group by MCM Research' (1992)

'Statistics on Alcohol: England, 2011' (NHS, Health and Social Care Information Centre)

E J Plant and M Plant, 'A 'leap in the dark?' Lessons for the United Kingdom from past extensions of bar opening hours', International Journal of Drug Policy Vol 16 (2005), pp 363–368

M Roberts and A Eldridge, 'Expecting "Great Things"? The Impact of the Licensing Act 2003 on Democratic Involvement, Dispersal and Drinking Cultures' (University of Westminster for the IAS, 2007)

R Room, 'Disabling the public interest: alcohol strategies and policies for England', Addiction, Vol 99 (2004), pp 1083–1089

M Tuck, 'Drinking and Disorder: A study of Non-Metropolitan violence', Home Office Research Study No 108 (HMSO, London, 1989)

'Time for Reform: Proposals for the Modernisation of our Licensing Laws' (White Paper, April 2000)

Chapter 66

'Calling Time: The Nation's drinking as a major health issue' (Academy of Medical Sciences, 2004)

M L Alaniz, R S Cartmill and R N Parker 'Immigrants and violence: the importance of neighborhood context', Hispanic Journal of Behavioral Sciences 20 (1998), pp 155–174

T Babor, R Caetano, S Casswell, G Edwards, N Giesbrecht, K Graham, J Grube, L Hill, H Holder, R Homel, M Livingston, E Österberg, J Rehm, R Room, and I Rossow, *Alcohol: No Ordinary Commodity – Research and Public Policy* (Oxford University Press, 2nd ed, 2010)

A Baigorri, R Fernándezand Giesyt, *Botellón: Un Conflicto Postmoderno (Botellón: A postmodern conflict)* (Ed Icaria, Barcelona, 2004)

A Britton, and M McKee, 'Relation between alcohol and cardiovascular disease in Eastern Europe: Explaining the paradox'. Journal of Epidemiology and Community Health 54 (2000), pp 328–332

B Borschos, 'Evaluation of the Swedish drunken driving legislation implemented on February 1, 1994' presented at the 15th International Conference on Alcohol, Drugs and Traffic Safety, Stockholm, Sweden, 22–26 Sept 2000

H Carter, *The Control of the Drink Trade: A Contribution to National Efficiency 1915–1917* (Longmans, Green & Co, 1918)

G E G Catlin, *Liquor Control* (Henry Holt & Co, New York and Thornton Butterworth, London, 1931)

P Chatterton and R Hollands, *Urban Nightscapes: Youth Cultures, Pleasure Spaces and Corporate Power* (Routledge, 2003)

T Chikritzhs and T R Stockwell, 'The Impact of later trading hours for Australian public houses (hotels) on levels of violence', Journal of Studies on Alcohol 63(5) (2002), pp 591–599

E L Collis, 'Discussion on alcohol as a beverage and its relation to certain social problems: alcohol and industrial efficiency', British Medical Journal 2 (1922), pp 244–248

P J Cook, 'The effect of liquor taxes on drinking, cirrhosis and auto fatalities' in M Moore and D Gerstein (eds), *Alcohol and Public Policy: Beyond the Shadow of Prohibition* (National Academy of Sciences, Washington, DC, 1981), pp 255–285

P J Cook and M J Moore, 'Violence reduction through restrictions on alcohol availability', Alcohol Health and Research World 17 (1993), pp 151–156

P G Dillon, *The Much-Lamented Death of Madame Geneva* (Justin, Charles & Co, Boston, 2003)

S Dunstan (ed), 'General Lifestyle Survey Overview: A Report on the 2010 General Lifestyle Survey' (Office for National Statistics, Newport, 2012)

M Ezzati, A D Lopez, A Rodgers, S Vander Hoorn, C J L Murray, and the Comparative Risk Assessment Collaborating Group, 'Selected major risk factors and global and regional burden of disease', The Lancet 360 (2002), pp 1347–1360

J Freyssinet-Dominjon and A-C Wagner, *L'alcool en fête — manières de boire de la nouvelle jeunesse étudiante (Party drinking: ways of drinking of the new student youth)* (L'Harmattan, 2003)

J Goodliffe, 'Can the civil law implement alcohol policy?' Alcohol Alert (No 3, 2003), pp 20–22

K Graham and S Wells, 'Somebody's Gonna Get Their Head Kicked in Tonight!: Aggression Among Young Males in Bars – A Question of Values?', British Journal of Criminology 43 (2003), pp 546–566

T K Greenfield and J D Rogers, 'Who drinks most of the alcohol in the US? The policy implications', Journal of Studies on Alcohol 60 (1999), pp 78–89

P Grover (ed), 'Preventing Problems Related to Alcohol Availability: Environmental Approaches – Reference Guide', Prevention Enhancement Protocols System No 3 (Substance Abuse and Mental Health Services Administration, Center for Substance Abuse Prevention, Rockville, MD, 1999)

Ö Hemström, 'Per capita alcohol consumption and ischaemic heart disease', Addiction 96 (Supplement 1, 2001), pp 93–112S

B Hibell, B Andersson, S Ahlström, O Balakireva, T Bjarnasson, A Kokkevi, and M Morgan, 'The 1999 ESPAD Report: Alcohol and Other Drug Use among Students in 30 Countries' (The Swedish Council for Information on Alcohol and Other Drugs, 2000)

D Hobbs, P Hadfield, S Lister and S Winlow, *Bouncers: Violence and Governance in the Night-time Economy* (Oxford University Press, 2003)

H D Holder, *Alcohol and the Community: A Systems Approach to Prevention* (Cambridge University Press, 1998)

R T Jewell and R W Brown, 'Alcohol availability and alcohol-related motor vehicle accidents', Applied Economics 27 (1995), pp 759–765

'Justices' Clerks' Society Good Practice Guide' (1999, amended 2001)

K Kypri, C Jones, P McElduff and D Barker, 'Effects of restricting pub closing times on night-time assaults in an Australian city'. Addiction 106(2) (2011), pp 303–310

B Hawkins, C Holden and J McCambridge, 'Alcohol industry influence on UK alcohol policy: A new research agenda for public health', Critical Public Health 22(3) (2012), pp 297–305

J Henstridge, R Homel and P Mackay, 'The Long-term Effects of Random Breath Testing in Four Australian States: A Time Series Analysis' (Federal Office of Road Safety, Canberra, 1997)

B Howard-Pitney, M D Johnson, D G Altman, R Hopkins and N Hammond, 'Responsible alcohol service: A study of server, manager, and environmental impact', American Journal of Public Health 81 (1991), pp 197–199

E Lang, T Stockwell, P Rydon and A Beel, 'Can training bar staff in responsible serving practices reduce alcohol-related harm?', Drug and Alcohol Review 17 (1998), pp 39–50

E A LaScala, F Johnson and P J Gruenewald, 'Neighborhood characteristics of alcohol-related pedestrian injury collisions: A geostatistical analysis', Prevention Science 2 (2001), pp 123–134

A-M Laslett, P Catalano, T Chikritzhs, C Dale, C Doran, J Ferris, T Jainullabudeen, M Livingston, D Matthews, J Mugavin, R Room, M Schlotterlein and C Wilkinson, *The Range and Magnitude of Alcohol's Harm to Others* (Alcohol Education and Rehabilitation Foundation, Canberra, 2010)

M Livingston, 'A longitudinal analysis of alcohol outlet density and assault', Alcoholism: Clinical and Experimental Research 32(6) (2008)

M Livingston, 'A longitudinal analysis of alcohol outlet density and domestic violence', Addiction 106(5) (2011), pp 919–925

M Livingston, 'Alcohol outlet density and harm: Comparing the impacts on violence and chronic harms', Drug and Alcohol Review 30(5) (2011), pp 515–523

P S Meier, 'Polarised drinking patterns and alcohol deregulation: Trends in alcohol consumption, harms and policy, United Kingdom 1990–2010', Nordic Studies on Alcohol and Drugs 27 (2010), pp 383–408

P S Meier, R Purshouse and A Brennan, 'Policy options for alcohol price regulation: the importance of modelling population heterogeneity', Addiction 105(3) (2010), pp 383–393

J Nicholls, *The Politics of Alcohol: A History of the Drink Question in England.* (Manchester University Press, 2009)

S Nordlund, 'Effects of Saturday closing of wine and spirits shops in Norway', Paper presented at the 31st International Institute on the Prevention and Treatment of Alcoholism, Rome, Italy, 2–7 June 1985, SIFA Mimeograph No. 5/85. (National Institute of Alcohol Research, Oslo)

T Norström, 'Assessment of the impact of the 0.02% BAC-limit in Sweden'. Studies on Crime and Crime Prevention 6(2) (1997), pp 245–258

T Norström, 'Outlet density and criminal violence in Norway, 1960–1995', Journal of Studies on Alcohol 61 (2000), pp 907–911

T Norström (ed), 'Alcohol in Postwar Europe: Consumption, Drinking Patterns, Consequences and Policy Response in 15 European Countries', (National Institute of Public Health, Stockholm, 2002)

E Österberg, 'Recorded Consumption of Alcohol in Finland, 1950–1975', report no 125 (Social Research Institute of Alcohol Studies, Helsinki, 1979)

S Owens, 'Pubs, clubs and restaurants: The impact of the new Licensing Act together with a difficult trading environment and other new legislation on capital and rental values of UK nightclubs', Journal of Retail and Leisure Property 5 (2006), pp 341–353

K Poikolainen, 'Increase in alcohol-related hospitalisations in Finland 1969–1975', British Journal of Addiction 75 (1980), pp 281–291

T Ragnarsdottir, A Kjartansdottir and S Davidsdottir, 'Effect of extended alcohol serving-hours in Reykjavik' in R Room (ed) *The Effects of Nordic Alcohol Policies: What Happens to Drinking and Harm when Alcohol Policies Change?*, Publication No 42 (Nordic Council for Alcohol and Drug Research, Helsinki, 2002), pp 145–154

D Raistrick, R Hodgson and B Ritson, *Tackling Alcohol Together: The Evidence Base for a UK Alcohol Policy* (Free Association Books, London and New York, 1999)

J Rehm and R Room, 'A case study in how harmful alcohol consumption can be', The Lancet 373 No 9682 (2009), pp 2176–2177

R Room, 'Alcohol control and public health', Annual Review of Public Health 5 (1984), pp 293–317

R Room, 'The impossible dream? Routes to reducing alcohol problems in a temperance culture', Journal of Substance Abuse 4 (1991), pp 91–106

R Room, 'Alcohol consumption and social harm: conceptual issues and historical perspectives', Contemporary Drug Problems 23 (1996), pp 373–388

R Room, 'Classic texts revisited: George EG Catlin, Liquor Control', Addiction 99 (2004), pp 925–927

R Room, 'Disabling the public interest: alcohol strategies and policies for England', Addiction, Vol 99 (2004), pp 1083–1089

R Room, 'The impotence of reason in the face of greed, moral cowardice, and selfish ambition', Addiction 99 (2004), pp 1092–1093

R A Shults, R W Elder, D A Sleet et al, 'Reviews of evidence regarding interventions to reduce alcohol-impaired driving', American Journal of Preventive Medicine 21 (2001), pp 66–88

J Simpura, 'Trends in alcohol consumption and drinking patterns: Sociological and economic explanations and alcohol policies', Nordisk Alkohol & narkotikatidskrift 18 (English Supplement, 2001), pp 3–13

O-J Skog, 'Public health consequences of the J-curve hypothesis of alcohol problems', Addiction 91 (1996), pp 325–337

D I Smith, 'Effectiveness of restrictions on availability as a means of preventing alcohol-related problems', Contemporary Drug Problems 15 (1988) pp 627–684

R J Stevenson, B Lind and D Weatherburn, 'Relationship between alcohol sales and assault in New South Wales, Australia', Addiction 94 (1999), pp 397–410

L Stewart and K Conway, 'Community action to reduce rural drink driving crashes: encouraging sustainable efforts in changing environments' in S Casswell, H Holder, M Holmila, S Larsson, R Midford, H M Barnes, P Nygaard and L Stewart (eds), 'Fourth Symposium on Community Action Research and the Prevention of Alcohol and Other Drug Problems: Based upon Kettil Bruun Society Thematic Meeting' (Alcohol and Public Health Research Unit, University of Auckland, NZ), pp 233–246

T Stockwell, M C Auld, J Zhao and G Martin, 'Does minimum pricing reduce alcohol consumption? The experience of a Canadian province', Addiction 107(5) (2012), pp 912–920

Strategic Task Force on Alcohol, 'Interim Report' (Department of Health, May 2002)

T L Toomey, G R Kilian, J P Gehan, C L Perry, R Jones-Webb, and A C Wagenaar, 'Qualitative assessment of training programs for alcohol servers and establishment managers', Public Health Reports 113 (1998), pp 162–169

A C Wagenaar and H D Holder, 'Effects of alcoholic beverage server liability on traffic crash injuries', Alcoholism: Clinical and Experimental Research 15 (1991), pp 942–947

A C Wagenaar, and T L Toomey, 'Alcoholic policy: Gap between legislative action and current research', Contemporary Drug Problems 27 (2000), pp 681–733

E Wallin, T Norström and S Andréasson, 'Alcohol prevention targeting licensed premises: a study of effects on violence', Journal of Studies on Alcohol 64 (2003), pp 270–277

J Warner, *Craze: Gin and Debauchery in the Age of Reason* (Four Walls Eight Windows, New York, 2002)

M Wicki and G Gmel, 'Hospital admission rates for alcohol intoxication after policy changes in the canton of Geneva, Switzerland', Drug and Alcohol Dependence 118(2–3) (2011), pp 209–215

York Health Economics Consortium, 'The Societal Cost of Alcohol Use in Scotland for 2007' (Scottish Government Social Research, Edinburgh, 2010)

Index